A Library
of Literary
Criticism

A Library
of Literary
Criticism

A Frederick Ungar Book

CONTINUUM • NEW YORK

MODERN BLACK WRITERS

Supplement

Compiled and edited by

STEVEN R. SERAFIN

1995
The Continuum Publishing Company
370 Lexington Avenue
New York, NY 10017

Printed in the United States of America

Library of Congress Cataloging-in-Publication Data
(Revised for vol. 2)

Modern Black Writers.

(A Library of literary criticism)
"Vol. 2 is a supplement to MODERN BLACK WRITERS
compiled and edited by Popkin (1978). It is published
by: New York: Continuum. And is edited by Steven R.
Serafin"—CIP info.
Includes bibliographical references and index.
1. Literature—Black authors—History and criticism.
2. Blacks in literature.   I. Popkin, Michael.
II. Serafin, Steven.
PN841.M58   809'.889   76-15656

ISBN 0-8044-3258-9
ISBN 0-8264-0688-2 (acid-free : v. 2)

INTRODUCTION

The legacy of black writing in the twentieth century extends from the emergence of authors who shared a similar commitment to literary endeavor and artistic purpose to the prominence of contemporary authors who have achieved critical reputation of international stature. Accentuating the importance of this extraordinary achievement, in 1986 the Nigerian author Wole Soyinka became the first African to be awarded the Nobel Prize for literature. The Afro-Caribbean author Derek Walcott, born in St. Lucia, was awarded the same prize in 1992, and two years later American author Toni Morrison became the first black woman to receive the award. Bound together by the heritage of a common past, black writers throughout the world constitute a vibrant and essential component within the context of modern literature, acknowledged by the unprecedented interest by scholarly and general readers alike in their lives and their work.

As an intricate part of an evolving literature that unifies Africa with the African peoples of the diaspora, the modern black writer embodies the essence of what the Kenyan author Ngugi wa Thiong'o has described as "our struggle for a cultural identity." It is this struggle that connects early African authors—Thomas Mofolo from Lesotho, B. W. Vilakazi and S. E. K. Mqhayi from South Africa—with African-American authors, such as Charles W. Chesnutt and Paul Laurence Dunbar, and Afro-Caribbean authors, such as René Maran from Martinique and C. L. R. James from Trinidad; authors associated with the Harlem Renaissance movement, notably Langston Hughes, Jean Toomer, Countee Cullen, Richard Wright, and Zora Neale Hurston, with the Négritude poets—Léopold Sédar Senghor, Birago and David Diop from Senegal, Aimé Césaire from Martinique, Léon-Gontran Damas from French Guiana, and Jacques Roumain from Haiti; the generation of authors coming to attention in the late 1950s and 1960s—including, among many others, Chinua Achebe, Gabriel Okara, Cyprian Ekwensi, Christopher Okigbo, and Amos Tutuola from Nigeria, Okot p'Bitek from Uganda, Michael Anthony from Trinidad, George Lamming from Barbados, Tchicaya U Tam'si from the Congo, Claude McKay from Jamaica, Shaaban Robert from Tanzania, Edouard Glissant from Martinique, René Depestre from Haiti, Peter Abrahams, Mazisi Kunene, Es'kia (Ezekiel) Mphahlele, and Alex La Guma from South Africa, James Baldwin, Ralph Ellison, John Oliver Killens, Amiri Baraka, and Gwendolyn Brooks from the United States—with the present generation of authors shaping the future of black writing: Kofi Anyidoho from Ghana, Daniel Maximin from Guadeloupe, Njabulo Ndebele from South Africa, Patrick Chamoiseau from Martinique, Festus Iyayi, Ben Okri, and Niyi Osundare from Nigeria, Nuruddin Farah from Somalia, Caryl Phillips from St. Kitts, Paule Marshall from Barbados, Beryl Gilroy from Guyana, Michelle Cliff and Olive Senior from Jamaica, V. Y. Mudimbe from Zaire, and Rita Dove, August Wilson, Terry McMillan, Charles Johnson, and Alice Walker from the United States.

This long-awaited supplement to *Modern Black Writers* is designed to complement the original volume (published in 1978, compiled and edited by Michael Popkin) by providing an enlarged collection of critical excerpts from a diverse selection of authors from Africa, the Caribbean, and the United States. The authors included in the supplement are all known primarily for their work in either fiction, poetry, or drama, illustrating the emphasis of the Library of Literary Criticism series on the creative writer rather than the writer of nonfiction. In discussing the trend of contemporary African and Caribbean writers to probe the various facets of postcolonial life, critics Bernth Lindfors and Reinhard Sander write that in carrying out this task,

> African writers in particular have frequently attracted the censure of their governments and have been imprisoned or forced into exile. Those able to continue writing in such circumstances have developed fresh perspectives on the vulnerability of their societies to economic and political pressures exerted by the outside world, which has resulted in writings that examine the black experience in the context of global power struggles. Close linkages of thought and feeling unite politically committed African, Caribbean, and African-American authors. Their novels, plays, and poems increasingly transcend parochial, domestic concerns and address wider international issues that have an impact on the entire black world. Since African and Caribbean writers are citizens of postcolonial societies, they often seek answers to the same vexing sociopolitical questions. They are drawn together by history and geography as well as by race.

Similar to the original volume, the supplement addresses the prominent role of women in the evolving nature of twentieth-century literature. Black women have emerged as distinctive literary voices or have come to the forefront of creative activity in their respective cultures. They are active in all genres and write in European languages as well as indigenous languages and dialects. As noted by critic Andrée Nicole McLaughlin: "The literary upsurge by black women in the second half of the twentieth century unveils a renaissance of the spirit inspired by those who have refused to surrender. Those who have resisted their oppression. Those who have undertaken to remake the universe to own their future." Responsible for a new reality rooted in diversity and equality, McLaughlin writes, "women of the intercontinental black women's literary renaissance are redefining themselves as well as language, images, ideas, and forms of expression within frameworks of cultural continuity." This "unwinding thread" of creativity connects the work of Maya Angelou and Audre Lorde with Ama Ata Aidoo from Ghana, Zee Edgell from Belize with Micere Githae Mugo from Kenya, Merle Collins from Grenada with Flora Nwapa from Nigeria, Lorna Goodison from Jamaica with Bessie Head from South Africa, Mariama Bâ from Senegal with Simone Schwarz-Bart from Guadeloupe. In her lecture when accepting the Nobel Prize for literature, Toni Morrison referred to the creative process as "this thing we have done—together," paying tribute to the contribution of all black women to the development of literature.

The supplement contains select criticism for 125 authors, forty-three women and eighty-two men, originating from thirty-two countries. Twenty-seven authors treated in the original volume of the series are included in the supplement based on their continued level of productivity. Those included for the first time represent authors with established literary reputations as well as authors who have emerged more recently and who have made a significant literary contribution. Whenever possible, if one author has written on the work of another, a selection of the criticism is reprinted in the volume. Those writing in English or French constitute the majority of authors included in the supplement, but there is some representation of authors writing in Portuguese and Swahili as well as other African languages and dialects. In accordance with the editorial policy of the Library of Literary Criticism, Caribbean or Latin American black authors writing in Spanish or Portuguese are treated within the context of Latin American literature. It is important to establish that numerous authors of substantial merit could not be included in this supplement due to the constraints of space. As black authors throughout the world continue to influence the development of modern literature, there will be increasing demand for extended critical treatment of their works.

The authors included in the supplement are arranged alphabetically, with the critical excerpts for each author arranged chronologically. The listing of Authors as Critics should be used in conjunction with the Index to Critics. The list of Works Mentioned includes all works cited in the text, followed by the year of publication. In the case of works originally written in a language other than English, a literal translation of the title is provided as well as the English translation, if any, and the year of publication.

The criticism reprinted here has been selected from a comprehensive range of sources. A dagger at the end of the credit line indicates a translation from French; otherwise, all criticism was published originally in English or reprinted in English translation. Although a significant amount of criticism was published in periodicals that are now either in a state of reorganization or defunct, the editor acknowledges the importance of those that continue to provide a venue for critical awareness concerning black authors, notably *African American Review*, *Ariel*, *Callaloo*, *Canadian Journal of African Studies*, *Commonwealth Essays & Studies*, *The Journal of Commonwealth Literature*, *Présence Africaine*, *Research in African Literatures*, *Studies in Twentieth-Century Literature*, *West Africa*, *World Literature Today*, and *World Literature Written in English*, among others.

The editor wishes to express his appreciation to the Wexler Library, Hunter College of the City University of New York, and to the Schomburg Collection of the New York Public Library. He acknowledges the assistance of the scholars cited as advisers and consultants in preparing the volume, especially the generosity of time and expertise provided by Hal Wylie and by the editor's friend and colleague Wole Ogundele. Jason Berner was the editorial associate for the supplement. Editorial assistance was provided by Elizabeth Haddrell, Carolyn Lengel, Lisa Tolhurst, Genevieve Trous>sereau, Greta Wagle, and Theresa Wyre. The editor is especially grateful to Werner Mark Linz, publisher of Continuum, Evander Lomke, the managing editor, and Rob Baker of Watersign Resources.

S. R. S.

AUTHORS INCLUDED

Achebe, Chinua
Aidoo, Ama Ata
Amadi, Elechi
Angelou, Maya
Anthony, Michael
Anyidoho, Kofi
Armah, Ayi Kwei
Awoonor, Kofi
Bâ, Mariama
Badian, Seydou
Baldwin, James
Bambara, Toni Cade
Baraka, Amiri
Bebey, Francis
Bemba, Sylvain
Bennett, Louise
Beti, Mongo
Bradley, David
Brathwaite, Edward Kamau
Brodber, Erna
Brooks, Gwendolyn
Brutus, Dennis
Césaire, Aimé
Chamoiseau, Patrick
Cheney-Coker, Syl
Childress, Alice
Clarke, Austin C.
Cliff, Michelle
Clifton, Lucille
Collins, Merle
Condé, Maryse
Depestre, René
Diallo, Nafissatou Niang
Dove, Rita
Edgell, Zee
Emecheta, Buchi
Farah, Nuruddin
Fauset, Jessie
Gaines, Ernest J.
Gilroy, Beryl

Giovanni, Nikki
Glissant, Edouard
Goodison, Lorna
Harper, Michael S.
Harris, Wilson
Head, Bessie
Hearne, John
Heath, Roy A. K.
Hodge, Merle
Iyayi, Festus
James, C. L. R.
Johnson, Charles
Jones, Gayl
Juminer, Bertène
Kincaid, Jamaica
Kourouma, Ahmadou
Kunene, Mazisi
Labou Tansi, Sony
La Guma, Alex
Lamming, George
Liking, Werewere
Lopes, Henri
Lorde, Audre
Lovelace, Earl
Maillu, David
Mais, Roger
Mapanje, Jack
Marechera, Dambudzo
Marshall, Paule
Maximin, Daniel
McMillan, Terry
Métellus, Jean
Morrison, Toni
Mphahlele, Es'kia (Ezekiel)
Mtshali, Oswald
Mudimbe, V. Y.
Mugo, Micere Githae
Munonye, John
Mwangi, Meja
Naylor, Gloria

Ndao, Cheik Aliou
Ndebele, Njabulo
Neto, Agostinho
Ngugi wa Thiong'o
Ntiru, Richard
Nwapa, Flora
Ogot, Grace
Okot p'Bitek
Okri, Ben
Osofisan, Femi
Osundare, Niyi
Ouologuem, Yambo
Phelps, Anthony
Phillips, Caryl
Rabéarivelo, Jean-Joseph
Reed, Ishmael
Reid, V. S. (Vic)
Rive, Richard
Robert, Shaaban
Rotimi, Ola
Rubadiri, David
Salkey, Andrew
Sanchez, Sonia

Schwarz-Bart, Simone
Sembène Ousmane
Senior, Olive
Sepamla, Sipho
Serote, Mongane (Wally)
Serumaga, Robert
Shange, Ntozake
Sow Fall, Aminata
Soyinka, Wole
St. Omer, Garth
Sutherland, Efua
Taban lo Liyong
Tati-Loutard, Jean Baptiste
Tchicaya U Tam'si
Tlali, Miriam
Walcott, Derek
Walker, Alice
Warner-Vieyra, Myriam
Wilson, August
Wynter, Sylvia
Zadi Zaourou, Bernard
Zobel, Joseph

AUTHORS BY COUNTRY

ANGOLA

Neto, Agostinho

ANTIGUA

Kincaid, Jamaica

BARBADOS

Brathwaite, Edward Kamau
Clarke, Austin C.
Lamming, George
Marshall, Paule

BELIZE

Edgell, Zee

CAMEROON

Bebey, Francis
Beti, Mongo
Liking, Werewere

CONGO

Bemba, Sylvain
Labou Tansi, Sony
Lopes, Henri
Tati-Loutard, Jean Baptiste
Tchicaya U Tam'si

COTE D'IVOIRE

Kourouma, Ahmadou
Zadi Zaourou, Bernard

FRENCH GUIANA

Juminer, Bertène

GHANA

Aidoo, Ama Ata
Anyidoho, Kofi
Armah, Ayi Kwei
Awoonor, Kofi
Sutherland, Efua

GRENADA

Collins, Merle

GUADELOUPE

Condé, Maryse
Maximin, Daniel
Schwarz-Bart, Simone
Warner-Vieyra, Myriam

GUYANA

Gilroy, Beryl
Harris, Wilson
Heath, Roy A. K.

HAITI

Depestre, René
Métellus, Jean
Phelps, Anthony

JAMAICA

Bennett, Louise
Brodber, Erna
Cliff, Michelle
Goodison, Lorna
Hearne, John
Mais, Roger
Reid, V. S. (Vic)
Salkey, Andrew

Senior, Olive
Wynter, Sylvia

KENYA

Maillu, David
Mugo, Micere Githae
Mwangi, Meja
Ngugi wa Thiong'o
Ogot, Grace

MADAGASCAR

Rabéarivelo, Jean-Joseph

MALAWI

Mapanje, Jack
Rubadiri, David

MALI

Badian, Seydou
Ouologuem, Yambo

MARTINIQUE

Césaire, Aimé
Chamoiseau, Patrick
Glissant, Edouard
Zobel, Joseph

NIGERIA

Achebe, Chinua
Amadi, Elechi
Emecheta, Buchi
Iyayi, Festus
Munonye, John
Nwapa, Flora
Okri, Ben
Osofisan, Femi
Osundare, Niyi
Rotimi, Ola
Soyinka, Wole

SENEGAL

Bâ, Mariama
Diallo, Nafissatou Niang
Ndao, Cheik Aliou
Sembène Ousmane
Sow Fall, Aminata

SIERRA LEONE

Cheney-Coker, Syl

SOMALIA

Farah, Nuruddin

SOUTH AFRICA

Brutus, Dennis
Head, Bessie
Kunene, Mazisi
La Guma, Alex
Mphahlele, Es'kia (Ezekiel)
Mtshali, Oswald
Ndebele, Njabulo
Rive, Richard
Sepamla, Sipho
Serote, Mongane (Wally)
Tlali, Miriam

ST. KITTS

Phillips, Caryl

ST. LUCIA

St. Omer, Garth
Walcott, Derek

TANZANIA

Robert, Shaaban

TRINIDAD AND TOBAGO

Anthony, Michael
Hodge, Merle
James, C. L. R.
Lovelace, Earl

UGANDA

Ntiru, Richard
Okot p'Bitek
Serumaga, Robert
Taban lo Liyong

UNITED STATES

Angelou, Maya
Baldwin, James
Bambara, Toni Cade
Baraka, Amiri
Bradley, David
Brooks, Gwendolyn
Childress, Alice
Clifton, Lucille

Dove, Rita
Fauset, Jessie
Gaines, Ernest J.
Giovanni, Nikki
Harper, Michael S.
Johnson, Charles
Jones, Gayl
Lorde, Audre
McMillan, Terry
Morrison, Toni
Naylor, Gloria
Reed, Ishmael
Sanchez, Sonia
Shange, Ntozake
Walker, Alice
Wilson, August

ZAIRE

Mudimbe, V. Y.

ZIMBABWE

Marechera, Dambudzo

AUTHORS AS CRITICS

The following is a listing of authors included in this book who are also quoted as critics on their colleagues. See the Index to Critics, which begins on p. 802, for complete details.

Achebe, Chinua
Anyidoho, Kofi
Armah, Ayi Kwei
Bemba, Sylvain
Brathwaite, Edward Kamau
Chamoiseau, Patrick
Condé, Maryse
Dove, Rita
Farah, Nurrudin
Harris, Wilson
James, C. L. R.

Jones, Gayl
Lamming, George
Morrison, Toni
Mphahlele, Es'kia (Ezekiel)
Ngugi wa Thiong'o
Okri, Ben
Osofisan, Femi
Osundare, Niyi
Salkey, Andrew
Soyinka, Wole
Taban lo Liyong

PERIODICALS USED

Where no abbreviation is indicated, the periodical references are used in full.

ACLALSB	ACLALS Bulletin (Mysore, India)
AfrQ	Africa Quarterly (New Delhi, India)
	Africa Report (New York)
	Africa Today (Denver)
	African American Review (Terre Haute, Ind.)
	African Literature Today (London)
AfrSR	The African Studies Review (Atlanta)
	L'Afrique Litteraire (Paris)
	Afriscope (Yaba, Nigeria)
	ALA Bulletin (Edmonton, Alberta)
	American Imago (Baltimore)
AL	American Literature (Durham, N.C.)
Ariel	Ariel: A Review of International English Literature (Calgary)
BA	Books Abroad (later World Literature Today, Norman, Okla.)
BALF	Black American Literature Forum (later African American Review, Terre Haute, Ind.)
BlackI	Black Images (Toronto)
	Bim (Christ Church, Barbados)
	Boundary 2 (Durham, N.C.)
	Callaloo (Baltimore)
	Canadian Journal of African Studies (Toronto)
CanL	Canadian Literature (Vancouver)
CarQ	Caribbean Quarterly (Mona, Jamaica)
CE&S	Commonwealth Essays & Studies (Dijon, France)
CLAQ	Children's Literature Association Quarterly (Battle Creek, Mich.)
CLAJ	CLA Journal (Atlanta)
	College Literature (West Chester, Penn.)
CLS	Comparative Literature Studies (University Park, Penn.)
	Concerning Poetry (Bellingham, Wash.)
CL	Contemporary Literature (Madison, Wisc.)
CBAA	Current Bibliography on African Affairs (Washington, D.C.)
	Dictionary of Literary Biography (Detroit)
	The English Academy Review (Wits, South Africa)
EinA	English in Africa (Grahamstown, South Africa)
ECr	L'Esprit Createur (Baton Rouge, La., later Lexington, Ky.)
	Europe (Paris)
FemSt	Feminist Studies (College Park, Md.)
FR	The French Review (Champaign, Ill.)

	The Gar (Austin, Texas)
	The Griot (Berea, Ky.)
	Imprévue (Montpellier, France)
IFR	International Fiction Review (Fredericton, New Brunswick)
	Jamaica Journal (Kingston)
JAC	Journal of American Culture (Bowling Green, Ohio)
JASt	Journal of American Studies (New York)
JCS	Journal of Caribbean Studies (Lexington, Ky.)
JCL	Journal of Commonwealth Literature (Hull, U.K.)
JWIL	Journal of West Indian Literature (Bridgetown, Barbados)
	Kunapipi (Aarhus, Denmark)
	Language Quarterly (Tampa)
	Legon Journal of the Humanities (Legon, Ghana)
LitC	The Literary Criterion (Bangalore, India)
LHY	Literary Half-Yearly (Mysore, India)
LitR	Literary Review (Madison, N.J.)
MassR	The Massachusetts Review (Amherst, Mass.)
	Matatu (Amsterdam)
	MELUS (Amherst, Mass.)
MQR	Michigan Quarterly Review (Ann Arbor, Mich.)
MD	Modern Drama (Downsview, Ontario)
MFS	Modern Fiction Studies (West Lafayette, Ind.)
MLS	Modern Language Studies (Providence, R.I.)
	Le Monde (Paris)
	Mosaic (Winnipeg, Manitoba)
	Neohelicon (Budapest)
	New African (London)
NBR	New Beacon Review (London)
NLH	New Literary History (Baltimore)
	New Statesman & Society (London)
NYRB	The New York Review of Books (New York)
NYT	The New York Times (New York)
NYTBR	The New York Times Book Review (New York)
NYTM	The New York Times Magazine (New York)
	Notre Librairie (Paris)
	Nouvelles du Sud (Ivry, France)
	Obsidian II (Detroit)
	October (Cambridge, Mass.)
	Okike (Nsukka, Nigeria, later Enugu, Nigeria)
PMQ	Pacific Moana Quarterly (Hamilton, New Zealand)
	Parnassus (New York)
PA	Présence Africaine (Paris)
PMLA	Publications of the Modern Language Association (New York)
PMQ	Pacific Moana Quarterly (Hamilton, New Zealand)
RAL	Research in African Literatures (Bloomington, Ind.)

	Review of African Political Economy (Sheffield, U.K.)
RCF	Review of Contemporary Fiction (Normal, Ill.)
	Review of National Literatures (Whitestone, N.Y.)
	Revista/Review Interamericana (San German, Puerto Rico)
SHR	Southern Humanities Review (Auburn, Ala.)
SQ	The Southern Quarterly (Hattisburg, Miss.)
SoR	Southern Review (Baton Rouge, La.)
SAF	Studies in American Fiction (Boston)
SSF	Studies in Short Fiction (Newberry, S.C.)
StTCL	Studies in Twentieth-Century Literature (Manhattan, Kan.)
	Theatre (New Haven, Conn.)
	Theatre Journal (Baltimore)
TRI	Theatre Research International (Oxford)
TWQ	Third World Quarterly (London)
TLS	The Times Literary Supplement (London)
	Ufahumu (Los Angeles)
VV	Village Voice (New York)
VQR	Virginia Quarterly Review (Charlottesville, Va.)
VLS	Voice Literary Supplement (New York)
WA	West Africa (London)
	Women's Review of Books (Wellesley, Mass.)
WLT	World Literature Today (Norman, Okla.)
WLWE	World Literature Written in English (Arlington, Tex.)
YFS	Yale French Studies (New Haven, Conn.)
YR	Yale Review (New Haven, Conn.)
	Zaire Afrique (Kinshasa, Zaire)
	Zambezia (Harare, Zimbabwe)
ZAA	Zeitschrift fur Anglistik und Amerikanistik (Berlin)
ZNHF	The Zora Neale Hurston Forum (Baltimore)

ACHEBE, CHINUA (1930–   )

NIGERIA

Chinua Achebe's *Things Fall Apart* demonstrates a mastery of plot and struc-ture, strength of characterization, competence in the manipulation of language, and consistency and depth of thematic exploration which is rarely found in a first novel. Although he has never quite been able to sustain this exceptionally high standard in subsequent novels, the general level of performance remains consistently impressive and he assuredly deserves his place as one of the most accomplished African writers. In the history of the anglophone novel, Achebe comes next to [Cyprian] Ekwensi in chronological importance, but his work is much more comprehensive in scope than that of the latter, who confines himself almost entirely to contemporary situations. All the shaping forces which com-bined to stimulate the growth of modern African literature in the 1950s are dis-cernible in Achebe's work. . . .

Novels like *Things Fall Apart* and *Arrow of God* in which the author sets out to demonstrate the beauty and validity of traditional life and its destruction by an alien civilization must inevitably have a very high sociological content, since the nature of the society must be thoroughly documented before its col-lapse is shown. This need partly dictates the structure of *Things Fall Apart* and *Arrow of God*, the first parts of both novels being comparatively leisurely por-trayals of Igbo society, whereas the second halves move much more rapidly, showing the forces which bring about the collapse. It also accounts for the high sociological content of the earliest African novels. However, a novel is not a sociological document; readers go to novels not for sociological information, but for impressions of life powerfully realized. Sociological information will therefore appear tedious to most readers unless it is expertly handled in the novel, that is, unless it is made to appear part of the vibrant life of the people the author is describing and does not seem to be sociological lore per se. Novelists like Achebe and [Elechi] Amadi have proved themselves very adept at the incor-poration of sociological material. Again and again we ask ourselves why it is that after reading hosts of novels which have been made tedious because of the preponderance of unassimilated sociological material, we can come back to Achebe's *Things Fall Apart*, half of which consists of sociological lore, and still be captivated by it. The answer is simply that in this novel the sociological does not call attention to itself as being purely sociological; it is presented as part of the life and activity of the people and is almost always related to some aspect of human character. At times the sociological is introduced as part of the detail which makes the book realistic and interesting. In chapter two for instance, the traditional fear of the darkness and of dangerous animals, and the various super-stitions concerning them, are incorporated into the general tension of the announcement of the meeting. When in chapter three Nwakibie invites his wives to drink Okonkwo's palm-wine in their due order, the process is saved from looking like pure sociological information by the attention to detail and the concentration on the words and gestures of the participants, so that a sense of drama is generated and the whole seems to be part of life as it is lived among the Igbos. Even the songs have a relevance they do not have in the works of less accomplished novelists. For instance, the song the women sing after Okonkwo's success in the wrestling match is relevant to that contest and to Okonkwo's character, and the contest is itself presented as part of the lives and feelings of the people. Then the childhood song Ikemefuna remembers as he is on his way to his death heightens the poignancy of the events all the more.

In fact, in *Things Fall Apart* the presentation of the sociological goes hand in hand with the development of Okonkwo's character. In the very deepest sense of the words, *Things Fall Apart* is a novel which shows the interrelationship of environment and character, one of Achebe's main aims being to demonstrate the way in which Okonkwo's character has been molded by his environment. At every single point in the narrative, Achebe tries to relate every belief, every activity of his society to some aspect of Okonkwo's character. If the novel is structured in such a way that at the end of the first part we have a powerful picture of the society that will collapse in the second part, it is also structured so that at the end of the first part the growth of Okonkwo's character has been perfectly traced and his personality established as one of the leading men in his clan; and it is that personality which will be largely in decline in the second. In this novel there is a masterly manipulation of plot and structure and a judicious deployment of the sociological, which ensures that the development of Okonkwo's character and the presentation of his society are coextensive and contemporaneous.

Eustace Palmer. *The Growth of the African Novel*
(London: Heinemann, 1979), pp. 63, 72–73

In depicting the disintegration of Igbo culture in both *Things Fall Apart* and *Arrow of God*, Achebe does not give us a partial or biased view of the historical epoch he is dealing with. He makes use of a wide variety of characters to represent different points of view and social groups. In *Arrow of God*, for instance, Ezeulu, Nwaka, and Akuebue represent the chief priest and elders of traditional society; Captain Winterbottom and Clarke are representatives of colonial administrators with different personalities, while Brown, Goodcountry, and Onachukwu stand for various approaches to the evangelization of Africans. Thus we are able to see how political, religious, tribal, and personal factors all contributed to the crumbling of the traditional social structure. Although the encroachment of the white man's civilization and political power features as the principal catalyst in this change, Achebe does not exonerate his ancestors from blame. Ezeulu's pride and unbending character and his personal conflicts with Nwaka are partly responsible for what happens. The author consequently succeeds in presenting a truthful and balanced account of reality and is able to capture the mood of the epoch. His method is that of objective realism.

Achebe typifies what has become the commonest version of African realism. His linear plots are not only an imitation of the African traditional story, but also coincide with the structure of nineteenth-century European realist fiction. And, just as the nineteenth-century European realists presented a critique of capitalism in non-Marxist terms, Achebe attacks cultural imperialism and postindependence corruption in what may be termed "moderate" terms. He certainly presents a progressive view of history. He aligns himself with anticolonialist forces in *Arrow of God* and *Things Fall Apart* and is critical of the rampant corruption and misdemeanors of the emerging African ruling class in *No Longer at Ease* and *A Man of the People*, but he only goes so far and no further. He does not present a Marxist or in any way radical view of social problems, but he succeeds in giving us a truthful account of what he portrays. His characters are typical and the circumstances under which they operate are natural and convincing. In the two "Old World" novels where he gives a truthful account of Igbo society without glossing over its weaknesses and despite his declared intention to dispose of "the fundamental theme," his art becomes a model of the triumph of realism over the claims of nationalism.

Emmanuel Ngara. *Art and Ideology in the African Novel*
(London: Heinemann, 1985), pp. 111–12

[Achebe's] novels either deal with the African past or refer to the presence of the so-called dark continent. They attack the colonist's view that the "blackman . . . had slept in a dark continent until the Livingstones and Stanleys woke him into history," without idealizing the precolonial era. According to a statement in the *Times Literary Supplement* in 1965, "*Things Fall Apart* is probably already as big a factor in the formation of a young West African's picture of his past, and of his relation to it, as any of the still rather distorted teachings of the pulpit and the primary school." As becomes evident in *A Man of the People*, Achebe is nevertheless also highly critical of the political and social development in postindependent Africa. . . .

Reflecting the social and political reality in postcolonial Africa, *A Man of the People* discloses in literary terms that the federal system installed by the British colonial government was too shaky to guarantee the necessary stability for the independent African nations. . . .

While Achebe's earlier works expose the author's concern for a revaluation of the African past and the search for a national identity, consequently conveying a rather constructive spirit, *A Man of the People* shows an entirely different Achebe. The novel can both be understood as the literary expression of historical change and the changed historical perspective of the author. The "national movement" which was based on the ideological alliance of the masses and the new African elite falls apart immediately after independence. Now it is no longer the opposition between the colonial power and the African population which dominates the political scene but the diverging interests of the black bourgeoisie and the mass of the people. Under these circumstances Achebe's sympathy for the underprivileged among his countrymen seems the

only adequate reaction of a writer who claims to be a social critic, the highly
negative presentation of Africa's new rulers in *A Man of the People* the only
appropriate expression of his critical awareness. This is also mirrored in a
change of the narrative perspective. In his last novel, Achebe introduces the
first person narrative which implies a greater, if not even more skeptical, distance between the author and his character. . . .

   In *A Man of the People* the situation is profoundly changed by the intervention of the military which may be regarded as Achebe's fictitious solution to
a problem that many Nigerian intellectuals actually hoped for. How closely
Achebe had anticipated the political development became evident when, only
nine days after *A Man of the People* was published in 1966, a real, but in the
end unsuccessful, coup d'état created further political chaos in Nigeria. Achebe,
accused of having supported the rebels, was put into prison. Considering these
circumstances, it may not be a surprise that a great number of critics have only
praised the anticipatory quality of *A Man of the People* while they have at the
same time overlooked its literary merits.

Wolfgang Klooss. In Hedwig Bock and Albert Wertheim, eds.
Essays on Contemporary Post-Colonial Fiction
(Munich: Max Hueber, 1986), pp. 24, 38–40

Anthills of the Savannah is as different a novel as each of Achebe's has been
from the one preceding it, or others that have come after it. But this [one] is
tidier, with a narrative structure that is earthly, and a language which, on the
whole, is spare, and a telling that is direct. Now and again, there is a stylistic
stutter. Often the points in the novel are made in a roundabout way or else in a
cryptic manner, and sometimes the reader becomes the proverbial man who's
lost a camel for which he looks in a milk container. Nevertheless, this is a most
charming novel, a book of metonyms, a rich treasure of transferred meanings.

   We're back to where the story of *A Man of the People* was interrupted, in
1966, by the army takeover of power in Nigeria. Only we are not in Nigeria, but
in a fictitious country called Kangan Republic, where in a recent popular referen-
dum, the head of state, an army general, has failed to be elected president-for-
life, because one of the provinces of which the land comprises says "no." The
name of this province will ring hatefully in the general's ears, and Abazon will
have become his obsession. Anyway, the Kangan Republic is much smaller than
Nigeria and is misruled by a general with the abbreviated name of Sam, a general
who has the touch of the clown, and the wit of a simpleton, and who . . . refers to
himself as the Big Mouth, literally a translation of the Somali nickname for
Siyad Barre, Somalia's generalissimo for the past seventeen-plus years. There
are endless references to other African tyrants, some by name, some not. . . .

   Abazon may be seen as a symbol of dissent to a dictatorship, but it is also
a rural Africa which has no muscle to show to the metropolis-concentrated form
of bourgeois authoritarianism. In fact, it is much more that. In Somalia, we know
what happens when a given province challenges Siyad Barre's authority: the
lifeline to the region is severed, no boreholes are dug, no development projects

are financed, no teachers are any longer transferred to this area, etc., etc., etc., precisely the very measures described in *Anthills*.

Nuruddin Farah. *WA*. September 21, 1987, pp. 1828, 1830

More people have read Chinua Achebe than any other African writer. This is no less true outside the continent than it is within it. And this is constantly reflected in the fact that more critical attention is paid to his novels than to the work of any other writer. Find someone who has read but one African literary work, and the odds are that the work will be Achebe's *Things Fall Apart*. The reasons for this are not hard to surmise. Achebe writes in a style that is at once accessible to the individual who knows nothing of Africa and intensely compelling to even the most knowledgeable Africanist. He was one of the first writers to effectively dramatize the most important historical, political, and cultural issues facing Africa, and he has remained among the best. Moreover, he is a consummate artist; he always tells a good story. . . .

By turns Achebe has been both praised and condemned for his didacticism. Regardless of how it is judged, perhaps the least controversial statement anyone could make in the field of African literature is that Chinua Achebe is a didactic writer. By his own statements and through his work, Achebe clearly shows his belief in the role of the artist as teacher. The pejoration of the word "didactic" in Western criticism, however, makes this statement rather misleading for many readers. Achebe's artistic concerns are with presenting a holistic view of the ethos of his people in an entirely vital, dynamic mode that is expressive of his culture in terms of form no less than content. His works progress in a linear manner and are set in an historical framework that reveals the persistence of cultural continuity despite internal and external threats to the society. Yet, as [Wole] Soyinka noted, there is never a mere photographic rendering of the world he gives us. We confront an ethical consciousness, an authorial presence that leads us into the societal structures of Igbo life and proceeds in a realistic, linear, and historical manner, while revealing the depth and breadth of strategies open to the individual and society for coping with reality. Achebe's works are didactic, but not in the manner of a facile, two-dimensional realism where all ethical choices are clear cut.

Richard K. Priebe. *Myth, Realism, and the West African Writer*
(Trenton, N. J.: Africa World Press, 1988), pp. 47–48

Achebe is . . . not exclusively a narrator of a nation's course through history and its individuals' personal destinies, but he also delightfully, if thoughtfully, offers us an insight into the inevitable relationship between folklore and literature, between African and European—specifically, Nigerian and British—values, and the tragic consequences of such a relationship. For those individuals who are caught up in this conflicting relationship, life offers no ease; for them, things fall apart. The center cannot hold.

The clash of traditional and modern values is easily plotted in Achebe. What is less evident, and therefore needs our focus, is that for Achebe's characters, the tragic choice between opposing values inevitably turns out to be a conflict between the spoken and the written word, between the folklore of the clan and the literature of the foreigner. This clash does not result in a simple victory or defeat. Achebe is too sensitive to the general ironies and ambiguities of life to offer a clear black-and-white solution. The conflict produces, instead, something akin to Greek tragedy: the rise and tragic fall of an individual caught between two impossible choices. . . .

Abdul R. JanMohamed, in his recent study, *Manichean Aesthetics: The Politics of Literature in Colonial Africa*, concludes that a basic ideological function of African literature is to negate European influences and thus restore the old culture. Achebe, in my opinion, does this by juxtaposing the two cultures in such a way as to reduce them to their most basic level—the word either sung, spoken, or written. The final word on the clash of cultures is not yet in, and may never be in; meanwhile, Achebe shows, that those who must make peace with the past and the present and the future, must not lose sight of the word. For, in the beginning was the word. And in the end too.

Raman Singh. Neohelicon. 16, 2 (1989), pp. 159–60, 167

Chinua Achebe dedicated his first three novels, *Things Fall Apart*, *No Longer at Ease*, and *Arrow of God* to helping the African people regain their sense of personal dignity, which they lost in their contact with colonialism. In the process of demonstrating such a fundamental commitment, he took a historical look back to the pattern of life in his characters before and after their confrontation with Europe. The internal weaknesses of their society are also exposed in order to present a balanced picture of that confrontation. The tragic flaws of old Okonkwo and Ezeulu, and the moral vacillation of Obi Okonkwo are sympathetically portrayed by the author, although these characters are held responsible for their contributory roles in their individual tragedies. But despite the instances of human weakness, miscalculations, power tussle, and clashes between human wills and the dictates of the gods, the prevailing tone of these works is still that of the type of optimism that follows well-wrought tragic work. The human errors responsible for the tragedies are restricted to the tragic heroes and a few identifiable characters whose corporate errors do not contribute to a sense of total loss and doom. Rather, there is hope that a new society will be built from the broken pieces of the past. Despite Ezeulu's sad end, traditional sanctions remain operative and continue to judge the actions of men.

The apparent tone of pessimism for which Achebe has been accused begins with *A Man of the People*, which is set in postindependence Nigeria. Like Achebe's former novels, it is deeply analytical. It mercilessly exposes the nature and roots of the bribery, corruption, and apathy which had come to typify Nigeria of the 1960s. Despite its comic exterior, the author's disillusionment is the most consistent aspect of the novel. Neither Nanga the crook nor Odili the idealist is spared Achebe's biting satire. Achebe's commitment resides exactly in his concern for the society and his criticism of all segments of it, both the corrupt and those who condone their corruption through general apathy. Such criticism constitutes the negative form of commitment, the type which exposes and criticizes in order to effect change. This mood dominates most of Achebe's later works, both poetry and criticism, written after the Nigerian Civil War.

Virginia U. Ola. In Jonathan A. Peters, Mildred P. Mortimer, and Russell
V. Linnemann, eds. *Literature of Africa and the African Continuum*
(Washington, D. C.: Three Continents Press, 1989), pp. 133–34

Twenty-two years have elapsed since *A Man of the People*: years that have seen worse things in Africa than that book prophesied. And then, in 1987, Achebe published *Anthills of the Savannah*. Set in an African country whose young, recently established military ruler has just sought confirmation from the people in his aim to become president-for-life, it seems to take up just where *A Man of the People* left off. Technically, too, it pursues the development already evident in the other books: it is as different from them, that is to say, as they are from each other. Indeed in this difference lies its continuity. . . .

Achebe's commitment here is to a history made vital and actual in language, and aware of itself as such. History is not, as it was in *Things Fall Apart*, there in the past to be known and told about: it comes into being in the minds and feelings of those involved in it. It is the product of the words which form it. That, I think, is why there is no fixed standpoint in *Anthills*, no single storyteller and no single story: the face of history has become a crowd snapshot, with its own very real claim to objectivity. And this takes us back to *Things Fall Apart*. For if there is an important linear development in Achebe's attitude to history, a movement from involved detachment to detached involvement, the more important development is circular. *Things Fall Apart* was also, it will be remembered, a mixed, imbalanced form.

Anthills of the Savannah is involved in the genesis of history. What takes place here does so inside the characters who tell their story. They, mentally and emotionally, are struggling to find guidelines through the morass of violence and fear which has taken the place of corruption in their society. . . .

For the anthills [of the title] are symbols, things which speak and, speaking, link past and future: ". . . like anthills surviving to tell the new grass of the savannah about last year's brush fires." And the novel itself is now symbol, not discourse. It is not about anything, nor does it have any purpose, beyond itself: it *is*, it has become, history. A history neither reported now, nor interpreted, but presented as the thing-in-language of a high objectivity. . . . History, we are told in this novel, is learning a language; it is learning that one is not alone. For in it we assimilate the events that made and make us. History and myth have been deconstructed: they have once again been liberated into language.

Joseph Swann. In Geoffrey V. Davis and Hena Maes-Jelinek, eds.
Crisis and Creativity in the New Literatures in English
(Amsterdam: Rodopi, 1990), pp. 197–98, 200–1, 203

Achebe is read and discussed more than any other African novelist, and his works have come to constitute important interpretative spaces in the development and critique of the postcolonial condition and its aesthetic. Nevertheless, Achebe has suffered the misfortune of being taken for granted: the intricate and deep structures that inform his narratives are rarely examined, except on an elementary introductory level, and the ideologies that inform his narratives and his theoretical reflections rarely seem to have the influence one would expect from Africa's leading novelist. . . . [His] writings and thought must be placed in their proper perspective, placed in relation to both some important literary precursors and within the nationalist tradition that produced him. Only then can we begin to understand why the kinds of narratives Achebe inaugurated have acquired so much ideological import, why he is indispensable to understanding the colonial and postcolonial condition in Africa. . . .

Achebe's seminal status in the history of African literature lies precisely in his ability to have realized that the novel provided a new way of reorganizing African cultures, especially in the crucial juncture of transition from colonialism to national independence, and his fundamental belief that narrative can indeed propose alternative worlds beyond the realities imprisoned in colonial and postcolonial relations of power. In other words, Achebe was possibly the first of our writers to recognize the function of the novel not solely as a mode of representing reality, but one which had limitless possibilities of inventing a new national community. In Achebe's works, questions of national identity are closely related to narrative strategies; fiction allows the writer to express a different vision and perspective. . . .

Indeed, the historical significance of Achebe's works lies in his ability to evolve narrative procedures through which the colonial language, which was previously intended to designate and reproduce the colonial ideology, now evokes new forms of expression, proffers a new oppositional discourse, thereby countering the "permanence of vision" embedded in colonialist discourse. . . . And in seeking a new form of expressing African culture, Achebe and his contemporaries were also seeking a way out of the prisonhouse of colonialism. For these writers to evoke a new African identity—which is one of Achebe's declared goals and persistent themes—these writers had to take the colonial project into account; they had to interrogate its vision, ideologies, historical claims, and its theory of Africans. In Achebe's case, the imperative to confront the colonial project in its totality arises from the belief that "colonization was the most important event in our history from all kinds of angles . . . most of the problems we see in our politics derive from the moment when we lost our initiative to other people, to colonizers." Significantly, Achebe's return to the colonial archive is motivated by the need to imagine the future: taking colonialism into account (both in terms of writing about it and interrogating its claims) "will help us to map out our plans for the future."

Simon Gikandi. Reading Chinua Achebe
(London: James Currey, 1991), pp. 1–4

AIDOO, AMA ATA (1942–   )

GHANA

Among contemporary Ghanaian dramatists, male and female, only Ama Ata Aidoo compares with [Efua] Sutherland in exploiting oral literature, especially folk drama, in modern theater. Like . . . Sutherland, Aidoo has taught extensively in her field. She graduated from the University of Ghana in 1964, and subsequently attended a creative writing program at Stanford University in the United States. Since then she has taught as a research fellow at the Institute of African Studies in the University of Ghana, and as visiting lecturer in other African universities and in American colleges. Both as writer and teacher she has always demonstrated a special interest in the kind of oral literary traditions that so strongly influence her own plays.

As Aidoo has remarked, her ideal form of theater is one that capitalizes on the dramatic art of storytelling. This kind of theater, she feels, would actually be a complete environment in which the usual amenities of eating and drinking would be combined with storytelling, poetry-reading, and plays. In Aidoo one encounters a tremendous confidence in the integrity and inclusiveness of the oral tradition. She perceives the tradition of storytelling as one that actually combines techniques and conventions that are often separated into distinctive genres, especially in the Western literary tradition. The storyteller's art is therefore a synthesis of poetry, dramatic play-acting, and narrative plot. This art is social in the most literal sense. The artist is physically and morally located in the center of her, or his, audience, and the story itself reflects and perpetuates the moral and cultural values of the audience. Consequently when Aidoo talks of a theater that, ideally, duplicates the oral tradition, she is emphasizing the inclusiveness of that oral tradition—and the extent to which the art and function of the storyteller's performance become direct extensions of the storyteller's society. . . .

Each Aidoo story bears the idiosyncracies of her protagonist and reflects the manner in which each protagonist is conceived as a performer offering judgments and justifying actions by way of a personal performance. Thus even in a rare Aidoo poem we can see her consistent strategy as a short story writer at work. For example, in "Last of the Proud Ones" the language is carefully subordinated to the powerful personality and voice of the old woman who speaks in the work. As the last survivor of her generation, she is contemptuous of the new-fangled ways, and the strange inventions, of the modern (Westernized) world. A diet of bread and cheese is therefore an unspeakable abomination, and she will have nothing to do with it. The stuff, she snorts, "reeks, reeks / the odor of stinking fish!"

It is important to emphasize that Aidoo consistently applies this technique—the short story as oral performance—to all of her short stories, irrespective of whether or not they are drawn directly from the nonliterate milieu of her rural characters or from the literate and literary traditions of Western narrative forms. This consistency suggests that she is able to apply a method that she cultivates out of her own oral tradition to a modern, literate medium. This ability is significant because it represents an achievement that is often discussed but rarely achieved in African literature—the integration of traditional oral techniques with Western literary forms.

Lloyd W. Brown. *Women Writers in Black Africa*
(Westport, Conn.: Greenwood Press, 1981), pp. 84–85, 100–1

The play *Anowa* is set in what is now Ghana a hundred years ago, in about 1870. It tells the story of an exceptional woman who had an inquiring and willful mind, as well as insights and an understanding well beyond that of her peers. Neighbors said that she should have been apprenticed to the priestesses of the local cult; but since she was the only child of her parents, they hoped for a normal married life for her and a continuation of the family. Against her mother's wishes she willfully marries Kofi Ako, the young man of her own choice, and walks out of her parent's home swearing never to return. . . .

Anowa is a traditional tale, a legend of the Akan. Aidoo has returned to the folk story to find what might be meaningful in it for contemporary society. She brings to the story, as she considers it again, issues which she sees as crucial for any thinking African today: exploitation of men, of women; concepts of personal responsibility, in general, and of the intellectual in particular. Can the old tale particularize any of these issues? And once she has found meaning, she can then try to reach the form that will give that meaning substance. It is the very opposite to Sutherland's approach to the oral tradition.

Anowa must surely be one of the most profound African plays to have been written so far. And yet it is not popular, in my experience, even among students, especially men, who insist that Anowa herself is a witch and needs to be slapped by her husband. Ama Ata Aidoo's reputation as a dramatist rests upon her earlier and much less complex play, [*The*] *Dilemma of a Ghost*, which is about a young professional Ghanaian who returns from the United States with a black American wife. She is a child of slaves, say the women of the community, and they intend to shun her.

Michael Etherton. *The Development of African Drama* (London:
Hutchinson University Library for Africa, 1982), pp. 227–28, 237–38

In *No Sweetness Here*, [Aidoo] addresses the theme of the African and African-American relationship in the short story entitled "Other Versions." While the tale actually concerns the bond of love between a young Ghanaian student, Kofi, and his mother, who has been a significant influence in his being able to continue his education, the young man also comes to realize that he shares an affinity with black Americans and, even more, that many African-American women are of the same pattern as many African women: they are lovely in their selflessness, sharing, and caring.

The beginning of "Other Versions" recounts Kofi's unhappiness over his mother's insisting that he should give a portion of his money to his father whenever he receives any. Our protagonist believes that if anyone shared his money, it should be his mother because she is the one who has made all the sacrifices. But his mother never accepts money for herself. As the story progresses, Kofi is successful in his studies. Consequently, he is awarded a scholarship to America to further his education.

Shortly after arriving in the United States, he is invited by a white family for dinner. While at the home of this family, our narrator is jolted into the realization that he feels more akin to the black cook whom he meets when Mr. Merrow, his host, is taking the two of them home, than he does to the white family: "You know what sometimes your heart does? Mine did that just then. Kind of turned itself round in a funny way." Kofi achieves a shock of recognition.

His consciousness grows when, as the young student tells us on another occasion (perhaps the next evening or two), he is on his way home by subway. He sees another black woman and he associates her with the cook who had been in Mrs. Merrow's kitchen. The young Ghanaian says that he became confused but, at any rate, he put his hands in his pocket, took out his scholarship dollars, crumpled them up and passed them to her, saying: "Eh . . . eh . . . I come from Africa and you remind me of my mother. Please would you take this from me?" Just as his mother who had been so unselfish, the black woman motions him to sit down beside her and she says: "Son, keep them dollars, I sure know you need them more than I do." The young student then reflects: "Of course, she was mother. And so there was no need to see. But now I could openly look at her beautiful face." The story ends with the emphasis on the mother-son relationship, and although the young narrator says "there was no need to see," he *has* seen. He has recognized some specific commonalities between Africans and African-Americans.

Mildred A. Hill-Lubin. *PA*. 124 (1982), pp. 195–97

Our Sister Killjoy, like Aidoo's short stories, deals with so many problems. . . . [Its] success depends largely on the ability of the author to lend all the problems equal spikes. In that regard Ngugi [wa Thiong'o] and Sembène [Ousmane] come to mind—writers who are fully aware in their works that a campaign for social justice is meaningful only when all disadvantaged people in human society receive undiscriminating attention. It is that same principle which makes Aidoo's works feminist literature with a difference. . . .

The three major sections of *Our Sister Killjoy* merge into each other in whorls. The concerns are the same and the examples used to support those concerns are similar as we shift from one geographical focus to the other. In the final major section, there is greater introspection because of the literary approach—a confrontational "love letter" from Sissie to an imaginary male partner. The letter suggests a way out of the morass—communication between man and woman. . . . Such dialogue based on a mutually comprehensible language would then form the secret springboard for the solution of *all* the spiritual and material problems bedeviling the black world.

Aidoo has dealt with women's problems with arresting wisdom and grace. The conservative dissenter and the radical sympathizer will probably find her approach stimulating. Aidoo's forte is her tremendous *feeling* and honesty of sentiment in expressing those issues. Her works ring like the unimpugnable scold of a justly aggravated parent. . . . Aidoo's identification extends beyond "underprivileged womanhood and the arrogance of manhood" to include a variety of social problems across geographical boundaries. Without doubt, like her feminist mouthpiece in her play, *Anowa*, Aidoo has learnt and heard that "in other lands a woman is nothing." Despite that knowledge, "everything counts" in the way she assembles her materials in her short stories and novel, *Our Sister Killjoy*, to register a feminism reasonably in tune with social realities.

Chimalum Nwankwo. In Carole Boyce Davies and Anne Adams Graves, eds.
Ngambika: Studies of Women in African Literature
(Trenton, N. J.: Africa World Press, 1986), pp. 155, 158

The Dilemma of a Ghost is a domestic comedy dramatizing the well-known literary theme of the cultural complex of the African been-to, that is, the African who has been overseas. Ato Yawson, the hero, a young Ghanaian man, returns home from America after his education with an Afro-American wife, and the problem that arises is that of reconciling his acquired Western way of life with that of his native home. By his education and marriage, Ato's life and that of his relations have become diametrical, and it becomes his responsibility to harmonize the two.

The two outstanding areas where conflict arises are the rites of stool veneration and the childbearing ideal of marriage perpetuated by Ato's relations. He can no longer regard these ideals in the same light as his relations, but even when he wants to pay lip service to them, his wife pulls him to the opposite stand. Moreover, he lacks enough tact to handle the situation, showing himself utterly unequal to the challenge. At the end of the play it is his mother who leads Eulalie, his wife, into the old section of the house while he remains dazed and unreconciled.

The physical setting reflects the opposing poles of the drama. It is an old family house with a new annex. The illiterate, traditionalist members of the family live in the old section while the annex is reserved for Ato, the new man. This device is not a mere dramatic fancy, but a true reflection of similar situations that arise in Ghanaian life. The ambivalence of the plot is dramatically clinched at the end of the play when Ato, in his bewilderment, is torn between going to the annex and going to the old section. This is symbolic of his inability to resolve his dilemma. Another device to dramatize the theme is the underlying dream-story of the ghost, derived from Fanti folklore, which parodies the story of Ato; for Ato has become a ghost, his true native personality having been negated by his Westernization.

Richard K. Priebe. Ghanaian Literatures
(New York: Greenwood Press, 1988), p. 178

[*Our Sister Killjoy*] traces the experience of Sissie, an African student in Europe. Her realization of the damage the West has inflicted on her culture is foregrounded in the text. At the end of the novel, Sissie returns from Europe to

Ghana, confident in her anti-Western nationalism, although she is stigmatized for her stance by her own peer group, who belong to a culturally disaffected, Westernized elite.

The second part of the novel is dominated by Aidoo's account of the friendship between Sissie and the German lesbian Marija. Although when Sissie first meets Marija it is immediately apparent that the German woman is married and has a child, it is also clear that Marija's approach to Sissie is neither casual nor disinterested. . . .

As the friendship grows, Aidoo indicates the comfort it offers Sissie, who is otherwise socially isolated in the West. In Marija's house Sissie talks about Africa, or each sits with [her] own thoughts. Marija gives Sissie plums from her garden, and Aidoo invests this gift with symbolic resonance. The physical appearance of the fruit is stressed, with their feminine shape and smoothness and skin color "almost like [Sissie's] own." . . . For Marija, the plums are a way of reaching Sissie, of touching her sensibility, and in their physical appearance, they are a homage. For Sissie the gift represents what the friendship gives more generally, a validation of female qualities in which she can find comfort and self-substantiation. . . .

Aidoo's account of a homosexual relationship differs from that in many African novels because it is so detailed and avoids a monothematic, pejorative treatment. It is closely related to the novel's primary thematic development, in that it shows Sissie—black and heterosexual—still able to maintain sympathy for Marija and to perceive common ground between Marija's position and her own. . . .

There are, then, two elements here: Sissie empathizing with Marija as female; Sissie seeing her own stigmatization reflected in Marija's. The relationship between these two factors is made clearer in the last section of the novel. Having been abandoned in London by a man she loves—and who loves her, but is alienated by her "anti-Western neurosis," Sissie comments: "I shall be lonely again. O yes, everyone gets lonely some time or other. After all, if we look closer into ourselves, shall we not admit that the warmth from other people comes so sweet to us when it comes, because we always carry with us the knowledge of the cold loneliness of death?" In the end Sissie's loneliness derives from her stigmatization not only by the West but, more damagingly, by her peers in her own society. Marija's loneliness, meanwhile, is that of a lesbian, who must seek relationships with other women outside the margins of her community. While Aidoo's approach is nonpejorative, it is predicated on the assumption that Marija's condition is a marked term, that it is defined by what, in the context of African literature, must be read as highly nonrepresentative characteristics. As for Sissie, the disadvantage she faces is more acute than that faced by a black man or even by a more representative black woman. She is a black woman isolated from her community because of her political convictions. Her loneliness is similar to Marija's then, in having a double origin, the result of a very narrowly determined condition.

Chris Dunton. *RAL*. 20, 3 (Fall 1989), pp. 431–34

There is much to be said for Ama Ata Aidoo's latest book, *Changes* [*A Love Story*], and the way in which she brings out the cultural complexities of this love story based in Ghana. Her heroine Esi brings to the fore the dilemmas faced by women whose education and Western influences conflict with their cultural background. The issues of marital rape, the struggle for independence, jealousy and tradition, are all featured in this [consciousness] raising novel. Yet while the story possesses all the ingredients for a riveting read, this is hindered by Aidoo's rather ponderous and cumbersome style, which prevents it from realizing its full potential.

Esi, a slim, attractive, well-educated woman, is clearly seen by her close friend and family to have made a drastic and foolish decision when she leaves her husband. The constant pressure he inflicts on her to leave the job she loves, have more children and become a "proper wife," represent some of the common dilemmas faced by the modern African woman. As a result, Esi feels suffocated and trapped, unable to make him understand her feelings. Aidoo tentatively raises the issue of marital rape, which prompts Esi's separation from her husband, but never really dwells on the subject. It is as if both Esi and the author realize that in an African society there could not possibly be an "indigenous word or phrase for it."

What Aidoo does tackle particularly well is the complexity and potential danger in trying to fuse modern ideas with traditional methods. When Esi later meets and falls in love with Ali, an intelligent, successful, and married man, she decides to become his second wife. Ironically it is her traditionalist family and friend who try to dissuade her, but to Esi the position of second wife appears to be the perfect way to continue her independent lifestyle as a career woman without the burden of a full-time husband and household to look after. Unfortunately as she later finds out, the reality of her situation is far different.

Bola Makanjuola. *WA*. April 1–7, 1991, p. 474

In 1985 the College Press of Zimbabwe published the first collection of Aidoo's poetry, *Someone Talking to Sometime*, which contains some of her older poems that have appeared in anthologies and other poetry collections and some new ones. The two parts of the collection—"Of Love and Commitment" and "Someone Talking to Sometime"—total forty-four poems. . . .

Someone Talking to Sometime reiterates various themes articulated in Aidoo's other works. In characteristic Aidoo fashion, criticism is blended with affirmation, and tragedy and pain are toned down with wit and humor. Political corruption is humorously depicted in "From the Only Speech That Was Not Delivered at the Rally": the insanity and collapse of order in contemporary Africa are suggested by the image of being overtaken "by / winter at the height of an / equatorial noon." Highly condemnatory poems, such as "Nation Building" and "A Salute to African Universities" and those in the "Routine Drug" sequence, are balanced by more affirmative poems—"Of Love and Commitment," "Lorisnrudi," and "For Kinna II." Aidoo employs a conversational style to lend humor to the essentially tragic nature of existence and to invest the poems with the enduring quality of the blues.

Ama Ata Aidoo has established herself as a versatile and impressive writer for adults, and she has also written stories and poetry for children [*The Eagle and the Chickens and Other Stories* and *Birds and Other Poems*]. Her most recent work, *Changes: A Love Story*, is a novel that presents a critical look at options in love and marriage for contemporary African women. Through the female character Esi, who is an educated, ambitious, career-oriented Ghanaian, Aidoo explores such issues as marital rape and career choices, and their impact on love and marital relationships, highlighting the role of compromise. She scrutinizes through fiction the age-old institutions of monogamy and polygamy.

Naana Banyiwa Horne. In Bernth Lindfors and Reinhard Sander, eds.
Dictionary of Literary Biography. 117 (1992), pp. 38–39

AMADI, ELECHI (1934–)

NIGERIA

Elechi Amadi's treatment of the supernatural is remarkable but not unique. Nearly all African novelists portray man as existing in mutual cooperation with other men, and in communion with the gods. This communion and cooperation between the human and the divine is important, and indeed, indispensable, for the realization of what [Wole] Soyinka describes as "cosmic totality," a relationship compounded by fellow men and supernatural essences, a relationship that is particularly vital for the African world-view.

However, in no other Nigerian novels have the gods been more dominant than in those of Amadi. Here the gods, uncanny, implacable, and ubiquitous, are not only an essence but a presence, woven as it were into every aspect of human relationship. In *The Concubine*, the sea-king intervenes even before the beginning of the story, and throughout remains the paramount but unseen force manipulating human life and orchestrating the painful course of men's tragic drama. The dreaded Ogbunabali breaks in halfway through *The Great Ponds*, and thereafter his power dominates human thought and action and pilots the very movement of the story. Consequently, in a vein reminiscent of early Greek tragedy and Victorian fiction, fatalism and its episodic surrogates of coincidence, omens, and premonitions loom large in the narrative.

Niyi Osundare. In Eldred Durosimi Jones, ed.
African Literature Today. 11 (1980), p. 97

Amadi's *The Slave* explores that which is central, relevant, and essential in the reclamation of black history and rehabilitation of black dignity, the presentation of a community pulsating with life of a self-sufficient and rich culture. . . .

In *The Slave*, form and content are both mutually expressive of the whole with the language as the abstract vehicle for expressing the myths, legends, art, and a whole way of life of a people. My interest is to see how Amadi presents through African aesthetics the complex interplay between the individual and his community. *The Slave* narrates the story of Olumati, grandson of the late village wrestling champion, Wakwakata, who returns to Aliji from Amadioha's shrine to reclaim his father's deserted inheritance. He struggles very hard to make a living and win recognition through palm-wine tapping and trapping. What success he experiences is largely due to the love of his sister Aleru, the constant help of his friend and brother-in-law Nyeche, and his own secret ambition to succeed and marry Enaa, the village beauty, whose *mgbede* or traditional seclusion parallels the duration of the novel. Aleru dies in her first pregnancy and sorrow devastates her brother and husband alike. His handicaps are many, and the last straw for Olumati is to learn of Enaa's betrothal to the village carver, Wizo, at the *mgbede* outing. Heartbroken and disconsolate, Olumati gives up the struggle and flees back to Amadioha's shrine at Isiala.

Amadi's language as vehicle for articulating the artifacts of a rich culture exhibits a remarkable fresh and symbolic texture, full of imagery, allusions to legends, to gods, feasts and festivals. . . .

Art in African aesthetics gives concreteness to religious beliefs and attitudes. Art in all its forms: music, dancing, carving, painting, and decorating are all collective and utilitarian, expressing collective emotions, enhancing the communal and corporate, celebrating communal beauty and creativity, and together heightening the aesthetic quality of life. In *The Slave*, Amadi skillfully welds together all the artistic tendencies and creativity of his community around the unifying traditional rite of puberty or *mgbede*. Since marriage and procreation are so central to communal survival, it is little wonder that the entire community is involved with Enaa's *mgbede*. She is the image of African beauty: tall, stately, graceful, and a virgin. Nyeche, Eze Minikwe's son, who refuses Enaa because she is taller than him, admits that she is "a formidable girl, an Eze's daughter in style if not in fact."

Amadi is careful, not just to describe for us the beauty of *mgbede* but by weaving exciting natural dialogues between Enaa and the various visitors to her *mgbede* hut, we not only learn more about each character, but also through their eyes, gaze our fill at the intricate and delicate woman's world. Above all, the *mgbede* is but a physical symbol of communality. Enaa's girlfriends and age-mates have decorated the *mgbede*; age-mates of her brother have helped in rethatching the roof; everyone seems to have contributed gifts and food towards giving Enaa a two-year luxury treatment before marriage. In addition, the carver, Wizo, has spared no efforts nor talent in carving, free of charge, the best of stools and masks for Enaa's *mgbede*. . . .

African aesthetics becomes flesh and blood in Enaa. There is in her beauty a smoothness of skin, a joy of living, a lightness of heart, a grace and a style, that is in a special way African, superb in its uniqueness, excellent in its grandeur.

Ebele Keo. LitC. 23, 1–2 (1988), pp. 145–46, 148–49

The perpetual thwarting of man's most cherished desires and the disjunction between intention, action, and result; the role of chance and the gods in the affairs of men; man's mistaken understanding of his relationship with that which is other-than-man; and his helplessness before an overwhelming, blank, cosmos; these are the themes that all Elechi Amadi's three novels, *The Concubine*, *The Great Ponds*, and *The Slave*, explore. All three have the same large subject of past rural life in the southernmost part of Nigeria (the author's own area), a life that knew nothing about the white race. In this rural world, life is tranquil and moves on an even, traditional keel. But "even keel" only in the sense that it had yet to experience the disruptive presence of the missionary or colonist, for there abound frictions between one villager and another or a god, and between two neighboring villages. Except in the second novel, Amadi places such frictions within the fictional context of an unchanging universe.

The three novels are simple in construction, the stories told in the stark manner of mythical narratives. They convey the mystery at the core of human existence, once and for all foreclosed to man and always defeating his efforts at self-realization. This vision is manifested in the ironic plot of each novel and complemented by the enigmatic standpoint of the omniscient narrator. The cosmic blankness and the author's strict objectivity combine to limit any critic's effort at interpreting the novels; but if only for the evocation of pristine African life, their unusual thematic focus and ironic plots, Amadi's novels deserve more critical attention than they have so far received. Equally important is his smooth blending of elements from oral forms of narrative—myth, romance, folktale, legend—with that most characteristic mode of the novel, realism. . . .

Elechi Amadi's novels remain neglected and, when remembered, misinterpreted. If the neglect is understandable on account of their not contributing to the great debate on Africa's political present or future, the misinterpretation is harder to explain. In plot manipulation, narrative technique, and language, Amadi's art is a model of simplicity, while the stories themselves have the uncomplicated movement and clarity of daylight. Paradoxically, these qualities have misled his few critics into imposing their own, oftentimes arbitrary, meanings. No wonder that no two of Amadi's few critics agree on the meaning of any of his works.

Wole Ogundele. *WLWE*. 28, 2 (Autumn 1988), pp. 189–90

In Elechi Amadi's first two novels, *The Concubine* and *The Great Ponds*, myth enjoys only a haphazard relationship with history. Myth combines forcefully with mores to create an African ahistorical world that must delight every anthropological critic. . . .

One crucial aspect of Amadi's work that also deserves close attention is the activities of those ubiquitous beings in the traditional African landscape, the medicine men—recognized as *dibias* in the Igbo world-view. Their absence would vitiate the power of any claims to the ambience of a traditional African society. . . . In *The Great Ponds* and *The Concubine* these *dibias* live up to their position in traditional African societies. They attempt always to reinforce in various ways the occult vitality in nature, especially when human life is at stake. It is in these efforts that we also sometimes find those disagreeable elements that readers find unacceptable in Amadi's works.

There is something about Amadi's not talking about errors of government in his first two novels. This is not to say that there is something intrinsically wrong in an artist adopting that posture; however, sometimes (because of the nature of subject matter) it becomes imperative for an artist to recognize the necessity for some kind of ideological matrix or historicity in favor of the society whose mores are being represented. With reference to Amadi's *dibias*, the degree to which they succeed in manipulating nature and the critical and derisive comments attendant on their visions, practices, and failures suggest a certain kind of artistic levity with negative effects on the pictures being painted. Even though everything points to the practices of these *dibias* being cosmologically related to the outlook of the society, their exposure to crucial circumstances that challenge the veracity of their practices would not recommend them positively to any reader's judgement.

Chimalum Nwankwo. In A. L. McLeod, ed. Subjects Worthy Fame
(New Delhi: Sterling Publishers, 1989), pp. 88, 91

Many critics have underlined Amadi's mastery of the English language and his skill in representing the supernatural in his novels. But few have studied the interaction between theme and style. Amadi's first three novels are set in traditional Africa before the coming of the white man. The supernatural is often introduced as one of the possible causes for the mysterious events that take place. Yet there is always more than one possible interpretation. Doubts remain concerning the natural, supernatural, rational, or irrational nature of the causes for these happenings. The reader has difficulty choosing between different explanations. . . .

It may appear that the notions of fantasy and realism are antithetical for the very reason that fantasy allows for the presence of doubts and maintains some hesitation in the reader, while "realism" aims at stating some "truth." Yet, if we take the example of Amadi's novels, fantasy and realism are not incompatible. The writer merely diversifies the values and meanings of the world he describes, thus multiplying levels of reading. Amadi works from the inside and leaves the reader free to pick up the contradictions and ambiguities in the events presented to him. Through using realism, he prevents the reader from relegating the characters to mere objects of superstition. In fact realism conditions the reader's hesitation between the natural and the supernatural. . . . Amadi does not try to make a stand against the rational skepticism of any reader. Instead he tries to present events as they appear to the characters in the society and at the moment in time concerned. He allies realism and fantasy and, thanks to the coherence of his style and themes, creates the illusion of the plausible.

Alfred Kiema. CE&S. 12, 2 (Spring 1990), pp. 86, 89–90

Sunset in Biafra is a personal account of [Amadi's] experiences as a detainee during the [Nigerian Civil War], having been branded a saboteur and imprisoned by the Biafran forces. Through his chronicle we are provided a portrait of the experiences of non-Igbo minorities residing in Biafra: the repression, the abuses, the dangers of being too slow and unenthusiastic to embrace the cause. Whereas Amadi's civil war diary basically portrays the secessionist leaders as a militarily incompetent and intransigent group leading young Igbos to their slaughter, his portrait certainly seems to legitimize the horror which appears as a backdrop in [Flora] Nwapa's works.

The fear of voicing one's opinions about the war because of the threat of detention, of being branded a saboteur—the experience of the protagonist in Nwapa's *Never Again*—was only too real for Amadi. . . . The abuses that civilians suffered occurred on both sides of the conflict, and in the aftermath of the war, somehow lives had to be pieced together again, if at all possible. This concern is the theme of Amadi's civil war novel *Estrangement*.

The backdrop for this novel is the early days after the war has ended and Nigerians are returning to the cities they had fled earlier. Although the defeat of Biafra is not mentioned, we know by reference the historical context for the novel. *Estrangement* is a love story played out in the ruins not only of cities and villages but of lives irreparably damaged during those thirty months. A husband returns to Port Harcourt from refuge in Biafra only to find that his wife has been involved with a soldier and has given birth to this other man's child. The permanent estrangement that occurs when the husband rejects his wife is symbolic of the gulf between the pre- and postwar lives. For although each searches for a familiar place in previously abandoned homes, picking up where they left off is virtually impossible. Too much has changed the players in the drama. . . .

Although much of the novel reflects the efforts of ordinary people getting back to business as usual, for Ibekwe and Alekiri, their lives will not cross again. The activity of those surrounding them as well as their own efforts to salvage the rest of their lives apart from each other only heightens the gulf that wartime circumstances created, a permanent estrangement.

Maxine Sample. MFS. 37, 3 (Autumn 1991), pp. 452–53

ANGELOU, MAYA (1928–   )

UNITED STATES

Maya Angelou's autobiography [*I Know Why the Caged Bird Sings*] . . . opens with a primal childhood scene that brings into focus the nature of the imprisoning environment from which the self will seek escape. The black girl child is trapped within the cage of her own diminished self-image around which interlock the bars of natural and social forces. The oppression of natural forces, of physical appearance and processes, foists a self-consciousness on all young girls who must grow from children into women. . . . The self-critical process is incessant, a driving demon. But in the black girl child's experience these natural bars are reinforced with the rusted iron social bars of racial subordination and impotence. Being born black is itself a liability in a world ruled by white standards of beauty which imprison the child a priori in a cage of ugliness. . . . I'm my own mistake. I haven't dreamed myself hard enough. I'll try again. The black and blue bruises of the soul multiply and compound as the caged bird flings herself against these bars. . . . If the black man is denied his potency and his masculinity, if his autobiography narrates the quest of the black male after a "place" of full manhood, the black woman is denied her beauty and her quest is one after self-accepted black womanhood. Thus the discovered pattern of significant moments Maya Angelou superimposes on the experience of her life is a pattern of moments that trace the quest of the black female after a "place," a place where a child no longer need ask self-consciously, "What you looking at me for?" but where a woman can declare confidently, "I am a beautiful, black woman.". . .

Maya Angelou's autobiography comes to a sense of an ending: the black American girl child has succeeded in freeing herself from the natural and social bars imprisoning her in the cage of her own diminished self-image by assuming control of her life and fully accepting her black womanhood. The displaced child has found a "place." With the birth of her child Maya is herself born into a mature engagement with the forces of life. In welcoming that struggle she refuses to live a death of quiet acquiescence. . . .

Once [Angelou] accepted the challenge of recovering the lost years, she accepted the challenge of the process of self-discovery and reconfirmed her commitment to life's struggle. By the time she, as autobiographer, finished remembering the past and shaping it into a pattern of significant moments, she had imposed some sense of an ending upon it. And in imposing that ending upon it, she gave the experience distance and a context and thereby came to understand the past and ultimately to understand herself. . . .

Her genius as a writer is her ability to recapture the texture of the way of life in the texture of its idioms, its idiosyncratic vocabulary and especially in its process of image-making. The imagery holds the reality, giving it immediacy. That she chooses to re-create the past in its own sounds suggests to the reader that she accepts the past and recognizes its beauty and its ugliness, its assets and its liabilities, its strength and its weakness. Here we witness a return to and final acceptance of the past in the return to and full acceptance of its language, the language a symbolic construct of a way of life. Ultimately Maya Angelou's style testifies to her reaffirmation of self-acceptance, the self-acceptance she achieves within the pattern of the autobiography.

Sidonie Ann Smith. SHR. 7 (Fall 1973), pp. 367–68, 374–75

In many ways, *I Know Why the Caged Bird Sings* resembles Richard Wright's *Black Boy*. The setting is a small segregated town in the rural South; the parents have sent the children to live with relatives, one of whom owns a general store; Maya and her brother are forced to attend church, where they amuse themselves by making fun of the more zealous members of the congregation; the preacher comes to dinner and eats all the chicken; there is constant friction between the blacks and the poor whites; the fact of her oppression gradually intrudes on the writer's consciousness when she observes what happens around her—the hypocritical speeches of the white superintendent in their segregated school, the refusal of a white dentist to fix her teeth after her grandmother had salvaged his business; her brother helps fish a decomposed Negro body out of the pond while whites stand around and tell malicious jokes; the local sheriff gives them casual warnings whenever the Klan is about to go on a rampage; and finally, she migrates to a Northern city. Maya Angelou's complex sense of humor and compassion for other people's defects, however, endow her work with a different quality of radiance; she does not have Wright's mortal seriousness, or his estrangement, and does not take his risks. . . .

The distance in Maya Angelou's work is achieved by her sense of humor. She has the power of joking at herself, of re-creating the past in a comic spirit without belittling the other people involved and of capturing the pathetic and tragic overtones of the laughter without being overwhelmed by them. Frightened of a ghost story about the dead Mrs. Taylor, a woman who had always screamed her orders in the store because she was half deaf, Angelou remarks, "the thought of that voice coming out of the grave and all the way down the hill from the cemetery and hanging over my head was enough to straighten my hair." As in Langston Hughes, the humor is often a way of shattering racist images by using them. She knows that the "superstitious" dread Negroes are supposed to have for graveyards is the butt of racist jokes and has felt the perpetual torture of trying to make her hair conform to white standards of beauty; both experiences are subdued, and controlled, by the comic purpose. It is the fear, and the author's ability to laugh at her insecurities, that we remember most—the caged bird's mastery of her song.

Stephen Butterfield, *Black Autobiography in America*
(Amherst: University of Massachusetts Press, 1974), pp. 203, 209

When Maya Angelou started her autobiographical series in 1970 with *I Know Why the Caged Bird Sings*, she naturally chose her childhood as the organizing principle of her first volume. The story of *Caged Bird* begins when the three-year-old Angelou and her four-year-old brother, Bailey, are turned over to the care of their paternal grandmother in Stamps, Arkansas, and it ends with the birth of her son when she is seventeen years old. The next two volumes, *Gather Together in My Name* and *Singin' and Swingin' and Gettin' Merry Like Christmas*, narrate Angelou's life along chronological lines for the most part, and one would expect that her most recent addition to the autobiographical sequence, *The Heart of a Woman*, would proceed with the account of her career as entertainer, writer, and freedom fighter. In many ways, Angelou meets her readers' expectations as she follows her life forward chronologically in organizing the newest segment in the series. Yet it is interesting to note that at the beginning of *The Heart of a Woman*, as she continues the account of her son's youth, she returns to the story of her own childhood repeatedly. The references to her childhood serve partly to create a textual link for readers who might be unfamiliar with the earlier volumes and partly to emphasize the suggestive similarities between her own childhood and that of her son. Maya Angelou's overwhelming sense of displacement and instability is, ironically, her son's burden too. . . .

In *The Heart of a Woman*, Angelou deliberately strives to capture the individual conversational styles of her relatives and friends. In a sense, her friends and acquaintances become "characters" in the story of her life, and like any good writer of fiction, she attempts to make their conversations realistic and convincing. With some of the people who figure in her autobiography, there is no objective measure for credibility other than the reader's critical appreciation for life itself. If the conversant in question is not well-known beyond the scope of the autobiography, Angelou need only ensure that the dialogue attributed to the individual be consistent with his character as delineated in the text itself. Yet many of her friends and associates were either highly successful celebrities or popular political figures, and the conversations recorded in her life story have points of reference beyond the autobiographical text. In other words, readers can test the degree of verisimilitude in the recorded dialogues with either firsthand knowledge or secondhand sources of information about the celebrities' lives.

It is highly probable, for example, that many of Angelou's readers are already familiar with the rhetorical styles of Martin Luther King, Jr., and Malcolm X, and the popular lyrics of Billie Holliday. In fact the lives of these three people in such accounts as *Why We Can't Wait, The Autobiography of Malcolm X*, and *Lady Sings the Blues* have in many ways become part of our contemporary folk history. Angelou adds a personalized quality to her recollections of conversations with these individuals and many others. The record of their conversations in *The Heart of a Woman* brings them to life again, because the autobiographer is sensitive to and even somewhat self-conscious about the accurate reconstruction of their individual styles.

Since memory is not infallible, fictionalization comes into play whenever the autobiographer reconstructs or, perhaps more correctly, re-creates conversation. While the autobiographer relies on invention, he or she creates the illusion of an infallible memory that records exactly the feel of a place and the words spoken there.

Carol E. Neubauer. BALF. 17, 3 (Fall 1983), pp. 123–25

The first three days Angelou spends in Ghana serve as a microcosm for the dream-nightmare opposition at work in the book [*All God's Children Need Traveling Shoes*] as a whole. In 1962, at the age of thirty-three, Angelou and her seventeen-year-old son Guy arrive in Accra full of expectations. Suddenly, tragedy scuttles Guy's plans to begin attending the University of Ghana and Angelou's intentions to go on to a job in Liberia. . . . As a result Angelou stays in Ghana to care for Guy, getting a job as an administrative assistant at the university. *All God's Children* describes the two years she spent in Ghana before leaving to take a position as a coordinator for Malcolm X's Organization of Afro-American Unity.

Two major topics dominate the book: first, the Afro-American expatriate community's relations with both Africans and the Black Movement in the United States; second, Angelou's personal quest for connection with Africa. The two topics occasion the use of a number of romantic images. . . . Angelou spends most of her time with the Afro-American community, whom she calls the

"Revolutionary Returnees." These Afro-Americans view Africa romantically, as a home, a heaven, and a mother. For example, because of their African descent, the Returnees believe they have a filial claim to Africa. . . . However, very early in the book the possibility that the expatriates are living in a dream world, having to invent connections with Africans rather than actually experiencing them is suggested: "We had come home, and if home was not what we had expected, never mind, our need for belonging allowed us to ignore the obvious and to create real places or even illusory places, befitting our imagination." . . .

Thus it seems that the connection Angelou and other Afro-Americans in Ghana have sought will not be realized, that she will depart from Africa disillusioned and alienated. . . . But then, right before leaving, she has an experience that reverses everything. While driving near Keta, Angelou has presentiments of something strange attaching to the region. She refuses to drive over a bridge and later learns that bridges in the area a hundred years previously were so poorly constructed that many people lost their lives because of them. A little further on a woman addresses her in Ewe, begins to wail upon learning that Angelou is an American, and shows her to other women who react the same way when they hear where she is from. Not only do Angelou's face and voice resemble those of people in the area, but during the slave trade some of the inhabitants of the region were transported to the New World. Angelou clearly believes that the elusive connection has at last been made: "I had not consciously come to Ghana to find the roots of my beginnings, but I had continually and accidentally tripped over them or fallen upon them in my everyday life." This realization comes just in the nick of time, for her stay in Ghana and the book itself end soon afterward. Angelou closes *All God's Children* with sentences that imply that her romantic quest for an African homeland has been successful: "Many years earlier I, or rather someone very like me and certainly related to me, had been taken from Africa by force. This second leave-taking would not be so onerous, for now I knew my people had never completely left Africa."

Although not a lie . . . this ending seems too easily manufactured at the last minute to resolve the problem of the book. The fact that Afro-Americans came from Africa was never in question. Angelou and other black Africans journeyed to Africa to establish viable and ongoing connections; despite Angelou's memorable epiphany at Keta, this is not accomplished. . . . Angelou experiences disillusionment and alienation in Africa. However, instead of stressing the nightmare side of Africanist discourse as her predecessors do, Angelou represses these feelings, refuses to relinquish her romantic image of Africa, and opts for the dream side of Africanist discourse.

John C. Gruesser. BALF. 24, 1 (Spring 1990), pp. 15–16, 18

A study of the work of Maya Angelou, autobiographer and poet, shows how the writer uses autobiography to define her quest for human individuality, identifying her personal struggle with the general condition of black Americans and claiming a representative role not only in relation to black Americans, but also in relation to the idea of America. Thus, through a study of her work, one gains a closer access to American cultural history. I find no precedent in American letters for the role Angelou has chosen and developed for herself. That is to say, I know of no American writer who has decided to make her or his major literary and cultural contribution so predominately in autobiographical form.

Through the device of autobiography, Angelou has celebrated the richness and vitality of Southern black life and the sense of community that persists in the face of poverty and racial prejudice, initially revealing this celebration through a portrait of life as experienced by a black child in the Arkansas of the 1930s (*I Know Why the Caged Bird Sings*). The second delineates a young woman struggling to create an existence that provides security and love in post-World War II America (*Gather Together in My Name*). The third presents a young, married adult in the 1950s seeking a career in show business and experiencing her first amiable contacts with whites (*Singin' and Swingin' and Gettin' Merry Like Christmas*). The fourth volume (*The Heart of a Woman*) shows a wiser, more mature woman in the 1960s, examining the roles of being a woman and a mother. In her most recent volume, Angelou demonstrates that *All God's Children Need Traveling Shoes* to take them beyond familiar borders and to enable them to see and understand the world from another's vantage point. . . .

Maya Angelou's significance as an autobiographer rests upon her exceptional ability to narrate her life story as a human being and as a black American woman in the twentieth century. In doing so, as one critic has observed, Angelou is performing for contemporary black and white Americans many of the same functions that an escaped slave like [Frederick] Douglass performed for nineteenth-century audiences through his autobiographical writings and lectures. This is [to] say, both Douglass and Angelou function as articulators of the nature and validity of the collective heritage as they interpret the particulars of a culture for a wide audience of both black and white Americans. Moreover, Angelou illuminates the black experience in an American context and in meaningful relation to the parallel and converging experiences of white Americans. In doing so, she provides her audiences with a fuller realization of the black American consciousness within the larger context and demonstrates that, as people who have lived varied and vigorous lives, black Americans embody the quintessential experiences of their race and culture.

Dolly A. McPherson. *Order Out of Chaos: The Autobiographical Works of Maya Angelou* (New York: Peter Lang, 1990), pp. 5–6, 128–29

It was the culmination of a number of factors at the end of the 1960s that led to the outpouring of writings by Afro-American women. First, the inherent shortcomings of the nationalism of the Black Power Movement; second, the increased social and economic pressures that led to the rapid deterioration of the urban centers of America; third, the rise of the feminist movement that made Afro-American women more conscious of their particularity; and, fourth, the increasing tensions in black male-female relations. . . . All of these factors led to a special kind of problematic to which the Afro-American woman had to address herself, adding a new and dynamic dimension to American literature. . . .

It is out of these conditions and in response to these specific concerns that Maya Angelou offered her autobiographical statements: *I Know Why the Caged Bird Sings, Gather Together in My Name, Singin' and Swingin' and Gettin' Merry Like Christmas, The Heart of a Woman,* and *All God's Children Need Traveling Shoes.* Although her last two works examine the manner in which the events of the 1960s impacted upon her life, they were produced in a time when some of the social and political fervor of the 1970s had abated and thus allowed for a more sober assessment. Needless to say, the political currents of the time are more prominent in the last two segments of her statement. As a statement, Angelou presents a powerful, authentic, and profound signification of Afro-American life and the changing concerns of the Afro-American woman in her quest for personal autonomy, understanding, and love. Such a statement, because of the simple, forthright, and honest manner in which it is presented, is depicted against the larger struggle of Afro-American and African peoples for their liberation and triumphs. It is a celebration of the struggle, survival, and existence of Afro-American people.

Selwyn R. Cudjoe. In Henry Louis Gates, Jr., ed. *Reading Black, Reading Feminist* (New York: Meridian, 1990), pp. 284–85

ANTHONY, MICHAEL (1932–   )

TRINIDAD

It is now over ten years since Michael Anthony, then resident in Europe though a native of Trinidad, wrote *The Year in San Fernando.* That novel matters wherever Commonwealth literature is discussed and has made Anthony quintessentially the novelist of growing-up. In *The Games Were Coming* and *Green Days by the River,* he looked further into the processes of maturation. In all three novels the uncertainties of childhood and adolescence are placed in a community split socially and racially, uncertain whether its future is rural or metropolitan. An awareness of landscape is an integral part of Michael Anthony's descriptive method—look at the seasonally changing Mount Naparaima which features in the first two novels—[but] his central interest always focuses on the frail consciousness of the child himself. . . .

Anthony's attitude to the family is important not just in *The Games Were Coming* but in the two other novels as well. Each of the novels concerns a fundamentally affectionate family, and in this way contrasts with the more unloving parent-child relationship of the short story "Drunkard of the River," in which young Sona loathes his foul-mouthed father. Even there Anthony stresses, through the absence of a right relationship, the value to an individual of a happy home life. *The Year in San Fernando* can be read as an evaluation of a home background. A child who is well integrated into his family finds himself suddenly deprived of his security by being sent from his small village to the city of San Fernando. During the year he spends there he is really seeking to re-establish the security he has lost. . . .

To speculate on a writer's future development is seldom valuable. There is, however, one feature in *Green Days by the River* which is more marked than in the previous novels, and that is the attention to racial distinctions. Rosalie is, after all, a "dougla girl, the slang everyone used for people who were half Indian and half Negro." Mr. Gidharee is Indian and Shellie [is] Creole. Anthony has said: "I don't want to write any race novels, I just don't want to. It's not in my nature. I feel that race novels usually carry the banner of trying to solve the problem." Sociological conclusions have never been part of his equipment in writing a novel; indeed, the subtlety of his art resides partly in the very absence of stated judgments. Nevertheless, there is enough evidence of an interest in the social side of Trinidadian life—the racial groups, the drifting youth, the piety of simple people and the indifference of those who are more sophisticated, even the state of hospitals in Port of Spain—to suggest that if Michael Anthony feels refreshed by his return to the Caribbean after many years' residence in England, he will perhaps direct his perceptions towards the contemporary affairs of his island.

Alastair Niven. *CE&S.* 2 (1976), pp. 45–46, 51, 61–62

Cricket in the Road [*and Other Stories*] is important for understanding Anthony's work because it provides insight into his art and his views on the task of the writer and his relationship with his work. No critic disputes the fact of the predominance of the use of a child or an adolescent as the narrator. [Paul] Edwards and [Kenneth] Ramchand see this as producing a "peculiarly 'open' state of consciousness" which brings about the fusion of unusually disparate elements of experience. This forces the reader to live the experiences of the narrator and creates intensity. . . .

Another aspect of Anthony's art made manifest in this book is his preoccupation with the idea of belonging and the need to appreciate one's surroundings. This feature is not readily discernible since it is couched in what seems to be an extolling of the virtues of living in the country as opposed to the town. In "Sandra Street" the beauty and freedom of this section of the street, where fowls can run wild and the hills can be admired, are revealed to the boy, Steve, by the teacher. The boy in "The Valley of Cocoa," in whom the laborer Willis had fostered a longing for the city, comes to appreciate his valley even more after the machinery salesman compared city and country lifestyles. . . . The message becomes crystallized in "The Holiday by the Sea" which deals with the relationship established between the countryboy Joe and the doctor from Port-of-Spain. At first the doctor is "enchanted by the idyllic scene around him" and both he and Joe are in their element; but the former soon becomes fed up and longs for his office. The fact is that he is as out of place here as Joe is when, innocent to the fact that the doctor's affair with Mayaro was temporary, he visits the latter in his office: "Joe cut such a ridiculous figure that the young doctor could hardly believe his eyes. And yet this was the same child that had fitted in so well with Mayaro by the sea. At this moment, with the doctor's head filled with medical problems, Mayaro was only a dream, in spite of the boy sitting there."

Dexter Noël. *IFR.* 5 (1978), pp. 61–62

[In *Green Days by the River*] life for Shellie and his harassed parents is severe and even cruel at times. In Anthony's fiction life does not resemble what one commentator thinks is a characteristic of West Indian life—"easy-going, happy-go-lucky, laissez faire." Rather, the pragmatic businessman of the short story, "The Patch of Guava," is speaking for several of Anthony's men and women when he says: "This world is blood and sweat and pressure, not poetry." . . . Anthony's men and women cannot be weak or fragile if they are to survive. Anthony has drawn several examples of the strong character. Of these, three are particularly engaging. The drunkard's wife in "Drunkard of the River" is constantly victimized by her husband's brutalities. Nevertheless, every Saturday night she courageously waits for his coming. In time she ages prematurely; but still she perseveres. The source of her strength is her indefatigable love for a man who "had only turned out badly." In "The Distant One" another sturdy mother is the family's bulwark against threatening poverty. While her son is away in England trying to make his fortune, she resolutely keeps the family together. When it becomes clear that the son, from whom much relief is expected, will never return to salvage the family, her response is characteristically resolute: "Okay, let him stay there. We'll live without him." Like Ruben's mother, in [Earl] Lovelace's *While Gods Are Falling*, she is deserted by her husband and left "alone to battle with the children in this town." When her son is arrested for murder, she can only shake a defiant fist at what seems to be a malevolent world. In 1955 the BBC's "Caribbean Voices" accepted Anthony's first short story, "The Girl and the River." It is certainly one of his finest pieces, and the girl is an excellent example of the sort of strong personality we have been noticing. The story is reminiscent of [William] Wordsworth's "Resolution and Independence." In both poem and story the central figure resists the hardships of living with a doggedness that stuns the narrator. There are other interesting parallels. Anthony's ageless ferryman (the ferry "had been plying the wide river even before the village itself sprang up, in those remote times when men said the river was too wide to take a bridge") reminds us of Wordsworth's equally aged leech-gatherer. Both narrators, seeking solitude and respite from troublesome thoughts, accidentally encounter the central figures. In Anthony's story Mr. Danclar is ostracized by the village, and as his bridge nears completion, insomnia and dejection attack him. Both narrators, we notice, come upon the central figures in lonely, isolated, and austerely beautiful settings. The severity of the leech-gatherer's life matches the girl's (and her father's) equally hard life. The building of the bridge has deprived the girl's father of his job as ferryman, and she is forced to join him in the languid isolation of Ortoire. Anthony stresses the girl's poverty; but his interest is largely in her admirable perseverance, her gentle acceptance of her hard lot, her infectious sympathy for her father's depression, her stoicism. Noticing the huge heap of clothes she must wash by hand in the stream Mr. Danclar, rather astonished, asks: "You could do all this today?" "Might, but if not, I'll have to come back tomorrow," she replies with a dry matter-of-factness. The severity of the girl's life ("I did not know that she washed other people's clothes so that she and her father could live!") gives Mr. Danclar much pause. It may even have made him less complacent. Wordsworth's narrator, we remember, is shocked to find in "that decrepit man so firm a mind." Anthony has shown us a young woman of equally firm mind tenaciously and cheerfully surviving.

Harold Barratt. *ACLALSB*. 5, 3 (1980), pp. 66–67

In any discussion of the challenges and achievements of the English-language fiction of the West Indies, one writer to whom few would deny a place is Michael Anthony. His short stories and novels have been praised for their clear yet evocative style, believable characterization, and realistic dialogue, and he has been compared to Nadine Gordimer because of his "scrupulous regard for the truth." Although recognized for his sensitive depiction of the landscape and people of Trinidad, his native land, Anthony is not a regional writer in the narrow sense of the term. He is, rather, a writer at times able to convey the general significance of the particular: "His memory-sharpened evocations of particular place and time verify some basic, universal truths of the human condition."

Several of Anthony's early works have given him some claim to fame in an area of fiction especially important in the West Indies, the fiction of childhood. More than a description of youthful adventures and escapades, the literature of childhood records the emotional growth of a young person becoming increasingly aware not simply of himself as an individual but also of his ethnic or national identity. Moreover, the account of a youth's maturation may be presented as a microcosmic counterpart to a broader development—the awakening of a whole society to its cultural identity. . . . [To] chart Anthony's movement towards an expanded awareness of his responsibility as a West Indian writer, one needs to gain a clear picture of the relationship between his earlier fiction, that of the 1950s and 1960s, and the works published in the 1970s, especially his most recent novel, *Streets of Conflict*, in which racial tension is so crucial. Specifically, it is important to discover why the view of reality conveyed in Anthony's highly regarded works dealing with childhood and adolescence has given way to the flawed vision of reality in *Streets*, which a prominent student of West Indian literature has called a "half-hearted attempt at the themes of social and racial injustice," a "failure."

Richard I. Smyer. *WLWE*. 21, 1 (Autumn 1982), p. 148

There are . . . admirable qualities in Anthony's fiction. Not the least of these is the sensitivity of his characters. They are largely vulnerable people, sensitive to a fault, uncommonly imaginative, infectiously warm. Anthony is particularly interested in the sensitive youngster, and in his short stories he has drawn several fine examples as a sort of preparation for Shellie, the boy hero of *Green Days by the River*.

Dolphus, Leon Seal's brother [in *The Games Were Coming*], is the precursor of this type of sensitive youngster. He is precocious, imaginative, and perceptive, and his type can be found in many of Anthony's short stories. In "Enchanted Alley," for instance, we note the ease with which the boy narrator establishes rapport with the Indian vendors. His imagination is fired by the vibrant life of the street which calls up "feelings of things splendored and far away." In "The Valley of Cocoa" we meet young Kenneth who fills his days with dreams of Port-of-Spain. He, too, befriends adults with an ease that belies his age. Roy, the boy-narrator of "Hibiscus," endures his somewhat overbearing aunt with mature forbearance. He also possesses a wit we might expect in an older person. In *The Year in San Fernando*, Francis reacts to the city, which is constantly shifting and changing chameleonlike, with a delicate imagination. As he tells us about it, he manages to transform what is trite into something quite uncommon. Francis's ability to extract beauty from what is seemingly bland never cloys. At the peak of the cane crop the sun and the relentless fires of burning cane blister the city, but even in this time of heat and irritability Francis finds and is touched by the beauty of the fires. And when the heavy rains of the wet season pound the city, he is able to extract from this disconcerting season the quiet beauty no one seems to notice. Francis reminds us of young Steve in the short story, "Sandra Street." Steve comes to see a strange enchantment in the hills around him. Even mango blossoms lose their triteness and become "rain-picked flowers."

Green Days by the River is an in-depth examination of a sensitive youngster's development from innocence to maturity. As an innocent in Eden, Shellie is particularly receptive to the changing moods of his idyllic world, and everything, even the most trite event in nature, thrills his sensitive heart. He is an affectionate, easily moved young man. He also shares his mother's volatile emotions, but when she rushes home to greet his father, who has been hospitalized, he shows a restraint and understanding that emphasize his sensitivity. . . .

There is, finally, the excellence of Anthony's prose. It is a prose of compelling sparseness. Sometimes it is an emotionally charged prose; but it is never glib or slick. Anthony writes a supple prose which is often characterized by a nice blending of tone, rhythm, and idea. If we regard a writer's control of language as one of his most valuable gifts, then *The Games Were Coming* is Anthony's finest novel because his control is sure and unflagging. In this novel Anthony, we may say, sets out to match his hero's self-discipline with his own artistic discipline. Although Anthony's prose has the rhythm of conversational speech, it has the tightness of poetry as well. The clarity and simplicity of his prose also remind us of [Ernest] Hemingway's, and indeed *A Farewell to Arms* seems to have acted as a sort of fictional catalyst for Anthony. This novel moved him deeply, and he set out to write a prose as lucid as Hemingway's. But Anthony's is not a derivative prose. It is essentially his. Nor does he try to express himself like anyone else.

Harold Barratt. *Bim.* 66–67 (1983), pp. 161–62

All That Glitters is simultaneously a detective novel and a novel about youth along similar lines to *The Year in San Fernando* and *Green Days by the River*. In addition, by introducing the notion of "open consciousness" into the detective format, Anthony radically reshapes the elements of detective fiction to fit his personal vision. He also challenges many of the social assumptions of the predominantly British classic mystery novel by subjecting them to a distinctively West Indian perspective and lays bare the spiritual weaknesses of the colonial system and its legacy in Trinidad. He capably resolves not one but two puzzles which he poses in the classic tradition, and the detective novel elements unquestionably play a major role in the work as a whole. . . .

As the title suggests, the themes that are illuminated through Anthony's puzzle resolutions are related to the old expression "All that glitters is not gold." Anthony refurbished the expression by exploring its multiple implications, some of which are obvious but many of which are not. His novel thus makes a profound search for enduring values, attempting to separate the merely glittering from the truly golden in society. . . .

Given the elaborate patterning of both plot and theme in Anthony's novel, there seems little room left for the open consciousness that was so refreshing in his previous books about boys, yet enough remains to give a touch of both originality and complexity far beyond that of the majority of classic mysteries (though in line with that of the best hardboiled mysteries and of many other experimental mysteries). This originality and complexity, along with the considerable technical skill and wisdom displayed throughout, provides the reader with a golden experience to ponder when all the glittering plots of Sir Arthur Conan Doyle or even Agatha Christie have been put aside as shallow.

Steven R. Carter. JWIL. 2 (1987), pp. 43–44, 46, 48–49

Michael Anthony has written five novels, numerous short stories, books for children, and assorted histories of Trinidad and Tobago. His fiction is widely read as prescribed texts at all levels of education, and he has made a major contribution to the remarkable emergence of a distinctive and vibrant West Indian literature. Examining the lives of those who survive in poverty and hopelessness, he shows candor and a sensitive understanding of their silent desperation, and he explores areas sometimes considered too banal for serious literary treatment. Anthony's best work shows a finely tuned understanding of his native society. . . .

Anthony is particularly interested in the growing consciousness of sensitive youngsters, and he has created several. Dolphus in *The Games Were Coming*, for instance, is a precursor of the type that Shellie in *Green Days by the River* more fully embodies. Dolphus is hypersensitive to the throbbing life around him, and Anthony conveys the excitement of the carnival and the coming games largely through Dolphus's sensibilities and resourceful imagination. At one point Dolphus recognizes that one must "suffer to become pure." An equally imaginative youngster, Alan, son of staid parents, appears in Anthony's *King of the Masquerade*, which, although written for children, is a trenchant defense of the carnival and an attack on the pretensions of Trinidad's middle class. . . .

Several reviewers adopted severe and patronizing attitudes toward Anthony's work in the mid-1960s. Since then, more perceptive critics have noted the quality of his uncluttered prose and his valuable explorations of the physical and metaphysical contours of his society.

Harold Barratt. In Bernth Lindfors and Reinhard Sander, eds.
Dictionary of Literary Biography. 125 (1993), pp. 4, 6–7

ANYIDOHO, KOFI (1947–   )

GHANA

The creative writing clubs established in secondary schools and training colleges across Ghana in the 1960s, and the new avenue provided by public
readings and recitals of poetry have together contributed to the emergence of
many new poetic voices in Ghana. One of the most notable is the winner of the
first prize in the 1976 VALCO Literary Awards contest, Kofi Anyidoho. Like
Kofi Awoonor, an Ewe, Anyidoho has absorbed much traditional Ewe poetry;
but they both constitute extensions of that mode, for their individual stamp is
discernible in their verse. In the case of Anyidoho, this is represented by a
toughness of texture, an ability to explore variations of a single theme. . . .

Anyidoho's is poetry of the speaking voice. More than Awoonor but definitely less than [E. Y.] Egblewogbe, he reveals a tendency to the elegiac. . . .
The theme of death and destruction is pervasive; the mood is predominantly
gloomy, the tone somber. But Anyidoho's treatment of funereal themes does
incorporate sometimes a critical detachment from the subject, a hint almost of
macabre humor and satire. . . .

Even in poems with foreign settings, Anyidoho shows little joy. Invariably,
we are given tragic forebodings, a sadly depleted patrimony, the agony of a wanderer struggling to get back home. . . . Anyidoho leaves an impression of
moroseness, although he is not as fatalistic as Egblewogbe. He lacks Awoonor's
occasional explosions of joy, even in his lighthearted excursions into abuse.

Jawa Apronti. In Kolawole Ogungbesan, ed.
New West African Literature (London: Heinemann, 1979), pp. 40–41

Kofi Anyidoho's letters from America are now reprinted as "My Mailman
Friend Was Here," part four of *A Harvest of Our Dreams*, his second volume of
verse which Heinemann [has] recently issued. The book confirms one's impression of his stature. Anyidoho returned from America more than a year ago, was
in London in November, but his chosen abode, his own plot of rootedness, is
Ghana, where he now lectures in the English department at Legon. More precisely, however, it is Wheta, that village of talent which, in the Volta region,
nudges Keta into the sea. It is here that his art begins, and, so he would have us
believe, ends. . . .

Anyidoho belongs to a generation which has lived to see its political hopes
betrayed again and again, by Kwame Nkrumah (who remains a beguiling memory)
by [Colonel I. K.] Acheampong, possibly even by [Jerry J.] Rawlings. It is in a
threadbare Ghana that he must now ply his craft, drawing deep at wells of
disappointment fed, as he never ceases to remind us, by ancient springs. If Ayi
Kwei Armah is the prose chronicler of Ghana's decline, Anyidoho is its pallbearer.
The poignancy of his accompanying dirge is at times almost unbearable. . . .

This volume contains three principal groups of poems. "Elegy for the
Revolution," a sequence first published separately by the Greenfield Press in

1978, and here reprinted at the end of the book, recounts the fading hopes of the last years of the National Redemption Council. Immediately before it comes a group of poems from the [United States], many of them contrasting the Ghanaian and American revolutionary legacies, the dearth that lies at the foot of the Thanksgiving table.

Other revolutions make fleeting appearances, notably Iran's, thus occasioning an arguably misjudged salute to Khomenei. [It] is with the most recent pieces, however, that the volume begins, poems which address themselves to the current dilemma of a people plighting their last troth in a regime which has promised to pluck the talisman of regeneration even from the Devil's jaws. . . .

In the face of all discouragement, Anyidoho holds his vision steady. For behind the despair is a calm grounded on the bedrock of a tradition he will not forsake. And, if the future is hazy, here is a writer who knows that for him there is but one way through, guided by the elder poets of whose rippling chants *A Harvest of Our Dreams* can provide but a distant echo, dimmed by the perplexities of our time.

Robert Fraser. WA. March 4, 1985, pp. 420–21

Much of the funereal gravity of [Ayi Kwei] Armah's vision of history finds its way into the inflections of Anyidoho's [*Elegy for the Revolution*]. The "Revolution" of the title was the overthrow in January 1972 of the democratically elected civilian government of Dr. Kofi Busia by Colonel I. K. Acheampong, whose National Redemption Council had itself, six years later, lost every shred of credibility with which the Ghanaian people had once endowed it. . . .

The typographical highlighting of key phrases, the tone of curdled regret, the oblique use of autobiographical anecdote are all typical of the method of this first collection which shows Anyidoho, surely the brightest representative of his generation, still searching for an exact personal idiom in which to do lyrical justice to his sense of dereliction. In the meantime, the poem operates by brilliant flashes: the two dogs circling one another like politicians sniffing the rump of opportunity, the "young veteran," already senile in hopeful scheming, and the pig which serves as a sardonic sacrifice to the doomed journey ahead. It is the "old peasant hoe in hand," who has already lived through so many violent, remote changes and in whose name the insurrection has nominally been staged, however, who earths the poem. At the time of writing the poet was a mature student of linguistics at the University of Ghana, where he had gone after several years of teaching Ewe and English. The pieces which eventually found their way into *Elegy for the Revolution*, published during the author's postgraduate studies in Indiana, are hence Accra poems invoking a ruined urban landscape. It is from Anyidoho's home district of Wheta in the Volta region, towards which his art would increasingly turn, however, from which these pieces derive their value system and their stubborn independence of thought.

Anyidoho possesses what can only be called a subversively provincial eye. At the very moment when the metropolitan demagogues are at their most deceptively strident, his attention will fix itself on the despised, silent northern servant as he reports for duty from his rudimentary backyard quarters in order to dance attendance on the argumentative employer who takes himself for the vanguard of the new revolutionary elite. . . .

Like all of his contemporaries Anyidoho grew to maturity against the distant rumblings of the Algerian War of liberation and the independence struggles in Asia and Africa. By the age of twenty-nine, when the majority of these poems were written, he had already lived long enough to see most of these aspirations reduced to tatters. Under the first impact of disappointment, his early poetry veers between the satirical and elegiac in a way that is not always satisfactory. . . .

Much of Anyidoho's most potent verse evokes [a] sense of isolation among kinfolk, the knowledge that he will always bear the birthmark of a hounded destiny. . . .

But Anyidoho's poetry is only dissenting in the quite special sense allotted to those who know that all human hopes and designs are prey to inscrutable and divisive forces. In the strongest of his pieces, the sensation of being set apart by a remorseless inner mania nevertheless constantly seems to aspire toward definitive political declaration.

Robert Fraser. West African Poetry
(Cambridge: Cambridge University Press, 1986), pp. 301, 303–4, 339

[Anyidoho] possesses a certain ardor of thought and feeling which is the result of a young mind with solid convictions, solid insights, and solid values. Perhaps this is why his poetry is dominated by a complex range of moods. One can say he writes "mood poetry," a concept not unrelated to mood expressions associated with jazz. It is not also by coincidence that "Earthchild" (the title poem in his third collection [*Earthchild with Brain Surgery*]) was written under the influence of jazz and expresses a variety of complex tones and moods. Similarly, in *A Harvest of Our Dreams*, the total atmosphere is dominated by shades of brooding cynicism. This edition, it must be pointed out, also incorporates his first collection of poems (*Elegy for the Revolution*), and therefore one can trace in it a certain development in the poet's consciousness of "mood poetry.". . .

[It] would be totally wrong to think that Anyidoho's poetry is all fire and storm. Certainly, it is not all anger and frustration, significant though these are in his works. There is a relieving dimension of serenity and quietude, a serenity which celebrates those quiet moments of the human frame and the tender emotions which possess it or give it life. Human emotions of love, tenderness, loneliness, and anxiety are depicted as potentially explosive, equally destabilizing. However, the difference here is that the poet exercises a control of craftsmanship in his shaping of ideas and emotion, particularly in bending these to the beauty of words.

Kofi Agovi. PA. 142 (1987), pp. 168–70

Anyidoho's books of poems, *Elegy for the Revolution*, *A Harvest of Our Dreams*, and *Earthchild* [*with Brain Surgery*], speak of and with sentiments and sensations that recall, to some extent, those of Ghana's older writers, like the poets Kwesi Brew, Kofi Awoonor, and Atukwei Okai, and the novelist Ayi

Kwei Armah. In light of this, it is significant that Anyidoho includes in his texts epigrams from the writings of his older compatriots. . . .

In the aftermath of independence, poetic concepts of nationality would bring forth, first in Brew and Awoonor and, subsequently, in Anyidoho, a multiplicity of images of harvest. . . .

Whether one is reading the long poem "Soul in Birthwaters," "A Piece of Hope," "Festival of Hopes" [in *Elegy for the Revolution*], or "Seedtime," "A Harvest of Our Dreams," "Akofa," and "Moments" [in *A Harvest of Our Dreams*], or "My Song" and "The Rise of the New Patriot" [in *Earthchild*], one is confronted with a poetry that breathes with extraordinary metaphors of hope. Indeed . . . it is a poetry that brings a new dimension to the phenomenon of hope and the expression of it. Thus, to take examples at random from the poems "Back to Memory," "Upon the Harvest Moon," and "The Passion-Gulf," all from *Elegy*, which reader of English poetry ever heard of "a festival of hope," "once upon a hope," or "boatfuls of hope"? Yet these and similar linguistic surprises or transgressions abound in Anyidoho, and serve to enrich thought, sentiment, and expression: they enable a creative link to be established between poet and ancestral time, a time of freedom and of fulfillment. The essence of that Motherland time is continuingly underscored by other verbal innovations, namely a succession of images and metaphors: covenant, dawn, hunting, laughter, and umbilical cord. These and other figures of speech, essentially the heartland of Anyidoho's creativity, are ethnic-oriented and earthbound. In other words, they allow a certain textual delirium to prevail and to give the sensation of oneness with earth in general and with the natural, animistic elements and mythologies of the poet's [homeland] in particular.

J. Bekunuru Kubayanda. *Legon Journal of the Humanities.* 3 (1987), pp. 63–64

AncestralLogic & CaribbeanBlues reinforces the qualities for which Anyidoho is well known. Focusing on Africa and Africans of the diaspora, the poet appropriately uses African folklore for the formal, linguistic, and imagistic reinforcement of his Afrocentric ideas. . . .

The poet's preface, "IntroBlues," sets the sad tone for poems about the condition of Africans both in the diaspora and on the home continent. The poems are divided into three major sections: "CaribbeanBlues," "AncestralLogic," and "Santrofi Anoma." They move from travel abroad to the African home, from the historical and geographic to the philosophical. This also corresponds with a movement from the past to contemporary issues.

The "CaribbeanBlues" section opens with a remembrance of the Taino, a native Caribbean group wiped out by the European settlers. Written in 1992 on the five-hundredth anniversary of the so-called discovery of the Arawaks by Christopher Columbus, these poems evoke memories of pain for both the native Caribbeans and the Africans brought there as slaves. Writing mainly travel poems, the poet moves through the Dominican Republic, Haiti, and Cuba. He says, "The Haitian *Batey* / Is a living Wound / In the throat of the Sugar Mill." In the Dominican Republic he hears a Bakongo voice in the drums. There is irony suggested in the discrepancy between the natural beauty of the Caribbean region and its turbulent, sad history. The poet pays tribute to the heroic struggle of the oppressed people of the area.

"AncestralLogic" contains perhaps the two most moving poems in the collection. The speaker of "Lolita Jones" is an African-American who chastises Africans for not acknowledging the great pan-African achievement of Kwame Nkrumah. This poem in black American English evokes strong pan-African sentiments. "Air Zimbabwe: En Route Victoria Falls" treats European colonization of Africa and its aftermath.

The third and final section deals with topical issues ranging from "DesertStorm" to military rule and political development in contemporary Africa. The poems here do not move so much as do those of the two earlier sections, maybe because the events are still very close and also because there are many philosophical statements. Santrofi, the dilemma bird of Akan mythology, seems to reflect the current plight of Africans. Dedicated to Jack Mapanje, who was perhaps still in jail at the time the poem was written, "Santrofi" relates the dangers of being an artist in Africa, a fate suffered by, among others, [Wole] Soyinka, Ngugi [wa Thiong'o], and [Kofi] Awoonor. "Husago Dance" deals on a personal level with the existential theme of life and death. . . .

The collection represents a major development in Anyidoho's poetic career. The language is witty and strong, the images drawn from African folklore and environment give concrete form to the poet's Pan-African ideas, and the expression of Pan-African experience and perspective is most fulfilling in its orality, passion, and use of African (Ewe) proverbial and other oratorical figures.

Tanure Ojaide. WLT. 68, 1 (Winter 1994), pp. 191–92

ARMAH, AYI KWEI (1939–   )

GHANA

Ayi Kwei Armah's first three novels, *The Beautyful Ones Are Not Yet Born*, *Fragments*, and *Why Are We So Blest?*, sought to expose political and social corruption not only in contemporary Ghana but in Africa as a whole. On the other hand, his fourth novel, *Two Thousand Seasons*, delves into the past and in one majestic sweep of Africa's history seeks to demonstrate how those pure African values and traditions which used to exist in an almost prehistoric past were destroyed through the exploits of Arab predators and European destroyers. The similarity with [Yambo] Ouologuem is obvious; but where the anti-Négritudist Malian author seeks to dispel all the myths about African history, declaring that black notables, no less than Arab and European conquerors and imperialists, were responsible for the historical degradation of the continent, Armah adopts an essentially Négritudist position, the net effect of his presentation being the total condemnation of the Arabs and Europeans as the destroyers of the pristine values of a pure Africa. It is true that even in Armah's work there are indications that the black people had started losing "the way" before the advent of the predators and destroyers; indeed there is a suggestion . . . that their subjugation by the imperialists was itself the consequence of the black people's loss of the way. But the venom Armah directs at the imperialists, a venom unequalled in African literature, and the constant reference to the imperialists as the destroyers, indicates that he lays the blame squarely at their door. It would be a remarkable twist of fate if the anglophone writers begin their flirtation with Négritude at precisely the moment when the francophones seem to be abandoning it; for this exercise in racial retrieval, this attempt to rediscover a glorious African past unadulterated by all those forces associated with the imperialists, is now to be detected, not just in Armah, but to a certain extent in Ngugi [wa Thiong'o] and in some of [Wole] Soyinka's recent pronouncements.

Eustace Palmer. The Growth of the African Novel
(London: Heinemann, 1979), pp. 221–22

Armah's stance against corruption, neocolonialism, and imperialism is not couched in terms that can in any sense be called moderate. It is decidedly militant or radical in the sense that it is expressed in vigorous, harsh, passionate, and uncompromising terms. Armah is a revolutionary but he is not a Marxist writer. No informed reader can deny that *Two Thousand Seasons* is influenced by Marxism. . . . It can be argued, for instance, that his ideological stance is consonant with socialism insofar as he takes a clearly partisan line—he is decidedly on the side of the oppressed. It is also arguable that the view of African history presented in *Two Thousand Seasons* is consistent with historical materialism. According to the Marxist conception of history, man has passed through various stages of social development from primitive communalism through slave societies, feudalism, capitalism, and socialism to the highest and final stage which is yet to be achieved—communism. In Armah's book African history passes through similar phases. The first stage is marked by an idealized form of egalitarianism when the people followed the way—this is the phase which inspires the prophetess Anoa. She wants the African people to return to the values of that period. The next decisive stage follows the period of contact between Africans and the Arabs. It was this phase which marked the rise of zombis, askaris, and other forces of oppression. It was also through the influence of the Arabs that kings like Koranche arose to oppress the people. The period of contact with Arabs is followed by the coming of the destroyers from the sea who bring with them capitalism, colonialism, and the slave trade. This phase is followed by the neocolonial phase when leaders like Kamuzu have replaced colonial rulers. Then comes the stage of an armed liberation struggle which gives rise to hopes of a genuine return to the way. This final stage is the millennium which the African people should hope for and fight for. It is a stage which parallels [Karl] Marx's vision of a classless society under communism.

Emmanuel Ngara. Art and Ideology in the African Novel
(London: Heinemann, 1985), pp. 112–13

Looking at the portraits of the women and the roles they play [in his novels] is one way of tracing the measure of resolution Armah finds in each text as he moves towards a greater understanding, or a more articulate explication, of the central problems he is exploring in all his works. For Armah, all oppression (whether social, political, or cultural) is a form of disease, and the source of all division among mankind. In each of his texts the same two fundamental problems are explored—the conflict between the private and social worlds in modern Africa and the crisis of divided loyalties this creates, as well as the difficulty, for the sensitive individual, of ordering the oppression and chaos of contemporary life into a comprehensible framework which takes account of the past as well as the present.

So far as the portraits of women are concerned, in all five novels [*The Beautyful Ones Are Not Yet Born*, *Fragments*, *Why Are We So Blest?*, *Two Thousand Seasons*, and *The Healers*] the division between parasites and prophets is stark. True to Armah's equation of things white with evil, and black with spirituality, the parasites are either Westernized African women, or, as in the case of Amy Reitsch in *Why Are We So Blest?*, both Western and white. The prophets are those women who are seen as being true to the aspirations of black African people, true to the ancient "way" that has long since been forgotten. In the two earliest novels, the female parasites are the mothers, wives, and sisters of the heroes. That is, they are always attached to the hearth. [It] is these "loved ones," as they are called, who are portrayed as the burden on the soul of the struggling and suffering hero. They are, whether intentionally or not, seen as the oppressors. They make demands, generally material ones concerned with keeping up social appearances, which always provoke a storm of conflict in their men. Pitted against them are the liberating prophets. This conception of them springs primarily from the literal role they play in the fourth novel, *Two Thousand Seasons*, the only work in which women ever initiate any action. In that novel, the voices of the prophets are female, and, at several crucial moments in the history being recounted, it is the women who save the nation, often in battle against the men. Yet, though their roles are not always so prominent, the other novels do contain women who are, in great and small ways, contending with oppression—their role being to understand their men in adverse circumstances, and, wherever possible, guard them and give them solace. They are liberating prophets in the sense that, even when powerless, they have a vision which can protect their men and at least steer them in the direction of some kind of salvation.

Abena P. A. Busia. In Carole Boyce Davies and Anne Adams Graves, eds.
Ngambika: Studies of Women in African Literature
(Trenton, N. J.: Africa World Press, 1986), pp. 90–91

To approach Armah's daring experimentation with the techniques of African oral narratives from the critical assumptions governing discussion of the European novel is to mistake both the formal design and the spirit of the book. Few novels create deliberately unmemorable characters who are merely functions of a collective will or ramble episodically over vast spans of time in pursuit of racial destinies. Even fewer novels start from the premise that certain groups, nations, or races and their colonial underlings have engrossed most of the human vices and are wholly predictable because helpless before the evil of their own natures. Abandoning critical investigation for partisan invective, Armah makes no claim to criticize his "destroyers" and "predators" and their African quislings but simply hurls abuse at them, more after the fashion of the Ewe *halo* than that of Western satire. These features are, more often, the stock-in-trade of epic, saga, and chronicle, both in the African oral tradition of the griot and in its written European equivalents: namely, those Homeric and Norse marathons which similarly trace the migrations of whole peoples and celebrate the founding of nations and empires. Doubtless, some Western scholars would claim, however, that the latter use stock epithets with more ironic discrimination and with a more novel-like, fair-minded openness to the variety of human experience than are to be found in *Two Thousand Seasons*.

Armah's self-consciously staged griotlike discourse is concerned to correct the method of narrating African history as well as the history itself. There are, therefore, some significant departures from storytelling traditions. The author's avowedly anti-elitist standpoint shuns the griot's customary glorification of the matchless deeds of past heroes, which is derisively parodied by [Yambo] Ouologuem and, as Isidore Okpewho has observed, rejects the supernatural along with the superhuman and denies the narrator's single creative personality any domineering proprietorship over the events narrated. Armah's discourse makes communal and egalitarian ideals not only potentially realizable in the contemporary world but so certain to be achieved that the goals can be described as having already been won. His world-view is essentially secular and humanist. His narrative strategy emphasizes the griot's self-effacing assumption of a common identity with both the specific audience which his tale is designed to educate and the characters of the tale itself. Thus *Two Thousand Seasons* is not only *about* reciprocity; its technique *enacts* reciprocity between the storyteller, his tale, and his listeners.

Derek Wright. *JCL*. 23, 1 (1988), p. 95

Ayi Kwei Armah's novels . . . are built around historical frames, and thus we can easily move in the direction of an ethical, even a literal analysis of thematic structure. Essentially, all his novels deal with individuals caught in the web of economic, cultural, and political forces dominating colonial and postcolonial Africa. To the extent, however, that we try to see these forces in terms of some European-African axis, we oversimplify and misread what Armah is doing. . . .

Ayi Kwei Armah's second novel, *Fragments*, contains what appears to be a perversion of the monomyth. Baako, the hero, is educated in the United States, an area which his people see as "a region of supernatural wonder." He returns to them with "a decisive victory"—namely, his degree—which gives him "the power to bestow boons on his fellow man." Baako himself does not perceive his journey in this light, but his family and friends do. The power he sees himself as possessing is a spiritual one, having nothing directly to do with the material benefits his people desire. Simply recognizing variations of the monomyth in Armah's work is not a useful exercise, but it is significant that much of his writing deals with characters who live on the margins of society in opposition to the values by which those inside society live their lives. In *The Beautyful Ones Are Not Yet Born*, "the man" confronts the futility of being good in a corrupt world. In *Fragments*, Baako confronts the futility of existing as a bearer of a spirituality the world has lost, and Modin, in *Why Are We So Blest?*, confronts it in revolutionary action. To paraphrase James Joyce, each of these heroes goes forth to encounter the reality of experience and forge in his soul the uncreated mythos of his race. . . .

Leaving aside for the moment Armah's heroes, we can see that the structure, or more accurately, the anti-structure of the societies he has rendered in each of his novels is a photographic negative of a well-ordered society. Without any idealization, in *Arrow of God* and *Things Fall Apart*, Chinua Achebe has depicted societies in which we could conceive of living; in *The Beautyful Ones Are Not Yet Born* we see a society from which we could desire only to escape. . . .

Ultimately, of course, there is no way of proving that Armah should not be read literally, but to do so means we must deny not only the rich symbolic complexity of his work, and thus his poetic genius, but also his African sensibility, the very particular way in which he sees the world as dynamic configurations of complementary opposites. In other words, we can look at the landscape of the man, the madness of Baako, or the sadistic torture of Modin as correlating directly to the real world and inducing us to accept an essentially nihilistic philosophy; or, we can look at these negations as symbolic action directed against an existing order, as essentially revolutionary, and hence inducing us to accept an apocalyptic orientation. If we accept Armah's images as symbolic action, it does not mean that we must totally discount their literal implications. The torture of Modin at the hands of the French soldiers can, and in fact should, be seen as a very real extension of white racism. But if we simply look at these images without also rationally discounting their literal reality, understanding that the work is fiction and not life, we can see them only as a monotonous, though grotesque, catalogue of negatives and fail to catch the vitality they have on an artistic level.

Richard K. Priebe. *Myth, Realism, and the West African Writer*
(Trenton, N. J.: Africa World Press, 1988), pp. 21–24, 30

[The] integral structure [of *The Healers*] is based on mythmaking, through which it attains symbolic proportions. In fact, Armah superimposes on its history of the Asante Empire a mythic level which is crucial to a full understanding of the novel. Since "a myth always refers to events alleged to have taken place in time" and "explains the present and the past as well as the future," the two intentions of myth and history are compatible. *The Healers* demands mythic interpretation, but it is informed by no classical European myth. In fact, Armah had already used myth, on a limited basis, in his earlier novels. In *Two Thousand Seasons* and *The Healers*, however, he embarked on a full-scale program of mythmaking. *The Healers* makes several references to traditional beliefs and practices, and habits of thoughts or behavior, which derive their origins not from the Greco-Roman myth of course, but from the African background. The novelist's overt purpose in mythmaking is to offer a dynamic impetus to the formation of a new social order and a new political ideology in which the collectivity, as opposed to individual achievement, competition, or manipulation, plays a leading role. In the writing of *The Healers*, Armah's imagination was unmistakably mythopoeic; mythmaking serves as an intensification of mood, a clarification of characters, and as a form of perception which brings his material to artistic concentration and endows his scenes with depth and liquidity. Armah's mythmaking thus exhibits both the "philosophic" and the artistic properties of myth in general. It proposes an admittedly individualized version of a people's ethical and cosmic vision, and it does so with narrative forms typical of myth's arbitrary plot (here the journey or quest), characters of heroic grandeur, and nature's complicity in the drama.

Armah's mythic didacticism is governed by two complementary arguments, one destructive, the other constructive. The first is "demythification." In presenting the rivalry and fragmentation of the Asante Empire and its failure to prevent British conquest, Armah demolishes currently prevailing myths which eulogize the government and society of that period. For its purpose, the novel relies on history—recorded fact in abundant detail—for support.

The constructive or positive myth is illustrated by Armah's dexterous interjection of a new, idealized society in which the only path to a harmonious and lasting survival is that of a communal consciousness and the total integration of individual feelings with collective life. Such a society is represented by the community of "healers" and their inspirational work in the novel.

Ahmed Saber. In Jonathan A. Peters, Mildred P. Mortimer, and Russell V.
Linnemann, eds. *Literature of Africa and the African Continuum*
(Washington, D. C.: Three Continents Press, 1989), pp. 5–6

Ayi Kwei Armah is a mythmaker. Mythmakers make myths. They do not tell of past actions: They create fables to explain the past. They reorder past events to become meaningful to a people. They create the past linking their history with it. . . .

If [the creative artist] is a mythmaker, he first creates a destiny for his people. Then all defeats are interpreted as battles lost during the course of the long way whose final victory would belong to his chosen people. His people could be as rude, uncivilized, as the Trojans. They could be chased out. And, after traveling the seas, some of them could land near Rome: fatherless and motherless. They could be bastards, outcasts, what-have-you. Wolves would be invented for their foster mothers. The future glory of Rome, at a later date, would be attributed to them. Destiny is the controlling theme: a future glory whose quest makes the momentary sufferings one goes through insignificant and bearable.

This is why *Two Thousand Seasons* was invented for us. African governments have failed us, every one of them. Those which were around when *The Beautyful Ones* was written, had failed us. Failed us in terms of not matching aspirations with performances. Now, twenty years later, they are none the wiser.

Taban lo Liyong. *JCL*. 26, 1 (1991), pp. 14–15

Armah may have learned in a roundabout way that African writers who discuss "their work and themselves quite willingly, sometimes even eagerly" seek for something far less trivial than fame and its privileges: they cry out for their message of hope, often the African point of view, to be heard in no uncertain terms. Armah, however, has properly taken his place among writers who, in [D. S.] Izevbaye's words, "create taste for [their] own type of literary compositions by prescribing literary criteria and standards which are often more valuable in the appreciation of [their] own works than for the criticism of other works." A possible grouping of Armah's work of this category could be: the review essays "The Definitive Chaka," "The Caliban Complex," and "Battle for the Mind of Africa"; incidental responses to criticism of his work, including "Larsony or Fiction as Criticism of Fiction" and "The Lazy School of Literary Criticism"; sociopolitical theories, as elaborated in "African Socialism: Utopian or Scientific?" and "The Festival Syndrome"; and such items as "One Writer's Education" and "Interview with Dimgba," which basically provide biographical insights on the writer.

Such a classification, though, is neat and simplistic; it is only valid as a convenient tool of analysis, because all the writings are linked by an obsessive preoccupation with the question of Africa's future. Armah isolates the colonization of the mind of the African—with all the attendant inferiority complexes—as the most devastating legacy of colonialism, an approach that is cultural, as opposed to the materialist view, which lays emphasis on economic exploitation. These are the issues with which the writer is concerned in his novels and short stories as well.

Ode S. Ogede. *WLT*. 66, 3 (Summer 1992), p. 439

AWOONOR, KOFI (1935–   )

GHANA

In politics and philosophy, as well as in the theory and practice of literature, Kofi Awoonor is a syncretist. He amalgamates all experiences, whether personal ones or the collective experiences of Africa, in order to produce a single vortex of images. Africa for him is a continent and a notion that draws into itself, appropriating and adapting, the whole of human life and history. . . .

In a note in his first volume, *Rediscovery, and Other Poems*, Awoonor (or George Awoonor Williams as he was then) says that he began writing in 1949. The notion of cultural synthesis is, however, one that came gradually to him. His first published adult poetry, "The Sea Eats the Land at Home," "Songs of Sorrow," and "Song of War," was largely derived from Ewe dirges, laments, and battle songs, which he learned in part from his grandmother, Afedomeshi, and translated into English. "Songs of Sorrow" has many lines of virtual translation from the work of Henoga Vinoko Akpalu, the originator of the modern style of Ewe dirge. It begins by talking about Dzobese Lisa, the Creator God or Fate of Ewe belief. The immutable fate destined for each person is said by the Ewe to be like the chameleon, whose sudden changes and foul-smelling feces are a significant metaphor for fate. Obviously regarding these poems as apprentice work, he chose not to include them in *Rediscovery*. In that volume, however, and in his second, *Night of My Blood*, several poems draw on the two early "Songs," incorporating whole long passages from them. Some other poems, Awoonor tells us, were first written in Ewe and subsequently translated into English. . . .

The first stage of Awoonor's progress towards cultural synthesis was . . . to rely heavily on Ewe oral poetry as his main source. The second was the bringing together in a single poem of material from the Ewe tradition and the European tradition in which he had been educated. Material from the two strands is set down side by side to emphasize a clash of cultures. Gerard Manley Hopkins, W. B. Yeats (in mythic and political ideology as well as in the creation of a mysterious mood of cosmic immanence), and T. S. Eliot are the major modern writers from whom he draws, but there is also a pervasive influence of the Bible.

Awoonor's first and second volume both contain several examples of each of the first two stages of his work. . . .

Night of My Blood contains one long poem, "Hymn to My Dumb Earth," that Awoonor regards as representing a third phase in his development, the synthesis of cultures rather than the juxtaposition of them as in the second phase. Here the material from each culture reinforces rather than opposes that of the other. Bud Powell, the jazz pianist; the crucified Christ; the childless villager; the man saddened by the venal politics of independence all merge into one, in much the same way as several of the disparate characters in [T. S. Eliot's] *The Waste Land* merge into Tiresias.

K. L. Goodwin. *Understanding African Poetry*
(London: Heinemann, 1982), pp. 93–95

When his apprentice volume *Rediscovery, and Other Poems* appeared under the Mbari imprint in 1964, many of the pieces were recognized by Ewe speakers as reworkings of Akpalu lyrics. In some quarters he was even accused unofficially of a mild form of plagiarism. The charge is unjust, since the book's title is clear acknowledgement of a debt owed to a long and distinguished tradition within which textual ownership has little meaning. When seven years later a selection from the pieces in *Rediscovery* was interspersed among other poems composed in the interval to form the volume *Night of My Blood*, Awoonor's intention became clearer. As a young poet he had sat at the feet of the Anlo masters, attempting to render the sentiments of their tonal verse in the strains of an imported, accentual tongue. Later he felt able to proceed beyond "rediscovery" and extend the dirge tradition into a medium for comment both political and private.

Though the Akpalu versions in *Rediscovery* were in some cases very close to the originals, their indebtedness to Ewe tradition was the result of influences imbibed during childhood rather than of deliberate research. It was not until after their publication and the inception of many of the poems included in *Night of My Blood*, that, in the rainy season of 1970, Awoonor was able to make a visit to Wheta systematically to investigate the sources of his own inspiration. The study which resulted, *Guardians of the Sacred Word*, is both a remarkable sourcebook and a prolonged meditation on the social position and skills of the vernacular Ewe poet or *heno*, translations from the work of three of whom he was able to include. Though a general reliance on an indigenous form has long been recognized as a feature of Awoonor's achievement, it was not until the comparison of related texts thus made possible that the exact extent of his indebtedness became clear. . . .

Awoonor's views as to the relationship between a modern artist and his community are explained with some care both in his historical survey *The Breast of the Earth* and in interviews which he has given from time to time. His statements here show him to be as wary of sentimental oversimplification as he is of a cynical denigration of tradition. Africa is involved in a continuous process of cultural transformation—she continues to "expand, change, adapt"—and yet the way in which she responds to these challenges reflects deeply her own complex personality. In the slow, unravelling process of "growth and elimination" undergone by every modern African community, the poet has a vital role to play, for it is only through the disruptive consciousness of the poet, revealed in blinding flashes, that the zigzagging direction of the future may be seen. Thus, though relating to a community in some respects more complicated than that of the village, the contemporary literary artist may revive within himself the function of the *heno*: he too may be scorned and ignored, but only through him, as through the indigenous cantor, may the community dimly define itself. . . .

Ride Me, Memory, the volume which he published while in the United States, contains a set of "American Profiles" to balance the "African Memories" with which the book closes. Prospect of return therefore balances retrospect, and the biting edge of the collection falls midway between the two. Awoonor was very far from the first West African poet to give us his verse impressions of God's Own Country. . . . But Awoonor's case was exceptional because he was in possession of an especially portable talent. Though emphatically grounded in a local tradition, Awoonor appears to carry his Ewe soul around with him in his hand luggage.

Robert Fraser. West African Poetry (Cambridge:
Cambridge University Press, 1986), pp. 158–59, 161, 290–91

Like [Christopher] Okigbo, Awoonor writes from the perspective of the poet-prodigal and, therefore, from within the context of the psychological myth of the journey. In his first major collection, *Night of My Blood*, almost every poem explores some aspect or nuance of the journey. The sense of alienation is everywhere, beginning with the lament in the first poem that "my god of songs was ill." It continues as the poet wonders in the middle of the collection "why could I not eat with elders / though my hands are washed clean in the salt river." And it is there in the last poem, in which the poet, hearing the fetish drums in the distance, realizes that "they do not sound for me." "I Heard a Bird Cry" is the major poem in the collection, and it confronts the central ironies in the myth. The poet regrets leaving the hearth although he would not have become the poet if he had not undertaken the journey. And he returns to find "the fallen walls of my father's house," walls which he, the reluctant Westernizing voyager, must rebuild. Here and elsewhere the journey becomes Awoonor's African version of the doctrine of the fortunate fall. But the collection does not have an autobiographical design. The two subsequent volumes do.

Ride Me, Memory is a slight collection of very personal poems arranged around a specific point in the cyclical journey. That is, the poet speaks from America, the farthest outward point in the journey; his is the voice of exile, "alien here among the muddied fields." The first section of the collection called "American Profiles," explores the world to which the Westernized African is drawn. There are pictures of Harlem, "the dark dirge of America," and of SUNY Stony Brook, where ineffectual white liberals appear as "Joshuas without trumpet or song." Perhaps the most important lesson the exiled poet learns is the lesson of blackness, which is the lesson of past pain and future triumph—the historical myth, if you will. In "An American Memory of Africa," the climactic poem of the collection, he discovers that Sharpeville and Memphis are the same in their suffering, their promise of "the hurricanes and eagles of tomorrow," and their color. Cut off from the Gulf of Guinea, he becomes a different kind of African by discovering the larger Africa of the historical myth and by discovering his relationship to those who inhabit it: Dennis Brutus, the "professional exile"; Maya Angelou, the "large savannah princess with the voice of thunder"; and Langston Hughes, "bagman of black rebirth." The second section, "African Memories," evokes the Africa to which the transformed African must return—an Africa of broken pots and "our fallen homestead." Wandering "here where there is winter / birdsong and a yellow moon," he realizes that his is the paternally bestowed mythic task; he is "the one who must resurrect / ancient days.". . .

The House by the Sea continues the autobiographical design. It is divided into two sections: section one, "Before the Journey," contains poems of and from America, continuing the mood and mode of *Ride Me, Memory*. Like the poet, the poems wander America restlessly recording passing experience. The personal twists and turns in exile as he encounters what he calls the "gothic beds of American vulgarity." In the second section the poet returns home to Ghana and, in fairly short order, to Fort Ussher prison, the fort functioning as a powerful symbol of the dislocating and suffocating present in which the Westernized African is forced to dwell, cut off from the past and from nature—from what Awoonor calls "the hills / and the sea nearby." In this confusing present he completes the cyclical journey—his and his generation's—by promising the future. He promises his condemned friend, Kojo Tsikata, "a garland / for your wounded knees," and he promises Ghana and Africa to "plait my hope / into poems." And then in "The Wayfarer Comes Home," the last poem in the collection and one of the great mythic poems of modern Africa, he fulfills his promise. He completes the journey by recalling the past, reacting to the present, and prophesying a future. By promising to "stalk the evil animal" and by predicting victory, he reaffirms the historical myth. In this affirmation he *achieves* his past, his home, and his purpose.

Thomas R. Knipp. In Eileen Julien, Mildred [P.] Mortimer, and Curtis Schade, eds. *African Literature in Its Social and Political Dimensions* (Washington, D. C.: Three Continents Press, 1986), pp. 47–48

The formal structure of Kofi Awoonor's *This Earth, My Brother* is probably as puzzling to the African reader as it is to the non-African reader. In strictly formal terms the book is more like a prose poem than a novel, though for purposes of general discussion it is not worthwhile quibbling about the label. Despite the extremely thin narrative thread which runs through it, *This Earth* relates to a tradition of expressionistic experimentation that can be traced from James Joyce to the present, though it is questionable how far this alone would lead anyone. Nor is it necessarily helpful to learn that the author himself has insisted on his work being thought of as a poem. The final judgment will of course be left to the reader. But classification per se, whether by the artist or his critics, is a rather useless game if it fails to reveal perceptions into the situation the artist has presented, and there is little beyond the obvious that a formal analysis of this novel will yield to the critic who does not take into consideration the formal elements that come from Eweland as well as those which come from England. . . .

Yet in discussing his poetry, Awoonor has said that he has been influenced primarily by the tradition of the Ewe song, "especially the Ewe dirge, the dirge form, the lament, and its lyrical structure with the repetition of sections, segments, lines, along with an enormous, a stark and at times almost naive quality which this poetry possessed." In fact, the images, motifs, and themes we find in the novel are very close to those Awoonor has employed in his poetry. . . . The assertion that *This Earth, My Brother* is a prose poem may thus have some critical relevance.

Richard K. Priebe. Myth, Realism, and the West African Writer
(Trenton, N. J.: Africa World Press, 1988), pp. 65–66

While he shows a deep interest in the oral tradition of African poetry, Awoonor has also enriched his work through his understanding of Western literature. Excerpts from Dante form an important motif in *This Earth, My Brother*, and many poems in *Night of My Blood* owe something to English writers from Shakespeare through T. S. Eliot. . . . Awoonor's poetry is exciting because it offers (at its best) the creative fusion of two cultures.

His poetry is also exciting because it transcends particular cultures. This universality is especially expressed in the recurring archetype at the core of *Night of My Blood*: the journey, which as quest for meaning and identity is a pattern implicit in Western poetry since Homer. Awoonor develops the motif in several ways. There is the historical migration of the Ewe people chronicled and mythologized in "Night of My Blood," and there is the recent traumatic journey of the African people out of a technologically primitive culture of their own into the welter of modernization and Westernization. This development is viewed as a journey of the dispossessed in "Exiles." Conversely, there is the journey of "rediscovery" undertaken by those Africans who (like Awoonor, in "Desire") seek to regain the wisdom of their ancestors. The most important refinement in Awoonor's use of the motif involves the journey as voyage, with its cluster of associated symbols, the canoe, the river, the estuary, the sea. The boat as a symbol of the journeying soul is an archetype in the works of such English Romantics and moderns as [Percy Bysshe] Shelley, D. H. Lawrence, and Malcolm Lowry. We don't need to invoke the European tradition, though. The symbolism of the Ewe mythology of death and beyond is clearly the source of the boat image in many of Awoonor's poems.

L. R. Early. In Richard K. Priebe, ed. *Ghanaian Literatures*
(New York: Greenwood Press, 1988), pp. 104–5

As the title page indicates, *Until the Morning After* is a selected volume of poems taken from four previously published collections: *Rediscovery*; *Night of My Blood*; *Ride Me, Memory*; and *The House by the Sea*. There are also nine new poems. The reader is thus provided with an overview of Kofi Awoonor's development as a poet and as a human being. His early lyrics invoking the mysteries of the natural world and welcoming the heritage of the Ewe people gradually give way to wider perspectives, but his early and eloquent "sorrow songs" continue, although they move into the dark world of power politics. . . .

Related to the urgency of freedom now is Awoonor's emphasis on brotherhood, perhaps best expressed in the poem "All Men Are Brothers." Doubtless his feelings about this fundamental need deepened when his brother writers and his brothers in Amnesty International succeeded in their efforts to obtain a trial for him after he had languished in prison for many months. Though convicted of harboring a fugitive, he was pardoned and freed. It seems evident that the "iron clang of door" still echoes in his thoughts, for there is genuine indignation in his new poems when he warns against leaders like Idi Amin and the "leeches who live on the fat of a lean land." *Until the Morning After* should increase Awoonor's already large audience and further enhance his international stature.

Richard F. Bauerle. *WLT*. 62, 4 (Autumn 1988), p. 715

Awoonor's allegory [*This Earth, My Brother*] teems with people, places, incidents, thoughts, emotions, actions, evasions. It follows (pursues may be more apt) the hero from the very orgasm of his conception through his feverish life. It takes off without warning to any part of the world and makes unscheduled stops where it pleases. Yet despite such wide-ranging techniques Awoonor never falls into preciousness or superficialities. What he unfolds before us may be fleeting but it is always sharp and never, one is convinced, unimportant. And it is not a succession of haphazard impressions either, despite the seeming arbitrariness of its sequences. There is a cumulativeness, indeed an organic, albeit bizarre, development towards the ultimate failure. But here is no existential futility; at every stage there is a misty hint of a viable alternative, of a road that is not taken, of a possibility that fails to develop. The central failure is African independence, whose early promise is like the butterfly that the child Amamu caught in the fields of yellow sunflowers wide as the moon, and it flew away again. He searched for it for days and found others that looked like it; but no, it was gone. Or his childhood love for the shadowy cousin who died at twelve of a mysterious pain that chewed her intestines, a love he was to spend his life searching for and not finding—certainly not from his been-to wife Alice, nor even from his more understanding mistress, though she tried harder. . . .

Through this teeming allegory we catch glimpses of the hero Amamu at significant moments in his life. The phrase "catch glimpses" is in fact misleading, since we know that even in those sequences that are most remote from him per-sonally—for example, in the invocation of the poet killed in battle, [Christopher] Okigbo, or the assassinated freedom fighter, Eduardo Mondlane—it is Amamu who is stretched on the rack and also Africa, whose story his life parallels in its purposelessness and self-destructiveness.

The question that one must ask at the end of Awoonor's book is: What then? He hasn't given any answer, and doesn't have to. But of late, many writers have been asking such questions: What then? What does Africa do? A return journey womb-wards to a rendezvous with golden-age innocence is clearly inade-quate. Amamu's father may have acted insensitively, but on balance he was right to show impatience at all the lachrymose farewells before the boy's first depar-ture from his mother's hut to the greater world beyond. Shoving aside the wailing women, he had brusquely and with a curse hoisted the boy into the lorry waiting to take him on a dusty journey to the coast and the future. The future is unavoid-able. It has to be met. What is not inevitable is malingering purposelessness.

Chinua Achebe. Hopes and Impediments: Selected Essays
(New York: Doubleday, 1989), pp. 122, 125–26

Awoonor's recent book of poems Until the Morning After, which won the 1988 Commonwealth Poetry Prize for the African area, consists in part of selections from his earlier work, and in part of new poems, some of which are translations of works originally composed in Ewe. The nine works in this section titled "New Poems," in theme, subject matter, style, technique, and language, reiter-ate many of Awoonor's basic preoccupations. The first few are in part laments over "life's tears" or "life's winds and fate." But as always with Awoonor and the Ewe dirge tradition, there is hope beyond death. . . .

Between the publication of The House by the Sea and that of Until the Morning After almost ten years elapsed. At least part of the explanation for the paucity of Awoonor's creative writing since his release from prison must be sought in a decisive change in his life, leading increasingly to direct participa-tion in national politics. . . .

Whether Kofi Awoonor returns to his earlier preoccupation with imagina-tive writing or not, he has already secured a safe place within the canon of African literature, both for the quantity and the quality of his work. In particular his poetry is notable for its intense lyricism. He is classed with a select group of African poets who have been most successful in bringing African aesthetic norms to bear on their writing in English, a group that invariably includes Mazisi Kunene, Okot p'Bitek, and Christopher Okigbo. The contribution of these poets to world literature lies in the great poise and power with which they can take a second language with its own literary heritage and peculiar linguistic structures and yet use it so as to capture effectively the rhythms, the essential imagery, and the often elusive thought patterns of their first language and culture.

Kofi Anyidoho. In Bernth Lindfors and Reinhard Sander, eds.
Dictionary of Literary Biography. 117 (1992), pp. 89–90

BÂ, MARIAMA (1929–1981)

SENEGAL

Her Western education notwithstanding, [Mariama Bâ] would like to be considered as an "average Senegalese woman," "a woman of the house." [*Une Si Longue Lettre*] is her first novel and it is filled with autobiographical elements, expressing as it does the novelist's desires and dilemmas, tracing her life in a society caught between the established order of the past and the exigencies of the present. A traditionalist at heart, Bâ aspires to be a revolutionary. A maternal retiring figure through and through, she aspires to be a pioneer in female emancipation. Her family upbringing and the Koranic training have imbued her with the absolute law of "divine wish": man is woman's overlord. Added to that is Bâ's fatalism. Destiny is a fixed reality, impossible to avoid. . . . However, such fatalistic tendencies are contradictory to the tenets of the white man's school where Bâ learned how to manipulate the French language. Submissiveness in the face of suffering is discouraged and the victim is told to demand total reform of the social order. Her "letter" is written in the form of a notebook kept by the heroine named Ramatoulaye. Married for thirty years to Modou by whom she has twelve children, Ramatoulaye has been separated for five years from her husband who repudiated her and left her for a much younger woman. Her "letter," ostensibly addressed to a bosom friend, a divorcee working as an interpreter in the Senegalese embassy in [the United States] and due to return home very soon, is written immediately after Modou's death. It is a reflection of life in a psychological ghetto of mental torture and social disorder, where woman is a slave and a beast of prey. Divorce is a rarity but separation and infidelity are common. The life of the couple, far from being a haven of contentment and consideration, is a hell of conniving criminals and common cretins. According to Bâ, two camps are precisely delineated: the victimizer, the slave-master, the ruler of this hell on earth, is Man; the victimized, the slave driven at times to the point of mental exhaustion, is Woman.

Femi Ojo-Ade. In Eldred Durosimi Jones, ed.
African Literature Today. 12 (1982), pp. 72–73

Ramatoulaye, the author of the long letter to her childhood friend Aïssatou, in Mariama Bâ's novel [*Une Si Longue Lettre*], presents [the] dilemma of a middle-aged woman in all its complex social, moral, and emotional implications.

She composes her letter over the first months following her husband's sudden death. During the compulsory seclusion imposed on a Muslim widow, she has time to review the thirty years of her married life and the formative years when she and Aïssatou were among the pioneers of girls' secondary school education. The epistolary form justifies the introspective analysis of the narrator's inner conflicts, lending authenticity to her honest heart-searchings. As the narrative progresses, we learn of the experiences of these two intelligent, responsible, generous-minded women, the impositions society has made on them, and the choices they make regarding their own destinies. Both defy convention and family opposition by marrying for love, without dowries, across caste barriers. Both women's happiness is suddenly disrupted by the introduction of a second wife. Aïssatou refuses the customary compromise, leaves her husband, and obtains a well-paid post at the Senegalese embassy in [the United States], enabling her to live independently and bring up her four sons. Then Ramatoulaye's husband casts an uxorious eye on his daughter's pretty schoolfriend, Binetou, who is under pressure from her family to accept the "old man." He has bribed them with the offer of a new home in a smart suburb, a car, a monthly income, and a pilgrimage to Mecca. Binetou is thus presented, not only as Ramatoulaye's rival, but also as a victim, a sacrifice on the altar of her parents' greed. After long and agonizing reflection, Ramatoulaye resolves to accept her husband's polygamy, much to the indignation of her eldest, emancipated daughter, who is horrified at her father's betrayal and her mother's obligation to share him with a seventeen-year-old. In spite of her education, her lucid intelligence, her love of life, Ramatoulaye retains a strong sense of the traditional role of Muslim women and the old moral values. She rejects Aïssatou's solution of divorce, partly because she still loves her husband and partly to maintain a stable home for her children. Five years later, she is a widow and discovers that her husband died penniless and deeply in debt, that her home is mortgaged, and that he had forgotten . . . all that he owed to her lifetime of devotion and had succumbed to the rapacity of his new in-laws and his adolescent bride. Only then does Ramatoulaye reflect bitterly on marriage, which for a woman means the amputation of her whole personality, her dignity, making her "an object to be used by the man she marries, his grandfather, grandmother, father, mother, sister, brother, uncle, aunt, cousins and friends." But, in spite of disappointments and humiliations, although exploited by her husband and manipulated by his family, Ramatoulaye never loses her inner dignity, and she emerges from her anguish with her principles strengthened and her moral stature enhanced. We are sure she will succeed in shaping a life for herself. . . .

Une Si Longue Lettre is the first truly feminist African novel, skillfully weaving the accounts of individual suffering and dilemmas into the exposition of her thesis: the issue of woman's status in Senegal today. Showing astonishing maturity of style and construction, it is a cry from the heart of a Muslim woman in a society in transition, voicing the social and religious constraints that weigh heavily on her. It also echoes women's protests against exploitation everywhere in the world and is a call to feminine solidarity.

Dorothy S. Blair. *Senegalese Literature: A Critical History*
(Boston: Twayne, 1984), pp. 137–39

Abandonment in the novels of Mariama Bâ is predominantly a female condition. It is both physical and psychological, and it transcends race, class, ethnicity, and caste. . . . The forces in society that set in motion the process that culminates in abandonment and the resultant impact of such a process on the abandoned femäle are conceived by Mariama Bâ to be enormously out of proportion to each other. The whim or accidental fancy of the male and the calculated machinations of a female elder, translated into reality either willingly or reluctantly by the male, place upon the female a burden infinitely heavier than the cause of that burden. The response to this unexpected burden takes one of two forms: reluctant surrender and bear the burden while lamenting and exposing social and other kinds of ills, or categoric refusal to shoulder the burden and opt for freedom through various means. In either case, the female will and determination to live and to retain the integrity of her moral principles usually predominate. Herein lies the faith and confidence of Mariama Bâ in a better future for women in particular, and humankind in general.

Posed in this manner, the problematic of abandonment in the novels of Mariama Bâ begins to take on the characteristics of a power struggle in which both sides, male as well as female, invoke canons of indigenous traditions as well as adopted nonindigenous values (conceived of as "universal") to justify or contest attitudes, beliefs, and actions. More specifically, the novelist concentrates on the question of the misuse and distortion of power and privilege in a sociocultural milieu in which one segment of the population—male, acting independently or under pressure from outside forces (usually revenge or profit-motivated parents)—readily acknowledges but selfishly and deceptively perverts privileges bestowed upon it by tradition to the detriment and disadvantage of the female segment. The two possible responses to this selective adherence to tradition—selective because it acknowledges privileges yet shirks responsibilities and obligations that come with such privileges—defines the nature, the intensity, the parameters, and the outcome of this power struggle. In light of this, one can right away dismiss the stereotype of the docile traditional African woman who mutely and passively surrenders to the whims and dictates of the African man. The very idea of a response suggests some measure of consciousness, consciousness which, in the case of Mariama Bâ's heroines, is translated into various kinds of concrete actions designed, in most cases, to counteract the potentially devastating condition of physical and psychological abandonment.

Power struggle, then, is to be seen not so much in terms of victory/defeat, since it is the kind of struggle that yields a no-win situation, but it is to be looked at from the perspective of the impact of the experience on the individual and the latter's ability to examine, articulate and utilize the transformative capabilities of such an experience of struggle. The heroines in *Une Si Longue Lettre*, Rama, Aïssatou, and Jacqueline, are a living testimony to the positive transformative capabilities of a negative experience born of the problematic of abandonment. Each one emerges from basically the same experience stronger and better placed to more clearly understand, cope with, analyze, and articulate the problems, challenges, and aspirations of not only women but of society. Such is the nature of the dialectical mind of Mariama Bâ. On the other hand, the white French heroine of *Un Chant écarlate*, Mireille de la Valée, exemplifies the tragedy and destruction attendant to the problematic of abandonment.

Her response is qualitatively different from that of the heroines of *Une Si Longue Lettre* even though the experience that elicits the response is the same. Here, Mariama Bâ introduces the pivotal role of culture in response formulation and execution in the face of a given problematic.

Mbye Baboucar Cham. *CBAA*. 17, 1 (1984–1985), pp. 30–31

One of the key concepts that emerges from Mariama Bâ's novels is that of choice. This is most striking in *Une Si Longue Lettre* where the recurrence of words like . . . [the choice, to choose, I have chosen, I have decided, my decision, I wished, I did not wish to] is in itself indicative of the importance of choice for Mariama Bâ. In *Un Chant écarlate*, even though words pertaining to choice are less recurrent, crucial choices are constantly being made throughout the novel. The act of choosing is shown as being pivotal in human experience. It is indeed a powerful act which gives shape and direction to human existence. . . .

It is important to focus on the choices made by female characters in *Une Si Longue Lettre* because women are definitely at the center of the novel. . . . Ramatoulaye is portrayed as a strong, dignified woman who is confronted with a number of options throughout her life; she is therefore called upon to make vital choices. . . .

In this novel Mariama Bâ affirms that ["Each woman makes of her life what she wishes"]. This affirmation is very reminiscent of Jean-Paul Sartre's pronouncements on choice. Indeed, in *L'Être et le néant* and, in more simple terms in *L'Existentialisme est un humanisme* Sartre posits that human beings are nothing else than what they make of themselves. They are the sum total of their choices and through the act of choosing, they create themselves. Sartre, then, views choice as essential for the creation of self. Even though Mariama Bâ does not go as far as to make choice a metaphysical concept like Sartre who thinks that human beings are condemned to choose, she does consider choice to be of vital importance, to be the ultimate affirmation of self. It is indeed through choice that Ramatoulaye and Aïssatou find the strength and courage to face problems that overburden women, to overcome what threatens to deny the self. It is also through choice that they arrive at self-realization. However, this is not achieved without pain, without conflict. . . .

Un Chant écarlate deals with choice in a very different way. Here all the characters are called upon to make choices and they are all affected by each other's choices. . . .

All the characters in *Un Chant écarlate* make important choices. Ousmane chooses to marry Mireille, and to remain faithful to his culture. He also chooses to marry a second wife even though his father who is a staunch Muslim married only one wife. . . .

Mireille, on the other hand, chooses to study in Dakar so she can see Ousmane; she also chooses to be converted to Islam without measuring the implications of such a conversion. She also chooses to remain faithful to her own culture. Her efforts of adaptation to Senegalese lifestyle are short-lived and frustrated by antagonistic forces. . . .

Even though the concept of choice underlies both novels, there is an essential difference in the way it is treated. In *Une Si Longue Lettre* there is no doubt that Modou, Binetou, Tante Nabou, and Mawdo make choices that affect others. However, the emphasis is clearly on the two main protagonists, Ramatoulaye and Aïssatou. Here, choice is essentially seen as it affects the individual lives of these two women, as it allows for growth, as it activates the development of consciousness. In *Un Chant écarlate*, on the other hand, choices affect not only the individuals who make them but also the people who are close to them.

Irène Assiba d'Almeida. In Carole Boyce Davies and Anne Adams
Graves, eds. *Ngambika: Studies of Women in African Literature*
(Trenton, N. J.: Africa World Press, 1986), pp. 161–62, 165, 168–69

Mariama Bâ did not attack tradition and custom blatantly, but she expressed her disapproval of certain glaring abuses of tradition which impede progress. While she demonstrated an unflinching faith in the freedom of choice and the personal nature of marriage and romantic love, she also expressed her belief in the gain that the community in the modern context—the nation—would reap from the success and the attainment of happiness by individual couples. For her, family success depended on the harmony of the founding couple, and in turn, it was the grouping of all these successful and happy families that would constitute the nation. . . .

One could argue that there was nothing new in this idea in the African context, for it was in the interest of the community in general that the family would initiate ties that would ultimately lead to the union in marriage of young men and women. What was new, however, was the notion that marriage was above all based on the choice and initial attraction of the two principal partners. . . .

Bâ was the first African writer to stress unequivocally the strong desire of the new generation of Africans to break away from the age-old marriage customs and adopt a decidedly more modern approach based on free mutual choice and the equality of the two partners.

In her two novels, she pointedly showed that the extended family's action could invariably make such relationships fizzle out in bitter failure. And while never indulging in outright condemnation of the traditions of her society, she denounced the contemporary abuses of these traditions.

Edris Makward. In Carole Boyce Davies and Anne Adams Graves, eds.
Ngambika: Studies of Women in African Literature
(Trenton, N. J.: Africa World Press, 1986), pp. 274–75, 278

A social history, [*Une Si Longue Lettre*, translated as *So Long a Letter*] deals very specifically with the struggle for social transformation. Ramatoulaye, the widow who writes, becomes conscious of the fact that, in the face of all the uncertainties and changes in her life, she is working out her salvation by addressing herself to a woman who is a sister spirit. In the course of the narrative, we watch a woman in her fifties being transformed, preparing to begin life anew.

The world of Mariama Bâ's novel is the contemporary African state, and her story takes place against the background of the creation of that civic state.

Bâ gives us a Muslim woman living in a patriarchal culture whose religious tenets and social conventions, at least as they are institutionalized and practiced, serve to keep women subject. Bâ then creates for us a contemporary woman challenged by the impact of the modern city and state from whose debris she reclaims herself and her children; having helped build the still patriarchal state, she must reclaim herself from it. . . .

In this work Ramatoulaye shifts from a notion of woman as subject female to one of the *complementarity* of man and woman as the vital unit of that national whole in which she locates the liberated woman. In this movement, Bâ strikes at the heart of the motherhood issue . . . by placing mothering firmly *within* a definition of the liberated female self and symbolically rewriting the history of maternal alienation from the modern state. In the same way that griots draw us forward to the present in their narratives, Ramatoulaye recollects the histories of women from *her* perspective and finds a place for them in her account of their new world. This novel writes women back into history by making it herstory also. It creates a heroine for whom the making of the modern state becomes also the making of a modern woman who survives and lives in that state and . . . becomes a mistress of her words, and worlds.

Abena P. A. Busia. In Joe Weixlmann and Houston A. Baker, Jr., eds.
Studies in Black American Literature,
(Greenwood, Fla.: Penkevill, 1988), Vol. III, pp. 27–29

Setting her novel [*Une Si Longue Lettre*] in Dakar about twenty years after Senegal's independence from France, Bâ evaluates from a contemporary perspective the outcome of the nationalist and feminist movements of the late 1950s. The world of the novel is that of Dakar's established professional class, the members of which in their student days were in the vanguard of these progressive movements. What she reveals is the betrayal by this same privileged elite of the hopes and aspirations of both. While Bâ's focal concern is the female experience, the national fate that provides the backdrop enlarges the scope of the novel, and the undermining by bourgeois materialism of the nationalist ideals of liberty and equality serves as a vehicle to illuminate the compromising by women as well as men of the feminist ideal of a marriage contract based on parity between the sexes. . . . [The] unhappiness of Ramatoulaye, the work's central character, is a result not only of her victimization by the male social order but also of her continuing complicity in the process.

Crucial to an understanding and assessment of this novel is an appreciation of the narrative framework Bâ has so carefully and skillfully elaborated. The story is told in the first person by Ramatoulaye in the form of a letter-diary that she addresses to her friend Aïssatou and writes following the death of her husband Modou. Working within the genre of pseudo-autobiography, Bâ has her heroine tell her story, not directly, but with subconscious evasion and revelation. While Bâ's exploitation of the ironic possibilities of her narrative mode provides the novel with much of its meaning and flavor, it is in the narrative setting created for the telling that the informing force of the novel lies. Ramatoulaye writes her letter during the four months and ten days of secluded mourning prescribed by

Islam for widows. In this Islamic practice, Bâ found her archetypal image of female experience. . . . Ramatoulaye's physical confinement during this period of mourning in the house she once shared with Modou replicates her psychological confinement in a debilitating stereotypical view of a woman's role.

Florence Stratton. *RAL*. 19, 1 (Summer 1988), p. 159

Ramatoulaye is a paradox, a conservative in revolt. She may endorse the European headmistress's exhortation to leave the bog of superstition, custom, and tradition, a call that equates African tradition with superstition and consigns both to the rubbish heap, but a part of her remains cautious, conservative, and "patriotic." The harshness and contempt reserved for the lower class that Binetou and her mother represent, and the very different treatment accorded to Mawdo's royal mother and Nabou, has already been mentioned. The latter are associated with Africa's heroic past: the retributive violence of the warrior, his reckless courage, his dusty combat, and thoroughbred horses. Of course, it is courage conceived of in aristocratic rather than in democratic terms. Like Camara Laye, Ramatoulaye regrets that traditional crafts decline into mere tourist art as the young artists choose European-run or European-modeled schools. In nonindustrialized countries, formal schooling and "paper qualifications" are sure avenues to well-paid jobs in the public sector. And as the individual rises, so does the extended family. Formal education is one means to an upward economic and social mobility, but traditional Ramatoulaye sees in young students only that lack of sensitivity to honor that leads to physical retaliation and assault. She who spoke about the bog of tradition also applauds the fierce resistance put up by old virtues against the inroads of imported vices. During the Algerian war of independence, the French attempted to compel Algerian women to discard their veils, but they clung to them: what was traditional was also national and, therefore, to be protected and preserved against foreign attack. Polygamy, which Ramatoulaye opposes, is sanctioned by Islam, a traditional religion, unlike Christianity. This is yet another contradiction and tension in devout, traditional, feminist Ramatoulaye. The conservative aspect of her character is also revealed in some of her opinions: for example, that cleanliness is one of the essential qualities of a woman and that a woman's mouth should be fragrant: but don't these qualities apply to men as well? Unwittingly, she casts women in the role of sex objects, attracting and seducing men into marriage. In spite of the decline in the conduct of young women, Ramatoulaye will not give her daughters immunity in pleasure. The price of sin is an unwanted pregnancy; such a pregnancy indicates theft, theft of virginity and of family honor. A woman who exposes any part of her body, like a woman who smokes, exposes a jaunty shamelessness.

And so Ramatoulaye the rebel becomes afraid of progress. . . . Ramatoulaye's caution and skepticism seem to extend to Aïssatou, her dear and faithful friend: Has Aïssatou, because of her stay in the United States, become too Westernized? Will she insist on eating with a fork and knife, rather than with the hand? Will she wear trousers? And so Ramatoulaye continues to write her letter even after hearing that her old friend will return home on holiday, to write even on the very day before Aïssatou's arrival. The letter has now become a diary, a form suggesting greater loneliness, beginning and ending with oneself.

Charles Ponnuthurai Sarvan. *MFS*. 34, 3 (Autumn 1988), pp. 459–60

[Marriage] remains a tangential concern in [Sembène Ousmane and Aminata Sow Fall] when compared with its place in the two novels Mariama Bâ wrote before her death in August, 1981. In the first novel, *So Long a Letter*, her protagonist, Ramatoulaye, "writes" a long letter to her friend Aïssatou—both of them victims of marriages that eventually went sour halfway. Ramatoulaye is shocked to learn of her husband's new desire for Binetou, their daughter's friend who used to spend part of her holidays with them. Part of the strangeness of Modou Fall's new appetite is located in the fact that the two of them had lived together as husband and wife for twenty-five years, and their marriage blessed them with twelve children. This horde of children and their mother are abandoned by Modou in preference for a younger woman. Aïssatou, on the other hand, considers her doctor-husband's second marriage as a breaking of faith in their relationship. She blames Mawdo for succumbing to his mother's long stratagem meant to humiliate her daughter-in-law by dangling before her son the sapling Nabou. Mawdo easily falls for this luscious bait, marries the teenage girl and expects Aïssatou to compromise and stay on. But she will not. Rather than accept Mawdo's second marriage, she decides to start life anew and alone. She will not bend her head in silence and accept a destiny that oppresses her. Aïssatou leaves with her four sons and takes to her studies, training as an interpreter and eventually finding a job at her country's embassy in America.

[*Un Chant écarlate*, translated as *Scarlet Song*] is a little variation of Bâ's concern in her first novel. Here the focus is still marriage, but this time it has been given a wider and more intensive scope. Two worlds—the worlds of the black man and that of the white—are brought together in a mixed marriage, which fails like the matrimonial unions of the African couples in *So Long a Letter*: the Mawdo-Aïssatou, Modou-Ramatoulaye, and Samba-Jacqueline relationships. Ousmane Gueye and Mireille de la Vallé first met in a Dakar university when the latter's father was a French diplomat in the Senagalese capital. Monsieur de la Vallé who had been identified with moving speeches addressing the necessity to demolish racial barriers, has no problems in deciding Mireille's fate in Dakar as soon as he knows that she is cultivating the love of an African boy. He immediately flies his "adventurous" daughter to Paris, their home, where she continues her study. But Mireille will later marry this boy in Paris to the unrelenting anger of her parents. However, when the mixed couple return to Africa they discover too late that there is a wide hiatus between theory and practice, ideals and reality. The two come face-to-face with consuming cultural clashes that soon help to diminish the intensity of their original passion for each other. Unknown to Mireille, Ousmane makes plans for a second marriage, to a childhood friend called Ouleymatou. But when Mireille learns about the affair, she becomes schizophrenic, kills the only child of their marriage, Gorgui, and then attempts to murder her unfaithful husband.

In the two novels, Mariama Bâ consistently attacks the idea of polygyny, which is for her indeed a humiliation of women. None of her major female characters accepts it, and where it appears some of them do, it is because of the blind alley in which they find themselves—the confines of marriage or the limited opportunities available to them outside of it. Ramatoulaye and her co-wife Binetou in *So Long a Letter* and Ouleymatou in *Scarlet*, who are apparently undisturbed by the multiple marriages of their husbands, clearly bargain from weak positions.

J. O. J. Nwachukwu-Agbada. *MFS*. 37, 3 (Autumn 1991), pp. 562–64

BADIAN, SEYDOU (1928–   )

MALI

[Seydou Badian's first novel *Sous l'orage*, reissued as *Sous l'orage (Kany)*] was completed in Montpellier in 1954, and was published nine years later. . . .

The story itself is simple. . . . Kany, daughter of Benfa and Téné, is in love with a young man, Samou, who lives with his mother, Coumba. They are two childhood friends who went to the same school. But their love is opposed by their parents, who are bound to traditional customs: the father, Benfa, has decided long ago to marry his daughter to the old businessman Famagan. Obviously the youg girl is supposed to blindly obey her father's wishes, which represent the ancestral wishes, but her personality and education prevent such a blind submission. She formally opposes Benfa, thereby creating a very serious conflict between father and daughter, a conflict of generations.

This pseudo-novel unfolds by using archetypes, therefore it is distracting to give room to a central character, since neither Benfa nor his daughter really occupy the foreground. Neither is described from the inside or the outside. Since one does not know Kany's exact age, her height, or her manner of dressing, and is thus deprived of any physical reference and of any emotional link with the past, . . . the reader concludes that by virtue of this deprivation, the author wanted to expose a character, not create a woman. . . .

[The themes] reflect the major preoccupations of the author, anxious about the destiny of his country as well as the upholding of the grand ancestral realities. Africa cannot remain as it is, nor can it reject the totality of its past. The difficult amalgamation cannot be achieved without problems. This is typified by the latent conflicts suggested in this novel, where tradition rules but where the opportunity of an outside pragmatism, necessary for a new lease of equilibrium, is also revealed.

S. M. Battestini. *Littérature Africaine Seydou Badian* (Paris: Fernard
Nathan, 1968), pp. 32–33, 37†

Without being polemical, [*Sous l'orage*] is strongly didactic and it is a contribution to the literature of Négritude: devoid of satirical elements, it is a novel of ideas rather than of character and incident. . . .

The tone of the whole of Badian's novel is that of a moralizing tract addressed to the people of Sudan, with independence round the corner, and the responsibility for organizing their own society in sight. The situation of the action, and every episode is thus chosen with a view to exposing or illustrating an idea or principle. Badian places his characters first in a small town in the Sudan shortly after the end of World War II. On Kany's refusal to accept the marriage plans, she is banished with her sympathetic brother Birama to their father's distant birthplace. The journey in the train allows for a discussion between a carefully selected group of passengers, who express their grievances and points of view in a contrived academic dialogue. The sojourn in the primitive village brings the "city youngsters" into contact with African rural life, where they are taught by their uncle Djigui to understand and appreciate the best of the old traditions. There is also vague and inconclusive reference to the continued existence of secret societies, a pretext for a lesson in the ancient tribal beliefs. The melodramatic introduction of the epidemic of cerebrospinal meningitis, inadequately motivated, and unlinked to preceding or subsequent events, is used to show the reactions of the old and superstitious who think that disease is the result of a curse.

Seydou Badian clearly has an important message to convey to his compatriots and he has chosen the *roman à thèse* for the purpose. Although the novel will not have been read by large numbers of these, as it is written in a European tongue, he can justify himself by the fact that his lesson is addressed in the first instance to the young intellectuals, the product of Westernized schooling and white progress. As the ones who will take over responsibility when colonization comes to an end, they are advised to retain the best of the wisdom of Africa and keep a nice balance between the old and the new. The message comes over clearly; on this level the work is irreproachable. It is more open to criticism, if it is to be assessed as a contribution to original creative literature, in the genre that the author has adopted. The characters are not treated with profundity and so make little impact on the reader; the situations are contrived and the solution not psychologically motivated. But these reservations will fall away for those who place Badian's novel solely in the category of illustrative sociology.

Dorothy S. Blair. African Literature in French
(London: Cambridge University Press, 1976), pp. 240–42

Le Sang des masques is an original work. Its originality resides primarily in the presentation of the subject and the perspective offered by Badian on contemporary African society. It is a novel of adventure, conflict, and dizzying intrigue.

In this novel, Seydou Badian is not attracted by traditional exoticism; but instead poses the everyday problems of Africa. The conflict of values constitutes the backdrop of the novel on which village and city intrigues are grafted. The universe of the two young heroes is divided into two distinct cultural zones. Will they succeed in bridging the gap that separates them? The two protagonists, Bakari and Nandi, originally in the camp of traditional culture, are literally thrown into the other cultural sphere by the pressure of events. Bakari goes to the city with his father's blessing. . . .

After an absence of three years, Bakari returns to the village. But the village has changed; indifference and hostility are prevalent. His childhood friends abandon him and he only encounters enemies. Veiled internal battles, for the conquest of power, place people in opposition to one another. Evil and greedy creatures like Bantji want to subjugate the others through words and magic. . . .

Bakari fights the forces of evil and conquers them thanks to the myth of courage and chivalrous virility still honored in the village. . . . And through dance, he wins the heart of Nandi. . . . The two are tied together by bonds of a loving friendship and spiritual complicity. . . . To assure his complete supremacy over the village, Bakari confronts and destroys the forces of deception and quackery represented by Bantji.

Bakari and Nandi meet in the city where they are torn from their milieu and their culture and assaulted by the values of the big city. . . .

And the only value the city holds is money. . . . Nandi is ill-treated and abandoned by her spouse . . . [and] finally returns to the village, disgusted by all that she saw and experienced in the city: a violent husband, women with loose morals, and the excessive power of money. The novel ends with the image of Nandi tracing in reverse the path taken by Bakari. She is in search of a more just and humane society, sheltered from violence, greed, and corruption. . . . Can the return of Nandi help preserve the purity and authenticity of ancient values? An element of doubt remains about this. One of the last sentences in the novel contains a message which is in effect an invitation to the creation of a new African culture. The co-penetration of ideas is inevitable in the real world. . . .

Le Sang des masques is a personal reflection by the author on the socio-cultural and economic upheavals that traverse modern Africa.

Christophe Dailly. *PA*. 101–2 (1977), pp. 293–95†

After *Sous l'orage*, the . . . novel in which the solution to the problems of contemporary Africa was to be found in a slow and ever-negotiated collaboration between the young and old, Seydou Badian [released] in 1977 another novel, *Noces sacrées*, in which he unequivocally asserts the values of ancestral tradition. This work, set in the colonial period, might seem curiously backward and paradoxical if it did not express a concern increasingly shared at present by some African writers and critics: namely that of preserving endangered traditional values and ethos. . . .

Noces sacrées is essentially the story of the moral evolution of a Westernized African doctor—of note is the fact that Badian himself is a doctor—who is led by strange circumstances to rediscover the depths and intrinsic value of his traditional culture. After numerous encounters which ultimately reveal to him the superiority of Africa over the West in matters of philosophy, religion, as well as technology, the hero returns willingly, through ritual initiation, to the world of his ancestry. . . .

Noces sacrées is particularly rich in accurate elements taken from the oral tradition. Even allowing for poetic license on the part of the author, this novel is unquestionably rooted in the Bambara magico-religious reality, as described by ethnographers. This aspect is indeed most significant for the message of the work: the Westernized African protagonist does undergo an initiatory return to the real, cultural sources of ancestral tradition and not merely the ever-archetypal return to the world of childhood. Moreover, the African tradition clearly demonstrates its universal relevance by receiving the two whites, Besnier and Mlle Baune, into its midst during an initiatory ceremony. This simple episode confirms the fact that the Western reader is equally and directly concerned by and implicated in the story. . . .

In conclusion, this novel, haunted by the N'domo and other occult powers, appears as an attempt to reassert a tradition and beliefs in danger of extinction. Like Birago Diop some twenty-five years earlier, Seydou Badian warns his compatriots against "the temptation of the West," the temptation to discard indiscriminately as obsolete the values and beliefs of the ancestral tradition. One may even wonder why Badian has chosen to set his novel in the colonial period rather than in the present. Might the author be suggesting that at the time of its most absolute supremacy, Europe was already supplanted, morally and technically—since precisely in the African view the moral and the technical go hand-in-hand by the specific nature of African power? As for the imposed involvement of the reader in the story, we would appear to be in the presence of yet another specifically African trait, transposed from the oral tradition: each listener/reader is an active witness, deeply committed by the word uttered by this descendant of the griot's Kouyate clan, whose name is Seydou Badian.

Jacques Bourgeacq. *PMQ.* 6, 3–4 (July-October 1981), pp. 158–59, 161

[*La Mort de Chaka*, translated as *The Death of Chaka*] is a play of ideas rather than a comic entertainment with socially critical overtones. [Badian] had already served for nearly a year as minister of rural development and planning in Mali when he began writing it. Like many young intellectuals in Africa, Badian was a committed socialist who resented the humiliations imposed upon the continent by a history of colonialist oppression. To comprehend such feelings, one has merely to recall the disdain in which Europeans held African civilization until very recently. As late as 1962 [when *The Death of Chaka* was originally published as *La Mort de Chaka*], the well-known British historian Hugh Trevor-Roper publicly proclaimed that there was no history in Africa before the arrival of Europeans—only darkness. In view of such attitudes, Badian's preface takes on a heightened significance, for in referring to the historical Chaka, king of the Zulus in southern Africa and brilliant organizer of a 400,000-man army, he is offering evidence to support his conviction that there was not only history before the arrival of the white man but there were also great heroes who succeeded in forging political order from chaos. On one level, then, the play promotes an African sense of pride in history, for by depicting the Zulu leader as a noble idealist and linking him with the creation of a new nation, Badian is ascribing epic proportion to a story that had been treated in a negative fashion by European historians, who tended to regard the historical Chaka as a bloodthirsty tyrant.

Badian's choice of an historical subject thus reflects a desire to recover the truth and to refute ethnocentric commentators like Trevor-Roper. . . .

The Death of Chaka is essentially a dialogue of conflicting perspectives. First, Chaka is presented through the eyes of his rebellious generals. Although there is an undercurrent of recognition for his accomplishments, these men are disturbed by what they interpret as Chaka's arbitrary cruelty and self-aggrandizing tendencies. Beneath the surface of their comments, it becomes apparent that some of them are also jealous of him. And they are all tired of the continuous effort that he demands from them. The specific occasion for their discussion in the opening scenes is Chaka's announcement that the Zulu will attack a coalition of hostile tribes in the south in order to consolidate their previous victories and to remove the last major threat to their control in the area. In addition, the generals resent the fact that Chaka had recently removed them from their command of specific regiments (*impis*) and would henceforth assign them to their positions only shortly before the battle. The immediate objective of the generals is to prevent the battle from taking place, for they regard it as untimely and unreasonable.

As their conversations progress, however, they gradually persuade themselves that it is necessary to eliminate Chaka, whom they accuse of being mad and increasingly bloodthirsty. Their arguments appear credible, and the reader of the play is predisposed to judge Chaka unfavorably. Yet when Chaka himself appears on the stage relatively late in the play, their image of him is utterly discredited, and they themselves are revealed for what they are—petty, self-serving plotters against the legitimate authority of a genuine leader. Badian adopts this approach for a very good reason. Because the truly decisive socialist leaders of independent African nations are frequently maligned by local elites and by conservative interests in the industrialized world, he desires to make the case against such leaders appear plausible so that when it is revealed as fraudulent, the audience will gain insight into the way people are duped in the real world by similar, apparently valid arguments. The drama of Badian's play lies not in the action, but in the conflict of ideas. His major purpose in drawing upon the story of an early nineteenth-century African hero is to raise the level of consciousness about what needs to be done in the present.

Richard Bjornson. Introduction to Guillaume Oyônô-Mbia and Seydou
Badian. *Faces of African Independence: Three Plays* (Charlottesville:
University Press of Virginia, 1988), pp. xxiv, xxvii–xxviii

Badian . . . presents, in *The Death of Chaka*, a tragedy of human nature unrelieved by any comic interludes and revealing the shattering interplay of self-confidence and jealousy on a patriot and nation-builder. . . .

Badian's Chaka is a patriot who is single-minded about the need to establish his people over other peoples in the area. He is conceived as gentle but very powerful, whether present or absent from the scene. Thus Badian does not deal with the controversial historical Chaka on whom many writers are so divided. The patriotism and commitment of Chaka is for Badian like the biblical Charity which "covereth a multitude of sins." "Hard" realism indicates that empires, civilization, and colonies have always been established at the cost of human lives and that the benefits of having them have invariably been reaped by the future generations. The play and its characters are hardly well developed but its message is unmistakably sympathetic to Chaka's patriotic leadership.

The Death of Chaka is a people's tragedy as much as it is that of the individual. The Zulu nation has lost the chance [of] political greatness and the struggle to regain it will never be easy for the descendants of Chaka. The voice of the people in the play is represented by that of a lone Zulu maiden, Notibel, who denounces her fiancé, Dingana, and pledges total allegiance to Chaka. As it were she is the ear of the people. In the first tableaux, when the mutiny against Chaka is being hatched, she enters uninvited. "I have overheard everything. There has been talk of bloodshed," she says and warns the generals not to desert Chaka no matter what happens. Also in the second tableaux she comes in under similar circumstances saying "Ndlebe, I overheard everything. I am disappointed," and thereafter she resolves: "I was Mapo's sister. I was Dingana's fianceé. Now I am neither Mapo's sister nor Dingana's fianceé. I am Chaka's daughter. Like everyone else, I am a Zulu." Following this declaration of loyalty which is supposed to be that of other Zulus, Ntiobe's political commitment becomes complete. Like Ebrahim's Kinjekitile, the hero of the play of that name, the future now belongs to the people.

J. Ndukaku Amankulor. Ufahumu. 17, 2 (Spring 1989), pp. 164, 168–169

BALDWIN, JAMES (1924–1987)

UNITED STATES

James Baldwin's late novel *If Beale Street Could Talk* . . . gives [a] graphic portrayal of the dread of intimacy. The work, a quasi-detective story on the surface, is divided into two parts, the first entitled "Troubled about My Soul," and the second, disproportionately short one, entitled "Zion." By virtue of such a structure, Baldwin suggests an introspective, even a spiritual bearing in the face of an action that is heavily social, with its exposé of police malice and its outcry against the destructive misery of the black and Puerto Rican poor.

But Baldwin earns his spiritual emphasis. Virtually every significant action in the text, except the rape which is falsely attributed to Fonny, the male protagonist, arises from an engagement of souls between two people. These engagements may be hostile, as is that between Fonny and the white policeman, Bell, who feels his power and life assumptions threatened by Fonny, and who accordingly contrives to pin the rape on Fonny.

The title of the second section, "Zion," suggesting recovery from the troubles of the soul and attainment of spiritual freedom, may be somewhat ironic. It seems evident that Fonny will be exonerated, on the grounds that the damning lineup was loaded against him (he was the only black man and the culprit was very dark in hue), and the victim cannot maintain her complaint, having at once lost her baby and her mind. But if we dwell a moment on this positive development, it gives rise to problems. The exoneration pivots on a technicality, and sustains itself on the destruction of another's spirit. The victim of the rape has looked into the same pit and mirror of vulnerability and violation as Fonny, and has been unable to stand it. She is the second minor character, Fonny's friend Daniel being the other, who comes too close to human cruelty, violation, and degradation. Whereas Fonny and the female narrator, Tish, prove that familiar, pedestrian life precludes ecstasy, Señora Sanchez (the rape victim) and Daniel find that the familiar preserves them from intimacy with horror.

The structure of the text, with a slow, tortured unfolding of social and spiritual distress giving way to a swift, revelatory brightness, tempts us to think of Fonny and Tish as looking into the pit of horror and, like the poet in [William] Blake's *Marriage of Heaven and Hell*, emerging not just unscathed but with a vision of heaven.

Michael G. Cooke. *Afro-American Literature in the Twentieth Century:*
The Achievement of Intimacy (New Haven, Conn.:
Yale University Press, 1984), pp. 199–200

While exile constitutes a spiritual loss, chaos, and struggle, the African religious tradition also embodies within itself resources and renewal power. It is within this context that we look at James Baldwin's *Go Tell It on the Mountain*. One may question how this work can be cited as a continuation of African traditional religion when it reads so Christian and postulates the view that the primary concern of the characters is to get their souls "right" so they can meet God in Heaven. Nevertheless . . . it uncovers the African-American's adaptation of Christianity. James Baldwin himself, in writing this book and in many of his works, attests to his ambivalence about black religion. Because of his own search for identity and his earlier belief that when blacks were brought to America they were stripped of their cultural heritage, his earlier works attempt to place black religion solely in the area of Christianity. By doing so he is unable to accept black religion because he identifies Christianity with oppression and the lack of love in the world. However, when he does isolate aspects of black religion, as he does in *Go Tell It on the Mountain*, Baldwin realizes that there is something else in it. He sees a beauty, strength, morality which he finds difficult to repel.

Mildred A. Hill-Lubin. In Kofi Anyidoho, Abioseh M. Porter, Daniel [L.]
Racine, and Janice Spleth, eds. *Interdisciplinary Dimensions of African*
Literature (Washington, D. C.: Three Continents Press, 1985), pp. 204–5

Baldwin transmutes the messianic myth into that of an artist-priest whose visionary powers allow transcendence of oppression so that she or he can ultimately change history. To Baldwin, the personal and racial past are inseparable; therefore, to grasp racial history, one must first confront personal history. Beyond knowledge lies change, and within each sensitive intellectual lodge the tools for transforming history. *Go Tell It on the Mountain*, like [Ralph Ellison's] *Invisible Man*, exemplifies distrust of collective effort in favor of individual action. Moreover, although Baldwin's work anticipates the urge to explore and reconstruct history, an urge permeating Afro-American literature of the 1960s, 1970s, and 1980s, *Go Tell It on the Mountain* does not reckon with African history or culture.

The introspection Baldwin demands of his [readers] prohibits him from employing the romance, with its de-emphasis on subjectivity. Instead, he turns to the confessional mode to convey his protagonist's guilt, confession, and transcendence. By using flashbacks disguised as prayers to present personal histories, Baldwin underscores the spiritual dimensions of those histories, at the same time focusing on the points of congruence between the personal and racial past. Finally, one must applaud Baldwin's recognition of the centrality of religion in black life and his ingenuity in employing a fictional mode that clearly suggests spiritual and religious concerns.

Jane Campbell. *Mythic Black Fiction: The Transformation of History*
(Knoxville: University of Tennessee Press, 1986), p. 101

In truth, the way of life reconstructed in most of Baldwin's novels is informed by a biblical imagination that is almost as bleak as that in [Richard Wright's] *Native Son*. In *Go Tell It on the Mountain*, the Grimes family has only a tenuous grip on reality due to the religiosity of the storefront Pentecostal church. In *Giovanni's Room* the subject of black culture is displaced by the moral and social problems of white homosexuals in Europe. In *Another Country* a tortuous series of racial and sexual encounters—white vs. black, homosexual vs. heterosexual, North vs. South, European vs. American—drives jazz musician Rufus Scott to suicide but becomes the rite of passage to self-understanding for his jazz-singing sister Ida and the social rebels of modern America who affirm bisexuality as the highest form of love. In *Tell Me How Long the Train's Been Gone*, Leo Proudhammer contends with his private and public demons—heart condition, white mistress, black militant lover, racism, and the stultifying influence of his family—as he claws his way to salvation as a black actor. In *If Beale Street Could Talk*, Tish and Fonny, the blues protagonists, are able to endure and transcend the agony of harassment in the ghetto and prison through love (personal and familial) and art (black music and sculpture). And in *Just Above My Head*, Hall Montana, the first-person narrator-witness and older brother of the gospel-singing protagonist, testifies about the agonizing realities of human suffering and the ecstatic possibilities of love in the lives of those touched by his brother's journey on the gospel road.

As fascinating and ambitious as these novels are, only *Go Tell It on the Mountain*, *If Beale Street Could Talk*, and *Just Above My Head* illuminate the matrix of shared experience of black Americans. But like Wright, Baldwin focuses sharply on a single dimension of black culture. His emphasis, however, is not political but spiritual and sexual, not the terrifying possibilities of hatred, but the terrifying possibilities of love. In contrast to Wright's unrelenting narrative drive, Baldwin's short stories and novels are memorable for the soul-stirring eloquence and resonance of their pulpit oratory and black music as they plumb the depths of our suffering and the possibilities of our salvation.

Bernard W. Bell. *The Afro-American Novel and Its Tradition*
(Amherst: University of Massachusetts Press, 1987), p. 219

The attitudes of Baldwin's characters to the black church vary dramatically from novel to novel—from survival with a high price in *Go Tell It on the Mountain*, through social protest in *Another Country*, to all-out rejection in *Tell Me How Long the Train's Been Gone*, back to a saving or damning role, depending on the character, in *If Beale Street Could Talk*, to a decidedly political function in his last novel *Just Above My Head*. Despite these different viewpoints in the novels, James Baldwin the man knows that those who hollered in black churches paid a price that began the liberation of the present generation, and his role as writer is to "excavate the role of the people who produced" him.

The final picture of *Go Tell It on the Mountain* is of an island of people united by their common faith in a God who promised to reward them for obeying His edicts. Around them is the sea of ghetto filth that threatens to engulf them with the "vices of perdition." They are returning home after an all night "tarry service" that had become an initiation ritual—a conversion event. The final picture encompasses the novel's principal preoccupations. During the hours preceding the "tarry service" we are witnesses to the Grimes' family battles that turn around guilt, poverty, wife-beating, and even sibling rivalry. These they leave to journey to the central location of "The Temple of Fire Baptized," to engage in rituals that affirm the beliefs that give meaning to their lives. The black church becomes a raft to which each of the characters clings. . . .

To date, Baldwin is the only black American novelist to write a serious novel exclusively around the rituals of the black church. For him as for [Arna] Bontemps and [Alice] Walker, the black church was a mystical body during slavery, but he goes beyond that to show that what was essentially beneficial in slavery had been transmitted unchanged to a nonslave era, with damaging results. The exorcism of pain and the promise of the glories of heaven treated in [Langston] Hughes and [Richard] Wright are also evident here. But the moral strength of a Vyry [in Margaret Walker's *Jubilee*] or an Aunt Hager [in Hughes's *Not Without Laughter*] is missing—even in a character like Deborah. Baldwin waited until *The Fire Next Time* and his later novels to express much of what he felt was negative about the black church. In *The Fire Next Time* he feels the black race would be better served if, instead of holding Sunday school classes and calling on the Lord, blacks organized rent strikes. Having been a preacher, he realized that what was deemed to be the Holy Spirit was simply theatrical conjuration; moreover the preachers knew it. It was only the congregation that was fooled. He chose, however, not to show these feelings in *Go Tell It on the Mountain*. In *Just Above My Head* Baldwin focuses on the political possibilities of the black church, especially in its use of the spirituals to strengthen the determination to fight injustice, just as in an earlier era those same spirituals had helped blacks to surmount injustice.

H. Nigel Thomas. *From Folklore to Fiction: A Study of Folk Heroes and Rituals in the Black American Novel* (New York: Greenwood Press, 1988), pp. 143–44, 151

Since James Baldwin passed away in his adopted home, France, on the last day of November 1987, the many and varied tributes to him, like the blind men's versions of the elephant, have been consistent in one detail—the immensity, the sheer prodigality of endowment. . . .

When at last I met Jimmy in person in the jungles of Florida in 1980, I actually greeted him with *Mr. Baldwin, I presume!* You should have seen his eyes dancing, his remarkable face working in ripples of joyfulness. During the four days we spent down there I saw how easy it was to make Jimmy smile; and how the world he was doomed to inhabit would remorselessly deny him that simple benediction.

Baldwin and I were invited by the African Literature Association to open its annual conference in Gainesville with a public conversation. As we stepped into a tremendous ovation in the packed auditorium of the Holiday Inn, Baldwin was in particularly high spirits. I thought the old preacher in him was reacting to the multitude.

He went to the podium and began to make his opening statements. Within minutes a mystery voice came over the public address system and began to hurl racial insults at him and me. I will see that moment to the end of my life. The happiness brutally wiped off Baldwin's face; the genial manner gone; the eyes flashing in defiant combativeness; the voice incredibly calm and measured. And the words of remorseless prophecy began once again to flow. . . .

[Neither] history nor legend encourages us to believe that a man who sits on his fellow will some day climb down on the basis of sounds reaching him from below. And yet we must consider how so much more dangerous our already very perilous world would become if the oppressed everywhere should despair altogether of invoking reason and humanity to arbitrate their cause. This is the value and the relevance, into the foreseeable future, of James Baldwin.

Chinua Achebe. *Hopes and Impediments: Selected Essays*
(New York: Doubleday, 1989), pp. 171, 173–76

BAMBARA, TONI CADE (1939–   )

UNITED STATES

Contemporary black writers seem to view urban life as lovable only when the ancestor is there. The worst thing that can happen in a city is that the ancestor becomes merely a parent or an adult and is thereby seen as a betrayer—one who has abandoned his traditional role of adviser with a strong connection to the past.

Toni Cade Bambara has written two collections of short stories and one novel. She is a New Yorker, born and educated in that city with an intimate and fearless knowledge of it, and although the tone of most of her stories is celebratory, full of bravura, joyfully survivalist, the principal fear and grief of her characters is the betrayal of an adult who has abandoned not the role of providing for, but the role of adviser, competent protector. Of the sixteen stories in *Gorilla, My Love*, only two stories cannot fit that description. . . .

In her novel, *The Salt Eaters*, the theme is totally explicated. A would-be suicide is literally and metaphorically healed by the ancestor; the witch woman, the spiritual sage, the one who asks of this oh so contemporary and oh so urban daughter of the 1960s, "Are you sure you want to be well?" Here is the village, its values, its resources, its determination not to live, as Stevie Wonder has put it, "just enough for the city," and its requisites for survival only. The village is determined to flourish as well, and it is that factor that makes it possible for Velma to rise from the ancestor's shawl and drop it to the floor "like a cocoon."

Toni Morrison. In Michael C. Jaye and Ann Chalmers Watts, eds.
Literature & the Urban Experience: Essays on the City and Literature
(New Brunswick, N. J.: Rutgers University Press, 1981), pp. 40–41

The Salt Eaters, like one complex jazz symphony, orchestrates the chordal riffs introduced in the short stories of Toni Cade Bambara collected, so far, in two volumes: *Gorilla, My Love* and *The Sea Birds Are Still Alive*. The improvising, stylizing, vamping, re-creative method of the jazz composer is the formal method by which the narrative genius of Toni Cade Bambara evokes a usable past testing its values within an examined present moment while simultaneously exploring the re-creative and transformative possibilities of experience. The method of the jazz composition informs the central themes and large revelation of the world of Bambara's fiction. In that world, time is not linear like clock time; rather, it is convergent. All time converges everywhere in that world in the immediate present; the contemporary, remote, or prehistorical past, and the incipient future are in constant fluid motion. Thus, a play of oppositions and the points of juncture between the past and present form a pattern of summons and response shaping the design of *Gorilla, My Love*, *The Sea Birds Are Still Alive*, and *The Salt Eaters*.

The meaning of ancestry and, consequently, the meaning of modernity is the primary focus of the Bambara narrator. The central vision of both the short and long fiction fixes a view of ancestry as the single most important inquiry of personhood and of community life. But ancestry, in the communities revealed in *Gorilla, My Love*, in *The Sea Birds Are Still Alive*, and in *The Salt Eaters*. is no mere equivalent of the past. Rather, ancestry is the sum of the accumulated wisdom of the race, through time, as it manifests itself in the living, in the *e'gungun*, and in the yet unborn. Often, in the narrative world of Toni Cade Bambara, the search for ancestry is the unconscious quest of the central character as it is for Velma of *The Salt Eaters*, or it is the conscious quest as for Jewel in "The Survivor" of *Gorilla, My Love*. And, in the title story of *The Sea Birds Are Still Alive*, the ancestral theme and one of its sharpest images is sounded in the musings of a boat pilot: ". . . it's not the water in front that pulls the river along. It's the rear guard that is the driving force."

Eleanor W. Traylor. In Mari Evans, ed. *Black Women Writers (1950–1980): A Critical Evaluation* (New York: Doubleday, 1984), pp. 65–66

Demonstrably, women are at the novel's [*The Salt Eaters*] center. Other aspects of it, too, are very *female*—references to "the moony womb," "the shedding of skin on schedule," and the synchrony of Palma's and Velma's menstrual clocks; the sister love between Nilda and Cecile who wear each other's hats; Obie's precise description of Velma's orgasm as "the particular spasm . . . the tremor begin[ning] at the tip of his joint" which it had taken him two years living with her to recognize; M'Dear's teaching that the "master brain" was in the "uterus, where all ideas sprung from and were nurtured and released to the lesser brain in the head." Such intimate attention parallels Bambara's larger interest in "black women and other women, particularly young women," in "that particular voice and stance that they're trying to find." . . . Like them, Bambara searches for a "new vocabulary of images" which, when found, is "stunning . . . very stunning."

First at the beginning, and then finally at the end, of studying the novel, one must reckon with its initially strange name. Of the three working titles which Bambara used to help her stay focused—"In the Last Quarter," "The Seven Sisters," and "The Salt Eaters"—this is the one she retained. . . . The title . . . calls into the subconscious images related to the folk concepts of "swallowing a bitter pill" and "breaking bread together." There are many allusions to salt in the novel, but they are not as numerous as references to some of the other major symbols. While the image of "The Salt Eaters" condenses the essence of this grand work, it does not reverberate all of its colors.

[Akasha] Gloria T. Hull. In Marjorie Pryse and Hortense J. Spillers, eds.

Conjuring: Black Women, Fiction, and Literary Tradition

(Bloomington: Indiana University Press, 1985), pp. 230–31

Toni Cade Bambara's stories focus on the ways gender roles, ideology, family, and community condition the experiences of black women. She portrays initiation as a painful but frequently rewarding ritual. Like [James Alan] McPherson, she seeks to take her characters from a state of certainty to a state of doubt, but unlike him, she does not so clearly define the conventions of that certainty. She implies that the realm of woman is more organic and less overtly confrontational than that of man. Nonetheless, a dialectic is clearly at work, one that is in some ways more complex since it adds to generational, racial, and cultural oppositions the polarity of male-female. While Bambara says that she is "much more concerned with the caring that lies beneath the antagonisms between black men and black women," she does repeatedly examine the nature of those antagonisms. Moreover, like [Ernest] Gaines and McPherson, she finds in folk material the means for her characters to resist fixed, dehumanizing identities, whether sexual, racial, or cultural. And also like these male writers, she tends to leave her characters at the edge of some new experience rather than with a sense of the completion of action and thus the resolution of oppositions. . . .

The stories of *Gorilla, My Love* are largely devoted to the lessons offered girls and young women within their local community or through representatives of the larger black folk community. Whether the lessons are learned or not, the tendency is to assume that the older members of the group have insights to pass along. Even in "The Johnson Girls," where the women are all young, the forms they use to share their experiences are the traditional forms of black expression. What happens in *The Sea Birds Are Still Alive*, a second collection of stories, is that Bambara expresses some doubt about the validity of folk experience in the process of trying to link folk wisdom to feminist, and to some degree nationalist, ideology. This doubt grows out of a more overt ideological perspective in these stories. The central, often narrating characters are pitted on the one side against very hopeful political activists and on the other against the harsh conditions of the black community. Bambara moves the central figures from their doubt toward an acceptance of revolutionary action. But in the process her characters must raise important questions about ideology that cannot be easily answered. Ultimately, and despite the apparent intentions of the author, the acceptance of ambiguity, which is the condition of folk reality, seems a more powerful narrative force than the positive identity of ideological imposition. The results are uneasy narratives that sometimes must strain to make their points.

> Keith E. Byerman. *Fingering the Jagged Grain: Tradition and Form in Recent*
> *Black Fiction* (Athens: University of Georgia Press, 1985), pp. 105, 114–15

Like her works in other genres, Bambara's short stories primarily aim at truth speaking, particularly as *truth* is related to the semiotic mediation of black existential modalities. Of primary importance are the construction and representation of an organic black community and the articulation of black nationalist ideology. Nevertheless, her two short story collections, *Gorilla, My Love* and *The Sea Birds Are Still Alive*, are marked by dissonance and ruptures; in both volumes, Bambara's insertion of themes related to the desires of black women and girls disrupts and often preempts the stories' primary focus on classic realism and nationalism.

In *Gorilla*, Bambara's use of the young girl Hazel as the primary narrator results in a decentering of the stories. In each narrative, a subtext focused on issues with which girls and women are confronted threatens to displace the racial discourse that is in the dominant text. The stories in *Sea Birds*, which are generally more explicitly political than those in *Gorilla*, directly inscribe the tensions between racial and gender politics. The stories in *Sea Birds*, then, signal a pre-emergent feminist consciousness. In this collection, more complex development and representations of black women of "the community," increased marginalization and deconstruction of mythologies centered on black males, and the general highlighting of feminine and feminist issues indicate a heightening of tensions between gender and racial politics.

> Elliott Butler-Evans. *Race, Gender, and Desire*
> (Philadelphia, Penn.: Temple University Press, 1989), pp. 92–93

The question of identity—of personal definition within the context of community—emerges as a central motif for Toni Cade Bambara's writing. Her female characters become as strong as they do, not because of some inherent "eternal feminine" quality granted at conception, but rather because of the lessons women learn from communal interaction. Identity is achieved, not bestowed. Bambara's short stories focus on such learning. Very careful to present situations in a highly orchestrated manner, Bambara describes the difficulties that her characters must overcome. . . .

Bambara's stories present a decided emphasis on the centrality of community. Many writers concentrate so specifically on character development or plot line that community seems merely a foil against which the characters react. For Bambara the community becomes essential as a locus for growth, not simply as a source of narrative tension. Thus, her characters and community do a circle dance around and within each other as learning and growth occur.

Bambara's women learn how to handle themselves within the divergent, often conflicting, strata that compose their communities. Such learning does not come easily; hard lessons result from hard knocks. Nevertheless, the women do not merely endure; they prevail, emerging from these situations more aware of their personal identities and of their potential for further self-actualization. More important, they guide others to achieve such awareness. . . .

Toni Cade Bambara's stories do more than paint a picture of black life in contemporary black settings. Many writers have done that, more or less successfully. Her stories portray women who struggle with issues and learn from them. Sometimes the lessons taste bitter and the women must accumulate more experience in order to gain perspective. By centering community in her stories, Bambara displays both the supportive and destructive aspects of communal interaction. Her stories do not describe a predictable, linear plot line; rather, the cyclic enfolding of characters and community produces the kind of tension missing in stories with a more episodic emphasis.

Her characters achieve a personal identity as a result of their participation in the human quest for knowledge, which brings power. Bambara's skill as a writer saves her characters from being stereotypic cutouts. Although her themes are universal, communities that Bambara describes rise above the generic. More fully delineated than her male characters, the women come across as specific people living in specific places. Bambara's best stories show her characters interacting within a political framework wherein the personal becomes political.

Martha M. Vertreace. In Mickey Pearlman, ed. American Women
Writing Fiction: Memory, Identity, Family, Space (Lexington:
University Press of Kentucky, 1989), pp. 155–56, 165–66

BARAKA, AMIRI (1934–   )

UNITED STATES

In [Amiri Baraka's] *Dutchman* the theme of the outsider has racial reverberations. The typical American outsider is the black educated man, difficult to place in the social ladder. He is doubly an outsider as he no longer belongs to the blacks, separated as he is in his aspirations and because of the potpourri nature of his culture, a factor that is reflected in the mythical and historical background of the play. Vis-à-vis the whites, he is considered an Uncle Tom, meek, aping white ways, and so desirous of their women. [Baraka] initially portrays this Uncle Tom stereotype in his portrayal of Clay, only to blast it in his exploration of the hidden aspect of the Uncle Tom—the revolutionary aspect. Thus, Lula and the American society which she represents experience a psychologically unbalancing phenomenon in [Baraka's] presentation of the erstwhile easygoing Uncle Tom. His Uncle Tom is an iceberg whose destructive potentialities are so well hidden that they take their victim by surprise. Lula the liberal thinks she knows Clay; but his tirade is unexpected, arousing primitive instincts for self-protection in her. For Lula and the society to maintain their equilibrium, society must connive at getting rid of the outsider, as we see in Clay's instance. His character is not individualized, emphasizing the democratizing quality of black art. Clay is the chosen black representative, and his role, with its suffering and pain, is for the benefit of all black men. Indeed, one can envisage a black audience reacting to his tirade with punctuations of "say it, brother," "right on," "soul brother," etc., as he puts into words what had been in black minds. He is a typical black, educated middle-class man, one of many on the journey through American history. The antagonist is Lula, whose confrontation with Clay represents that great, unconsummated stereotypic romance between the white woman and the black American man. Receiving an inkling of the unseen reaches of this outsider, she unleashes her violence in typical frontier fashion, for these are the frontiers of the black-white relation, with its ignorance, its pretensions, its sexuality, its deceptiveness, its violence and blood bath.

Lula seems to have won this round but it is only seemingly so. Clay, however, has lived fully in his moment of outburst and, like [Ernest] Hemingway's Francis Macomber, he is a hero who has enjoyed a triumph though it is short-lived. Lula's murderous career indicates what she is—a mad criminal—as she waits to tackle her next victim. Her violence against Clay or all black men is a representation, from [Baraka's] point of view, of the emasculating nature of the relationship between white women and black men. Her use of a knife demonstrates symbolically black penis envy; it adequately illustrates the psychological and sexual undertones in the relationship. The disturbing nature of [Baraka's] portrayal is consequently obvious as he dismisses one popularly held opinion after the other.

Chikwenye Okonjo Ogunyemi. In Eldred Durosimi Jones, ed.
African Literature Today. 9 (1978), pp. 29–30

The plays by Afro-American writer LeRoi Jones . . . who has used the African name Amiri Baraka ("blessed prince") in his civil and literary life since 1968, illustrate the political and artistic changes Baraka's writing underwent in the past twenty years. . . . The early works reflect, and in some ways herald, the gradual change in mood from the bohemian life of the Beat Generation in the 1950s to the new race consciousness and political flamboyance of the 1960s, the later plays show Baraka's commitment, first to black cultural nationalism and, in the case of the last play, to Maoism.

Baraka's first drama, *The Eighth Ditch* (*Is Drama*), published and performed in 1961, is indicative of the interference of the "social" with the lyrical world of a poet's imagination who is obsessed with a narcissistic self-division into two personae, one "46," a young middle-class Negro boy scout, and his counterpart, guide, and seducer, "64," an older underprivileged black boy scout who introduces himself with the Melvillean salute "Call me Herman," and who is full of blues and allusions. The pure physical expression of which 64 and 46 seem capable in isolation is threatened and debased when other boy scouts in the camp find out about their homosexual affair.

This brief lyrical drama anticipates central structural elements of Baraka's later drama. Viewed on the literal level, the drama represents the two protagonists' inability to maintain a truly intimate sexual relationship, since they are confronted with the threatening presence of "others." At the end of the play, "46" is no longer a lover; for the benefit of the other boy scouts, he has been reduced to a commodity, an object. As in the later plays, *The Toilet* and *Dutchman*, the dramatic conflict originates with the assumed hostility of the not very well characterized "others" (boy scouts, classmates, or subway riders) toward the sensitive protagonists, a hostility which perverts love into abuse, into violence, or into the very act of killing. . . .

The Toilet, first performed in 1962, is set in an urban high school and deals again with loving self-expression in terms of homosexuality. The one-act play contrasts the homosexual relationship of two protagonists with the hostile and threatening, all-male outside world. Again, homosexuality is viewed positively by Baraka both as an outsider-situation analogous to, though now in conflict with, that of blackness, and as a possibility for the realization of "love" and "beauty" against the racial gang code of a hostile society. But there is also a new element of race consciousness in the play. . . .

Among Baraka's . . . plays performed at the Black Arts Repertory Theatre/ School was *Experimental Death Unit No. 1.* . . . The play is a short "black" continuation of *Waiting for Godot*. Two white bums from the Theater of the Absurd, Duff and Loco, philosophize in Barakian lyricisms about life and art, beauty and intelligence, when a black prostitute appears on the Third Avenue scene. Duff and Loco make perverse propositions to the woman who is in need of money and entices the two men. The two men begin to make love to the woman in a hallway, when the black group for which the play is named comes marching in, behind a "pike on the top of which is a white man's head still dripping blood." The group leader orders Loco, Duff, and the black woman killed; the white men's heads are cut off and fitted on two poles. The bodies are pushed into a heap, and the experimental death unit marches off. . . .

The difference between the play's decadent victims and their black executioners is further developed in the later play, *Home on the Range*. . . .

Death Unit and *Home on the Range* are attempts at de-brainwashing a black audience, and at exorcising Baraka's literary past, by ridiculing absurdist drama as an expression of white degeneracy. Against this degenerate white world, Baraka poses the orderly military violence of the black execution squad and the power of black music and dance. The references to Robin Hood movies and to Frankenstein as well as the very title of *Home on the Range*, are indicative of another familiar technique, which Baraka now uses to reach black audiences:

he continues his adaptations of American popular culture, even in the process of inverting its mythology.

The most famous example of a black nationalist popular culture play is *Jello*, a drama written for, and performed at, the Black Arts Repertory Theatre/ School. *Jello* is a parody of the Jack Benny radio and television show; in the course of *Jello*, Eddie "Rochester" Anderson, Benny's chauffeur-servant, appears in a new, revolutionary role. Rochester lets his hair grow long, is "post-uncletom" in appearance, and demands his "back pay" from Jack Benny. Although the miserly Benny does, eventually and reluctantly, part with his $300 in petty cash, Rochester still wants more: "I want everything you got except the nasty parts." Perhaps as an elaboration of these "nasty parts," Benny is later accused of advocating "art for art's sake." While Rochester knows everything about Benny, Benny knows nothing about his chauffeur and "friend." In the key speech of the play, Rochester almost becomes another Clay; he voices his moral grievance, which, of course, exceeds the demand for back pay, and criticizes the medium which the play parodies, that "evil tube." . . .

A Black Mass continues the technique of inverting elements of American popular culture; it parodies *Frankenstein* as one-dimensionally as *Jello* parodied the Jack Benny show. *A Black Mass*, however, is also a black ritual which incorporates the mythology of the Nation of Islam into a black nationalist play which questions the functions of art and creativity. . . .

Slave Ship: A Historical Pageant, one of Baraka's most interesting plays of the black nationalist period, attempts to raise the political consciousness of black audiences by first showing historical models of black oppression and then breaking them on stage and inviting the audience to join in the ritual. Baraka's only endeavor to write a historical play—beyond the mythmaking of *A Black Mass*—interprets black history somewhat statically, as a chain of similar oppressive situations, in each of which blacks are the victimized group. On stage, the lower boat deck of the middle passage is transformed, first into slave market and "quarters," and finally into a contemporary black ghetto. At the same time, the whites on the upper tier change their functions—from captain and sailors to slave dealers and plantation owners, and finally, to white business men. Between the two groups of white oppressors and black people is the middle-class Uncle Tom, who is at first a shuffling "knee-grow" aboard ship, later betrays Nat Turner's rebellion to his slave-master, and finally appears in a reverend's suit as a parody of Martin Luther King.

Werner Sollors. In Hedwig Bock and Albert Wertheim, eds.
Essays on Contemporary American Drama
(Munich: Hueber, 1981) pp. 105–6, 110–13, 117

It is difficult to find in [the so-called New Black Theater] a play which could be called an allegory in the strict sense; however, there are several that could be termed allegorical. [Amiri] Imamu Baraka's play, *Great Goodness of Life (A Coon Show)*, is an example. Reminiscent of [Franz] Kafka's *The Trial*, a middle-aged postal employee (bureaucrat) named Court Royal is arrested and charged by an anonymous voice (omnipotent Whiteman) which never reveals itself. The characters, some visible and some not, all represent something beyond their surface roles. Court's lawyer, for example, appears on stage with wires attached to his back and a huge wind-up key stuck in the side of his head. He babbles, slobbers, and grins as he recommends in exaggerated sheepishness that Court simply plead guilty and accept his fate without resistance. He is the overdrawn mimicked symbol of the Uncle Tom who stands ready to sell Court down the river at the mere suggestion of the anonymous White Voice. On the surface, he is a lawyer, but there is a second and more important meaning to be read beneath and concurrent with the surface story. This second meaning is made obvious to the audience through the use of blatant symbols like the wind-up key in the side of the lawyer's head, which tells us immediately that he is really the Uncle Tom of the story.

As the lawyer exits, another character variously named Young Voice, Young Boy, and Young Man enters. He is strong, young, and black, and speaks tough and cryptically. He wears only black. He, like the lawyer, demands that Court plead guilty, but for entirely different reasons. To Young Voice, Court is a "guilty, stupid nigger" because he has worked hard all his life and caused no trouble. Young Voice, who is obviously the play's militant antagonist, is also a captive of the unseen White Voice. In the end, Court is asked by that voice to shoot Young Voice in a blood rite that will set him free and turn his soul "white as snow." After only a brief hesitation, he shoots Young Voice, who dies, but not before saying in his last breath that Court is his "Papa." Court is stunned for a second, but quickly recovers, singing that his soul is "white as snow."

On the surface, we have the story of a weak man who kills his own son rather than resist the pressures of an evil power. In the second and concurrent meaning, we have a middle-aged black, a representative of an older generation, who is so intimidated and filled with fear of the white man that he is unable to stand up for the life of his own son. Filicide, an unthinkable sin, becomes preferable to resisting the omnipotent white man. Through allegory, the play achieves the suspense of drama as well as the implicit communication of a nationalistic value system.

Shelby Steele. In Errol Hill, ed. The Theatre of Black Americans
(New York: Applause, 1987), pp. 33–35

Baraka's revised aesthetic led him in at least two clear "social" directions, yielding first the agitprop dramas of *Four Black Revolutionary Plays* and *Jello*. With the exception of *A Black Mass*, these works conform closely to the requirements set forth in "The Revolutionary Theatre." In *Experimental Death Unit No. 1*, *Great Goodness of Life*, and *Madheart*, black victims are parodied, castigated, or shown in horrible deaths. Duff and Loco, the white characters of *Experimental Death Unit No. 1*, are appropriately crushed by the bullets of the Black Liberation Army—not before they have been rendered patently grotesque by their dialogue and actions, however. *A Black Mass* stands out from the company because its tone and language are elevated to match a sophisticated ideational framework. The conflict between Jacoub and his fellow "magicians" in the black arts is one between the restless, empirical inventor and the mystical artists who feel their oneness with all things. Finally, Jacoub creates both time and a hideous white beast who adores it under the following sanction: "Let us be fools. For creation is its own end." *A Black Mass* employs the demonology of the Nation of Islam, but in Baraka's hands its story takes on the character of a lyrical, mythopoeic exchange designed to guide the energies of the new Black Arts Movement. The play is dedicated to "the brothers and sisters of The Black Arts."

> Houston A. Baker, Jr. *Afro-American Poetics: Revisions of Harlem and the Black Aesthetic* (Madison: University of Wisconsin Press, 1988), pp. 131–32

Among contemporary writers, no one has been more provocative, politically and otherwise, than Amiri Baraka. . . . In the political sphere, Baraka has been as notorious for his radical transformations as for his radical stances. Bohemian aesthete, new left polemicist, black cultural nationalist, and Marxist-Leninist-Maoist, Baraka has declared his politics uncompromisingly at every phase of his career. More importantly . . . he has always insisted on an integral relationship between political and aesthetic commitments. I have written elsewhere on the major phases of Baraka's career and how his politics have shaped his creative work. The purpose of the present essay is to examine Baraka's use of popular cultural motifs and his understanding, at various points of his career, of how political meaning imbues the icons of popular culture. . . .

Throughout *Preface to a Twenty Volume Suicide Note*, Baraka uses the icons of popular culture . . . both as objects of criticism and articles of faith. The same is true in his second collection of poems, *The Dead Lecturer*, except that these poems express the central existential crisis of Baraka's life, and his formulations present polarized extremes with a tone more shrill and less coy. He still sifts through the artifacts of popular culture in search of adequate articles of faith, but the sense of satisfactory resolution expressed in "In Memory of Radio" eludes him here. . . .

The turning point for Baraka came with his reinvestigation of Afro-American history, which helped him to transcend the dogmatic cultural nationalist assumption that the past offers only a dreary chronicle of abject slavery, cowardly capitulations, and false consciousness. At the same time, his study of Mao and rediscovery of Langston Hughes made him recognize the existence of a long and powerful international tradition of politicized art. These discoveries made it possible for Baraka to reconceive the relationship between the artist and existing culture. As a cultural nationalist, Baraka had assumed that the artist must destroy the corrupt existing culture in order to create a new, more humane culture. Now, he began to recognize the tradition of struggle embedded within existing culture, and this recognition entailed the possibility of an art grounded in that tradition of struggle. Such an art could celebrate as well as criticize; it could embody the complexities of real historical experience. Perhaps most importantly, it would allow the poet to write as a voice within a tradition and not just as a lonely pioneer, attempting by the naked force of rhetoric to lead his audience away from reality and into the promised land of utopian "blackness."

David Lionel Smith. In Adam J. Sorkin, ed. *Politics and the Muse: Studies in the Politics of Recent American Literature* (Bowling Green, Ohio: Bowling Green State University Popular Press, 1989), pp. 222, 225–26, 231–32

Baraka's deep concern with tradition is part of a pervasive concern among black intellectuals with identifying and codifying an existing tradition. . . .

Underlying or overt, the concern with tradition and traditions . . . counterpoints both political and aesthetic radicalism, and it locates unequivocally in Baraka's major poem *In the Tradition*, which he has both published and recorded (with music). Dedicating it to "Black Arthur Blythe," the alto saxophonist (whose 1979 record album lent the poem its title), Baraka calls it "a poem about African American history . . . a cultural history and political history." If a single work could sum him up "at a certain point," he says, it would probably be that poem. It incorporates his spirit, his energy, his musicality, all that he ever learned about and contributed to the visual and aural elements of modern poetry. . . .

Baraka's new book, *The Music*, clearly locates in its very title his focus for present and future. It is black music that has provided the lens, the cohesion, and the communication he has been pursuing as he "investigates the sun." This anthology of recent work, of [his wife] Amina's poetry and his own poetry, essays, and "anti-nuclear jazz musical," reveals a second and relatively new emphasis: Baraka as a poet/musician of praise—a lover of "The Music" (by which black music is understood) and the family of black musicians who create and interpret it, and a lover of his own family, itself consanguine within it.

D. H. Melhem. *Heroism in the New Black Poetry* (Lexington: University Press of Kentucky, 1990), pp. 220–21

Rebelling against conventional linguistics, Baraka's "I Love Music" uses no capital letters for proper nouns. This conscious subversion promotes a vision of freedom from stultifying categories of expression. Just as Baraka notes, in the essay "Greenwich Village and the African-American Music," that the "music was trying to get away from the restrictions of tradition without reason," so too his poetry was attempting, through subversion of conventional forms, to return to African rhythms, to reclaim the primacy of improvisation and the primordial construct. . . .

In the essay "Expressive Language," Baraka articulates the need for a new speech to undermine hierarchies of Western meaning; and he searches for this voice in African rhythms. Baraka feels that the twisting of meanings by dominant language forms has been a cause of great confusion and ignorance, both on the part of the dominated and the dominator, the latter having convinced himself that his distortions are justified and are, in effect, solid reasoning and no distortion at all. The Slave Trade was blessed by the religious and political leaders in Europe because, to them, the African was a heathen whose enslavement was therefore a natural punishment by God for his sinful nature. Projective verse as used by Baraka . . . attempts to tear down the hierarchical language structures which have consolidated that illusory view of Western superiority by over-esteeming and inflating Western importance.

Anthony Kellman. *Ariel*. 21, 2 (April 1990), pp. 54–55

"The Screamers" is like a free-form jazz solo. Many readers find it difficult because of its adroit blurring and blending of visual and temporal details, its shifts in time, setting, and emotional sequences; its fragments of biography, history, and sociopolitical commentary. Reading the story, then, is like solving a puzzle of space, time, character, chronology, event, and description. There are jazz-dada-surrealist shifts in accents; scenes and themes are introduced, reiterated, and amplified in solos within solos, where jazz is both meat and meteor, providing the substance and movement of the story. . . .

Although "The Screamers" challenges Western tradition in its obscuring and fragmenting of detail, it nevertheless maintains the complications of a traditional beginning: conflict and establishing the circumstances of character, society, and historical situation that must be resolved. As Baraka continues his jazz improvisations on divisiveness and solitude through the "slow or jerked staccato," the narrator makes initial efforts at communion, but it is only a communion of perception and intellect, not of feeling; he like the others remains a "valuable shadow, barely visible . . . Chanting at that dark crowd." Throughout the story, notes run together in a musical collage of identities and images: "Big hats bent tight skirts" in a "mingled foliage of sweat and shadows." The narrator is aware of the poorer blacks' misperceptions of him as "that same oppressor" and acknowledges his own arrogant and disordered misinterpretations of their mystery. . . .

In his use of jazz as metaphor and model for narrative and dramatic strategies, Amiri Baraka in "The Screamers" fashions a form that shows the integration of the artistic and social imagination. The story doesn't entirely resolve social dilemmas and paradoxes of consciousness, but it is successful as a blending of aesthetic and moral function in a new mode, and it provides a breakthrough and a greater feeling of fictional boundaries through its use of jazz as subject, tonal structure, and aesthetic-ethical model.

Gayl Jones. *Liberating Voices: Oral Tradition in African American Literature*
(Cambridge, Mass.: Harvard University Press, 1991), pp. 115–18, 122

As Leroi Jones, Baraka found himself out of his ethnie in a literary world that fetishized his ethnos. He never had a chance to view his ethnoculture with mere wonder, or nostalgia, or love. He found himself among a hundred white agents of articulation of a perceived black ethnoculture. Baraka's brief early years as a black bohemian are replete with this false agency. His ethnicization is directed by them—it is joyous, full of libido, and critical of the black bourgeoisie. Norman Mailer's "White Negro" lacked anger, sexual violence, black nationalism, or Marxism; he was a black man as the Beats wished to find him. The Beats wanted simply "jazz as orgasm." At first Baraka provided it. Although the host society plays a role in the process from ethnogenesis to ethnicization in any ethnie, in the case of Baraka it is possible to say that attention was so great, and the black community so oppressed and silenced, that reverse ethnicization occurred, created by the Beats, in which Baraka was handed highly ideological material. In the beginning he takes an almost primordial approach to this manufactured culture. . . .

Thus Baraka confronts the pervasiveness of his ethnos in American culture and consciousness, as it is portrayed, sublimated, stolen, and examined by the majority. Baraka sees that blacks are, on the one hand, rendered historically inarticulate, and on the other, accorded by the majority with a deep and pivotal place in American culture. Baraka challenges, in these poems, the right of people outside the ethnos to influence ethnicization. He becomes an agent of articulation to challenge others who would claim the role; he becomes indeed a guerrilla of articulation.

Steve Harney. JASt. 25, 3 (December 1991), pp. 371–72, 377

BEBEY, FRANCIS (1929–   )

CAMEROON

Each of the short stories in the collection entitled *Embarras & Cie* is followed by a poem which echoes the theme, sometimes personal, sometimes traditional, in which fantasy, humor, reverie and serious reflections all meet. [Francis] Bebey is a very articulate artist, completely at home in a Western cultural environment in which he mainly lives. But he retains a deep loyalty to the artistic traditions of his origins in Cameroon. The humor, the fantasy and the lighthearted irony of much of his writing belie his seriousness as a disciple of an enlightened neo-Négritude school, less portentous than its predecessors and stripped of all militancy, which the situation in any case no longer demands. . . .

In the eight short stories of *Embarras & Cie* (the title comes from one of the poems inserted between the tales), the author speaks in his own name, sometimes recounting a brief personal experience, sometimes an incident purporting to have occurred in his native Cameroonian village, or have been told to him by a fellow traveler. For the most part they are as light and transparent as gossamer and as smoothly textured as velvet—woven out of gentle raillery, mock self-deprecation, pseudo-naïveté, and disarming understatement. But under cover of this reassuring bonhomie, Bebey shoots off little barbed shafts and sometimes the gossamer is the web woven by a spider hidden in its heart to catch its prey. His exposition of a sorcerer's difficulties in making ends meet in this enlightened age is innocent enough, or his mockery of marriage customs and the one-up-manship of rural African society in "Le Mariage d'Edda," where the whole hierarchy of status symbols is revealed, ranging from a brick house to the ultimate in coveted possessions—a tropical pith helmet. But the dart sinks deeper in "Jimmy et l'égalité," aimed at the ambiguous position of the Westernized Negro—the "Black Frenchman"—and at the whole master-servant relationship of black Africa, inherited from the colonial era.

With only two works of fiction to his name, Bebey showed that he was an accomplished prose writer as well as a poet. With his sure sense of the ironic effects to be drawn from the simplest, colloquial language, with his humorous tolerance of human foibles, spiced at times with subtle malice, Francis Bebey's writing in his first novel [*Le Fils d'Agatha Moudio*] and short stories has the same impact of that of his countryman Bernard Dadié. Like him, too, he manages to imply criticism without dogmatism or any overt attacks. If he trails a wisp of Négritude after him, it is a Négritude freed from any complexes, any protest, any hatred or even cynicism. It is compounded of a concern for honesty—which means for him writing as an African—and a preoccupation with getting through to his reader.

Dorothy S. Blair. *African Literature in French*
(Cambridge: Cambridge University Press, 1976), pp. 171, 289–90

A Western reader, scrutinizing the novels of Francis Bebey, may be struck by their apparent lack of narrative consistency. It is as if the author had set out quite systematically to flout all the rules handed down by Flaubert, Henry James, and Ford Madox Ford. Objective narration and its attendant qualities of neutrality, impartiality, and *impassibilité* are thrown to the winds as Bebey's narrators become either his direct spokesmen or enjoy a bonanza of self-indulgence, interpreting the facts, pronouncing judgments, offering advice, and digressing at length on a host of subjects ranging from the trivial to the intellectually abstract. Far from adhering to the convention which requires that a story be told from one point of view, these same narrators adopt any stance convenient to their immediate purposes—omniscient author, author-participant, author-observer—within the confines of the same novel. In short, a dominant characteristic of Bebey's work is its polytonality.

Although familiar with Western novelistic techniques, having studied literature at two French *lycées* (La Rochelle and Louis le Grand) and at the Sorbonne, Bebey chooses quite consciously to discount them in favor of a more instinctive approach. . . . This insouciance produces a form of expression closely allied to that of the oral folktale as delivered by the traditional Doualan *conteur*. An examination of his three novels—*Le Fils d'Agatha Moudio*, *La Poupée ashanti* and *Le Roi Albert d'Effidi*—will demonstrate the point and highlight certain defects in Bebey's artistry.

Le Fils d'Agatha Moudio may be viewed as the unhappy tale of a simple, good-hearted young fisherman, Mbenda, who is constantly victimized by the social system and the mischievous appetites of those around him. He ends up saddled with two wives, both of whom have been unfaithful to him and may well continue to be so, and two children, neither of whom is his. To crown all, he seems perfectly resigned to his fate. A similar sense of tragedy hangs over *La Poupée ashanti*, set against the urban backdrop of Nkrumah's Accra. It is the drama of an attractive, intelligent and courageous girl who is seduced in primary school, denied an education, almost killed in a street demonstration, constantly badgered by her domineering grandmother, ultimately brainwashed into spending the rest of her life as a market vendor, and married to a husband whose values and educational level are so markedly different from her own that their future connubial happiness must be regarded at best as uncertain. Bebey's most recent novel, *Le Roi Albert d'Effidi*, brings us the bittersweet tale of a successful middle-aged businessman who is almost destroyed by his political and marital ambitions. Albert's new and dangerously young wife, Nani, is unfaithful to him. He loses an election after a particularly turbulent campaign involving the virtual destruction of his car and his self-respect. Finally, his wayward wife returns to him, and Albert, setting aside his political ambitions and some of his long-held beliefs, returns to his neglected shop.

In their sense of tragedy, these novels are worthy of Balzac. Yet Bebey, for all his cynicism, is basically an optimist in regard both to Africa and to humanity in general. And, equally important, he has a wry sense of humor. He could no more make tragedies out of his stories than could Molière out of *Le Tartuffe*. To have done so would have been to sacrifice their delightful irony, their lightness of tone, their earthiness and ring of truth. It would also have been to violate Bebey's own nature. Such considerations help explain his choice of narrative stance.

Norman Stokle. In Kolawole Ogungbesan, ed.
New West African Literature (London: Heinemann, 1979), pp. 104–5

La Poupée ashanti is, at least on the surface, the most conventionally political of Bebey's works, Set in Accra, Ghana, shortly before Le Docteur's (read: Dr. Nkrumah) accession to the presidency of the new republic, it deals with the marketwomen and their political organization, with the country's leader himself, and includes a large political march and demonstration midway through the novel. And yet the main interest does not lie in politics. Despite the political background, it is essentially the love story of Edna, a young marketwoman, and Spio, a young and somewhat idealistic bureaucrat, which moves the plot. The political issue which is intertwined with this personal relationship centers on the marketwoman who has lost her seller's permit because the man to whom her daughter is engaged has been arrested for being a member of the opposition party in Parliament. This issue and, more generally, that of Le Docteur and the principle of his one-party state, are the subject of heated discussion between Edna, her aunt, and her grandmother, Mam, the leader of the Marketwomen's Association. These political issues are of serious interest now, and at the time Le Docteur (Nkrumah) was coming to real power, topical as well. But a close reading of the text produces two interesting discoveries: first, these key political issues are downplayed by stylistic means and are thus shown to be of less than central importance; second, the novel never resolves these issues, an unusual situation in the highly polemic world of African fiction.

W. Curtis Schade. *StTCL*. 4, 2 (Spring 1980), p. 163

In Francis Bebey's *Le Fils d'Agatha Moudio* we have a . . . humorous account of a love affair, opposed by the man's mother and, thus, by the village as a whole. Set in a fishing village during the colonial period, it offers its own version of the conflict between traditional and Western views of love and marriage. Agatha Moudio's love for Mbenda, a local fisherman, dates from the day when he forced the white monkey-hunters to pay for using the village's forest. By sprinkling salt on the fire, she causes a big rain storm, enabling her to spend the day undisturbed with Mbenda in his hut. They are in love, but Maa Médi, Mbenda's widowed mother, has no intention of allowing her son to fall into the clutches of a loose woman such as Agatha Moudio. As a way to block their relationship, Maa Médi prepares to marry her son to Fanny, whom his father had named, on his deathbed, as Mbenda's future bride. Powerless to oppose the will of his mother and the elders, he continues to see Agatha while the bargaining goes on with Fanny's people. In chapter seven Fanny becomes his wife, and in the next chapter we learn that she is pregnant—but Mbenda, thinking her too young, has never slept with her! Great commotion ensues as the truth is made known, but the birth of a daughter smooths things over. After further intrigues, including Agatha being driven to the city in the white monkey-hunter's car, we learn that Mbenda now has two wives, for Agatha, back in the village after her excursion to the city, has been installed in his hut by her aunt. The village is upset about this, feeling her to be a source of trouble, but, strangely enough, Fanny does not seem to mind at all.

Agatha Moudio is pregnant and is certain that it will be a boy. The village, joyous that some of its men who had been sent to prison are about to return, becomes kinder towards her. The child is born, a boy as predicted, but he is white. The reaction on Mbenda's part is first perplexity, but then joyful acceptance. . . .

While the central conflict is once again the question of who governs the marital relations of the younger generation, it is posed in a far more gentle, more humorous light than in the other works dealing with this theme. The traditional ways are upheld for only the best of motives, the central characters are all essentially likeable people, and the resolution at the end is a peaceful merging of the will of the village with the will of Mbenda and Agatha to love each other.

W. Curtis Schade. In Carolyn A. Parker and Stephen H. Arnold, eds.
When the Drumbeat Changes (Washington, D. C.:
Three Continents Press, 1981), pp. 49–50

Cameroon has had a tradition of producing fine satirists—Mongo Beti, Ferdinand Oyono—and now Francis Bebey, whose third novel is . . . now available in English translation. Warm, genial, comic, the book reflects Bebey's own humor and breadth. Bebey finds harmony in his own life as guitarist, poet, composer, novelist, and musicologist. [*Le Roi Albert d'Effidi*, translated as *King Albert*] reflects this balanced perspective. Set in the Cameroon of the late 1950s, the novel centers on the coming election of a delegate to represent three villages in a parliament for a newly independent nation. Each village claims supremacy for possessing either the highway or the church or the school. Village champions emerge: "King" Albert, successful, middle-aged merchant, hence capitalist; Toutouma, former railroad worker and trade-unionist, hence communist; and Bikounou, minor bureaucrat, the younger generation's upstart and individualist. . . .

Bebey keeps up plot suspense to the very end, for as one hilarious episode favors one champion, the next works to the advantage of another. Though all the principal characters suffer from their frailties, they are the more lovable by being so human. Bebey's sense of the ridiculous is most evident in dialogue, where often the seemingly naive comment contains an ironic twist. The villagers are proud to have learned church response in Latin. Accustomed to European visitors who are linguistically inept, they accommodate the white man's god in whose image he is made: "God understands only Latin, and he never learned our language at school."

The novel has depth: it presents not only delightful satire but also incisive commentary on cultural changes occurring in many Third World societies. The whimsy will amuse the Africanist and the newcomer to African literature alike.

Charlotte H. Bruner. WLT. 56, 3 (Summer 1982), 559–60

For Francis Bebey, change is necessary in African society today. But there is also need to control undesirable aspects of change in order to preserve certain desirable values in the traditional culture. This intention is reflected in the conciliatory measure which he proposes in his novel *Le Roi Albert d'Effidi*, in which traditional values are meaningfully adapted to serve the needs of modern Africa. The novel was published in 1976 by Editions CLE in Cameroon. *Le Roi Albert d'Effidi* attempts a reassessment of the African ancestral past showing its wealth and the extent to which tradition can be comfortably accommodated to the modern world. . . .

There is a conscious attempt in the novel to reaffirm African personality and culture. African food, hospitality, languages, music, and dance figure here prominently. The traditional set-up and beliefs which in the past secured peace, stability, and progress in the community are critically examined in the light of the needs of modern Africa. From an assessment of traditional standards in terms of such substantial goods as food, clothing, and shelter, the author passes to less tangible services such as those connected with education and social welfare. He extends his inquiry to the realm of the human spirit and shows the general sense of the individual and what constitutes social well-being in a traditional African society.

The author draws our attention to modern political campaigns, unheard of in the traditional past, marked by violence and conflicting ideologies which often end in disaster. The dangers of this unfortunate development in Africa in the name of modern politics are outlined by the author, and there is little consolation in telling the victims and the silent millions of modern Africans that the fire of discord has been lit by their own countrymen. *Le Roi Albert d'Effidi* pleads for a critical appraisal and rehabilitation of African traditional values. Francis Bebey appears convinced that traditional values are not necessarily incompatible with modern progress. He calls for caution in matters of change and modernization. With him there is a great need to conduct careful research about the probable effects of alternative courses of action before taking a final decision on them.

Elerius Edet John. *Language Quarterly*. 23, 3–4
(Spring-Summer 1985), pp. 42–43

Although Francis Bebey belongs to the same generation as Ferdinand Oyono and Mongo Beti, he did not begin to write seriously until the mid-1960s. His view of the world was shaped less by a resentment against colonialist oppression than by a desire for reconciliation, for he believed people could transcend the injustices of the past by accepting what cannot be changed and by committing themselves to a society based on love and productive work. Inspired partly by the Christian humanism he absorbed as the son of a Protestant pastor and partly by his respect for traditional African wisdom, Bebey's dream of reconciliation expresses his belief in a spiritual reality that gives meaning to human existence. When people lose contact with this reality, he contends, they begin to act in selfish, cruel, and hypocritical ways that prevent them from living in harmony with each other. Couched in a tone of comic irony, all his writings subtly reaffirm this sense of moral idealism.

All the major characters in his novels confront the opposition between modern and traditional values, and each of them ultimately synthesizes a hybrid world-view not altogether different from [Léopold Sédar] Senghor's "*métissage culturel*." In fact, Senghor himself once told Bebey: "you have done what I expect of an African artist—rooted yourself in the black African tradition while welcoming all available influences from abroad. This is how we shall develop from folklore to great works which are truly African." The traditional component of Bebey's world view is crucial to his synthesis of values, but it is not tied to outmoded beliefs, and he insists it must be freely chosen by Africans in response to their present needs, not imposed on them from the outside. . . .

This same impulse toward reconciliation is apparent in the balance Bebey seeks to strike between individual demands for self-realization and African principles of communal solidarity, between scientific knowledge and traditional wisdom, between productive work and the joy of living. It also emerges in the forgiveness and tolerance that allow the characters in his novels to overcome their resentments against each other and to establish relationships based on love and trust. In a sense, the dilemma they confront in defining their self-images is similar to that of newly independent African countries like Bebey's own Cameroon, and the endings of his novels suggest that these countries could articulate a viable sense of identity in the same way that his principal characters do—through hard work, willingness to accept what cannot be changed, forgiveness of past offenses, and commitment to a morally idealistic vision of peace and harmony.

Richard Bjornson. In János Riesz and Alain Ricard, eds.
Semper Aliquid Novi: Littérature Comparée et Littératures d'Afrique
(Tübingen: Gunter Narr, 1990), pp. 205–6

Although couched in a tone of comic irony, [Bebey's] writings subtly affirm a moral idealism that reflects his faith in the spiritual dimension of human life while implicitly condemning those who turn their backs on it.

In traditional African society, an awareness of this higher reality was embedded in cultural practices and artifacts that Europeans transformed into museum pieces with economic value. However, as Bebey attempts to show in his long poem *Concert pour un vieux masque*, their real value lies in their ability to convey the communal spirit, the vitality, and the sense of awe with which Africans had traditionally confronted the harshness and mystery of life. One of the best-known Cameroonian singers and composers, he had originally presented *Concert* as a song, but when its message was misinterpreted by one of his listeners, he expanded it into a narrative poem that recounts the story of a mask that an old Angolan chief had presented as a token of friendship to a white Brazilian. Many years after returning to his homeland, the Brazilian forgot the chief's proviso that the mask not be sold or given to anyone else, and he allowed it to be exhibited in the local museum; however, during its first night in a display case, it mysteriously broke in half.

The mask in the poem symbolizes the human values that had found expression in African cultural practices. The old chief's generosity made these values accessible to the Brazilian, but because he lived in a materialistic society where people did not comprehend the real significance of the mask, he eventually betrayed its gift of knowledge. His betrayal denies the original function of the object that incarnates traditional spiritual insights, but it does not invalidate the insights themselves. In fact, the words of Bebey's poem endow them with new meaning and communicate them to a much larger audience.

Richard Bjornson. *The African Quest for Freedom and Identity: Cameroonian Writing and the National Experience* (Bloomington: Indiana University Press, 1991), pp. 262–63

BEMBA, SYLVAIN (1934–   )

CONGO

[An] important dramatic procedure is borrowed from the tradition of the character *sine qua non* in oral literature, the griot or the singer of the tale as presenter of the performance. This character is frequently used in French-language theater. . . . [and Sylvain Bemba] makes use of this formal aspect in different ways in two of his plays. In *Un Foutu Monde pour un blanchisseur trop honnête* the griot's function is limited to providing a framework and an opening comment, and serving as a linking element between two acts of the play, a biting satire of the corruption that seems to have infected the whole population. The *blanchisseur*, Raphaël, embodies goodness and respectability, and is therefore alienated, since all the others are corrupt. . . .

We do not encounter the presenter again [after the introductory passage] until the end of the first act. He remains outside developments on the stage. In another play by Bemba, this role does not remain restricted to that of providing a framework. In the character of the *amuseur public*, the storyteller is integrated *within* the action and he plays a considerable role. He continually comments on the action, followed by reactions from the public, in this case the other characters on the stage. . . . In *L'Homme qui tua le crocodile*, it is the rich N'Gandou, whose name means "crocodile," who as a businessman terrorizes and exploits a whole district until a teacher from the local school rebels and the crocodile receives his just deserts. In this tragicomedy, as Bemba calls it, the *amuseur public* of the district where N'Gandou lives tells the people the fable of the crocodile who wants the river all to himself. It is clear to whom he is referring and the other characters, the people of the district, enthusiastically repeat certain sentences from the storyteller's tale at every turn, exactly as in a performance in the oral tradition. . . . In the ensuing scenes the actual struggle against N'Gandou unfolds. Here the teacher plays an important part. The *amuseur public* keeps the people (on stage and in the audience) informed about developments, and following the arrest of N'Gandou, warns them to remain alert because—and this is the moral—new N'Gandous can always appear, each exploiting the people in his own particular way.

In Bemba's play the *amuseur public* acts precisely as he has from time immemorial in Congolese "reality." It begins with a death vigil (*veillée mortuaire*) at which a great number of people are present. The *amuseur public* is also there, as is customary. Cards or draughts are being played. The *amuseur* is the first character to speak; the group answers and already responds to his jokes and commentary. . . . Thus his role is clear from the beginning. He introduces the play, but does not stand outside the action: he functions on the same level as the other characters.

Mineke Schipper. *TRI.* 9, 3 (1983–1984), pp. 226–28

In *Rêves portatifs*, the projectionist Ignace Kambéya, the unfortunate spouse of Marie Kabongo, is a twin who lost his brother when he was five years old. Responsible for a murder, imprisoned at the dawn of independence, he is the "vanished one," the one who will return to haunt, divide, and separate the actors and players of the political debates that animate Inoco. His absence will have multiple repercussions.

Twins constitute a connection—a pair, a separation—that is concrete and alive. It is thanks to the character of Ignace Kambéya that Bemba can unfold in the novel connections of sequences, of characters, of actions, and of objects. Ignace is the one whose disastrous itinerary disrupts the sense of the festivities of independence, unties and divides the knot of ulterior events. Moudandou, on the other hand, is the one who never stops to bind, tie, chain, and trap.

We already know that in the first part of *Le Soleil est parti à M'Pemba*, Félix Gamboux kills N'Gampika, his younger brother. In the same first part we learn that Gamboux has become "*un tara bwolo*, father of twins." It is these twins that we rediscover in the second part of the novel. All the connections (the groups of coincidences and the game of relations) gravitate around the theme of the destiny of the twin couple. Otto Rank explains, in *Don Juan et le double*, that the motif of twins is a concretization of the motif of the double—the twin couple, supernatural and heroic, appear to be united beyond life and death by the immortal connection which they incarnate. If in the first part of *Le Soleil est parti à M'Pemba* Félix Gamboux kills his brother, in the second part of the same novel, Albert N'Gambou and Ronald N'Gampika are twins whose relationship is that of two beings inaccessible to one another. . . .

The twin connection Ronald and Albert form leads them towards a dangerous meeting in a dangerous place. To some extent, this new death is only the recommencement (repetition, reiteration) of the murder perpetrated by Félix Gamboux in the first part of the novel. . . .

The narratives and plays of Sylvain Bemba (re)constitute a typology of characters, a typology of the forms of aggression and a typology of the systems of reading. The typology of the systems of reading discloses the links and divergences between reading methods. The typology of the forms of aggression reconstitutes . . . certain "independent forms of violent acquisition of living creatures: war, hunting, fishing." The typology of the forms of aggression is inseparable from a classification of techniques. The typology of characters reveals the different connections, like that of the role of doubles and of twins, distributions and incarnations of passions and forces. . . .

Sylvain Bemba establishes a constant interaction between the existence of machines and the theme of the double (the presence of twins). The twin has an extension beyond himself (he belongs to a human connection) and the machine is an extension of the human body. The machine (pole of an extension, or prosthesis) makes possible the doubling of the real, and provokes accidents and disappearances.

Ange-Séverin Malanda. PA. 130 (1984), pp. 95–97, 100–1, 110

In Sylvain Bemba's *Une Eau dormante*, Olessou the fisherman, who dared to rise in protest against the village chief and the owner of the pond in which Olessou is fishing, is rescued from sure death by Ecombo-Veritas, a young man whom villagers consider to be half crazy and who is an allegory rather than a human character. In any case, he is the figure that the author needs to demonstrate the victory of justice and kindness over arbitrary acts, inequality, and evil. The author's move in this case is in consonance with the concept dating back to the Age of Enlightenment: it is possible to reorganize society through the favorable influence of an ideal character.

Bemba's comedy is extremely original because it offers two ways toward a happy outcome. The first way: Olessou, who is ordered by the chief to fight Sosso, the pond owner, in public, is saved from death by Ecombo-Veritas, who led the village youth to his rescue. The second version: Olessou overpowers Sosso in the fight. The melodrama of the situation is growing proportionately to Olessou's resistance to the efforts of Oluo, the village thief, and Sosso to subordinate him to their will. At first they try to talk the fisherman out of opposing them; then they intimidate him, abduct his wife, and finally decide to kill him. The features of "villains" in Oluo and Sosso, both of whom are retrogrades and selfish men, are so overemphasized and pointed and the righteous Olessou is so lonely (the action takes place in the colonial period and the authorities are on the chief's side) that it requires a double happy ending to "justify" the survival of the protagonist: this does not arise from the development of the plot.

It is interesting to hear Bemba's arguments in justification of the obviously artificial character of the happy endings in his plays. On the one hand, he relies on the eternal moral code of the people: Olessou cannot be defeated because he embodies justice, kindness, and reason. On the other hand, the playwright explains the intervention of supernatural forces in the characters' struggle against evil by the fact that it reflects a psychological stereotype of mass consciousness—the popular belief in the presence of the irrational and magic in reality. "I am trying to express in a dramatic form what Congolese people hide under the cover of myth," Sylvain Bemba said in an interview with a Congolese literary journal in 1977. "If the fantastic did not combine with the real most closely, if it was not intertwined with the fiber of our social existence, I would never dream of introducing it into my plays."

Nina D. Lyakhovskaya. RAL. 18, 4 (Winter 1987), pp. 464–65

In the works of Sylvain Bemba, the world of the imaginary is activated by elements like dream, the restoration of speech, and the meeting of the forbidden. The principal element is the voyage, the passage from one state to another, the ultimate test that leads to life. *L'Enfer, c'est Orféo* is the passage of the frontier, Orféo's voyage toward the maquis for regeneration. There, he rediscovers a sense of creatures and things. *Rêves portatifs* is the journey towards the life of others through image. Dreams are lived in an obscure room and projected on a white wall. The reinvented life unfolds to the rhythm of the salivation of Ignace the projectionist. It is a voyage through independence. *Le Dernier des cargonautes* is a novel of constant departure: departure from home for a rupture of moral values, departure for France to a confrontation of other battles, and expulsion for a return towards a collective village conscience. In *Léopolis*, the American Nora makes the cycle of return to the quest of a past prefiguring the future. She rediscovers *Léopolis*, the city of lions, and reconnects with the life of the great assassinated leader, Fabrice M'Pfum. It is the voyage towards the dimension of myth, similar to that of Patrice Lumumba. . . .

Bemba's narrative technique simultaneously incorporates several techniques of this sort. Man becomes the master of the universe when he dreams. If he stops dreaming, he dies. His literature appears like a transgression that destroys and creates at the same time. The work is then a product of diverse controlled circumstances, which the pathways of the imaginary allow to roam free, face to face with the self of the author, his biography, his story, his readings, his character, his habits, his human and ecological environment, and his philosophy. . . .

By an assiduous practice of the process of distancing, Sylvain Bemba has built some of his plays around pedagogical and demonstrative irony. *Une Eau dormante* provides the outline and *L'Homme qui tua le crocodile* is the perfect example. The urban decor covers the dealings of a usurer, with the symbolic name of the cayman, with Henri Balou the teacher, punctuated with the comments by a public entertainer. The author also rediscovers traditional, oral theatricality with this buffoon, philosopher, and implacable observer who enjoys the immunity of tolerance. This view of urban Africa is accentuated in *Embouteillage*, shown several times at Brazzaville, in *Un Foutu Monde pour un blanchisseur trop honnête*, *Eroshima*, and *L'Étrange Crime de Monsieur Pancrace Amadeus*. It is represented by the poetry of the social fantastic, popular language, satire and the detailed recreation of the jokes of the characters. . . .

The theater for Sylvain Bemba is, without contest, the nocturnal return to the community around the fire, replaced by projectors. It is the return to communion. With the principal protagonist, the community gets rid of its anxieties and, through a cultural identity, becomes a collective social character. . . .

For Sylvain Bemba, the novel today is the privileged space for the demonstration of the mechanisms of domination and exploitation through creatures of flesh and blood. . . .

All the characters in his novels live in a renewed state of solitude, because, often, the traveler finds himself alone, having left behind him his past experiences.

In Congolese literature, Sylvain Bemba's writings are probably the most prolific and also those in which social fantasy verges most directly with realism, and the magic of words is linked to that of things, in a rational didacticism. This type of writing revalorizes even more a culture made up of parables and a variety of bizarre and symbolic elements. The bizarre gives us a vantage point from which to view historic, political, and social truths. The characters glide through the bizarre with the weight of concrete, realistic truths in order to become transformed into living memories.

The work of Sylvain Bemba records the greatest tragic possibilities, from humor to death, thus summarizing our multidimensional dreams, whose dimensions become movements which contain the plenitude of body, time, space, and word.

Caya Makhélé. Notre Librairie. 92–93 (1988), pp. 97–99†

Sylvain Bemba . . . is one of the most recent African writers to have achieved an international reputation, first in the theater, then through four novels that seem to puzzle readers. Critics also seem somewhat put off by his works, since they have received little sustained analysis, although Bemba's name is often seen in general discussions of the new African writing. Bemba mixes modern literary technique and complicated psychological and sociological concepts with elements drawn from African folklore, legend, tribal history, and religion in a quite original way. The supernatural aspects of African tradition are crossed with modern fantasy and science fiction in the manner of Third World "marvelous realism" to dig deeper into the double identity of the colonized person.

The theme of dancing masks provides a key to Bemba's main characters and to his literary methodology and style. The image of dancing masks is very close to the central concept behind all of Bemba's work. The masks worn by the characters, the roles they play, are less a disguise or protection than a symbol, a

projection of the self, a label, an "identity," serving to relate the individual, especially the inner self (emotions, the subconscious), to the ideal self, the collective
self, the historical self, the timeless self. Obviously masks are ambiguous, overdetermined, and kaleidoscopic, constantly shifting in valence, like the moods of
the mythological gods with whom they are allied; but like all mythic elements
they have a positive significance, weaving a web of references while educating
those who witness their dance. . . .

Bemba is fascinated with the problem of identity and with central African
history. There is always a doubling. In [Le Soleil est parti à M'Pemba] he presents
two sets of twins, the second set sons of one of the brothers in the first. We can
thereby contrast two generations and the difference between urban and rural settings. All Bemba's characters undergo striking transformations as we see them in
different settings, playing different roles, assuming various identities, especially
when they go to France. The Lumumba- and Schweitzer-like characters come to
assume the mask of "hero" or ideal self; like the numerous political-leader characters, they come to represent the group and a kind of "collective self." In Soleil we
are also given the classic case: the buffoon masker, playful, a clown, who uses a
magic phonograph to do a rapid-rerun of recent African history to unmask the evils
and distortions of colonialism and their vestiges in the postcolonial world. . . .

Bemba wrote his first novel, Rêves portatifs, at the age of forty, in 1979.
The central concern is the relation of film to freedom. Bemba hangs all the
diverse happenings on the story of a projectionist who has inadvertently gotten
tangled up in drug dealing, just as the country of Palms is coming to independence. The rather rambling narration depicts not only the microcosm of the
movies, but also nightclubs, jails, courts, journalism, politics, clinics, and bush
hospitals. The author attacks all the cultural changes that accompany the birth
of a new nation, which in itself might be seen as a manifestation of the mask
theme; in running up the new flag the nation puts on a new mask. . . .

Le Dernier des cargonautes, the least substantial of Bemba's novels,
relates to the mask theme in emphasizing changing identities in development of
character. It combines the apparent simplicity of a Gidean récit with elements
of medieval hagiography. It somewhat resembles [Albert] Camus's Etranger in
focusing on the vicissitudes of the life of an exceptional Everyman who is also
something of a Christ figure; he resembles both [Patrice] Lumumba and
[Albert] Schweitzer to some degree and is named "Emmanuel." . . .

Bemba's most recent novel, Léopolis, represents something of a new
departure and demonstrates a new mastery. The fact that it was published in an
inexpensive paperback edition indicates that the publisher believed it might
attract a larger audience. This seems paradoxical, since the aspects that characterize the new "popular" literature in Africa have always been present in
Bemba's work; but in this novel Bemba combines them with irony and some of
the Brechtian distancing elements to create a work to be read on many levels.
One may read it as a combination adventure tale, detective story, love story,
and historical romance, or see it as a gentle mocking of the quest for the epic.

Hal Wylie. WLT. 64, 1 (Winter 1990), pp. 20–23

BENNETT, LOUISE (1919–   )

JAMAICA

Any discussion of Caribbean popular culture must notice the work of the Jamaican, Louise Bennett. Her unique gift is that she is both a folklore scholar and a brilliant popular entertainer, and while the qualities of Caribbean popular culture are evanescent before the recording of the conventional researcher, Bennett is able to physically recreate her findings in performances that reveal the idiom, the gestures, the stress and the flow of the personalities and private dramas of the people. Her use of dialect can be amusing, but is not necessarily so. In "Bans O' Killing" she places herself . . . in the tradition of poets who have used dialect for serious purposes, as the straightest route to the inner life of the ordinary people. Bennett would not claim either the depth of feeling or the lyrical impulse of the greatest dialect poets, and in a volume the length of her first major book of collected poems, *Jamaica Labrish*, there was inevitably some weak material. On the other hand her claim that dialect be taken seriously is not only valid, it is borne out by many of her own successful pieces. Through dialects she catches conversational tones that illuminate both individual and national character. . . .

Most of Bennett's verse is in a loose ballad form that focuses, without restricting, the rapidly shifting moods and attitudes of the character she assumes. . . .

Because Bennett uses essentially the natural speech idiom of the people, and because she is guarded from pretension by self-critical folk wit, she can . . . cover a range of subjects unrivalled by more conventional poets, without striking a false note. Further, her verse is a valuable aid to the social historian. Her selection of themes reflects the concerns of Jamaican life; the public ones—federation, street peddlers, bodybuilding contests, Paul Robeson's visit to Jamaica, emigration or an infuriating telephone system; and the private—the yard gossip or the death of a pet turkey watched by a hungry neighbor. More important, she approaches her theme by way of the attitude an ordinary person feels towards it, and it is this that makes an historical event meaningful. This is particularly important in the West Indies, where the private attitudes behind public events are so complex, a tension between national pride and self-satire, between knowledge, ignorance, and common sense.

Louis James. Introduction. The Islands in Between: Essays on West Indian Literature (London: Oxford University Press, 1968), pp. 15–17

I do not believe that Louise Bennett is a considerable poet. But a poet, and, in her best work, a better poet than most other Jamaican writers she certainly is. She does not offer her readers any great insight into the nature of life or human experience, but she recreates human experience vividly, delightfully, and intelligently. She is rarely pretentious—the most common fault in West Indian poetry; she is not derived from other poets—she has her own interesting voice; and she is invariably sane. . . .

I think her most central difficulty is choice of subject. Many of her poems are a sort of comic-verse journalism; she is quick to tackle the topical, which is only natural, as she published her early and some of her later poems in newspapers. One willingly says goodbye to numerous poems about new governors, new pantomimes, Paul Robeson's visit, a test match victory, and so on, where interest has not survived the topicality of the subject. As in the same period of her topical poems she wrote others of more lasting interest, we can hardly complain: we can only regret that so much of the journalism has been published in book form. It would be a service to her readers if Bennett would present a *Collected Poems*, dropping all the ephemera and choosing the best of the others. . . .

Louise Bennett, then, is a poet of serious merit, although like all poets, she has her limitations. Like most poets she is . . . developing. And she is so much more rewarding a poet than many to whom we in Jamaica give the name, that it seems reasonable to expect more of those who claim an interest in poetry to give her more attention. She is sane; throughout, her poems imply that sound common sense and generous love and understanding of people are worthwhile assets. Jamaican dialect is, of course, limiting (in more senses than one); but within its limitations Louise Bennett works well. Hers is a precious talent.

Mervyn Morris. In Edward Baugh, ed. *Critics on Caribbean Literature: Readings in Literary Criticism* (New York: St. Martin's Press, 1978), pp. 137–38, 143, 147–48

In the case of Louise Bennett [the] performer's role has its source in her relatively early involvement in the theater. Hence during the late 1940s she studied at the Royal Academy of Dramatic Art, then worked with several repertory companies in England before returning to teach drama in Jamaica. As both performer and composer she is comparable with the calypsonian in that she relies less on the explicit statement about the ironic deception of the grinning mask, and more on the suggestive contrast between diction and rhythm, on the one hand, and on the other hand, the implications of her themes. But when she does offer explicit statement it does shed very useful light on the ironic import of those rhetorical devices which she and other artists in the oral tradition exploit.

Her most important, and comprehensive, collection of poems, *Jamaica Labrish*, offers several examples of such explicit statements. In "War-Time Grocery," composed during World War II, the scarcity of food gives rise to the warning that "happy" talk and laughter among frustrated shoppers are definitely deceptive. And in "My Dream" the political unrest of those hard times and the resulting pressures for independence feed a discontent which is barely disguised: "Dog a-sweat but long hair hide i' / Mout a laugh, but heart aleap!" The witty, trenchant proverbs drawn from the colloquial language of the folk both explain and exemplify the idea of a mask. The proverb in "My Dream" is comparable in this regard with the very similar technique of "Dutty Tough" where wartime hardships persist, despite appearances to the contrary, like the dry toughness of rock-hard dirt in drought: "River flood but water scarce yaw, / Rain a-fall but dutty tuff!" And in proverbs like these Louise Bennett . . . discovers the precise, built-in

antitheses through which the folk verbalize their sense of conflict and social contradictions, and which the poet adopts as a ready-made mode of ironic statement.

But in developing the ironic implications of the performer's grinning mask
Bennett goes beyond explicit statements of this kind. She also relies on the
evocative contrast between her subject matter and her *manner* of statement. In
"Dutty Tough" the elaboration on hard times lends itself to a raucous liveliness,
even to farcical embellishment. . . . Altogether then, the playful raucousness of a
Bennett poem is based on the same tactic which informs the calypsonian's
irony—the traditional function of laughter and play as disguise and resistance in
the language of the folk.

Lloyd W. Brown. West Indian Poetry (Boston: Twayne, 1978), pp. 106–7

The poems in Bennett's collection *Jamaica Labrish*, spanning approximately
twenty-five years, cover a broad spectrum of dramatic personalities and events.
The poems are classified in four groups: "City Life," "War-Time," "Politics,"
and "Jamaica—Now an' Then." Some of the subject matter is so topical that not
all historical details are easily accessible to the contemporary reader. But the
majority of poems constitute a kind of comedy of manners in which those
recurring rascals of Caribbean societies—social climbers, petty crooks, displaced colonials, to name a few—come decidedly to grief.

One kind of social climber whom Bennett satirizes ruthlessly—for obvious reasons—is the character who feels impelled to deny any connections with
the Creole culture. Several poems in the collection poke fun at this character
type with varying degrees of gentleness. "Dry Foot Bwoy" satirizes a Jamaican
of peasant stock who has travelled to England, perhaps to study, and has
returned with an English accent and a bad case of linguistic amnesia. He can no
longer converse with his former acquaintances, much to their annoyance, for he
disclaims knowledge of Jamaican Creole. . . .

Similarly the poem "Noh Lickle Twang!" makes fun of a woman who is
embarrassed because her son, newly returned from the United States after six
months abroad, doesn't have even the slightest trace of an American accent. He
cannot, therefore, be shown off to the discriminating neighbors, who, once he
opens his mouth will think that he's surely been to Mocho—the archetypal
Jamaican village that epitomizes social gaucheness. The depth of the young
man's failure must be measured against his sister's success in acquiring the
semblance of an American accent after having had only one week's exposure to
American expatriates. The fact that her parents cannot understand her is the
proof of her sophistication. So the poor mother bemoans her unhappy lot.

The tone of Bennett's satirical poems is not always as light as the poems
cited above would suggest. In some poems in which Bennett confronts the demean-
ing poverty of the Jamaican worker—more often, nonworker—the comic vision
seems inadequate to express the sustained pathos of intense poverty. The pain of
deprivation cannot always be sublimated in laughter. The pair of poems . . . "Me
Bredda" and "My Dream," demonstrate the differences of tone that Bennett can
employ in examining the same subject matter. In both poems the persona is that of

a female domestic servant, who, in Jamaica, has been a ubiquitous symbol of middle-class exploitation of cheap peasant labor. But whereas "Me Bredda," in true comic spirit, vigorously affirms the supremacy of Good over Evil, "My Dream" articulates the burgeoning political engagement over the oppressed in colonial Jamaica. . . .

The strength of Bennett's poetry . . . is the accuracy with which it depicts and attempts to correct through laughter the absurdities of Jamaican society. Its comic vision affirms a norm of common sense and good-natured decorum. The limitations of the poetry are partially the inevitable consequences of having used Jamaican Creole as a poetic medium. For what the experiments in Creole—whether St. Lucian, Trinidadian, or Barbadian, for example—have indicated is that there are subtle nuances of thought and feeling that are at times best expressed in Creole, at times in English. The poet who relies exclusively on either medium reduces the expressive range of his/her art.

Louise Bennett, having chosen to write exclusively in Jamaican Creole, cannot easily answer the charge of parochialism and insularity. But what she loses in universality she gains in vivid particularity.

Carolyn Cooper. *WLWE*. 17, 1 (April 1978), pp. 322–25

Characteristically, the Louise Bennett poem is a comment in Creole on "the now" of Jamaican lives, often on something topical. It offers insight into, and corroborative evidence of, people's responses to particular events. To make sense of the poem, we sometimes need to know of the occasion that provoked it; and the topicality was often an important factor in the initial impact. Lloyd Brown makes the important point, however, that many of the poems survive their original contexts because "by virtue of their style their focus is less on the specific topics of the 1940s (food shortages, high prices, the war itself) and more on the continuing modes of perception they dramatize."

The modes of perception being dramatized are often themselves subjected to critical irony. The form most often employed by Louise Bennett is the dramatic monologue; and what Philip Drew wrote of [Robert] Browning's also applies to Louise Bennett's: "In poem after poem the vital point to observe is . . . that the speaker understands himself and his own situation less thoroughly than the reader, who nevertheless derived all his understanding from the poem." Poems by Louise Bennett often provoke in us that "combination of sympathy and judgment" which Robert Langbaum has identified as a common response to the dramatic monologue. . . .

Whether in print or in performance, many of the poems are remarkable as social commentary and as works of art. They deal with a variety of topics, including problems of colonial education, the vagaries of politics, economic hardship, bureaucratic humbug, strategies of survival. The poems in general promote acceptance of Jamaican culture; they draw on the customs, beliefs, language of ordinary Jamaicans, the living tissue of Jamaican life. They are critical of gossip. They expose people ashamed of being Jamaican or ashamed of being black. They ridicule class and color prejudice, but are more concerned to tackle

black self-contempt or to express pride in being black. They undermine pretension of various kinds.

Mervyn Morris. In Daryl Cumber Dance, ed. *Fifty Caribbean Writers*
(Westport, Conn.: Greenwood Press, 1986), pp. 37–38, 41

The work of Louise Bennett of Jamaica was . . . important in establishing a
unique Caribbean literature and a distinctive woman's voice within it. The language and speech of Caribbean women had always played an important part in
contesting slave and colonial domination and so was an important tool in the
struggle for liberation. As a consequence, the articulation of the Jamaican experience in the exceptionally flexible and pliable medium of the dialect offered
enormous possibilities for its use as a literary language. Because "all linguistic
communities evolve systems of power relationships enforced by and repeated in
language," it was not inconsistent that a great amount of interest was displayed
in the literary possibilities of the dialect during the 1940s, when discontent with
colonial rule in Jamaica reached new heights. Bennett's work challenged the
privileged status accorded to the poetic tradition of white discourse in
Caribbean letters, empowering the voices and expressions of the masses of
Caribbean people. Bennett used the power of Jamaican speech to explore the
complexity of the Jamaican experience and, in so doing, forced the members of
the upper and middle classes to face their own linguistic and class biases. Her
use of oral and scribal forms, as she forced the language to accommodate itself
to express the poetic sentiments of the people, was an important breakthrough
in Caribbean literature.

Selwyn R. Cudjoe. Introduction. *Caribbean Women Writers*
(Wellesley, Mass.: Calaloux, 1990), pp. 25–26

Though Bennett maintains the old view of the working-class woman as more
than a match for her oppressors at the level of language, her poems tend to
show women using men as surrogates for their aggression and, at a first glance,
she seems to follow the bias of Jamaican men in her presentation of women as
apolitical. In "Uriah Preach" for example, Bennett recounts the vicarious pleasure taken by a Jamaican woman in the accomplishments of her children and
especially in her son's ability to use his occasional ascent to the pulpit to lambast the family's enemies. . . . In "Me Bredda," an irate woman who has failed
to get a job as a domestic servant forces her would-be employer to placate her
with two weeks' wages by threatening to call in her imaginary brother to settle
the matter physically. . . . Here again the woman shifts the responsibility for
physical confrontation to a male figure, implying that the woman herself no
longer considers the threat of her own action sufficient to terrify the housewife
she abuses.

    Though Bennett often works through apolitical female figures who are
more likely to react to the cut of a politician's clothes than what he says, she
often expresses a womanist perspective on topical issues and her poems take
note of social reforms intended to improve the position of women. In "Bans O'

Ooman!," for example, she celebrates the founding of the Jamaican Federation of Women in the 1940s aimed at bringing together women of all classes, describing the clothes and social status of the women who flock to support it as "high and low, miggle suspended." Poems like "Solja Work" show the consequences of a local military presence for Jamaican women.

Bennett is one of the first creative writers to register the increase of female oppression which was one of the consequences of the male assertion of racial and political power during the nationalist movement of the 1940s and 1950s. Her poem "Pinnacle" satirizes the new chauvinism of men towards women as it manifested itself within the Rastafarian movement, which in other respects has had such a profound and in many ways beneficial effect on Jamaican attitudes to language, race, and spiritual values. Written after the brutal destruction of one of the first Rastafarian communities by the Jamaican government, the poem delights in the humiliation of one of the male members of the sect who had formerly used his Rastafarian convictions to terrorize his woman. . . . Bennett's satirical resources however are limited to what she can authentically express through the resonances of a specific social reality and way of speech, so that in her dramatic monologues she can only be as positive about women as she thinks the character through whom she speaks is in real life. . . . This presentation of the female point of view elucidates Bennett's own method in her early poems, by which she is able to assert a sense of female strength under the guise of using male surrogates and seeming to acquiesce in ideas about female weakness. The fact that she feels constrained to work through such masks, however, gives an indication of the extent to which the attitude to women in Jamaican society had become that expressed in the song she quotes in her poem on Jamaican women: "Oman a heaby load!"

Rhonda Cobham. In Carole Boyce Davies and Elaine Savory Fido, eds.
Out of the Kumbla: Caribbean Women and Literature
(Trenton, N. J.: Africa World Press, 1990), pp. 217–19

More than any other single writer, Louise Bennett brought local language into the foreground of West Indian cultural life. From the 1940s, when she began contributing to the annual pantomime in Jamaica, Bennett's storytelling had a substantial influence on the literary credibility of dialect. But it was not an unqualified credibility. From the beginning, Bennett was aware that language is not a simple matter and that the unfamiliar has its own appeal—especially when linked with an assumed superiority. And she dealt with the equivocation of these attitudes with relentless irony. One of her poems tells of the dismay of a mother whose son has come back from the United States with no change in his speech, no heightening of his language. . . . The appeal of artifice, of strangeness—the superiority that distance or difference (in the right direction) generates—are satirized here even as the poem itself relies on this appeal, for its own cleverness is implicated in the satire. . . .

The acceptance of dialect in poetry, as in other forms of communication, was partly a matter of fashion. The popularity of Louise Bennett, whose work was on radio and in the newspapers as well as on stage and in books, helped create the fashion, and provided encouragement to other poets and storytellers.

J. Edward Chamberlin. *Come Back to Me My Language: Poetry and the West Indies* (Urbana: University of Illinois Press, 1993), pp. 95–97

BETI, MONGO (1932–   )

CAMEROON

At the age of twenty-two, while still a student at [Aix-en-Provence], Mongo Beti [born Alexandre Biyidi-Awala] offered his first novel to *Présence Africaine*. After publishing a key chapter in the review, they decided to issue the whole book, though Beti himself already had doubts about it. *Ville cruelle* was duly published by Éditions Africaines in 1954, under the pen name of Eza Boto. The author has since indicated his opinion of the novel by jettisoning this nom de plume and taking that of Mongo Beti for all his subsequent books. . . .

Ville cruelle . . . combines a novelettish plot with a brilliance of observation and a quality of pain which we associate with a major novel. Strangely enough, it was precisely by the more controlled and skillful use of exclamatory, naïve monologue that Mongo Beti developed some of the most effective passages in his second novel, *Le Pauvre Christ de Bomba*. With this book, published only two years after *Ville cruelle*, the writer emerged as a formidable satirist and one of the most percipient critics of European colonialism. For now the naïvety of his hero, instead of being presented subjectively, becomes the pure mirror through which we see the greed, the folly and the tragic misunderstandings of a whole epoch in Africa's history. Used in this more distanced way, the monologue becomes a weapon of devastating satiric force.

Le Pauvre Christ de Bomba is written entirely in the form of a diary, the diary of an acolyte who accompanies his master, the Reverend Father Superior Drumont, on a missionary circuit through the land of Tala. Tala is a remote district of Cameroon which has been deliberately abandoned by Drumont for three whole years because of its "backsliding." He is now revisiting all the stations in the hope of finding the thirsty souls crying out for solace. In fact, of course, he finds nothing of the kind. The men of Tala have forgotten God and turned to bicycles. Even the women have fallen short on their cult payments. The churches are broken and empty, but the bars are full and the new money from cocoa is beginning to flow through the land, for we are now in the late 1930s. Drumont is an austere man of obstinate courage, choleric and impatient, moving with all the authority and confidence of twenty years' missionary work in Africa. But even his faith wavers before the spectacle of Tala. As the circuit progresses he questions himself and his purposes more and more deeply. For the first time he enters into dispute with his parishioners and listens to their arguments, instead of quelling them with his own energy and authority. Meanwhile the young administrator Vidal, who is also touring Tala, continually appeals to him as an ally. Is he not a fellow white and a Frenchman? Vidal assures him that all will soon be well, for a road is to be built through Tala by forced labor: The sufferings of the road gangs will soon fill the churches to bursting, as they have already done in those areas which lie along the main routes, under the heavy hand of the administration. The whole system of forced labor is a true friend of the Catholic Church, for is not contentment the great enemy of religion?

Gerald Moore. *Twelve African Writers* (Bloomington: Indiana University Press, 1980), pp. 194, 197–98

After a long period of silence, Mongo Beti published three novels within a short time. Seen together they convey the sense of an epic sweep materialized by their extension in time and space. The first novel, *Remember Ruben*, starts with a problem of genesis. Mor-Zamba, the hero of the novel, is a foundling. His quest for identity through the history of the Cameroonian people is partially fulfilled when, at the end of the novel, he learns from his friend Abena, that he is the son of the brutally deposed but long-lamented chief of Ekoundoum. He then decides to return to Ekoundoum to begin the work of transformation which the community yearns for. *Remember Ruben* covers forty years of the history of Cameroon, through World War II to independence in 1960.

Perpétue [*et l'habitude du malheur*], the second novel, continues the story to the 1970s. The novel takes the form of an investigation into the causes of Perpétue's death. The investigation is conducted by her brother, Essola. Essola is a former militant of the Union des Populations du Caméroon a political party headed by the nationalist leader Ruben Um Nyobe, whose name provides the title for two of Beti's novels. After having served a long jail term in the prisons of the dictator Baba Tura, Essola is released on condition that he join the dictator's party.

Although [*La Ruine presque cocasse d'un polichinelle*] is a sequel of [*Remember Ruben*], it does not dwell in the semilegendary time of Mor-Zamba's childhood. It focuses on the first years of independence and shows an independent Cameroon caught in a total state of anarchy and violence. By responding to the popular call from Ekoundoum, Mor-Zamba acquires the ultimate characteristic of the epic hero. By liberating the people of Ekoundoum from a despotic chief he regains his full identity and returns to the community.

One of the pillars that sustain epic action is the reliance on myth as the leading light in the grand time swing proper to the epic narrative; *Remember Ruben* is an epic narrative both by the life it depicts and the style in which it does this. Time, as we shall see, is limitless, inexhaustible, and dense. The plot freely multiplies itself into a multitude of subplots born out of each other and resulting in an illusion of endlessness, through a psychological intensity that derives from the intensity of the life portrayed. Epic action develops into epic time; the action often plunges into the remote past, the apprehension of which is sometimes made possible through a name, a character who is both remote and close, and whose unmediated presence seems totally overwhelming. That character whose existence finds a place in countless stories illustrating every moment in the life of the community is the link that bridges the gulf between history and the unfathomable time of origins.

While setting up the framework of the epic story the narrator of *Remember Ruben* appeals to Akomo, the ancestral creator of the Essazam nation: this he does in order to conjure up the most fundamental pillar of the community and bring forth a time span of unlimited extent. A careful reading will show that all the elements proper to the epic form the foundations of this narrative. These elements include a mystic reference, the characterization proper to the epic hero, and divine presence often expressed in prophetic terms throughout the narrative. It will also appear to the reader that all these three major elements which set the tone for epic action are structurally interrelated in the dynamic progression of the novel.

Kandioura Dramé. *Ufahumu*. 12, 2 (1983), pp. 45–46

Unlike Beti's other recent exile writing, *Les Deux Mères* [*de Guillaume Ismaël Dzewatama*] resembles the typical novel being written and published inside Africa today, studying marriage patterns and the evolving roles of women. Guillaume Ismaël has two mothers because his father, finding himself in a confused situation, tries to reconcile the two halves of his split personality by adding his French mistress as wife number two to his extended African family. Instead of bridging the gap, this aggravates all the problems. Seeing the tensions from the point of view of the African boy and his good-hearted, idealistic but naive white mother throws into relief the melodrama and pathos of modern Africa and all its ironies. The reader wonders who has the most colonized mentality in this swirl of alienations juxtaposing races, generations, classes, sexes, and roles.

Beti seems to be placing himself in the new "popular" literature in Africa. The psychological penetration and the realism seemingly derived from the auto-biographical elements, however, plus the artistic use of ambiguity here, lend depth to the new genre. This is a curious love story, full of drama, harmonizing the political and literary in Beti.

Hal Wylie. *WLT.* 58, 1 (Winter 1984), pp. 151–52

The early works of Mongo Beti with their biting satire and unrelenting criticism of the colonial situation in Africa, demonstrate a large degree of consistency in narrative tone. Detachment, cynicism, and distortion are features of that tone and the regularity of these features gives evidence of a patterning principle that blueprints these works. It circumscribes the relationships of characters who for the most part deal ineffectively with their changing environment. It also determines the manner and form of the narration, at times resulting in a narrative space literally charged with cynical distortions of the facts being related. The contours of this patterning principle, as it molds the reactions and movements of actors in the fictional realm, strongly evoke the paradigm of neurosis: Impulses to act get short-circuited or stem from invalid motivations. Works constructed in this way suggest a relationship between neurosis and the human potential for acting and reacting creatively. . . .

Mission terminée opens with the revelation that Medza has failed the oral examination for the *baccalauréat* degree. He masks his frustration and indignation with a cultivated response for anyone who might inquire: "J'ai été recalé comme il se doit." It would be unacceptable for Medza to appear to have lost control of his situation, so he must remain flippant at all costs. This characteristic flippancy surfaces again when he engages in a brief sarcastic exchange with the driver of a transport vehicle. The agony in the faces of the other passengers mirrors the inappropriateness of Medza's remarks and laughter. For the moment he manages to retain mastery of his situation, but his sense of inadequacy becomes obvious as the novel progresses. Having been fueled by his most recent failure, it is not erased by the conscious efforts at nonchalance he displays. . . .

If neurotic responses can function creatively, as with Medza in *Mission terminée*, the creative impulse can also degenerate into a neurotic mockery of itself. We see examples of the latter in *Le Roi miraculé* where Beti deals with a society experiencing the most painful kind of cultural decline. Its members are forced to adjust as best they can, but suffer necessarily from an insecure ontological orientation: previously held practices and explanations (conventions) no longer make sense of life, and the resulting ontological insecurity breeds neurotic personalities, passive dependence, and confusion. All of the characters are in fact troubled, including the narrator. As Thomas Malone points out, these characters are caught up in a humiliating game with life. Beti heightens the effect this widespread neurotic anxiety will have on the reader by allowing it to permeate throughout all levels of the work. By exploring the neurotic potential of the creative function, he transforms neurosis into a creative tool.

JoAnne Cornwell. FR. 60, 5 (April 1987), pp. 644–45, 648–49

Although it is Mongo Beti's first novel and it is not difficult to point out its weaknesses, *Ville cruelle* is in fact a more substantial work than a cursory reading might suggest. On the surface the story line is strong and clear, although its components are often awkward and contrived. The hero, Banda, wishes to marry before his sick mother dies, so he goes to the nearby town of Tanga to sell his cocoa crop, intending to use the money he receives for it to pay the customary dowry. He is however cheated by the colonial officials who have to inspect the crop before it can be sold; they claim it is substandard and confiscate it in order to sell it for their own gain later. Banda then meets Odilia, whose brother Koumé is in hiding after taking the law into his own hands in an attempt to obtain his wages, which his white employer has not paid for months. Banda offers to hide Koumé in the forest, but Koumé is drowned while crossing the river separating Tanga from the forest. Banda takes Odilia to the safety of his own village, where he leaves her with his mother, while he returns to put Koumé's body where it will be quickly found by the police and so forestall any harassment of the dead man's family. Banda finds a large sum of money in Koumé's pocket which would more than compensate for his own loss that same morning. On his return home he decides it will be more honest to give the money to Odilia, who has a stronger claim to it. He then finds a suitcase lost by a Greek trader and his wife who have been driving up and down the countryside all day looking for it. When he returns the case to them, Banda receives a reward exactly equivalent to what he expected to gain from his cocoa crop. So, in financial terms, all's well that ends well. With the blessing of his mother (who dies soon after), Banda marries Odilia, for whom he does not have to pay a dowry. Banda, who hates his village and had sworn to leave it when his mother died, now moves to Odilia's home village, where he is very happy, still dreaming of fulfilling his long-held ambition to work in the capital city, Fort-Negrè.

The plot is filled out with examples of the evils of colonialism, and it is here that the evocative quality of Beti's descriptions begins to reveal his talent as a writer. The second chapter, in which he describes the town of Tanga, is one of the most striking in the novel, and the only part of it translated so far into English. Beti portrays Tanga, and symbolically colonial life, as being divided in two—the two Tangas constitute two worlds and two destinies: on the one side of the town live the whites, whose world is that of the commercial center, while on the other side live the blacks, separate and exploited. The whole emphasis of the white world is on money, which takes precedence over all other considerations and which is slowly corrupting the moral values of the blacks who are themselves becoming obsessed with the same greed, expressed in the way the impoverished inhabitants of the shantytown of Tanga-Nord dream of the wealth that tomorrow will bring them; expressed in the dishonesty of the inspectors who condemn perfectly good cocoa beans to enrich themselves; . . . expressed above all through the novel's hero, who dreams of going to live in the town and who is obsessed by the need for money, so that his problems are only resolved when he is the lucky recipient of a windfall. On this level of the narrative, Beti seeks to show not only the injustices of colonial society, its hypocrisy and its morality based on self-interest, but also the total lack of concern for the welfare of the township blacks, the breakdown of social order, and the frightening instability of the world of the urban African. . . .

However, Beti is as critical of traditional society as he is of colonialism; he sees the former's male element as just another expression of the will to dominate. Indeed, Beti, through his hero Banda, stresses that male African society, typified by the elder, is even more repressive in its way than colonialism. . . . Banda has decided to leave his home village as soon as his mother dies and go to the town to escape the domination of the "old men." The town, for all that it reflects the worst that is to be found in colonialism, is preferable to subjection to the authority of the "old men" of the village. The "old men" are the "fathers" of the community and individually and collectively act as the "fathers" of the orphaned Banda. Paternity and authority are associated in Banda's mind, and are together rejected, because the sole effect of authority is to give power to those who exercise it and to repress the freedom of the individual. Beti's heroes cannot tolerate the loss of their personal freedom, even though acknowledgement of the collective will as expressed through the elders is widely held by African writers, particularly of Beti's generation, to be a fundamental value of traditional African society. Banda is therefore a "loner"; he tries to justify this with the excuse that he is the victim of a will to exclude him, both on the part of the "old men" and of "fate." . . .

Beti equates the male, the paternal, with superficiality and with the clumsy verbal and physical bullying that accompanies authority founded on an absence of thought or feeling. The other side of the novel explores the female, the maternal, and sees it as exerting a different kind of authority which functions from within and is founded chiefly on the emotions. As far as the structure of the novel is concerned, the penetration beneath its surface-level criticism of colonial and African society coincides exactly with the contrast the author makes between the male and the female, the paternal and the maternal, external and internal authority, between gesture and emotion, speech and silence.

Clive Wake. In János Riesz and Alain Ricard, eds. *Semper Aliquid Novi:*
Littérature Comparée et Littératures d'Afrique
(Tübingen: Gunter Narr, 1990), pp. 297–300

After the appearance of *Main basse* [*sur le Cameroun*], Beti published five novels, a documentary account of his difficulties with the Biya government, and countless articles. For more than a decade, he has kept alive *Peuples Noirs/Peuples Africains*, one of the few independent progressive journals with a focus on Africa. Throughout this flurry of publication, Beti was motivated by many of the same considerations that had prompted him to write *Mission terminée*, *Le Pauvre Christ de Bomba*, and his other preindependence novels. By juxtaposing the true historical situation with the self-serving myth that had been fabricated to disguise the beneficiaries of the collaboration between vested interests in France and Cameroon, Beti hoped to prod his readers into a critical consciousness that would enable them to liberate themselves from the new forms of oppression being imposed on them. As in his earlier work, he argued that Africans themselves must forge the image according to which they shall be known in the world, for only then will they be able to control their own destiny.

By repudiating the false images of Africa promulgated by a new alliance of oppressors, Beti contended, Africans could expose the fraud perpetrated on them by the illusory promises of political independence. Convinced that this alliance retains its power by cultivating a resigned acceptance among the people, he concluded that revolutionary social and political change is possible only if a heightened sense of awareness can be communicated to the general public in countries such as Cameroon. From this perspective, the act of writing becomes a gesture that sweeps away false images and lays the groundwork for a rational understanding of contemporary Africa in its socio-historical context. On the basis of this understanding, Africans can participate actively in this struggle for freedom and identity that, according to Beti, each people must undertake for itself.

The people in this case are the people who live within the boundaries of a single country. In contrast to Beti's earlier fiction, his writing after 1972 focuses on questions specifically related to national identity in Cameroon, although the situation there is sufficiently typical that his descriptions of corruption and oppression have considerable relevance to other African countries as well.

Nevertheless, his allusions to people, places, and events in Cameroonian history make it evident that the novels, essays, and documentary exposés he wrote in the 1970s and 1980s are part of a larger attempt to reestablish the true story of Cameroonian independence and to offer it as a counterimage for the false one that had gained currency because the country's privileged class and its French allies controlled access to the mass media. His five novels from this period— *Perpétue et l'habitude du malheur, Remember Ruben, La Ruine presque cocasse d'un polichinelle, Les Deux Mères de Guillaume Ismaël Dzewatama,* and *La Revanche de Guillaume Ismaël Dzewatama*—are thus designed to provoke a rethinking of what national identity might mean in a free and independent Cameroon.

> Richard Bjornson. *The African Quest for Freedom and Identity: Cameroonian Writing and the National Experience* (Bloomington: Indiana University Press, 1991), p. 326

BRADLEY, DAVID (1950–   )

UNITED STATES

David Bradley ranks among the most sophisticated literary stylists of his generation. His two novels present subtle and original perspectives on issues that traditionally have concerned significant Afro-American writers: the meaning of community, the effects of racism, the shape and substance of history. His first book *South Street*, went out of print soon after publication and has yet to receive the attention it merits. But his award-winning second novel, *The Chaneysville Incident*, has established Bradley's reputation among major contemporary authors. . . .

South Street explores the inner life of the Philadelphia ghetto, with particular emphasis on its three social and cultural centers: Lightnin' Ed's Bar and Grill (the corner dive owned and managed by genial but formidable Leo), the Elysium Hotel (headquarters of Leroy Briggs, a bloodthirsty, womanizing numbers runner), and the Word of Life (the nondenominational, theatrical showcase of a church over which a lecherous charlatan, the Reverend Mr. J. Peter Sloan, presides). With insightful characterizations, strikingly accurate dialogue, and irreverent wit, Bradley examines the kind of communal relationships that bind people of the street to each other. . . .

The Chaneysville Incident is the story of a young man's search for the meaning of his father's life and death. The protagonist, a young, black, Philadelphia-based professor of history named John Washington, does not know that this is what he is after when he returns home to western Pennsylvania to nurse (and then to bury) his ailing surrogate father, Old Jack Crawley. But Jack's death prompts him to visit his parents' home and study Moses's (his late father's) exhaustive collection of manuscripts and journals. This research helps him to understand his father's suicide and its relation to the death of . . . thirteen fugitive slaves years before. Moreover, the process of describing his findings to his white psychiatrist girlfriend, Judith, shows him what the true meaning of history is.

Valerie Smith. In Thadious M. Davis and Trudier Harris, eds.
Dictionary of Literary Biography. 33 (1984), pp. 28–31

It is as much a search for meaning as for being that inspires the trend toward reimmersion in Afro-American literature. The historian-protagonist in *The Chaneysville Incident* stands as a candid embodiment of this fact. John Washington's central act of closeting himself to study his dead father's carefully placed materials actually takes up the Afro-American motif of hibernation and makes it over into a preparation for understanding, not (as with [Ralph] Ellison) for action. . . .

The pressure toward understanding . . . precedes John's election of history as a career. It may indeed have caused it. In grade school he had discovered that ignorance equals humiliation, and that a little knowledge (outdoing [Alexander] Pope) comes close to being deadly, while total knowledge serves as a source of power. But the equation of understanding and power becomes less certain as the subject matter becomes larger and more complex. The only power John Washington really possesses at the end of his story is the power (admittedly not negligible) to shift the quest for understanding to Judith, and to us.

In effect Bradley has set up a circular reading of *The Chaneysville Incident.* The action ends by driving back to its beginning, to the aborted quest for knowledge of, and through, history, and to the surprise revelation of the will. Presumably, even though the "next man" cannot count on that prop, the cycle will somehow lead on to the dramatically vivid but intellectually irresolute fire in the snow and that to the thought of "someone else" who will "understand," and thus to the beginning again.

John Washington's reimmersion ends, but reimmersion must go on in perpetual resumption, at once revelatory and frustrating, at once emancipating and insufficient. The reader becomes John Washington's heir, the "next man" who however dares not burn the tools of his trade, having been enjoined to use them—that is, now, the book—in endless repetition. In this light, we might almost see Truman Held as immersing himself in Meridian's sleeping bag [in Alice Walker's *Meridian*] and then instantly making the reader his heir, with assurance no greater than John Washington holds out.

In the beautifully cadenced scene containing the pivotal quarrel between John and Judith . . . the latter all but enunciates the problematical status of understanding in the new concern with reimmersion in Afro-American literature.

Michael G. Cooke. *Afro-American Literature in the
Twentieth Century: The Achievement of Intimacy* (New Haven,
Conn.: Yale University Press, 1984), pp. 214–16

Through use of the monomyth, Bradley . . . illustrates a firm conviction in the power one gains from personal history. His narrator, John Washington, leaves the urban North to return to the rural setting he came from. . . . John leaves home with a tangible goal: to bury his old friend, Jack; but he . . . finds himself completely obsessed by the desire to unbury his family history. During most of his quest, John's state of mind might be described as mad, in the sense of a transcendent awareness that ignores the distractions society attempts to impose. Bradley's opening passage suggests the Call to Adventure, as John receives a telephone call from his mother conveying John's boyhood mentor's wish that John come to his bedside before Jack dies. Lest the reader underestimate the nature of this call, John, the narrator, underlines its mythic significance: "Sometimes you can hear the [telephone] wire, hear it reaching out across the miles; whining with its own weight, crying out from the cold, panting at the distance, humming with the phantom sounds of someone else's conversation. . . . whining, crying, panting, humming, moaning like a live thing." With this haunting passage, reflective of Bradley's love of the oral narrative, John draws us into his vaguely supernatural vision. Ignoring, or perhaps compelled by, the midnight hour, he takes the next bus, thus beginning his quest; both reluctant to answer the Call to Adventure and driven to do so, John spurs himself on with hot toddies. John's departure from his adopted home, urban academia, takes him back to a region whose mythic significance is underlined by the names of its various locales: the County, the Town, the Hill.

After Jack's funeral, John realizes he has been summoned for reasons more complicated than a burial. He resists the wiles of three trickster figures: the Judge and his son, emblematic of the white power structure, who in archetypal fashion function to dissuade John from completing his journey, and John's mother, who has colluded with this white power structure. Returning to old Jack's cabin, and aided by the tools of historical scholarship, pens and notes that acquire a magical dimension because he believes they will help him untangle his personal history, he begins the second stage of his journey and the second major part of *The Chaneysville Incident.* Like Milkman [in Toni Morrison's *Song of Solomon*], John feels driven to merge himself with elemental reality; he abandons all but the most meager comforts Jack's dwelling provides. During this phase of his quest, John enters a state of mind akin to the holy madness of a mystic, leaving the corporal world almost entirely. Suffering through a number of grueling initiatory trials, including a deer hunt, John finally enters fully into the depths of the underworld: his creative imagination. The final section of *The Chaneysville Incident* begins when John emerges, having gained liberation as a result of immersing himself in his history and fusing that history with African philosophy. Finally, Bradley's hero returns to his urban community fortified with knowledge that transcends the historical facts that academia prizes. Until his quest, John Washington, an historian, has persistently avoided discussing the history of the region where he grew up, an area he has refused to visit for years. Before his quest, Milkman Dead has come to accept the notion that he is incapable of flight, a notion that denies his spiritual link with the past. Consequently, he has become shallow, inhibited, and incurious about his history. Both of these men, having spent years evading their personal histories, end up affirming them, typifying the strenuous journey from denial to celebration of Afro-American history.

Jane Campbell. *Mythic Black Fiction: The Transformation of History*
(Knoxville: University of Tennessee Press, 1986), pp. 139–40

The Chaneysville Incident unfolds one new dimension after another—historical, political (micro- and macro-), linguistic, interpersonal, intrapsychic, spiritual. There is also an integral, unintrusive, and illuminating consciousness of the process of "making" with language. There is the history John tells us, but also the histories of the history. Indeed, assembling and telling the history is what constitutes John's heroism. John's task involves all the processes of writing history—gathering and sorting information, reconstructing sequences and simultaneities, and confronting the gaps. The task also leads him to another modality of knowing—though to get there, he must drop his scientific/obsessional ways. The focus of the history itself is on racial conflict from slavery to the present as seen through the microcosm of one line of descent—that of John's father, Moses Washington. A central concern of the history is with black rebellion and subversion, to be seen and treated as autonomous people. At the interpersonal level, the novel focuses on the tensions between generations, races, and sexes. The history and present moments of John's relationship to Judith has its own distinct tensions; and these tensions are brought up against the origins of John's side of the antagonism and ambivalence: Jack Crawley, John's surrogate father, the last father in the line. Jack Crawley teaches John many invaluable skills; he tells two or three of the best stories in the novel (about the great trickster, Moses). At his funeral we learn how generous he has been—he without family. But he also prohibits John from the white world and the sexual world. John has entered both.

The world John grew up in, the one he now lives in and the one he returns to are fraught with tension. The focus of this paper is on how that tension manifests itself within the character, particularly how it is mapped onto his body. Specifically, I focus on the symptomatic pain in the belly of John Washington. The conflicts generating the pain and anxiety are rooted in the hero's historical quest, in the history he discerns, in the primitive rage developed within his family with its rage, and his fear of the gaps of history and relationships. The resolution of the symptomatic pain, the interpersonal knots, and the historical problems emerge almost simultaneously, interdependently, precipitated by one another. The ending brings us to the birth of the narrative, the possible inception of new life, a new paternity, and an understanding of heroic suicide and spiritual birth. The hero, at least for the moment, succeeds in leaping the gaps between male and female, black and white, past and present, present and future.

Martin J. Gliserman. *American Imago*. 43, 2 (Summer 1986), pp. 99–100

In his second novel, *The Chaneysville Incident*, David Bradley has presented a narrative text in which authenticated historical material is so charged with the expressive claims of fiction as symbolic action that the book may today already claim a unique position within Afro-American fiction—a narrative tradition well-known for its concern with history. As Bradley's statements in the short preface to the novel make explicit, he places himself within a collective endeavor for the ten years it took him to conceptualize and finish the book. Bradley has drawn on archival research (his own and that of others) into family, community, and group history in order to invest the quest for personal and cultural self-definition of the central narrator John Washington with as much historical context as possible. . . .

In terms of the historical material, Bradley's novel tries to present a comprehensive perspective on the formative experience of black Americans (that is, on slavery and the desire for self-realization) and on the necessity of recapturing their past. On the fictional level this quest is presented as a process of self-scrutiny and self-therapy for the precarious self-concept of a representative individual, John Washington. . . . The deliberate breaking-up of the narrative structure . . . points to Bradley's being heir to fictional techniques in the mainstream tradition of American literature. Bradley is trying to fuse not only black and white narrative traditions (thus claiming a non-segregated heritage), but also more fundamentally the documentary and imaginative reconstruction of the black experience in America, while at the same time raising positive questions about the interrelation of history and fiction. . . .

This is the main thrust of Bradley's novel: history can only become meaningful through active imaginative appropriation of its raw material, which is to say by an act of imaginative completion, by the fictional reconstruction of the unfinished story-line of history. The three major protagonists of the novel—C. K., Moses, and John Washington—together establish a fictional lineage with strong reference to factual history, but all enhanced and projected onto a more than life-size fictional screen in order to articulate central thematic concerns of Bradley's dramatized version of black history in the context of America. C. K. and Moses Washington are passionately concerned with defensive as well as offensive (or militant) social and political power, with survival as the prerequisite for an outspoken (C. K.) or tacit (Moses) demand for gaining the power to have their say in shaping the national or local world they live in. Their heir John Washington has shifted his struggle for survival to the psychological and class level—he has to fend off both the destructive influence of white racism, and its equivalent of internalized self-hatred, as well as the suffocating norms of middle-class respectability embodied by his mother and her lineage. On the militant level, John (clad in the contemporary armor of the university professor) has shifted his ancestors' bid for power to the intellectual or cognitive sphere, with power becoming the control over and mediation of knowledge. As historian he partakes in exemplary fashion in the business of image-making and image control which has already been at the heart of black-white antagonism in America, and around which the novel in its continuing dialogical quest keeps moving, sometimes in contracting, sometimes in expanding circles, including a possible future as represented by Judith, and easily shifting from present to past since all time levels remain closely interconnected in the unremitting questioning attitude of John's mind.

Klaus Ensslen. *Callaloo*. 11, 2 (Spring 1988), pp. 280–81, 286

BRATHWAITE, EDWARD KAMAU (1930–   )

BARBADOS

[Edward Kamau] Brathwaite's trilogy, *Rights of Passage*, *Masks*, and *Islands*, constitutes an epic of sorts on the black West Indian's history and culture. . . .

Rights of Passage concentrates on blacks in the Americas, moving from the West Indies to the United States and back. The second book, *Masks*, reverses the Middle Passage voyage by returning the reader to Africa. Finally, *Islands* is both a return to the contemporary West Indies and a symbolic retracing of the original voyage of enslavement. The odyssey or journey motif of the trilogy dramatizes the nature and function of the artistic imagination in the black experience: art is a journey through time as well as space; it is an act of memory, discovering and imitating the cycles of history, and in the process both creating and demonstrating a heightened new awareness of the past in the present. Consequently the work song with which *Rights of Passage* opens exemplifies art as an act of memory. . . .

[*Masks*] is also rooted in the strategy of developing a full awareness through the cyclical course of memory and art. Here the persistent journey motif describes the West Indian's cultural pilgrimage to West Africa. That pilgrimage is a literal and physical one. But it is also psychic, linking the West Indian's modern return to his Akan beginnings with the period in which his ancestors were torn from West Africa by the slave trade and with that even earlier period when those precolonial ancestors sought new homes for the first time in West Africa. The total effect of this simultaneous perception of time cycles is to reemphasize time itself as an essentially cyclical, or circular whole. It is therefore appropriate that the work opens with a ceremony of libation that celebrates the cycle of time in the year that has "come round / again." Moreover, this impression of a cyclical wholeness also rests on the continental dimensions of Africa, the cultural affinities between its distinctive regions, and most important that cyclical perception of time and experience which the poet shares with his Africans: "all Africa / is one, is whole." . . .

The circular movement of art and memory also takes us back, in the other direction, to the Caribbean starting point of *Rights of Passage*. And this return is the main subject of *Islands*, the final book of the trilogy. The major divisions of this work are centered on the growing consciousness with which the West Indian returns from the memories of, and journey to, Africa . . . . "New World" therefore represents both the New World ambience of the West Indian and the new possibilities that are inherent in the West Indian's recreated consciousness; "Limbo" recalls the legendary roots of the dance as an exercise for slaves immediately after disembarkation from the slaveships, and in so doing it celebrates the West Indian endurance despite slavery; "Rebellion" offers reminders of the old plantation systems, emphasizes their continuation under new, postcolonial disguises, into the present, and by virtue of those reminders its title becomes a prophecy or threat; "Possession" picks up the rebellious, transforming energies of "Rebellion" by offering the contrast between islanders as possessions and islands as symbols of a new dignity or integrity: "possession" as spiritual possession (in the manner of folk religions from Africa and the West) therefore celebrates the new, aggressive consciousness within Brathwaite's West Indian. And in a fitting conclusion to the circular structure of the trilogy as a whole, the carnival dance of "Beginnings" recalls the folk songs and dance with which *Rights of Passage* opens: in this concluding section the dance celebrates the beginnings of a national consciousness that has been derived from the total experience, or historical "rites" of the Middle Passage.

Lloyd W. Brown. *West Indian Poetry*
(Boston: Twayne, 1978), pp. 140–42, 149–50, 153

In his early work Brathwaite conceives of the poetic imagination as a superior way of perceiving the world. The poetic reconstruction of the world could redeem reality from its fallen state. In [an] early poem in *Other Exiles* Brathwaite expresses the need for "words to refashion futures like a healer's hand." The same line recurs in [*The Arrivants: A New World Trilogy*] . . . as the poet is attempting to liberate the region from its sterile fallen state. The poet's public voice has its roots in this early recognition of the role of art as a means of discovering unconscious figurative meanings behind the concrete and the visible. What was essentially a private literary quest for the young Brathwaite later becomes the point of departure for an aesthetic exploration of the Caribbean that transcends the historical stereotype of pluralism and fragmentation.

Even though Brathwaite situates himself in a new vanguard of West Indian writing, his actual career and experiences are not unlike those of the generation of the "first phase." Born in Barbados in 1930 he follows the familiar pattern of metropolitan exile and an eventual return to the West Indies. He receives his higher education in Cambridge in the early 1950s and becomes in his own words "a roofless man of the world" before returning to the Caribbean. As is the case with most artists who underwent this sequence of experiences, the odyssey served to heighten the poet's sensitivity to the dilemma of alienation which plagued West Indian intellectuals in exile.

During this period of exile Brathwaite's work reflects his various experiences. For instance, "The day the first snow fell" is basically about the poet's disappointment at discovering his estrangement in Britain from a world which he thought he could possess. The frustration normally expected at this point in the career of the exiled artist, when all worlds appear strange to him, never really emerges in Brathwaite's work. We have an important departure from the sense of dispossession that comes with exile, in the poet's eight-year stay in Ghana [from 1955 to 1962]. It is here that he discovers the sense of the sacred so crucial to the poetic imagination. He discovers a world which he cannot adopt but one which seems to retain a communion with the mysterious and numinous which is absent in the historically disadvantaged New World. His awareness of the customs and language of the Ghanaian people is seen in his adaptation of *Antigone* to a Ghanaian context in *Odale's Choice*. This does not represent an original project since the adaptation of classical drama to local situations was not unknown, but it does show a closeness to the environment in which he found himself, which is central to his dramatization of this experience in his trilogy.

J. Michael Dash. In Bruce King, ed. *West Indian Literature*
(Hamden, Conn.: Archon Books, 1979), pp. 214–15

The Arrivants trilogy is essentially a record of the stages of Brathwaite's life from feelings of exile, through the years in Africa, to the discovery of his African heritage in the New World and the resulting sense of community. It is a creation of a mythology for the black West Indian to replace earlier images of the self created by white prejudice, colonialism, and European history. *Rights of Passage* . . . is a *Wasteland* based on the various roles and postures ("Uncle Tom," "Spider," "the Negro") of the descendants of Africans taken to the New World. It is partly a lament for a lost world: "We kept / our state on golden stools—remember?" It begins with an evocation of the past: "Drum skin whip / lash" and examines the life of the black man in the Americas and Europe.

The second part of the trilogy, *Masks*, celebrates the life Brathwaite found in Africa, particularly among the Akan in Ghana. Africa is a land of history remembered, music, dance, ancestors, customs and especially religion. The poem "The Making of the Drum" concerns the sacrifices that sacramentalize ordinary objects in African life. [The second section of the poem] "The Barrel of the Drum" is a catechism praising the holiness of the wood from which the drum will be made. [Sections 3–5] "The Two Curved Sticks of the Drummer," "Gourds and Rattles," [and] "The Gong-Gong" are among the various musical objects given a religious significance. The "Path-finders" poems treat of African heroes and places of the past. [The "Limits" poems recall] the movements of the West African tribes from their supposed home in Egypt, across the Sudan, until they settle on the coast, where the voyage to the New World and slavery will begin. "The Return" [poems treat] of Brathwaite himself in Africa. . . .

The poems in *Islands* . . . reject the imitation of European culture in the West Indies and treat of restoration, the recognition of African roots which will contribute towards the making of a new authenticity in the New World.

Bruce King. *The New English Literatures: Cultural Nationalism in a Changing World* (New York: St. Martin's Press, 1980), pp. 131–33

The load of black experience which is central to the thought in Brathwaite's trilogy as well as in his other volumes, *Other Exiles, Days & Nights, Black + Blues*, and his more recent volume *Mother Poem*, is conveyed through sets of archetypal patterns which center around the sea as a redemptive as well as exiling elemental force, the journey which is at once specific and universal, and the earth as the base of cultural roots, the womb of life and the ultimate abode to which we retire at death. The result of this schematization of symbols and images is the constantly compelling concatenation of antithetical references to life and death, dryness and wetness, departure and arrival, exile and rediscovery, disintegration and restoration, hope and despair.

Samuel Omo Asein. *WLWE.* 20, 1 (Spring 1981), p. 100

The first significations of the centrality of African deities in Brathwaite's poetry occur in his reference to fire and its associated images in *Rights of Passage*. . . . The recurrent images of fire in this first book point the way forward to the motif of Ogun (the Yoruba deity of war and creativity) in *Islands* while Anancy (the Akan creator god) who also becomes one of the prominent deities in the New World and, therefore, in *Islands*, is signalled through multifaceted allusions which recall the spider's (*anancy*) complex and intricate webs. Both Ogun and Anancy eventually emerge as the two presiding ancestral African deities in *Islands*, with the other African deities making infrequent but essential appearances. By choosing Ogun, the warrior and craftsman, and Anancy, the cunning spinner, as the expressive images of the New World situation, Brathwaite leaves us in no doubt as to the fact that he is set to articulate the spirit of creative struggle which has enabled the New World African to cope with and even overcome the debilitating effects of transplantation and enslavement.

Islands opens with a consideration of godhood in the New World. In "Jah," the first poem in *Islands*, Brathwaite focuses on both Western and African concepts of God and, in the process, establishes the tangible physical and subliminal links between Africa and the New World. He borrows organic and musical images (music is the intensive language of communication between man and the gods) to express these links: Nairobi's male elephant's trumpeting is taken up in the black music of Havana and Harlem; the orchestra of seven elephant-tusk horns used to relate history on state occasions in Africa (*Masks*) is echoed in the history-laden jazz of the black New World; and the slave ship's riggings are manifested in the new prisons of the steel bridges and skyscrapers of the white New World. The first part of this poem suggests that the Western god has become so debased and commercialized that he is synonymous with the cities' neon lights. The second part makes an almost equally devastating assessment of the African deities in the New World. In addition to being separated from Jah because there is "no sound . . . no ground to keep him down near the gods," Brathwaite suggests that the African deities "have been forgotten or hidden" because "the land has lost the memory of the most secret places." Anancy now prefers to peep "over the hills with the sunrise" and to "spin webs in the tree," and Ogun of the fiery temper is transformed into voiceless volcanoes. These views are, however, summations of the general views about African gods and cultures in the New World. Brathwaite is not necessarily in agreement and . . . he, at the worst, may be willing to concede only that the African deities are in a state of suspended animation. That he opens *Islands* with a consideration of the idea of godhead is in itself an indication that he considers it a very important index in any analysis of the New World African's psyche.

Funso Aiyejina. WLWE. 23, 2 (Spring 1984), pp. 398–99

For the poet Edward Brathwaite, himself a historian, history becomes a tool for the discovery of self. His trilogy, *The Arrivants*, focuses on the black man of the New World and defines his condition as "homeless" and "historyless." The European writers of West Indian history, far from having written for the black man, have vigorously suppressed his humanity and identity. Brathwaite is concerned therefore with the rediscovery of an African past and identity that will remove from the black man of the New World the sense of "loss" and dereliction which would be his lot from a different historical perspective.

The journey across Africa in *The Arrivants*, with its biblical echoes of the chosen people crossing the wilderness to the promised land, functions . . . by remaining, in image and symbol, central to our experience of literature. The African place names (Ougadongou, Chad, Timbuktu, Volta) ring like bells in the volume *Masks*, and create a sense of possession or repossession of a rich alternative historical reality. This sense is reinforced by rituals, such as the making of the drum, the dance of possession in "Adowa," the solemn dirge in Tano. . . .

History . . . which includes folk history and ritual, pervades Brathwaite's later volumes of poetry, imparting a distinct historical resonance to landscape, character and image in *Mother Poem* and *Sun Poem*. For Brathwaite, man's identity is determined by his past, but he must discover/re-create that past, rather than accept the crude "given" of the colonial tradition. In *Sun Poem* Brathwaite shows how this is accomplished, for even where the poetry appears lyrical and autobiographical, the historical resonances, as Gordon Rohlehr points out, are very much present.

Mark A. McWatt. West Indian Literature and Its Social Context
(St. Michael, Barbados: Cave Hill, 1985), pp. 43–44

Mother Poem and *Sun Poem* are the first two poems in Edward Brathwaite's . . . poetic trilogy. Both poems are set in the post-Emancipation period on the island of Barbados. . . . Like *Rights of Passage*, *Masks*, and *Islands*—the poems of Brathwaite's first trilogy, *The Arrivants*—*Mother Poem* and *Sun Poem* are poems of multiple voices. *Mother Poem* traces the history of Barbados through the voices of working-class or folk women, a female slave, children, and a debt collector, agent of the capitalist merchant; these voices are interspersed with the at times ideologically committed descriptive, at times directly protesting voice of the visionary poet, evaluating the folk women's uncritical consumption of white bourgeois materialism, religion, and education (the last of these for their children), and the expedients associated with the socioeconomic conditions imposed on working-class married and family life by the plantation and its owner, the white mulatto merchant. The text is determined to give articulation to the often publicly silent dreaming of the folk women, to "slowly restore [their] silent gutters of word-fall" through the impersonations of art. *Sun Poem* traces the history of Barbados through the loss or perversion of male dreaming. The voices of the poem are many: the voice of the rainbow; the inner and speaking voices of Adam, the archetypal folk boy; the voices of Adam's sister, male playfellows and childhood sweetheart; the voice of an emasculated black male; the historical voices of a slaver and a follower of the slave rebellion leader, Bussa; and the at times ideologically committed descriptive, at times directly protesting voice of the visionary poet and historian. The poem carries in itself and in its connections with *Mother Poem* the implication that the plantation, the merchant, and female dreaming cause the loss or perversion of male dreaming and emasculation—as one male puts his dilemma in the poem: "i gettin smaller . . . is de sun dyein out of i vision." Both *Mother Poem* and *Sun Poem* close on a note of hope, with the rediscovery of the power of nam, the "soul, secret name, soul-source, connected with *nyam* (eat), yam (root food), *nyame* (name of god)," a rediscovery which the text insists will enable the present generations of black Bajans to find their Afro-West Indian roots, their folk/maroon heritage, and so become "the first potential parents" to "contain the ancestral house" threatened and made insecure by lack of solid foundations in the soil of landscape and history.

Sue Thomas. *Kunapipi.* 9, 1 (1987), pp. 33–34

Clearly the Afro-Caribbean writer who is most strongly influenced by black America is Edward Brathwaite. Born in Barbados and educated at Cambridge, he is a poet of international distinction. His formidable knowledge of the histories, cultures and literatures of the peoples of the African diaspora and his uncompromising cultural nationalism make him especially receptive to influences, both Afro-American and African. The elements of black American influence that are discernible in Brathwaite's poetry fall into two categories: allusions to aspects of Afro-American culture and incorporations of the blues forms and jazz techniques.

Brathwaite's intricately allusive poetry is replete with references to various aspects of black American culture, both classical and popular. A notable feature of his allusiveness is his frequent references to Afro-American cultural heroes. The evocations of those names not only constitute a leitmotif that reinforces his themes, but the individuals whose names are alluded to become symbols that undergird Brathwaite's concept of a Pan-African identity. For example, his anthology *Other Exiles*, has poems titled after Count Basie, Miles Davis, [John] Coltrane, and Charlie Parker; each of these poems provides a sensitive assessment of the titular hero's enriching contribution to the black musical tradition. To Brathwaite they are more than celebrities who represent the essence of black musical genius; they are spiritual guardians of the black civilization. In *Sun Poem*, for instance, he suggests that Aretha Franklin's voice, Coltrane's inventiveness, and Jesse Owens's athletic prowess are manifestations of Ogun, the Yoruba god of invention. In *X/Self*, his most recent volume of poetry, he has a poem titled "Julia." The title refers to the 1960s television series, "Julia," with Diahann Carroll, which was the first prime-time show in American television history with a black woman as a major character in a nonmenial role. The poem contains allusions to Bill Cosby, [Muhammad] Ali, Tina Turner, the famed Apollo Theater of Harlem, and the Montgomery bus boycott that signaled the advent of the Civil Rights Movement in the South. In *The Arrivants* he employs innumerable Afro-American cultural referents—to Malcolm X, James Baldwin (whom he calls Jimmy Baldwin, with affectionate familiarity), Martin Luther King, Jr., Ralph Ellison, among many others.

Emmanuel S. Nelson. *JAC.* 12, 4 (Winter 1989), pp. 55–56

In *Middle Passages*, as in much of the earlier work, it is not unexpected that Brathwaite would see the loss of self as the *X* or unknown quotient of personality; thus, the poetic effort becomes the dramatic quest to reclaim that self as personhood. In the end the *X* self becomes the dynamic and positive other half of the individual in the resulting flux originally cast in the form of placelessness: the void is then transformed through the sense of all the innate and inherent possibilities embedded in the human being as real *self* with one's dignity intact. Perhaps in so powerfully identifying this aspect of his poetic drive, Brathwaite curtails the purely intuitive self as imaginative expression. . . .

The various [poems] in *Middle Passages* attest to the range of history and ideas, beginning with the acknowledgment of language in "Word Making Man" and continuing with "Colombe," "Noom" (suggestive of African religion), "Duke" (Duke Ellington playing piano at seventy), "Flute(s)," "Veridian," "The Visibility Trigger," "How Europe underdeveloped Africa" (a familiar theme), "Stone" (for Mickey Smith, the dub poet), "The Sahell of Donatello," . . . "Soweto" (dedicated to the Mandelas), "Leopard," "Letter Sycorax," and "Irae." Although the sections are short, it is important to identify them as a way of tracing the organic poetic impulse, as the images flow and intertwine to reveal their inner selves through naming history with the voice of acknowledgment and protest.

Cyril Dabydeen. WLT. 67, 2 (Spring 1993), p. 426

BRODBER, ERNA (1940–   )

JAMAICA

Erna Brodber has, in a sense, *always* been a creative writer. Before starting secondary school, she had already earned the grand total of seventeen shillings and sixpence in prize money for three short stories, published in the children's section of the Jamaican paper, the *Weekly Times*. Since then, she has been involved with theater, had poetry and short stories published in Caribbean journals, and written one acclaimed novel. . . .

The opening of *Jane and Louisa Will Soon Come Home* situates the reader in . . . [a] close-knit rural community, isolated but secure. "Mountains ring us round and cover us, banana leaves shelter us and sustain us." Here also is the extended family of small farmers, and here also "everybody is related," with the life of one impinging upon the life of others. The community is an entity in itself and, much like the "chorus of people in the lane" in Roger Mais's *Brother Man*, it speaks with one tongue: "the voice belongs to the family group dead and alive." That the dead ancestors are as vital a part of the community as the living is made clear early in the novel by the comparison of the white plantocracy's dead, safely "tombed and harmless" with the black peasant dead, imaged in terms of continual growth and influence on the living: "Our dead and living are shrouded together under zinc, sweet potato slips and thatch. Step warily— one body raises itself into a mountain of bodies which overtop to form a pit or a shelter for you." Community and communal ancestors, then, have power that can be positive ("a shelter") or negative ("a pit") for the individual. . . .

Despite the differing interpretations of a work that, by its very nature, invites complex and various readings, critical evaluation of *Jane and Louisa* has tended toward unanimous eulogy, particularly in its formal status as a new milestone in Caribbean creative writing. [Rhonda] Cobham hails the novel as "probably the most exciting piece of prose fiction by a West Indian author to appear in recent years," and [Jean Pierre] Durix makes the significant claim that "probably no one else in the West Indies, apart from Wilson Harris, has revolutionized the art of fiction as much as Erna Brodber in *Jane and Louisa*."

Evelyn O'Callaghan. In Daryl Cumber Dance, ed. *Fifty Caribbean Writers* (Westport, Conn.: Greenwood Press, 1986), pp. 73–74, 80–81

Jane and Louisa Will Soon Come Home makes selective use of the author's experience in mediating a variety of themes. Discussion of this novel so far has concentrated on Nellie's experience as a reflection of that of the Caribbean woman, with considerable attention also being given to stylistic and structural aspects of the novel and to the central image of the kumbla. Brodber's concern with communal ancestry has also been noted, and it has been generally recognized by her critics that Nellie's search for autonomy represents more than a search for a personal direction. The main purpose of this further examination is to show how she uses Nellie's experiences and those of other women whom she depicts to allude to specific incidents or events in her society's history, going back as far as the immediate postemancipation period. The portrait of the society is strengthened both by the parallel between Nellie's circumstances and those of the society and the way in which the outlook of the women portrayed relates to particular periods of Jamaican social history. The Caribbean woman's behavior, as Brodber has described it, has been formed very much in the same way as that of the slaves: to avoid conflict and to promote survival. In responding to experience in the way they do, she demonstrates, women become accomplices in their own oppression. Wittingly and unwittingly they create myths and perpetrate deceptions by which they are themselves controlled. Parallels with the colonial society caught up in the hoax of history are thus suggested. Furthermore, Nellie's attempt to free herself from the safe "womb" of inherited ideas evokes extreme schizophrenia comparable to the confusion and disaffection created within the social organism attempting to reorient itself. The new level of awareness which she achieves, through her re-examination of the past, is far removed from that of her grandmother, Granny Tucker. Nellie's changed outlook may be compared with that of the ex-colonial society in the 1970s, which has come to view its colonial heritage dispassionately.

Joyce Walker-Johnson. *JWIL*. 3, 1 (January 1989), pp. 47–48

The landscape of Erna Brodber's *Jane and Louisa Will Soon Come Home* is largely that of rural Jamaica, a setting in which family ties are complicated by the sinuous bonds of color and class: a context within which an oral tradition of long-time story, family history, and pure gossip flourishes alongside the world of books and distant town. Brodber's narrative method exemplifies an interpretation of scribal and oral literary forms: a modernist, stream-of-consciousness narrative voice holds easy dialogue with the traditional teller of tales, the transmitter of [the Anancy] story, proverb, folk song, and dance.

Brodber's experiment in form is underscored by the writer's deliberately ingenuous assertion that *Jane and Louisa Will Soon Come Home* was not conceived as a novel: she set out to write a case study in abnormal psychology. But literary critics have appropriated the work, recognizing in its dense patterns of allusive imagery, its evocative language, and its carefully etched characterizations, the sensibility of the creative writer. The "functionalist" intention of the social psychologist appears divergent from the "structuralist" analysis of the literary critic. But Brodber's "faction" can be categorized within a neo-African folk aesthetic of functional form: literature as wordhoard, the repository of the accumulated wisdom of the community, the creative medium through which the norms of appropriate social behavior can be elaborated metaphorically.

The Afro-Jamaican folk ethos of *Jane and Louisa Will Soon Come Home* is evident in the organizing metaphors of the work, derived from the folk culture, and in its primary theme: the healing of the protagonist Nellie, who travels to "foreign" to study, and returns home to a profound sense of homelessness, from which she is redeemed only when she comes to understand the oral accounts of her fragmented family history, and the distorted perceptions of female identity and sexuality that she has internalized in childhood. The therapeutic power of the word is the subject and medium of Brodber's fictive art.

Carolyn Cooper. In Carole Boyce Davies and Elaine Savory Fido, eds.
Out of the Kumbla: Caribbean Women and Literature
(Trenton, N. J.: Africa World Press, 1990), pp. 279–80

Erna Brodber did not set out to write a novel but rather to present a case study to teach the dissociative personality to her class in human growth and development. The case study incorporated some of the issues that concerned her and her students such as male-female relations, black liberation, and the women's movement. The decision to publish this material was made by her sister, teacher-poet-critic Velma Pollard. . . .

Nellie Richmond, the protagonist of *Jane and Louisa Will Soon Come Home*, is born into a virtual Garden of Eden, where "mountains ring us round and cover us, banana leaves shelter us and sustain us." Nellie's world is protected from everything; not even the sun can get in: "Outside infiltrated our nest only as its weave allowed." But this Edenic existence is short-lived for growth brings with it a series of exposures and revelations that shatters Nellie's sense of herself. She becomes aware of color and class divisions in her family and in her community, recognizes the "shame" and "filth" and precariousness of being a female; has to face "it" (alternately menses, female sexuality, everything associated with being a woman), which sets her apart from everybody, including her favorite neighbor, Mass Stanley, and all the boys who had been her playmates; has to face physical development ("Have you ever seen a new sucker trying to grow out of a rotten banana root? My whole chest was that rotten banana root and there were two suckers"); has to submit to sex (recalled with shame and disgust in images of a "long nasty snail," a "mekke mekke thing"), simply because "you want to be a woman; now you have a man. . . . Vomit and bear it"; has to accept that as a woman "the world is waiting to drag you down: Woman luck de a dungle heap"; and has to acknowledge that "the black womb is . . . an abominable scrap heap thing." . . .

It adds up to more than our heroine can bear, and she suffers total psychic collapse. Her condition is sometimes described as a loss or lack of balance. Nellie's Aunt Becca warns her of the precarious position of women in the world, concluding, "Learn that lest you be weighed in the balance and found wanting." Nellie's fear of losing the balance, of being found wanting, is a critical part of her dilemma and is reinforced in the many descriptions of her sensing herself spinning wildly; like Anancy caught in his own trap and convinced by his own words, "spinning around in the woods," she is "twirling madly in a still life." The importance of maintaining the balance is demonstrated in the experience of her neighbors: Mass Stanley's son David had to be cast out of his home because he disrupted the balance when he wanted to be a bull (man) in the same pen with his father. Mass Stanley's grandson Baba, on the other hand, "never disturbed their balance."

Nellie's ailment is frequently described as a cold, often icy, lump. This contrasts with the warmth of her original Eden: "Ever see a fowl sitting on eggs in cold December rain. We knew the warmth and security of those eggs in the dark of her bottom." When, because of the onset of puberty, the boys in her neighborhood no longer tussle with her, she laments, "What kind of coldness in this hot sun." After her first sexual experience she speaks of having to live in "an ice cage" and of the "dry ice [that] works my body to a bloodless incision." She learns that displays of anger must be "frozen with a compress of ice"; she characterizes her life as having "passed through a seasoning of ice."

Daryl Cumber Dance. In Selwyn R. Cudjoe, ed. *Caribbean Women Writers* (Wellesley, Mass.: Calaloux, 1990), pp. 170–71

Jane and Louisa Will Soon Come Home takes its title from a common children's song, the basis of a ring dance performed some evenings by little boys and girls in the yard or at the beach, anywhere outdoors, usually with adults helping out. Brodber takes the words and makes them into social commentary, then into talismans, then into mythic concentrations of the whole complex of Caribbean experience: childhood, city and country, the extended family, social mores and biases, sexual emergencies, political structures, and travel and study abroad (with all that these entail of culture shock and culture clarification and culture enlargement and culture reaffirmation). . . .

The text is replete with images of enclosure, refining, revising, compounding, enriching one another and the mind of the central speaker. We find enclosure as imprisonment ("I was being choked. . . . I needed out"), and as potential site of germination and growth ("immaculate egg," and the image of menstruation as a thing in its own space).

The kumbla is the ultimate image of enclosure in *Jane and Louisa*, and it is used with structural brilliance to resolve the contradictions and anxieties of the garden—the claustrophobia and paranoia and disgrace (since menstruation raises the danger of sexual capture and pregnancy, with its terminal confinement). The kumbla is the space of the self and space for the self, and is as versatile in form as our needs may be various: beachball, eggshell, light bulb, calabash, shell, parachute, womb, and, of course, the omnipresent ring of the title song. Where the garden gives space, the kumbla goes one better by giving both space and time—its only requirement is that one not stay in it too long, for fear of turning albino from lack of sun. The kumbla is the space-time for an apocalypse that is not yonder and happenstance in character, but the sum and product of experience that is illumined in our embrace.

Michael G. Cooke. *JWIL*. 4, 1 (January 1990), pp. 36–37

In Brodber's novel [*Myal*], the powerful grip of obeah—the debilitating obverse of therapeutic myal, is imaged most dramatically, and ironically, in the attempted theft of Anita's spirit by Mass Levi, a deacon in the Baptist church. Mass Levi, suddenly become impotent, appropriates the spirit of the young girl in order to regain sexual potency: a particularly perverse manifestation of the sexual exploitation of woman. The Kumina Queen, Miss Gatha (in collaboration with the Baptist minister, Simpson; the necromancer, Ole African, and somewhat surprisingly, the English wife of the white Jamaican Methodist minister, Brassington) draws the malevolent possessing spirit from the girl on to her own person.

Brodber's quiet shaping of this act of exorcism focuses on the intimate, human scale of this potentially sensationalist complex of circumstances. The spirit's power is manifest, but it is its containment (the healing) and the ordinariness of faith in the spirit world that is Brodber's point. This is not a lurid voodoo tale. . . .

There *is* a voodoo doll in Brodber's fiction . . . but its significance in the total architecture of the novel is not only that it is a literal artifact in the practice of obeah; rather, like the crumbling fertility doll that Baba mockingly carves for Nellie in *Jane and Louisa Will Soon Come Home* (Brodber's earlier novel), it becomes an icon of the zombification of diminished woman who is robbed of her possibilities: the alabaster baby. This is Ella's story, as well as Anita's. In Brodber's subtly shaded rural world, the reader focuses less on the "strangeness" of events and more on their import for characters who fully believe in a cosmology where the natural and the supernatural, the demonic and the divine regularly consort.

Carolyn Cooper. In Susheila Nasta, ed. *Motherlands* (New Brunswick,
N. J.: Rutgers University Press, 1992), pp. 71–74

In her essay "Fiction in the Scientific Procedure," Brodber sees a continuity between her scientific and her literary projects. Both Brodber's social science and her fiction attempt to understand the social world as a *system* of relations. However, they differ from that "objective" narrative which [Edouard] Glissant condemns. For whereas the latter narrative erects binarisms, Brodber reveals a commitment to *overcoming* binarisms—notably the self/other, science/art, objectivity/subjectivity dualisms. Thus, she writes of a "twinning of fiction and science." And her commitment to a realist epistemology also leads her away from formal realism. Like Glissant, then, Brodber doubles the meanings of objectivity, science, and realism.

In her attempt to understand Jamaican society, Brodber grapples with the bitter (post)colonial phenomenon of "prejudice against blacks in a country of blacks. The enemy was a ghost that talked through black faces." Her novel, *Myal*, is in many ways a literalization of that metaphor. The novel is erected around the mulatto child Ella O'Grady. It spans the years 1913–1920, Ella's fourteenth to twenty-first year. As a story of education and coming to consciousness, the novel functions at least partly in the tradition of the *bildungsroman*. However, it does not proceed in the linear fashion of the traditional *bildungsroman*, but through a complex series of halvings and doublings. At the beginning of her story—though not at the beginning of the novel—we see Ella reciting [Rudyard] Kipling's "The White Man's Burden." It is quite literally the colonizer's voice that speaks through her. At the time, she is unaware of the implications of a colonial text that describes her people, a colonized people, as "half devil, half child." She does, however, know the pain of being a half-caste; like her mother, she knows what it is like to be a "long face, thin lip, pointed nose soul in a round face, thick lip, big eye country." With her racial doubleness born of a forcible colonial coupling, Ella is not-quite-black-enough for most blacks to be comfortable with her; she is just-black-enough to be exotic and exciting to her white American husband; she is not-quite-white-enough to be worthy of carrying his children. We can reconstruct the novel as tracing Ella's development, from unconscious quiescence to the colonial text, through complicity with the text, and recognition that "the half has not been told," to resistance to the text. . . .

[The] narrative strategy of doubling serves several purposes: it evokes the cultural and racial heterogeneity of Jamaica; it figures the reconnection of mind and body, the restoration to wholeness of people who have been split in half; it is the means by which texts are hybridized and appropriated; and it signals the possibility of reversal and renewal. *Myal* thus shares with postmodernism the vocabulary of doubleness, ambivalence, hybridity, and textual proliferation. However, unlike much postmodernist discourse, it retains a commitment to the categories of truth and error, knowledge and ignorance. . . . *Myal* dramatizes the difficulty of knowing; it does not assert the impossibility of knowing. The novel's suggestion that texts can yield knowledge about the world returns us to the metaphors of light and vision of Glissant's realism: "And the draining brought clarity so that Ella could, after a time, see not only Mammy Mary and them people clearly but she could see the things around them." The "truth" towards which Ella moves is that the colonialist narratives offer an inadequate amount of reality: "It didn't go so," she realizes.

Myal's proliferation of narratives does not, then, assert the equivalence of all texts. Its multiple narratives are not unconnected and discrete; they are related and conflicting. Indeed, doubling becomes a strategy for resisting and refusing colonialist narratives; it permits us to read the colonialist narrative in another light, as it were. The subjectification of the colonized depends on this ability to re-vision their reality, to provide an account of it which brings to light their possibilities. *Myal*'s project of reconstruction is thus tied to the project of recognition. The novel's faith in a poetics of doubleness, a "twilight poetics" that walks the border between obscurity and illumination, derives from the belief that it is at their borders that texts first fray, and it is there that the fabric of colonial narratives is most liable to be torn.

Shalini Puri. *Ariel*. 24, 3 (July 1993), pp. 98–99, 112

BROOKS, GWENDOLYN (1917–   )

UNITED STATES

Gwendolyn Brooks is the only black woman poet to have achieved public and critical recognition before the 1960s. Her first book of poems, *A Street in Bronzeville*, was published in 1945. It was perhaps only "natural" that the white male literary establishment that published her, reviewed her, and gave her fame (poetry prizes, grants, and the Pulitzer Prize in 1949 for *Annie Allen*) should consider her an "exception," or, more commonly, should consider her neither black nor woman but poet: an American poet who happened to be Negro. Reviews of her work from that early period either ignore the question of race and sex . . . or take special issue with the matter of universality in poetry. . . .

It was only "natural" that Brooks's early poetry be largely defined by its acceptability. While she never whitewashed her subject matter (her poems have always been about black people, and frequently black women), her style—the manner in which she presented those subjects—was what [Don] Lee calls "European," demonstrating her preoccupation with a formal elegance and dexterity directly in the tradition of English literature. Brooks could always be topical or colloquial ("At Joe's Eats / You get your fish or chicken on meat platters"), but such localness was carefully embedded in the universal. . . .

Like the white women poets of her generation, Brooks may write about women, but rarely will she include herself among them. She never achieves either the personalism or the engagement that I have identified with the "feminine" poet. Yet there is a difference between her presentation of women and that of the white women poets who are her contemporaries: in Brooks's poetry—and, indeed, throughout the poetry of black women—there is a pride in womanhood that does not exist in the poetry of white women until recently. The white woman poet set herself apart from "women": she was special, because she was a poet. She was not and must not be like those motherly, housewifely, essentially weak creatures whose lifestyle she repudiated for the sake of her art. The black woman, on the other hand, as wife and mother has been many things but never weak. Her very strength has caused the black male of the 1960s and 1970s to label her Sapphire: to call her a cause of his own lack of manhood. Indeed! Gwendolyn Brooks, like the black women poets who have followed her, has always expressed pride in the black woman.

Suzanne Juhasz. *Naked and Fiery Forms: Modern American Poetry by Women. A New Tradition* (New York: Octagon Books, 1978), pp. 145, 149, 153–54

Gwendolyn Brooks's style of poetic realism has undergone developments that conform its use to her changes in both general and racial outlook, and to the evolving state of her consciousness. . . .

The consciousness producing *A Street in Bronzeville* was one making its first compassionate outreach to the broad range of humanity. On the one hand, it represented the mastered past: the author's old neighborhood and youth. On the other hand, it represented an intense getting acquainted with the present which was pressurized by the raw currents of Chicago's racial practices, and by World War II. Optimism prevailed, however, since the war situation had produced both threatening violence and some evidence that a broadened democracy would be born from it. In the poet's early work, one result is a deceptively simple surface. Syntax is most often either in close correlation with the usual subject plus verb plus object or complement pattern of a familiar prose sentence or within calling distance. Wielding this syntax is a friendly observer giving one a tour of the neighborhood or quick views of situations. Thus abrupt beginnings sound pretty much the way they do in our communications with friends with whom we share clarifying reference points. . . .

The style of *Annie Allen* emerges not only from the fact that the poet of the highly promising first book naturally expects to present greater mastery of craft in the second but also from a changed focus in consciousness. In her first book Brooks's emphasis had been upon community consciousness. In her second her emphasis is upon self-consciousness—an attempt to give artistic structure to tensions arising from the artist's experience in moving from the Edenic environment of her parents' home into the fallen world of Chicago tenement life in the roles of young wife, mother, and artist. Her efforts, however, were not an attempt to be confessional but an attempt to take advantage of the poetic form to move experiences immediately into symbols broader than the person serving as subject. A thoroughgoing search of the territory and the aspiration for still greater mastery of craft called for a struggle with language, a fact which would require the reader to make also a creative struggle. . . .

In *Bronzeville Boys and Girls*, a volume for juveniles, Brooks's skills effectively work together to comprise a language of poetry that describes for the child his or her experiences. Poems with bouncy rhymes are intermixed with those of more subtle and varied sound patterns. Emphasis upon the monosyllabic word at the end of end-stopped lines and other places, varying lengths of lines, repetition, and other devices sustain an interesting poetics which unpatronizingly presents the childhood world. "Ella" reveals something of the magic maintained, even down to a simple use of paradox in the first two lines: "Beauty has a coldness / That keeps you very warm. / 'If I run out to see the clouds, / That will be no harm!'"

In *The Bean Eaters* and certain of the new poems of *Selected Poems*, developments in style, for the most part, are responses to experimentations with loosened forms and the mileage one can gain from very simple statements. In *Annie Allen*, Brooks had loosened up the form of the sonnet in "The Rites for Cousin Vit," with the use of elliptical syntax, the pressures of colloquial speech, and the cumulative capacity of all the poetic devices to create the impact of hyperbole. Cousin Vit was simply too vital to have died; thus Brooks interjects into the language of the sonnet the idiomatic swing and sensuality of the street: that Vit continued to do "the snake-hips with a hiss. . . ." In *The Bean Eaters* she again loosened up sonnet form in "A Lovely Love" by adapting the Petrarchan rhyme scheme to the situation of the tenement lovers, intermingling short and long complete statements with elliptical ones, and managing a nervous rhythm which imposes the illusion of being a one-to-one imitation of the behavior of lovers. The diction of the poem is a mixture of the romantic ("hyacinth darkness"), the realistic ("Let it be stairways, and a splintery box"), and the mythically religious ("birthright of our lovely love / In swaddling clothes. Not like that Other one"). Although the elliptical structures are more numerous and informal in "Cousin Vit," the rhythm of "A Lovely Love" seems to make that poem the more complex achievement.

Another technical development is the poet's bolder movement into a free verse appropriate to the situation which she sometimes dots with rhyme. The technique will be more noticeable and surer in its achievement in the next volume, *In the Mecca*. But the poem "A Bronzeville Mother Loiters in Mississippi. Meanwhile a Mississippi Mother Burns Bacon" gives the technique full rein, except for the rhyming. The lines frequently move in the rhythms of easygoing conversation or in the loose patterns of stream-of-consciousness, as the poet portrays the movement from romantic notions to reality in the consciousness of the young white woman over whom a young black boy (reminiscent of the slain Emmett Till), has been lynched by her husband and his friend. The dramatic situation determines the length of lines, and the statements vary in form; short declarative sentences, simple sentences, phrase units understandable from their ties to preceding sentences, and long, complex structures. Additional sources of rhythm are repetition, parallel structures, and alliteration. . . .

With the publishing of *To Disembark*, it is apparent that Gwendolyn Brooks's change in outlook and consciousness has crystallized in an altered and distinctive style that offers the virtues of its own personality without denying its kinship with an earlier one. Most dramatic are the speaker's position in the center of her kinship group and the warmth and urgency of her speech. As indicated, the tendency of the language is toward a new simplicity. It can be seen in poems which, on the surface, remain very close to a traditional style of poetic realism but always evidence the fact that they proceed from an artist who is choosing from a wide range of resources. It can be seen in poems which will still, in particular passages, place language under great strain. Such patterns create also a recognizably new voice in the poetry.

George Kent. In Mari Evans, ed. *Black Women Writers (1950–1980): A Critical Evaluation* (New York: Doubleday, 1984), pp. 88–89, 92, 96–97, 104

Brooks, in her poetry, seldom endows women with the power, integrity, or magnificence of her male figures. The passive and vulnerable Annie Allen, the heroine of her Pulitzer-Prize-winning poem [*Annie Allen*], is deserted by her soldier husband and left pathetically mourning her fate in her little kitchenette, "thoroughly / Derelict and dim and done." Sometimes Brooks's women manage to be "decently wild" as girls, but they grow up to be worried and fearful, or fretful over the loss of a man. They wither in back yards, afraid to tackle life; they are done in by dark skin; and, like "estimable Mable," they are often incapable of estimating their worth without the tape measure of a man's interest in them. . . .

Rereading *Maud Martha* is a necessary step in revising the male-dominated Afro-American canon not only because this unusual text requires a different set of interpretative strategies but because it suggests a different set of rituals and symbols for Afro-American literature and a different set of progenitors. Current feminist theories which insist that we have to learn how to read the coded messages in women's texts—the silences, the evasions, the repression of female creativity—have helped me to reread *Maud Martha*, to read interiority in this text as one of the masks Maud uses to defend herself against rage. But if she cannot rely on the spoken word for help, she certainly appropriates power in more concealed ways—she writes her husband out of the text mid-way, she reduces her mother to a vain, pretentious fool, and she assigns her beautiful sister to a static end in a compromising marriage—thus the victim becomes superior to her victimizers. The reconstruction of scenes in which condescending others (white women and black and white men) are shown dominating Maud, while the reader is aware of her internal resistance, is another indirect way of giving Maud power. . . .

If *Maud Martha* is considered an integral part of the Afro-American canon, we will have to revise our conception of power and powerlessness, of heroism, of symbolic landscapes and ritual grounds. With his access to middle-class aspirations, to a public life and to male privilege, is the Invisible Man [in Ralph Ellison's *Invisible Man*] as easily defined out of existence as the physically vulnerable and speechless Maud? Yet, in spite of her greater powerlessness, she is not at the end of her text submerged in a dark hole, contemplating her invisibility in isolation. She is outside, in the light, with her daughter by the hand, exhilarated by the prospect of new life. Her ritual grounds are domestic enclosures, where we have rarely looked for heroic gestures; her most heroic act is one defiant declarative sentence; and yet she has changed in enough small ways for us to hope that "these little promises, just under cover" may, as she says earlier in the novel, in time, fulfill themselves.

Mary Helen Washington. In Henry Louis Gates, Jr., ed. Black Literature
and Literary Theory (New York: Methuen, 1984), pp. 255–56, 260

Gwendolyn Brooks has experimented with a variety of prosodic, syntactic, and narrative strategies. Her writing career has been remarkably rich in forms and ideas. Her creative practice has involved the ongoing articulation and formation of a variety of texts that express a shifting, exploratory, and ultimately performative consciousness. In terms of art, she has never been wary of "the fascination of what's difficult"; but in terms of social justice, she has always addressed a range of America's social problems. In short, at the nexus of Brooks's art lies a fundamental commitment to both the modernist aesthetics of art and the common ideal of social justice.

Nowhere is this dual commitment more apparent than in the multiplicity of voices in her works. If the reader finds echoes of T. S. Eliot and Countee Cullen in her poetry, there are also equally strong folk vernacular voices punctuating her forty-year literary career. Her three early works, *A Street in Bronzeville*, *Annie Allen*, and *The Bean Eaters*, present a wide range of poetic forms, including blues poems, ballads, experimental free verse, quatrains, Petrarchan sonnets, and Chaucerian stanzas. Her subsequent publications, *In the Mecca*, *Riot*, *Family Pictures*, *Beckonings*, and *To Disembark*, are written primarily in free verse and show her increasing concern with social issues, yet the variety of speakers continues. In fact, as the diversity of Brooks's achievement becomes apparent, our initial impression is one of a talent that does not need the unifying edge of a single, stylized voice or of a unique aesthetic with which to assert itself against tradition.

Yet Brooks's talent defines itself against the weight of tradition: She consistently utilizes the past while creating new constructs. Her variations on several traditions, several systems of values, give her poetry continuity within change, making it both difficult and original. She keeps before the reader that which is traditional at the same time that she modifies the tradition to accommodate her unique and developing sensibility.

Maria K. Mootry. In Maria K. Mootry and Gary Smith, eds.
A Life Distilled: Gwendolyn Brooks, Her Poetry and Fiction
(Urbana: University of Illinois Press, 1987), pp. 1–2

Although [Brooks] is currently serving as one of the most engaged artistic guides for a culture, she is more justly described as a herald than as an uninformed convert. She has mediated the dichotomy that left Paul Laurence Dunbar (whose *Complete Poems* she read at an early age) a torn and agonized man. Of course, she had the example of Dunbar, the Harlem Renaissance writers, and others to build upon, but at times even superior talents have been incapable of employing the accomplishments of the past for their own ends. Unlike the turn-of-the-century poet and a number of Renaissance writers, Brooks has often excelled the surrounding white framework, and she has been able to see clearly beyond it to the strengths and beauties of her own unique cultural tradition.

Gwendolyn Brooks represents a singular achievement. Beset by a double consciousness, she has kept herself from being torn asunder by crafting poems that equal the best in the black and white American literary traditions. Her characters are believable, her themes manifold, and her technique superb. The critic (whether black or white) who comes to her work seeking only support for his ideology will be disappointed for, as Etheridge Knight pointed out, she has ever spoken the truth. And truth, one likes to feel, always lies beyond the boundaries of any one ideology. Perhaps Brooks's most significant achievement is her endorsement of this point of view. From her hand and fertile imagination have come volumes that transcend the dogma on either side of the American veil. In their transcendence, they are fitting representatives of an "Effulgent lover of the Sun!"

Houston A. Baker, Jr. In Maria K. Mootry and Gary Smith, eds.
A Life Distilled: Gwendolyn Brooks, Her Poetry and Fiction
(Urbana: University of Illinois Press, 1987), p. 28

In contemporary poetry, the world of the poem is often conceived as a beleaguered fortress against the real world; to enter one is to depart from the other. This limits the material of reality for the work and requires a choice between the two as means or end. Whether weighted toward solipsism or manipulation, the tendency results in an exclusive poetry, usually offered with matching poetics and criticism. The art of Gwendolyn Brooks makes no such dichotomy. It includes the world, its poetic emblems, and us. We are not merely to be ranked and shaped with the raw data of existence. We matter, in the vital properties of our thought, feeling, growth, and change, so that the poem becomes an interaction in a mutual process, socially resonant. . . .

Brooks's religious faith is ambivalent regarding the supernatural, yet it is deeply humanistic. Her apocalyptic imagery has a counterpart of stability, but its force is dynamic; its permanence, change. "Divorce"—from nature, as decried by [William Carlos] Williams and followers like Charles Olson; from God, as mourned in [T. S.] Eliot; from excellence in art, as scorned by [Ezra] Pound; from mind, as chided by [Wallace] Stevens—is transformed by Brooks into a concern with divorce from human dignity. Her work cries out against the subjugation of blacks, which may have inflicted more physical than spiritual damage, while it has hurt whites spiritually. Brooks embodies *caritas*, expressed in the poetic voice as it articulates a racial and communal vision. Hers is a unified sensibility, pragmatic and idealistic, shaped, in part, by the needs which it ventures to meet. . . .

[Brooks] belongs to that select category Pound called "the inventors," the highest classification of poets who create and expand formal limits and, thereby, taste itself. Development toward a genre of contemporary heroic poetry, offering distinctive style and language, may be considered Brooks's outstanding achievement. Various types of heroic, exemplified by several other black poets, are examined elsewhere. Yet Brooks's heroic, direct though subtle, comprehensive in sensibility and range, whether "grand" or "plain," socially responsive and evangelically fused, makes her work a paradigm of the genre. The unique authority with which she speaks to her people is based in mutual affection and esteem and a historically viable sense of kinship. Her call to black pride, even when chiding or dismayed, has a familial intimacy. This kind of rapport hovered over the Fireside Poets who supported the Union during the Civil War. For the earlier tradition of literature in English, the configuration is Miltonic and

Romantic, the poet as artist and activist. For the native tradition of the American and African American folk preacher, it is sermonic and communal.

D. H. Melhem. Gwendolyn Brooks: Poetry and the Heroic Voice
(Lexington: University Press of Kentucky, 1987), pp. 236–38

Gwendolyn Brooks's feminine landscape is clearly demarcated as heterosexual territory. Males are never far away from its female centers of attention, even when the male presence is overwhelmingly implicit and memorial, as it is in "The Anniad" and various other poems in the volume, *Annie Allen.* The poet's particular address to communities of women in her audience is persistent in the canon across four decades of work, reflecting the storm and stress of this period of African-American women's political consciousness with the 1981 publication, *Primer for Blacks: Three Preachments*, "To Those of My Sisters Who Kept Their Naturals." Brooks's work interweaves the female and her distinctive feelings into a delicate tissue of poetic response to the human situation, defined by a particular historical order—the African-American personality among the urban poor in the city of Chicago between World War II and the present of the poem. Within this body of work, the female voice, for all its poignant insistence, is a modified noun of vocality, danced through a range of appetite and desire that does not stand isolated from a masculine complement. If poetry is our teacher in this instance, not entirely estranged from theory, but subsuming it, then the "feminine" is manifest as an emphasis, neither hostile to "masculine" nor silenced by it. We are rather reminded now of an image of Jungian resolution with the circumferences of double circles overlapping to form an altered distance through the diameters of both. It is only by virtue of a perversion in the seeing that the overlapping circles can declare any independence whatsoever. They relinquish their imagined uniqueness to an enlarged order of circularity, as the peripheries of both now involve us at the center of each. Getting the point does not necessarily require that we embrace the idea, or the "man," but that we acknowledge it as a viable figure in the universe of female and "feminine" representability. This involved image of circularity renders a geometry for poets, and those are the depths and surfaces that claim our attention at the moment.

In Brooks's poetic order of things, the "feminine" is neither cause for particular celebration nor certain despair, but near to the "incandescent," it is analogous to that "wedge-shaped core of darkness," through which vision we see things in their fluid passage between dream and waking reality, as multiple meanings impinge on a central event. The poet's novelette *Maud Martha* does not exhaust Brooks's contemplation of the "feminine," but provides a point of illumination and departure concerning an important phase of her long and distinguished career as an American poet. If not chronologically central to the canon, *Maud Martha*, beside "The Anniad," is experienced by the reader as an "impression point." . . . *Maud Martha* brings to closure the poems in *A Street in Bronzeville* and *Annie Allen*, while it prepares the way for *The Bean Eaters* and, from the 1960s, the stunning poetry of *In the Mecca*.

Hortense J. Spillers. In Henry Louis Gates, Jr., ed. Reading Black,
Reading Feminist (New York: Meridian, 1990), pp. 249–50

BRUTUS, DENNIS (1924–   )

SOUTH AFRICA

The poetry of Dennis Brutus is the reaction of one who is in mental agony, whether he is at home or abroad. This agony is partly caused by harassments, arrests, and imprisonment, and mainly by Brutus's concern for other suffering people. Thus Brutus feels psychically injured in some of his poems. When he traverses all his land as a "troubadour," finding wandering "motion sweeter far than rest," he is feeling the pinch of restiveness resulting from dislodgement. All the factors that make life uncomfortable are assembled . . . banning of "inquiry and movement," "Saracened arrest," and "the captor's hand"; and against them Brutus takes to roaming in freedom, "disdaining," "quixoting" (i.e. pursuing an ideal honor and devotion), singing all the time. His fight is purely psychological, not physical, for he puts up an attitude which his oppressors would least expect and which would disconcert them.

The emotional tension is palpable; to find "motion" sweeter than "rest" is in fact to have no rest. The conceit is as effective here as that used by John Donne when he wrote "Until I labor, I in labor lie," in the poem "Elegy: Going to Bed." Like W. B. Yeats, Brutus is pursuing his mask, his anti-self, or that which is least like him. His expression of love-emotions towards the land is a dramatization of his want of love. Thus instead of a "mistress-favor" he has "an arrow-brand" to adorn his breast. Brutus is therefore seeking for "something that is dear to him, but something that is out of reach."

R. N. Egudu. *Modern African Poetry and the African Predicament*
(New York: Barnes & Noble, 1978), pp. 53–54

Of the major [African] poets writing in English, the one who is least "Africanized" and the most alienated from the indigenous traditions of his homeland is Dennis Brutus. His style and tone, though they have shifted somewhat over his career, always draw on European rather than African models. His subjects, on the other hand, are largely drawn from experiences in South Africa, though they are seen as exemplifications of problems common to all humanity. . . .

The first poem of *Sirens, Knuckles, Boots*, "A troubadour, I tráverse all my land," concerns the adventurous clandestine life he led before his arrest, defying banning orders, evading the Saracen scout cars used by the police, giving the African National Congress sign of the upraised thumb. It is a poem that, like "Nightsong: City," combines the political and the sexual: he is for instance, in the first quatrain, exploring and investigating both the land and the body of his mistress, or in the sestet being pulled away from his "service" of her by "the captor's hand." The troubadour image works well at the beginning, for medieval troubadours commonly engaged in illicit love affairs, spiced with the ever-present danger of discovery and punishment. Such an interruption to freedom and pleasure was, however, unlikely to be at the hands of the Saracens. The lord of the castle was the one likely to be captured by Saracens while he was away fighting in the Crusades; the troubadour was a minstrel who took advantage of the lord's absence at the wars to woo the castle ladies. To this extent, then, the troubadour image was suggestive of a life of pleasure during a state of war, or irresponsibility and fecklessness. This may be one reason why Brutus did not develop it fully: it held too many contradictions and unwanted overtones. In this poem, however, he ignores the problem and ends up with the troubadour snapped off like a frayed end . . . wearing no lady's favor but only [a] prison uniform branded with an arrow. . . .

The remaining early poems appended to the first section of *A Simple Lust* fall into the same categories as the poems of *Sirens, Knuckles, Boots*. There is a plangent elegy, "For a Dead African," more meditative than the somewhat brassy "At a Funeral," and opening with the memorable line "We have no heroes and no wars." The date of "Lutuli: 10 December 1961" is the day Chief Albert Luthuli, or former chief as the South African government would have it, was due to receive the Nobel Peace Prize in Oslo, after grave doubts that he would be permitted to leave South Africa. . . . Its imagery of the masterful African lion roaring might be compared with the autumn imagery of "Autumn comes here with ostentation." All but one of the other poems combine individual love with love for the country. The sense of love (both for a woman and for the land) easing his pain of loneliness and desperate, restless seeking is poignantly expressed here. In "I might be a better lover I believe," he yearns for a secure, lasting relationship, replacing the present situation where neither woman nor land can be Brutus's or the rightful owner's. In "When last I ranged and revelled," he admits, though "wryly," that he is now "the slave of an habituated love," irrespective of present appearances or conditions. Brutus's characteristic blue or green imagery for love continues to operate in these additional early poems. . . .

The original publication of *Letters to Martha [and Other Poems from a South African Prison]* included some early poems and some poems written after "Letters to Martha," without any clear indication of which were which. Several reviewers found the sequence confusing, with the result that the poems were rearranged in four more-or-less chronological groups in *A Simple Lust*. The first group, "Early Poems," ranges from the mid-1950s to the first half of 1963, before he was imprisoned. In style they range from the clotted polysyllables of "Longing" to the simple vignette of "Train Journey." Brutus speaks of personal loneliness in "No, I do not brim with sorrow" and "Longing," and expresses the familiar need for comfort in "Nightsong: Country" and "The Mob." "The Mob," though occasioned by an attack by whites on a group of people demonstrating against the Sabotage Bill, is much more general in implication than the description "occasional" poem would suggest. Brutus has in fact said "I try to avoid 'occasional poetry,' because I have a guilt about it." The text of "The Mob" mourns his countrymen (in language drawn from biblical laments), and sketches the outline of a hostile mob of "faceless horrors," but it hardly alludes to the circumstances and not at all to the reason for protest and reaction. . . .

Stubborn Hope has poems from the years immediately before his imprisonment until well into the 1970s. "When they deprive me of the evenings" looks forward with apprehension to his inevitable imprisonment. "I remembered in the tranquil Sunday afternoon" refers to his imprisonment while awaiting trial. He thinks of Federico García Lorca, the Spanish poet arrested and assassinated in 1936 who also liked to think of himself as a troubadour. The poem is suffused with typical García Lorca images: plaza, church, bullring, tropic light, salt sea, wild orange, frangipani. . . .

Another theme continued in *Stubborn Hope* is that of elegies on the death of friends and admired leaders. The earliest in the volume is "I remember the simple practicality of your reminiscences," from the London years. It celebrates the life of Che Guevara, the freedom fighter in Cuba and South America. He was one of the eighty-two who, in November 1956, under Fidel Castro's leadership, sailed on the barely seaworthy yacht *Granma* to begin the Cuban revolution. Discovered by Batista's soldiers before they landed, only a remnant of the force remained to struggle to safety in the mountain chain of the Sierra Maestra. Though wounded in the landing, Guevara was one of only twelve survivors who reached the mountains and helped to set up the nucleus of a guerrilla army. His death in Bolivia in 1967 was greeted with dismay by radicals, especially youthful ones, throughout the world, and, as Brutus notes at the beginning, it produced some very emotive poetry in stark contrast to the "simple practicality" of Guevara's *Reminiscences of the Cuban Revolutionary War*. Brutus, always skeptical of claims to heroism, especially his own, characteristically speculates on whether this book is as "meretricious and falsified" as T. E. Lawrence's *Seven Pillars of Wisdom*, but decides that the undoubted sufferings of Guevara authenticate his account. . . .

Since the publication of *Stubborn Hope*, his published poetry has followed no new lines. There are, for instance, travel poems like "Berlin Notes" or "Crossing the Atlantic" and elegies like "In Memoriam: Solomon Mahlangu." Over the last thirty years, Brutus's poetry has in fact changed little. He began with a wide range of available styles and his career has concentrated at various times on one or another of them. His earliest poems are bejeweled metaphysical artifacts in imposed forms. His poems in the year after his release from Robben Island mostly adopt a rhetorically shaped simple style. And in 1973 he went to the extreme of minimalism. But he has always been able to write in various styles and his precepts have remained constant: determination, unremitting struggle, fortitude, patience, hope (both political and spiritual), tenderness, passion, vulnerability, and skeptical self-examination.

K. L. Goodwin. *Understanding African Poetry*
(London: Heinemann, 1982), pp. 1, 4–5, 8–10, 23–25, 27

In his collection, *Letters to Martha*, Dennis Brutus gives a hint of his attitude towards his prison material: "I cut away the public trappings to assert / certain private essentialities." It is the private angle of prison life with its humanistic emphasis which the public figure, Brutus, examines urbanely and objectively and with a remarkable ironical distancing. This apparently calm exterior, a recognizable black South African pose in racial politics, covers up an inner turmoil and seething. In one dramatic vignette, he presents himself as unprotected, but we perceive an inner resilience that only the spiritually strong can possess when opposing a contemptible but powerful enemy. . . . His courage in the unequal struggle is the mark of his victory and heroism. He can therefore afford to be matter of fact when reporting the deplorable conditions under which he and the other prisoners find themselves on Robben Island. . . . [As if] indignities and deprivations are not enough, the prisoners, these descendants of a race of slaves, are psychologically demoralized by being chained together in pairs. Brutus's choice of aspects of prison life to emphasize demonstrates his acute awareness of the humiliating experience that is prison life, its emasculation of the black South African in a hideous system that remains apparently unchanging.

Brutus touches on the perennial conflict between the warder and the jailed, a relationship that the reader readily extends to the apartheid rulers and the black populace. . . . The factual reporting allows the reader to make even extreme associations, between the situation reported and the brutality of the Nazis towards the Jews, for example. It is intended to arouse the moral awareness of the international community, to get us to view seriously the individual scenarios that take place in South African prisons, and by extension, in South Africa itself. Brutus's strategy is to engage in a quiet, unobtrusive, and insistent attack on his enemies, in an approach that is compatible with Martin Luther King's philosophy of political nonviolence. Part of his attitude is a modesty and humility that will not jubilate over victory in any form. . . .

Brutus maintains a detached mood and achieves self-effacement with the use of imprecise pronouns like "one," "you," [and] "your" instead of "I." His objectivity lends an air of truth and sincerity to his account as he explores the degeneration of the human mind in prison through observing various prisoners and their ways of coping with their terrible status. Deprived of basic necessities of life like sex and music and prevented from watching objects of nature like stars and the carefree bird, some prisoners take recourse in psychosomatic illnesses or fantasizing. Others move towards "Coprophilism; necrophilism; fellatio; / penis amputation." Sodomy is rampant. Many find peace from their cares in the very private world of the insane. Yet through it all, with patience and without self-praise, Brutus not only survives the numerous hardships, the lot of the prisoner, but, like Malcolm X, matures through contact with so much hideousness and suffering. . . .

By handling the subject of prison life, mulling over it, seeing its corrosive effect on both the jailer and the jailed, Brutus grapples through it with the existential human predicament that man finds himself in. His message, even if ultimately didactic, as most good literature is, is humanistically convincing and artistically enunciated.

Chikwenye Okonjo Ogunyemi. Ariel. 13, 4 (October 1982), pp. 67–69, 71

Brutus has written few "militant" poems, or to be more precise, if he has written any, he has published very few of them. This is not surprising in a man who loves fine poetry and who has declared that it is immoral for the artist to introduce propaganda into his work: militant poems are often declamatory, or else they want to convince at all costs. But this is not Brutus's aim, and he has sometimes been reproached for it. Thus, during a public reading of his poetry (in Chelsea in August 1971), when he was criticized by a member of the audience for rarely writing "political" poems, Brutus retorted that it was true he had no intention of saying in so many words "apartheid is detestable," but: "This is apartheid as we live it; it is for you to draw the inescapable conclusions." . . .

Poems from Algiers is a slim volume comprising nine poems of varying length and a commentary running into several pages: the poems were written in Algeria during the first Pan-African Cultural Festival, the commentary a few months later. In a very significant way, the collection brings together Brutus's personal reflections, expressed with great frankness, and his self-questioning concerning his "representativeness" and hence his sense of belonging. But representative of what? And his belonging to what world? In this Mediterranean climate which is so close to that of the Cape, the thoughts he evokes mingle and become confused: does he belong to a clearly defined African or South African world? Or is he, in his fundamental solitariness, the unattached poet who is, by that fact, universal? Hence the poem that opens the collection, "And I am driftwood," a meditation on his destiny as an exile which opens out onto the mystery of man as a whole, and not only of the man Brutus. . . .

Thoughts Abroad, published in the same year but under a pseudonym to enable it to be sold in South Africa, opens with a very fine poem which, seven years after *Sirens [Knuckles, Boots]*, establishes the link between past and present. . . .

Indeed, it is in this collection that the song of exile comes across most powerfully, beneath the overcast skies of London or the bright skies of India with, at each stage and perhaps because of his freedom of movement, the memory of the men who are still in prison. . . .

The collection also reveals Brutus's wider commitment to the problems of his fellow men, whatever the color of their skin. The work of destroying deceptive appearances which so far he had restricted to South Africa he now carries out wherever he feels it necessary to dispel ambiguity. So, on a visit to Bristol, the former center of the slave trade, of the "triangular" trade which to a large extent made it possible for Britain to accumulate the capital necessary for its technological development, Brutus addresses [a] poem to the Quaker owners of Cadbury's. . . .

Since *A Simple Lust*, which essentially brings together the poems contained in *Sirens*, *Letters to Martha*, *Poems from Algiers*, and *Thoughts Abroad*, Brutus has published two slim volumes [*China Poems* and *Strains*]. . . .

In summarizing our view of this writer who is inseparable from the life of his country and his century and whose future development is difficult to predict (for Brutus is sixty), it may be best to stress those characteristics which show his originality.

As a man who has protested and as a poet, Brutus clearly deserves to be called a committed writer. With him, the marriage of poetry and commitment is possible and complete only because he is involved in two types of quite separate activity: political and parapolitical activities, and poetry. The former enable him to serve in his capacity as a citizen; they are the outlet for his need to act and to speak out. As a result, it has been possible for him to keep his poetry relatively free of propaganda, since he has had the opportunity to make his ideals known in another way. It is no secret that Brutus dreams of being able to devote himself entirely to poetry: the fact that he has postponed the realization of this dream clearly shows that he gives his social and political responsibility priority.

It would, however, be to misunderstand him and the significance of his present struggle against the Nationalist government especially to view his commitment as a limited one.

Jacques Alvarez-Pereyre. The Poetry of Commitment in South Africa
(London: Heinemann, 1984), pp. 138, 141–44

Much has been written about the poetry of Brutus, especially his images of pain, his prison poems, and his portrayal of the apartheid society. My aim . . . is to identify the poetic mask in the poems, describe it, and show its ramifications. . . .

The troubadour mask is extended and complicated after *Sirens, Knuckles, Boots*; *Letters to Martha*; and early exile poems. The later poems represent an alienated exile, still a troubadour in his being a poet of the open road. There is a close correlation between the poetic personality and the man in Brutus's poetry. The poet is familiar with his country and the world and speaks of human suffering because of sociopolitical injustice from the wealth of his individual experience as a sage and philosopher in his struggle to free the oppressed. Brutus uses this mask of a troubadour with ambivalence, but his position remains a valid poetic standpoint. . . .

A Simple Lust and *Stubborn Hope* clearly present the poet who is a fighter for justice at home and abroad, struggling to realize his poetic aims. The troubadour image is consistent in all of the poetry of Brutus. The poet is variously a wanderer, an exile, a dreamer, a bird, a sea-voyager; and in all these aspects he is pursuing an ideal. The poet is committed to his struggle and leaves no one in doubt as to which side he stands for: he fights as a spokesman and a representative of the oppressed and the victims of injustice in South Africa and elsewhere. As a troubadour he uses movement and the road to establish his wealth of experience and give credibility to his sayings. He is thus a witness and a victim of the injustice he fights against. The idea of being on the road has universal meaning as the road involves the quest for an ideal. The road also makes the experiences of the poet universal and human as it designates life. The poet's exile brought him the realization that there is evil everywhere, but there is an intensification of it in his country which he loves in spite of the apartheid system.

Tanure Ojaide. Ariel. 17, 1 (January 1986), pp. 55–56, 67–68

Brutus's peaceful response to the apartheid system is informed by a formidable academic intelligence which explores the possibilities of a more humane and passionate approach to the problems of existence. For instance: in "Postscripts," he speaks of the "mosaic of your calm and patient knowledge." In "For My Sons

& Daughters," he says that despite "adult bitter years" and "loneliness," "my affection enables me to penetrate the decades and your minds / and . . . I hope to shape your better world." The spirit of love, forgiveness and fortitude, which Brutus evinces here, recalls the Biblical injunction which upholds "brotherly love" in the face of provocation and injustice. Although he has been misconstrued by some critics who think that this is a sign of weakness, the fact remains that the device enables him to come to terms with the conflicting emotions of "love" and "hate" in his poetry. On this score, Brutus deserves credit for writing with a rational intention and for making the objective reader perceive the serious purpose behind his irony.

Isaac I. Elimimian. *LHY.* 28, 1 (January 1987), pp. 77–78

The poetry of Dennis Brutus is one more evidence that the "artist has always functioned in African society as the recorder of mores and experiences of his society and as the voice of vision in his own time." The South African reality is one that cannot allow any sensitive writer in South Africa to remain aloof except, of course, as he wishes to be irrelevant. . . . It is no wonder then that the writings of not only Brutus but most other South African writers focus primarily on that monstrous epitome of man's inhumanity to man—the apartheid system in South Africa. For Brutus, "a writer must write about what he sees around him and he must write truthfully about it; or he must come to terms with what is ugly in it and pretend that it is not there or that it is not bad." It is a happy thing that Brutus has chosen the first option. Because of this he has emerged as the foremost writer in Africa who has greatly contributed to that bid to overthrow the pernicious apartheid regime and white supremacy by the power of the pen. . . .

His poetry . . . is a direct response to the unsavory demands which a horrible sociopolitical situation makes on his personality. Every page of his poetry bristles with images of searing pain, spilling blood, contorting hearts or wracking nerves. In his poetry words are charged with lethal colors. From Brutus we read poetry that shocks, stimulates, agitates, activates and educates us about the South African society. In fact Dennis Brutus's poetry is inseparable from South African reality. He is the altruistic voice of the people, who has gone through all the experiences which any colored South African may undergo. To read his poetry is to read an artistic rendition of a sociopolitical discourse of the South African situation. . . . Brutus wants to say something and urgently too about the economic, social, residential, and educational deprivations meted to the South African majority in the civilized world and he feels that his life and the lives of millions of South African citizens depend on what he has to say.

Jasper A. Onuekwusi. *LitC.* 23, 1–2 (1988), pp. 59–60

CÉSAIRE, AIMÉ (1913–   )

MARTINIQUE

Twenty years after [the] final edition appeared, forty years after [Aimé] Césaire began to write the poem, it is increasingly apparent that his *Cahier d'un retour au pays natal* is the product of a complex dialectic between the poet and his text, between the poet and his experience. In this sense, the poem appears not only as the beginning of the young writer's career, but also as a series of guideposts to his subsequent development. If we are to fully appreciate and understand this evolution from a personal to a more collectively-oriented consciousness, we can do no worse than to follow the signs in the four versions of Césaire's most widely-read work.

Thomas A. Hale. In Carolyn A. Parker and Stephen H. Arnold, eds.
When the Drumbeat Changes (Washington, D. C.:
Three Continents Press, 1981), p. 192

The greatness of Césaire was not only that he stole his master's language and turned it into a weapon but that his long quest for a submerged identity gave him a deeper consciousness, enabling him to clearly understand the dialectics of master and slave. The true power of his miraculous weapon was that they gave the oppressed the warm vision of a possible humanism. . . .

Césaire says no to any kind of "racist anti-racism." He knows that racism is the logic of the exploiter and will be nothing but a mystification in the hands of the oppressed. He is against racist battle cries for he understands that the question is not so simple, that colonial problems cannot be analyzed in terms of color alone and that the instinctual "death to the whites" has to transcend itself in order to give way to a higher level of consciousness. . . . In his numerous collections of poems, essays, and particularly in his plays, Césaire has tried to study the painful process of decolonization with its pitfalls and tragedies. With [*La Tragédie du roi Christophe*, translated as *The Tragedy of King Christophe*] and [*Une Saison au Congo*, translated as *A Season in the Congo*], he has been searching for a solution to the chaos created by the neocolonial domination, for a lesson to learn from the tragic destinies of Christophe and Lumumba, for a philosophical and political understanding of decolonization seen in a global perspective. From his first work to his latest writing, we can observe a progression from the personal plane to the universal, from cultural to political consciousness and the beautiful metamorphosis of his Negro cry into a song, a love song for the whole human race, a song capable of forging a "blood transcending fraternity" rising from an immense "bush-fire of friendship."

Guy Viêt Levilain. In Ileana Rodriguez and Marc Zimmerman, eds. *Process of
Unity in Caribbean Society: Ideologies and Literature* (Minneapolis, Minn.:
Institute for the Study of Ideologies and Literatures, 1983), pp. 159–60

Like the laminaria, the algae that tenaciously cling to rock, Aimé Césaire, with his latest collection of poems [*Moi, Laminaire* . . .], reiterates his lifelong political and poetic commitments: Négritude, a name he coined designating one of the powerful ideas of the century; and surrealism, whose ideology and esthetics gave impetus to his writing and thought. There are of course new intonations too. Age, disillusionments, the wear and tear of living wedged between human wretchedness and the splendors of nature that mockingly promise happiness, violent destruction—all have taken their toll. . . . Departure, suffered and anticipated, its potential relief as well as affliction, is a much-modulated motif. There are homages to friends departed: Wifredo Lam, Léon Damas, Miguel Ángel Asturias. There are also old scores to be paid off, obsessions to be laid to rest. . . .

But if life takes away, it also enriches. . . . And indeed, the Césairean afflatus explodes with verbal energies, profuse vocabulary, tortuous syntax, startling images. But next to this intensity, there is also playfulness, sometimes a cheap jingling rhyme, sometimes a facetious wordplay. And as so often before, Césaire celebrates the Martinican landscape: the mountains, mangroves, ravines filled with marvels and significations, visited by the island's inevitable scourges, the hurricane and the earthquake. The volcano serves as a polysemous metaphor for the island, its people and the poet himself.

Juris Silenieks. WLT. 57, 4 (Autumn 1983), p. 678

As Césaire defines the past suffering of his people, the beauty and uniqueness of his land, and his dreams for both the people and the land, he experiences a catharsis which allows him to become the psychological leader of his people. He challenges himself to take on this role, he rejects hatred as a way of dealing with the white world, and he insists on love. . . .

In looking at the evolution of francophone poetry, and more particularly Caribbean poetry, it is clear that Césaire's is the voice of the awakener. He summons those who follow to act, to affirm their Négritude. He explores the negative emotions any victim feels for his oppressors, but he doesn't dwell on them. He dwells rather on the potential within the victims themselves, because he is eager to respond to the sense of humanity he has discovered, he is eager to press forward.

Ann Armstrong Scarboro. Concerning Poetry. 17, 2 (Fall 1984) pp. 123–24

Cahier d'un retour au pays natal is admirable in the power of its images and in its inexorable movement from detached observation to commitment to struggle. A turning point occurs when Césaire turns from generalized description from on high (we can almost see him floating above Martinique in a French balloon) to a moving description of his own home and family. . . . And it is soon after this moving tableau that Césaire affirms that "my tongue will serve those miseries which have no tongue, my voice the liberty of those who founder in the dungeons of despair." He goes on to affirm that "life is not a spectacle, a sea of griefs is not a proscenium, a man who wails is not a dancing bear." . . .

Throughout the [*Discours sur le colonialisme*, translated as *Discourse on Colonialism*], Césaire quotes at length from racist works by Christian humanists, but he either has not read or refuses to acknowledge the great socialist writers and philosophers of Europe. The only writer he speaks of with admiration is [Comte de] Lautréamont, a nineteenth-century poet and precursor of surrealism, known for a single work, *Chants de Maldoror*. Césaire admires his nightmare visions of the putrid capitalist system. Césaire's *Discourse* is grim and deeply pessimistic. This is not a dialectical analysis. The concluding paragraph on the mission of the proletariat seems tacked on; there is nothing in the rest of the work to indicate that the proletariat is developing and struggling or that the working class even exists.

April Ane Knutson. Ideology and Independence in the Americas
(Minneapolis, Minn.: MEP Publications, 1989), pp. 47-48, 55

[Césaire] has made the study of international blackness his lifelong vocation. Léopold [Sédar] Senghor credits him for having articulated and defined the concept of Négritude, which concept, in spite of the attacks aimed at it today, essentially meant the understanding by blacks of the implications of their blackness. In 1939 Césaire pointed the way in his autobiographical poem, *Cahier d'un retour au pays natal*. In this outstanding work he unweaves the skeins of black suffering, vomits the self-hate that according to colonialism should have been his lot, and embraces his Africanness with a commitment to sing it, proclaim it, and beautify it. In so doing, he proclaimed himself the enemy of colonialism. In 1955 came the renowned masterpiece *Discours sur le colonialisme*. Moreover, Césaire was prepared to be more than a verbal antagonist: he became politically active. I feel that this experience with politics endowed him with many of the insights he brings to *A Season in the Congo*.

A Season in the Congo dramatizes several facets touching on the Congo in particular and Africa in general. The coming of the Belgians put an end to the great political and social traditions of the Congo. In their wake came social and ethical decay to the point that at independence colonialism had poisoned most of the leaders into believing that they were to be the new overlords to begin the oppression of their people exactly where the Belgians left off. In the case of the different ethnic groups, each felt that it alone should be the principal benefactor of independence. Because most of the characters are shown to be motivated by personal gain, men of Lumumba's vision and integrity, with a vocation to bring about African unity and restore African dignity, are a minuscule minority. But even such a character is insufficient, for leaders like Lumumba, granted the Machiavellian nature of the West, must be able to supersede the West in its political duplicity. (Perhaps a cunning leader had to be as ruthless and vain about power as Césaire portrays in another play, *La Tragédie du roi Christophe*.) Africa has the traditions, the wisdom, the structures for its potential unity, but does not have in place the altruistic leaders with a sufficiently broad vision to cement those structures. Finally, this play demonstrates that a writer attempting to portray African reality can enrich his work significantly by incorporating into it many of the forms germane to African languages—the metaphor, the proverb, the fable, etc.

[H.] Nigel Thomas. In Jonathan A. Peters, Mildred P. Mortimer, and
Russell V. Linnemann, eds. Literature of Africa and the African
Continuum (Washington, D.C.: Three Continents Press, 1989), p. 91

Césaire's Martinique background is just as germane to an understanding of his approach to escape as [V. S.] Naipaul's Indian affiliation is to his. The remnants of the once extensive French Caribbean empire have, in the twentieth century, been officially drawn into the political structure of the French republic. Martinique is an "overseas department" of France, and theoretically is on equal footing with other administrative regions of metropolitan France. Martinique is represented in the French National Assembly, and Césaire himself has served as a deputy. Again in theory, there is no racial discrimination in Martinican society, since all Martinicans are citizens of France. Indeed, ever since the heyday of colonialism, the French have held to the ideal of their "mission civilisatrice," a movement to bring the "natives" the benefits of French culture. In the thinking of the French colonialist, even the blackest African could be considered French—and claim all the rights of a Frenchman—as long as he adopted French culture. Such a person was called an "évolué" as if to emphasize that, in assuming the mantle of Frenchness, he had become truly human.

On one level, this philosophy and the political integration it spawned were beacons of enlightenment. People in the British and Dutch West Indies could only look longingly at those in the French Antilles who seemed to have arrived at a plateau of metropolitan acceptance undreamed of in their own territories. But on the other hand, this policy, well intentioned though it may have been, had the vicious effect of relegating local culture ever further to the shadows. For the French West Indian, there *was* no culture but that of France. An English-island intellectual like Naipaul could *choose* to try to adopt English culture; a French-island intellectual was either French, or he was a savage.

For a self-aware Martinican of the late colonial period, this situation was intolerable. Césaire, for example, saw perfectly well that while he might be accorded an official status of Frenchman, he was certainly *not* French in the truest sense. His Frenchness was but a mask of culture. It is no accident that Martinique also produced the radical philosophy of Frantz Fanon. While Césaire, unlike Fanon, was able to play all along with the system for most of his long and productive career, he was never unaware that the mask of the évolué was a betrayal of his deepest self.

Michael V. Angrosino. In Philip A. Dennis and Wendell Aycock, eds.
Literature and Anthropology (Lubbock: Texas Tech
University Press, 1989), pp. 122–23

CHAMOISEAU, PATRICK (1953–   )

MARTINIQUE

Patrick Chamoiseau is emerging as one of the prominent writers and cultural leaders of Martinique today. Though his oeuvre, comprising poetry, drama, and fiction in French and in Creole, is not immense, it has earned him critical and popular acclaim. Chamoiseau is also a co-author [with Jean Bernabé and Raphaël

Confiant] of a cultural manifesto of sorts, *Éloge de la créolité*, that proposes to dislodge Caribbean writing from the impasses of Négritude.

Antan d'enfance, dealing with childhood memories, is an illustration of some of the tenets of *créolité*. Recognizing the problematics of autobiographical writing, especially when the subject is early childhood, Chamoiseau settles for an interesting compromise: the point of reference is "le négrillon" (the little black boy), who is endowed, as it were, with an adult consciousness: "From our past nothing remains, yet we keep it all." In sequences both humorous and laden with feeling, Chamoiseau re-creates childhood scenes from "the age of fire," when insect burning is the boy's principal preoccupation, to "the age of the tool," when the insects are mercilessly cut up. The little boy has a special relationship, defiant and affectionate, with Man Ninotte, his mother and the resourceful mistress of the household, whose courage and wisdom permit the family to survive the apocalypse of devastating hurricanes and stand firm on the treacherous grounds of the marketplace. Papa, on the other hand, is the "maître ès l'art créole" and the paragon of *créolité*, who easily orients himself among the various linguistic codes in the confluence of cultures of the region.

A rich panorama of sociocultural life in Fort-de-France is evoked with scenes from La Savane, the city's "Central Park," where politicians and merchants of love cross paths, and with scenes from the shops of the Syrians and the Chinese who ply their trade with pride and deceit. Chamoiseau arranges these scenes in a rich mosaic pattern, without chronological subordination, with different rhythms and tonalities, admixing French with suggestions of Creole vocabulary and syntax, thus demonstrating the vitality of cultures that thrive on intercontamination.

Juris Silenieks. *WLT.* 65, 3 (Summer 1991), p. 535

Chamoiseau takes liberties with French which not one of his French contemporaries could even imagine ever taking. It's like the license of a Brazilian using Portuguese, of a Latin American writer using Spanish—or, if you prefer, the freedom of a bilingual who refuses absolute authority to either of his languages and who has the courage to disobey them both. Chamoiseau does not compromise between French and Creole by mixing them up. His language is French, but French transformed—not creolized French (no Martiniquais speaks as he writes), but Chamoisified French: he endows his style with the casual charm of the rhythms and melody of speech (but not, please note, with its syntax or limited vocabulary); he grafts many Creole turns of phrase onto it: not for the sake of "naturalism" (to bring in "local color"), but for *aesthetic* reasons (for humor, quaintness, or for semantic precision). Above all, however, he takes the freedom to bring into French unaccustomed, unconventional, "impossible" expressions and neologisms (freedoms which French is less able to enjoy than many other languages). Chamoiseau effortlessly turns adjectives into nouns, nouns into adjectives, adjectives into adverbs, verbs into nouns, nouns into verbs, and so on. Yet none of these infringements leads to a reduction of the lexical and grammatical richness of French: there is no shortage of learned and rare words, and even that most academic of French verb forms, the past subjunctive, holds its own. . . .

At first glance, *Solibo Magnifique* may seem to be only an exotic novel of place, centered on a folktale-teller, a character that can only be imagined here. But it is not. Chamoiseau's latest novel deals with one of the major events in the history of culture: the meeting of oral literature in decline and of written literature in the making. In Europe, the place of this meeting is Boccaccio's *Decameron*. The first great work of European prose could not have come into being had there been no storytellers skilled at oral entertainment. . . .

"Hector Biancotti, this talk is for you," runs the dedication at the head of *Solibo Magnifique*. Chamoiseau underlines that it is *talk*, not writing. He sees himself as the direct descendant of the oral storytellers, and describes himself not as a writer, but as a "word-maker." On the supranational map of cultural history, he would place himself at the point where the spoken voice hands on the baton to literature. In this novel, the fictional storyteller called Solibo tells him: "I was a talker, but what you do is to write and to say that you come from talk." Chamoiseau is a writer come from talking.

But . . . Chamoiseau is not Boccaccio. He is a writer who has the sophistication of the modern novelists and it is from that position (as an heir of [James] Joyce and of [Franz] Kafka) that he holds out his hand to Solibo and to the oral prehistory of literature. *Solibo Magnifique* is thus a place where two times meet. "You give me your hand over a great distance," Solibo says to Chamoiseau.

The story: in a square called Savane, in Fort-de-France, Solibo is talking to a few chance listeners, among them Chamoiseau. In the middle of the talking, he drops dead. The aged Congo knows: he died of word-strangulation. The explanation hardly convinces the police, who seize upon the incident and labor hard to find the culprit. Interrogations of nightmarish cruelty ensue, during which the deceased storyteller's character is drawn and two suspects die under torture. In the end, the autopsy rules out murder. Solibo died inexplicably; maybe he really was strangled by a word.

The last pages of the book consist of what Solibo was saying when he dropped dead. This truly poetic, imaginary speech is an introduction to the aesthetics of orality: what Solibo tells is not a tale, but spoken words, fantasies, puns, jokes, it is freewheeling *automatic talking* (like automatic writing). And since it is talking, "language before writing," the rules of written language have no purchase here, so there is no punctuation: Solibo's talk is a flow without commas, periods, or paragraphs, like the poetry of Robert Desnos or Molly Bloom's monologue at the end of [Joyce's] *Ulysses*, like Philippe Sollers's *Paradis*. (Another example to show how at a particular point in history, popular and modern art can meet on the same path.)

Milan Kundera. *NYRB*. December 19, 1991, pp. 49–50

Solibo Magnifique establishes that the cultural dependence of the Caribbean people brought on the escheat of a tradition that is fundamental to their identity. As Paul Zweig writes in *The Adventurer*, the storyteller is the founder of civilization, and his disappearance puts the survival of the community in danger. That is why the recovery of the spoken, in one form or another, is indispensable and urgent to prevent its complete dissolution by exterior forces. "Collective memory is our emergency," declare the authors of the *Éloge de la créolité*. Chamoiseau not only saves it from ruin, but he perpetuates it in another form, walking on "the edge between the oral and the written," as Edouard Glissant so correctly emphasizes in the preface to *Chronique des sept misères*. Through the many narrative voices mixing French and Creole—a "linguistic space" that he manages remarkably well—Chamoiseau brings the Caribbean reality to life without complacency and with irresistible humor. Using a reworked syntax, he causes to emerge a new abundance of imagery, sonorities, metaphors, even a complete poetics of Creoleness. He also manages to impart to his discourse the verbal energy that attracted him so much to Solibo, because he anchors the "new" language to everyday reality, the movement of life experience.

The storyteller instinctively reveals the imaginary world of his community. "The writer" Chamoiseau, once his function as "marker" is complete, tries to consciously identify this imaginary realm; following the example of Solibo, he is "on alert." To capture the complexity of the cultural reality, he must free himself of the unicity of one linguistic practice; he therefore constructs his tale with the help of the French language, which he changes, enriches, and amplifies with the multilingualism that is Creole. "We believe that a creative use of intellect might lead to an order of reality capable of preserving for our Creoleness its fundamental complexity, its diffracted referential space" write [Jean] Bernabé, Chamoiseau and [Raphaël] Confiant. Chamoiseau splendidly communicates the complexity of his culture by exploding language.

Marie-Agnès Sourieau. *Callaloo*. 15, 1 (Winter 1992), p. 136

Texaco, the third novel of Patrick Chamoiseau, traces the dual figures of a woman and a country: Marie-Sophie Laborieux (born around 1913, the daughter of a freed slave and founder of the Texaco district in Fort-de-France) and Martinique. The author of *Chronique des sept misères* and *Solibo Magnifique* has a grand ambition in this novel: to help the readers understand two centuries of the history of his country. . . .

One is carried by a tide of words and sensations. Wielding incantation as well as humor, having the sense of caricature as well as that of detailed descriptions, Chamoiseau narrates the story of an entire people. From this is derived the splendid portrait of Marie-Sophie, [a] "femme-matador" who knew to create a neighborhood in order to find an identity. . . .

Texaco, like any important novel, is a language, a style, and a reflection on literature. Chamoiseau defines himself clearly as a "keeper of words," situated near the complex and fragile frontier which separates oral and written literature. . . .

[To] love and defend Chamoiseau because of a penchant for the exotic . . . would be a serious mistake. Far from being a renewal of the French novel from the margins or from the outside . . . Chamoiseau's literature is an affirmation of belonging to French culture in all its diversity.

Who are the authors that Marie-Sophie reads and of whom she talks? Montaigne and Rabelais in the first place. And it is from their thoughts and their words that she draws her strength and her pugnacity. She learns very quickly, coming in contact with texts, to make a distinction between literature and the colonizer, between a culture that has always "welcomed" and a people—who, moreover, dislike their own culture—often sadly narrow-minded, revanchist, and hardened. To like Chamoiseau for the exotic is to perpetuate the mentality of the colonizer. It is to refuse this proclamation: "We declare ourselves Creoles. . . . Our history is a fabric of histories."

Josyane Savigneau. *Le Monde.* September 3–9, 1992, p. 12†

Chamoiseau's first published work, *Manman Dlo contre la fée Carabosse*, does seem to hold out the possibility of resistance. . . . The play dramatizes the conflict between the colonial powers and its culture, symbolized in the figure of the wicked fairy Carabosse taken from Creole folklore, and the dominated culture, symbolized by the water-spirit Manman Dlo and the forest-spirit Papa-Zombi, who, together with other denizens of forest and water, set out to counter the colonizing project of Carabosse and her assistant Balai. From the outset, Carabosse is associated with the written word and Manman Dlo and her allies with the spoken word (*la Parole*); Carabosse's initial effect is to reduce to silence all those spirits which previously had filled the island with unfettered speech and song. Gradually, however, Manman Dlo and Papa-Zombi muster the necessary resources of speech with which to confront Carabosse and her scribe Balai before unleashing the natural forces of wind and water which finally sweep her out of the island. On the surface, *Manman Dlo* is a straightforward nationalist allegory, notable for its optimistic assessment of the strengths of the dominated culture in the face of the dominant colonial system. Looked at more closely, however, the play reveals a fatal flaw which lies in the uncertainty of the origins and status of the Creole counterculture. By stressing Manman Dlo's African origins, the play seems to endow that counterculture with an identity anterior to and wholly separate from that of the colonial culture it is called upon to combat: it is as though Manman Dlo and her fellow spirits had occupied the island for eons prior to the arrival of Carabosse and the written word. But, though they may be of African *origin*, Manman Dlo and Papa-Zombi are only in the Caribbean because Carabosse, in her guise as slave-trader, brought them there. Creole culture, like the Creole language itself, may be *anti*-colonial in character, but it is in no way *ante*-colonial. On the contrary, Créolité is a product and consequence of colonialism which, no matter how much it derives from non-European sources, is impregnated—some might say contaminated—at every point with the culture of the colonizer. It is different from, but in no way separate from, the dominant culture and, to that extent, is to be contrasted to the "traditional" cultures of black Africa or the Islamocentric cultures of the Maghreb which, for their part, are both anterior and exterior to the European colonial cultures superimposed upon them. Positing the Creole counterculture as entirely separate from the colonial culture certainly allows the play to be brought to a (wholly unhistorical) triumphant conclusion, but at the price of seriously distorting the relationship between "great" and "little" traditions in the French West Indies. Chamoiseau partially acknowledges that this is so in a final scene in which Manman Dlo hands over to her daughter Algoline the magic wand which Carabosse has left behind her in her flight from the island, urging her to *assimilate* the magic powers it embodies, including the formidable and enigmatic power of writing, with a view to transcending the opposition of Word and word, of speech and writing, that the play has dramatized. Where the writer himself stands in all this remains unclear. He is a son of the Word, dependent on it for his very being, but transcribing the spoken into the written exposes him to the charge of exploiting the very Word he would capture and celebrate. Like so much else, *Manman Dlo* raises this problem, the crucial theme of *Solibo Magnifique*, only to drop it: small wonder that, asked today about this product of his apprenticeship, Chamoiseau merely shrugs his shoulders and smiles.

Despite its simplistic and misleading presentation of the relationship between colonial culture and Creole counterculture, *Manman Dlo* clearly lays out the tripartite structure of Chamoiseau's imaginative universe. On the one hand, invariably associated with rationality, order, and the written word (French), is the world of the powerful who are not always necessarily white or French but can in assimilated Martinique include individuals of each and every racial category. Opposed to this, and commonly linked with fantasy, magic, the elemental forces of forest and water and, above all, with the spoken word (Creole), is the world of the powerless, usually men and women of African or Indian origin, who must somehow survive on terrain which, originally defined and regimented by the whites (*békés-France* and *békés-pays* alike), has progressively been invested by colored and black supporters of the dominant ideology of assimilationism. Straddling these two worlds and mediating between them is the writer or "marker of words" (*marqueur de paroles*) as Chamoiseau chooses to call himself, who belongs to neither world and both and whose interstitial position clearly resembles that of the *djobeurs* and other liminal figures whose lives form the subject of Chamoiseau's first novel *Chronique des sept misères*. The novel uses the vegetable market at Fort-de-France as a complex metaphor for the transformation of Martinican society from before World War II, through the three years of domination by the Vichy regime, to departmentalization in 1946 and the subsequent disintegration, becoming apparent in the early 1960s and accelerating in the 1970s, of the traditional Creole culture under the pressure of imported French goods, French lifestyles, French thought patterns, and, not least, of the French language itself.

Richard D. E. Burton. *Callaloo*. 16, 2 (Spring 1993), pp. 469–70

Nominally a novel, *Texaco* expands the traditional notions of the genre. It could qualify as an oral history of epic proportions. It is the narration by an African Martinican woman, Marie-Sophie Laborieux, to the author, who calls himself the "marqueur de paroles" but whom Marie-Sophie occasionally addresses, with obvious relish, as "Oiseau de Cham." The author, as he explains in the postface, first took copious notes, then resorted to a tape recorder, trying "to write life." The narrative, in mock imitation of archeological periodization, is divided into four epochs, which represent African Martinican building materials: straw, crate wood, fibrocement, and concrete. In terms of European historiography, the time span would encompass the years from circa 1823 to 1980. Biblical allusions enlarge the scope of the narrative. It begins with the sermon, not on the mount, but before old rum, and ends with resurrection—i.e., with the author's endeavor to resurrect life, "écrire la vie." . . .

Marie-Sophie, following a series of vicissitudes in her personal life, becomes willy-nilly the spokesperson for the slum dwellers. She pleads with the authorities (including "notre papa Césaire," then and still today the mayor of Fort-de-France), organizes demonstrations, and, when [Charles] De Gaulle comes to visit the former colony, prepares a sumptuous feast to show him how hospitable Martinicans can be. The general, perceived as a savior figure, does not come, however. Marie-Sophie engages in a titanic struggle against the owner of the land, a *béké*—i.e., a Frenchman born in the colonies. The people persevere, and in the end, as Christ makes another appearance, the authorities recognize the squatters, install electricity, and incorporate the settlement. Even the vicious *béké* is reconciled with his enemies.

Needless to say, the novel acquires epic dimensions. Fact and fiction intertwine to weave a narrative wherein myth and history complement each other. *Texaco* evokes an ethos and also a vision which, though localized, reaches out far beyond the region.

Juris Silenieks. *WLT*. 67, 4 (Autumn 1993), pp. 877–78

CHENEY-COKER, SYL (1945–   )

SIERRA LEONE

The Creoles of Sierra Leone, who furnish their country with a disproportionate share of its cultural and political leaders, are descendants of the "recaptives" who were rescued from slave ships during the British suppression of the slave trade. The Creole ancestry of [Syl] Cheney-Coker is the source of much of the strength as well as many of the weaknesses of his poetry [in *Concerto for an Exile*]. Its rough rhythms, harsh diction, and extremes of self-revelation clearly reveal antecedents in [Arthur] Rimbaud, but its most important derivation is the ideal of Négritude. In his weaker poems Cheney-Coker's ambivalence about his Creole heritage betrays him into rhetorical rage against the Creole's oppression of the pure African, who personifies Négritude. . . . At worst, he falls into expressions of passionate self-loathing. But his best poems objectify a violent inner conflict between Africa ("the centrifugal mother") and his own feelings of unworthiness, stated in terms of his "foul genealogy," a Christian upbringing . . . and other "Afro-Saxon" impurities, including an unfortunate love affair with an Argentine woman "to whom I offered my Négritude / that señorita who tortured my heart." The sequence of poems leads finally to a breakthrough to a wisdom understood in terms of recovery from this romantic failure, a repudiation of exile ("agrophobia's sickness"), and a powerful affirmation of the value of poetry.

Robert L. Berner. *BA*. 48, 4 (Autumn 1974), pp. 835–36

Unlike [Sarif] Easmon who sees membership of the Creole group as a cause for congratulation, Cheney-Coker sees it as a cause for regret, since it reminds him of the Creole history of slavery, suggesting degradation of the black race and alienation from one's roots. The preface to his collection of poems subsumes his major themes—his sense of frustration and disillusionment, his rejection of institutionalized religion, the betrayal of his love, his disgust with himself, and his awareness of the erosion of his original black personality. A dominant motif in his poetry, which he claims is largely influenced by the Congolese poet Tchicaya U Tam'si, is the figure of the Argentinean woman with whom he fell disastrously in love. Since he sees the history and present predicament of Sierra Leone and Argentina as being basically similar, he had hoped, through his love, to bring the two continents together in a common cause. The woman therefore becomes the symbol of betrayal of love, personal despair, and loss of hope for the regeneration of an ailing Third World.

In poems such as "Hydropathy," "Freetown," "Absurdity," and "[The] Masochist," Cheney-Coker presents what he feels is the tragedy of his Creole ancestry. . . . His ancestry is one of the devastating effects of the slave trade and he sees himself as the polluted product of a violent and filthy rape. The consequence is a feeling of disgust with himself; he becomes "the running image" and "the foul progeny" of his race; the rot of his country, and even the vultures will be afraid of his corpse. But the meaning of their ancestry is lost on some of his countrymen who "plaster their skins with white cosmetics to look whiter than the snows of Europe" and who plead: "make us Black Englishmen decorated / Afro-Saxons / Creole masters leading native races." Several poems present his disgust with the Christian religion. He often refers to Christ as the Eunuch who lied to him at Calvary. . . . "Misery of the Converts" and "I Throw Myself to the Crocodiles" similarly present a Christianity that has taken sides with the oppressor against the downtrodden. Other poems, like "Toilers," consist of social comment pointing to the neglect of the toiling masses by the powers that be, and contrasting the opulence of the latter with the squalor of the former.

Eustace Palmer. In Bruce King and Kolawole Ogungbesan, eds. *A Celebration of Black and African Writing* (London: Oxford University Press, 1975), pp. 255–56

Cheney-Coker has provided us with a poetic preface to his volume *Concerto for an Exile.* He first describes his poems as "Venomous songs!," but later qualifies this statement by saying that "song by itself is no fertile language for death." . . . Personal and passionate poetry will investigate the poet's own mind; his feelings, beliefs, prejudices, and obsessions—what he calls the "tree of agony wickedly planted in my soul." It is a poetry which puts before us the history of the man and his society and which makes critical statements about that society. The poet's weapons—evolved as shock tactics—are violent words and violent, surrealist images. We are challenged to respond and, in our turn, we the readers challenge the poet to create art; poems, as opposed to verse and mere statements. . . .

Cheney-Coker is at his best, as a poet, in poems like "Toilers," "Freetown," "My Soul O Oasis!," "Environne," "Agony of the Dark Child," and "Myopia." He is at his best, that is to say, when he rigorously controls his poetic images and uses them organically in his poems. The poem "Environne" opens surrealistically and the surrealism is necessary in order to shock the readers out of a possible complacent attitude to the past history of Africa. . . . The poem "Storm" deals, in part, with the conflict between the privileged and underprivileged in modern African societies. The image of the storm is established in the poem as the image of revolt. The character of the storm is evoked economically, but powerfully. . . . The poem "Toilers" depends upon a contrast between the inherent "fruitfulness" of Africa— especially traditional Africa—and the spiritual and physical blight which seems, to the poet, to affect most modern societies on the continent. What Cheney-Coker calls "black opulence" rules the roost to the detriment of the poor. The title of this poem is ironical; everyone is either toiling for nothing or for the wrong things.

All of these poems are intense and personal, but the best of them evoke feelings and aspirations common to all men. The poem "Freetown" works like this and so too does the poem "Guinea." Here, Cheney-Coker captures what we might call the spirit of revolutionary fervor.

M. J. Salt. In Eldred Durosimi Jones, ed. *African Literature Today.* 7 (1975), pp. 159–61

The Graveyard Also Has Teeth is a very edifying and interesting collection of poems of even texture and yet multifarious themes. This is the second book by [Cheney-Coker]. . . . The title derives from the Creole. In Sierra Leone, when mourners are deeply shocked by the death of a beloved, they show their sorrow and pain at the graveyard by shouting hysterically: "Eh, the grave yard bet (bites) me, eh, it bet (bites) me!" This title thus implies artistic creations of sadness, of agony, of pain full of cryptic and folded meanings.

The collection may be profitably viewed as a panorama of verse brilliantly folded with layers of diverse meanings, perceptions and sensibilities expressed within compressed images. The author obviously regards his poems as enigmas to be solved by the reader. These attributes might make the work appear too exacting but once the right intellectual effort is made, understanding comes easily and the reader sees the poet's landscape, shares in his creativity and in his experience. . . .

Bursting with creative energy, [Cheney-Coker] is sensitive and serious, bold and imaginative, speaking the voice of laughter through tears, of mourning, of anger, wisdom and truth. The collection consists of verse with familiar themes, situations and characters. The poems in this group, which include "Song for the Ravaged Country," "Talons in the Flesh of My Country," "The Executed," "Haemorrhage" and "Putrefaction," seem to be fairly direct descriptions or narratives with a delightful but modest poetic complexity. The themes and situations are easily reflected in the titles, making elaborate comments unnecessary. But lurking behind the paradoxical simplicity of the lines are strong, complex images of birth, initiation, growth and death.

These recurrent images, which help the poems in the collection to achieve an organic unity, seem to symbolize the human life cycle (including the poet's), its genesis, vicissitudes, fear, aspirations, and the search for the meaning of life or eternal good. It is in response to this that the poet embarks on his search, probing himself, the reality of his environment as well as that of our collective unconscious. . . .

Syl Cheney-Coker is a fascinating poet who blends theme, idiom, and syntax delightfully. The poems exude an admirable intricacy of language ordering. Significance is given to commonplace statements, events and situations through ironic emphasis. Over the years, the poet has tightened up his style and expression. His present collection is in places fierce, fluent, and tense. He is a nationalist, a poet of anger: he is angry with cheats, fakes, dupes, dictators, with life and death; angry with the world and with himself. . . .

Cheney-Coker's verse is powerful. Indeed, he is one of the best, if not the best poet that has come out of Africa in the last decade and is one of the most original and gifted African poets alive today.

Segun Dada. In Eldred Durosimi Jones, ed.
African Literature Today. 13 (1983), pp. 240–41

In his third book of verse Syl Cheney-Coker devotes nearly all the fifty-plus poems to the development of a single theme. Whether the locale is his homeland of Sierra Leone or Chicago, his resonant voice speaks for the wretched of the world. He hears "a million muted cries" from Palestine, from Beirut, even from Japan, where babies are dying from mercury poisoning.

The unifying symbol of the collection is announced in the title, *The Blood in the Desert's Eyes.* These words become the title of the fourth poem, reappear in varied transformations now and again, and finally occur as the last line of the final poem. Literally, the desert is slowly encroaching on the fertile savanna of the poet's country, rendering the soil sterile and forcing the people from their homes. This deadly event is emblematic of the drying up of human concern for those in need the world over. In "Song on the Chinese Flute" Cheney-Coker speaks of the desert's eyes as "lenses" through which we can better see the hungry millions to whom we need to "hold the cup of hope."

Richard [F.] Bauerle. *WLT.* 65, 2 (Spring 1991), p. 350

Divided into four books of four chapters each, *The Last Harmattan of Alusine Dunbar* sketches in broad historical strokes the founding of a West African settlement, the inevitable ramifications of development, and the devastating pains of growth when the idyllic is inevitably shattered by infiltration. The history of past and present "harmattans" is prefigured in the planetary movements of the visionary Alusine Dunbar's herniated testicles: the arrival of the black pioneers seeking freedom after the American revolution; the introduction of Christianity and Western education; the arrival of the British spoilers and the beginning of the "eruscient expropriation of land" for exclusive clubs where "Africans and dogs are not allowed"; the arrival of the Arabs and their cunning entrenchment (by the British) as major players in the settlement's economy in partial payment for their "accidental" discovery of the diamond; and finally, the evil of and destruction by black despots. Alas, the pathos which circumscribes life! Unrelenting harmattans with "the remorseless demons humans create in their lives," which allow "the leopards to go after the goats," will now replace the previous "harmattans" of historic and legendary kings.

Contrary to the criticism that character development is generally lacking in the African novel, Syl Cheney-Coker weds symbolism with humor and pathos to create memorable characterizations. There is Suleiman the Nubian (later Alusine Dunbar), the vagabond visionary whose herniated, optical testicles presage an age of endless bitter strife and colonial/neocolonial oppression. There are the revolutionaries—Thomas Bookerman, Sebastian Cromantine, Gustavius Martin, Emmanuel Cromantine, and Garbage—all pioneers of black freedom and witnesses to the historical force of the harmattan's ill omen.

Pamela J. Olubunmi Smith. WLT. 65, 4 (Autumn 1991), pp. 755–56

The Last Harmattan of Alusine Dunbar encompasses in its epic sweep the African experience in slavery, colonialism, and neocolonialism. The world of its action stretches from the antebellum southern United States of America to an imaginary country in West Africa called "Malugueta," a thinly disguised present-day Sierra Leone, or even Liberia. . . .

The four books which constitute the core of this novel chronicle the futility and ephemeral character of human power as wave after wave of the slave master and slave transmutating into master to initiate and perpetuate oppression. From America to Africa, the story is the same. In a book teeming with a beautiful cast of well-realized characters, quite a few should be noteworthy, especially those whose pedigree constitute the fabric of what becomes, for Malagueta, a national heritage. . . .

The Last Harmattan of Alusine Dunbar is an unusual African novel with startling freshness, and there are a number of things which make it so. First, it is a novel of marvelous realism which comfortably takes a path most African writers have timidly avoided. And this is ironic because the African imagination powered with a unique cosmology and a dynamic eschatology appears more fertile for this kind of expression than that of any other culture. Second, even though the work is nationalistic in its ethnic sentiment, it is without that stridency and abrasion with which many activist writers mar their works. The novel is history, fantasy, magic, legend, and political testament unfolding before the eyes with the easy gait of the classic of adventure. Third, the author's intelligence and the intensity of verbal expression sustained for nearly 400 pages is no mean feat by any measure considering that in a work of that nature it is imperative for credibility to remain unflagging. And credibility does remain unflagging whether it is in the use of slave plantation Creole dialogue or in the clarity with which everything is described from the concrete to the sundry magical and inexplicable presences.

Chimalum Nwankwo. AfrSR. 35, 1 (April 1992), pp. 134–35

CHILDRESS, ALICE (1920–   )

UNITED STATES

By using features from both written and oral traditions, Alice Childress is one black American writer who succeeds in adding a unique dimension to her work.

In her collection *Like One of the Family: Conversations from a Domestic's Life*, Childress makes use of traditional metaphoric language and written form, but she uses the storytelling forms of black folk tradition to give Mildred, her major character, the means for telling her own stories and interacting with the audience. Usually in literary works in which the author relinquishes the reins of narration to a character, there is still a sense of an authorial presence. An author will create a semblance of removal for the purpose of evoking a particular response from readers, but [he or she] may still sense a direction for [his or her] sympathies. In such cases, an author's ostensible absence from a scene suggests that the character has a life of his or her own, and a consciousness uncontrolled by the author. However, Childress's knowledge of folk forms allows her to succeed to a greater extent than most authors because she totally effaces herself from the narrative, and Mildred indeed seems to have a consciousness of her own.

Obviously we know that Alice Childress wrote a book called *Like One of the Family*. Beyond the title and the author's name, however, we never see the presiding presence of Childress. Once a reader opens the book, he or she ceases to be a reader and becomes a part of an audience. As members of that audience, we are never allowed to verbalize the fact that the author, Childress, is in control of the volume. We are simply confronted with a character, whose name we later learn is Mildred. We are never introduced to her or given any background information about her or presented with another character who tells us anything about her. The form of the collection allows us to see Mildred and no reality beyond that. We meet her, interact with her, and must rely upon her for whatever we experience in the book. As a character, Mildred completely controls her storytelling environment as well as the form in which her stories are presented. Mildred is not only the principal actor of the story, though; she quickly assumes the role of artist by embroidering the series of events in which she acts or has acted. She does her own kind of mythmaking without any apparent manipulation from Childress. While Mildred manages to incorporate forms of black folk storytelling, she nevertheless keeps her stories within the broad guidelines of the conscious creation of literature.

Trudier Harris. *BALF*. 14, 1 (Spring 1980), pp. 24–25

[In *Trouble in Mind*] Childress demonstrated a talent and ability to write humor that had social impact. Even though one laughed throughout the entire presentation, there was, inescapably, the understanding that although one was having an undeniably emotional and a profoundly intellectual experience, it was also political. One of Childress's great gifts: to have you laughing, not at the characters, but with them. It is a rare gift that does not come easily. Humor is of serious import, not a thing to take for granted. One gets the feeling that the writer loves the people she writes about. Love of life and people, accent on struggle, humor as a cultural weapon. . . .

Childress's drama *Wedding Band*, a play about an ailing white man and a black woman living together in a Carolina town, details the black woman's struggle against the racist attitudes of the town and against the members of the white man's middle-class family who are outraged by the relationship. Childress's other writings had seemed to have a total and timely relevance to the black experience in the [United States]; *Wedding Band* was a deviation. Perhaps the critic's own mood or bias was at fault. For one who was involved artistically, creatively, intellectually, and actively in the human rights struggle unfolding at the time, it is difficult, even in retrospect, to empathize or identify with the heroine's struggle for her relationship with the white man, symbolically the enemy incarnate of black hopes and aspirations. Nevertheless, again, at the heart of *Wedding Band* was the element of black struggle, albeit a struggle difficult to relate to. As usual, the art and craftsmanship were fine; the message, however, appeared out of sync with the times.

Her novel *A Hero Ain't Nothin' But a Sandwich* was adapted for a film production. It is the story of Benjie, a thirteen-year-old drug addict. There are some awesomely beautiful and powerful moments in this novel. One that comes immediately to mind is the poignant scene in which Butler Craig, the "stepfather," saves spaced-out Benjie from falling from a Harlem rooftop, even as the boy begs his stepfather to let him go. "'Let go, Butler . . . let me die. Drop me, man!' He's flailing his legs, trying to work loose my hold, hollerin and fighting to die. 'Let me be dead!'" . . .

Alice Childress is a tremendously gifted artist who has consistently used her genius to effect a change in the world: to change the image we have of ourselves as human beings, black and white. Her primary and special concern has been the African image. She knew that black was beautiful when so many of us thought that Black Beauty was the name of a storybook horse, a figment of a writer's fantasy. Her gift has been used as an instrument against oppression; notwithstanding, she is always the consummate artist, telling her story powerfully and artistically. Her writing is always realistic, avoiding somehow the indulgence of wallowing in quagmires of despair and pessimism. After all, life is a short walk. There is so little time and so much living to achieve. Perhaps her greatest gift, along with her satiric bent and the thematic accent on struggle, is the leitmotif of love for people, particularly her own people. I have come away from most of her writing feeling mighty damn proud of the human race, especially the African aspect of it. Portraying it with great fidelity in all of its meanness, its pettiness, its prejudices, its superstitions. Childress captures most of all its capacity to overcome, to be better than it is, or ever could be, its monumental capacity for change.

John O. Killens. In Mari Evans, ed. *Black Women Writers (1950–1980): A Critical Evaluation* (New York: Doubleday, 1984), pp. 129, 131–33

Alice Childress posits [an] idealized friendship between a black and a white woman in *A Short Walk*. The friendship between black Cora Green and white May Palmas happens simply and spontaneously because of the proximity of their apartments and because of the respect each has for the other. Cora says, "May is my first close friend-girl of any race—my closest friend since Papa died. Like him, she also knows how to look at matters and trace meanings and feelings down to the core." Married to a Filipino and consequently ostracized by her mother, May is familiar with the pain caused by racial prejudice and counts on love, as she tells Cora, to conquer all. However as no racial tension exists between the two women, race is not a subject for discussion between them. Always supportive of each other, May sees Cora through her decision against abortion and through childbirth, and Cora sees May through [attempted] suicide and loneliness when her husband is jailed. They struggle together against their common poverty, and they take a common delight in food and music. Through the repeated exchange of gifts, Childress suggests that their friendship is ritualistically sealed forever. Although Childress confronts racist and sexist dilemmas in describing Cora's relationship with other characters in *A Short Walk*, the friendship between Cora and May, which continues until the end of Cora's life, in its lack of conflict and growth, might seem an unrealizable model. Yet in her representation of May's apartment as a meeting place for the countries and races of the world and of Cora's parties as a center for people from all walks of life, all classes, and all sexual preferences, Childress seems to be emphatically suggesting that it is possible for human beings to accept their national, sexual, individual, and racial differences and to live together with peace and pleasure. The central theme of Childress's novel seems to be expressed in Cora's explanation of the basis of her friendship with May, ". . . she's my friend. I love her for good and sufficient reason. It's not ever easy, but I try to accept people just as they come wrapped. . . . I treat white folks according to how they act, not by how they look."

Elizabeth [A.] Schultz. In Marjorie Pryse and Hortense J. Spillers, eds.
Conjuring: Black Women, Fiction, and Literary Tradition
(Bloomington: Indiana University Press, 1985), pp. 81–82

One very modern thing Childress did in her plays was to break down the binary oppositions so prevalent in Western society—black/white, male/female, North/South, artist/critic—with their implications that one is superior to the other. Such breaking of these categories is a major interest in much modern criticism as well as feminist theory today. . . .

By 1969 the racial situation in this country had shifted considerably, and *Wine in the Wilderness* reflects Childress's feelings about some of the new racial stereotypes. In the midst of a racial riot in Harlem, a black liberal couple brings Tommy, a thirty-year-old woman who works in a factory, to the apartment of Bill, a thirty-three-year-old artist, to serve as a model for the final panel of a triptych he is painting called "Wine in the Wilderness," portraying three aspects of "black womanhood." One painting is chaste "black girlhood," the second is majestic "Mother Africa," and the third will be a contemporary "lost woman," a "messed up chick" to serve as warning to all ghetto women. Tommy warms up to Bill when she thinks he likes her, but when she finds out the kind of painting he is actually planning to make, she tells him that he likes blacks in the abstract but that "[You] don't like flesh and blood niggers." Bill changes the triptych to embody more realistic images of the blacks he knows. . . .

Many of the characters and ideas in *Trouble in Mind* are as fresh as and perhaps more generally recognizable than they were thirty years ago. Both the character, Wiletta, and author Childress are actively protesting the few and false images of black women written by white men with "blind spots." Wiletta, along with the other black actress in the play, Millie, jokes about the roles they have had to play. . . . In the second act, the director, Manners, is dissatisfied with Wiletta's performance and directs her by saying, "We're dealing with simple, backward people but they're human beings." Wiletta quickly points out, "'Cause they colored, you tellin' me they're human bein's. . . . I know I'm a human bein'. . . ." Childress, in writing the roles of Wiletta and Millie, has provided some alternative images of black women, three dimensional characters with weaknesses and strengths.

Gayle Austin. *SQ*. 25, 3 (Spring 1987), pp. 53, 55–57

In the first act of *Wedding Band*, a scene of reading and performance occurs that lies at the center of a feminist interpretation of the play. Mattie, a black woman who makes her living selling candy and caring for a little white girl, has received a letter from her husband in the Merchant Marine and needs a translator for it. Her new neighbor, Julia, the educated outsider trying to fit into working-class surroundings, reads the sentimental sailor's letter aloud. After her performance, in which the women listening have actively participated, Mattie tells Julia that, in addition to his love, her husband gives her what is more important, his *name and protection*. These two standards of conventional love are denied Julia because her lover of ten years is white; and even Mattie learns that because she never divorced her first husband, she is not now legally married and cannot receive marital war benefits. Neither woman enjoys a man's name or his protection, in part because the chivalry implied in such privilege was unattainable for blacks in the Jim Crow society of 1918 South Carolina. The women in *Wedding Band* learn to depend on themselves and each other rather than on absent men, a self-reliance born painfully through self-acceptance. . . .

Set chronologically midway between the poles of Reconstruction and [the Civil Rights Movement], *Wedding Band* describes an era when lynching presented one answer to demands for equality in the South, while Harlem flowered as a mecca for black culture in the North. In the 1960s, white women and black men's sexual relations generated tension in the black community, but miscegenation as the white master's rape of his slave retains deeper historical ramifications for black women. Childress's drama, subtitled "a love/hate story in black and white," takes place on the tenth anniversary of Julia and her white lover in the backyard tenement to which Julia has moved after being evicted from countless other houses. Determined to get along with her nosy but well-meaning neighbors, Julia seems to have won a guarded acceptance until her lover, Herman, visits her. He has brought her a gold wedding band on a chain, and they plan to buy tickets on the Clyde Line to New York, where Julia will proudly and legally bear Herman's name. But Herman succumbs to the influenza epidemic, and in the second act he lies in Julia's bed waiting for his mother and sister to take him to a white doctor. Julia's landlady has refused to help because it is illegal for Herman to be in Julia's house, and she cannot appear to sanction Julia's immoral behavior. Herman's mother sides with the landlady in preserving respectability even at the cost of her son's life, and she will not carry him to the doctor until it grows dark enough to hide him. In the last scene, Herman returns to Julia with the boat tickets, which she refuses to take because his mother has convinced her that blacks and whites can never live together. Finally she appears to relent so that Herman can die believing that Julia, even without him, will go north.

The secondary characters, however, more than the two lovers, underscore the drama's didactic politics. They are types, but not stereotypes, and their separate dilemmas and personalities describe the injustices blacks have endured in the South. The landlady, Fanny, the neighbors Mattie and Lula, Lula's adopted son, Nelson, and the abusive white traveling salesman give the stage community a historic idiosyncrasy missing from Julia and Herman's relationship. Fanny has proudly joined the middle class by acquiring property and exploiting her tenants (in 1918 a relatively new possibility for black women) in the name of racial uplift. As homeworkers, Mattie and Lula exist bound to a variety of semi-skilled, low-paying jobs to feed their children. Nelson, as a soldier in the newly desegregated United States army, assumes that when the war is over he will be given the rights of a full citizen, even in South Carolina. He is a forerunner of the militant youth who would later provide the impatient voice to the nascent Civil Rights Movement of the late 1940s, and whose dreams of integration would be realized only partially in the 1960s.

These characters who inhabit Miss Fanny's backyard tenement underscore the vexed issue of difference as explored by the feminist scholars cited above. Julia's problem throughout the play is less her white lover than her reluctance to see herself as a member of the black community. Although a mostly white theater audience would see her as a different sort of heroine because of race, her black neighbors perceive her as different from them for issues more complex than skin color. She assumes that her racial transgression with Herman will make her unwelcome among the women she wishes to confide in, but her aloofness from their day-to-day interests also serves as a protective shield. In this, Julia is similar to Lutie Johnson in Ann Petry's *The Street*, written in 1946. Both characters are ostensibly defined by their unequal relations with men, but their potential for salvation lies in the larger community that depends on the stability of its women. Lutie Johnson is so determined to move off "the street" in Harlem she thinks is pulling her down that she refuses to join the community Harlem offers her, a community that in some ways defies the white society keeping it poor. Neither poor nor uneducated, Julia finds herself defying the black community by asserting her right to love a white man, but this self-assertion is, in a larger sense, a more dangerous defiance of the white community. She wants her love story to be one of individual commitment and sacrifice, but it is that only in part. Julia's refinement in manners, education, and financial independence, which are middle-class, traditionally white attributes, make her and Herman available to each other. But theirs is, as the subtitle insists, a "love/hate" story, in which interracial love cannot be divorced from centuries of racial hate.

Catherine Wiley. In June Schlueter, ed. *Modern American Drama:*
The Female Canon (Rutherford, N. J.: Fairleigh
Dickinson University Press, 1990), pp. 184, 187–89

CLARKE, AUSTIN C. (1934–   )

BARBADOS

[Austin C.] Clarke's major themes are similar to those of most West Indian novels during the last thirty years—black awareness, national identity, the hateful ambiguities of the West, and the heroic potential of the black peasant. But the emphases and contexts through which he develops these topics are shaped by his experience of the Afro-American consciousness that has been gaining momentum during his stay in Canada and the United States. He has, in effect, helped to contribute a North American dimension to the characteristic identity motif of the West Indian novel; and as the major West Indian writer on the continent at the present time, he provides an invaluable perspective on an aspect of British Caribbean literature that has too often been minimized or ignored in the past. His significance in this respect is increased by the fact that he is among the few West Indian artists of any note to have lived and worked in North America, for any considerable time, since the beginning of the new "black revolution." In fact "revolution" is the major theme of his first novel, [*The*] *Survivors of the Crossing*. It presents the abortive attempts of Rufus, a sugar-plantation laborer, to effect an economic and political revolution in Barbados. He tries, unsuccessfully, to break the repressive powers of a white establishment by using the strike as his main weapon, and when that fails, resorts to equally ineffective terrorist tactics. But in spite of the very obvious political motif of the work, the real import of the revolution in *Survivors of the Crossing* is cultural and emotional, rather than constitutional. Hence the portrayal of Barbados in the mid-1960s as a politically deprived society, lacking even the fundamentals of a labor union movement, is an ironic rather than literal anachronism. All the constitutional, political, and economic trappings of the West Indian independence movement have been reduced, by Clarke, to the level of relative insignificance, in the face of the black apathy and self-hate that have traditionally stunted cultural and racial self-identity. The native government and its leaders are conspicuously absent from the main plot of *Survivors of the Crossing*, and are occasionally just referred to in passing as rather vague and irrelevant details of the background. The real powers in Rufus's world are the white plantation owner and a white-controlled police force, both exercising their influence through native sycophants. Rufus fails, then, not only because of his opponents' power and his own incapacities, but also because of the hostility or indifference of other blacks who actively or passively support the status quo. Whippetts, the black schoolteacher in Rufus's village, is a representative figure in this context; his violent hatred of Rufus and his contempt for members of his own race not only make him an effective opponent of the ill-fated revolution, but also demonstrate the educational and class barriers to an effective kind of racial self-identity in his society. . . .

The identity theme with its attendant conflicts also appears in Clarke's next novel, *Amongst Thistles and Thorns*. Both the coherent structure and psychological complexity of this work attest to the rapid development of Clarke's narrative techniques. He treats his racial and cultural subjects on a less exclusively external level than he has Rufus's political misadventures: the moral and emotional conflicts become more coherent and psychologically interesting by being presented as the experiences of a single character whose introspection provides the work with a kind of subjective unity.

Amongst Thistles and Thorns portrays a weekend in the life of Milton Sobers, a young schoolboy in Barbados, who runs away temporarily from both school and home. Milton's truancy is developed as a psychological quest, a search for identity that has racial as well as psychological overtones. He has run away from a sterile educational system represented by a servile and sadistic black teacher, an impersonal and detached white inspector, and the irrelevant offerings to a white "motherland" during the colonial rites of Empire Day. At the same time, he is detached from the society of his village, for only his father, Willy-Willy, shares his interest in the topic closest to his heart—Harlem. Milton's Harlem assumes the dominant symbolic proportions it has in [Claude] McKay's *Home to Harlem*, and his daydreams of the famous black community at once testify to the importance of American symbolism in Clarke's fiction, and indicate the unifying subjectivity with which Clarke is developing his themes. . . .

Psychologically Clarke's themes evolve a stage further with the incisive irony of *The Meeting Point*. Familiar clashes with the external world of the status quo persist, but the more interesting conflicts are wholly internal: the actual process of self-identification is itself being more closely scrutinized, and is revealed as a painful, and often unresolved, series of conflicts *within* each awakening consciousness—the tension between nascent blackness on the one hand, and the old self-hate or apathy, on the other. Moreover, this is the fundamental ambiguity that proves to be the source of much of the novel's irony.

The Meeting Point is the story of Bernice Leach, a Barbadian immigrant working as the maid of the Burrmanns, a Jewish family in Toronto. The title of the work is itself ironic, for the novel dispels, rather than confirms, the optimistic connotations of the familiar phrase. "Meeting Point" really indicates, not reconciliation and harmony, but the collision of hostile attitudes: the black sensitivity of Bernice and her friends meeting the coldness and antipathy of Canadian society.

Lloyd W. Brown. *JCL*. 9 (July 1970), pp. 90–91, 93, 95–96

Bertram Cumberbatch, better known as Boysie, the protagonist of *The Bigger Light*, has, after years of scrounging and scraping, achieved what by his standards is great material success. . . . Boysie's wife, Dots, has also progressed—

from being a servant in a rich, suburban household to being a nurse's aide in a hospital. *Her* progress is not so much a case of material advancement as of a greater feeling of independence, of movement away from a servile condition. It is the nagging sense of servile status that, among other things, qualifies Boysie's success. For his "business," as he calls it grandly, is that of office cleaner, which he euphemistically refers to as "janitorial service"—and *he* is the only member of his so-called firm. His awareness that, in spite of his outward success, he has not essentially changed his condition of servility, is shown when he reflects: "Imagine! Most men and women too, go out every morning to work, wearing business clothes, nice clothes. And I go to work at night, wearing old clothes, as if I am a blasted cockroach!" In order to counteract this sense of inferiority, and to feel that he is truly a part of the country which has given him material security, Boysie tries to make himself over into a Canadian. This means denying his blackness and West Indianness. He stops going to the Mercury Club, a West Indian meeting place, and burns all his records of West Indian music and jazz, except for Miles Davis's *Milestones*. His cultural and psychological confusion is further reflected in the fact that he later regrets, secretly, not having also kept back The Mighty Sparrow's "Congoman," a calypso about "three white women traveling through Africa" who are ambiguously eaten by savages, the savages thereby becoming the envy of the calypsonian. Boysie's attraction to this calypso shows that deep down inside him he still feels a need to assert himself as a black man, to enjoy a sense of "black power." And, of course, the meaning of the calypso for him and the sense of power which it gives him are inseparable from its language.

Edward Baugh. *ACLALSB*. 5, 3 (December 1980), pp. 3–4

Clarke's closeness to [his protagonist, the poet-politician John] Moore in *The Prime Minister* creates some doubt as to how clearly he himself perceives Moore's failure. Yet Clarke raises some important issues through Moore. What is the poet's role in an ex-colony? Should he try to provide leadership through his poetry or through political action? Or should he divorce his writing from society entirely? *The Prime Minister* remains pessimistic about the ability of literature to effect change, though it is ambivalent about the power of the written word. No one reads John Moore's poetry, but the newspaper runs the country. Is Clarke suggesting that the writer who genuinely wishes to contribute to his country's real development (as opposed to the development of underdevelopment) should turn to journalism or music, to the popular forms that are reaching the people because they employ their language? But if he is, then why does he continue to write novels? Because he is trying to change the novel form, to make it more accessible as a popular genre, reflecting political concerns and challenging "literary standards of the colonization period." The powerful writing in *The Prime Minister* records the language of the people, particularly Kwame's speeches. As John Moore recognizes in a rare moment of insight: "The speech had ceased to be a political harangue and had become a work of art. . . ." Its strength mocks the false sentimentality of John Moore's lyrical evocations of "the blessed woman with her black beauty." If one could be sure that Clarke meant his readers to see John Moore as a false poet, then all would be well, but Clarke carries ambiguity to the point of confusion. . . .

Clarke's concern in *The Prime Minister* is to find a creatively violent language to challenge the old Miltonic rhythms that still hold John Moore's imagination in sway, but Clarke himself seems moved by some nostalgia for these European forms and by some fear of where violence in the language may lead him, so that *The Prime Minister* leaves us in limbo.

Diana Brydon. *CanL.* 95 (Winter 1982), p. 184

In Austin Clarke's *Amongst Thistles and Thorns* a sonorous dialect is used simultaneously for comic effect and to register social protest. In one episode, Nathan feels that he is qualified to describe the limiting society to his woman Ruby: "I have come to a damn serious understanding during my travels in and around this blasted past tense village." The conversation occurs when Nathan and Ruby are considering sending their son to the high school. Nathan argues that there is no hope of any but the least-considered white-collar jobs for the educated black man. . . . The zest with which Nathan puts this case and the rhythmic insistence of his language might be thought to distract from the force of the protest. But this would be true if direct protest were Clarke's sole intention. In fact, Nathan is an irresponsible character and his intention is to regain the favor of Ruby by attacking the things that threaten to thwart the boy. There is a protest element in his speech which is part of an authorial intention, but it is emphatically in the background.

Kenneth Ramchand. *The West Indian Novel and Its Background*
(London: Heinemann, 1983), pp. 110–11

In Clarke, the realist and the idealist are always in a state of tension, comparable with the dual images of Canada and the Caribbean in his work. Indeed those dual images, those ironically balanced views of the real and the idealized, are themselves symptoms of the moral tension within Clarke's own artistic imagination. In essence, Clarke's art is rooted in tension, in his deep but inspired ambivalence towards his two societies—their myths, ideals, and cultural traditions. This all results in a network of finely balanced ironies in the comparison and contrast of the two, and in reenacting the conflicts within each of them. The complex of ironic analogies and contrasts goes beyond cultural groups as such. Clarke also focuses on individual attitudes and the relationships which symbolize their immediate cultural milieux while representing universal experiences—especially in matters of race, sex, material ambitions, and political power. . . .

The tensions between satiric outrage and idealistic vision have remained fairly constant throughout Clarke's career as a writer. From a moral point of view, the differences in tone and mood are often more apparent than real. Hence, the ebullient atmosphere that seems to characterize an early work like [*Amongst Thistles and Thorns*] does not really disguise the brooding tragedy of lost innocence. And the moral idealism which envisions the corruption of innocence as tragedy is identical to the grim short stories which have recently savaged

Canadians; for the latter, too, have corrupted their own ideals. Given this basic constancy in Clarke's moral viewpoint, we must look to his choice of topics for a sense of overall pattern in his work. The pattern is basically chronological: the choice of topics shifts from peasant poverty in Barbados, in the earliest fiction, thence to immigrant experiences in Canada, and finally, the probing analysis of Canadian and Caribbean nationhood.

Lloyd W. Brown. *El Dorado and Paradise: Canada and the Caribbean in Austin Clarke's Fiction* (Parkersburg, Iowa: Caribbean Books, 1989), pp. 7–8

After the publication of *The Prime Minister*, Clarke turned his hand to what he perceives to be the first volume of his memoirs, *Growing Up Stupid under the Union Jack*, in which he recounts his early experiences in rural Barbados, concluding with his leaving Combermere School for Harrison College, Barbados's prestigious senior high school. The many dramatic scenes, the lively dialogue, and the narrative pace invite the reader to parallel this memoir with Clarke's novels. Clarke renders vividly details of time, place, customs, and habits. And he evokes, not just recalls, his moods and feelings. The work points up how much *Amongst Thistles and Thorns* issued from Clarke's own boyhood experiences.

After a gap of five years, Clarke published in quick succession two volumes of stories: *When Women Rule* and *Nine Men Who Laughed*. Of the eight stories in *When Women Rule*, five have the familiar working-class West Indian protagonist struggling to find his place in Canadian society. These stories are about men rendered impotent as much by their inhospitable environment as by wives, friends, and their own self-hatred. The other three are about working-class white Canadians, who, like the protagonist of "The Collector," resent the incursion of immigrants, yearning for a time when Canada was "pure." . . .

Clarke's novel *Proud Empires* looks back at the Barbados politics of the 1950s. Boy, a thirteen-year-old high school student, prepares for a scholarship examination in the middle of a national election, which proves to be a rite of passage for him. It opens his eyes to the corruption and treachery of island politics. But Clarke is less concerned with Boy's development than with the reprehensible conduct of the politicians and the distorted values of the middle class. At the end of the novel Boy, who has gone to study in Toronto (where inevitably, like Clarke's other immigrant characters, he experiences racism), returns to the island and allows himself to be persuaded to enter politics. But Boy's experiences are so cursorily given and his character so sketchily portrayed that it is not clear exactly what he has learned about politics and what he can contribute politically. Characteristically *Proud Empires* has many fine episodes and scintillating dialogue, employing the rhythm and idiom of Barbados English, which helps considerably to bring the characters to life. The novel confirms that Clarke's strength as a novelist lies not so much in his probing the psyche and inner development of his protagonists as in capturing the subtleties of the social and political behavior of his Barbadian characters whether at home or abroad.

Victor J. Ramraj. In Bernth Lindfors and Reinhard Sander, eds.
Dictionary of Literary Biography. 125 (1993), pp. 32–33

CLIFF, MICHELLE (1946–   )

JAMAICA

Michelle Cliff's *Claiming an Identity They Taught Me to Despise* deals head-on with the identity issue even to the expressive titling of her book. It is a lyrical, somewhat autobiographical exploration into identity with gender and heritage composing this identity. Landscape, history, family, events, places, all become features of her exploration. The movement of the book mirrors the migratory pattern, beginning in the Caribbean and childhood and moving to adulthood and America. The sections entitled "Obsolete Geography" and "Filaments" particularly typify this theme. In the first, we get an extended catalog of Caribbean fruits, vegetation, details of day-to-day experience like the waxing of parlor floors, the burying of umbilical cords, the slaughtering of domestic animals. Much of the identification with "home" comes from the rural grandmother who maintains continuity with homeland and whose entire being conveys the multi-faceted composition of Caribbean society. We see her, however, caught up in the conflict of being privileged, yet poor, white-skinned but culturally Caribbean. Her mother is a distant, intangible, liminal presence in her life. The contradictions of surface appearance versus reality, of camouflage and passing are explored. . . . The hybrid Creoleness that is essentially the Caribbean, the necessity of accepting all facets of experience, history and personhood in the definition of a self become integrated in her consciousness of her own identity. Personal history, family history, and a people's history and culture all converge.

Carole Boyce Davies. In Carole Boyce Davies and Elaine Savory Fido, eds.
Out of the Kumbla: Caribbean Women and Literature
(Trenton, N. J.: Africa World Press, 1990), pp. 63–64

Bodies of Water is peopled with misfits, the lonely and forgotten, but the feel of [Cliff's] stories is more monotonous than [Pauline] Melville's [in *Shapeshifter*], and the cruelty of life more relentless. Her style is less quirky, but the stories are rich and sensual nonetheless, full of sights and sounds and smells: "Her room, her pink expanse, smelled of urine and bay rum and the wet sugar which bound the tamarind balls. Ancestral scents."

History, both personal and political, underpins many of the characters and their actions. "A Hanged Man" is a beautifully crafted evocation of the days of slavery and the human confusion engendered by brutality: a woman awaits "fifty lashes and charge to account." The man to be paid for beating her has hung himself from his own whipping post—an incident Cliff has based on historical fact. In this story, as in others, the author abandons sequential narrative in a way that seems casual but is, in fact, minutely calculated. In "Screen Memory," an actress recalls her upbringing in a series of bright, eclectic pictures. The thread is hard to follow but the style is apposite for a tale of remembrance and loss. The reader is left with strong visual images, and a vague impression of pain. Many of the protagonists are looking back at the past, towards the future or around the present. There are insights into life cycles; birth, aging, death; a young girl forced to care for her grandmother "Resented the old woman as a portent—this is what little girls turn into." Alongside rich physical description, Cliff also uses scene setting as comment. "Election Day" shows two women in a queue for a polling booth as Ronald Reagan is about to be returned to office. The story has no overt political content, but the situation of the women is a wry note in the social tragedy they discuss.

Louise Doughty. *TLS*. February 23, 1990. p. 203

From beginning to end, *Bodies of Water*, Michelle Cliff's first collection of short stories, is shadowed by dark but subtle images of the child immigrant, sometimes the first-person narrator of these wonderfully rich and disturbing tales. This Jamaican-born author seems to understand, as perhaps only one who was a child immigrant herself can, the complex pain of the child whose parents have sent her away to another country for her own good. . . .

Each story in this collection tells a tale of abandonment, sometimes motivated purely by callousness, sometimes by racism, sexism, or homophobia, sometimes for the good of the child. Regardless of the reason, it is the abandonment that leaves such individuals damaged and scarred; these are the people Cliff celebrates. She presents them not as passive players in their dismal fates, but as people who struggle (though more quietly than not) to escape their condition even when escape is not possible. . . .

These bodies of water lapping against the shores of our common world remind us of human indifference and cruelty, but tell us too of the courage of those we would harm and of their will to survive. Michelle Cliff uses spare and taut language that sharply underscores the harsh realities of the worlds she recreates. *Bodies of Water* is a remarkable collection, a testimony to human endurance and the triumph of the spirit.

Elizabeth Nunez-Harrell. *NYTBR*. September 23, 1990, p. 22

A nun avenges seventy-five years of abuse by torching her family's Winnebago; a black woman bleaches herself into a checkerboard sideshow freak; a Vietnam vet wearing a hat of yesterday's news wanders in a forest of shell-shocked men: such is Michelle Cliff's landscape of fragmented souls in her short-story collection, *Bodies of Water*. . . .

Many of the stories feature abandoned children and disoriented adults, somehow set apart by a deeply wounding experience. Operating on a continually shifting foundation, where broken homes are more the rule than the exception, the characters often violate traditional social mores in their restless search for validation and wholeness. Rich intertextual references enliven the stories and illustrate how an individual's history can encompass many lives, as references from one "life" intrude into another. In "A Woman Who Plays Trumpet Is Deported," set in the 1930s and 1940s, an African-American female musician travels to Paris, where "They pay her to play. She stays in their hotel. Eats their food in a clean, well-lighted place. Pisses in their toilet. . . . No strange fruit hanging in the Tuileries."

The narrative voices in *Bodies of Water* are quietly scattered, carefully avoiding certain disclosures, and Cliff's writing not only accommodates but even simulates this quality. Her sentences are choppy prose-poems, alternately flowing with the ease of free association and halting as pain becomes too sharp for conscious articulation: the effect is a sort of syntactical breakdown reflecting the internal state of her characters. If the reader is often puzzled and must struggle to piece together these narratives, it is a confirmation of Cliff's success at portraying characters who mystify even themselves.

Laura Frost. *RCF*. 11, 1 (Spring 1991), pp. 317–18

Cliff's first novel [*Abeng*] is concerned with the deconstruction of the Eurocentric phenomenon in Jamaica as a prelude to unearthing the repressed Afro-Caribbean experience in the island. Thus the reconstruction of elided black identities and African fragments long lost in the colonial archive is as urgent as the deconstruction of modernism and modernity. . . .

The uniqueness of Cliff's aesthetics lies in her realization that the fragmentation, silence, and repression that mark the life of the Caribbean subject under colonialism must be confronted not only as a problem to be overcome but also as a condition of possibility—as a license to dissimulate and to affirm difference—in which an identity is created out of the chaotic colonial and postcolonial history. In writing about the ways in which Caribbean subjects strive to subjectify themselves within the commodified space and time of colonial modernity, Cliff finds discursive value in the very fragmentation that other commentators have seen as the curse of West Indian history. According to Cliff, fragmentation can indeed function as a strategy of identity since the colonized writer struggles "to get wholeness from fragmentation while working within fragmentation, producing work which may find its strength in its depiction of fragmentation, through form as well as content." . . .

Through deliberate strategies of intertextuality, Cliff reifies the linguistic and ideological conflicts that arise when colonialist discourse is challenged by the vernacular, when official versions of history are questioned by the silent history of the poor and powerless. By establishing the antagonistic relationship between linguistic forms (especially the oral and the written), and through the interpolation of time frames and the spatialization of historical events, she represents both the value and limits of fragmentation as a condition of history and as a strategy of representation. Furthermore, as a narrative of turbulence and crisis, *Abeng* is not intended simply to evoke the value of otherness, but also to provide a genealogy of the loss of value and speech in the colonial subject. By dispersing the historical narratives of colonialism, Cliff recenters, and gives value, to margins and edges. . . . [A] narrative whose goal is to disorient the reader from entrenched forms of modernism, *Abeng* finds its power in its parasitic and subversive relationship to previous texts, which it appropriates and then spits out, clearing a space for alternative systems of representation.

Simon Gikandi. *Writing in Limbo: Modernism and Caribbean Literature*
(Ithaca, N.Y.: Cornell University Press, 1992), pp. 233–36

Clare is clearly the protagonist of Michelle Cliff's 1987 novel *No Telephone to Heaven*, yet a large early section of the book focuses equally on Clare's mother Kitty who is Jamaican-born and never wants to live anywhere else. While still in Jamaica, Kitty marries Boy Savage and has two daughters. But then Kitty's mother, Miss Mattie, dies, and Boy seizes the opportunity to move his family to New York. For Kitty, the new life is a living death. She misses the climate, the foods, the music and patois, the customs and traditions of Jamaica. With no warning and no explanation, Kitty moves back to the islands, taking Clare's dark-skinned sister with her but leaving Clare and her father, both of whom can presumably make lives for themselves because they can "pass for white."

For Clare, however, Kitty's abrupt rejection is traumatic. She is left unmothered, while still a child, "not feeling much of anything, except a vague dread that she belongs nowhere." Between Clare and her father a gulf exists that only widens with time, Boy Savage having embraced his adopted country when he arrived in Brooklyn and completing his rejection of all things Jamaican by eventually marrying a white New Yorker of Italian descent. After Kitty dies, Clare's sister comes to visit in New York. But there is no bond between the two young women, and Clare is unable to find out from her sister why their mother took one of them and left the other, Clare, without so much as a word of farewell or explanation. Feeling rootless and alone, Clare begins an odyssey that takes her from New York to London and eventually across Europe, with intermittent returns to Jamaica. As Cliff writes about her protagonist, "There are many bits and pieces to her, for she is composed of fragments. In this journey, she hopes, is her restoration."

During her brief trips to Jamaica, Clare stays with relatives on her father's side of the family. These relatives are in fact quite proud of her when she moves to London and enrolls in university there, and they always encourage her to make the best of this wonderful opportunity. Clare, though, thinks sardonically of her motives: "Choosing London with the logic of a Creole. This was the mother country. The country by whose grace her people existed in the first place." At the same time Clare's only true friend in Jamaica, a transvestite who calls himself Harry/Harriet, tries urgently to persuade Clare that she must return permanently to Jamaica, her true home. She resists Harry/Harriet's urging, yet she finds London no more hospitable than New York: "I feel like a shadow," she says, "like I could float through my days without ever touching . . . anyone." Still resisting a return to Jamaica, Clare becomes involved with a black man from Alabama, a Vietnam veteran who carries a leg wound that will never heal. Together, both of them fleeing demons that they can hardly name, they embark on a cross-European journey. As might be expected, they are unable to succor each other. After a miscarriage, and seriously ill from a resulting infection and fever, Clare returns to Jamaica for good. At this time, she is thirty-six years old.

The Jamaica to which Clare returns is ravaged by poverty, crime, and civil insurrection. Yet in the midst of all this, Clare begins to find her roots. She finds the way to her grandmother's house, now in ruins but also belonging to Clare. Nearby is a river where, as a child, she watched washerwomen at work, slapping the clothes on rocks worn as smooth as silk. Here, too, she often swam, and in remembrance she does so again: "The importance of this water came back to her. Sweet on an island surrounded by salt. She shut her eyes and let the cool of it wash over her naked body, reaching up into her as she opened her legs. Rebaptism."

This was not, though, a place where Clare came alone as a child. Thus she remembers that this river place was where her mother, Kitty, "was alive, came alive," and Clare thinks, "I was fortunate I knew her here." But then she stops, corrects herself: "No, I was blessed to have her here. Her passion of place. Her sense of the people. Here is her; leave it at that."

Indeed, "here is her" for Clare Savage. In returning to her mother's land, Clare finds her mother. Equally important, she finds herself. At one point an old island woman thinks that Clare *is* Kitty, and this seems to Clare an appropriate sign that the years and miles separating mother and daughter are diminished. In response to a question as to why she returned, Clare says, "I returned to this island to mend . . . to bury . . . my mother . . . . I returned to this island because there was nowhere else. . . . I could live no longer in borrowed countries, on borrowed time." Having found her mother and herself, Clare goes on to make a personal and political commitment to Jamaica and its people. For the first time since leaving Kingston many years ago, Clare has found the place where she belongs.

Ann R. Morris and Margaret M. Dunn. In Susheila Nasta, ed. *Motherlands*
(New Brunswick, N. J.: Rutgers University Press, 1992), pp. 232–34

Michelle Cliff chooses the *abeng* as an emblem for her book [*Abeng*] because, like the conch, the book is an instrument of communication whose performative function seems to be valorized. The story she tells is meant to inform Jamaicans and non-Jamaicans alike, and she goes to great lengths to demystify the past in order to imagine, invent, and rewrite a different collective and personal history for the protagonist. The narrative weaves the personal and the political together, allowing the protagonist Clare Savage, who is but a thinly disguised alter ego of the author, to negotiate the conflicting elements of her cultural and familial background. She thus succeeds in reclaiming the multifaceted identity her family and society had "taught [her] to despise," namely, her mixed racial heritage, her femininity, and her homosexuality.

The narrative sets up an uneasy and duplicitous relationship with its audience. It begins with the standard disclaimer, "This work is a work of fiction, and any resemblance to persons alive or dead is entirely coincidental," despite its clearly autobiographical themes, which echo and repeat similar themes treated from a first-person perspective in Cliff's poetry and essays. But *Abeng* discloses far more about the author than does the poetry, while engaging the reader in a dialogue that confronts the fictions of self-representation. It would seem that, for Cliff, the third person is a self-protective device that creates sufficient distance, and thus helps her deal with the burden of history. Acts of disclosure are always painful, and since Cliff admits that she has labored "under the ancient taboos of the assimilated," the "hegemony of the past" cannot easily be broken by a straightforward act of self-portraiture. Like German writer Christa Wolf and Chinese-American writer Maxine Hong Kingston, Cliff uses postmodern fictional techniques that, in the words of Sidonie Smith, "challenge the ideology of individualism and with it the ideology of gender."

Françoise Lionnet. In Sidonie Smith and Julia Watson, eds.
De/Colonizing the Subject (Minneapolis:
University of Minnesota Press, 1992), pp. 323-24

The contemporary West Indian novel reflects a somewhat different sensibility than its predecessor: a significant percentage of today's West Indian writers are women, and they have recast the familiar project of articulating a national identity to reflect their specific experiences as women. Michelle Cliff's novels are critical to working out the problems of race and gender in this regard because they reflect her search for an Afrocentric identity through her planters and slave owners; thus, the search for a black history/identity is intimately bound up with a latent feminism as well as with a revolutionary social consciousness. . . .

No Telephone to Heaven builds upon *Abeng* by deconstructing the reductive gender/race ideology in the former so that it is not solely white, male, European culture which is the focal point of conflict but language itself, wherein gender and geopolitical categories are both created and fixed in memory. To attempt to imitate the "reality" of these categories thus becomes a futile project. In the final analysis, it is discourse which creates meaning; by creating an alternative "reality" in a narrative structure which both extends and engages West Indian and European representations, the text attempts not an imaginary nor an imitation universe but a new kind of reality.

Belinda Edmondson. Callaloo. 16, 1 (Winter 1993), pp. 182, 190

CLIFTON, LUCILLE (1936–   )

UNITED STATES

There is a particular sort of movement rhetoric—it could belong either to the black movement or to the women's movement—which subverts the ambiguity of literature. Lucille Clifton avoids it much of the time. It must be a difficult thing to be a black writer in an age which demands political polarization of everyone—especially those who belong to oppressed groups. At times that demand for ideological clarification must interfere with a writer's freedom to be herself in all her complex selfhood. Lucille Clifton's definition of blackness is an organic part of her consciousness and therefore rightly pervades her work, but when she takes to self-conscious black mythmaking, she loses the subtlety which is her greatest strength. . . .

Whatever disappointments I have with *Good News about the Earth* spring mostly from that. Too many poems are agitprop, not art. Too much socialist realism. On second reading, when the shock of Lucille Clifton's perfect lines has been absorbed, some of the poems seem to collapse. The poems about the Panthers, Malcolm X, Eldridge Cleaver, Bobby Seale, Angela Davis, [and] Richard Penniman are artfully written, but they are not much more durable than the headlines which inspired them. They have practically no substance in and of themselves and rely principally upon the gut response of the reader. There is a place for writing like this—both as entertainment and as inspiration. Certainly it moves people, but then so do the most banal popular songs and so do angry slogans.

The question of politics and literature is ancient, and I do not pretend to be able to solve it here. I value Clifton and other black writers for reinterpreting black history, and thus reinterpreting American history, for daring to deal with their own internal racism and self-hatred, but I often feel they do not press their self-knowledge far enough. Surely there is *more* to say about the fantastic history of black/white relations in America (and the world over) than "white ways are the ways of death." A writer is supposed to be first of all a *knower* and a *self-knower*. If a poem contains no more *knowing* than an editorial, something is missing.

Erica Jong. Parnassus. 1, 1 (Fall-Winter 1972), pp. 86–87

Lucille Clifton, in her third collection of poems, *An Ordinary Woman*, plays on [a] collective sense of déjà vu, by using the power of everyday objects. She records the riddle of the ordinary with deliberate irony. In the first poem in the book, "In Salem," the "black witches know" that terror is not in weird phases of the moon or the witches' broom or the "wild clock face." . . . This is an extraordinary "ordinary" poem, a homely and particular source of history, of memory, the bread rising as the witch burns and the sinister association made and given its full measure of terror and truth in the emphasis on *ordinary*—the word and the state of mind. . . .

Lucille Clifton seems bent on examining in this book the states of mind, the personal commentary and paraphernalia that become momentous and historical. Her talent is for "news," facts that bloom into profundity or glamour, at best and worst respectively. Her language has flex and determination. She is an *intensifier*, steeped in what [Wallace] Stevens termed the "lentor and solemnity" of commonplace objects. In "At Last We Killed the Roaches," all these elements come together to render a poem like a scream sealed in the walls, a family curse falling with the dead roaches. . . . In one sense, the mnemonic becomes moral. Cleanliness instead of *reminding* us of godliness *is* godliness. Clifton knows this distortion well: if "such cleanliness is grace," then the slaughter of the roaches becomes the bondage and slaughter of the black race—the "tribe was broken" and it was "murder."

Yet despite this awareness, she occasionally, perversely, sets the same demon to work for her. The clock is thrown out the window, but we do not see time fly. It's just not enough, sometimes, the mnemonic: mentioning collard greens and Moses and Ms. Ann—although the words are touchstones and the phrases reverberate with the authority of common use (the ordinary), they remain strung out and glittering in air like a failed incantation.

Carol Muske. *Parnassus*. 4, 2 (Spring-Summer 1976), pp. 111–13

Lucille Clifton is a soft-spoken poet. She writes verse that does not leap out at you, nor shout expletives and gimmicks to gain attention. A public poet whose use of concrete symbols and language is easily discernible, Lucille Clifton is guided by the dictates of her own consciousness rather than the dictates of form, structure, and audience. She is not an "intellectual" poet, although she does not disdain intellect. She simply prefers to write from her heart. Her poetry is concrete, often witty, sometimes didactic, yet it can be subtle and understated. Her short-lined economical verse is often a grand mixture of simplicity and wisdom. Repeated readings of her work show her to be a poet in control of her material and one who is capable of sustaining a controlling idea with seemingly little effort. Clifton is a poet of a literary tradition which includes such varied poets as Walt Whitman, Emily Dickinson, and Gwendolyn Brooks, who have inspired and informed her work.

Lucille Clifton writes with conviction; she always takes a moral and hopeful stance. She rejects the view that human beings are pawns in the hands of whimsical fate. She believes that we can shape our own destiny and right the wrongs by taking a moral stand. . . .

Her children's books are her most prolific literary product, and no analysis of her work could ignore their overall importance. Her books for children introduce themes, ideas, and points of view that may sometimes find their way into her poetry. It is important to note that she does not greatly alter her style as she moves from one genre to another. Her language remains direct, economical, and simply stated. She does not patronize the children for whom she writes. She gives them credit for being intelligent human beings who do not deserve to be treated differently because of their age. Being the mother of six children must certainly give her material for her books, but it is her respect for children as people and her finely tuned instincts about what is important to them—their fears, their joys—that make her a successful writer of children's literature.

Audrey T. McCluskey. In Mari Evans, ed. *Black Women Writers (1950–1980): A Critical Evaluation* (New York: Doubleday, 1984), pp. 139–40

[Clifton] is effective because, despite consciously limiting her vocabulary, she has defined her audience. She is not out to impress, or to showcase the scope of her lexicon. She is communicating ideas and concepts. She understands that precise communication is not an easy undertaking; language, at its root, seeks to express emotion, thought, action. Most poetry writing (other than the blues) is foreign to the black community. It is nearly impossible to translate to the page the changing linguistic nuances or the subtleties of body language blacks use in everyday conversation; the black writer's task is an extremely complicated and delicate one. But . . . Clifton does not write down to us, nor is she condescending or patronizing with her language. Most of her poems are short and tight, as is her language. Her poems are well-planned creations, and as small as some of them are, they are not cloudy nor rainy with words for words' sake. The task is not to fill the page with letters but to challenge the mind. . . .

Her originality is accomplished with everyday language and executed with musical percussion, pushed to the limits of poetic possibilities. Lucille Clifton is a lover of life, a person who feels her people. Her poems are messages void of didacticism and needless repetition. Nor does she shout or scream the language at you; her voice is birdlike but loud and high enough to pierce the ears of dogs. She is the quiet warrior, and, like the weapons of all good warriors, her weapons can hurt, kill, and protect.

Haki Madhubuti. In Mari Evans, ed. Black Women Writers (1950–1980):
A Critical Evaluation (New York: Doubleday, 1984), p. 154

Despite the considerable achievements of *Good Times*, *Good News About the Earth*, and *Generations*, it is with the publication of *An Ordinary Woman* and *Two-Headed Woman* that Clifton strides to center stage among contemporary African-American poets. These two fine collections parse the female sector of African-American life and give vivid testimony to the terse brilliance which alerted readers of her early work to Clifton's enormous potential. Not only do they explore a broad swath of rarely examined experience; they do so in an appealing personal voice with an attractive infusion of self-revelation and wit. By now, all the major contemporary African-American women poets have written verse about women's lives: the mother-daughter dyad, heterosexual relations, oppressive standards of female beauty, and loneliness are common themes. The verse is often autobiographical, its saturation in African and African-American culture is explicit, and its tone varies from aggrieved to nostalgic to exultant. Several things set Clifton's work apart from the strophes of others. First, she has written more poems about women's lives than any other African-American poet except Gwendolyn Brooks. Second, she has consistently done so in the African-American demotic with sinewy diction, a confiding voice, and stark imagery.

With the Kali poems in *An Ordinary Woman*, Clifton makes a bold innovation in poetic presentation of African-American women. Rather than limning heroic embodiments of female power and triumph, or depicting lifelike women victimized by parents, racism, poverty, and sexism, Clifton invokes an aboriginal ebony-faced Indian goddess associated with blood, violence, and murder. Since the paternal slave ancestor Clifton celebrates in her memoir, *Generations*, came from Dahomey, with its well-known tradition of heroic women, Clifton could have crafted poems around an African-based tradition. In turning to Kali, however, she frees herself from the feminist tendency to see women as hapless victims and explores the psychic tensions of an introspective modern woman negotiating the dramatic changes in contemporary attitudes about culture, race, and gender at the same time that she juggles the roles of daughter, sister, artist, wife, and mother. Written in standard English, these lyrics differ from Clifton's earlier work in syntax and diction; they are also tighter and more forceful. Like her earlier work, however, they also employ short lines, few rhymes, brief stanzas, and recurring images of women's blood and bones. . . .

The thematic connections between *Two-Headed Woman* and Clifton's previous verse are immediately apparent. The opening "Homage to Mine" section demonstrates her continuing attention to family and friends and religious themes. In other ways, however, Clifton's latest volume of verse marks some sort of threshold experience for her. Unlike most other African-American women poets of the 1960s and 1970s, Clifton's marriage has been stable, and she has had six children. None of her verse articulates either the strains between men and women or the loneliness which often characterizes the work of other female poets, and her sons and daughters have been sources of pleasure and affirmation for her.

Andrea Benton Rushing. In Diane Wood Middlebrook and Marilyn
Yalom, eds. *Coming to Light: American Women Poets in the Twentieth
Century* (Ann Arbor: University of Michigan Press, 1985), pp. 217–19

Fortunately for the world of young people's literature, there are those authors who broaden our realms of experience by representing and exploring African-American culture. Lucille Clifton is one of the most prolific and accomplished of this number. In this context, her work is especially impressive when viewed as an entire oeuvre. Each book works in concert with the others to illuminate aspects of the communities, largely African-American, in which the characters live their lives. Everett Anderson's is one of the lives which is documented through a series of books. An examination of the Everett Anderson stories reveals the range and richness of this youngster's life and of the series book itself. This is especially true when examined within the context of the secondary function (intentional or not) of Clifton's telling of story: the exploration of Afro-American community and consciousness.

Dianne Johnson[-Feelings]. *CLAQ.* 14, 3 (Winter 1989), p. 174

Although Clifton, as a children's author, is perhaps best known for her Everett Anderson stories, I find her finest books to be *The Black BC's, The Times They Used to Be,* and *All Us Come Cross the Water.* The latter book, published in 1973, best demonstrates the fact that Clifton's "children's" writings are of a piece with her poetry, dignifying the lives of blacks through acts of memory and attention and through a well-wrought vernacular. *All Us Come Cross the Water* begins "I got this teacher name Miss Wills. This day she come asking everybody to tell where they people come from." The main character of the story is called Jim by his teacher, but he calls himself Ujamaa. Like Clifton, he searches for information about his own lineage, consulting Big Mama: "Big Mama is my Mama's Mama's Mama's Mama. She real old and she don't say much, but she see things cause she born with a veil over her face. That makes it so she can see spirits and things." Like Clifton's own family, Big Mama's family came over from Whyday in Dahomey. And like Clifton, whose own spare poetry requires careful attention. Big Mama can be cryptic. . . .

   As both her poetry and *All Us Come Cross the Water* illustrate, ownership is linked to language and to naming. Telling the story, choosing the dialect, and picking the name are acts of power with direct consequences in terms of dignity and autonomy. Clifton's acts of naming are *not* the transcendental "perfect fits" imagined by Ralph Waldo Emerson, whose Adam-poet gives the "true" and "original" names to the creatures of the earth. It seems to me that Emerson's ideal is imaginable *only* from a position of power and privilege, not from within a family and a race where names are imposed as a brand and an exercise of power by someone else. Clifton's position as namer gets written in "the making of poems." . . .

In her newest poems, Clifton's revisionary history focuses more insistently on women. In one poem, she rewrites woman's power relationship to God, concluding "i am the good daughter who stays at home / singing and sewing. / when I whisper He strains to hear me and / He does whatever i say." Earlier in her writing, Clifton found herself "turning out of the / white cage. turning out of the / lady cage." . . . Thus, her newest poems continue her work in defining and affirming "us."

Hank Lazer. SoR. 25, 3 (Summer 1989), pp. 766–69

COLLINS, MERLE (1950–   )

GRENADA

The testimony of [Merle Collins's] poetry is one of transformation in attitudes, in ideas, and in language. A new freedom and love as woman, as Grenadian, as poet, flashes through her words. The joyous reception . . . given to such poems as "Callaloo" show how much she speaks for the people. The reflections on girlhood in the context of neocolonial cultural oppression, through the empathy with her grandmother in "The Lesson" and more directly in "The Butterfly Born," reflect the militancy of the Grenadian woman and her participation within the process of building the revolution. Yet the nourishment of the past is also acknowledged through the use of the patois, which is beginning to be legitimized and reincorporated into the language of the Grenada Revolution through the intervention of poets like Merle Collins.

Chris Searle. Words Unchained: Language and Revolution in Grenada
(London: Zed Books, 1984), pp. 135–36

It is right and appropriate that this collection of poetry [*Because the Dawn Breaks!*] is dedicated to the Grenadian people. For the poems—their tone, language, content, and vibrant commitment—belong first and foremost to Grenada: the beauty of her landscape; the challenges of her history; and the grandeur of her people. So in the poems one hears not just the voice of Merle Collins, but that of the people of Grenada talking about their struggles, and in particular about their five years' experience of revolution and revolutionary transformation. The poems embody, and celebrate, the people's visions, dreams, and hopes during those momentous years of hovering on the brink of

tremblingly new and full eternity. And above all is the celebration of beauty—
the beauty of the *new* emerging from the *old*. I remember, says the poet, the
form of the past foretelling the shape of things to come.

What is that past? It is one of slavery and colonialism and what goes with
them: the exploitation, the oppression, the deformation of spirit. Blackness is
denied: Africanism is denied; the very landscape of Grenada becomes a matter of
shame. Blackness, Africanness, lower-class origins reflected in a mirror become,
particularly for the petit bourgeois educated, a threat to the self-esteem of those
"caught in the strange dilemma of non-belonging." The history celebrated in
books and the media is that of the colonial conquerors. Gairyism perpetuated this
and more. The meek, the exploited, and the oppressed were supposed to wait for
compensation in heaven. Blessed are the meek. Deliverance will come from the
big houses on the hill!

But that very past is one of continuous resistance by the meek, [Frantz]
Fanon's wretched of the earth, for whom "struggle is the loudest song." It was
out of that fierce and continuous struggle that came the 1979 Grenada Revolution. Merle Collins's poetry captures in telling images and clear languages
the new horizons, the new possibilities opened up by the revolution. . . .

The revolution then embodies the dreams and visions of an awakened
people. Not surprisingly, the image of the dream is the most dominant in the
entire collection. In this Merle Collins joins another Caribbean revolutionary
poet, Martin Carter, who celebrates the grandeur of all the struggling of the
earth who sleep not to dream, but dream to change the world.

It is her consciousness that change is inevitable, that movement is not
always along a straight line, and her commitment to the collective dream of
Grenadian masses for a world in which they own the earth and the sweat that
works the earth, that makes Merle Collins, the poet, not despair when the revolution suffers a double blow: the disintegration of the leadership and the invasion of Grenada by United States imperialist forces.

Ngugi wa Thiong'o. Introduction to Merle Collins.
Because the Dawn Breaks! (London: Karia Press, 1985), pp. vi–viii, x–xi

Merle Collins's poetry identifies its constituency as the comrades in the struggle. It derives its artistic validity from its ability to inspire and support the revolutionary impulse. It is poetry to be read out loud to an audience that has shared
the writer's private turmoil, if only at a distance. This sense of commitment to a
cause that goes beyond aesthetic self-assertion has made the author ruthless in
her exclusion of artistic extravagance. The poems' shared images are carefully
chosen and sparingly used, giving a sense of unified purpose to the work as a
whole—a quality that is often missing in poetry anthologies. One sees the influence of Edward Brathwaite in the poet's choice of rhyme scheme and line
arrangement as well as the insistence of an oral dimension to the work. The
influence of Ngugi [wa Thiong'o], with whom Merle has worked closely in her
present exile, can also be traced in the clarity of her language and the unapolo-
getically political dimension of her art. . . . This anthology establishes Merle

Collins unequivocally as a poet deserving of a place among the poets of Caribbean heritage. She updates the political commitment of Martin Carter since she has at her command the oral and literary techniques that a new generation of poets since Brathwaite (Kwesi Johnson, Keens-Douglas, Grace Nichols, Michael Smith) have been developing. I can only hope that readers and educators inside and outside of the Caribbean will give this volume the attention it deserves both artistically and as a political statement. In an era of drowned dreams, [Collins's] poetry offers a lifeline.

Rhonda Cobham. NBR. 2–3 (November 1986), pp. 76–77

The novel [*Angel*] is set in Grenada and spans about thirty or forty years prior to and including the revolution of March 13, 1979 and its aftermath of the United States' invasion four years later. Collins traces the events in the life of Angel McAllister, a young black Grenadian woman whose parents work in the early years of their marriage, as agricultural laborers on the cocoa plantation of the DeLisles, members of the white planter elite. (The McAllisters had recently returned from Aruba to which they had earlier emigrated from Grenada to find work in the oil industry). Collins seldom clutters her narrative with dates, and one needs to have some knowledge of the chronology of historical currents in Grenada in order to place events in the novel properly in time. Angel's earliest memories are of the burning down of the DeLisle plantation sometime in the late 1940s or early 1950s. This event occurs during the activism of the fledgling labor movement which has been trying to secure more equitable remuneration and improved working conditions for agricultural laborers on the cocoa estates. There is repeated reference to a charismatic labor organizer named "Leader" (Collins's deliberately flimsy, pseudonymous allusion to Eric Gairy, later the Prime Minister overthrown in the revolution) who is the popular driving force behind the growing labor unrest, but who is dogged by rumors of dishonesty in his union's financial dealings. . . .

Perhaps the most compelling aspect of this novel is Merle Collins's willingness to reach deep down into the gut of the survival instinct often characteristic of the most desperately poor. That instinct manifests itself most clearly in her characters' readiness to work at all costs, even in the most humiliating conditions, at greatest inconvenience to themselves—often for the least remuneration. Both Doodsie and Allan go to Aruba to take advantage of labor opportunities presented there by the oil industry. When times are especially hard, Doodsie is prepared to engage in domestic labor, run a small goods shop, and plant her little plot. . . . Allan becomes part of the exploited migrant labor force in the United States, picking fruit and vegetables for meager wages, having to bear prolonged absence from his family, and missing the conviviality of native Grenadian life. In his loneliness, he writes Doodsie from Florida: "We dont see a lot of people besides who we working with." Their friends, Ezra and her husband, are also migrant laborers, and as soon as he is old enough, Simon, Angel's younger brother, leaves the island to work in the United States.

Another strong point of the novel is that it reflects Collins's keen ear for her native Grenadian dialect, a talent which she uses to full narrative advantage in the work. The lilting cadence of the dialogue enters one's consciousness as much through the ear as through the mind. Collins is so accurate, so meticulous in her attention to the most minute details of phonetic reproduction that it is easy to imagine even the tone of voice accompanying the spoken words of the dialogue. At times, Collins's authorial voice merges with that of her characters, adopting the dialect form, and expertly submerging narrator and reader in the swirl of events taking place in the novel. . . .

The work's weakness derives from Collins's attempts to comment on too many aspects of Grenadian social oppression in too limited a narrative ambit. The novelist tries to address questions of racial inferiority, male domination, women's liberation, political oppression, and generational differences. The result is that the narrative pace lumbers as the author, somewhat gratuitously and heavy-handedly, injects an element of propaganda into Angel's utterances, Angel's education making her character a perfect vehicle for such talk. Thus, her remarks to her mother immediately prior to the invasion, manifest a hollow shrillness rather than the perceptive instruction which the author may have intended. . . .

These flaws apart, however, *Angel* is undeniably a literary hymn of praise to the ingenuity and survival skills of Grenada's working poor. In the final analysis, when politicians' promises ring hollow in the ears of the oppressed, as had happened so tragically in Grenada, there will be the comfort of storytellers like Merle Collins who record with love and respect for posterity the people's triumphs and tears.

Brenda DoHarris. ZNHF. 4, 1 (Fall 1989), pp. 25–28

In *Angel*, three generations of women experience the changes that Grenada undergoes under [Eric] Gairy's regime and the New Jewel Movement. "The Revolution has given me a theme," Collins tells us, "and has also developed a greater awareness of self and pride of being." The revolution was also instrumental in validating the Creole language and affirming its power through popular culture. It effected a reevaluation of the language and a reconceptualization of the curriculum which Grenadians initially resisted, as we see in the chapter that deals with the elections for the teachers' union, with secret campaigns "to ensure that Angel and those who shared her views did not get on to the executive."

Collins's novel explores the function of education, reading, and writing in nation formation and decolonization. The Caribbean child's encounter with language through the colonial school drove a wedge between the "real" world she saw about her and the world of the school and its curriculum. While the reality of the colonizers' books is made to supplant the reality of the island, Collins traces the evolution of Angel's consciousness until she ultimately rejects the world the colonial school has created. Like Annie John [in Jamaica Kincaid's *Annie John*], Angel devours Enid Blyton's adventures and the love stories her friends bring in. Angel's name is with time perceived as inadequate as she becomes darker, for in all books the children read "angels [are] white." Rather than concentrating on Sunday service, Angel thinks up all sorts of stories about faraway places: "In her mind, she went off sometimes by boat, sometimes by plane. . . . She never arrived anywhere in these daydreams; but she was often travelling." In Angel's case, however, the revolution creates a discursive space in which she can posit herself as a subject in the new Grenada, and she is able to see through the "mist.". . .

The many different ways in which Collins conveys the evolution of both Angel's and Grenada's consciousness help create the documentary effect of the narrative—we get the truth from many angles of vision and through different channels—which makes the novel not only less teleological but more politically effective. Another evolutionary movement is figured in both the content and the form of the letters that the characters exchange throughout the novel. The epistolary validates Creole as a written language, and the letters ultimately serve to represent the unity of the Caribbean peoples in diaspora. As they trace the characters' movement among islands and to the United States, in search of better economic conditions, they ultimately help the reader to perceive them not only as an extended family, but as constituting a Caribbean community. The letters also allow Collins to articulate in the voice of the people the significance of the events that are occurring in the society: their own writing and interpretation of history. . . .

Providing a site of resistance to narrative closure, the female voices in the novel have their own genealogy in relation to the independence movement and the critical response to that movement articulated in the black power and socialist movements. But Angel's vision is not enough to maintain a critical distance from Party doctrine, whereas Doodsie knows better. . . . If the novel presents unity from a woman's perspective, it does not exclude men. The words and actions of Angel's brothers help us see that it is not only from a female perspective that totalitarian structures can be recognized. It is in the very paradox of unity and fragmentation that the novel reaches history, as [Patrick] Taylor suggests, neither as utopia, nor as tragic failure, but as the hope and possibility of a new future. . . .

It is also significant that Angel returns to Grenada to perform a ritual wake. Although she feels "a little bit stupid" about what she is going to do, to light a candle and sing the song they always sang at wakes, with her good eye, in "her mind's eye," Angel sees that the spirits are sympathetic. As a communal form, the wake is a way for the living people to deal with the reality of death and the loss of a loved one. Angel sees the "figures circling the room," and she tells her Sunday school teacher, who has been dead for ten years, that the spirits are "either gone, or they [are] sympathetic." The wake at the end of the novel functions as a symbol of past traditions which Angel must retain if she is to have an awareness of her community and her heritage. Angel is lighting a candle not only for the part of her self that was lost with the blinding of her left eye—the Angel that got carried away with party arrogance and detachment from the people they were supposed to be accountable to—but to all Grenadians who lost their lives trying to keep the revolution alive.

Maria Helena Lima. *Ariel.* 24, 1 (January 1993), pp. 45–48, 51–52

CONDÉ, MARYSE (1937–   )

GUADELOUPE

[Maryse Condé's early plays *Dieu nous l'a donné* and *Mort d'Oluwémi d'Aju-mako*] are concerned with the manipulation of social mores and myths by individuals seeking political power and influence. Her three novels, *Hérémakhonon*, *Une Saison à Rihata*, and *Ségou* [*les murailles de terre*], attempt to make credible on an increasingly larger scale the personal human complexities involved in holy wars, national rivalries, and migrations of peoples. . . .

Condé, in her fiction as well as in her criticism, reflects her concern for the art of writing. Though her characters are not self-portraits, their remarks appear often to echo her experience and her critical opinions. For example, in her short story, "Three Women in Manhattan," she sympathizes with each of three writer-characters. She finds irony in Eleanor's dislike of having to exploit the spurious antebellum glories of the Old South in order to please white critics in America. She understands Vera's frustration in finding no public for her romantic period novels of Haiti's glorious past. She recognizes Claude's frustration at having to address a foreign readership in a European tongue. . . .

It is not that there has been a change in Maryse Condé's basic understanding, nor even in her narrative skills, that one is impelled to view *Ségou*, her latest novel, as a truly remarkable book. . . . Indeed, the ability to make the truth of fiction compatible with the data of historical events is discernible in all her writing. . . . She is unwilling to accept a popular belief or to reject it just because it is popular, she is willing to refrain from drawing inferences and theorizing on the basis of inadequate or confusing evidence, and she has a persistent curiosity which sharpens her powers of observation. This same analytical intelligence and critical integrity are evident also in her many essays and scholarly critiques; they have often put her into bold relief against a popular attitude, as did her article "Pourquoi la Négritude? Négritude ou révolution?" when presented to the colloquium in 1973. In that essay she refuted as ill-founded Léon Damas's enthusiastic perception of a healthy, triumphing Négritude, citing Haiti as a prime counterexample, among others. . . .

Upon reading *Ségou*, at least one difference from the two previous novels is immediately clear: its magnitude. The magnitude is not wholly one of the number of pages (nearly five hundred), but also of the years covered (sixty to eighty), of the localities involved (perhaps a dozen different nations or kingdoms), of the number of major historical and fictional characters extensively developed (over a dozen), of the major historical events integrally involved (the march of Islam over north central Africa, the later years of the slave trade, the "repatriation" in West Africa of Brazilian slaves, etc.).

Charlotte [H.] and David [K.] Bruner. WLT. 59, 1 (Winter 1985), pp. 9–12

Maryse Condé's world of fiction possesses, besides its diversity, the quality of commanding attention by its power of conviction. The realism of the framework, the psychological verisimilitude, and the plausibility of the situations contribute to the development of a fiction which succeeds in creating the illusion of reality. The primary topics treated in these novels, such as cultural alienation, the political climate in young African nations, the penetration of Islam and European imperialism in the Sahel of the eighteenth century, link everything to a psychological, actual, or historic reality and by consequence to an easily identifiable referent.

Maryse Condé often uses the motif of alienation in her works; therefore, it is not surprising that exile, which is part of the same thematic, also occupies an important place. In *Hérémakhonon*, Veronica feels exiled from her native milieu in Guadeloupe, and from the cultural French milieu, in spite of successfully adopting its customs. And despite her ardent desire to be part of the African culture, she feels excluded from that culture too. Rihata, in *Une Saison à Rihata*, is perceived as the definitive, irremediable place of exile. In *Ségou: les murailles [de terre]*, the concept of exile is intrinsic to the very subject of the novel, which deals with a period of great mobility and cultural transition on the African continent. . . .

These are the direct, obvious, and literal expressions of exile. . . . In addition, certain techniques contribute equally to conveying this notion of exile; among them, three metaphors, that of the absent mother, the adoptive mother, and the seductress.

Maryse Condé frequently evokes the figure of the mother. This is not surprising considering the symbolic ties between the earth and the mother: the homeland and the mother both suggest the origin, the source of life, the first place of growth. However, in her works the theme of the mother presents a special interest, because of the perspective in which it is presented. In fact, the relationship of the child to the mother is, in the majority of the cases, marked by trauma. The mother is rarely the one who nourishes and protects the child, or whose presence and actions provide a safe haven for the child. On the contrary, the motifs of absence, death, defection, and ambiguity are most often associated with the maternal figure.

The theme of the mother is inscribed in a structure of absence-presence, which also dominates the organization of the motifs associated with exile, forced separation, regret for a lost homeland, recourse to the imaginary or to memory in order to try and re-create it, in short, conjuration of absence by the illusion of presence. In the eyes of her dispersed sons, Nya, the archetype of the mother, and Ségou, the cradle of the family, are closely linked. It is their combined memory that nourishes the nostalgia they feel and that revives their desire to return to the place of their origins.

There exists another figure, complementary to the previous one, that of the adoptive mother. . . . Both the adoptive mother and the land of exile shelter the exiled, the disinherited. However, an unalterable fact exists: being just adoptive mothers, they can only play a borrowed role.

Nevertheless, in *Ségou: les murailles*, the land of exile is endowed with different characteristics than those associated with the adoptive mother. It wears the traits of a seductress who uses her charms to attract the exiled. When the latter yields to his fascination and tries to be accepted by her, she rejects him by invoking his foreign origins, which she denigrates haughtily. The refusal which he suffers marks the perpetuation of his exclusion.

These three figures—the missing mother, the adoptive mother, and the seductress—are distinct from each other due to the nature of their representative content. However . . . these metaphors invite an identical interpretation by virtue of their antithetical structure whose respective poles are: absence and presence, identity and alterity, and attraction and rejection.

Arlette M. Smith. FR. 62, 1 (October 1988), pp. 50–55†

The narrator in *Hérémakhonon*, Veronica, not only speaks incessantly of sex, it is her sexuality and her sexual activity that define her very essence. Moreover, the narrative act is inscribed within a masculine/feminine configuration of desire since it postulates a daughter-to-father or woman-to-lover discourse. In other words, the text is presented—at times alternately, at times simultaneously—as a conversation with and a search for the father ("le marabout mandingue") and as a conversation with and a search for the lover. The father is, of course, the lover par excellence, the ultimate object of desire. . . .

Because of his attempts to deny her an active sexuality, the father, in addition to being her idol, is also Veronica's nemesis. This is because . . . Veronica, even as an adolescent, is conscious of her body as a locus for pleasure and of herself as a sexual being. . . . Because it is proscribed, Veronica, from the very beginning, imagines the sexual act as a liberating one and the sexual partner as giving access to a certain independence. Her first experience is then a deliberate act of defiance and separation from the family and especially from paternal restriction. . . .

She realizes that to make love is always to make a political choice. . . . As an adult, she continues to envision the sexual act as liberating. The African revolutions for independence, she contends, were in fact revolutions for sex. . . . Furthermore, revolutions and sex are so intertwined in her thinking that it is difficult for her to determine finally if, in general, one engages (in) sex in the name of the revolution or if one engages (in) the revolution in the name of sex. . . .

Veronica, who as an adolescent had been surprised "en plein coit ou presque," is labeled by her father "putain" and, for different reasons, she is labeled "intellectuelle de gauche"; but it is the first label only—the one with which, as an adult, she is insulted by her students—that she accepts and in which she gradually appears to take pride. For since she equates sexuality with (masculine) independence, Veronica esteems the prostitute for daring to attempt to usurp the masculine prerogative by striking a pose—albeit illusory—of independence and power.

Arthur Flannigan. FR. 62, 2 (December 1988), pp. 306–8

Maryse Condé's novel, *Une Saison à Rihata*, set in a fictitious African country, opens with a description of the protagonist's house: it is cut off from the rest of the town, a picture of neglect and decay, damp, mildewed, a crumbling reflection of its former colonial glory. The appearance of the house offers a striking parallel to the situation of the family and in particular to that of its *Antillaise* mistress, Marie-Hélène—a stranger in exile and at odds with her surroundings in an alien and hostile society. A brilliant, middle-class woman, married to an African, she had hoped to heal the divisions in herself by a return to her ancestral homeland. Marie-Hélène's life in Africa, however, is characterized by shattered hopes and unfulfilled dreams. She finds herself banished to an isolated and stagnating provincial town and responds to being rejected by Africa by withdrawing from life and from those around her. The journey back has not recovered the lost mother, the mythical Africa, the ancestral homeland. Like [Aimé] Césaire's poet, the Antillean heroine fails to find what she expected. She becomes more cut off, more exiled from herself. The rejection of Africa leads to a corresponding withdrawal from all everyday reality, expressed metaphorically by her physical isolation: Her room becomes her refuge where she rejoins her rejected West Indian homeland through the medium of the dream and the imagination.

Elizabeth Wilson. In Carole Boyce Davies and Elaine Savory Fido, eds.
Out of the Kumbla: Caribbean Women and Literature
(Trenton, N. J.: Africa World Press, 1990), p. 48

The story [of *Traversée de la mangrove*] is apparently simple. A dead man is discovered at Rivière au sel. This dead man is Francisco Alvarez Sanchez. He had landed in this part of Guadeloupe, reclaimed a house that everyone feared—one of those haunted houses that abound in Creole cultures of the Caribbean—and settled there, provoking the disruption of several lives. We will learn of these disruptions during his wake, as the people of Rivière au sel gather to contemplate his mysterious corpse and his equally mysterious death. And all those attending this dead man will, from chapter to chapter, tell about him, about their relationship with him, and about the part they played in his life—now gone. These recollections at the wake will reveal to us the multiple facets of Francisco Sanchez—subjective, incomplete, moving, and forgotten facets, even for the person recollecting them. And, slowly, these facets will reflect, not a character clear and sharp as in a Western novel, but a mysterious man who may have come from Cuba, or most certainly from Colombia; who was a son of Guadeloupe, though he really was not; and who feared something no one knew—maybe this very death that would mysteriously strike his lineage at a specific age. Through the testimony of Moise, Mira, Aristide, Man sonson, Carmélien, Désinor, Dinah, Dodose Pélagie, the historian Emile Etienne, and others, we see Francisco Sanchez foretell his own death, await and flee it at the same time, and also write about it—because he is a writer—in a novel that no one will read and which, of course, is entitled *Traversée de la mangrove*.

The wake is for us a melting pot of Creole culture, of its speech, of its orality, and it gave the extraordinary pretext that would allow plantation slaves to gather without spreading the fear that they were plotting to revolt or to burn down a plantation. I even have the feeling that the Creole language, in its whispers, that the Creole culture, in its ruses and detours, and that the Creole philosophy, in its underground, clandestine, and fatalist character, all were shaped in the wake's contours; there, too, was shaped our most painful subjectivity. The wake also is the space of the storyteller, our first literary figure, the one who, in the silence, gave us his voice, and who, facing death in the night, laughed, sang, challenged, as if to teach us how to resist our collective death and night. It is in this culturally powerful space, then, that Maryse Condé's novel evolves, revealing the mysterious reflections of Francisco Sanchez, a strange Caribbean vagabond. This revelation will not follow a straight narrative line, but rather the sinuous contours of the tale—or, more accurately, of several tales. It will not be traced in linear logic, but in the many detours and byroads constructed in the wandering utterances of each person at the wake—wandering and personal utterances, deeply rooted in a language to which we will return. It is difficult for the Creole language to ignore, in its growth, this space of the wake, and thus it is not surprising that Maryse Condé anchors her novel in this space, at the heart of our history and culture, and of our memory.

Patrick Chamoiseau. Callaloo. 14, 2 (Spring 1991), pp. 390–91

Maryse Conde's historical novel about the black witch of Salem [*Moi, Tituba, sorcière*, translated as *I, Tituba, Black Witch of Salem*] furnishes Tituba with a social consciousness as contemporary as the motivating impulse behind the novel, which drives Condé to retrieve fragments of an intentionally ignored history and to reshape them into a coherent, meaningful story. It is the same consciousness that has motivated contemporary women of African descent—both scholars and artists—to explore the infinite possibilities of our lost history.

As Condé offers to Tituba the possibility of filling the silence and voids with voice and presence, we who are Tituba's cultural kin experience the possibilities of our own history. Via an active, constitutive voice, Tituba leaps into history, shattering all the racist and misogynist misconceptions that have defined the place of black women. Tituba's revenge consists in having persuaded one of her descendants to rewrite her moment in history in her own African oral tradition. And when Tituba takes her place in the history of the Salem witch trials, the recorded history of that era—and indeed the entire history of the colonization process—is revealed to be seriously flawed.

Angela Y. Davis. Foreword to Maryse Condé. I, Tituba, Black Witch of
Salem (Charlottesville: University Press of Virginia, 1992), pp. xi–xii

In her newest novel, *Les Derniers Rois mages*, Condé tells the saga of three generations in the family of an African king exiled by the French from Benin to the island of Martinique but who ultimately returns to Africa—specifically, Algeria—to die. She skillfully interweaves the king's life, African customs, the past magnificence and grandeur of the king's panther clan, and the lives of his descendants, scarred by his majesty. The narrator is Djéré, the king's son by a local servant girl, who has been brought up at court, imbued with the legends and myths of Africa, and loved and pampered by all. That brief childhood spent with the exiled king casts its shadow over his entire life, and he cannot accept the fact that he and his mother are left behind when his "ancestor" goes back to Africa after six years. He resorts to writing a diary, recording like the griots of old all his reminiscences and the many stories and events told him by his father. This diary will later help his own offspring endure the daily hardship, poverty, disappointment, and scorn they will suffer from the inhabitants of Guadeloupe. . . .

Condé deftly interplays the various geographic settings of her novels—Martinique, Guadeloupe, America, and Africa—jumping from one continent to the other as her protagonists, from the former African ruler down to Spéro, muse about their lives. She provides her readers with descriptions of the local inhabitants, their way of life, their manner of spending time, their customs. The cultural clash which Spéro, the last of the "magician kings," experiences in the American South is subtly presented. The king's descendant becomes a looked-down-upon Negro in a milieu in which blacks, though officially equal, have yet to win truly equal footing with whites. An entire gallery of characters are sketched, both successes in life and failures, as Spéro comes in contact with them all. The relative material opulence of his domestic life, ensured by his industrious wife, does not satisfy him. He is emotionally dry and often longs for Guadeloupe, brooding about the past and his ancestors.

The novel is well written. The language is rich, and the text luxuriates in the islands' natural beauty, the blueness of the surrounding sea, the blooming of various tropical flowers and trees, and the variety of faces.

Nadezda Obradović. *WLT*. 66, 3 (Summer 1992), p. 564

As with [*Moi, Tituba, sorcière*], Condé opens *Les Derniers Rois mages* with a historical disclaimer to play upon readers' conventions of disbelief. When the French captured the last prince of the Fon dynasty of d'Abomey, known as Béhanzin, in early 1894, they were able to establish their protectorate of Dahomey. Béhanzin was deported to Martinique and died in Algeria in 1906. . . . Much as with Tituba, she thus assures us that, although we know the novel deals with an actual historical personality, the fiction will include conjecture and the imaginary. Condé again uses a multiple-point-of-view narration, concentrating primarily on the descendants of the African "king" but also on an African-American woman, Debbie. It is indeed Debbie's investigation into her African past that leads her to the French Caribbean and attracts her to Spéro, much as Veronica sought out her "nègre avec aïeux." The problem with Spéro's heritage, like that of his father Justin and grandfather Djéré (the child left behind in Martinique by the African king), is that the "royal" past provides neither glory nor power. The descendants of the original king have maintained only dreams of the past; they are, in fact, relatively lazy drunkards who "n'[ont] jamais rien fait de leurs deux mains." Exiled on his South Carolina island, Spéro epitomizes his ancestor's exile as well as that of African slaves exiled in the Caribbean. As she has remarked elsewhere, however, Condé affirms that, "Fait indéniable, l'exil crée des liens même factices." The spiritual link to his ancestor, both real and imaginary, offers him a fertile terrain for his primary activity: dreaming, as evidenced in both sections of the novel which open upon the supine Spéro, awaking from a recurrent dream. Whereas the women of the novel are active in their pursuits of the history of black people—his wife Debbie frenetically collects the oral histories of local African-Americans, and their daughter has left for the ancestral lands of Benin—one might wonder if, in portraying the young Anita (who echoes Veronica Veronica), Condé is not ultimately valorizing the role of men like Spéro. After all, she herself is "just a dreamer," she says, exploring "a certain past" and "a certain history" with her "imagination" and "intuition." . . .

The specificity of what Maryse Condé often portrays as a particularly Caribbean "identity problem" is emblematic of universal phenomena; through the "insular" realities of her characterized individuals, she presents in microcosm the universal conflicts of our splintered and multifaceted associations with and within the disparate elements of a modern, multicultural world. As exemplified by her transformation of the legacies of Tituba and Béhanzin, Condé shows us that a search for both individual and collective histories is limited only by the frontiers of our liberating imaginations.

Thomas C. Spear. WLT. 67, 4 (Autumn 1993), pp. 729–30

DEPESTRE, RENÉ (1926–   )

HAITI

René Depestre belongs to the second generation of Négritude poets. He was born in 1926 in the port town of Jacmel, in southern Haiti, and spent his early childhood there. Depestre's father died when he was a small child, leaving [his] widow to bring up a large family on slender means. For his secondary studies, Depestre went to the Ecole Tippenhauer in Port-au-Prince. As a teenager he met and much admired Jacques Roumain—both for his writings and the political ideals he represented. Depestre, who had known deprivation firsthand, wanted to see the continuing misery of his country and his people relieved. By the time he was twenty he had published two books of stirring, patriotic verse, *Etincelles* in 1945, and *Gerbe de sang* in 1946. He had also become editor-in-chief of a small, revolutionary newspaper, *La Ruche*, and was a leader of the group responsible for the overthrow of the Elie Lescot government in 1946. As a gesture of gratitude, the then new president of Haiti, Dumas Estimé, in 1947 awarded the young Depestre a scholarship to continue his education in France.

In 1950 the Estimé government fell, and was followed by the Magloire regime. Five years later, Duvalier took over the presidency and remained in power until his death in 1971, when he was succeeded by his son.

Depestre never returned to his homeland to live. In the 1950s he traveled a great deal in Europe, sojourning here and there on both sides of the Iron Curtain, frequently appearing at leftist-oriented international youth festivals, such as those in Berlin, Moscow, [and] Algiers, to speak and to read his poems. He also traveled widely in Central and South America, visiting Haiti briefly again in 1959. At least once, the intervention of a fellow poet of quite different political persuasion, Léopold [Sédar] Senghor, is said to have saved the "boilingly militant" Haitian—who had become a communist during his early years abroad—from being imprisoned for his political activities.

For some twenty years Depestre's poetry has continued to appear in France: *Végétations de clarté*, in 1951; *Traduit du grand large*, in 1952; and *Journal d'un animal marin*, in 1965—all published by Seghers. *Minerai noir* and *Un Arc-en-ciel pour l'occident chrétien* were published by Présence Africaine in 1957 and 1967 respectively. The last two books appeared since Depestre's emigration to Cuba.

Ellen Conroy Kennedy. The Négritude Poets
(New York: Thunder's Mouth Press, 1975), pp. 89–90

Un Arc-en-ciel pour l'occident chrétien [translated as *A Rainbow for the Christian West*], published in 1967, reveals the personal evolution of René Depestre as well as the synthesis of his poetic metamorphoses. Although it grows out of his earlier poetic collections . . . and although it reflects the bitterness of his exiles from Haiti and Cuba and then his joy on return, *Un Arc-en-ciel pour l'occident chrétien* has an intensity and a comprehensiveness of vision that mark it off from all his earlier works. Here he articulates a new humanism by transforming the dead past into living actuality. Traditionalism interacts with a prophetic, progressive impulse, and the facts of individual experience become expressive of larger, more universal possibilities. . . .

Seeking to join forces with world movements in revolutionary poetry, he creates a literature both rich in revolutionary action and in the spiritual qualities of his psychic inheritance. Through a confrontation of that past mythic tradition with the present, he aspires simultaneously to revitalize the past and transform the present.

The drama of *Un Arc-en-ciel pour l'occident chrétien* consists of this confrontation. The title itself is a key to Depestre's purpose. The symbol of the rainbow, connecting heaven to earth, dramatically embodies the interdependence of the earthly and the eternal. In the role of Haitian *houngan* (priest) he will descend to the dark stagnation of a sterile South (the parlor of an Alabama judge), steal the fire from the white man's "false gods," and, possessed by the sacred gods of voodoo, he will communicate their eternal truths to the alien white world. Within this work are gathered many connections. Relative to his previous poetry, it combines the black militancy of *Minerai noir* and the lyricism of *Journal d'un animal marin*. The constituent parts of his past creation are altogether transformed, yet never left behind. All that he articulated in his earlier poetry is now manifested through the essential, unifying elements of voodoo. It is through the external form of this indigenous dramatic rite that Depestre communicates that which acts in all traditions to liberate and he finally realizes his dream of twenty years. His last article during "The Debate over National Poetry" expresses his hope that he can create an original poetry, "a realism universal and human by content and Haitian as to its expressive contours." And, relevant to this debate, he rejects the supremacy of either the form or content, external tradition or individual freedom of inventiveness. For poetry, as ultimate synthesis, must unite and thus surpass these apparent contradictions. . . .

Although Depestre necessarily passes through annihilation and negation in his descent, the final shaping of the created mythology of *Un Arc-en-ciel pour l'occident chrétien* involves the revelation of both worlds, black and white, as mutually interrelated and interpenetrating. The structure of the entire work can be seen as the blacks' continuous movement forward: "I go forward barefoot / In the grass of my Négritude," passing through a transcendence of the limits of place in order to enter the civilization of the universal. Not content simply to delve into voodoo's past to find coherent, indigenous elements to countermand white attempts to falsify and dissociate, he also works to construct out of its basic principles a universal humanism. Thus, the dramatic phenomenon of continuous transformation, which is the major thrust of this collection, structurally manifests itself as a tense dialectic into which all stages of opposition finally disappear. Through self-transformation Depestre has articulated a new vision that completes the dramatic action of *Un Arc-en-ciel pour l'occident chrétien*. But in the

"Prélude," the beginning of this collection, we get a fierce sense of the self that is to undergo this transformation—this "personal surpassing."

Joan Dayan. Introduction to René Depestre. *A Rainbow for the Christian West* (Amherst: University of Massachusetts Press, 1977), pp. 3, 39–41

After publishing his earliest verse in Haiti in 1945–1946, Depestre was forced into exile by François Duvalier because of his political opposition to that dictator. He lived in Paris in the 1950s and in Cuba from after the revolution until recently, when he began to work for UNESCO in Paris and New York. All his poetry about the United States predates his residence there, however, so he does not write from firsthand experience. In his poetry, Depestre focuses on the manifestations of North American life most publicized in the Soviet and Cuban press which have touched him most deeply as a leftist, a Caribbean, and a black, namely racism, capitalism, imperialism, and militarism. . . .

Depestre identifies in the United States another variety of perversion, a collective sterility and alienation from the rest of humankind. In "Poème à hurler sous les fenêtres de la Maison Blanche," he probes North Americans' profound and neurotic desire for cleanliness, and discovers a need to cover corruption and callousness. . . . This black Haitian, writing in a Cuba sharply divided between the races in its prerevolutionary period, attributes white North America's moral insensitivity and hygienic compulsivity to guilt stemming from its role in the slave trade. The psychological portrayal elaborated by Depestre shows white America trapped in a syndrome of the denial of historical reality . . . and in a desperate attempt to suppress its detractors who tell the painful truth. . . . Depestre's picture of the United States as monolithically racist seems to constitute an appeal to francophone "Third-Worlders" to mark that nation as a whole—not just a particular group or set of policies—as their inherent enemy, and as irremediably so. It has none of [Ernesto] Cardenal's subtlety, no sense of part of white America's being victimized by another segment of white America in the context of racism. That Depestre's racially based historical analysis flies in the face of Marxist theories of social science seems not to deter his pursuing that propagandistic course.

Henry Cohen. *Revista/Review Interamericana*. 11, 2 (Summer 1981), pp. 220–21, 224–25

René Depestre is an essayist of the first rank. The essay in his hands successfully combines political immediacy and lasting literary values. [Karl] Marx's idea of human reality as essentially dialectical and historical is used as a base of vision of our times that is both analysis and synthesis, the creation of a jumping-off platform for Third World action. *Pour la révolution: pour la poésie* tries to rally Third World peoples by relating literary men to political leaders like Ho Chi Minh. Depestre works systematically to produce ideological "antibodies" (resistance to imperialism) and new myths to encourage and motivate Third World activists to seize the initiative from capitalistic media forces which impose alienated forms on colonized peoples. Battlefields for his essays include

Présence Africaine, Africasia, L'Action poétique, Casa de las Americas, and other periodicals circulating in Africa and Latin America.

In poetry, short story, and now novel form, Depestre has effectively used imagination to inspire hope and faith in oppressed peoples, to pass on a vision of a better way of organizing society, a vision of a new culture and liberation. He has shown that revolt does not have to be sacrifice and pain, that activism and eros are related, that healthy sexuality involves commitment to ethical and political values. He struggles to demonstrate to Third World leaders that sexual revolution should be part of their anti-imperialistic struggle. Depestre uses fantasy in political writing in a new way, as in his new novel *El Palo Ensebado,* published originally in Spanish and later, in revised form in French as *Le Mât de cocagne,* where surrealism and social realism, sex and revolt are mixed in a most curious style. The protagonist, an ex-senator and leader of resistance forces in Haiti who was transformed into an impotent zombie after his partisans and relatives were tortured and killed, has decided to act, to "dezombify" himself after many years of tending a little shop in Port-au-Prince. He will prevail by climbing the *mât de cocagne,* the greased Maypole, and winning the national prize at the annual celebration used by the dictator and his *Tontons Macoutes* to further demonstrate that "dezombification" and revolt are still possible. In the ensuing cat and mouse game the ex-senator and the dictator use voodoo to strengthen their resolve, the dictator baptizing the *mât de cocagne* with his own blood to make it even more directly his phallic symbol "screwing" the people (Depestre's own characterization).

Hal Wylie. In Carolyn A. Parker and Stephen H. Arnold, eds.
When the Drumbeat Changes (Washington, D. C.:
Three Continents Press, 1981), pp. 282–83

The most striking aspect of the novel [*Le Mât de cocagne*] is the use of the fantastic in what is essentially a realistic depiction of historical figures, set in a frame of real moral, social, and political problems. Surrealistic qualities are present, as is the influence of J. S. Alexis's theory of "Marvelous Realism." Depestre also reflects [Bertolt] Brecht's ideas on socialist writing. *Le Mât de cocagne* is a step forward in the evolution of a twentieth-century literary formula through which leftist writers can criticize and make political points while entertaining. Brecht's theories may perhaps be more easily applied in the Third World than to a capitalistic world where literature and entertainment are dominated by Hollywood and Madison Avenue. Theater (as [Antonin] Artaud and Brecht conceived it) is more alive in the "underdeveloped" world than in America or Europe, in the new countries where oral literature is still a living tradition, where there is still a feeling of community and where the village or town still has an organic quality. The "marvelous" has not been distorted by commercial interests and is still in touch with everyday life through myths and legends. The marvelous lives in the streets in a way the marvels of *The Exorcist* cannot. Depestre's brightly colored literary effects are analogous to those of Haitian "primitive" painting. Using voodoo and folklore that has an aura of the "sacred," Depestre creates modern fiction that reveals the exploitation of peoples and land produced by a regime which systematically sells out to outside financial interests. The rapaciousness of such regimes is evident in the trade in Haitian blood and cadavers dramatized in the novel.

Hal Wylie. *WLT*. 55, 1 (Winter 1981), p. 164

In the heart of *Un Arc-en-ciel pour l'occident chrétien*, Depestre exalts his Négritude by attacking the white colonial structure in a series of voodoo mystery poems. His use of the voodoo makes this work particularly relevant to Haitian culture today, because it "is the religion of the common people. It is a unifying force, an integrated system of beliefs, binding Haitians to their African heritage and creating a sense of collective responsibility to themselves—an indissoluble spirit of solidarity." The intensity created by the juxtaposition of the voodoo myths with the white culture is very powerful indeed.

Depestre thrusts the clichés whites have formulated about blacks into the intimate parlor of a "genteel" white family in Alabama, forcing the reader to acknowledge the existence of the clichés. He strips these scenes of the cloak of false courtesy sometimes characteristic of interaction between the races. There is a magnetism in the tension Depestre produces and a fascination in the horror of the prejudices he unveils for us.

Ann Armstrong Scarboro. *Concerning Poetry*. 17, 2 (Fall 1984), p. 125

Depestre sees much good in Négritude. . . . But he also seems to be proposing an alternative, *le négrisme*, an interesting concept that may, however, be equally or more vague or confusing. Depestre presents it in the initial essay in *Bonjour et adieu* [*à la négritude*]: "Les Aventures du négrisme en Amérique latine." He cites Monica Mansour's book *La Poesia negrista* as the definitive source. It seems that Depestre may be stretching a concept which was a precise delineation in referring to a literary school in Spanish- and Portuguese-speaking Latin America, but which becomes amorphous when extended beyond Latin America. Depestre does not give a short, simple definition of *le négrisme*; instead he lists a number of defining factors. . . .

It seems that Depestre considers *négrisme* the dialectical gropings to counteract the racist definitions that developed out of the "colonial adventures of capitalism." It is a literature sympathetic to the plight of the enslaved or colonized black which attempted to humanize his image or identity by showing how the world looked from his point of view. The romantics, the abolitionists, and especially the avant-garde played an important role before black writers came to the fore.

Why does Depestre go to such length to further complicate an already confused conception by introducing yet another term to the francophone world? Besides the philosophical and political objections to Négritude already noted, he feels very ill at ease with any conception built on race. He feels that race is a delusion produced by the mystification used by the early stage of capitalism to justify the imposition of slavery and colonial conquest. He obviously feels that in the long run any philosophy built on race is counterproductive. He begins his book by stressing the need for a "pan-human identity." He prefers "Americology" to Négritude, defining Americology as a study . . . that goes beyond race, culture, and language to demonstrate the creativity of "*créolité*" and "*marronnage*" or "*métissage*" (cultural cross pollination or hybridization) in producing American cultures. *Négrisme* offers several virtues or advantages. It is a historical reality that can be studied objectively, phenomenologically, independent of a priori definitions of race. It is open-ended in inviting all to participate. It relates well-known francophone and anglophone literary and philosophical events to those in the Hispanic Caribbean and in Latin America. It is necessarily dialectical and represents an effort to "deracialize" social relationships, so that political and economic factors can be seen. *Le négrisme* thus necessarily demands syntheses with political conceptions, and also philosophical and literary formulations, such as Marxism, socialism, surrealism. Depestre seems to feel it is less bound to the mid-twentieth-century moment of history and more future oriented.

> Hal Wylie. In Kofi Anyidoho, Abioseh M. Porter, Daniel [L.] Racine, and
> Janice Spleth, eds. *Interdisciplinary Dimensions of African Literature*
> (Washington, D. C.: Three Continents Press, 1985), pp. 47–48

Exiled from Haiti in 1946 at the age of twenty, [Depestre] writes a poetry that turns on the tension between an unattainable past and an unsatisfactory present. Depestre's transits through politics and places—a trek that takes him from Haiti to Paris to Cuba and then back to Paris—is most clearly conveyed by his presentations of woman. No matter where he is, his select muse remains the same: his chosen "moyen de connaisance," she moves through these places with a peculiar redundancy. This redundancy becomes even more striking when the reader notes the poet's own progress from dream-dimmed Marxist adolescent (*Etincelles*) to the role of poet-houngan (*Un Arc-en-ciel pour l'occident chrétien*) to Cuban revolutionary (*Poète à Cuba*). But perhaps this progress is only apparent, for the series of poetic stances somehow land Depestre back in Paris (where he now works for UNESCO), still using the elusive idea of woman to gain a voice that expresses insurmountable longing but never assuages it, that claims a desire for change but never brings it about. In this strangely static "progression," the very naming of woman becomes not an inspiration for revolutionary engagement, but an excuse for self-indulgence. We are left finally with a poet before his "douce Hélène de la connaissance"— a revolutionary who has, perhaps unknowingly, crafted his own exclusive cult of Beauty.

Ostensibly in praise of women, Depestre writes *Alléluia pour une femme-jardin*. . . . In this collection of stories, Depestre articulates the paradoxical use and abuse of woman's image in the Caribbean. . . . She is certainly not [W. B.] Yeats's "white woman whom passion has worn" nor that Hérodiade fashioned to embody the rigors of a [Stéphane] Mallarmé in pursuit of *poésie pure*. For the black poet whose writing is determined by specific cultural and political constraints, the woman comes to be the muse of Négritude. She seems the means of transit from solitary thought to a poetic that promises to be at once lyrical and engaged; and she offers the poet the opportunity to turn personal love song into public exhortation. Yet like [Léopold Sédar] Senghor's famous "Femme noire," who offers herself as the taut "tamtam" to be played upon by her "vainqueur," Depestre's woman betrays something awry in this poet's apparently anti-idealizing thrust. Depestre has long argued against what he calls Senghor's "totalitarian Négritude," his cult of a vague "essence noire" that mystifies the African people and serves the interests of a dominant social class. But in his attempt to recapture the singular identity of his Caribbean brothers, Depestre in fact dispossesses the female in his culture. The conversion of woman into motive for text exacts a cost on his poetry: the more Depestre uses the woman as conduit to revolt, the less "revolutionary" his poetry becomes. Whereas Depestre, the canny theorist of Négritude, demystifies the "false identity" determined by such taxonomic divisions as black or white—what he calls an ontological disguise—Depestre the lyricist remains trapped in a curious "bovarysme." His desire to desire, turning his love objects into various images at his disposal, recolonizes the very semantic traps that colonial semiology has fabricated and that he has spent his life endeavoring to expose.

Joan Dayan. FR. 59, 4 (March 1986), pp. 582–83

Words like "hope," "future," and "freedom" acquire a new force in Depestre's triumphant vision of a world reborn. In presenting himself as a "nègre aux vastes espoirs" pursuing a dream of hope and freedom in *Etincelles*, Depestre indicates the scale of the political commitment envisaged by his generation. In presenting himself as an *enfant terrible* and acknowledging his debt to Arthur Rimbaud, Depestre clearly placed high value on the figure of the outsider, whether in the benign image of the child or that of the vengeful *poète maudit*. . . . In 1946 Depestre transformed Rimbaud's "Mauvais sang" into his *Gerbe de sang*. The pagan carnality already apparent in Depestre's early work is somewhat different from the earnest purposefulness of [Jacques] Roumain's poetic temperament. Nevertheless, the influence of Roumain's sensibility is unmistakable. This early verse anticipates the preoccupation in Depestre's entire oeuvre with a celebration of cultural encounters and a sustained assault on all systems that inhibit individual freedom, whether class, church, or state.

In inventing himself through his poetry, Depestre, whether as a "petite lampe haitienne" or "animal marin" in *Journal d'un animal marin* and *Poète à Cuba* or as virile houngan in *Un Arc-en-ciel pour l'occident chrétien*, projects himself as the marginalized figure ever watchful on the periphery and capable of brief moments of triumph against the forces of "zombification." His poetic wanderings in Paris, Brazil, Cuba, and Jamaica are not construed as painful exile but rather as a ubiquitous adaptable self drawing on a cross-linguistic and cross-cultural reality. Depestre's ideal of "geolibertinage" is quite different from the idea of *marronnage* in the discourse of Négritude. The latter signifies individual salvation through escape. The former suggests a discovery of self through contact, in which the other becomes a liberating partner. In elaborating a poetics of rootlessness, in reacting against the inhibitions of Négritude's authenticity, Depestre had a liberating effect on poets in Haiti in the 1960s. . . .

Depestre's voice dominates Haitian poetry from the mid-1940s to the early 1960s. His continuous exile from Haiti, except for a brief period in 1958, and the terrors of [François] Duvalier's regime led him to despair for Haiti which he described in *Le Mât de cocagne* as a "zoocracy." Port-au-Prince emerges as a world of vermin and dust where only the living dead survive. His twenty years spent in Cuba would also lead to disappointment. Depestre became by the 1970s the incarnation of the poet as refugee, a condition shared by various writers who for various reasons are no longer rooted in a single community. This experience has led Depestre in recent times to rethink the whole question of exile. In favoring the word "errance" (errancy) over the word "exile" Depestre insists on the positive potential for self-transformation inherent in the condition of the poetic refugee.

J. Michael Dash. Callaloo. 15, 3 (Summer 1992), pp. 749–50

Determined by varying uses of exile, Depestre's writings can be read as a formidable tension between an unattainable past and an unsatisfactory present. His desire to make art out of a remembered Haiti, though sometimes imprisoned by memory, marks all of his works with a consistency that can only be called obsessive: a quest that keeps turning in on itself. As "navigator of forbidden seas"—with the slaves' sea journey from Africa to the New World ever in mind—Depestre journeys through a series of landscapes, increasingly solitary, from Dahomey to the United States, to South Africa, to Cuba, to Brazil, to France, all "far from Jacmel." . . .

When the metamorphoses of [*Hadriana dans tous mes rêves*] can be perceived as "mixing the horrors of death with the laughter of carnival," "blasphemous rites" and "saturnalia" coincident with "the vengeful magic of voodoo," then what kind of attitude or belief is formed about that land named Jacmel, Haiti? How can readers hearing news of another coup, another massacre, expect anything else from such a bizarre people? Some reviewers have stressed that the unbridled love-death scenes of this "crazy story" in the "hot tropics" are not to be found in "our pale, reasoning, Christian latitudes." "Too much, it's too much, will judge indomitable Cartesians! We are here in voodoo land." With such inevitable difference established, we need go no further. The phallic butterfly Balthazar can pierce sleeping virgins throughout Jacmel, Erzulie can lasciviously lift her dress, the black gods can copulate around Hadriana's coffin, but readers do not have to worry about the human context out of which these images are wrenched. For where are the humans in this "island of dreams"? One reviewer makes the link between the improbable and the actual. Talking of the strange life-in-death of Hadriana, whom Depestre describes as "the Creole fairy," "the white little angel," he writes: "Pseudodeath or pseudolife? Why look for an answer when the incredible belongs as naturally to the destiny of Haitians as the fatality of dictators."

Joan Dayan. YFS. 83, 2 (1993), pp. 157–58, 167–68

DIALLO, NAFISSATOU NIANG (1941–1982)

SENEGAL

One can consider [Nafissatou Niang Diallo's *Le Fort maudit*] from a dual perspective. It can be considered as a novel of destiny, of fatality—a sort of tragic drama whose vicissitudes lead to the fall of the individual. It can also be read as a social testimony, because, through the narration of real and fictitious events of the past—the action takes place in Senegal in the nineteenth century—a certain number of African customs and traditions are evoked.

A tragedy in five acts, it is like the works from the classical period. The first act, the longest, which coincides with the entire first part, is situated in the kingdom of Cayor. . . . This first act is written in great detail. It appears as if the author did not wish to make an impressive evocation of plenitude but desired rather to narrate in detail that which ordinarily remains in the shadows. This she does in order to show the indelible mark of these happy years on the heroine. For this reason, the rhythm of the first part is slow and melodious, an expression of a peaceful existence, a tranquil reflection of a well-balanced life.

In contrast, the second part of the novel presents a rocky and quicker-paced rhythm: although much shorter, it corresponds to the last four acts of the novelistic tragedy that is *Le Fort maudit*—that is to say, the drama reaches a climax. . . .

Le Fort maudit is indeed a tragedy in that a total confrontation takes place and in that Fariba Naël Ndiaye can be considered as the maleficent agent (physically, he is cold and hard, and morally, he is egoistic, cruel, and sly, truly a "diabolical" being) of an inescapable fatality, who has come to destroy the happy destiny of Thiane, changing it into misfortune. All the psychological traumas of the latter (the rape of her mother, the death of all her near ones) are themselves at the origin of the metamorphosis of the heroine. They inaugurate a new phase in her life as evidenced by her physical and moral evolution: beauty and irony disappear completely, whereas certain harder traits become accentuated. Traits that become a headstrong and stubborn child grumbling against inaction are changed thereafter by an inextinguishable thirst for vengeance and by a hatred which triumphs over her to the point of illness. . . .

The very construction of the novel confirms this circularity of the heroine's destiny, because *Le Fort maudit* begins with a kind of prologue, by the evocation of the death of Thiane, the narration of which is repeated at the end of the work. Posed as a hypothesis, this death is also the conclusion of the novel—the image of the cycle, of the spiral whirlwind of this human adventure.

The story of a destiny, *Le Fort maudit* also stands as a testimony to a certain number of telling traits of Negro-African civilization. Without necessarily having an ethnographic design, Diallo has admirably portrayed traditional life on whose behalf she makes an apology through her praise of the kingdom of Cayor.

Undoubtedly, the writer's pen is somewhat critical with regard to polygamous life. . . .

Other than this custom, traditional life seems to have only virtues and positive aspects. . . .

Such is the purity of traditional civilization that it seems to engender only good. If Baol is the opposite of Cayor, a kingdom without morality and harmony, it is because it has abandoned all its traditions. Its degeneracy, as attested by its bloodthirsty delirium and its disregard for the community spirit, is in some manner corroborated by its fascination "for the marvels of Western technique."

We then understand that the crushing defeat of Cayor by Baol could symbolize total dispossession—of life, of the nation and traditions. . . .

Thus Diallo's novel is inscribed in a certain thematic lineage of African literature. Through the detour of history and by recourse to a story, the novelist embarks on the discovery of Africanity. One is aware that this search for identity remains one of the most fecund themes in the writings of once colonized people. This inexhaustible theme is marvelously personified here and makes *Le Fort maudit* more than a pleasing fiction to read. It makes it the spiritual biography of a tree in search of its roots.

André-Patrick Sahel. *L'Afrique Litteraire.* 63–64 (1982), pp. 83–85†

A witness of the reactions of the postindependence generation to the strictures of the caste system is Nafissatou Diallo who, in her autobiography, *De Tilène au plateau [une enfance dakaroise]*, tells how she is determined to marry the handsome stranger with whom she has fallen in love with no knowledge of his family's origins: "Even if he was a sorcerer, a griot, a jeweller," she insists, "you wouldn't make me respect your darned traditions!" Fortunately, these young victims of love at first sight are of equal noble birth and there are no obstacles to their union. . . .

Diallo's *De Tilène au plateau* offers a very different chronicle of Dakar society of the same period as that covered by [Amar] Samb. The title of this autobiography, translated as *A Dakar Childhood*, refers to the district of the Dakar Medina where the author was born in 1941, and the Plateau, the smart residential part of the capital. The details that Safi gives of her home and childhood are probably typical of life in a high-caste family at that time, with the protocol of an Islamic home and day-to-day domestic activities. The story begins with the account of the little Safi playing truant from the Koranic school and her eventual admission to the French primary school. She graduates from the Lycée to enter the Training School for Midwives in Dakar, and the book ends with the death of her beloved father, her marriage, and subsequent departure for France. However, this bald outline gives little indication of the story's charm and universal appeal. Safi reveals herself as a mischievous, rebellious child, turning into a coquettish, petulant, somewhat arrogant adolescent, always in hot water at home and at school, always the ringleader in all manner of pranks which she recounts with simple, honest recall. The chapter describing her father's final illness, her grief at his death, and eventual resignation to this loss is a sincere and moving expression of a personal emotion and universal experience.

Nafissatou Diallo's style is simple and straightforward, eschewing literary effects and giving the impression of spontaneity and honesty of composition. She recounts her childhood pranks with lively humor and describes the storms of rebellious adolescence with insight and no self-indulgence. The reader who wishes to know about urban Islamic life in the 1940s and 1950s will find much of great informative interest. But the essence of the book's appeal, which to my mind will make it a minor classic, is the universality of Safi's story with which girls of all cultures and backgrounds can identify. And without setting out to moralize, it tells how a normal, high-spirited girl develops into a mature, responsible career woman, wife, mother, and talented writer.

Dorothy S. Blair. Senegalese Literature: A Critical History
(Boston: Twayne, 1984), pp. 12–13, 120

In African and Caribbean literature, the 1980s have brought forth new writings, not only by new writers in first novels, but new themes. A new motif of girlhood is emerging and proving to be significant enough to warrant extended fictional treatment.

Nafissatou Diallo's *De Tilène au plateau: une enfance dakaroise* is a forerunner of this new genre, even though the author denigrates her effort. . . .

Translated as *A Dakar Childhood*, [it] is a barely fictionalized autobiography. Diallo calls the work a tribute to her progressive but severe and patriarchal father. She recognizes that her father was ahead of his time in urging her education and in causing his untraditional views to prevail in the family: "I was the first girl in the family that Grandpa in his old age had finally allowed to go to school." It was a French school. Nonetheless, she underwent a strict Muslim upbringing at home. When she met the son of a Koranic schoolteacher, danced with him, and kissed him goodnight, she suffered such a severe beating from her father afterward that she could not leave her room for a week. She continued her education, however, finished high school, and went on to study midwifery. She married at twenty and finished her career preparation.

A few years later, mourning her father's death, she recalled her childhood sentiments: "Father dominating everything—And so I thought that one day I would write about him. He had been neither a politician nor a caliph, only a man of honor. . . . I would tell this to his children, to his grandchildren; why should I not tell it to the world? Why should I not say to the world . . . that it is the unimportant modest folk who support and carry the weight of the great?" Her tribute is straightforward. The chronology of her childhood is specific in remembered detail. She does not pretend to criticize her cultural milieu or to interpret the events of her own life as significant beyond personal narrative. But she treats themes which subsequent writers will amplify: the need for motherly understanding, the importance of education for women, the imprint of puppy love on adolescence, the quickly changing mores for women living today. Her goal is modest: "I am not the heroine of a novel but an ordinary woman of this country, Senegal. . . . So here are my memories of my childhood and adolescence. Senegal has changed in a generation. Perhaps it is worth reminding today's youngsters what we were like when we were their age."

Charlotte H. Bruner. *CLAJ*. 31, 3 (March 1988), pp. 324–26

Diallo's second novel, *Awa, la petite marchande*, is . . . for young people. Juvenile literature is of particular importance in Africa, where it often replaces traditional stories and legends as a source of moral instruction. This work is written in the first person and is what Bede Ssensalo calls a "pseudo-autobiography," for if one did not know it was fiction, one would take it to be autobiography. As a result, the reader identifies closely with the heroine, Awa. She is nine years old at the beginning of the novel and is the second of six children in a poor fisher family. After his father and brothers were drowned, however, her father, Salif, left fishing and now works as the cook of a Lebanese shopkeeper, for which he is despised by the rest of the extended family. To supplement the limited family income, Awa's mother, Yacine, sells fish. When the father loses his job through illness, Awa is forced to leave school, which she loves, and become a fish seller too. Nobody in the extended family helps them and their situation becomes desperate. Finally, a friend has Salif hospitalized and when he is cured, finds a job for him and Awa with the ex-governor who is returning home. The last third of the novel takes place in France, which is presented as the land of opportunity. Salif and Awa both make good: Salif learns to read and write and obtains a diploma in mechanics; Awa completes her primary education. After three years, during which they have been sending money home, they return to Senegal to a new villa and bright prospects for the future.

Despite its fairy-tale character, this novel is interesting for its didactic intent and its social criticism. Diallo presents Awa as a role model for young people, particularly girls, to show that hard work at home and at school brings its reward. Related to this is her desire to arouse sympathy for poverty, to demonstrate that it is not necessarily the fault of those concerned, and to advocate education as a way of escaping it. (It would have been difficult, perhaps impossible, however, for Awa and Salif to succeed without leaving for France.) Her depiction of Senegalese society is not a flattering one. Money is the most powerful force, corruption is widespread, and there is a general contempt for the poor. One cannot even rely on one's family for help. Friendship though does exist, and without it Awa's family would have sunk into penury and her father would probably have died. Diallo comes out clearly in this novel against polygamy: in fact, the only shadow which hangs over the ending is the possibility, because of the improved status of the family, that Awa's mother will have to accept a co-wife or wives: "Allait-elle connaître la vie infernale de la polygamie?" Awa asks herself. Diallo also criticizes the forced marriage of young girls to old men. Thus through *Awa, la petite marchande* Diallo hopes to contribute to a change in attitudes which will lead to an improvement in the status of women and to a more egalitarian society.

When we look at Nafissatou Diallo's literary production as a whole, we can see that she became acutely aware of her responsibilty as a woman writer. Although her works are different in form, they are not fundamentally different in intent, for each presents as a role model a young woman who has to make basic choices about her life. On an artistic level, there is a remarkable similarity between her energetic and determined heroines, who, if one compares them to Safi [in *De Tilène au plateau*], all appear to be projections of Diallo herself. The author's relationships with her father and grandmother also reappear in a thinly disguised form in her novels. With each book, however, her didiactic purpose and feminist consciousness seem to evolve. It is significant that her final work is for young people, perhaps because they are the most open to change. It may be that she had come to see her didactic role as more important than her artistic vocation. Some critics would call this a degeneration. And yet in the African context, where literature is expected to be *engagée*, this evolution could be interpreted as a full acceptance of one's social duty. Nafissatou Diallo was only forty when she died, however. Who knows what else she would have written, had she lived?

Susan Stringer. In Ginette Adamson and Eunice Myers, eds.
Continental, Latin-American and Francophone Women Writers
(Lanham, Md.: University Press of America, 1987),Vol. II, pp. 169–70

DOVE, RITA (1952–   )

UNITED STATES

[With] the consistently accomplished work of thirty-three-year-old Rita Dove, there is at least one clear sign if not of a coming renaissance of poetry, then at least of the emergence of an unusually strong new figure who might provide leadership by brilliant example. Thus far, Rita Dove has produced a remarkable record of publications in a wide range of respected poetry and other literary journals. Two books in verse, *The Yellow House on the Corner* and *Museum*, have appeared from Carnegie-Mellon University Press. A third book-length manuscript of poetry, "Thomas and Beulah," is scheduled to be published early in 1986 by the same house. Clearly Rita Dove has both the energy and the sense of professionalism required to lead other writers. Most importantly—even a first reading of her two books makes it clear that she also possesses the talent to do so. Dove is surely one of the three or four most gifted young black American poets to appear since [Amiri Baraka] ambled with deceptive nonchalance onto the scene in the late 1950s, and perhaps the most disciplined and technically accomplished black poet to arrive since Gwendolyn Brooks began her remarkable career in the 1940s. . . .

In many ways, her poems are exactly the opposite of those that have come to be considered black verse in recent years. Instead of looseness of structure, one finds in her poems remarkably tight control; instead of a reliance on reckless inspiration, one recognizes discipline and practice, and long, taxing hours in competitive university poetry workshops and in her study; instead of a range of reference limited to personal confession, one finds personal reference disciplined by a measuring of distance and objectivity; instead of an obsession with the theme of race, one finds an eagerness, perhaps even an anxiety, to transcend—if not actually to repudiate—black cultural nationalism in the name of a more inclusive sensibility. Hers is a brilliant mind, reinforced by what appears to be very wide reading, that seeks for itself the widest possible play, an ever expanding range of reference, the most acute distinctions, and the most subtle shadings of meaning. . . .

As a poet, Dove is well aware of black history. One of the five sections of *The Yellow House* is devoted entirely to poems on the theme of slavery and freedom. These pieces are inspired by nameless but strongly representative victims of the "peculiar institution," as well as by more famous heroic figures (who may be seen as fellow black writers, most of them) such as Solomon Northrup, abducted out of Northern freedom on a visit to Washington . . . and the revolutionary David Walker. . . . In these works and others such as "Banneker" in the later volume, *Museum*, Dove shows both a willingness and a fine ability to evoke, through deft vignettes, the psychological terror of slavery. She is certainly adept at recreating graphically the starched idioms of the eighteenth and early nineteenth centuries, at breathing life into the monumental or sometimes only arthritic rhythms of that vanished and yet still echoing age. Her poems in this style and area are hardly less moving than those of Robert Hayden, who made the period poem (the period being slavery) virtually his own invention among black poets. Dove's special empathy as a historical poet seems to be with the most sensitive, most eloquent blacks, individuals of ductile intelligence made neurotic by pain, especially the pain of not being understood and of not being able to express themselves.

Arnold Rampersad. Callaloo. 9, 1 (Winter 1986), pp. 52–54

Rita Dove has always possessed a storyteller's instinct. In *The Yellow House on the Corner, Museum,* and the forthcoming *Thomas and Beulah,* this instinct has found expression in a synthesis of striking imagery, myth, magic, fable, wit, humor, political comment, and a sure knowledge of history. Many contemporaries share Dove's mastery of some of these, but few succeed in bringing them together to create a point of view that, by its breadth and force, stands apart. She has not worked her way into this enviable position among poets without fierce commitment. . . .

Museum begins with travelogues, which prepare the reader for travel poems that eclipse the personal by introducing overlooked historical detail. "Nestor's Bathtub," a pivotal poem in this respect, begins with the lines "As usual, legend got it all wrong." This announces a dissatisfaction with the conventional ordering of events and an intention to rejuvenate history by coming up with new ways of telling it. In successive poems ("Tou Wan Speaks to Her Husband, Liu Sheng," "Catherine of Alexandria," "Catherine of Siena," "Boccaccio: The Plague Years," and its companion piece, "Fiammetta Breaks Her Peace"), Dove adopts a variety of personae that bear witness to the struggles of victimized women in societies in which men are dubiously perceived as gods.

This strategy continues into the book's second section, though the subjects and personae are primarily male ("Shakespeare Say," "Banneker," "Ike"). . . . As in *The Yellow House*, in *Museum* Dove focuses on characters, and chooses characters to speak through, from the historical rosters of those whose lives have been the stuff of fable. Toward the end of this section, her identification with historical and mysterious male-female consciousness is most complete in "Agosta the Winged Man and Rasha the Black Dove." In this poem she tells the story of a pair of German circus performers, an inscrutable deformed man and an equally inscrutable black woman who dances with snakes. These characters are performers, who like the poet, look at the world in unique ways. . . .

The poem that follows, "At the German Writers Conference in Munich," examines and exploits this preoccupation from another angle. In the poem another art—another way of performing—is described. The calm, stiff characters of a tapestry are not outwardly grotesque as are the characters in the preceding poem. Nevertheless, they appear to be out of step with their woven environment, existing as they do in a world of flowers. The two poems, together, illustrate a brilliant shifting of focus, a looking out of the eyes of characters, then a merciless looking into them.

The third section of *Museum* contains a focusing down of this strategy in a tight group of family poems in which the father is the dominant character. He is perceived by the innocent narrator as the teacher, the bearer of all that is magical in the world. . . . Whether he is making palpable an impalpable taste or miraculously rescuing roses from beetles ("Roses"), or deftly retrieving what is magical from a mistake ("My Father's Telescope"), he is clearly the narrator's mentor, inspiring a different way of meeting the world. . . .

But even in this tender, celebratory section, Dove includes one poem, "Anti-Father," which satisfies her self-imposed demand that she tell all sides of the story. . . . The innocent narrator, not a knowledgeable woman, reverses roles here, contradicting the father but offering magical insight in doing so.

The closing section of Rita Dove's second volume summarizes all that has preceded it, and in two remarkable poems, anticipates *Thomas and Beulah*.

Robert [E.] McDowell. Callaloo. 9, 1 (Winter 1986), pp. 61, 64–66

[*Thomas and Beulah*] engages history, in this case, personal history . . . and refers obliquely to twentieth-century American history, but from the family album snapshot on the cover through the appended "Chronology" (first item: "1900: Thomas born in Wartrace, Tennessee"), we read this book as a family chronicle. However, the poems themselves are not about an individual's *relationship* to her history, nor about the weight of history. They are, more, history allowed to speak for itself. The title page tells us that the "poems tell two sides of a story and are meant to be read in sequence." The history contained in *Thomas and Beulah*, indeed, is found in the unfolding story—or juxtaposed stories—told of the youth, marriage, lives, and deaths of two people. We even forget that the poems are historical, in part because they mix past and present tense, in part because of the frequent use of the past and present progressive, and in part because of the vividness of the characters revealed. . . .

It is worth adding that most of the language in *Thomas and Beulah* could have been spoken by the people whose story is told, which is to say that the poems do not seem to impose on their subjects. Rather, they slowly build a context for the objects, images, and scraps of reported speech and song that appear and keep reappearing. This is an impressive achievement, although it also means that the poems have more power taken together than individually. To give one . . . example: when Thomas watches the "shy angle of his daughter's head," sees his son-in-law swallow, and feels for the first time "like / calling him *Son*" ("Variations on Gaining a Son"), attentive readers confronted only with this poem will recognize the oblique reference to fishing and to the commonplace, "hooking a man." But it is only in the context of the other poems about Thomas, about his own marriage, about his more literal fishing trips (in "Lightnin' Blues" and "One Volume Missing"), and his desire for a son that these lines have their full impact. This is, of course, an appropriate way to reimagine and represent the lives traced in the book, since they are lives not fully examined by those who live them. The marriage of Thomas and Beulah, in particular, is clearly one where communication is tacit, contained precisely in repeated phrases and motions that have gained meaning over the years. The poems recreate both the accretion of meaning and the taciturnity, perfectly right for this subject, although, given other subjects, one might want more.

Lisa M. Steinman. MQR. 26, 2 (Spring 1987), pp. 433, 435

Rita Dove's *Thomas and Beulah*, winner of the 1987 Pulitzer Prize, has a distinctive, ambitiously unified design. It traces the history of two blacks who separately move north, to Ohio, meet and get married in the 1920s, and go on to raise four girls, enduring many vicissitudes before their deaths in the 1960s. Arranged serially and accompanied by an almost essential chronology, the poems, we are told in a note beforehand, are meant to be read in order. Much as Michael Ondaatje has done in his poemlike novel, *Coming through Slaughter*, Dove reconstructs the past through a series of discontinuous vignettes which enter freely into the psyches of the two main characters.

It is important that the poems are arranged chronologically because we often need all the help we can get in clarifying many of the references. Even with the chronology as a guide, the poems sometimes seem unnecessarily obscure and cryptic. More often, however, the difficulty of the work is justifiable because the insights are exactly as subtle as they are oblique. In exploiting the virtues of ellipsis, Dove evidently has faith we will have gumption enough to stare a hole in the page until our minds leap with hers across the gaps. . . .

One of the great strengths of this book is the depth of Dove's sympathetic understanding not only of Beulah but also of Thomas; she manages to convey the inner savor both of Thomas's early ebullience and of his later frustration and despair at not being allowed a part in the world equal to his considerable sensitivity. The mandolin provides him with a creative outlet, but it becomes the bittersweet outlet of the blues. . . .

In her forays into the black vernacular, Dove chooses not to be phonetic; instead, she concentrates on diction and speech rhythm and does so with dialectical pizzazz, as in the conclusion to "Jiving.". . . Here, the juxtaposition of two voices and styles highlights the virtues of both. It's difficult to make such switches in the level of diction while still maintaining a plausible narrative voice; yet Dove most often succeeds. Because she has thoroughly imagined her characters, Dove can handle her vernacular material convincingly from a decided stylistic remove.

Peter Harris. VQR. 64, 2 (Spring 1988), pp. 270–72

The events in *Thomas and Beulah* are narrated in strict chronological order, which is detailed in the appended chronology. The subjection of story time to historical time, unusual in modern narratives, gives Dove's sequence a tragic linearity, a growing sense that what is done cannot be undone and that what is not done but only regretted or deferred cannot be redeemed in the telling. The narrative runs from Thomas's riverboat life to his arrival in Akron and marriage to Beulah, to their children's births, his jobs at Goodyear, his stroke and death. Then the narrative begins again with Beulah: her father's flirtations, Thomas's flirtations and courtship, their marriage, a pregnancy, her millinery work, a family reunion, and her death. In the background, the Depression and the March on Washington mark respectively the trials of the couple's and their children's generations.

The sequence of *Thomas and Beulah* resembles fiction more than it does a poetic sequence—[William] Faulkner's family chronicles in particular. Dove's modernist narrator stands back paring her fingernails like an unobtrusive master or God. The cover shows a snapshot, of Thomas and Beulah presumably, and the volume may be considered as a photo album, or two albums, with only the date and place printed underneath each picture. Thomas and Beulah are probably Rita Dove's grandparents; the book is dedicated to her mother, Elvira Elizabeth, and the third child born to Thomas and Beulah is identified in the chronology as Liza. But whether the couple is actually Rita Dove's grandparents is less important than the fact that all evidence of their relation has been removed. Any choice of genre involves an economy of gains and losses. Objective, dramatic narration—showing rather than telling—has the advantage of letting the events speak for themselves and the disadvantage of dispensing with the problematics of narrative distortion and a camera-eye or God's-eye view. *Thomas and Beulah* tells it like it is and assumes it is like it tells us.

John Shoptaw. In Henry Louis Gates, Jr., ed. Reading Black,
Reading Feminist (New York: Meridian, 1990), pp. 374–75

As a black person living in the predominantly white societies of the Old and New Worlds, having entered an interracial and intercultural marriage (her husband is a German writer), and trying to forge an autonomous poetic voice against the background of a male dominated Euro- and Afro-American literary tradition, Dove has often crossed social and literary boundaries, violated taboos, and experienced displacement, e.g., living "in two different worlds, seeing things with double vision," wherever she has stayed (the United States, Germany, Israel). Talking to Judith Kitchen and Stan Sanvel Rubin about her European experiences which inspired her second book, *Museum*, Dove admits that she had a sense of displacement while she was in Europe, and that she expressed this sense through various characters and situations in *Museum*. She remarks, however, that her stay in Europe broadened her world view and contributed to her growth as a person and an artist. . . . Dove's complex experiences in the United States and abroad (Europe, North Africa, Israel) have affected both her vision and her poetic method. Although she deals with the problems of racism and sexism, she does not adopt the polemical voice of either a black nationalist or a feminist poet, and therefore she does not let indignation, anger, and protest control her verse. Although she focuses on the black experience in many of her works she goes beyond the definition of black literature which reflected the black ideal that prevailed since the late 1960s: "Black literature BY blacks, ABOUT blacks, directed TO blacks. ESSENTIAL black literature is the distillation of black life." Her poem "Upon Meeting Don L. Lee, in a Dream," included in her first book, *The Yellow House on the Corner*, expresses her reaction to the black nationalist aesthetic. The poet Don Lee, one of its major representatives, is described as "always moving in the yellow half-shadows," as a man with "lashless eyes," surrounded by a chorus of chanting women dressed in robes and stretching "beaded arms to him." After setting the stage and introducing the black male poet in a kind of priestly role, Dove creates a dialogue between him and the first-person speaker who is obviously her mouthpiece; and then, through a cluster of surrealistic images, she suggests the decay of the ideology that Don Lee embodies. . . .

By combining fact and fiction, biographical and autobiographical with historical events over a period of sixty years, as well as characters and values from different races and classes (low-class American blacks, middle-class white Americans, French aristocrats, etc.), by identifying with both male (Thomas) and female (Beulah) consciousness, by creating a background of black music, and by describing Southern Thomas's journey north and the wanderings of unemployed men during the Depression, Dove balances opposites, bridges conventional divisions (private-public, white-black, high-folk culture, male-female, rural South-industrial North, low-high class, America-Europe, past-present, etc.), and she transcends boundaries of space and time in *Thomas and Beulah*. Her international characters and settings in *The Yellow House on the Corner*, *Museum*, and *Grace Notes*, the journey motif that runs through them, her references to artists and artifacts since the ancient times, her individual portraits of real or mythical men and women from the United States and other countries, as well as the instances of love, struggle for freedom and dignity, and sensitivity to beauty, but also of violence, disease, decay, and death that she observes everywhere—all of them enable Dove to expand her range of reference even more. She appropriates, defies, subverts, and reconstructs the traditional male-centered poetic discourse to convey her own complex vision. She speaks with the voice of a world citizen who places her personal, racial, and national experience within the context of the human experience as a whole, and celebrates its richness and continuity. She also speaks with the authority of an artist who claims the world's civilizations as her rightful heritage.

Ekaterini Georgoudaki. *Callaloo*. 14, 2 (Spring 1991), pp. 419–20, 429–30

The discipline of writing *Thomas and Beulah*, a family epic in lyric form, required Rita Dove to focus, as never before, her talent for compression. How to get years of her grandparents' joy and anguish into spare lines without presuming to sum up for them; how to telescope distances of place, background, dreams, without narrating—these were some of the problems she solved so brilliantly in that book. The past shed its patina as bits of voice and image shone through to bespeak whole epochs and regions. The book moved us by its understatement, the major ally of compression, and by its sympathetic imagination, that refused to make Thomas and Beulah stereotypes, the mere objects of our pity or nostalgia.

In *Grace Notes* Dove returns to the range of subjects and settings that characterized her first two books (she is remarkably broad in the scope of her references without ever being showy). All the features we have grown to appreciate in this poet arise here in their finest form: descriptive precision, tonal control, metaphoric reach within uncompromising realism. Moreover, she has brought these talents to bear upon a new intimacy and moral depth, served by memory and imagination working together. . . .

The poems of [the second section] deal with being not in its social and autobiographical dimension but in its ontological dimension of origin and destiny, first things and last things, though as always in terms of the local, the familiar. In "Ozone" the poet returns to the dual idea of wound and flight, the hole in the ozone a kind of cosmic wound out of which we yearn to escape, to pursue a star to its vanishing point. Yet we "wire the sky so it won't fall down," comforting ourselves and protecting ourselves from self-annihilating dreams. Section three comes down from this height to explore the poet's present life and her ties to others, especially her young daughter. But the poems of this section are informed by the ultimate questions asked in the section before: what unites us, where does our identity begin and end, what is the meaning we derive from our bodies? . . .

Many of [the poems in the fourth section] take the implicit form of dialogue as they attempt to define a stance toward the world. In "Ars Poetica" she considers one writer's desire to merge with the elemental, another's desire to master it. Her own way of putting herself on the map is to be "a hawk," a traveling "x-marks-the-spot." This attitude reemerges in "Dialectical Romance" where, in arguing against a definition of God she imagines "a program so large there could be no answer except in working it through." In "Stitches," about an accidental gash sewn up in the emergency room, the difference is emotional and within herself—the part that feels pain, experiences alarm and watches the seamstress Fate "pedaling the needle right through," and the part that stands outside and laughs "in stitches" over the ironies of her life. One part of the poet finds the laughter distasteful in the midst of pain . . . it is answered by the part that finds in wit a choice of resistance. . . . The ways we find to rise above our vulnerability, above the wounds we suffer, is Dove's constant theme. How to cope, especially, with prejudice, is the theme of "Arrow," about the poet's response, and that of her students, to the racial stereotyping by an "eminent scholar" in a lecture, and the sexism of the poet he discusses. The arch poet-teacher assures her students "we can learn from this," though she herself is burning from the poison of the scholar's "arrow.". . .

It is to the castoff, the "truly lost," the "lint" of the world that Dove turns in the final section of *Grace Notes*. What vitality is left for Genie, "born too late for *Aint-that-a-shame?*" Quite a lot, it seems, dream of "a breezeway and real nice wicker on some astroturf." For Billie Holliday and women like her, caged canaries, the bitter message is: "If you can't be free, be a mystery." There are grace notes even for the castaways and their cool view from the edge wields a strange kind of power over us, though hardly a power one envies. Zebulun, the wretched Jewish dyer, purifier of purple pigment from juice of snail, cries out to God: "You gave my brother countries; / me you gave the snail! / God answers: / After all / I made them dependent on you / for the snail." This is ambiguous comfort, as is the unwanted, homely (despite the glorious press) revelation of the Roman on the road to Damascus.

In a volume of poems full of resistance, offering ways of coping with and transcending wounds, these last poems have the eerie placidity of surrender; they remind us that our vulnerabilities are real and often untranscendable. The volume which began with black American adolescence, its fears and aspirations, ends in an Old Folks Home in Jerusalem, ancient, mythical desert place where the pangs of difference, worldly hope, even survival are no longer in question. "So you wrote a few poems" almost cuts the wing, coming as it does from the scene of Jews enduring their final suffering. But the last words of the volume are not simply bleak: "Everyone waiting here was once in love." The invisible wings of the human spirit continue to flutter.

Bonnie Costello. Callaloo. 14, 2 (Spring 1991), pp. 434–38

[The] strength of [Dove's] first novel, *Through the Ivory Gate*, is her prose, her ability to describe and suggest. The novel's heroine, Virginia King, is a gifted musician and actress. She takes up a temporary post in an elementary school in her hometown of Akron, Ohio, a homecoming that provokes a flood of memories. As Virginia helps the schoolchildren to develop a puppet show, she remembers her own childhood—the early days in Akron, her family's move to Arizona, her university studies, her love for a fellow student called Clayton.

The story is gentle and the style plain, at its best describing the sky over Lake Erie, a neighbor's homemade pastries, the décor of a restaurant or the face of a long-lost aunt. It is a happy book, about the pleasures of living. The author has a talent for sanguine observation.

The novel moves, as does memory, through association. One chapter starts in Akron, with Virginia playing the cello. She remembers events in class that morning, and is reminded of her own childhood. She remembers lying on a bed and listening to the Arizona rain. She thinks about the children's puppet show, with its magic football and drum majorettes. This cues different memories of becoming the only black drum majorette in her high school. We get flashbacks within flashbacks. . . .

The book deals sparingly but effectively with the issue of race. Virginia becomes a mime artist and puppeteer partly because there are few parts for black actresses. When she gets her first straight-A report card, a white school friend pushes her over and calls her a nigger. The book begins powerfully with the young Virginia's first encounter with a Sambo doll and the confusions this causes her. . . .

These themes of fantasy, childhood, and oppression are brought together, perhaps a touch too explicitly, in a scene toward the end. Virginia dreams she is lecturing on the subject of Sambo to an audience of adult heads screwed onto children's bodies. "The first thing to bear in mind about Sambo," she begins, "is that Sambo is all of us. We all want to make merry, to wear bright colors and sing in the sun all day." The oppression of a race is seen in the context of the oppression of children and of joy.

Geoff Ryman. NYTBR. October 11, 1992, pp. 11–12

EDGELL, ZEE (1941–   )

BELIZE

[Zee Edgell's novel] *Beka Lamb* is a competently written work which in no way reflects the magical realism of its Latin American neighbors. If anything, it is a solid specimen of the traditional novel, employing flashback to recount the sad ending of a likable seventeen-year-old who finds herself pregnant out of wedlock. The villain of the piece is a rather self-satisfied young member of Belize's Hispanic population; the novel's weight is thrown heavily in favor of the black Creoles. Beka's own triumph over her tendency to lie—the declared main action of the novel—does not engage the reader to the same degree as does Toycie's story.

The story of Toycie's fall from virtue is really a frame from which to hang a considerable amount of information about the everyday life of Belize's newly emergent urban middle class, a population still too close to poverty to have developed a set of bourgeois assumptions. Despite Edgell's understandable desire to explain contemporary Belizean events, despite the highly traditional form of the novel, and despite the material of yet another West Indian novel of childhood, *Beka Lamb* could signal a significant change of pace in the West Indian novel because it bypasses what have become the pieties of the times. Beka's engrossment in her milieu calls to mind the novels of Michael Anthony, novels singularly devoid of a sense of estrangement. Anthony's characters are totally integrated West Indians, so absorbed in life's little moments that they bring to West Indian fiction a quality of sweetness rare in the literature of commitment. While Edgell's conservative style may somehow be a function of Belize's position outside the mainstream of West Indian affairs, she cannot be accused of naivete as she has lived in Jamaica, Britain, Nigeria, Afghanistan, Bangladesh, and the United States.

Elaine Campbell. *JCL*. 22, 1 (1987), pp. 142–43

Set within the framework of a colonial society, a society aspiring to independence, *Beka Lamb* examines the dialectical relationship between that society and the individual. The personal stories of the girls Beka and Toycie are used as ways of examining the colonial society. The relationship between Toycie and Emilio in particular suggests the exploitative colonial one. And Beka's journey to self-assurance compares with her country's move to independence. In addition, the traditional ways are shown in conflict with the values promoted by the Church and educational institutions. The result is dramatic change whose impact, emphasized by the constant references to "befo' time" and "tings bruk down," is seen in the disintegrating society, its former wholeness and stability eroded by the colonial experience. But disintegration is only part of the life cycle. Edgell's heroine learns this truth, and by implication independence is therefore a real possibility for her country. . . .

Central to this novel is the close relationship between Beka and Toycie, which not only points up the support that women provide for each other but also reveals the experiences of the adolescent female. Edgell presents both Beka and Toycie as adolescents in the quest for identity. Through them she explores different facets of female adolescent experience—their awakening sexuality, relationships, fantasies, and fears. The friendship between Toycie and Beka defines and charts both girls' growth into and beyond their specifically adolescent crises. Toycie also functions as Beka's alter ego. She lives out things that remain mere possibilities for Beka, showing quite clearly how Beka, like so many things in her country, "could bruk down." Toycie and Beka also seem initially to represent a body-mind dichotomy, but Beka is shown as resolving this split as she moves toward unity. . . .

In *Beka Lamb*, Edgell portrays the importance of adolescent girls' private relationships. And while she admits to the tension that society creates she demonstrates that finally it is the girls' personalities and their means of resolving conflicts that determine their growth. The mother-daughter relationship in its various forms also provides central support for the adolescent. There is a direct relation between its presence and the adolescent's definition of self. In addition, Edgell examines stereotypical female means of coping—emotional and passive. Such ways are shown as negative: heroines who practice them fail to attain wholeness. In contrast, there are strong and independent women who through an active creativity impose their will on the world. Edgell has affirmed that emotionality and passivity are not the only feminine ways of coping.

Beka Lamb offers us a more complex picture of the female adolescent. Through Toycie and Beka, Edgell examines the conflicts she faces with her awakening sexuality and society's increasing expectations. Such expectations are often ambiguous. They acknowledge her visible growth and supposed maturity but not her sexuality. Beka and Toycie are thus most vulnerable in that area. Miss Flo makes oblique references to Beka's sexuality and Miss Ivy's confession helps her. But generally, the adult women remain silent about their daughters' sexuality. And while Edgell does not claim that biology controls a girl's perception of self and the choices she makes (that is, that biology is destiny), she does take into account the pressure society exerts on a woman to conform to its image of femininity, especially during adolescence. Like other women, Beka must confront and surmount these pressures to achieve selfhood.

Lorna Down. *Ariel*. 18, 4 (October 1987), pp. 39–40, 50

Toycie in Zee Edgell's *Beka Lamb* is . . . driven to madness. Toycie, a vibrant, brilliant, ambitious seventeen-year-old is Beka Lamb's best friend. Through Beka's recollection we learn of the childhood pastimes and ambitions of Toycie, a student at St. Cecelia Catholic Academy—a sophisticated high school for girls. From Beka's grandmother, Ivy, we learn that the academy previously accepted only girls from the higher social strata of Belize; thus it is a singular achievement for Creole girls like Beka and Toycie to attend this bastion of educational grandeur controlled by the expatriate Sisters of Charity. In Caribbean life, earning a secondary school certificate is an honor, and earning one from a prestigious secondary school is an immediate passport to a better standard of living. For this reason, relatives, friends, and neighbors take exceptional pride in the Creole girls who attend the academy. In fact, they see this gesture as a step toward the end of the history of discrimination that is associated with the school. Toycie had seen many girls terminate their education at the elementary level; hence, her primary obsession is to graduate from high school and repay her aunt who had reared her since she was three years old. Her other obsession is to promenade along Fort George, admiring the beautiful homes of the wealthy. Toycie has another reason for wanting to stroll by Fort George: her boyfriend, Emilio Villanueva, who attends St. Anthony Jesuit College, works at [a] Fort George hotel. Emilio is a pania; that is, he has a mixture of Maya Indian blood and Spanish blood. Beka dislikes their liaison and warns Toycie about being "involved" with a pania, since panias scarcely ever marry Creoles, but Toycie continues the friendship believing that Emilio loves her and will marry her as he claims. . . . [Regardless] of Beka's disapproval, she continues to be Toycie's steadfast confidante, not once reporting the secret meetings between Toycie and Emilio, especially the nocturnal ones at the cay during the summer vacation.

When Toycie returns to school after the summer vacation, she has lost the gaiety and enthusiasm that seniors display at the beginning of their final year. She seems despondent and distracted. Often she "stares into space in a trance as if waiting for some signal that would restore her to normalcy." She tries to compose herself, but when unable to stifle a vomit while at worship, she is sent home by Sister Virgil.

Later Toycie confides in Beka but refuses to tell her aunt, Miss Eila, that she is pregnant. Yet Miss Eila seems to have surmised the problem for she matter-of-factly remarks about Toycie's illness. . . . Having no one else to turn to, Toycie decides to inform Emilio, thinking that he would marry her. . . . Emilio does not marry Toycie; in fact, he claims that he wouldn't and he couldn't because he could not be sure that after marriage she would be faithful to him—although he had no reason for doubting her fidelity. The pregnant Toycie was expelled from school despite pleas for another chance from her aunt and Beka's father. . . .

Toycie's expulsion triggers the second phase of her decline. The girl who was "so brave, so encouraging to others, whose eyes were usually lively with anticipation of tomorrow's promise" now looks at her friend with dull resignation, too nauseated, too disoriented to recognize or appreciate anyone's concern or sympathy. The girl who formerly spent hours to "titivate" before going on her stroll now sits disconsolately with her hair in disarray. Her blazing spirit now gives way to rocking back and forth in her aunt's chair. . . .

Everyone is saddened by Toycie's condition and departure [to the country]. The effect on Beka is twofold: she is inspired to work harder and she no longer depends on her family's praise as her motivation. Beka wages a personal one-girl vendetta for her friend and when the news arrives that Toycie, after wandering off in a storm, is killed, Beka realizes that now more than ever, she must excel not only for herself, but also for Toycie.

Enid Bogle. *ZNHF*. 4, 1 (Fall 1989), pp. 11–13

[In *Beka Lamb*], published shortly after Belize's independence, the devalorization of colonial modernism and its authority is achieved through an appeal to figures and tropes of difference and ambivalence. As they are represented in language and ideology, such figures express the kind of diversity which according to [Edouard] Glissant allows Caribbean peoples to repossess their historical spaces. In Glissant's words, "Diversity, which is neither chaos nor sterility, means the human spirit's striving for a cross-cultural relationship, without universalist transcendence. Diversity needs the presence of peoples, no longer as objects to be swallowed up, but with the intention of creating a new relationship. Sameness requires fixed Being, Diversity establishes becoming." The colonial power fixes the colonized as objects of labor and/or appendages of the colonizing culture. Rewriting the Caribbean national allegory thus demands a narrative strategy that confronts the objects and historical forces blocking the desire for that diversity that establishes becoming. As a strategy of individual and national identity, ambivalence disperses the fixed sites of colonial cultural production; in semiotic terms, as Julia Kristeva says, it "implies the insertion of history (society) into a text and of this text into history.". . .

[A] novel that begins with its ending often promotes a moment of interpretation which is definite and conclusive; the reader is supposed to follow the incidents related in the flashback from the vantage point and certain knowledge denoted by narrative closure. But this is not the case in *Beka Lamb*: we are not certain that Beka, by winning the coveted essay contest, has initiated the decisive transformation of moral character and social class which her family and community expect. On the contrary, Beka's ostensible transformation is presented by the narrator as if it were merely the subjective (and possibly erroneous) assumption of her family—"It seemed to her family . . ."—a mode of representation clearly intended to create doubts about the given significance of the essay contest and the colonial economy of meaning with which it is associated.

The very notion of a radical shift in Beka's character and position in the community is further undermined by the problematic expression of temporality in the novel. We are told, on one hand, that "before time" (that is, in the past), Beka had no hope of winning the essay contest because "the prizes would go to bakras [whites], panias [mestizos], or expatriates." A new consciousness is hence dawning on Belize, and the Creole majority is now being recognized as a powerful force. On the other hand, however, this "new" consciousness cannot be apprehended except in relation to the past. In fact, as we read the novel and retrace Beka's struggle to establish her identity within the social order of colonialism (represented by the school) and the as yet unrealized dream of national culture (expressed by her grandmother and other nationalists), we begin to realize that the essay contest is loaded with ironic implications. Initially represented as the sign of historical transition—from past to present, Creole to bakra, colony to nation—the essay instead draws our attention to the difficulties of forging new identities and expropriating colonial modernism and its discourse. The essay marks the gap between an unrealized identity and the realities of colonial domination and repression; it becomes a synecdoche of what is referred to euphemistically as "these hard times.". . .

[If] writing after colonialism is posited as a means of mastering the linguistic codes of colonial modernism, it is because the alternative to writing, as Edgell suggests in *Beka Lamb*, is madness or social death. Indeed, in this novel, both Beka and her friend Toycie provide contrasting forms of dealing with displacement: Toycie engages life at its most fundamental and spontaneous level—that of eros and sexuality—and thus triggers the process that leads to the mental institution and her eventual death; Beka strives to master writing, leading to the award that restores her self-esteem. But mastery of writing is not, of course, presented as a simple and singular process of liberation; on the contrary, it is cast as the result of a painful reflection on how the self (and its cultural community) are constituted in, and constitute, language. For even where the facts have been collected, there is still the problem of organizing them into a coherent narrative; it is only when all the disparate parts of the essay have been organized that the self has mastered the appropriated forms of representation. Thus the essay Beka writes is an allegory of her own struggle to rewrite herself in a world dominated by often hostile signifiers. Ironically, once she has won the essay contest she has moved closer to the colonial orb, and hence aggravated her self-alienation in the process that was supposed to pull her out of the prisonhouse of colonialism.

Simon Gikandi. Writing in Limbo: Modernism and Caribbean Literature
(Ithaca, N. Y.: Cornell University Press, 1992), pp. 218–20, 230

EMECHETA, BUCHI (1944–   )

NIGERIA

Buchi Emecheta, an Igbo woman living in London with her five children, has joined the vanguard of contemporary women writers such as Flora Nwapa, [Ama Ata] Aidoo, Grace Ogot, and Bessie Head with the publication of her five novels: *In the Ditch, Second Class Citizen, The Bride Price, The Slave Girl*, and *The Joys of Motherhood*. Currently, she is in the process of writing her sixth novel, *Destination Biafra*, which chronicles the happenings of the Nigerian Civil War. More so than her female predecessors, Emecheta documents the experiences of the modern African woman in her novels. She chronicles their struggle for equality in a male-dominated world.

Formerly, images of African women were drawn exclusively by African men who idealized them in their writings. Their one-dimensional, romanticized images of the African woman, primarily as mother, is contrary to that illustrated by Emecheta in her novels. Rather than simply portraying the African woman symbolically as part of the warm and secure African past, she offers faithful portrayals, patterns of self-analysis and general insights into the female psyche, ignored by, or inaccessible to, African male writers. Emecheta's perspective on African women in Nigerian society is therefore a welcome occurrence. Male writers lack the empathy, sympathy, and consciousness of their female characters' psyche. They do not know what it means to be an African woman in an

African society. This explains why the multidimensional role of African women is not accurately reflected in modern African literature. In any event, the importance of Emecheta's works does not lie in her attempt to address a group or fill a gap. Her writings introduce new themes in African literary history: the emergence of self-conscious feminism—women's liberation and the celebration of the black woman. She is an advocate of women's liberation and is of the opinion that male writers make African women their housemaids or prostitutes in their books. Therefore, "all women suffer oppression and need to be liberated." Emecheta's female characters epitomize the difficulty of being a black woman in a changing Nigerian society, particularly in the early twentieth century. Her novels center around the extraordinary courage and resourcefulness of Nigerian women which often prevent black families from disintegrating. She reports the problems and pleasures of the black female and not only does she include her personal experiences but also those of other women in her home town of Ibuza, Nigeria. It is in this way that the young author writes to raise the images of Nigerian women to a level commensurate with historical truths.

Marie [Linton] Umeh. *PA*. 116 (1980), pp. 190–91

The story of *The Bride Price* is a study of the relationship between the collective traditions of the communal will and Aku-nna's own strength of will (and in this regard she is the fictional counterpart of the autobiographical Adah Obi). This is the central theme on which Emecheta focuses her novel. The result is a tightly organized structure which is a decided improvement over the episodic fitfulness of *In the Ditch* and which fulfills the promise of *Second Class Citizen* where the development, decline, and last-minute salvaging of Adah's individuality provides the narrative with a definite coherence and an element of suspense. In *The Bride Price* the concern with narrative suspense and development occasionally lends itself to the rather melodramatic scenes of Aku-nna's abduction and subsequent elopement. But on the whole, it works to Emecheta's advantage, delineating Aku-nna's growth from an inexperienced and naive childhood into a knowing and rebellious womanhood. The narrative development is heightened by the pervasive sense of a malevolent and increasingly menacing destiny, from the sudden death of Aku-nna's father to her own deathbed terror of an avenging deity. Emecheta's central theme also benefits from the manner in which the tightly controlled narrative flows for the most part through Aku-nna's consciousness and at regular but limited intervals through external viewpoints (of mother, uncle, cousins, and future husband) which focus directly on Aku-nna herself (as daughter, bride-price bait, age-group member, and wife respectively). Within this subjective context Emecheta's narrative presents both the communal will and Aku-nna's personality simultaneously by emphasizing the manner in which Aku-nna grows up into womanhood. Her growth is, simultaneously, the development of her own personality and will, and her perception of the rituals, the values, and the institutions through which her community celebrates its traditions and exercises its will. In turn, these rituals and their attendant sense of proper form permeate Emecheta's narrative form with a definite sense of proportion. Her fictive structure is beginning to become a direct symptom of her thematic concerns.

Lloyd W. Brown. *Women Writers in Black Africa*
(Westport, Conn.: Greenwood Press, 1981), pp. 49–50

Now that Emecheta has won acclaim, she has determined to make London her home base and writing her main endeavor. She faces, therefore, the constant problem for the expatriate and exiled writer. What authentic background can she draw from her fiction? What audience shall she address? Her personal experience in contemporary Nigeria becomes increasingly remote. In 1980 she accepted a fellowship at Calabar, which she uses as a locale for *Double Yoke*, a brief college novel in which the male protagonist, Ete Kamba, cannot overcome his traditional, adverse reaction to the knowledge that his girl has given herself before marriage, even to him. Emecheta met some absurd criticism for centering her novel on a male protagonist.

In her latest novel, *The Rape of Shavi*, Emecheta undertakes a futuristic science-fiction type of narrative. A planeload of British scientists seeking escape from an "inevitable" nuclear holocaust is grounded in a traditional African country. The technological and economic changes they provoke leave the African nation much worse off than before. A return to past traditionalism for either group, however, is not satisfactory either.

In 1982 Emecheta published her major work to date, *Destination Biafra*. Different from any of her others, it is larger and more substantive. Here she presents neither the life story of a single character nor the delineation of one facet of a culture, but the whole perplexing canvas of people from diverse ethnic groups, belief systems, levels of society—all caught in a disastrous civil war. Though she herself at the time was a student in London, out of the fray, she has compiled family histories, eyewitness accounts, and political documents to tell this story. Her personal anguish at the loss of many relatives and friends—particularly of an aunt and uncle who died trying to escape the bombing of Ibuza, and an eight-year-old namesake who, with a tiny sister, died of starvation—is apparent. Her outrage at the greed, corruption, and sadism of many of the antagonists on all sides fitly demonstrates the illogicality of seeking to explain the war. She felt the book "had to be written." In relief, she wrote: "I am glad this work is at last published. It is different from my other books, the subject is, as they say, 'masculine,' but I feel a great sense of achievement in having completed it."

Charlotte [H.] and David [K.] Bruner. *WLT.* 59, 1 (Winter 1985), p. 11

Double Yoke is a love story told in the blues mode. The story laments a loss; yet it sings a love song. Its theme of the perilous journey of love, is a major preoccupation in author Buchi Emecheta's dramatic work. On an equally fundamental level, *Double Yoke* describes the tragic limitations of Nigerian women in pursuit of academic excellence and the anxiety of assimilation. Similar to her early novels, *Double Yoke* assesses the predicament of women in Africa. By describing the sexual and cultural politics in Nigerian society, Emecheta again campaigns against female subjugation and champions her case for female emancipation. Nko, the author's intellectually oriented heroine, provides some insight into the psyche of modern African women who are encumbered by traditional African misconceptions attached to the university-educated female.

Firstly, *Double Yoke* is a love story but with tragic implications. Buchi Emecheta is at her best in describing the anxiety lovers often experience because of mutual distrust at one time or another and the inability to reconcile their difficulties. According to the author, love, if betrayed, is directly responsible for the misery that afflicts the human soul. The tale of the terrifying journey of the possibilities and failures of love is then at the dramatic center of *Double Yoke*. . . .

There is satire too in *Double Yoke*. As well as the clash between the old and the new, there is a clash between the genuine and the false. In the character of Reverend Professor Ikot, pretentious and immoral university professors in Nigeria are attacked. Ikot, like the true trickster figure, is shrewd, cunning, and loquacious. Posing as a religious leader and educator, he dupes others but is rarely duped himself. His strong archetypal appeal, ability to outwit others and articulate his ideas enable him to exercise power and control over people. Even when caught in the act, he exploits the situation and emerges a winner. Note how he handles his confrontation with Ete Kamba in one of the most dramatic scenes in the book. Playing on the intelligence of his people, he fabricates a story knowing full well what the policemen want to hear. Emecheta, pointing to the exploitation of students on university campuses and the abuse of Christian teachings, protests against the corrupt, opportunistic nature of contemporary Nigerians. Rather than working towards the acquisition of souls or imparting knowledge to students, Ikot preoccupies himself with "getting a piece of the cake." Almost risking his chances of being the next vice chancellor at Unical, he shamelessly destroys the lives of both Nko and Ete Kamba.

Finally, Ete Kamba exemplifies primacy of the group ethic over individual self-interests, which is so embedded in traditional African society, by sympathizing with Nko upon hearing of her father's death. Ete Kamba begins to realize that despite their inexperience they have to resolve their problems for no other reason than because they love each other. Ete Kamba and Nko choose to grow from their blunders and bear their double burden together. Ete Kamba's deep feeling of affection for Nko, despite a certain myopia which blinds him to manifest ambiguities within himself, helps him to understand that no one knows very much about the life of another. This ignorance becomes vivid, if you love another.

This ending is not altogether convincing even in these modern times. It then becomes obvious that author Emecheta is ascribing her personal modes of thought even though they may be way ahead of her audience. Most of us are still very conservative. In the fusing of the old and the new traditional African society's intolerance of one's right to choose one's destiny rather than consider the common good seems to be strengthened. In spite of this, *Double Yoke* is quite entertaining while it explores several political and social issues common in African literature. Emecheta's simplicity of style covers her exploration of these important issues in strikingly new and provocative twists.

Marie Linton Umeh. In Carole Boyce Davies and Anne Adams Graves, eds.
Ngambika: Studies of Women in African Literature (Trenton, N. J.:
Africa World Press, 1986), pp. 173, 178–79

In 1980, Emecheta put out her second children's book, *Nowhere to Play*. The plot is based on a story by her twelve-year-old daughter Christy and involves the same family that appears in *Titch the Cat*. However, this story takes place five years earlier in the London public housing estate, near Regent's Park in Rothay's Albany Street. Like the wife Emecheta portrayed in her second novel, *Second Class Citizen*, the children of the housing project are second-class juveniles with no place to play. In each of the five chapters, the little neighborhood gang, made up of Irish Catholic, East Indian, and Nigerian children, seeks an open area nearby in which to play. Each time they are refused or ejected. Their mothers have forbidden them to cross the busy streets to go to the park after a car accident to Dan and a near miss for June occurred the year previous. So the summer holidays find the group "Chased from the Green" in chapter two, "Expelled from the Crown Bushes" in chapter three, "Knocking Dollies Out of Bed" in chapter four (after they ran through the flats knocking on all the doors), and finally "Frightened from the Church" in chapter five.

The incidents are commonplace. The adults' rejection of the children is neither unkind nor malicious. The youngsters are an irresponsible group, naturally needing space and freedom to express their high spirits. They care for and tease each other. Little Irish Moya lags behind the others, hampered by her skirt, worn because her father doesn't believe women should wear trousers. She shrieks at a bee, and the others have to go back to cajole her to follow the group again. "Were you trying the Tarzan call?" they tease.

Emecheta's easy style and natural dialogue are well suited to these stories. The children portrayed are loving, caring, and uninhibited. Emecheta is neither sentimental nor poignant. The children do need a place to play; the adults do need their own privacy as well. But there is not the threat of crime, sadism, drugs, or pornography. The children are healthy, lively, and lovable. Their adventures bring a chuckle not a grimace.

Charlotte [H.] Bruner. *AfrSR.* 29, 3 (September 1986), p. 135

The novels of Buchi Emecheta, an Igbo woman writer, explore the varying definitions of womanhood and motherhood as experienced by her women protagonists in Nigerian society. A fundamental purpose of womanhood, [that is] to flower into motherhood, is rooted in the paradoxical relationships of both the traditional structures of patriarchy and the modern structures of urbanization. Emecheta is concerned equally with the dual issue of the biological control of women whereby sexuality and the ability to bear children are the sole criteria which define womanhood; and the economic control of women within the colonially-imposed capitalist system whereby women are placed at a disadvantage graver than they had faced in precolonial economic structures. Capitalism which brought the mixed blessings of urban development and modern ways of life, did not change traditionally accepted modes of oppression, such as bride-price and polygamy, and, in fact, often reinforced them. . . .

Emecheta's women protagonists are depicted as belonging at every stage of their lives to some male figure—as a female child grows from girlhood to womanhood to motherhood, she is controlled and owned by her father, her husband, then her sons. Her biology defines her womanhood; only as a mother is she culturally believed to be a complete human being. Mothering as a concept, involving such invisible tasks as household chores, is inculcated throughout the period of her socialization. She learns to make sacrifices for her brothers and to look after the younger children. In Igbo society it is the father and not the mother who is believed to be one's "life, shelter" remarks the narrator in Emecheta's novel *The Bride Price.* . . .

In Emecheta's next and finest novel, *The Joys of Motherhood*, womanhood is defined exclusively as motherhood. The chapter headings interestingly trace the ups and downs of the protagonist Nnu Ego's fate, all revolving around her success and failure as a mother: "The Mother," "The Mother's Mother," "The Mother's Early Life," "First Shocks of Motherhood," "A Failed Woman" and so on to the last chapter, "The Canonized Mother." Emecheta vividly charts Nnu Ego's history as mother starting from Nnu Ego's mother, developing into Nnu Ego's present life consumed by demands of constant childbearing, culminating in her death at forty. By the conclusion of the novel one recognizes the irony of the title—the joys of motherhood are experienced by Nnu Ego as the sorrows of motherhood. Emecheta seems to find no escape for women from the bonds of biology.

Ketu H. Katrak. *JCL.* 22, 1 (1987), pp. 159, 163, 166–67

[In] *The Joys of Motherhood*, more than in any of her other novels so far, Buchi Emecheta achieves success in her handling of her theme and language both of which are characterized in the tradition of African narrative art, by precision, subtlety, and a sense of inviolable mission. *The Joys of Motherhood* is not only an ironic commentary on the destinies of African womanhood, it is also a parable on the misplaced values of life in general in Africa as elsewhere. The irony becomes more biting as the story progresses. Nnu Ego has placed all her hope for joy and success in her children, yet she is continually disappointed. The final irony in the novel is devastating. Directly contrasting with what society and Nnu Ego's own beliefs have promised her, she finds no joy in her grown children. The spoiled boys have become selfish, egotistical men, due in large part to Nnu Ego's own attitudes toward her male children. Nnu Ego is given a fancy funeral, but it is too late. While dying, as in her life, she did not have the support or comfort of her children. . . .

Through an examination of imagery, figurative language, omniscient commentary and irony it is possible to understand the growth of Emecheta as a writer in her three novels: *The Bride Price, The Slave Girl*, and *The Joys of Motherhood*. Buchi Emecheta presents the plight of the African woman in a culture

involved in a clash between traditional society and Western influence. In spite of
the author's pessimism as an artist, and despite the stereotyped male characters,
these novels exhibit strong artistry which makes Buchi Emecheta one of the best
storytellers in modern Africa.

Ernest N. Emenyonu. *JCL.* 23, 1 (1988), pp. 140–41

Emecheta's interest in the story of the slave woman dates at least from the time
she was writing *The Bride Price*, as passing reference is made to a similar incident. However, it was not until *The Joys of Motherhood* that Emecheta discovered the possibility of fully integrating the story into the larger narrative, for
although the story is told in detail in *The Slave Girl*, the incident itself is only a
minor character's recollection of a brutal event that she witnessed in her youth.
Nonetheless, the slave woman's story is not extraneous to the meaning of *The
Slave Girl*. The image of woman as slave pervades the novel, and it is the struggle of its heroine, Ojebeta, to come to terms with her bondage, to accommodate
herself to the fact that "all her life a woman always belonged to some male,"
that provides much of the biting irony that is so characteristic of all of
Emecheta's work. In addition, as will be shown, the slave woman's story does
serve as a paradigm for much of the female experience in the novel, although
this seems to occur at the level of subconscious artistry.

This practice of experimenting with an idea before fully developing it
appears to be one that Emecheta has adopted as part of her creative strategy. In
The Bride Price, with the same kind of casualness with which she inserts the
slave woman's story into *The Slave Girl*, she introduces the *ogbanje* myth of
the Igbo into her text. This she seizes on in *The Slave Girl*, making it the
novel's single most important source of energy. However, even with *The Bride
Price* a careful consideration of the function of this myth in its creative adaptation is essential to an understanding and appreciation of the work. The heroines of both novels are identified as *ogbanje*, the Igbo term for spirit-children,
children believed to be destined to die and be reborn repeatedly to the same
mother unless a means can be found to break the cycle. In its cultural form the
ogbanje myth is a "myth of infant mortality" common to many West African
societies. In *The Bride Price* Emecheta translates *ogbanje* to mean "a 'living
dead,'" and in both novels she uses the ambiguous status of such children to
represent the state of her sex in a society that denies the female any measure of
self-determination.

In *The Slave Girl*, with evident conscious intent, Emecheta employs this
image as her archetype of female experience. In addition, the *ogbanje* myth
determines the form of the novel, the subgenre to which it belongs. *The Slave
Girl* is a *bildungsroman*, but one of a peculiarly female type: a story of entrapment. Ojebeta's journey through life is a journey from autonomy and self-assertion into dependency and abnegation, from the freedom and fullness of girlhood
into the slavery and self-denial of womanhood. On the figurative level of meaning, it is an *ogbanje*, "a 'living dead,'" that Ojebeta is to become.

Florence Stratton. *RAL.* 19, 2 (Summer 1988), pp. 147–48

Emecheta has been rightly identified as having perpetuated and reinforced certain negative stereotypes about Igbo culture and Africans in her writing. This is perhaps the symbolic equivalent of the false self, an attitude which both revenges hurt feelings about the mother through attacking her culture and makes peace with the new and alien environment. In *The Slave Girl* Ojebeta asks, after her mother's death, "Why did she leave me behind with no one to look after me?" She is sold into domestic servitude by her brother (a story which Emecheta identifies as her own mother's in *Head above Water*), and there follows the story of her growth to maturity in the household of "Ma" Palagada. There are many times when the mother role becomes a crucial element in relations between Ojebeta and the world: from the opening question of Okoline at Ma Palagada's market stall, "Where is your mother?," to the promise of Ojebeta's husband-to-be, to be father to her as she will be mother to him. As a result of the shift from one home to another, because of her mother's death and the selling, Ojebeta must "learn to be somebody else." The false self is created for the false mother, to hide the real self which can no longer grow in harmonious relation to the real mother.

Elaine Savory Fido. In Susheila Nasta, ed. *Motherlands*
(New Brunswick, N. J.: Rutgers University Press, 1992), p. 340

[In *The Family*] Emecheta returns to the London black immigrant milieu that she knows so well, but for the first time the main character is not a Nigerian but a West Indian. The theme is incest, and although this is new in Emecheta's work, it lends itself to the well-known scenario of girls and women oppressed by men and fighting for self-respect. The book starts off in Jamaica. Gwendolen is left behind with Granny, as first her father and later her mother leave for the "Moder Kontry" and settle in London. While in Granny's care, Gwendolen is sexually assaulted by Uncle Johnny, who misuses his position as old family friend. The village blames Gwendolen, but luckily her family sends for her, and she goes to London. Her arrival in London gives Emecheta the opportunity to describe immigrant slum conditions through eyes that are innocent of the social meaning of such observations. Gwendolen's family is at the bottom of the social scale, illiterate and unable to cope with the complexities of British society, but they are surviving and gaining pleasure and support from a primitive church community. Granny dies and the mother goes back to Jamaica; during her absence the father starts an incestuous relationship with Gwendolen, who is sixteen. She becomes pregnant, but she also meets a white boy and starts a sexual relationship with him. The outcome of all this is optimistic if slightly confusing. The father commits suicide; the mother is partially reconciled with her daughter. Gwendolen lives with the baby in a council flat and is happy, and the boyfriend remains a friend, despite the shame of the paternity of the baby. This modern ending rests on a new set of relationships formed on the basis of personal choice rather than on blind acceptance of the established pattern of race and family relationships. There seems to be an implicit suggestion that this alternative mode of social organization might avoid a repeat of the experiences of the main character.

Despite variations and contradictions in Emecheta's work, critics—both approving and disapproving—tend to be drawn to her novels for their ideological content. Her criticism of aspects of African cultural tradition invites the charge of being a traitor to her culture, and her feminism, though mild in Western eyes (she refuses to be called a feminist), has enraged some male African critics to a vitriolic attack on her books, which they claim misrepresent Igbo society. . . . As a role model for other women she is important, and, despite certain stylistic limitations, she represents a new and vigorous departure in fiction about women in and from Africa.

Kirsten Holst Petersen. In Bernth Lindfors and Reinhard Sander, eds. *Dictionary of Literary Biography.* 117 (1992), pp. 164–65

FARAH, NURUDDIN (1945–   )

SOMALIA

The title [of Nuruddin Farah's first novel, *From a Crooked Rib*] is taken from a Somali traditional proverb: "God created Woman from a crooked rib; and any-one who trieth to straighten it, breaketh it." The proverb is well known to Ebla, and the novel traces her progress as experiences teach her its implications and, finally, its limitations (no doubt a man coined it). Even before the novel begins, she has made her first steps towards thinking and deciding for herself, and has run away from her grandfather, despite her sense of duty and perhaps love, or pity, for him—something unheard of in the nomadic, pastoral society in which she has grown up. . . . Like a Jane Austen heroine, and many others too, she is endowed with qualities of mind and disposition which distinguish her from everyone around her and for which no explanation is given. She is just innately exceptional: "She thought of many things a woman of her background would never think of." She wants her actions to correspond to the meaning of her name, Ebla: graceful. . . .

In transferring from the crude but time-honored selfishness of her igno-rant grandfather to the knowing, modern selfishness of the city, Ebla unwit-tingly tests her ambition to be "graceful" to the uttermost. Against a (by now) familiar background of squalor, corruption, double-crossing, and crass greed, she succeeds in mating innocence with experience, and constructs a scheme of self-reliance under which both she and others benefit (not profit) from her goodness of nature. She may have made little headway in the writ-ing of her name, but she has learned to articulate her principles, if only to herself. . . .

It has become something of a cliché to praise Farah's ability to portray female sensibility "from the inside," and certainly the plight of women in an anachronistic society is one of his chief preoccupations, but the remarkable achievement in his account of Ebla is the access it gives us into that particular kind of mind, irrespective of sex: a mind in the process of self-formation. It is in the later novels, set in the postrevolution era, that the portraits of individuals are juxtaposed with the portraits of a society in the process of self-deformation.

D. R. Ewen. In G. D. Killam, ed. The Writing of East and Central Africa
(London: Heinemann, 1984), pp. 194–96

The African writer who has done the greatest justice to female existence in his writing, in the number of female characters he projects and the variety of roles accorded them as well as in the diversified attitudes toward life represented, is the Somali author Nuruddin Farah. The perspective from which Farah projects his women is almost unique within the context of African creative writing. With the possible exception of [Sembène] Ousmane and [Ayi Kwei] Armah, whose women possess some vision on which they base their actions, Farah seems virtually alone among African writers in depicting the progress which women have made within the constricting African social landscape. Problems there may be, and for some they are insurmountable. Nevertheless, a good many women are succeeding in scaling the hurdles; and Farah exhibits them, together with their achievements and the challenges with which they are confronted. So pervasive and consistent is his espousal of the female cause that he has been described [by Kirsten Holst Peterson] as "the first feminist writer to come out of Africa in the sense that he describes and analyzes women as victims of male subjugation."

Farah's championing of the cause of women is part of his crusade against tyranny and victimization not just of women, but of all who are denied their legitimate rights—social and political, private and public. . . . With his novels *From a Crooked Rib, A Naked Needle, Sweet and Sour Milk*, and *Sardines*, we are introduced to yet a new trend in the large corpus of modern African creative writing, particularly the novel. The central feature of this new trend is the demythification of the traditional and communal concept of African life, the generally glorified African past, which overidealized the beauty, dignity, and excellence of African culture. Farah, like [Cyprian] Ekwensi and [Wole] Soyinka (in his novels), is completely immersed in the present. His novels offer an incisive picture of contemporary African realities compounded with vestiges of tradition and elements of modernism. He sees his function as the molding of opinion (through authentic information) against social and political oppression. He champions the cause of individual freedom and exposes such aberrations as nepotism, misused tribal allegiances, female suppression, and stifling materialism, which are responsible for the debasement of humanity and the standard values of the modern African. . . . *From a Crooked Rib* discusses the feminine plight and the general odds which weigh against the female in a traditional Islamic cultural environment. The first two books of his proposed trilogy, *Sweet and Sour Milk* and *Sardines*, give prominent places to women and highlight the repressive and horrifying aspects of the Somali military regime. . . .

The realistic feature of Farah's portrayal of women is that they are seen to take active part in various forms of life around them. Even when they are cast in the traditional mold, like Qumman [in *Sweet and Sour Milk*] or Idil [in *Sardines*], they are active in those areas where they are permitted to operate. Qumman's solicitousness over her dying son and her decision about drugs and medication clearly indicate that she is a vital element in the Keynaan household and in Somali society. She organizes the religious rituals involved with Soyaan's funeral rites, arranging for the presence of the sheikhs and watching over the corpse. More than this, Farah illuminates the changing role of women in a changing society. He even shows some of the men discussing the plight of women. Both Soyaan and Loyaan [in *Sweet and Sour Milk*] advocate a new relationship between men and women which will recognize woman's essential humanity. For such a commitment to the cause of women, Nuruddin Farah is unique among African creative writers.

[Juliet] I. Okonkwo. *WLT.* 58, 2 (Spring 1984), pp. 217, 221

Farah's political novels have great relevance for the growing reaction against the debilitating developments in most postindependence African societies. Thematically, they are significant not only in their Somali or African context, but also in all societies where oppressive regimes have become entrenched. In an age in which people have become more politically conscious, national politics have progressively assumed more complex dimensions in the African continent, and Farah's novels present an incisive picture of contemporary politics and politicians. He leaves one in no doubt about his attitude to the maneuverings of the Jomo Kenyattas, the Idi Amins, the Bokassas, and the Siyaad Barres of Africa. Although his novels manipulate a deep political consciousness, he is careful not to adopt an ideological stance as Ngugi [wa Thiong'o], [Ayi Kwei] Armah, [Wole] Soyinka, or Sembène Ousmane have done. He seems committed to the mirroring of the foibles, cruelties, and imperfections of men in society; and this has contributed to his success. . . .

Sweet and Sour Milk and Sardines present the terror and inhumanity which are the hallmarks of a tyrannical and dictatorial fascist state. The novels register with suffocating intimacy the brutality, suspicion, [and] mental and physical degradation which are consequent upon unstable totalitarian governments operated by megalomaniacs with a lust for unbridled power. In Sweet and Sour Milk, the General, who is also the head of state, had declared that he is the country's constitution, and possesses the right to pass laws and sign decrees at will. The General employs all the resources he can muster to keep the people in abject subjection and a state of humiliation. There is no longer the tragicomedy of revolutionary rhetoric in the midst of gross underdevelopment, as found in Farah's previous novel, A Naked Needle. A Naked Needle had quietly registered the revolution ushered in by a bloodless coup.

Juliet I. Okonkwo. Africa Today. 32, 3 (1985), pp. 57–58

In Sweet and Sour Milk, the opening novel of his trilogy, Farah shows the "fine ear of the people" put to sinister use. When the novel opens, Loyaan realizes that the recent death of his twin brother was not a natural one. Soyaan had written and kept in safe keeping a secret memorandum entitled "Dionysius's Ear." In it Soyaan seeks to discredit the military dictator, known as the General, who rules the Somalia of Farah's novels. The General's despotic methods are compared to those of Dionysius the Elder who controlled Syracuse in the fourth century B.C. Dionysius had a cave dug in the shape of the human ear where he kept those who resisted him. When they whispered their secrets to each other, their words were carried along underground passages to the ears of chosen listeners. Soyaan argues that the General "has had an ear service of tyranny constructed" and that he has selected illiterates as "ear servants.". . .

In Sardines, the middle novel of the trilogy, Dulman, who as singer and actress is an exponent of the oral, admits that she has been caught (her name implies that she is a victim) between oral and written forces. Her early success was the result, she believes, of the Somali attachment to their oral traditions. "One can communicate," she says, "with the hearts of Somalis only through their hearing faculties." Dulman distrusts the written word which she associates with the General's era. He "made his people read and write" and she becomes his victim when her name is written on a wall.

Farah explores different responses to the spoken and written word throughout his trilogy but never more so than in *Close Sesame*. Here the transition from an oral to a written society defines the historical background for his central character. Deeriye, the sixty-nine-year old protagonist of *Close Sesame*, has been a freedom fighter all his life. Born and raised [a] devout Muslim in the Ogaden, he was imprisoned when young and newly married for defying the Italian colonial power. In 1972, the year Somalia became officially literate, Deeriye was imprisoned again, but this time for defying the enemy within, for openly criticizing the first public executions ordered by the General.

Fiona Sparrow. *JCL*. 24, 1 (1989), pp. 165–66

Close Sesame is the third book in the trilogy *Variations on the Theme of an African Dictatorship*. The connecting theme in the novels is arbitrary power, that of the president, the police state, or the patriarchal family, as seen by some of the oppressed, young intellectuals, or women. In the third book, the approach is paradoxically centered on an old man, a traditional and pious character, and from this unexpected angle, the debate on the legitimacy of rebellion against an unjust ruler will take a new dimension. Through him, time and history will be the main subjects of *Close Sesame*, as well as giving shape and texture to a complex narrative technique.

Close Sesame being part of a trilogy, this in itself gives a temporal dimension to the experience of reading, as we meet again characters who have matured or changed from *Sweet and Sour Milk*, *Sardines*, and even *From a Crooked Rib*. The other novels, set in the contemporary world and in a recognizable political system revolved around fictitious events. This time, fictitious elements are secondary to the urgent choices to be made in a context anchored in reality with dates and known facts. By examining how fiction and historical facts are organized and balanced in the book, we can see how the scope and craft of Farah as a novelist are evolving and also how the text can function as fiction *and* comment on Somalia's history, past and present, for its various readers. . . .

In its treatment of history, *Close Sesame* is committed, but not didactic. The novel gives us too much a sense of the complexity of human interaction for that. Farah in his exile of thirteen years writes to his people, clearly stressing the need for reflection and action. Yet the book, with its direct historical references, far from being a pamphlet, is more a meditation on time and history. The subject is Somalia, but the scope of the book can be extended to the whole of postcolonial Africa. It can be read also, more generally, as a dramatization of the human consciousness of the past and of time fleeing. The subject is very ambitious, but in presenting a protagonist who was a national hero and is a mystic, the book presents us both with a sense of eternity as felt in repeated moments of prayers, and of the sequences of human conflicts and achievements. Some of the best passages, blending the awareness of the minutiae of daily life

and the feel that there is an overall meaning to human endeavor . . . are passages
of poetry, close to the poetical vision and rhythm of the great oral intertexts.

Jacqueline Bardolph. *JCL.* 24, 1 (1989), pp. 193, 205–6

With this sweeping gesture of irreverence ["Living begins when you start
doubting everything that came before you."] Nuruddin Farah announces his
break with the past in the epigraph to his novel, *Maps*. Farah focuses the cryptic
iconoclasm of Socrates's "everything" on the ambiguity surrounding the gender
assignation of his novel's protagonist, Askar, and the uncertainties about the
integrity of the boundaries that define the nation state, Somalia. These unstable
categories of gender and nationality are situated in a contrapuntal relationship,
so that each term, in the course of the novel's development, comes to subvert or
complicate the meaning of the other. . . .

   [The] transformation of the anti-imperialist struggle in Africa into a
nationalist movement exacerbated a crisis of individual and collective identity
that is staged in the African novel. Critics have seen these two levels of trauma
in terms of an allegorical correspondence between the psychic crisis of the
(usually educated) individual and the sociopolitical crisis of the modern nation
state. However, I think we can also read the crisis of individual identity as a crisis of gender and sexual identities that parallels and intersects with the sociopolitical manifestations of disorder, and it is this process of destabilization that
Farah's *Maps* enacts. Farah's refusal to accept the categories of gender and
nation as sacrosanct or independent of each other is not without precedent in
modern African literature. Novelists writing as early as Camara Laye and from
ideological perspectives as divergent as Ngugi [wa Thiong'o] and [Chinua]
Achebe, [Wole] Soyinka and [Ayi Kwei] Armah, can be seen as contributors to
a debate about the efficacy of an identity built around contested "natural" categories when read from the vantage point of Farah's text. Conversely, the ways
in which these writers have approached the question of identity elucidates
Farah's method and the context for his concern in *Maps*. . . .

   Farah is unremitting in his insistence that there can be no easy certainties
or identities in the Somali situation or about the historical events that have produced it. At every turn in the narrative we are challenged to call our assumptions into question: about imperialism (the "imperial" powers in the Somali
conflict today are other African countries); about our sense of the "natural" justice of the nationalist cause, even where a nation state like Somalia can boast a
specific rather than generic identity. Ultimately Farah calls into question the
most cherished myths of modern African identity—from the "natural" moral
superiority of oral pre-technological cultures over literate cultures (Ethiopia has
had a written tradition for centuries, the Somali language had no orthography
until 1972); to the unquestionable nature of ethnic or nationalist loyalties, and
the inevitability of certain gender distinctions. . . .

   Farah's destabilization of national and sexual boundaries forces a remap-
ping of the terrain that would take more fully into account the complexity of the
modern nation state in Africa. In the process, the evocation of "traditional"

truths as the paradoxically static yet organic point of departure for the nation state is replaced by a sense of the dynamic interaction and internal contradictions of both the traditional and the modern in today's African nation. Such a strategy could in [Mikhail] Bakhtin's terms truly challenge a Western paradigm of linearity and consolidation; not merely by endlessly pulling out the deconstructionist's rug from under the feet of the dominant/imperial culture, but by confronting and accepting the way in which any act of identity within human culture situates itself in relation to the fluctuating social forces that constitute its specific historical moment.

Farah's text offers no answers, but it challenges us to resist the reflexive urge to pin down a single version of the African reality as "true" without first attempting to take seriously the conflicts, tensions, and absences inherent in any narrative of the past or present. His stance makes it possible to reread many of the earlier narratives of the nationalist era in ways that escape the paternalism inherent in Western notions of "otherness," as well as the uncritical assertion of essence that underlies much of the discourse around nationalism and sexualities in modern African fiction.

Rhonda Cobham. RAL. 22, 2 (Summer 1991), pp. 83–84, 94–96

Nuruddin Farah announced the imminent arrival of his novel *Gifts* in 1986, shortly after the publication of his extraordinary novel of the Ogaden War, *Maps*. However, readers then had to wait (surprisingly, for this prolific novelist who had published six novels in fifteen years) until 1992 for the book's African publication, by a Zimbabwean press, and until 1993 for its European distribution. . . .

Farah's new novel is, first and foremost, a love story. Duniya, a twice-married thirty-five-year-old single parent, slowly succumbs to the loving gift offerings of the once-married Bosaaso, recently returned from America. Duniya is that familiar figure in Farah's fiction: the Somali woman imprisoned by patriarchal Islamic tradition, her position negotiated by men. At the outset of her marital career she is herself a "gifted" property, given by her father in a customary marriage to a man three times her age, and one of the subsequent "givens" of her destiny is to be controlled by the uncles, half-brothers, and husbands whose charge she is in and in whose houses she is temporarily accommodated. Woman, as she says, is a "homeless person." Duniya moves from her father's house into her aging husband's and from there into a tenancy to the journalist-landlord Taariq, who makes her his live-in companion and then his wife, and who turns out to be a drunken and demanding husband. After the divorce from Taariq, she takes a tenancy to her petulant half-brother Shiriye, but she quarrels with his wife and moves out to live with Bosaaso. Even the alternative pied-à-terre provided by her expatriated brother Abshir at the end of the book to help her preserve her independence is but another male gift; and as gifts have conditions and built-in dependencies, Duniya has grown wary and distrustful of them and has cultivated a habit of looking them in the mouth.

The personal story is foregrounded, however, against a larger social and political canvas and opens out into the wider perspective of international gifts from First to Third World countries, each chapter ending with a newspaper snippet about American and United Nations aid to famine-stricken nations in the Horn and other parts of Africa. Political gifts to nations, like personal gifts to people, bind together donor and recipient in ways which change their relationship. Either may be given with the best or worst of motives and results. They may express affection, compassion, loyalty, or penance; meet contractual obligations; assert superiority and dominance or create dependency; or angle to get something in return, in the hope (though hardly in the case of Africa) that yesterday's recipients will become tomorrow's donors. And since shortages both of food at the national level and of love at the domestic one are man-made (famine, the result of maladministration, "is a trick up the powerful man's sleeve"), one effect of outside aid to remedy them may be to bolster corrupt power and influence, whether of an Ethiopian emperor or a domestic patriarch. . . .

[Death] notwithstanding, *Gifts* is a sunny and radiant novel, its gentle, teasing humor a welcome relief after the dark menace and shrill psychological agonies of the *Dictatorship* trilogy, and its disciplined clarity of style refreshing after the somewhat mannered esoterics of *Maps*. This is Farah's first African-published book, and it is clearly aimed at a broader and more African-based readership; thus the learned epigraphic allusions to Western literature which open the chapters in the earlier books have been replaced by captions briefly summarizing the events that follow. This is a new, different Farah, interspersing his narrative with the familiar poetic dream literature and oral folklore of Somali tradition but in a much more accessible form than before. *Gifts* is a poetically evocative as well as (politically) a mildly provocative work, and is full of unexpected echoes, startling insights, and subtle quirks of characterization that will continue to delight Farah's readers.

Derek Wright. WLT. 68, 1 (Winter 1994), pp. 195–96

FAUSET, JESSIE (1882–1961)

UNITED STATES

Without polemicizing, [Jessie] Fauset examines [the] antagonism [of social conventions], criticizing the American society which has institutionalized prejudice, safeguarded it by law and public attitude, and in general, denied the freedom of development, the right to well-being, and the pursuit of happiness to the black woman. In short, Fauset explores the black woman's struggle for democratic ideals in a society whose sexist conventions assiduously work to thwart that struggle. Critics have usually ignored this important theme which even a cursory reading of her novels reveals. This concern with exploring female consciousness and exposing the unduly limited possibilities for female development is, in a loose sense, feminist in impulse, placing Fauset squarely among the early black feminists in Afro-American literary history. It is this neglected dimension of Fauset's work—her examination of the myriad shadings of sexism and how they impinge upon female development—that is the focus of this discussion. A curious problem in Fauset's treatment of feminist issues, however, is her patent ambivalence. She is alternately forthright and cagey, alternately "radical" and conservative on the "woman question." On the one hand, she appeals for women's right to challenge socially sanctioned modes of feminine behavior, but on the other, she frequently retreats to the safety of traditional attitudes about women in traditional roles. At best, then, we can grant that Fauset was a quiet rebel, a pioneer black literary feminist, and that her characters were harbingers of the movement for women's liberation from the constriction of cultural conditioning. . . .

Fauset's oblique and ambivalent treatment of women's roles in "The Sleeper Wakes" and in *There Is Confusion*, respectively, is less apparent in her next three novels, *Plum Bun, The Chinaberry Tree*, and *Comedy: American Style*. She continues her exploration of women's roles, their lives' possibilities, and her criticism of social conventions that work to restrict those possibilities by keeping women's sights riveted on men, marriage, and motherhood. These domestic and biological facets, Fauset suggests, while important, are just one dimension of a woman's total being, one aspect of her boundless capacities and possibilities. Seen in this light, then, fairy-tale illusions about life give way to mature realities, and women, instead of waiting for their imaginary princes, aggressively take charge of their lives and move toward achieving authentic selfhood.

The idea of Fauset, a black woman, daring to write—even timidly so—about women taking charge of their own lives and declaring themselves independent of social conventions, was far more progressive than critics have either observed or admitted. Although what Fauset attempted in her depictions of black women was not uniformly commensurate with what she achieved, she has to be credited with both presenting an alternative view of womanhood and a facet of black life which publishers, critics, and audiences stubbornly discouraged if not vehemently opposed. Despite that discouragement and opposition, Fauset persisted in her attempt to correct the distorted but established images of black life and culture and to portray women and blacks with more complexity and authenticity than was popular at the time. In so doing, she was simultaneously challenging established assumptions about the nature and function of Afro-American literature. Those who persist, then, in regarding her as a prim and proper Victorian writer, an eddy in a revolutionary literary current, would do well to read Fauset's work more carefully, to give it a more fair and complete appraisal, one that takes into account the important and complex relationship between circumstances and artistic creation. Then her fiction might finally be accorded the recognition and attention that it deserves and Fauset, her rightful place in the Afro-American literary tradition.

Deborah E. McDowell. In Marjorie Pryse and Hortense J. Spillers, eds.
Conjuring: Black Women, Fiction, and Literary Tradition (Bloomington:
Indiana University Press, 1985), pp. 87–88, 100

Jessie Fauset, whose fiction falls to some extent within the romance genre, makes greater use of the Cinderella Line as narrative strategy than does either Alice Walker or Toni Morrison. Olivia Cary, the unpleasant central character of

Comedy: American Style, resembles the "typical mother" in marriage novels— Mrs. Bennett in [Jane Austen's] *Pride and Prejudice*, for example. The subtext of Fauset's novel follows the Cinderella Line: Olivia dreams her light-skinned daughter Teresa marries a princely (white, rich) husband. The achievement of Olivia's dream, however, is thwarted by the larger, racial issue which informs the novel, the issue of "passing." Jessie Fauset, whose novels espouse essentially middle-class values, nevertheless offers, particularly in *Comedy: American Style*, a critical perspective of these very values. This ambivalence results in a subversion of the Cinderella Line. Teresa, who has passed at her mother's insistence, marries not a prince but a pauper. At the end of the novel both mother and daughter, defeated in the marriage quest, are left without a culture and without a language, in the threadbare clothing which signifies an unhappy ending. . . .

As a woman writer writing *as* a woman, if not *for* women, Fauset was likely to notice the aesthetic relationship between skin and clothing. This kind of thing is important in the daily lives of most middle-class women and, I would guess, of many middle-class men. By including chestnut hair and puff sleeves in her fictional world, Fauset is only being true to the tradition of American realism. But these concerns are not merely gratuitous. . . . Fauset uses clothing as a way to articulate not only the racial differences between mother and daughter but also the hierarchy of class/race which she then addresses throughout the novel: the desperate, white-identified mother; the middle-class daughter caught between her mother's notion of "a cruder race" and her own desire to be like her peers; the black-identified Marise in her "glowing, gay colors"; the naturally gifted, light-skinned Phebe, who is already accumulating capital.

Fauset also captures here the excitement of adolescent anticipation, the thrill of choosing for oneself what one is to wear and not to wear. Thus Teresa is transformed, through clothing, from "mouse" to warm, young black woman. As she puts her "nice narrow feet" into "bronze slippers," she becomes reminiscent of Cinderella on her way to the ball—in this case a neighborhood party. It is in fact Teresa's crowning moment. For later she meets a young black man, falls in love, and is humiliated by her mother, who forces her into a disastrous marriage. The Cinderella Line has reversed itself irrevocably.

Mary Jane Lupton. BALF. 20, 4 (Winter 1986), pp. 410–12

Fauset's four novels, *There Is Confusion, Plum Bun, The Chinaberry Tree*, and *Comedy: American Style*, contain numerous shared perspectives with [Edith] Wharton, especially on issues confronting women. Fauset's critique of the economics of marriage for women, of fairy-tale illusions of love and salvation, of mother-daughter conflict and alienation, of the tension between class and gender for privileged women (a theme only partially plumbed in both authors), and of the deep rivalries and divisions that sever bonds between women, all bring to mind Wharton. Further, although no one to my knowledge has explored the similarities and contrasts between the two authors, quite specific echoes and parallels exist. The marriage of Fauset's Teresa Cary in *Comedy: American Style* to a conservative, economically straitened Frenchman, complete with tyrannical mother—a marriage which entombs the young American heroine in a suffocating Old World contract which she totally misjudged—has a strong parallel in Undine Spragg's disastrous French marriage in [Wharton's] *The Custom of the Country*. Likewise the suicide in this bitterly satiric Fauset novel of a kind, gentle young man who puts a revolver to his head because of the heroine's rejection of him recalls Ralph Marvell's death in Wharton's equally scathing novel. Fauset's portrait of the casual, careless sexual predation of a privileged educated young white man in *Plum Bun* bears very interesting comparison, it seems to me, with Wharton's portrait of Lucius Harney in *Summer*. Indeed, the whole issue of marriage for profit in *Plum Bun* evokes several Wharton novels—*The House of Mirth*, *Summer*, *The Custom of the Country*. . . .

A major theme in both authors is the agonizing break between mothers and daughters experienced by women at the turn of the century, the drama specifically of a daughter leaving her mother's world, even renouncing it, and the bitter split that consequently exists between the two worlds, one of the daughter, the other of the mother. In Wharton, think of the distance between Lily Bart [in *The House of Mirth*] and her mother, Undine Spragg and hers, Charity Royall [in *Summer*] and hers. Likewise in Fauset, Joanna Marshall [in *There Is Confusion*] strikes out on her own, Angela Murray [in *Plum Bun*] radically cuts herself off from her mother's world, and Olivia Blanchard does the same. Similarities abound; the younger generation in the work of both authors seeks freedom and self-determination, especially economic and sexual, in ways their mothers never dreamed of. But there are also basic differences. In Wharton the mothers of her most interesting rebellious young women—Lily, Undine, Charity—represent a world that should be left behind, a past that is confining and suffocating. They represent an impoverished past for women—whether it is the spiritual poverty of Lily's mother or the literal misery of Charity's. They evoke a negative past from which the daughters rightly rebel.

In Fauset, in contrast, the rejected mothers represent a positive world: one of purpose and group pride born of struggle. They are a strong confident group whose lost, confused daughters have much to gain from coming back home to them. Unlike Edith Wharton, that is, for Jessie Redmon Fauset the generation of mothers whose daughters came to maturity in the two or three decades before 1920 do have an important life-giving vision to offer. It is based on the corporate value of community action and rootedness, female friendship, solidarity with men in the race struggle, membership in a church, and commitment to the bonds of family. This dramatic contrast between the impoverished inherited maternal world in Wharton and the rich one in Fauset leads inexorably to the conclusion that it is not just class or personal history or gender but also and perhaps most important race which leads Edith Wharton to her bleak, hopeless endings. Had she been a black American writer of comparable generation, education, and class, she would have had behind her, as Fauset did, a generation of strong inspiring mothers to offer support and wisdom—even if their daughters, as we see in Fauset, were too foolish to listen to them.

Elizabeth Ammons. *College Literature*. 14, 3 (Fall 1987), pp. 211–12, 214–15

Fauset responded to an emerging black urban working class by a mediation of her authorial position as a class perspective. She represented in her fiction a middle-class code of morality and behavior that structured the existence of her characters and worked as a code of appropriate social behavior for her readers. Fauset's intellectual contribution was the development of an ideology for an emerging black middle class which would establish it as being acceptably urbane and civilized and which would distinguish it from the rural influx. Unlike earlier women novelists, Fauset did not consider the aftermath of slavery and the failure of Reconstruction as a sufficient source of echoes and foreshadowings for her new relation to history. Fauset represented this new history through a generational difference, a difference figured as a recognition of the need for the protagonists to revise the irrelevant history of their parents, a history tied to the consequences of slavery.

Hazel V. Carby. *Reconstructing Womanhood:*
The Emergence of the Afro-American Woman Novelist
(New York: Oxford University Press, 1987), pp. 166–67

Like Jane Austen, Jessie Fauset is concerned with the commonplace details of domestic life, and at her best, as . . . critic Sterling A. Brown has observed, "succeeds in a realism of the sort sponsored by William Dean Howells."

In the foreword to *The Chinaberry Tree*, Fauset reveals her social and artistic preference for depicting "something of the homelife of the colored American who is not being pressed too hard by the Furies of Prejudice, Ignorance, and Economic Injustice," and who as ". . . naturally as his white compatriots . . . speaks of his 'old' Boston families, 'old Philadelphians,' 'old Charlestonians.' And he has a wholesome respect for family and education and labor and the fruits of labor. He is still sufficiently conservative to lay a slightly greater stress on the first two of these four." By stressing the genteel tradition and everyday rituals of the urban black elite, Fauset limits her presentation of truth and reality to the class of people she knew best. . . .

The moral of her novels is that the respectable, genteel black American "is not so vastly different from any other American, just distinctive." In *There Is Confusion* dark-skinned Joanna Marshall and light-skinned Peter Bye overcome color prejudice and achieve success by confronting the truth of their family backgrounds and committing themselves to education, hard work, respectability, and each other. Even so, neither the characters nor the author-narrator has much sympathy for commonplace minds or people. In *The Chinaberry Tree* adultery and illegitimacy overshadow the lives of three black women in a small New Jersey town. Fauset is more concerned with the realistic details of Aunt Sal and Laurentine's daily routine and their ability to rise above the ostracism of their community than she is the narrowness of small-town notions of respectability. As the central unifying metaphor, the chinaberry tree is a sentimentally contrived symbol of the illicit love of Aunt Sal and Colonel Holloway and of the shadowy past that unites Sal with her illegitimate daughter, Laurentine, and illegitimate niece, Melissa. Unlike Howells, Fauset does not shrink from the unpleasant aspects of the black bourgeoisie as she approvingly reveals that their morals and manners are not appreciably different in kind from those of the white bourgeoisie.

Bernard W. Bell. *The Afro-American Novel and Its Tradition*
(Amherst: University of Massachusetts Press, 1987), pp. 107–8

Though the emphasis in Harlem Renaissance writings was professedly on things "Negro," Fauset's poetry, with few exceptions, was both conventional in form and curiously silent on questions of race. Except for two or three experimental pieces, her roughly two dozen published poems are unremarkable imitations of Western poetic conventions in spirit, form, and theme. Her two predominant themes are nature and unrequited love, both timeworn, "universal" poetic subjects, which she treats with a casual matter-of-factness. Seldom is there a concrete reference to race, gender, or any of the controversial political and social issues of her day that readers might take as evidence of a "black woman's" signature.

If readers look for such a signature merely in the presence and number of references identified narrowly with race and gender, then Fauset's poems will disappoint. In an era when many black writers were celebrating their racial origins and distinctiveness and calling for representation of those origins in the arts, Fauset was writing poetry whose indebtedness to the Western literary tradition is everywhere apparent. . . .

Critics have been severe in their assessments of Fauset's poetry, especially of its "Western" predilections, impugning in the process her consciousness of and commitment to her race. Viewed from a different perspective, however, her "universal" (read "Western") lyrics of love and nature can be said to make problematic the very idea and category of "Western" seen in opposition to "black." Behind all of Fauset's work, both as editor and as writer, is a sensibility, catholic and global in its reach, that complicates simplistic orthodoxies. For her, "blackness" was not synonymous with "African-American" but included black people the world over. Hence, the French references in her poetry are not necessarily evidence of a flight from blackness but, rather, of her awareness of "the French connection" to a number of French-speaking blacks in other parts of the world. As Fauset herself had noted in her translation of Haitian poets, "Both France and the classics are the property of the world."

Deborah E. McDowell. In Lea Baechler and A. Walton Litz, eds. *Modern American Women Writers* (New York: Scribners, 1991), pp. 126–27

GAINES, ERNEST J. (1933–   )

UNITED STATES

Ernest J. Gaines's most recent novel, *In My Father's House*, published in 1978, was not widely reviewed. The notices that did appear were respectful but a bit gingerly and unenthusiastic in tone, as if the reviewers did not quite know how to respond to the book. The relative neglect of the work, in comparison to the more compelling *The Autobiography of Miss Jane Pittman*, is understandable. But it is unfortunate in view of the fact that *In My Father's House* is an important work, showing significant development in Gaines's art and thought, especially in light of his depiction of and reaction to the 1970s.

One reason for the lukewarm response to *In My Father's House* is the voice Gaines uses. In fact, according to his own testimony, he had trouble completing the novel because it employs an omniscient narrator, while he wrote most of his earlier works in the first person. His use of omniscient narration led to a phenomenon much noted by reviewers—a severe detachment, a distance between story and narrator. The reader does not get as personally involved with Philip Martin as he does with Miss Jane or Jim Kelly or the narrators of the stories in *Bloodline*. Yet are not detachment and the consequent irony precisely what Gaines aimed to create in *In My Father's House*? He does not intend for the reader to become intimately involved either with the characters or with the story.

Gaines's distancing of his readers—and himself—from this novel may not indicate a change in his philosophy, but it does, I think, reflect a change in his attitude toward his characters' potential development. Considered in sequence, Gaines's first three novels show a gradual development in his characters' ability to grow, change, and prevail. All the characters in *Catherine Carmier*, his first novel, are victims of social or environmental forces, while in *Of Love and Dust* Jim Kelly and Marcus Payne achieve growth through fighting the inertia of Southern black life and, within limits at least, gain the capacity to shape their lives. Gaines's sense of this power on the part of his characters culminates in the depiction of Jane Pittman, who prevails over seriously adverse circumstances. The *Autobiography* reconciles the dichotomies of the earlier novels: past and present, young and old, man and woman. In *In My Father's House* the reconciliation falls apart. Discussing the novel while he was still writing it, Gaines contended that it does not reflect a change in his views: "I cannot write only about Miss Jane and man surviving. And I cannot write only about man failing. I write about both." Certainly his works do portray both survival and failure, but I think *In My Father's House* questions the emphasis on black progress reflected in the *Autobiography*, and . . . suggests that Gaines feels that a modification of the positive conclusion of the *Autobiography* is in order.

Frank W. Shelton. *SoR*. 17, 2 (April 1981), pp. 340–41

The prime characteristic of the pseudo-autobiographical novel . . . is the author's deliberate attempt to convince the reader that the events described actually occurred. The pseudo-autobiographical novel employs all the elements of the autobiography. It reads as an autobiography and is often presented as such. In Ernest Gaines's [*The Autobiography of Miss Jane Pittman*], for example, the word "autobiography" even occurs in the title. Indeed, unless the reader knows facts to the contrary, there is very little to indicate that such a work is not a verifiable autobiography. . . .

As in all autobiographies, *The Autobiography of Miss Jane Pittman* has one main character. Miss Jane, the narrator, is the central figure around which the story evolves. All the other characters are minor and are seen through her eyes. They are important to the story only to the extent that they illuminate Miss Jane's character. As a consequence, the facts or historical events of the story are related through the context of her experience. . . .

The book is written in the form of a series of tape-recorded interviews of a black woman who was once a slave. In his attempt to simulate the autobiographical form, Ernest Gaines went out of his way to demonstrate Miss Jane's dependence upon what William Howarth calls an "essential control" in autobiography, memory. Due to her age, however, many times her memory fails her. . . . In fact, in the introduction to the book, the schoolteacher who "conducted" the interviews talks about the difficulties caused by the lapses in Miss Jane's memory; at some points she was said to forget everything.

Another strategy Ernest Gaines employed to make his book look like a real autobiography was to model it after a major subgenre of the Afro-American autobiography, the slave narrative. In the tradition of this mode, the ex-slave would risk recounting his life only after he was safely out of the slave states. Similarly, the fictional Miss Jane tells her story from a position of relative impunity. When she agrees to talk to the schoolteacher, she is already over a hundred years old. Her life has run its course and is only a few months from its glorious end. The incidents she narrates, including the bold and militant act of drinking from a fountain marked FOR WHITES ONLY, are of no consequence to her future life.

Bede M. Ssensalo. In Eldred Durosimi Jones, ed.
African Literature Today. 14 (1984), pp. 94–95

The interaction between the community and the individual, along with its role in the shaping of human personality, is a primary concern of Ernest J. Gaines in much of his fiction. It is in probing the underlying community attitudes, values, and beliefs to discover the way in which they determine what an individual will or has become that Gaines gives poignancy to the pieces in his short-story collection *Bloodline*. Because his fiction focuses on the peculiar plight of black Americans in the South, Gaines must consider an additional level of significance—the strong communal bonds characteristic of Southern black folk culture. In these stories, black folk culture, with its emphasis on community-defined values and behaviors, shows signs of deterioration, while

Western individualism and the development of more personally-defined values appear as catalysts in the demise of the black folk world-view. In such a cultural climate, the spiritual and emotional well-being of both the community and the individual is threatened. Faced with the necessity to act and finding traditional solutions no longer viable, the characters in Gaines's stories struggle desperately to restore some semblance of normalcy to their worlds. The dramatic conflict endemic to the stories in *Bloodline* arises out of the efforts of various characters to reconcile their individual needs with community prerequisites. Two of the stories in *Bloodline*, "A Long Day in November" and "The Sky Is Gray," are particularly illustrative of the conflict between community perspective and individual needs. The conflict in these two stories further illustrates the importance of the changes taking place within Southern black culture to the development of the social consciousness of children. While the action of the stories revolves around two young boys, the resolution of the conflict resides with their parents.

John W. Roberts. *BALF*. 18, 3 (Fall 1984), p. 110

The fictions of Ernest J. Gaines reflect and refract the place, history, traditions, folklore and folkways, situations, and people of his native South. . . .

His first published major work, *Catherine Carmier*, has two principal characters, Catherine and Jackson, who in order to confirm and demonstrate their feelings for each other, must break away. Catherine must break from an emotionally incestuous relationship with her father, Raoul, and the intraracial discrimination that he represents; and Jackson, from the expectations of his elders, personified by his Aunt Charlotte, that he remain there to be "the one," their Moses. The time of the novel is set during the stirrings of what would develop into the Civil Rights Movement. Gaines followed this novel with *Of Love and Dust*, an exploration of the protocols of interracial sex and love in a time of rigid taboos, before the social revolution in the South in the 1950s and 1960s. The novel's tensions develop as the protocols are violated or prove ineffective as lust becomes love. The result is that the delicate equilibrium that makes for overtly peaceful coexistence among the ethnic groups—black, white, and Cajun—is upset. His next book, *Bloodline*, is a collection of shorter fictions, each about a black male in a conscious or subconscious movement toward identity, self-esteem, maturity, dignity. . . .

Gaines's fictional people are generally well-realized and unfailingly human characters capable of humor and high seriousness, of foolishness and wisdom, of indifference and compassion, of jealousy and uncompromising, sustaining love. His central characters are usually Negroes. In depicting them and their conflicts and struggles, Gaines is not a hostile, combative writer; his fictions, at least on the surface, do not have as a major purpose indictment and condemnation of whites and racism. Rather, with great warmth, he celebrates the indomitable strength and resilience and moral reserve of black people. Trapped in circumstances of place and history and custom, his protagonists do not capitulate; they adapt to or deflect adversity as they bide their time or revolt. Most importantly, they endure. . . .

The fiction of Ernest J. Gaines demonstrates his thorough factual and experiential knowledge of his native, regional South. More importantly, his fiction demonstrates his penetrating understanding of the complexities and subtleties of universal human nature that affect and are affected by these regional realities.

Theodore R. Hudson. In Louis D. Rubin, Jr., ed. The History of Southern Literature (Baton Rouge: Louisiana State University Press, 1985), pp. 513–15

In *A Gathering of Old Men*, Gaines returns to the territory and narrative techniques of his earlier works. He tells the story of a group of old black men who, though denied dignity all their lives, have a final opportunity to assert their manhood. The chance comes when a Cajun field boss, Beau Boutan, is killed in front of the shack of Mathu, the only man in the community to have consistently stood up to both the Cajuns and the whites. As soon as word spreads of Boutan's death, the black men begin arriving on the scene, each carrying a recently fired shotgun that could have been the murder weapon. Much of the novel is devoted to the "confessions" of these men, each of whom tells the sheriff why he had sufficient motive for the crime. These voices, plus a few others, are, as in "Just like a Tree," the bearers of the narrative. In effect, Gaines again creates a communal history of black life in rural Louisiana.

That history is violent, oppressive, and dehumanizing. The story told by Uncle Billy, the oldest of the men, is typical. . . . Though the beating that caused [his son's strange] behavior occurred years earlier, the pain clearly remains just as acute as when the violence took place. A perpetual present has been created, because the anguish is lived with daily. Billy does not simply relive that original violence; he lives the history generated out of that act. In this sense, the assault continues every moment of his life. . . . [Each] trip to Jackson is another act of violence, another assault on the humanity of Billy and his wife. To kill Beau Boutan is not to seek revenge on his father for the treatment of Billy's son; it is to exact justice for continuing criminal behavior. Killing Beau does not balance the books, according to some talionic code; such a principle would implicitly suggest that Billy's suffering could be canceled. The murder neutralizes nothing; it is simply a refusal to allow the crimes of the racists to be erased. Each story told by the old men serves a similar purpose: to expose the marks that have been made on them throughout their lives and to attempt, for the only time in their lives, to get recognitions of their own definitions of reality. The "ink" for their self-marking is the blood of Beau Boutan; the script written by each is, like Uncle Billy's, the story of his own bleeding.

Keith E. Byerman. Fingering the Jagged Grain: Tradition and Form in Recent Black Fiction (Athens: University of Georgia Press, 1985), pp. 98–99

The action in Gaines's fiction takes place in the quarters, homes, jails, saloons, stores, yards, and fields; in the city of New Roads (named Bayonne and St. Adrienne for Gaines's mother, Adrienne Gaines Colar) and on False River (St. Charles River, for his brother Charles); at gates and public gatherings; and on the roads and in other places. In its infinite details, the world of the fiction of

Ernest Gaines encompasses the countryside, the villages, and the town of New Roads in Pointe Coupée Parish. . . .

Gaines concentrates on Pointe Coupée/St. Raphael Parish as a center of meaning in order to "record" the lives of the people he knew as he saw them, and to use their experiences to construct a myth that articulates the struggles of a static world fiercely resistant to change. St. Raphael Parish is like William Faulkner's Yoknapatawpha and James Joyce's Dublin: it equals the modern world. To understand the Gaines canon, we must explore its symbolic geography. We can begin with the quarters, the focal place and central metaphor of his parish. To examine the quarters community as a phenomenon in Southern history, and as a physical, social, and political entity in Gaines's work is to tell much about the symbolic, temporal reality of his fictional world. . . .

As a symbolic space, the quarters, in the hands of Ernest Gaines, takes on epic dimension; like William Faulkner's Yoknapatawpha, it is a microcosm in which humankind, undaunted in its Sisyphus-like struggle, wills to prevail. Through the quarters as a center of meaning, Gaines, on the one hand, explores facets of a particular Southern experience which, on the other hand, becomes symbolic of modern human experience in its questions about the individual, the family, the community, and the past. Gaines's quarters and the rest of his St. Raphael Parish are also unlike Faulkner's north Mississippi county; Gaines's quarters . . . is not fixed geography with characters who appear in more than one narrative. Instead, Gaines's quarters, like the rest of his St. Raphael Parish, is a fluid concept which he shapes and reshapes as he creates each narrative. Together the narratives do not recount the doings of a single community; rather they record the spiritual, social, economic, political strivings of a people in the act of becoming. Although it is a dying physical entity in historical reality, the quarters in Gaines's fiction is a ritual ground of communion and community to which Gaines, the man and the artist, returns again and again for perception and sustenance.

Charles H. Rowell. *SoR.* 21, 3 (Summer 1985), pp. 734–35, 749–50

Historians, like many nonhistorians, tend to be interested in causes as well as effects. Gaines, the novelist-historian, in [*The Autobiography of Miss Jane Pittman*] is not satisfied merely to attempt the re-vocation of a past essentially as it was. . . . [He] seeks a meaning in that past, an indication of how and why it assumed the form it has today. He broods, indeed, over what may be gained from his didactic scrutiny of history with much of the intensity and fervor with which [William] Faulkner peers into the southern past in [his] Yoknapatawpha novels. This brooding, this peering, in *Pittman* appears hardly to be an exercise in futility. Quite to the contrary, the results from it may well be, in *Pittman*, the crowning achievement of a major piece of fiction. . . .

In the final analysis Gaines wrote *Pittman* to insist to his readers that a credo common among American whites and the injustices that credo has occasioned American whites to perpetrate upon American blacks has accounted almost as unequivocally for the major problems of black America as, according to St. Augustine, the Good Lord accounts for the City of God. Why does a woman of Jane's human stature, a woman who has so much to give, who, though barren, can play so well the surrogate mother of two remarkable men, whose sense of humor is matched in its abundance, its acuteness, and its lack of sour self-defensiveness, only by her propensity for compassion, who is respected by all who get to know her well, be they black or white, or magnates or nonentities, and who has lived so long that her age alone has made her a fondly beloved figure truly admired in her community—why does such a person find herself calumniated as she is in America? How has her life been so unnecessarily (as well as, sometimes, so venomously) circumscribed? And why is she, even at her advanced age, treated by whites as if she were still a child? Is she responsible for the indignities heaped upon her? If she is not, who is? And has a system, a prescribed routine, rather than individuals reacting to their own observations and following their own leads, been her bane, and if a system, what is its nature and what, principally, the thing that makes it work? Jane's problem, and the one she shares with all black Americans, Gaines does say in *Pittman*, is indeed with a system. That system works, along with other reasons, Gaines does also say, because of its simplicity. And it has worked so well that not only whites contribute to its success. So do blacks. And if that system is to end, whites must free themselves of their willingness to maintain its vitality, but so, also, must blacks.

Blyden Jackson. In J. Gerald Kennedy and Daniel Mark Fogel, eds.
American Letters and the Historical Consciousness (Baton Rouge:
Louisiana State University Press, 1987), pp. 268–69

In the Louisiana Bayou area that he calls Bayonne, Gaines reveals the actions, impulses, and provocations that produce the body of ideals of the culture. Most criticism of his works acknowledges the keen ear, the sensitivity in rendering dialect, and the superb handling of voice in his fiction. Another acknowledgement which should be made is Gaines's mastery of the ethical precepts in the culture of his area in western Louisiana—precepts derived from plantation tradition and from reactionary elements that bring about changes. When these changes have occurred in his work, they have occurred at great sacrifice by men who may be called *deliverers* by virtue of the trials they undergo and the far-reaching implications of the results.

The courage of characters who accept responsibility for change creates the dynamic flow of Gaines's fiction and this courage is often of a sacrificial quality. Social changes won by those willing to take risks are the vehicles through which Gaines reveals his high regard for sacrifices made in social activism. The gains per se are given little attention, while their motivation and implementation are the points of focus. It can be demonstrated that the experiences of certain characters in Gaines's stories propel them to an activism that most often leads to a sacrificial death. These characters can not accept the "safer" rules of the system and in resisting conformity endanger themselves. . . .

Through his heroic deliverers Gaines demonstrates the ethical precepts of their milieu. In the stratified Bayonne community these precepts occasionally clash. The principles of conduct which through tradition seem good and morally obligatory for the planters are not good for Cajuns and blacks. Gaines's heroes are those blacks who perceive their duty to their community and attempt to bring about change. In each instance they build upon heroic actions of the past. Phillip Martin follows Martin Luther King's example, and the old men in *A Gathering of Old Men* follow the fallen ones who preceded them. Combined with this is a respect for the wisdom of the elderly and an instinctive hope for the future. Gaines's heroes learn that the bonds of continuity that link generation to generation and father to son are good and hence worth any sacrifice that will retain or atone for that relationship. The sense of duty is the force which is constantly evolving while linking the past with the present. Gaines has succeeded in defining it through several characters who exemplify responsible action in their environment. In instances in which their adventures end in death, they leave their wisdom, from which others can draw strength. When they survive and return to society, they are stronger in the mythic sense of the indestructible being. They are all purveyors of duty in the community and their actions set in motion changes which benefit the society. This duty, transmitted at great cost, is the lifeline to which Gaines's characters cling as a necessity for surviving in the world with dignity.

Audrey L. Vinson. *Obsidian II.* 2, 1 (Spring 1987), pp. 35–36, 46–47

Near the end of Ernest J. Gaines's novel *A Lesson Before Dying*, set in the fictional town of Bayonne, Louisiana, in 1948, a white sheriff tells a condemned black man to write in his diary that he has been fairly treated. Although the prisoner assents, nothing could be farther from the truth in that squalid segregated jail, which is an extension of the oppressive Jim Crow world outside.

A black primary schoolteacher, Grant Wiggins, narrates the story of Jefferson, the prisoner, whose resignation to his execution lends credence to the lesson of Grant's own teacher, Matthew Antoine: the system of Jim Crow will break down educated men like Grant and prisoners like Jefferson to "the nigger you were born to be."

Grant struggles, at first without success, to restore a sense of human dignity to Jefferson, a semiliterate, cynical and bitter twenty-one-year-old man, who accepts his own lawyer's depiction of him as "a hog" not worthy of the court's expense. The social distance between the college-educated Grant and Jefferson appears as great as that between the races, and class differences often frustrate their ability to communicate. It does not help that Grant has intervened only reluctantly, prompted by his aunt, a moralizing scold and a nag, and by Jefferson's godmother, Miss Emma. . . .

Despite the novel's gallows humor and an atmosphere of pervasively harsh racism, the characters, black and white, are humanly complex and have some redeeming quality. At the end, Jefferson's white jailer, in a moving epiphany, is so changed that he suggests the white-black alliance that will emerge a generation later to smash Jim Crow to bits.

Carl Senna. *NYTBR.* August 9, 1993, p. 21

GILROY, BERYL (1924–   )

GUYANA

I enjoyed and learned much from *Frangipani House*, an elegantly written and heartening novel by one of our distinguished women novelists (Sylvia Wynter, Merle Hodge, Marion Glean, Erna Brodber, Joan Cambridge, and Michelle Cliff are some of the others who readily come to mind). Beryl Gilroy's Mrs. Mabel Alexandrina King (affectionately called Mama King by friend and frightened foe), old, ill, but splendidly her own woman, is put away by her family in Frangipani House, a Dickensian rest home on the outskirts of Georgetown. It's the kind of place that the city folks point to and say, "Over yonder—Frangipani House! People dies-out dere! They pays plenty to die-out inside dere! Death comes to the lodgers in Frangipani House!" . . .

Beryl Gilroy's aptly, understatedly honed, symbolic inference, together with her driving social conscience, makes of all Guyana an allegorical Frangipani House, and certainly one either to escape from or be changed radically.

Andrew Salkey. WLT. 61, 4 (Autumn 1987), p. 670

In Georgetown, British Guyana, during the late 1940s there was a retirement home for upper middle-class ladies called "The Gentlewoman's Home." It was a chintzy, exclusive place, set aside for elderly whites, and near-whites, of "good" background but impecunious circumstances. Beryl Gilroy's *Frangipani House* with its "sleepy-headed windows dressed in frill bonnets of lace . . . sleek and comfortable on the town's edge" recalls that genteel establishment. But hers is a fictional home for working-class black women in colonial Georgetown, and sets out to give dignity to the lives of those forgotten "relics of work-filled bygone days," consigned to Frangipani House by relatives glad to be directly rid of them. The story revolves around Mrs. Mabel Alexandrina ("Mama") King, an ailing grandmother in her seventies who shows remarkable energy and resourcefulness. The author, in attempting to give Mama King dramatic stature, makes her a kind of picaresque, poor black Caribbean Queen Lear. Discarded by her "pelican" offspring, she begins to fear madness, fantasizing about her past and brooding on the ingratitude of her family. She escapes from the home in the company of a group of itinerant Hindu beggars . . . is attacked by "choke-and-robbers" and falls into a coma from which she awakes in [a] hospital. Surrounded by her now concerned offspring, all wanting to take care of her, she chooses to go with her granddaughter, Cindy, who is pregnant. The novel ends with the birth of Cindy's twins (Mama King having taken over from the starchy midwife) and the reestablishment of the old woman as loved matriarch.

The novel's intention—to protest against the institutionalizing and isolating of the elderly—is admirable, but badly served by a hyperbolical, self-conscious style: "Every step to hospital was like an orchestral instrument contributing its part to a symphony of pain . . . pain tailored by fate to fit her frail body." When the women in the home decide to sing a hymn, one of them says: "I'll call the others. Let us blend our voices in a thick, heavenly sound." The brown, middle-class "matron" is a kind of dragon lady . . . and while the beggars' natural good-ness is contrasted with uncaring middle-class attitudes, "the unstirring contentedness of their lives" to which Mama King is admitted, comes across as pseudo-pastoral nostalgia. The novel is effective, however, in its rendering—through a dialect voice—of Mama King's inner life, her memories of the past. Through the unwinding of the reel of memory, "my whole life pass before me—like a film at a picture show." The picture of colonial Guyana that emerges (of the hard but vital life of the black working class and of the color-based, hierar-chical society in general) is imaginatively and powerfully evoked.

Michael Gilkes. *TWQ*. 9, 4 (October 1987), pp. 1371–72

Most West Indian fictions about migration have been concerned with an indi-vidual's adjustment to a new social environment and have been written in the autobiographical mode. *Boy-Sandwich*, however, expands the range of this type of writing by considering the experiences, aspirations, and reactions of three generations of [a Guyanese] family long settled in Britain, though it retains the form of an autobiographical narrative embellished with astute social observa-tions and penetrating analyses of interracial and interpersonal behavior.

The narrator is an eighteen-year-old boy . . . burdened with the responsi-bility of caring for his institutionalized grandparents, who have lived in Britain longer than most of their neighbors and who are Empire loyalists who have worked hard, paid their taxes, been frugal, and raised a family that includes a grandson now ready to go up to Cambridge. As the protagonist Tyrone Grainger comments, "I was the filling and they were the slices of bread." Such figurative language abounds in the novel; in fact, the texture of the style is a delight in a time when language is not always valued and crafted in fiction. The bananas in an old people's home are described as "like fingers covered with large neglected sores," and an elderly inmate is said to be "tucking pain away in his body like a coin in his purse." Fear is "a solid rock inside people's hearts." Dialect, not always handled convincingly, is here used with great skill as an elucidation of character and role; it is neither an entertainment nor a decoration. Language, perhaps more than any other element, differentiates the three generations of the family and the family from others.

A. L. McLeod. *WLT*. 64, 1 (Spring 1990), p. 348

Mama King, the heroine of *Frangipani House*, is a sixty-nine-year-old black Guyanese peasant, who after many years of hard work, her faculties still intact, finds herself discarded by her loved ones. She . . . is unique in West Indian fic-tion, embodying that indomitable urge—so often stifled by male conditioning and female self-effacement—the Caribbean woman has for self-realization and freedom of expression. . . .

In Gilroy's novel, Mama King, who has worked so very hard and has unstintingly provided for her children and grandchildren, is installed in a tiny room in Frangipani House to spend the remainder of her days, with forty-two other black women, "waiting, waiting, waiting for 'the call from heaven.'" The ambivalence of the institution is strongly imaged at the outset. . . .

The "iron gate" that encloses and incarcerates is "finely wrought"; the windows are dressed to resemble the inmates of the house; the hibiscus flowers, always beautiful, are of course ephemeral; and the mammee apple tree is as sterile as the matron and as the life that obtains within the institution. Frangipani House provided, on the one hand, "constipated self-seeking care," and, on the other hand, an "answer to a prayer from children who prospered abroad and who wanted superior care for their parents." The irony of the images above is reinforced in "prayer," "prospered," and, most of all, in "superior."

Although Mama King had been ailing for a considerable time with malaria, then quinsy, then pleurisy, she . . . is still remarkably alert and strong. The well-publicized philanthropy of her youth, her emphasis on her personal independence, her sense of pride in self, and five hundred dollars a month, provided by her solicitous daughters, earn her the dubious privilege of "the room by the garden," which has a fair-sized glass window on one side. At first Mama King, nursed by the strangeness of the routine, by the ordered rhythm of institutional life, and the cleanliness of everything around her, regains her health. With the return of health comes the desire to be free, as she . . . begins to be overwhelmed by a feeling of being trapped. The urge to be vital, mobile and free reasserts itself powerfully, and she spends the rest of her sojourn thinking of ways of escaping Frangipani House. . . .

Mama King chooses to flee the sterile security of Frangipani House for the warm fellowship of a group of beggars led by Pandit Prem. Although one cannot be absolutely sure about the racial composition of the group of mendicants, one can reasonably assume that they are Indo-Guyanese. And it is quite significant that Mama King, an Afro-Guyanese can confess, "I free and happy with Pandit them." Gilroy, consciously, it seems, has set up what appears to be an ethnic hierarchy, in which groups are judged according to the way they treat their old folk. Token and Cyclette pay for "white people care" for Mama King in Frangipani House. This care is "ordered," and clean, but cold, sterile, and expensive. Opposed to this is the African tradition in which the old have a place and function.

Roydon Salick. CE&S. 14, 2 (Spring 1992), pp. 98, 100, 104

Stedman and Joanna is a well-written and, above all, convincing account of an interracial love affair set in eighteenth-century Surinam (and in fact received an award in Gilroy's native Guyana for historical fiction). Divided into three parts—"Before Joanna," "Joanna, My Love, My Life," and "The Sea Change"—the novel chronicles John Gabriel Stedman's life from his gaming and womanizing youth, through his adventures and coming of age in Surinam, to his decline in Europe. . . .

Among other themes and motifs, the novel examines the debilitating effects of slavery: the sexually abused slave woman, the failure of Christianity, the cruel mistress, the horror of the black codes, and the maroons who fought against colonial powers for independence. Running throughout the novel is the suggestion that death—of one sort or another—accompanies the institution of slavery. . . .

What remains the crowning achievement of the novel, however, is the depiction of the love between Joanna and Stedman. It is a love that transcends color and class. Even though Joanna is never fully able to discard her "coat of deception" (the multifaceted personas she must adopt as a black slave woman), she enjoys with Stedman an enviable love. One is tempted to compare the work with Barbara Chase-Riboud's *Sally Hemmings*, whose story opens in 1787, ten years before the death of Stedman. Although both novels offer fictionalized accounts of historical personages, Gilroy is more convincing in the ethics that inform the individual lovers.

A. S. Newson. *WLT.* 67, 1 (Winter 1993), p. 219

GIOVANNI, NIKKI (1943–   )

UNITED STATES

Nikki Giovanni is a product of the thunderous and explosive 1960s, endowed with a powerful and inquiring mind absorbed with the black America of that decade—our vision of ourselves. And, like a painter's brush, her life depicts what black America can see and feel. . . .

[Giovanni] has absorbed her atmosphere—she knows her world from chief to thief. In "Nikki-Rosa" she wrote five words that stated to the world a new commitment, "Black love is Black wealth," and made one quixotic judgment: "[They'll] probably talk about my hard childhood and never understand that all the while I was quite happy." The world of Nikki Giovanni is very real, sometimes too real for comfort, too naked for delight. A person who enters that cavern of poetic adventures can never be the same again. But she asks no more of her readers than of herself. In *Gemini* she raked her emotions bare to write of the death of her grandmother—moved from her home of eighteen years for a cutoff of a cutoff, knowing that neither she nor her mother would ever be able to read that essay without crying, without wondering if more could have been done.

Ida Lewis. Foreword to Nikki Giovanni. *My House*
(New York: William Morrow, 1972), pp. x–xii

A poet may be musician, preacher, articulator of a culture, but she or he is also a dreamer. In a series of poems about herself as dreamer, Giovanni explores the conflicting and confusing relations between her roles as poet, woman, and black.

In "Dreams," she describes her younger years—"before i learned / black people aren't / supposed to dream." . . .

A few years later, in "The Wonder Woman," she must deal with the fact of having become that sweet inspiration. "Dreams have a way / of tossing and turning themselves / around," she observes; also that "the times / make requirements that we dream / real dreams." . . . The wonder woman is a totally public personage who cannot—must not—integrate her personal needs and experiences into that role if they do not coincide. Giovanni makes this clear in poems about female stars, like Aretha Franklin, and in poems about herself, such as "Categories.". . .

"Categories" goes on to question even black/white divisions (political and public), if they can—and they do—at times violate personal reality, describing in its second stanza an old white woman "who maybe you'd really care about" except that, being a young black woman, one's "job" is to "kill maim or seriously / make her question / the validity of her existence."

The poem ends by questioning the fact and function of categories them-selves . . . but, in doing so, it is raising the more profound matter of the relations between society and self. The earlier "Poem for Aretha" . . . begins with a clear sense of the separation between public and private selves. . . . Again Giovanni explains the significance of the musician/artist to society: "she is undoubtedly the one person who puts everyone on / notice," but about Aretha she also says, "she's more important than her music—if they must be / separated." (It is signif-icant that the form of both these poems is closer to thought than speech. No answers here, only questions, problems.)

One means of bridging the gap between public and private is suggested in "Revolutionary Dreams." . . . "Militant" and "radical" are poised against "nat-ural" here, as they were in "Categories." But this poem makes the connection to gender: the "natural dreams," of a "natural woman" who does what a woman does "when she's natural." The result of this juxtaposition is "true revolution." Somehow the black woman must be true to herself as she *is* to be both a poet and a revolutionary, for the nature of the revolution itself is in question. . . . In the poems of *Black Feeling, Black Talk/Black Judgement* and of *Re: Creation*, the doubts are present, and possibilities for solution occur and disappear. However, *My House* as a book, not only the individual poems in it, makes a new statement about the revolution, about the very nature of political poetry, when the poet is a black woman. . . .

My House is divided into two sections, "The Rooms Inside" and "The Rooms Outside." The inside rooms hold personal poems about grandmothers, mothers, friends, lovers—all in their own way love poems. "Legacies," in which the poet describes the relationship between grandmother and granddaughter, is a very political poem. . . . Black heritage is explained in personal terms. The little girl in the poem recognizes an impulse to be independent, but the speaker recog-nizes as well the importance of the old woman, of her love, to the grandchild in achieving her own adulthood. Although the poem ends by observing that "nei-ther of them ever / said what they meant / and i guess nobody ever does," it is the poem itself that provides that meaning through its understanding. . . .

It is fitting to the purpose of *My House* that its final poem, which is in "The Rooms Outside," is "My House.". . .

The first stanza follows Giovanni's familiar oral structure. Phrases stand against one another without the imaginative extensions of figurative language: word against word, repeating, altering, pointing. A love poem, to one particular lover. It starts in a tone reminiscent of both "Beautiful Black Men" and "All I

Gotta Do"—the woman is there to adore her man: "i only want to / be there to kiss you"; "as you want"; "as you need." But although the gentle tone persists, an extraordinary change is rung with a firm emphasis on the personal and the possessive in the last three lines: "where i want to kiss you," "my house," "i plan." She is suiting his needs to hers as well as vice versa. . . .

In bringing together her private and public roles and thereby validating her sense of self as a black woman poet, Giovanni is on her way towards achieving in art that for which she was trained: emotionally, to love; intellectually and spiritually, to be in power; "to learn and act upon necessary emotions which will grant me control over my life," as she writes in *Gemini*. Through interrelating love and power, to achieve a revolution—to be free.

Suzanne Juhasz. *Naked and Fiery Forms: Modern American Poetry by Women. A New Tradition* (New York: Octagon, 1978), pp. 165–71, 174

Nikki Giovanni has . . . been called the "Princess" of black poetry because of her regal attitude toward her race in championing its right for real equality for every individual: she was a strong advocate of individualism during a period when the trend in the black community was away from individualism toward the mass. At the same time, she realizes the necessity for universal recognition of the talent that lies in her race for achievement in the artistic, scientific, and political worlds—for the wealth of love to be found in the individuals who compose it. If there appears to be a dichotomy in her thinking it is because the poet is as realistic as she is idealistic: she understands that changes are won by both individual pragmatism and functional unity. . . .

Like Gwendolyn Brooks, Nikki Giovanni has happy memories of her childhood. Her parents, like Brooks's, had a struggle to make ends meet, but they always managed to celebrate Christmas and the birthdays of their two children, Nikki and her sister Gary, with secret preparations and surprise presents, so that those days became events to look forward to, and happy memories. If her parents quarreled—again like Brooks's—it was over finances; but in the Giovanni household, the arguments were complicated by the fact that "Gus," Nikki's father, who held down three jobs at one point, was always trying to increase their income further by various investments that failed, or he would have to sell treasured stock to make the mortgage payments; then he would be depressed, and turn to drink. But it didn't matter so much because everybody was together; they were a family, and though there might be differences of opinion and disapproval, there was always love, a strong feeling that gave richness to the poorest home. A key phrase in "Nikki-Rosa" contains words that became famous in connection with Giovanni: "Black love is Black wealth," and from a number of poems in [*Black Feeling, Black Talk/Black Judgement*] . . . this poet is concerned with love, family love and relationships, as much as she is concerned with the oncoming "Black Power through Revolution." Poems like "Nikki-Rosa" and "Woman Poem," and "Knoxville, Tennessee," all contain recollections of happy moments in her childhood in contrast to polemic poems like "The True Impact of Present Dialogue, Black vs. Negro," which begins, "Nigger / can you kill / can you kill / can a nigger

kill a honkie?" an idiomatic chant presenting a call to action, action against acceptance of white supremacy; or, "Our Detroit Conference—for Don L. Lee," another
chantlike poem, employing a play on the words "bitter" and "black" to display the
deep resentment felt by the people of her race in regard to the injustices of the past.

Jean Gould. *Modern American Women Poets*
(New York: Dodd, Mead, 1984), pp. 330–31, 333–34

Giovanni's books after [*Black Feeling, Black Talk/Black Judgement*] did more
than repudiate violence. As critic Eugene Redmond pointed out, they offered
her views from a new perspective: that of the rite of passage toward womanhood. The growing-up motif is a common one in literature, especially among
women writers. It has provided some of their most memorable work and, in
Giovanni's case, a unifying theme in her work.

In *Gemini*, she is the feisty woman child who, to the consternation of her
mother, defies middle-class convention and gets suspended from Fisk
[University]. She traces her relationship with her older sister, that evolves from
shameless idolatry to the realization that love "requires a safe distance." In
these essays we are introduced to other members of her family, including a wise
and warm grandmother and a newly born son, who reappear in later books.

As the title suggests, *My House* continues this theme, and Giovanni
explores the legacies passed from generation to generation; and the lighthearted
pleasures of love and mischief. Sex sans politics does allow more playfulness. . . .

The evolvement away from the political poems had a significant impact
on her career. Her work became distinguished from that of others in her generation at a time when it was propitious to stand out from the rest. By the early
1970s, the black movement was in disarray, factionalized, and largely reduced
to internecine bickering. Giovanni, however, could still maintain an appeal
across ideological lines. . . .

If there is a median in [her] career, it came in 1975 with the publication of
The Women and the Men. Pursuing the rite-of-passage theme eventually leads
to becoming a woman; an adult, graced or burdened with the responsibilities of
maturity. *The Women and the Men* recognized a coming of age. For the first
time, the figure of the woman-child is virtually absent. In "The Woman" section, the dominant theme is the search for identity, for place, in the community
of black women. In the poem "The Life I Led," whose title is already suggestive, the poet even envisions her physical aging process: "i know my arms will
grow flabby / it's true / of all the women in my family." The free-spirited love
poems are grounded in the concern that "my shoulder finds a head that needs
nestling.". . .

In each of Giovanni's books, there is a poem or two which signals the
direction of a subsequent book. In *The Women and the Men*, "Something to Be
Said for Silence" contains the lines "somewhere something is missing / . . .
maybe i'm just tired"; and in "The December of My Springs," another poem,
Giovanni looks forward to being "free from children and dinners / and people i
have grown stale with."

The next book, *Cotton Candy on a Rainy Day*, recognizes the completion of a cycle. "Now I don't fit beneath the rose bushes anymore," she writes, "anyway they're gone." The lines are indicative of the mood of this book, which talks about a sense of emotional dislocation of trying "to put a three-dimensional picture on a one-dimensional frame," as she wrote in the title poem. She has evolved to be that creature which often finds itself estranged from the history which created it: a bright black female in a white mediocre world, she notes in "Forced Retirement." The consequences are an emotional compromise to a bleak reality, for compromise is necessary to forestall inevitable abandonment. Although the men in her life "refused to / be a man," Giovanni writes in "Woman," she decided it was "all / right." The book is immersed in world-weary cynicism, as the lines, "she had lived long and completely enough / not to be chained to the truth" suggest.

Paula Giddings. In Mari Evans, ed. *Black Women Writers (1950–1980): A Critical Evaluation* (New York: Doubleday, 1984), pp. 212–15

The most significant development in Giovanni's career has been her evolution from a strongly committed political consciousness prior to 1969 to a more inclusive consciousness which does not repudiate political concern and commitment, but which regards a revolutionary ethos as only one aspect of the totality of black experience. Her earlier political associates and favorable reviewers of the late 1960s often regarded her development after 1970 with consternation, as representing a repudiation of her racial roots and of political commitment, without perhaps fully understanding the basis for her widened concerns and interests. Giovanni's shift in interest from revolutionary politics and race as a collective matter towards love and race as they affect personal development and relationships brought strong reviewer reaction. . . . The problems involved in studying the relationship between this shift in her poetry and the somewhat delayed shift from favorable to less favorable criticism, as her artistry grew, are complex. And they are further complicated by the fact that, at the very time the negative reviews of her poetry markedly increased, her popularity with readers surged dramatically ahead. . . .

Studying the relationships between the positive and negative reviews and between the opinions of reviewers and popular audiences is made more difficult by an anomaly presented by Giovanni's *Black Feeling, Black Talk/Black Judgement*: two thirds of the poems in this 1970 volume are brief, introspective lyrics which are political only in the most peripheral sense—that they mention a lover as someone the speaker met at a conference, for instance. The remaining third, poems which are strongly political and often militant, received practically all the attention of reviewers. Critics ignored almost completely the poems that foreshadow nearly all the poetry Giovanni was to write in the next thirteen years. In short, the wave of literary reviews that established Giovanni's national reputation as a poet also established her image as a radical. Yet, by the summer of 1970, when these reviews began to appear, Giovanni had been writing solely nonpolitical, lyric poetry for a year. The label "the poet of the black revolution" which characterized her in the popular media was already a misnomer in 1970, when it began to be popularly used. . . .

It is my contention that Giovanni's rejection of the pressure to write primarily a didactic, "useful" political poetry was not only a sign of her integrity but an inevitable sign of her development. A truly comprehensive criticism of her work must be willing to recognize both her continuing commitment to the attainment by black people of power in America and a commitment to personal freedom for herself as a woman and an artist. Critics need not only to see the importance of politics in her life but to perceive also that a commitment to politics, pursued with ideological rigor, inevitably becomes constricting to an artist. That Giovanni still writes political poetry can be understood by attending to the anger which she expresses in each volume at the oppression of blacks, women, and the elderly; she continually deplores also the violence which oppression spawns. She illustrates the conflict between ideological commitment, exacted by political beliefs, and the demands of the artistic sensibility which tend to find such commitment confining and stultifying. She illustrates in her own work and career the same arc that the poets of the [W. H.] Auden generation in England illustrated: the passing beyond a doctrinal basis for one's poetry to a work responsive to an illuminating of the whole of the individual's experience. Giovanni's case is both complicated and made clearer by her connections with the Black Liberation Movement, which has not yet won all its objectives, particularly her affinities to the work of those closely tied to Marxist-Leninist ideology and Pan-African goals. . . .

In her poetry Giovanni has chosen to communicate with the common reader, as well as with artists and critics; consequently, she has used graphic images from everyday Afro-American life and stressed the "orality" of her usually short poems, often by assimilating into them the rhythms of black conversation and the heritage from jazz, blues, and the spirituals—reflecting these origins both in rhythmic patterns and borrowed phrases. She has tended to focus on a single individual, situation, or idea, often with a brief narrative thread present in the poem. Her choice of such simple forms has meant that academic critics might well be less interested in her work than in that of the more complex and intellectualized poets most often associated with modernism, such as T. S. Eliot, Ezra Pound, and W. H. Auden. She avoids the allusions to classical literature and mythology, the relatively obscure symbolism, the involved syntax, the densely-packed idiom, and the elliptical diction often characteristic of such poets. If the verbal and structural forthrightness of Giovanni's poetry in some measure accounts for the paucity of academic criticism of it, this elemental quality accounts also for her popular acclaim by thousands who come to hear her read her work. Like a folksinger, she senses the close relationship of poetry with music, since her poetry, like music, depends on sound and rhythm and is incomplete without oral performance and without an audience.

Margaret B. McDowell. In Joe Weixlmann and Chester J. Fontenot, eds.
Studies in Black American Literature
(Greenwood, Fla.: Penkevill, 1986), Vol. II, pp. 143–44, 151–53

Nikki Giovanni has, with special force, made the case for the relation of autobiographies to changing political conditions. She attacks the assumption "that the self is not part of the body politic," insisting, "there's no separation." Giovanni believes that literature, to be worthy of its claims, must reflect and seek to change reality. And the reality black people have known has left much to be desired: "It's very difficult to gauge what we have done as a people when we have been systematically subjected to the whims of other people." According to Giovanni, this collective subjection to the whims of others has resulted in the alienation of black Americans from other Americans. For as black Americans "living in a foreign nation we are, as the wandering Jew, both myth and reality." Giovanni believes that black Americans will always be "strangers. But our alienation is our greatest strength." She does not believe that the alienation, or the collective history that produced it, makes black experience or writing incomprehensible to others. "I have not created a totally unique, incomprehensible feat. I can understand Milton and T. S. Eliot, so the critic can understand me. That's the critic's job."

Personal experience must be understood in social context. Its representation is susceptible to the critic's reading, regardless of whether he or she shares the personal experience. Giovanni rejects the claim that black writing should be the exclusive preserve of black critics—that it is qualitatively different from white writing, immune to any common principles of analysis, and thus severed from any common discourse. There is no argument about the ways in which the common discourse has treated black writing, especially the writing of black women: shamefully, outrageously, contemptuously, and silently. The argument concerns who can read black texts and the principles of the reading. For, as [Wole] Soyinka said, if the denial of bourgeois culture ends in the destruction of discourse, the refusal of critical distance ends in the acceptance of an exceptionalism that portends extreme political danger. Giovanni explicitly and implicitly makes the main points: the identity of the self remains hostage to the history of the collectivity; the representation of the self in prose or verse invites the critical scrutiny of the culture. Both points undercut the myth of the unique individual and force a fresh look at the autobiographies of black women.

Elizabeth Fox-Genovese. In Henry Louis Gates, Jr., ed. Reading Black,
Reading Feminist (New York: Meridian, 1990), pp. 183–84

GLISSANT, EDOUARD (1928–   )

MARTINIQUE

[Edouard] Glissant's continuous inquiry into the meaning of the Caribbean past constitutes one of the salient features of his literary work and philosophic thought. Rejecting the main thrusts of Négritude, its nostalgia for Africa and its overreaction to white racism, as inadequate for the situation of the Afro-Caribbean, Glissant proffers the concept of Antillanité. Among other things,

Antillanité encompasses a lucid apprehension of the Caribbean past experience and a projection of a future course toward the shaping of a distinct regional collective consciousness and destiny. The function of the Afro-Caribbean writer is to commit himself to the "decisive act, which, in the domain of literature, means to build a nation." Nation-building exacts a vision that can "perceive of the consciousness, the one and only operative, of our being." Furthermore, Glissant maintains that "for those whose allotted share of history is only darkness and despair, recovery of the near and distant past is imperative. To renew acquaintance with one's past is to relish fully the present." A conscious collectivity is bound together by the heritage of a common past. . . .

In one of Glissant's early works, the play *Monsieur Toussaint*, the celebrated Haitian Maroon, Mackandal, is among the six dead who surround Toussaint and signify a temptation, a potential, a conflicting loyalty Toussaint is faced with. Mackandal expects Toussaint to avenge him for his violent death with massacres of whites and destruction of their property. But Toussaint, the nation-builder who wants the new order in Haiti to be based on peace, justice, and prosperity, refuses to yield to the temptation of requiting violence with violence. For the lawgiver, administrator, and proprietor Toussaint, Mackandal's insistence on equal retribution can lead only to the impasse of self-perpetuating violence. On the other hand, Toussaint, imbued with the ideas of the Enlightenment and the French Revolution, remains estranged from the ethos of his people, and the Haitian Revolution, propelled by its own revolutionary dynamics, bypasses him and abandons him to his tragic solitude. The confrontation between the Maroon and the builder or the intellectual is further amplified in Glissant's novels.

The first novel, *La Lézarde*, deals with the postwar scene in Martinique at the time of the first elections, when the island became a French overseas department. The plot of the novel revolves around a group of young radicals who plan the assassination of a turncoat in order to prevent the betrayal of Martinican aspirations to the metropolitan interests. To execute the plan and cover their tracks, the radicals inveigle a young shepherd, Thaël, who has been living up in the mountains like a latter-day Maroon, into drowning the traitor. In the course of their political pursuits the young activists visit Papa Longoué, a *quimboiseur* of Maroon lineage, who has refused to compromise with the modern times. He leads an isolated life on the mountain slopes, gathering his herbs, cultivating ancient African mysteries and wisdom. He is the last link with Africa, reliving in his memories passed from generation to generation the Middle Passage, the arrival of Africans in the New World, the days of *marronnage*. As a final gesture of adamant refusal, on his deathbed Papa Longoué forbids his friends to take his corpse down to the cemetery for burial.

Papa Longoué embodies negation in its ultimate form. Thaël, however, signifies an evolution of the Maroon prototype. Like Papa Longoué, Thaël leads a solitary life up in the mountains surrounded by legends and prophecies. But unlike Papa Longoué, he accedes to the request of his friends from the plain to descend from the heights and commit himself to political action in solidarity with the people. When Thaël returns to his mountain abode with his new bride, Valérie, following the elections won by the people's candidate, he assesses his adventure: "We left the mountains, we drank from the Source." But the ultimate significance of his incursion into the life of the plains people remains ambiguous. Valérie is killed by his dogs, who had grown hungry and furious during his absence—in a way, a reminder of the punishment that slave owners inflicted upon runaway slaves. The final scene of the novel offers no resolution to the ambiguity of Thaël's adventure. As his faithful dogs are licking his hands, Thaël can only think of the ways he would kill them to avenge Valérie's death. The meeting of the mountain Maroon and the plainsman, the past and the present, the old traditions and modern mentalities signals the need for further rapprochement, but at the same time a kind of atavistic curse hangs over those who commit themselves to incautious action. Glissant's second novel, *Le Quatrième Siècle*, projects much further the trajectory of the Maroon's evolution in the face of the choices between the sterility of negation and the uncertainties of compromise.

Juris Silenieks. In William Luis, ed. *Voices from Under:*
Black Narrative in Latin America and the Caribbean
(Westport, Conn.: Greenwood Press, 1984), pp. 119–21

Edouard Glissant's most recent volume of poetry, *Boises*, is dedicated "to every country which is diverted from its course and suffers the failing of its waters." The dedication, the book's subtitle (*Natural History of an Aridity*), and the concluding words of the final poem—"So we must retrace the dried watercourse and descend into many absences, to wind along to the place of our rebirth, black in the rock"—all refer us to the major themes of Glissant's work: the need to recapture, but also to transcend, a vanished, unrecorded history; and the struggle to preserve a sense of cultural identity in the face of metropolitan French policies that discourage and inhibit the onward flow of a specifically Caribbean tradition in Martinique and Guadeloupe. . . .

Along with the image of the parched and devastated land, that of the dried watercourse, with its suggestions of drought and sterility, has come to haunt Glissant's latest works. Its meaning is twofold: as the river is a traditional symbol of the passage of time, its ceasing to flow denotes the absence of a sense of history and continuity in the French Caribbean islands today; and the failing of the water also represents the inroads of modern industrialization, a destruction of the landscape that is itself symbolic, in the author's eyes, of the destruction wrought upon his race first by slavery and then by economic and cultural imposition. Slavery, with its enforced separation from African roots, began a long process of physical deprivation and emotional impoverishment. . . . This historic loss of identity is paralleled by a divorce between man and the land today which is, for Glissant, symptomatic of the state of alienation that characterizes his country: the feeling of dispossession, the moral disarray. The situation has been aggravated by the policy of assimilation to France which has sundered, for French West Indians, the connection with a meaningful African past and has disregarded the folkways of their slave ancestors. Glissant's second novel, *Le Quatrième Siècle*, is an imaginative reconstruction of the Caribbean past as it would have appeared to all those living through it, with major emphasis upon the viewpoints of two interwoven families whose African ancestors arrived on the same ship: one, Longoué, to escape immediately and take refuge in the Maroon forests; the other, Béluse, to accept his fate as a plantation slave. Members of these families appear in his other novels: *La Lézarde* [translated as *The Ripening*], *Malemort*, and *La Case du commandeur*. . . .

The Ripening records a moment in the history of Martinique when it seemed that the breach between the land and its inhabitants could be healed, that with the assumption of departmental status the island could hope for real progress and fruitfulness; in the novel the river is depicted as curving around the town as if "to enfold a portion of humanity, to reassure its people and help them." On the contrary, in *Malemort*, the title of which is a medieval word meaning cruel and tragic death, the predominant mood is a compound of grief, cynicism, and disillusionment. The author sardonically exposes the contradiction between the lip service officially paid to the notion of fostering a sense of Caribbean cultural identity, and the true attitude of metropolitan France towards the islands: "Of course there are problems here but a Frenchman's a Frenchman, whether he's a Breton, an Alsatian or a West Indian." The crushing of independent private initiative and self-development is rendered in microcosm by the failure of a modest local attempt to create a commune which would have brought a few families back to the land. The area is requisitioned by a metropolitan company whose giant tractor charges noisily backward and forward, ripping the earth apart, fouling the freshwater pools and "ravaging all this dream of land reform." The tractor's blind attempt to uproot three tall ebony trees echoes an earlier moment in *Le Quatrième Siècle* when Saint-Yves Béluse (a descendant of the African who accepted slavery), desiring, like his former masters, to exploit the land, plans to uproot and sell the wood of three ebony trees, seeing only their commercial value and not the fact that they have looked down upon the lives of his ancestors and are a precious link with the past. Such indifference to the landscape is indifference to the meaning and importance of history. On the other hand, care for the landscape and attachment to it are, for Glissant, essential means whereby a community cut off from its original roots and ties may slowly come to know its new country and take root in it, regaining through the landscape a lost sense of historical continuity and nationhood, "*suffering* the land and becoming worthy of it." . . .

[Glissant's] deft intertwining of poetic fiction and political thesis is in keeping with [his] conviction that the function of his art is not merely to reflect the Caribbean environment, but to support and illuminate the stages of its growth, to testify to the slow formation of a nation whose existence is not yet recognized even by its own nationals, and still less by those who contest its right to independence.

Beverley Ormerod. *An Introduction to the French Caribbean Novel*
(London: Heinemann, 1985), pp. 36-39

Le Discours [antillais] frightens as much as it fascinates. Western intellectuals, especially the French, have a need to organize, classify, and order the world. Glissant's multiplicity of themes, at times dealt with in a systematic fashion, at other times in a fragmentary fashion, his series of blank spaces, his theoretical texts, his poetic texts, his accounts of experiences, and his other texts, give the reader the sensation of being dragged over a precipice.

Le Discours reveals another facet of this poet, critic, novelist, and playwright: an unflagging researcher with an admirable production of theoretical writings, engaged in blazing new trails (or in following old ones from a new perspective) in search of clues that may better explain the reality of his country. The importance of *Le Discours* (and the difficulty in its reading) lies also in its great diversity. By discussing a whole variety of topics in the most diverse manners in a sequence not always clear to the reader, Glissant demonstrates that the study of a situation as original and complex as that of Martinique demands an entirely new approach. He is aware of the fact that "no method is ever innocent," and one of his main concerns is to escape the pitfalls of Cartesian logic and academic formalism, the great danger for Antillean intellectuals. . . .

It seems to me that one of the key concepts of Glissant's analyses is that of *dispossession* (the subtitle to book one of *Le Discours*). This concept also appears under the names of "lack," "absence," and "privation" and forms part of an economic and political but also philosophical consideration. On the other hand, considering that Glissant's literary project is fundamentally concerned with the land, the history, and the language of his people, as became apparent in 1969 with *L'Intention poétique* . . . one may say that Martinique, according to Glissant's criteria, is the locus of threefold dispossession: of place, of history, of language.

Diva Barbaro Damato. WLT. 63, 4 (Autumn 1989), p. 606

Glissant's last novel, *Mahogany*, establishes itself not only as the confirmation of an ancient and exemplary coherence—the rigorous coherence revealed by the continuity of the project in Glissant's poetry, novels, and theoretical works— but also as *détour*, humorous and playful recollection, and threefold *marronnage*: once again, *marronnage* of language, *marronnage* of structures and laws governing the narrative (since the character becomes creator), and lastly, *marronnage* by the chronicler, regarding the official Text of History, and, as such, a *marronnage* of Time. This enlightening and necessary reflection of the novel's discourse upon itself is also a well-reasoned and playful duplicity of the narrative, since, as we are told: "Whether sung or chanted, the depth of time comes back up to the surface. The rigidity in elucidating History yields to the pleasure of telling stories."

This game involving the author and the narrator and the character's autonomy toward his creator demonstrate the necessary complexity of a relationship that would not only be from self to the Other but from self to self. In the same way that *Mahogany* shows the reflection of the literary discourse upon itself, it also seems to indicate the possible reflection of the community upon itself, this reflection being the only guarantee of true progress, despite uncertainty, chaos, and misery. . . .

[It] often seems that Glissant's words, already so far ahead of us, await us like the words of someone who divined there in the depths that which we have yet been unable to see. These patient, obstinate, rigorous, brilliant, and burning words also affirm, as we are told in *Mahogany*, that "in this country of Martinique, those who search pass on to those who speak, who named them but did not recognize them. Thus we move forward to the edge of the world."

Priska Degras. *WLT*. 63, 4 (Autumn 1989), pp. 618–19

It seems fitting to discuss the Antilleanity of Edouard Glissant, as this appears to be the most obvious aspect of his personality and his entire work. Born and raised in Martinique, the French Antilles, Glissant has devoted all his life and creative activity to the quest for the Antillean identity. . . .

Glissant's impassioned attachment to the Antillean land could only lead him to use his talent as a writer to describe its landscape, which is always related to the people. . . . This means that different parts of the island of Martinique correspond to different historical events or activities of the people, as illustrated in *La Lézarde* or *Le Discours antillais*. In both cases Glissant gives the reader a guided tour from the top of the mountain—which happens to be in the North—to the sea, which is in the South, and along the way he comments upon every pertinent face of the landscape. The mountain, with its thick forest and intricate fern trees that stop sunlight, was the privileged refuge of the Maroons. It is the symbol of the past, of faithfulness to Africa and refusal of servitude. The center, called the *plaine*, with its sugar cane fields, its decaying sugar and rum factories, was once entirely occupied by the plantations and the slaves, who would first land at the Dubuc mansion, now in ruin, before distribution to their masters. The junction of the mountain and the *plaine* is made by the Lézarde River, whose winding brings us next to the city and the people who use it for their laundry and their bath. In recent years its delta has been used for airport traffic and various enterprises, which has caused the crabs to disappear. Finally, comes the southern part bordering the coast, with its coconut trees, whose trunks were used to cross the sea by those slaves who unsuccessfully tried to join Toussaint L'Ouverture in his revolt. The beaches and other parts of the island are now put at the disposal of tourist companies and their customers, a modern substitute for the plantations. In *Mahogany* Glissant parabolically compares Martinique to a colonial museum, a showcase not only for the everyday visitors but also for researchers such as sociologists and psychiatrists, who may be inquisitive about the possibility of such a human phenomenon. . . .

In a systematic and didactic way, Glissant will undertake to rewrite the history of the Antilles in his autobiographical novel *Le Quatrième Siècle*, published in 1964 and honored with the Charles Veillon International Award. Under the pretext of writing the first official history of his island, Mathieu, a young activist who may represent Glissant himself, asks an elderly *quimboiseur*—a witch-soothsayer and griot—to tell him what he knows about the topic. He expects that the old man, Papa Longoué, who can encompass the past, the present, and the future, will also provide information for his own political activities and will help him at the same time discover his own identity along with public truth. This historical novel turns out to be the chronicle of several families, including two black, two white, and one mulatto. The two black families stand for Africans like the Longoués, who refused slavery and started a community of Maroons, and others like the Béluses, who were assigned to plantations by their acceptance of enslavement. Eventually these two lines will converge as components making up the Caribbean people. Similarly, the white families, the La Roches and the Senglises, will serve as types. In between, the development of the Targin family illustrates the mulatto class that usually derives from miscegenation between white masters or overseers and female slaves. It is recorded that this new group grew away from the others and remained a floating element within society. This explains the development of the divisions of class and color which were to persist within the Antillean population even after emancipation.

Daniel [L.] Racine. *WLT*. 63, 4 (Autumn 1989), pp. 620–22

Among Glissant's earliest published works, *Les Indes*, a six-part epic poem that relates Caribbean history from Columbus's voyage to the European conquest and slave trade, illustrates the poet's relationship to collective memory and the Antillean landscape. *Les Indes* begins as an epic, promising praise for European adventure and discovery. . . . Despite the joy and optimism, accentuated in the poem by alliteration and the inversion of syllables (*lyre d'airain* / *l'air lyrique*), sailors who embark on Columbus's ships experience fear of the unknown, boredom at sea, and risk death from disease, all trials the Africans will face in turn. The opening of new space for Europeans ("Sur Gênes va s'ouvrir . . .") will result in closed space, confinement for the Africans who, unlike the European sailors working freely on deck, are shackled and brutalized in the ship's hull. Glissant's epic becomes an "anti-epic" even before the poet depicts the horrors of the slave trade, for Columbus's discovery of the Caribbean islands opens the way for exploitation as conquistadores, seeking riches, arrive to plunder. . . .

Glissant's most recent collection of poetry, *Pays rêvé, pays réel*, attests to his continued commitment to unearth the past in its complexity, contradictions, and opacity. A long poem divided [into] eight sections, it bears traces of the legacy of Columbus's voyage; annihilation of the Caribs, Middle Passage, slavery, marronage, all inform the poet's view of the past and the present. However, Glissant now rejects chronological organization, discarding the linear narration of the epic poem. Instead, he posits two time-frames, a *pays rêvé*, the atemporal oneiric landscape of a mythic Africa, and a *pays réel*, the Martinican landscape of his fiction. Each evokes a cast of characters: *pays rêvé* depicts mythical Africans that include Ichneumon, the storyteller, Milos, the blacksmith, and Laoka, an African goddess; *pays réel* presents protagonists of his earlier novels, Mathieu, Thaël, and Mycéa, political radicals intent on transforming Martinique's social and political structure. Thus, Glissant moves toward dissolving two boundaries, one between dream and reality, the other between poetry and prose.

An important distinction between poetry and prose lies in the special relationship each has to memory. In his study of Glissant's work, Daniel Radford explains that . . . Glissant's poetry probes inner consciousness in a way that his prose, constrained by time, geography, and grounded in realism (albeit poetic realism), cannot. Transmitting the historical reality of conquest and slavery in the Caribbean, *Les Indes* does not lend itself to the evocation of an oneiric landscape of mythic ancestors. *Pays rêvé, pays réel* moves beyond the epic to explore cultural identity as a concept embracing both the unconscious and the conscious—myth, dream, and reality in all their contradictions and opacity. Furthermore, unlike *Les Indes*, it does not deal with historical incidents but rather allows historical images to emerge from the collective unconscious. . . .

Written three decades after the epic, *Pays rêvé, pays réel* is far more pessimistic than *Les Indes*, which pays tribute to rebels who used their creative energy to combat the destructive powers of European conquerors. The more recent poetry is haunted by the fear that this energy has been depleted, that Martinican creativity is drying up just as the Lézarde River has become an insignificant stream. . . .

In the process of recovering a lost past marked by the earlier choice between dependency and flight (the slave either submitting to the colonial plantation order or fleeing to the *mornes*), Glissant finds a reflection of yesterday's dilemma in French Caribbean reality today, as Martinicans decide between dependency (social security handouts at home), or flight (emigration to France). Ironically, flight, which as *marronnage* once preserved identity, now often leads to further alienation. Sustained by the collective memory of indigenous resistance to colonial conquest and domination, the poet, despite his pessimism, remains firmly committed to using his own creative energies to articulate the collective voice of his people. Clearly, Glissant has not abandoned the hope that the energy which sparked former resistance will continue to flow.

Mildred [P.] Mortimer. *ECr.* 32, 2 (Summer 1992), pp. 67–68, 72–75

GOODISON, LORNA (1947–   )

JAMAICA

We need to remember, as we discuss Lorna Goodison's work, that she is an artist as well as a poet. The keenness of her observation, her certain demarcation of shapes, her canny sense of physical and sociological textures are undoubtedly related to that other cousin sensibility. Poems like "Guyana Lovesong," which carefully vignettes that country, object of a visit by hurt persona; "On Houses," where the houses image the need for the soul to repose in relationship, in a loved and familiar Otherperson; "Port Henderson 6 AM," which celebrates dawn— "the horse of the morning / spectacular"—as seen from that place; "Wedding in Hanover," which describes the ritual of the country bride bathing with her young woman friends (the "elected virgins") at the river . . . are all imbued with this clearness, brightness, nice perpetual acuity. Even the romantic "Moonlongings" in which the poet fantasizes about traveling on the moon to her sleeping lover, paints a vivid picture, muted though the tones may be.

It is this painterly self that gives us the surrealist "Sketches of Spain," "Xercise for Tony Mc," "The Day She Died," "Saggitarius," and "Whose Is That Woman?" The first of these in particular not only combines objects to make a picture of the orderly derangement of another world, but creates in addition a mood with the haunting quality of the music of Miles Davis, to whom it is dedicated. . . .

Lorna Goodison's use of language is exciting in its versatility; it is married to the range of content of the poetry and deployed with the confidence which perhaps resides only in the supposed "matriarchs" who (our men tell us) make these societies. The poetry rejoices in this place and the myriad facets of life experience which it offers. The exhilaration of beating the would-be robber and rapist in "For R & R in the Rain" is the excitement of overcoming the impulse to violence in these societies. For the present, at least, it is truly a woman's triumph.

Pamela Mordecai. *Jamaica Journal*. 45 (1981), pp. 39–40

Sooner or later, as the work of a poet assumes volume and personality, a few key images are likely to emerge, which serve as distinguishing marks, signatures of a sensibility. So we notice, for example, in Goodison's work, developing from *Tamarind Season*, a fascination with imagery of water and wetness—rain, river, sea. This water imagery signifies variously fertility, creativity, the erotic, succor, freedom, blessing, redemption, divine grace, cleansing, purification, and metamorphosis. In "On Becoming a Mermaid," for example, the woman imagines herself undergoing, through the agency of the buoyant element, "a sea change into something rich and strange" and self-possessed, liberated from the tyranny and ache of sexuality. "Jah Music bubble[s] up through a cistern"; Keith Jarrett, the pianist, is a "rainmaker," slaking the soul-drought of the poet far from home; and she cries, after the example of Gerard Manley Hopkins, "In this noon of my orchard / send me deep rain."

Then there is the continuous extending of linguistic possibility, which has been one of Goodison's most distinctive features. She has been steadily refining her skills at sliding seamlessly between English and Creole, at interweaving erudite literary allusion with the earthiness of traditional Jamaican speech, images from modern technology with the idiom of local pop culture. This process is the perfecting of a voice at once personal and anonymous, private and public. It may reach a kind of maturity in *Heartease* and will be an important factor in the increasing "largeness" of her work, as that work fuses private and communal pain and resolution. . . .

The deepening of the pain, and a corresponding discovery of new resources of resilience and a redemptive joy of life, are features of Goodison's development as a poet. Combined with the widening and subtilizing of her resources of form and expression, they have ensured that her work has indeed been getting "larger," and that her voice, personal and unmistakable as it is, is increasingly, and whether she knows it or not, the voice of a people.

Edward Baugh. JWIL. 1, 1 (October 1986), pp. 20–21

[Lorna Goodison's] two volumes of poetry to date, *Tamarind Season* and *I Am Becoming My Mother*, show a progression towards harmony. Less polemical than [Christine] Phillips (although some poems, like "Judges" in *Tamarind Season* are very strong), Goodison is a very skilled craftswoman of sounds. In "Judges" the point is partly the rhythm, which beautifully mirrors the Jamaican voice. . . .

[Some] of Goodison's poems find the crossroads between gender and race, and are neither strongly polemical nor primarily sensuous and resolving of issues. In "England Seen," for example, there is a very good sense of humor about Icylyn "chief presser hair," who goes "afro" in the summer, and the poem plays with the anxieties of women about looks (particularly here of black women in a white society). Middle-class aspirations are comically treated. . . .

Goodison occasionally treats class as a theme (as also do Phillips, [Olive] Senior and [Esther] Craig). In Goodison, voice of the dialect or Creole speaker is much more often interwoven into the texture of the line than it is in the other writers who tend to write either in one linguistic mode or the other in different poems. Goodison's humor is a medium for dealing with potential confrontation. . . . But for the most part, she is a poet of sensuous language, who is, to judge from her newest work, like *Heartease*, both technically confident and moving towards harmony and healing.

Elaine Savory Fido. In Carole Boyce Davies and Elaine Savory Fido, eds.
Out of the Kumbla: Caribbean Women and Literature
(Trenton, N. J.: Africa World Press, 1990), pp. 37–38

With two books of poems to her name, *Tamarind Season* and *I Am Becoming My Mother*, Lorna Goodison has already been the subject of an article by Caribbean poet and critic [Edward] Baugh which indicates that she is working upon a long sequence poem called *Heartease*. Her first book indicated some affiliations with the experimental jazz-oriented writing which characterized the work of one of the most interesting young male poets, Anthony McNeill's *Credences at the Altar of Cloud*. *Tamarind Season* contains one piece called "Xcercise for Tony Mc," while both volumes have a number of poems about jazz musicians. Her second volume, though, has allowed Goodison to evolve more of her own voice and concerns, particularly in relation to the experience of being a woman. Here she has made an affiliation with the great Russian poet Anna Akhmatova as a model of that activity so many of the Caribbean women poets see as central: acting "as a person who could speak for everybody, for people, for ordinary people, for people suffering." . . . Baugh sees this as an identification of the communal with the personal. Again, part of this process involves a reclamation of history. Like Jean Breeze in her "Soun de abeng fi Nanny," Goodison has a poem celebrating Maroon resistance leader Nanny, heroine of Jamaican national culture. She is, as . . . Baugh points out, one of a lineage of powerful female figures, public and private, in Goodison's work, including Rosa Parks of the Alabama bus boycott, Winnie Mandela, and Goodison's own mother, as in the powerful "For My Mother (May I Inherit Half Her Strength)." . . . The historical continuity of this female experience is central to Goodison's stated commitment to "write about women more than anything else, the condition of women," and she does so with a continual insinuation of hope and promise. "We Are the Women" ends with a familiar image from Afro-Caribbean ancestry, the buried navel string of the newborn child, the guarantor of future safety. . . . "Bedspread" presents an imaginary monologue by Winnie Mandela addressed to her imprisoned husband from the bright Azanian colors of the quilt woven in the past by "woman with slender / capable hands / accustomed to binding wounds" and ingrained with "ancient blessings / older than any white man's coming." It is a process of weaving the future which continues, the poem argues, despite the long confinement of [Nelson] Mandela and offers the certainty of change.

Goodison also has a number of poems about children and child care, a crucial area of concern for Caribbean women. . . . Goodison has a sharp awareness of the emotional complexities of such issues. She manages to present the ambiguities of hope during the present time while keeping faith with the progressive potential of the future and particularly the role of women in that transformatory process. It is this commitment that allows the woman speaker of her title poem to see herself as giving birth to herself, and becoming her mother in a double sense. In this awareness, Lorna Goodison is representative of much of the freshness and vigor to be found in Caribbean women's poetry. Given the recent emergence of these writers and the fact that most of them are at the very beginnings of their poetic developments, they promise a very bright future and new directions for Caribbean literature itself.

Bruce Woodcock. In Gina Wisker, ed. Black Women's Writing (New York: St. Martin's Press, 1993), pp. 73–75

The evocative power of Lorna Goodison's poetry derives its urgency and appeal from the heart-and-mind concerns she has for language, history, racial identity, and gender (and these are not as separate and consecutive as I have listed them, but rather as alternating and interwoven as they usually occur in the hurly-burly of human existence).

In the exceptionally engaging and indeed enticing selection of the poet's work recently issued by the University of Michigan Press [*Selected Poems*], which includes spiritual, humanistic, and political themes ranging from the southern Caribbean to North America, there are poems that depict the inconsolable condition of women struggling against the aridities of "love misplaced" and the resulting social inequities and enforced loneliness ("We Are the Women," "Mulatta Song," "Mulatta Song II," "Jamaica 1980," "Garden of the Women Once Fallen"). There are also the lyric narratives, in part expressed in the demotic, in part in the Creole standard, that extol, commemorate, and offer us lasting metaphorical strophes and images of human excellence and achievement

("To Us, All Flowers Are Roses," "Guyana Lovesong," "For Don Drummond," "Jah Music," "Lullaby for Jean Rhys," "For Rosa Parks," "On Becoming a Tiger"). And by the way, I consider "Heartease I," "Heartease II," and "Heartease III" to be among the most thematically important and sensitively written lyric demotic compositions in the collection (and surely among the finest of their kind in Caribbean poetry in English).

Then there are Goodison's mother poems, contemporary elegies, odes, and praise songs, substantially contemplative and emotional *yet* unsentimental, and which at once instruct and delight heart and mind and are some of the most memorably tender statements in the book ("I Am Becoming My Mother," "Guinea Woman," "The Woman Speaks to the Man Who Has Employed Her Son," "Mother the Great Stones Got to Move"). Altogether, these are the poems I like best, the ones that reveal the poet's regional and at the same time her universal sense of compassion. Of course, my all-time favorite Goodison poem is "For My Mother (May I Inherit Half Her Strength)," a resonant *cri de coeur* in support of the primacy of motherhood and family unity.

Andrew Salkey. *WLT.* 67, 4 (Autumn 1993), pp. 876–77

Goodison's is first of all a woman's voice, grounded not just in sorrow, but in resolution and independence; the voice of a woman who in her own litany is daughter, sister, mistress, friend, warrior, wife, and mother; the voice of a woman for whom home is a place where simple things are central, a place located here and now with pigeons roosting over the door and tomatoes growing in the garden, a place that nourishes the spirit and imagination. . . .

Goodison's poetic imagination includes both men and women, in Jamaica and elsewhere, with whom she shares a life of struggle and of freedom. But she grounds her imagination at home. In the poem "We Are the Women," she confirms her special bond with other West Indian women, past and present, notable and unknown. Silver coins and cloves of garlic, the precious and the commonplace, come together here in a ritual witnessing whose apocryphal character represents a collective wisdom outside the canon, unauthorized but true, the shared secrets of resistance and restoration. . . . The complementary images of rooting and burying, and of the land and the sea (the anchor to our navel strings), bring together here the whole history of slavery: the drowning at sea and the death on land and the harrowing legacy of sexual exploitation; the hiding away of secrets and the determination of those entrusted with them to give voice to new hope and to give birth to a new generation of . . . conquerors who will finally set their people free. . . .

Goodison's inspiration comes from a deep understanding of her experience as a West Indian woman. Images of that inspiration are drawn from the traditions of European literature, but they are transformed by Goodison not only into distinctly West Indian terms but also into her own. Literary tradition has given us the image of a female muse as the source of poetic inspiration. Goodison's muse is not some woman of shadowy power and intermittent presence, as a tradition dominated by men would have it, but is instead the figure of a man, overwhelming and unreliable at times (as muses tend to be), and created as a woman's image of inspiration. She writes about her muse in all the ways that are familiar to readers of European literature . . . except that her muse is different, inspiring her desires and dreams—and occasionally prompting her dismay—as a woman as well as a poet. She finds his image in the peace of God, and His wrath; in the preciousness of her son to her, and the fears she holds for him; in the power of love, her sometime destiny and her despair. Her muse is an image of otherness, a power beyond and within herself, both of her own devising and determined by her literary heritage. . . .

Through all the divisions and deceptions, there is a deep reserve of hopefulness in Goodison's work, sustained by the links she has forged between the poetic and the personal. There are risks here, mainly of self-conscious ingenuity and sentimental indulgence. But she takes them openly, with almost cavalier disregard for the different conventions of life and literature, in order to challenge our customary distinctions between reality and the imagination, and to bring a spirit of reconciliation back into poetry. In "My Last Poem (Again)," written several years later, she negotiates between images of love to which she has in a sense become hostage, and between the men who are figures of fear and hope to her—as a woman and as a poet. . . .

At the heart of Goodison's poetry is a profoundly religious sensibility, embracing a purpose that both transcends human understanding and is part of everyday life. There is much pain in her poetry, beginning with a recognition of the sorrow and suffering that are part of the heritage of all West Indians. But out of this heritage comes the dignity of a "Survivor," representing all those whom grace has touched . . . which in some measure should be all of us. . . .

Goodison, like [Edward Kamau] Brathwaite and [Derek] Walcott, writes poems of possibility—the possibility of understanding the past and present experience of West Indians, the possibility of sharing their heritage of pain, and the possibility of peace and light and love. Their poetic testaments are simply and unmistakably their own, bringing together the Old World of European and African inheritances with the New Land and literature of the West Indies.

J. Edward Chamberlin. *Come Back to Me My Language: Poetry and the West Indies* (Urbana: University of Illinois Press, 1993), pp. 196, 203–4, 207, 209–10, 212, 216

HARPER, MICHAEL S. (1938–   )

UNITED STATES

[Naively] I set out to write an omnibus essay-review, insufficiently aware of how many laminations and concentricities inform Michael S. Harper's complex and coherent oeuvre. . . . This is very likely the finest poetry now being written in a woebegotten and woebegone country—perhaps the best since John Berryman—and the serious reader had better buy or at least read all of it at once. . . . First, a clarification and an admonition. Clarification—Harper is a black poet; Harper is an American poet. Asked if he saw any contradiction in terms, he replied: "None at all. They are two aspects of the same story." In the same interview he spoke of his responsibility (calling, vocation) to connect "black idioms and black tradi-tional motifs" with "American institutions, the American lexicon, the American landscape." Beyond that, Harper writes toward "a totally new aesthetic, a totally new world-view" not yet existing, and a place never before conceived. In other words, "a poet has a responsibility to his people. And when I say people, I mean all people." To start with, Harper wants to re-create America, substituting for the Declaration of Independence ("a document written for a handful of men to pro-tect their interests and commodities") what he calls "the democratic Promise." Like John Coltrane, Harper makes his way by "extension and overextension.". . .

Admonition—Harper's aesthetics are not easy, either for himself or for his reader. His key verbs are *to do* (action) and *to go* (process). But he must always move against the resistances of American history, which stand in nearly total contradiction to his poetics and politics. It is not only a matter of breaking cages (Harper's metaphor for preconceptions), nor of overt racial oppression.

Edwin Fussell. Parnassus. 4, 1 (Fall/Winter 1975), pp. 5–6

With the publication of his sixth book of poems, *Nightmare Begins Responsibility*, Michael S. Harper has begun to receive the kind of thoughtful, critical attention he has always deserved. Reviews of *Nightmare* and "reconsiderations" of his entire canon have poured forth, not just in newspaper book columns, but also in journals like the *New Republic*, *Parnassus*, and *New Letters*. Rarely content sim-ply to quote a powerful line, reviewers like Laurence Lieberman are writing extra-ordinary praises such as "Michael Harper is uniquely creating in his poetic art an indispensable . . . segment of the American moral conscience." We need to hear this; we need to be assured (or informed) that, despite occasional evidence to the contrary, poets still mine the human predicament, especially in its American con-tortion, not to relish it but instead to retrieve and to present artfully its moral and spiritual teachings. What interests me, and is the concern of this essay, is how Harper's studies of his kin figure fit into this; how kinship is for him a recurring metaphor for poetic process, the artist's obligations to traditions, and for living a life morally and well.

In pursuing these questions, I find myself less concerned with portraits, even though they are often considerable efforts like "Reuben, Reuben," and more attentive to poetic sequences or series. My search is for evidence of kinship-in-process, and sequences of poems, possibly because they *are* sequences, seem to yield up what I'm after. In *Dear John, Dear Coltrane*, for example, "We Assume: On the Death of Our Son, Reuben Masai Harper," "Deathwatch," and the aforementioned "Reuben, Reuben" are three extraordinary portraits of Reuben and Michael, the sons "torn away." Taken by themselves, they are powerful statements of horror fused to love. . . . But to receive the fuller, more variegated expression of kinship suggested by these portraits we must return them to their surroundings, to the landscape Harper has meticulously seeded with other poems. There are no "labeled" sections to *Dear John*; it is the only Harper volume not predivided by numbers or titles. But moving backward from the Reuben/Michael portraits to "American History," and forwards to "After the Operations," we discover that the poems grouped therein have a certain unity. As they sustain each other we gain a context, present and historic, in which to receive the dead sons and their grieving kin.

Robert B. Stepto. MassR. 17, 3 (Autumn 1976), pp. 477–78

For Michael Harper the mission of poetry is bound up with eloquence and the magic of the spoken word, the oral tradition. Harper is a poet whose vision of personal and national experience is worked out in the Afro-American grain— the tradition of pain and rejuvenation expressed in the sorrow songs, the blues, and folktales, the whole range of Afro-American oral tradition, a tradition, it is important to remember, which also touches formal American/Afro-American rhetorical patterns, from Abraham Lincoln and Frederick Douglass in the nineteenth century to Martin Luther King in the 1950s and 1960s. Harper is alert to the possibilities of rhetoric and the complexities of that ancient and American rhetorical tradition whose purpose was to challenge, vex, please, persuade, and, at last, illuminate the audience. He is a poet not of paradox but of the paradoxical, of simplicity in the midst of complexities, affirmation in the midst of tragedy—but affirmations so aware of the incongruities of eloquence that his voice intensifies the sense of tragedy and devastation. . . .

At forty, Harper has written a dozen or more extraordinary poems, poems long-lived and stunningly original, poems that transform his stance as an American/Afro-American poet into a reality with the power of illumination. *Images of Kin* is a collection of Harper's best and most representative work. Beginning with *Healing Song [for the Inner Ear]*, a selection of recent, previously uncollected poems, and "Uplift from a Dark Tower," Harper's important poem stalking Booker T. Washington's connection with the Trask family and its Yaddo estate, *Images of Kin* reverses chronological lines and travels back through Harper's prolific earlier volumes: *Nightmare Begins Responsibility*; *Debridement*; *Song: I Want a Witness*; *History Is Your Own Heartbeat*; and *Dear John, Dear Coltrane*.

Arranging and organizing one's poems can be a difficult and perplexing task, particularly this early when the writer's trajectory may not yet be clear. In the case of *Images of Kin*, Harper seems to have been governed by an urge to see, feel, and make known the past in the present moment—understandably, given his emphasis on healing and transformation. Nevertheless, in my view the cutting edge of the current work is somewhat diluted by its being presented first. In the sense that [William Butler] Yeats called poetry a quarrel with ourselves it may be that some of the current poems need the dramatic declaration and details of the early work, particularly *Dear John, Dear Coltrane* and *History Is Your Own Heartbeat*. Not that Harper's early poetry is always simple and direct. It is not, and neither is the later work inaccessible or uncompelling, but I think that even the best of the current poems ("Tongue-Tied in Black and White," "Bristol: Bicentenary Remembrances of Trade," and "Smoke," for instance) are richer for the contexts worked out and made familiar in earlier poems. The moments of controlled eloquence in the current poems might have a greater impact if the collection were arranged chronologically.

John F. Callahan. BALF. 13, 3 (Fall 1979), p. 89

Certainly a commitment to kinship gives Harper a scope and freedom of position, as well as a substance and fineness of relationship, that [James Weldon] Johnson does not imagine, nor [Richard] Wright and [Ralph] Ellison, for all the sweep of their works, approach. Kinship and, with it, a fuller range of psychopolitical complexity may have come into [Ellison's] *Invisible Man* through Mary, who embodies patience, compassion, and practicality. But the inflated and drifting ambition of the invisible man will not let him operate on Mary's level. He is with his oratory what Ras is with his weaponry, a believer in grand and instant solutions. Only on this level does Ras, the creator of the riot, prevent the invisible man from going back to Mary. To go back is *physically* within his compass, but psychologically he is blocked by his persistent grandiosity. With Wright the case is even more problematical. Wright offers overpowering accumulation, without overpowering range.

But there are signs that Harper's scope and his orientation to kinship may come largely from the will. A note of harshness, an air of impatience not tempered by humor, a kind of vulnerability pitched near dark resentment and rage: these belie the grace and strength kinship would seem to connote. The metamorphosis of "The Families Album" is forced and problematical: "this old house which was hers / made her crooked back a shingle, / her covered eye this fireplace oven." "Sambo's Mistakes: An Essay," which is evidently inspired by A. J. Langguth's *Jesus Christs*, does not reflect the elastic irony of its source, but falls into a dehumanized, rigid violence. One is only arrested for the moment when, after a detailed account of Sambo's difficulties and disabilities, the poem comes up with its one-word litany of Sambo's "Strengths: guns." Uncomplicated by strength of principle and of heart, the strength of guns is tantamount to anarchy.

Michael G. Cooke. Afro-American Literature in the
Twentieth Century: The Achievement of Intimacy
(New Haven, Conn.: Yale University Press, 1984), pp. 121–22

In *Nightmare Begins Responsibility*, Harper presents, as an introduction, a set of aphorisms entitled, "Kin." The sentences are set forth as a basic chord structure of the songs he will perform throughout the book. As such, they are useful to the reader, enabling one to keep in mind just what themes are important to the writer, and they are useful in determining whether the writer fulfills his self-imposed intentions. Several of these aphorisms are especially pertinent as descriptions of the vocation of the *Poet* as Harper sees himself. . . .

As a human being, Harper believes that "life's terms" must be met; and as a poet, Harper argues that the existing techniques and traditions of poetry must be confronted. It is enough to master the forms, because in mastery the artist demonstrates power. But something must be added to nature, to life, to the "available realistic or legendary material." The world in which Michael Harper lives is not significantly different from the world of Paul Laurence Dunbar or John Coltrane. That world is the real and legendary *America*, a world where the souls of black folk are continually threatened with dreams which turn into nightmares. For Harper, technique is natural, the easy part of poetry. What he wrestles with in his poetry is what he sets out for himself in his declaration of intentions: understanding and conscience. Harper's methodology derives from the music of his maturity. If the dream becomes a nightmare, if the legend is a lie, say so; confront the wall head-on, swallow the fire straight, with no soothing "chaser."

Joseph A. Brown, SJ. Callaloo. 9, 1 (Winter 1986), pp. 210–11

The poems [of *Debridement*] are about a black soldier who won the Congressional Medal of Honor for heroism in Vietnam but then, when he returned to civilian life in Detroit, was unable to cope with a paradoxical combination of fame and poverty and was eventually shot to death while trying to rob a suburban grocery store. The sequence is not, as it might appear at first reading, just an attempt to rewrite Vietnam according to a different myth—i.e., the myth of America as oppressor, which stems, of course, from slavery, the central fact of black American history. Such an approach would be just as reductive, just as false to the particulars of human experience, as the myth of the liberator. Instead, the sequence attempts to heal the mythological wound of Vietnam by replacing the possible closed myths with what Harper calls an "open-ended myth," a myth that takes into account the contingencies of human experience and tries not to distort the particulars of that experience. Thus, the sequence is in part critical: It analyzes the collision of mythmaking discursive strategies through which our understanding of Vietnam has been generated, and it dramatizes the mythological machinery through which cultural and historical "truths" are systematically maintained by a sort of cultural blindness and historical amnesia. But the sequence is also creative: By remaining always conscious of the poem's status as a mediating and therefore potentially reductive or distorting mythical discourse and by constantly exposing the reductiveness and distortions of the established myths which infiltrate the sequence, Harper offers in *Debridement* a new sort of history, a new sort of mythology—a language of "open-ended myth" capable of articulating between the brutal human reality of warfare and the broader cultural meanings of that violence.

Kyle Grimes. BALF. 24, 3 (Fall 1990), p. 419

"Uplift from a Dark Tower" offers the simultaneous compressing and magnifying of personal and historical experience, a sense of the paradox and modal possibilities of jazz and blues. "Uplift" is complex in its narrative texture and pluralistic visions. Clearly in the jazz tradition, the poem is defined by its metaphoric variations, its sense of the poet as articulator or articulate hero, its simultaneity and multiple thought contexts as it breaks out of the traditional confinements of landscape, personality, and history; the poet, like the jazz musician, "seizes . . . the territory.". . .

In Harper's poetry, jazz is not a metaphor for battles and dilemmas of self but for the resolution in journeys of the spirit. The African-American's own music has a unifying effect, which brings a sense of wholeness to the individual, not in solitude as Hermann Hesse's *Steppenwolf* or James Joyce's [*A Portrait of the Artist as a Young Man*], but in communion (or if solitude, then communing solitude). One also sees the potential of the jazz perspective for reintegrating the whole of American experience in a "rainbowed" text. For the African-American artists the music is universal, complex, and multileveled in its identities. They claim for their music the "thousands and thousands" of possibilities that the Steppenwolf would claim for his own. It is music that renders visible the "spirit of a people" and can also have cosmic dimensions, music that "strengthens and confirms."

The poet's vision from the dark tower, then, like the jazz musician's, "conjures being," reclaims the whole. It is a modal perception. As defined by Harper, "The African Continuum is a *modal* concept which views the cosmos as a totally integrated environment where all spiritual forces interact . . . the music that provides images strong enough to give back that power that renews." His own "Uplift from the Dark Tower" is such music.

Gayl Jones. Liberating Voices: Oral Tradition in African American Literature
(Cambridge, Mass.: Harvard University Press, 1991), pp. 44, 53–54

HARRIS, WILSON (1921–   )

GUYANA

Its constantly evolving character notwithstanding, a remarkable unity of thought conveys this considerable opus [*Palace of the Peacock*]. Two major elements seem to have shaped [Wilson] Harris's approach to art and his philosophy of existence: the impressive contrasts of the Guyanese landscapes, with which his survey expeditions made him familiar, and the successive waves of conquest which gave Guyana its heterogeneous population polarized for centuries into oppressors and their victims. The two, landscape and history, merge in his work into single metaphors symbolizing man's inner space saturated with the effects of historical—that is, temporal—experiences. The jungle, for example, is for Harris both outer and inner unreclaimed territory, the actual "landscape of history" for those who only survived by disappearing into it and a metaphor for that inner psychological recess to which his characters relegate both their forgotten ancestors and the living whom they dominate. It contrasts with the savannahs and is itself full of contrasts. Though teeming with life, much of it is invisible to the ordinary "material" eye, just as those who, willingly or not, lead an underground existence and remain unseen save to the "spiritual" (imaginative) eye. The jungle's extrahuman dimensions suggest timelessness and offer a glimpse of eternity, while the constant renewal of the vegetation confirms its existence within a cyclical time pattern. In Harris's words the jungle "travels eternity to season"; and the Amerindians, who move to and fro between that secret primeval world and the modern areas where they can find work, subsist, as he writes in *Tumatumari*, "on a dislocated scale of time." They are an essential link between the modern Guyanese and the lost world of their undigested past, and must be retrieved from their buried existence in both real and symbolical *terra incognita* if Guyana (and the individual soul) is to absorb all its components into a harmonious community. . . .

Harris's fiction began to appear at a crucial time for both the nascent West Indian fiction and the novel in English since, in the 1950s and early 1960s, the trends in English and American fiction indicated that many inheritors of established traditions had ceased to believe in them. The dissolution of values and forms due to the combined action of history and science had left artists in a void similar in kind to that experienced with more tragic intensity by West Indians throughout their history. With a few notable exceptions, English and American novelists reacted to this loss of certainty by either seeking refuge and renewing their faith in realism, or turning experimental fiction into an art of the absurd, technically brilliant and [innovative] but often undermining the very purpose of art. Wilson Harris is among the very few West Indian writers who pointed out the irrelevance of both trends to a "native" art of fiction. While insisting that the disorientation of the "diminished man" in formerly strong societies had been experienced for centuries by the conquered populations in the Caribbean and the Americas, he warned particularly against the influence on West Indian writers of the postwar European art of despair. His own "art of compassion" does not involve, as has sometimes been suggested, a withdrawal from history in order to transcend it. It is, on the contrary, intensely concerned with the impact of history on the ordinary "obscure human person" and expresses a passionate denial of what has been termed the "historylessness" of the Caribbean; it shows that people exist by virtue of their silent suffering as much as by celebrated deeds or a materially recognizable civilization, of which incidentally obscure men are the unacknowledged executors.

Hena Maes-Jelinek. In Bruce King, ed.
West Indian Literature (Hamden, Conn.:
Archon Books, 1979), pp. 179–82

If Wilson Harris has any direct forebear, it is T. S. Eliot with his meditations on time and tradition, and his fragmentation of narrative into a mosaic of dissociated images and symbols expressive of the chaos of modern culture and the individual mind attempting to piece together an encompassing vision out of personal disorder. While the allusions, techniques, symbols, and even occasional phrases are similar, Harris differs from Eliot in trying to create a new world myth of process whereas the American poet sought to lose himself in an impersonal tradition, salvaged from the ruins of the Old World. Harris refers to fossils not as records but as gateways to an imaginative participation in the culture and events of the past. It is only through such an extension of the imagination that rigidly fixed cultural and racial boundaries, with their social superiorities and animosities, can be destroyed, and the many peoples of the New World can renew their contact with each other, recognizing that their shared history involves more basic experiences than are accepted by such stereotypes as colonizer, slave, or exterminated Indian. . . .

The four novels in the *Guiana Quartet* roughly form a chronological sequence from the days of conquest (*Palace of the Peacock*), the period of slavery and Indian indenture (*The Far Journey of Oudin*), the establishment of a frontier society and law (*The Whole Armour*), and the imposition of a modern state on the land (*The Secret Ladder*). As the setting approaches modern times and notions of reality, with linked cause and effect, it becomes more necessary to show the primitive truths of experience that are hidden to the compartmentalized mind. The attack on what we might call scientific thought is also a freeing of the imagination from the boundaries imposed by colonization and Europe on the New World. Thus the role of Cristo in *The Whole Armour* both has analogies to the role of Christ in the Christian scheme of redemption and is different as is fitting to a New World context. Underlying the novel is an awareness of basic myths of death and renewal: Abram is killed by a tiger; Cristo is made by Magda to disguise himself in Abram's garment, then he kills the tiger and wears his skin. In his tiger skin he returns to the village and initiates a chain of events that changes the lives of important characters within the story. Sharon, formerly a frigid "snow-maiden," becomes Cristo's lover in the jungle. Cristo is hunted by the tiger and by the law as a murderer. His death or sacrifice is part of the tragedy of renewal in a world of process. Such sacrifice is necessary: "Cristo would be free in the end, it seemed to state, in an armor superior to the elements of self-division and coercion. Magda fell on her knees and prayed. There was nothing else to do."

Bruce King. *The New English Literatures: Cultural Nationalism in a Changing World* (New York: St. Martin's Press, 1980), pp. 109–10, 112–13

For Wilson Harris, "exile," deliberately sought and accepted, becomes the necessary first step in the development and growth of the creative imagination. And it is the sense of exploration, of self-discovery (as part of a dynamic "drama of consciousness") that marks his work. His early novels, from *Palace of the Peacock* to *Heartland*, deal with this main theme of the spiritual journey of the hero who has to discover, by trial and error, an "authentic" existence. In *Palace of the Peacock*, Donne, the leader of a boat crew on a journey up river in the Guyana interior, is on a quest that has many significances, the chief of which is the search for illumination or true selfhood. All the characters die, yet experience a rebirth or reawakening in the process. Theirs is also a circular journey, like Sir Gawain's, from outer, encrusted personality to naked, inner self. . . .

In the later novels, this theme of the journey toward selfhood is extended to include and emphasize the idea of the imprisoning quality of personality and the positive value of "*identitylessness*" of a "liminal" state, as a means toward a genuine resensing of the world. The need for a rejection of preconceptions and biases about social and political freedom, about history and tradition, becomes paramount.

In *Tumatumari*, Prudence, as the prevailing consciousness in the novel— the figure of Mnemosyne, the Greek Muse of Memory (as well as the embodiment of the rootless, historyless, identityless condition of West Indian society)—makes an imaginative journey back through history through the labyrinth of memory. It is an "adventure into the hinterland of ancestors.". . .

In *Black Marsden* the hero, Clive Goodrich, sees the landscape of Scotland as inextricably interwoven with that of his native South America: tropical and Mediterranean civilizations merge in spite of contrasts because he himself has gained freedom from his own, imprisoning "I" which tends to "fix" other people, other cultures in static frames like the eye of a camera.

Later still, in *Companions of the Day and Night* the hero, "Idiot Nameless," is literally without identity, the nameless, archetypal fool. The book is a sequel to *Black Marsden*. Clive Goodrich receives from Marsden a confused collection of manuscripts, sculptures, and paintings—"the Idiot Nameless collection"—the work of an unknown man, a tourist, whose dead body has been found at the base of the Pyramid of the Sun in Teotihuacan in Mexico. The novel is a flashback as Goodrich edits the writings which begin to reveal "doorways through which the Idiot Nameless moved." He gradually enters the Nameless collection and becomes aware of "the mystery of companionship . . . and . . . frightening wisdom" they embody. . . .

[*Da Silva da Silva's Cultivated Wilderness; and, Genesis of the Clowns*] carries forward this theme of the "interior journey" with great technical skill and imaginative power. The hero of *Da Silva* is married and lives in a Holland Park flat in Kensington. He is a composite man. Born in Brazil of Spanish, Portuguese, and African stock, orphaned early, he survives cyclone and flood to be adopted by the British Ambassador. Growing up in England with access to his rich benefactor's library, he gradually becomes convinced that his "parentless" condition obliges him to create, to "paint" himself and his world anew. Seeing everything in terms of his art, he discovers new "illuminations" and "unpredictable destinies" within the most apparently solid and uniform people and events. As his "canvases" multiply, the range of his awareness widens. Relationships with Jen, with Manya (the model with "a reputation for chaos"), with schoolmistress Kate Robinson, with Legba Cuffey (composite rebel slave leader/West Indian barman/Haitian folk god), gain in complexity. The bare framework of his life becomes a crowded canvas of interlocking past and present lives as he "cultivates" the apparently static wilderness of identity, historical fact, and urban existence.

Michael Gilkes. *The West Indian Novel*
(Boston: Twayne, 1981), pp. 145–46, 149

The Eye of the Scarecrow occupies a privileged place in Wilson Harris's fiction: chronologically, in the sequence of the author's novels, it opens a "second phase" after the Guyanese cycle. Stylistically, it explores new modes of expression and presents some difficulty for a reader who has not yet become acquainted with Harris's work on language. More so than previous works, *The Eye of the Scarecrow* is rooted in history and based on recognizable places: the East Street house in Georgetown where the narrator spends his youth was built on the site of a plantation which was in turn owned by nationals of the main successive colonizing powers. In the background of the plot we find evocations of the great strike of 1948, which was a decisive step towards political awareness and a prelude of independence for Guyana. Here dates relate the story to actual events. Yet, as always with Wilson Harris, history and time are used unconventionally. . . .

Memory is so important for the writer not because it merely enables one to relive forgotten moments but also because of its creative potential. The narrator of *The Eye of the Scarecrow* sees himself as if he "were a ghost returning to the same place (which was always different), shoring up different ruins (which were always the same)." In this interplay between difference and identity lies the center of the artist's quest when he realizes that well-known and commonplace objects have unexpected aspects, whereas the most unrelated elements can be put into mysterious dialogue and resonance. Reflection is the first stage of recognition in the same way as surprise and disorientation are preliminary to more profound knowledge. To see the world—and oneself—in reverse is a necessary step to genuine awareness in Harris's world. The creator discovers—and helps the reader to accept—that radically different facts, people, or ideas can echo one another and pertain to a common logic. For him, deconstruction reconstructs, the distinction between the two processes being that the first applies to static structures whereas the second helps to elaborate transformational and more fruitful patterns. . . .

In *The Eye of the Scarecrow*, paradox is more than ever an instrument of discovery. The movement which Harris sees at the heart of resonance and meaning becomes "the flight of stillness." In a novel mingling plot and self-reflexivity, the author progresses in cyclic fashion. Events, characters, and ideas echo one another; but the importance does not lie in the static repetition of self-contained elements. In each mirror-pattern, the image evokes the model without reproducing it exactly. Thus the creator shows the necessity for both relationship and "exile." . . . The artist considers that genuine identity does not lie in traditional harmony. On the contrary it opens onto difference of a radical kind.

Behind every shape lurks a shadow; behind consonance one may perceive dissonance. The artist, demonlike, lifts the veil on new perspectives. He dons the raiment of the scarecrow to open our eyes and become our own vicarious gauge of experience, our engineer of depth.

Jean-Pierre Durix. *WLWE*. 22, 1 (Spring 1983), pp. 55, 68–71

In his recent fiction Harris becomes more and more interested in the novel as a form of art akin to painting. In *Da Silva [da Silva's Cultivated Wilderness]* and *The Tree of the Sun* much of the plot arises out of a picture which Da Silva, the protagonist, is painting in his studio. The artist is created by his work as much as he creates it. The novel brings to light a subtle sort of mutuality which enables the characters to reach unsuspected dimensions and discover hidden layers of history. This passion for visual effects also leads Harris to experiment with graphic representations inserted in his texts. This starts in *The Waiting Room* but becomes even more noticeable in *Ascent to Omai* with a series of eight concentric circles around a point called "Stone/Epitaph One." Each circle is given the name of one of the major metaphors of the novel (Madonna, Baboon, Raven, Parrot, Iron Mask, Rose, Whale, Petticoat). The graph illustrates Harris's particular use of language. All-important but separate images are brought into forced contact, thus engendering new forms and meanings, which symbolically exemplifies Harris's general theory of art as an attempt to overcome fixed polarities. The work of the writer causes a shock similar to the fall of a stone in a pool. The energy fans outward and then inward again when it has rebounded on the edges. The elements—here the different ripples—are animated by a current which causes them to react to each other and to be transformed by the different collisions. Harris suggests that images can be given one-sided equivalents only on a superficial level. With his bold couplings of apparently disparate units he suggests that one can reactivate seemingly sterile representations.

Jean-Pierre Durix. *WLT*. 58, 1 (Winter 1984), p. 21

Among the novels of Guyanese author Wilson Harris, *The Secret Ladder* is generally considered different from the others because of its relative clearness and straightforward narrative. . . . However, despite its apparent simplicity, *The Secret Ladder* already poses the problem of the functioning of the imagination in a subtle way which has frequently been overlooked.

The novel unfolds along a seven-day period, an echo of the creation of the world in Genesis. Art is thus equated with the essential activity which consists in giving shape and meaning to chaos. The title certainly contains an allusion to Jacob's dream in the Bible. Writing for Wilson Harris means the abolition of the barriers between the material world and what, for want of a better word, I will call "otherness." The novel is a dreamlike experience in which the reader, like Jacob, is promised some kind of revelation, the annunciation of visionary possibilities. . . .

The narrative structure of *The Secret Ladder* follows a relatively straightforward line, both in the succession of events and in its temporal organization. The plot unfolds in a linear way and is conveyed to the reader through an alteration of dialogues and narrative interventions. The third-person narrator describes settings, suggests moods and frequently interprets the characters' thoughts. . . . The voice which speaks through this third person might appear omniscient. Yet the only certainties which it provides concern the impossibility to *know* anything for sure, to distinguish appearances from the hidden life which binds the elements in creation. Its comments are never definite except in unmasking prejudices. They provide paradoxical representations which, far from closing the plot, question any possibility of exhaustive meaning. Wilson Harris leaves few opportunities for the reader to "translate" images into one-sided equivalents. Metaphors become significant only through the networks of ever-changing relations which they form. Even if the world of *The Secret Ladder* is less puzzling than that in *Palace of the Peacock*, the reader can rely only on the narrator's intervention to guide him through a maze of complex evocations. The latter becomes a guide who lets the former into a less and less recognizable land where certainties vanish one after the other. The reader is like Dante following a sort of Virgil whose words become more and more mysterious. Through the device of "omniscience," the narrator of *The Secret Ladder* proves that omniscience does not exist.

Jean-Pierre Durix. *Ariel.* 15, 2 (April 1984), pp. 27, 35–36

In his two previous collections of critical essays, *Tradition, the Writer and Society* and *Explorations,* [Harris] presents the reader with a vision of a new society which underlies his aesthetic concepts, and with his notions about the function of the writer. His latest critical work, *The Womb of Space: The Cross-Cultural Imagination*, will again serve as "an indispensable guide to Harris's understanding of his own novels," but it is much more than that. It is an attack on the traditional critical establishment, for which "literature is still constrained by regional and other conventional but suffocating categories."

Utilizing a genuinely comparative approach, Harris juxtaposes and analyzes the work of two dozen writers from Europe, Africa, the Americas, Asia, and Australia and finds that on a cross-cultural level "each work complexly and peculiarly revises another and is inwardly revised in turn in profound context." The writers he discusses include William Faulkner, Edgar Allan Poe, Ralph Ellison, Jean Toomer, Juan Rulfo, Jay Wright, Jean Rhys, Paule Marshall, Djuna Barnes, Patrick White, Aimé Césaire, Derek Walcott, Christopher Okigbo, Edward Brathwaite, Mervyn Peake, Emma Tennant, Claude Simon, Raja Rao, and Zulfikar Ghose. Each of these writers, Harris contends, has unknowingly (intuitively) been attempting to free himself or herself from the shackles of cultural homogeneity, since homogeneity "as a cultural model, exercised by a ruling ethnic group, tends to become an organ of conquest and division because of *imposed* unity that actually subsists on the suppression of others."

Reinhard Sander. *WLT.* 59, 3 (Summer 1985), p. 477

The action of *Carnival* centers around the psychic journey of the narrator Jonathan Weyl, who, under the guidance of his "interior-guide" Everyman

Masters, travels back in time from his present-day domicile in the imperial center, London, into the "Inferno" of Guyanese history of the 1920s. He there witnesses a series of actions, each of which portrays emblematically one way in which the colonial encounter can be allegorized, but each of which, in itself, provides an inadequate "reading" of colonial history and the investments of power within it. To use the language of the novel itself, each separate action constitutes a "frame" within which at least two kinds of meaning operate. In the first instance, there is an absolutist and blinding meaning that "conscripts the imagination" and binds the characters to some kind of overwhelming pattern of perception—fear, desire, anger, and so on—that seems imposed from an outside source. But behind this, there is a second kind of meaning that teases itself into the interstices of the narrative and that can be "glimpsed through barred gate and segmented mask"—the kind of meaning the text associates with the concept of "Carnival evolution." Here, "sovereign" forms of perception that inhere in the hierarchical structures of tradition are shown to contain decentering or fissuring impulses that can erupt into consciousness and thus liberate vision from its material restraints into the imaginative reaches of what Harris calls "a kind of far viewing." The two kinds of meaning are in dialectical relation to one another, each exerting pressure on the kinds of meanings Weyl, Masters, and the characters within the tableaulike episodes will derive; and because the two levels of meaning can never come together, there always remains a slippage of signification which engenders new characters, new episodes, and new meanings as the narrative proceeds. The pattern of the novel is thus incremental, each frame in the narrative generating new patterns of association that qualify the meanings of the preceding frames, and each in turn being modified and disrupted by the frames that develop out of it. . . .

Much of what takes place in Harris's writing, or in his speech for that matter, seems baldly modernist: its gnomic obscurity, its search for "new" forms, its Romantic highbrowism, its syncretic drive, its apparent subjectivism—all of them elements which modernism's detractors see as contributing to "a tyranny of the creative imagination over the public." Where such a profoundly unsocial characterization falls short in regard to Harris's work is in the kind of cultural *work* his fictions, as *postcolonial* documents, seek to perform. The canonical center, if nothing else, is *textual*, and as a site for the operations of a dominant discourse it has consistently worked to textualize or "prefigure" colonial space as a projection of its own metaphysical, social, and cognitive systems—that is, as a term within a European cultural thematics, unmarked by any measure of difference save that constituted by the concept of "lack." But by rewriting signs of the canon into fictive structures of *difference*, Harris's text functions discursively as what Homi Bhabha identifies as a "hybrid object": that is, as a peculiar agent of replication within which the authoritative symbol is both retained and resisted. . . . *Carnival*—like the true and false shaman figures within it, whose immeasurable blows on the mudshore flats initiate the novel's dialectical action—both *dis*figures and *re*figures the discursive space of power upon which tradition actuates. It reoccupies the theater of textuality and replaces its authoritative signs with dialogic fictions whose narratives, at even the minutest level of representation, are always double. And it subjects the absolutist monuments of history to the gaze of an ex-centric and non-complicit reading practice which seeks not only to transform inherited codes of recognition into new ways of "reading" tradition but also to deconstruct those monuments through the discursive reoccupation of the ground upon which their shadows fall.

Stephen Slemon. Ariel. 19, 3 (July 1988), pp. 59–60, 69–70

Though *Carnival* seemed like a climax in [Harris's] opus, *The Infinite Rehearsal* probes even deeper into the labyrinths of self and nature to present as facets of the same allegorical quest the survival of modern civilization and the creative process of fiction writing. Significantly, it is a "rewriting" of the ever-modern myth of Faust, who longed to reach heights accessible to God only and thereby pierce the mysteries of creation but paradoxically attempted to do so through a pact with the devil. There can be no such pact in Harris's novel because good and evil are not separate moral categories. Like Harris's earlier fictions, this novel reads as a dialogue between the living and the dead, close and distant voices, or sovereign and lost traditions. The first-person narrator, Robin Redbreast Glass, is dead but speaks through W. H., his "adversary," with whom he nevertheless shares "an approach to the ruling concepts of civilization . . . from the ruled or apparently eclipsed side of humanity." Since his Da Silva novels, Harris has entered his own fiction as a character "in search of a species of fiction" as if the fiction preexisted, a "living text" brought to the fore through a polyphonic narrative in which both he and the existences or "agents of personality" he creates are vessels rather than the omnipotent author and sovereign characters of realistic fiction. Tenuous, even uncertain facts underlie Glass's narrative. He introduces himself as a "gravedigger in a library of dreams and a pork-knocker [a gold and diamond prospector] in the sacred wood [echoes of Dante and [T. S.] Eliot]." He drowned in 1961 at the age of sixteen with his Aunt Miriam, his mother Alice, and a small party of children, actors in Aunt Miriam's childhood theater in which she staged plays "revising the histories of the world," in order to revise also the deprivations she called "*illiteracies of the heart and mind.*" Only Peter and Emma were saved. Glass and W. H. are each a fictionalized character in the other's narrative, and each claims to have been in bed feverish with flu when the accident occurred, after which W. H. occupied Aunt Miriam's little theater while Glass set out for the "sacred wood" "in the multitextual regions of space." Actually, the shipwreck in which Aunt Miriam, the female creator, and her young actors drowned can be read as the shipwreck of civilization. Both Third- and First-World catastrophes are evoked as the Guyana strike and riots of 1948 (also the hub of the historical reconstruction in *The Eye*), the destruction of earlier Western civilizations, the two World Wars, Hiroshima and Nagasaki, the civil war in Lebanon, and the Chernobyl disaster.

Hena Maes-Jelinek. In János Riesz and Alain Ricard, eds.
Semper Aliquid Novi: Littérature Comparée et Littératures d'Afrique
(Tübingen: Gunter Narr, 1990), pp. 159–60

HEAD, BESSIE (1937–1986)

SOUTH AFRICA

Like many other black South African writers, Bessie Head lives in exile from South Africa. Her chosen place of exile is neighboring Botswana, where she has lived since 1964, in her words, "as a stateless person," who is required to register with the local police. Her three novels are set in Botswana, and her themes reflect the exile's prevailing sense of homelessness. But in its most profound sense, Head's fiction draws significantly upon the experience of being a non-white in South Africa, for the denial of civil rights to the South African non-white encourages Head's sense of homelessness in much the same way that the system of apartheid fragments the individual's sense of personal integrity. Physical exile and the permanent status as a refugee in Botswana are not distinguished, in Head's fiction, from the stateless condition which South Africa represents for nonwhites living in that country. Indeed, Head's personal background confirms this symbolism. She was born in an asylum for the insane to a white woman who had been placed in the institution for having dared to become pregnant by Bessie's black father, and her enforced condition as orphan is an intrinsic part of a continuing experience which has denied her a national identity in southern Africa, especially in Botswana and South Africa.

Head's racial experience as a South African "colored" (to borrow the quaint South African designation for racially mixed persons) has encouraged a profound alienation from prevailing ethical traditions and from many existing social institutions. This rebelliousness goes hand in hand with a certain skepticism about what she sees as the special disadvantages of women. This skepticism inspires a search, in her novels, for humane sexual roles and political values within a harmonious social order. In her fiction, the limitations of the woman's role and self-image, and the historical dispossession of the nonwhite are the very essence of a pervasive social malaise. In Head's view, that malaise assumes the proportions of a far-ranging moral crisis: racism, sexism, poverty, and entrenched social inequities are both the special ills of her world in southern Africa and the symptoms of a universal moral disorder. This revulsion at the moral wasteland of her world has also inspired an intensely moral idealism, one that assumes the force of a crusade in her fiction, sparking the quest for a more creative and less power-hungry sense of self. Head's work as a writer is closely integrated with her personal life in Botswana, for she has chosen to live in a rural village, working in a farming cooperative in which political refugees of all kinds and colors attempt to develop a thriving community out of Botswana's unpromising terrain—creating, in Head's words, "new worlds out of nothing."

Lloyd W. Brown. *Women Writers in Black Africa*
(Westport, Conn.: Greenwood Press, 1981), pp. 158–59

[Head's] three novels all deal with the reorientation of the exile to a new, somewhat hostile society. The autobiographical basis evident in the experience of her lead characters gives credence to her fictionalized and hence, generalized, exile-portraits. The progression from the position of affirmation of *When Rain Clouds Gather*, her first novel, to the uncertain, thin hope of survival through individual inner strength of her latest, *A Question of Power*, mirrors Bessie Head's own unrewarded struggle for acceptance in her new community.

It is significant that her first exile figure, Makhaya, in *When Rain Clouds Gather*, is a male. He achieves satisfaction in meaningful work with Gilbert, the English engineer, as they initiate land reclamation in Botswana. He achieves marital satisfaction and intellectual companionship with Paulina, a passionate and vigorous woman who leads the village women in making agricultural experiments. His success is paralleled for the village, Golema Mmidi, itself. This tiny community triumphs over its evil overlord through group action. The villagers, in common concern, defeat the chief's persecution of Paulina. Makhaya shares in this fulfillment. So, despite the poverty, the unremitting labor, the tragedy of a child shepherd's death, Makhaya—and the reader— achieve affirmation. This affirmation has its basis in shared human concern. . . .

In her second novel, *Maru*, her personal identification with the fictionalized woman's position, suggested earlier in her characters of Maria and Paulina in *Rain Clouds*, is clear. In *Maru* the first central female character, Margaret Cadmore, is an Englishwoman teaching in Africa. She adopts and educates an abandoned Bushman child and gives the child her name. The second Margaret Cadmore becomes the main protagonist of the novel. This Margaret is light-skinned—a suspicious color—just as Bessie Head in South Africa is identified as "colored." Neither character nor creator is a member of the black majority— of South Africa, of Botswana, or of the African continent itself. . . .

A Question of Power reflects a variety of emotional crises resulting from stress upon this sensitive writer. Even the name of the lead character, like the nursery rhyme refrain—Elizabeth, Betty, Betsy and Bess—evidences the self-identification of the writer with her lead character. Head takes the reader through Elizabeth's emotional breakdowns which immediately follow her exile and then recur later and provoke her dismissal from her teaching assignment. "Something was going drastically wrong with her own life. Just the other day she had broken down and cried . . . 'I'm not sure I'm quite normal any more.'" Shortly thereafter, Elizabeth receives the school board report: "We have received a report that you have been shouting and swearing at people in public. Such behavior is unbecoming to a teacher. We are doubtful of your sanity, and request that you submit to us a certificate of sanity within fourteen days of receipt of this notice." The hospital suggested is too far away, the situation humiliating, the other teachers hostile. The conditions of conforming to accepted social patterns in what is basically still a conservative man's world in a black African society almost defeat her. "She fell into a deep hole of such excruciating torture that, briefly, she went stark, raving mad." Her hallucinations deny her sexuality and her Africanness.

Charlotte H. Bruner. In Carolyn A. Parker and Stephen H. Arnold, eds. *When the Drumbeat Changes* (Washington, D. C.: Three Continents Press, 1981), pp. 263–64, 268–69

Bessie Head, in a volume of short stories entitled *The Collector of Treasures* [*and Other Botswana Village Tales*], is concerned with ideas similar to those in her novels. This time she makes use of incidents that have been related to her, and of Botswana history, legend, and myth, as the basis for her fiction. She explores the meaning and values of traditional life and as usual goes right to the heart of everything that she examines. What is it for instance, she wants to know, that prevents a city-reared girl, significantly named "Life" in the story that takes its name from the character, from finding her niche in the village community? Or rather, why is it that the rest of the people do not find the everyday round of village life deadly dull—"one big, gaping yawn"—in its unbroken monotony? The answer lies in contact between people. . . .

The help people give each other . . . brings meaning to a hard life. When in the title story, Dikeledi, who has killed her husband, is befriended by another inmate in prison and thanks her for all her kindness, the woman replies, with "her amused, cynical smile": "We must help each other . . . This is a terrible world. There is only misery here." The treasures that are collected by Dikeledi in this story—one towards which the other stories lead, as the author tells us, "in a carefully developed sequence"—are "deep loves that had joined her heart to the heart of others."

Ursula A. Barnett. *A Vision of Order* (London: Sinclair Browne, 1983), pp. 198–99

Bessie Head's reputation as a writer rests on three novels, a collection of stories, and a book on Serowe village. The three novels . . . form something like a trilogy. In each of them the novelist exhibits strong disapproval for the misuse of power by any individual or group. This dislike is evident in the way she dramatizes the process of the abdication of power which gets more complex from the first novel to the last. By the time the reader gets to the end of the third novel the novelist's message is clear: the naked display of power by the racists in South Africa or any other bigots elsewhere can lead only to disaster. There is no way of avoiding the rewards of oppression, whether it is of blacks by whites, whites by blacks, whites by fellow whites, or blacks by fellow blacks. The wise thing to do is to conceive of power in a progressive evolutionary manner. But, given man's insatiable lust for power, this is hardly possible. The novelist considers at length the psychological basis for power and finds that this has been largely eroded in a world dominated by conflict and the desire for political ascendancy. It is because of this stated position that Bessie Head is, for example, said to express "an indiscriminate repugnance for *all* political aspirations in *all* races."

The collection of stories, *The Collector of Treasures*, affords the author a chance to display her mastery of the art of storytelling. She understandably concentrates on the position of women and takes every opportunity to project a feminist point of view. She needs all the artistic talent displayed in her previous works to succeed with *Serowe: Village of the Rain Wind*. Here she combines imaginative writing with the fruits of a year's research study to produce work of great distinction. She succeeds magnificently in her reconstruction of the village life of Serowe. The daily occupations, hopes, and fears of the ordinary people of the village come alive in the reader's mind mainly because of the opportunity given the inhabitants to tell their own stories. The conception of history here is edifying—history is made out of the preoccupations of the common man, not out of the lofty ideals, cruelty, or benevolence of the wealthy and powerful. This reflects the concern for the underprivileged and oppressed masses of the people which is easily discernible in Bessie Head's writings.

Oladele Taiwo. Female Novelists of Modern Africa
(New York: St. Martin's Press, 1984), pp. 185–86

Bessie Head is a crusader for sexual and social justice for all men and women. Her favorite theme is the drama of interpersonal relationships and their possibility for individual growth and regeneration. She explores not only social harmony but also what is unique in each individual who contributes to it. In the realization of this task she employs an imaginative power and an original grasp of style which match her forceful moral vision. In all this, the woman's identity is fundamental; for it is still easy to encapsulate the central issues of all Head's novels into the vital issues of power and identity. . . . She truly approaches her characters as individuals and, with her usual sensitivity and thoroughness, journeys through the innermost recesses of their lives. The product of this exploration is the emergence of that uniqueness which makes each of them special. To Bessie Head, South Africa typifies power in its ugliest form, and the revulsion with which she views such a moral wasteland has aroused in her a special reverence for human life and dignity.

Head's characters are refugees, exiles, victims, all of whom are involved in a very personal and private odyssey of the soul from which they finally emerge regenerated, as well as spiritually and psychologically enriched. These characters inhabit the harmonious new worlds which operate in her novels; but like Ngugi [wa Thiong'o], she seems to imply that it is only from the interaction of both men and women in relationships of mutual love and respect that such a society can be created. Like Ngugi also she has a number of solid, resilient, and resourceful women in her novels. Through them she explores the limitations of women's roles, their disadvantages and their bruised self-image, and celebrates their occasional successes. . . .

Head's three novels can be seen as a systematic study of women's roles and handicaps in society, especially an unjust one like South Africa. She has also x-rayed their emotional, psychological, and spiritual endowments in the context of a human society, sane and accommodating. Her women are invariably thrust into a hostile landscape from which they must grow and realize their identity. There are passionate women like Dikeledi and Paulina; reserved women like Maria and Margaret; wise old women like Mma-Millipede; silent but self-confident women like Brigitte; loud and pushy women like Camilla; and frightened and mentally tormented women like Elizabeth. Even weird Thoko has a special value in this landscape. Head assesses the Botswana woman's worth by the degree of inner strength, individuality, and drive with which she is able to rise above the brutalizing and restrictive roles assigned her by an unimaginative society. The degree of humility and sincerity with which she adapts herself to a strange people and society contributes to the harmonious coexistence of all in her environment. In exploring their day-to-day activities Head does not fail to point out that quite often these women perpetuate their own problems through mental conditioning and their acceptance of social norms and taboos and also because of unfounded interpersonal jealousies. For all, their lives are a constant struggle and movement towards self-discovery.

Virginia U. Ola. *Ariel*. 17, 4 (October 1986), pp. 39–40, 46–47

Bessie Head's novel *A Question of Power* raises the problem of how one can write about inner chaos without the work itself becoming chaotic. . . . Bessie Head writes of the human "capacity to endure the excruciating." Appropriately, the novel is set in a village called Motabeng, "the place of sand." Motabeng suggests a lack of certainty and firmness. Like life and the world, all is loose, shifting and changing. Yet we search for little rocks and patches of firm ground in the sand; for permanence within the wider impermanence; for value within the ultimate valuelessness. . . .

The central character in *A Question of Power* is Elizabeth, and the novel covers a little more than a year in her life (around 1970) a time when she experienced a nervous breakdown and was committed to an asylum. The hallucinatory is real to Elizabeth and therefore presented as factual. The reader is placed within her world, and experiences something of Elizabeth's bewilderment and strain. Such a subject was foreshadowed in *Maru* where the characters, while being individuals, also represent forces. That novel confronts the mystery and power of man, the extraordinariness within the apparently ordinary. People were "horrible" to Maru because he could see into their thoughts and feelings, see their very bloodstreams and hear the beating of their hearts. The novel goes beyond psychology and dreams to the psychic and the supernatural. Not only are Maru and Moleka aspects of one person, but within the half of Maru there are further divisions such as between his compassion and idealism on the one hand, and his cruelty and cunning on the other. The interest in psychic states, Margaret's nightmares, her awareness of something within her "more powerful than her body could endure" all prepare us for the fracture which is the subject of *A Question of Power*. . . . To say that *A Question of Power* is about one "fall" or breakdown is to oversimplify the novel. The work describes a series of defeats and successes and, in this way, more truthfully represents the pattern of human life. "The dawn came. The soft shifts and changes of light stirred with a slow wonder over the vast expanse of the African sky." But dawn and night alternate, and in the experience of some the nights are more frequent and longer.

Charles Ponnuthurai Sarvan. In Eldred Durosimi Jones, ed. *Women in African Literature Today* (Trenton, N.J.: Africa World Press, 1987), pp. 82–84

African literary criticism . . . often denies that Head's work can be understood as expressing any kind of Western-influenced feminism. But few can dispute that, if feminism is broadly defined as the insistence that women have suffered systematic social injustice because of their sex, Head's work, particularly *The Collector of Treasures*, has a discernible feminist content. She clearly delineates the oppressiveness of tribal life for women, compounded by urbanization. But Head herself refuses to be labelled as a feminist, and close reading of her work indicates that her attitudes about women are ambivalent. A consistent pattern in her fiction is for the female hero to endure trials only surmountable through the intervention of a godlike man. Most of Head's presentation of *good* relations between the sexes (which has been diminishing in her work) embodies a sentimental ideology of romance. A woman like Life, who acts "with the bold, free joy of a woman who had broken all the social taboos," gets murdered in the end. And Head's presentation of sexuality, especially in *A Question of Power*, betrays such anxiety and distaste that one suspects she has displaced racial and ethnic self-doubts and dilemmas on to sexuality as well. Just as the greatest insult a colored can receive, in her work, is to be taunted as a half-caste, the most disgusting epithet for women who transgress norms is a "he-man": ". . . it was meant to imply that something was not quite right in her genitals, they were mixed up, a combination of male and female." This dread concerning one's sexual make-up and capacity for a healthy sexual relationship pervades *A Question of Power*, which attempts to exorcise Elizabeth's fear that, like [Doris] Lessing's Mary Turner, she suffers from "something not quite right . . . something missing somewhere."

In Head's work, moreover, a distaste for homosexuality also conveys a considerable malaise about sexual identity and capacity. It would seem that the reconciliation of opposites, whether psychologically or in social relationship with another, is something she envisages with difficulty. Such a conflation of writer and implied author is, of course, risky, more often than not mistaken, and perhaps intrusive. But Head has repeatedly stressed that *A Question of Power* is autobiographical: "A private philosophical journey to the sources of evil"; "my only truly autobiographical work." Enlightened feminism neither fears nor hates men, but elements of these attitudes frequently occur in Head's work. Lloyd Brown is one of only two critics to have noticed that "the imaginative power with which [Head] can describe hatred, death, and poverty . . . fails her when the subject is largely one of love or sexual passion"; the other being the ever-perceptive [Lewis] Nkosi.

Susan Gardiner. In Cherry Clayton, ed. Women and Writing in South Africa: A Critical Anthology (London: Heinemann, 1989), pp. 231–32

The present anthology [*Tales of Tenderness and Power*] represents the second collection of Bessie Head's shorter writings. They cannot all be classified as short stories in the usual use of that designation: some are fictional or semifictional, some historical stories. But most of them have one thing in common. They are closely rooted in actual events. The only purely fictional story is "The General." Even in "Chief Sekoto Holds Court," the incident described is probably based on fact, though Head has shaped the events to her own purpose. All the others are stories clearly related to or identifiable with personal, national or historical events, or we have her word for it that the story is based on fact. . . .

Often choosing a mundane event as her starting point . . . Bessie Head proceeds to give her story a subtle lift, even universal significance as she, the teller of tales, intrudes with humorous comments or her own view of things. Often she introduces an element of tenderness to the original event. She was easily moved by a generous action and responded quickly to real goodness, which she continued to believe does exist, especially in the lives of ordinary people. Yet she had, as well, a sharp nose for the power people, whom she exposed at every opportunity. . . .

Bessie Head always retained her individualism. Though feeling strongly about racism and sexual discrimination—and having gained by the bitterest experience a considerable knowledge of both problems—she would never allow herself to be totally identified with either African nationalism or feminism. Her vision included whites and blacks, men and women. What she feared was the misuse of power, what she strove towards was human goodness and love. The idea of the basic goodness and decency of the ordinary person never left her. Though she became increasingly susceptible to the evil around her as she grew older, including the constant misuse of power at local, national and international levels, she clung bravely to her ideals.

Gillian Stead Eilersen. Introduction to Bessie Head. Tales of Tenderness
and Power (London: Heinemann, 1989), pp. 10, 14–15

The publication of [Head's] eulogistic social history Serowe: Village of the Rain Wind in 1981 and her "major obsession, the Khama novel" A Bewitched Crossroad in 1984 (research for both of which had begun in the early 1970s), was the culmination of a long, hard battle for acceptance. Her death in 1986 was premature, a foreshortening of what could otherwise have been a long and rewarding relationship as a citizen with her adoptive country Botswana. . . .

The generic classification of the pieces in [A Woman Alone: Autobiographical Writings] poses a challenge to the literary critic. They span a number of overlapping genres: letters, journalism, autobiography, fictional sketches, essays, forewords, explanatory notes on novels. Were one to assume these generic markers to denote discrete and insular categories, it would appear possible to label the pieces in the present volume accordingly. At the end of this exercise, however, one would be left with a number of alarming and messy anomalies: how could "Snowball: A Story" be classified a fictional sketch when three quarters of the piece is devoted to the author's reflections on her day-to-day life in District Six? And why does the piece "An African Story" (so misleadingly titled) fall into neither of the categories "fictional sketches" or "journalism," or even wholly into "autobiography" for that matter? Its title promises fictional narrative, and indeed it begins like a story, but then quickly becomes autobiographical, even anecdotal, and ends with a philosophical reflection on the future of South Africa. And this indeterminacy characterizes almost every piece included in the present volume.

The truth is that the majority of the pieces assembled here defy classification. At their two extremes they represent autobiography and (very nearly) pure fiction. Most of them are however strung somewhere between these two extremes, and each (with a few exceptions) represents an amalgam of self-reflection, semi-fictional narrative, journalistic reportage, and cultural comment. The significance of each piece (and the justification for its inclusion in the present volume) is that it reveals something about the extraordinary life of the author Bessie Head.

Craig MacKenzie. Introduction to Bessie Head. *A Woman Alone:*
Autobiographical Writings (London: Heinemann, 1990), pp. xii–xiii

Parameters are required for appreciating *A Gesture of Belonging*. It contains only letters to [Randolph] Vigne: [Vigne] compensates for this with an introduction and commentaries. We see that Head needed Vigne as a father. She is a quivering being: her insights are in terms of dreams, the soul, etc. At moments she seems to receive messages like a radio. Her notion of God is eccentric, profound. "I think I can say, with authority, that God in the end, is not an old man in the sky or invisible, but certain living individuals whom I adore," she states. The most valuable letters give insights into her novels. "*A Question of Power* is stark, bleak tragedy from beginning to end," she says. "It is written at two levels. The everyday level involves a development project. The people I work with come in and keep moving steadily and sanely through the book, just as beautiful as they are in real life. The second level is a journey inwards into the soul, with three soul characters, who are really disembodied persons, the concentration is on arguments of power, good and evil and it is really in the form of dream sequences which had a thread of logic, the sort of logic of war."

Bessie Head was all "right brain," it seems. No wonder she liked Tayeb Salih's *Wedding of Zein*. Her imagination gives her trouble where ordinary, logical people do fine: she goes through sheer terror when she has to open a bank account and issue checks. She is blind where others see. "Friends come and go for strange reasons," she says. After she left Iowa, she wrote to Paul Engle that when most people looked back on their trail, they saw achievement and order; she saw only chaos. I was astounded she did not accept that much of the chaos was of her own making. So it is not surprising that, seeking balance, she identifies with her male protagonists, noting that they also have the female element in them.

Peter Nazareth. *WLT.* 66, 2 (Spring 1992), p. 391

HEARNE, JOHN (1926–   )

JAMAICA

From the outset John Hearne established himself as a writer of considerable technical competence. *Voices under the Window*, an intensely dramatic story of political intrigue and revolution, is written with the disciplined craftsmanship and skill one seldom looks for or finds in a writer's first novel. It seemed to augur well for his future and his second novel, *Stranger at the Gate*, more than fulfilled earlier promise and consolidated Hearne's reputation. It was here, in this second book, that he contrived the stage that was to be the setting for all his later novels. Like [George] Lamming, he mapped out an imaginary island in the Caribbean. This he called Cayuna. But it was not a mere sketchy or fanciful province of the imagination. It was a re-creation and extension of his own Jamaica and to the evocation of life on this stage, the life not only of its humans, but of its beasts and birds, its landscape and its legends, Hearne brought to bear a care and skill that seems to be the stamp on everything he has written. . . .

Hearne's characters spring from every level of Cayunan society, a society which like every society in the Caribbean is a dynamic mixture of the light and dark races and bloods. They are boldly and convincingly drawn. And the technique of unfolding these characters is cinematic. They move before you like on a swiftly spooling reel of action film. They move, too, towards the same dark end and defeat: Roy McKenzie, the dedicated communist leader in *Stranger at the Gate*; Jojo Rygin, the violent but big-hearted animal in *[The] Faces of Love*; Eleanor Stacey, the young lover in *The Autumn Equinox*—they storm through the pages with hope that bitters into futility through some kind of treachery and betrayal.

Ivan Van Sertima. Caribbean Writers
(London: New Beacon Books, 1968), pp. 14–15

From [Hearne's first novel], *Voices Under the Window*, the reader is aware that the writing is not typical of the main current of West Indian literature. [George] Lamming has said that the West Indian novel is peasant; Hearne's are uncompromisingly middle class, and concerned with an intellectual's moral dilemma. Mark Lattimer in this first work is a "white" middle-class Jamaican lawyer. Like Roy McKenzie in *Stranger at the Gate*, or Jim Diver in *Autumn Equinox*, Mark has devoted himself to "the common people.". . .

The neat structure of this fable is held within a fast-moving, accomplished piece of storytelling that largely compensates for the somewhat wooden characterization. And if the moral design seems over-neat, it is interesting to note the questions it raises and leaves unanswered. Lattimer becomes politically involved, and all the overt implications are that such involvement is good. But do Lattimer's politics have any real significance, as politics? Speaking of his work to Brysie, his colored mistress, he declares "the slogans were taking me over . . . after a while (the people) aren't souls any more. They're the New Jamaica or some crap like that." And again, "To do anything worthwhile you have got to do it *alone*." His death occurs when he happens to be in Coronation Lane on political business, but Hearne makes it quite clear that he was not killed because he was on political work; his death is a chance, meaningless tragedy that might have occurred if he had never joined the People's Party, and had been in Kingston for some other reason. The hero's conscience impels him to the "committed" life, but how far has this any objective meaning? . . .

Behind the meticulous observation we find in Hearne's novels lies his intense nervous energy. The eye hungers for detail after detail. When description gives way to narrative, one has the sense of a brake being let off a high-powered car under full throttle. The scene of the hurricane in *The Faces of Love* is one of the most powerful scenes in Caribbean fiction. The same nervous energy can be seen in his characterization. Like his seeing eye, his characters, too, exist in a heightened state of self-awareness and intensity. Even laughter is said to "spurt," shyness to be "fierce," and people are "deliberately casual." Their humor is muscular, their stalwart wit indomitable. In bed with a dark barmaid, the hero of *Land of the Living* makes bright remarks about a French play. Their intense entities are formalized and made larger than life by their moral purpose in the story. This can be a major limitation. Until *Land of the Living*, their actions are predicted by Hearne's direction; there is little sense of spontaneous human action, the discovery of new and unexpected moral perspectives. At its best, however, Hearne's method gives his characters a sense of heightened significance, the moral drama they play out gains power and meaning from its definition.

Barrie Davies. In Louis James, ed. *The Islands in Between: Essays on West Indian Literature* (London: Oxford University Press, 1968), pp. 109–11, 114–15

Hearne always remains frankly a middle-class "campus" novelist of a type familiar in America. Indeed, modern American fiction and short-story writing in the *New Yorker* or *Atlantic Monthly* tradition are the dominant influences in Hearne's narrative style, plot-making, and dialogue. He also displays an American relish for the material impedimenta of middle-class living; cars, long drinks, and cigarette lighters gleam and sparkle from his pages. The setting is not so much urban as suburban; for few prosperous Jamaicans, and Hearne's main characters are always prosperous, choose to live in central Kingston. Even in *Land of the Living* his Central European refugee hero, a professor at the university, is consciously making a sortie into another world in his affair with the black bar-keeper, Bernice. It is almost with a sigh of relief that he abandons this secret liaison and turns to a public, socially accepted involvement with the drunken Joan Culpepper, who at least has the merit of being a member of his own set. Thus in Hearne's work the values and social habits of the professional middle class and the masses coexist in the same island but are held consciously apart; any fuller contact between them is conducted deliberately, is never free from tension, and can be broken off at any time as a release from this tension. . . . The impulse towards democratization which Elsa Goveia has detected in West Indian literature appears to be absent from Hearne's carefully shaped novels. Rather, he is intent on reporting West Indian experience, from a certain viewpoint, to an international English-speaking bourgeois readership. For such a readership his books hold no difficulties of form or style such as [George] Lamming, [Roger] Mais, or [Wilson] Harris may present; they are essentially familiar, and their generally favorable critical reception in the West belongs with this quality. Whereas many exiled West Indian writers create out of their memories of folk experience, Hearne, who lives mainly in Jamaica, reports with more immediacy in time and place but from an angle which somewhat detaches him from the mainstream of popular life.

Gerald Moore. *The Chosen Tongue* (New York: Harper and Row, 1969), pp. 93–94

The West Indian who comes near to being an exception to the peasant feel is John Hearne. His key obsession is with an agricultural middle class in Jamaica. I don't want to suggest that this group of people are not a proper subject for fiction; but I've often wondered whether Hearne's theme, with the loaded concern he shows for a mythological, colonial squirearchy, is not responsible for the fact that his work is, at present, less energetic than the West Indian novels at their best. Hearne is a first-class technician, almost perfect within the limitation of conventional storytelling; but the work is weakened, for the language is not being *used*, and the novel as a form is not really being *utilized*. His novels suggest that he has a dread of being identified with the land at peasant level. What he puts into books is always less interesting than the *omissions* which a careful reader will notice he has forced himself to make. He is not an example of the instinct and root impulse which return the better West Indian writers back to the soil. For soil is a large part of what the West Indian novel has brought back to reading; lumps of earth: unrefined, perhaps, but good, warm, fertile earth.

George Lamming. In Edward Baugh, ed. *Critics on Caribbean Literature* (New York: St. Martin's Press, 1978), p. 26

In *The Autumn Equinox*, John Hearne frames his fictional state of Cayuna with different stages of revolution in Haiti and Cuba. Cayuna harbors the deluded remnant of the reactionary government in Haiti, but the actual state of the new revolutionary government there is not set forth. With Cuba, the Castro revolution is in progress, and Cayuna becomes an innocent base for revolutionary propaganda. Since the government and politics of Cayuna receive no substantial attention, we are thrown out of the novel in two directions: first, we ask what makes Cayuna (née Jamaica) so innocent of revolutionary impulses, and so immune to the ferment all around; and, second, we wonder how to place the historical Haiti and Cuba in the interpretative scheme of *The Autumn Equinox*. . . .

The rational despair of *The Autumn Equinox* is embodied in Nicholas Stacey, the man who refrains from resenting or resisting his lot, as bastard, as abused stepchild, as betrayed brother, as neglected heir. His one chance to see and occupy an unconventional world, that is, one not defined by an authority seated in his disfavor, all but paralyzes him. Old Nick, who has so little of the devil in him, does not so much share as submit to a boundary-shattering engagement with Teresa Galdez, his first wife's sister (intimations of incest partly explain the inaction of the characters, as action is taboo and implicitly directed against the self). He tries to compensate by "adopting" Teresa's daughter, Eleanor, but he is comfortable only as long as she is docile, or in other words a child. He is baffled by her emergence as an independent young woman, and accordingly seeks to send her away or to co-opt her into his business. Her tacit revolution is stymied by her gratitude, her love for him; she finds it easier to let Jim Diver go than to go away from Nick. The unspoken law of familiarity thus yields another version of the ubiquitous indecisiveness of West Indian literature in the revolutionary situation.

Michael G. Cooke. *YR*. 71, 1 (Autumn 1981), pp. 32–34

John Hearne's *The Faces of Love* and *Land of the Living* are good examples of novels which reveal the state of racial complacency and the sense of community in the West Indian psychological makeup. In both novels Hearne depicts a multiracial society and illustrates that the nature of love has little or nothing to do with racial origins. In both novels love affects the lives of people who pay, at best, only superficial attention to their racial makeup. The characters are aware of themselves and each other as persons, without having to undergo the process of racial identity (or even the search for it). Still, their sense of community is strong, and in their interactions they confront complex social and political issues without calling attention to the possible connections between these issues and race.

In *The Faces of Love* Rachel Ascom, the black daughter of a German woman, treats material values as the only mirror which can reflect her essence and thereby validate her existence. The possibility of pride in either aspect of her racial makeup never pierces her consciousness. "I am nothing, you see," she tells Fabricus, who is one of her many past lovers and the narrator of the novel. "I come from nothing and none of you people will ever forget that when I make a mistake. Everything I become I've got to show. That's why I buy such good clothes. Every time I spend ten times what I should on clothes it's like a standard I set myself."

Because of her deep-seated insecurity, Rachel "uses love as a compensatory exercise of power." While her black lover, Jojo Rygin, is in prison, Rachel initiates a romantic relationship with a white Englishman, Michael Lovelace. Soon after, Jojo is released and Rachel begins to manipulate the love triangle. The forceful and ebullient Jojo feels sure that his coming wealth will be sufficient grounds for Rachel's choosing to marry him. Meanwhile, Michael, a newcomer to the West Indian scene, undergoes no psychological changes as a result of his participation in the activities of this West Indian community—he is the editor of the island's leading newspaper, *Newsletter*. He is affected only by his love for Rachel, which seems, like himself, unconnected to any particular cultural reality (his or Rachel's). In fact, Hearne intentionally contrives an interracial and intercultural love triangle and then proceeds, presumably just as intentionally, to avoid confrontation with the possible implications of such a situation. Indeed, such implications are irrelevant to Hearne's thematic concerns.

Melvin B. Rahming. The Evolution of the West Indian's Image in the Afro-
American Novel (Millwood, N. Y.: Associated Faculty Press, 1986), pp. 78–79

Hearne's first five novels end with the affirmation that integration is possible for his educated, middle-class characters, and this integration is based upon the strength of one's immediate relationships with others; the uneasy guilt of Mark Lattimer has been replaced with the intimate world of Stefan and Joan. Yet the peace seems an uneasy one, since basic questions, such as whether the social structure of Cayuna will survive the disparities within it, are left unanswered. Moreover, the underlying tension that exists is presented by Hearne himself: the texture of his novels allows for the darker sides of West Indian society to be presented by such characters as Johnson in *Stranger at the Gate*, by Heneky in *Land of the Living*, and by the riot in *Voices under the Window*, for example. Overall, however, the vision is positive: after *Voices*, the resolution of the novels is consistently toward the comic. . . .

It is with this in mind that one turns to examine the world of *The Sure Salvation*, published twenty years after *Land of the Living*. There are several departures from the patterns established in Hearne's earlier novels: the context is no longer contemporary West Indian society; the setting carries symbolic and allegorical overtones; and Hearne has altered the narrative style to allow himself to wander through an unprecedented number of intimately presented characters. In viewing the work from the aspect of integration, one is struck by the reversal of the positive note established by the earlier works. Isolation and fragmentation are paramount; each character, as Edward Baugh writes, revolves on his own "particular, obsessive, flawed center of self." This point is more importantly illustrated by the relationship between the two most powerful men on board, Hogarth and Alex, since a personal betrayal is the result of five years of working together in what Hogarth thought was mutual trust. Yet it is not only the individual failure of each that work against the type of friendship Hearne has described in positive terms in earlier works. At the central point of betrayal, Hogarth launches into a denunciation that goes beyond the immediate and personal to a racial and social statement with a hint that the breakdown is predestined, a fact of their difference in race. . . . Hogarth and Alex both exit unreconciled and separate, Hogarth to trial and prison, Alex very much alive on the very mainland on which he has planned to establish his kingdom. There are no real heroes in this novel, though it is Hogarth who comes closest to the protagonists of earlier novels. It is a significant break in the pattern that this time it is the protagonist who is left on the outside with nothing achieved: the darker side has finally triumphed.

David Ingledew. In Daryl Cumber Dance, ed. Fifty Caribbean Writers
(Westport, Conn.: Greenwood Press, 1986), pp. 202–3

John Hearne's novel, *The Sure Salvation*, focuses upon the traumatic historical events which have given birth to what is now the West Indies. The action occurs on a barque ironically named the *Sure Salvation* which is being used to take an illegal shipment of slaves from Africa to Brazil in 1860. Hearne's depiction of the bewildered sensibility and horrific condition of the slaves is remarkably unsentimental; he captures both their plight and their peculiar dignity in a fashion so objective as to render their abominable physical condition and spiritual malaise as distanced. A peculiar mist or opaque glass seems to stand between them and our perceiving eye. Hearne realizes that the cruel fact of slavery is a grotesquerie that the human consciousness can only approach or conceive in vague shadows or tearful glimpses if we are not to despair of humanity's future by succumbing to the cruel legacies of the past. This rendition, strangely enough, simultaneously heightens and diminishes the suffocation and immobilization which the slaves are made to suffer. . . .

In *The Sure Salvation*, John Hearne shows that the erosion of self—the reality of individuality in the process of becoming the void of self—is itself an illusion if it is seen in terms of immediate and total loss. Rather, there is a *metamorphosis* of self, an evolution of consciousness which is necessitated and compelled by human endurance even in the furnace of apocalyptic occurrence.

Daizal R. Samad. *WLWE*. 30, 1 (Spring 1990), pp. 11–12

HEATH, ROY A. K. (1926–   )

GUYANA

The fiction of Roy A. K. Heath includes, so far, several short stories and four novels: *A Man Come Home, The Murderer, From the Heat of the Day*, and *One Generation*. The readers of these works tend to be struck immediately by certain aspects of the author's style. Reviewers are quick to home in on Heath's extremely realistic portrayal of his fictional world: the city of Georgetown, Guyana and outlying towns and villages, and the language, activities, and concerns of the characters. . . .

Apart from the ironic, there are hints of a tragic mode in the novels as well. In all four novels the main protagonists are relentlessly thwarted in their plans and modest aspirations, and they are eventually destroyed—three of them end up dead and the other insane. These characters can command, on occasion, the tragic gesture, but for the most part we watch them flailing helplessly in their domestic webs and we do not really see in them the stature or self-knowledge of the tragic protagonist—they are more victims than heroes and it appears as though their ironic presentation diminishes or qualifies the sense of tragedy. . . .

From the Heat of the Day is the first [novel] of a projected trilogy, of which the second, *One Generation*, has also appeared. The trilogy is about the events and fortunes of the Armstrong family and the first novel takes us back to the 1920s, to the point where Armstrong is courting Gladys. He is from a village and of a status socially inferior to that of his wife, whose family lives in the desirable Queenstown section of Georgetown. . . .

[*One Generation*] is divided into two quite distinct parts; the first part completes the business of *From the Heat of the Day*, in that it is concerned with the decline and death of Armstrong and the rising to full maturity of his two children—especially Rohan. The second part concerns the brief and tragic life of Rohan after his father dies.

Armstrong's decline is almost baroque in its horror, and is an ironic reversal of his earlier life. Here we find him bullied by his children, forced to appear in rags because his children seek to prevent him from spending all his pension on drink by insisting that he buy his own clothes, contracting filaria which causes his feet to swell, developing a horrible personal odor which can't be obliterated, and, finally, falling into the clutches of a stern woman of some dubious religion who ministers to his illness and to what is left of his soul. All the fates he strove to avoid befall him in the end, emphasized by the force of Heath's irony and in turn emphasizing the extent to which any control he may have exerted over his life in the past was transient and illusory. He dies the victim he always was; we are not even spared such final details of his degradation as the fact that the horse that drew the hearse "defecated copiously" as Armstrong's coffin was removed from it. Nevertheless, to emphasize that even at the point of death there is a simultaneity of the ridiculous and the grandiose, in a flourish of "atmospherics" reminiscent of [Edgar] Mittelholzer, there's a terrible storm on the night of Armstrong's death.

Mark A. McWatt. In Erika Sollish Smilowitz and Roberta Quarles
Knowles, eds. *Critical Issues in West Indian Literature*
(Parkersburg, Iowa: Caribbean Books, 1984), pp. 54–56, 58, 62–63

Through seven novels in ten years, Roy Heath has laid claim to being *the* chronicler of urban life in Guyana. In *Orealla*, his latest work, set in 1927, the sights and sounds and smells and gossipy surface of life in Georgetown are convincingly rendered by Heath: the gorgeous tropical flora, the tones of the Stabroek tower clock, the stench of the open sewage in trenches dissecting the city, the "Creolese" spoken by Heath's lower-class characters. Along with these things he effectively exposes the inhumane aspects of caste and color conventions in Guyana.

In addition, Heath often writes beautifully; there is, for instance, the long dreamy paragraph . . . about Ben, his central character, recollecting his childhood at Skeldon and thinking of freedom and "that calm the aboriginal Indians had always known, that had never ceased to elude him." This elusive contentment is embodied in his friend Carl, the detached, independent, nonmaterialistic Amerindian who eventually forsakes Ben and drifts back to his home settlement of Orealla.

Robert E. McDowell. *WLT*. 59, 2 (Spring 1985), p. 310

Roy Heath's first published novel, *A Man Come Home*, is an unusual work of West Indian fiction in that it does not have any large historical or sociological view or argument to present; rather, it encloses the reader within a very powerfully evoked world of the range yards and the poorer housing areas of Georgetown, Guyana, and it concentrates on the actual processes of life and experience within this context.

The "man" referred to in the book's title is Bird Foster, but neither he nor any other character in the novel achieves the status of hero or even main protagonist. Heath presents instead members of the Foster family—and their yard-dwelling friends and neighbors—and concentrates upon portraying their relationships and experiences in a thoroughly convincing way. As one critic has remarked, the novel "projects a sharp sense of time lived, giving the texture of experience so subtly that the reader is enchanted into accepting the world of the novel as his own." . . .

It is perhaps appropriate that *A Man Come Home* should be the first novel published, for in this book Heath displays most of the major themes and concerns that dominate the later works. Already in this novel one has the sense of the family or household and its domestic concerns as somehow central to the

work's design and the locus of curiously powerful emotions and conflicts. It is
the context of actions that are frequently tragic in their consequences. Heath
exposes the accumulated animosities and frustrations within the domestic situation as well as the sudden explosions of violence that they ultimately precipitate.
In this novel, for example, we see the gathering mistrust and animosity between
Foster's mistress Christine and their daughter Melda as the girl (the last child)
grows older and more independent. When Melda announces that she is pregnant
and refuses to discuss it with Christine, Heath portrays, in his powerful, understated technique, how the mother's anger and anxiety overflow into violence. . . .

In *The Murderer* the novelist's focus is somewhat narrower, the psychological portrait of Galton Flood more intense and relentless. There is no doubt
here that Galton is the central figure of the work, and while the reader still finds
himself firmly in touch with the urban landscape of Georgetown, he also finds
himself inside the mind of Galton. Heath probes far more insistently into the
shaping influences and motivation of his main character than he did in *A Man
Come Home*. What we find, as this relentless exploration proceeds in the novel,
is something that we would have suspected from the earlier work: that the
domestic household and the interweave of relationships therein can be sinister
and frightening and their effects destructive in the extreme.

Mark A. McWatt. In Daryl Cumber Dance, ed. *Fifty Caribbean Writers*
(Westport, Conn.: Greenwood Press, 1986), pp. 209–11

Roy Heath is a contemporary West Indian novelist whose work commands serious attention. It provokes interesting speculation about where he fits in the tradition of the West Indian novel developed in the 1950s by writers such as Edgar
Mittelholzer, George Lamming, Samuel Selvon, V. S. Naipaul, and Wilson
Harris. Since 1974 when his first novel, *A Man Come Home*, was published, he
has produced six other novels, three of which, *From the Heat of the Day, One
Generation*, and *Genetha*, make up his ambitious Guyana trilogy. . . .

Heath's fiction is not overtly concerned with the theme of nationalism, or
of the search for a West Indian identity, or of the heritage of colonialism, or of
independence and its aftermath. He is not especially interested in history, at
least not in the manner of Mittelholzer. He does not see history as a simple
series of cause and effect because characters are often not sure why they have
acted in a certain way. For Heath, human motives are usually complicated and
often contradictory. His people have to struggle to survive in society because
they are poor, and because they are separated from each other by considerations
of class and sex. They have difficulty understanding their own natures and the
urges that both drive and inhibit them.

On the one hand, this tendency to ignore so many of the themes that are
central to West Indian writing might suggest that Heath is out of touch with the
important issues in the life of the area, possibly because he is an expatriate. On
the other hand, it might indicate that he is so self-consciously Guyanese and
West Indian that he can see the struggle to survive in the Caribbean as not simply
a regional problem but as a form of anguish shared in differing degrees by people

everywhere in all periods of history. Heath deals with the materially poor and the dispossessed, but one senses from his fiction that the state of dispossession is not peculiar to the poor and is the inevitable condition of life in general. . . . Freedomlessness is an affliction of all his people. Genetha, the central character of the last novel of Heath's trilogy, speaks for them thus: "For me that's the problem. Freedom and the secret of a settled mind."

In this trilogy, Heath uses a structure that is episodic—indeed this is true of all his novels—and in *From the Heat of the Day*, the narrative often switches abruptly from the relationship of the husband and the wife, to examine relationships Armstrong has with his men friends with whom he goes drinking and whoring, and with the whores whose company he seeks out. Sometimes the relationships of Gladys and her servants, Esther and Marion, are focused on. This method of short, jerky chapters emphasizes the fragmented, paranoid states of the people in Heath's world. The general impact of this method, however, is one of concentration rather than diffusion because the episodes with Armstrong and his friends, and Gladys with the servants repeat with variations what is going on between husband and wife.

Anthony Boxill. *WLWE*. 29, 1 (Spring 1989), pp. 103–5, 108

Roy Heath's latest work [*Shadows Round the Moon*] is described as "the first volume of his autobiography": it ends (like V. S. Naipaul's *Miguel Street*) with his departure for England at about age twenty.

The initial half has . . . reminiscences of colonial life and Caribbean culture, with occasional reproductions of Guyanese dialect conversation; but the observations seldom transcend the superficial, and the reconstruction of personal experiences does not take on a dimension exceeding the purely individual. Nevertheless, there are some insights into the social life of the sole anglophone country of South America. . . .

The second half of the volume makes amends for the shortcomings of the first: there are several perspicacious observations on religion, family relationships, and colonial administrators, and postcolonial manners and aspirations are occasionally alluded to. Here too are to be found examples of the author's skill at inventing impressive similes: "The first pleasure at being chosen for a post in the Treasury wore off like a woman's make-up in a persistent downpour" is one: another is "The psyche, like an ancient book whose pages rustle at night and disturb our sleep." Equally interesting, however, are the dicta on Guyanese society, where the "town, the graveyard of all cultures" is subjected to as much criticism as "the civil service," which "represented the ambition of a class, which saw in it a guarantee of material security." Some of these views are supported; unfortunately, no support is offered for the view that the 1832 abolition of slavery "was absurdly attributed to the efforts of the antislavery societies."

A. L. McLeod. *WLT*. 64, 4 (Autumn 1991), pp. 753–54

[In *Shadows Round the Moon*] Heath suggests that his fascination with the hidden and the grotesque arose as a reaction against the prohibitions of a Creole society riddled with "secrets and secret places." His protagonists characteristically pursue restless dreams of freedom and independence, but their quest leads them in an ironic cycle, into themselves and the patterns of their past. Heath's employment of a constantly shifting viewpoint suggests the impossibility of an individual seeing himself clearly or comprehending his relation to others. The greatest strength of Heath as a writer, perhaps, is his ability to convey the complexity of the individual, through a loose, episodic narrative strategy that conceals as much as it reveals. His style, occasionally florid and artificial in the earlier novels, has grown increasingly controlled and ironic: it is a style, comments another contemporary Guyanese writer, Wilson Harris, "that truncates emotion." . . .

The Guyana of Heath's sixth novel, *Kwaku; or, The Man Who Could Not Keep His Mouth Shut,* is a country in a state of collapse, with rampant "choke-an'-rob," a tottering rural economy, and the omnipresent governing party. For Kwaku Cholmondley, a shoemaker in the village of "C," the only defense is an air of idiocy, though Kwaku is privately convinced of his special mission in life, "a journey to be undertaken." Pursuing respectability, he marries Miss Gwendoline, who bears him eight children, yet Kwaku gains no reputation until—forced to leave the village after a plague of locusts destroys its one cash crop—he attains success as a healer in New Amsterdam.

There Kwaku has little more going for him than a few garlic concoctions, a sense of ritual, and the common touch. He is convinced of his worthlessness, though to the villagers in "C" he has become a man of reputation. His insecure need to command respect leads to his downfall: he fails to fulfill a rash promise made to a fisherman, who retaliates by blinding Miss Gwendoline with an obeah curse. Back in New Amsterdam, Kwaku's herbal practice languishes, he is beaten up by his own sons, and he ends up touring the rum shops, capering for dollar bills. The narrative tone of *Kwaku* passes skillfully, almost imperceptibly, from comic to tragic, yet Kwaku is, finally, a heroic character, loyal to his family to the end and able to cope with misfortune by accepting it, even as his country "seemed to be sinking under its weight of debt and ambitions.". . .

The bride in Heath's *The Shadow Bride* is Mrs. Singh, who has come to Guyana from South India as bride to a wealthy, if disreputable, Guyanese. Once free of her husband—gossip has it she poisoned him—she becomes an authoritarian figure in her household, determined to control her son, Betta, and the assortment of servants and "hangers-on." Like many of Heath's characters, Mrs. Singh is trapped in images of the past: her nostalgia for her Indian home is so strong she raises Betta apart from other children, until he complains that he knows more of Kerala than Guyana. . . .

Betta's journal, which he has begun in order to record his medical studies, becomes a means of self-exploration, through which he understands the way he is intricately bound not only to the East Indian community at its point of crisis, as thousands of East Indians desert the estates for the city with the end of indenture, but to his mother, whose crisis he had failed to recognize: "he had seen fit to ignore his mother's plea for help, he, who did not hesitate to speak of ideals." If mother and son are both confined by their past, Betta, fortified by a disintegrating but still powerful communal tradition, is able to recognize and accept the irony of his motivations without submitting to despair: "He could not," the novel concludes, "have acted otherwise." . . .

Heath's eight novels have added a new dimension to the literary map of Guyana, complementing Wilson Harris's fantastic journeys into the Guyanese hinterland. Heath has become a novelist of international stature by remaining in compassionate contact with the world he knows best. . . . His work may be "indelibly Guyanese," but it belongs also to "the small group of works that make the reader understand more about the nature of human suffering and violence."

Ian H. Munro. In Bernth Lindfors and Reinhard Sander, eds.
Dictionary of Literary Biography. 117 (1992), pp. 199, 201–3

HODGE, MERLE (1944–   )

TRINIDAD

Crick Crack, Monkey, which was first published in 1970, belongs to a group of West Indian novels, such as [Michael Anthony's] *The Year in San Fernando* and [Geoffrey Drayton's] *Christopher* which deal with the theme of childhood. The central character, Tee, moves in two worlds—the world of Tantie and the world of Aunt Beatrice—and those two worlds are bound together in a coherent and unified way by the response of the central character, who is also narrator, to the experiences of both worlds. The child, Tee, moves in a context in which there is strong opposition between certain social and cultural values, and, as narrator, she recounts the intensely personal dilemmas of her life in that context. This she does with a remarkable depth of insight and with a vivid evocation of childhood memories. The reader is made to share in the diversity and richness of Tee's experiences without being able to discern at times where the child's voice with a child's perception of things slides into the adult voice and vision of the omniscient author. Child vision and adult vision are made to coalesce at several points in the novel.

The two worlds of childhood which Tee inhabits result from the nature of her domestic circumstances. Her father, who has emigrated to England, is the brother of Tantie, and her deceased mother is sister to Aunt Beatrice. Tee oscillates between these two spheres of existence and emerges as a deeply disturbed being—a plight derived from the essential conflict of Creole middle class and Tantie's world. The conflict externalized in these two classes of society generates acute feelings of ambivalence within Tee. Both in form and content the novel is indeed a response to the inner pressures of a profoundly felt and complex experience. The vivid exploration of the child's inner world confers on the novel its essential strength. The child's feelings, thoughts, and actions, as she responds to the social and cultural environment in which the novel is set, reflect the authenticity of remembered experience.

Roy Narinesingh. Introduction to Merle Hodge. *Crick Crack, Monkey*
(London: Heinemann, 1981), p. vii

Merle Hodge's *Crick Crack, Monkey* was the first major novel by a postcolonial
West Indian woman writer to problematize and foreground questions of difference and the quest for a voice in a social context that denied social expression to
the colonized self and hence cut it off from the liberating forms of self-expression which define the Caribbean narrative. For Hodge, this emphasis on voice as
a precondition for black subjectivity in a colonial situation was necessitated by
both ideological and technical reasons. First of all, in the plantation societies of
the Caribbean, the voices of the oppressed and dominated slaves and indentured
laborers survived against the modes of silence engendered by the master class.
For these slaves and laborers, then, the preservation and inscription of a distinctive voice would signify the site of their own cultural difference and identity.
Second, the voice was, in radically contrasting ways, an instrument of struggle
and a depository of African values in a world in which the slaves' traditions
were denigrated and their selfhoods repressed ([Edward Kamau] Brathwaite;
[Edouard] Glissant). In terms of narrative, the recovery of voice becomes one
way through which unspoken and repressed experiences can be represented.

In Merle Hodge's novel, then, the voice is a synecdoche of the unwritten
culture of the colonized, the culture of . . . Tantie and Ma, and its privileging in
text signifies an epistemological shift from the hegemony of the written forms;
alternatively, the negation of the spoken utterance through education and assimilation is a mark of deep alienation. When Tee opens her retrospective view of
her childhood at the beginning of *Crick Crack*, she discovers that the past cannot
be narrated without a cognizance of the voices that defined it. The voice is
shown to be both central to the subject's conception of her past and as a paradigm that defines the context in which her multiple selves were produced. At the
opening of the novel, a moment in which the birth of a new baby is superseded
by the death of the mother, the world appears to Tee merely as a relationship of
voices: "a voice like high heels and stocking," "an old voice . . . wailing,"
"some quavery voices," "a grumble of men's voices." Tee's subsequent alienation in the colonial world is prefigured by her inability to identify with these
fetishized voices as easily as she identifies with the voice of Tantie and Ma.

Simon Gikandi. *Ariel*. 20, 4 (October 1989), pp. 20–21

Merle Hodge . . . explores the tension between the African-Caribbean and met-
ropolitan cultures. Unlike the majority of other novels addressing this question,
Crick Crack, Monkey examines the African-Caribbean woman's cultural identi-
fication. In Hodge's novel, Cynthia, or Tee, must choose between Aunt
Beatrice's attempts to imitate British upper-class society and language and
Tantie's more honest acceptance of Creole manners and dialect.

Living in a society colonized by Europeans, Beatrice has become what O. R.
Dathorne calls an "expatriate of the mind," denying the worth of locally evolved
culture to identify with a foreign tradition. Tee, whose mother has died, is the
object of a long custody battle between her Aunt Beatrice, who attempts to identify with the metropolitan culture, and Tantie, who accepts the indigenous black
culture. Her acceptance of the black Creole cultural tradition is based on the

recognition that imported cultural values evolved in a different environment and historical experience.

Although Tee feels more comfortable with Tantie, the young woman's later contact with Beatrice's values makes it impossible for her ever again to identify completely with the black Creole culture. When the potentially positive bonding between Tantie and Tee is disrupted and Beatrice wins custody of Tee, the girl suffers a gradual cultural displacement. At the novel's end, when Tee goes to her father's house in London, she has already internalized the racist values of the white colonials. Although Hodge does not offer a convincing alternative to the ambivalent balancing of two cultures, she does offer in Tantie a positive model of strength and endurance. She and the other women characters survive, physically and psychologically, because they have formed strong ties with other women in their families or communities. The potentially healthy relationship of Tee and Tantie is unfortunately interrupted by Beatrice's intrusion of values from the dominant culture.

Laura Niesen de Abruna. In Selwyn R. Cudjoe, ed. *Caribbean Women Writers*
(Wellesley, Mass.: Calaloux, 1990), pp. 92–93

Tee's journey in *Crick Crack, Monkey* is not one of personal development but rather of psychological disintegration. The breakdown of her character begins imperceptibly in Tantie's home. Although Tantie's household provides an anchor for the sensitive infant, it is terribly flawed. The presence of a tantie marks the absence of a mother. Tee's first handicap is orphanhood.

Chapter one ends with Tee's awareness of the absence of her mother and father, the former by death, the latter by exile: "Then Papa went to sea. I concluded that what he had gone to see was whether he could find Mammy and the baby."

The orphaned child has only her adopted home to serve as her moral exemplar and formal education at school to be her teacher. Both fail her. Tantie's world is a morally broken environment full of indecencies and obscenities. There is first the problem of Tantie's many lovers who offend Aunt Beatrice's sense of uprightness: "And then what about all those men, did we like all those men coming," Aunt Beatrice questions Tee and Toddan; and second there is the problem of physical and verbal violence that Tee has to endure.

On one hand, Tantie's world gives Tee negative moral values, and on the other the education system alienates her from herself and her culture. By the end of primary school, Tee has developed a schizophrenic personality characterized by self-hate and an admiration for all things foreign thanks to colonized teachers like Mr. Hinds and a British-oriented curriculum that symbolically starts with "A for apple." It is at this time that she creates her double, Helen, the epitome of the British child she would like to become: "Helen wasn't even my double. No, she couldn't be called my double. She was the Proper Me. And me, I was her shadow, hovering about in incompleteness."

Tee's journey through life, like the picaroon's, is marked by loss of innocence, by petty theft, and finally by self-contempt. Having rejected self and family, she has no alternative but to flee her country.

Ena V. Thomas. In Selwyn R. Cudjoe, ed. *Caribbean Women Writers*
(Wellesley, Mass.: Calaloux, 1990), pp. 212–13

Crick Crack, Monkey shares with the nationalist novels of the late 1960s and early 1970s a sense of postcolonial angst, even despair. Both in its construction of female roles and in the way in which its structure revises the terrain upon which quest narratives like [George] Lamming's [*In the Castle of My Skin*] inscribe themselves, Hodge's novel transforms the narrative conventions by which it is contained. . . .

"Crick-crack monkey" is part of a call and response chanted at the end of folk tales in the southern Caribbean. . . . The "crick-crack" probably imitates the breaking of a branch as the self-opinionated monkey falls out of the tree and slips on the skin of a pomerac fruit. But the literal meaning of the phrase is less important than its symbolic function as a marker separating the fantasy world of the story from the "real" world of the storyteller and her audience. The child protagonist, Tee, shouts this response to end the Anancy stories her grandmother tells during holidays in the countryside where, she imagines, the magic of an earlier world not yet deformed by the demands of growing up survives. But the tag is also used in the novel by city youths as a means of challenging the stories told by Manhattan, a member of their circle who claims to be an expert on the American way of life. . . .

Hodge utilizes the deflationary technique associated with the tag implicitly in other contexts to emphasize the hiatus between fantasy and reality in the options open to Tee. Thus, the fantasy world of respectability and pseudowhiteness associated with Tee's prim Aunt Beatrice is undermined when Tee's younger brother, Toddan, shatters the teatime idyll with his earthy insistence that he must make "ca-ca." Tee's raucous, big-hearted Tantie, is undermined by similar devices, in spite of the positive, caring values which distinguish her from Aunt Beatrice. Sexual independence in Tantie's life has degenerated into sexual promiscuity; freedom from social taboos has degenerated into alcoholism. This is why the decision of one of her older wards, Mikey, to fight for her honor on the street touches Tantie so profoundly. Mikey's intervention on her behalf is the answer to the "crick-crack" challenge of the boys on the bridge to the myth of Tantie's respectability. However, his heroic stance does not change the fact that Tantie's lifestyle is in many respects as inauthentic as that of Aunt Beatrice and that it offers Tee no viable alternative in her search for a role model. . . .

Crick Crack resembles the novels of many male Caribbean writers in that it offers us no way of resolving this contradiction between sterile middle-class fantasy and sordid lower-class reality. But the fact that Hodge sets up the problem by recourse to an oral form suggests that its resolution may be achieved through the folklore associated with Tee's grandmother. . . . [It] is important to note that Hodge uses the crick-crack tag self-reflexively, to provide the deep structure of the text and to critique the narrative to which it gives shape.

Rhonda Cobham. *Callaloo*. 16, 1 (Winter 1993), pp. 46–48

IYAYI, FESTUS (1947–   )

NIGERIA

Festus Iyayi's *Violence* provides us with an alternative view of man in society as well as a new formal option in the Nigerian novel. Its sustaining ideological premise, which also provides it with a title, is the materialistic contention that in a society where relationships among men are governed by the laws of capitalist production and its attendant jungle ethics (eat or be eaten!), the various injustices which the oppressed masses have to suffer amount to variations on a grand theme of violence. . . .

Iyayi depicts a world in which man's philosophical options and moral choices are determined by the objective forces of economic relations in society. Consequently, the view of man and society that prevails in *Violence* derives from the Aristotelian axiom that man is *Zoon politikon*, a sociopolitical animal, who, in being a product of social determinism, is nevertheless an active product and, to that extent, is also the principal agency of change and progress in society. This conviction would seem to unite Aristotelian political philosophy with traditional African social philosophy with its emphasis on communalism.

Accordingly, the immediate social setting of the novel is played up to a position of prominence. The sociohistorical context is unmistakably real, nearly anarchic, and can be easily located in postwar petro-dollar Nigeria. The characteristic features of this milieu are carefully presented as atavism, aggressive individualism, limitless acquisitiveness, and conspicuous consumption. In the immediate locale of the action which is thinly disguised as Benin, the capital of Nigeria's Bendel State, the most noticeable fact of social existence is the coexistence of abject penury with scandalous affluence. More importantly, Iyayi is at pains to capture the prosaic reality and the raw immediacy of the material conditions under which the exploited classes live. The situation is such that the poor even have to sell pints of their own blood to those of the sick who can afford the giveaway price . . . in order to ensure the next meal for their family. Medical facilities, jobs, decent shelter, and food are luxuries which only the rich can afford.

It is against this horrifying social spectacle that the different characters derive their identity as either exploiters or victims of exploitation. The principal contrast, in terms of material conditions, is between Obofun and his wife, Queen, on one hand and the Idemudias on the other. The former are wealthy hoteliers and government sponsored contractors while the latter are a poor couple driven by poverty and unemployment to the periphery of society, a situation in which they can hardly afford the next meal and have to live on pittances and handouts from benevolent neighbors.

However, the implications of Iyayi's ideological standpoint for characterization in this novel are not exhausted by this simple positing of two couples living in contrasting material conditions. Far from simplifying the problematic of the novel in a polarization of characters, Iyayi weaves into them certain psychological attributes which add up to a negation and indictment of the capitalist ethos which is a central theme. Thus, although materially rich, Obofun and his wife fail to achieve mutual fulfillment in their "marriage of convenience." The emotional content of their marriage has been corroded by their pursuit of money and business opportunities. Consequently, they both degenerate morally to a point where Obofun resorts to lechery and womanizing while his wife, in her endless quest for easy profit, becomes more of a glorified prostitute. . . .

The tragic essence of *Violence* lies more [in] the anarchic social setting and blood-curdling experiences which it constitutes as its central problematics. But its formal integrity lies in the peculiar kind of resolution which it forges for its tragic dialectic. Here again, Idemudia as the hero of this "tragedy" is also the carrier of its peculiar aesthetic proposition. In spite of his poverty and marginalized condition, he does not acquiesce or succumb to oppression. At different moments in the novel, he revolts against the indignities meted out to him by society on account of his material limitations. At the height of his humiliation in the hospital because of his inability to pay the exorbitant bills, he resolutely declares: "I am going to escape somehow from this so-called hospital in which I am being held as a prisoner . . . I am going to continue to struggle, to fight."

Chidi Amuta. CE&S. 7, 1 (Autumn 1984), pp. 99–101, 104

[In *Violence*] the working people, represented by Idemudia and others who gather at Iyaso Motor Park, are constantly looking for work. Here again, people are forced to sell their labor power to the local bourgeoisie in order to survive. In most cases they are employed merely on a daily basis, so there is no job security. Since the surplus value created is to be shared between the local and the foreign masters, Idemudia and his comrades are grossly exploited as manual laborers in off-loading cement bags and as workers with building contractors. . . .

[The] working people are presented as individuals who believe in struggling for their liberation—as fully conscious human beings who are prepared to face their problems with courage. At the same time, they are not presented as infallible heroes but also have their human weaknesses. Idemudia, for example, is tempted to propose sex to Queen even though he realizes that this might adversely affect the ongoing struggle between Queen, the contractor, and Idemudia's own labor union. . . .

In Festus Iyayi's novel a balanced picture is given, both of the working people and of the exploiters. Neither social class is infallible. They both show a degree of human failing and human strength, although it is abundantly clear that Iyayi is on the side of the working people. As a radical writer he is not complacent towards the plight of those who have only their labor to sell. But he does not legitimize Idemudia's attempt at beating his wife; neither does he approve of the (understandable) "sexual methods" of Adisa, who searches for money to pay off Idemudia's hospital bill. . . .

Iyayi's concept of art tallies with that of [Frantz] Fanon. In his novel, he sees working people as people always in the process of asserting their existence through struggle. They face the future with determination. At the same time, a balanced view is given of the members of the neocolonial comprador class. They are also portrayed as human beings, but as human beings debasing themselves and others in their efforts to appropriate the surplus value created by the working people. On the whole, Iyayi's concept of art is progressive and Fanonist.

Tunde Fatunde. In Georg M. Gugelberger, ed. Marxism and African
Literature (Trenton, N. J.: Africa World Press, 1986), pp. 111–14, 116

[*Heroes*] is one of those artistic texts which carries within it a clue as to how its author intends it to be read. A key to understanding the novel lies in the words of one of its characters, Sergeant Audu, a Federal soldier fighting on the Asaba front during the Nigerian Civil War. Several of Audu's men die heroically in an ambush, abandoned by their officer, who had arranged to be driven away to safety. At this point, Audu remarks bitterly: "After the war, many generals will write their accounts in which they will attempt to show that they were the heroes. . . . They will tell the world that they singlehandedly fought and won the war. The names of soldiers like Otun, Emmanuel, Ikeshi and Yemi will never be mentioned. . . . The soldiers pay for the unity of this country with their lives and yet, what happens? . . . Always the generals get the praise. Always they are the heroes." . . .

Iyayi's attack on bourgeois historiography in *Heroes* is incisive and convincing. His main character, the young journalist Osime Iyere, is initially a firm supporter of the Federal cause. He accepts the Federal government's contention that the war must be fought and won in order to protect Nigerians from the tribalistic attitude and greed of the Igbos. As the novel progresses, however, the contradictions in this argument begin to appear. When the Federal army arrives in Benin to "liberate" the town from the Biafrans, Osime observes that, far from protecting the inhabitants, they slaughter civilians just as indiscriminately as the Biafrans had done earlier. At the Asaba front, the Federal officers indulge in endless rounds of parties as the rank and file are sent into battle to die. In Lagos, far from the battlefront, the head of state and commander in chief of the armed forces, General Gowon, remains oblivious to the carnage in Asaba as he celebrates his wedding with the vulgar insensitivity typical of his class.

These contradictions provide dramatic evidence of Iyayi's thesis that the war originated less in tribal sentiment than in class interests: indeed, he succeeds in reducing the war to a greedy squabble between factions within the ruling class. As Osime reflects, ordinary Igbos, as opposed to those of the ruling class, "never had any quarrel with the Hausas or the Yorubas until the politicians and generals allowed their lust for power and greed for profit to run riot." Osime insists that the real basis for solidarity is not tribe but class. He points out to a fellow journalist: "The fact is that the ordinary Igbo man has a great deal more in common with the ordinary Hausa and the ordinary Yoruba than he has in common with the Igbo businessman and general and politicians."

Similarly, members of the ruling class, irrespective of tribal origin, are, in the final analysis, bound together by mutual interest.

What is needed in order to change this situation, Iyayi tells us, is a "third army," an army whose role would be ideological in that it would fight ruling class propaganda and enable ordinary Nigerians, be they Igbo, Yoruba, or Hausa, to recognize their common interests and reject the divisions that their respective ruling classes seek to promote between them. The combined forces of the Nigerian people would then take up arms to destroy the entire ruling class, irrespective of tribal considerations. Iyayi sums up his message in a striking image of Gowon and Ojukwu, seeming enemies but in reality fellow members of the ruling class, fleeing together from the Nigerian people, because, in the war to end all wars, "they would be on the same side, where they actually do belong."

Fírinne Ní Chréacháin. RAL. 22, 1 (Spring 1991), pp. 43–45

The relationship between the historical event and its fictional representation, situated as it is in the vast mine-pitted terrain of "realism," is an extremely complex one, and this study of *Heroes* will focus on just one dimension: the selection and handling of particular historical events by the artist as a means of intervening in the making of history. . . .

The task which Iyayi explicitly sets himself in *Heroes* obviously has much in common with that of the radical historian: to expose the ideological bias of bourgeois historiography and, by adopting the perspective of the exploited majority, by rewriting history "from below," to reveal the class interests that are the motive force of history. This project is expressed with remarkable economy in the novel's title: in a single word, Iyayi signifies his determination to substitute one set of actors for another, to replace the generals, the "heroes" of bourgeois historiography, with the "unknown soldiers" who represent the masses and are the heroes of radical history. Iyayi is equally explicit in stating the purpose of radical history and radical art. The exposure of ruling-class self-interest is a step towards liberating the exploited from the dominant ideology, and ultimately towards mobilizing them against the ruling class. As Osime tells the soldiers, "I want you to know the truth, and knowing the truth helps until there are so many who know the truth that you can do something about it." . . .

Central to his art is the judicious use of the *typical*, of what people will recognize as characteristic of the society, in terms of events and the agents shaping them. For Iyayi, the Asaba-Onitsha crossing, in which hundreds of ordinary Nigerians from all over the country lost their lives but which brought no benefit to the Nigerian masses, is clearly such an event. Similarly typical is Gowon's wedding, which came to symbolize all the callousness of a corrupt regime. Iyayi knows that any reference to Gowon's wedding is capable of stirring the memories of Nigerians of his own generation, of reawakening old resentments against the ruling class and the upper echelons of the military which are part of it. For those too young to remember the war, the artistic combination of the Asaba tragedy and the wedding provides a paradigm which exposes the contradictions, not just of a war they did not experience, but of the cruel realities of their own lives today.

Fírinne Ní Chréacháin. *JCL.* 27, 1 (1992), pp. 48–50, 56–57

The Contract opens with the return to Nigeria of Ogie Obala, the son of a wealthy businessman, from his studies overseas. Iyayi takes full advantage of his protagonist's initial shock of arrival, the frenzy he sees all around him, to introduce his theme. In the taxi bearing him home, Ogie is subjected to a diatribe by the driver on the importance of money in the society to which he has returned. . . . Arrived home, his father is quick to confirm the driver's outburst, though without the former's bitterness and outrage. . . . When [Ogie] visits [his girlfriend Rose Idebale] a week after his arrival, he tells her that he will be joining his father's firm. His job will be to award government contracts. The whole issue of contracts is at the heart of large-scale corruption, if only because of the amounts involved. The commonly accepted practice is for the awarding firm to automatically demand ten percent commission of the value of the contract as a matter of course, and for the interested parties to bid against each other on that basis. Rose is only too well aware of the damage this is doing to the country. . . .

[The] theme of *The Contract* is corruption and its corrosive effect on one man's soul: "I have eaten the apple," Ogie says, and so he has. In this context, Ogie's death is merely a diversion because it absolves the writer from the necessity of examining the full implications of the moral depths he has plumbed. But this is precisely what the novel demands. Physical death is by no means the worst thing that can happen to a person; far worse is the death of the soul that comes with eating the fruit of sin. This is what Rose meant, after all, when she declared, "How could you fight it alone and hope to come out of it alive." She meant that he was heading for a spiritual annihilation that she has daily witnessed in those around her, but which she firmly rejects as a possible option for herself.

Rose, like Idemudia in *Violence*, is the person who will not be corrupted; who will hold herself aloof from the prevailing squalor and follow only the dictates of her conscience. It is for this reason that she rejects Ogie's proposal of marriage. . . . This is not bravado for its own sake. Even when she discovers that she is pregnant by him, and that her pregnancy could easily be her passport out of the rathole to which her poverty condemns her, she remains faithful to her beliefs.

Adewale Maja-Pearce. *A Mask Dancing: Nigerian Novelists of the Eighties* (London: Hans Zell, 1992), pp. 79–80, 84–85

JAMES, C. L. R. (1901–1989)

TRINIDAD

[C. L. R.] James said that he wrote *Minty Alley* "purely to amuse myself one summer." For some time he had been interested in the literary possibilities of "yard" life, and had published a short story, "Triumph," which dealt with the picturesque life in a Port-of-Spain "barrack-yard." James had actually decided to live in such a yard in order to experience the life of its inhabitants at first hand: "I went to live there, the people fascinated me, and I wrote about them from the point of view of an educated youthful member of the black middle class." In *Minty Alley*, James drew on this experience to illustrate not only what he saw as the natural joie de vivre of the slumdwellers, their ability to transcend repressive surroundings, but also the possibilities for mutual enrichment which might come from a middle-class involvement with, and understanding of, the "yard" folk. Mr. Haynes, a young, middle-class Negro orphaned by the death of his mother, decides to look for cheap lodgings in a slum yard to escape both loneliness and the expense of living in his parents' large, mortgaged home. His faithful servant, Ella, tries to dissuade him, but he persists, and takes a room in No. 2 Minty Alley, where he becomes involved in the life of the yard community. The others respect his higher social status as an educated man, a householder, and a white-collar worker and he uses his position as "father-confessor" and ombudsman to the residents to keep the unstable yard relationships from becoming too explosive. He enjoys this new life, gaining a measure of maturity during the process (thanks partly to an affair with young Maisie, the fiery-tempered beauty of the yard), and is very unhappy when, owing to the death of Benoit, one of the yard's most vital characters, and the insoluble conflict between Maisie and her aunt, Mrs. Rouse, the bereaved landlady of the yard, the community disbands and the property is sold. Haynes goes back to his dull, middle-class life, which had been temporarily heightened by the experience of No. 2 Minty Alley, which itself, inevitably, undergoes change, becoming a respectable, residential area.

As this summary of the plot suggests, *Minty Alley* . . . is intended by its author to be a sympathetic study of slum life from a middle-class viewpoint. . . . James's stance is one of subjective involvement. He attempts this through his black character, Mr. Haynes, who functions as an extension of his author's voice and sympathies. From the outset James is clearly an advocate for lower-class vitality as opposed to the dullness and snobbery of middle-class life.

Michael Gilkes. The West Indian Novel (Boston: Twayne, 1981), pp. 28–29

In *Beyond a Boundary*, James describes his departure for England in 1932 as a necessary step in what was to be a literary career: "I had a completed novel with me. But that was only my 'prentice hand. Contrary to accepted experience, the real *magnum opus* was to be my second novel." James was to distinguish himself internationally as an imaginative political theorist, and as a sensitive commentator on the West Indian social and cultural scene, but no second novel ever came to be written. The first was *Minty Alley*. . . .

Minty Alley is more than just a novel of the yard narrated from an unusual point of view. And Haynes is not simply a narrative device. The novel is really about the mutually impoverishing alienation of the educated West Indian from the people. James allows Haynes's economic necessity to coincide with the character's "need to make a break" from the protecting world of middle-class mother and faithful family servant. The young man's growing involvement with, and appreciation of, the inhabitants of the yard are made to correspond with the degrees by which he comes to have his first sexual affair with Maisie, the yard's young firebrand. It is a function of the author's lack of sentimentality, that Maisie should leave for the United States by the end, rather than hang about in the hope of leading the affair with Haynes to a conventional conclusion. But Haynes has had his awakening. His returns to the respectable house that has replaced the old Minty Alley are as much an ironic comment on the rising West Indian bourgeoisie as a wistful backward glance at what is being lost.

Kenneth Ramchand. *The West Indian Novel and Its Background*
(London: Heinemann, 1983), pp. 69–71

James wrote his fiction well before he was thirty. He had always been a voracious reader, feeding his insatiable curiosity with a wide variety of material. In his twenties, he was intellectually stimulated by the young artists and thinkers who were changing the direction of West Indian culture. "La Divina Pastora," brief and complete as a miniature portrait, was his first success. Then came "Triumph," which he still considers one of his finest works, and finally the novel *Minty Alley*. All concern the grassroots people, whom James considered the lifeblood of the culture.

"La Divina Pastora" is the story of Anita Perez, whose shy but affluent lover Sebastian Montagnio visits nightly but cannot break through his inhibitions. He smokes while Anita knits or sews and her mother sits on the ground just outside chatting away in patois. Marriage to Sebastian (or somebody) is Anita's only chance to escape her daily labor in the cocoa fields, and that hope is fading with Anita's fading beauty. The routine is broken when Anita visits her aunt in Siparia and presents her case at the altar of the renowned saint La Divina Pastora. Anita leaves as a sacrifice her only ornament, a little gold chain. Upon her return, Sebastian, jarred by her unprecedented absence, becomes more demonstrative and even asks to take Anita to the cocoa-house dance. Discounting the influence of La Divina Pastora, Anita wishes she had her gold chain back to wear to the dance. By the end of the dance, a coolness has arisen between the lovers. Later, undressing for bed and telling her mother about the dance, Anita suddenly falls silent, then faints—for on her table, in its accustomed place, is the little chain.

Brief though it is, the story is perfectly crafted. It is an interesting balance of realism and mysticism. The objective narrator neither denies nor affirms the powers of La Divina Pastora but merely tells concisely what happens. The ending leaves many questions unanswered—which is, of course, the way of our lives and of good fiction. The basic *fact* of the story, the dominant thought with which the reader is left, is the impact of generations-long poverty.

"Triumph" portrays life in the urban barrack yards. Again the story focuses on the plight of impoverished women, whose only resource ultimately is their sexuality. In "Triumph" Mamitz has lost her lover and is therefore destitute since, like the other women in the yard, her survival depends upon her ability to maintain a relationship with a man. Her friend Celestine, suspecting that their enemy Irene has put a curse on Mamitz, performs Obeah rites, after which Mamitz attracts not one but two lovers. Popo is a flashy playboy who soon moves on. Nicholas the butcher is a steady type who pays Mamitz's rent and supports her well. When Popo returns for a brief but impressive fling, Irene hastens to tell Nicholas, who rushes to the scene. Fortunately, Popo has left. The ensuing quarrel is classic, but Mamitz convinces Nicholas of her fidelity. Her triumph is the dramatic display of the money Nicholas has given her, nailed in small denominations to the double doors of her house, proclaiming to the yard-world the defeat of the enemy Irene.

Eugenia Collier. In Daryl Cumber Dance, ed. Fifty Caribbean Writers
(Westport, Conn.: Greenwood Press, 1986), pp. 232–33

Although C. L. R. James's *Beyond a Boundary* is not autobiography in the traditional sense, it is more than a cricket memoir by a major West Indian writer. It is a complex narrative, rich in personal insight, seasoned with cricket history, cultural mythography, and Marxist polemics. In answer to the perennial question *what do men live by?* James, theorist, historian, Pan-Africanist, and pamphleteer, spins an intriguing, idiosyncratic tale of West Indian cultural emergence within the context of a national sport. He employs cricket as a metaphor for a nascent West Indian community from which, as an expatriate and "British intellectual," he is estranged. The center of interest is the self and its relationship to the surrounding world; as autobiographer, sentimentally tied to both [William Makepeace] Thackeray and [William] Hazlitt, James self-consciously reshapes the past into a pattern of stages where he mediates a battle between the "old world" of tradition and the "new" one of revolt. . . .

Beyond a Boundary is a carefully crafted account of the author's past as seen through the veil of exile. It is a journey into a childhood marked by Victorian sensibility, an errant view of early adulthood spent at the heels of cricketers and at the shrine of ancient learning, a journey that led to the seat of empire where sports and politics became integral pawns on the playing fields of a class war.

Consuelo Lopez Springfield. CarQ. 35, 4 (December 1989), p. 73

James's speeches, like the brilliant orations of [Edmund] Burke and [Benjamin] Disraeli, abound in messianic images. As a Marxist Milton or modern Moses, he embraces a romanticized past. His historical vision portrays the world's proletariat as a legion of saints struggling against the monstrous forces of capitalist evil to achieve a new society. Images of rebirth contrasted with those of decay suggest a choice: redemption through a baptism of fire—socialist revolution—

or spiritual death. If James were to travel through time to a distant past, in nineteenth-century England he would feel at home. In the House of Commons, before the leading speakers of the day, he would oppose the rights of privilege and property. In speeches noted for their ardor and keen sense of the sweep of history, he would juxtapose the dominant image of the masses as mindless barbarians to show that their conscious activity is democracy in motion. Popular struggle, James tells audiences, will destroy the corruption and disillusionment of our age. "The world now lives in a state of despair such as it has never known before," James warned Trinidadian union delegates. To change the destructive course of events, he urged them to "take over the destiny of this country, your own destiny, and shape the society along the lines that you desire, making possible what has been denied to you all these years." . . .

In his speeches before audiences in four main geographical areas of the globe, James's pride in his own accomplishments as a scholar and as a political figure underlines ethical appeals. But his humility, his acknowledgement that contact with ordinary people enables him to understand history, attests his firm belief in creative interaction. Discussing *[The] Black Jacobins* with an audience of West Indians in 1966, James declared, "It is only of late years with my acquaintance with the West Indian people and actual contact with them, political and in some degree sociological, that I have learned to understand what I wrote in this book." His words recall a younger James reporting on cricket matches, interacting with the "common folk" of his native land, and learning, from them, of social ties and obligations. In turn, James assured them that their rebellious history, pregnant with democratic zeal, insures their continued efforts to resist oppression. "If we want to know what the ordinary population can do, let us know what they have done in the past," he told them. "The Negro people in the Caribbean are of the same stock as the men who played such a role in the history of their time," he argued; "we shall be able to do whatever we have to do." On the pages of history, ordinary people have left an indelible mark, James reminds us; human emancipation lies within the struggle towards democracy in our own daily events. His efforts to reveal the conflicts inherent in our times through the portholes of our pasts help to persuade us that our boldest aspirations can be forcefully enacted. Our common history is his rhetorical tool; and, on the basis of his trust in humanity, he wields persuasive power.

Consuelo Lopez Springfield. CarQ. 36, 1–2 (June 1990), pp. 89, 94–95

Now, the reader of *Beyond a Boundary* will already sense modernist strategies of subversion and defamiliarization in the mixed generic conception at the heart of James's discursive strategy. Indeed, a reader encountering James's text for the first time can be forgiven for wondering how a history of cricket in the West Indies provides one of the central paradigms in my study—the notion that the Caribbean self must of necessity move from a position of silence and blankness to a cognizance of its own marginal status in the colonial economy of representation as a precondition for the recentering of the colonial subject in history.

James must have pondered the same question when he wrote this book because he initiates his discourse with an epigraph that, rather than assuring the reader that he or she is in the familiar territory of the Caribbean *bildung*, goes out of its way to confuse the terms by which we read this text. In this succinct and carefully crafted epigraph, James is emphatic that his text is "neither cricket reminiscences nor autobiography"; rather, he offers us a document in which generic boundaries are collapsed and the distinction between facts and fiction, discourse and narrative, is rejected. The autobiographical form James adopts in the book is not a means toward writing a coherent history of self, but a structure for framing displacement in a temporal sequence "in relation to the events, the facts and the personalities which prompted them."

Simon Gikandi. *Writing in Limbo: Modernism and Caribbean Literature* (Ithaca, N. Y.: Cornell University Press, 1992), p. 44

JOHNSON, CHARLES (1948–   )

UNITED STATES

Perhaps closest to [Ralph] Ellison's novel [*Invisible Man*] in overall mythic design is Charles Johnson's *Faith and the Good Thing*. Faith, cautioned by her dying mother to get herself a "Good Thing," begins a Platonic search in the cave of life for Truth, an Arthurian quest for the Grail, or, like the African Kujichagulia, a climb toward the peak of Mount Kilimanjaro and the source of knowledge. Traveling from rural Georgia to urban Chicago, she embraces numerous roles and ideologies—her mother's fundamentalist Christianity, middle-class materialism and opportunism, a streetwalker's self-sacrifice, an artist's solipsism. As she passes from one ideology to another—ever hopeful—she also finds herself involved with a variety of people, most of whom exploit her for their own ends, few of whom see her according to her own needs and complexity. Burned by an apocalyptic fire at the novel's conclusion, she becomes a wraith: seen and not seen, a visual symbol of her former existence and an obvious analogy to Ellison's Invisible Man. Faith's invisibility differs, however, from that of Ellison's protagonist, for throughout her travels she has been in touch with the unseen world—not the unseen world of Plato's perfect forms, Kujichagulia's absolute answers, or the nightmares of Ellison's protagonist, which are no alternative to his waking world; she is in touch with memories, or more accurately, the spiritual presences of three human beings who persist in haunting her; they keep alive the faith in her, the faith which gives her her name and identity, the faith that believes that the search itself is its own end. These familiar presences are "the living dead," and only when Faith stops searching, momentarily convinced she has found the "Good Thing" in a materialistic middle-class life, and joins "the dead living," do they cease to appear before her. Following [a] fire and a hospital internment—events which also force Ellison's protagonist to new perspectives on himself—they are restored to her, however, as she herself becomes one of them.

Indeed, as Faith, the wraith, returns to the swamp from which she had started her journey, she is reincarnated as the Swamp Woman. In his cellar Ellison's hero gains perspective on his personal agonies by reviewing in a dream sequence the ambiguities of his own life and of black Americans from the days of slavery; similarly, Faith's sufferings seem to give her access to the werewitch's esoteric and folk wisdom, her knowledge of Western and African philosophical and cabalistic systems as well as her consciousness of the terrible history of oppression. Like Ellison's protagonist's, Faith's journey has also been cyclical, returning her to her own past—the swamp and the Briar Patch of her own mind—as well as to the historical past, represented by the conflation of her experiences with the Swamp Woman's lore. By Faith's return to the swamp as well as by the old crone's marvelous subsequent assumption of Faith's guise and her return to the world to continue Faith's search, Johnson demonstrates his commitment, however, to myth rather than history, for he seeks to guarantee its truth by suggesting its endless repetition. Finally, Faith, like Ellison's protagonist, contemplates the possibilities of the mind to conceive a pattern for living; she, living in a state of faith rather than of paralysis, imagines both progress and responsibility beyond the control of history. . . . Finally, then, unlike Ellison's protagonist, she envisions a way to reconcile the many with the one.

In the conclusion of his novel, Johnson informs us that Faith's way will not be a solitary one. Not only do we learn that she is preparing to relate Aristotle's Illusion and "Stagolee's great battle with Lucifer in West Hell" to two children who seek her out in the swamp as she herself had once sought the werewitch, but we are also reminded that we ourselves have been children throughout the novel, listening to Johnson relate Faith's own tale. Ellison, too, somewhat perfunctorily, reminds us in the last sentence of his novel that we have also been an audience for his protagonist's story when he queries, "Who knows but that, on the lower frequencies, I speak for you?" Johnson's repeated imperative reference to his readers as "Children" and Faith's preparations for her young visitors suggest, however, a more than rhetorical involvement with others; the "Good Thing" is not only the search itself but also the fact that the search is everyone's, and that we are on it together. For other black writers following in Ellison's footsteps, the "Good Thing" is even more emphatically the involvement with others as well as one's personal search.

Elizabeth A. Schultz. *CLAJ.* 22, 2 (December 1978), pp. 106–8

Since most contemporary novels involving race are scandals of contrivance, unwheeled wagons hitched to cardboard horses, it's a particular pleasure to read Charles Johnson's *Oxherding Tale*. This is his second novel and . . . it separates him even further from conventional sensibilities. In [*Faith and the Good Thing*], Johnson told the tall tale of a black girl's search for meaning—What is the good life? What is good?—and soaked it through with skills he had developed as a cartoonist, television writer, journalist, and student of philosophy. This time out, he has written a novel made important by his artful use of the slave narrative's structure to examine the narrator's developing consciousness, a consciousness that must painfully evaluate both the master and slave cultures.

The primary theme is freedom and the responsibility that comes with it. Given the time of the novel, 1838 to 1860, one would expect such a theme, but Johnson makes it clear in the most human—and often hilarious—terms that the question of freedom in a democratic society is essentially moral, and that social revolution pivots on an expanding redefinition of citizenry and its relationship to law. The adventure of escape only partially prepares Andrew Hawkins, the narrator, for the courage and commitment that come with moral comprehension. Andrew's growth is thrilling because Johnson skillfully avoids melodramatic platitudes while creating suspense and comedy, pathos and nostalgia. In the process, he invents a fresh set of variations on questions about race, sex, and freedom.

Stanley Crouch. *VV*. July 19, 1983, p. 30

Charles Johnson's *Oxherding Tale* . . . extends convention by showing an interracial romance that is not doomed to failure or fraught with unhappiness, and in doing so signals a new direction for a vexed issue in American fiction. *Oxherding Tale* shows an interracial relationship that quietly and matter-of-factly succeeds. Set in the antebellum South, *Oxherding Tale* conflates and juxtaposes past and present in Andrew Hawkins, the contemporary narrator. His origins are comic: one night, after sustained drinking, plantation-owner Jonathan Polkinghorne and his slave, George Hawkins, swap wives and the outraged Anna Polkinghorne becomes pregnant with Andrew. After a series of bizarre adventures and philosophical explorations—the novel is an entertaining mixture of picaresque and slave narrative forms (what Johnson calls "genre crossing")—Andrew decides to pass for white to escape to freedom. . . .

The plot of *Oxherding Tale*, though it is complex and entertaining, is, as Andrew points out in the opening sentences, "mere parable" for deeper concerns of individual identity and spiritual development. Passing for white gives Andrew the opportunity to begin again, to "reconstruct his life from scratch." As he admits later, he "milked the Self's polymorphy to elude, like Trickster John in the folk tales my father told." Throughout the narrative, Andrew is many things: slave, student, lover, teacher, husband, nineteenth- and twentieth-century man combined, philosopher, and writer. Andrew the narrator comments on the literary conventions as he experiments with them. He is hardly a "character" in the traditional sense of the term since he serves for Johnson more as a palimpsest: a fluid repository for metaphysical musings and literary echoes and experimentation. In one of his essayist asides (another metafictional defamiliarizing device), Johnson clarifies this strategy: "The Self, this perceiving subject who puffs on and on, is, for all purposes, a palimpsest, interwoven with everything—literally everything—that can be thought or felt." Thus Andrew's decision to pass for white resonates at more than just the level of physical survival and expands into phenomenological issues of freedom and identity.

Jonathan Little. *SAF*. 19, 2 (Autumn 1991), pp. 143–44

Oxherding Tale acknowledges the marginalization not only of black men but of women, black and white. Johnson explores questions of race and gender by locating them within a complex, experimental network of slave narrative conventions, Afro-American tropes, eighteenth-century narrative strategies, literary constructs of the first-person narrator, and philosophical constructs of the Self and of freedom—all of which are subsumed in Johnson's version of Zen Buddhism. Johnson has described his book as "a modern, comic, philosophical slave narrative—a kind of dramatization of the famous 'Ten Oxherding Pictures' of Zen artist Kakuan-Shien" that represent a young herdsman's search for his rebellious ox, which symbolizes his self. . . .

Johnson's attitude towards women tends towards a glorification of the Eternal Feminine, an attitude which can (and, in this book, several times does) flip over into the concomitant terror of women as all-encompassing and all-powerful. The fact nevertheless remains that Johnson makes a strong attempt to understand feminist issues and to inscribe them in his book. And his technical innovations—particularly the shifts in narrative and temporal perspective—help break the bounds of canonical (Western androcentric) literature.

Jennifer Hayward. BALF. 25, 4 (Winter 1991), pp. 689–90

Since the 1974 publication of his first novel, *Faith and the Good Thing*, Charles Johnson has repeatedly called for a revitalized Afro-American literary aesthetic. Decrying what he terms black fiction's largely "splintered" perspective, Johnson suggests that Afro-American writers concentrate on the new goal of achieving "whole sight," a broadened literary outlook that embraces (to quote Clayton Riley) the "entire world—not just the fractured world of American racism and psychic social disorder." We know more, Johnson claims, than oppression and discrimination. Contemporary black writers not only need to project a new vision into the preexisting tradition of literature, but must at the same time invent the very fictions that will embody it. Johnson's project thus requires first a rebirth and then a rebuilding of Afro-American literature. . . . [*Oxherding Tale*] is an explicit response to his own call. *Oxherding Tale* is necessarily informed by, while at the same time re- (or even de)forming, several precursive literary strategies, including the slave narrative and the Eastern parable. Through its self-consciously postmodern, cross-cultural blend of (principally) Afro-American tradition and the philosophy of Zen, *Oxherding Tale* attempts what Buddhists call opening the "third eye," or what Johnson sees as the final aim of serious fiction: namely, the liberation of perception.

William Gleason. BALF. 25, 4
(Winter 1991), p. 705

A freed slave, a roguish fellow, stows away on a ship in New Orleans to avoid creditors and a forced marriage, not realizing the clipper is bound for Africa to capture slaves. Put to work as a cook, he encounters a crew of misfits, a cruel and brilliant captain, legendary tribesmen, storms, and rebellions, and is transformed by the journey.

So goes the tale of *Middle Passage*, which won the National Book Award for fiction . . . and brought a flurry of attention to [Johnson]. . . .

In *Middle Passage* and his two other published novels . . . he sought to develop "an Afro-American philosophical fiction," he said, adding, "I feel we don't have enough of that in black American literature." He then cited important exceptions: works by Jean Toomer, Richard Wright, and Ralph Ellison, "Those were the writers I was most inspired by," he said.

The ex-slave and lyrical narrator of *Middle Passage*, Rutherford Calhoun, has been well educated by his former master, and can speak of, say, someone's "Sisyphean" love and of an "Icarian, causa sui impulse."

But the real philosopher on board, said Mr. Johnson, is the captain, Ebenezer Falcon. He is based loosely on Sir Richard Francis Burton, whose contradictions fascinated the author. "He was an explorer, an imperialist, a translator, a quasi-genius," he said, "and also the biggest bigot in the world."

As for the slaves, captured members of a tribe called the Allmuseri, "They live and *breathe* philosophy," Mr. Johnson said. "I wanted to make them the most spiritual tribe ever. What I admire about them is their profound connectedness to everything around them. They are biologically related, but what truly unites them is their shared vision, their values."

Eleanor Blau. NYT. January 2, 1991, p. C9

Rutherford Calhoun, the narrator of *Middle Passage*, begins his career as a thief. Stealing, for Rutherford, is more than just an occupation; it is a philosophy, indeed a phenomenology. He treats the world as a mine of property from which to hoard "experiences"—as "if *life* was a commodity, a *thing* we could cram into ourselves." Rutherford then meets the Allmuseri, who are themselves being stolen from Africa in the summer of 1830, and finds that his life and his philosophy are indigent. As he learns about their philosophy, their history, their language, he finds himself, for the first time in his life, in a position of wanting to possess something that, by definition, could only be *had* if it is not possessed. "As I live, they so shamed me I wanted their ageless culture to be my own . . . ." During the course of the Middle Passage, Rutherford discovers several things. First, he learns that a culture cannot be possessed because it is an unstable entity. The Allmuseri, he learns, "were process and Heraclitean change . . . not fixed but evolving." He also learns, though, that bonds and connections are a matter of surrendering to another order of being, and are not simply determined by racial or biological destiny. . . .

Eventually, and after a course of adventures rivaling the plots of [Herman Melville's] *Moby-Dick* and "Benito Cereno," Rutherford surrenders to that order and discovers that "experience" is not a property belonging to a "subject" but rather an intersubjective process by which subjects are formed and transformed. . . . In the end, the exposure to the Allmuseri . . . leaves [Rutherford] and his world altered. "The voyage had irreversibly changed my seeing, made of me a cultural mongrel, and transformed the world into a fleeting shadow play I felt no need to possess or dominate, only appreciate in the ever extended present." This is, essentially, the phenomenology of the Allmuseri. . . .

In his meditations on artistic creativity, Charles Johnson has noted that there is a "curious, social, intersubjective side of art [which] is, as the best aestheticians report, central to the artistic personality and the creative process." Part of Johnson's achievement is to promote this intersubjective aspect of art and describe the immense benefits obtaining for us if we act on this desire to inhabit fictional worlds which challenge our parochialism. But the greater part of Johnson's achievement is to enact intersubjective relations in the making and to discover in the phenomenology of the Allmuseri a theory and a symbol for the postmodern condition discernible in much of the fiction written by those Johnson calls "Americans who happen to be black." The discovery of the Allmuseri has been, one suspects, at least one of the reasons that his most recent novels have not only enjoyed a fate different from his first six, but have broken new and very fertile ground in the field of African-American letters.

Ashraf H. A. Rushdy. *African American Review*. 26, 3 (Fall 1992), pp. 376–77, 393

JONES, GAYL (1949–   )

UNITED STATES

[Gayl Jones's first novel] *Corregidora* is a bizarre romantic story that exposes the intimate life of the main character, Ursa Corregidora, with such candor and immediacy that its narrative texture seems like a screen onto which her unique psychological history is projected. The novel is a carefully controlled creation of storytelling in which the process of communication develops from the author's determination to relay the story entirely in terms of the mental processes of this character, and thus without any authorial intrusion. The narrative itself is composed of two stories that are so closely related that they are inextricably intertwined. One concerns the course of ordinary external events in a small town in Kentucky, while the other evolves from Ursa's personal recollections. Together they create the illusion of an actual record of a living person.

Ursa Corregidora is black and obviously female. These characteristics neither typecast the novel into a racial or feminist category, nor do they detract from the universality of the protagonist's plight. Rather, they enhance the psychological intensity of Ursa's evolving portrait as well as serve to enrich the novel's narrative texture by relying on symbols and allusions that naturally arise from her racial and mythic histories. In this manner the story achieves subtle psychological form and universal meaning. Without the historical references and allusions, Ursa would lack important interpretative potential beyond the fictional world which she inhabits. She would be merely an unusual aberration of human character rather than a distinct personality encountering situations imbued with human paradox.

The external drama of *Corregidora* involves Ursa's estrangement from her husband, Mutt Thomas, who in a jealous rage pushes her down a flight of stairs in the spring of 1948. Her injuries result in her having to have a hysterectomy. She is extremely bitter about her condition, especially since she has a family obligation to bear children, an imperative first impressed on her by her great-grandmother in order to preserve the details of her slave heritage. She divorces Mutt and, as a result, seems to be left with no alternative but to live out her life alone like all the Corregidora women before her. Perhaps she would have remained content to have done so were she not frightened by a lesbian encounter while convalescing at the home of a friend, Cat Lawson. This experience makes her worry whether men will still find her desirable, or whether she will eventually succumb to homosexual embrace. In order to quell her fear, she marries the first man who shows an interest in her—Tadpole McCormick, the owner of the club where she sings. Their marriage is short-lived, and Ursa soon finds that she is again alone with her fear. After twenty-two years of uneventful living and singing the blues in another club just across town, Mutt returns, and they are reunited.

Claudia C. Tate. BALF. 13, 4 (Winter 1979), p. 139

Corregidora provides a clear account of the ambiguities of childbirth under slavery and provides as well a vision in which the traditional African celebration of childbirth is joined to a New World rebellion against history. Ursa Corregidora, the singer whose life the novel portrays, is the fourth-generation descendant of a Brazilian slave and a Portuguese plantation owner. She has grown up in the American South in a household shared with her mother, her grandmother, and her great-grandmother. They pass on to Ursa their common fund of memories, extending back to the sexual abuse suffered by her great-grandmother and grandmother under slavery in Brazil. Corregidora, the great-grandmother's owner, had fathered Ursa's grandmother and later hired both women out as prostitutes (to white men only). Ursa's mother was the product of incest between Corregidora and his own daughter. Corregidora's sexual abuse of his female slaves makes a mockery of the traditional African point of view in which sexuality and childbirth were seen as inseparable and sacred. Yet in the great-grandmother's vision "making generations" is nevertheless celebrated because, as in traditional Africa, descendants ensure a continuity of time. Ursa's great-grandmother wants this continuity so that the white slaveowner may not repudiate his own past. She tells Ursa, "When they did away with slavery down there [Brazil] they burned all the slavery papers so it would be like they never had it." "Making generations" is part of her plan to make this burning of records futile. . . . In Ursa's great-grandmother's vision, one's children and one's children's children thus counter the fragmentation of time that is fostered by the white repudiation of the past.

Bonnie J. Barthold. Black Time: Fiction of Africa, the Caribbean and the
United States (New Haven, Conn.: Yale University Press, 1981), p. 125

Corregidora espouses action, but remains a book of delay and avoidance and denial. It is at bottom a book about meaning, or attempted understanding. It continually rings changes on the idea of "pretending not to know what's meant," or not knowing and yet not asking, or being "afraid to ask more." As a result its exploitative sexual action remains strangely verbal; that is, it comes across as something that violates speech taboos more than human bodies or standards of personal integrity or moral principles. Intimacy is not at issue, though intimate things are at work. The meaning of these actions accordingly remains obscure, and the actors thwarted in two spheres. In like manner the engagement with the past proves less a matter of reimmersion than of arrest and obsession. (There is an immersion scene of sorts, but it involves the literal drowning of the runaway adolescent slave, with the cruel notation that after three days his body rose; we find no redemption here.) . . .

Ursa Corregidora herself illustrates the basic quandary of the text, that movement seems impossible until meanings are known, and meaning seems available only through movement. The emphasis on sex results from the fact that it so readily stands as a synecdoche for movement. But sex itself is a movement toward a larger goal than the "generation" that is specified. We need to see generation as merely instrumental, the real objective being *propagation*, that is, the spreading of the word, not just the multiplication of seed.

The past, as Wilburn Williams, Jr. notes, offers "possibilities of inspiration and renewal," but it also "can exert a malignant influence on the present." The Corregidora legacy is supposed to inspire a verdict but it only perpetuates itself inertially, with a faintly malignant influence. The only "verdict" that actually appears in the novel is tainted by its prevailing and reductive sexuality. . . .

In only one aspect of *Corregidora* does its obsessive and somewhat cryptic activity evolve into a measure of understanding, a measure of available meaning. That aspect is the blues. Ursa Corregidora is a blues singer whose experience of losing her baby (and her womb) at her husband's hands leads to a new style and voice for her, and to a new level of success. The blues can be taken as a subtheme of the novel. The meaning and work of the blues become all but a formal topic, receiving explicit discussion and analysis. The amplifying presence of the blues seems to give historic depth, validity, dignity, and power to Ursa's experience and to her being. And yet it is important to recognize that the same temporal alteration or denaturing that besets the Corregidora issue also infects the blues subtheme in the novel. Though at one point Ursa sings to Mutt before they make love, the blues cannot be said to break out of the condition of an isolated phenomenon of a nightclub. The novel may abound in blues-worthy incidents or situations, but its action rather deploys than absorbs the blues.

Michael G. Cooke. *Afro-American Literature in the Twentieth Century:*
The Achievement of Intimacy (New Haven, Conn.:
Yale University Press, 1984), pp. 218–19

The action in *Eva's Man* begins where [*Corregidora*] left off and envelops us in the despair of one woman's failure to achieve redemption. In fact, the unrelenting violence, emotional silence, and passive disharmony in *Eva's Man* are the undersides of the blues reconciliation and active lovemaking in *Corregidora*. Eva Medina Canada poisons her lover Davis Carter and castrates him with her teeth once he is dead. Important to our brief study here is that Eva never gains control over her voice, her past, or her identity. Instead of wielding language as useful evidence for justice and regeneration as Ursa has done, Eva is defeated by words and brandishes first a pocket knife against Moses Tripp, then uses arsenic and teeth against Davis. Eva never comes to terms with her past; she chooses to embrace received images of women as femmes fatales. Ursa and Eva are further separated by their vastly different capacities for love.

In relation to Jones's concern with opening avenues for reconciliation between the sexes and breaking down barriers erected against it from both self and society, it is important to see *Eva's Man* and *Corregidora* as companion texts. Primarily through their attitude toward language and fluency with idioms necessary for personal deliverance, we encounter one woman's fall and another's rise. The clear contrast between them makes Ursa appear as Eva's alter ego and reveals Jones to be a gifted ironist: Eva, surnamed Canada, the promised land for fugitive slaves, contrasts with Corregidora, Brazilian slave-master. Yet it is Ursa who actually frees herself from bondage and Eva who succumbs to it. Eva has imprisoned herself in the debilitating stereotypes of Queen Bee, Medusa, and Eve long before she is locked away for her crime. And Eva remains only dimly aware of her own responsibility in being there. . . .

Eva remains imprisoned literally and figuratively by her silence that simply increases her passivity and her acceptance of the words and definitions of others. Elvira, more like Tadpole and Mutt in *Corregidora* than the rejected lesbian Cat Lawson, tries to get Eva to talk and, by talking, to assume full responsibility for her acts. Eva's silence is more abusive than protective and inhibits her from developing her own "song" or voice about self and ancestry. Silence also blurs more truth than it reveals and Eva, unlike Ursa with her foremothers, is unable to gain the larger historical consciousness necessary to end individual alienation. Moreover, Eva's guilty silence, her inability to use language, makes her unable to hear others. Eva fails to grasp Miss Billie's important advice about the past and being true "to those people who came before you and those people who came after you." Miss Billie, angered and exasperated by her own daughter's lack of interest in marriage (in making generations), tries to elicit some response from Eva: "You got to be true to your ancestors and you got to be true to those that come after you. How can you be true to those that come after you if there ain't none coming after you?" Eva's deafness to this historical responsibility renders her even more deaf and inarticulate about her own redemption. The prison psychiatrist warns: "You're going to have to open up sometime, woman, to somebody." . . . When she finally talks, Eva confuses fantasy and reality, no longer able to distinguish between them. Ironically, language fails Eva; it has atrophied from disuse. And Eva's sexual coupling with Elvira happens in prison. Eva has failed to free herself or to speak anything more significant than the chilling "Now" at the novel's close which announces her solo orgasm.

Melvin Dixon. In Mari Evans, ed. *Black Women Writers (1950–1980):*
A Critical Evaluation (New York: Doubleday, 1984), pp. 245–47

[Gayl Jones] creates . . . radical worlds. Not only are the societies depicted . . . thoroughly and directly oppressive, but she also denies readers a "sane" narrative center through which to judge world and narrator. Most frequently, her narrators have already been judged insane by the society; and this assessment, given the teller's actions and obsessions, seems reasonable. But we cannot therefore assume that we have entered a Poesque world of confessors of personal guilt or madness, for it is equally apparent that society has its own obsessions and that its labeling of the narrators as mad facilitates evasion of the implications of those obsessions.

Given the irrationality of both narrator and world, the reader must rely on the text itself to provide whatever sense is to be made of the story. Jones's stories and novels work because they effectively give voice to those who have suffered. By structuring the experiences, the texts become blues performances, rendering as they do stories of the convolutions and complications of desire. Patterns of repetition, identification of sufferer and solo performer, and use of the audience as confidant—all characteristics of the blues—suggest that the worlds of [her protagonists], no matter how disordered, are worlds of human experience.

> Keith E. Byerman. *Fingering the Jagged Grain: Tradition and Form in Recent Black Fiction* (Athens: University of Georgia Press, 1985), pp. 171–72

It is no simple task to summarize the stories and sketches that Gayl Jones's *White Rat* comprises. They enact moments and mindscapes that resist not only the narrator's moralization of experience, but the reader's quest for "hidden meaning." In part, the difficulty resides in the characteristic absence in her fiction of authorial intrusion and judgment. Jones prefers to write in the first person, giving the impression that "it's just the character who's there." In constructing the interiority—the psychology—of her characters, Jones, in effect, allows them to speak for themselves. Yet, at the very heart of her stories are silences, silences that speak eloquently to the pleasure of her text. In a Pinteresque fashion, Jones's work resonates with both the plentitude and paucity of language in human relationships in the modern world. Her stories both thematize and formalize silence as a stratagem that reveals the discontinuities and breaks in the connections and bonds between individuals. Sometimes these silences are expressed by a recalcitrant refusal to speak, and, at other times, by an eruption of speech that displaces that which is left unsaid.

> Mae G. Henderson. Introduction to Gayl Jones. *White Rat* (Boston, Mass.: Northeastern University Press, 1991), pp. x–xi

JUMINER, BERTÈNE (1927–   )

FRENCH GUIANA

In addition to more than one-hundred scientific publications, [Bertène] Juminer has written three novels [*Les Bâtards, Au seuil d'un nouveau cri*, and *La Revanche de Bozambo*]. He has also written a play, adapted from the latter novel, entitled *Archiduc sort de l'ombre*. . . .

With the exception of Léon-Gontran Damas, Juminer is the best known—and his works the most accessible—of the contemporary French Guyanese authors. . . .

Juminer's first novel *Les Bâtards* [translated as *The Bastards*] is to a great extent autobiographical, being inspired by the author's two-year assignment at a hospital in the town of Saint-Laurent in his native [French Guiana]. During this period, Juminer was particularly struck by the almost total alienation of the educated, black elite from the great majority and their "local" culture—and by the quality, or the lack of it more precisely, of many of the French administrators. Juminer found that these individuals were nothing like the Frenchmen he had known and usually respected in France. Accordingly, his novel centers around the intertwined stories of the two main characters, Robert Chambord and Alain Cambier, as well as a subordinate, but very interesting character, Turenne Berjémi (an anagram of the author's name), all of whom are educated and to a high degree assimilated into French culture. They are, needless to say, aware of, and responsive to, their own culture which is first and foremost black. Their consequent intermediate position between these two cultures is indicated by the title *The Bastards* and their predicament as unusual beings emphasized by such an opprobrious term.

Au seuil d'un nouveau cri is an intriguing, didactic novel, which is skillfully structured into complementary parts, "Le Cri" [translated as "The Cry"] and "L'Echo" [translated as "The Echo"] dealing, respectively, with the black man's past and his present, vis-à-vis oppression. "Le Cri" recounts an epic myth in which slaves revolt against the tyranny of their masters and gain their freedom. "L'Echo" is a contemporary portrait of the problems of the black man, with an exhortation to him to rise, as did his ancestors, to wrest freedom from the clutches of the oppressors.

In terms of mood, structure and style, [*La Revanche de Bozambo*, translated as *Bozambo's Revenge*] is a radical departure from Juminer's two previous novels. Here the mood is satirical. An absurd world is created in which there is a reversal of roles between Europe and Africa (a reversal brought about ironically by Europe's continuing ability to maintain a genuine peaceful coexistence between its two dominant political ideologies: capitalism and communism). The situations brought about by the reversed role create a great deal of comic relief, for it is Juminer's contention that laughter—be it ever so bitter—is beneficial, for it offers the black man a temporary release from the ever present tension created by his oppression and, at the same time, it puts the oppressor into a perspective which blows away the cant and mystification of Western colonial claims.

Paul L. Thompson. Introduction to Bertène Juminer. *Bozambo's Revenge*
(Washington, D. C.: Three Continents Press, 1976), pp. ix–x, xii–xiv

It is in [*Au seuil d'un nouveau cri*] that Juminer deals with the phenomenon of a special mutual attraction, and presents a black man-white woman couple in a society that rejects such a combination violently. The situation is presented through fiction, and it is through the thoughts of Juminer's principal character that he analyzes it, building a theory to explain it. . . .

In the second part of the work, "The Echo," Juminer proposes his world view and his explanation of the special black man-white woman mutual attraction only suggested in "The Cry." The narrator, still addressing the hero as "*tu*," reflects on the problem of the omniscient, omnipotent colonists, who specifically prevent the

hero's being a man. They depend for their power source on a world they themselves have created, a world in which everyone and everything is devoted to them.
However, it seems that in the white man's organization of the world the white
woman has finally rebelled and upset things. For a long time, she was a slave,
"whose only compensation was derived from a well-organized mythology, in
which one saw a knight risk his life for a beauty, a prince marry a shepherdess.
Reality remained no less bitter and unacceptable." The white man had allowed no
meaningful place in his society for the white woman, and now, militant, she
demanded it. The more like the white master she became, the more he feared her.
Unwilling to abandon his former privileges altogether, the white man threw himself
into colonialism as compensation. Meanwhile the colonized man, assumed here to
be black, became increasingly depersonalized as the result of the white man's educational system. In the course of time he realized the need to rebuild society from
the bottom up, and it is in the struggle toward a common humanity that the educated black man encountered the white woman: "One need not look elsewhere than
to this comradeship in misfortune for that affinity, conscious or unrecognized,
existing between the militant white woman and the colored intellectual."

[Elinor] S. Miller. *BALF*. 11, 1 (Spring 1977), pp. 25, 29

The novels of Juminer are important because of his use of the ideology of revolutionary struggle and the influence of Frantz Fanon that can be seen in his works.
Frantz Fanon's influence upon Juminer is best manifest in the latter's second novel,
Au seuil d'un nouveau cri, in which Juminer goes back into the history of the
Caribbean and draws upon the revolutionary struggle of the maroons in "The Cry"
. . . and the contemporary communist cell which is set in Paris in the second part of
the work, "The Echo." The work is also significant because Juminer fuses Fanon's
theory of the cathartic nature of revolutionary violence into the portrayal of his
characters in a technique which this author has called sociopsychological realism.

On the other hand, *Bozambo's Revenge* is written from the perspective of
revolutionary struggle conducted at the level of guerrilla warfare as the central
theme. Juminer calls this work a novel, but it can best be described as an allegory, i.e., a figurative treatment of colonialism by the transformation of symbols (white is black and black becomes white; Europe becomes the colonial
backwater and Africa the metropole), a system of "cultural reversals" as one
critic has called it. *Bozambo's Revenge*, therefore, operates as a symbolic narrative which imparts to us some information about the colonial situation without
giving us a sense of the multidimensional nature of the colonial experience, or
the peculiar psychological conditions which this experience creates and the
implications of the colonial situation on the ever evolving nature of . . . contemporary life. Indeed, in trying to turn "colonialism inside out" as the subtitle suggests, he pares away all of the rich complexity of the colonial experience.

Selwyn R. Cudjoe. *CarQ*. 25, 4 (December 1979), p. 2

Dakar [Senegal] and its surroundings, a few years after independence, is the
scene of [*Les Héritiers de la presqu'île*]. Bob Yves Bacon (whose real name is

Mamadou Lamine N'Diaye), a young Senegalese, has established his profession of "détective privé, diplômé de l'Académie de Paris et du New Jersey" [private detective, graduate of the Academy of Paris and of New Jersey], and is attempting to assert his rather exotic practice. . . .

Cases are rare, but Alassane Ibou N'Diaye solicits his services in order to untangle a conjugal imbroglio that is embarrassing him greatly. We don't learn much about the resolution of this matter, the story having been pushed to the background in order to make room for the development and analysis of the character of Bob Yves Bacon. . . .

If [the plot] surprises by lack of intensity, it is because it is appropriate to go beyond it to find in the novel an investigation of the interior, based on the suggestion of an imaginary and aesthetic universe rather than a totalizing and definitive vision. . . .

This space is a two-faced Africa, where Bob Yves Bacon evolves. His pseudonym is a reminder of the West: of Europe and America simultaneously. The country, the city, the man, and the places become indistinguishable and only symbolize the path of a people and a man in search of themselves. Bob Yves Bacon, in rejecting his given birth name and in choosing a profession that is nonexistent and useless in Senegal, has resolutely chosen the West and refused the traditional reality of his country. . . .

The characters who surround Bob Yves Bacon also represent one or another facet of Senegalese city life. Ibou, the keeper, Nafissatou, who knows the value of money, and Mado, who is trying to express himself as a woman—each one . . . shows a possible way and allows the ambiguity of the detective to emerge. With this little fresco, Juminer gives us sociological observations rather than psychological comments. . . . In fact, each protagonist appears as an element of the symbolic quest of Bob Yves Bacon, a stage of the initiatory course, until the affirmation of his authenticity, when he exclaims at the end "Je suis Sénégalais, je m'appelle Mamadou Lamine N'Diaye!" [I am Senegalese, my name is Mamadou Lamine N'Diaye]. . . .

The novel, a simple stylistic effort, does not innovate much on the level of composition. The two levels of the narration—the immediate and the profound—are blended closely. Nevertheless, one deplores, on several occasions, the rather obvious desire to present clichés of characters, places, and society. . . .

Thus, the heirs take possession of their patrimony, i.e., of their buried self. They are heirs twice over—of ancestral Africa as well as Europe—and they have appropriated, in an equitable manner, the wealth of their double inheritance. . . . In reality, *Les Héritiers de la presqu'île* describes to us a different experience, but isn't the important thing the fact that it speaks to all who are exposed to it?

Isabelle Gratiant. *PA*. 121–22 (1982), pp. 430–31†

During the past twenty-five years the Caribbean-French and the Afro-French worlds have witnessed some extraordinary political, economic, and social changes which have motivated concerned black writers of French expression to look at old themes from a new perspective. Even though the familiar message and the themes remain in *La Revanche de Bozambo*, Juminer deviates some-what in this third novel from his grave and austere tone in the previous novels and produces a diverting work which is a combination of fantasy and morality. Less complex perhaps and shorter than its two predecessors, *La Revanche de Bozambo* allows Juminer greater freedom to call attention to controversial dis-cussions on racial imperialism and the timeless evils of colonialism.

La Revanche de Bozambo is written in the third person, and its plan of action is heightened by the proficiency of an omniscient narrator who sees all, hears all, and anticipates all. In addition to allowing the reader to share the privi-lege of seeing what is contained in the minds of each of the characters, the narra-tor intrudes into the action at intervals and supplies a good measure of wit and wisdom, thus augmenting the entertaining power of those aspects of the tale which he is obliged to relate or explain. On one level we are placed in contact with a world saturated with political and social satire where the relationships between blacks and whites are exploited. In this particular fantasy of the author, Africa becomes the colonizer and Europe the colonized; the whites are the natives and the blacks are the imperialists in this novel of reverse colonialism. . . . There is no sentimentality in this situation, for the blacks are not what one would call "forgiving" masters. In exchanging conditions, morals, style of living, prejudices, and racism with the whites, they are equally merciless in their treat-ment of them. In this farce of reversed functions, the blacks usurp the roles of *adorables créatures* or villains, roles historically enjoyed by the whites. Thus, present-day Europeans are forced to hear the raw truth about themselves and, in the novel, to submit to all the traditional and imaginable humiliations inflicted upon them by a racist society dominated now by Africans. Contemporary black society is satirized in its turn by the author's use of components based on white or European norms. Through the role-playing of the black colonizers, both whites and blacks are mocked to a degree when Africans are made to assume the odious mentality of European imperialists. Consequently, we discover the employment of satire as an offensive and a defensive weapon when, through personal inter-vention, the narrator's subjective attitude is exposed creating a contrast with his objectivity.

Robert P. Smith, Jr. CLAJ. 26, 1 (September 1982), pp. 25–26

[A] forceful treatment of satire and caricature is found in Juminer's novel, *Bozambo's Revenge*. . . . [The] situation presented is a skillful sleight-of-hand, a fantastic farce which draws on all the registers of a successful comedy, but whose often ferocious humor serves a twofold purpose: to remind the reader of colonial rule and to point out the many humiliating experiences the native trav-eler from Africa or from the Caribbean countries was—and still might be—sub-jected to upon arrival and during his stay in Paris.

Juminer presents a hypothetical situation: after having colonized the Light Continent, blacks are now the ruling class. The novel takes place in a big city called Bantouville (once called Paris), which African genius has created from swamps bordering the banks of the Sekuana River, which the natives still call the Seine. The protagonist is Anatole Dupont, a young Provençal, who arrives in Bantouville for the first time. He has come to further his education. . . .

Juminer leaves no stone unturned. He introduces well-known characters and events, transformed to suit his purpose, in order to captivate the reader with his fantasy. Thus we learn that thirty years ago university students had formed a "White-is-beautiful" movement, and that Colonel Bozambo's secretary, while looking for the file of Anatole's uncle (a known agitator), came across the file of a certain D'Egoulles (de Gaulle). Even literature becomes a part of the satirical network: The narrator mentions the "thrilling book" *Uncle Jules' Hovel* by Koumba Couli-Cagou, Vivi Oumarou's account of the white hero Laclôture, and quotes from Lamine Zamba's *Record of a Return to the Land of My Ancestors*— "My whiteness is neither a bombax nor a baobab." . . .

The novel's principal plot, laid out in a scenario familiar to countries ruled by a military government, is the preparation of a coup d'etat; Colonel Bozambo's revenge is directed against his own people, fellow government officials whose conduct—both public and private—had been a great embarrassment to the state. Juminer's biting satire is directed against both blacks and whites. His perspective of Paris is not necessarily "darker" in the sense that it expresses more bitterness, or a greater resentment; he sees the city as a conglomerate of power and its abuses, irrespective of the color of the people who find themselves in command. Though his approach is quite different from that of many other francophone writers, he shares with them the experience of a French colonial education, as well as years of study in France. More important still is that for him . . . Paris has been a magnet.

Ingeborg Kohn. In Jonathan A. Peters, Mildred P. Mortimer, and Russell V. Linnemann, eds. *Literature of Africa and the African Continuum* (Washington, D. C.: Three Continents Press, 1989), pp. 107–9

KINCAID, JAMAICA (1949–   )

ANTIGUA

The magic of [Jamaica Kincaid's] *At the Bottom of the River* comes from its language. It is as rhythmic and riddlesome as poetry. Lovely though the words are, they often read like a coded message or a foreign language. Throughout *At the Bottom of the River* the reader is left wondering how to decipher this writing. The decoder comes in the form of Jamaica Kincaid's novel *Annie John. Annie John* was published in 1985, two years after *At the Bottom of the River*. Its chapters had all appeared as individual stories in the *New Yorker*. *Annie John* tells the same story as *At the Bottom of the River*, that of a girl coming of age in Antigua, but uses straightforward novel talk and presents few comprehension barriers to the reader. *Annie John* is a kind of personification of *At the Bottom of the River*. It fleshes out the fantasy and philosophy of *At the Bottom of the River's* poetry, and between the two books there exists a dialogue of questions and answers. They ultimately read as companion pieces or sister texts. . . .

Since *Annie John* tells the same story as *At the Bottom of the River*, it is instrumental in illuminating the difficult text of the latter. It fills in the spaces. It replaces the fuzziness of *At the Bottom of the River* with facts. For example, Annie is an exceptional student and at fifteen is accelerated to a class with girls who are two or three years older than herself. Once this specialness is clearly defined in *Annie John*, the intense imagination and inventiveness of *At the Bottom of the River* is easier to understand. Then a strange thing happens, however. Annie, at fifteen, has a nervous breakdown. The same breakdown occurs in *At the Bottom of the River* in the story "Blackness," but the language in "Blackness" is so clouded and intentionally sparse that the point is almost completely missed. The story reads as a mere mood piece, with passages like, "In the blackness, then, I have been erased. I can no longer say my own name. I can no longer point to myself and say 'I.'" . . .

Compared to *At the Bottom of the River*, *Annie John* reads like a photo album. Though it is immensely helpful in translating *At the Bottom of the River*, *Annie John* looks at the surface of things and lacks rationale, explanation, motivation. *At the Bottom of the River* acts as the cerebral text for the pictures in *Annie John*. Together the two books allow the reader to develop one cohesive story.

Wendy Dutton. *WLT*. 63, 3 (Summer 1989), pp. 406–7

Some of the finest fiction from the West Indies has been written by Jamaica Kincaid. Her collection of short stories, *At the Bottom of the River*, makes interesting use of dream visions and metaphor as the imaginative projections of family life and social structure in her West Indian society. In these stories Kincaid explores the strong identification and rupture in the daughter-mother relationship between the narrator and her mother. The process is mediated through metaphor and, when it is threatening, through surrealistic dream visions.

Each of these stories demonstrates tensions in the daughter-narrator resulting from a prolonged period of symbiosis between mother and child, especially because the mother views her daughter as a narcissistic extension of herself. In "Wingless," the narrator dreams the story as a mirror of her own situation and then imagines herself as a wingless pupa waiting for growth. The narrator uses a dream vision to mediate her sense of helplessness as a child dependent on her mother's care and attention.

In this dream, the mother is perceived as powerful, even more potent than the male who attempts to intimidate and humiliate her. Thus an incident of potential sexual violence becomes an easy victory for the mother. . . . The strong mother threatens death to those who confront her. But there is also a wonderful parable here of the integrity of the woman who shields herself from assault by refusing to listen to the tree-satyr who is trying to assert his power over her.

The story that best demonstrates the daughter's ambivalent relationship with her mother is "Girl." The voice is the girl's repeating a series of the mother's admonitions. . . . The first of the mother's many rules concerns housekeeping. Unlike the girl's father, who can lounge at the circus eating blood sausage and drinking ginger beer, the woman is restricted to household duties. The many rules are experienced by the narrator as unnecessarily restrictive and hostile. The mother's aggression is clear in the warnings of the price a girl will pay for ignoring her mother's advice. The penalty is ostracism—one must become a slut, a fate for which the mother is ironically preparing the daughter. The mother's obsessive refrain indicates hostility toward her adolescent daughter, activated when the girl is no longer an extension of herself but a young woman who engenders in the older woman feelings of competition and anger at losing control of her child. Her anger may also result from the pressures felt by every woman in the community to fulfill the restrictive roles created for women. Of the ten stories in the collection, "Girl" is the only one that is told as interior monologue rather than dream and thus seems to be the least distorted vision. The ambivalence of the mother-daughter relationship is presented here in its most direct form. The reasons for their mutual distrust are very clearly stated: resentment, envy, anger, and love.

Laura Niesen de Abruna. In Selwyn R. Cudjoe, ed. Caribbean Women Writers
(Wellesley, Mass.: Calaloux, 1990), pp. 93–94

The works of Jamaica Kincaid, with their forthright acceptance of Caribbean identity (and of course the fact that she has legally renamed herself "Jamaica") present an explicit identification. . . . Having already accepted Caribbean identity, she can then pursue the meaning of her woman self as she does in "Girl"; her inner personal self as she does in "Wingless" and "Blackness," which is a clear redefinition of the concept of "racial" blackness; her relationship to the landscape and folklore, as she does in "In the Night" and "Holidays"; and all of these in the title story "At the Bottom of the River." Both *At the Bottom of the*

River and *Annie John* explore the female self in the context of landscape and Caribbean folk culture. Central to both books also is perhaps the best presentation in literature so far of the conflicted mother-daughter relationship.

Heritage and identity are intrinsic to the narrative and have as much significance as the gender issues with which she begins *At the Bottom of the River*. "Girl" begins with a catalogue of rules of conduct for the growing Caribbean girl/woman. These merge into surrealistic images of the Caribbean supernatural world but conclude with the woman-to-woman motif which recurs throughout both texts. In *Annie John*, a similar landscape is created. Here, the maternal grandmother, Ma Jolie, clearly an ancestral presence, is characterized as a mysterious healer who appears on the scene at a time when her granddaughter is experiencing a terrible psychological dislocation which is manifesting itself in physical illness and disorientation. Much of this dislocation is located in Annie's attempts to understand and define herself against her mother. *Annie John* differs from *At the Bottom of the River* in that it is an autobiographical narrative which . . . functions as a decoder of much that is unexplainable in the mysterious world of the first work. But in both, the necessity to identify with, yet separate oneself from, the mother is a central issue. "My Mother" in *River* pursues this maternal identification/separation fully. There is a need for bonding as there is for separate space. The ability of each to separate and thus grow ensures harmony.

Carole Boyce Davies. In Carole Boyce Davies and Elaine Savory Fido, eds.
Out of the Kumbla: Caribbean Women and Literature
(Trenton, N. J.: Africa World Press, 1990), pp. 64–65

[Jacques] Derrida in *Positions* speaks of the necessity of ridding oneself of a metaphysical concept of history, that is linear and systematic. His claim is for a new logic of repetition and *trace*, for a monumental, contradictory, multileveled history in which the *différance* that produces many differences is not effaced. Jamaica Kincaid's *At the Bottom of the River* and *Annie John* represent examples of writing that break through the objective, metaphysical linearity of the tradition. At the same time, her voice manages to speak up for her specificity without—in so doing—reproducing in the negative the modes of classical white patriarchal tradition. Kincaid's voice is that of a woman and an Afro-Caribbean/ American and a postmodern at the same time. This combination is therefore not only disruptive of the institutional order, but also revolutionary in its continuous self-criticism and its rejection of all labels. Perhaps we could say that it is a voice coming *after* the struggles of the women's movement first for recognition and then for separation; the voice of the third "new generation of women" as [Julia] Kristeva defines it: an effort to keep a polyphonic movement in process in the attempt to be always already questioning and dismantling a fixed metaphysical order, together with a determination to enter history. Her narrative, in fact, is a continuous attempt to turn away from any definitive statement and to utter radical statements. . . .

The main theme of her writings is the inquiry into the feminine role and racial difference. Kincaid criticizes the very existence of sexual and racial difference, rather than the modes of their existence: there's no place left for reform; the change that is invoked is not one of guards, but of structure.

Giovanna Covi. In Carole Boyce Davies and Elaine Savory Fido, eds. *Out of the Kumbla: Caribbean Women and Literature* (Trenton, N. J.: Africa World Press, 1990), pp. 345–47

We have known for some time that Jamaica Kincaid writes with a double vision. From one point of view, her early fiction and sketches in *The New Yorker*, her collection of dream visions, *At the Bottom of the River*, and her novel *Annie John* all concern the coming-of-age narrative of a young woman in Antigua. Much of Kincaid's fiction, especially the intensely lyrical prose poetry of *At the Bottom of the River* and the autobiographical novel *Annie John*, focuses on the relationship between mother and daughter and the painful separation that occurs between them. Careful examination of the psychoanalytical implications of these relationships will surely open up the meanings of these texts. A psychoanalytic analysis from a feminist perspective, one examining mother-daughter bonding, would point out that the narrators in Kincaid's fiction resist separation from the mother as a way of denying their intense fear of death. The fear of separation is further complicated in *Annie John* because the narrator leaves the island for Britain with the clear intention of making a break with her environment. Both she and her mother, who is also named Annie, have left their respective mothers and their own homes to seek a more comfortable life elsewhere. The process of Annie's leaving her mother is mirrored in the process of leaving the island. Displacement from an initial intimacy with her mother's realm is reflected in a growing away from the environment until, at the end of the novel, Annie can only dream of leaving her own home for England.

Laura Niesen de Abruna. In Susheila Nasta, ed. *Motherlands* (New Brunswick, N. J.: Rutgers University Press, 1992), pp. 273–74

With *Lucy* Jamaica Kincaid continues a story of West Indian female development. Whereas the earlier *bildungsroman*-style works *At the Bottom of the River* and *Annie John* dealt with the adolescent years of a girl in the Caribbean, the new book presents a single learning year—the nineteenth—in the life of a character called Lucy, in the new setting of the United States. Lucy is an immigrant engaged to work as an au pair for a wealthy white couple and their four young daughters. Her year is complexly lived with its attendant difficult times, but it provides Lucy with learning experiences that enable her to manage the cultural change and her passage. By the end of the year she can appreciate the commitment of sisterhood (with her employer, for instance), has negotiated a social world of friends and lovers, and has embarked on an independent life provided for by a job as a photographer's helper. She has, moreover, survived the separation from her West Indian mother and upbringing, tasting an independence she has craved for many years. However, the persistence of unreconciled ambivalence toward her mother, guilt about her recently deceased father, and fears concerning her uncharted future becloud this newly gained freedom. The end of the work thus suggests a problematic future, though the fact that Lucy identifies herself as a writer—the act of inscribing her name, Lucy Josephine Potter, across the top of a journal notebook signifies this—indicates a self-authenticating, defining, and authorizing gesture of significance.

Evelyn J. Hawthorne. WLT. 66, 1 (Winter 1992), p. 185

Lucy is a novel which interrogates and refuses Euro-American theories of many kinds, from those old "fairy tales" of history, fiction, anthropology, to more contemporary notions of psychology and ecology. Lewis's and Mariah's interpretation of the world around them is constantly contrasted with that of Lucy, and their "axioms" are constantly relativized by her different views. The yellow of the daffodils (those flowers which "looked simple, as if made to erase a complicated and unnecessary idea") is associated throughout with the yellow of Mariah's hair and that of her clonelike children. It is a yellow substance "like cornmeal" which forms the ground on which Lewis chases her in her dream. The yellow of cornmeal conjures slave provisions and slavery and is associated with the colonialist "daffodil complex" Lucy strives to articulate to Mariah. But to Lewis and Mariah the significant aspect of the dream is the pit with the snakes. "Dr. Freud for Visitor," Mariah archly remarks to Lewis, and both the stress on this particular aspect of the dream and the naturalization of a particular European interpretation of dreams exposed as culturally grounded *theories* which Lewis and Mariah regard as fact. Like the earlier "fixtures of fantasy" historically instilled in colonial subjects, these new "fixtures" are interrogated in *Lucy* by the different and often more complex interpretations offered by Lucy herself.

This "alternative" reading of a "classically Freudian" dream, emphasizing racial oppression over sexual psychology, does not of course deny the importance of gender oppression or the complex sexualities complicit in race oppression. But in *Lucy*, Lucy uses her sexuality against these oppressions, just as she uses the body to reclaim self-identity from the capture and abuse of the black female body within the European "book." If Lucy could not openly rebel against the recitation of [William] Wordsworth in Antigua, in New York she increasingly rejects new European theories about her sexuality and her body offered by Mariah. She interrogates contemporary Euro-American feminism against the background of her own experience, wondering why Mariah relies on books to explain her life. . . .

Mariah's simplicity and "innocence," her reliance on books, is contrasted early in the novel with another kind of body/script interaction. Relying on "theories" to explain her life, Mariah has little grasp of the way words enter and mark colonized bodies, and this is part of her "simplicity." Lucy understands the interpellative and body-marking (and body-erasing) power of text, but contrasts and counteracts its potential power with that of the body itself. Mariah's faith in her books is equated with her "yellow" simplicity, and her apparently perfect body is contrasted with that of Sylvie, Lucy's mother's friend who has been in jail. Sylvie has a mark like a rose on her face, a scar from a bite she received in a fight with another woman. This mark "bound her to something much deeper than its reality, something she could not put into words."

Helen Tiffin. *Callaloo*. 16, 4 (Fall 1993), pp. 919–20

KOUROUMA, AHMADOU (1927–   )

COTE D'IVOIRE

Ahmadou Kourouma's *Les Soleils des indépendances* has not yet been evaluated at its true worth, although the review *Études Françaises* of Montreal recognized its quality and awarded it their annual literary prize. It is a novel that is profoundly African in style and subject, inspiration and expression. It could be considered the first real African novel, in which the fact that it is written in French seems almost incidental. It might almost be deemed to manifest those values that Jean-Marie Abanda Ndengue calls *Négrisme*, which he defines as the result of a fruitful marriage between the culture of the Negro-African world (Négritude) and those values introduced by the values of Western colonization—whether military, economic, political, or cultural. In the case of Ahmadou Kourouma, we find a Malinké who has adopted the most popular literary form of the modern Western world—the novel, and mastered the literary language of the former colonists; but he writes a French which seems the spontaneous, indigenous tongue of Africa, such as only Birago Diop had used before for his *Contes d'Amadou Koumba*, and [Léopold Sédar] Senghor for his poems, and composes a novel which owes little to traditional Western European models. His language is neither the labored high-school exercise of African novelists of mediocre talent or inadequate literacy, nor the polished, flexible medium of the best of his compatriots. Like Senghor and Diop he has—probably unconsciously—emancipated himself from the attitude of awed respect for the French vocabulary and syntax bearing the seal of the Académie Française. He has evolved a rich, spontaneous expressiveness that seems the natural idiom of his Musulman, Malinké hero, Fama Doumbouya, expostulating, vociferating, vituperating, or merely meditating in his own vernacular. . . .

Superficially, the theme of *Les Soleils des indépendances* seems to be . . . that of a childless marriage, which is not only a personal tragedy but also a source of social inferiority in an African society. But Fama's barren union is only one aspect of his tragedy; moreover, it is treated with . . . profundity, originality, psychological insight, and elaboration of dramatic and episodic detail. . . . The true subject, of which Fama's sterility is only the individual symbol, is the collapse, with no hope of regeneration, of the only society into which he was fully integrated. This is an extension of the "Things-Fall-Apart" theme, originally illustrating the catastrophic impact of colonization on African rural society, now applied ironically to the disillusionment and eventual tragedy that independence brings to those for whom the colonial era was a time of prosperity and privilege.

Les Soleils des indépendances is a novel symmetrically structured in the shape of a parabola. The first of the three parts presents Fama at the nadir of his social humiliations and personal despair at the impossibility of his twenty-year-old monogamous marriage to Salimata ever bearing fruit. In part two, his fortunes rise to a summit, with the possibility of his reintegration as the honored chief of his native village and the promise of a nubile young bride who seems capable of being "as fertile as a mouse." Part three tells of Fama's decline and death after vicissitudes worse than he had ever anticipated in the miseries of his earlier existence. The tragic equilibrium of the novel is likewise assured by the presentation of Fama as the victim of circumstance and of his own character. Irascible and arrogant, susceptible and superstitious, intractable and uncompromising, born to riches, honor, autocracy, and ostentation, ambitious but politically naïve, he is incapable of accommodating himself to poverty, compounding with sycophancy, or quite simply of understanding the realities of his present existence. For Fama Doumboya, last legitimate descendant of the princes of Horodougou, a region of the fictitious "Ebony Coast," the colonial era had been a time of prosperity, in that it favored the free-trading enterprise in which he was engaged. Independence has brought Fama nothing but an identity card, a membership ticket of the single party in power, poverty, and the humiliation of a life of quasi-beggary. Too old to return to the land, the last prince of Horodougou is unfortunately completely illiterate, so [he] could hope for none of the perquisites of power in the new regime. The man whose totem was the royal panther is reduced to earning his living as a "hyena," a "vulture," that is a professional assistant at Musulman funeral rites, which even with independence are long and complicated. . . .

Les Soleils des indépendances is not a novel that can be neatly tagged and docketed like many earlier French-African works of fiction. It is not simply a political, sociological, psychological, or anthropological study. Fama Doumbouya is manifestly the victim of a changing world to which his inculcated principles, lack of formal education and inflexible temperament prevent him from adapting. But his story is not simply that of a society in transition, the novel of metamorphosis. Similarly, while the author throws light on social custom, details of the female excision, consultation of sorcerers, these passages are not included for their exotic interest and to enrich the local color, but are closely integrated into the psychological study of Salimata's predicament. Like many creative black writers of the last decade, no longer committed to the anticolonial cause, nor to any partisan issues, Ahmadou Kourouma can permit himself ironic comment on contemporary African politics and politicians, without passing final judgement on the situation. He merely suggests, with objective and lucid intelligence, that all is not a utopia in the territories illuminated by the suns of independence. The conclusion to be drawn is consistent with the Muslim African inspiration and texture of the novel: no political change can bring Paradise on earth to mortal existence plagued by: "Colonization, District Commandants, Epidemics, droughts, Independence, the single party and revolution . . . all kinds of curses invented by the devil."

Dorothy S. Blair. African Literature in French
(London: Cambridge University Press, 1976), pp. 300–4

Even a cursory reading of *Les Soleils* [*des indépendances*] would identify the society in the text as distinctly Malinké. Thus the novel may be said to be about the Malinkés. But, like every novel, it mediates that referential society through the obliquities of language and narrative. While the social reality that appears in the novel is most meaningful when related to the Malinké society outside the text, this verbalized society is both the result of representing and a way of seeing the outer social world. Ahmadou Kourouma is himself a Malinké, steeped in the traditions of his people. But he is also a well-educated Ivoirian with a modernist outlook; he is an actuary by profession. Kourouma chooses to express his observations about his people through a created self (often the narrator), or sometimes more subtly through a fictional character like Fama. He maintains a critical distance between his people and himself, by adopting a satirical tone. . . .

Clearly, the novel's main focus is the capitalist Ebony Coast, although the novel is not more ideologically biased against capitalism than it is in favor of socialism. In highlighting the plight of Fama, an impoverished *dioula* living in a slum in the Ebony Coast's capital, Kourouma is not primarily interested in the class of northern *dioulas* living in the capital. It is revealing that Fama is no longer a prosperous *dioula*, but a jobless Malinké. True, he likes to think of himself as set apart by birth and profession from the beggars, the blind, the maimed who can hardly conceal their misery, but the novelist shows him as belonging very much to the pariahs of society. In fact, Fama's condition provides Kourouma with the opportunity to raise one of the central issues in the novel: what has independence really brought to the ordinary man? In a powerful authorial interpolation, Kourouma himself provides an answer. . . . Fama is one of these pariahs who crowd the little slum markets in search of alms. The one thing that they are sure of getting in plentiful supply is "lagoon water . . . rotten and salty as well as the sky, either dazzling with fierce sunshine or loaded with rains which fall on the jobless who have neither shelter nor beds." They have nothing else to do except "roam about, stink, pray and listen to the rumbling of their empty stomachs." Nobody seems to care for them, certainly not the affluent corrupt elite "who could afford to have cloths made out of bank notes." It is the novel's unrelenting focus on the lot of the "wretched" which adds ideological substance to its criticism of the postindependence era. . . .

Les Soleils is a complex novel which calls for "plural" readings, the kind of novel which frequently frustrates the critic's imperialistic attempts to domesticate or "naturalize" it with his reading strategy. However, from whatever angle one reads it, one cannot miss two of the novel's axes: its critical celebration of traditional African culture and its criticism of postindependence African politics. It is one of the most authentically African novels, and possesses a remarkably original perspective. Without being uncritical of tradition, *Les Soleils* views independent Africa mainly through the critical lens of a traditional African nurtured on the culture and worldview of his people. It speaks about Africans, not without affection, but without excessive indulgence. Above all, it speaks to Africans with an African voice.

Kwabena Britwum. In Kolawole Ogungbesan, ed. *New West African Literature* (London: Heinemann, 1979), pp. 80–81, 87–89

[*Les Soleils des indépendances*] reveals many aspects of the engaging artistry of the griot—master storyteller, trustee of the lore, the genealogy, and the wisdom of traditional African societies. It is by virtue of its flawlessly oral quality that here, more than in any other African novel, the reader encounters the shape and sound of oral performance. As [Martha] Cobb found in her study of the literature of the slave diaspora, "the verbal techniques of oral art are embodied in a *concrete* speaker-audience relationship." The textual voice that emanates from Kourouma's work relies upon two devices highly reminiscent of the *call and response* format of oral performance—alternance between first and second person, and a special fondness for the exclamatory and interrogative mood. The surprising effect that these produce in Kourouma's novel is to elicit the readers' *response*. They help to sustain a dynamic and flexible relationship between the narrator and the audience.

Kourouma achieves almost immediately that ambiance of ease, of relaxed familiarity, indeed of intimacy so readily identifiable with the storytelling setting, so indispensable a factor in the relationship between storyteller and audience. From the first sentence, the narrator transforms the isolated reader into an "audience" and then proceeds to enlist his sympathetic cooperation. Although the narrator is occasionally reminded that there are non-Malinké present . . . the general tenor of the narrative, strengthened by asides like "Que voulez-vous?," "Dites-moi," and "Mais attention," reveals a close bond, indeed almost a kinship between the Malinké narrator and the listeners gathered around. The narrator who says *je* plays no role in the events of the story yet is decidedly well informed, as only an insider could be, concerning the particular Malinké milieu depicted. He is equally knowledgeable about the protagonists Fama and Salimata, although the perspective he enjoys is not solely that of an omniscient narrator, nor does he identify exclusively with any single character. Rather, the point of view indicated by textual voice qualities—the inflections, the intonations, the idiom—is at once that of a distinct narrative *je*, Fama, Salimata, *and* the social group to which they belong. . . .

Kourouma brings new dynamism and energy to the traditional role of the narrator. By the same token, he alters the role traditionally reserved for the readers, by making them sense that they are directly and physically present in the narration. In *Les Soleils des indépendances* it is the narrative voice that so beguiles the listener. No technique or device in the oral performer's arsenal is absent. Their skilful manipulation, in conjunction with the poignant and tragic story of one man's fate, ensures Kourouma's novel a place of distinction in recent African fiction.

Rosemary G. Schikora. FR. 55, 6 (May 1980), pp. 812–13, 817

By focusing upon Fama, the disinherited Malinké prince, Kourouma breaks the pattern of writers who portray cultural hybrids in African literature. Indeed, by presenting an illiterate protagonist in a society where literacy is a prerequisite to joining the ruling elite, Kourouma explores the psychological and sociological effects of marginality in a context that differs from the earlier works of

writers like Camara Laye and Cheikh Hamidou Kane. Whereas their protagonists struggle to integrate newly acquired European language and technology
with traditional African social and spiritual values, Kourouma portrays the
plight of the individual who has been left behind. Unskilled in modern technology as well as illiterate in French . . . Fama cannot join the ruling elite in the
new era of the "suns of independence." He represents the disgruntled displaced
masses lured from the village to the city by promises of opportunity only to
encounter an ever-deepening poverty.

Fama lives in a topsy-turvy world. In fact, "le monde renversé" becomes a
metaphor for the protagonist's condition. In Fama's mind, independence is the
root of all evil, responsible for his misfortunes and those of his society as a
whole. With the coming of independence to his country, the hereditary Malinké
prince of Horodougou has been deprived of all his former privileges. The reader
initially encounters Fama in the capital city, far from his village of origin; here
the prince without a kingdom is reduced to accepting handouts as praise-singer
at Malinké funerals. In addition, he is plagued by sterility, believing incorrectly
that his wife, Salimata, is responsible for the couple's lack of an heir.

In *Les Soleils des indépendances*, Kourouma uses elements of oral tradition to alter the relationship between the narrator and the reading public, and to
stretch the limits of conventional French syntax. . . . Kourouma thus assumes
the narrative voice of the griot, and although limited by the written word on the
printed page, he attempts to re-create both the spontaneity of oral performance
and the characteristic interchange between performer and audience.

Mildred [P.] Mortimer. *RAL*. 21, 2 (Summer 1990), pp. 36–37

[*Monnè, outrages et défis*] is the story of Djigui Keita, King of the Soba nation
in the Mandinka region. When Samory invited him to raze his own city to the
ground and to join with Samory in fighting against the French intruders, Djigui
decides to confront the "Nazarenes" (i.e., Christians) because he assumes that
the magic he inherited from his ancestors, the protection of Allah, and a hastily
built wall will be sufficient to repel them. In contrast to his expectations, he was
defeated by the French troops and obliged to swear allegiance to the new rulers
of the territory. Thus begins the long life of *monnè* that destiny imposed upon
him—a life that he lived, helpless and bitter, until the eve of independence.

Deprived of the reality of power, Djigui Keita, king of a conquered people,
witnesses, along with his griot and his court, the "pacification" of the territory and
the establishment of a colonial administration in which civil servants eventually
replace the military. Naturally, the king's collaboration is required to assure the
smooth functioning of the *indigénat*, forced labor, and the recruitment of soldiers
after the outbreak of World War I, but the colonial regime actually plunges the
people of Soba into a state of misery and despair. Torn between the suffering of
his people and the endless demands of the white administrators, Djigui ignores the
true meaning of the projects with which he is being associated. . . .

Kourouma's novel dramatizes the incommunicability that emerges in the
numerous misperceptions and misunderstandings that characterize relationships

between the colonial administration and the "natives." This incommunicability is linked to a cultural incompatibility, to a conflict between divergent ambitions and dreams, but also to the impossibility of mutually comprehensible linguistic communication. Just as Malinké means nothing to the French, French means nothing to the Malinké. Under these circumstances, the interpreter can allow each party to understand whatever seems suitable to him.

Through the act of writing, Kourouma reacts against this impossibility of mutual understanding. This is what justifies his project, begun in [Les] Soleils and continued in Monnè, of Africanizing the French language. In his second novel, Kourouma seems less daring than in the first, but his desire to imprint French with the mark of African culture through the use of words (as in the title) remains dominant. His technique includes syntactic nonconformity; a wit that enlivens the narrative and manifests itself in rustic humor, imagery, and metaphors (often with sexual connotations); proverbs; fantasy; and, above all, the joy of storytelling that is so characteristic of oral cultures and so aptly illustrated in the pompously sententious chapter headings in Monnè.

Guy Ossito Midiohouan. RAL. 22, 2 (Summer 1991), pp. 232, 234

Going beyond the justly acclaimed brilliant demonstration of the use of African voice and point of view in his first published novel, Les Soleils des indépendances, Ahmadou Kourouma achieves, with Monnè, outrages et défis, a masterpiece of literary creation in the French language. Kourouma confirms his position in contemporary international literature, while offering an injection of sorely needed vitality to the French novel.

Monnè is admirable in all its dimensions: for the depth of its underlying ideas and the breadth of its historical vision; for virtuosity in style, sense of humor, and razor sharp sense of reality; for a heart of gold beating in a warm, upright body; for comprehension without complacency; for that heady mixture of humor and wisdom laced with just a soupçon of healthy vulgarity that makes Africa so exasperating. Ahmadou Kourouma speaks out, speaks straight, speaks true as only a man who has earned his voice by the sweat of his mind, body, and soul, and at the risk of his life can speak.

Kourouma's brilliant transformations of French linguistic usage and literary methods are part of an audacious project which should be appreciated in the context of the stubborn persistence of academic constraints on literature published in France, where the taboo against "writing what is spoken" is maintained against all good sense, and the written form must be elaborated within a closed system of canons d'écriture which discourage convincing experiments in raising voice to literary heights.

At the same time, Kourouma transgresses the taboo against the liberal use of foreign words, integrating an extensive Malinké vocabulary into the body of his text. These Malinké words, accents, and rhythms are not props to convince readers—African or other—that they are in the presence of an African novel; on the contrary, they are essential to the structure of the work, to its philosophical, sociological, and historical ambitions. In the same way, the African music of Kourouma's syntax is determined by the necessity to communicate a particular mental structure which is not French. As a result, Kourouma succeeds in creating a literary version of recent African history as seen and experienced from a Malinké point of view.

Nidra Poller. *RAL*. 22, 2 (Summer 1991), pp. 235–36

In [*Monné, outrages et défis*], Kourouma attempts to re-create the ample universe of an epic past. Like *Sarraounia* (by Abdoulayi Mamani), *Tchaka le Zoulou* (by Thomas Mofolo), *Soundjata ou l'épopée mandingue* (by Djibril Tamsir Niane), his epic echoes the foreign presence in Africa, the indigenous resistance and the shattering conquest of the continent. The story, narrated in the style of a griot, evolves around Djigui Keita, the affable king of Soba and the ally of Samory, *mandingue* emperor. Djigui decides to turn a deaf ear to the retreat order given by the emperor, whose army has massacred a French battalion, and to face alone the troops marching under the command of Faidherbe. As defense strategies against the advance of the "Nazarenes," this king turns to his ancestors and to Allah, while fortifying the town of Soba with a wall, the *tata*. But the French army, without striking a blow, capture it. Thus follows the submission of the *mandingue* empire, the implantation of the colonial regime and the clash of cultures. The king, Djigui, wishing to ensure the perpetuity of his dynasty, begins to corroborate with the occupant, resulting in the eruption of murderous violence in the *mandingue* kingdom, orchestrated by social and political powers. Throughout the narration, the peasants appear in hostile and sordid spaces: the south, lice-infested swamps, abandoned and deserted villages. One also finds them in social institutions like mosques, forced labor yards, and battlefields. The population, subjected to taxation and exploitation, travels henceforth through an *unnamable* time punctuated by "monnew" and anxiety.

This critical period of African history allows Kourouma to demonstrate the ancient values incarnated by marabouts, prophets, griots, and fetishists, all of whom are partisans of traditional power. But the presence of foreigners in the *mandingue* space establishes a new (spoken) word and a new power, because in traditional Africa, saying word means saying power. Thus the structures of a new society impose themselves through protagonists like the governor, the general, the captain, the commander, the marksmen. To this list is added the interpreter who has henceforth become a buffer, an agent of peace instead of an "established crook." The Cote d'Ivoire writer rehabilitates the interpreter throughout his novel. As for the Nazarenes, they start the disorganization and the destruction of all the operating forces in the ancient space.

The work gives an important place to the religious dimension. The spiritual experience of Fama, the fallen prince of *Les Soleils des indépendances*, is matched by that of Djigui, the dispossessed king. Incessant Islamic prayer, the immolation of victims to the spirits of ancestors are, for the latter, rites for the protection against the invading Nazarenes. All this is evidence of religious syncretism and of the permanent alliance between Islam and animism on which Christianity is grafted. In this perspective, the work can be viewed as a quest for God.

And there is no lack of mystical resonances. Djigui, for having disowned and rejected the alliance of Samory and then having collaborated with the foreigner, is forced to assume the tragic consequence of his choices. He resorts to lies and deception with his Nazarene collaborators; the construction work of the railway lines initiated by his new allies remains incomplete. Later, Béma, his own son born of a wife unworthy of the king allies himself with the Nazarenes, falsifies his father's signature and dethrones him. The fallen king is outraged by this treason. . . . He falls and dies on the way to Toukoro. . . . The dead are metamorphosed into phantoms who haunt the activities of the collaborators. The entirety of events marks the fantastic in the novel and is inscribed in the disintegration of traditions and the ruin of the ancient world. The downfall of the king, Djigui, seems to correspond to that of his people who are abandoned to slavery, forced labor, and colonization.

Kourouma has not done away with the crude language that characterized *Les Soleils des indépendances*. The traditional African aesthetic—proverbs, local talk, chants, poetry and music, words and dialogue—dominate the attentive gaze that he poses on the *Crépuscule des temps anciens*, on *mandingue* history, and on African history. *Monné, outrages et défis* remains a magnificent celebration of life, of the 125-year period that would have been the reign of Djigui. The novelist knew how to marry the real and the imaginary and to bring to light the experience of the African people in their encounter with the outside, in their national and international politics, in their conflicts, in their corruption, in their suffering, in their oppression, in their religiosity, and in their disorder. The historian, the sociologue, the ethnologue, the linguist, and the fan of African studies will each find a great source in *Monné, outrages et défis*.

Eronini E. C. Egbujor. *Canadian Journal of African Studies*. 26, 3 (1992), pp. 544–45†

KUNENE, MAZISI (1930–   )

SOUTH AFRICA

Many of [Mazisi] Kunene's shorter poems seem like chips from the creation epic. They take up some of the same concerns and use the same cosmic imagery. "From the Ravages of Life We Create," for instance, focuses on the emergence of creation from destruction, the renewing process of life, the interrelationship of grief with joy. Each of the images says almost the same thing, but each defines the concept in some particular way. Suns are "torn from the cord of the skies," to mingle in shame with fallen leaves, but the cord itself remains and the combination of winter suns and leaves offers a hint of the process of natural decay that feeds the next generation of life. The "wedding party" image of fecundity is mingled with "the moon disintegrating," a suggestion of renewal only through decay, whether the decay is in inanimate nature or a woman's monthly cycle. The power of man as it is found in the searching intellectuality that can never rest is again asserted, and the poem ends in a

splendidly original image combining the notion of man's power and his limitations, the good and the evil that he is capable of: even a plague of locusts "with
broken wings" can shelter the earth from the intense heat of the sun. . . .

Kunene draws on Zulu oral traditions not only in these poems on epic
subjects but also in his elegies, which, as he points out in the Introduction to
Zulu Poems, use the traditional device of understatement. Understatement of
the grief felt by the poet is achieved by adopting an almost lighthearted sense of
grievance against the dead person. The magnitude of death may be scaled down
to seem equivalent to the embarrassing absence of the guest of honor from a
feast, for which the poet reproves the dead one. "Elegy for My Friend E. Galo"
chides the friend for dying "without my knowing" while the poet was out collecting firewood, buying expensive cattle, and preparing stories for the celebration. At the end, however, there is a bitterer tone, as the poet turns from the
imagery of the feast to that of predatory locusts and "the discordant symphony
of naked stars": what had been made to seem casual absence from a celebratory
occasion is now recognized as part of the universal mortality of man and nature.
"An Elegy to the Unknown Man Nicknamed Donda" is addressed not to the
dead man but to the poet himself, as he muses on what he should do in his grief.
He decides to take the elephant's advice to follow Donda into death, "the place
of the setting sun." Death is again understated: here it seems to be just an
everyday journey where one might meet an uncomprehending traveler. The
ending this time recognizes not the universality of death, but its personal quality: one man's grief is another man's idle curiosity. In both these poems, the
feeling is personal. In "Elegy for Msizi," however, the voice is largely a communal one, representing the grief of the Bhele clan. Msizi's fame and achievement are matched by the magnitude of grief felt for him, and the poet ends with
a prophecy of the clan's future greatness. . . .

To compose a national epic demands both historical skills and literary
courage of high order. Kunene's *Emperor Shaka the Great: A Zulu Epic* was a
long time in gestation, not only in the sense that some of the materials used are
over two centuries old but also in so far as Kunene's own composition spanned
many years. In [a] 1966 interview with Alex La Guma . . . he said that he was
writing this work, in Zulu, partly because he considered Shaka "a great political
and military genius" and partly because he hoped, through a national epic, to
"express the general experience of mankind," emphasizing "the oneness and the
unity of man." This second reason is, in fact, a belief that he attributes to Shaka
himself many times in the epic, for he presents Shaka as wishing neighboring
peoples to live in peace (though under a strong unified leadership) and as
respecting the customs (though not the acquisitiveness and ill manners) of
white traders. A third reason lying behind Kunene's demanding and ambitious
work is the respect he has for Shaka's court poet, Magolwane, "one of the
greatest of African poets, indeed I would say one of the greatest world poets."
To Magolwane he ascribes a revolution in Zulu poetry, including the introduction of political and social analysis, penetration of character, philosophical
ideas, and abundant imagery (notably of ferocious animals). A great deal of

Magolwane's "epic" or "poem of excellence" about Shaka (other writers call it a "praise-poem" or "praise-song") is in fact incorporated in Kunene's work. . . .

Kunene's shorter poems of the 1970s, many of them collected in his *The Ancestors & the Sacred Mountain*, concentrate on three main subjects. One large group is concerned with the liberation by bloodshed of South Africa, another looks forward millennially to the time after liberation (and sometimes looks beyond South Africa to the world and, indeed, the universe), and a third concerns the ecstatic nature of poetry. In these poems and the smaller groupings (such as the poems about individuals, the laments, the poems on motherhood, and the personal poems) the sense of the ancestors, observing and encouraging, is always present. In addition, some poems are directly about the ancestors or forefathers. They represent for Kunene the whole company of those "who have made their contribution to human welfare and progress," as he says in the introduction to *The Ancestors*. It is to them and not to inventors of material improvements that the Zulus look for standards, guidance, and inspiration in continuing social life, and they treat them as a collective repository of wisdom rather than as a group of individual heroes. . . .

For Kunene, then, the social and cultural history of the Zulus as incorporated in the cult of the ancestors, can provide guidance, inspiration, and vision on every moral and political matter. Personal grief, insecurity, and even rage are swallowed up in a communal experience capable of producing the most intense ecstasy. The poet is possessed by a sexual and religious frenzy that authenticates and gives certitude to his message. Yet unlike the possession of, say, the Romantic poets, this is possession of a spokesman who has a social duty to announce truth to the clan. In this respect, it is like the traditional possession of the singer of an epic who ascribes the glory of the tale of the tribe to divine inspiration.

> K. L. Goodwin. *Understanding African Poetry*
> (London: Heinemann, 1982), pp. 175–78, 196–97, 200

The poems for Kunene's first volume in English, *Zulu Poems*, were taken from a larger selection he had originally written in Zulu, and were translated by the poet himself. His subsequent work in epic poetry was also first written in Zulu, though there is little chance of its being published in South Africa today. Kunene's allegiance as a poet, however, is to an African world-view rather than a particular African language. His purpose in translating, and therefore promulgating these poems among a larger audience, is to encourage a return to oral tradition in literature. . . .

Kunene's second epic, *Emperor Shaka the Great*, was published in 1979, again written first in Zulu and then translated by the poet himself. Running to more than 17,000 lines, it is a monumental work. It is the story of the great warrior king who united several Nguni tribes to form the Zulu nation. Again this is not an academic or chauvinistic attempt at historical or heroic preservation, but an imaginative interpretation of African philosophy. Kunene tries to replace what black South Africa lost under conquest: the feeling for the continuity of history, not as an object lesson for modern times, not as stimulus for nostalgia and pride, but as part of one's own life. He demonstrates how we live in the past and present, and thus shape our future. Through the knowledge of Shaka's vision, Kunene tells us in the introduction, many may understand the dreams and realities that have shaped the destinies of the peoples of Africa. In this respect it may possibly stand beside some of the world's great epics. This is something time will decide and it is impossible to make decisive comments so soon after publication of a work of this kind. Many rereadings will be required, together with a thorough study of the historical, linguistic, and philosophic background. Also a reading in the original language is probably essential, even though Kunene's translation into English, is, as always, impeccable.

Ursula A. Barnett. *A Vision of Order* (London: Sinclair Browne, 1983), pp. 104, 108

[*Zulu Poems*] was in no sense an urban poetry like that which was to be written in the townships from the middle of the 1960s: it did not reflect the African's confrontation with the white city and its restrictions; it contained no descriptions of the black ghettos or of humiliating contact with the whites. Several of the poems have a pastoral setting; they are concerned with nature, love, and friendship, with the cycle of seasons and the generations. Yet Kunene is not at all indifferent to what is going on in the world, especially in his own country, or to the clash of cultures. How could he be when for so long he traveled the world to bear witness against apartheid and concerned himself with the problems of the Third World?

But, by temperament and because . . . he has other platforms from which to express his political views, his poetry has no trace of the language of protest. He avoids the purely anecdotal and the abstract and seeks within his own culture the images, symbols, and metaphors which through their concreteness attain the universal. A quite definite elevation of thought runs through his poems and gives them their life, a combination of dignity and lyricism—a lyricism which is at times contained but which at others expresses itself with force and passion. Indeed, his criticism can be sharp. . . .

Committed Kunene certainly is, but in the best sense of the word. Beyond the "situation" itself, it is in the values of his own culture, through recourse in the first instance to his own language, that his commitment and resistance are expressed. Evidence of this is to be found in the lengthy introduction to *Zulu Poems*, which is a fascinating guide to his own civilization and an invitation to attempt a deeper understanding of his poetry. In spite of the geographical separation, the poet has remained in complete communion with his people. It is with the firm conviction that those who follow him will take up the torch that he writes "To the Killer.". . .

Through his attachment to his mother tongue and to his African values, Kunene foreshadows the tendencies that will emerge fully into the open with black consciousness. He is not concerned with a love for the past or a return to a parochial view of culture harmful to the political battle of the present but with the urge to regain his dignity and force the white man to acknowledge the African, the "other," he has so long ignored and humiliated.

Jacques Alvarez-Pereyre. *The Poetry of Commitment in South Africa*
(London: Heinemann, 1984), pp. 126–28

To Kunene, man is a multifaceted being with an expandable psychological universe which reaches out to various directions: the Earth, the Sun, the Moon, the Pleiades, the gods, and the Supreme Creator. The Earth is his focal point of operation, having within its folds the interrelated worlds of man (with its tangled historical experiences), water, plants, animals, and inanimate objects. Man relates harmoniously to these various elements because of the symmetry holding the components of the cosmos together. In other words, he forms part of the rhythm generated by the interaction of the forces of society and the cosmic system, which move cyclically in an ever-expanding process of life-death-rebirth. He is free when he operates in harmony with the forces and in chains when he is alienated from them. There is thus an interrelationship between human freedom and the cosmological canvas of man's existence.

This world-view permeates the creative consciousness of the African artist who generally stresses realism since man is basically earthbound, inextricably tied up to the destiny of society. Subjective effusions of emotions give way to more or less intellectualized expressions of group values. Literature therefore deals with "concrete events, concrete situations, and is firmly rooted in traceable social events. As in Chinese literature, the abstract is incidental."

This vision of African cosmology informs the metaphorical universe of *Zulu Poems*, which can be studied in three parts: the nature of the power structure of the apartheid regime, the African resistance to it, and Kunene's call for a universal brotherhood of man. . . .

Kunene . . . draws heavily from the African oral tradition in defending African civilization against the ravages of colonialism. And in doing so, he deploys the resources of Zulu cosmology in fighting against apartheid which he portrays as a horrendous system run by individuals who have dehumanized themselves by cutting themselves off from the fold of mankind through their subjugation of a segment of the South African population which, by cosmological design, forms an integral part of the South African society.

Kunene writes with a buoyant spirit and shows that life has glamor despite the determination of the Afrikaner settler regime to make it perpetually unbearable for the African. A nonconformist who is spiritually uncowed, he holds in contempt the self-proclaimed mission of the white racists to ensure the psychological enslavement of the African. He knows quite well that racism "is a dangerous superstition which has been used to define economic privilege and maintain exploitation." Accordingly, through his embodiment of the spirit of resistance of his people, he suggests in *Zulu Poems* that the apartheid regime will eventually succumb to the pressures of opposition mounted against it.

Chidi Maduka. *The Griot*. 4, 1–2 (1985), pp. 60–61, 70–71

[The] trend of Kunene's embellishment of Shaka [in *Emperor Shaka the Great*] is towards the exculpation of the public figure, and towards the "understanding" of the individual. The poet writes from the perspective of the ruling family, stressing Zulu—and by extension, African—values and continuities, and, as ruling families are apt to do, emphasizes nationalism. The pedagogical implication of the poem, looked at in Kunene's terms, is that it may broaden and deepen the understanding of the "children" it is addressed to. It does not aim at philosophically simplistic comprehensibility such as [the Nigerian critic] Chinweizu advocates, nor proletarian immediacy such as we find in Ngugi [wa Thiong'o]'s recent work. Yet events in South Africa as I write do *render* the themes of *Emperor Shaka the Great* relevant to the immediate experience of its readers, especially the actual children who are stoning the police and being shot in the townships. The poem is in Zulu (originally) and deals with a Zulu hero, but Shaka can no longer be seen as only Zulu since to a large extent he is now an African figure who transcends ethnic boundaries, and Zulu is a language many non-Zulus speak. The poem has an obvious relation to the modern quest for black unity in South Africa, for organization and martial courage at a time when the conflict is becoming more violent, when anti-apartheid parties are still not united, and when a significant number of blacks man the armed forces and the police. . . .

We learn from this poem to see Shaka from a particular point of view, one possibly very close to his own view of himself; but we do not passively "swallow" this, as Kunene the propagandist would perhaps wish. Kunene the *poet* goes deeper and is more compelling. He does affect his readers, but how this relates to their everyday political and personal lives remains very obscure. The ancient question (which we find also in Shakespeare, whose ideology is not so far from Kunene's) about the difference between poetic and other kinds of communication comes back to us again. . . . [Although] African poets, and other literary artists and critics, have emphasized the pedagogical role of the writer, they have not yet sorted out what this role consists in, what kinds of communication are possible, what literary discourses are like and how they mesh with educational systems, political movements, and so on. There is always a difference between what you may wish to teach me and what I may wish to learn from your trying to do that.

John Haynes. *Ariel.* 18, 1 (January 1987), pp. 48–50

LABOU TANSI, SONY (1947–   )

CONGO

[Sony Labou Tansi's] *Je Soussigné Cardiaque* presents the drama of a school-teacher, Mallot, who refuses to submit to the master of the place where he has just been appointed. . . .

Refusing to submit to the whims of this ridiculous despot, just as he had earlier refused to submit to other insupportable powers, Mallot is obliged to leave the village with his pregnant wife and daughter.

Fighting against destiny—his destiny—even though he does not wish to be a hero, Mallot revolts. He asks for a certificate of incapacity, obtains it, and, thus hoping to escape the trap of the net, goes to the ministry in order to meet the Director General of Education. There, too, he meets with defeat.

Thus, from refusal to revolt, he, who three times and in different ways declared his independence and his desire to be free, finds himself in prison. This is how he appears in the first scene, which introduces the narration of his revolt seen in the form of a dream. It is in his cell that we find him in the last scene. "Mon papa a raté sa Nelly" [My father failed his Nelly], he says to his daughter before the soldiers in charge of his execution come to fetch him.

Bernard Magnier. *PA*. 120 (1981), p. 98†

Sony Labou Tansi's novel [*La Vie et demie*] opens with a scene of such intensity as is rarely achieved in literature: The tyrant of an African kingdom has just seized his most active opponent.

From the first pages of the novel, we enter into the style and language particular to this young author: a violent, stormy style scattered by lightning flashes of serene poetry, and a language dramatically altered by his triumphant Africanness.

We penetrate into the universe of this novel, midway . . . between the cruelest of political realities and its universal and mythic transposition. Martial, the symbol of immortal liberty, is sadistically massacred by the tyrant who cannot overcome his indestructible refusal. Along with the rest of her family, Chaïdana, Martial's daughter, has to feed on the corpse of the assassinated father.

The cruelty of the tyrant rebounds on him. Chaïdana, endowed with "a corpse and a half," is henceforth her father. She takes up the battle using other, less political means of which Martial, the hero, disapproves. He reproaches her throughout the novel by means of symbolic and memorable slaps. As for the tyrant, who is marked by the seal of "the black of Martial," the indelible color that reveals his crime, he slowly loses his reason, subjected to the terrifying appearances of the hacked-up corpse of his enemy. Martial, after his death, has definitively opted for a charismatic and quasi-messianic personality, appropriate for galvanizing the oppressed masses. His prophetic phrase: "I don't want to die this death," becomes the symbol of active revolt, whereas the "black of Martial" becomes the forbidden color.

Using her incomparable, "formal" beauty, Chaïdana assassinates all the members of the government and becomes the tyrant's own wife, wife of her father's assassin. Slowly, her vengeance grows, and the hatred of this overfull, almost double body invades the heroine, and she feels raped by the incestuous phantom.

Following a monstrous pregnancy, Chaïdana gives birth to triplets, two boys and a girl, also called Chaïdana.

Sony Labou Tansi's novel abandons the tone of sarcastic criticism that is found in the first part and henceforth moves to a rhythm of an African "shamanist" mystique. . . .

The entire last part of the novel is almost impossible to summarize. It is a bloody, disorderly chronicle, marked by the seal of the tragic insanity of the leaders of total derisive power. "Martial's People," the opponents, tortured, mutilated, and decimated, continue to resist. . . .

The author succeeds, with a single sentence, in situating his narration in the antediluvian past. "Thus was born the Nile." However, he does not succeed (does he wish to?) in making us forget that the fable and the tale offer, in colonized countries with oral traditions, symbolic and sarcastic reflections of social reality.

Nevertheless, he takes care in warning us that the tale is not a tract: "The day that I will be given the opportunity to speak of a somebody today, I will not take a thousand paths, especially a path as torturous as the Fable."

In any case, as an African, he chooses African images that deal with the universal contradiction between opposition and revolt, tyranny and battle, in his culture.

Inventor of language, of myths, and a caustic contemporary griot, Sony Labou Tansi undertakes, in this novel overflowing with a healthy and corrosive humor, an astonishing dialogue with the human.

Ina Césaire. *PA.* 129 (1984), pp. 163–65†

Labou Tansi lacks the stature of his Nigerian counterpart [Wole Soyinka] but has nevertheless produced an impressive body of plays and novels. With subtlety and grace of style, his latest novel, *L'Anté-peuple*, eases us into a world of deceptive assurances. Dadou, a director of a girls' training school, finds himself the object of a student's infatuation. Gradually and inexorably, with that same sense of obsession which characterizes the more heavily allegorical novels *The Voice* [by Gabriel Okara] and *La Plaie* [by Malick Fall], Dadou falls into patterns of self-destructive behavior and, equally passively, falls victim to a sequence of disasters which spring as much from the failings of men as from the workings of a malevolent society. The hint of a fallen universe that lies behind this social decadence is repeatedly echoed: realism yields to satire, defined by the image of a world far worse than that of our experience.

At times, and not always with complete success, we leave the flow of mimetic narration for a heightened, poeticized series of reflections whose effect is to break the sense of a chain of experienced events and to install in its place a symbol for experience. There is, as a consequence, the haunting feeling of unreality, an unreality disturbingly echoed in many strains of Congolese or Zairoese literature—notably in the works of [V. Y.] Mudimbe, but also in Henry Lopes and Tchicaya U Tam'si. What this recent body of works has constructed is the image of an upended society, often electric and dangerous, as in the most modern mechanism of power and its dynamics in contemporary Zaire, of life flickering in the muscled rhythms of the crowded streets, bars, and nightclubs—but especially in the wrenching malaise of despair. The course of events which complete Dadou's decline are eventually cast into the mold of a prehistory in which the *anté-peuple* are left awaiting some divine intervention to put an end to a desperate state of affairs apparently beyond the powers of human beings to repair.

Kenneth [W.] Harrow. *WLT.* 58, 2 (Spring 1984), p. 316

Sony Labou Tansi burst on the literary scene in 1979 with the astonishing novel *La Vie et demie* and continues, with each succeeding work, to confirm his prodigious talent. Set in an indeterminate African country sometime after independence from its colonial occupiers, his fourth novel [*Les Sept Solitudes de Lorsa Lopez*] pursues (albeit somewhat more diffusely) the theme of profound disenchantment with the new indigenous regimes which have replaced the former European ones. Rather than depict a bloodthirsty and grotesque tyrant opposed to the forces of decency, as he did in *La Vie et demie* or in *L'État honteux*, the novelist here establishes a moral dichotomy in the opposition between the high-principled coast and the brutal and venal interior of his nameless and troubled land.

Even here, however, the people of the coastal city and former capital Valancia have undergone a kind of degradation since the transfer of the capital inland to Nsanga-Norda. A series of murders, beginning with the unspeakable, atrocious crime committed by the eponymous Lorsa Lopez, are met with silence born of fear by a population that once prided itself on its integrity and love of truth. In the end, it is above all the women of Valancia, led by the remarkable Estina Bronzario (the name describes the woman), who possess the strength to stand up to the despotic authorities of Nsanga-Norda. Though the latter ultimately have Bronzario assassinated because, as she explains, "of the privileged relations we have with the truth," the ruthless forces of guns and money receive their just deserts as the sea completely inundates Nsanga-Norda. . . .

[No] summary of events can possibly capture the extravagant nature of the author's fertile imagination or his inspired verbal inventiveness. Infused with vigorous and colorful dialogue, neologisms and enumerations, startling images, humor, and trenchant satire (a parrot is tried for murder), the whole takes on mythological dimensions in a larger-than-life Estina Bronzario or in cliffs that cry out their anguish before man's inhumanity to man. Like those cliffs, Sony Labou Tansi shouts ("mon écriture sera plutôt crié") his distress but also his abiding hope (he sees despair as an "absurdity") in this parable of cowardice and courage.

Fredric Michelman. *WLT*, 61, 1, (Winter 1987), p. 142

In undertaking the reading of Sony Labou Tansi's novel *L'Anté-peuple*, we propose two essential objectives: firstly, to respect the work keeping in view our position of an observer unfamiliar to African, albeit francophone, literature, and [secondly] to establish a significant rapport between the work studied and us.

It is in this manner that we will attempt to express all that we derive from this novel and to learn of the degradation of a social system which plunges an individual into the absurdity of an existence ruled by impulses that emerge onto a chaos that is uncontrollable. Nevertheless, the same individual fights against disorder in order to establish the triumph of the supreme values emanating from him and which is the quest of the truth governing the entire work. . . .

All social life is regulated by a series of laws and tacit and non-tacit rules. Its occurrence is harmonious if the rights and social duties are a means to better maintain peace and security. . . .

It is easy to establish the transgression of these elementary laws. The rationale is supplanted by emotion, truth by lies; in short, the protection of the individual loses its consistency without the ability to master the law fundamental to existence.

Let us follow the path of the characters who are victims of this diversion of the law. By order of entry into the narration, it is Dadou, Yealdara, Maître Malvoisi, and the prison director. . . . Whether it is the director of a school, a sociologist, or a lawyer, each of these characters finds himself confronting a system rendered absurd and ridiculous due to its inconsequence. Dadou, for example, fights against emotion by forbidding himself from succumbing to the advances of Yavelde. Yealdara, revolted by the injustice that has befallen Dadou, renounces the privileges offered to her by her family and leaves them. Maître Malvoisi has no apparent reason to defend his client except the concern to see justice done. . . . As for the prison director, because he is suspected of sympathy for Dadou, he is accused of a completely imaginary conspiracy and when given the alternatives of imprisonment or escape, he can only choose the latter. . . .

Facing these characters who act in good faith are those individuals who, thanks to their power, adapt the laws to suit their fancy, thereby bringing about the downfall of certain others.

Characters whose behavior is dictated by impulsive and tyrannical personal interest are, among others, Yavelde, Nioka Musanar, and the berets. Yavelde, for example, cannot understand how her director can refuse her advances. Incapable of understanding his point of view, she seeks to avenge herself by abusing her social privileges, which are considerable if one recalls that her uncle is the commissioner of the zone. In Machiavellian fashion, she commits suicide after having accused Dadou of forcing her to have an abortion. . . . As for Nioka Musanar, he plays a direct role in the future of the defendants, who are equally condemned to their destruction. . . .

Dadou, Yealdara, the director, and the others whose lives are deeply compromised, are not beings limited by their actions. On the contrary, they serve as the arm of the lever of a movement which will reestablish justice and truth in general. This victory over the irrational is purely imaginary since it is the result of a dream, but it is a dream filled with hope. . . .

Sony Labou Tansi is above all a novelist; it is with a stormy imagination in the service of self-respect that he takes us into his domain, which is that of language. The language is that of an embittered man who denounces in all forms hypocrisy, mediocrity, and impulsiveness. However, we could not understand the message of the novelist if he did not make reference to a reality that flows from experience. Henceforth his work is the privileged moment where experience passes through the aesthetic of language. In the same way, the narration returns to life through us, the readers, who capture it as narrated time. It is from this point that we pass from fiction to reality. This leads us to believe that Sony Labou Tansi, by the madness of his words and situations, leads us to put an end to a degraded and corrupted reality in order to reinvent a new world.

Nadine Fettweis. Zaire Afrique. May 1989. pp. 247, 249–51, 260†

The form and language of *La Vie et demie* are . . . indicative of contemporary trends in African fiction that [takes] neocolonialism as its focus. With regard to narrative form, we note that Sony Labou Tansi refers to his narrative in the *avertissement* as a fable, a form both didactic and "ideal." That is to say, the narrative manifests no conventional sense of what is realistic. Following the example of [Gabriel] García Márquez and of many tales of the oral tradition, *La Vie et demie* "dwells in possibility," a fertile ground for that very imagination so beset by Katamalanasia. Thus Sony Labou Tansi proposes tyrants who, in their crassness, are of the same ilk as Ubu Roi and who, in their enormity, are of the same size as Gargantua. The narrative abandons the canons of realism that governed fiction in the 1950s and 1960s. . . .

As for the language of *La Vie et demie*, its subversive character resides, first of all, in its abundant irony. . . . [It] is obvious that the regime's language, in view of itself and of Katamalanasia, self-destructs for the reader (as for the citizens) when it is held up to "ce qui existe." The novel plays on the incongruency between Katamalanasian reality and terms and phrases such as "le *Guide Providentiel*" or "on interdit la douleur sur toute l'étendue du pays." The narrator's pervasive neologism, *excellentiel*, is equally trenchant.

Yet there is a still more sophisticated arsenal of verbal and narrative procedures that convey the bankruptcy of Katamalanasia. *La Vie et demie* juxtaposes logic and illogic, measure and the immeasurable, seriousness and folly. This alternation is manifested verbally in the text's absolute precision, on the one hand, and its repetition *ad nauseum*, on the other. The text obeys both these apparently opposing impulses, and yet, for the purpose of Sony Labou Tansi's fable, they are complementary, for the first suggests a matter-of-fact, ordinary reality, while the second gives the narrative its dimension of the fantastic. Indeed, the presence of both impulses suggests the tension between narrative as (empirical) chronicle and as (ideal) fable and thereby recalls the problematic of contemporary African fiction to which Ngugi [wa Thiong'o] refers. The tension between verbal empiricism and extravagance is sublimely comic and absurd. . . .

La Vie et demie is thus a discourse about the betrayal of discourse. But the untrustworthiness of language does not become a source of profound disillusionment and doubt as it does in the theater of the absurd and poststructuralism. Because language disorder is contextualized in Sony Labou Tansi's novel, verbal *délire* suggests neither that language is ontologically empty nor that life is metaphysically problematic. Indeed, many texts by African and diaspora writers caution against blind faith in discourse that serves power: the racist, colonial discourse ([Ferdinand] Oyono, [Aimé] Césaire), a capitalist or religious discourse (Sémbène [Ousmane]), the male discourse ([Buchi] Emecheta). Yet for all these writers, there is faith in language and discourse: texts, like *La Vie et demie*, that demonstrate the unbelievability and violence of colonial and neo-colonial discourses, are texts which also believe in their own words, the power of their words to portray truth, to be heard or read, to make a difference.

Eileen Julien. RAL. 20, 3 (Fall 1989), pp. 379, 382

Labou Tansi's creative voice is one of the most vital of this decade in African letters. A playwright and theater director in Brazzaville, his literary production also includes four novels, all written since 1979: *La Vie et demie, L'État honteux, L'Anté-peuple*, and *Les Sept Solitudes de Lorsa Lopez*. With the English translation of *L'Anté-peuple* in 1988, his fiction is reaching an even broader public. In each of the novels, Labou Tansi continues to expand the conventions of the postmodern novel. . . .

In *Les Sept Solitudes*, the heroine and her community must now confront a postcolonial bureaucracy with its residue of dishonor, corruption, and political abuses. In this fictional world, male discourse—the discourse of authority and power—destroys both history and women. Not only is the wife of Lorsa Lopez brutally killed; the collective history of the people is also destroyed. The capital city and all its monuments and historic artifacts are moved, "decapitalized" for the seventh time, to a new seat of government in another city. Countering this dissolution is the mediating voice of the heroine, Estina Bronzario. She creates history, rather than destroys it, and binds it to stability, continuity, and social cohesion—the values prized by traditional societies. . . .

Labou Tansi sets *Les Sept Solitudes de Lorsa Lopez* in a generic mode appropriate to a politics of resistance, to the mode of exuberant satire. Yet he also draws on the conventions of several other literary traditions, especially the fable, fantastic literature, and oral literature, with their repetitions, cycles, incantations, and Rabelaisian accumulations. When compared with *L'Anté-peuple*, the severe linearity of male discourse that shaped the latter work appears to give way at the level of structure and narrative voice to a resistant, feminine discourse. The latter discursive mode allows Sony Labou Tansi to achieve what he sets out to do. . . .

Thus, Labou Tansi opts for a position familiar to the critics of contemporary aesthetic discourse. He rejects a neocolonial paradigm of centrality that "takes the rest of the world as its body, extension and periphery." He prefers instead a new center, one peopled by those who can "name" and "breathe," for they are the ones who also know liberation. Yealdara of *L'Anté-peuple* gives us an intimation of what it means to be able to name and breathe in new ways. With *Les Sept Solitudes de Lorsa Lopez*, the centrality of Estina Bronzario and her capacity to rename is beyond question. The two novels demonstrate in quite distinctive ways how the structure and resolution of the narratives have been informed by women, in one instance through the prism of male discourse, in the other through women's liberating discourse of resistance.

Louise Fiber Luce. FR. 64, 5 (April 1991), pp. 739, 745–46

LA GUMA, ALEX (1925–   )

SOUTH AFRICA

The landscape of [Alex La Guma's early fiction] is invariably urban and unrelentingly sordid. Not for him is there any escape to the white suburbs or to the noble landscapes where one can momentarily forget the South African tragedy. And for his characters too, there is often only the escape of death. Their poverty and abandonment have no other end. *A Walk in the Night* begins as the story of Michael Adonis's aimless journey through District Six, but in the course of the narrative we have a sense of all its characters locked in similarly random and wasting motion. Willieboy's own journey ends in the back of a police truck and Doughty's at the end of a bottle. Adonis is clearly destined to drift into violent crime and towards a violent end. Foxy and his depraved gang move through the plot like a sinister chorus, looking vainly for Sockies. Only the orphaned Joe, the most destitute of all, has any sense of dimension extending beyond Hanover Street, with its filthy alleys and the illusory promise of its neon signs. But he is unable to convey his sense of this to the damned spirits who walk the dark labyrinth of these streets. His sense of wonder is as lost upon them as his sense of nature. . . .

Whereas many of [La Guma's] short stories exhibit an ironic humor, *A Walk in the Night* is a somber work, as dark as the streets through which its action is threaded. Those exhibiting random acts of charity, like Adonis, are also capable of random acts of violence. Constable Raalt is capable of little else but brutality, through which he channels all his rage at his inadequacies as a husband. The young police driver will, we are sure, soon pick up the brutal attitudes and corrupt practices of his senior. The only glimpses of a fuller humanity are in the marginal characters of Frankie Lorenzo and his wife (who play no part in the action) and Joe. . . .

Unlike the ironic commentary which characterizes the early stories the increased scope of the novel brings from the author a greater degree of commitment. If *A Walk in the Night* shows us characters caught up in an inexorable fate, *And a Threefold Cord* indicates more possibilities of choice and development, even though its actors are sunk lower still in poverty and abandonment than those of the earlier book.

Structurally, the new novel also differs considerably from its predecessor. *A Walk in the Night*, as befits its title, is confined to the events of a single night as well as those of a single district. But, although it starts by following the footsteps of Michael Adonis, it soon broadens out to show us other actors who are likewise "doomed to fast in fires," so that the center of the narrative's attention is continually shifting. *And a Threefold Cord* offers the same concentration of venue and concerns the events of a few days only, but it is more exclusively centered upon the consciousness of Charlie Pauls. In this sense, it may be said to have a "hero." All the other figures who appear in the book, from the Pauls family through their African and colored neighbors to Susie Meyer, the poor-white wreck George Mostert and the white policeman felled by Charlie's heavy fist, are connected with his movements around the shantytown in the brief time span of the plot. . . .

As already suggested, each of La Guma's novels establishes a distinctive, closed world and confines its actions entirely within it. This confinement reaches its logical conclusion in his third novel, *The Stone Country*. The panorama of fiction can be internal as well as external, and we need not traverse the steppes of Russia or the battlefields of Napoleonic Europe to encounter examples of every sort of human personality in action. It is a true if sad comment on twentieth-century literature, that many of its finest novels have accepted the walls of a prison, a labor camp, or a hospital as the limits of a sufficient world; for the prisoner or patient at least knows precisely what he longs for, which is often more than the free man can boast of. . . .

In 1979, after a silence of seven years, La Guma published a short novel which marks, in some respects, a return to the manner of his short stories and of *A Walk in the Night*. Whereas *In the Fog of the Seasons' End* traces a developing situation which begins with the arrest of Elias and ends with his death and the safe departure of the young guerrillas, *Time of the Butcherbird* centers upon a single episode. That episode is the murder—or perhaps the execution—of the nationalist politician Hannes Meulen. We sense its approach from almost the first page; thereafter we merely follow the gradually converging movements of Meulen and his assassin until their explosive encounter. . . .

Time of the Butcherbird is remarkable not only for the density with which it recalls rural South Africa after thirteen years of exile and for the sureness of its touch with all the inhabitants of the wretched little *dorp*, but for the poetic interpretation of landscape and action. This is particularly evident on the first page and the last, and in all those intervening sequences which involve Murile with the old shepherd Madolena. The story ends with these two setting out across the scorched *veld*.

Gerald Moore. Twelve African Writers (Bloomington:
Indiana University Press, 1980), pp. 108–11, 113, 118, 120

La Guma's writing career began in 1956 when he joined the staff of a progressive newspaper, *New Age*, for which he wrote striking vignettes about life in Cape Town. However, when he was forced to abandon journalism in 1962 because shortage of funds forced the newspaper to reduce drastically its staff, La Guma became completely isolated from his community; his house arrest precluded any re-employment and participation in the social and political life of his country, and because he was a banned person, all his novels were published outside South Africa. *A Walk in the Night* was published in Nigeria, *And a Threefold Cord* and *The Stone Country* in Berlin, *In the Fog of the Seasons' End* in New York, and *Time of the Butcherbird* in London.

His novels graphically depict various facets of South Africa's disfranchised population: his first novel draws a portrait of the precarious and alienated life in the slums of Cape Town; his second records the dignified attempt of shantytown dwellers to survive amidst hunger, apartheid, and the winter; *The Stone Country* depicts life in a South African jail; his fourth and best novel [*In the Fog of the Seasons' End*] . . . describes a few days in the life of a man working in the political underground; and the latest novel [*Time of the Butcherbird*] depicts the poverty to which rural black South Africans are consigned and their powerful desire to seek revenge for their oppression. In spite of their diversity, all these novels have one fundamental factor in common: the marginality of life for the nonwhite in South Africa. Although not all his novels take up the theme of marginality, they inevitably end up commenting on and indirectly depicting the material, social, political, and spiritual poverty to which apartheid relegates the darker, "inferior" people. Thus La Guma's novels constitute a transformed, fictive version of his own marginality, which initially consists in his social and political disfranchisement and then is followed by his enforced internal isolation and later "voluntary" external exile. His personal experience of exclusion from a full and free life is only a more dramatic version of the exclusion experienced by all nonwhite South Africans. His novels, then, represent the effects of the manichean bifurcation imposed by apartheid. . . .

[*In the Fog of the Seasons' End*] extends and clarifies the different preoccupations of his earlier novels. What had previously been an opposition between the assumption that individuals have a right of access to certain basic forms of self-fulfillment and the *deprivation* of this right, with the major stress falling on the latter, now becomes an overt and explicit struggle between the colonized nonwhite and the colonizing white sections of the South African population: the initial overt statement of the issues involved in this fight, in the form of a brief debate between a political prisoner, Elias, and a major in the secret police, is followed by the story of a sustained struggle between the police and one cell of an underground revolutionary movement which is attempting to depose the South African government. Yet since the depiction of this struggle necessarily involves some cloak-and-dagger scenes, La Guma cautiously avoids sensationalism by understating the drama, by making his characters weary rather than elated, and by ironically equating the precarious conditions of the fight to the unreality of "gangster" and "western" films, which will restore one to the normal world of complex reality at the end. He is perfectly able to eschew a romantic view of revolution, for by the end of the novel one is left with a feeling of an arduous and political struggle that will probably kill all the protagonists and continue into the next generation.

Abdul R. JanMohamed. *Boundary 2.* 11, 1–2 (1982–1983), pp. 273–74, 279–80

La Guma's *In the Fog of the Seasons' End* does not trace the whole evolution of the black man on the continent but, through Beukes (the main character of the novel), La Guma strives to show every African's effort to overthrow the invaders' rule. Beukes and his companions are not just fighting for the liberation of South Africa: they embody the courage and determination of freedom fighters all over the continent. Various battlefields such as Namibia, Angola, Mozambique and so on are still lingering in our minds. La Guma, in focusing on Baukes's urban guerrilla warfare does not intend to put the first stages of African history (slavery and colonization) into brackets but to underscore . . . that the question of the total liberation of Africa is no longer vested in supermen or heroes but in the common people. . . .

[In *In the Fog of the Seasons' End*] the characters . . . show [a] high sense of solidarity in their fight against the apartheid system which indistinctively casts individuals of different social strata—doctors, dentists, teachers, factory workers, messengers, taxi drivers—in the same mold only because they are black. They all contribute to some extent (and according to their particular skills) to the success of the underground movement: most of them for political reasons and some for sentimental ones. The patent illustration of the second category of fighters is revealed through the portraits of Henry April, the van driver who serves as a link between the nationalists "inside" and "outside" the country, and of Tommy, the dancer, who nevertheless takes part, in his own way, in the fight. . . .

Christophe Dailly. PA. 130 (1984), pp. 124–25, 128

Since La Guma's novels are written about a society which has made racial divisions mandatory, it is to be expected that they will contain references to race-based ideologies which create different perspectives of the same experience. In both *In the Fog of the Seasons' End* and *Time of the Butcherbird*, English-speaking whites regard the countryside as something entirely apart from them. For Edgar Stopes it is *bundu* inhabited by "bloody Dutchmen . . . not like us, modern, up-to-date." In the earlier novel when Beukes sits wounded outside a suburban garden in a white suburb, he listens to the conversation of young white English speakers inside. One characterizes Frikkie as a farmer who smells of sheep all the time; another defends him: "Don't be silly, he doesn't go near the farm." That brief spat operates within a single ideological framework. Frikkie is condemned because he is rural; he is defended because he keeps as far away from his farm as he possibly can. It is implied in the context that Frikkie is rich and he is defended precisely because his money does not come from his own labor. He is acceptable because it is only money which links him with the land. Far from turning to the land for some saving perspective, the rejection of the land by Edgar and these young whites is total. If we are going to look in the novels for conventional expressions of pastoral it will certainly not be among La Guma's English-speaking characters. In the novels they are represented as being entirely urban. . . .

The conventional location of pastoral art—the countryside—is more obviously present in *Time of the Butcherbird* than in [*In the Fog of the Seasons'*

End]. . . . Although some of the novel is set in Johannesburg, its principal setting is a drought-stricken rural area where both the Afrikaner community and
Hlangeni's people (as the whites call them) respond in their different ways to
the drought. For the blacks the ordinary problem of survival in the few hectares
which have been left them becomes even more acute. For the Afrikaners, the
drought provides an opportunity to assert their sense of community in their
prayers for rain and allows the dominee to claim the drought as a manifestation
of God's anger and to pronounce judgement on the evils of the cities. "There is
corruption in our cities," he says and goes on to assert that for the Afrikaners
the land itself is Jerusalem, the source of values to a chosen people. The New
Jerusalem, together with Arcadia and Eden, are conventional alternatives to the
corrupt city of Western pastoral. As the novel demonstrates, however, in the
random racist brutality of the countryside there is a far greater corruption than
anything the dominee could dream of in the cities. For both communities, invo-
cations of the past are central to their communal lives. The ubiquitous pictures
of the Great Trek and the Boer War, memories of fighting the British or mas-
sacring a group of San serve to recall the Afrikaners to a past which is heroic in
their mythology, and can provide the decadent present with a new sense of purpose. For Hlangeni the past is recalled with simple nostalgia. He has submitted
to orders that he and his people should move from the land and now confronted
by his powerlessness, stripped of his traditional authority, "He tried to force his
mind back to another time, a far-off youth, when he had dreamed of warriors."
Hlangeni through dream and then again through dream lives at two removes
from his warrior inheritance. But as he steps from his dilapidated house, it
seems for a moment that he will draw from the past an informing inspiration for
the present. The absence of a praise-song which once would have announced
his presence provokes in him "a twinge of pride" at the heritage which should
be his and he speaks with an uncharacteristic authority.

Anthony Chennells. In Emmanuel Ngara and Andrew Morrison, eds. *Literature,*
Language and the Nation (Harare: Baobab Books, 1989), pp. 42, 45–46

Alex La Guma, writing as a committed, active (rather than former) communist, out
of the experience of a political activist inside his own country and outside it in
exile, goes some way to detach himself from . . . ideological conventions. In his
novel, *In the Fog of the Seasons' End*, there is a genuine attempt to eradicate the
personality cult and the notion of the heroic leader figure. The revolution he
depicts is not a heroic epic of platforms and seething masses, romantic imprison-
ments, and popular deliriums, but a silent back-street affair of secret assignments,
dreary trudging about with leaflets, and a constant haunting fear of detection,
betrayal, and the repulsive and shameful realism of the torture cells. His main characters, Beukes, Tekwane, and Isaac, are drained of much of their individuality in
the interests of their functions as revolutionary units. La Guma is much too skillful
a writer to present them as cardboard stereotypes, mouthpieces for didacticism and
propaganda. The reader is always in full possession of their humanity, of their
placement in a network of relationships—Beukes with his wife and child, Tekwane

with his widowed mother, Isaac, more superficially, with his workmates—but this is all background detail. . . . Background in terms of the subject matter, in that these networks are only mentioned fairly briefly, but background also in terms of characterization, for all these men have deliberately cut themselves off from connections in order to dedicate themselves entirely to their political activities, free from the distraction of domestic demands. (The impossibility of reconciling the two is emphasized in the presentation of Bennett, distracted from the simplest obligations by a demanding wife and his own fear for the safety of his family.)

Yet for all their single-minded dedication, none of these figures emerges as the romantic hero of the revolution: theirs is a drab and unexciting struggle, with little prospect of early success and no possibility of individual glory or power. La Guma underlines this subordination of the individual to a cause most emphatically in his account of the day of the strike, where he picks out various symbolic figures and charts their normal activity—the Washerwoman, the Bicycle Messenger, the Outlaw, the Child—to emphasize the outrageous cruelty at the hands of the police, among the crowd gathered outside the police station. La Guma not merely makes no effort to conceal the artificiality of his literary device here, but actually stresses it typographically by his use of capital letters. For these four are more significant as representatives of their people, oppressed to the point of senseless obliteration, than they could ever be as individuals.

This combination of diverse stylistic devices reveals the extent of La Guma's literary skills enabling him to present the social and objective historical significance of events without divorcing his main characters from everyday reality or humanity. If he had attempted to individualize the victims of police brutality on the day of the strike it would have confused the reader and blurred the dialectical message: but if he had attempted to subordinate the characterization of his main figures to his dialectics it would have emptied his message of all power to evoke a response from the reader. Beukes, Tekwane, and Isaac are cogs in the machine of the movement, but they are sentient cogs, feeling not only in their capacities as functionaries, but also in their individual consciousness, the bruises suffered by the movement as a result of organized repression. And their attempts to try to heal the breaches, to put things together again so that the party can function, are attempts to heal their own psyches and find mechanisms to deal with their own hurts and fears. They work like moles in the dark, groping blindly, but testing each move, each contact first.

Jane Watts. *Black Writers from South Africa*
(New York: St. Martin's Press, 1989), pp. 214–15

LAMMING, GEORGE (1927–   )

BARBADOS

George Lamming is the most outspoken nationalist of the generation of West Indian novelists who grew to maturity in the turbulent 1930s and 1940s. His six novels chronicle the sweep of West Indian history, from the colonial setting of *In the Castle of My Skin* through the achievement of independence in *Season of Adventure* to a postindependence uprising in *Water with Berries*. His most recent novel, *Natives of My Person*, is the culmination of his work, reaching back to the beginnings of colonialism and, through allegory, suggesting the underlying, recurrent patterns of Caribbean history. Each of his novels is both complete in itself and part of a continually developing vision linked to the changing political scene in the Caribbean, with its urgent problems of political and psychological decolonization, and to Lamming's evolving understanding of the human condition.

His earliest writing, the poetry and short prose he wrote before emigrating to England in 1950, expresses primarily a rejection of West Indian society and politics. From 1946 to 1950, while living in Trinidad, he devoted himself to the creation of an "artistic personality" through poetry. Romantic and ethereal in the earliest poems, the persona soon came into conflict with West Indian colonial society. In 1948, Lamming describes a Trinidadian "Dutch party," with the poet on one side, brooding on the "permanent disease of society," and the "glittering chatter" of the party on the other. The West Indies in Lamming's poetry is a spiritually sterile prison for the creative spirit: "islands cramped with disease no economy can cure." In the short story "Birds of a Feather," his young protagonist dreams of a "way of escape." The colonial politics of the time are seen as an exercise in futility. . . . Lamming speaks of retreating from "the multitude's monotonous cry / For freedom and politics at the price of blood," to an aesthetic world where the spirit can "Live every moment in the soul's devouring flame."

Emigration to England marked a turning point in his attitude towards the West Indies. A black West Indian in an unfriendly city, he discovered not creative freedom, but alienation. . . .

His experience in England showed Lamming the need to define himself not only as an artist but as a West Indian. The poems he wrote before beginning work on *In the Castle of My Skin* return to the society he had earlier rejected. "The Boy and the Sea" celebrates the freedom of boyhood, and "The Illumined Graves" introduces a central motif of his later work: the living seeking communion and reconciliation with the dead on All Souls' Day.

Ian [H.] Munro. In Bruce King, ed. *West Indian Literature*
(Hamden, Conn.: Archon Books, 1979), pp. 126–27

In George Lamming's partly autobiographical *In the Castle of My Skin*, young G feels himself to be part of the communal village experience; he and his friends are close to the land and the "folk." But as the boy grows up he discovers himself to be more and more an individual, a stranger in his own society. His gradual alienation from friends, from the village, and finally from the island environment is more than a case of "growing up," of leaving the world of childhood behind. And it is not finally a question of class nor even of education, but of sensibility. For G has the questing, sensitive awareness of the creative artist. And in his development the natural, undifferentiated world of the village and the

world of literature and art inevitably draw apart. The gulf looms, even where . . .
there is no irresistible cultural pull toward Europe. G's overriding concern
becomes the need to *preserve* this new identity, his integrity as a private individual, "the you that's hidden somewhere in the castle of your skin." It is a self-
protective measure in a society that apparently can no longer contain or nourish
the individual mind. Near the end of the book, G, a high-school product by now,
cannot find acceptance with the villagers, nor can he relate meaningfully to his
new status. . . . Yet G, at the end of the book, recognizes that the reason for his
sense of alienation is not simply the high school. . . . Emigration, exile, is the
obvious next step. But in the next novel, *The Emigrants*, there is another disillusionment and the inevitable return, the subject of *Of Age and Innocence*, which
embodies an act of repossession of the native landscape, a reorientation of feeling through the experience of Fola in the *tonelle* during the ceremony of souls.
But San Cristobal is an imaginary island, where the Haitian voodoo ceremony
can effect a "return to roots" alongside the music of the steel band as a message
of the society's indigenous cultural health. Even if one accepts, through Fola's
"conversion," the cultural return to the "folk," one is left with that other
dilemma: that of the artist, Chiki, who feels that his creative talent is drying up.
Caught between his peasant origins—the world of the *tonelle*—and his
European-oriented Christian education, he cries because he is afraid that his creative growth is stunted. . . . This is a persistent symptom of a psychological and
cultural division which still needs to be exorcised. Indeed, in *The Pleasures of
Exile* Lamming explicitly sought exile to *confront* that other culture, the world
of Prospero, in an attempt at self-definition. This was a head-on, articulate
tackling of that deeper, cultural schizophrenia. For Lamming it is important that
Caliban and Prospero should meet again within a new horizon. . . .

   In the Castle of My Skin is generally regarded, like V. S. Reid's *New Day*,
as a "classic" of West Indian fiction. It is one of the earliest novels of any substance to convey, with real assurance, the life of ordinary village folk within a
genuinely realized, native landscape: a "peasant novel" (it is Lamming's term)
written with deep insight and considerable technical skill. *Castle* is also a partly
autobiographical novel of childhood, and, like *New Day*, celebrates the particular feeling of a particular community through the author's ability to re-create
the sights, sounds, and even odors of his native Barbados. The assertion of a
rooted, indigenous life merges with the theme of a lost, rural innocence to suggest comparison with other, more famous "childhood" novels: with James
Joyce's *A Portrait of the Artist as a Young Man*, for example, where Stephen
Dedalus's love/hate relationship with his native Ireland ends in voluntary exile;
or with Mark Twain's *Adventures of Huckleberry Finn*, that early assertion of
American literary independence, native wit, and lost innocence.

   New Day, Huckleberry Finn, and *A Portrait of the Artist* all celebrate, in
different ways, "the prototype of the national experience"; but in Lamming's
novel there is no such celebration. No sense of a national consciousness
emerges. To Lamming's young hero, G, Stephen Dedalus's vow "to forge in the
smithy of my soul the uncreated conscience of my race" would have sounded

remarkably like arrogance; and Huck Finn's confident, existential *American-ness* would have seemed impossibly precocious. Nor could he have seen himself, like Reid's Johnny Campbell, as a member of an illustrious, proud family. G's ninth birthday, with which the book opens, is a sad reminder of his own shaky sense of identity. . . .

The consciousness which develops is that of the private individual within the framework of his own little village community. Even *other* village communities remain largely outside the young G's focus. His is a gradual, often painful growth toward a personal view of the immediate community: it is a much narrower stage than Reid provides for his drama of the events of the great 1865 Morant Bay rebellion (there is, by contrast, only a timid riot in *Castle*), yet the "inner" action is equally urgent. For Lamming's villagers are acquiescent colonials whose acceptance of their island as a "Little England" is uncritical; and it is an acceptance that leaves them without authentic identity whether they know it or not. When Trumper (recently returned from America) speaks of "his people," G (whose name we never discover) thinks he means the villagers. "You ain't a thing till you know it," snorts Trumper, "and that's why you and none o' you on this island is a Negro yet." But Trumper's return and his conversation with G occur during the last few pages. The idea of national or racial consciousness as a goal remains peripheral, outside the range of G's experience.

Michael Gilkes. *The West Indian Novel* (Boston: Twayne, 1981), pp. 86–87, 123–24

In the six novels he has published since 1953, George Lamming identifies colonialism as the political institution that has shaped the structure and direction of West Indian society. He has striven consistently as a writer to portray the development of this society in its totality. He describes the complex motivations and interrelationships of the West Indian community within the framework of its political history. Each novel explores a stage in, or an aspect of, the colonial experience, so that the novels are finally the "unfolding of a single work." Each individual novel is originally related to Lamming's political concern with how the structure of power reflects colonial history and how this in turn affects the intimate details of private and public life in a representative community.

There are two distinct movements in this body of work that mark a clear progression in thematic and artistic method. There is a well-coordinated continuity in the first four novels, from *In the Castle of My Skin* to *Season of Adventure*, that gives these volumes epic stature. Together they describe the struggle of the West Indian people to be free of the political, economic, and cultural domination that characterized their history. Lamming describes the breakdown of colonial rule and the emergence of an independent republic in the Caribbean, followed by the fall of this republic and the emergence of the second republic in a continuing struggle to break free of the psychological and political thrall of colonialism. He begins with the initial promise and failure of the emerging labor movement of the 1930s in *In the Castle of My Skin*. This is the prelude to *The Emigrants* in which Lamming describes, with deep sympathy and understanding, the attitudes and the motivations of thousands of West

Indians who emigrated to the "Mother Country" after World War II. In *Of Age and Innocence* he describes the return of the emigrant to the Caribbean and the sudden growth of independence movements in the 1950s. *Season of Adventure* is Lamming's last direct fictional statement on the now largely independent, self-governing Caribbean. It marks a high point in Lamming's fiction with the unqualified promise of Gort and Fola, the folk artist and the middle-class revolutionary who ties her educational advantages to the African and peasant values of Gort's drum. In Gort and Fola, the masculine and feminine principles in the society are identified in productive harmony with each other, as an oppressed working class struggles for freedom from the inherited bias and injustices of the postcolonial regime. This is Lamming's concluding and most optimistic statement about the future of an independent Caribbean. Revolution is seen as a continuing process with certain guarantees of success in the Gort/Fola alliance. . . .

Season *of Adventure* marks the end of one movement in Lamming's work. He explains that "there was at that moment no further point for me to go without in a sense going beyond what has actually happened in the society." For twelve years Lamming published no further novels. Then in 1972, his last two novels were published simultaneously: *Water with Berries* was released in London in October, and *Natives of My Person* was released in New York in the same month. The shift in focus and artistic method immediately set these novels apart from his earlier efforts.

In *Water with Berries* Lamming turns his attention to those West Indians, artists in particular, who never re-entered the mainstream of life in the Caribbean. He examines the continuing drama of conflict and rejection that attends West Indians domiciled in Great Britain. Interestingly enough, this is the shortest of Lamming's novels. It offers a much reduced canvas of characters and makes them carry the burden of the book's comment on the immigrant experience. The relative compactness of the novel is clearly tied to its allegorical design and marks a new development in the writer's artistic method. The allegorical structure of *Of Age and Innocence* had been heavily underscored with a wealth of descriptive detail about his characters and their fictional setting. It would seem that working with Great Britain as a known setting in *Water with Berries*, as opposed to San Cristobal, Lamming no longer felt he had to chart the history and structure of the society in the convolutions of an elaborate plot. In *Water with Berries*, as few as eight characters, and the interrelationships among them, sustain the multiple levels of allegory that comprise the novel's statement about the conflict between immigrant and native Briton.

Natives of My Person, with its very different setting and European cast, confirms Lamming's continuing concern to define the scope of the colonial experience. In this instance, he explores the crises of late sixteenth-century and early seventeenth-century Europe which inspired Europe's annexation of the New World. . . . In *Natives of My Person* Lamming goes back in history to describe the genesis of colonialism. He describes a sixteenth-century voyage that was the beginning of plantation society in the West Indies. But while the historical fiction is complete within itself, the novel is also a sustained allegory of the structure of power in postcolonial countries. In this novel, Lamming returns to the elaborate architecture of the first four novels as he once again attempts to chart a whole society in the full complexity of the historical moment. But he considerably limits the multiple demands of setting and custom that weight his earlier fiction by structuring this novel around a real and symbolic ship's journey. This is by far the most finely executed of his novels, and especially impressive in that it penetrates the consciousness of another race, another culture, and a distant moment in history.

Sandra Pouchet Paquet. *The Novels of George Lamming*
(London: Heinemann, 1982), pp. 116–18

Season of Adventure is, in a way, an imaginative projection of the "true meaning of Africa for the West Indian people and their intellectual classes." The novel opens with echoes of two distinctly folk idioms—the steel drum and the religious Ceremony of the Souls—both of which recall continental African practices. The steel drums and their music recall the African drums whose music is used as the "intensive language of transition and its communicant means, the catalyst and solvent of its regenerative hoard." The Ceremony of the Souls on which the novel is based is a voodoo religious ceremony practiced in Haiti by "peasants who have retained a racial, a historic, desire to worship their original gods." The Haitian peasants regard this ceremony as a solemn communication in the process of which they hear the secrets of the dead at first hand. During the ceremony, the dead return to offer, through the medium of the priest, a full and honest report on their relation to the living. The African antecedent of the Ceremony of the Souls is the Masquerade Cult (the Cult of the Ancestors) which manifests in concrete and imagistic terms the African rendezvous with the past.

In San Cristobal, the recently independent fictional West Indian island on which *Season of Adventure* is set, all signs of the past and the living links with aboriginal civilizations are denigrated by the small ruling middle-class elite, who perpetuate an educational system which displays a fear of any affirmation of ancestral heritage as a tool for shaping a revolutionary future. Members of this elite group are enthralled by foreign values and systems; they shy away from their African and slave pasts and the need to use these for creating a viable alternative to their inherited colonial power structure. The only survivors of their systematic denigration of the past in this island are the Ceremony of the Souls and the steel drums. Fola, the middle-class mulatto heroine of the novel, is taken by Charlot, her European teacher of History to the *tonelle* to witness a Ceremony of the Souls. As Fola watches the women dance feverishly, she, in a moment of inspiration/possession, recognizes the ancestral link between her and the worshippers, between her West Indian island and Africa. She is shaken out of her middle-class entombment and becomes aware of the need to take the all-important backward glance into her and her society's past in order to possess the future.

Funso Aiyejina. In Eldred Durosimi Jones, ed.
African Literature Today. 14 (1984), pp. 119–20

[George Lamming] has become a successful literary figure in the English-speaking Caribbean. Although he achieved early success in England, Lamming has opted not to remain an exile like his contemporary, [V. S.] Naipaul. He lives and works in the West Indies, where he is now as famous as a vigorous and influential polemicist as he is as a creator of fiction. Lamming was among the first prominent anglophone Caribbean writers to espouse the cause of black consciousness in the 1960s, and he has argued eloquently for a regional identity. He has been a vocal and scornful critic of Naipaul and others who have remained in permanent exile; his objections have rested less on their physical removal from the Caribbean than on their unwillingness to deal directly with West Indian subject matter.

And yet Lamming himself has been caught up in the typical West Indian need to escape to an ideal, although his evocation of that ideal is quite different from that of either Naipaul or [Aimé] Césaire. Like so many West Indian writers, Lamming returns to childhood, and his very first novel, *In the Castle of My Skin*, still stands as the classic of the quite numerous genre of West Indian childhood narratives.

Lamming's view of childhood, and the uses for which he mobilizes his image of youth, are, however, quite different from the common run. His distinctive tone is part of the source of his power as an opinion leader. Other famous Caribbean childhood novels, such as the Barbadian Geoffrey Drayton's *Christopher* or the Trinidadian Michael Anthony's *The Year in San Fernando*, take what might be the expected approach of dwelling on the innocence of childhood and the creation of a kind of magical, special world sheltered from adult fears and responsibilities. These novels are written in the first person, and preserve the point of view of the young boys who narrate them. Lamming, on the other hand, infuses his first-person narrative with the voice of the wise adult. The little village that is the setting of *In the Castle of My Skin* is not a place of refuge; the changes that were to happen in the course of time are already reflected in Lamming's descriptions of it as it was when he was a child.

Lamming is explicitly political in a different way from the other childhood escapists. Lamming has affirmed his belief that as an artist his responsibility is to his own consciousness, to his society, and to the "community of man," not necessarily in that order. Lamming expresses a particular disdain for the West Indian bourgeoisie, because in his view only the "peasants" (including, in his later formulations, the urban proletariat) are the true bearers of pure folk culture. It should be noted that Lamming's reference to "the folk" extends beyond those people who live in the West Indies. His use of the term is global, symbolic, inclusive, as was Césaire's use of "black." By the same token, the middle class is an artifact of colonial exploitation. He does not, therefore, depict the "coming of age" of his four young heroes as a psychological process. Rather, he sees the maturation of his protagonists essentially as a microcosm that symbolizes the evolution of rural, peasant society and the growth of consciousness among the formerly oppressed and ignorant peasantry. The village in *Castle* is "growing painfully . . . into political self-awareness," and Lamming's political aims generally serve to push his account of the boys' adventures to the background, so that he can concentrate on detailing "the complex shiftings in the community at large."

The common problem is the confusion of West Indian identity. The solution again is to clear the heads of people so that they can start fresh. Naipaul did so by first setting up the romantic allure of the sophisticated world of the metropole, and then debunking even that myth; Césaire did it by exalting the race that transcends the locality and its specific sufferings. Lamming does it by equating the clear-headed, straightforward approach of childhood with the earthbound good sense of the immemorial peasant. The "folk" could be seen as "the ground of psychic wholeness and source of new community." He was not one to mourn the passing of the old order. Rather, he wished the people to greet the coming of the new order with the unabashed, can't-put-nothin'-over-on-us common sense of the common people. The peasants were no less confused than the intellectuals about their identity, but, Lamming suggests, they did not let their confusion hold them back. His was therefore a plea for the unashamed acceptance of local history and culture. His was among the first strong voices to suggest that the West Indies themselves had something valuable to contribute to the identity of its people.

Michael V. Angrosino. In Philip A. Dennis and Wendell Aycock, eds.
Literature and Anthropology (Lubbock:
Texas Tech University Press, 1989), pp. 125–27

In *The Pleasures of Exile*, the reconsideration of the relationship between the margin and the center takes textual form; in many ways, the experience of exile is about reading and rereading the colonial narrative of history and the canonical text. In such texts, especially in the gaps his reading exposes, Lamming seeks his space of representation and identity. In reflecting on the meaning and ideological implications of rewriting the colonial experience, Lamming also questions certain doctrines of European modernity: the historical beginnings it is supposed to engender, the gift of language it is supposed to proffer, and indeed the assumption that in the modern world (the colonial world) a common identity is shared by the colonizer and the colonized. As a state of limbo, exile becomes Lamming's carnivalesque space of representation. According to Joyce Jonas, in this space where he is no longer bound by old laws concerning representation or interpretation, Lamming functions as a trickster. . . .

The need to counter the Apollonian fiction of empire seems to explain Lamming's desire to valorize the disruptive and diachronic functions of narrative. As he notes in regard to *In the Castle of My Skin*, he uses methods of narration in which things are never as tidy as critics would like: "There is often no discernible plot, no coherent line of events with a clear, causal connection." Indeed, rather than appeal to a holistic world that might counter . . . loss and displacement . . . Lamming develops narrative strategies that underscore the converse process: his novels are primarily about a destabilized world of childhood and adolescence (*In the Castle*), of emigrants displaced in the place they hoped to claim through language and tradition (*The Emigrants*), and of the failure of the nationalist dream of a national culture that transcends race and class (*Of Age and Innocence*). Such persistent themes suggest that Lamming has accepted displacement as a strategic narrative possibility that allows the writer to deconstruct the colonial vision and to introduce the narrative of Caribbean history into the text. So although Lamming's early works are intended to evoke a narrative of decolonization and liberation, as several critics have argued, such a narrative is not possible until the writer has overcome the obstacles that block the realization of a national community of language and culture and of nationalism as a state of belonging. As a result, there is explicit tension between the author's desire for a grand narrative that will restore coherence to the Caribbean social body and the mechanisms of psychological blockage generated by colonialism. If Lamming's early novels are motivated by the desire to "return a society to itself"—as he told graduating students at the University of the West Indies in 1980—then these narratives have had to seek a detour around the "hidden forms of censorship" in the dominant culture.

Simon Gikandi. Writing in Limbo: Modernism and Caribbean Literature
(Ithaca, N. Y.: Cornell University Press, 1992), pp. 57–58, 72–73

The Emigrants is a novel about Caliban in exile in more ways than the obvious physical exile of the characters themselves. The tragic sense of life is seen in its theme. A shipload of West Indians goes to England. They are filled with the excitement of travel and the anticipation of finally seeing the country that has for centuries dominated their islands. Instead of feeling at home, however, they are shocked to discover that they are considered outsiders in England. Torn between nostalgia for what they have left behind and the necessity to cope with what confronts them, they suffer the anguish of exile.

There is first of all the sheer physical suffering caused by a climate that is bitterly different from that of the Caribbean. Second, it is confusing to confront a white majority who are employed in a wide variety of jobs that the newcomers have traditionally associated with menial labor at home. Did white people actually do manual work? They had seen only white landlords who were served, not who served. This demands a refocusing of ideas. Third, while each of the immigrants is ambitious to prove himself, theory is easier than practice. It is difficult to keep any sense of identity. Terror stalks the exile, filling him with a sense of disintegration and disillusionment. . . .

Water with Berries was published more than fifteen years after *The Emigrants*, but again the theme is exile fraught with the terror of utter alienation. In the earlier novel, the reader interprets the situation of the uprooted West Indian from the viewpoint of Prospero and Caliban. In the later book, the author himself draws an explicit parallel, making it a kind of reverse allegory of *The Tempest*.

Lamming acknowledges in *The Pleasures of Exile* that he may be accused of blasphemy because he deliberately uses Caliban as a symbol of the West Indies. This is an accusation that can be refuted: for symbols, after all, can be plucked from thin blue air. However, matters become complicated when he goes further and chooses *The Tempest* as the symbolic *structure* for *Water with Berries*. Even the names of his characters echo those of Shakespeare's play. One woman is called Myra; another is Randa; a third is compared to Ariel. It is now that we are faced with the problem that confronts him. For if Shakespeare has become such an important frame of reference, it suggests the problematic nature of cultural entrapment. And does this not dramatize the tragic sense? Lamming tries to escape the influence of the "mother country" but cannot liberate himself from its stranglehold.

Margaret Paul Joseph. *Caliban in Exile: The Outsider in Caribbean Fiction* (New York: Greenwood Press, 1992), pp. 59, 65–66

LIKING, WEREWERE (1950–   )

CAMEROON

A relatively recent appearance in African theater is the Cameroonian writer Werewere Liking. She was conscious of how rich in possibilities African theater itself was and was amazed that, despite this, French-language theater in Africa remained so strongly oriented to the old-style European theater where classical dramaturgy sets the tone. . . .

The myth on which one of her plays, *Une Nouvelle Terre*, is based answers the question of the origin of the Bassa in the Cameroon: what were the beginnings of this people, how did they establish themselves in the Cameroon? Bassa tradition sings of two brothers, Koba and Kwan, their courage and tenacity and their arduous, testing journey. Leaving their original home territory, they cross, miraculously, the mythical *White River* (the Nile?) on a "Likogui leaf." Eventually, they arrive at the "Stone with the Hole," Ngok Lituba, in the central southern area of the Cameroon. Here was the birthplace of the Bassa, in the impenetrable cave. Here "une nouvelle terre" ("a new land") began. They developed into a powerful and prosperous people. With the passage of time things did not go well for them. Because of this a ritual was needed through which they could rediscover the purity of the myth, the uncorrupted mythical setting in which the original powers acted positively on the society. That purity can only be re-created through catharsis. The cause of the destruction of good in the society had first to be found. That must happen through group activity, and for that an old Bassa ritual is used in *Une Nouvelle Terre*. . . . [The] original myth, which was meant to explain the origin and bond of the Bassa with their tribal lands, is linked by the author with the complex problems of modern society. She achieves this by means of an entirely different element of Bassa tradition, namely the initiation rite of the Ngué masked figure, which works as a theatrical process. . . .

In the dramatic works of Werewere Liking, written in French, rituals and other old customs occur which are clearly the product of thorough preliminary research. Researched material has thus been used in different and new ways in the theater. In . . . *Une Nouvelle Terre* a ritual based on one of the three existing initiation rites of the Bassa is used. Here an important role is played by the masked Ngué figure. . . . [The] artist, the "Ndinga," initiates the restoration of harmony, along with the child, carried by the masked Ngué figure and in whose name he speaks. The accompanying rhythm is always recognizable because it returns each time the Ngué speaks. Finally, thanks to the ritual, harmony is restored. The village receives new hope, a new ideal, new energy, a new future. Symbols play an important role in the play. . . . Thus, contact with the other world is re-established; the initiation ritual constitutes the most essential element, enriched with the positive achievements of the present. A new village comes into being, thanks to the creative word of the Ndinga. The oral "text" of the myth and the use of the traditional Ngué initiation ceremony both contribute to the thematic coherence of this modern French-language play, about which there is much more to say than is possible here.

Mineke Schipper. *TRI.* 9, 3 (1983–1984), pp. 219–21, 225–26

[*Spectacles rituels*] contains two ritual dramas by the Cameroonian writer Werewere Liking, together with commentaries on these by Marie-José Hourantier, who staged their first productions, in Abidjian, in the early [1980s]. In her introductory essay Hourantier refers to traditional ritual as a model "one may examine endlessly" in order to regain contact with "certain primordial ideas." The theater derived from this is intended to question contemporary social rules and codes, to examine a world which most people find no longer responds to their needs. The plays expose wounds, dramatize states of unease and self-blame, and above all, seek to accuse: to find the proper targets to blame for social injustice and to exorcise these.

[In *Les Mains veulent dire*] a mentally ill woman is interrogated as to the cause of her sickness. She, and a child who doubles her responses, act as truthtellers: they are special and valuable because they are so open in revealing their distress. The woman's husband can understand no reason for her illness. . . . Women's experience is central to the play, but the accusations are also aimed at a society which is ordered, in any case, to serve only a few. Some of the speeches which specify social injustice have a scorching impact; the play might benefit from more of these, from more direct reference to the base, since it's here it takes off in full air-breaking flight. . . .

The second play, *La Rougeole-arc-en-ciel*, is shorter but more ambitious, using a disturbingly dense and fragmented language to present deliberate caricatures of alienation. . . . [As] Hourantier explains it, the plays are intended to have a healing effect, drawing their audience through a process of interrogation, accusation, and exorcism, and so providing a renewed sense of viability and wholeness. The idea of therapeutic drama might need to be approached carefully; there is a danger, for example, of patronizing men and women who can identify pretty confidently the political initiatives which would heal their lives, but are denied the power to effect these. All the same, these plays mark an interesting and provocative experiment.

Chris Dunton. *WA.* November 13–19, 1989, pp. 1894–95

[In] less than fifteen years Werewere Liking has become a significant dramatist in Cameroon because her innovative ritual aesthetics steers clear of the prevailing extroversion of contemporary drama. Her experimental plays represent a major breakaway from the mainstream of current dramatic expression. From the beginning she asserted her presence with a vision and artistry that recoiled from Eurocenteredness. Evincing a taste that was completely antipodal to the prevailing cosmopolitan trend, she set out to probe the deeper layers of her specific cultural experience. While concentrating on the exploration of her people's traditional modes of thought, she has still been able to tackle the most pressing problems of her time, thanks to the extreme flexibility of her ritual matrix. And although the uniqueness of her vision is yet to gain recognition, it could help establish a dramatic tradition of longterm goals if it were to command followership. Indeed, the distinctively traditional canons that underlie her dramatic style are pointing the way to the future development of a theater of national significance, since they are more relevant to the country's insistent preoccupation with cultural identity. . . .

When Werewere Liking came to the fore in 1978, she was bent on showing more loyalty and reverence to the aesthetic tradition of her ancestors, by reorganizing the past not in terms of "modern" perspectives, but according to its own laws. This did not, however, mean that she was going to uncritically extol her Bassa cultural past, but simply that she was setting out to explore its well-tried formulae and techniques to see what originality they could lend her work. Although in her particular case . . . the traditional self dominates the alienated one, she does not reject her duality which finds expression in the way she harmoniously integrates into her drama some elements inherited from Western theatrical forms and thought so as to reflect more faithfully, through her own experience, the cultural situation of all contemporary Africans. The paramount difference here is that, for the first time on Cameroon's stage, the society is seen as evolving from a traditional vantage point: there lies the profoundly innovative nature of Liking's ritual drama. . . .

La Puissance de Um concerns the death of Ntep Iliga, a leader of a Bassa clan. Responsible members of the community are convened by Ngond Libii, the widow, to proceed to the ritual burial. Instead of letting the ceremony follow its normal course, the widow surprisingly refuses to act the role prescribed by tradition. She first claims responsibility for her husband's death and shows impatience to get rid of his corpse. From the burial ritual that was going to take place, what we now see developing is a trial ritual. Then, suddenly, she shifts the accusation from herself to the whole society which she holds responsible for producing mediocre males [like] her late husband who was notoriously callous, improvident, profligate, alcoholic, and lazy, yet passed for a successful descendant of the clan in his lifetime! . . .

Une Nouvelle Terre . . . starts with a deceptive conflict involving a man, Nguimbus, and his wife, Soo. It opens in an apocalyptic world where institutions and people (apart from a handful of miraculous survivors) have been wiped out. Man and wife are faced with the alternative of escaping or accepting to leave with the general chaos: where the former favors a timid policy based

on inaction and silence, the latter rejects mediocrity and compromise. But a
smooth transition is made from the couple's divergence to the scrutiny of the
powers that be. It is the existing political system, headed by a self-seeking,
ruthless, and grabbing Chief whose authority on the people passes through a
gun-wielding Cop, which has generated tyranny, oppression, misery, that ultimately lead to chaos in the society. . . .

The third play, *Les Mains veulent dire*, dramatizes a therapeutic ritual
organized to cure an insane woman. Kadia, the high priestess called to preside
over the ceremony, discovers that the woman suffers from self-guilt originating
from ill-digested Christian teachings and from marital infidelity. But it is
mostly her option for mundane, shallow appearances (under the husband's insti-
gation) which has led to failure in her marriage, sterility in her life, and finally
to madness. In the subsequent search for a scapegoat, the husband is found
guilty of exploiting his wife's financial generosity and psychological immaturity; but he tries to cover up his own failure as a husband by having her publicly
certified. What appears as madness is in fact the woman's escape into self in
order to avoid further victimization. This play re-enacts the ritual quest for personal identity, independence and wisdom. . . .

The flexible medium of Liking's drama is not only firmly rooted in African
soil, but it also reflects contemporary situations. Her whole technique is not to
restrict the reader, but to make his/her mind function on a wider environment in
which moments of intense poetic expression—provided by chorus-figures who
comment [on] the action—constantly alternate with ordinary speech. The overall
impression is that of a forceful and vital idiom which makes all characters—and
more so the rural people, who are neither naive nor gullible like the majority of
their counterparts in African drama—very much alive before us with the issues
that concern them. Even political jargon is dragged in without the author
indulging in didacticism, for she uses parody as an element of her style to torture
"empty" words. . . . By doing so she stresses "modern" verbal insignificance.
Through her controlled rendering in which seriousness and humor appear in
shifting perspectives, Liking distances herself from the void of political sloganizing and journalese, a thing which her contemporaries, bent on imitating reality,
can hardly achieve. Yet her ritual method is not argumentative, nothing is
demonstrated, no judgments are passed. What seems to count more is the manner
rather than the meaning. The semiotics of the theater expectedly plays a role
equal in importance to that of verbal expression in the drama. More than ever,
the reader is forced to enter into a permanent dialogue with a variety of objects,
symbols, gestures, bodily marks, and costuming whose "words" though needing
no arguments, are central to the understanding of the author's complete meaning.

Jeanne N. Dingome. In János Riesz and Alain Ricard, eds.
Semper Aliquid Novi: Littérature Comparée et Littératures d'Afrique
(Tübingen: Narr, 1990), pp. 317–21, 324

In plays such as *La Queue du diable*, *Du Sommeil d'injuste*, and *La Puissance
de Um*, Liking assumes that a re-enactment of repressed fears and hostilities

will enable actors and spectators to coalesce into a community that emotionally repudiates the false values behind such feelings. For example, the mimed flash-backs in *La Queue du diable* reveal the truth about a man's incest with his daughters and the hatred that inspires his wife with a desire to kill them. The death of her son impresses upon her the horror of the situation she has helped create. A chorus of wailing women comments on the fate of women in their society, and actors planted in the audience cite proverbs in judgment of the events being enacted in front of them.

In *Du sommeil d'injuste*, an ailing chief is portrayed by two actors—one playing the actual individual lying on the sickbed, the other portraying the per-sona he presents to the public. Throughout the play, the public persona refuses to recognize that he is terminally ill and continues to believe that he can control the world through an exercise of will. Although his "nation-building" policies have brought the people to the verge of starvation, he insists that everyone pre-tend to be happy. In the end, the figure on the bed arises, gazes into the mirror, and collapses dead on the floor. By participating in the process by which the truth emerges in spite of people's attempts to repress it, the spectators of both plays presumably open themselves to the cosmic force that can endow their lives with purpose, meaning, and joy. In this state of mind, they become capa-ble of recognizing and repudiating the false consciousness that has been foisted upon them by petty dictators like the terminally ill chief.

A similar movement toward heightened awareness characterizes *La Puissance de Um*, in which a woman initially refuses to mourn her dead hus-band because he never created anything with his own hands during a life gov-erned by outmoded customs and the obsessive pursuit of wealth and pleasure. As she begins to reflect, however, she and the rest of the community realize they are all responsible for the man's death. Living at the crossroads of modern and traditional cultures, they now understand that his assimilation of corrupt norms was merely a symptom of what was happening to the entire village, for it too is menaced with fragmentation and purposelessness. By acquiescing in his false constructions of reality, the other villagers helped obscure the truth that could have liberated them from this malaise.

Richard Bjornson. *The African Quest for Freedom and Identity:
Cameroonian Writing and the National Experience*
(Bloomington: Indiana University Press, 1991), pp. 450–51

Writing primarily as a dramatist, Werewere Liking incorporates both initiation and collective healing in her works of ritual theater, such as *Une Nouvelle Terre*. Indeed, this is the basis for [Pierre] Medehouegnon's acknowledgement of her as a pioneer of ritual theater as a subgenre. However, as the following discussion intends to demonstrate, Liking, in her two novels, *Orphée-dafric* and *Elle sera de jaspe et de corail*, provides a rebuttal to Medehouegnon's opinion of the unsuitability of other, nontraditionally African genres for the adaptation of traditional ritual in literature. As we have said, for Liking the imperative fac-ing African societies and African people in contemporary times is for a renascence stimulated by first purging themselves of the destructive behaviors inherited from traditional society or sown by the colonial experience. Replacing these with behaviors and attitudes based in an Afrocentric discourse relevant to contemporary reality, the purged organism can grow healthy. As the two novels under consideration demonstrate, Liking makes a case for the urgency of a cultural/philosophical self-reassessment and regeneration to rescue "Africa strangled, endangered, betrayed."

In the two novels under consideration, ritual is the basis of both structure and content. *Orphée-dafric* not only incorporates initiation but is also based on a myth. As is obvious from the title, Liking has adapted the Greco-Roman Orpheus myth to a contemporary story of an African's quest for enlightenment. Acknowledging the frequent occurrence of the Orpheus quest also in the lore of African societies, Liking finds a symbolic descent into hell necessary for Africa to extract itself from the infernal state into which it has fallen. So, referring to a Bassa ordeal by fire, Liking unites the universal myth with the particular ritual, "tropicalizing" the myth in the process by incorporating very specific Bassa/Cameroon cultural material, for example, retaining the name of Orpheus for her (peasant-class) hero while giving the Bassa name "Nyango" to her (middle-class) Eurydice counterpart. At the other end of the mythology-reality continuum from *Orphée-dafric* is Liking's second novel *Elle sera de jaspe et de corail.* . . . Its genre label of "chant-novel" suggests its ritual nature, proposed for the healing of a socially and morally diseased African village, and, by extension, of Africa in general. . . .

Liking's Orpheus story takes the form of a double-frame narrative: a nuptial-night dream within the external story of a marriage celebration, with its ritual nuptial kayak ride, [and] wedding night consummation of the marriage. The initiation is effected through the structure as well as the content of the narrative. Following the same initiation schema described by Medehouegnon for [Amadou Hampaté] Bâ's novel *Kaydara* and Liking's play *Une Nouvelle Terre*, Orpheus is taken through the three stages of novitiate, disciple, initiate. Since Orpheus's initiation is executed entirely in the course of a dream, its duration of nine years is artistically telescoped into the twenty-four-hour wedding night slumber, which is punctuated by sessions of ecstatic lovemaking. Orpheus, dreaming that Nyango drowned during the nuptial kayak ride on the White River, is compelled to go to search for her in the unknown land of the ancestors. Thus, Nyango's love is the driving force that propels him on the odyssey toward the ultimate understanding. . . .

The "chant-novel" *Elle sera de jaspe et de corail* illustrates the healing ritual through its polymorphous form. This ritual character of the work is signalled by the author's own genre designations "(*journal d'une misovire*)," as well as in the publisher's "*chant-roman.*" Structurally, the work flows between first- and third-person narrative befitting the style of a diary, generously interspersed with poetry, theatrical dialogue, theoretical commentary, dream-state action—within the framework of the text's "action," which is the writing of a journal. The journal-writer, or diarist, is performing a function analogous to that of the *historian* described by Liking in the healing ritual: "For it is he who, through his *chant* and his music, *will narrate and move the event forward,* even mythify it. Relative to the total event, *he is the 'script.'* He notes everything: the incongruity of the most meaningful and most dissociated objects brought together in a ritual, the most absurd and contradictory audience attitudes, the most deep-seated conflicts, the most imperceptible and unperceived suggestions of the crowd" (emphasis mine). In addition to the participation in the ritual by the diarist as "historian," we hear the voice of the community in the form of two of its intellectuals, and the inter-mittent voice of the unseen spirit, *La nuit noire.* Thus, Liking's text is the ritual cast in a literary form. Not simply a matter of the ritual as content of the novel, the ritual becomes, here, the genre fitted to the content.

Anne Adams [Graves]. *Callaloo.* 16, 1 (Winter 1993), pp. 155–56, 158–59

LOPES, HENRI (1937–   )

CONGO

La Nouvelle Romance by Congo-Brazzaville's Henri Lopes is a cacophony of sound, the song of modern Africa with all its discordant notes and jarring rhythms. It is a vignette of marriage that is used by the author as a foil to portray the clashes which occur every day in the life of the young African. Lopes pre-sents life as a whirl of dualisms: man and woman, husband and wife, married and unmarried, white and black, colonial and independent, East and West, Europe and Africa, communist and noncommunist, Mercedes and any old car, café-crême and café-au-lait. Underscoring the theme of disharmony, he shifts the action in each chapter from one character to another and from one place to another. To heighten contrasts, he uses language—formal French, casual French, translations of traditional expressions, slang, street jargon, and popular terms borrowed from English. He makes frequent use of flashbacks, and once, to emphasize the hero-ine's dilemma, he uses an extended flashback within a flashback. . . .

La Nouvelle Romance is the first novel to come out of francophone Africa that addresses the challenge posed by women's liberation to young Africa; but while affirming the need for change, the author leaves unanswered the question whether the result will be harmony or heightened discord. The work also directly attacks abuses and corruption in government and debates political philosophies, a fact that is of particular interest, since the author himself has been minister of education and prime minister of his own country. Although its conclusion tends toward the didactic, *La Nouvelle Romance* is an excellent lit-erary work which provides a poignant picture of the universal dilemma of the young educated wife of the twentieth century.

Philip A. Noss. *WLT.* 52, 2 (Spring 1978), p. 329

The novelistic work of the writer and Congolese statesman Henri Lopes, like that of Sembène Ousmane and earlier the poetry of Aimé Césaire, constitutes a veritable mirror in which contemporary African society is reflected. This society is described and analyzed with a merciless lucidity: its principal characters are the African elite who have taken the place of the white colonizers. Students, politicians, officials, revolutionary militants, educated women, etc.—all can see their images there, recognizing themselves and either shaking with anger or laughing secretly. It matters little. This is involved (*engagée*) literature that wishes to be both soul-searching and conscience-awakening.

Henri Lopes does not take pleasure in the role of an impartial observer, who from above the clouds contemplates with a critical eye "this hideous spectacle" (Césaire's words) of an Africa simultaneously young and old, entangled in its own contradictions, whose intellectual elite is not only its sole responsible party but also its only hope. On the condition that Africa becomes aware of its responsibilities and accepts its role fully, the author also recognizes himself as part of this intellectual elite, simultaneously as actor and accomplice of the African drama whose spectacle he unravels from his first collection of short stories, *Tribaliques*, to his recent epistolary novel, *Sans tam-tam*, and including the captivating *La Nouvelle Romance*.

Yumba wa Kioni. Zaire Afrique. 132 (1979), p. 77†

Henri Lopes is one of Congo-Brazzaville's most recognized prose writers. What has become his literary signature is a single-minded attention to—almost a preoccupation with—the ideological parameters of the problems that affect the social, economic, and political progress of contemporary African society. His short-story collection, titled *Tribaliques*, recipient, one year after its publication, of the Grand Prix Litteraire de l'Afrique Noire, includes stories such as "L'Honnête Homme," "La Fuite de la main habile," and "Monsieur le député," whose very titles imply an exposition of some of the self-acknowledged nemeses of African nations today. By effecting a tone of familial frankness Lopes engages the conscience of the members of his African family, warning, exhorting, nagging the family members to do some housecleaning.

In addition to the above-mentioned *Tribaliques*, consisting of eight short stories, published in 1971, Lopes's oeuvre includes three novels, *La Nouvelle Romance*, *Sans tam-tam*, and *Le Pleurer-rire*. Depicting commonly found situations from all strata of contemporary African life, Lopes's works evoke such subjects as the pressures of tribal differences on individuals' lives in a now highly mobile society; the questions of management of a state's industrial resources; the means and ends of popular education; or the sociology and psychology of the changing relations between men and women. In a significant portion of his work—seven out of ten total pieces—women and/or women-focused issues take a central place in the narrative. . . .

The presentation of the experience of the African woman is one of the qualities that makes Henri Lopes's work important in the literature of contemporary Africa. Factors such as the high frequency of women as narrators or focal characters, and topical content covering the broad spectrum of issues of the African woman's experience make the novels and short stories of this unfortunately little-discussed writer a literary forum for African women's consciousness. By virtue of the quantity of attention Lopes devotes to women, the urgency for integration of women's issues into the African social process is made unequivocal. Lopes's women characters articulate their own self-consciousness. Even the fact that some of them are not able to articulate their self-consciousness is a part of their statement through the author as spokesperson. This situation is, however, representative of the contradictions surrounding women's relationships with all the other agents affecting their lives.

While the context of Lopes's creative practice is the family of African people, the context within which his works is set is quite frequently specifically Congolese but with situations drawn along broader African lines. The use of the homebased setting enables Lopes to be self-critical of Africa in general, with the attention directed at his own country. The problems, issues, contradictions which Lopes points to are presented unmistakably as African, not Congolese particularly. Thus from his own ideological stance Henri Lopes presents, in his work, the issues of social change in African society. The issues of women's status have a high place on his agenda for social change in Africa.

Anne Adams Graves. In Carole Boyce Davies and Anne Adams Graves, eds.
Ngambika: Studies of Women in African Literature
(Trenton, N. J.: Africa World Press, 1986), pp. 131–32, 137–38

This novel [*La Nouvelle Romance*] is at the same time the story of a football player who accedes to diplomatic functions and, in parallel, that of the maturation and liberation of his wife.

A modest employee in a bank, Bienvenu Nkama, known especially under the nickname of Delarumba, is a notorious football virtuoso. Married, he has no children with his legitimate wife, but has gathered and brought under his conjugal roof those children that he has had with his different mistresses. At this level, in fact, Delarumba leads such a dissolute life that his profession feels its effects: one fine day, he loses his job for the third time due to his repeated latecomings. . . .

Learning the very same day of his firing that the diplomatic work pays better than any other career, and that there is a vacancy in his country's embassy in Bonn, Delarumba puts all his efforts into soliciting and obtaining this post. . . . But his behavior does not improve much; he continues to sleep out, shows himself to be capable of embezzlement, impregnates a young Belgian whom he refuses to marry, and finally is caught redhanded while trafficking drugs. For the last two reasons, Belgium declares him persona non grata and expels him from its territory. But immediately on his return to his country, the president of the republic receives him and names him cultural consular to Washington.

Parallel to the lapses of conduct of Delarumba and his capricious posts, we witness the sad and progressive maturation of Wali, his spouse. The most obvious proofs of this maturation are her decision to study and that of leaving her husband in order to continue in Paris the studies undertaken at Brussels. Oriented at first toward personal liberation, her studies become at the end of the novel the sine qua non condition of the revolution. That consists of destroying the monolithic and phallocentric society in order to replace it with another, more just, welcoming, and dynamic. It is this renewal that is suggested by the title of the novel.

Makolo Muswaswa. Zaire Afrique. 30 (1990), pp. 230–31†

Throughout his short stories and four previous novels . . . Henri Lopes has dealt extensively with the role of women in contemporary Africa. With his latest novel, *Sur l'autre rive*, he goes one step farther: his first-person narrator and protagonist *is* a woman. It is her voice which takes us back in time on a painful inner journey, constituting the central portion of the narration.

Living at present under a fictitious identity on the island of Guadeloupe, Marie-Eve has a chance meeting with a shadowy figure from the past. This encounter releases a torrent of memories of another life (recalled in an extensive flashback) that she had attempted to erase forever. Well over a decade earlier, Madeleine (the narrator's true name), a talented and apparently happily married Congolese painter, suddenly vanishes from her home in Brazzaville, leaving behind a pile of charred canvases. She is assumed, to the astonishment of her family and friends, to have drowned herself in the Congo River. She had in fact been trapped in a sexually dysfunctional relationship with her insensitive husband, and, more serious from a traditional African point of view, she is childless. Prior to her disappearance, during a short vacation in Gabon which was ironically to have been a kind of second honeymoon for the hapless couple, she inadvertently meets a Nigerian chief with whom she had a torrid affair some years before. This event impels Madeleine to relive—in what amounts to a flashback within a flashback—their passionate but ultimately ill-fated liaison. She had, on more than one occasion, yearned to be delivered from her unhappy existence, but this stirring of the embers of her one true encounter with love sweeps away any remaining vestiges of restraint.

Soon after her return from Gabon, Madeleine flees, dissolving into another identity a continent away. Her motivation for so drastic an act (she could have chosen divorce) continues to elude her to the end. Her unhappy marriage and the constant intervention of her husband's extended family in their personal affairs are certainly provocation enough for her need to escape. (Lopes reminds us here that the struggle between tradition and modernism is still often unavoidable, even in an urban African setting at the close of the twentieth century.) But, try as she may, she cannot explain why she chose a solution so desperate as to be tantamount to a kind of suicide. She can only speak vaguely of an "irresistible [inner] force" and is haunted by the question, "Was this an act of courage or cowardice?" What *is* clear is that she can never completely "drown the landscapes of her memory," and a certain melancholy pervades the existence of this fugitive from the past, ostensibly fulfilled by her art and the love of the man with whom she now shares her life.

Although the novel does not contain the daring linguistic and structural innovations of the author's remarkable *Le Pleurer-rire*, it is illuminated by moments of pure poetry and is nonetheless audacious for the challenge it raises: can a man pour himself into the psyche of a woman and speak authentically in her voice? The sensitivity with which Lopes has allowed his narrator to weave her memories and feelings into a touching tapestry of the heart leads this reviewer at least to answer in the affirmative.

Fredric Michelman. WLT. 68, 1 (Winter 1994), pp. 187–88

LORDE, AUDRE (1934–1992)

UNITED STATES

[Audre Lorde's] *The Black Unicorn*, is a big, rich book of some sixty-seven poems. . . . Perhaps a full dozen—an incredibly high percentage—of these poems are searingly strong and unforgettable. Those readers who recall the clear light and promise of early Lorde poems such as "The Woman Thing" and "Bloodbirth," and recall as well the great shape and energy of certain mid-1970s poems including "To My Daughter The Junkie On A Train," "Cables to Rage," and "Blackstudies," will find in *The Black Unicorn* new poems which reconfirm Lorde's talents while reseeding gardens and fields traversed before. There are other poems which do not so much reseed as repeople, and these new persons, names, ghosts, lovers, voices—these new I's, we's, real and imagined kin—give us something fresh, beyond the cycle of Lorde's previously recorded seasons and solstices.

While *The Black Unicorn* is unquestionably a personal triumph for Lorde in terms of the development of her canon, it is also an event in contemporary letters. This is a bold claim but one worth making precisely because as we see in the first nine poems, Lorde appears to be the only North American poet other than Jay Wright who is sufficiently immersed in West African religion, culture, and art (and blessed with poetic talent!) to reach beyond a kind of middling poem that merely quantifies "blackness" through offhand reference to African gods and traditions. What Lorde and Wright share, beyond their abilities to create a fresh, New World art out of ancient Old World lore, is a voice or an *idea* of a voice that is essentially African in that it is communal, historiographical, archival, and prophetic *as well as* personal in ways that we commonly associate with the African griots, *dyeli*, and tellers of *nganos* and other oral tales. However, while Wright's voice may be said to embody what is masculine in various West African cultures and cosmologies, Lorde's voice is decidedly and magnificently feminine. The goal of *The Black Unicorn* is then to present this fresh and powerful voice, and to explore the modulations within that voice between feminine and feminist timbres. As the volume unfolds, this exploration charts history and geography as well as voice, and with the confluence of these patterns the volume takes shape and Lorde's particular envisioning of a black transatlantic tradition is accessible.

[Robert] B. Stepto. Parnassus. (Fall/Winter 1979), pp. 315–16

For Lorde, as for many women of color, [the] celebration and assertion of female identity has been a key survival technique, a way of combatting a subtle but potent enemy: silence. As Lorde tells us in *Zami [A New Spelling of My Name]*, she did not speak until she was five years old, and when she finally found a voice, she talked in poetry—first by reciting verses she had memorized, then "when I couldn't find the poems to express the things I was feeling, that's when I started writing poetry." To Lorde, poetry represents a refusal of "dishonesty by silence"; her foremost goal as a black woman poet then becomes "the transformation of silence into language and action"—a transformation essential if women are to overcome what Adrienne Rich has called "the terrible negative power of the lie" among them. Silence is a destructive quality, Lorde asserts, because "it's the nameless. As Adrienne has said, 'what remains nameless eventually becomes unspeakable, what remains unspoken becomes unspeakable.'" To speak the unspeakable is thus a key task for Lorde as for Rich, to revision herself and other women. . . .

Another primary aspect of the "poet warrior's" task is paying tribute to the women from whom she gleans her power, "re-creating in words the women who helped give me substance." In Lorde's writing of the last twenty-five years, we find four main sources of creative inspiration, all female. First, she celebrates as muses the women who make up her own family: her mother, her mother's West Indian female relatives, and her sisters, literal or figurative. Second, she pays homage to the women lovers who have "helped sustain" her, and to her own erotic power, which she considers a vital creative force. Third, she seeks sustenance from African goddesses, mythological women whose names and legends survive in black cultures as tributes to a strong matriarchal legacy: Yemanja, Mawulisa, Seboulisa, the "Women of Dan," her African warrior sisters. Finally, Lorde names as muses and acts as a mouthpiece for those women who have been victims of a racist, sexist, homophobic society—her "sisters in pain." Many such women have been violated, murdered, silenced, yet it is for and by them that the poet-warrior is empowered to speak. If women, black or white, are to survive, Lorde insists in "Meet," they must bring to bear on behalf of one another their passionate convictions, their powerful eroticism, their terrible anguish, their fluid and mutual identities.

Mary K. DeShazer. *Inspiring Women: Reimagining the Muse*
(New York: Pergamon, 1986), pp. 170–71, 173

Lorde began her published work in 1968 . . . with *The First Cities*. When she arrived via five volumes of verse and a growing reputation at *Between Our Selves* and *The Black Unicorn*, she had gone from merely writing poetry to casting wise and incantatory magic. . . . *The Black Unicorn* is a majestic voicing of statements and propositions whose applications are further worked out in her later book, *Our Dead Behind Us*. Much of the struggle of defining and instating herself was done in the earlier volume, so that now she can simply put herself in motion, acting and being who she is. And because we know—and she knows that we know—where she is coming from, there is no need for her to repeat herself. At this hard-earned point, we can read Audre Lorde in her own light. . . .

Lorde's seemingly essentialist definitions of herself as black/lesbian/ mother/woman are not simple, fixed terms. Rather, they represent her ceaseless negotiations of a positionality from which she can speak. Almost as soon as she achieves a place of connection, she becomes uneasy at the comfortableness (which is, to her, a signal that something critical is being glossed over) and proceeds to rub athwart the smooth grain to find the roughness and the slant she needs to maintain her difference-defined, complexly constructed self. *Our Dead Behind Us* is constant motion, with poem after poem enacting a series of displacements. The geographical shifts are paralleled by temporal shifting in a "time-tension" which Mary J. Carruthers sees as characteristic of lesbian poetry. . . . The ubiquitous leave takings [in the poems] are not surprising—"Out to the Hard Road" ("I never told you how much it hurt / leaving"), "Every Traveler Has One Vermont Poem" ("Spikes of lavender aster under Route 91 / . . . I am a stranger / making a living choice"), "Diaspora" ("grenades held dry in a calabash / leaving"). . . .

Lorde's tricky positionality—as exemplified by her relationship to home and poetic lines—also extends to community, which she likewise desires, but problematizes and finds problematic. An early poem, "And What about the Children," alludes to the "dire predictions" and "grim speculations" that accompanied her interracial marriage and mixed-race offspring. . . .

However uneasy her identity may be, it is imperative for Lorde that she read the world as a meaningful text and not as a series of interesting and elusive propositions. For her, to "read" is to decipher . . . the signs of the times, to decode—as the lesbian/gay community does—the submerged signification of the visible signs, and to sound out clearly and "to your face" uncompromising truth as she sees it, in that foot-up, hands-on-hip loudness that is self-authorized black female jeremiad, sermon, and song. From the beginning, her vatic voice has defined her moral and didactic arena—in the same way that her presence claims its territory on the stage or in a photographic frame. She and Adrienne Rich, especially, have been criticized for their heavy seriousness. However, with so many dead behind her, Lorde is too busy pulling the bodies from bars and doorways, jungle tracks and trenches to find time for unrestricted poetic laughter. Her task is to foreground the carnage in a valiant effort to make such senseless dying truly a thing of the past.

[Akasha] Gloria T. Hull. In Cheryl A. Wall, ed. *Changing Our Own Words* (New Brunswick, N. J.: Rutgers University Press, 1989), pp. 153–56, 159–62

Audre Lorde's *Zami* . . . explores the struggle to define a self amid the overwhelming Caribbean culture of the household. The conventions of autobiography allow for the centering of a self caught in the conflicts of a Caribbean/ American household which eschews any thought of private individual space: "a closed door is considered an insult." Nevertheless, there is an engagement with Caribbean folk culture through the recalling of folk healing, songmaking, the notion of "home." Above all, she is able to make an explicit connection between her lesbianism and the fact that Carriacou women have a tradition of "work[ing] together as friends and lovers." By accepting "Zami," a word still identified negatively in the

Caribbean, she is like Michelle Cliff, "claiming an identity" she was taught to despise. The definition of "Zami" is a bold epigraph to the work. And the tension in accepting identity seems to be finally resolved here. Her essay "Grenada Revisited," for example, is one of the best evaluations of the Grenada invasion and, as I see it, a fitting conclusion to *Zami*. Buttressed by concrete images of Grenada, pre- and postrevolution, she concludes with a tribute to the strength and resilience of the Grenadian people. . . .

The heritage/identity question is definitely established in the Grenada essay as is the woman-identification in the acceptance of the term "Zami." But Lorde's expressed connectedness has its impetus from revolutionary Grenada and the sense of possibility which it held. Clearly then, for Lorde, cultural iden-tification has to be addressed along with an overtly, antihegemonic discourse. She therefore moves the discussion, beyond a singular Pan-African identifica-tion to a fuller acceptance of a gender-identified relationship with history and an ideological consciousness of the meaning of Grenada's thwarted revolution within the context of power, powerlessness, and empowerment.

> Carole Boyce Davies. In Carole Boyce Davies and Elaine Savory Fido, eds.
> *Out of the Kumbla: Caribbean Women and Literature*
> (Trenton, N. J.: Africa World Press, 1990), pp. 62–63

Zami is a Carriacou word "for women who work together as friends and lovers." Just as the title implies, *Zami* is woman-identified from the outset and thor-oughly suffused with an eroticism focusing on women. Lorde connects her les-bianism to the model her mother, Linda, provided—her pervasive, often intimidating, strength; her fleeting sensuality when her harsh veneer was lifted— and also to her place of origin, the Grenadian island of Carriacou, where a word already existed to describe who Linda's daughter would become. . . . [In] *Zami* relationships between women are at the center of the work. Here they are com-plex, turbulent, painful, passionate, and essential to the author's survival.

Although Lorde continuously explores the implications of being a black lesbian and she has an overt consciousness about her lesbianism . . . she does not define lesbianism as a problem in and of itself. Despite homophobia, particu-larly in the left of the McCarthy era; despite isolation from other black women because she is gay; and despite primal loneliness because of her many levels of difference, Lorde assumes that her lesbianism, like her blackness, is a given, a fact of life which she has neither to justify nor explain. This is an extremely strong and open-ended stance from which to write about black lesbian experi-ence, since it enables the writer to deal with the complexity of lesbianism and what being a black lesbian means in a specific time and place. Lorde's position allows black lesbian experience to be revealed from the inside out. The absence of agonized doubts about her sexual orientation and the revelation of the actual joys of being a lesbian, including lush and recognizable descriptions of physical passion between women, make *Zami* seem consciously written for a lesbian reader. This is a significant point because so little is ever written with us in mind, and also because who an author considers her audience to be definitely affects her voice and the levels of authenticity she may be able to achieve. Writing from an avowedly black lesbian perspective with black lesbian readers in mind does not mean that a work will be inaccessible or inapplicable to non-black and nonlesbian readers. Works like *Zami*, which are based in the experiences of writers outside the "mainstream," provide a vitally different perspective on human experience and may even reveal new ways of thinking about supposedly settled questions.

> Barbara Smith. In Joanne M. Braxton and Andrée Nicola McLaughlin, eds. *Wild Women in the Whirlwind: Afra-American Culture and the Contemporary Literary Renaissance* (New Brunswick, N. J.: Rutgers University Press, 1990), pp. 238–39

The struggle to claim her racial, sexual, feminist, and warrior identities forms the core of Audre Lorde's poetics and politics. . . .

Many of Lorde's early poems contain images of women as warriors: "warrior queens" ("Harriet"); "like a warrior woman" ("Chorus"); "like my warrior sisters" ("125th Street and Abomey"); "Assata my sister warrior" ("For Assata"). At times the epithet *warrior* becomes an emblem of hope for future generations: "I bless your child with the mother she has / with a future of warriors and growing fire" ("Dear Toni Instead of a Letter"). For Lorde, the term *warrior* evokes centuries of history of African women's resistance to white authorities and other forces of suppression. Foremost among such warrior women were the legendary Amazons of Dahomey, about whom Lorde writes in "The Women of Dan." Here she enacts a strong revisionist impulse, for she insists that women's warring be not stealthy but open, visible. . . .

Dangerous to others but not to herself, the poet names her new weapons, erotic heat and poetic words, a combination vital for continued growth and vision. . . . Like Mawulisa, a peace-loving Dahomean goddess about whom she often writes, Lorde resists war as a deceptive, vindictive enterprise. She refuses to be silenced or to destroy unnecessarily. Instead, she openly warns contemporary oppressors of her watchful presence and embraces her warrior identity through a passionate, ritualistic celebration with her sisters of Dan. . . .

"Sisters in Arms" illustrates the complexity of Lorde's most recent use of the warrior construct; in fact, it interweaves related images of the poet-warrior, the war correspondent, and the warrior muse. Sexuality and political struggle intersect, as Lorde describes sharing her bed and her arms (in both senses of the word) with a South African woman who learns that her fifteen-year-old daughter has just been brutally murdered near Durban, her body "hanging / gut-sprung on police wheels." The poet feels agony and helplessness. . . . So Lorde does what she can—buys her lover a ticket to Durban (ironically, on her American Express card) and comforts her physically before her departure.

Written retrospectively, the poem reveals Lorde's fury at both the South African government's continuing atrocities against its black people and the *New York Times*'s scant coverage of what it euphemistically deems the "unrest" there. As a war correspondent, she reports graphically the horrors the *Times* chooses to hide: "Black children massacred at Sebokeng, / six-year olds imprisoned for threatening the state . . . / Thabo Sibeko, first grader, in his own blood / on his grandmother's parlor floor." The newspaper's evasions and these terrible truths haunt Lorde as she gardens haphazardly and recalls moments of intimacy and pain with her South African sisters. . . . Lorde knows that the sisters who lay in one another's arms may also bear arms together one day, stronger for having shared erotic experience: "someday you will come to my country / and we will fight side by side?" Since she cannot go to South Africa, Lorde invokes in her stead the African warrior queen Mmanthatisi, who led the Sotho people during the *mfecane*, an earlier black South African uprising. As this warrior muse "dresses again for battle, / knowing the men will follow," the poet chronicles her preparations, dreaming of Durban and the possibility of revolutionary change.

Mary K. DeShazer. In Suzanne W. Jones, ed. Writing the Woman Artist:
Essays on Poetics, Politics, and Portraiture (Philadelphia:
University of Pennsylvania Press, 1991), pp. 266–68

In her essays collected in *Sister Outsider*, Audre Lorde performs a complex act of cultural revisioning wherein she reappropriates the ground of creativity for women of all kinds. She does so by envisioning a figure of "the black mother who is the poet . . . in every one of us," and linking her with an "erotic" lifeforce that she finds necessary to creative work. The figure revises well-known Greek myths that represent the erotic either in terms of the male god Eros, whose passions are sexual, or Aphrodite whose activities are seductive. It also revises the Jungian tendency to associate women with Eros, understood as psychological relatedness in opposition to Logos, the principle of abstract thought supposedly embodied by men. Neither exclusively physical in orientation nor wholly concerned with relationship, Lorde's female figure of the erotic potential that lies within both women and men is a deep-seated capacity for joy and excellence that she hopes women will realize in order to effect social change. . . .

Lorde's figure of an erotic wellspring provides the basis for belief in female authority because it removes the necessity for certification of one's ideas by the dominant group. The creative impetus is in all of us in our capacity for feeling. Lorde speaks of creative process as a matter of tapping or honoring the "deep place" from which perception comes; rationality, she says, serves feeling and knowledge by building roads from one place to another, but "Perceptions precede analysis just as visions precede action or accomplishments." The figure of the black mother within allows us to stop questioning our perceptions before they have a chance to become poems.

Lorde's figure of the black mother poet, then, symbolizes the belief in one's own authority to create, and her association of it with the erotic, with Eros in female form, is a potentially useful strategy for rethinking women's relationship with love, a concept that has often worked in Western culture to prevent women from realizing creative as opposed to procreative potential. Lorde's figure addresses the root problem of women's motivation for creative activity. If a woman believes that the source of creativity lies within her, perhaps she can more readily marshal her resources to combat the external conditions of her life.

With the help of figures such as Lorde's . . . figures that refuse to freeze and ration creative energies—perhaps women can not only survive as artists but also re-envision survival itself as a matter of reclaiming what has been repressed and nourishing the capacity to change.

> Estella Lauter. In Suzanne W. Jones, ed. *Writing the Woman Artist:*
> *Essays on Poetics, Politics, and Portraiture* (Philadelphia:
> University of Pennsylvania Press, 1991), pp. 398, 415–16

Audre Lorde terms *Zami: A New Spelling of My Name* a "biomythography," a combination of autobiography, history, and myth. I have chosen to discuss it here because it is the one extended prose work of which I am aware that approaches black lesbian experience with *both* verisimilitude and authenticity. *Zami* is an essentially autobiographical work, but the poet's eye, ear, and tongue give the work stylistic richness often associated with well-crafted fiction. . . . Because *Zami* spans genres and carves out a unique place in African-American literature as the first full-length autobiographical work by an established black lesbian writer, it will undoubtedly continue to be grouped with other creative prose about black lesbians.

The fact that *Zami* is autobiographical might be assumed to guarantee its realism. But even when writing autobiographically, an author can pick and choose details, can create a persona which has little or nothing to do with her own particular reality, or she might fabricate an artificial persona with whom the reader cannot possibly identify. A blatant example of this kind of deceptive strategy might be an autobiographical work by a lesbian which fails to mention that this is indeed who she is; of course, there are other, less extreme omissions and distortions. Undoubtedly, Lorde selected the material she included in the work, and the selectivity of memory is also operative. Yet the work is honest, fully rounded, and authentic. . . . The candor and specificity with which Lorde approaches her life are qualities that would enhance black lesbian writing in the future.

> Barbara Smith. In Chandra Talpade Mohanty, Ann Russo, and Lourdes
> Torres, eds. *Third World Women and the Politics of Feminism*
> (Bloomington: Indiana University Press, 1991), p. 122

For feminist academia Lorde is particularly effective as a token: since she is black, lesbian, and a mother, her work compactly represents that generally repressed matter towards which white feminists wish to make a gesture of inclusion—but since Lorde conveniently represents so much at once, she can be included without her presence threatening the overall balance of the white majority vision. As a token of particular identities, moreover, Lorde is included as one who speaks for the marginal, not for the mainstream. Paradoxically, in other words, Lorde occupies diametrically opposed positions in two literatures: in one her words are consumed for the light they can shed on the mainstream of black female possibility; in the other her work stands alongside, but is not read as directly bearing upon the mainstream, white feminist consciousness. It is my project here to challenge both these ways of reading Lorde, to suggest that *Zami* produces a way of seeing that has significance as a commentary on how the black community as a whole both lives and theorizes itself, and that Lorde's textual practice also has the power to address not merely the problems of identity politics but also the issues of lesbian aesthetics. . . .

Lorde's biomythography *Zami* initially constructs a lesbian existence that has needs and features in common with the lesbian myth produced by white Anglo-American novelists. Her sexual coming out is described within a series of metaphors for recognition familiar from that tradition: making love is "like coming home to a joy I was meant for"; the act of lesbian sex is naturalized through being presented as a return to an original knowledge that the protagonist has temporarily forgotten: "wherever I touched, felt right and completing, as if I had been born to make love to this woman, and was remembering her body rather than learning it deeply for the first time." This is a country of the body rather than of a people. Audre's community as a young lesbian in New York is defined by sexuality, and it is a community that attempts the utopian separation and newness of a lesbian nation: "We were re-inventing the world together"; "we had no patterns to follow, except our own needs and our own unthought-out dreams." Yet membership in such a community is purchased at the price of nonrecognition of blackness; Lorde repeatedly describes Audre's "invisibility" to the white lesbian community as black; she is admitted only under the assumption of sameness. The lesbian community believes in itself as obliterating difference, "that as lesbians, we were all outsiders and all equal in our outsiderhood. 'We're all niggers,' [Muriel, Audre's white lover] used to say." Yet in Lorde's analysis the lesbian community is not elsewhere but is rather a microcosm of the world outside, as her description of the lesbian bar the Bagatelle shows. . . . In the white model, the real world recedes before the lesbian community's power to redefine: one reclothed oneself in a new identity and a new way of relating. It is one of Orlando's freedoms in Virginia Woolf's imaginary biography that s/he is able effortlessly to switch between costumes; her sexual fluidity is signaled by this flexibility, and in the same moment it indicates a crucial aspiration: the capacity both to switch between costumes and to cross-dress stands for freedom from gender imprisonment. George Sand said of her experience of cross-dressing, "My clothes knew no fear." But for Audre a rigidly stratified dress code, each item signifying a particular class or role position, expresses not freedom of play but her imprisonment within a system of hierarchized differences. The "uncharted territory" that she finds in trying to discover new ways of relating in "a new world of women" is not just uncharted but inaccessible: there is no pathway for the black lesbian that leads from the actual lesbian community, where class distinctions are precisely observed and race is unmentionable, to lesbian nation. It is from this experience that Lorde constructs the "house of difference" that she finally articulates as "our place"; it is a refusal of the aspiration to unity that lesbian nation encodes. The "house of difference," then, is a movement away from otherworldliness. It accepts the inevitability of a material world where class, race, gender all continue to exist. It is, therefore, a step back towards acknowledging the necessity of reasserting ties of identity with the black community. . . .

Lorde's challenge to current aesthetic inquiry lies in her assertion of an abiding connection between individual and social identity. This is how she is able to maintain a connection between political subversion and textual subversion, a link that in contemporary discussions of a lesbian aesthetic seems to have become an abyss. Unlike that of the postmodern lesbian subject, Audre's identity is never established only by the transgressions of the bedroom: it is from the bedroom that Audre and Kitty emerge, and it is from this "lesbian narrative space" that Audre goes out to refigure the black family of Harlem as including her; but the reconstruction that happens in the street is as crucial as that conducted in the mythic bed.

Anna Wilson. In Sally Munt, ed. *New Lesbian Criticism: Literary and Cultural Readings* (New York: Columbia University Press, 1992), pp. 77–78, 81–82, 89–90

[The] title poem [of *The Black Unicorn*] uses its controlling trope to construct a poetics of identity; the black essence of coal is deployed in a new guise in the feminized figure of the black unicorn. . . . As an allegory for Lorde and for the black woman poet, the unicorn is at once angry and erotic, regendered and recolored, reaching the site of deepest female power. Insofar as the political agendas in the poem generate spaces for identities made doubly absent in dominant cultural and literary discourse, they also reflect the dangers of their re-empowerment. *The Black Unicorn*, although reclaiming an alternative mythos for black women poets, is cognizant of the problems attending its mythmaking. . . .

Even as *The Black Unicorn* examines the complexities of political agency in poetry, the history of Lorde's publications maps the socioeconomic boundaries of literary institutionalization. As her volume of poetry wrestles in the interstices between speaking local resistance and grand narratives for change, Audre Lorde's identity as poet enacts its histories between literary academia and grassroots audiences. Her various speeches and essays became available in the late 1970s and through the 1980s mainly through small press broadsides and alternative journals for an otherwise marginalized readership. Dominant literary discourse perpetuates and legitimates the absences. Lorde's poems appear in none of the better known feminist anthologies, edited, as Jan Clausen points out, for a feminist but also primarily heterosexist and white community of readers. . . .

The hierarchy operating among presses publishing Lorde's work and the chronology of early and late publications significantly charts the "growth" of [an] unknown poet to a name increasingly better known. Although her poetry is still noticeably "unread" within English departments, Lorde has become a feminist and lesbian name to be cited as her activist prose engages women's studies and African American studies programs. The presses publishing her poetry bear ironic witness to her double status in literary and mainstream feminist discourse. Her first two volumes of poetry, *The First Cities* and *Cables to Rage*, were published by Diane di Prima's Poets' Press and Paul Breman, small presses catering to the needs of relatively unknown writers. As the black community took up her work, her publishers changed. The Broadside Press in Detroit, a small press oriented to a black readership, published her next two volumes, *From a Land Where Other People*

Live—nominated for a National Book Award for Poetry—and *New York Headshop and Museum*. As her name came to be recognized in select literary and activist audiences, Eidolon Editions published *Between Our Selves* in a special edition of eleven hundred copies. This pattern of small presses, however, changed as Norton published Lorde's next three volumes of poetry, *Coal, The Black Unicorn*, and *Our Dead Behind Us*, as well as a volume of her selected poems, *Chosen Poems, Old and New*. Norton, of course, is the same press that underwrites the literary canon in the United States with its Norton editions and anthologies, basic texts for students in English literature. Publication of her poetry by Norton indicates that Lorde is now available in academic bookstores. Lorde's work is not usually found in the poetry sections, but is probably available in black studies or women's studies sections—another ironic gloss on Lorde's literary status as activist writer.

Sagri Dhairyam. FemSt. 18, 2 (Summer 1992), pp. 237, 239–40

LOVELACE, EARL (1935–   )

TRINIDAD

[In *The Schoolmaster* Earl Lovelace] catches so surely the essence and color of the region in northeast Trinidad where the real Kumaca and Valencia are to be found, and renders us so susceptible to his fictional landscape (and, incidentally to its source—a visit seems a logical extension of the literary experience), that we might think nothing is wrong with Kumaca. The fictional village, however, has its human derelicts: the old man Miguel Paponette living on memories of those days only he can remember when he owned the king of all gamecocks; Francis Assivero who has lost his lands and his standing, now works as a cocoa picker on another man's estate, and, according to his son "dies daily inside himself, because Mama is looking at him and does not complain, and because he knows the man he was, and remembers, and goes again and again to the shop of Dardain." Then there is the boy Robert languishing in a dark hut with the poliomyelitis there is no one to diagnose or relieve, for Kumaca has no doctor and the track that leads to the nearest medical attention is sure to be too uncomfortable for the patient to be carried out. Finally, there is Ignacio Dardain, the economic serpent in the village, slowly undermining the old ways while exploiting them.

Kenneth Ramchand. Introduction to Earl Lovelace.
The Schoolmaster (London: Heinemann, 1979), pp. vi–vii

In Lovelace's *The Schoolmaster*, Pauline Dandrade makes this pithy remark: "Kumaca not even in the world." The smallness of Lovelace's Kumaca matches the impotent smallness of the West Indies, and Pauline's remark, we may say, is a metaphor for the West Indian's search for identity and a significant place in the world. Of course the search for these things has always been important to all human beings; but given the nature of the West Indian past, this search has been a matter of chronic anxiety for the people living in the tiny, impoverished islands. This search is at the heart of *The Schoolmaster*. It is also the central theme of Lovelace's *While Gods Are Falling*, his first novel, and *The Dragon Can't Dance*, his latest work. Walter Castle, hero of the first novel, faces a daily struggle to extricate himself from the squalor and crime of a Port-of-Spain slum where "life has no significance beyond the primary struggles for a bed to sleep in, something to quiet the intestines, and moments of sexual gratification." One thinks of Calvary Hill, the dunghill setting of *The Dragon Can't Dance*. Here the pervasive nihilism can only be alleviated by the sensual excesses of Carnival, furtive sex and occasional violence. To a man, the residents of Calvary Hill are desperately searching for "the tune that will sing their person and their pose, that will soar over the hill, ring over the valley of shacks, and laugh the hard tears of their living." . . .

The need for selfhood is given special emphasis in *The Schoolmaster*. Benn's confrontation with Captain Grant, his rich, white employer, underscores this need rather effectively. Benn's wizened foal, which he buys from Grant and then nurses to vibrant health, [is] an emblem of his self-worth. Grant knows this, and he blackmails Benn: he can sell the animal back to the Captain or lose his job. Benn can defy Grant and lose his job, or he can grovel "like a little field nigger." Instead, he gives Grant the beautiful animal ("just like am a white man myself"), against the Captain's vigorous protests. It is too much for the utterly abashed Grant. The next day he shoots the animal, symbolically, of course, killing Benn. Like Francis Assivero, another villager, Benn is trapped by the severity of the . . . existential situation. His donkeys are Father Vincent's only transportation between Zanilla and Kumaca, and this gives him a temporary importance. Once the road is built, however, this fragile importance will end, and he will have to scratch out a living planting and selling yams. From time to time this brings him close to despair; but his spirit, like Walter's, cannot be cowed. Benn's determination to be somebody in the face of humiliation and degrading poverty ennobles him. [In *The Dragon Can't Dance*] Aldrick, too, does not give in. After serving stiff jail terms for their abortive rebellion against poverty and the nothingness of their existence, the rebels, Aldrick excepted, return to Calvary Hill thoroughly chastened. For them Calvary Hill has become "the Hill of accommodation." Not so for the recalcitrant Aldrick whose brooding rebelliousness is too implacable to be quelled by forces who "want us to surrender because we can't win." Lovelace rather ironically sets Aldrick's unappeased restlessness against Philo's final, tawdry victory—the bedding of Cleothilda, sometime beauty queen, but now a dried-up, old prune.

Harold Barratt. ACLALSB. 5, 3 (December 1980), pp. 63, 66

In his fourth published novel, *The Wine of Astonishment*, Earl Lovelace charts the history of a Spiritual Baptist community from the passing of the Prohibition Ordinance in 1917 until the lifting of the ban in 1951. The choice of subject matter reflects Lovelace's continuing awareness of the vital role of the artist in the decolonization process. Beginning with the publication of his first novel, *While Gods Are Falling* in 1965, one can discern in Lovelace's fiction an ongoing commitment to "the task of re-education and regeneration" which, Chinua Achebe has suggested, is one of the first duties of the writer in a postcolonial society. It is a commitment that has consistently influenced the direction of Lovelace's creative energy, encouraging him to explore in his works those experiences which have shaped the social and psychological development of the black West Indian community. . . . As a syncretistic religion, born out of Africa's encounter with Europe in the New World, Lovelace sees in the Spiritual Baptist system of faith and worship, in their "Africanization of Christianity," a living example of the creative and regenerative impulses inherent in the black Creole cultural tradition. The conflict between the Bonasse Spiritual Baptists and the established authorities is therefore conceived as only one other episode in the centuries-old struggle between Prospero and Caliban; and it is this which accounts for the symbolic significance of the church in the world of the novel. In tracing the history of this particular community, Lovelace is reflecting on the more general experience of the black man in the Caribbean. The novel therefore returns us to the now familiar black West Indian world of deprivation and oppression, but with the important distinction that, here, the image of the black West Indian as courageous victim is superseded by the image of the black West Indian as authentic hero-figure.

In *The Wine of Astonishment* Lovelace moves away from the third-person narration of his earlier novels, electing instead to relate the events from the point of view of a middle-aged peasant woman who is, herself, a member of the Baptist church. The change has certain obvious advantages. Lovelace's Eva is cast in the tradition of those clear-thinking, resolute, and spiritually resilient mother-figures who have always peopled the world of Caribbean fiction. Thus, although her sympathetic "inside" view of the Shouter Movement conflicts sharply with the recorded perceptions of the wider society, the associations which she provokes dispose the reader to prefer her authority to that of the establishment's colonial regime. And this authority is further enhanced by Lovelace's linguistic skill which, from the outset, encourages the reader to believe that he is in fact listening to the artless, unstructured narrative of a simple peasant woman.

Marjorie Thorpe. Introduction to Earl Lovelace. The Wine of
Astonishment (London: Heinemann, 1982), pp. viii–ix

The search for a hero-figure constitutes the basis of Earl Lovelace's four published novels. At a time when major writers throughout the Western world appear to be convinced that the age of heroes has long passed, this may seem a somewhat romantic undertaking; and particularly so in the West Indies where, some have argued, there has never been an age of heroes. "What have we to celebrate?" is the question that has been asked. To urge our capacity for survival and endurance does not always seem enough. Our literature is full of those who have suffered and endured. But what of the man who attempts to move beyond endurance? the man who stands up against his fate and battles it, and whose defeat only serves to counterpoint that greatness of spirit, that dignity and wholesomeness which we associate with the hero-figure? The need to explore the experience of such a man carries Lovelace from crowded city slums to remote country districts, takes him as far back as the prewar years and ultimately brings him into contact with every aspect of Trinidad society. More important, however, it leads him to re-examine the values which form the foundation of his Creole world, and to attempt in his novels a definition of heroism within the context of the modern West Indian society.

An important aspect of these novels is the distinction which is made between those false heroes whom the society esteems, and the true hero-figures whom the novelist seeks to celebrate. Lovelace's false heroes all enjoy some measure of authority within their particular communities, although the sources of this authority are varied. It may be based on a character's economic success, or it may be a consequence of his superior social status; it may be associated with political eminence, or it may even be the authority of force. But whatever its foundation, two features always emerge: first, that authority carries with it no moral responsibility; and secondly, that it is authority which finds its most usual expression in vulgar display and egocentric action.

Marjorie Thorpe. In Erika Sollish Smilowitz and Roberta Quarles
Knowles, eds. *Critical Issues in West Indian Literature*
(Parkersburg, Iowa: Caribbean Books, 1984), pp. 90–91

Earl Lovelace is as engaging a polemical ironist in his novels . . . as he is in his new and very impressive collection of three plays. Apart from noting Lovelace's accuracy for confronting social-political inequities and inconsistencies with durable irony and Selvonian satire, I must mention the playwright's extraordinary lyrical gift, his splendid rendering of Trinidadian demotic speech, and his well-honed crafting of nicely differentiated dialogue passages.

Jestina's Calypso [in *Jestina's Calypso, and Other Plays*] is the story of an affectionate deception, in which Jestina uses the photograph of her beautiful hairdresser friend Laura to impress a pen pal in the United States. A deeply acrimonious comedy, its central meaning moves easily from personal pathos to metaphorical neocolonial suggestion.

The New Hardware Store is the portrait of a petit-bourgeois "realist," who is tyrannical with his staff and whose black conservative credo can be summed up in his own words: "This is just an island. We only part of some thing that they directing from another region. You could change that?" The political *picong* barbs against the store owner are the most deadly in the volume, and in all three plays picong abounds.

My Name Is Village is a musical based on a lighthearted didactic narrative. An aging carnival stickman and his son are surrounded by a welter of contradictions: the drama derived from their differing generational points of view; the tug of their village and the pull of the city; recognition versus anonymity; style and fancy up against mediocrity and dullness.

Andrew Salkey. *WLT.* 59, 3 (Summer 1985), p. 480

The main preoccupation in Earl Lovelace's fiction is liberation: he thinks that it is dangerous to move ahead without a proper understanding of its true meaning.

Liberation is not merely winning political independence or discarding the yoke of imperialism; it involves true transformation. Decolonization of the mind is a preliminary step towards liberation. As Frantz Fanon says, "decolonization cannot be successful without any period of transition. It is a nonviolent phenomenon." Lovelace thinks that reclamation of the self is an important step in achieving liberation that needs to be qualified by vision, and that vision is something that does not burst out from a vacuum but needs to be informed by contemporary awareness. He is also of the opinion that the greatest responsibility of the people is in electing good leaders, and that they should see that power is not concentrated in the hands of a few. Therefore, he says, the greatest task of the artist lies in educating the masses—not only at the political level but also at the social and cultural levels. The artist believes that the people should first be made to feel proud of themselves and be made to realize, to discover, their mission on earth. These are the principal concerns of Earl Lovelace, and they are to be discerned most clearly in *The Schoolmaster*, *The Wine of Astonishment*, and *The Dragon Can't Dance*. . . .

A powerful and moving novel like *The Wine of Astonishment* also raises philosophical questions about the meaning of life. It chronicles the different ways in which the members of a small community adhere to their identity as they find themselves caught up in the corrupt machinery of political life. Bee, a major character, is disappointed after meeting Ivan Morton, who is elected to the village council by a small congregation of Baptists in the Trinidad village of Bonasse to fight for their cause. But they soon realize their mistake, for Ivan is seen to follow the same route as the authorities. The changed Ivan admonishes Bee not to worship the spirit; he associates spiritual religion with primitive backwardness and barbarism. Bee, after the embarrassing confrontation with Ivan, decides not to send his elder son to high school because the school promotes colonial values. The narrator of the book does not share Bee's disappointment, for he is clearly more optimistic; he persuades Bee to have patience with the world and not to quarrel with it: "The world is not a market place where you quarrel over the price you have to pay. God fix the price already, and if we could pay ours, we have to be thankful. Things have meaning."

The last sentence of this statement, "Things have meaning," seems to be the thesis of the novel, besides illuminating the importance of the need to reconcile and compromise with the world.

Lovelace's persistent preoccupation with the discovery of the meaning of life is continued in his brilliant novel *The Dragon Can't Dance*. Carnival, the novel's theme and organizing principle, is a grand occasion for communal fantasy. The poverty of men and women alike is gloriously overcome for two days in the year when Carnival gives them identity and stature. But such an identity, according to Lovelace, is a dubious one, and the author engages himself in the task of articulating the values that his society should uphold. Aldrick, an important character in the novel, in the process of growth and self-education sees clearly the conflict between his role as the dragon in the Carnival and his essential manhood. He discovers that "He had been cheating himself of the pain, of love, of his living" and that two days of dancing as the dragon is but a poor substitute. In a gradual process of growth he outgrows the pleasure, joy, and zeal of participating in Carnival.

K. T. Sunitha. In A. L. McLeod, ed. *Subjects Worthy Fame*
(New Delhi: Sterling Publishers, 1989), pp. 124–25

Earl Lovelace's works begin with the Trinidadian folk . . . but considered outside of their setting, they reflect the drama of any people emerging from colonialism and facing the subtler temptations of international enterprise that seeks to recolonize them. But having said that, one must still affirm that Lovelace's characters are rooted in a landscape to which they have a spiritual and linguistic affinity. So complete is the synthesis that one is tempted to refer to it as pantheistic. . . .

All four of Lovelace's novels deal explicitly or implicitly with the community's role in conferring dignity on the individual. The reader is invited to think of community as a mirror in which the individual sees his/her values and beliefs reflected and as ramparts within which the individual feels secure. In all four novels, Lovelace presents us with threatened communities and agglomerations of people adrift, frantically in search of salvation, but he explores this theme most profoundly in *The Wine of Astonishment*. Here the forces, both colonial and indigenous, that conspire to destroy the community are pictured as they shave away with each onslaught a little more of the communal resolve. . . .

Lovelace's other novels (and even his plays) treat this theme in various ways. In *The Schoolmaster*, Dardain calmly introduces the capitalist values and quietly robs the villagers of their land. When the schoolmaster, Mr. Warrick, arrives, he adds to the rapine. Before the community gets around to killing Mr. Warrick he has already done irreparable damage to its most sacred values, has already destroyed its pristine way of life.

While Gods Are Falling and *The Dragon Can't Dance* present us with the victims of progress totally alienated from one another in a world where wealth is accorded primacy. In the first of these novels . . . we witness the characters in a community setting where wealth has no other value than to foster drinking and gambling rituals. According to Lovelace, such characters do not value money because they do not have it. But we also meet them in the slums of Port-of-Spain deeply suspicious of one another, long after the forces of progress had caused them to be uprooted from their rural traditional communities. The novel concludes with the vision that community is possible among the uprooted. In *The Dragon Can't Dance*, Lovelace returns to the theme of community among urban dwellers. This time he reveals in great detail the origins of the principal characters and shows that their deepest longing is for a community to which they can contribute and in which they can feel comfortable. As Angelita Reyes notes, Lovelace shows that the ritual of Carnival, for as long as it lasts, generates that communal feeling; when it ceases the games of economic and class power resume. But Carnival too ceases to have that bonding effect when it becomes appropriated by capitalist concerns to glorify business and sell products. The final vision, which belongs to Philo the calypsonian, is that a Babbitry, a formulaic material quest, infects Trinidad.

H. Nigel Thomas. *WLWE*. 3, 1 (Spring 1991), pp. 1, 6

One of Lovelace's major themes is the idea of "personhood." In order to be free, man must first discover himself and his place in relation to his world. It is only through such awareness that he can then relate to the larger world of which he is a part. By affirming that every man belongs to the community of mankind, Lovelace refutes the notion of a First and Third World. Like his fellow West Indian writers, he shows the danger of imposing Western standards on Caribbean societies, which robs them of their heritage and their identity. Lovelace also dispels the myth which portrays the slave as a victim, without the strength to survive. He warns his fellow West Indians against such customs as Carnival, which confer illusory power to men while luring them away from their fundamental duties and responsibilities to each other.

Jestina's Calypso is the poignant story of a homely black woman, who believes that her Trinidadian pen pal, now living in New York, is going to marry her. As she prepares herself for his arrival, she becomes the laughing-stock of the village. The young man arrives, sees Jestina's face, and immediately takes a flight back to New York. Fundamentally, there is nothing wrong with Jestina's aspirations "to want to be, to be a whole person, somebody with a journey in front of [her]," but her stubborn belief is at once tragic and noble. Lovelace speaks of it as that complex "courage, and guts and wickedness," the kind that makes "Little Man, the stickfighter," fight to his death. . . . But unlike her Trinidadian pen pal, who went to America to fulfill his dreams at the price of losing his own identity and values, Jestina stayed. "You are here," Laura tells her, "swayed, unbroken, you have survived, Jestina." Unlike those who parade their emptiness, playing illusory kings and queens, Jestina drops her pretense and dares to face her own ugliness. In this act lies her beauty. Redemption, Lovelace teaches, lies in the courage to seek oneself by breaking away "from all the lies heaped on your life." This advice comes from Prettypig, who is enacting Jestina's response to her disappointed pen pal, from a woman whose name symbolizes Jestina's beautiful ugliness.

In *The New Hardware Store* Lovelace shows the tragic emptiness of people who have not been able to break from the lies luring them away from basic human decency. Survival, to some, means material success, a lesson Mr. Ablack, the new owner of the hardware store, has learned well. In his vocabulary are the words, "hustle," "scheme," "bribe," "smile," "bow," all having to do with his ultimate goal, "Now is the time to produce production. Productivity." To others, it implies playing roles: Rooso, the nightwatchman and advertiser for Ablack's hardware store, is also a clown, entertaining people by making them laugh at him and giving them a chance to feel superior. Like the masquerader, who is no more than the mask he wears, Rooso will be remembered as the calypsonian but not as the man: "and you wouldn't even remember my name was Rooso." Yet, like Aldrick of *The Dragon Can't Dance*, he becomes the hero of Lovelace's play because he changes, and in the process *becomes*. He realizes that his roles, as perfect as they may be, are only illusions: "I had to dance the stickman dance, I had to . . . kick my feet in a Bongo . . . I play slave, guerrilla. I follow the crowd, play marcher, play servant, savage, skylarker." At the end of the play, his undressing before leaving Ablack is symbolic of the stripping of his roles in order to face the naked self. It is only then that he becomes a man ready to fulfill his responsibility to himself and to others.

This is also the lesson Cyril Village gives his son, Roy Village, in *My Name Is Village*. Roy Village wants to be "a big man" with the power of a Jab Malassie in a world of progress, the features of which the Town Tester enumerates to the Yes Men: "speed," "Color Television," "tall building." For this, he rejects his father's identity of "old stickman" who doesn't want to "get dirty" and is "meek and mild." But by the end of this short play, Roy has learned from his father that true greatness cannot be imported; it is right at home in the world his people have made for themselves: "This is we world because is we who love it and with we hands make things grow out of it."

Pierrette M. Frickey. In Bruce King, ed.
Post-Colonial English Drama: Commonwealth Drama since 1960
(New York: St. Martin's Press, 1992), pp. 230–32

MAILLU, DAVID (1939–   )

KENYA

Capitalizing on the song school, [David] Maillu has produced a . . . series of
works using the dramatic monologue technique, be it in the form of a letter, as
in *Dear Daughter*, or verse, as in his three-decker *The Kommon Man*. . . .

Totally disregarding form, he talks to the reader directly; matter becomes
all-important. The values he portrays are common to most of these novels.
Their market is largely urban and so, too, is their setting, with all the attendant
social attitudes brought about by rapid urbanization along a Western pattern—
rootlessness, cynicism, materialism, and escapism. The parallels with nineteenth-century Britain are striking. Of the general process Louis James has
written that "the essentially rural lower-class culture which expressed itself in
ballads, broadsheets, and chapbooks, was fragmented when the worker moved
into the towns." While Maillu's works can in no way be termed traditional they
do contain fragments of that tradition in his fondness for aphorisms like "the
chameleon can change its colors but it cannot change its behavior" and "when
two bulls fight, it is the grass that suffers most." Edward Hinga still recalls the
traditional fine for sleeping with an unmarried woman but is embarrassed by
elders judging his affairs. . . .

There are gratuitous, graphic descriptions of sexual intercourse in
Maillu's work as when Maiko has sex with his secretary, Ema, to ensure her
promotion, but this is followed by a short poem decrying the practice. Again
the Kommon Man vividly imagines his wife's affair with Makoka but the whole
trilogy is a condemnation of her materialist-inspired actions. The sexual content
in these novels is certainly ambiguous. Maillu, for example, has many serious
points to make about the state of society and, in part, *The Kommon Man* is
intellectually demanding. Is the sexual content then the carrot to entice the ordinary reader to serious thought on the problems of urban life or is the philosophy
a rather lengthy afterthought and conscience salver? Maillu's stand is not
unequivocal. . . .

[If] the ordinary reader turns to . . . Maillu's *The Kommon Man*, combing
through the trivia, soft porn, trite moralizing, and cynicism, he may find the
hymn of the common man which speaks as clearly of social injustice as does
Okot p'Bitek's *Song of Lawino*, but with less anger and more cynicism.

Elizabeth Knight. In Eldred Durosimi Jones, ed.
African Literature Today. 10 (1979), pp. 178, 182, 184, 188

In the 1970s David Maillu emerged as the most significant popular writer in
Kenya. This he accomplished not by writing school books for local branches of
international publishing houses nor by soliciting the patronage of government-
subsidized Kenyan publishers but by establishing his own firm, Comb Books,

and inundating the market with novelettes and volumes of verse he himself had written, published, and then energetically promoted. His first "mini-novel," *Unfit for Human Consumption*, the costs of which had been underwritten partly by a loan from a friend and partly by a trade agreement with a distributor, had sold so well that he had been able to invest the proceeds in a second book, *My Dear Bottle*, a poetic apostrophe to the consolation of inebriation. This too had been swallowed up quickly by a pop-thirsty reading public, and Maillu had plowed the profits back into the firm just as quickly, bringing out in the next year another mini-novel, *Troubles*, and another humorous soliloquy in verse, *After 4:30*, as well as reissuing the first two sold-out titles. By repeating this kind of pyramiding procedure, Maillu in four years was able to publish twelve books he himself had written (including a Swahili translation of *My Dear Bottle*), reprint the best-selling works several times, and publish four books by other Kenyan authors who had similar stories to tell. . . .

When Maillu first appeared on the East African literary scene, he introduced an innovation that no other writer in his part of the world had exploited so fully: he talked dirty. True, Charles Mangua had done this a little earlier in Kenya in two extremely popular novels, *Son of Woman* and *A Tail in the Mouth*, but Mangua wrote humorous picaresque tales in which a streetwise hero talked tough and dirty. Maillu may have learned something from Mangua, but his own civil-servant heroes were not roughshod rogues but middle-class victims of biological urges that ultimately destroyed their careers; they talked weak and dirty. . . .

If we compare Maillu's latest works with those he wrote and published during Comb Books' brief heyday, one change becomes apparent immediately: the dirty talk is gone. His heroes may be sexually active but they are not sexually obsessed, and their physical interactions with members of the opposite sex tend to be described with restraint, even reticence. This is true not only in the two novels he has published in the Macmillan Pacesetter Series, *For Mbatha and Rabeka* and *The Equatorial Assignment*, but also in *Kadosa*, the first novel brought out by David Maillu Publishers Ltd., and in *Tears at Sunset*, the yet unpublished novel written for the Koola Town Self-Help and Community Development Scheme. Moreover, carnal love has no place in *Jese Kristo*, a morality play performed at the Kenya National Theater in October and November of 1979 and published in the program prepared for that production, or in *Hit of Love*, a one-hundred page poem issued by David Maillu Publishers Ltd. in a bilingual (English-Kikamba) format. . . .

Maillu's success in adapting to new popular formulas is evident in the first two Pacesetters he has written. *For Mbatha and Rabeka* is built on a classic love triangle. Mbatha, an idealistic primary-school teacher, is planning to marry Rabeka, his beautiful childhood sweetheart who teaches at the same village school, but while she is in Nairobi recovering from a liver ailment, she meets Honeycomb Mawa, a panel beater foreman with Bodyliners Limited, who shows her the town in his Saab sportscar, wining and dining her at all the top establishments in the Rift Valley and escorting her to high-class international parties. Rabeka, dazzled by the urban glitter and impressed by Mawa's sophistication and wealth, begins to long for life in the fast lane. . . .

Maillu's second Pacesetter, *The Equatorial Assignment*, was an African adaptation of the James Hadley Chase type of thriller. Benni Kamba, Secret Agent 009 working for the National Integrity Service of Africa, is pitted against beautiful Konolulu, known professionally as Colonel Swipta, an agent for a multinational European organization intent on destabilizing Africa for the benefit of the Big Powers. NISA has its headquarters at a Saharan desert outpost run by the brainy Dr. Triplo, and Colonel Swipta works at a mountain station called Chengolama Base run by the unscrupulous and equally brilliant Dr. Thunder. Benni Kamba's mission is to infiltrate Chengolama Base and destroy it before Dr. Thunder can launch his secret weapon, a missile called Thundercrust that would obliterate NISA. Agent 009 accomplishes this by making romantic overtures to Colonel Swipta, killing her after gaining her trust, and then detonating the Thundercrust on its launching pad, thereby destroying Chengolama Base. The good guys win; the bad guys die. . . .

This is light fiction written with a light touch. Unlike *For Mbatha and Rabeka*, *The Equatorial Assignment* does not deal with semiserious social issues or with real people in recognizable situations. It is escape literature pure and simple, an indigenous variant of an extremely popular foreign genre. Benni Kamba is an African James Bond. . . .

Literary critics have not been very generous in their assessments of Maillu's work. No one has lavished praise on him, and few have admitted finding any redeeming value in what or how he writes. The general feeling among serious academics appears to be that such literature is beneath criticism for it is wholly frivolous, the assumption being that a scholar should not waste his time on art that aims to be truly popular. Yet Maillu cannot be ignored in any systematic effort to understand the evolution of an East African literature, for he has extended the frontiers of that literature farther than any other single writer. One may regard his writing as undisciplined, unrefined, uncouth, and outrageously excessive, but it is precisely because he has been spectacularly audacious and unmannerly that he is important. He has broken most of the rules of good writing and has gotten away with it, thereby releasing an embryonic literary culture from the confining sac of conformity to established conventions of taste and judgment. Maillu, a primitive pioneer and intrepid trailblazer, has liberated fenced-off aesthetic territory. Now that he has pushed the boundaries of decorum back, others can stake out their own claims in the same untamed wilderness.

Moreover, Maillu is important because he possesses tenacity and resourcefulness. He has learned to survive by adjusting to new circumstances and imposing his will on the world about him. He has taken risks that the prudent would have eschewed and has discovered through trial and error, as well as trial and success, just how far he can carry others with him. One has to admire his courage both as a publisher and as an author. Perhaps no one else would have persisted so long in the struggle when buffeted continually by the criticism that everything he produced was unfit for human consumption.

Bernth Lindfors. *Kunapipi.* 4, 1 (1981), pp. 130, 132–34, 136–37, 141–42

Maillu's works could be easily dismissed as being too pornographic and form-less. The author may not be given any credit for the few creative devices that sympathetic critics glean out of these works because such devices are purely accidental and the currency and importance of the themes in contemporary society are vitiated by low artistic taste. That Maillu's writing is amateurish is a truism; that within his fictive world there are the two opposed camps of art and action is apparent. These two camps are opposed because Maillu appears to have sacrificed intellectual and scholarly obligations in order to bear the self-imposed sociopolitical burden of the writer as a teacher, which the limits of his literary education do not permit. A criticism of these works implies examining how far Maillu succeeds in marrying morality and aesthetics, content and form—an exercise which raises aesthetic questions. . . .

He refuses to be bound by conventional forms. He adopts the poetry format in writing *After 4:30*, *My Dear Bottle*, and *The Kommon Man* . . . but his style is essentially a prose style. It is hard to classify his writings as poetry or prose; rather, it is safer to use the looser and noncommitting term, works. This is because, apart from the two letters, *Dear Monika* and *Dear Daughter*, and the mini-novels, his works . . . could be classified as books of poems or short stories. Whether or not they qualify as any of these classes is another matter. Their format disqualifies them as short stories; and when pitted against some other poetry written in East Africa, they may not pass as good poetry. The ones arranged in verse are essentially disjointed items of colloquial utterances. They lack the terseness, texture and complexity of language which create the images, metaphors and symbolic meaning which characterize good poetry. . . .

His works, for what they are worth, cannot be appreciated more than those of a writer pandering to popular taste by portraying Nairobi as a city of self-destructive sex. They could be enjoyed as a change made in East African literature, which, until the emergence of Okot p'Bitek, was primarily concerned with hackneyed culture conflict and colonialism. But if Maillu refuses to tow the lines of writers like Ngugi [wa Thiong'o] and others who stuck to the conventional forms they learned from British and American literatures, his refusal should have prompted him to create new and mature fictional techniques and style that would challenge the ones the older and established East African writers adopt. His themes may be topically relevant to East African society, to the social problems facing Africa as a whole. The books serve as his contribution to the social reform. Maillu's success in publishing these works, in spite of his not-too-high literary education, might be considered a promise of his greater future achievements. But since he adopts the same style, point of view, and discusses the same redundant theme in all ten works—a fictional mode which eventuates in amateur-ish, unliterary, and monotonously repetitious works—we question his seriousness and commitment as a social reformer. The contemporary African societies are too educated to accept *any* and *every* writing as literature. Genuine experiments in language and form will continue to be conducted in African literature, but certainly the age of "Onitsha market literature" is fast becoming an anachronism.

Kalu Ogbaa. *Ufahumu*. 10, 3 (Spring 1981), pp. 57, 59, 66

If nothing much has been heard about Maillu in West Africa, it is because writing of the type he does and publishes is regarded with a certain amount of disdain by academic critics. For the man in the (East African) street, however, Maillu's name is a household word. He is by far the most popular writer in East Africa, even though Ngugi wa Thiong'o is the Kenyan writer best known to the outside world. These two Kenyan writers address two largely disparate audiences and their work may indeed be regarded as complementary. . . .

Maillu is a fairly careful craftsman when it comes to vocabulary and characterization. But he has a penchant for repetition not only of themes but also of incidents and reflections. His reputation has so far been based on his exploration of sexual relations between men and women, and yet in private life he is neither frivolous nor a libertine. On the contrary, he is ascetic and prefers the peace and quiet of his suburban Langata residence west of Nairobi to the hurly-burly of city life. The serious strain in Maillu is clearly portrayed in a supernatural novel *Kadosa* which is due to appear soon. While he traces the origin of the ideas of *Kadosa* to [Mikhail] Bulgakov's *The Master and Margarita*, there is much in Maillu's forthcoming work to indicate originality in plot and characterization.

To date, however, his reputation has rested on works dealing with the lives of city prostitutes and layabouts. He has been criticized . . . for displaying a limited and unidimensional view of human character, especially female character. In his defense, he has argued that whatever vulgarity one can point to in his work can also be found in real life.

E. O. Apronti. PMQ. 6, 3–4 (July–October 1981), pp. 162–63

David Maillu is a writer who deserves greater attention from serious critics than he currently enjoys. His lighthearted style and his "vulgar" language probably account for the . . . [critical] neglect of his writing, nevertheless his social vision is much more profound than readers may realize, for he addresses himself to some of the most serious problems facing independent Africa today. . . . *After 4:30* can be summarized as a book on women's liberation. The protagonist of the novel, the typist, is a highly conscientized proletarian woman who is bitterly critical of male ideology on the question of the place of women in society. . . .

In this male-dominated society, women find themselves oppressed and exploited at work, at home, everywhere. Male executives make use of their positions as bosses to demand sex from their typists. Unless she submits to her boss's sexual desires, a typist has no hope for promotion. And junior men, subjected to such treatment by the same women, lord it over their wives at home. In a male-dominated bourgeois society, wives are at the beck and call of their husbands. Those women who marry wealthy men pay for the luxury of their homes with misery and tears. . . .

In *My Dear Bottle* the protagonist is not a militant feminist, but a male drunkard. The drunkard is a member of the working class and is a failure in life. His world is a world of wishful thinking, but try as he may, he cannot emulate his boss who is himself a member of the wealthy bourgeoisie and enjoys all the advantages that accrue to those who belong to that class, including the use of big cars like the Mercedes Benz. In many ways, the drunkard is the male equivalent of the typist in *After 4:30*. Like the typist, he is a spokesman for the less privileged section of the population, and he is similarly far from idealized. He makes it clear that if he were in power he would indulge in corrupt practices. Nevertheless, what he says about what he would get up to were he a minister is meant to be a reflection of the corruption of those in the upper echelons of society. Thus Maillu takes a drunkard, who himself has faults, and criticizes the injustices of society through him. . . .

In the final analysis, however, Maillu's novels cannot be described as "socialist art." His final word on socialism is pronounced by the drunkard's learned friend who is critical of both capitalism and socialism. The major criticism against communism, or what he calls "another form of capitalism where a chosen élite must control the entire population," is that its rulers exercise their power through fear. Though he is a radical writer who sides with the workers and the less privileged sections of society, his position is no more than that of a social critic; he does not examine the possibility of collective bargaining for the workers, or define the problem in terms of the class struggle. However, the point must be made that Maillu's writings draw their strength from proletarian culture and should find a place among the works of those who are committed to the cause of the less privileged classes of bourgeois society. He may with some justification be condemned as a "pornographic jester," but his style should not obscure the fact that he raises questions capable of pricking the consciences of those in positions of power and authority.

Emmanuel Ngara. *Art and Ideology in the African Novel*
(London: Heinemann, 1985), pp. 55–58

MAIS, ROGER (1905–1955)

JAMAICA

By his life, even more than by his work, Roger Mais grew into something of a legend. He was a man of violent sympathies, passionately dedicated to the vision of a new Jamaica, and when in 1944 he was sent to prison for his writings, a part of all protesting Jamaicans served the term with him. The political ferment of the 1940s—its early enthusiasm, its ultimate phase of treachery and disillusionment—was to leave a graver mark on him than on any other of the island's writers. His novels, paradoxically enough, are completely free of the political issues that dominate the work of Vic Reid, yet it was his fierce participation in the national struggle that sparked his creative personality; it was from this he drew the inspiration for works of a raw but vivid and moving power.

Poet, painter, and playwright, one of Jamaica's most fertile and talented short-story writers, Mais came to the novel rather late, and in his first book, *The Hills Were Joyful Together*, he crystallized all the indignation and sympathy of a remarkably intense life. Unlike the shapely and rounded short stories of this period his novel is a jagged creation, but what is lost in form on the bigger canvas Mais compensates for by the release of dramatic energy. In this first book he gives us a portrait of the Jamaican lower-class life, a tenement yard embracing the lives of twenty-five people. The result is something vital, eloquent, and disturbing.

His second book, *Brother Man*, is a more finished, mature, if less powerful, work. The rhetoric and the turbulent spirit of *The Hills* is here again but Mais is more restrained and the drama now is touched with pathos. It is the story of Brother Man, a messianic but convincingly human figure, who holds up the ideal of the Christian life against the challenge of a brutal environment. The people tolerate him as long as they can trade on his eccentricities. But in the end the rival power and influence of the obeah man, Brother Ambo, asserts itself and Brother Man is framed and disgraced, stoned by his followers and abandoned. Mais attempts here to create a character of almost Christlike proportions. The lines of Brother Man's life parallel those of his model in many significant details—the years of wandering and preparation before his mission among the people, the healings and fastings, the going up into the hills for meditation and prayer, the eventual betrayal by one of his own followers, and mortification at the hands of the very people he had sought to save. What emerges, however, is a crude, though compassionate, portrayal. It is not informed by the difficult spirit of tragedy that would have lifted it out of the sentimental context in which it moves and remains.

Black Lightning, his last novel, is a complete departure from the first two in setting, mood and intention. The portraits of vigor which had redeemed the limitations of these earlier books are less in evidence. It is a work of subdued tone, at best femininely tender. Mais had actually begun to collapse, both as man and artist. When the advance copy of his last novel was sent out to him from London he lay in bed, dying. He had sought, as he said in his own words, "to write the story of man, the eternal protagonist amid eternal process—man whom I met at the top of a hill in St. Andrew, Jamaica, dirty, hungry, and in rags." One would like to think, in tribute to his memory, that, in some modest but memorable way, he succeeded.

Ivan Van Sertima. *Caribbean Writers*
(London: New Beacon Books, 1968), pp. 20–21

Mais drew the mystical element in his writing from the rhythmical, figurative style of both [the] Bible and Jamaican patois. He used words to reach behind the symbols of language and objects to the nameless reality beyond symbols, the timeless Word of St. John's Gospel. So that when in Mais, words fail, the reader is usually left not with a sense of emptiness, but of vision outreaching vocabulary.

This is true of both the language and main character of *Brother Man*. Here, Mais is again exploring the microcosm of the slums. But he is concerned with a wider concept and the enclosed yard gives place to a Kingston slum street. Surjue [in *The Hills Were Joyful Together*] was destroyed against both tenement and prison wall. Is there any way for human values to survive in the modern human predicament? His answer is one of the utmost daring. He developed Ras, the figure of the gentle Good Samaritan and observer in *The Hills*, and created Brother Man, John Power. John Power has human features. He is the focal point of the community, the healer of mind and body, the religious leader, and the helpful undemanding neighbor. He strengthens, through his own understanding and stability, the mentally unstable Cordy. . . . Mais insists on Brother Man's basic humanity when he shows Power finally taking [the prostitute] Minette in total, unashamed love. Yet Mais uses his portrait of a Rastafarian cultist—the Rastafarian greeting, "Peace and Love, Brother Man," comes at once to mind—only as a fulcrum between the human and the ideal. We learn something of John Power's thoughts, but very little of his motivation, because as his name implies, he unites in himself Everyman—hence the common name, John—with the ultimate motivation, Power. In him the humanity that gleams fitfully, fragmented, in the various characters of *The Hills*, comes together. And his significance moves beyond that of John Power the Healer and Leader, to that he assumes in the final confrontation with the hysterical, violent mob that cannot endure his goodness. He is Mais's vision of the reincarnate Christ. This is no escape into sentimental mysticism from the political realities. Mais's conviction of spiritual values was too absolute.

As with *The Hills*, sociological or ethical values are inadequate for a criticism of *Brother Man*, because physical conditions are interpreted under the eye of the artist. Human and artistic values, for Mais, meet, each illuminating the other. In a sense, the personality of Brother Man is a work of art beyond the levels of normal literature, exploring the artistic pattern of life itself. And so the artistic faults in the book also imply a limitation of the vision. At times the physical, human presence of Brother Man loses its definition. The Word is no longer incarnate. The plot, too, is uneven and episodic, diverted by a multiplicity of subsidiary characters. When moving on a plane of such heightened symbolism, any deviation into mechanical narration or portraiture jars heavily. But at its key points the novel is usually successful, as in [its] biblically simple hint of resurrection after virtual crucifixion.

> Jean Creary. In Louis James, ed. *The Islands in Between: Essays on West Indian Literature* (London: Oxford University Press, 1968), pp. 56–58

Mais was a poor dramatist, but the dramatic elements in his first novel, *The Hills Were Joyful Together*, do not consist only in the stagelike use of its yard setting, with glimpses of a more "private" life through the doors and windows opening upon it, but also in the long exchanges of dialogue between a constantly varied selection of its inhabitants. Mais even begins his book with a cast list and follows this with a description of the yard which amounts to a stage direction. The choice of a cast which embraces whores, cardsharpers, thieves, layabouts, and drunkards is not without its twin dangers of patronage and sentimentality. . . . With Mais's characters, however, we have said nothing when we have said "whore" or "cardsharper." In this sense they are the very opposite of stagey. And because they all retain the capacity to surprise, because they retain through all their suffering and degradation something of their autonomy as human beings, Mais manages to remain completely inside his story. A setting

of this kind may be chosen by writers in search of folk authenticity or of a sanction for their political radicalism. In such cases they can hardly avoid calling
attention to their astonishing knowledge of low life, or wagging an invisible finger at their comfortable readers. Because the characters in Mais are so abundantly alive he avoids these perils also.

The inhabitants of the yard in *The Hills Were Joyful Together* may be
divided into those who accept their lot with a certain amount of philosophy and
those who seek to escape it through drink, sex, evangelical religion, or crime.
Prominent among the first group is Ras, the angular, bearded Rastafarian bar-
row-pusher who is the yard's only peacemaker. The others either seek or avoid
trouble, but seldom attempt to quell it. Ras makes his presence and his values
felt gradually as the plot advances, as acts of folly or violence involve more and
more of the yard-dwellers in tragedy. The group of active escapists is dominated by Surjue, a man whose sense of right and wrong may not accord with
that of the law but who possesses nonetheless a particular kind of personal
integrity and valor. Surjue and his woman Rema are deeply in love, but he is
restless and looking for a break. His gambling crony Flitters finally induces him
to go on a "job" and, when the police catch them on the roof, runs off leaving
Surjue to take the rap. Angry though Surjue is with Flitters, he refuses to tell the
police the names of any of his accomplices. To do so would be to violate his
own curious sense of honor, but he has no qualms about arranging for Flitters to
be hunted down and murdered by his underworld acquaintances. The same
unyielding defiance brings terrible treatment to Surjue after his conviction,
making him the favorite victim of the more sadistic warders. Hearing that Rema
is going mad in her loneliness, Surjue resolves to escape and see her. Again he
is unlucky; just as he is about to haul himself to the top of the wall he is shot
and killed by the guards. . . . Surjue's death ends a novel whose small cast has
already been ravaged by similar tragedies, many of them resulting from heed-
lessness or from the violence which continually wells up in their random relationships. Surjue never knows that Rema has died before him, burned helplessly
in a fire she herself has started in a crazy effort to drive off her delusions.
Surjue's own escape plan had involved the deliberate starting of a fire to panic
the warders and set them running in the wrong direction. Despite this sardonic
coincidence, Mais does not appear to invoke a Hardyesque fate to account for
such things. They simply happen, especially to those who court disaster like
Surjue by trying to make their own rules.

Gerald Moore. The Chosen Tongue (New York: Harper & Row, 1969), pp. 86–88

[*Brother Man*] is Mais's "best" published work because it brings together in
one minor classic, all the aspects of his instincts and talents. . . . The problems
of urbanization . . . in *The Hills Were Joyful Together*—growth of slums,
increase of crime, alienation, cul-de-sac sense—were now much more evident.
But the city had also started to absorb this sense, making it part of its survival
style. Bedward, the August Town pentecostal preacher, had already laid the
basis for a millennial mythology with his attempt to ascend into heaven. More

quietly, and more significantly, he had also given his flock a sense of their own unique cultural identity. His ideas spread through the city, giving strength to the countless "revival" Afro-Jamaican churches thumping at the crossroads and backstreets of the corporate area. Among these were the Rastafari, a remarkable, bearded "Israelite" group who date their foundation from the coronation of the Emperor Haile Selassie I of Ethiopia, the former Ras (Prince) Tafari, and a statement attributed to Marcus Garvey prophesying this. The shoemaker, Brother Man (John Power), hero of this novel, is a member of this sect. "Brother" and "Man" are appellations characteristic of them: "I-re, brother," "Hail the man," "I-man," etc. . . .

Brother Man is perhaps too Christlike to be always "true"; unlike the ideal of the Rastas, he is not fully enough grounded in reality. But this is a tendency Mais shows in all his novels. What he does achieve in *Brother Man*, however, is the depolarization of his rural and urban norms into a single equator, and the condensation of his moralizing tendency into a single mask. The novel is in this sense a "humanist" triumph, if by this term we understand an emphasis on humane elements within an alienating environment. Had Mais not limited so severely his characterization and thematic variations, we might have had a major novel by any standard. . . .

Yet in writing this novel, Mais moved towards certain important formal and stylistic interventions which make it far more important than its limitations would suggest. In fact, as we begin to examine *Brother Man*, the first thing that strikes us is the remarkable coincidence of "style" and "formal structure"; a coincidence, indeed, which we associate more with poetry than with prose fiction. By "style" I mean the way—action flow—the book is written; its use and movement of language. By "form," I refer to how the work is built: its "archistructure." Both these are unusually clear in *Brother Man*.

Edward [Kamau] Brathwaite. Introduction to Roger Mais.
Brother Man (London: Heinemann, 1974), pp. x–xii

Mais's technical achievement in his novels seems to me to have been underrated by most critics who have ignored or criticized his style and concentrated on his passion and social anger. Although he has been justly criticized for lapses into sentimentality and prolixity . . . the accuracy and directness of his descriptive writing has rarely been matched in the West Indian novel to date. But the heart of Mais's achievement is not technical. What he did was to present a view of Jamaican life from inside, an uncompromising and complete picture of the suffering and misery of day to day existence in the Kingston slums. His novels celebrate the strength and spirit of the Jamaicans who inhabit [the] slums, and show the impoverished existence of those who, ironically, ought to be heirs to the most beautiful island in the West Indies. In this Jamaica there are no tourist pictures of gleaming beaches and blue, forest-clad mountains. These novels reflect a world whose unremitting demands shut out everything but the immediate daily grind. Poverty, crime and dirt are ever-present realities; race and color the sources of conflict and petty snobbery; while sexual passions alternatively assuage and irritate his characters' restricted feelings. In his first novel, *The Hills Were Joyful Together*, Mais details the lives of the inhabitants of a Jamaican yard. In a manner reminiscent of the tenement plays of Sean O'Casey he abjures narrative and plot in favor of a fragmentary, imagistic series of scenes in which each character is introduced as an aspect of the life of the yard. In a sense the yard itself is the subject of the novel, a setting which so permeates and governs the actions of its inhabitants that their lives are insepara-ble from the conditions it imposes on them. Gradually a series of patterns emerge defining conditions which are the springs of individual lives. Zephyr, the warm-hearted whore; Euphemia, the seductive wife of Shag who awakens to sexuality through an unwanted bur irresistible physical passion for the no-good Bajun Man; Shag himself, a dying man, whose pent-up violence is released viciously and pointlessly by circumstances which he can barely com-prehend; all these and others interact in a story whose motivation is in the phys-ical and economic conditions they must all endure.

Gareth Griffiths. A Double Exile: African and West Indian Writing
Between Two Cultures (London: Marion Boyars, 1978), pp. 116–17

[In *Black Lightning*] Jake, the blacksmith of a tiny, rural village by day and a sculptor by night, is both a society-oriented artisan as well as a private artist. He stubbornly refuses the advice of the village elders, who feel that, as an educated man, he ought to look for a more suitable job. . . . His commitment to a social role, however, leaves only the nighttime for his woodcarving, an artistic urge that he clearly cannot ignore, and about which he feels some anxiety. Jake, working on his Samson figure by the light of a lamp held by young Miriam, has a sudden sense of panic. . . . But the moment passes, and he is able to resume his work. . . . Indeed, Jake's nocturnal carving has an obsessional note, for he iden-tifies with the Samson-figure, seeing himself as a strong man threatened by weakness, the need to depend on others. The community-minded Jake is really a lonely and proud individual at heart, and his jealously guarded carving repre-sents this private, artistic self. As the work proceeds, Jake comes to be more and more dependent on others. His wife, Estella, deserts him (a "betrayal," one feels, that is intended to remind us of Delilah's treatment of Samson), and his friend-ship with the accordion-playing hunchback, Amos, becomes more complex. . . .

Jake's carving represents a Promethean *hubris* which creates within him a sense of secret guilt. Jake knows that it was not merely Samson's betrayal by Delilah that brought humiliation, blindness, and death, "but what must have lain secretly underneath . . . that the Bible never gave any clue of at all." In the cli-mactic scene in the book when, during a thunderstorm, he takes an apprehen-sive Amos to see the carving in the loft, the link between the Samson-figure and Jake is clear. The figure has become that of the blind Samson, leaning on the shoulder of a boy. Worse, it has begun to resemble Jake. . . . Like Milton's tragic hero in *Samson Agonistes*, Jake, convinced that he has been blinded for his sin of pride, broods inwardly. Estella returns to the village, but it is too late. Jake destroys his carving and, finally, himself. Unable to reconcile the demands of social awareness—his blacksmith's job —with the more urgent demands of his art, he chooses self-destruction as a means of escape from an insoluble crisis of loyalties.

Mais, like his character Jake, began his career with a sense of social duty: the need to champion the cause of the despised and neglected black urban poor. As the development of his work suggests, however, the split between his role as spokesman for a community and his concern as an individual artist continued to grow.

Michael Gilkes. The West Indian Novel (Boston: Twayne, 1981), pp. 37–40

It is possible that if Mais had lived he may have written stranger and more complex fictions that may have revisioned the trauma of violence that afflicts his work. In some degree his work was crudely influenced by Hollywood cinema as Kenneth Ramchand, I think, makes clear. Nevertheless . . . there is a seed of forces in his narrative that carries the thrust of potential revisualizations of violence in *The Hills Were Joyful Together* and his last novel *Black Lightning*.

The Hills Were Joyful Together is shot through by great violence, tight and hideous lives, slums and prisons: emotional claustrophobia. And yet the violence is overshadowed by an elusive sensation that the characters wrestle with fate, with a sky god, who overshadows them and sculpts or carves them out of the hills. Such a view is justified, I think, in *Black Lightning* where parallel forces, violence and creativity, loom unmistakably. The sculptor Jake carves a compulsive Samsonian figure who strikes back from the sky with black lightning. Jake is smitten and blinded. Jake's coming death by his own hand is a parody of the sky god, the parody of creation that succumbs to despair, save that Jake's fall is threaded into a miraculous therapy that heals the inner or psychical malaise that afflicts Amos, Jake's half-crippled friend who "lives" the activity of the stricken yet striking sculpture. Amos can do nothing to save his blind master and friend but in absorbing into himself the blow that the wood receives under Jake's hand, and in coming "alive" as if he is Jake's carving, he brings an element of differentiation into the parody of the sky god—to which Jake succumbs—in the renewal of his own life, a renewed inner dimension, or psychical body.

Wilson Harris. In Robert Sellick, ed. Myth and Metaphor (Adelaide:
Center for Research in the New Literatures in English, 1982), pp. 6–7

We cannot come to *Black Lightning* with the same expectations we bring to [Mais's] two earlier novels. . . . This work does not follow in the tradition of social realism found in those works. If we look for a crowning achievement to mark the end of Mais's life, then we may be disappointed and puzzled by this novel. Mais would have been untroubled. He was by all accounts not an easy man; his business was asking questions, not answering them. He was obsessed with the question and cared little for the audience's attitude. We know many of the social concerns and questions which preoccupied him, for his writing is devoted to these issues. Yet he constantly goes beyond the predictable boundaries; at the end of his life he was more involved with painting—a more enigmatic, less didactic art than writing, John Hearne, a close friend of Mais's, felt that this was the direction which Mais would have taken, had he lived. Certainly there is much in *Black Lightning* to show us that it was created by a consciousness keenly aware of shape, outline, lighting, color, and texture. It is the product of a painter's eye. It has something of the frozen energy of pictorial art which conveys emotion directly; it strives to appeal to us in ways beyond the reach of words. . . .

The direction taken in *Black Lightning* is inward, but it is not a study of character. The protagonists are simply sketched; we know very little about them beyond the immediate role played by each. This is one of the problems of the novel. We do not know what any of them looks like, save for the broadest generalizations: Amos is a hunchback with a monkey face; Bess is middle-aged and fat; Jake is "tall, powerfully built"; Glen and Miriam are young. The plot, too, is simple and deals baldly with a tragedy in a small village. We know nothing of the antecedents of the main actors in this tragedy, and the tragic act itself—Jake's suicide—is handled with explicit explanations from Jake's wife, Estella, that only deepen the mystery. What we have in this novel is the story of a respected, able man, talented and sensitive, who loses his wife, his talent, and his health, who is then struck blind by lightning and, filled with a despair which no one can dispel, takes his own life. We must ask ourselves whether this chain of events is credible as presented: is a wife's desertion enough to set off such a tragic decline? Is Jake a conventional tragic hero brought down in prideful despair? These are the views that the plot insists upon, but in the end we hesitate. At a deeper level than that of plot, we are moved by a tension and terror not openly explored in plot or characters. At the end of the novel we find ourselves shaken, yet we can hardly say why. The effect of *Black Lightning* is to point us inwards to levels of our being where language hardly works but where the raw energy of consciousness exists. This is the level of forgotten nightmares and unspoken dreams; of the unconscious reaction, the sudden anger, fear, or joy; it is where memory lives, not in sharp detail but in wordless, unimaged feelings. It is the level of myth, symbol, and pure emotion. . . .

Lightning is the symbol of divine energy, creativity, and justice. Black lightning suggests a diabolic opposite. Lightning maims or kills the body; black lightning maims or kills body and soul. Jake, artist-blacksmith, servant of his people, greatest of his kind, destroys his humanity because he finds it intolerable. His only ostensible sin is that of being stronger, better, and wiser than his peers. For this he exacts a terrible revenge on himself. His self-hatred is uncomfortably close to the self-destructiveness which is one part of the Jamaican consciousness, and his heroic stature drives this home to us. His self-hatred being what it is, small wonder that Amos and Estella never consider following him into the woods. They are as much victims and objects of that passion as Jake himself is.

Mais is plainly fascinated with the opposition of creativity and destruction, and of the creator as destroyer. This can be seen in the imagery and symbolism of his two other novels, but in neither does he go so far as to speculate on how the creator might be brought to destroy himself.

Jean D'Costa. Introduction to Roger Mais. Black Lightning
(London: Heinemann, 1983), pp. 7–8, 21–22

A God-conscious island, Jamaica could not consider nationalism without giving attention to its religious traditions. Mais's works incorporate this essential religious background, though the views he proffers could not have populist appeal, nor could they be agreeable within nationalist discourse.

Christianity and obeah form the core of the belief systems that Roger Mais inherited from his Caribbean (Jamaican) culture; of the two, Christianity plays the major role. This twofold heritage, pointing to the European and African components of the culture, is evidenced in Mais's subject matter and themes, and especially with respect to Christianity, in the archetypes and language that he uses. Of these two belief systems, Christianity is the most pervasive presence in his three published novels—*The Hills Were Joyful Together*, *Brother Man*, and *Black Lightning*. The majority of the novels' characters, for instance, overtly express a Christian faith. The role of reformer and social critic in *The Hills* is given to a prison chaplain; *Brother Man* and *Black Lightning* have protagonists who are fashioned according to biblical archetypes. In contrast, the folk belief of the Jamaican masses, obeah, seems to be treated with skepticism by this writer of middle-class origins.

Evelyn J. Hawthorne. *The Writer in Transition: Roger Mais and the Decolonization of Caribbean Culture* (New York: Peter Lang, 1989), p. 87

MAPANJE, JACK (1944–   )

MALAWI

Among African poets writing in English, [Wole] Soyinka stands out as having created a "human voice" for his poetry. But that voice (and the trait is not always endearing), tends always towards magniloquent self-dramatization, towards bardic posturing. [Mongane] Wally Serote ranges conversationally, and with quite frequent success, across the Johannesburg scene, but his idiom is not wholly self-made—it is that of someone who has listened to a lot of jazz talk, read a good deal of "black protest" verse. Stressing . . . that other kinds of achievement in verse than this may be equally, sometimes more, valuable, I am still convinced that Jack Mapanje offers something good which one finds nowhere else on the continent.

Mapanje, in his early thirties, teaches in the Department of English at Chancellor College, Zomba, Malawi. Some ten years of adult writing have produced enough for one slimmish volume. This doesn't mean that he is a sluggish person. His teaching is mostly in linguistics and in "oral literature"; he defends the claims of the latter to serious attention with great energy and erudition. He writes poetry not only in English but also in Chichewa, Malawi's other official language. . . . Mapanje is fully aware of the actual and potential status of African languages as an alternative medium. He does not think that he is going to solve Africa's problems by writing verse in English. Almost uniquely, he accepts his actual small audience—other staff and students at Chancellor, a few poetry lovers elsewhere in Malawi, and any enthusiast (like myself) from out-side who may happen to drop in on the conversation. He does not attempt to shout across the Zaire river and the Sahara, nor direct a megaphone at the slums of South Africa. He writes for people whose faces he sees or remembers, and a high proportion of his poems carry dedications to his friends.

Angus Calder. ACLALSB. 5, 3 (December 1980), pp. 137–38

Only a small proportion of the contributors to the Heinemann African series are poets, and a single new volume of poetry is therefore a publishing event of some importance. With this volume [*Of Chameleons and Gods*] the Malawian poet Jack Mapanje deservedly joins the ranks of such distinguished poets as Okot p'Bitek, [Dennis] Brutus, [Christopher] Okigbo and [Léopold Sédar] Senghor.

We are warned in the poet's introduction that not all the poems will be eas-ily accessible. Mapanje explains that "where voices are too easily muffled" it is difficult to "find a voice (or voices) as a way of hanging on to some sanity," and as a result the poems sometimes "seem to be too cryptic to be decoded." Notes and a glossary help explain specific objects, places, and legends, but a knowl-edge of political affairs is also sometimes required. This presents less difficulty when Mapanje writes of events in the neighboring states in the south and east—Steve Biko, Soweto, and Wiriyamu are household words in Africa—but recent events in Malawi are not as well known. Nevertheless, the intention is clear. As a poet who is deeply versed both in oral tradition and in his English academic background, Mapanje successfully uses African and contemporary myth and imagery to comment on the state of affairs in Malawi. The tone is somber or ironical, and hope for the future dims in the face of events. In the final poem of the volume Mapanje speaks of the futility of "occasional verse" when, in the "year of the child," "Skeletal Kampuchea children staring, cold / Stubborn Irish children throwing grenades" are "objects too serious for verse.". . .

Mapanje's deep love for his own country is demonstrated not only by his bitterness and despair over shattered dreams and "bloated images," but also by the setting and imagery of the poems. The rich landscape of Malawi sets the emotional atmosphere of the poems: "the soft beaches" of the "golden lake," the arid Namizimu Mountains, the gliding Shire River which "mystifies our golden lives," the luscious fruit of the land. The terms used to describe the beauty of the land stand in contrast to the metaphors for man: cockroaches, "toxic frogs," "green hounds." Mapanje's voice is original yet free of artifice. Quietly but strongly it emerges from the turbulent center of Africa.

Ursula A. Barnett. WLT. 56, 4 (Autumn 1982), pp. 737–38

"We Wondered about the Mellow Peaches," which is included in Jack Mapanje's collection of verses entitled *Of Chameleons and Gods*, excites curiosity and arouses interest. But, at first reading and out of context, it does not reveal much in the way of coherent meaning.

Who is the "generous" Alberto referred to in the second line? Why does the opening sequence bring together a selection of attractive sounding fruit desserts with a reference to "township / Lambs brutally chopped"? What is the significance of the allusion to Chilobwe? Why does the poet return to Alberto in the seventh line? How could "whiskers" map moves and pay bills? For a few lines after these enigmas, the reader seems to be on firmer ground when the poet speaks of wasting his "melodious song," which is, presumably a reference to Mapanje's feelings about his earlier poetry. But when he moves on to indicate *what* he has wasted his song *on*, then the clouds of obscurity settle once more—and, in Malawian terms, there is a regular *chiperoni*. Who or what are "parochial squirrels / And hammerheads"? What are they doing "running messages / Up and down bowing peach trees"? How can the Range Rovers to which they bring "Flashy girls with mellow peaches and vermilion / Strawberries" be "lascivious"? What does the poet mean by regretting not having "erected an edifice," not having set up "votive slabs" and not chalking "the rude walls"? What does he imply by the reference to the chameleon having "lost grip of his own colors"? Which years are referred to as "the restive decade"? Why do the last two lines of the poem make important sounding observations about "conspiracies and goats" and at the same time dismiss the observations as "fuss"? Finally, what on earth does the poet mean by tugging at our sleeves and, in a chuckling whisper, recalling—quite groundlessly—that "we all wondered about the mellow peaches"? . . .

Mapanje writes as a mature student of the oral tradition and of the English language. He writes, under the suspicious eyes of security officers and the censorship board, for his friends and fellow countrymen about events which have affected him and his people. Circumstances have introduced a degree of obscurity into his work, but he communicates with an alert, attentive, "home" audience by employing the conventions of riddling and by using a consistent, resonant system of codes.

James Gibbs. *JCL.* 22, 1 (1987), pp. 31–32, 43–44

When Jack Mapanje . . . entitled his collection *Of Chameleons and Gods,* he confessed that he was being advisedly "cryptic" in his poetry since he was writing about situations which forced him to adopt such a style. The choice of title and style are significant in that Mapanje's poetry can be claimed to be as illusive as the animal that is their trademark. The poet himself reveals in the introduction that the identification is a conscious metaphor: "one is tempted like the chameleon . . . to bask in one's brilliant camouflage." The illusiveness of the verse is also deliberate and one way of approaching its underlying meaning is, of necessity, to go through the mythological background of the chameleon informing the poet's inspiration. . . .

The need for taking such a mythological excursion is felt not only in the title but also because the volume's central, most profound, and one of its longest pieces, "If Chiuta Were Man," borrows heavily from Malawi's creation myths featuring the animal itself. The argument posited . . . is that the ambiguities revealed by the chameleon in lore and life are similar to those observed in Mapanje's poetry. . . .

In "If Chiuta Were Man," Mapanje borrows extensively from the cluster of creation myths centered on the chameleon. The earliest published version has the chameleon and the salamander as the two messengers. The second pub-lished version from an unidentified ethnic group has the chameleon and the lizard carry the two messages: that men would never die at all, and that even if men died they would rise again thereafter. The effect on man is the same. The third version gives a partial reason why conflicting messages were given from the same sender(s). It was two old men who, entrusted with holding the sun up high lest it fall and bring death to living things, sent the chameleon and the lizard separately and independently of each other.

The three versions above place the chameleon and the lizard as central to the message of life and death. Once the messages are delivered, the narratives end with an explanation of why men hate the chameleon and/or the lizard. Two other published versions . . . however, extend the narrative to explain what hap-pened to man, animal, and god to bring about a separation, or such punishment as death. In the fourth version, the chameleon reports to God (Mulungu) the discovery of a pair of human beings in his fish trap. God advises the chameleon to watch what the human pair do next. This narrative then describes the inven-tion of fire and the driving out of God and animals from the place of creation. The animals flee into the forest while God climbs to the sky on the spider's web. Mapanje uses the second part of this narrative in his poem. The fifth ver-sion was also useful to Mapanje since it contains more details not only of the fire making but also the actual coming down together of man, animal, and god to live together on earth and the subsequent cataclysm.

Steve Chimombo. JCL. 23, 1 (1988), pp. 102, 105–6

[Mapanje] appeals first for a return to "traditional literature and modes of thought as the source of metaphor and inspiration." In suggesting this, Mapanje is not, as it may appear, advocating a nostalgic or neotraditional literature of drums and masks and fly-whisks and rain-shrines. He means that he wishes the new generation of young Malawian artists to have available, even when writing in English, something of the range of devices and density of metaphor the oral poet shares with his audience. At the center of his argument is a long section on the art of riddling, a subject that has long fascinated him. Riddling, he argues, is at the heart of all new metaphors. The "rebellious nature of the riddle" lies in the fact that it surprises the audience into realizing the things that are not "pat-terned as they appear." . . .

Mapanje firmly rejects the notion, still current in some discussions of writing from East and Central Africa, that oral modes are simple and unsophis-ticated or that wit and polish and complexity in a writer are signs of Western influence. To Mapanje, the language of the oral poet is sophisticated and mis-chievous, dense with history refined to metaphor, yet capable of dynamic effects of communication precisely because those metaphors are understood and have achieved currency. To re-create in Malawian English a language of such local resonance, recapturing the toughness and complexity of oral poetry and especially its capacity for intellectual rebellion, has become his literary pro-gram. From this perspective, the coded metaphors of his poems contributed to meetings of the Writer's Group in the early 1970s were not primarily the product of circumstances in which the Group came together. They were the offspring of a marriage of the English language with a Malawian oral aesthetic. . . .

The profoundly oral nature of Mapanje's style needs little demonstration. The poems are dominated by the speaking voice, usually in the first person and the present tense. They shift line by line both in tone and syntax, from bald statement to quiet reflection to satiric jibe to open interrogation. They are intensely dramatic with strong beginnings and forceful endings and incorporate a good deal of direct speech. These effects are, of course, an achievement of artifice. Mapanje is not in practice an oral poet with his audience present before him. He writes his poems in several drafts, working through as many as a dozen versions before hitting on the form and the images appropriate for what he wishes to say. But the direction of these revisions is always toward greater immediacy of impact and variety of tone, the illusion of orality. Equally demonstrable is the extent to which Mapanje has adopted the oral poet's stance of public spokesman. Poem after poem uses the first person plural "we" in a manner not available to post-Romantic European poets. Of the forty-seven poems in *Of Chameleons and Gods*, no fewer than eighteen end with questions and [a] further eleven with exclamations. It is the stance of the praise poet, telling the chief what no one else will say and licensed by the medium of which he is master.

To his audience in Malawi the poems are packed with references to the people, places, and events of the country's recent history. A reading of the landscapes of Malawi is also a reading of ethnic tensions and political rivalries. Mapanje's poems represent not history as code but history as drama, evaluation, and judgment. They address the agenda which has been set by President Banda since the events of the cabinet crisis of 1964 and they seize back President Banda's own appropriation of the past by offering an alternative account of history, custom, and tradition. In the process, they become the best guide available within Malawi to events over the past generation. In a country where intellectual and moral enquiry have been savagely repressed, Mapanje's satire challenges like a conscience.

Leroy Vail and Landeg White.
Review of African Political Economy. 48 (1990), pp. 30–31, 38

A key point about Mapanje is his village background with which he has maintained strong links. Thus, rural life and the lakeshore area of Mangochi often feature in the poetry. This happens in "Messages," "Requiem to a Fallen Son," "The Sweet Brew at Chitakale," "The Palm Trees of Chigawe," "These Too Are Our Elders," "Visiting Zomba Plateau," "Epitaph for a Mad Friend," "In Memory of Matthew, 1976," and "An Elegy for Mangochi Fishermen." By and large, however, these poems reflect rural life as a backcloth to some other theme: they do not regularly foreground that life for its own sake, though it is clearly valued. But the poet's overseas experience stamps the verse too, as happens in a series of expatriate poems which often present not just an African view of Britain but also a springboard for contrast and comparison of British life with the African home scene.

There is a reliable freshness in Mapanje's work, an air of spontaneity and a feeling that each venture elicits new technical responses. And a tertiary training in education and language rather than literature perhaps explains why the poet, though familiar with the canon of English literature, shows no firm allegiance to any outside tradition of which he sees himself a part. Rarely does he consciously echo British and world literature and in this differs from his local colleagues or from other African poets such as [Dennis] Brutus, [Wole] Soyinka, [Christopher] Okigbo, [Michael] Echeruo or [Jared] Angira. One cannot imagine his quoting an entire [John] Donne sonnet within a personal poem, as [Felix] Mnthali does to great effect; nor see him, as we are asked to see Angira in *Juices*, appearing among glittering company at a party given by Chaucer! But then it is worth noting that, while writing mainly in English, Mapanje has also written a good deal in the vernacular and that he is deeply conversant with local oral tradition. . . .

Though a lively mind and open sensibility draw him to many subjects, certain issues predominate. Fundamental . . . is emotional and psychological survival and the therapeutic role that writing plays in this as it does for [Frank] Chipasula, [Steve] Chimombo, [Edison] Mpina, and Mnthali. A prolific use of questions and exclamations reflects a mind striving by turns to probe, jest, and assert, and to create space for free movement. One topic receiving repeated treatment is the modern response to tradition which he feels lacks proper respect. Too often what happens is mere debasement; of, for example, dancing styles, music, carving, and indeed of all the various ways in which the dead are remembered. Another concern, widely shared, is the demoralizing effects of urban life on former villagers. And like all his local contemporaries he worries about a blighted promise and wasted talent, frets about a censorship which must stifle artistic effort, and deplores injustice meted out to humble people endlessly beset by fear of drought and sickness. He is concerned about family and friends, about those who suffer in neighboring states such as Mozambique and South Africa.

Adrian Roscoe and Mpalive-Hangson Msiska. *The Quiet Chameleon: Modern Poetry from Central Africa* (London: Hans Zell, 1992), pp. 47–48

Each section of *The Chattering Wagtails of Mikuyu Prison* concerns a phase in Jack Mapanje's life, and each has a particular tone. A characteristic mood is struck for the opening section by "Kadango Village, Even Milimbo Lagoon Is Dry," in which the poet, on returning to his family home in Malawi, is confronted by evidence of hunger. In a series of lightning sketches Mapanje conveys telling impressions, and by loading the language he makes words work for him, nudging the reader toward inescapable conclusions. The repressive government has, it seems, added misinformation to misery by smothering all news of this suffering: "Our fat-necked custodians despatch another tale."

The poem which gives the second section its title is built around a reaction to scenes on a maternity ward and is characteristically angry. On the ward the poet sees "Sixty inmates of spasming women top & tail / On thirty beds." He describes the "inmates" as "atoning for the ghost / Revolution twenty years ago." As if these scenes, and the inability to talk openly about them, were not enough, there is the prospect of a visit from the man who has been called "a black tin god." In that part of the world where Father Christmas wears a homburg to "visit the sick at Christmas, some caesareans will," the poet writes, "be / Prematurely discharged." Others will be "jostled into / Neat lines, clapping their praises" so that, as far as Hastings Banda is concerned, there will be "one patient per bed." . . .

Jack Mapanje's virtues are his clarity of vision, his accessibility, his honesty, and his stubbornness. He has written thoughtful and thought-provoking poems, which are undoubtedly the work of a word artist able to sketch relevant images and of a wordsmith quick to hammer out telling phrases. The country's "ghost revolution" is now history, and Mapanje was among the gravediggers. The "fat-necked custodians" have used up all their credit, and Mapanje is among the chattering wagtails who now speak of what went on in Banda's Malawi.

James Gibbs. *WLT*. 68, 2 (Spring 1994), pp. 411–12

MARECHERA, DAMBUDZO (1952–1987)

ZIMBABWE

The House of Hunger—a novella, poems, and short stories—is an unrelenting depiction of the stunning effects of poverty and its concomitants of cruelty and pain. As significant as its Rhodesian locale is the novella's adumbration of a species of poverty which can only be known in those countries where racial oppression is a way of life. . . .

The House of Hunger . . . is a controlled explosion of passions. [Dambudzo] Marechera is wonderfully aware of the direction of his work as he leads the reader through new and terrible realms of human suffering. The newness derives from his adamant refusal to imitate the structure and narrative method of the traditional English fictional forms, and, instead, to thrust his reader into a world of distorted experience for which most will have no frame of reference. The distortions are of time and place, the normally consoling solidity in the "backgrounds" of most fiction. Here the dislocation of both dimensions is skillfully contrived to suggest the continuous disconnectedness of the protagonist from the very tactile and earthbound world—of which he is a part and yet not part. Living as he does a fragmented life, the protagonist of this tale, a boy in a Rhodesian township, charts his crazy existence by reference to violence, pain, and revenge. He is exposed from the beginning to brutality as a way of life—a father and brother whose mode of life is physical assault against women; a mother so desperate with her own physical and mental pain as virtually to ignore this urgently needful son; a world beyond the family that offers more vice and cruelty in the form of bullying the weak and being beaten by the strong—a world which is secure only for the traitor and the whore who have grasped its terms. The white world, in larger terms responsible for the chaos, is regarded for much of the time as a kind of disgusting irrelevance. Yet the novella is redolent with a deep black rage against the whites who have confined the African spirit into these houses of hunger where the only release is intestinal violence. . . .

The House of Hunger defies the traditional reduction into story and neatly plotted parts. While these elements are present they are so subtly intermixed into the brittle mosaic that any attempt to extricate them leaves scars on the surface of the work. The misery and madness, pain and want are present in every line simultaneously. The story is only one hard subterraneous vein in this flinty landscape of despair. The novella describes the growth into awareness, madness, and maturity of the protagonist. What lends it its power is the imagistic precision with which it is told, the rhapsody of violence and rage with which it is woven together. Its images, the stuff of real poetry, take their form from the elemental world, and by the poetic force with which they are yoked to the life here described, they crowd the mind with a tangible reality.

Derek Cohen. *Canadian Journal of African Studies.* 15, 2 (1981), pp. 337–39

Though Marechera's work is written against the background of preindependence Zimbabwe, it represents a considerable development in African literature. His work is not pure anticolonial protest, as one might have expected from preindependence Zimbabwe. He writes in a deeply introspective vein and shows a keen interest in unveiling the psychic responses of his protagonists. There is an almost total absence of celebration, romanticizing the African past or glorifying the African personality, such as one finds in the literature of the Négritude movement; none of the exclusive preoccupation with the iniquities, as such, of the white racist minority regime or the guerrilla struggle, as in South African literature or in the early fiction of East Africa. Marechera's work also differs in tone from the gentle prodding irony and satire (largely corrective or reconstructive in intention) of the postindependence novel, especially in West Africa. His expression of disillusionment in his work is deeper even than [Ngugi wa Thiong'o's] or [Ayi Kwei] Armah's; its cynicism more complete than anything [Wole] Soyinka has ever been accused of. There is an element of resignation and a devil-may-care type of attitude in his work. But on closer examination this apparent resignation and the frivolity and recklessness of his characters mask their extreme sensitivity and vulnerability. Their perverse behavior also manifests a kind of assertiveness that can be seen as some form of defensive mechanism against life's utter senselessness and brutality, against all the chaos in their families and the disarray in the nation, which threaten Marechera's characters and infect their whole personalities. . . .

The title story of *The House of Hunger* . . . is written against the background of discontent. It is an expression of disillusionment with both the past and the present, and is written without any illusions about the future. The novella deals with the misery and the sordidness of life in his home and in Rhodesia in general, which is dubbed "the House of Hunger" and from which the central character of the story seeks to escape, as Marechera himself was to do.

Mbulelo [Vizikhungo] Mzamane. In Eldred Durosimi Jones, ed.
African Literature Today. 13 (1983), pp. 203–5

[Marechera] is so preoccupied with violence that the social dimension of his stories fragments into a kaleidoscope of personal protestations. There is virtually no social framework into which his narrative settles. His attempt at psychological realism is a break from both sociopolitical realism and the more conventional stance of the narrator in other Zimbabwean fiction. *The House of Hunger* is not about the processes of alienation or the dynamics of opposing cultures and traditions. The stories allude to an image of a house. The village house, home, and center of cultural consciousness, is metamorphosed into the African mind in Zimbabwe. It is beset by spiritual drought. "Capitalists," "imperialists," and "the bloody whites" are for Peter what have "held the House of Hunger in a stinking grip." Rather than validate this as [Stanlake] Samkange's *The Mourned One* did, Marechera writes a fiction in which the assertion of feelings becomes the substance of the narrative. Hence the varied modes of his fiction are more obtrusive and telling than those found in other Zimbabwean writers. The political dimensions of experience in Zimbabwe are taken for granted in a way that the narrator's violent response to his place in that society is less interesting for its causes than its startling manner of protest. In the title story the narrator, emerging from an abrasive domestic background, goes for a drink with an acquaintance, Harry. They meet his friend Julia in the bar. On the surface that is the story. But beneath this thin series of events are several layers of consciousness which constitute the inner imaginative life of the narrator. By various techniques—stories within stories, patterns of imagery (stitches, stains, blood, breaking)—the fiction establishes the territory of the narrator's mind. Weariness and disillusion with life, protest at missionaries, black informers, whites, education, repeated physical violence, sexual perversion, are markers on a drought-stricken landscape. . . .

Marechera breaks away from most trends in Zimbabwean fiction by accenting the intensity of the inner world of his narrators. The sociohistorical and political context that so concerns other Zimbabwean writers is there as a world with which the narrator has difficulty making contact. His starting point is the opposite to that of other writers. "The silent but desperate voices inside me" have a problem not with understanding that external world but in putting words to it. At one level *The House of Hunger* illustrates the devastating effects of growing up in colonial Rhodesia, but the vision of that devastation is not presented in social realist terms. Here the black narrator is left almost speechless while in the internal world of his consciousness there is a hyperactive verbal iconoclasm that leaves nothing standing but its fictions about itself. Marechera's verbal dexterity outstrips that of most African writers but, as his recent book *Black Sunlight* indicates, his serious concerns with the metaphysics of creativity, and with language itself as a violent instrument, take his fiction beyond the accepted bounds of "African" literature. The writing is sometimes obscure, and his identity crisis as a black Zimbabwean living in exile has thrown him into the searing problems that surround a writer's relation to reality.

T. O. McLoughlin. In G. D. Killam, ed. *The Writing of East and Central Africa*
(London: Heinemann, 1984), pp. 110–11

Marechera's first book, *The House of Hunger*, won *The Guardian* Fiction Award in 1981. It is a collection of stories about a brutalized personal life and a society ground by the white penal system of then Rhodesia. And, if he treats the white with complete cynicism, it is no more nor less than how he treats all experience. Nothing gets special treatment; it is informed by a consistent vision, which puts the book into the class of one that had to be written. . . .

Marechera is by no means the complete artist yet. In his second book, *Black Sunlight*, he perversely exaggerates all the qualities praised in his first book and renders up a concoction. Nonetheless, he is the first black Zimbabwean writer to enjoy freedom, not freedom, of course, in a purely political sense, but freedom of experience and access to his material, without the obstructions and shibboleths of the past. His handling of the theme of the white is my touchstone to this judgment. It is the climate in which *the* great Zimbabwean writer will emerge (who might be the matured Marechera himself). And, it is one which the whites were not able to achieve for themselves, for all their privileges. After all, excepting the single figure of Doris Lessing, they were not able to produce a writer of international stature in ninety years.

Colin Style. Ariel. 16, 3 (July 1985), pp. 62–63

Marechera's philosophy derives from his extreme individualism, rejecting any kind of rules and constraints. While he strongly disapproved of colonial rule, he is equally critical of the government of independent Zimbabwe. This creates a lot of enemies for him. He, in turn, feels like a misunderstood lone campaigner. . . .

Behind his vacillating face—his "black mask," as he so often refers to it in his stories—is a permanent storm, a battle of contradictions which threaten to blast his mind. *Mindblast* [*or the Definitive Buddy*] illustrates this explosion of mind, soul, senses, concepts, and reason. . . .

He remains between the two worlds of Africa and Europe, between the experience of physical poverty and cultural wealth, between colonialism and racism and the rebellion against them. . . .

The world for Marechera is split up, shattered into many pieces which he cannot put together. He himself is split. This motif one finds frequently in his work, especially in *The House of Hunger*. His own distorted mirror image stares back at him like a jeering monkey, or the actual split of the personality into twin brothers where the one does and says things which the other finds embarrassing and beyond his control. His writing is full of contradictions and paradoxes. It disturbs the mind, it disrupts realities and patterns of thought so far taken for granted. At the same time, it creates pictures of striking beauty and lucidity, opening new horizons and dimensions of feeling, of grasping, of sensing life. This distinguishes him from all other African writers and gives him a special significance in modern African literature.

Flora [Veit-] Wild. New African. 223 (April 1986), p. 52

Metaphor in Marechera attempts to artistically contain chaos. In the absence of significance, of correspondence, of relationships, which means the death of culture, we have "sharp howling winds scattering grit." The drought is psychological and spiritual sweeping away normal referential language. The narrator typifies the collapse of inner and outer coherence. Metaphor in *The House of Hunger* is singular in anglophone African literature not for any yearning after authentic culture but as a protest at its absence. . . .

The metaphoric narrative of Marechera—"the drought had raised its great red hand"—exemplifies the argument that metaphor operates by a radical departure from the normal functions and relations within language, and between language and the world referred to. Metaphor is a Janus figure that makes nonsense if you look from one point of view and remarkable vision from another. It shatters literal sense. To start with the relation between the metaphor "hand" and the object which that term designates in normal usage is destroyed. . . .

Metonymy is rejected by Marechera because the conditions for the accepted or authentic manner of vision within his culture—semantic homogeneity, metonymy—have disappeared. The incoherence in life calls for a radical departure from the normal linguistic manner to a mode that attacks and distorts language itself.

In this light *The House of Hunger* and *Black Sunlight*, his second novel, are unique cultural statements within Shona society, no less authentic for being in English or for their verbal pyrotechnics. Such writing could continue in Zimbabwe, it might be argued, if the liberation war had not ended, or if the writer had profound ideological differences with the governing mores of independent Zimbabwe. History has ruled out the first possibility, but the second, if Marechera's latest book, *Mindblast*, is a fair indication, is still open to dispute.

T. O. McLoughlin. *Nouvelles du Sud.* 4 (1986), pp. 85–86

Dambudzo Marechera is an outsider. He cannot be included in any of the categories into which modern African literature is currently divided: his writings have nothing in common with the various forms of anticolonial or antineocolonial protest literature, nor can they be interpreted as being an expression of the identity-crisis suffered by an African exiled in Europe.

Marechera refuses to identify himself with any particular race, culture, or nation; he is an extreme individualist, an anarchistic thinker. He rejects social and state regimentation—be it in colonial Rhodesia, in England, or in independent Zimbabwe; the freedom of the individual is of the utmost importance. In this he is uncompromising, and this is how he tries to live. . . .

In *Black Sunlight* Marechera fuses the diverse forms of self-expression and lifestyle of London's "alternative" scene: when he wrote the book, in 1979, he was living in a huge commune of artists, drug addicts, meditators, and individualists of all kinds. In a process of philosophical and poetic self-discovery, the book explores the relationship between Marechera's concept of the total freedom of the spirit as it can be manifested in art, and the political action which aims at gaining this freedom—anarchism. Marechera discusses in many different ways questions of reality, of man's capacity to perceive reality, of illusion and delusion, and of the task of the artist in relation to all these. . . .

At the same time, *Black Sunlight* is a poeticized confrontation with the theories of the futurists . . . and the surrealists, whom it quotes and itself tries to emulate in their *écriture automatique*. Like them, Marechera seeks the liberation of language from the fetters of syntax, a free "stream-of-consciousness" similar to that of James Joyce. In *Black Sunlight*, different planes of consciousness, recognizable stories and dreamlike visions, memories, and reflections continually blend, flowing into images which are no longer recognizable to the intellect, but which the reader must feel and imagine.

This novel also presents Marechera's dichotomous view of women. On the one hand, the various female characters—from the anthropologist rescuer to the individual woman terrorists—are depicted as being very positive, self-assured, independent, having a positive attitude toward life, and are strong, stronger even than the men. Blind Marie, the photographer's wife, as the symbol of sensibility, is wild and unspoiled, rooted in her own "black sunlight." . . .

Mindblast [or the Definitive Buddy] is a miscellany of three plays, a prose narrative, a collection of poems, and a park-bench diary. In a more accessible style than in his first two books, Marechera describes with wit, intelligence, and vivid imagery his view of the newly independent state of Zimbabwe: the materialism, the political intolerance, the stupidity and corruption, the socialist slogans, how a few become rich while the masses become poorer. At the same time, the author's own existence as an artist preys on his mind, full of hate, self-pitying, or ironic; he is out of place, made to feel an outsider, misunderstood, despised, taken for a madman. . . .

For Zimbabwe, with its lack of public criticism, *Mindblast* represents an important contribution. However, overall, the book suffers from a viewpoint which is too abstruse for the ordinary reader to identify with: the egocentric existence of the poet acted out in the bar and saloon. The most powerful literary statement is to be found in the poems. Unfortunately, Marechera's poems—apart from those in *Mindblast*—have never been published in a single collection, only sporadically in anthologies and journals. Strongly influenced by T. S. Eliot, they illustrate in a concentrated form the extraordinary creative power of Marechera's writing. With a highly unusual choice of words and their contextual associations, through the juxtaposition of opposites to the point of paradox, through the combination of the contradictory, he creates unexpected, inspired, shocking images of great intensity.

Flora Veit-Wild. *Zambezia*. 14, 2 (1987), pp. 113, 117–19

The House of Hunger is . . . a depiction of not only social deviances but also spiritual and physical exhaustion of the individual in a callous society. Marechera sees even sex as an instrument of domination and also as a function of white domination. *The House of Hunger* which serves as a metaphor for these stories epitomizes the prison nature of township life. There is so much hatred, violence, and horror that one wonders at the impossibility of sane minds retaining their sanity. The characters stumble from one absurdity to another, from one hopeless situation to another and most times they disintegrate in a blaze of horrifying activities.

Frustration is also another aspect of Dambudzo Marechera's writings that is significant. The characters who are nonconformists are seen by a majority of the people as eccentric iconoclasts. In the short story entitled "The Writer's Grain," he tells the story of a writer whose works are found wanting and whose personal life is about breaking up. This frustration makes the writer become almost mad with bitterness. Furthermore, in *Black Sunlight* . . . the author uses a principal character known as Christian, a press photographer who moves through the society to depict the frustrations of the people. It is through the personal frustration of Christian that Marechera records glimpses of the prevalent chaos and social disorder. The novel is also suffused with incidents of sex and violence. The result of this aimless destruction reflects the general aimless direction of the people. Marechera writes: "In our wake, smashed institutions, smashed minds. Smashed traffic signs. Smashed courtrooms. Smashed armories." . . . The author presents these signs of destruction as imaginative photographs of a society doomed to violence.

The third novel, *Mindblast* [*or the Definitive Buddy*], which does not rise up to the standards set by *The House of Hunger*, is equally concerned with a society in disarray. Most of the characters are also replicas of the numerous deranged, embattled, bitter characters that people the stories of Dambudzo Marechera. However, it is in the use of language that the author succeeds in drawing the greatest attention to his work. The South African writer Mbulelo Mzamane feels that his narrative technique incorporates an interesting avant-garde experiment. In confirmation, Juliet Okonkwo presents the most interesting assessment of Marechera's style when she states: "Marechera displays genius in the manipulation of words and ideas. He communicates mostly in images and makes language do new things through the application of words and expressions to actions and thoughts which are normally strangers to each other. His usual comparisons come from the habit of seeing the relatedness of many things." It is this ability that makes his loss to the literary world very painful.

Ezenwa-Ohaeto. ALA Bulletin. 14, 1 (Winter 1988), pp. 7–8

All of Marechera's narratives, including *The House of Hunger*, the novel *Black Sunlight*, and his text collection, *Mindblast, or the Definitive Buddy*, demand much from the reader. The main reasons are the writer's mixing of narrative modes or genres, and what I would like to call his technique of fragmentation. None of his prose, not even the very short "The Slow Sound of His Feet" . . . is either pure fiction or pure autobiography, but both. None of his stories are told in a realistic or nonrealistic manner throughout but move back and forth constantly between different modes. Finally, the author attacks the concept of linear time that we ascribe traditionally to narrated fiction. As a result, past, present, and future experience, reflection, and nightmarish dreams merge in Marechera's work and can hardly be distinguished. Such narrative strategy naturally questions the unity of the mind and the progress of time, two fundamental presuppositions of most postcolonial writing, whose intention it is to overcome the experience of dispossession and not to confirm its lasting continuity after independence. Marechera challenges these assumptions, and by breaking away from conventional ways of storytelling, he does not merely dabble in formal experimentation—as some of his critics maintain—but radically questions the view held by many postcolonial writers that it is not only possible, but morally obligatory, to reinstate a sort of status quo that is considered to represent one's identity.

Marechera's persona, his first-person narrator in "The Slow Sound of His Feet," is unable to restore a life that is both meaningful and worth living. His experience is one of loss and, toward the end, perhaps one of temporary escape. The young student tells us how he loses first his father, then his speech, and finally his mother. Even his sister, appearing in one of his nightmares, seems dead.

These events are presented so that we cannot be sure whether the student dreams them or actually experiences them. Though he repeatedly uses phrases like "mother woke me up," "I woke up," "when I woke up," or "when I opened my eyes," the borderline between waking and sleeping-dreaming, between the outer and inner world, is crossed and recrossed so subtly that we feel the whole episode is one long moment of reminiscing in which memories, dreams, and momentary thoughts and feelings coalesce into a state of profound loss and alienation. . . .

Marechera paints a harrowing picture of individual suffering and of a totally isolated and alienated young man, a person who bears much resemblance to the author himself: his father, too, was killed in a car accident, the author suffered from a stutter, had lost his teeth, and had been brutally beaten up as a student. . . . [The] loss of speech and language symbolizes the destruction of man as a human and a social being; it is a loss that counts more than that of one's parents. . . . Marechera's student is reduced to someone who is merely able to record sense impressions: "The hot flush of it shook us in each other's arms. Outside, the night was making a muffled gibberish upon the roof and the wind had tightened its hold upon the windows. We could hear, in the distance, the brass and strings of a distant military band." The loss of one's language stands for the destruction of the mind, and if the unity of the mind is destroyed, the world can neither be re-created nor can a vision of it be projected into the future. Marechera's narrative technique symbolizes his view of a world fallen apart and torn asunder.

Dieter Riemenschneider. RAL. 20, 3 (Fall 1989), pp. 405–7

The posthumously published volume *The Black Insider* . . . consists of the title text, three short stories, and two poems, preceded by editor Flora Veit-Wild's introduction, wherefrom we learn that a number of unpublished manuscripts— six novels, five plays, over a hundred poems, and several essays—were left behind by the late author. . . .

"The Black Insider," written in 1978, is "an important and unique literary contribution to the question of what exile has meant for a whole generation of Zimbabweans," states the editor. The story is autobiographical. In the shadow of war a variegated group of people is encapsuled in a dilapidated old building, where they pass their days in squalor and poverty and utter degradation, alienated, color-aware, uprooted from their culture. . . . Throughout, Marechera shrewdly and thoughtfully depicts the poverty, disillusionment, failure, alienation, squalor, and, above all, loneliness of a black intellectual highly disappointed by society: "I am the rape / marked on the map / the unpredictable savage / set down on the page / the obsequious laborer / who will never be emperor." He consciously plunges into intoxication, finding there a temporary relief: "It had been hell, the whole week. Alone in his flat eating semolina and soya beans. Trying to write his weekly poem. Feeling suffocated by the stale gas-fire air in the room. Trying to think out the pattern behind the deeds (or lack of them) in his own life."

Nadezda Obradović. WLT. 65, 3 (Summer 1991), p. 538

Published posthumously, *Cemetery of Mind* easily brings to mind Christopher Okigbo's *Labyrinths* in many ways. With Dambudzo Marechera's death, African literature lost a young star whose meteoric appearance has left an illuminating trail. Though better known for his collection of short stories entitled *The House of Hunger*, Marechera in fact deserves far more praise as a poet. He is highly imagistic, fresh, shocking, and delightful despite the pervading angry and sad mood in his poems. . . .

Compiled by Flora Veit-Wild, who has done an excellent job of assembling the poems, *Cemetery of Mind* is divided into twelve sections—a quasi-epic form to reflect the struggles of the poet at home and abroad. The poetic voice grows more agonized, darker, grimmer, and more intensely passionate as the poet becomes increasingly defiant at finding neither Britain nor Zimbabwe hospitable. The growing morbidity is accentuated by hunger, homelessness, drink, sex, and disease. Marechera writes on political and social issues, but as he becomes more personal, love and death become major preoccupations before the "darkling complexion of the horizon."

The poet's words are finely honed, the lines elegantly crafted. It is most satisfying that the free spirit and wandering mind of the poet are disciplined in his craft. This tension is never lost on the careful reader. In Marechera, opposites meet, not just the black-white love relationship but also in flowers and metal, beauty and ugliness. It is the conflict within, reinforced by these images of opposites, that gives enduring strength to *Cemetery of Mind*. Marechera has very strong opening and concluding lines, which not only make the poems memorable, but impress the experiences themselves indelibly on the reader. For instance, he closes "Landscape Gardens" with the line "They win whose silence is a grenade blast." . . .

To read *Cemetery of Mind* is to be cast under a spell, to be transported from the physical into the realm of the soul. Marechera's unconventional life immensely enriched his poetry. By the time one has read the poems, one can only exhale and wonder about the poetic genius of such a young man. The consolation is that the poetic charmer will live forever in our minds.

Tanure Ojaide. WLT. 68, 2 (Summer 1994), p. 417

MARSHALL, PAULE (1929–   )

BARBADOS

As a first-generation West Indian-American and the author of three novels and a collection of short stories, Paule Marshall gives evidence in her work of a marginal duality similar to that felt by immigrants. While not herself an immigrant, Marshall grew up in an immigrant community whose legacy to her and her work is a share of its alienation. Marshall's first novel, *Brown Girl, Brownstones*, may explain the source of that marginality. The basic conflict of this novel, between the protagonist's mother and father, overshadows the protagonist's coming of age and her search for identity. The mother has accepted the crass values of the upwardly-mobile Barbadian immigrant community in which the family lives, while the father maintains a dreamer's futile pride in the cruel face of American racism and disappointment. Their daughter, Selina, vacillates between these two extremes, neither a Barbadian nor an American, but a permanent and unhappy outsider. The novel ends with her escape to Barbados, where, we presume, her alienation will continue—if not deepen.

In her second book, the collection entitled *Soul Clap Hands and Sing*, Marshall explores the alienated marginality seen in Selina through different characters. The four stories comprising the collection are set all over the Americas: in Barbados, Brooklyn, British Guiana, and Brazil. Each story focuses on an elderly, marginal man, and the point at which he realizes the extent of his alienation. Despite the implication of the volume's title, a line borrowed and modified slightly from [W. B.] Yeats's "Sailing to Byzantium" ("An aged man is but a paltry thing, / A tattered coat upon a stick, unless / Soul clap its hands and sing, and louder sing / For every tatter in its mortal dress"), the concern of the stories is not with the age of the men who are their protagonists, but with their souls. Each of the protagonists has lost, as he has gained partial admission into the dominant culture or the ruling class, his soul—his faith in God, in his fellows, and in himself. . . .

Each of these stories is a story of marginality, a story of the pain of the immigrant, the returned immigrant, the upwardly mobile individual who has forfeited his place in a society which is rapidly changing. Each is critical of, yet at the same time sympathetic to, the plight of these old men for whom Soul has long since ceased to sing. Paule Marshall has not, as many of her readers seem to think, merely set up straw men like coats on sticks to be knocked down by the force of her political argument. There is no character in these stories who is without blame, who is completely human and responsible. This fact, and the fact that her sympathies are divided between the old men and the characters through whom they receive their visions, indicate that she understands and shares something of their marginality.

Marilyn Nelson Waniek. Callaloo. 6, 2 (Spring–Summer 1983), pp. 46, 55

At first thought, *The Chosen Place, the Timeless People* seems the least typical of Paule Marshall's novels. Each of the other novels is focused upon the experience of single individuals; however far-reaching the implications, Marshall's vision in these works moves outward from the situation of a woman in a problematic family situation. *Brown Girl, Brownstones* and *Praisesong for the Widow* are fictions of the private life, while *The Chosen Place, the Timeless People* seems, in contrast, to be primarily a fiction of the public life. The novel's length, its range of psychological themes, the international and interracial cast of characters, and—most distinctively—its economic and political dimensions make it seem a very different kind of novel indeed.

But second thoughts, as they often do, complicate all these seemings. For one thing, there is a social, even a political, dimension to both *Brown Girl, Brownstones* and *Praisesong for the Widow*. In each of these novels, a woman explores her connection to the world—the *umbilicus* is the family, that most personal of social institutions. Both Selina and Avey achieve a new relationship to their families that is more fulfilling to them as human beings in a larger social world. Further, it seems to me, all novels by significant writers share thematic concerns that are constants—concerns, if not obsessions—which along with other qualities of craft and vision lift an author's work above the level of the commercially viable. *The Chosen Place, the Timeless People* does not lie outside the continuing concerns of Paule Marshall. Quite to the contrary, this second novel develops very similar concerns to those which are more readily seen in the earlier and later novels.

The vehicle of the author's most charged concerns in each of these works is the female protagonist. The size and complexity of *The Chosen Place, the Timeless People* has obscured, for many readers, the similarities between Selina Boyce in *Brown Girl, Brownstones*, Merle Kinbona in this novel, and Avey Johnson in *Praisesong for the Widow*. These three protagonists comprise, in fact, a history of human psychosocial development. Marshall's gallery of portraits carries our attention from childhood to old age. Selina Boyce is the image of woman experiencing the "identity crisis" of youth; Avey Johnson is the figure of the mature woman dealing with the "crisis of integrity" which accompanies the final stages of development. In these same Eriksonian terms, Merle Kinbona, the vexed and difficult protagonist of *The Chosen Place, the Timeless People*, is an image of the crisis of the middle years, the "crisis of generativity." Paule Marshall's longest and most complicated work of fiction has at its center a figure of human consciousness coming to grips with the need to be a cause, the need to make things happen, but in a world where such efforts are all but impossible to achieve. Like the portrait of Selina which began the set, and the portrait of Avey which seems to complete it, Marshall's portrait of Merle is both richly psychological and richly social. But in *The Chosen Place, the Timeless People* the relationships between the psychological and social dimensions of the character are developed within a denser context of ideas, actions and ideologies which are particular to the middle years of persons—and societies.

Joseph T. Skerrett, Jr. Callaloo. 6, 2 (Spring–Summer 1983), pp. 68–69

In two of her three novels to date, Paule Marshall undertakes an in-depth study of the West Indian society at home (in *The Chosen Place, the Timeless People*) and

abroad (in *Brown Girl, Brownstones*). Being the daughter of West Indians and having spent a part of her adult life in the West Indies, Marshall is undoubtedly better
acquainted with the nature of West Indian life than any other Afro-American novelist. This more than superficial acquaintance serves her in good stead as a novelist, for it is the basis of her ability to create credible West Indian characters and to
affect a peculiarly West Indian atmosphere, as that atmosphere is created by West
Indians in Harlem and as it shapes island life in the West Indies. . . . [For] the first
time, we have an Afro-American author who demonstrates, without caricature,
how racial complacency affects the West Indian lifestyle. It is because of her grasp
of the West Indians' sense of community and racial complacency that Marshall is
able to exploit a wide range of West Indian sensibilities, especially in *Brown Girl,
Brownstones*. She is not apt to be swept away by idealism . . . when she follows a
character along the road to racial identity and cultural relevance. Nor is she apt to
distort by easy symbolism . . . the subtle but trenchant tensions which attend the
stable but struggling personality or the personality in the state of metamorphosis.
To discuss the characters and themes of her novels is to reveal the essential "West-
Indianness" of the author.

    Brown Girl, Brownstones traces the development of Selina Boyce, daugh-
ter of a Barbadian couple living in Brooklyn. Through Selina's observation and
participation in the lives of the West Indians who board at her parents'
Brownstone home, Marshall is able to synthesize her interest in individual characters with her interest in the dynamics of this Barbadian community. As Selina
matures, so does her and the reader's understanding of the individual and
domestic forces which shape her life and the lives of her parents. . . . Selina is
caught in the middle of a temperamental and ideological clash between her
mother (Silla) and her father (Deighton). She gradually understands that a life
of hard work and unfulfilled dreams has transformed Silla into a self-centered,
scheming, possessive, and vindictive woman whose tenderness is buried somewhere under the debris of her Barbadian past. . . .

    In the characterizations of Silla and Deighton, Marshall demonstrates a
battle of wills that is universal in its implication. In terms of sheer survival Silla
wins, but only because she replaces love of self and love of family with love of
the values of white middle-class society. Deighton loses because he has to fight
in an environment where his personal armor (love, tenderness, and casualness)
is turned against him in a world where aggressive and materialistic competition
is glorified. But Silla and Deighton are both losers in the sense that the essential
humanity of each is eventually destroyed.

Melvin B. Rahming. *The Evolution of the West Indian's Image in the Afro-
American Novel* (Millwood, N. Y.: Associated Faculty Press, 1986), pp. 110–12

[In *Praisesong for the Widow*], Marshall continues to explore the dynamics of
the West Indian cultural landscape, and its African heritage. The very title of
the novel attempts to celebrate cultural transition and African continuity.

    In traditional Africa, the praise-song is a chant or poem-song which dra-
matizes the achievements of an individual or community within the realm of

history and extended family. Performed by the griot or griotte, the oral historian, genealogist, and musician, the praise-song is a highly developed "genre" in African oral literature. It is both a sacred and profane modality. In Marshall's invocation of praise-singing we see how the sacred overlaps with the profane reality. Avey Johnson's praise-song fulfills a vital function: it allows her to create a new opportunity for spiritual empowerment as she learns a new understanding of social propriety. . . .

A summary of *Praisesong* shows that Avey Avatara Johnson is a comfortably middle-class, self-conscious, elderly widow, who during a Caribbean cruise with two friends abruptly decides to leave the ship. When the ship docks for a few hours on the Caribbean island of Grenada, she disembarks and plans to fly back to her home, New York City. Significantly, her trip has been jolted by dreams of her long dead Great-Aunt Cuney of Tatem, South Carolina. Destiny intervenes, and she misses the plane to New York only to get involved in the annual festival of the "out-island" people—people of the smaller island, Carriacou—who live and work in Grenada. The excursion back to their native land (Carriacou and by way of myth/ritual, Africa) is in fact their annual rite of rejuvenation, their rite of the eternal return, their transhuman communication with the African past and its sacred forces. The Big Drum ceremony is the enactment of their African past, their native land. The dance creates temporal space between reality and the spirit world. By going to Carriacou and experiencing the intensity of neo-African ritual dancing and music, Avey Johnson rediscovers her own sense of place as an American of African ancestry. She rediscovers what it means to bond with people and with the spirit, and not with *things*. As she leaves Carriacou, she resolves to renew her ties with her own ancestral and spiritual home, Tatem, South Carolina.

Avey Johnson's classical journey occurs on two levels: she is, in essence, the heroine embarking on a quest for spiritual enlightenment and renewed strength to deal with the human world. The journey becomes a validation of Avey's American social consciousness. By the middle age of life, Avey has settled for the illusion of El Dorado; that is to say, she has given in to the complacency of upper-middle-class living and values. However, the spiritual void in her life began even before the death of her husband. By dividing the novel into four sections, with the ritual-implied titles of "Runagate," "Sleeper's Wake," "Lavé Tete," and "The Beg Pardon," Marshall demonstrates how the journey motif is inherent to Avey's spiritual and social awakening. Through transhuman communication, Avey reestablishes order out of her own chaos.

Angelita Reyes. In Adam J. Sorkin, ed. *Politics and the Muse:*
Studies in the Politics of Recent American Literature (Bowling Green,
Ohio: Bowling Green State University Popular Press, 1989), pp. 185–87

Paule Marshall's project in this deceptively simple novel [*Praisesong for the Widow*] is a bold one. This novel becomes a journey not only for Avey, but for her readers, for to appreciate the widow's experience's fully, the reader must journey with her in the same active process of recognizing and reassembling cultural signs. . . .

Marshall's concern is to take us through a journey of self-recognition and healing. Her text requires of us that we have a knowledge of "diaspora literacy," an ability to read a variety of cultural signs of the lives of Africa's children at home and in the New World. Marshall articulates the scattering of the African peoples as a trauma—a trauma that is constantly repeated anew in the lives of her lost children. The life of the modern world and the conditions under which Afro-Americans have to live, the sacrifices they must make to succeed on the terms of American society, invariably mean a severing from their cultural roots. As Avey learns to her cost, this is tantamount to a repetition, in her private life, of that original historical separation. This is a sacrifice too high. To understand the nature of the journey and the magnitude of the sacrifice, it is necessary not simply to mark the passage of Avey's journey, but to become fellow travelers with her. It is not only Marshall's heroine, but Marshall's readers as well, who need to acquire "diaspora literacy." For to do so is to be able to see again the fragments that make up the whole, not as isolated individual and even redundant fragments, but as part of a creative and sustaining whole.

Thus the first task for the reader is to learn, like the widow whose journey we experience, to recognize the cultural signs of a past left littered along our roads of doubtful progress. The crucial factor about *Praisesong* is that it is a novel about the dispossession of the scattered African peoples from their past and their original homeland and, in the present, from their communities and each other. The boldness of Marshall's project here is to take us through a private history of material acquisition and cultural dispossession, which becomes a metaphor for the history of the group, the history of the African in the New World. The challenge therefore is not to look at literacy or cultural artifact as abstraction, but as a concrete aspect of our lives, where our meaning—our story—becomes what we can read and what we can no longer, or never could, read about ourselves and our lives. The act of reading becomes an exercise in identifications—to recognize life experiences and historic transformations that point the way toward a celebration, a coming together attainable only through an understanding and acceptance of the demands of the past. . . .

Praisesong for the Widow is a tribute in praise of the homecoming of a woman who succeeds in making an awesome physical and spiritual odyssey. Avey's epiphany is presented to us as an arduous progress through a partially familiar landscape littered with cultural artifacts as clues. The widow's narrative becomes a map, with music, song, dance, dress, and ritual as the cultural registers we need to decode to follow her across the terrain to journey's end. But journey's end is Africa. By the end of her journey, Avey has symbolically reversed the diasporic journey and that wrenching Middle Passage. Through Avey's life, Africa is once more reinvented with worth, the continent is no longer fractured from human history but restored to consciousness with valid meaning. Through the healing of one of Africa's lost daughters, a scattered people are made whole again, and the question "What is your nation?" is no longer a bewildering and devastating mystery.

Abena P. A. Busia. In Cheryl A. Wall, ed. Changing Our Own Words
(New Brunswick, N. J.: Rutgers University Press, 1989), pp. 196–99

Marshall is one of the few Afro-American women writers who focuses on the relationship between black people in the United States and the West Indies in her literary work. . . . In *Brown Girl, Brownstones*, Marshall portrays a girl growing up within the West Indian community in New York. Her second novel is set on an imaginary island in the Caribbean. In *Praisesong for the Widow*, Marshall describes a journey through the West Indies.

Important themes in Marshall's work are the relationship between the individual and the community, relations between women and men, ritual, dance and the influence of the past on the present, often symbolized by older characters such as Miss Thompson in *Brown Girl, Brownstones*, Leesy Walkes in *The Chosen Place, the Timeless People*, and both Great-Aunt Cuney and Lebert Joseph in *Praisesong for the Widow*. . . .

Analyzing the objects in *Praisesong for the Widow*, one can trace one of the most important lines of the story as follows: as a child, Avey hears the story of the landing of the slaves, the Igbos, in Tatem, from her great-aunt Cuney who had learned it from her grandmother. By narrating this story again and again, great-aunt Cuney entrusts Avey with the mission to keep the memory of the past alive. . . . We can explain in Greimasian terms that Avey is the subject, Great-Aunt Cuney the destinator, and the object is to carry out a mission. Although the precise meaning of this mission still escapes her, little Avey feels that she has been given a task. . . .

In the course of the story, the subject Avey neglects this particular object—the mission—and tries to acquire other objects, like social ascension and material wealth. The destinator here is society, not a personified sender. The norms and values in this society are determined by white people. . . .

In their struggle for social ascension, Avey and Jay have to accept the norms and values of the dominant group in society. They neglect their own cultural heritage. They become successful members of the black middle class, but underneath the surface, Avey always has the feeling that they have given up some essential part of themselves. At the end of the story, the subject reaches the initial object, that is, fulfillment of the mission. Avey sets out to make the history of the African in the United States known.

Lucia Nankoe and Essa Reijmers. In Geoffrey V. Davis and Hena Maes-
Jelinek, eds. *Crisis and Creativity in the New Literatures in English*
(Amsterdam: Rodopi, 1990), pp. 492–94

Paule Marshall's three novels—*Brown Girl, Brownstones*; *The Chosen Place, the Timeless People*; and *Praisesong for the Widow*—successively illustrate stages of the historically grounded female quest . . . the decision to investigate the historical past, difficulties in assimilating it, and a purposeful incorporation of historical past into the present self. . . . Selina is exasperated by her family's expectations of her, including both her probable occupation and her relationship with the tribe. Initially rejecting the heritage embodied in her mother . . . [she] eventually brings both her mother's and another older woman's knowledge to the task of self-construction. . . . Selina, at the end of *Brown Girl, Brownstones*, embarks for the Caribbean islands of her progenitors. In *Chosen Place*, Merle Kinbona . . . [experiences] pain and confusion at the overwhelming historical oppression that has constructed the present. Lacking [the] ability to escape to another context, she is forced to find the materials for reinterpretation of self and history in her immediate surroundings. Like *Brown Girl*, this novel ends with the beginning of a journey. Merle's departure for Africa, unlike her earlier voyage to England, takes her to a site that may invigorate while it discloses its mixed histories; it incorporates the origins of free black cultures, the historical past of slavers, the personal past of an unforgiving husband, and the future in the form of Merle's daughter. . . . [The] form of Merle's life has not yet coalesced, but reinterpretation of history . . . can construct a fuller version of the self. Completing the cycle, *Praisesong* links the acceptance of tribal history to the full experience of one's personal history. When Avatara almost simultaneously rediscovers both, she emerges as an avatar of her ancestral women griots. . . . Avatara knows both form and content of her historical message for the present. Unlike the earlier novels, *Praisesong* ends with the female quester's return home.

In her depictions of female quests, Marshall follows [Zora Neale] Hurston in making storytelling central. Listening to stories motivates some questers. Telling stories helps to heal others. Above all, the sense of community involved in the participatory interchange of teller and audience strengthens the questers' identities. In *Brown Girl*, with its adolescent quester, older characters generally tell stories to younger ones. In *Chosen Place*, the middle-aged exchange stories. Selina must absorb the narratives of her parents and their generation, and Merle must draw out and contribute to the flow of personal stories in her mostly middle-aged circle. Merle's search for her daughter, however, implies subsequent participation in the intergenerational pattern: questers do not choose one pattern or the other, but participate in each at different stages in their lives or in different roles during the same stage. *Praisesong* exalts the intergenerational narrative by making it Avatara's vocation. Both her process in claiming it and her conception of storytelling purposes, however, diverge from those of Marshall's earlier novels and from a large portion of other African-American fiction. All three of Marshall's novels emphasize the integral relationship of storytelling and the female quest. Collaboratively constructing stories, both tribal and individual, furthers the development of both community and individual. The quester must find an empowering, participatory audience to help her articulate her own destiny within its larger destiny.

Missy Dehn Kubitschek. Claiming the Heritage: African-American Women
Novelists and History (Jackson: University Press of Mississippi, 1991), pp. 69–72

Paule Marshall's new novel, *Daughters*, is the story of Ursa Mackenzie, a woman born in the West Indies, educated at an Ivy League college in the 1960s, and active in the Civil Rights Movement until joining the white corporate world as vice president of the National Consumer Research Corporation. She has a boyfriend she doesn't like and a best friend who feeds and scolds her. She calls herself young, restless, and upwardly mobile. . . .

While *Daughters* is primarily Ursa's story, it's also the history of a group of other women who are in direct or remote ways connected to her. Attempting to trace how, exactly, Ursa came to be in such a dazed, silent state, Marshall explores the lives of the women who surround her: her father's mistress, Astral Forde; and Celestine, her father's maid. She also moves far back in history, to a time before Ursa was born, reviving the voices of her real and spiritual grandmothers. Like Ursa, some of these women have made one compromise too many; they have seen too much personal and political disappointment. In many ways, *Daughters* is a feminist novel, not so much about empowerment as about inertia, exhaustion, and the struggle to recover will. . . .

Daughters is structured as a series of uncanny parallels between New York and the West Indies, between past and present women. We're asked to see Ursa as an incarnation of Astral Forde, whom we also see going in for an abortion, or of Congo Jane, an ancient revolutionary who also "loved pretty things." After a while this method seems simplistic; the plot grows heavy with forced echoes. By making her women mirror one another, Marshall seems to hope they will be seen as descendants of one vast, overarching spirit-of-woman, an unbroken daughter-chain.

Emily White. *VLS*. November 1991, pp. 6–7

For Paule Marshall, the transformation of the instruments of Western culture under the power and influence of the folk is a primary condition for the production of black culture in the New World. In her principal works, the folk return not only to disturb the dominant version of history and culture, but also to promote an Afro-American modernism that, by sustaining the tension between the persistent ancestral voice in black cultures and imposed European forms, seeks to affirm an indigenous language of history and self in the space of the other while unraveling the ideological and political necessity that justifies a Caribbean narrative. . . .

Moreover, the question of how to represent and understand colonial modernism and its narrative of history is of the utmost importance to Marshall; it provides the ideological and theoretical underpinning for most of her major works. If her texts seem to keep on returning to the terms by which the colonized can articulate the past, it is because she believes that the present order of oppression and reification can only be reversed if its material conditions—and what she might consider to be the necessity of history—are fully comprehended. But Marshall's novels are unique in another sense: they probe the rules by which the black experience in the New World can be interpreted and represented. These novels struggle with the linguistic and psychological blockage that hampers the hermeneutical act, the rules of overdetermination that often make it impossible for the reader to gain access to those original meanings that have been repressed in the Middle Passage of the black experience. Marshall's major works thus strive to provide a metacommentary on the painful coexistence of European modernist institutions and the dynamic survivals of the African experience in the islands. In addition, Marshall's subjects often make narrative turns toward the Caribbean landscape in an attempt to capture what she aptly calls "thoughts and feelings about the Middle Passage," and to elaborate "the psychological damage brought on by history."

Although Marshall perceives history in terms of its effects, rather than as what Fredric Jameson . . . calls "a reified force," her novels—like those of her contemporary, George Lamming—also strive to unmask the necessity of alienating history and even to provide a theoretical justification for an alternative episteme. Indeed, underlying Marshall's well-known concern for the nightmare of history and its alienating necessities is the desire for an ideal (and hence modern) version of the black experience which both transforms African culture and transcends the colonial tradition. . . . The roots of Caribbean modernism can actually be traced to the paradoxes and contradictions [Sylvia] Wynter recognizes in the Africans' attempt to adapt themselves to the Caribbean landscape while transforming its nature. . . .

In effect, folklore and popular culture played a central role in the transplanted Africans' quest for an indigenous language that could help them transcend reified history. According to Wynter, "Folklore was the cultural guerrilla resistance against the market economy." This resistance constitutes a key subtext in Marshall's novels: it is represented by the stories told by Barbadian immigrants in *Brown Girl, Brownstones*, the indigenous Carnival sustained by the peasants of Bournehill in *The Chosen Place, the Timeless People*, and the national dances of Carriacou replayed by the displaced descendants of African slaves in *Praisesong for the Widow*. Whereas colonial history is represented as painful and alienating, a servant of the plantation system and the market economy, the voices of the subaltern affirm the history of the Africans, and the forms that history takes, as the "absent cause" that is shaping a Caribbean national culture.

Simon Gikandi. Writing in Limbo: Modernism and Caribbean Literature (Ithaca, N. Y.: Cornell University Press, 1992), pp. 169–71

MAXIMIN, DANIEL (1947–   )

GUADELOUPE

L'Isolé Soleil is primarily a history book in which Daniel Maximin retraces or reconstitutes, with great precision, the evolution of the West Indies, especially Guadeloupe, from the period of slavery till the current time. It begins with the statute of departmentalization in 1946 . . .

The precision of information on which Daniel Maximin relies, the depth of the painting he traces, and the multitude of the aspects he evokes make *L'Isolé Soleil* a veritable historical account and, in addition, confer on this book an obvious epic dimension. . . .

This reference to history is insistently accompanied by a questioning of the nature of history and its effect: in short, the significance that it is capable of assuming.

At the very heart of the text, a chasm opens up—like a sort of challenge—that constantly troubles the comprehension of the reader.

This effect is derived primarily from the manner in which Maximin inextricably links the particular destinies of some heroes—historic and novelistic—with that of an entire people. . . .

The chasm is due equally to the difficulty that we experience in grasping the truly significant events of Caribbean history. Events that involve the characters are relentlessly alternated with those of diverse cataclysms—volcanic eruptions, earthquakes, cyclones—which mark the narration, including the aerial catastrophes which seem to echo back to the gods, and in one of which Louis-Gabriel, the father of Marie-Gabriel, dies. . . . There is in this elaboration of human events and geological accidents, a certain expression of the revitalization of history and the efforts deployed by man in order to master it. Pessimism? Not necessarily. Rather, it is a fascination in the face of that which, seen from a certain spatio-temporal level, is based on both the tragic and the ridiculous.

To this is finally added a number of developments in which the author, through the dialogue lent to his protagonists, proceeds to evaluate this history, searching in particular to define its specific effects. On this level, one is aware of the manner in which Maximin does not limit his approach of the past to positive information habitually represented by objective facts, events, chronology, and biography of the actors involved. He shows that history exists beyond the familiar terrain of historians. It also exists at another level, in the conscience—and more still without doubt, in the unconscious—of the West Indians of today. He underlines its symbolic dimension. . . .

The men and women that Maximin places on the scene are torn between two contradictory demands. On the one hand, they wish to bear witness to the violence that played in the theater of their country and to describe fully the rich culture of their people; on the other hand, they wish to affirm and live out their own individualities, even at times to extremes. They believe that nobody, under whatever pretext, however noble it might be, has the right to deprive them of this individuality.

How to be oneself? What to do so that life, thought, and action are not confined within a system of preestablished categories that are as frustrating as they are fascinating, especially those of race and sex? Such is the problem that each one of them finds himself confronting. . . .

The realization of such a project is evidently not without agony. In particular, it supposes that the dual image of father and mother ceases to occupy definitively, in the conscious and the unconscious of the subject, its former abusive place.

Oral and written literature are testimony to the fact that the heroism of the fathers and the fecundity of the mothers constituted an anchor which allowed the Caribbean people to conserve their integrity in the face of the formidable force of destruction that was slavery. . . .

In reading these texts, one must have noted a preoccupation that constantly animates the two young people: *life*. Life, which in order to develop, with all its concealed potential, has to escape definitively the stifling shade of parental authority and of the heroes of Caribbean history.

With regard to this plan, one is aware of the manner in which Maximin alternates, throughout his novel, two distinct images of birth which clearly contradict one another. On the one hand is the "Negro" birth, linked to the canonical theme of African fecundity. . . . On the other hand is the painful but exalting birth of the individual who attempts to give shape to his existence, outside of any preexisting category. . . .

The biological and institutional link, which is strongly coded on the cultural level, is thus substituted by a relation in which liberty occupies a crucial space. . . .

It is obviously in relation to this theme of birth and life that one must situate the totality of reflection of the different protagonists, throughout *L'Isolé Soleil*, on the power of art and literature.

In this respect, one cannot avoid being struck by another opposition, no less fundamental, that is articulated in the novel: literature and music. Both are dreaded and desired because of what one can call their power of life and their capacity to allow the birth of life.

Bernard Mouralis. PA. 121–22 (1982), pp. 418–20, 423–26†

Lone Sun is the first novel published by Daniel Maximin, a high school teacher and radio journalist born in Guadeloupe, who has lived most of his life in Paris. *L'Isolé Soleil*, the title of the French edition published by Le Seuil, is both typical of a first work of fiction—it is a novel about the writing of a novel—and an unusual achievement in the familiar genre of the *Kunstlerroman*. Its highly allusive style, and its delight in associative wordplay mixed with elusive autobiographical details, show the strong influence of modern poetry. The novel's vast scope aims at the recuperation of the lost history of an entire people, the black diaspora of the Caribbean. A complex narrative texture invites the reader to participate in an elusive puzzle composed of fragments of narratives, dreams, diaries, legends, folktales, and oral history. Its main characters, who are trying to become writers, often exchange pieces of work in progress, along with technical advice.

Read exclusively on an aesthetic level, it is as though the youthful exuberance and overflowing talent of the author did not know when to stop, to impose limits. The richness of the language presents a challenge to the uninitiated reader and, more importantly perhaps, to translators faced with puns in French, English—and sometimes a curious private mixture of Italo-Spanish—and the rhythmic and thematic influence of black music, in particular, Afro-American and Afro-Cuban jazz. Fragments of Antillean folktales, folk characters, and bits and pieces of Creole aphorisms and proverbs are woven into the plot. But the patient reader is amply rewarded, for Maximin has been careful to provide textual clues. Privately encoded images answer each other. Often, one character will take the trouble to explain them to [another]. For example, the twelve proverbs that punctuate the narrative are elucidated very early on in Jonathan's notebook and serve as a guiding thread. In a narrative governed by clusters of images that bind the present to the past, the surface playfulness is an introduction to more serious political considerations. . . .

When reading Maximin, it is often hard to determine where life ends and fiction begins. Often, his most serious and far-reaching passages start with a small detail from real life. For example, he has claimed that the novel's title comes from a memory of his adolescent years. Playing with words, he discovered that the French language could simultaneously pun upon the words for *lone* and *sun*, turning *soleil* into *isolé*, a fact he makes clear at the end of the passage by the same title, "Lone Sun." . . .

Lone Sun develops a dual plot line, presenting itself as a dialogue between history and literature; thus, it continues the inquiry started by C. L. R. James. But it is also a cautionary tale that situates Maximin fully within his own generation. Marie-Gabriel, whose father has just died, searches among the great men of the past for a hero to write about and finds one unmentioned in the history books, Louis Delgrès. Adrien warns Marie-Gabriel against the paralyzing effect of hero-worship, whether of her real father or her putative one, cautioning her against "those who have left us nothing but their death as a stunning memory." . . .

This multivoiced narrative strategy carries over into the linguistic registers in order further to decenter the exploded writing self. The full impact of the original depends a good deal on what I would call a systematic "surprise effect"—grammatical as well as semantic—the better to remind its French readers that Creole, too, is a foreign language not entirely assimilable to French cultural codes. This makes translating Maximin a nearly impossible task, and demands of his editors a higher than usual amount of tolerance. *Lone Sun* refuses a unifying narrative voice because such a voice would in turn imply a unified, homogeneous audience.

Clarisse Zimra. Introduction to Daniel Maximin. *Lone Sun*
(Charlottesville, Va: Caraf Books, 1989), pp. xi–xii, xxxiii, l, lvii–lviii

In *L'Isolé Soleil*, Maximin tells us that the individual on his or her own path must look inside as deeply as possible to find his or her own voice if he or she wants real freedom: "Brise ce premier miroir et écoute bien le silence de ton double devant ta main qui saigne et ton regard aveugle" [Break this first mirror and listen carefully to the silence of your double standing before your bleeding hand and blind gaze]. Valorizing the inner voice and creating the framework for journeys—journeys by both "le même" and "l'autre" [the one who is the same and the one who is similar]—are among [Simone] Schwarz-Bart's and Maximin's most meaningful contributions. The inner journey is essential to a literature of liberation, because only through such an exploration can the individual, and the collectivity, become free. . . .

If Creoleness is to succeed, the "acceptation de soi" must characterize the group's attitude toward itself as well. *L'Isolé Soleil* exemplifies this vision more fully than [Joseph Zobel's] *La Rue cases-nègres* and [Schwarz-Bart's] *Pluie et vent sur Télumée Miracle*, because it affirms French Caribbean historical and literary figures, showing how extensive this heritage is. Maximin's second novel, *Soufrières*, affirms the group more completely, because it focuses on the group experience of enduring the eruption of Guadeloupe's volcano, La Soufrière. . . .

The relationship of *La Rue cases-nègres*, *Pluie et vent sur Télumée Miracle*, and *L'Isolé Soleil* to history, presents another shift in emphasis. José tells the story of his own life and his grandmother's *prise de conscience*, anchoring his text in realistic details. Schwarz-Bart depicts Télumée's quest for internal harmony, showing how she eventually exemplifies the wisdom of her community as she achieves individuation or self-understanding. Clearly, Zobel, Schwarz-Bart, and Maximin all use real history to present the negative experience of colonial life. However, [Maximin] explores the resonance between the past and the present much more fully.

Maximin's protagonists journey to self-understanding and rebirth, but they engage as well in a quest to find the historical roots of the collectivity. The history of the collectivity is merged with Marie-Gabriel's personal story, because she re-creates herself in telling [her mother] Siméa's story, and Siméa's story re-creates part of the collectivity's story. Making a double point about truth, Maximin shows that although a full-blown history written by Caribbean people cannot exist because those who would write it died long ago, the truth of the people's resistance to oppression can be affirmed by reading between the lines of colonial history books. This revisioning of French Caribbean history, which reflects the polyvalent dimension of contemporary life, fulfills the impetus of Caribbeanness and Creoleness, because it repairs gaping holes and redefines part of the fabric of Caribbean reality.

Ann Armstrong Scarboro. *Callaloo*. 15, 1 (Winter 1992), pp. 15–16, 19–21

The project at the heart of Daniel Maximin's *L'Isolé Soleil* . . . is the rewriting of Antillean history—the reinscription of the other America seen through the tormented mind and soul of the educated savage, Caliban, inheritor of his master's tongue. . . .

Maximin's *L'Isolé Soleil*, like the narratives of his compatriots Maryse Condé and Edouard Glissant, takes as its subject the rewriting of a history of his home islands; it seeks to wrest from the occupier the history of Guadeloupe—from the reconquest of the islands by the French under General Richepanse in 1802, and the reimposition of slavery, to the present-day clashes between the French occupiers and the Antilleans, who persist in demanding independence. . . .

Siméa, the mother of Marie-Gabriel (the principal character/narrator), makes annotations in the margins of the copies of *Tropiques* sent to her from Fort-de-France. In the April 1942 number, Suzanne Césaire has contributed an article entitled "What is a Martinican," followed by a nine-page extract from Léo Frobénius's *History of African Civilization*. Siméa remonstrates with Suzanne Césaire for seeking their "black essence" in the writings of a white ethnologist, just as her comrades have called on white psychoanalysts, political thinkers, and poets to help to define them. "Will we always need *them* and their *reasons*? What's the use of rejecting their reason only to adopt their science? It's up to us to invent a future, without expecting much from the African past and the European present." She adds that "identification [of the Antillean with the European] is the enemy of identity," and that Suzanne Césaire should speak of all the Antilleans, not solely the Martinicans.

These very principles—the invention by the Antilleans of their own future and the cultivation of a sense of Antillean community—guide the project of Maximin's/Marie-Gabriel's narrative. The epigraph of that narrative speaks of the nightly eruption of cries of "joy and misery, chants, poems of love and rebellion choked in the throats of men and women undressed of their anguish, writing to each other from island to island, a story in the shape of an archipelago traced by our four races, seven languages and dozens of bloods." The refrain of silenced cries reverberates throughout postcolonial literature—in the motives of muteness, of aphasia, of the unarticulated words of the Other's history/story that, "hidden in the depths of silence," under the words of the oppressor's history/story, seek to enunciate themselves. This other history, this other story, is the "intractable" (*intraitable*), as Jean-François Lyotard terms it, the repressed, the stifled, the unsaid, existing below the level of words. *L'Isolé Soleil* takes on the task of expressing the inexpressible.

The narrative proper opens with a narrator whose identity initially remains unrevealed, and who describes events on the birthday of the seventeen-year-old Marie-Gabriel. As she climbs a mango tree, she discovers in a cavity a ring engraved with the name "Angela," put there, we are told, two centuries earlier by Jonathan (later, we'll be told, a ring belonging to a young girl under the care of Marie-Gabriel's mother, Siméa, during World War II). Marie-Gabriel awaits her father who, returning after several years' absence in Paris, will die that same day as the plane explodes over Guadeloupe. . . .

A journal entitled "Désirades" that [Marie-Gabriel's] father was carrying with him on his return to the island, and which he intended to give to her, perishes with him in the explosion. Absent father, absent journal, absent cries—the life of the Guadeloupeans is marked by absence, like the Martinican crowd in Fort-de-France, described by Aimé Césaire as: "this noisy crowd, so astonishingly passing by its cry . . . passing by its cry of hunger, of poverty, of revolt, of hate, this crowd so strangely chattering and mute . . . this strange crowd that does not crowd. . . ." Such is the state of mutism inflicted upon the Antillean whose story has been appropriated by the Other, but it all the more describes women's voices muted in male history.

On the one hand, we find in *L'Isolé Soleil* a cluster of metaphors built around the notion of absence; on the other, a lexicon rife with metaphors of solarity, explosion, fire, detonation, and eruption. Over everything rises Soufrière, the active volcano that holds over the island the omnipresent threat of a fiery cataclysm. While Western novelists paint the Antilleans as children falling off to sleep, their heads filled with childhood memories and magical tales, while record jackets of calypso recordings sold in Parisian shops speak of "the gay, carefree temperament of the Caribbean islanders," Marie-Gabriel equates her people with "sleeping volcanoes" that need to be awakened. It is they who will explode.

John D. Erickson. Callaloo. 15, 1 (Winter 1992), pp. 119–21, 128

The quest to understand the past in order to know oneself and one's culture is at the heart of both novels by the contemporary Guadeloupean novelist Daniel

Maximin, *L'Isolé Soleil*, and *Soufrières* (*Sulphur Mines*, or in the singular, *La Soufrière*, the name of the volcano that dominates the island of Guadeloupe). In these two novels, he reserves a prominent place for references to literature as well as to other forms of art, such as painting and music, which often seem to be the key to developing that understanding. Beyond being simply gratuitous allusions to other works of art, these references constitute an essential part of the framework of the two novels. They also speak to the nature of the human experience and to the role of art forms in that experience. Specifically, the use of art forms in *L'Isolé Soleil* and *Soufrières* reflects the freedom of the human spirit and the desire to communicate the relationship of the past to the present, and to give tentative and renewable form to the life of individuals in the Caribbean. . . .

Soufrières is the story of five different days over the span of five months, leading up to the eruption of the volcano La Soufrière on the island of Guadeloupe in 1976. However, the title, a plural noun, shows that the novel is more than simply the story of one specific volcano's eruption. It is also the record of the essential background of Caribbean life brought to the surface by the narrative, the story of the hopes and desires of various individuals, including Adrien and Marie-Gabriel from *L'Isolé Soleil*, each with his or her own personal "bubbling volcano," each needing to come to an understanding of the past before being free to face the future with confidence.

Though the subjects of the two novels seem at first glance different, they are in fact very complementary, and we can see the second as a continuation of the first in several ways. First of all, both have as their point of departure a specific and real historical event. Secondly, the major characters in *Soufrières* were already present in *L'Isolé Soleil* as those who reflected on the historical events of the preceding centuries. And thirdly, apparent in both novels is these characters' preoccupation with writing, with the interplay of literature and history, and with the goal of using that interplay to help them understand themselves and their place in the twentieth century. . . .

The infusion of hope helps one understand the past, and Maximin suggests that the hope which helps understand the past can also help modify the future. The three lines that end the novel are presented as a poem, and juxtaposed as they are with the old Creole round that the tape recorder sings sweetly to Elisa, who finally feels that she has found her place in the world ("nicely positioned between sky and earth"), they can be taken as representing an old Creole song, suggesting hope and healing just as the old traditional songs instilled identity and understanding: "When the thread of the days / follows the needle of hope, / it patches up destiny."

As Siméa expresses in her journal: "A page of poetry . . . will always be able to express . . . the essence hidden in a passing moment, an eternity of dreams, an instant of true life." Writing, along with other art forms, is able to capture eternity, linking meaningfully for individuals and for countries the events of the past, the experiences of the present, and the hopes of the future.

Understanding the contemporary culture of the Caribbean and developing an awareness of the Antillean identity depends on the interplay between history and writing about that history. Writing, the act of placing words on paper in the various forms we see in these two novels, encourages not only reflection, but also action. But most of all, writing by the characters in Maximin's novels is an affirmation of their self, of their community, and of their culture.

Lauren W. Yoder. In Helen Ryan-Ranson, ed.
Imagination, Emblems, and Expressions (Bowling Green, Ohio:
Bowling Green State University Press, 1993), pp. 109–11, 124–25

MCMILLAN, TERRY (1952–   )

UNITED STATES

Terry McMillan's first novel, *Mama*, opens with the elaborate plans of its memorable title character, Mildred Peacock, to defend herself against an attack from her alcoholic husband Crook. Mildred's self-protective scheme, almost militaristic in its multiple options and tactical flexibility, serves as an accurate reflection of the survivalist mentality that compels her subsequent adventures and misadventures. . . . *Mama* delineates Mildred's ultimate rejection of a fearful existence as victim of an abusive man, her resilience in the face of much—perhaps too much—adversity, her ability to fend for herself and her five children in both the urban wasteland of Point Haven, Michigan, and in a materially seductive Los Angeles, and her general resolve to gather her rosebuds whenever the opportunity presents itself.

If viewed in a cursory way, McMillan's novel seems, in its figuration of an unquestionably resourceful black female protagonist, consistent with the impulses of the emerging black women's literary tradition. However, *Mama* is, in the final analysis, more accurately read as what Hortense Spillers's essay "Cross-Currents, Discontinuities: Black Women's Fiction" calls a moment of "discontinuity" in the tradition, one in which the author "reaches behind her most immediate writing predecessor[s]" and embraces not the lyrical mode of contemporary Afro-American women writers such as Paule Marshall, Toni Morrison, and Alice Walker, but the clearly realistic models of black female precursors such as Ann Petry. In its rather self-conscious rejection of the examples of these immensely influential writers, McMillan appears intent on protecting herself from unjustified considerations of indebtedness to these contemporaries.

In its purposely stark, unlyrical delineation of an unredeemed and unrepentant female character (whose most significant psychological transformation is her ability to tell her oldest child Freda that she loves her), *Mama* stands boldly outside of the mainstream of contemporary black women's fiction. Unlike the tradition's most representative texts, *Mama* offers no journeys back to blackness, no empowering black female communities, no sustained condemnation of American materialism or male hegemony. What it does provide, in its largely episodic depictions of the travails of Mildred and her family, is a moving, often hilarious and insightful exploration of a slice of black urban life that is rarely seen in contemporary black women's fiction.

Michael Awkward. *Callaloo*. 11, 3 (Summer 1988), pp. 649–50

Terry McMillan's new novel is a love story waiting to explode. The lovers of *Disappearing Acts* are both intelligent and good-looking, both possessed of dreams—but Zora Banks is an educated black woman, and Franklin Swift is an unschooled black man. It's Brooklyn, it's 1982, and it's clear from page one that the two of them are sitting in a minefield and something's going to blow.

McMillan's first novel, *Mama*, was original in concept and style, a runaway narrative pulling a crowded cast of funny, earthy characters. *Disappearing Acts* is also full of momentum, and it's a pleasurable, often moving novel. In this intricate look at a love affair . . . McMillan strikes out in a whole new direction and changes her narrative footing with ease. But *Disappearing Acts* is also a far more conventional popular novel than *Mama* was. Despite its raunchy language and its narrative construction (Franklin's voice and Zora's alternate), its descriptions, its situations, even its generic minor characters are often predictable. I say this with some surprise, because it seems to me that Terry McMillan has the power to be an important contemporary novelist.

Much of the predictable feel of the story has to do with Zora Banks's narrative. Zora, who reaches her thirtieth birthday in the book, has come to New York from Ohio; she is a musician who makes her living teaching in a junior high school but feeds her soul by writing songs. She dreams of landing a recording contract, and seems on her way to that goal when she falls hard for Franklin Swift, separated and the father of two, who is working on the renovation of her apartment building. The progress of their love affair is punctuated by construction layoffs for Franklin: as his resentment escalates, so does Zora's frustration. She becomes pregnant, and by the time their son is born they are both enraged and near desperation. . . .

I have my doubts about the ending of *Disappearing Acts*, but I'm a hardhearted reader; I leave you to your own conclusions. Nevertheless, I admire the risks Terry McMillan has taken in making Franklin Swift come to such intense life. I imagine she'll make a long and challenging career of taking such chances.

Valerie Sayers. *NYTBR*. August 6, 1989, p. 8

Even though Zora and Franklin are last-week contemporary, they are also like classic folklore characters come to life in Brooklyn. She's the wily black woman of yore, the smart-talking Eve who's always got a little something on the rail for the lizard, as we used to say. She's also a sophisticated shopper who likes fancy cheeses and bottled water, and she says "shit" all the time. Zora has all the tugs of feminism versus the feminine that a modern black woman who's read [Alice] Walker and [Ntozake] Shange is supposed to have. She's not unlike Zora Neale Hurston's sassy folk women—characters *Cosmo* would never dare to pop-psychoanalyze.

Complicated as Franklin is supposed to be, he is a savvy urban John Henry—he don't take no tea fo' the fever. An intellectual Tina Turner meets a hardhat Ike. They are both bricks, and though they may chip each other, they ain't never gonna blend. They live and work in New York City, but are in a very insulated world; their problems are completely personal. Their relationship is doomed by mutual expectations and ended by an outburst of gratuitous male violence. Let's just say it wasn't needed for the love affair to fall apart.

These two are as they are; like other folk-heroes, they don't change much or drag skeletons out of the closet, and they learn their lessons the hard way. They've been created by years of past mythologizing, drawn their images from popular culture, black and white. They are black, sho' nuff—the last thing I would say about McMillan's people is that they ain't black—but they're black in big, bold strokes. And that means her work will continue to raise questions among African-Americans about the fuzzy line between realism and popular misconception. And at the same time, McMillan is, as she said, less race-conscious. She confines herself to the day-to-day life struggle, as told from behind the mask Claude McKay so poignantly described. McMillan uses, almost exclusively, the performance side of black character, emphasizing the most public, most familiar aspects of us. If you smell a little song-and-dance in the self-sufficient ribaldry, it's there.

Thulani Davis. VLS. May 1990, p. 29

The four women in *Waiting to Exhale* are black, but aside from that distinction (and the fact that the author brings a wicked wit to this often sentimental form of fiction), no new literary ground is broken. But going over the old ground is still great fun with . . . McMillan's characters for company. Savannah Jackson, a public-relations executive, is, like the others, in her mid-thirties. She is cool, competent, and shrewd, the strongest of the group. But her private relations with men are singularly unsatisfying. "What I want to know is this," she asks. "How do you tell a man—in a nice way—that he makes you sick?"

Savannah decides she's had it with cold Denver. Her college roommate, Bernadine Harris, who is living the ideal black urban professional life, complete with an entrepreneur husband, two children, pastel-perfect interior decor, and a BMW, urges her to come to Phoenix. It's warm. It's beautiful. It's the good life. But by the time Savannah arrives, Bernadine's marriage is in ashes and her husband has flown off—with his beautiful, young, and exceedingly blond bookkeeper.

As Gloria, hairdresser to them all, notes: "I don't know which is worse, trying to raise a teen-age son or dealing with a husband who leaves you for a white woman." Gloria is worried about her sixteen-year-old son, Tarik, a smart, talented kid who, overnight, has turned sullen, secretive, and stunningly hostile.

She should relax. Gloria is a great mother, a straight-talker. ("I never really expected you to come up to me one day and say, 'Yo, Ma, I'm doing the wild thing now,' but my Lord, Tarik. This is just one reason why I've always wanted you to have a father. Let me ask you something. And don't lie to me. Are you using condoms?") She is also a shrewd businesswoman and a loving friend: a super woman. But Savannah, Robin, and Bernadine are distressed that she is hiding behind a wall of fat, endangering her health as she protects herself from men, from love—from the possibility of pain.

Pain? Robin, the eternal optimist, is the expert. She looks for love in all the wrong places and, naturally, never finds it. . . .

Terry McMillan's heroines are so well drawn that by the end of the novel, the reader is completely at home with the four of them. They observe men—and contemporary America—with bawdy humor, occasional melancholy, and great affection. But the novel is about more than four lives; the bonds among the women are so alive and so appealing they almost seem a character in their own right. Reading *Waiting to Exhale* is like being in the company of a great friend. It is thought-provoking, thoroughly entertaining, and very, very comforting.

Susan Isaacs. *NYTBR*. May 31, 1992, p. 11

McMillan frequently draws from her own life for her fiction. Critics often object to her simple characters and dialogue-driven plots. Nonetheless, they regard her as an important chronicler of 1990s black life. The four central women in *Waiting to Exhale* are all members of Black Women on the Move, a networking organization in Phoenix. Besides Robin, there are Bernadine, Savannah, and Gloria—respectively the wife of a successful entrepreneur, a TV public relations executive, and a hair salon owner. The novel's emphasis on brand names—BMW, Coach leather, Calvin Klein, and Perrier—has earned the author the title of "the black Judith Krantz," but this is indicative more of how unfamiliar whites are with successful blacks than of the novel's content. Except for Bernadine, who is truly affluent, these women are only solidly middle class—it is their delight in their success that makes them seem richer.

Daniel Max. *NYTM*. August 9, 1992, p. 22

Written for and about educated black women, *Waiting to Exhale* reflects the growing numbers of successful African-Americans who have fled the drugs and violence of the ghettoes for fashionable neighborhoods, while trying to preserve a uniquely black cultural heritage. McMillan's characters believe in black solidarity. To act like a white is an act of betrayal. "White folks" hover disconcertingly on the novel's margins.

Waiting to Exhale's four protagonists live in Phoenix, Arizona. Apart from being black, female and thirtysomething, they have one thing in common: "None of us have a man." And they're holding their breath until they get one. Savannah wants to feel "important to somebody," though she's not yet desperate: she's just "thirsty," not "dehydrated." Bernadine has been betrayed by her acquisitive husband, who traded her in for a new trophy-wife, his twenty-four-year-old (blond) bookkeeper. Gloria has given up waiting for a man who can make her toes curl and takes comfort in God, her hair salon, a promiscuous adolescent son, and much too much food. Robin's toes curl for "pretty men with big dicks," but she's hung up on an unscrupulous cad and doesn't know a good man when she sleeps with one. *Waiting to Exhale* chronicles these women's bedroom capers in their exhaustive—and exhausting—searches for Mr. Right.

He's hard to come by. Black men prove to be "'Stupid.' 'In prison.' 'Unemployed.' 'Crackheads.' 'Short.' 'Liars.' 'Unreliable.'" And worse. McMillan's generalized male-bashing has understandably alienated some black men. Her portrayal of women may be more sympathetic, but it is equally shallow. Her characters' preoccupation with deodorants, douches, and dates soon grows wearisome. And the attention McMillan draws to male-female rifts within the African-American community seems at odds with the black solidarity she otherwise implicitly approves.

But whether her views are politically correct or not, McMillan has hit a nerve. Many African-American women identify with her heroines. Using the vibrant street-talk McMillan grew up speaking, her protagonists tackle sexual issues that most women can relate to.

It may in part be concern to avoid accusations of racism that has prevented some critics from putting this book firmly where it belongs—among the glitzy, commercial women's novels. Its one true importance is that it appeals to a market that American publishers have previously overlooked—the new black middle class.

Frances Stead Sellers. *TLS*. November 6, 1992, p. 20

MÉTELLUS, JEAN (1937–   )

HAITI

Like [Émile] Zola, the poet and novelist Jean Métellus . . . has chosen to depict [in *La Famille Vortex*] a slice of life from his native country through a single family. For narrative economy, he condenses the transcription of an extraordinary, wide, and complex reality. A well-to-do family with seven legitimate children, the Vortexes are presented with their ups and downs amidst the Haitian struggle for power. Their social actions and democratic aspirations are drowned in the miasma of military and police brutality. Left alone in their comfortable countryside villa, Solon and Olga Vortex live only for their reunions with their grown children, particularly at Christmastime. Except for the absence of their daughter Astrid, a musician whose career has exiled her to the United States, they are shown enjoying this opportunity for the last time in 1949 before the "hemorrhage of exile."

The oldest son Edward, a military officer who shares his father's poetical talent and his mother's honesty and Indian features, has to follow his patron President Estimé to New York after a coup d'état. And because Edward's brother Louis (an English teacher) has also been a supporter of the deposed president, he is rushed to France by another brother, Bishop Joseph, after being beaten up and incarcerated by the officers of General Férére, now in power. A sister, Sylvie, who teaches at the school of hotel management, will soon follow her brothers into exile. Socially committed, she is shocked by the poverty of the slum areas she visits in Port-au-Prince and raises questions about the insultingly luxurious parlor of a neighboring prostitute that is frequently visited by high-ranking officials of the military government. Accused and threatened for "social provocation," she is forced to flee to France. Her twin brother Sylvain, a physician, is also a leader of a labor union and the Popular Democratic Party. Thanks to his popularity, he manages to survive through Estimé and Férére until his followers raise him to power. But before he can implement his democratic program, he is ousted by a violent military coup and compelled to embark to New York. This does not prevent his brother Joseph from becoming cabinet counselor to the new president. A fighter for Haitian priests' promotion to the church hierarchy, he is also a champion of unity between the clergy and the government. But for voting against a law to dissolve existing organizations, including Christian ones, he is irrevocably destituted and forced, in his turn, to leave for France. Ludovic Vortex is then the only child remaining, but one wonders for how long, as he is harassed by military police searching his house for some pretext on which to arrest him. . . .

Rather than elaborating on characterization, *La Famille Vortex*, which exemplifies a society offering itself to history, focuses on the interactions of a human aggregate indissociable in its eddies and frictions. The behavior of its characters is briefly described more to indicate the weave of history in the making than to provide psychological analysis. Most of Haiti's conflicting world is skillfully presented in physical, social, political, ethical, and spiritual terms. The contrasts between different strata of Haitian life are enhanced by the author's alternation of realistic and poetic descriptions in stylistic levels more akin to classical or colloquial Hexagone French than to a francophone dialect (with some rare exceptions).

Daniel L. Racine. *WLT.* 57, 3 (Summer 1983), p. 502

Beyond the central theme of injustice or racism, and beyond the very Haitian references, the diverse parts of [*Hommes de plein vent*] are linked by the extraordinary poetic power of expression, a grounding in body images that permits the author to write: "j'arrache de mes entrailles un chant illimité" [I tear out from my entrails a limitless song]. . . .

At the beginning of [this] collection, as in our modern history, we encounter the figure of Christopher Columbus, a man of thought who wished to encounter "vies épaisses de promesses" [lives full of promise]. His greed to conquer is the manifestation of a poetic attempt: a refusal of limits, and of lands bogged down by conventions. His is then the figure of the poet itself. . . .

Writing poetry that is *engagée* [committed], where good or bad "ideas," which take the place of poetic value, are affirmed, is common practice. But being able, in a flamboyant affirmation of a vision of historical reality, to accede to a poetic expression that seizes with an unequaled density, is quite rare. The author, however, is successful at this.

When he evokes the Ku Klux Klan, the brutal madness of the fanatics of hatred appears before our eyes in all its horror. . . .

In the entire work, the coherence, the force, and the splendor of images organized in waves and in glowing rhythms attest to the reality of a poetry in which the usual analytical dichotomies are no longer pertinent. . . .

In *Hommes de plein vent*, we find words whose arresting vehemence, enriched with images, provokes us to think of the writings of the prophets. The text restores an essential and sacred function to language, a song of power, pain, and hope that revives the hearts of men and immerses us in the acute consciousness of a world tormented and ravaged by history.

This is a poetry for living, but for living tall and grand. Aesthetes and critics armed with the scalpels of analysis will find their share in it, but the value of

Métellus's work lies elsewhere. It is not the obvious literary quality of the work that is essential, but all that this quality demands and makes possible, because poetry draws from, and inscribes in its violence, the truth about man and life. . . .

The poetry of Jean Métellus is not a poetry of self but of the world. If language is essential to it, it is not so much as language, but as a living force that must communicate itself. The founding images are those of a vital movement. Words become the medium of a natural impulse. . . .

Here then is a poetry which, far from being separated from the body, seems on the contrary to be its emanation and its very sign. The importance of the physical world and of the senses is an adequate indication. It is, in fact, in his astonishing images of carnal vitality that Jean Métellus demonstrates his superiority.

Alain Deschamps. Nouvelles du Sud. 1 (1985), pp. 87–89†

Having established himself as one of Haiti's foremost new writers, with four novels and three volumes of poetry, Jean Métellus has now turned to the theater with a four-act play narrating the fall of the Indian kingdoms to the gold-hungry Spaniards in the 1490s. *Anacaona* . . . is a rather odd mixture of old and new, verse and prose, epic and tragedy, history and fable, and black and Indian cultures. Métellus has found an obviously interesting historical figure, the poet-queen from a peace-loving culture, given power by her older brother seemingly paralyzed by an intuition of looming disaster, married to a somewhat opportunistic warrior from an inimical group. She must make the final decision: to fight or bargain.

Having already seen the massacres produced by the superior arms of the Spanish, and also the results of the Spaniards' treachery, Anacaona hesitates; her indecision in the long debate with her advisor Yaquimex reflects classical notions of tragedy. The tension between the roles of poet and queen dramatizes the struggle between individual and historical forces. Ultimately, however, the play seems neither tragedy nor epic, but more of a poetic reverie, an attempt to realize the impossible, to make this Indian queen accessible to the twentieth century.

Hal Wylie. WLT. 61, 3 (Summer 1987), p. 480

Les Cacos . . . shows us once again how history can be enlivened and made fertile by the art of an author. Perhaps one must be more precise and say that the author reveals to us, in all the diverse meanings of the word, that which certain dictionaries and historical essays tell us with far too much discretion. . . .

The novel adds to history to the extent that it shows us, in a setting alive with authentic events and precise facts, human beings in their everyday reality. We see these *cacos*, i.e., these revolutionaries, not as perfect heroes of an intrepid and pompous guerrilla, but as the inhabitants of this country, attached to their land, their customs, their beliefs, their language also, and with their faults, their courage, their weakness, their certitudes, and their hesitations. . . .

One of the great originalities of this work lies in this, the detailed, lively, and flavorful painting of psychologies and attitudes. The novelist helps us to capture the historic truth of an epoch in the hearts and in the spirit of the protagonists, in the subtle detail of their reflections and their reactions. References to current life are numerous, in measure with novelistic necessity and avoiding the falsity of exoticism or local color. . . .

Religion and beliefs, in their expression and popular practices, play a very important role in thoughts as well as social and political attitudes. Here we touch upon a sort of poetic or even magic realism—either in the emotion or in the irony that allows us to better understand Haiti and Haitians. The language of the narration also helps us, either by the rather developed quotations of the Creole language, with its French translation, or by the very French of the writer, subtly impregnated with this essential linguistic reality.

One then understands that the life and tragic destiny of the few principal heroes, *les cacos* Alexandre and Thémistocle whom we follow in their daily life, to the maquis and to combat, are not the only elements of the novelistic plot. It is true that their characters are numerous, but, in truth, it is an entire people in the diversity of their pain and their combat, that Jean Métellus is describing to us.

Pierre Gamarra. *Europe*. 67, 722–23 (June 1989), pp. 174–76†

In *Charles Honoré Bonnefoy*, the title, like a nameplate on a door or a desk, introduces an exemplary man of science who has "la passion d'enquêter, de comprendre, d'expliquer." Faithful to his name, he truly is a man of good will, dedicating his whole life to the pursuit of truth, observing, and probing, in a constant dialogue with the human body.

The first ninety pages of the novel cover a single day in June, the day when, after thirty years as head of neurology at La Salpêtrière Hospital in Paris, Bonnefoy, at seventy, is supposedly retiring and holds his last public consultation, lionized by students and colleagues. It is far from being the end for Bonnefoy (or the novel), however. The septuagenarian regards his retirement as the beginning of a new life, continuing with renewed vigor to pursue his lifetime interests. . . . Bonnefoy is in love with life, in all its aspects, including intellectual stimulation, and is ready (the very next day) to embrace new responsibilities at a public assistance hospital near Paris, always "au service de la vérité," even if it means for him, at the end, a broken nose!

The novel is written mostly in dignified classic French (using *vous* and the preterit), as befits a well-bred man always wearing a three-piece suit. He has refined tastes (fine cuisine and fine books), and is fond of quoting to himself, as he goes on his walks, such authors as Dante, [Agrippa] d'Aubigné, [Jacques Benigne] Bossuet, [Louis] Bourdaloue, Saint-Simon, and Mme. de Sévigné. Bonnefoy is not an isolated case, one of the characters remarks, but rather "une sorte de quintessence de ce milieu." Specialized terms deriving from cases studied by the neurologist naturally abound in the novel. . . . There is a long monologue in the form of a professor's farewell speech, and large chunks of doctor-patient dialogues interspersing description/narration. The book is a serious one, written by a moralist and expressing his philosophy, particularly about aging and the public image of old age, which he fights to change through his own example.

Charles Honoré Bonnefoy, like its protagonist, exudes an appetite for life, "une grande joie de vivre." Like Métellus, Bonnefoy is an artist and a poet in his appreciation of nature, as seen in flowers, fruit trees in bloom, gardens. He has an impressionist's love of light and "tastes" colors like a Haitian primitive painter. He too likes to paint, as he likes to cook or to caress the books he collects, celebrating "the motionless poetry of the printed page." A man of the intellect, he is also a man of the senses.

Danielle Chavy Cooper. WLT. 65, 4 (Autumn 1991), p. 754

Jean Métellus is probably Haiti's most active author at present. Trained as a linguist but currently working as a neurologist in France, Métellus published several novels—including *Jacmel au crépuscule*, *La Famille Vortex*, *Une Eau-forte*, and *L'Année Dessalines*—as well as several volumes of poetry and one play in the 1980s. These works have made a name for him even though little scholarship has yet been devoted to them.

Readers have already encountered members of the Vortex family in other novels. [In *Louis Vortex*] Louis recapitulates, in many ways, the story of his father, but brings us up to the 1950s; it seems likely that he also reflects the existence of the author, for the theme, clearly delineated here, is exile. Indeed, this work is more an essay, or meditation, upon the problem of being obliged to live far from one's childhood roots, than it is a real novel. The fictional character of Louis Vortex serves to allow a certain detachment necessary for analysis of the particular patterns of stress and alienation experienced in exile.

Like Vortex, Haitian literature has a bifurcated existence today; there are almost two separate literatures, one inside and one outside the country. In *Louis Vortex* Métellus suggests that Haiti itself has come to have the same double existence: within/without. . . . Many writers live in exile, and studies have been written on the way this reality influences their writings; but few care to discuss their feelings about exile. Métellus shows in Vortex why the exiled person finds himself in a double bind which becomes almost a kind of bad faith. When Louis starts to develop new roots in France, he is accused by his friends of betraying his family and homeland. Métellus is original in analyzing the dialectics between the two countries, old and new, and the resulting psychological complexities.

Exile involves several kinds of alienation, each dramatized in certain episodes of *Vortex*. Louis is first seen as numb, but he is eventually drawn into three involvements that remake him. His friendship with Nadine becomes a love affair, a substitute for his wife and family left behind in Haiti. His fervent Catholicism lands him a teaching job at a Catholic school; religion and vocation become one. Later, he turns from religion to political faith, resigning his job in order to devote himself completely to the overthrow of the oppressive regime.

Louis's authentic self, however, is hard to find. We know he is a Don Juan, a lover of fine food, and a smooth talker. Eventually his penetrating analysis distances him from his activist friends as he sees their opportunism, personal agendas, and illusions. Here Métellus seems to be using the 1950s as an allegory for the confused political situation of 1992; the events of the return of Louis's friend Regis to Haiti are more plausible in the post-Duvalier context; the "collective fury" reflects the *déchoucage* (retribution) and "necklacing" of the last five years.

Louis finally decides to abandon the hope of return and to accept exile, sending for his wife and children. The rhetorical bent of the novel leads to the justification of integrating oneself in the host society. Many will find this a painful message, but the logic of Métellus's essay-novel is quite forceful.

Hal Wylie. *WLT*. 66, 4 (Autumn 1992), p. 759

MORRISON, TONI (1931–   )

UNITED STATES

If metaphor, and much of [Toni] Morrison's writing in general, represents a return to origins, it is not rooted in a nostalgia for the past. Rather, it represents a process for coming to grips with historical transition. Migration to the North signifies more than a confrontation with (and contagion of) the white world. It implies a transition in social class. Throughout Morrison's writing, the white world is equated with the bourgeois class—its ideology and lifestyle. This is true of *Song of Solomon*, where Macon Dead's attitudes toward rents and property make him more "white" than "black." It is true of *Tar Baby*, where notions of bourgeois morality and attitudes concerning the proper education and role of women have created a contemporary "tar baby": a black woman in cultural limbo. And it is made dramatically clear in *The Bluest Eye*, whose epigrammatic introduction and subsequent chapter headings are drawn from a white middle-class "Dick and Jane" reader. In giving voice to the experience of growing up black in a society dominated by white, middle-class ideology, Morrison is writing against the privatized world of suburban house and nuclear family, whose social and psychological fragmentation does not need her authorial intervention but is aptly portrayed in the language of the reader: "Here is the family. Mother, Father, Dick, and Jane live in the green-and-white house. They are very happy." . . .

In Morrison, everything is historical. Objects, too, are embedded in history and are the bearers of the past. For those characters closest to the white bourgeois world, objects contain the residues of repressed and unrealized desires. For Ruth Foster in *Song of Solomon*, the daughter of the town's first black doctor and wife of the slumlord, Macon Dead, a water mark on a table is the stubborn and ever-present reminder of her husband's remorseless rejection. The bowl of flowers around which their hatred crystallized is no longer present; only its sign remains, an opaque residue indelibly written into the table. If, for the bourgeois world, experience is capable of being abstracted to the level of sign, this is not the case for the world of the marginal characters. To cite an example from the same novel, Pilate, Ruth Foster's sister-in-law and in every way her antithesis, enjoys a special relationship to all levels of natural experience—including a specific shade of blue sky. Now, color does not function as a sign in the way that the water mark on the table does. While it bears a concrete relationship to a real object (the blue ribbons on Pilate's mother's hat), it is not an abstract relationship in the way that the water mark stands for the bowl of flowers. For Ruth Foster, the water mark is an "anchor" to the mental and sexual anguish imprisoned in the sign. In contrast, when Pilate points to a patch of sky and remarks that it is the same color as her mother's bonnet ribbons, she enables her nephew, Milkman (Ruth Foster's overly sheltered son), to experience a unique moment of sensual perception. The experience is liberational because Pilate is not referring to a specific bonnet—or even to a specific mother; rather, the color blue triggers the whole range of emotions associated with maternal love, which Pilate offers to anyone who will share the experience of color with her.

In contrast to the liberational aspect of *Song of Solomon*, Morrison's . . . novel *Tar Baby*, registers a deep sense of pessimism. Here, cultural exiles—both white and black—come together on a Caribbean island where they live out their lives in neatly compartmentalized bourgeois fashion: the candy magnate, Valerian Street, in his stereophonic-equipped greenhouse; his wife, cloistered in her bedroom; and the servants, Ondine and Sydney, ensconced in their comfortable quarters. Daily life precludes the "eruption of funk," a lesson poignantly taught when Margaret Lenore discovers the bedraggled wild man, Son, in her closet. While Son's appearance suggests Rastafarianism and outlawry, any shock value stirred by his discovery is canceled when he, too, proves to be just another exile. Except for one brief incident, when Ondine kills a chicken and in plucking it recalls a moment from her distant past when she worked for a poultry butcher, there are no smells, tastes, or tactile experiences to summon up the past. Rather, there is a surfeit of foods whose only quality is the calories they contain.

In contrast with Morrison's earlier novels, the past in *Tar Baby* is never brought to metaphoric juxtaposition with the present. Rather, it is held separate and bracketed by dream. When Valerian Street, sipping a brandy in his greenhouse, lapses into daydream, his recollection of the past, which in essence contrasts entrepreneurial capitalism to modern corporate capitalism, does not intrude upon his present retirement. The past is past, and the significant historical transition evoked is perceived as inaccessible and natural. . . .

As Morrison sees it, the most serious threat to black culture is the obliterating influence of social change. The opening line from *Sula* might well have been the novel's conclusion, so complete is the destruction it records: "In that place, where they tore the nightshade and blackberry patches from their roots to make room for the Medallion City Golf Course, there was once a neighborhood." This is the community Morrison is writing to reclaim. Its history, terminated and dramatically obliterated, is condensed in a single sentence whose content spans from rural South to urban redevelopment. As throughout Morrison's writing, natural imagery refers to the past, the rural South, the reservoir of culture which has been uprooted—like the blackberry bushes—to make way for modernization. In contrast, the future is perceived as an amorphous, institutionalized power embodied in the notion of "Medallion City," which suggests neither nature nor a people. Joining the past to the future is the neighborhood, which occupies a very different temporal moment (which history has shown to be transitional), and defines a very different social mode, as distinct from its rural origins as it is from the amorphous urban future.

Susan Willis. In Henry Louis Gates, Jr., ed. *Black Literature and Literary Theory* (New York: Methuen, 1984), pp. 264, 268–71

Sula is the story of black women. . . . The story begins with a description of the Bottom, a black slum of the Southern town Medallion; and with the story of a World War I soldier who is released from an army hospital while still having problems with hallucinations, is arrested for his peculiar behavior, and is finally sent home to the Bottom, which he had not seen since going into the army. He seems to be crazy, and doesn't know what has happened to him. He establishes an annual holiday in the Bottom called National Suicide Day: on this day every year people can let out their anger and their violence acceptably. He lives alone, and generally celebrates the holiday alone. He supports himself by catching fish twice a week and selling them. This is how the book begins. It begins this way to register that the people in it, and the work they do, and the life they lead, are not normal. But this is the life of the vast majority in the South; from 1971, when the book was published, until this very day.

We are introduced to two girls: Sula and Nel. They are very good friends. The level of their lives is very low, and they go through much together. There is something harmonious between them. They are not separated even by the accidental death of a small boy who drowns while playing with them; even by the bizarre incinerations of two of the people Sula lives with. They grow up around, and in spite of, the daily poverty and tragedy. Nel gets married to a man named Jude. Sula sees that he is a handsome, hard-working, well-meaning young man. She helps with the wedding and reception, and then leaves town.

Ten years pass between the wedding and the beginning of the next chapter: 1927–37. Nel is still with Jude; they are living well, and have two or three children. Sula returns well-dressed, sophisticated, and college-educated. She and Nel seek to rediscover that friendship which they had before, but Sula is unable to accommodate herself to the old society. One day, Nel comes home to find Sula and Jude together in the bedroom, and Jude leaves her that day. Sula does not particularly want Jude; she begins sleeping with men in the town and is further distanced from the other townspeople. She becomes, at one point, really attached to a man; but it is, of course, at that point that he leaves her. . . .

Now, this black woman has gone to all of these most important towns and places of social life in the United States, found them no good, and has gone back to Medallion. That is a very bold thing to write about. [Morrison] tells us why Sula returns—because everywhere she goes the men and the problems and emptiness with them are always the same. The important thing about that is that it could, and would, be said by women on every level of society in the world today, from the highest to the lowest. This woman could not find a man who would treat her as another human being, and she got tired of it and went back to her hometown. So on the one hand, the friendship between women, that is so often ignored, is really of great importance; and on the other hand, no matter how hard she tries, she just learns that friendship with a man is impossible.

Toni Morrison is saying that in this society, with the lives they lead, this is what happens to men and women; this becomes characteristic of the love relationship. I find it astonishing and revealing that Morrison should insist that this tremendous insight come from a poor black woman, on the lowest level of

American society. She is also saying that the real fundamental human difference is not between white and black, it is between man and woman.

C. L. R. James. *At the Rendezvous of Victory: Selected Writings*
(London: Allison & Busby, 1984), pp. 264–66

There is nothing in the history of the belletristic relationship between the West Indian and the Afro-American to prepare the reader for the portrait of Elihue Whitcomb in Toni Morrison's *The Bluest Eye*. And although his is undoubtedly a negative portrait (perhaps the most insidious of all the West Indian portraits in the Afro-American novel—the most insidious because through a process of intellection he refines his profound emotional and spiritual illnesses almost beyond recognition), the reader cannot justly resign him to the status of a stereotype. Like his illnesses, he is multidimensional and, unlike the West Indian stereotypes, there is nothing in his make-up or in the tone of the narration to suggest that the portrait is meant as an attack on that small group of inbred West Indian mulattoes on whose idiosyncrasies and vagaries the portrait is based. To find possible prototypes to the deracinated but highly stylized consciousness of Elihue, the reader must look outside the parameters of Afro-American literature, perhaps to the narrator of Orlando Patterson's West Indian novel, *An Absence of Ruins*, or even to the narrator of Dostoevsky's *Notes from Underground*. But unlike Dostoevsky or Patterson, Morrison allows the reader to approach her character through the limited omniscience of a narrator. It is because of the emotional, moral, and aesthetic detachment of the narrative voice that the reader is able to see Elihue in all his transcendent corruption without calling judgments into play, without, that is, making an attempt to label Elihue.

Melvin B. Rahming. *The Evolution of the West Indian's Image in the Afro-American Novel* (Millwood, N.Y.: Associated Faculty Press, 1986), pp. 54–55

In theme and style Toni Morrison's novels are a fine example of vintage wine in new bottles. Her exploration of the impact of sexism and racism on the lives of black women in her gothic fables provides a more complex and, perhaps, controversial vision of the personalities and bonding of fiercely alive modern black women than the idealized images of most writers of the 1960s. Particularly in *The Bluest Eye* and *Sula*, she distills history and fact with the poetic freedom and gothic vision of modernist and postmodernist writers. Her sharp eye for the concrete details and telltale gestures that evoke a sense of place and character in the fables and *Song of Solomon* are complemented by a wonderful gift for metaphor and metonymy that are as penetrating in their insightfulness as they are arresting in their freshness and suggestiveness. Her characters are eccentric and maimed as a result of their experience as black men and women in an environment that rigidly defines their humanity by economic, sexual, and racial myths, but still they persevere in their efforts to cope with or triumph over the obstacles in their path to self-esteem, freedom, and wholeness. Thus Pecola is destroyed psychologically, Sula dies an outcast among her own, and Milkman follows the path of his African ancestor, but both Claudia and Nel survive the terror and tragedy of their friends' lives, achieving in the process a precarious adjustment to the worlds of Shirley Temple and the Bottom. Pilate's moral victory is even more Pyrrhic. Because Morrison probes the awesome will to live of her characters in order to suggest the truth of their psychic experience and the complexity of their humanity, her gothic fables . . . are a quintessential blend of realism and poetry, bizarreness and beauty, revelation and lyricism.

Bernard W. Bell. *The Afro-American Novel and Its Tradition* (Amherst: University of Massachusetts Press, 1987), pp. 276–77

Morrison transforms myths of American materialistic culture with the earned wisdom of a people grown wise through suffering. At once polemical and mythic, her novels juxtapose unrelenting realism and the transcendent authority of mythic truth. A source of the mythic substructure of her fiction is most certainly the Bible, if not the conventional interpretation of its meaning. Acknowledging her upbringing in a highly religious family whose "resources were Biblical," Morrison has noted that her family combined the Bible with other sources. "They did not limit themselves to understanding the word only through Christian theology." Her novels similarly reflect an amalgamation of mythic matter, depicting a world couched at times in seemingly contradictory truths: rebels becoming heroes, good creating evil, gardens that oppress, sins that redeem. They preserve the essential truth of myth by ironically modifying or reversing more orthodox assumptions of meaning. . . .

Though by no means imitating the Romantic poets, Morrison creates a parallel view of a fortunate Fall: the necessary and potentially redemptive passage from a garden state of debilitating innocence to painful self-knowledge and its consequences. But whereas Romantic writers tended to see the Fall more essentially as personal experience than the embodiment of communal myth, Morrison sees the fortunate Fall as a return to the true community or "village" consciousness. The victorious end for her involves not only the escape from the white man's Eden, but the discovery of the black consciousness muted in a white society. Certainly Morrison understands well what the Romantics learned long ago, that in a society operated by an oppressive order, not to sin in the conventional sense perpetuates an immoral justice. In such a world, innocence is itself a sign of guilt, because it signals a degenerate acquiescence. Not to fall becomes more destructive than to fall. Those of her characters who accept the debunked values of the dominant white culture construct or escape to spurious Edens: the quintessential white middle-class "Dick-and-Jane" house, as well as Geraldine's imitation of it, and the pretentious Fisher estate where Pauline Breedlove evades her blackness in *The Bluest Eye*; the proper if sterile Wright house in *Sula*; the Deads' house and the "nigger heaven" Honoré Island in *Song of Solomon*; the white man's paradise Isle de Chevalier in *Tar Baby*; the deceptive Sweet Home in *Beloved*.

And those who disrupt these Edenic worlds play the ambiguous role of serpent in a specious paradise. Morrison's novels often present us with conventionally evil characters, outsiders in a decadent, white-dominated culture, Cains and Liliths in the guise of Cholly Breedlove or Sula Peace or Guitar Bains or Son Green or Sethe Suggs. On the one hand, characters of potential violence or cruelty and, on the other hand, rebels against a morally deficient system, each one tells us in unequivocal terms that evil can be redemptive and that goodness can be enslaving. In the language of existential theology, those who sin against the flawed order become the agents of experience and so run the risk of freedom. Those who do not are often doomed to spiritual stasis and moral entropy. For Morrison herself has stated, "Evil is as useful as good," and "Sometimes good looks like evil; and sometimes evil looks like good." . . .

In Toni Morrison's fiction, characters one way or another enact the historical plight of blacks in American society. She offers no apology for her black female perspective. Though the black experience frames and informs her fictional narratives, it in no way reduces their universality. For all their complexity and diversity, the novels are woven together by common themes: the passage from innocence to experience, the quest for identity, the ambiguity of good and evil, the nature of the divided self, and especially, the concept of a fortunate fall. Morrison works the gray areas, avoiding simple-minded absolutes. Guitar tells Milkman at one point that "there are no innocent white people," but Milkman knows that there are no innocent blacks either, least of all himself. Blacks as frequently as whites inflict extreme physical and psychological violence on blacks: the Breedloves torment each other, and Cholly rapes his daughter; Eva Peace burns her son, and Nel and Sula betray the other self; Milkman callously rejects Hagar, and Guitar kills Pilate; Son takes revenge on the childlike Cheyenne, and Jadine abandons Son; Sethe murders her daughter, and Beloved demands uncompromising payment—and of course much more. There is no doubt, though, that underlying all these manifestations of cruelty is the pernicious racism of American culture which wields its power to pervert and distort the moral center. Clearly, Morrison wants us to see the most insidious form of evil in the malevolent ability of racism to misshape the human spirit.

Terry Otten. *The Crime of Innocence in the Fiction of Toni Morrison*
(Columbia: University of Missouri Press, 1989), pp. 2–5, 95

In *The Bluest Eye* and *Sula*, two of Morrison's early works, the apparent dominance of an "ideology of the aesthetic" directly conflicts with subtextual eruptions of feminine and feminist issues. Through complex strategies of representation, shifts in perspectives, and fragmented stories of feminine or feminist desire, the Morrison narrative, in spite of its apparent single voice, is marked by ideological ruptures and dissonance. . . .

The Bluest Eye depicts the struggle between two warring factions. The Dick-and-Jane frame has as its referent not only the primer but the cultural values of the dominant society. It is read and deconstructed by the lived experiences of the Breedloves. Juxtapositions of the two narratives not only reinforce the dominant theme of the novel but illuminate the novel's textual processes. Contrasts between the Dick-and-Jane world and the "real" world of the Breedloves are structured around several sets of binary oppositions: white/black, affluence/poverty, desirability/undesirability, order/chaos, valued/devalued. The "truth" of the authoritative discourse is challenged by the internally persuasive discourse. The comfortable home of the Dick-and-Jane myth is contrasted with the squalid living conditions of the Breedloves; the Dick-and-Jane family has its counterpart in the misery and violence that seem normal among the Breedlove clan; the Dick-and-Jane myth celebrates familial love, while rape and incest are rife in the Breedlove household.

The conflict is transparent, but the focus on the aesthetic and the struggles between the discourses suppress other issues in the text. The resulting text is marked by ideological dissonance and rupture. . . .

Critical readings of *Sula* have focused on the novel's extensive treatment of the relationship between Sula and Nel, a relationship generally assumed to reveal the work's specific feminist dimension. Yet closer readings show that the Sula-Nel relationship, although one of the novel's dominant themes, is contained within a larger textual enterprise. Moreover, that larger enterprise determines the relationship and is the dominant focus of the novel.

Central to *Sula* is the construction of myth, and through its strategies of narration, the form of the novel becomes dominant. The attention to minor details to effect the real, the graphic descriptions of individual acts, the detailed incorporation of folklore—all constitute the larger theme in which the Sula-Nel narrative is enclosed. . . .

The Bluest Eye and *Sula*, then, are narratives marked by tensions and dissonances generated by contending discourses. The primary focuses—the production of "literariness" and the semiotic and mythological construction of a black "village" or community—are disrupted by the insertion of feminine desire, which takes the form of embedded narratives that relate stories of the oppression of women, ambivalent, and ironic characterizations and representations of males, and shifts in narrative perspective that allow specific mediations by the external narrator.

Elliott Butler-Evans. Race, Gender, and Desire
(Philadelphia: Temple University Press, 1989), pp. 63, 68, 81, 89

A decade before Michael Jordan made black synonymous with a brand name, Toni Morrison used [one] of her novels to demonstrate the futility of affirming blackness with a white label. In *Song of Solomon*, Morrison depicts the anguish of Hagar, who wakes one morning to the realization that the reason for her boyfriend's lack of interest is her looks. . . .

Morrison reveals her sensitive understanding of how commodity consumption mutilates black personhood when she has Hagar appear before her mother and grandmother, newly decked out in the clothes and cosmetics she hauled home through a driving rainstorm: her "wet ripped hose, the soiled white dress, the sticky, lumpy face powder, the streaked rouge, and the wild wet shoals of hair." If Hagar had indeed achieved the "look" she so desperately sought, she would only have been a black mimicry of a white cultural model. Instead, as the sodden, pitiful child who finally sees how grotesque she has made herself look, Hagar is the sublime manifestation of the contradiction between the ideology of consumer society that would have everyone believe we all trade equally in commodities, and the reality of all marginalized people for whom translation into the dominant white model is impossible.

Morrison's condemnation of commodity consumption as a hollow solution to the problems of race, class, and gender is as final and absolute as are Hagar's subsequent delirium and death. Unable to find let alone affirm herself, unable to bridge the contradiction in her life by way of a shopping spree and a Cinderella transformation, Hagar falls into a fever and eventually perishes.

Susan Willis. In Cheryl A. Wall, ed. *Changing Our Own Words* (New Brunswick, N. J.: Rutgers University Press, 1989), pp. 178–79

Sula is too complex to be classified because Toni Morrison writes from an African point of view—an African aesthetic. Names are a vital connection to life in traditional African culture, and Sula is an African name. In the Babangi language, it means any one or a combination of the following: to be afraid, to run away, to poke, to alter from a proper condition to a worse one, to be blighted, to fail in spirit, to be overcome, to be paralyzed with fear, to be stunned. In the Kongo language Sula means electric seal—a meaning which is highly applicable to the critical thrust of this analysis. Knowing the Africanness of the major character's name adds a dimension that clarifies much of the mystery of the novel for the reader and places a demand on the critic to search for a blueprint for the novel based upon an African world-view—a blueprint that is sorely needed for African-American fiction as people of African descent wrestle with problems of identity, as we move into the twenty-first century. . . .

Sula is Morrison's most complex work in reference to traditional African culture. This is true because the African presence and cultural rootedness is woven into black American culture without contrivance and with such extraordinary subtlety that neither the characters nor the reader are immediately aware of it; just as most of us are oblivious to the fact that after some three hundred plus years in America, African tradition continues to manifest itself in our lives. Black people in the Bottom of Medallion, Ohio, consider Sula and Shadrack pariahs of their community, and do not recognize their African presence.

Vashti Crutcher Lewis. In Joanne M. Braxton and Andrée Nicola McLaughlin, eds. *Wild Women in the Whirlwind: Afra-American Culture and the Contemporary Literary Renaissance* (New Brunswick, N. J.: Rutgers University Press, 1990), pp. 316–17

In Toni Morrison's *Beloved*, a constraining definition of motherhood is a major component of the overwhelming historical past in which Sethe is mired. An extremely rich book, *Beloved* contains myriad themes—relationships between black men and women, the differing oppressions of more-brutal and less-brutal slave masters, the effects of printed materials on African-Americans of the nineteenth century, the characters and motivations of white abolitionists, and the nature of black spiritualities. This argument does not seek to explicate the entirety of the novel but, instead, to highlight a central theme. Morrison shows black women's construction of motherhood under slavery; then Sethe's paralysis because she is hampered by the limitations of this idea in the very different conditions of freedom; and finally, *Beloved* shows the joining of the past and the future to mother Sethe and offers a liberating vision of motherhood.

Beloved delineates African-American women under slavery who refuse to mother children not conceived in mutual desire and who fiercely defend those who are. Sethe's mother, for instance, "threw away," without naming them, all her children resulting from rape on the Middle Passage and the plantation. Similarly, when Ella bears a child fathered by one of a father-son pair who confine and rape her for years, she refuses to nurse it, and it dies soundlessly after five days. As Nan, shipmate and friend to Sethe's mother, informs her, Sethe lives because she results from a union in which her mother "put her arms around" a black man, because the possibility of a child is chosen rather than imposed. After Sethe kills her daughter rather than allowing her to be reenslaved, she puts only "Beloved" on the tombstone, not the child's given name. In this novel, then, the very existence of any African-American person testifies to mother love and acceptance.

Missy Dehn Kubitschek. *Claiming the Heritage: African-American Women Novelists and History* (Jackson: University Press of Mississippi, 1991), pp. 165–66

The black community in *Beloved* thinks of the erratic behavior of white people as "a far cry from what real humans did," neatly inverting the stereotype Morrison chooses to pursue in *Playing in the Dark*, in which whiteness, in North American literature, is what is human, and blackness is a deviance, exciting, regrettable, or unmentionable. "Until very recently," Morrison says, "and regardless of the race of the author, the readers of virtually all of American fiction have been positioned as white." We know a character in [Ernest Hemingway's] *To Have and Have Not* is white, for instance, "because nobody says so." We would, if we were in any doubt, know he is a man for the same reason, and we may not have progressed as far as we think since 1937. . . .

Morrison's case in these lectures is not angry and partial, as some have thought, but global and rather wishful. "Africanism is inextricable from the definition of Americanness," she says. It probably should be, on the grounds that a fudged acceptance of historical responsibility is better than a blank refusal. But is it? The proposition assumes that the guilt of whites with respect to slavery is as large as it ought to be, and that the secret power of blacks bears a relation to their suffering. This is a noble story, but it isn't a story Morrison tells in any of her novels.

The story she does tell in *Jazz* has a similar generosity, but it has a nuance and a complication the lectures lack. This is not only because good fiction says more than even the most intelligent discursive prose. The story itself is different. It concerns not the black haunting of white minds, but the slow and difficult liberation of black minds from black and white oppression, from complicity with the all-knowing master of ugliness.

Morrison's chief metaphor for this movement is in her title. This is not a novel about jazz, or based on jazz, and I think reviewers' comments about the improvisatory quality of the writing underestimate what feels like the careful premeditation of the work. Each chapter after the first, for example, picks up an image or other cue from the preceding one, and takes it into new territories: caged birds, hot weather, a hat, spring in the city, the phrase "state of mind," a look, a person, the words "heart" or "pain." This is musical and elegant, as if a tune were to be shifted into a new arrangement, but what it borrows from jazz is a sense of flight and variation, not a method of composition.

Michael Wood. *NYRB*. November 19, 1992, p. 10

MPHAHLELE, ES'KIA (EZEKIEL) (1919–   )

SOUTH AFRICA

[Es'kia] Mphahlele's fierce prose evokes all the strain of . . . [his] adolescence. Both structure and style in *Down Second Avenue* show the attempt to enlarge the normal limits of autobiography, so that the book will be both a record of events, more or less chronological, in the author's life, *and* an immediate, impressionistic evocation of certain typical moods and moments which don't belong at any special place within it, but must be allowed to spill their fear and anguish over the book as a whole. These are evoked in the sections called Interludes, which contain some of Mphahlele's most angry and electric writing in the book. The search for immediacy has muted the common tendency for the writer (especially the exile) to see even the painful events of youth and childhood through a certain softening haze. In the Interludes, we actually hear the steely clang of police boots in the yard, the thunder of hard knuckles on the door at dawn, the sirens, the cries, and the sickening blows which authority rains upon the unprotected. . . .

It was during . . . [his] years in Nigeria that Mphahlele achieved his greatest period of fertility as a writer. *Down Second Avenue*, presumably completed by 1958, was published in the following year. In 1961 the newly established Mbari Publishing House in Nigeria brought out a volume of his short stories entitled *The Living and Dead [and Other Stories]*. All of these stories, except the rather weakly melodramatic "We'll Have Dinner at Eight," had already appeared in such South African magazines as *Drum, Student, Standpunte, Purple Renoster*, and *Africa South*. But, although they are thus the harvest of his last four years in the republic, the opportunity to publish them in book form was peculiarly the kind of opportunity brought to Mphahlele by his departure. The following year, 1962, brought the appearance of his book of critical essays, *The African Image*. The years since 1962 have seen no comparable burst of creativity, surely the fruit of that "sense of release" of which Mphahlele wrote. His second collection of stories, *In Corner B*, published in East Africa in 1967, also contained hitherto uncollected stories from his South African days, as well as reprinting three of the stories already used in *The Living and Dead*. Mphahlele's main production since 1962, apart from various critical introductions, has been his largely autobiographical novel *The*

Wanderers in 1971, a revision of *The African Image*, and one further volume of essays, *Voices in the Whirlwind [and Other Essays]*, in 1972. . . .

Mphahlele . . . is the most important black South African writer of the present age, by virtue of his all-around achievement and his lifelong commitment to literature. Others may have equaled or excelled him in autobiography, or in criticism, or in the short story. But Mphahlele's contributions in all three of these fields add up to a career of major distinction. If he cannot give us the great black South African novel which has been so long awaited, it seems probable that no one at present can. The fragmentation of creative achievement into the poems and short stories in which black South Africa has been so prolific must be seen as the obverse of those conditions which make major fiction so difficult of achievement there. The corpus of Mphahlele's work remains rich enough, however, in qualities of insight, compassion, and intelligence.

Gerald Moore. *Twelve African Writers*
(Bloomington: Indiana University Press, 1980), pp. 46, 52, 65–66

Chirundu was completed some three years after *The Wanderers* but was not published until five years later. . . . This was the first work since [Mphahlele's] very first volume, *Man Must Live [and Other Stories]*, to be published in South Africa. The banning order, imposed on him in 1966, had recently been lifted, and the publishers immediately availed themselves of the opportunity to add the doyen of black South African literature to their list of authors. . . .

Chirundu concerns the trial of cabinet minister Chimba Chirundu, whose wife accuses him of bigamy. Chirundu contends that Bemba marriage laws, according to which he married Tirenje, look upon a marriage as having ended if a wife leaves her husband, and her family takes no steps to bring her back. Tirenje counters that the traditional marriage was subsequently registered under old colonial ordinance, the divorce rules of which supersede the traditional ones. Since no divorce proceedings took place, Tirenje claims, her marriage still holds and Chirundu's marriage to Monde is bigamous. Chirundu does not expect to win the case but is "out to fight a system." He says that the ordinance should recognize traditional marriage as something that cannot be superseded. He tells his advocate that he does not want to plead guilty, he wants to "speak up so that when the government gets around to marriage laws this inanity will not be repeated." Mphahlele sees the confrontation not as a clash between tradition and Western values as would at first appear. Rather, he is investigating the effect of a foreign culture on an African one and how one should deal with the resulting conflicts. Should all Western culture be discarded, he asks? Chirundu tries to discuss polygamy with Tirenje before their marriage, but Tirenje is too young and inexperienced to get her point across. . . .

Mphahlele's ideal modern Africa, which he presents in much of his writing, both fiction and nonfiction, is a synthesis of tradition and the best of what Europe has brought it. In the novel, Tirenje and Chirundu's nephew Moyo represent this ideal. In her school days, Tirenje falls under the influence of a young woman teacher, the first woman in her country to have obtained a B.A. degree, who tells her women students to wake up and fend for themselves.

Tirenje, described as firmly built, walking like a woman who knows where she is going, with an earthy tone to her voice and a steady look in her eyes, is contrasted with Monde, who is modern in a superficial way. She has gained her veneer of Western sophistication by mimicry.

Ursula A. Barnett. *A Vision of Order* (London: Sinclair Browne, 1983), pp. 145–47

In *Chirundu*, Mphahlele is primarily concerned with the nature of political power in ex-colonial Africa and the problem of adapting traditional cultures to modern social structures. The personal relationships of the main characters represent situations and relationships which exist between various groups in the society. Mphahlele examines the choices for the individual and the society as a whole, operating as they do between African and Western institutions. Social relationships, in this context, Mphahlele shows, become "largely incoherent, pulling against and contradicting each other." The situation which Mphahlele describes for a particular Central African territory may be regarded as a paradigm for all ex-colonial African societies which show social structures that are inconsistent in themselves because of social and political pressures which operate in contrary directions. . . .

The main characters in the novel, Chimba Chirundu, his wife, Tirenje, and his nephew, Moyo, belong to the Bemba ethnic group. The two important relationships depicted are Chimba's relationship with Tirenje, whom he marries both under Bemba customary law and British ordinance, and his relationship with Moyo, his sister's son. In *Chirundu*, the circumstances of the breakup of the marriage between Chimba and Tirenje symbolize the breakdown of relationships between previously allied groups in the society. It also indicates the loss of certain guidelines of conduct in the society, for in the context of which Mphahlele writes, the marriage relationship or kinship affiliation, as represented in that of Chimba and Moyo, provides stable guidelines of conduct for the individual. The metaphor of marriage or kinship to describe other types of alliances is thus, in this instance, culturally derived.

The conflict in the novel arises from the circumstances under which Chimba takes a second wife. By marrying his second wife, Monde, under British ordinance, Chimba becomes guilty of bigamy which does not exist under Bemba customary law. The conflict of interests arising from Chimba's bigamous contract supplies the background for dealing with the theme of power and the conflict between the politicians and their grassroots supporters, who, like Tirenje, are abandoned by the politician who is busy consolidating his power.

Joyce Johnson. *Kunapipi*. 6, 2 (1984), pp. 109–10

In *Chirundu* there are obvious parallels with "mainstream" African fiction. At one level *Chirundu* is concerned, as are many postindependence African writers, with the dynamics of the emerging state, the impact of power on leadership, the attempt to reconcile technical and traditional modes, and the complexities of inherited economic structures. . . .

Yet the relationship between "African" and "South African" occurs at a deeper level. Mphahlele's attempt to relate African and South African themes arises partly out of the peculiar circumstances of Zambia in the late 1960s and his choice of Zambia as setting. Independent since 1964, Zambia has been hailed as Africa's second chance after Ghana. Yet such independence was belied by Zambia's insidious relationships with its southern neighbor, South Africa. In choosing Zambia as setting, Mphahlele recognizes the interaction between Zambia and South Africa, their close geographic proximity and interconnected histories. . . .

Chirundu is not, as one critic suggests, "part of established Pan African literature," but a novel that reveals a dialogue between South Africa and independent Africa immediately to the north and identifies concerns common to both societies. The ambiguities of Zambia at the end of the 1960s render it an intriguing setting for such a venture.

Dorian Haarhoff. EinA. 13, 2 (October 1986), pp. 39–40, 44

There is one writer in whose work it is possible to trace, over a period of forty years, both the problems of literary production experienced by South African writers and the stages in the development of an appropriate critical approach: for Ezekiel Mphahlele functioned as artist and critic throughout that period, encountering in his creative and confronting in his critical work the alienation of consciousness and the appropriation of discourse, while his later criticism records the efforts of black writers towards reappropriation.

While it would distort the corpus of his writing to divide it, whether critical or creative, into stages, there are nevertheless certain identifiable features appearing progressively within it, which sometimes correspond to, and sometimes seem to be partially responsible for, precipitating changes in the attitudes of black writers. In his earliest years, his writing is white-oriented: he addresses a predominantly white readership, in the forms and language of white culture, to record his protests on behalf of his black brothers. The events and pressures leading to his exile, together with the distancing effect of that experience, produce a raised consciousness that eventually resolves itself into an identification with the general ideas and aims of the black consciousness movement, despite his removal from the scene of its inception and growth. Lastly, with his return to South Africa, he was compelled to confront the whole issue of the liberation struggle, which had finally and reluctantly moved beyond the long years of patient nonviolence. . . .

Mphahlele wrote his critical works during periods when he felt too barren and infertile to attempt creative writing. They became, I would argue, far more than his fiction or poetry, seminal forces in the development of South African literature. He used both versions of The African Image and Voices in the Whirlwind as a search for personal, intellectual, and cultural identity, and they helped the establishment of a communal cultural identity in his country. The resonances of his work can be traced throughout the black consciousness movement in South Africa and beyond it, into the 1980s, providing young writers with aspirations and goals, and helping them to develop the means—the literary skills, styles, and genres—with which to attain them. He is the grand old man of South African letters, to which he has contributed, inside and outside South Africa, for forty years. His criticism helped to launch a self-propagating cultural theory—feeding into the work of younger writers, then, years later, taking up what they produced and analyzing their contributions in such a way as to prepare the ground for further cultivation. . . .

Throughout his writing, creative as well as critical, the impact of Europe on himself and his community provides a leitmotif—a leitmotif which is given different emphases at different periods, at times being overshadowed almost completely by contemporary preoccupations, but repeatedly surfacing and always, after such a period of dormancy, having suffered a sea-change. His atti-tude to the effects of European culture and education were equivocal from the outset. He was always aware of the conflicts set up by its introduction into an African context even when he was most receptive to the potential benefits it brought with it. However, throughout his life the balance shifts consistently, to the point where he is acutely aware of the damage it has inflicted, though even then he recognizes that there is much to be salvaged from the wreckage.

Through the course of his three major critical works, we can chart a grow-ing awareness of his own emergence from a Western-style education. At the beginning when he embarked on English literature courses he was too involved, too subordinated to the structure, too much an agent of the power that had pro-duced him, to be conscious of the implications of its operations upon himself as an individual and upon the African community as a societal network. With his incursions into Négritude and black American literature, he gained the necessary distance from his own educational background to achieve his consciousness.

Jane Watts. Black Writers from South Africa
(New York: St. Martin's Press, 1989), pp. 57–58, 63

Afrika My Music takes up [Mphahlele's] life story where *Down Second Avenue* left off, and the greater part covers the years of exile. He tells of literary mat-ters in African countries in which he played a role, all seen from the viewpoint of a newcomer to these regions. The word portraits of writers such as Camara Laye, Ngugi wa Thiong'o, [Wole] Soyinka, [J. P.] Clark, [Christopher] Okigbo, [Kofi] Awoonor, and others are too brief to be revealing, but they give thought-ful glimpses of the people he met. The South African section takes readers only as far as his work in Lebowa. Mphahlele calls the first chapter "The Sounds Begin Again," but the sounds are not the "sirens in the night," the "thunder at the door," or the "wordless endless wail / only the unfree know," to which Dennis Brutus refers in his well-known poem "Sirens, Knuckles, Boots" . . . the first line of which Mphahlele chose as the title of this second autobiography. Neither are the sounds the earthy, vibrant ones he records in *Down Second Avenue*. They are the thinner, plaintive noises of a man whose homecoming was not a triumphant return to his roots. The picture he draws of modern South Africa is an impersonal one, which is available to readers in greater detail in many social documents. . . .

There is one more book-length work of fiction Mphahlele has written and published. *Father Come Home* is a historical novel for children that takes place in the early 1920s after the Native Land Act had been passed, driving Africans from large, fertile areas into small, arid reserves. As a consequence, men were forced to leave their families and work in mines. The story concerns the growth to independence of fourteen-year-old Maredi Tulamo, whose father has left the family and returns only many years later. Adventures occur when the boy goes off in search of his father, but he gets only as far as a farm where he remains to work. The white farmer is not an important character in the novel. White life has become peripheral again, as it was in Mphahlele's earliest fiction. The man is neither unkind nor cruel: "he was simply in charge of [the laborers'] fate. . . ." It is with life in the village that Mphahlele is primarily concerned, the suffering of the wives and mothers left behind, and the hardships and values of the community. The narration is filled with folklore and includes epics about warriors, sung by the stranger Mashabela, a musician, poet, and healer, who moves into the village.

Mphahlele draws on his own life as a herd boy in the northern Transvaal, where he suffered the pain of growing up without a father. There is psychological insight in the story of the boy whose life is ruled by a longing for his father, but when at last the father comes home, there is no fairy-tale ending. Maredi finds it difficult to relate to the man and has to learn to adjust. The story is told in simple language for children, but the touching plot and the vividly depicted geographical and historical background appeal equally to adults. The work fills part of a great need in South Africa for a children's literature that is meaningful for black children. . . .

Es'kia Mphahlele's vision of an African culture, with a creative energy strong enough to survive and renew itself perpetually, is responsible for his involvement in every phase of black life, literature, and education in South Africa. Because his vision is essentially a Pan-Africanist one, his legacy will survive the present regime in South Africa and will benefit future generations in his own country and beyond.

Ursula A. Barnett. In Bernth Lindfors and Reinhard Sander, eds.
Dictionary of Literary Biography. 125 (1993), pp. 104–7

MTSHALI, OSWALD (1940–   )

SOUTH AFRICA

Many people write poetry, but there are few poets in any generation, in any country. There is a new poet in Africa, and his name is Oswald Mbuyiseni Mtshali. . . .

Mtshali's relationship with his immediate world—his philosophical approach, if you prefer—is married successfully with his style. The most striking poems are often those where the verbal magic—in this case the creation of mood or sense of place—contains a sting that finally shrivels the verbal magic away, leaving a question or statement burning in the mind. . . .

The world you will enter through [his] poems is a black man's world made by white men. It finds its epitome in the ghastly vision of township dogs fighting over the corpse of an abandoned baby—surely one of the most shocking poems ever written, and yet a triumph, since it could have been achieved only by forging from bitterness a steely compassion, by plunging into horror deep enough to bring forth tenderness. If, in this world, the poet Mtshali belongs automatically to an elite, it is the dead-end elite into which black artists and intellectuals are thrust by any color-bar society. The daily circumstances of his life remain those of the majority population of South Africa. The image of bread recurs again and again in his work: even snow suggests the labor for bread—"Trees sagged and grunted under the back-breaking flour bags of snow." The fact that man cannot live by bread alone is seen as a need for the "rare bread, solitude" which he seeks to "feed my hunger to read / to dream, and to write."

This is the imagery of survival. Oswald Mtshali, ironist, knows all that threatens man, abroad as well as at home: the Berlin walls of distrust, and the "moats of fright around his heart." He knows, finally, that even man's apparent virtues threaten him, in some times and places.

Nadine Gordimer. Foreword to Oswald Mbuyiseni Mtshali. *Sounds of a Cowhide Drum* (New York: The Third Press, 1972) pp. xi–xii, xv

The themes of Mtshali's poetry derive inevitably from the deepest and bitterest personal experience of his life as a messenger in Johannesburg. But the events provoke not the anticipated rage of immediate resentment, they are absorbed into poetry, distilled in his lines into moods of wry irony, and a curiously sustained tender awareness that persists through the anger. . . . Perhaps it would not be fanciful to note in passing a partially equivalent agony to be found in the work of Wilfred Owen during [World War I]. He too had to find a mechanism in his writing to distill the brute blood experience of the gangrene of war into poetry suffused with the realization that pity and compassion are moods that allow the best response to such a confrontation with unimaginable horror. . . .

Mtshali's voice can of course be strident and declamatory "for that is the sound of a cowhide drum / the Voice of Mother Africa." Yet, he accepts equally the implications of his role as a poet, his obligation to strike that cowhide drum so that its reverberations are true and valid, and therefore as complex and varied in its tones as the human feelings it lauds. He recognizes that distaste does not preclude humor, that power may flicker in moments of delight, that a saint is a beast, and the noble are also fools. Mtshali is a poet and sees himself specifically as an artist. . . . [His] lines indicate a significant degree of introspection, of a personal vision of poetry that is different from debate about the public efficacy and function of his verse. Quite openly he declares that neither "curses" nor "praises" can deflect him from his dedication to his art. Mtshali sees the poet as "a mole burrowing," drawing not only upon outward experience but also upon his deep private spirit. There is an acceptance of his role, of the function of words, rather than the anxious concern for their validity. Poetry, in a sense, is taken for granted as a pure discipline that allows the inspection of circumstance. It is for this reason that in Mtshali's work, the violence is controlled by a poetic sensibility that utilizes the devices of poetic expression for the recognition of experience. Both tone and technique are at the service of art; and just because his verse is, in the entirely nonderogatory sense, "artistic," it is the more effective and passionate. For above all, Mtshali as a poet, is a worker in words that are rich, daring, suggestive, catching mood and scene into the concentrated explosion of work and experience that makes the imagery of poetry.

John Povey. Ufahumu. 4, 1 (Spring 1973), pp. 151–52

Mtshali is essentially the urban poet; his importance lies in having brought Africa in literature to the townships, thus making black literature once again an important medium in South Africa. . . .

Few people doubt . . . that the publication of *Sounds of a Cowhide Drum* had begun a new era in black South African poetry. Asked why he chose the title of the collection from the last poem, Mtshali explained that the cowhide drum is a symbol which can be used to express many moods and different occasions of his life. "When war is declared, drums are beaten in a particular way; and when a baby is born, another tune is played on the drum."

He succeeded because of his genius in putting . . . [the experience of black township life] into words. White readers found his poetry fascinating because it gave them a window into black life, and black readers identified with his projection of their thoughts. . . . Mtshali makes his impact by his astounding capacity for absorbing and reflecting impressions and reproducing these, not instinctively—the simplicity is deceptive—but with the deliberate awareness of the craftsman. . . .

Mtshali's greatest asset . . . was his ability to communicate, at a time when blacks were eager to find a spokesman and still willing to communicate with whites who were prepared to listen. By looking upon poetry as a form of communication rather than as the intellectual pursuit of crystallizing individual thought, Mtshali became an exponent of African culture. Moreover, Mtshali's writing moves with the rhythm of feeling to provide a particular emotional atmosphere which [H. I. E.] Dhlomo saw as essentially African.

Ursula A. Barnett. A Vision of Order (London: Sinclair Browne, 1983), pp. 33, 35, 51, 53

Oswald Mtshali, the distinguished South African poet, has also spent his time in exile in the United States. . . . In 1971, when he published his first collection of poems, *Sounds of a Cowhide Drum*, Mtshali exploded upon the South African literary scene—a distinct new voice marked by delicate lyricism. Since that time his fame has steadily increased.

Mtshali states in a note at the beginning of his new collection of poems that *Fireflames* . . . "had a long gestation period," and that each poem for him is "like a long-overdue baby." The analogy is an apt one, given the content of this new volume—especially the opening poems, which painfully describe family relations. In the midst of human tragedy, Mtshali believes that a sense of hope and faith will prevail, especially in the infant's cosmos: "A child is the angel of the world . . . a picture of righteousness."

The tone changes in many of the subsequent poems, where history is referred to as "spring cleaning," and Mtshali describes his sense of uprootedness twelve thousand miles away from his homeland. There are vivid poetic evocations of a number of martyred South African black leaders, a commemoration in Harlem of the Soweto uprising and, finally, bittersweet images of the author's experiences in New York City, made bearable by Harlem. . . .

Fireflames has been handsomely illustrated with woodcuts by eight South African artists. I wouldn't say that the poems within the volume are particularly radical or inflammatory, yet the volume was banned in South Africa after its publication in 1980—simply another example of the rampant censorship within the country. All this, of course, to Mtshali's country's detriment.

Charles R. Larson. *WLT*. 58, 3 (Summer 1984), pp. 383–84

Mtshali's poems are intended, in the first instance, for the fringe of the English-speaking white population that reads poetry. But, although this public may well be educated, it is no less ignorant of the real conditions of the African with whom it rubs shoulders without seeing.

When Mtshali demands the right to speak, when he reveals to the whites the "hidden face" of South African society, he is undertaking a political act of which only the black prose writers of the late 1950s and early 1960s who are now banned in South Africa were capable. Although he never presents the communities in a position of conflict, although he always adopts a restrained albeit firm tone, although he plays at being naive the better to attack, he nonetheless fulfills his role as the revealer of the truth, in other words, as a man of protest.

Rather than restrict himself to the more usual portraits, Mtshali prefers to sketch characteristic little scenes which enable him to reveal some fundamental features of the African's situation. Thus, he constantly switches from the swarming crowds of the township, where the African lives at night and [on] weekends, to the white city, where he works during the day: from the one to the other and vice versa, in the constant back-and-forth movement of the pendulum that is the underlying pulse beat of the urban life of South African blacks.

The dominant impressions conveyed by the township are all confirmed by the sociological surveys: hunger, poverty, fear, for the majority; a relative prosperity and violence for the rest. . . .

At the heart of the poems directed especially at the black community, Mtshali returns constantly, and in several cases fairly explicitly, to the same crucial idea: the chief enemy of the oppressed is not the white man but the black man himself—because of his passivity and his lack of courage and aggressiveness. He allows himself, in fact, to be exploited, to be reduced to the state of an animal, to accept the imposition of the fatality of color distinction in which white is the symbol of domination and monopoly, and all without the slightest protest. All he does is turn to prayer, drink, or drugs, which are of little effect against the weapons of the white man. In this way, he wastes his vitality and sweeps aside the heritage of his ancestors. In other words, Mtshali invites the Africans to radically change their thinking.

This is something that would have difficulty in getting past the censor if the message were clearly stated: even in a country where the potential audience for poetry is minimal, there are limits the regime would not allow to be exceeded. Mtshali was well aware of this, so out of necessity, as well as from personal preference, it seems, he veiled his thoughts and used "the language of the slaves"—a network of allusions, references and hints which are clear only to those who share his culture.

Jacques Alvarez-Pereyre. *The Poetry of Commitment in South Africa* (London: Heinemann, 1984), pp. 172–73, 179

[The] "new" wave of committed poetry was first made prominent by Oswald Mtshali. When his first collection of poetry, *Sounds of a Cowhide Drum*, was published, Mtshali was working as a motorscooter messenger in Johannesburg. The poetry, which was generally well received at its publication by both blacks and whites, deals with the familiar concerns of race and politics similar to those examined by older poets such as Dennis Brutus. But it is the manner in which these concerns are expressed that has made *Sounds of a Cowhide Drum* so successful. Mtshali's cynical and sarcastic attitude, his oblique and ironic use of vivid, suggestive similes and images, and the profound meaning that lies beneath the apparent simplicity of his poetry, all contribute towards their total effect. This technique, however, is said to have disgruntled younger, radical writers like Mbulelo Mzamane, who wanted to see "revolutionary fire" in Mtshali's poetry. . . .

While critics like Mbulelo Mzamane have attacked what they consider to be an overemphasis on this Blakelike innocence and simplicity, they have overlooked the fact that what at first appears to be a poem celebrating innocence and the rapport between the shepherd and his environment, becomes a biting critique of the system's inequality; this is entirely compatible with the indirect approach Mtshali sets out to adopt.

Mtshali's manner of protest is reiterated in another poem that also focuses on a child character, and the technique of rhetorical questioning is again effectively employed. Like the shepherd in "The Shepherd and His Flock," the boy in "Boy on a Swing" is a type character representing the suffering majority of blacks. Nadine Gordimer has perceptively described this singular representation that characterizes the "new" poetry saying, "'I' is the pronoun that prevails, rather than 'we,' but the 'I' is the Whitmanesque unit of multimillions rather than the exclusive first person singular."

Piniel Viriri Shava. *A People's Voice: Black South African Writing in the Twentieth Century* (London: Zed Books, 1989), pp. 71–73

It was in 1948 that the policy of racial discrimination was consolidated in South Africa and since then the legislation of the South African government has been geared towards a total repression of all categories of nonwhites. Among the several laws promulgated towards this end are the laws against franchise, laws against interracial marriages, laws for residential segregation based on color, pass laws, detention laws, and several other acts which have generated unabating violence. That these laws are designed to make various racial groups live mutually exclusive lives, to protect the whites, and to further exploit the nonwhites, especially the blacks, is graphically depicted by Oswald Mtshali. His portrayal in his collection of poems, *Sounds of a Cowhide Drum*, demonstrates that the legislation engenders restriction of movement and association, repression of thought and speech, and denial of educational opportunities to the blacks. . . .

Mtshali evokes and ridicules some of the laws which engender restriction of movement and association. They include: the separate Amenities Act for separate social facilities such as hotels, lavatories, parks, and post offices; the Immorality Act, for the prevention of sexual or marital relations among the different races; and the Pass Laws, which require the African to carry a document on him at all times for effective control of his movement and easy distribution of his labor.

In a colloquial style, Oswald Mtshali, in "Pigeons at the Oppenheimer Park," makes a sarcastic and concentrated evocation of the typical slogans and usual tactics of the evidently prejudiced law enforcement agent, and dares the white policeman to apply the laws to the contravening birds. . . . We are told that "these insolent birds . . . not only sit on White Only benches . . . the hallowed benches," but "they also mess them up with birdshit." The persona then sarcastically asks, "Don't they know of the Separate Amenities Act?" . . .

Mtshali's use of the bird imagery evokes the borderlessness of the sky, the birds' region, where they fly freely and this suggests the poet's longing for the spirit of such [an] environment which contrasts sharply with his own real world riddled with restrictions. . . .

Mtshali's diction is very effective in its evocation of the sacredness with which the blacks are expected to regard the things of the white man and [their] attendant restrictions. Words such as "hallowed," "chant," "holy," and "congregation" used to describe the park, its bench, its fountain, and its water are words usually associated with the worship of God. Their use in this context heightens the effect of his depiction of the disparity in the apartheid system. . . .

It is evident that Mtshali's poetry is evocative of the denial of the right of the blacks to express their thoughts freely and develop intellectual powers; it is also evocative of the censorship of the press, and the banning of committed literary works.

"Handcuffs" is suffused with images of somatic pain and repression of thought and speech. It is a concentrated evocation of the agony of a people in bondage. Ordinarily, handcuffs are instruments of restriction and repression; the poem's title is symbolic in that here they serve to evoke the effects on the blacks. . . . Mtshali depicts that the repression is so total and overwhelming that it encompasses not only the physical but also the intellectual and the spiritual creates certain urgent needs whose fulfillment it, at the same time, makes impossible. It is like beating a man and asking him not to cry. . . .

Mtshali in his "This Kid Is No Goat" evokes the irrelevance of the schools' syllabus to the needs of the blacks. He views the education given as misguided, with a strong inhibitory religious influence. The protagonist laments his brother's incapacitating education metaphorically, depicted in the latter's "clutching a rosary as an amulet against" discrimination and oppression. . . .

Consequent upon their inability to go to school, most black children spend their lives in the streets and rely only on raw life experience for their learning.

This leads to their acquisition of bad habits such as drunkenness, stealing, and other forms of violence which eventually drag them to jail. This feature is portrayed by Mtshali in "This Kid Is No Goat" where the protagonist's brother, denied the opportunity to go to school, has to enroll at "Life University" which connotes his complete reliance on the everyday raw experience of life for his learning, and the consequences of this are unfortunate. . . .

It can . . . be concluded that Oswald Mtshali's depiction of the horror of social discrimination in South Africa is vivid, effective, and comprehensive. Its comprehensiveness shocks the reader into awareness of the extent to which apartheid has brutalized the black populace and this constitutes a subtle indictment urging a revulsion against apartheid. Mtshali's colloquial style is gentle and refreshing, and his skillful wielding of metaphors and irony earns his portrayal the seal of poetry.

David Olusegun Agbaje. *LHY.* 32, 2 (July 1991), pp. 17–20, 27–28, 33–35

MUDIMBE, V. Y. (1941–   )

ZAIRE

The plot of [V. Y. Mudimbe's] *L'Écart* revolves around Ahmed Nara, a young and very brilliant historian who is working on a thesis on the Koubas. Throughout the novel, this character is a neurotic affected by emotional troubles. He is aware of this state of affairs but is incapable of getting rid of these problems. . . .

In this situation of existential anguish, Ahmed Nara, like the majority of contemporary African intellectuals, is a person with a self-analyzing consciousness. This role is played here by Dr. Sano, who is the double of Nara. He is also the expression of a secret split, a hidden disarticulation. He is living in the gap or in between, because he does not wish to conform to the norms accepted by all, and because of this, wishes to create a new path for himself.

Indeed, from the beginning of the novel, Nara is bored by the "dullness" of life, by the feeling of a vague, indefinable, and unnamable dissatisfaction. . . .

Apparently spineless, unwilling, and in addition obsessed, Nara lives for Aminata alone. The attachment to this woman is a consolation, a liberation. It is even a deliberate act. . . .

Although intensely in love with each other, Nara and Aminata discover a difference in race. . . .

Opposing Aminata and her friends, Soum in particular, is Nara, who declares his black identity, his Négritude. But, in opposition to this notion of race firmly established in Nara, Soum presents the notion of social classes going so far as to reject even Négritude, which he describes as "merde." He also has the firm conviction that one must lead the fight against social structures. He suggests to Nara adherence to the Communist party. . . .

Neither the thesis work, nor the domestication by Aminata, nor the appeal of his leftist friends to participate in their revolution can eliminate Nara's anguish. . . .

Finally, the gap or distance is in effect the distanciation with the community of men and the desire to change oneself first and then one's surroundings.

L'Écart does not limit itself to the analysis of the unhappy and stifled consciousness of an African intellectual, but reveals at the same time the difficulty experienced by this intellectual in living in a topsy-turvy world. A sociological reading of the novel shows us that Mudimbe talks in halftones of his own world. He sends back its own image to Africa. This is to say that *L'Écart* is not divorced from reality. Beyond the capture of the tortured consciousness of this African intellectual, there is a complete lucid political reflection on the situation of the continent.

Among the ills evoked are general unemployment, the quantitative and qualitative deterioration of teaching, the merciless exploitation of the weak by the strong, the exaggerated military parade, famine, the irresponsibility of political leaders, the silencing of the only political party, etc. . . . .

At the level of writing, we gather that there is a search for a new language that is reflected by the practice of broken-up style, often incomplete, and marked by frequent points of suspension. . . .

Almost nothing of the substance of the traditional novel remains: the classical well-punctuated style has disappeared.

The theme of *L'Écart* enriches the francophone, novelistic production of Zaire in particular, and of the Negro-African world in general, through a novel interrogation: the neurosis of an African intellectual who lucidly examines Africa eroded by corrosive ills. It is, then, a "committed literature that desires to give birth to souls that are awakened to their consciousness."

Mbuyamba Kankolongo. *Zaire Afrique*. 144 (1988), pp. 227–29, 232†

To read Mudimbe is to be brought into a discourse whose archeological field is broad and deep: breadth arising from the extensive reading in many schools of thought, indeed in many disciplines, varying chiefly over the hard and soft sciences, including also history and literature, and with certain "réflecteurs" prevailing—notably [Michel] Foucault, and to a lesser extent [Jacques] Lacan, [Louis] Althusser, and [Jean-Paul] Sartre . . . depth arising from the sense of an historical consciousness in which can be traced the evolution of a diachronic phenomenon that has been occurring ever since the first Portuguese missionary-explorer ever set foot in the Kingdom of the Bakongo in 1483, and maybe, in terms of a typology of the encounter, for a much longer time.

The point of entry into this discourse for us is not, however, in the continuation of contemporary European thought, or of one of its branches abroad, but in the formation of a text of the encounter between Europe and Africa whose meaning is elaborated largely in the language of the above-mentioned thinkers. Mudimbe acquaints us with the issue at hand at the outset of his two major works of critical enterprise, *L'Autre Face du royaume* and *L'Odeur du père*, by stating that he intends to raise the question of whether and under what conditions one can practice the social sciences in Africa. . . . As a social scientist, Mudimbe is particularly interested in raising the issues of political, existential freedom, and greater individual and social fulfillment in terms of the practices of the social scientists, and as the source of meaning for those practices, in their discourses. At the end of *L'Autre Face du royaume* we see that this problem is the pretext for examining the larger issue of the relationship between European and African discourses. The problematic element in this relationship is easily stated: How are the social scientists, the thinkers, the researchers in Africa, to produce today a discourse that will be productive in terms of Africa's needs and special conditions when the norms of the sciences, indeed of virtually all the disciplines being practiced in Africa are shaped by the Western tradition; and, indeed, it goes deeper than norms to encompass the entire discourse: its codes, its values, its assumptions on what constitutes truth, acceptability, worth in terms of information and research—all the unstated presuppositions.

Kenneth [W.] Harrow. In Stephen Arnold, ed.
African Literature Studies: The Present State/L'État présent
(Washington, D. C.: Three Continents Press, 1985), pp. 91–92

Mudimbe's novel, *Le Bel Immonde*, has a unique style in which the action stagnates a little, then rushes forward, and then returns to the original point. The crux of the plot is an affair between a powerful minister and a young prostitute. An affair that is transformed with the passage of time, from a simple fancy to a kind of romance, especially for the official who is married and father of a family. The attachment of the woman is all the more surprising, because one learns soon that she prefers Sappho's taboo to male warmth.

The destiny of the two characters is further linked by a political factor: the combat that the country is leading against the woman's ethnicity. Her father having died recently at the hands of the legal forces, the prostitute is recruited by the insurgents to serve as a spy against the minister. In the meantime, the latter, wishing to protect himself against the enemies, makes a sacrifice of his mistress's friend to the spirits of his ancestors. But he is suspected no less by his colleagues and, therefore, in order to demonstrate his good faith, he undertakes a mission in the region of the insurgency. Soon after the departure of her lover, the prostitute is arrested and questioned at length. In desperation, and in order to get out of this problem, she ends up betraying the minister, of whose death in a car accident one finally condescends to tell her. Free and quite relieved, she starts her life over as if nothing has happened. The novel returns to the starting point: a nightclub where the prostitute devotes her time to soliciting, all the while scouting for an eventual homosexual partner.

That's it as far as the plot of *Le Bel Immonde* is concerned. As for the rest, this novel with the ambiguous title is marked by an uncommon heterogeneity, which is translated on several levels. Firstly, the themes treated or evoked go from adultery to betrayal, while passing through lesbianism, transvestitism, love, death, human sacrifice, anthropology, and themes of a sociopolitical nature such as prostitution, malpractice, and rebellion. Furthermore, the entire ambience of the work seems to have the same bizarre nature: the nightclub scenes reappear constantly, whereas many other episodes seem to be experienced in a dreamlike state or in a state of semiconsciousness.

But it is especially at the level of structure that this heterogeneity is best represented. In fact, the composition of the novel shows different genres: about ten pages are devoted to the epistolary genre. One also finds a radiophonic discourse, a journal article, as well as numerous passages from the novel in the form of memoirs. Finally, the entire novel is punctuated by transitional poems that announce, the majority of times, the nightclub scenes. . . .

In conclusion, we can say that, in *Le Bel Immonde*, Mudimbe seems to participate in the inclinations of the new Western novelistic form. He distances himself from the traditional norms of the genre in treating heterogeneous themes, in creating anonymous characters with hazy and fleeting personalities, and through the blend of narrative modes.

Victor O. Aire. In Jonathan A. Peters, Mildred P. Mortimer, and Russell
V. Linnemann, eds. *Literature of Africa and the African Continuum*
(Washington, D. C.: Three Continents Press, 1989), pp. 153–54, 156†

[In *Entre les eaux*] Mudimbe presents Pierre Landu as one who embodies the extreme poles of an impossible purity. Pierre is a priest whose need to be true to his vocation leads him to join the revolution in his homeland, ostensibly Zaire. His narrative-confession is all the more appropriate given his dual identity as priest-revolutionary. He is a devout Christian from early youth, and completes his training for the priesthood in Rome in the Jesuitical seminary, the Angelicum. There, with his young, Italian friend, Fabrizio, he is seduced by the beauties of Italian culture, especially Medieval and Renaissance art, and Baroque music, while at the same time learning about the latest trends in Marxist thought; he is led to conclude that the true calling of Christ's ministry is best embodied, in our times, in Marx himself.

Despite his initiation as a youth in the religion of his ancestors, Pierre accepts Christianity. Yet he fails to find a way to harmonize his new religion with his traditional past. He remains torn, despite his early alienation from that past, because the new culture and religion which attract him are manifestly not his own, and because he cannot fulfill the expectations of his priesthood without denying his African priesthood and family. He is "entre les eaux," unable to be true to either path, aware of his failure to live up to either the imported ideals of Marxism or Christianity, or to fall back on the traditional way of life.

Kenneth W. Harrow. In Jonathan A. Peters, Mildred P. Mortimer, and
Russell V. Linnemann, eds. *Literature of Africa and the African Continuum*
(Washington, D. C.: Three Continents Press, 1989), pp. 164–65

V. Y. Mudimbe's second novel, [*Le Bel Immonde*, translated as *Before the Birth of the Moon*], is a very rich, very disturbing story about individual pain and loss in a young society's struggle for independence and nationhood. It is set in Zaire in the mid-1960s, a period which was arguably the country's most perilous and chaotic. Fourteen million people drawn from some two hundred ethnic groups struggled to bind themselves into a nation after generations of alternately brutal and paternalistic Belgian colonial rule. During those years betrayal, assassination, greed, deceit, and confusion were as common as equatorial rain. But Mudimbe spends little time discussing these crises on the macrocosmic scale. Instead he skillfully extracts from the historical panorama two very complex and troubled people—a government minister and a prostitute—who, through their protean love affair, tell us more about the pains of the young nation than could any history book. In the first of his four novels to be translated into English, Mudimbe shows what sociopolitical upheaval does rather than what it is.

Reginald McKnight. NYTBR. April 30, 1989, p. 43

Mudimbe's theoretical books, L'Autre Face du royaume and L'Odeur du père, and his novels, Entre les eaux and L'Écart, engage as their subject the enabling as well as the regressive elements in Western discourse, thereby liberating spaces in Africa from which more empowered discourses can be uttered. . . .

[Mudimbe] calls for a reformulation of discourse in Africa. He argues that "we Africans must invest in the sciences, beginning with the human and social sciences. We must reanalyze the claims of these sciences for our own benefit, evaluate the risks they contain, and their discursive spaces. We must reanalyze for our benefit the contingent supports and the areas of enunciation in order to know what new meaning and what road to propose for our quest so that our discourse can justify us as singular beings engaged in a history that is itself special." For Mudimbe, Africans must rid themselves of the smell of an abusive father, of the presence of an order which belongs to a particular culture but which defines itself as a fundamental part of all discourse. In order to produce differently, they must practice a major discursive insurrection against the West.

For Mudimbe, the most radical break with the West can be obtained only through a linguistic revolution in which European languages are replaced by African languages. Just as the originators of Greek thought set into motion a reorganization of knowledge and life through their transformation of ancient Egypt's use of science and methodologies, the West dominates the rest of the world today because it has appropriated Greek thought in its languages. In like fashion, for Mudimbe, at least "a change in the linguistic apparatus of science and production would provoke an epistemological break and open the door for new scientific adventures in Africa."

Mudimbe further argues that the other insurrectionist practice against the abusive father is obtained through the excommunication of Western ratio from African discursive practices that take place in European languages. In other words, Mudimbe calls for a reformulation of discourses inherited from the West and a subtle discursive technique aimed at deconstructing Western control over the rules that govern scientific statements. While working within Western languages, the new practice nevertheless departs from the traditional duplications of the Western canon in Africa and moves toward the construction of an African regime of truth and socially appropriated sciences. The new and cannibalizing discourse swells, disfigures, and transforms the bodies of Western texts, and establishes its order outside the traditional binary oppositions such as primitive/civilized, (neo)colonized/colonizer, slave/master, receiver/donor.

Manthia Diawara. October. 55 (Winter 1990), pp. 79, 88–89

Entre les eaux by V. Y. Mudimbe analyzes the inner conflict of an African priest whose theological training, including years of study in Rome, has made it impossible for him to relate to those to whom he is intended to minister. Seduced by Western culture—and by the relative comfort accompanying his status—he nevertheless sympathizes with the plight of the people and leaves his order to join a Marxist revolutionary leader in the forest. In spite of the action stemming from rebel forays, the real subject of the novel is the internal dilemma of the priest, Pierre Landu, as he tries to decide between his duty to his people and the obligation he feels to the church, between conscience and comfort, between Marxism and Christianity. Key to the novel's effectiveness and to the portrait of the alienated intellectual is the attitude of the revolutionary group toward the priest. Rarely trusted, constantly spied upon, Landu is regarded as the symbol of the social injustice and unwarranted privilege upon which the revolution is based.

Janice Spleth. *StTCL*. 15, 1 (Winter 1991), pp. 126–27

On the prefatory page of his first book of poetry, entitled *Déchirures*, Mudimbe exclaims: "J'aimerais crier contre les poèmes pour que surgisse l'indiscrète insistance de l'extase" ["I would like to cry against poems so that the indiscreet insistence of ecstasy may surge!"] . . .

Irony is not the least pregnant figure in *Déchirures*. In the fifteen stations, or tableaus, offered to the reader's contemplation through the poet's own mind's eye, multiple elements could be regarded as the climax of despair, horror, and alienation. The first three sections unroll like a nightmarish film or dream whose sequences lead the dreamer from night to midday through dawn and morning. In its turn, at the microcosmic level, each subsection mirrors the larger dream in which the apotheosis of a redemption and a resurrection bathed in warmth, light, and joy is evoked, or even announced, as the eventual outcome of the whole drama. . . . Constantly, however, in all three sections, the intensity of the pain felt by the speaking subject at the obsessive sight of the omnipresent wounds, lacerations, or sterile landscapes is prevalent. In section two, the first-person narrator, whose presence has been discreetly announced in [section one], steps into the drama as a full-time contemplator, but also as an actor. Not unexpectedly, following the heroic path traveled by many prophetic figures, this narrator speaks both from outside and within the drama. As the text develops, the speaker's status as both savior and victim asserts itself more and more strongly. . . . Remarkable in these sections are the associations between the lofty red cannas, evoked as a burgeoning forest of loved idols, and the red dancing Africa present in the speaker's blood (" . . . l'Afrique en danse rouge de mon sang"). Here, with authority, the speaker announces the resurrection of a blossoming land where he, again, will be able to love. Such a resurrection, however, remains encompassed within the humble vision afforded by writing. In fact, it is not easy to interpret such a line as "dans les brouillons maladroits de l'écriture" ["in the clumsy drafts of writing"]. Is the reader to assume that dream will never meet reality, that beauty, fecundity, and love will for ever remain a clumsy and tentative figure of speech? Or, on the contrary, is the reader to believe that the speaker is imparting to the word, if not the power to change the world, at least the power to plant the seeds of a new season?

The third section offers no relief to the reader's questioning. In this section, the speaker retreats to the contemplation of horror while seeking complete union with the sufferers. In [the first three subsections], various outside images, paintings, places, [and] milieus pass by the traveler's side like inconsequential mirages opposed to the "fertile eyes" of dream, a dream depicted through an interplay of alliterations and assonances in such a way as to suggest the sharpness of a blade and the torture of numerous lacerations: "Dans la rêve, le rêve effilé, si long et si lent des estafilades, des taillades" ["In the dream, the sharp-edged dream, so long and lingering with slashes and gashes"]. The fifteen remaining subsections bring the reader close to the infinite misery of the Kisangani tragedy. The desire to be one with the African brothers and sisters' suffering is translated in a striking and uncompromising figure of speech: "Pouvoir être cette meurtrissure, cette gangrène éternelle . . . " ["I wish I were that bruise, that eternal gangrene . . ."]. Towards the end of section three, the speaker recalls the responsibility incurred by the Christian Church in the various stages of the African holocaust. The reader is left with a burning figure/tableau: numbed with indifference, the guilty ones slumber before the "split veil," following the death of so many cross-bearers. . . .

Déchirures was written by a young man who, as stated on the prefatory page, worked on an obsessive thought (*idée fixe*) for ten years, in fact from 1961 to 1971, a thought expressed through "variations" and "repetitions." If, for this reader, the "idea" of a state of ecstasy—in which the split between body and "soul," self and other, secular and sacred, grief and bliss, art and life might become transcended through acts of love—is indeed provocatively powerful in the texts, the various exchanges evoked in the poems do not, however, culminate into the vision of one triumphant climax. Individual sections or poems do (such as the beautiful, heartlifting "Gloria" poems, section thirteen). If, on the other hand, one tried to assess the poems from another angle in which the writing and reading processes would also be placed within the context of an ecstatic journey, there again, the overall experience might not measure up to the ambition. Yet, going through these poetic pages one more time, this reader knows that many fragments from *Déchirures* have forever become part sof her knowledge of human history, part, also, of her grief and part of her bliss. . . . The next step should be to situate *Déchirures* in relation to the other two collections of poems. Obviously, a comprehensive and detailed study of Mudimbe's poetry and fiction is still needed. As years go by, it seems to me that Mudimbe has been increasingly purging his style of all unessential ornaments. To use a quick analogy, I would say that reading his latest work is like contemplating a face whose beauty would rely exclusively on its bone structure. If many of us have good reason to believe that Mudimbe will be remembered as one of the leading African theoreticians and scholars of his generation. I, for one, fervently hope that his rare gift as a creative writer, his rare style and dream, will elicit even more interest among future readers and critics.

Bernadette Cailler. *RAL*. 24, 4 (Winter 1993), pp. 15, 18–19, 26

MUGO, MICERE GITHAE (1942–   )

KENYA

Dedan Kimathi fought for the total liberation of the Kenyan people from foreign domination and oppression. He did not achieve this in his lifetime: the struggle continues, and Kimathi is the legitimate hero of the revolution. Ngugi [wa Thiong'o] and his colleague Micere Githae Mugo have collaborated in writing a play with a number of specific purposes. It is a "song of praise" for the feats of leadership and resistance of the most brilliant of the generals of the independence struggle who . . . are neglected, often repudiated heroes, their deeds for the most part not known by the present generation of young Kenyans. . . . The play [*The Trial of Dedan Kimathi*] is an attempt to restore the character of Kimathi to his legitimate place in the history of Kenya.

Secondly, the play establishes the connection with the masses in the present struggle by reasserting Kimathi's values. More than this the play is a self-conscious assertion of the part that literature should play in the revolution. . . .

The authors present a play in which time past and time present are made to merge in a continuous present where Kimathi on trial in Nyeri and the mythic Kimathi, who stands on the dock in the present-tense, debate the causes and prosecution of the continuing revolutionary struggle. Ngugi and [Mugo] state in their notes that "the action should on the whole be seen as breaking the barrier between formal and infinite time, so that past and future and present flow into one another." . . .

The authors achieve their purpose by employing a number of theatrical techniques and characteristics of the non-naturalistic theater. The play, which has an opening, three movements, and fourteen scenes, makes use of mime, dancing, drumming, singing, music, sudden blackouts, and artful changes in lighting. The authors further enhance the suggestion of a time continuum by creating characters whose conduct in time past is coincident with their current values and motives. Moreover, the characters are typed. There is nothing introspective about them. Positions have been adopted, and in the play they are debated and put on trial. Further, the authors employ language in such a way [as] to bridge the gap in time. Kimathi, for example, speaks a revolutionary language appropriate to his role in both past and present, but the vocabulary in scenes devoted to past time often uses a language inappropriate to the past time period, drawn from contemporary revolutionary rhetoric—but this is nevertheless effective in suggesting the coincidence of the struggle.

G. D. Killam. An Introduction to the Writings of Ngugi
(London: Heinemann, 1980), pp. 86–87

The playwrights use Kimathi's "trial" at Nyeri as a starting point. The core of the action of the play, the story element, concerns a peasant woman who separates a ragged urban youth from fighting a similarly impoverished girl, and then co-opts him in her efforts to get a gun to Kimathi in jail. The youth is not initially aware of the nature of the mission, but his and the girl's eventual understanding of the struggle and commitment to it lead to the climax of the play—the firing of a shot in the courtroom after Kimathi has had the sentence of death passed on him. The shot symbolizes the continuation of the struggle through the young boy and the girl.

The core of the play—a core of meaning as well as a storyline—has woven around it a cumulative portrait of Dedan Kimathi, developed through four symbolic trials, which are not to be confused with the "trial" staged by the colonialists in the Nyeri courthouse. These four symbolic trials take place in the cell in the jail, which itself is symbolic of a state of mind, or of a "wilderness." The play is in three movements, which we are advised to imagine as one single movement, with actions, events, incidents—all the parts of the play, in fact—moving along with great urgency. The four trials of Kimathi occur in the second movement.

Other elements of stylization in *The Trial of Dedan Kimathi* tend to reinforce this determination of the playwrights to explain the reasons why things happen in a certain way, and how they can be changed. Thus, the four trials which Kimathi undergoes are symbolic because they represent "temptations" to end the struggle; their apparent reasonableness has to be answered by a deeper analysis. . . .

There are other symbolic groupings on the stage. The courtroom scene occurs three times. It is the same event on the first two occasions, namely Kimathi's appearance before the white judge, which results in an adjournment. The third court scene—the climax of the play—is Kimathi's reappearance in court and the pronouncement of the death sentence upon him. Whites and Africans are symbolically divided in the courtroom. . . . In the final courthouse scene, the whites' side now contains, symbolically, the blacks whom we earlier saw as some of Kimathi's "tempters." The blacks' side, made up of people in very ragged clothes, consistently supports Kimathi whenever he speaks. The whites are settlers, and they react towards Kimathi with frenzied hate. With Kimathi in chains in the dock, challenging the white judge's right to try him, the scene visually shows how Kimathi brings the oppressors into confrontation with the oppressed.

Michael Etherton. The Development of African Drama (London:
Hutchinson University Library for Africa, 1982), pp. 168–69, 172–74

In Ngugi wa Thiong'o's and Micere Mugo's *The Trial of Dedan Kimathi*, time and space coalesce in a symbolic drama of growth and development. Past and present events surrounding the Mau Mau revolt are re-created on stage to provide an historical perspective to and continuity of the anticolonial movement in Kenya. Spatial shifts from distant guerrilla encampments in the Nyandarua forest to local prisons and courtroom installations in Nairobi emphasize the breadth and depth of the Mau Mau rebellion. The rapid montage design of the play overrides the accustomed cause-effect rational processes of the audience and consequently prohibits simplistic and limiting interpretations of staged events. In this structure, the characters are similarly transformed from their spatial and temporal individuality to symbolic, collective proportions.

The Trial of Dedan Kimathi is composed of two narrative plot movements: the first focuses on the capture, imprisonment, and subsequent trial of
[Dedan Kimathi]; the second features the transformation of two young Kenyans
from childhood to adulthood in a symbolic "rite of passage." Both of these plot
movements utilize the character of Kimathi . . . as a symbol of the Mau Mau
movement. . . .

Ngugi wa Thiong'o [and Micere Mugo use] the image of Dedan Kimathi
as a model against which the activities of the boy and girl are measured. Under
close scrutiny, they discover that their own attitudes and behaviors fall short of
the mark set by this standard bearer. Vowing to forsake their fallen world, they
pursue the path blazed for them by Kimathi. . . . Their imitation of his heroic
deeds identifies them as newly initiated freedom fighters. As such they themselves become metaphors of the continued spirit of anticolonial resistance and
rebellion in Kenya.

In this analysis, metaphor differs from symbol in that it represents a
unique creation of the artist within the given work itself. It comes to life as a
result of the insight of the artist and does not depend on the external culture or
literary background for its existence and emotive power. The artist is free to
manipulate it according to her/his own thematic designs. A symbol, however,
depends on and utilizes outside influences for much of its efficacy although the
artist can highlight particular details or associations to conform to her/his purposes. Every symbol, from its inception, is a metaphor. But it is a metaphor that
has been socially accepted and repeatedly used by others. The creative insight
and new associative meaning that sparked the first use of the metaphor is conventionally accepted as the meaning of the symbol. . . . Accordingly, in *The
Trial of Dedan Kimathi*, the unnamed boy and girl are metaphors for all the lost
youth of Kenya. Their transformation in the play becomes the model for others
to follow.

E. A. Magel. *Canadian Journal of African Studies.* 17, 2 (1983), pp. 239–40

As with [Ola] Rotimi's play [*Ovonramwen Nogbaisi*], the emotional appeal of
Dedan Kimathi consists in the spectacle of the sufferings of a blameless protagonist with whom the audience is invited to identify. Like Oba Ovonramwen,
Dedan Kimathi is the victim of an imperialism which he struggles heroically to
counteract but which finally destroys him: his only weakness is in any other
context a virtue—love and mercifulness to those closest to him, who nevertheless betray him. On trial for his life before a hostile court, Kimathi is like
Ovonramwen in his stoicism, which in no way, however, implies resigned submission. He refuses to be influenced by the attempts to seduce him away from
the cause he leads: like Ovonramwen, albeit in far more vehement terms, he
addresses his captors and accusers, indicting them for their crimes and exhorting the masses to continue the struggle.

[Mugo and Ngugi wa Thiong'o], like Rotimi, reinforce empathy with their
heroic protagonist through their portrayal of his enemies. The imperialists are
much more full-bloodedly villainous than in *Ovonramwen Nogbaisi*: they are

portrayed as hysterically racist, for example in the outburst of the white settler, whom the stage direction describes as "foaming with rage like a madman," in the court. Though Moor and his compatriots are depicted as callous in their humiliation of Ovonramwen, they are far from being the brutal torturers of *Dedan Kimathi*. The audience is invited to feel nothing but disgust and contempt for the whites and their black and Indian stooges, whose various attempts to "tempt" Kimathi are shown as obviously determined by economic considerations. Most emotive of all, perhaps, considering the Kenyan audience for which the play was originally written, is Kimathi's betrayal by his brother and close associates, despite his initially merciful attitude towards him. Kimathi's torture by the white colonialists and their allies doubtless stirs a black audience; but the spectacle of his betrayal and martyrdom by those who should be his cohorts in the struggle is likely to arouse the strongest emotions and establish an especially powerful empathy. . . .

The struggle for national liberation is thus invested by the Kenyan dramatists with specifically religious connotations, including a martyred redeemer. The affective power of the Christian myth, and of the sacrificial Christ-figure, is exploited to lend emotional and ethical force to the authors' call for a continuation, inspired by the memory of Kimathi, of the anti-imperialist struggle in Kenya. This struggle, and the values that it and its leading martyr embody, are shown as being ultimately successful.

Brian Crow. Ariel. 14, 3 (July 1983), pp. 25–27

[Mugo] and Ngugi [wa Thiong'o] were inspired by a woman they met when they visited Karumaini, Kimathi's birthplace. The defiant pride of the woman, who had been Kimathi's pupil at Karumaini Independent School, her continuing love of her former teacher and leader, and her insistence to the visitors that "Kimathi will never die" challenged Mugo to create the Woman of the play, a multifaceted individual presented as of almost equal importance to Kimathi himself. [Mugo], an actress, as well as a writer, educator, administrator, and political activist, played this central role of the Woman during the play's premier run.

We know from history that many Kenyan women supported, even fought alongside, the men during their struggle for national liberation. . . .

So, in one sense, [Mugo's] emphasis on the Woman can be seen as evidence of her commitment to socialist realism, an implicit assertion that classes and their historical conflicts, not gender, is the authors' main concern. The Woman functions historically in the play, as Kimathi does, carrying out acts of subversion; she operates politically by analyzing the exploitive colonial economic situation and eloquently announcing the Freedom Fighters' plans for recovery from imperialism. Linked to Wanjiru, a guerrilla "who fought like a tiger," she is a "mother, a fighter all in one." She becomes symbolic, moreover, of all the women of her class, not only those who actually helped the guerrillas; the authors state explicitly, "the Woman now represents all the working mothers."

Arlene A. Elder. Matatu. 3, 6 (1989), pp. 81–82

MUNONYE, JOHN (1929–   )

NIGERIA

[John Munonye's] novels are mainly domestic, centered around the family and its problems for the man, woman, and even the children. He . . . has quite often evoked the typical marital situation which normally results in polygamy, especially childlessness, but has in addition rejected polygamy as the solution for such a problem. In *Obi*, Munonye successfully dramatizes the pressures on a childless couple from family members and friends, especially the mother-in-law and in particular the *umuada*, a group which has heretofore not been treated in such detail. These are the married daughters of a family. Their place within the community or in any marriage contracted by one of their "sons" forms one of the sources of tension in *Obi* and *The Only Son*.

In *Obi*, the *umuada* are presented as the greatest single source of challenge to the fatherless hero of the novel, Joe. A further topic of the book is the clash between traditional religion and Christianity to which Joe and his wife, Anna, belong. Joe believes in total allegiance to his religion, while certain members of the society believe that when the issue of childlessness arises in a marriage, religion should be forgotten and a man should be free to take a second wife, especially if there is no male child to succeed to the ruling of the "Obi," the family house. . . . His immediate family, with their belief in the traditional religion and their hopes for him as their specially gifted son, also had their own ideas of what they expected Joe to be and do for the family. His allegiance and love for his wife contribute an added problem since he has the responsibility to shield her in a society where she is regarded as a stranger and a useless wife. . . .

In his third novel [*Oil Man of Obange*] Munonye examines the tragedy of a man who sacrifices everything, including his own life for the welfare of his children. The tragedy is intense because it is much more personal and domestic. The very little happiness in the hero's life comes from seeing his children healthy, happy, and successful at school. At his death a friend comments: "His life was a whole planting season. It is a pity he died so early, before the fruits of his labor began to appear." During his life, Jeri derives most of his courage from his daughter and receives most of his jeers from his only sister. Although Jeri is married, his wife is done away with early to make way for his only daughter Celia, whose development from a little child to a responsible young lady is easily traceable. This technique is a departure from the theme of *Obi*, which treats in depth the marital problems of a childless couple. Marcellina features simply as the typical quiet, hard-working, and understanding Christian wife of a God-fearing man. She encourages Jeri at his work, worries over his safety, and rejoices at his successes. These, in addition to serving as the focal point of a well-organized and happy family, are her functions. From Onugo we also hear that she is the only one whose advice her husband takes. As a good mother, she settles the little bickerings among her children and serves as a worthy representative of a husband whose unusual job of an oil man compels him to spend most of his time outside the home. But when Marcellina dies of a tetanus infection, her duties in the family are shifted to her only daughter, Celia. . . .

Although Munonye's novels contain a recognizable number of female characters, he exhibits the same unwillingness or inability of most West African writers to enter the minds of their female characters—the inability to create characters with conviction or surprises, not so easily predictable, and always shielded from the realities of a changing society. Hardly do these women characters show any awareness of their societies in the sense of projecting their talents or abilities beyond the borders of their homes or the market towards the betterment of the society as a whole. From the emotional point of view, they are also splendidly and consistently mediocre, always reacting with superhuman endurance to their problems. Anna is a good example of such a flat character. Only once does she break down weeping under the pressure of such a central and grievous problem heightened by a host of unsympathetic in-laws.

Marcellina is equally flat and weak in portrayal. Blessed by a happy Christian home, a devoted husband, and healthy children, she makes her brief sojourn in the book, dies, and is mourned by almost everyone in the village. Even in the case of Celia, the author fails to develop her in any recognizable psychological way. Her little growth is more from accident than design and even her own form of adolescent rebellion does not last longer than a week. She soon falls back into being the prim and proper young girl she has always been.

[Virginia] U. Ola. *Okike*. 21 (July 1982), pp. 78, 81–82, 85–86

Undoubtedly one of the most prolific novelists in Nigeria, with six full-length novels to his credit, Munonye is in danger of remaining in critical limbo for far too long. For a writer of his training and ambition to be totally ignored by the critics is disheartening. . . .

Oil Man of Obange is in a class by itself among Munonye's works; it is the one novel that deserves a second reading. Here, most of the flaws that encumber his other books are surprisingly absent. It has the high seriousness that is lacking in his other novels. The story it tells is timeless. There is skillful composition, a miniature canvas painted with intensity of feeling. In *The Only Son*, Munonye was playing the proverbial sedulous ape to [Chinua] Achebe's *Things Fall Apart*. *The Only Son* was a first novel with the usual flaws—formlessness, authorial intrusions into purely narrative passages, boring digressions that lead nowhere other than the privileged glimpses they give of the Igbo cultural milieu, and a lack of thematic depth. His second novel, *Obi*, was scarcely an improvement. His initial faults persisted, while new ones disturbingly intruded—no innuendo, no mystery, no foreshadowing, nothing left to puzzle the mind and tantalize the imagination—in other words a poor concept of plot. The conclusion one is forced to draw after reading *Obi* is that even though Munonye succeeds quite often in evoking almost the same situational scenes as Achebe, he falls far short of the latter in his handling of plot, in creating characters with the complexity and dignified stature of Ezeulu, and in his narrative technique. *A Wreath for the Maidens* reads almost exactly like [Cyprian] Ekwensi's *Survive the*

Peace. Both are topical novels about the Nigerian Civil War—shallow, reportorial, and doomed to die a natural death once the issues that keep them current fade into the limbo of memory. *A Dancer of Fortune* borders on farce, unrelieved by its great narrative skill or the profundity of its thematic concerns; while the latest novel, *Bridge to a Wedding*, which continues the odyssey of Joe and Anna in *Obi*, contains no exciting new developments worth noting.

But *Oil Man of Obange*, Munonye's third novel, has the makings of a classic, if we understand a classic as a work of art that is among the best of its kind. A classic, one must also add, starts with what is traditional in its genre but goes further, since ultimately it advances the whole tradition, dealing with eternal truths presented in such a way that it pleases generation after generation. *Oil Man of Obange* is such a work. . . .

[One] must observe that in *Oil Man of Obange*, Munonye has written a novel that might survive him. The canvas is small and compact, the style is lucid, even engaging; the action is emotionally charged and often gnaws at our hearts: the plot reveals proper foreshadowing and motivation. These are qualities which have eluded Munonye in most of his other novels. *Oil Man of Obange* marks a turning point for the better, in Munonye's novelistic technique.

Charles E. Nnolim. In Eldred Durosimi Jones, ed. African Literature
Today. 12 (1982), pp. 163–65, 173

There seems to be a consistent attempt by John Munonye to view and treat the heroes of his novels as individuals who break out beyond the framework and limitations of their community. These individuals feel no longer constrained by the conventions of their milieu. They are invariably individuals with problems, but who seem to be up against society in their attempts to find solutions to these problems. The various methods and ways of solving these problems constitute the distinguishing marks of these heroes. Whether we deal with Nnanna in *The Only Son*, who has to attend school against the wishes of his relatives and thus becomes isolated from his immediate community; or with Joe in *Obi*, who finds himself in conflict with the traditional group in his village on the issue of his marriage; or with Jeri in *Oil Man of Obange*, who leaves the traditional economics to embrace the Western one and becomes an oilman suffering alienation and isolation by so doing; or even with Ayasco in *A Dancer of Fortune*, who is forced by the circumstances of his trade to resort to intrigue, blackmail, and exploitation in order to survive and look after his family, we are all the time dealing with different manifestations of the individual trying to be himself, and to survive in an often hostile society determined to thwart the individual's efforts at self-realization.

Munonye's heroes generally are presented in isolation, facing their fate as they make their choices, often guided by certain moral sense which ultimately brings them to disaster. They and their problems present us with a series of faltering uneasy attempts to match the desires of the individual with the desires of the community. Most often, this delicate balance act falls apart as the tension flares up leading to the destruction of the isolated individual. . . .

Munonye is one of the African novelists concerned primarily with the traumas in the African society caused by Western cultures, and with their influence
on the individual's psyche. He depicts the frustrations, the disappointments, the
anger, the cynicism over unfulfilled hopes, and the inability of the individual
working alone to reverse these situations. The central question which the three
novels . . . attempt to answer is, what is the best attitude to take towards Western
cultures? The dialectic of these novels is that salvation and survival may well lie
in an integration of the old and the new. . . . Accordingly, the novels are not
tracts of antitraditional pose or pro-Western stance. They are the author's blueprint for the African's survival in the face of conflicting values. He is convinced
that the African situation demands and deserves serious and delicate consideration. To survive, the African cannot afford to close his eyes to the new ways, or
to refuse to draw inspiration from the solidarity of the past based on communalism. Mere individualism exercised outside the communal interest is bound to
falter because it is antithetical to the African way of life. Stated differently, the
question Munonye raises is not whether the principles of the new religion and
Western education are valid for Africa, but of finding out whether the Africans
are capable of overcoming the enormous obstacles of a changing universe.

Julius N. Ogu. *IFR*. 11, 2 (Summer 1984), pp. 90, 92–93

Bridge to a Wedding may lay no claim to being—artistically speaking—
Munonye's profoundest [work], but as a forthright document of his viewpoint on
the cultural/ideological implications of colonization for subject peoples, it is his
most significant. The terminal novel in a trilogy [including *The Only Son* and
Obi], it resolves the various dimensions of crisis, conflict, and alienation generated and compounded in the anteceding novels by the defection of a native son
to the alien institutions introduced by colonialism. Of course, in a panoramic
sense, it detracts from the completeness and autonomy of each of these novels,
forcing them to become the exposition and complication of a strange and torturous drama of which it is, itself, the denouement. More important for our purposes here, *Bridge to a Wedding* reiterates far more forcefully the idea (first
broached in *The Only Son* and amplified in *Obi* and even in *Oil Man of Obange*)
of apostasy as the key to the treasures of a brave new world of opportunity and
redefined social eminence, of the material and psychological accretions of colonialism as unfailing indications of commitment to progress. The fact that this is
Munonye's latest (and possibly last) novel, and that he felt compelled in it to
return to the theme of conflict of cultures, after moving in an Achebean trajectory from the ethnographical novel to satire, would seem to suggest that it might
be Munonye's defining position novel on the contact of Europe with Africa. . . .

The bridge, when built in *Bridge to a Wedding*, is more like one needed by
an offensive army to ensure the rapid success of a campaign than one necessary to
facilitate a peaceful interpenetration of the sensibilities of the village and the city,
the past and the present, the young and the old. The march over it toward "civilization" is attended by no ambivalence, no self-doubt, no complications, indeed no
contemplation of the ideological meaning of colonialism for subject cultures. This

is, perhaps, part of what [Charles] Nnolim means when he observes that in John Munonye's novels, there is "no casting around of a great soul athwart the mighty purposes of existence in a world full of insoluble tensions where the problem of 'how to be' becomes a burning question." Neither in this novel nor in *The Only Son, Obi,* and *Oil Man of Obange* does Munonye grapple with much apprehension regarding the "bounty" that is the advent of colonialism. In these novels Africa's subjugation by Europe seems simply to mark the dawn of a blessed new morning of glorious opportunity and civilization, rousing us with the bright promise of liberation from the inadequacies and injustices of ourselves and our past.

Azubike F. Iloeje. *RAL.* 16, 4 (Winter 1985), pp. 526–27, 538–39

Munonye has an excellent ear for human dialogue. He is able to capture the various verbal nuances which not only identify personalities, but also announce relationships existing between persons, whether cordial or hostile, distant or intimate. The characters establish their humanity through this ever-present infectious sense of humor, the exchange of repartee or abuse, and the use of proverbs fashioned out of their intimacy with forest and earth. This aspect is also underscored by his language, woven with a deceptive simplicity, with hardly any sustained "poetic" flights or complex metaphorical structures. Thus, language itself becomes a mirror of the social organization present in the world of the author's fiction, a reflection of tribal ethos and of the stream of traditional life in its uncomplicated flow.

[*Oil Man of Obange*], to my mind, is his most powerful novel. . . . Jeri, the hero, is the first truly modern hero in African literature: the picture of the simple, diligent common man struggling courageously to adapt himself without dishonor to the exigencies of the modern world, refusing to yield to poverty, traditional narrowmindedness, or the corrupting ethos of the new capitalist world. For a man alone, the problems Jeri faces are simply overwhelming: there is his polluted past composed of crises, feuds, and a costly vendetta; there is his poor, infertile land and the unpredictable antics of seasons: then comes the sudden death of his wife, leaving him alone with the burden of the children; then his accident and long convalescence and, finally, his robbery by thieves at a moment when, at the cost of heavy debts, he starts the process of retrieving himself again. Through all these misfortunes, until the end, he bears his cross with courage, resilience, and exemplary fortitude, making no long speeches or grand gestures, only loving his children, bearing his pain in silence; his old bicycle becomes the symbol of a larger plight, that of the oppressed but indomitable wretched of the earth, a symbol of their pathos and of their heroic destiny.

Femi Osofisan. *PA.* 139 (1986), pp. 175–76

To date, six novels by Munonye have been published. . . . In most, if not all, of these works, the average man locked in a grim, existential combat with the invariably hostile forces of society is a recurring motif. Indeed if [Chinua] Achebe can be described as the novelist of epic personages, the uncanny explorer of extraordinary souls, Munonye must be seen as the novelist of the common man par excellence. And it is precisely this immersion in the predicament of the ordinary folk and a faithful and sensitive rendering of their whims and follies which give Munonye's works their compelling realism and often faintly "naturalistic" quality. For example, few are the like of Okonkwo, the hero of Achebe's *Things Fall Apart*, and Ezeulu, the protagonist of his *Arrow of God*, but the Igbo society, and in fact the whole world, is teeming with only sons like Nnanna, sullen exiles like Kafe, and tragic speculators like Jeri. As a matter of fact, Ayasko, the protagonist of *A Dancer of Fortune*, derives his name from the traditional appellation given to that breed of itinerant dancers. . . .

Munonye's works teem with such characters: outcasts, lonely exiles, eccentric martyrs; and in his narratives, threatened abortion, secondary infertility, and outright barrenness cast a forlorn shadow. These in themselves serve as a powerfully symbolic projection of the human condition and they give Munonye's vision its bleak and pessimistic hue. What cannot be denied, however, is the fact that despite his often tragic view of the human condition, Munonye's sympathy is always with the underdog and the downtrodden.

It is only in *A Dancer of Fortune* that this sympathy for the oppressed is transformed from a passive and acquiescing element to an active and rebellious one. Here, the embattled individual rises to the occasion to beat the society at its own game of treachery and fraud. In this haunting work, fraught with social tension and unease, Ayasko, the hero, bides his time until he is strong and powerful enough to turn the tables against his tormentors. Munonye has very harsh words for those who may feel uneasy at this rather inelegant resolution of social conflict.

'Bayo Williams. *Obsidian II*. 2, 1 (Spring 1987), pp. 76–77

Perhaps, because of Munonye's acknowledged indebtedness to [Chinua] Achebe, and because major parts of his novels deal with plot and conflict situations reminiscent of Achebe's novels, critics of Munonye have tended to miss the point that Munonye's fiction offers a social vision almost antithetical to Achebe's. As I have stated elsewhere: there is "a distinctly un-Achebean optimism regarding colonialism and its implications that seems to inform Munonye's novels" of culture conflict. . . . I believe that there is a consistent pattern in Munonye's ethnographical novels, of either actual and ultimate (*The Only Son, Obi, Bridge to a Wedding*) or transcendental (*Oil Man of Obange*) vindication of the aberrancy and apostasy of the hero. When Charles Nnolim can say nothing more about the social perspective projected in Munonye's first novel than that in it the writer has been "playing the proverbial sedulous ape to Achebe's *Things Fall Apart*," I am convinced that it has escaped Nnolim's attention that, in many ways, *The Only Son* rewrites *Things Fall Apart*; its conclusions differ from, and at the same time, complement those of Achebe's first novel. In his ethnographical novels, Achebe primarily portrays the resistance of older Igbos to colonially induced change; Munonye, on the other hand, chronicles the receptivity of younger Igbos to change. Whereas the psychology of the stubborn resister is at the center of Achebe's novels, the psychology of the resolute defector is both fundamental and ascendant in Munonye's. . . .

The problem quite early in *The Only Son* is how to bring up Nnanna Okafo in a manner required and demanded by the existing precolonial Igbo society, a patrilineal, male-dominated, agrarian society organized on dependent femininity. The problem also concerns proffering him an effective program of education necessary for his proper integration within the social structure. The untimely death of his father has jeopardized the prospects of Nnanna's growing up in the prescribed manner. The novel opens in the 1920s, about thirteen years after the death of Okafo; both his widow and her only son are left, according to custom, in the custody of Amanze, Okafo's younger brother. The expected program of surrogacy, however, collapses as distrust, conflict, and suspicion descend on the extended family. Not only, Chiaku feels, has Amanze repudiated his responsibilities, he has also expropriated his late brother's estate, the rightful inheritance of Nnanna. . . . Here we have a kinship crisis centering on Chiaku's perceived sense of wrong and inequity in the allocation of patrimonial inheritance. We might suspect, at this early point, that a morality drama is in the offing, with good confronting evil, right deployed against avarice and theft. This predictable path towards the resolution of the conflict never develops in the novel; the factor of colonialism effectively nullifies . . . any hope of recovering the lost birthright in its precolonial form.

Azubike [F.] Iloeje. *WLWE*. 29, 1 (Spring 1989), pp. 8–9

MWANGI, MEJA (1948–   )

KENYA

Kill Me Quick was published in 1973 and was quickly given the President Kenyatta Award for Literature. Since then, Meja Mwangi has published two more novels and several short stories. His fourth novel is about to be published.

Like Ngugi wa Thiong'o, East Africa's first novelist, Meja Mwangi is a Kikuyu; as with Ngugi, Mwangi's second novel was published first; and like Ngugi, Mwangi has published two novels about the Mau Mau, *Taste of Death* and *Carcase for Hounds*. Thus comparison between Mwangi and Ngugi is inescapable. However, Mwangi is very different from Ngugi. . . .

Although Ngugi has set the pace for other East African writers, Mwangi confesses he finds Ngugi very difficult to read, if not unreadable. Questioned further, Mwangi says that he feels Ngugi is best able to write about the life and problems of people in or from the village, while he likes to write about the urban dispossessed, of which he himself is one. Ngugi's style reflects his concerns, just as Mwangi's style is swift-moving because it reflects the urgency of life in the city. . . .

Meja Mwangi makes no claims to being a political writer, or to understanding why things in newly-independent Africa have gone wrong, let alone providing solutions. In this respect, too, he appears to differ from Ngugi, who understands the forces at work, analyzes them, and suggests solutions. Mwangi makes statements that sound cynical. He says that there could not be another

Mau Mau movement, since so many of the people involved in the first one see that they gained nothing while others benefited. The end of *Carcase for Hounds* implies that the kind of brotherhood and justice General Haraka fought for can only be achieved in the life beyond. The death of the Mau Mau leader in *Taste of Death* leads finally to confusion, while the death of Kihika in Ngugi's *Grain of Wheat* does not diminish the continuing validity of his example and message for the people. However, we cannot leave the matter there and say that Ngugi believes in the future while Mwangi does not. The reverse side of Ngugi's "messianism" is, as he says at the beginning of *Secret Lives*, that he experiences moments of despair. It is hard to imagine Mwangi making such a statement.

Peter Nazareth. Afriscope. 6 (April 1976), pp. 25, 27

Meja Mwangi is certainly one of the most exciting . . . East African writers. He is already the author of two successful novels, *Kill Me Quick* and *Carcase for Hounds*, in which he amply demonstrated his characteristic qualities—a touching compassion for the social or political underdog, a quietness of tone which emphasizes rather than obscures the very serious problems being analyzed, and a remarkably controlled though unpretentious prose style.

Mwangi's latest novel, *Going Down River Road*, displays all these characteristics. Set in Nairobi's seething brothel, pub, and cheap nightclub area, the novel presents with commendable power and detailed demonstration the fortunes of the hero, Ben, against the background of all those social forces which we have now come to associate with the growth of modern African cities. Mwangi hits on the clever device of using the framework of the construction of the luxurious twenty-four-story Development Building as a means of presenting the experiences of the ordinary workers, whose lifestyles are in such stark contrast with all that the Development Building represents, but who must look forward to the completion of the building with apprehension since it would mean the loss of their jobs. Mwangi's exploration of urban problems is if anything, more detailed, more sensitive, and ultimately more convincing than anything that [Cyprian] Ekwensi has ever written. The squalor, degradation, and misery are tellingly presented through case histories such as that of Wini, Ben's girlfriend, who had a child at the age of fourteen and was forced into prostitution to keep herself and the fatherless child, but still possessed enough moral courage to see her through a secretarial course. She eventually gets a decent job, but is forced to abandon her baby and elope with her boss as a way out of the urban impasse. There is the sixteen-year-old prostitute who fornicates with Ben in the same room in which her friend is simultaneously having fun with another man, while her month-old baby screams in the corner. Such scenes give convincing social motivations of conduct while generating tremendous sympathy for the unfortunates who are trapped in the situation. Far from being titillating, the sexual details stamp unforgettably on the reader's mind the hopelessness of the masses in the struggle to survive. The prostitutes are dogged by a basic insecurity and the fear of hunger; the fun-loving teenage girls who are hired out by their boyfriends are so vulnerable to the sadistic whims of drunkards, thugs, and drug-addicts. Indeed, violence is never far

from the surface. It degenerates quite often into motiveless hatred and even murder. The inhabitants of the River Road area occasionally demonstrate a certain
comradeship in adversity and the reader is made to experience the warmth of
populist amusement spots such as Eden or the Karara center, but he still senses
the absence of real friendship which is ultimately attributable to the dehumanizing effect of the impersonal city where everyone is involved in the scramble to
survive. Mwangi does not flinch from presenting the grim realities of the housing
racket, the corruption of the politicians, the high cost of living and its consequences, and organized as well as petty crime.

Mwangi's preoccupation with the social realities of the city does not prevent him from creating some interesting characters and exploring some significant relationships. The hero, Ben, is the most fascinating of them all. A central
consciousness through whose eyes almost all the events and the other characters
are viewed, he survives in the mind of the reader as a kind of antihero whose
huge bulk and physical strength go oddly with his lack of resolution and real
guts. There is even a slight hint of some kind of emasculation in this young man
who, in spite of his sexual prowess, seems unable to father his own child or
have a lasting relationship with a woman and at the end adopts a child who
everyone knows to have been fathered by another man.

Eustace Palmer. In Eldred Durosimi Jones, ed.
African Literature Today. 9 (1978), pp. 105–6

[During the Mau Mau conflict] the whites . . . insisted that the Mau Mau were
nothing more than a group of destructive terrorist elements; the blacks argued
back with naked emotion that they were freedom fighters. But recently, whether
it be because the "freedom fighter" image has taken firm hold among the
Kenyan people, or because a new generation which did not experience the war
has grown to adulthood, the Kenyan "Mau Mau complex" seems to have disappeared. This can be clearly seen, for example, by looking at the cold objec-
tivism of Meja Mwangi's creative technique as he treats the Mau Mau
liberation struggle in his novel *Carcase for Hounds.* Mwangi's work deals from
the inside with the indomitable fighting spirit of the Mau Mau soldiers, who,
although pushed into the Aberdares Range by government troops, maintain
rigid discipline and finally, ablaze with love for their comrades and their sense
of mission, give their lives in a battle. The pursued and the pursuers (puppets of
the whites) are former comrades who had once shared food and friendship; as
we read we are reminded of Che Guevara, and the conflict of Vietnam flickers
through our minds. The tragedy of such conflict between brothers is pathetically
distressing. But in Mwangi's novel there is no longer a trace of the meanness
and sense of humiliation seen in Ngugi [wa Thiong'o]'s *Grain of Wheat.* What
one finds here is simply a refreshing, mechanical light dryness which amounts
to one kind of sublimation. In this sense the title of the book (from
Shakespeare's *Julius Caesar*) can also be read as biting satire aimed at the
insensibility and unashamed egotism of humans who fabricate a grand and glorious cause. . . .

Mwangi's approach in his works, of trying to describe the mechanism of the internal contradictions of contemporary Kenyan society in the process of modernization, clearly sets him apart from the older generation of writers in two ways. The first is that while Ngugi's main interest is in the fate of individual human beings, Mwangi has pinpointed his interest on social mechanisms. Secondly—and this is a phenomenon common to West and South Africa as well—such writers as Ngugi and [Chinua] Achebe turned their attention to the outside by focusing on the struggle against Western white culture at the time of independence. Now, in the 1970s, it is on interior questions that they are fixing their glance. . . . This tendency to portray the internal contradictions peculiar to African society is also proof positive that the inner-directed younger generation has grown up soundly. While talking with Mwangi, I got the feeling from the grandness of his conceptions, the broad range of his interests, and his flexibility, that he is a man of great latent talent. In order to understand his promise more fully, one should examine his novel *Kill Me Quick*. . . .

In the prizewinning story two young men, Meja and Maina, manage to graduate from middle school through the sacrifices of their families. Shouldering the expectations of their relatives, they dream of wreathing their homes in glory, and with hearts full of hope for success, they set out for Nairobi in search of good jobs. But with the high unemployment rate in Kenya it proves to be impossible to find work, and they are forced into living as drifting back-alley beggars. Finally they find employment on a white man's plantation with half-pay—that is, one man's wages for the two of them. Then one day suspected of thievery, they are given the sack. After finding their way once again to the back streets of Nairobi, they commit theft at a supermarket and in the resulting chase get separated. Maina then joins a gang which, with the slums on the outskirts of the city as its headquarters, plagues the busy sectors of Nairobi with pickpocketing and thievery. He thus commits one crime after another on the main streets, and in the meantime he falls in love with a beautiful but impoverished girl of the slums; this love, however, comes to nothing. Finally he is caught by the police and thrown into a solitary confinement cell. It is in prison that he again meets Meja. Maina is accused of murder, but Meja, knowing him, tries desperately to convince the other inmates of Maina's innocence. In the mutual trust and friendship of comrades, even in such wretched circumstances, there is evidence of human warmth.

What Mwangi wanted to write of in this novel was the social mechanism which twists the lives of innocent young men who want to live honestly, which drives them into ill-doing, and which can produce only tares and no good wheat. Here the internal contradictions of Kenyan modernization are exposed, and at the same time certain characteristics peculiar to East Africa are revealed. . . . What kind of a society can it be that forces a life without hope on a good people, that drives them into crime? We see here the figure of Africa laboring over modernization.

Satoru Tsuchiya. *WLT*. 52, 3 (Summer 1978), pp. 570–71

Meja Mwangi is certainly one of the most exciting of the new East African writers who have made social comment and analysis the dominant trend in the contemporary African novel. *Going Down River Road* must surely rank as his most important work so far, but in the two earlier novels—*Kill Me Quick* and *Carcase for Hounds*—he had already shown his characteristic qualities: a touching compassion for the social or political underdog, a quietness of tone which emphasizes rather than obscures the very serious social problems being analyzed, and a remarkably controlled though unpretentious prose style.

Kill Me Quick presents with great pathos and commendable realism the fortunes of two adolescents in modern urban Kenya whose hopes and aspirations, buttressed by a successful secondary education, are eventually dashed by the nature of the Kenyan political, social, and economic system. *Kill Me Quick* and *Going Down River Road* give a very detailed and convincing analysis of the causes of juvenile delinquency, prostitution, and big-time as well as petty crime. In doing so, Mwangi has staked his claim to a territory hitherto dominated by [Cyprian] Ekwensi, and he carries out his analysis with greater depth of presentation, strength of characterization, psychological understanding, and awareness of the implications of the issues he raises. . . .

Carcase for Hounds is about the activities of the Mau Mau during their struggle for the liberation of Kenya. Inevitably the novel has to concentrate on the presentation of life in the jungle. And Mwangi proves himself as much at home in the uncanny mysteriousness of the jungle as in the hustle and bustle of the city. Indeed, the powerful evocation of setting must surely rank among this novel's claims to attention. The jungle is unmistakably there—its power, its darkness, its mystery, its terror, its discomfort, and its luxuriance; and this evocation of setting is done not just to provide local color, but meaningfully to reflect the characters' moods and circumstances. . . .

These two novels are a fitting prelude to the Mwangi who is revealed in *Going Down River Road* . . . [which] explores the harsh realities of city life to a much greater depth than *Kill Me Quick*, and with a greater realism than Ekwensi's *Jagua Nana*. It is a novel which is also preoccupied with human relationships; indeed it presents with commendable power and detailed demonstration the fortunes of the hero, Ben, against the background of all those social evils which we have now come to associate with the growth of modern African cities. Mwangi does not flinch from details which would most tellingly present the squalor, degradation, and misery that characterize the lives of most of his characters.

Eustace Palmer. *The Growth of the African Novel*
(London: Heinemann, 1979), pp. 307–8, 311–12, 314

Meja Mwangi exorcized his particular Mau Mau ghost with the two novels *Carcase for Hounds* and *Taste of Death*. The latter traces the history of Kariuki, a soldier who fought in World War II, and who joined the freedom fighters because of the bullying tactics of the homeguard in his village. He takes part in the daring rescue from prison of the leader, several ambushes, is captured by the British, tortured, sentenced to death, then escapes to remain in the forest with two companions until independence. His story is interlaced with details of British attempts to destroy the freedom fighters by psychological and military means. Inspector Cowdrey plays a leading role in the former activities. He is the chief interrogator of Mau Mau suspects and is fanatical in his search for the leader whose capture he sees as crucial in defeating the Mau Mau. The demented Cowdrey leaves Kenya at independence, his wife having been brutally murdered, and his career and dreams shattered. *Carcase for Hounds* is more confined in both time and space covered. It concentrates on a few days in the lives of General Haraka and his gang, and D. C. Kingsley and his men who are out to capture them. Caught between the two are the frightened and confused villagers of Pinewood and Acacia Ranch.

In both novels, Meja Mwangi concentrates attention on the freedom fighters, or "forest fighters," as he consistently and with studied neutrality calls them. Unlike previous novels, his work also depicts in some detail the whites and civilians, giving a more complete picture of the struggle than, say, Ngugi [wa Thiong'o] and [Lennard] Kibera, who concentrate more on the civilians, or [Godwin] Wachira, who is concerned almost exclusively with the leading freedom fighter. Part of Meja Mwangi's uniqueness lies in this wholeness of vision, a characteristic that can be seen developing from the earlier *Taste of Death* to *Carcase for Hounds*. The former covers a long period of time—from the early 1950s to independence in 1963—and has a large cast of characters, but there is little depth of characterization or subtlety of plot. In part, this can be explained by the audience. The book is a secondary-school reader and, naturally, keeping the readers excited and involved overrides other artistic considerations. Characters tend to fall into stereotyped modes of behavior. Kariuki is the stock freedom-fighter hero. He leads daring rescues, is a crack shot, and does not break down despite terrible torture. Lieutenant Davis is the disciplined army officer who maintains a stiff upper lip throughout and gets through a Mau Mau ambush alive because of his reliance on strict military discipline. Cowdrey is the inherently racist white, caught up in the emergency in an attempt to preserve his privileged lifestyle.

While this tendency to stereotype may be expected of a young writer, there is some evidence of the more mature style that is to burgeon in *Carcase for Hounds*. There are little touches that add some life to the characterization. Lieutenant Davis's driver is an interesting example. British soldiers, if they are portrayed at all in fiction of this period, are either the leading officers masterminding operations and interrogations, or young privates raping and murdering villagers. Meja Mwangi adds some individuality and credibility to his portrayals. In contrast to the calm Lieutenant Davis, the anonymous driver is scared stiff at the nearness of death, intent only on escape and contemptuous of his superior's orders: "To hell with your orders. I am not going to sit here and be blown to hell because of your lunatic orders." Similar details of personality and social relationships appear, sparingly, in other portraits.

Elizabeth Knight. In Eldred Durosimi Jones, ed.
African Literature Today. 13 (1983), pp. 147–48

It is easy to see how the novels of Meja Mwangi, as they appeared through the years, were related in their tone and subject matter to the literary production of his country. The first two novels, in order of writing—*Taste of Death*, appearing in 1975, and *Kill Me Quick*—are in the same vein of angry realism and are both documents and pamphlets. *Kill Me Quick* follows two uprooted adolescents, school-leavers, barely surviving in the slum jungle of Nairobi. . . . *Taste of Death* is a Mau Mau novel which . . . shows both sides of the conflict as doomed to suffer and lose. Taking up the same subject, *Carcase for Hounds* moves further from fictionalized history; the narrative concentrates on the character of a rebel general, truly tragic in his mad pride, doomed to fail in his growing isolation in front of greater technological power. Although it owes a debt to the legend and the historical reports on people like [Dedan] Kimathi and Mathenge, this chief dying in his cave, insane and stoical, has the grandeur of romantic figures of fiction. *The Trial of Dedan Kimathi* by Ngugi [wa Thiong'o] and Micere Mugo will portray the dead general with a special effort to blend history and legend, facts and a political message for the present. Mwangi creates a lonely figure, a hero for our time with no message but chilly despair in an absurd world.

Going Down River Road, Mwangi's second urban novel, is also a great move forward from *Kill Me Quick*. There is less of the journalist's eye for striking facts, less lingering on the sensational and the exceptional. The thieving gangs of Mathare Valley have been replaced by a group of laborers who are building the new Nairobi. The unrelieved gloom of the first book is far less effective than the humorous tone in which the hero's sad journey through the city is related in the [second] book. The allegory in the building of the hotel (which stands for the New Kenya), the elements of burlesque and the sad scenes at the brothel, the nightmare visits to the bars—all merge into a strongly constructed whole, drawing in one's imagination the map of a city truer and more vivid than any single African city, or any big city, with all its lonely aimless lives.

This freedom to re-create, to transcend documentary appeal, this very personal narrative voice, with as good an ear for sharp dialogue, for handling of all minor characters, a feeling of pity which is never condescending, mark Mwangi as a writer of great stature with the promise of much good work to come.

Jacqueline Bardolph. In G. D. Killam, ed. The Writing of East and
Central Africa (London: Heinemann, 1984), p. 46

Mwangi's *The Bushtrackers* . . . is the "novelization" of a screenplay by one Gary Strieker. Though the story is set in Kenya it involves the Mafia, it has a black American villain and a white co-hero, and it presents a string of situations familiar from American thrillers in the less familiar setting of Tsavo Game Park. It is not mere hackwork. The story, however shallow, is told in a fast, extremely exciting way, and Mwangi excels himself in the evocation of the Kenyan bush. . . .

Mwangi's narratives are not perfect. Leaving aside the technical flaws in *Taste of Death* and *Kill Me Quick* on the grounds that such a young writer was bound to make mistakes . . . one must still acknowledge lapses in his more masterful later books. They are generally in what filmmakers call "continuity." *Carcase for Hounds*, on the whole a complete tour de force of gripping narrative, begins with two Mau Mau moving through the forest. They come to a river. The big one, General Haraka, tells his lieutenant, Kimamo, to cross first. The smaller refuses—"'No. You go first. I will cover you.'" The big one shrugs and goes first. Yet sixteen pages later we have a paragraph beginning "Haraka sighed. Kimamo, so reliable . . ."—and a couple of pages further on, "Kimamo was the man. Hard, brave . . ." How do we reconcile these thoughts with the apparent cowardice on Kimamo's part which we saw earlier? In *Going Down River Road*, Mwangi's fourth novel, there's a still more abrupt jump. Ben Wachira's girl has just left him to run off with her white employer. Ben gets violently drunk in the Karara Center, hits a prostitute with a beer bottle, then passes out on the floor. "Typical of Karara Center, no one gives a thought to the lonely drunk." The next chapter opens immediately, and at its beginning we see Ben entering the Karara Center again. "A tired drunken smile breaks over his rough bearded face. Good old Karara Center, stuffy as hell, warm as home. Here at least are people. People he understands, people who are people, human beings." . . .

[If] others, like myself, feel jolted on first, even on second reading of both those passages, then Mwangi's irony is not working properly. . . . But the point I want to make now . . . is that one feels such jolts with special severity because one is traveling so fast. Like a car splendidly driven at top speed, Mwangi's narratives make the road seem so easy that the odd pothole (over or round which a slower vehicle could be gently maneuvred) strikes the passengers, though so briefly, with surprise.

Angus Calder. In G. D. Killam, ed. The Writing of East and
Central Africa (London: Heinemann, 1984), pp. 178–80

The reader who is interested in a good, well-told story with a linear sense of time will find a ready-hearted accommodation in [*Striving for the Wind*]. It is an old-fashioned fabulation in the popular vein. It does not displace a good narrative with any of the off-putting cleverness that goes with postmodernist storytelling. As in his earlier novels, *Going Down River Road* and *Kill Me Quick*, Meja Mwangi is a self-conscious folk-performer who laces the wisdom of the village square with barroom banter; it's the narrative style of the city slick and the village wag rubbing shoulders on the page. As such, it has the normal accompaniment of stock characters: the good on one side, the evil on the other, and the fight to a finish drawn out between them. Except that Meja Mwangi does not allow the kind of easy resolution that transports the simple-minded.

Baba Pesa, the "Father of Money" in *Striving for the Wind*, is as much of a stock character as you can find, one of the lucky few who bought the farms abandoned by white farmers in the wake of the Mau Mau struggle. He has "hundreds of acres of land, woodlands, and grazing fields down in the valley, forests up in the hills where only the elephants and buffalos roam . . . cows and cars, goats and tractors and all the money in the world"; what more did he want? He is obviously not satisfied with the lot that he has acquired through further arm-twisting of the poorer neighbors; he wishes to take over all the farms on the next hill and the next and the next. His greed is fastened, almost as we first come across him, upon the land of his immediate, near-destitute neighbor, Baru. His reason is that he cannot bear to see Baru's hovels each time he looks over his fence from his veranda. But Baru will not let himself be intimidated into selling. He is the typical rural dweller, poor, uneducated, and at a moral distance from the moneyed ethic which sees neighbors as tools to be used rather than as fellow human beings to share snuff and wine with. Baru is as stubborn as the ox that drives his plough: he may not have a tractor or a Mercedes Benz car like Baba Pesa; he may be scratching a living, never having enough to pay fees for his son in the village polytechnic, but he is not going to give away his land and slouch landless into the desolation of city life like many with whom Baba Pesa has dealt. He bears abuse and ridicule like all the big and small people of Kambi village upon whom the Father of Money has trampled capriciously. . . .

The story barely manages to avoid being judgmental. Not that the author did not try. The measure of his success however is that he presents the rural poor without romanticizing their lives. Having drawn a line between the good and bad, he makes quite a visible effort to be evenhanded. Yet, it is clear where his hammer falls. This gives *Striving for the Wind* its point, making it one of those novels which manage, whatever their literary quality, to remove indifference to a social malaise. It does not relieve it of a certain wearisome familiarity; for one may well ask when the Baba Pesas of this world will stop getting away with so much? Surely, until there is an answer to the question every novel out of Kenya, no matter how apolitical, would continue to make one wonder about the difference between "permitted" literature and the literature which says the unsayable.

Odia Ofeimun. *WA*. 7–13 September 1992, pp. 1547–48

In *Striving for the Wind* . . . Mwangi tries to return to his roots as they were so powerfully displayed in *Kill Me Quick* and *Going Down River Road*. . . . Mwangi's attention is focused on a world of rural poverty and greed, a world he knows firsthand, in which the future of Kenya is continuously being debated between Baba Pesa (meaning "Father of Money") and his university dropout son Judas (Judas, the betrayer). Mwangi rejects the shifting spaces of his thrillers, focusing instead on a static, weary, and worn-out landscape; he rejects the idiom of the movies, seeking instead to capture the language of rural despair and the tyranny of the nouveau riche; the alienated authorial tone of the thrillers gives way to a profound voice that sustains the pessimism and angst of the rural poor.

So in *Striving for the Wind* readers see Mwangi at his most serious. But this novel is as dull as the land and people it represents, and by the time readers finish it, and as they reflect on the labor and pain Mwangi has put into it, they begin to realize that his real talents are not in this kind of "tractor" fiction, but in the phantasmal world of the thrillers and movies he loves so much. One cannot help but wonder what Mwangi has inherited from the movies tradition. On the one hand, the movies have endowed him with the palpable wealth of Americana—in habits and idiom—that is largely responsible for his artistic fluency and his engagement with his African popular audience, which lives and thrives on such material. On the other hand, however, this appropriation of Americana has impoverished him as a novelist in the areas in which he was strongest—his sense of the African landscape and its people, the language of the urban poor, and the discourse of contemporary politics. Mwangi's real talent is manifested in the novels in which he marries the techniques of the thriller with a profound exposition of the African scene.

Simon Gikandi. In Bernth Lindfors and Reinhard Sander, eds.
Dictionary of Literary Biography. 125 (1993) p. 119

NAYLOR, GLORIA (1950–   )

UNITED STATES

Gloria Naylor's *The Women of Brewster Place* is set in one of those vintage urban-housing developments that black people (who are, in truth, "nutmeg," "ebony," "saffron," "cinnamon-red," or "gold") have inherited from a succession of other ethnic groups. The difference is that while the Irish and Italians used it as a jumping-off place for the suburbs, for most of its "colored daughters," Brewster Place is "the end of the line": "They came because they had no choice and would remain for the same reason." But the end of the line is not the end of life. With their backs literally to the wall—a brick barrier that has turned Brewster Place into a dead end—the women make their stand together, fighting a hostile world with love and humor.

There's Mattie Michael, dark as "rich, double cocoa," who defied her over-protective father to take a man who was pure temptation, almost a force of nature—a Pan. Pregnant and disowned, she made the instinctive matriarchal decision (I mean that word in the mythic, not the sociological, sense) to live without a man and invest all her love back into her child. Left in the lurch by the grown, spoiled son who results, she becomes the anchor for the other women of Brewster Place.

There's Etta Mae Johnson, survivor and good-time woman, who comes home to Mattie when her dream of redemption by marrying a "respectable" preacher is sordidly ended. There's Ciel Turner, whose husband, Eugene, ominously resents her fertility: "With two kids and you on my back, I ain't never gonna have nothin' . . . nothin'!" There's Kiswana (formerly Melanie) Browne, idealistic daughter of middle-class parents, who has moved to Brewster Place to be near "my people." Cora Lee, a welfare mother, likes men only because they provide babies, but she can't cope with children once they are older. She is *almost* lifted out of the inertia of her life by the power of art when Kiswana takes her to see a black production of Shakespeare in the park. And finally, there are Theresa and Lorraine, lovers who embody the ultimate commitment of woman to woman and yet arouse unease or loathing in most of the other women of Brewster Place.

Despite Gloria Naylor's shrewd and lyrical portrayal of many of the realities of black life . . . *The Women of Brewster Place* isn't realistic fiction—it is mythic. Nothing supernatural happens in it, yet its vivid, earthy characters (especially Mattie) seem constantly on the verge of breaking out into magical powers. The book has two climaxes: one of healing and rebirth, one of destruction. In the first, Mattie magnificently wrestles Ciel, dying of grief, back to life. In the second, Lorraine, rejected by the others, is gang raped, a blood sacrifice brutally proving the sisterhood of all women. Naylor bravely risks sentimentality and melodrama to write her compassion and outrage large, and she pulls it off triumphantly.

Annie Gottlieb. *NYTBR*. August 22, 1982, pp. 11, 25

Gloria Naylor's second novel, *Linden Hills*, is a modern version of Dante's *Inferno* in which souls are damned not because they have offended God or have violated a religious system, but because they have offended themselves. In their single-minded pursuit of upward mobility, the inhabitants of Linden Hills, a black, middle-class suburb, have turned away from their past and from their deepest sense of who they are. Naylor feels that the subject of who-we-are and what we are willing to give up of who-we-are to get where-we-want-to-go is a question of the highest seriousness—as serious as a Christian's concern over his salvation. . . .

Naylor's tale is an allegory based on the physical and moral topography of Dante's *Inferno*. It covers four days in the life of a twenty-year-old black poet, Willie Mason, who lives in a poor neighborhood called Putney Wayne that lies above Linden Hills. Working temporarily as a handyman to earn money to buy Christmas presents, Willie passes through Linden Hills and, like Dante, analyzes the moral failures of the lost souls he encounters. By the time Willie escapes from the frozen lake at the bottom of Linden Hills and crosses to the safety of a nearby apple orchard, he has experienced a spiritual awakening. The "new" Willie has decided to give up his aimless drifting and to take charge of his life. He becomes, as his name implies, a decisive builder. He accepts responsibility for his life, he refuses to blame his problems on others or on fate, and he realizes that he can choose a middle way between the poverty of the ghetto and the depravity of Linden Hills. . . .

Linden Hills is an uncomfortable and dangerous book which pricks the conscience. It takes the reader on a perilous pilgrimage and forces him to consider the hidden cost of his choices. It strips him of the ease of innocence. Naylor has risked much by writing such a disturbing tale. Her readers may view her subject too narrowly. If they do, she could lose a black audience that feels unjustly challenged and a white audience that thinks the novel's hard questions are not meant for them. Naylor also risks offending modern sensibilities that regard an allegory about moral accountability too medieval for their tastes. But because Naylor knows who she is, where she has been, and where she wants to go, she dares to tell her tale and dares the reader to reckon with it.

Catherine C. Ward. *CL*. 28, 1 (1987), pp. 67, 69, 80–81

[What] happens if we resist the temptation to subsume into a narrative of sexual binarism the dispersed array of subject positions that *Linden Hills* frames— what happens, that is, if we respect another (nonmonistic) feminist injunction and refuse to impose a hierarchy of political signification? The question arises here because part of what distinguishes black women's fiction in the contemporary scene is a sense of a historical community and its peculiarities, sometimes antic, sometimes grim, but never quite reducible to a masterplot of victim and victimizer. At their best, these texts are porous to history and propose an articulation of power that is more decentered and nuanced than most of us are accustomed to. Attention must be paid: master narratives of sexual oppression, crucial as they are, can so easily render the sociopolitical subtext opaque.

And that is especially important in *Linden Hills*, which depicts the irruption of class politics into the terrain of race politics. . . . For any reading that subsumes the whole issue of class politics into a purely racial (or sexual) binarism will miss the novel's sedimented ambivalence. Linden Hills (in contrast to Putney Wayne, say) is indeed modeled after mainstream "white" affluence and appropriates its symbolics. But even in these resemblance effects it presents the confusing phenomenon of the black bourgeois, a socioeconomic disruption of an overdetermined alliance of color and poverty. To situate the narrative in the social real, we would want to ask whether black poverty remains a viable means of retaining difference in an age of mass culture. And we need also to ask about the politics of difference as such.

Henry Louis Gates, Jr. CL. 29, 4 (1988), pp. 617–18

Gloria Naylor's *The Women of Brewster Place* is a novel composed of seven connecting stories. In beautifully resonant language, Naylor makes strong sexual political statements about the lives of working poor and working-class black women and does not hesitate to explore the often problematic nature of their relationships with black men—lovers, husbands, fathers, sons. Loving and supportive bonds between black women are central to her characters' survival. However, Naylor's portrayal of a lesbian relationship in the sixth story, "The Two," runs counter to the positive framework of women bonding she has previously established. In the context of this novel a lesbian relationship might well embody the culmination of women's capacity to love and be committed to each other. Yet both lesbian characters are ultimately victims. Although Naylor portrays the community's homophobia toward the lovers as unacceptable, the fate that she designs for the two women is the most brutal and negative of any in the book. . . .

Many a lesbian relationship has been threatened or destroyed because of how very differently lovers may view their lesbianism, for example, how out or closeted one or the other is willing to be. Naylor's discussion of difference represents a pressing lesbian concern. . . .

In "The Two," however, Naylor sets up the women's response to their identity as an either/or dichotomy. Lorraine's desire for acceptance, although completely comprehensible, is based upon assimilation and denial, while Naylor depicts Theresa's healthier defiance as an individual stance. In the clearest statement of resistance in the story, Theresa thinks: "If they practiced that way with each other, then they could turn back to back and beat hell out of the world for trying to invade their territory. But she had found no such sparring partner in Lorraine, and the strain of fighting alone was beginning to show on her." . . .

In considering the overall impact of "The Two," I realized that because it is critical of homophobia, it is perhaps an effective story for a heterosexual audience. But because its portrayal of lesbianism is so negative, its message even to heterosexuals is ambiguous. A semisympathetic straight reader's response might well be: "It's a shame something like that had to happen, but I guess that's what you get for being queer." The general public does not want to know that it is possible to be a lesbian of whatever color and not merely survive, but thrive. And neither does a heterosexual publishing industry want to provide them with this information.

The impact of the story upon lesbian readers is quite another matter. I imagine what might happen if a black woman who is grappling with defining her sexuality and who has never had the opportunity to read anything else about lesbians, particularly black ones, were to read "The Two" as a severely cautionary tale. Justifiably, she might go no further in her exploration, forever denying her feelings. She might eventually have sexual relationships with other women, but remain extremely closeted. Or she might commit suicide. As a black lesbian reader, I find Naylor's dire pessimism about our possibilities to be the crux of my problems with "The Two."

Barbara Smith. In Joanne M. Braxton and Andrée Nicola McLaughlin, eds. *Wild Women in the Whirlwind: Afra-American Culture and the Contemporary Literary Renaissance* (New Brunswick, N. J.: Rutgers University Press, 1990), pp. 225–27, 231

The setting of *Linden Hills*, Naylor's second novel, makes it clear that she is creating a geographical fictional world similar to or in the manner of [William] Faulkner's Yoknapatawpha county. Her first novel is set in Brewster Place, her second in Linden Hills. Brewster Place and Linden Hills are geographically in the same area; both are inhabited by blacks, and in both novels, characters refer to each of these places as proximate neighborhoods, though quite different in their orientation. Linden Hills is a posh upper-middle-class settlement, Brewster Place the last stop on the road to the bottom in American society; where you live when you can't live anywhere else. The outside world perceives Linden Hills as a symbol of black achievement, while Brewster Place is seen as a manifestation of failure. Ironically, through her two novels' respective characters and structure, Naylor portrays Brewster Place as a black community (though flawed and vulnerable) held together primarily by women, while Linden Hills is characterized as a group of houses that never becomes a community, a showplace precariously kept in place by the machinations of one wealthy black patriarchal family. . . .

The Women of Brewster Place begins with an introduction about the history of that street, which is followed by a series of stories, each about a particular woman who lives there. The novel concludes with Mattie Michaels's dream-story about a block party in which all the women appear, as well as a coda which announces the death of the street. Created by city officials, it is destroyed by them. Although each of their narratives could be called a short story, the novel consists of the interrelationship of the stories, as a pattern evolves, not only because the characters all live in Brewster Place but also because they are connected to one another. With the exception of the lesbians in "The Two" . . . Naylor emphasizes the distinctiveness of each story by naming it after the specific woman on whom she is focusing, even as she might include that woman in another's story. By using this form, one that heightens the individuality of her characters so that they are not merely seen as faceless "female heads of households," while stressing their interrelationships, Naylor establishes Brewster Place as a community in spite of its history of transients—a

community with its own mores, strengths, and weaknesses. Even when that specific Brewster Place is destroyed, its characteristics remain, for most of its
inhabitants must move to a similar street. Brewster Place, then, stands for both
itself and other places like it. . . .

In *The Women of Brewster Place* and *Linden Hills*, Gloria Naylor's portrayal of her two neighborhoods demonstrates the effects of class distinctions on
the African-American community and how these distinctions are gender oriented. As well, when read together, her two novels present "solutions" idealized
during the last decade by important powerless American groups, solutions which
are characterized by Naylor, finally, as ineffectual routes to empowerment.

By creating a tapestry of nurturing women in her first novel, Naylor
emphasizes how female values derived from mothering—nurturing, communality, concern with human feeling—are central to Brewster Place's survival. . . .
The Women of Brewster Place was preceded by a decade of American feminist
writing that responded to patriarchal society's devaluation of women by revalorizing female principles. In reaction to the Western patriarchal emphasis on
the individual; on the splitting of human beings into mind and body; and on
competition, conquest, and power, these writers saw the necessity of honoring
female values. If women were to become empowered, it was necessary for them
to perceive their own primacy, their centrality to their society, as well as to analyze how dangerous patriarchal values were to a harmonious social order.

Barbara Christian. In Henry Louis Gates, Jr., ed. *Reading Black,*
Reading Feminist (New York: Meridian, 1990) pp. 348–49, 353, 363–64

Naylor's desire to write the experience of black American women was born
from an impatience with the critical establishment's assumptions that black
writers should provide "definitive" reflections of black experience. The emphasis on the definitive, she argues, denies the vast complexity of Afro-American
experience. In a conversation with Toni Morrison, she speaks of her struggle to
realize the dream of writing the lives of black women without falsification and
sentimentality, making visible those whom society keeps invisible. She dedi-
cates the novel [*The Women of Brewster Place*] to those who "gave me the
dream, believed in it . . . nurtured it . . . applauded it." . . .

Although *Brewster Place* is a novel about women and concentrates on
exploring the experiences of women, it does not enlist a dogmatic feminist ideology. There is little of [Alice Walker's] *The Color Purple*'s celebration and
rejoicing in the discovery of self, sexuality, and creativity in the face of male
abuse and repression. Celie [in *The Color Purple*] is encouraged to trade her
razor—she wants to slit Albert's throat—for a needle, the implement of her
autonomy and creativity. If *The Color Purple* mediates a feminist solution to
the problems of the oppressed Celie, Naylor's novel is far more tentative about
celebrating the efficacy of female friendship and supportive connection, but
there are no radical transformations; Naylor does not, as Walker does, draw on
feminist ideology as an agent of transcendence. Naylor calls attention to the
particular problems of black women without suggesting that such problems are

gender issues alone. When she says that she hopes the novel does not make a bitter statement about the men, she is, I think, voicing a concern that the problems she addresses will be oversimplified if they are seen only in terms of male-female relationships. . . .

Naylor's novel does not offer itself as a definitive treatment of black women or community, but it reflects a reality that a great many black women share; it is at the same time an indictment of oppressive social forces and a celebration of courage and persistence. By considering the nature of personal and collective dreams within a context of specific social, political, and economic determinants, Naylor inscribes an ideology that affirms deferral; the capacity to defer and to dream is endorsed as life-availing. Like Martin Luther King, Naylor resists a history that seeks to impose closure on black American dreams, recording also in her deferred ending a reluctance to see "community" as a static or finished work. There are countless slum streets like Brewster; streets will continue to be condemned and to die, but there will be other streets to whose decay the women of Brewster will cling. The image of the ebony phoenix developed in the introduction to the novel is instructive: The women rise, as from the ashes, and continue to live.

Jill L. Matus. BALF. 24, 1 (Spring 1990), pp. 50–51, 62–63

The rape scene in *The Women of Brewster Place* occurs in "The Two," one of the seven short stories that make up the novel. This story explores the relationship between Theresa and Lorraine, two lesbians who move into the rundown complex of apartments that make up "Brewster Place." Lorraine's decision to return home through the shortcut of an alley late one night leads her into an ambush in which the anger of seven teenage boys erupts into violence. . . .

In Naylor's representation of rape, the victim ceases to be an erotic object subjected to the control of the reader's gaze. Instead, that gaze, like Lorraine's is directed outward; it is the violator upon whom the reader focuses, the violator's body that becomes detached and objectified before the reader's eyes as it is reduced to "a pair of suede sneakers," a "face" with "decomposing food in its teeth." As the look of the audience ceases to perpetuate the victimizing stance of the rapists, the subject/object locations of violator and victim are reversed. Although the reader's gaze is directed at a body that is, in Mulvey's terms, "stylized and fragmented by close-ups," the body that is dissected by that gaze is the body of the violator and not his victim.

Laura E. Tanner. AL. 62, 4 (December 1990), pp. 574–75

The legend of Sapphira Wade, "a true conjure woman," forms the opening event of Gloria Naylor's *Mama Day*. In a story fraught with overwhelming psychic and physical intensity, Sapphira's (absent) presence is the single most powerful image in the book. The ramifications of her necromancy in 1823 are still being played out in the contemporary lives of her children's children's children on the island of Willow Springs. They are left to inherit the shimmering spirit of her memory and the unavoidable stature commanded by her mythic presence. . . .

A narrative voice uses "we," "ours," and "us" to retell the story of Willow Springs and involve the reader in its simultaneous recall of historical, spiritual, and physical events. The reader's voice is invited to join its community of tellers: "Think about it: ain't nobody really talking to you. . . . Really listen this time: the only voice is your own. . . . You done heard it the way we know it. . . . You done heard it without a single living soul really saying a word." This voice—ancient, aware, and able to bridge the subjective and objective worlds and to match imagination with magic—connects the story's disparate events and maintains its presence over all of them. In addition, the ancestral and narrative voices of the island's past and present generations as well as the personified island itself—its dust and purple flowers, the gardens and cemeteries, its abandoned houses and (re)membered rituals—gather to tell Naylor's story.

The ancestral voices in this story are primarily the voices of the island's generations. All of them mediate the text, bridging the events of Naylor's contemporary story of the lovers Cocoa and George with the haunting presence of Sapphira Wade, Cocoa's grandmother of five generations past, whose propensity for conjuring leaks into the present-day world. George is destined never to leave the island of Willow Springs, and Mama Day readies him for the paradise for which Cocoa, perhaps because she has been geographically disengaged from her place in the island's history, could not prepare him.

Naylor's novel emphasizes how a collective revision of an ancient community substantively inserts a metaphorical language into the text. This language carries a symbol system more weighty than the individual word. For example, at one point in the story, Miranda tries to remember her ancestor's name. But her failure to do so is a "loss she can't describe." Although she tries to use her psychic gift to discern the print on a damaged slip of paper where Sapphira's name is illegible, she can not read it. In her frustration, she falls asleep murmuring the names of women. It is the murmuring of the spoken text (rather than the effort to read) that enables Miranda finally to meet Sapphira Wade in her dreams. The importance of this oracular event is acknowledged at the point when Miranda is able to sense the being, the presence in this word: "Daughter." It is described as a "word [that] comes to cradle what has gone past weariness," and is the word that Miranda senses as the relational word of the oracular text. It also acknowledges the contradiction and paradox within the textures of this novel. There is enough metaphorical dislocation in *Mama Day* to contain the ambiguous histories of the spirit as well as the body. The text is implicated in this revision because the collection of tellers and listeners who organize its body and who include (in black women writers' texts) the reader as well, loses its alterity—its separation—at this juncture. In the same way that Miranda is cradled by the word that acknowledges her spiritual ancestor, the words of the text are incorporated into the generative spiritual body of Sapphira's linguistic acknowledgment.

Karla F. C. Holloway. *Moorings & Metaphors:*
Figures of Culture and Gender in Black Women's Literature
(New Brunswick, N. J.: Rutgers University Press, 1992), pp. 86, 126–27

Gloria Naylor, in *Bailey's Cafe*, addresses female circumcision in Africa (in this case, Ethiopia) as part of a larger examination of the sexual mutilations inflicted on women in contemporary society. . . . Naylor's characters are based on archetypes—mostly from the Bible—but . . . they are not universalized. The novel takes place in a blues cafe down a dead-end street at the tip of New York City. On this city block are Bailey's cafe, Eve's garden and boardinghouse, and Gabe's pawnshop. The novel's fluid time sequence culminates [on] New Year's Eve, 1949. As in her other novels, Naylor infuses day-to-day living with an alternate, magical reality. . . .

The stories of these characters vividly illustrate the range of bodily and psychic mutilation African-American women have experienced. The focal point of the novel is the introduction of "Mary (Take Two)," a fourteen-year-old, circumcised Ethiopian Jew named Mariam. Her story serves both to expose genital mutilation and to highlight relations between blacks and Jews. Young and slow-witted, Mariam has undergone infibulation and, though no man has touched her, is pregnant. She has magically traveled from Addis Ababa to New York after being expelled from her village for refusing to reveal the identity of her unborn child's father. Gabe, the Jewish pawnshop owner, announces her arrival to the rest of the street. He brings her to Eve to figure out how to help her. Eve learns her story and later repeats it in Bailey's cafe. The story of Mariam's circumcision is so gruesome that Bailey and the other men have to leave. Eve, in telling the tale, metaphorically describes it by cutting open a succulent plum.

Although she has been abused, Mariam, carrying new life, brings life and hope to the dead-end street. Naylor ends *Bailey's Cafe* as she did her first novel, *The Women of Brewster Place*, with a kind of miracle; readers familiar with her most recent novel, *Mama Day*, will find a special surprise.

Bailey's Cafe is Naylor's finest novel to date. Her rendering of life in a New York alley reflects the city's magic, its jazz, its violent stories, its streetlamp sparks of hope. It examines a broad spectrum of black women's lives while dealing with the complexities of a multi-ethnic American society still caught up in restrictive notions of color, gender and culture. It is more literary than polemical, bridging ancient stories and modern problems to create a context for the mutilations women have suffered and a space for curing their (our) souls.

Gay Wilentz. *Women's Review of Books*. 10, 5 (February 1993), pp. 15–16

NDAO, CHEIK ALIOU (1933–   )

SENEGAL

[In *L'Exil d'Albouri*, Cheik Aliou Ndao] takes his inspiration from real characters and an authentic episode in the nineteenth-century history of the Empire of Mali. The author, an English teacher at the William Ponty Normal School, has succeeded in composing an epic drama, free of any contemporary political inferences, somewhat in the [Pierre] Corneille tradition, with realistic elements. The language is elevated, the characters well opposed, the king's moral dilemma clearly and convincingly stated, and the action economically conducted to its inevitable historical climax.

Albouri, differing from the ruthless historical Shaka, and without the proselytizing mysticism of El Hadj Omar, is caught in a conflict between his sense of responsibility to his people and the concept of honor and courage. The situation is rapidly presented of the Djoloff Empire of Mali—which included present-day Senegal—on the dawn of invasion by the Spahi troops, armed by the French general, Faidherbe. Albouri decides on a strategic withdrawal to Ségou, the home of a friendly prince. The basic moral dilemma is then revealed in the confrontation between Albouri and the queen mother. To the challenge that retreat signifies lack of courage, he argues prudence, the superior arms of the enemy, and the necessity to save his people from slavery. . . .

Samba, a griot, in traditional fashion, speaks the epilogue, telling of the king's death from a poisoned arrow, his son's capture by the Mauritanians during the retreat before the Spahis, the final dispersal in the face of the colonial invasion of all the people who had accompanied Albouri into exile. The final words are a feeble afterthought—an attempt to infuse a committed message into a play that is rich with tragic conflicts and elements of fatality. Without them, *L'Exil d'Albouri* has all the essential criteria for good theater: by probing into the hidden motives of the king's actions, by not clearing him of the charges of human error, Ndao has achieved a work of tragic dimensions and psychological authenticity.

In 1973, when Cheik Ndao published *Le Fils de l'Almamy*, his second historical tragedy which he had written about 1967, he took up the promise of Samba's reincarnation, making the griot Maliba speak a short prologue, in which he repeats Samba's final words in the epilogue to *Albouri*: "The Word does not die." But this device adds nothing to the force of his new tragedy, for the message of the destiny of Karamoko, son of the Almamy Samory, and of Samory himself, is not a message of hope, but the conflict of two intransigent characters at the beginning of the twilight of the Samorian Empire.

Le Fils de l'Almamy more than confirms that Ndao is a tragic writer of impressive stature and originality, whose works have universal, moving appeal. This second work is even richer in characterization, more consistent in action, and economical in structure than the earlier play. It has a classic concision, a disturbing complexity of personalities caught in a critical moment of history, which makes them victims of circumstances, of interested ill-wishers, and of the clash of their own inflexible characters, in which one is doomed to destroy that which he loves, and at the same time shatter his own existence. It is the tragedy of the honor of a son pitted against the honor of a father.

The Almamy Samory Souré, the last warrior king of the Sudan to be subjugated by Faidherbe's armies, is painted as proud, uncompromising, intolerant, somber, and suspicious, but at the same time a great and courageous patriot, with his own concept of honor, synonymous with the glorification of his country and his people. Neither his limited experience nor his unlimited arrogance can allow him to conceive of his country's defeat by any but mysterious, supernatural forces. He is, by his very nature, receptive to the plots woven at court for the destruction of his son, Karamoko.

The play, as the title suggests, is the tragedy of Karamoko, a man born before his time, the only one to understand that Africa had not the means to confront the powerful war machine of Europe and to believe sincerely in the possibility of peace with Europe, when the tradition was one of uncompromising belligerency. He is the victim of his own vision as well as of the plots and machinations that his unconciliatory nature inspires at the court. It is also the tragedy of Sendi, his devoted wife who goes mad with grief at his terrible fate. Samory, persuaded that his son is a traitor, has his hut walled up for him to die Antigone's death. But it is first and foremost the tragedy of Samory himself, shown here not as the legendary conqueror, nor as the defeated emperor, but like his son, the victim of his own times and his own intractable, proud, and suspicious character. After carrying out the cruel judgment on his son, on whom he has laid such hopes for the continuance of his own glory and that of his dynasty, Samory gives orders to raise camp for the attack on the French and to quit the place of accursed associations: it is with the sense that his personal greatness, like that of his empire, is irrevocably doomed. . . .

In [his] first novel [*Buur Tilleen, roi de la Médina*], Cheik Ndao paints the portrait of the respected elder of an earlier society, who cannot adapt to changing customs and standards. . . . Gorgui Mbodj, a man of honor and principle, preferring personal humiliation rather than not uphold the proud traditions of his race and caste, makes himself and his family the victims of his stiff-necked intolerance. . . . Ndao makes only one indirect reference to the end of the colonial era, his story illustrating more specifically a sempiternal generation gap than a contemporary social evolution. Gorgui, the proud descendant of princes, had some years previously been banished from his region for affronting a district commandant who had humiliated him before his own subjects. Since then he has lived in poverty in the Medina, his only link with his proud past is his stallion Sindax, from whom he has refused to be separated; his only consolation for his wretched condition is to ride through the streets of the Medina in the afternoon, reliving the glory of the court of Walo. He has refused to sanction his daughter's marriage with a man of inferior caste and prefers to turn her out on the streets, in time-honored melodramatic fashion when she becomes pregnant.

There are clearly many predictable ingredients in the plot of *Buur Tilleen*, which culminates in Raki's death in childbirth together with that of her infant. On the other hand, the portrayal of the complex character of "Buur Tilleen" is authentic and moving. The conflict between his sense of honor and his real affection for his wife and child is presented with economy and understanding. In the end, when he reverts to animist practices to try and conjure the threat of death to Raki, we realize how irrevocably the pattern of his life has been rent, even before the final tragedy, and how real will be his remorse. Cheik Aliou Ndao has succeeded in portraying the tragedy—albeit on a small canvas—that ensues when noble aspirations go hand in hand with human weakness. He has attempted to make us enter more deeply into the emotions and dilemmas of Gorgui and his wife Maram by adopting the technique of the inner monologue for the opening passages which present the immediate crisis in their lives and the background of their past history. It is a pity that he is not consistent in using this narrative technique throughout, as it might have infused a little more life into the other protagonists, in particular Raki and Bougouma, the two lovers and representatives of the younger generation.

Dorothy S. Blair. *African Literature in French*
(Cambridge: Cambridge University Press, 1976), pp. 111–14, 311–12

Ndao's play *L'Exil d'Albouri* won the first prize at the Algiers Festival in 1969, and is perhaps the most striking of the historical plays dealing with the first contacts between African rulers and the white colonizer. Ndao has a good sense of dramatic economy and relevance, so that he is able to create scenes which are dramatically effective, and his dialogue moves the action forward rather than keeping it static, as so often happens in plays of this group. Another common difficulty is that of adequately portraying the psychology and particularly the motivation of the characters; in this respect Ndao is less successful. In *L'Exil d'Albouri*, Ndao puts forward a very interesting dramatic situation. Realizing that he cannot hope to defeat the French in battle, Albouri, contrary to what is expected of a warrior, decides to go into exile rather than be captured by the enemy, believing that this will preserve the honor and integrity of his country more effectively than subjection. The historical situation is relatively simple to portray, and at this level the play works well. The use of the griot as a commentator who will always be there and can project the significance of events beyond the immediate present effectively links the audience with the historical situation. The drama itself, however, is meant to spring from the conflict between Albouri and his brother on the one hand, and between Albouri's mother and sister (who agree with his decision) and his young wife (who is afraid of exile) on the other. There is also tension between Albouri and his wife, who complains she never sees her husband. These conflicts are sketched in rather than developed, and are therefore not as effective as they could have been in showing Albouri's dilemma. We are given the skeleton with far too little of the flesh. Motivation is at times lacking or even contradictory, as when Albouri, after expressing complete confidence in his brother in the opening scenes of the play, suddenly reacts to his brother's opposition to the exile proposition. . . . One could make the same criticism of a subsequent play by Ndao, *Le Fils de l'Almamy*. It deals with the conflict between the great Samory and his son, who has spent a year in France and returned convinced of the uselessness of resisting the white man's arms. One feels the need for a fuller treatment of the relationship between the father and the son and, once again, motivation is at times badly handled, as when Samory believes without hesitation a malicious story told him by one of his wives whom the king knows to be jealous of the favorite son. There is some question of a potion intended to create strife between father and son, but it is not clear how or even whether it is administered.

Martin Banham and Clive Wake. *African Theatre Today*
(London: Pitman, 1976), pp. 66–68

One of the most successfully staged plays presenting a Resistance hero of the late nineteenth century is Cheik Ndao's *L'Exil d'Albouri* which was awarded the Gold Medal for drama at the Algiers Festival of African Arts in 1969. Albouri Ndiaye ruled the Djoloff kingdom between 1875 and 1890 when, rather than live under foreign domination, he went into exile shortly before Colonel Dodds invaded his capital, Yang Yang. Albouri was the last free Djoloff king because his successor, Samba Laobé Penda, was dethroned and deported to Gabon and replaced by Albouri's son, Bouna, who was reduced to the rank of a chief in 1900. One of Cheik Ndao's purposes in this play is the rehabilitation of African history which had been distorted by the colonial notion of "pacification" that was transparent in the historical plays of the early Ponty repertoire. Ndao uses the technique of reversal to achieve his purpose. The sowers of discord are the Spahis led by their European officers who "have burnt thousands of villages; they wreak havoc and destroy the granaries. Worse than the year of the plague! They come with machines which spit fire and demolish our fortifications." Conquest, not peace, is the goal of the foreigners who by a combination of troops, treaties, and treachery seek to wrest control from the local rulers. In the face of this threat, Albouri is portrayed as an upright and lucid ruler, bold and proud but not foolhardy, a patriot who has the best interests of his people at heart. As a foil to the notion of the "precolonial night" Ndao underlines the fact that Albouri's lineage stretches back to Ndiadiane Ndiaye who founded the Djoloff kingdom in the fourteenth century. Thus the myth of pacification is destroyed as the focus shifts to Albouri's noble attempt to resist the invader and to preserve the independence of his people.

Although Cheik Ndao warns us in his prologue that historical fact and fiction are intermingled, his aim being to compose a work of art not a historical treatise, he is concerned with presenting a faithful picture of the social reality of the time. Contrary to the mistaken notion that the kings ruled as absolute despots, he depicts Albouri as governing in concert with his council of representatives of different social groups. A special role is reserved for Samba who opens and closes the play. Samba functions as a griot and as a depository of the traditional wisdom, albeit a stylized griot. Costumes, decor, instruments, and accessories are carefully noted with a view to expressing authenticity and are used functionally. Ndao eschews the folkloric tendencies of Ponty theater.

L'Exil d'Albouri is not, however, an uncritical panegyric of the past. In the conflict that opposes Albouri and Samba Laobé Penda, the latter represents the blind reproduction of traditional thought patterns and gestures of the past whereas Albouri incarnates the spirit of innovation. Samba Laobé Penda is obsessed with the symbol of the throne whereas Albouri is more concerned with effective independence. In creating the role of the Diaraf of the Slaves and in exposing Samba Laobé Penda, the Diaraf of Thingue, and their associates as people who under the guise of patriotism promote their own ambitions and class or caste privileges, Ndao seeks to project the values of social equality which should form the basis of contemporary society. He explicitly states in the prologue that his aim is "to assist in the creation of myths which galvanize the people and which lead to the future." His vision of a just and democratic society, faithful to the spirit of the best elements of tradition but open to new solutions in order to meet the challenges of the present, is subtly harmonized with his evocation of authentic Djoloff society in the late nineteenth century. The other historical plays that fall into this group generally develop in their own way the same three themes of authenticity, exemplary values embodied in the hero, and rehabilitation of the historical record.

Gary Warner. *TRI.* 9, 3 (1983–1984), pp. 188–89

If [Bernard] Dadié and [Guillaume] Oyônô-Mbia are the doyens of the satirical vein in black French theater, Cheik Ndao is the doyen of tragedy, or, rather, of dramatized history-with-a-lesson. The former want to change men by showing them their foibles, while Ndao exhorts men to realize the greatness within themselves through the example of the past. So it is, especially in his *Du sang pour un trône ou Gouye Ndiouli un dimanche.* The scene is the kingdom of Kawoon in the Saloum region of Senegal in the early 1860s. Lawbé Fall is king, seconded by the Queen Mother Linguère. The king's father, Macodou Fall, had long ago deserted his kingdom for the conquest of other lands and has lost his throne as a result. The whites however, are near, and Macodou has returned to the Saloum with the idea of uniting all its kingdoms into one. Macodou places himself at the head of the black brotherhood resistance composed of both animists and the Muslim Foutanké people. Lawbé and his counsellors learn of Macodou's return and of his intentions; they also discover that he has a marabout (i.e., a Muslim) in his retinue. Lawbé is mistrusted by his own advisers because of the blood connection, but he himself fears the threat to his own leadership represented by his father; he also condemns his alliance with the Muslim Foutanké. His opposition to his father reassures the Royal Council, which had been prepared to kill him, and there is battle on one Sunday at Gouye Ndiouli, hence the second title. Lawbé wins decisively though after that he plans to wage war on the Foutanké. In this manner the play ends, under the sad cloud of fratricidal war among black Africans, weakening the area for the onslaughts of the whites which are being prepared in the wings.

The most striking feature of the play is that it has no villains. If the village that harbored Macodou should have received permission from Kawoon before so doing, it acted so out of respect for him. If the council plots to kill Lawbé, it is for *la chose publique*, as too are Lawbé's wars on his own father and the Muslim Foutanké. His father is not at all villainous either, since he thinks that the whites are the menace. The role of griots in the play is most important and impressive. They are narrators, genealogists, moderators, counselors, entertainers, funambulists. Ndao is the first black [francophone] dramatist to humanize thoroughly the griot caste, which has over it a curse that derives from incestuous cannibalism in the past, reminiscent of the curse over the House of Atreus. Principally this is done via the wise "Maître de la Parole" . . . Niambali who, with his two wives, truly comes to life in these pages. One is impressed by the feeling of authenticity in this and just about every other detail of the play. *Du sang pour un trône* as written is perhaps more a dialogued novel than a stageable play; what is in effect a genre in itself, the dialogued novel is especially exemplified by Benjamin Matip's *Laisse-nous bâtir une Afrique debout*. The fact that Ndao reused a theme should not surprise. On the one hand there are such continental figures as Shaka, treated often, and on the other there are the more regional ones: Abraha Pokou (four plays), Lat Dior (three plays), and Lawbé-cum-Macodou.

Harold A. Waters. *TRI.* 9, 3 (1983–1984), pp. 201–2

Ndao stands apart from his contemporaries, David Diop and Lamine Diakhaté, by virtue of the strongly personal note that imbues his lyric poetry. Although his commitment to Africa's cause is irreproachable and the themes of liberty and country are evident in his first verses, he is primarily a sincere and sentient poet who weds the expression of his private sensibility to that of public issues. He writes . . . that his ambition has always been to remain faithful to himself, "to marry the idea to the form. I believe," he continues, "that the poet has the right and indeed the duty to rise up against injustice, but *artistically*, otherwise you are dealing with slogans. I also believe that sincerity must be the basis for the poem, and that we must not cheat. That is why I have not hesitated to sing of all the white women who have inspired me, in a period of exacerbated black nationalism.

Some of the poems included in *Kaïrée*, Cheik Ndao's first published collection, for which he was awarded the Prix des Poètes de Langue Française, date back to 1955. The rest were written between 1958 and 1961, a period of intense loneliness and nostalgia for Africa. Like [Léopold Sédar] Senghor in *Chants d'ombre*, he expresses the languor induced by the long European winters with "the endless silent rain of white locusts" eroding his insomniac nights. In "Paysages," he expresses his nostalgia in an evocative series of images, seeking to banish the autumn melancholy by clothing the European scene in the sights of Africa, with "hills reddened by the sun's wounds . . . furrowed by termites . . . baobabs tearing up the heavens." . . . Even in poems inspired by contemporary political situations, the remarkable play of images maintains the lyric harmonies and sensual qualities of the verse. This can be found in the song of the three mourners from "Larmes de flammes pour Lumumba," or the love song, "Poem for Laora," in which the artist's eye for color combines with the musician's ear for dancing rhythms to express the upsurge of his emotion. Elsewhere, in "Guinté" (the name of a Senegalese dance), the relentless stamp of feet, the singers' incantations, and the tom-tom's furious beat combine to conjure up monsters and jinni, as well as an irresistible erotic force. . . .

In 1970 he published a second book of poetry, *Mogariennes*, which owes its title to a pleasing conceit: it is formed from the prefix and suffix respectively of the names of two important towns which the poet visited in his travels to Mali in 1963: *Mo*pti and Bandia*gara*. So the poems of *Mogariennes* trace a personal itinerary and also pay homage to the women of Mali. We find similar personal themes to those of the earlier *Kaïrée*, but treated with more maturity and sureness of touch. The first poem, "Un Cygne sur la mer," dates from the school year 1962–1963 which Ndao spent in Wales as French teacher at Bishop Gore Grammar School in Swansea, where the "Child of the Savanna" finds empathy with a "Daughter of the Celts" and literary kinship with Dylan Thomas, while not forgetting the women of the Joliba River.

The untitled verses of the long poem, which gives its name to the collection, follow his pilgrimage from Europe back to Africa, from Dakar to Mali. The poet weaves a spell of proper names to conjure up the precolonial past of the great West African empires, and evokes the color and texture of places whose *genus loci* presides over his present travels as over his childhood experience. Although there are verses in this volume inspired by white women which are the pure expression of personal emotion, Ndao never forgets his identity as a black man committed to his African origins. The theme of his homeland is always present, even when he acknowledges the charm of Europe; like Senghor, he expresses the seduction that the landscape of France exerts over "The son / Of the sands of the russet grass / On the plains of Salum," who sends his greetings to the mountains of France.

Ndao returns to political themes in "Afrique II," which alludes to the illusory freedom that "independent" Africa enjoys under a neocolonial hegemony and to the continual struggle for even this incomplete freedom still being waged in Angola and Southern Africa. Finally, in "Hello Joe," he proves a master of Swiftian polemic. The pseudobonhomie of the title introduces the bitterly ironic note that infuses this attack on "G. I. Joe," the representative of all that is hateful in America's power-wielding throughout the world and repression of black and red men at home. He recalls a childhood terrorized by American soldiers in Senegal throwing beer bottles from jeeps, fracturing black skulls, raping girls on beaches, and shooting at women "to kill time." There follows violent invective against American intervention in Korea, Cambodia, and Vietnam, against the insidious support Wall Street gives to repressive regimes for the sake of multinational business interests, all expressed in a vitriolic parody of the Lord's Prayer.

The corrosive passion of "Hello Joe" is unique in Cheik Ndao's poetry, as if he had accumulated all his anger at injustice and repression throughout the world and vented it in this one long virulent outburst. Generally his lyricism is more suited to an elegiac mode, whereby themes of country, national heritage, African identity, and African history are refracted through the prism of personal experience to assume a more universal dimension.

Dorothy S. Blair. *Senegalese Literature: A Critical History*
(Boston: Twayne, 1984), pp. 90–91, 101–2

[In *Excellence, vos épouses!* the] opening crisis could have been lifted straight from the contemporary political diary of any African country. The Leader, in the latest surprise reshuffle, drops a faithful old Minister. It's one of those graceless jerk dances in which the Minister only happens to hear of his dismissal through the media.

The man sent on this express trip from grace to grass is a figure of touchingly familiar mediocrity. He's not burdened with excess intelligence, innate or acquired. His major claim to fame is that he was a founding member of the Party, one of the first riders on the independence wave. For that sole achievement our

Minister expects a lifetime of lucrative posts and sugared privileges, financed by a grateful, if beggared, nation.

The country has grown poorer since independence, but the elite has grown rich. Our friend the Minister, for instance, has children in Western universities, taking courses available in Dakar. He has enough money to maintain four wives, the last a Dakar University Pharmacy student about the age of his own oldest child. This pseudo-progressive girl, the ambitious first child of a large slum family, has a secret dream: she plans to use the amorous Minister as an economic cushion just for the time it takes to grab her degree, then cut him loose. That is merely one of the innumerable betrayals that give this novel its thematic substance. . . .

Rottenness . . . has been and remains the common denominator of the country's public life. Quite accidentally, though, our Minister has come to be perceived as the one Party big shot uninvolved in the elite's determined plunder of the nation. The reputation results from no surfeit of integrity. It's just that this Minister, from his modest background as an agricultural extension officer, has been slow to discover the golden road of international contracts and coded bank accounts. Temperamentally careful, he has a habit of covering up his dirt. A grateful Muslim, he deals with his sexual weaknesses by marrying the women who infatuate him. Sure, he tups the occasional female militant accompanying ministerial delegations on tours of European capitals and hotels. But after such slips he always feels a respectable amount of remorse, later.

Unfortunately for our Minister, though, the Leader, like the head of every irretrievably moldy government, needs a green symbol to cover up the general decay. The Leader has fixed on our unsophisticated Minister to play the oxymoronic part: paragon of Party purity.

Trouble arises in the form of a lean and hungry generation, clawing its way up the Party pyramid. Ambitious young activists dig up buried dirty secrets, using them to knock down old Party faithfuls blocking their path to power.

The Leader is thus informed of a buried scandal: while serving as public works minister, our fig leaf of a minister once cashed a bribe from a Scandinavian bidder for a national highway contract. What the Leader discovers, in effect, is that his beloved fig leaf is just as lousy as the general body politic. In righteous anger he tears it off and throws it away. That's how His Excellency the Minister is precipitated into the warm, hospitable ranks of the unemployed. . . .

Here is a threat of tragic outcomes, but the novel ends softly, on a comic note. Capricious as always, the Leader rehabilitates the fallen Minister. It was, after all, a round trip: from grace to grass to an awkward kind of grace again.

The Leader, dipping generously into the nation's empty coffers, has established diplomatic relations with a faraway country just to create an ambassadorial sinecure for our friend. The new ambassador, weak in geography as in all intellectual matters, has not the slightest idea what or where the new country is. No matter, the pressing issue is not to find out where in the world the embassy is, but to settle a matter of national importance: which of wives one, two, three, or four is to accompany His Polygamous Excellency?

Cheik Aliou Ndao starts his book as if he's getting ready to bite into his social subject. But when he opens his authorial mouth, we see he has taken care to remove his dentures. His intention is: to caress the subject with his gums, not to draw blood. A prudent, limited goal, well achieved.

Ayi Kwei Armah. *WA*. October 29, 1984. pp. 2171–72

NDEBELE, NJABULO (1948–   )

SOUTH AFRICA

Njabulo Ndebele argues that to be intellectually engaging, contemporary black writing must go beyond mere description: "It seems to me that a large part of the African resistance to the evil of apartheid has, until recently, consisted of a largely descriptive documentation of suffering. And the bulk of the fiction, through an almost total concern with the political theme, has in following this tradition, largely documented rather than explained." . . . The method that Ndebele advocates is what "literature" needs, but as long as blacks continue to expect literature to play a role in their struggle there will be controversy over what form writers should use.

Ndebele seems to have made his choice. His recent collection of stories, *Fools and Other Stories*, combines both explicit and implicit comment. The content of the stories, particularly that of "Fools," is similar to that of the short stories of the 1950s. Social, economic, and political concerns are revealed through various forms of township experience. . . .

Ndebele's subtle protest against the system appears towards the end of the story where the two protagonists, Zani and Zamani, attempt to "break up a picnic on the Day of the Covenant, Commemorating December 16, 1838, the day the Boers killed thousands of Black South Africans and dethroned their ruler, King Dingane." As blacks enter the picnic grounds, a Boer appears and picks a quarrel with Zani. An ugly situation ensues in which the angry Boer lashes at any black person in his way with a whip. The symbolic significance of the episode is revealed when Zamani, the schoolteacher, shows typically heroic, unflinching endurance as the Boer madly lashes at him. . . . Ndebele's calm portrayal of heroic and passive resistance in this episode is probably one of the most effective in black writing. Yet there is a built-in problem regarding his characters' level of political consciousness and the kind of resistance they embody. Zani, who, of all Ndebele's "fools," is the most "politically aware," comes across as an incautious idealist. His attempts at politicizing Zamani's young primary school pupils sound naive and politically immature. Although his idea of breaking up the picnic is seen as noble, the act itself is ill-planned. Zamani, who hesitantly supports the idea, is a blind fellow-traveler. Despite the fact that he is the central character in the symbolic episode cited above, Zamani's politics are riddled with indecision and sometimes utter confusion. His decision to take part in breaking up the pic-nic is a result of compassion for Zani and not political commitment. The princi-pal of Zamani's school (who has organized the picnic) . . . [cares] only about his own importance. The picnickers themselves are portrayed as a group of hedonists whose sole concerns are drinking, dancing, and lovemaking rather than the political boycott Zani is advocating.

Since Ndebele is aware of the flaws of his characters, one can only conclude that, like his poem, "The Revolution of the Aged," "Fools" is a story that deliberately sets out to celebrate passive, antirevolutionary resistance. "The veiled symbolism of this episode . . . is clear: apartheid will wear itself out in the end." . . . The society Ndebele depicts is in desperate need not only of political awakening, but also of a more effective form of resistance.

Piniel Viriri Shava. *A People's Voice: Black South African Writing in the Twentieth Century* (London: Zed Books, 1989), pp. 152–54

Njabulo Ndebele approaches politics indirectly by exploring subjective experience in *Fools and Other Stories*. Having articulated the need for black writers to move beyond the documentation of oppression, Ndebele avoids explicit discussion of apartheid until the end of the book [in "Fools"]. . . . The other, earlier stories are all told from the point of view of preadolescent boys in Chaterton township, but although his protagonists are often children, their problems prefigure the dilemmas of the student, the artist, and the intellectual in confronting conflicts of race and class. The time of Ndebele's narratives is unspecified until the last story, when we learn that it is 1966, ten years before the explosion of the Soweto youth. The choice of childhood and adolescence as a subject—culminating in the teenager Zani's groping toward revolutionary activity in the story "Fools"—is clearly related to the 1976 rebellion, and to the tragedy of youths' having to sacrifice themselves to political struggle.

Ndebele's stories do not project a unified black experience. They are stories of self-division, intellectual yearnings, and class division. The characteristic protagonist is a black child who is somewhat better off economically than the average township child. Thus in the first story, "The Test," Thoba feels challenged to prove himself physically by imitating the dominant boys in his group, boys from poorer families. Reproducing the hierarchies of the playground and the street, apartheid is almost nonexistent in "The Test," present only in the Dutch Reformed Church that marks the limit of Thoba's run in the freezing rain and in the persistent cough of Nana, a sickly boy whom the others protect. In "The Music of the Violin," a similar conflict is presented in sharper terms, as Vukani resists being forced to play the violin because of the humiliation that carrying the instrument brings him from classmates and the adolescent gangs on the streets. The class pretensions of Vukani's mother are underlined by her daughter, Teboho, a university student who accuses her mother of becoming a "white black woman." The intervention of Teboho saves Vukani from the agonizing personal isolation in which he experiences his need to reject the violin, alone in his room "as good as any white boy's." At the end of the story, Vukani's father stands up for him against Vukani's mother, who has also resisted allowing the father's relatives to visit, violating traditional African attitudes toward the extended family.

It is in the third story, "Uncle," that the problem of the relation of the individual—especially the artist and the intellectual—and the group is most fully examined. The uncle who comes to visit, although a jazz musician and somewhat suspect in his family, is the only positive adult role among the major characters in *Fools and Other Stories*. The uncle tries to give his nephew a sense of African pride, telling him to travel and know the places in his country so that "it will be your country. And then you must ask yourself: what can I give to all those places?" Stressing social responsibility, he tells the boy to develop goals, claiming that the ancestors "say that you do not really know what you want, and that is very dangerous for someone who is going to be a man." However, the uncle also indicates the value of isolation and apparent selfishness, sometimes ordering his own friends and the bewildered boy from the room when practicing. He explains: "The best way to avoid endless struggle . . . is to struggle very hard for a short period of time." In music, he tells the nephew, knowledge is a prerequisite for improvisation; without knowledge, "you'll soon tire of playing anything, because your playing will have no direction. Unlearned freedom frustrates; nothing elevating and lasting ever comes of it." Teaching his nephew about African history, Arabic culture, and the hope of regaining that history for Africans, the uncle is as at home on the street as in the library; he defeats the local bully whose girlfriend he has seduced, and his music is popular. . . . [The] uncle relates his skill and knowledge to the needs of the class he represents, but he is also an embodiment of Ndebele's demand for some distance between art and politics if art is to have relevance to either politics or itself.

Raymond A. Mazurek. SSF. 26, 1 (Winter 1989), pp. 75–77

Njabulo Ndebele's collection of stories *Fools [and Other Stories]* is a celebration of life in the black townships. The stories are set entirely within the world of the townships and white people remain a distant, almost irrelevant presence for the black characters. Within the collection there is a great diversity of characters, drawn from virtually every class and sector of the black township population. This is part of Ndebele's vision of a diverse, yet united black community. For all the violence in the township (the student activist Zani in the story "Fools" is stabbed, for example, and a young boy is viciously kicked by church elders in "Uncle"), Ndebele offers a view of this world which revels in its communalism and vibrancy.

The collection's best story, "Uncle," for example, ends with a scene of triumph in which people from all corners of the township gather together in an informal way to enjoy the music of a variety of performers. The work ends with the young narrator's delighted cry: "Oh, Uncle, everybody is here." Here one has an affirmation central to Ndebele's thinking about society (and one might add, to that of many black writers): namely the need to include and incorporate everybody within one's sense of community. And, obviously following from this, the necessity for socialist transformations within society that take into account the broad spectrum of needs of that society.

Interestingly, as in many works of black fiction since the students' uprising of 1976, the central characters or narrators in the majority of Ndebele's stories are young children or teenagers. Ndebele is clearly addressing himself, in the first place to a new generation of young black South Africans, the people for whom his vision of a unified community is of greatest relevance.

One senses throughout *Fools* that the small triumphs of the characters over a range of hardships in their everyday lives stand for the confidence of black people in their struggle against oppression. Again, it is in the story "Uncle" that Ndebele establishes most explicitly a connection between the actions and sayings of his characters and the broader context of black people's lives. Uncle's statements, in particular, have a resonance for the entire community. . . . This quiet, unobtrusive, often humorous form of guidance and illumination, indicating the future role for the black community in South African history and its celebration of communalism, are the most distinctive features of Ndebele's volume of stories.

Martin Trump. Rendering Things Visible: Essays on South African
Literary Culture (Athens: Ohio University Press, 1990), pp. 168–70

In the article ["*Turkish Tales*, and Some Thoughts on South African Fiction"], Ndebele develops a thesis about storytelling, and the relationship between storytelling and fiction writing. He takes his admiration for the stories of the Turkish writer, Yashar Kemal, as the basis for a diagnosis of what is wrong with fiction by African writers in South Africa. Kemal's strength lies in his understanding of the conventions of storytelling, and in his ability to draw on the oral storytelling traditions of Turkey in the composition of his own written stories. Kemal's stories are critical stories, exploring the predicament of an impoverished rural population dominated by a ruthless, if paternalistic, land-owning class of Aghas. Because Kemal understands the conventions of storytelling narrative so well, and because of his familiarity with local storytelling traditions, he can draw his reader into an "imaginative" yet critical reflection upon the social processes of rural Turkey.

What of local African writers? They are not like Kemal, says Ndebele. They also want to write critical stories. The apartheid laws, by which a minority white population holds a majority black population down in impoverished subjection, offer as pressing an occasion for critical reflection as the predicament of rural Turkey. Unlike Kemal, though, local writers show little regard for the conventions of storytelling, and little interest in the oral storytelling art that is so popular among the wider African population. Instead, in order to provide their stories with the desired critical character, they resort to sloganizing, and to a journalistic, rather than a storytelling, mode of narrative, presenting the reader with "evidence" of the cruelty of apartheid rather than composing a thought-provoking story. . . .

In this context, an inadequate conception of political commitment is prevalent among writers. Political commitment comes to mean, broadly, condemning apartheid and its agents, especially African "sell-outs," and sympathizing with the plight of the majority of the African population, who are the victims of this policy. It does not involve a serious analysis of the *culture* of this "victimized" population, of the themes that resonate in the daily lives of the people. It fails largely to connect with these resonances, to engage with them imaginatively or analytically.

Political commitment has overlooked culture; it has confined itself to a comparatively narrow range of attitudes and slogans, shared or debated among the intelligentsia. This is where Ndebele's conception of "storytelling" comes in as an antidote. Storytelling requires precisely the cultural insight or capacity for imaginative analysis—analysis which engages seriously with the resonances of popular experience—that has been wanting in the literature of African writers.

Storytelling is the antidote suggested by Ndebele for the ailing condition, as he sees it, of African fiction writing. This antidote arises out of a profoundly critical reflection on prevailing conceptions of how to express political commitment in literature. . . .

What characterizes each of Ndebele's stories is its prominent and sensitive treatment of the "inner life"—the intellectual and emotional processes—of the protagonist. This concern with the inner life, focused upon a strategic theme or incident, provides the principle of coherence of each story. It also differentiates Ndebele's stories from those which he criticizes for their sloganistic and journalistic ambience. Little of the fiction published by African writers in South Africa shows the same degree of concern with the exploration of the inner life that Ndebele exhibits. Clearly, it takes a lot of skill and insight into the craft of fictional narrative to compose the fascinating accounts of personal experience that distinguish the stories in *Fools*. Furthermore, the skill involved in composing these accounts is inseparable from the practice of cultural analysis.

Michael Vaughan. In Martin Trump, ed. *Rendering Things Visible: Essays on South African Literary Culture* (Athens: Ohio University Press, 1990), pp. 186–88

Writing under literary censorship after the Sharpeville crisis in 1960, Ndebele belonged to a group of poets whose "indirect approach" in condemning the government enabled them to publish their works. Despite their cautiousness, however, they were eventually forced into exile. Ndebele now teaches at the University College of Roma, Lesotho, a nominally independent country surrounded by South Africa. Although Ndebele relies on multiple meanings, he does so not to evade an issue, but to make his criticism even more effective, and only the most obtuse censor could fail to see his devastating indictment of apartheid in *Fools*. As much as his carefully nuanced descriptions generate a dizzying multiplicity of meaning, the political implications are definite, and to praise such a work for its "indeterminacy" is to engage in another form of repression. . . .

Ndebele daringly chooses to have *Fools* narrated by a black South African who, like [Feodor] Dostoyevsky's Underground Man, scarcely qualifies as heroic or even likable. Teacher Zamani, known as Tee, grovels, abases himself, hurts his wife, Nosipho, punishes himself, and rapes a student named Mimi, who bears his child. A few years after the rape, at the time of the story (1966), Tee meets Mimi's now eighteen-year-old brother Zani. Although Zani agrees with his mother that "When you look at [Tee] you see disgrace," they both seem to pity more than hate him. . . .

The two men . . . still have, as Zani would insist, a responsibility to bolster their respect for themselves and their fellow blacks as a prelude to taking back their government. By the end of the story, Tee has moved slightly toward reclaiming respect. When a stone hurled at Zani by a toadying black principal accidentally hits a passing car, a furious Boer emerges; to the Afrikaner, "The possibility of resistance to his power seemed as unthinkable . . . as the revolt of chickens." Yet Tee—chicken-hearted, oppressed, humiliated, further self-humiliating, and hurtful—does manage a revolt. He refuses to run, though the Boer whips him. He laughs, until, finally, the Boer weeps, taking on the frustrated, sadomasochistic powerlessness that has always been Tee's lot. . . .

Ndebele is well aware of this seeming dilatoriness of the literary sign, expanding and dawdling, but he is also careful to prod it to finally yield up its meaning. He grants that "The language of art is by definition a language that demands to be interpreted." In a sardonic and self-reflexive line in *Fools*, Ndebele further indicates his awareness that metaphor is a method that encourages thought but also produces dangers of evasiveness or delay. When the school board rehires Tee after only a three-month dismissal for rape, the delegation is too ashamed, of him and of themselves, to broach the subject directly. . . .

Zani sometimes resembles the despicable Tee because the younger man has to recognize humbly that his bookishness gives him "the obscenity of high seriousness." The sympathetic Zani also resembles Tee because the latter deserves some sympathy as a victim. The opposition between Tee and Zani is "deconstructed" occasionally not because signs somehow inherently contradict themselves but because Zani must recognize his limitations and Tee, his potential. Similarly, the polar opposition of Tee and the Boer is undone to show the parallel limitation of the men, since both have wept in sadomasochistic excess. This resemblance, however, does not dissolve all differences. The government is not excused and the system of apartheid represented by the Boer must be defeated. Yet the brief, shocking similarity of the Boer to Tee may prepare for a future healing, after blacks have taken majority rule, if a slight basis of kinship could be recognized between the races.

K. J. Phillips. *Mosaic*. 23, 4 (Fall 1990), pp. 88, 94–97, 99

NETO, AGOSTINHO (1922–1979)

ANGOLA

Agostinho Neto is one of the few lusophone African writers with an international reputation. He has spent much of his life in the struggle of his people to win independence. Whereas some Angolan intellectuals chose to live in Europe during the thirteen years of guerrilla warfare, Neto remained in his homeland organizing resistance to Portuguese domination. Moreover, Neto did not isolate himself from the great masses of Angolans living outside urban centers. He personally visited interior sections, eating with the people and frequently sleeping in their mosquito-infested huts. For Agostinho Neto his own life has taken on meaning only in conjunction with the lives of the oppressed people of Angola. . . .

In 1961 Casa dos Estudantes do Império in the Colecçao Autores Ultramarinos published a small volume of Neto's poetry under the title *Poemas*. A much larger selection appeared first in Italy in 1963 under the title *Con occhi asciutti*. This book was later published in Yugoslavia, Russia, and China. The first complete Portuguese edition came out in 1974 as *Sagrada esperança*, the title Neto preferred. It was awarded the Poetry of Combat Prize by the University of Ibadan in 1975. The forty-eight poems in this collection constitute nearly all of Neto's poetic work and cover a period from 1945 through 1960. . . .

Neto presents a gallery of victims in his early poems. Forced labor, hunger, loss of dignity, loss of hope, humiliation, even death, assault the body and spirit of the African living under colonialist domination. Life in the musseques is *ansiedade* (anguish). There is "saudade dos dias nao vividos" (nostalgia of days never lived) in "Sábado nos musseques." But Neto does not despair. In the very first poem of *Sagrada esperança*, "Adeus a hora da largada," he asserts his faith in himself and the people to create a new destiny.

Agostinho Neto does not often write of an individual love—that is a luxury; he writes about his love of his people, of his land and of liberty. And he writes primarily for his people. Unlike the francophone Négritude poets whose voices were heard more in Europe than in Africa, men like Neto, Costa Andrade, and António Jacinto brought their words to their own marketplace where the Angolan people came to know them. Many of Neto's poems have been put to music by soldiers who would sing these hymns of Africa. Poems such as "Havemos de voltar" and "Criar" are particularly well known. Ruy Mingas, among others, put out a record of Neto's poems and his songs can be heard in the streets of Luanda today, for in Neto's words the dreams of Angola are expressed.

Donald Burness. *Fire: Six Writers from Angola, Mozambique, and Cape Verde* (Washington, D. C.: Three Continents Press, 1977), pp. 19–20, 24, 33

Neto's poetry is seen by Donald Burness as one of combat. Militancy in Neto's poems, as in those of many other African writers of Portuguese expression . . . is a determining factor. Most lusophone African intellectuals, committed in the liberation struggle, would easily subscribe to Amílcar Cabral's view that the struggle itself was an act of culture. Their militancy, however, did not imply, as Neto's case so well illustrates, that they put aside the specific demands of the means employed. It is difficult to accuse Agostinho Neto of carelessness in his approach to poetry. Images and metaphors are judiciously set in the organic unity of the poem, so that the implicit message may be conveyed more effectively. All stylistic devices—anaphora, alliteration, enumeration, parallelism—contribute to intensify the rhythmic quality of poetry (seen as a counterpart of some black musical forms) and not to overcharge or smother the contents of the text. . . .

The theme of *identification* is present in one of Neto's most famous poems, "Mussunda amigo." The text is at the same time a melancholy recollection of a childhood and adolescence in common (the narrator remembers the time when he and his friend Mussunda used to buy mangos, or lamented "the destiny / of the women from Funda" with "clouds" in their eyes) and the expression of a deep confidence in the permanence of a sense of communion that nothing can destroy. The final statement, "We are," avoiding as it does the rhetoric of any exclamatory emphasis, echoes nonetheless a determined militancy, the idea that in spite of everything, of the ditch that colonialism put between the intellectual and the masses ("Here I am / Mussunda my friend / writing poems you can't understand"), they persist, they *are*, they affirm their existence simultaneously as an ontological and a historical barrier against which colonialist violence can do nothing. The African intellectual is fully aware of the contradiction implicit in his literary endeavors inaccessible to his illiterate countrymen; he knows, however, that there is always a point of convergence that makes them, after all, "inseparable."

Fernando Martinho. *WLT*. 53, 1 (Winter 1979), pp. 47–48

Neto's poetry is a perfect synthesis of history and art. ["Sábado nos musseques," translated as "Saturday in the Musseques"], for instance, tells of the deplorable condition of living in the slums. It begins with a straightforward statement: "Musseques are poor neighborhoods of poor people"—an expression most critics would consider too prosaic. But this manner of expression has worked and is consistent with Neto's objective, which is to educate his people and define their struggle in clear and precise terms. In this way, obscurantism, silence, and extinction are challenged. In "Saturday in the Musseques," Neto analyzes social life in a slum, showing that violence, oppression, brutality, alcoholism, sexuality, and other related social ills, are all symptoms of the anxiety in which the oppressed wallow. . . .

Neto's poetry is noted for its simplicity and directness. Its figurative expression is spare and unobtrusive, for Neto uses metaphor and symbols, not for ornamentation or deliberately as a poet seeking an effect would do, but as a man would use them in conversation or in silent musing. Everything comes naturally, as for example, his metaphors drawn from the medical profession: "no penetration of the germ of exploitation" [in "A Voz Iqual," translated as "With Equal Voice"], and "Injustice inoculated into the living system in which we revolve" [in "A reconquista," translated as "Reconquest"]. Neto's thoughts and feelings are communicated with ease and certainty, and so achieve maximum effects. . . .

Neto's poetry is for the people from whom it draws many of its virtues. Basil Davidson has noted that [*Sagrada esperança*, translated as *Sacred Hope*] . . . shows the poet's "vision of himself as not alone, but peopled with his own humanity, as having no personal 'career' outside the meaning of his people's life, as enjoying no worthwhile privilege save that of sharing in a necessary struggle for the future, shaking off the past, transforming the present." In many poems, Neto expresses his conviction that an individual cannot make a revolution without uniting with his people. This is a call to all people who need to change their condition. . . . Neto's use of poetry to propel revolutionary action and change, his clarity of expression that has made it possible for him to communicate with most of his people, regardless of their social class, and his sober confidence, are virtues, which other African poets will do well to emulate.

Ossie Onuora Enekwe. Okike. 18 (June 1981), pp. 3–6

The poetry of Agostinho Neto is often perceived as one of combat, revolutionary verse whose primary objective is to awaken the poet's compatriots, to help them become aware of their unenviable plight as a colonized people. This revolutionary element is dominant throughout Neto's opera. It is prevalent in the later poems in which the author already envisages an independent Angola, as one can easily deduce from such titles as: ["Havemos de voltar," translated as] "We Shall Return," "With Equal Voice," and ["O içar da bandeira," translated as] "The Hoisting of the Flag," as well as in the poems he started to write around 1945. Unlike the later verse, written in the advent of the eruption of the armed struggle and thus after Neto had been imprisoned for his poetry and political militancy, the earlier poems are works of social protest rather than of rebellion. . . .

["Adeus à hora da largada," translated as] "Farewell at the Hour of Parting" . . . is an outright and unqualified denunciation of Portugal's unwelcome presence in Angolan territory. Although the colonial power is never directly identified, it becomes emphatically clear that the poet deems it responsible for most of his society's ills, the most conspicuous of which is probably forced labor. Contract workers may well be the only people who are "burning" their lives in the coffee plantations of Angola and Sao Tomé, but Neto does not consider their ordeal more degrading than anybody else's and there are, as he shows in the poem, many other individuals getting burned by the fires of colonialism. Large segments of the populace feel alienated from life and attempt to get from alcohol, parties, and dancing what they are otherwise unable to acquire. Communication has broken down to such a degree that dialogue is almost impossible between parent and child. The whole nation seems to have fallen victim to a situation it obviously did not create and over which it has little or no control. The chaotic state of human relations, perhaps more than anything else, appears to be a vivid reflection of the extent to which society has disintegrated.

"Farewell," however, is not a pessimistic work. In fact, like most of Neto's poetry, it is infused with a dominant element of hope. The author does use "Farewell" as a means of exposing Portugal's policies in his native land, of showing how the people and resources of Angola are being exploited by a country that claims to be in a fraternal crusade to "civilize" Africa. As he does so, he evidently cannot avoid emphasizing the atrocities being committed in the name of religion or civilization. But he also utilizes the poem as a means to alert his compatriots to the realities under which they live as well as to rally them in an attempt to reacquire the autonomy they lost to Portugal or, rather, the sovereignty the Portuguese usurped from them.

A. R. Brás. Ufahumu. 11, 2 (Fall 1981–Winter 1982), pp. 82, 87

The poems collected in Sacred Hope span several years in Neto's career as well as various stages in the struggle for national liberation. Consequently, the themes range from [the] need to use valuable elements from the past to shape the future to reflections on the deprivations and sufferings of the people under colonial rule. . . .

For Neto, the historical experience of the people is the first condition of art, hence he writes from a position of absolute immersion in their plight. His voice is their voice and it reveals the various dimensions of their plight under colonial tutelage. In this respect, there is, in the poems, a strong sense of realism which is able to capture the subtle nuances of life among the common folk while constantly relating this to the relations of dominance and subordination which define the colonial equation. . . .

Much as he is engaged with the realities of the colonial "present," Neto's verse is also a means of positing a cultural antithesis to the hegemony of colonial values. Thus, the landscape of his verse is furnished by prominent landmarks in Angola in particular and Africa in general. The River Congo, the Kalahari Desert, and the Maiombe Forest become means of authenticating experience and reinforcing the poet's identification with his people and their roots. In this respect, Neto's verse shares with Négritude poetry a certain nostalgic re-creation of Africa and its vital rhythms. But for Neto, affirmation of racial cultural identity is a complement to liberation action, not a substitute for it. . . .

The poet cherishes freedom, not for its own sake and at all costs but in the context of his people's struggle to regain their dignity after the years of humiliation and denigration. Consequently, even in prison, the poet's attitude is one of stoic defiance and pride towards his persecutors. . . .

Yet in spite of the repression of armed tyranny, hope emerges as the dominant theme in most of Neto's poems. The constant reaffirmation of optimism and faith in the future is not just an anodyne to drown the pangs of present adversity but a way of imbuing the sacrifices implicit in the struggle for freedom with a sense of purpose. The struggle becomes a painful process of building for future success; looking forward to a time when the poet/combatant shall lose his anonymity and emerge distinguished in a new "catalogue of human glory."

Neto's poetry is characterized by a general contemplative tone which is unhurried, painstaking, and shrewd in its attempt not to compromise the organic proximity between the poet and his people. Consequently, the emotions which permeate and exude from his verse are those of patriotic heroism and sympathetic identification with those who bear the burden of oppression.

Chidi Amuta. The Theory of African Literature
(London: Zed Books, 1989), pp. 186–89

A space where the dark is tempered by the light, despair by hope, the past by the future, the individual's ambitions by the collectivity's determinations: this is the essential provision of Agostinho Neto's poetry. Combat poetry? This would be a reductive, even condescending characterization, and would tend to minimize the stature of one of the twentieth century's most important African poets. It is a perilous term for a perilous genre—a term, among others, we *might* apply, but one that seems in any case ineluctably associated with Neto's name . . . and one that therefore provokes us to see in him a nucleus around which critics have gathered other poets of this modern genre we call militant or guerrilla poetry. Neto's importance in relationship to this genre, and his poetic gifts apart from it, therefore call for a mainstreaming of his literary contributions. "Protest poetry" might, however, more aptly describe his ouevre; the term is certainly a somewhat better representation of his content than "guerrilla poetry" or "poetry of combat" would allow. But whatever the word used to sum up that content, it is best to see contextually how this talented poet fuses his ideologies with his structures, and intertextually, how he avoids the diatribes, the invectives, and the stereotypically strident rhetoric of most guerrilla poetry in a way scarcely imitated by his poetic "counterparts."

In his earliest poems . . . Neto establishes the juxtapositions of dark versus light, of despair versus hope, of individual versus collectivity; and these oppositions, especially that of the self versus the group, will be the leitmotif of his life's work, collected under the general title of *Sagrada esperança*, or *Sacred Hope*. And however Marxist his readers find the theme of confraternity inherent in such poems as "Farewell at the Hour of Parting" to be, the oversoul, the spareness, the structural as well as the grammatical and syntactic fusions, all subvert any tendency toward the doctrinaire that are potentially inherent in a bare ideological approach; and these traits consequently guarantee the poem's aesthetic success.

Janis L. Pallister. StTCL. 15, 1 (Winter 1991), pp. 137–38

NGUGI WA THIONG'O (1938–   )

KENYA

[Ngugi wa Thiong'o's] strength as a novelist proceeds from the way in which he encrusts his political vision with material derived from his own Kenyan background—the peasant values which are the real values as opposed to those new First World values which are taken on by the blacks who become the leaders in the postindependence circumstance. These are contemptible people so far as Ngugi is concerned because of the way they exploit their own kind and, secondly, for their repudiation of the heroes of the revolution who brought about those circumstances in which they are able to act as they do. Thus, Dedan Kimathi is Ngugi's legitimate hero: his vision was straightforward, unflinching, uncompromising, ultimately successful. But now he has been repudiated. . . .

Weep Not, Child, the first published novel but the second written, brings Ngugi to his central theme which is the struggle for Kenyan independence and the effect of the struggle on the lives of individuals within the Kenyan context. *Weep Not, Child* is less complex in its form than *A Grain of Wheat*, and less complex still than *Petals of Blood*. But the theme is the same where we find reference to various historical revolutionary activities before the Mau Mau independence movement got under way in the 1950s. In both *Weep Not, Child* and *A Grain of Wheat*, the causes and the prosecution of Mau Mau aspirations are dramatized. . . .

The materials of *Petals of Blood*, Ngugi's fourth novel, are related to those of the earlier novels but are more abundantly conveyed. In a novel almost double the size of *A Grain of Wheat*, he widens and deepens his treatment of themes which he has narrated and dramatized before—themes related to education, both formal and informal; religion, both Christian and customary; the alienation of the land viewed from the historical point of view and as a process which continues in the present; the struggle for independence and the price paid to achieve it. And to these themes he has added artistic representation of the betrayal of the independence movement and its authors, the nature and cost of modernity as this coincides with the emergence of a Kenyan middle class, and of the need for the creation of a cultural liberation struggle fostered by the peasants and workers. This is a political novel in the widest sense. . . .

Concern over the land is a central theme in the novel as it has been in the earlier ones. Ngugi is concerned about what has happened to the land: how the African has been alienated from the land first by the imperial colonialists who helped themselves to the land, paying into the pockets of a few whatever worth they consigned to it, and subsequently by a class of African landlords who, because of their connections with the forces of world capitalism, are able to manage the purchase price. And it is the question of how to reachieve the land that links the Kenyan people with the struggles of other movements in the Third World. The struggle has an historic as well as contemporary dimension and more than once in the book the unity of experience and purpose is conveyed in references to "Chaka . . . Toussaint . . . Samori . . . Nat Turner . . . Arap Manyei . . . Mondlane . . . Cabral . . . Kimathi . . . Nkrumah" and others.

G. D. Killam. *An Introduction to the Writings of Ngugi*
(London: Heinemann, 1980), pp. 14–15, 19, 96, 102

A Grain of Wheat is a . . . complex novel, both in style and language. The simple narrative technique has gone; we have moved very far from the structure of traditional stories; and though the texture of the language is in some cases thin, the simplicity of the earlier novels is frequently replaced by a complexity which surpasses what many other writers have written. . . .

A Grain of Wheat is above all a book which deals with the effects of great events of the external world on individual people. The events portrayed take place in the context of the Mau Mau war and the coming of Uhuru, but the writer focuses our attention not on the events as abstractions, but on their effects on the individual soul and the individual mind, and on person-to-person relationships. . . .

In terms of varieties of language, the novel is limited. In choosing Standard English, Ngugi has deliberately shunned the linguistic experiments of [Chinua] Achebe and [Gabriel] Okara, who both try to reflect African modes of thinking. In consequence, linguistic differentiation as a method of depicting characters is minimal in *A Grain of Wheat*. There is no noticeable difference between the language of Gikonyo and that of Mugo, Mumbi, or even Karanja. The question of their educational or social background is irrelevant. Whether educated or uneducated, Ngugi's characters speak meticulous English, the language of the author.

Whether the writer is translating or quoting his speakers verbatim are not questions that cross our minds as we read through the book. . . .

If any African novel has a claim to complexity, it is *A Grain of Wheat*. . . . Though the language itself is not labored and complicated, Ngugi's narrative technique is sufficiently complex to make the book one of the most sophisticated in the African literature so far published. If the narrative structure is complex, the response it calls forth in the reader is equally complex. The reader's attitude to characters and his impressions about the thread of events keep on shifting as the narrative shifts from one person to another, from one event to another, from one focus to another. He may dislike a character in one part of the novel; but in the next he may like him better, or at least learn to understand or accept the character's faults. The characters themselves get a better understanding of themselves and others, of their own motives and other people's motives, as the story progresses to its end.

Emmanuel Ngara. *Stylistic Criticism and the African Novel*
(London: Heinemann, 1982), pp. 81, 86, 97–98

Ngugi was arrested on New Year's Eve, 1978. The precise reasons for the imprisonment have never been revealed since no charges were laid.

Detained: A Writer's Prison Diary is Ngugi's "prison memoir," the record of his incarceration. The importance of *Detained* to an understanding of Ngugi's career, both in the direction it has taken since his release from prison and in accounting for the intellectual process which leads him to his present position, cannot be overemphasized. It described the purposes of the detainers and the effect of detention on the sensibility of the detained person. Committed to the struggle of alleviating the suffering of the generality of people, recognizing the connection between himself and his fellow detainees and, as well, other advocates in other cultures, the detained person must find the spiritual and psychological resources to withstand the punitive methods of his jailers. . . .

The political theme in the novel [*A Grain of Wheat*] is a leitmotif to the human interchanges the novel explores. *A Grain of Wheat* is Ngugi's most finished piece of writing in conventional fictional terms. Here his concern for individual sensibilities, shaped by but in important ways isolated from social issues larger than the individual, is conveyed. Figures in these novels are participants in the events which shape the destiny of the country by accident rather than choice, through ignorance rather than apprehension. Ngugi's compassion for their bewilderment is profound, the more so, perhaps, because of their ignorance.

And, as with the other novels, the ending forecasts the beginning of the next book. . . .

A Grain of Wheat . . . forecasts at its close the development of the political context in which Kenyan will be ranged against Kenyan, and in his recent writing, produced from 1977 to 1982, Ngugi evokes a wholly contemporary setting, theme, and treatment. The setting is the Kenya created out of [Jomo] Kenyatta's repudiation of his revolutionary sensibility and his collusion with former political rivals and international finance capitalists. The analysis [Ngugi] offers is presented in *Detained [A Writer's Prison Diary]*, the diary he kept in prison, in which he records the experience of being incarcerated for almost a year following the publication of *Petals of Blood* and the production of *Ngaanhika Ndeenda [Ithaako ria Ngerekano*, translated as *I Will Marry When I Want]*. . . .

   Petals of Blood is a pivotal work in the Ngugi canon, since it marks his last major piece of writing in English before he took the decision to turn to Kikuyu as his medium of expression. The novel is cast in the form of a crime thriller and opens with the murder of three industrial and economic leaders of the new Kenya—Chui, Mzigo, and Kimeria—and the arrest of the four principal suspects—Munira, Abdulla, Karega, and Wanja. . . . The narrative of the novel shifts backwards and forwards in time, adopting a variety of narrative and temporal perspectives—thus the present-time action of the novel takes place over about ten days; the lives of the principal characters are revealed over a span of twelve years; and, as an expanded canvas, moving backwards and forwards in time, the history of Kenya is conveyed from precolonial times (where Ngugi records the mythic basis of Kenyan society in ways with which we are familiar from the earlier novels) and especially from the beginnings of European exploitation of Kenya which began in the 1890s. . . .

   Petals of Blood is a novel about faith and the possibilities of the workers and peasants reasserting their traditional role as producers of the national wealth which they will have to create for their own use. The rhetoric of the novel is subsumed by Ngugi's harmonizing of the characters in the exemplary roles they are given. Rejecting a number of possible abstract solutions to the depressed state of the people, Ngugi places his faith in the militant unity of peasants and workers—whose collective voice is heard off camera at the close of the novel but who thunder into the fray in *Devil on the Cross* [first published in Kikuyu as *Caitaani Mutharaba-ni*].

G. D. Killam. The Writing of East and Central Africa
(London: Heinemann, 1984), pp. 124, 133–36

In *A Grain of Wheat*, Ngugi shows his socialist inclinations by focusing his attention on the common people and their predicament. The novel depicts the events leading to the coming of Uhuru, but the focus is not on the major events that are recorded in history books. [Jomo] Kenyatta is mentioned, but only as part of the history of the people of Kenya—Ngugi does not project the interests and views of outstanding figures like Kenyatta and other people in the upper echelons of society. The book talks about independence celebrations, but we are not shown the celebrations which took place in Nairobi, the capital city of Kenya. Rather, we are taken to an insignificant place out in the country— Thabai. Similarly, the characters we deal with are small village people and members of the peasant class—Gikonyo, Gitogo, Mumbi, Karanja, and, of course, their British overlords.

   We witness here colonial Kenya giving way to the independent Republic of Kenya which is the result of the sacrifices of the people of Kenya who suffered and died for freedom's sake. As the Bible quotation prefixed to the beginning of chapter 14 suggests, there was in Kenya "a new heaven and a new earth; for the first heaven and the first earth were passed away." But the crucial question is whether Uhuru has brought forth much fruit as a result of the people who died. In other words, has independence brought about a change of system for the better?

Emmanuel Ngara. *Art and Ideology in the African Novel*
(London: Heinemann, 1985), pp. 59–60

The only fictional work I have found which elevates female circumcision to a position of thematic central importance, *The River Between*, has the issue serve as battleground in the clash between conservative tribal elements and the patriarchal Christian church. . . .

Ngugi's novel, in any case, deals with female circumcision not from a feminist, but from a humanist and progressive standpoint, leading its readers gently and ironically to understand that male insistence on female "rites" is displaced impotence and is ultimately deconstructive. He shows, for example, how the brothers are mistaken in viewing circumcision as a still unsullied source of cultural integrity from which strength can be drawn in preparation for the battles ahead, to repossess the land. Ngugi further links this futile hope to renewal of the martial image, in turn tied to the vehement insistence on female mutilation. For without removal of the clitoris, without "purity," it is assumed that female sexual energy would threaten the tribe with destruction.

Tobe Levin. In Carole Boyce Davies and Anne Adams Graves, eds.
Ngambika: Studies of Women in African Literature
(Trenton, N. J.: Africa World Press, Inc., 1986), pp. 209, 211

Devil on the Cross is the story of Jacinta Wariinga, ostensibly narrated by the "Giccandi Player" or "Prophet of Justice" at the request of Jacinta's mother, "so that each may pass judgement only when he knows the whole truth." In many respects the pattern of Wariinga's life resembles that of Wanja in *Petals of Blood*. Both approximate to the exemplary tale of Kareendi, told by Wariinga as the story of "a girl like me . . . or . . . any other girl in Nairobi." Sexual exploitation and discrimination are dominant factors in Kareendi's life. She is given few opportunities to develop her potential and is constantly at the mercy of men for her livelihood. She is very often reduced to the cursed "cunt" Wanja protests about in *Petals of Blood*. . . .

Ngugi portrays sexual confrontation between men and women as part of the destructive rivalry on which contemporary Kenyan capitalism thrives, and through which injustices and inequalities are perpetuated.

The ending of *Devil on the Cross* is optimistic insofar as it offers possibilities of new social orders in the future, but it is not conclusively "happy." Both Wariinga and Gaturia go through enlightenment and liberation in the process of finding themselves and each other but, like the ill-fated lovers of Ngugi's earlier novels, they are to find that the larger social forces impinge on their personal relationship. The fact that there is no simple "happy" ending reinforces the point, made in *Petals of Blood*, that "La Luta Continua!" As Ngugi has said: "The problem of men and women cannot be satisfactorily solved under the present system. Sexual relations are the reflection of an unequal economic system." Wariinga refuses to settle down to marriage with Gaturia, because she discovers that her prospective father-in-law is her seducer, "the Rich Old Man from Ngorika." When Wangari delivers her condemnation of the thieves at the Devil's Feast, "her voice carried the power and authority of a people's judge." Wariinga also speaks with the voice of "a people's judge" when she condemns the Rich Old Man to die. Wariinga's execution of her oppressor, like Wanja's execution of Kimeria in *Petals of Blood*, is more than personal revenge. It carries the force of communal retribution and justice.

Both Wariinga and Wanja rise above the tale of Kareendi because they do not finally accept defeat and humiliation. Having come to the realization that there are more than the "two worlds" of "the eater" and "the eaten," Wariinga commits herself to the "third world": "the world of the revolutionary overthrow of the system of eating and being eaten."

Ngugi has tailored the content, form, and style of *Devil on the Cross* for his intended Kikuyu-speaking worker and peasant audience. His only concession to his foreign readers is to have made an English translation. Properly the work should be read aloud and communally in its original Kikuyu. An individual private reading of the English version can obviously not do justice to a work whose principal significance lies in its use of the Kikuyu language. But, in a novel which is so intimately concerned with Ngugi's individual and communal identity, it is also significant that images of women are such a prominent feature. Wariinga the female protagonist of *Devil on the Cross*, is the successor to a line of heroines who have become increasingly central to the structure and meaning of Ngugi's novels.

Jennifer Evans. In Eldred Durosimi Jones, ed. Women in African Literature
Today (Trenton, N. J.: Africa World Press, 1987), pp. 131–32, 136–37

A Grain of Wheat is situated on the border between a messianic and intellectualist field of vision, by the late 1960s representing decolonization as a failure, and a more concretely committed socialism, casting the decolonizing process in similarly radical but more soberly material and historical terms. The novel leaves the reader with an image of hope, embodied in Gikonyo's carving of a stool in the shape of a pregnant woman, but also with the fear that, as represented, the victory of British colonialism will prove to have been a Pyrrhic one. It would only be in his fourth novel, *Petals of Blood*—a novel that it would take him seven full years to write—that Ngugi would be able to find a less intellectualist register for his new political sensibility. And even here, in the formulaic quality of the final pages, in which the specter of proletarian internationalism is rather implausibly seen to be arising in the collective political imagination of Kenyan workers and peasants, there is the suggestion of a residual intellectualism.

Nevertheless, in several respects, *Petals of Blood* is definitive of the new politically committed writing that has emerged in Africa since 1970. Set mostly in the countryside, it portrays a community struggling against an environment that a combination of factors have contrived to render sterile and harsh: drought and desertification, colonial neglect and despoliation, postcolonial mismanagement and venality. To the members of this community, independence is only a word: its substantive impact on their lives has been virtually nonexistent. Between these villagers and an authentic independence there stand daunting obstacles—economic, historical, political, psychological. Yet through the whole novel there is Ngugi's insistence upon the transformability of existing conditions. Meaningful social change will come, he suggests: perhaps not tomorrow nor the next day, nor even the day after that, but still it will come, for "the peasants, aided by the workers, small traders and small landowners . . . [have] mapped out the path" for themselves to follow.

Neil Lazarus. *Resistance in Postcolonial African Fiction*
(New Haven, Conn.: Yale University Press, 1990), p. 213

Matigari ma Njiruungi, literally meaning "the patriots who survived the bullets," is the name of the protagonist in Ngugi wa Thiong'o's latest novel [*Matigari ma Njiruungi*, published in English as *Matigari*]. . . .

Matigari ma Njiruungi, who was Settler Howard Williams's servant during the colonial days, decides to end his exploitation by shooting Williams, who happens to be speaking on the telephone when Matigari reaches out for the settler's gun. It is John Boy, another servant, who saves his colonial master. Suddenly both Williams and John Boy wrestle with Matigari, but he escapes through the window. Thereafter the struggle between the two opponents continues in the forest, and after many years of hunting each other, Matigari, armed with an AK-47, eliminates his two enemies. Following his victory, he hides his weapons near a *mugumo* (fig) tree and is determined to occupy Williams's house, which he claims as his own. Upon arrival, however, he finds John Boy Jr. in occupancy, with the blessing of Williams Jr., from whom he has bought the house.

Throughout the novel Matigari is depicted as a disillusioned and frustrated revolutionary who, after killing his two enemies and thus contributing to the liberation of his country, finds himself grappling with the problems of postindependence neocolonialism. In his effort to understand his postcolonial country, he approaches many people, seeking to know how and where he can find truth and justice. . . . Before embarking on his search for those qualities, he endeavors to reestablish links with his family, whom he has not seen for many years while engaged in his country's fight for liberation from colonialism. Among the people he comes across as he searches for his family members are the young boy Muriuki, the trade-union worker Ngaruro wa Kiriro, the young woman Guthera, and the young man Macharia; it is with these people from different backgrounds that he discusses the socioeconomic and political problems plaguing his supposedly independent and free country. These individuals accompany and support Matigari as he seeks to regain what he regards as his rightful property: namely, Settler Williams's house. In his exertions to secure the house, Matigari is arrested and jailed; he later escapes with help of Guthera and is subsequently committed to a mental hospital, assumed by the authorities to be a lunatic. Nonetheless, he succeeds in escaping from the hospital as well, and rumor begins to circulate in the country about his greatness and superhuman (even divine) qualities; there are people who elevate his image to that of Christ and predict his return to save their country from exploitation and oppression. Thus, as the moment of Matigari's long-awaited return to Settler Williams's (now John Boy Jr.'s) house becomes imminent, throngs of people, including members of the security forces, surge toward the house. To facilitate his trip, Matigari seizes a Mercedes-Benz belonging to the adulterous wife of the Minister of Truth and Justice. He evades the dragnet of security forces who are in pursuit of this mysterious and elusive "criminal." The climax of the satire is reached when Matigari's pursuers at long last trap him and are certain of his impending capture.

Matigari's nonviolent approach to finding truth and justice for himself and his people proves increasingly futile, given the state's widespread violent repression of dissent and workers' strikes. He therefore resolves to resume armed resistance in order to establish justice based on truth, which he believes to be an essential cornerstone for the true liberation of his people. Toward the end he seeks to retrieve his AK-47, which he had hidden. However, he is unable to do so due to a trap by the security forces. He manages to elude his pursuers when he drives the car into Williams's house, from which he eventually escapes in the prevailing confusion caused by the car crash and the subsequent explosion and fire. In the ensuing manhunt Guthera is shot and severely wounded, but Matigari carries her as he slips through the security dragnet yet again. The novel concludes with Matigari still intent on resuming his struggle, especially after Macarie has retrieved the AK-47 for Matigari's use.

In sum, the novel is a powerful satire, couched in strong language intended to question the meaning and validity of postcolonial African claims to socialism in the midst of capital accumulations by the few, to democracy under a one-party system, to maintenance of law and order under political repression, to democratic institutions under authoritarian rule. In the Kikuyu . . . version of the novel, for instance, the author questions the democratic nature of the KKK, which is supposed to stand for Kiama Kiria Kirathana (meaning "the ruling party"). In the English translation Wangui wa Goro offers an excellent rendition of the Kikuyu original. Ideally, of course, the novel should be read in both languages for a full appreciation of the richness of Ngugi's latest important contribution to African literature.

Jidlaph Kamoche. *WLT*. 64, 2 (Spring 1990), pp. 348–49

Together, *Decolonising the Mind* and *Devil on the Cross* propose different approaches to the novel. First of all, Ngugi insists that a literary invention like "the novel" can be used, regardless of its origins, either to promote and reinforce repressive ideologies or to undo them. Second, he insists that novels can be produced and consumed in elitist or populist ways. Furthermore, Ngugi's essay and narrative suggest that orality can be an idiom out of which writers write and through which they target a specific audience rather than a set of traits or an atmosphere represented by writers to suggest an African identity. These two texts thus challenge the notion of the novel and of orality as essences. . . .

Ngugi depicts language, not surprisingly, as dynamic, differentiated, determined by one's class and one's gender; it is one of several registers of wealth and class. Levels of power in current society can be surmised by the foreign languages one knows and particularly by one's attitude toward them. Thus Wangari, the least powerful of the travelers in *Devil*, speaks only Kikuyu during the story—we guess that she does not speak English or speaks little of it. On the other hand, Mwireri wa Mukiraai knows English quite well; he has studied at foreign universities and is schooled in money-making schemes. Gatuiria, the young composer and student intellectual, also mixes English and Kikuyu but wishes, the narrator tells us, that his speech were rid of the foreign tongue. . . . The so-called modern thieves in the forum of the competition—attended by foreigners and for the benefit of these international visitors—speak English, of course. Language, like the number of women, cars, and guns a man owns, is a sign of status. Thus while choice of language and mode of language do not necessarily measure honesty, they are predictors of the dimensions of crime (when crime exists), since they correlate to one's class and access to international institutions: the names of buildings, banks, moneymaking enterprises are all in English. . . .

Now, "oral" language in any written text is obviously neither oral nor—were such a thing possible—a transcript of standard speech, characterized by rhythms, pauses, tones, and unconventional sounds. What is usually meant by the "orality" of . . . Ngugi [is] the proverbs, analogies, and the cadences of phrasing, which literary convention holds to be oral. In the case of *Devil on the Cross*, as Ngugi describes it, the intended audience and the probable means of distribution and consumption of the novel in Kenya seemed to require "oral" language. . . . *Devil* was written to be read aloud for people schooled in oral stories. Here, orality is not "preyed upon," a resource *for* the narrative, inside its frame, "possessed" by it. Oral language is thus not the object of representation that can be read as quaint and *passéiste* [of the past]. Orality here means the language and tradition in which the narrative is articulated, the medium in which Ngugi's audience will hear this story. Intended for telling or reading aloud, *Devil* does not showcase a neat orality. Proverbs, repetitions, riddles, "songs," and so on reveal the addressee and are not uniquely referential. . . .

Decolonising the Mind and *Devil on the Cross* suggest . . . that "oral tradition" is not the sign of a coveted set of values; it is rather a set of aesthetic conventions with which Ngugi's audience is conversant and from which he chooses several elements. Just as he chose multivoiced narration in preceding novels, here he chooses proverbs, parables, and the motif of the journey. *Devil* thus gains a particular currency and comprehensibility by associating itself with traditional storytelling, but it does not muster authority from traditional high genres. It cannot in any case rely on the questionable authority outside the protagonist (and, we infer, outside the narratives themselves), for Ngugi's novel proposes a caricature of power. As I read it, *Devil* does not conceive of orality as a source either of authority or of precious authenticity to be held and treasured. It does not use the "oral tradition" as a bulwark to inspire confidence or action by association with a people's past grandeur or wisdom and virtue. It is neither the "source of truth" nor an exemplary quality of African culture to be retreated into or represented textually; rather, it offers verbal means and procedures for constructing and analyzing an issue. *Devil* treats the same issues that are at the heart of other Ngugi texts, but it does so in parables. In so doing, it demonstrates that oral traditions are not synonymous with static codes and principles.

Devil is deconstructive and reconstructive in other ways as well. Not only does it take orality out of the past, but . . . it focuses on the constructedness of the order of things, their inner workings and tensions. Ngugi's exposition of the relationship between the Kenyan thieves and international capital is masterful, as is the revelation of their vulnerability in the jealous dispute about belly size and in the thieves' anger at being duped by one of their own who has stolen their unsatisfied wives and offered them counterfeit English schooling for their children. These cleavages in their ranks are analogous to the "appeals to tribe and religion," which the thieves themselves use to divide peasants and workers.

Eileen Julien. *African Novels and the Question of Orality* (Bloomington: Indiana University Press, 1992), pp. 142, 144–46

NTIRU, RICHARD (1946–   )

UGANDA

[Richard] Ntiru is a very society-conscious poet, and is always exploring and exposing something of the dichotomy that exists in the human situation, something of the shadow between the idea and the reality—in our attitudes and intentions and wishes and performance. On the whole he is much more in control of his material and expression in the shorter poem; in the longer poem he has a tendency to disappear into imprecision.

Ntiru's indebtedness to other literatures is a conscious one. There is undisguised borrowing from other poets: significantly from T. S. Eliot, but also from [William] Blake, Claude McKay, and others. Sometimes it is for the sake of parody, with very refreshing effect when it works, as in "Ojukwu's Prayer" (compared with Claude McKay's "If We Must Die"). In "Chorus of Public Men," which is modeled on T. S. Eliot's "The Hollow Men," Ntiru presents us with dissatisfied, worn-out men who are much more concrete than Eliot's shadowy personages. The social setting is much more immediate, and for the East African reader the poem may easily have more appeal than its prototype.

Timothy Wangusa. In Eldred Durosimi Jones, ed.
African Literature Today. 6 (1973), p. 50

[In *Tensions*, the] content, the themes, are African, but it is exceptional to find a particular atmosphere or sense of locale. Where in [J. P.] Clark and [Gabriel] Okara we have the rivers of Ijawland, where in Kofi Awoonor the Atlantic visibly washes the coasts of Ghana, where [Jared] Angira and [Onyango] Ogutu constantly reflect the shape and feel of Western Kenya and where Okot [p'Bitek], [Okello] Oculi, and [Joseph] Buruga reflect the rolling grasslands of Uganda, in the early Ntiru all this is lacking. The home landscape has either made no impression on him (which is unthinkable) or it represents an area of his memory drowned for the moment in a flood of academic and philosophic matter.

Nor does the humorous find much room in Ntiru's work. The mirth of a [Wole] Soyinka in his comic mode or the bitter laughter of an Okot or Angira are not heard. For Ntiru life seems a gloomy, rather joyless passage through time. There are serious flaws in man's vision and it would be immoral to laugh and let them pass. If modern man can wallow in wealth while his brother starves, he must be told about it; and this is how Ntiru's art is defined, for its basis is moral rather than sensual, its urge is to censure rather than to celebrate. Modern man is discarding a joyful response to the mystery of birth and cultivating the murderous practice of ripping children from the womb. He must therefore be upbraided for it. The world failed to understand the justice of the Biafran cause and must therefore be scolded.

Yet according to Ntiru's "Portrait of the Little Self," neither the poet nor his censure can change much, for this piece gives us a picture of frustrated ambition, cancelled initiative, useless speculation, and a web of those tensions implied in the volume's title. The poet can neither laugh nor cry to any effect. He can neither address society with profit nor usefully stay silent. What remains, according to the poem, is for the artist to lie in a narrow bed and contemplate the "silence beyond silence" of the grave. . . .

Ntiru is better elsewhere and it would be unfair to suggest that this poem is typical of *Tensions* as a whole. The more tangibly human, earthy subjects suit him better, even if he believes that his strengths run towards a more abstract style of verse. One example is "The Happiness of a Mother," written "for aborters and abortionists who take Malthus seriously." The joy of birth is described as something at once intensely private and personal, yet social too, and the point is made that life, even crippled life, is always better than the tomb. . . .

The image of poverty amidst luxury is apt to spark a strong response in Ntiru. The language of "The Pauper" is concrete and visual, and the whole portrait is edged with a coloring of human sympathy. The poor man leans "on a leafless tree / Nursing the jiggers that shrivel" his bottom. He trudges on "horny pads," "Gullied like the soles of modern shoes," all under the eye of an inscrutable God. . . .

"Morning Arrows," dedicated to Okello Oculi, upbraids the sun for unveiling each day a world filled with pain and frustration, shining a fierce light on every wart that scars mankind's face. This is a good imitation of the hectoring Oculian style, but gaining from its control under the reins of Ntiru's discipline. The rough and tumble energy is here, the bold phrasing and repetition; yet the poem enjoys a restraint, a submission to discipline and decorum that makes this essentially an Ntiru poem.

Adrian Roscoe. *Uhuru's Fire: African Literature East to South*
(Cambridge: Cambridge University Press, 1977), pp. 108, 110–11

The poetry of Richard Ntiru ranges over satire of situation, invective and raillery, ironic praise, direct moral exhortation, elegies and laments, disquisitions on love (rather than love lyrics), and mystical, symbolic, and prophetic scenes. Like Taban lo Liyong, Ntiru has a wide-ranging acquaintance with world literature, both imaginative and didactic. Like Okello Oculi, he expresses disgust for institutions and people as he lampoons them. Like Christopher Okigbo he aspires to a mystic communion with a symbolic virgin. . . .

The objects of his satire and castigation are both social and metaphysical. He rails against the venality of politicians, civil servants, large corporations, and all those who seek to control and oppress the human spirit. But he also expresses dissatisfaction with the gods for their indifference to suffering and injustice. The best of his poems are probably those that present a single scene of suffering or oppression and those that employ an anaphoric rhetoric to execrate abuses—that is, the poems that come closest to [David] Rubadiri models. The weakest are the Oculian diatribes that wander in focus and oscillate in tone.

"Introduction" is a good example of the narrative vignette. Its satiric object is the person who emphasizes status and appearance rather than worth and performance. Like many of Ntiru's works it is cast in the form of a dramatic monologue, spoken in a rather irritable, exasperated tone of voice. "The Latest Defector" is another vignette in monologue, this time more abstract in its diction and less sharp in its visual details. Its satiric target is the hypocrisy of sexual relations, with perhaps also the hint of a political application. "The Pauper" is addressed to a representative pauper, but more as a literary fiction than as a mimetic re-creation of an actual encounter. The satiric target is multiple: the godhead, society, tourists, politicians, and the author himself, for all are guilty of knowledge and even inquisitiveness unmatched by practical reform. . . .

"Ojukwu's Prayer," dating from the time of the Biafran War, is one of the best of the "literary fiction" type of dramatic monologues. . . . The structure is filled in with images of pseudo-philanthropic gestures, increasing in intensity from throwing a bare bone to a dog to being slaughtered by Russian bombs. One of the charitable gestures is the supply of high-protein manufactured food by Western relief agencies. This ill-informed policy is savagely ridiculed in "'Formula Two,'" a vivid descriptive account of the operation of relief agencies in Biafra. . . . The infilling images are of bones and skeletons as the poem builds up a scene of men, women, and children—or, rather, women with children in the front, sullen men resentful of their ignominy behind—lining up for "their rationed taste / of the wholesome high-protein relief meal." . . .

Ntiru's longer, more ambitious poems are less successful. They employ the high-pitched, strained tones of Okello Oculi combined sometimes with the surrealistic allegory of Bahadur Tejani. The allegory is fitful, being conveyed largely in isolated patches such as—to take examples from "The Secret of the Skeleton"—"the last hurdle / which is also the first hurdle / in the circular race" or "The Watchman of Dark Cave between Light and Darkness / lifted his Rod of Seven Eyes" or "Who would dally at the River of Continuity." Ntiru's characteristic intensity and his horror of sexual violence emerge strongly from this poem. But his imagemaking power is insufficient to sustain the kind of allegory of life and death that he aspires to. On its smaller scale, the failure is akin to that of Gabriel Okara in "The Fisherman's Invocation." But it is an honorable failure insofar as Ntiru is constantly pushing beyond the limits of what he knows he can accomplish.

[K. L.] Goodwin. In G. D. Killam, ed. *The Writing of East and Central Africa* (London: Heinemann, 1984), pp. 219–21

Richard Ntiru's intense poetic career provides the reader of modern East African poetry written in English with a very good example of the versatility of this tradition. He, like most of his contemporaries of this region, handles a rich variety of themes which range from the personal and descriptive to the near-abstract which, in his hands, find expression through fitting pseudo-existentialist linguistic structures. But most importantly, Ntiru is a poet who seems to be irresistibly attracted to the extra-personal public events which impinge on the lives of both his contemporaries and society at large. Thus, basically, in spite of the wide and varied thematic territory within which his imagination operates, the unmistakable poetic forte of Ntiru is the sympathetic appraisal of the social and political realities of his society. This focus is always directed toward the manner in which the new sociopolitical order ushered in by *uhuru* or political freedom from colonialism has affected or failed to affect the fortunes of the generality of the people in the society. . . .

The beauty of Ntiru's poetry lies mainly in some specific areas. In the first place, he is able to explore with a protean turn of mind each new topic he decides to focus his attention on in each new poem. This versatility he is able to achieve through a constant correlation of imagery, music, and thought, the three chief means by which, in the words of Ezra Pound, the language of poetry could be charged "with meaning to the utmost possible degree." In addition, his poetry displays both a keen ear for rhythm and a mature sense of the musical potential of words. All these qualities give the reader of the poet's work a pleasurable sense of a harmonious blend of euphony and sense.

A. Rasheed Yesufu. *CE&S*. 8, 2 (Spring 1986), pp. 94–95

Ntiru's dominant vision of human nature is that of futility, loneliness, insecurity, and ultimate meaninglessness. This view of human life in society is definitely influenced by his knowledge of modern European literary attitudes. This fact creates an initial problem for one who comes to his work with the singleminded expectation of finding the more popular perception of man held by his contemporaries in East Africa. The question an uninformed reader of modern African literature is bound to ask is, "Is it actually compatible to the African psyche and social nature to feel a sense of futility, loneliness, and insecurity in the midst of the much-avowed communalistic spirit of Africa?" The answer to this question is yes, because the society about which Ntiru writes is not the pristine type which thrived on a communalistic ethos. Rather, it is a world similar to those portrayed by Ayi Kwei Armah in *The Beautyful Ones Are Not Yet Born*, by Kofi Awoonor in *This Earth My Brother*, and by other writers who mirror the modern soul in its perennial confrontation with the disillusionment of its time. It is also a society which, according to [critic Rosette] Francis, has undergone "an accelerated degree of change that produces profound alterations and tensions." These changes in society, the way man reacts to them, and how he now behaves toward his fellow men account for his sense of futility, loneliness, and insecurity. Since, as [Alexander] Pope remarked in *An Essay on Man*, the proper study of mankind is man, Ntiru studies man in his society to investigate the actual nature of the human mind.

In order to give man a local dimension compatible with his reflection of his society, Ntiru often operates along a line similar to that of his contemporary Jared Angira. However, in place of Angira's bellicose Marxist dichotomy, Ntiru sees men in his society as divided into two economic classes. These classes are not exclusive, since one could easily move from the lower to the higher one, as in "Flashback." But it is always clear that he sympathizes with the "paupers" of his society. Hence, in spite of the absence of the revolutionary zeal of Angira's language, the tone of Ntiru's work is never mistaken in its purely moral concern. He is concerned not with revolution but with the exposition of human failure and the need to reverse its trend, possibly through a spiritual retreat. . . .

Ntiru . . . sees man's ultimate state as loneliness, since man's basic motivation in his interactions is neither love of others nor selflessness. The ultimate expression of this innate quality of man is made in "To a Late Rich Miser." In this poem we see that even the man of wealth will experience loneliness in his final hours on earth and eventually leave the world alone. The loneliness of the "late rich miser" here is symbolic of that of all men. He is someone who has enjoyed the gregarious pomp that high society can offer; but the time comes when all that becomes immaterial. At this time everyone—from the family to "the poor folk that has wealthed [him]"—has to withdraw physically. The miser, however, has a way of alleviating the pangs of loneliness. He thinks about his wealth, but eventually everything (including this) will slip away and leave him alone. . . .

It is this loneliness of man that Ntiru further captures in his image, in "The Pauper," of the pauper who, even though he is in the city center where beautiful cars reflect him and which is filled up with "beautiful people" and tourists, is still lonely. He sits, "alone on hairless goatskins" as the busy world hurries by oblivious of his plight. Ntiru seems to say that he is also the quintessential man.

Ntiru expresses the futility of human life by focusing on the inexorability of fate. He sees man as continuously progressing toward his predetermined fate; there is virtually nothing he can do to change the course of events already in motion as well as those which are bound to come to pass. These are the points which the poet makes in "The Prophecy." By the title he seems to suggest that human life is something of a vindication of a divine prophecy for man; that what constitutes one's fate is already part of a plan known to the gods. Hence he sees it as futile for man to attempt to control, in any way, his own or his fellow human beings' fate. . . .

Ntiru's poetry is that of the human condition; and in his moral sympathy with the seemingly hopeless situation of man in his world, the poet's vision is ultimately a bright one. However, one needs to trudge through a verbal terrain of disillusioning details in order to arrive at the thrill of a hopeful future which will be achieved through the sacrifice made by man. It is with regard to this dominant view that his work, in spite of the uncomfortable current of skepticism which runs through it, should be seen as that of a man who is in love with men and his society. In this perspective, his vignettes of degeneracy on the personal and societal levels become his own way of recommending an opposite way of life for a man; and his Heraclitian vision, predicated upon a fire of strife and tension, leads man to a vista of a New Jerusalem.

A. Rasheed Yesufu. *Ariel*. 18, 3 (July 1987), pp. 32–33, 37–39, 45

NWAPA, FLORA (1931–1993)

NIGERIA

In 1966, Flora Nwapa wrote *Efuru*, the first novel to be published by a woman writer in Nigeria, followed shortly afterwards by *Idu* and more recently by a collection of short stories. The first novel is set in rural Igboland. Efuru is a beautiful, wealthy and respected woman who, however, cannot bear children successfully or be happy in marriage. Her only child dies in infancy while her first husband deserts her and she feels forced to leave her second one. The reason for this unhappiness is that she has been chosen by a river goddess to be her companion and, as far as earthly companions are concerned, she must remain alone. . . .

Efuru is portrayed as a very independent character. Unconcerned with her parents' opinions, she chooses her own husband, a young man who has not even enough money for her dowry, and runs away to live with him. "Efuru and I have agreed to be husband and wife and that is all that matters." Having married the man of her choice, Efuru does not stop there and is no picture of meek obedience. She refuses to go to the farm and, instead, decides to trade. In contrast with her, Adizua, her husband, is almost a failure. He is so unsuccessful at farming that he joins his wife in trading but, once again, he is no good and Efuru is the brain behind the business. In every detail of her life, Efuru shows surprising determination and independence of character. She does not think twice about being seen everywhere with her husband, thus refusing the traditional pattern whereby the husband walks in front while the wife walks behind. In order to go trading, she decides to employ a maid to look after her baby daughter who is only eight months old. . . .

With Eneberi, her second husband, Efuru acts as an adviser. When he contemplates building a house of his own, she refuses, explaining that a canoe would be better at that stage. Later, she is so broad-minded that she accepts Eneberi's child from another woman under her roof, and she does not even blame him when she discovers that he has spent a few months in jail. It is not only in her marital relationship that Efuru shows surprising independence. She so believes in science and technique that she takes Nwosu, her maid's father, to a doctor-friend to have an operation on his male organ. Here again, Flora Nwapa carefully describes Nwabata, Nwosu's traditional wife, all in tears, refusing to allow her husband to go to [a] hospital where he will most certainly be poisoned by white witchcraft.

The complexity of Efuru lies in the fact that, although she shows such determination, she still remains strongly attached to traditions. She never questions polygamy ("only a bad woman would like to be married alone by her husband") and goes out of her way to find a second and third wife for Eneberi. But is it really logical that she should be more upset by her husband's absence at her father's funeral (i.e., an offense against tradition) than by the discovery of the reason for his absence (his imprisonment on a charge of theft)? If she is so levelheaded about taking a man to have an operation on his male organ, should she really be so upset at having bad dreams that she runs to her father who in turn takes her to see a *dibia*? This contradiction can only be accepted as representative of the dichotomy in Efuru's (and Flora Nwapa's) mind. As far as the physical world is concerned, she can accept Western techniques and progress; but as for the spiritual one, she does not get rid of her traditional habits and beliefs. Flora Nwapa makes it very clear, however, that she does not fully accept these powers of the *dibias*, since one of them is obviously mistaken in pronouncing Efuru guilty of adultery, which brings about the catastrophe and destroys her life. But the biggest contradiction is that Efuru, for all her qualities and gifts, considers her life as valueless since she fails to have a child. She can deliberately and willfully decide to leave her husband and therefore live by herself, but she cannot follow the logical consequences. She cannot find in herself enough resources to counterbalance her sterility and never thinks of devoting her energies to something else. To ask her to do so would be asking too much. If a woman rejects the view that the "birth of a child is a crowning glory," is she still an African? Flora Nwapa categorically refuses the cliché of the weak and obedient female slave, mere appendix to her husband's life; but she cannot go to the end of her analysis. The main objection, however, is that by making her heroine unique among her fellow villagers and by reporting the unanimously hostile and adverse comments of the other women on every one of Efuru's decisions and actions, Flora Nwapa gives, in fact, a disturbing picture of narrow-mindedness, superstition, malevolence, greed and fear in traditional Africa—a picture which might be contrary to what she has thought to defend.

Maryse Condé. *PA*. 82 (1972), pp. 133–36

Flora Nwapa's *Idu*, like her previous novel [*Efuru*], deals with the culture and lifeways of the Igbo and more specifically the fishing and farming residents of Oguta, who find occupation and pleasure in the Oguta Lake, and to whom the "fantasies" of the "woman of the lake" are a reality. These are the people about whom Flora Nwapa writes in these novels, but this is not enough to make her an authentic Igbo novelist. An Igbo novel (or Igbo literature as a whole) emanates from Igbo life and language. It embraces the social, political, economic, and emotional forms under which Igbo life is manifest. The evaluation of an Igbo work of art is essentially an appreciation of the validity of content as well as the appropriateness of technique. What the writer says about the Igbo is as important as how he says it. Neither alone can constitute his success, but the failure in both could mean his failure as an artist. Flora Nwapa's *Idu* is a successful Igbo novel by both standards. . . .

The realism of her themes and her ever-increasing sensitive use of language are two of Flora Nwapa's most enduring qualities as a novelist. Of the former, one might tend to say she is over-preoccupied with the concern for children in marriage in an age when the fear of overpopulation is acute and some ecologists are talking about "zero population growth"; but then among the Igbo (and I fear most Africans) "What we are all praying for is children. What else do we want if we have children?" One might tend to find Flora Nwapa's characters too talkative and gossipy, and her Ajanupas and Onyemurus too boring by virtue of the same organ that gives them distinction—their tongue—but these novels are mostly about women by a woman, and one should not take lightly the line in which Nwapa says, "You know women's conversation never ends."

Ernest N. Emenyonu. In Eldred Durosimi Jones, ed.
African Literature Today. 7 (1975), pp. 28, 32

Whereas [Ama Ata] Aidoo's short stories are based on the skillful manipulation of diverse narrative forms, Flora Nwapa's technique as short-story writer is more uniform. This uniformity is not really a shortcoming in the work of this Nigerian writer. *This Is Lagos, and Other Stories* actually owes much of its undeniable power to a consistently spare and taut style skillfully adapted to the writer's intense irony and to a brooding sense of tragedy throughout the collection. . . .

On the whole it appears that Nwapa's very choice of genre, as well as her choice of techniques within the selected genre, are interwoven with her most fundamental perspectives. Her perception of contemporary life in urban Nigeria demands a short-story format, one that does not depend to any significant degree on the kind of oral modes that are so integral to much of Aidoo's short fiction. It is a format which reflects the largely literate, Western middle-class world within which her women move (as in the case of Bisi or Amedi). That literate world's dominance in the lives of older, rural-oriented women like Mama Eze is emphasized by the uniformly literate method which describes *their* experiences. In Nwapa's hands the short story seems especially appropriate for brief, even deliberately unfinished glimpses of urban life. Thus many of the stories leave their protagonists in the middle of seemingly insoluble crises or, at best, in the face of disturbing and unanswerable questions. Taken together, these suggestively abbreviated vignettes suggest the fragmentary nature of the social experiences out of which they arise. In addition, the spare language which Nwapa sustains throughout suggests that thinness of spirit and that limited humaneness which the stories themselves attribute to the society as a whole.

The rural and largely traditional world of the older Nigeria, as it is envisaged by Nwapa, seems to require a different style—an expansive use of language reflecting the formal richness and ornate modes of traditional oral cultures. It seems to demand the detailed duplication of those social conventions intrinsic to everyday relationships in that milieu of elaborately defined roles. When Nwapa turns to that milieu, she selects the genre that most easily accommodates an expansive language and elaborate design, for these features reflect the complexities of a society that is always more ambiguous (fulfilling in some respects, while limiting in others) than the general meagerness of urban life.

Lloyd W. Brown. *Women Writers in Black Africa*
(Westport, Conn.: Greenwood Press, 1981), pp. 122, 134–35

Flora Nwapa . . . arrived on the [Nigerian] literary scene at a time when it was almost completely dominated by men. She was at first received with mixed feelings. Some received her works with admiration while others considered them as an unwarranted imitation of what the men were doing. It took some time for the works to be considered on their own merit. When finally this was done, it was discovered that she was writing in depth, at least initially, on topics which were better handled by a woman, even if her methods and approaches were not significantly different from those employed by other writers. Flora Nwapa's topics have been to some extent unique to her. Her reputation as a writer rests solidly on her achievements in *Efuru* and *Idu*. In these works she concentrates on marriage, mother care, home and family life, the status of women in traditional society, the hierarchical structure of Igbo society, and the place of the gods in the maintenance of peace and order in tribal communities. She creates a self-contained world in which her villagers live a full life based on their own customs and beliefs, with only minimum influence from outside sources.

She has since written two shorter novels—*Never Again* and *One Is Enough*, and also has to her credit two collections of short stories—*This Is Lagos* [*and Other Stories*] and *Wives at War* [*and Other Stories*]. These latter works have benefited from her personal experiences of the Nigerian Civil War, especially as they concern her hometown, Ugwuta. She writes with insight on the ravages of war—the loss of men and property, the psychological effect on the human environment and the abrupt large-scale disruption of a way of life. She also takes a great deal of interest in the moral laxity, social decadence, and the craze for wealth which result from the mass movement of people from their secure homebase to the comparative insecurity of the city. The point at issue is usually so well dramatized that the social risks being taken by groups and individuals become obvious for all to see. So effectively has the novelist diversified her literary interests in recent years that her versatility as a creative artist is no longer in doubt. . . .

Never Again is devoted to the ravages of war, especially its effect on human beings. In particular Flora Nwapa concentrates on the capture of Ugwuta by the federal troops during the Nigerian Civil War and its recapture by the Biafran soldiers. The work owes its dramatic impact to the way the author uses incidents at Ugwuta to highlight the nature and extent of the conflict between the two sides. Ugwuta is important because of its nearness to the Uli airstrip through which Biafra gets its supply of ammunition and other materials. Uli is the only reliable line of communication with the outside world. Once Ugwuta is captured, it will require only a little more effort on the part of federal troops to take Uli, which is so essential for the resistance. Given this importance, it is not surprising that the author devotes so much attention to the people's resolve not to see Ugwuta fall. . . .

Flora Nwapa successfully dramatizes the human dimensions of the war. The painful experiences of Kate, her husband Chudi, and members of their family are typical of the hardship which the war brings upon the citizens. They have fled Enugu, Onitsha, Port Harcourt, and Elele, and are thoroughly tired of moving from place to place. Now they are required without much notice to flee from Ugwuta. Kate and Chudi necessarily become skeptical about the ability of the secessionist army to contain the onslaught of the federal troops. For this they are called saboteurs by their friend Kal, who threatens to hand them over to the army. The situation is so confused that it is difficult to know when it is safe to talk or whom it is safe to talk to. . . .

The author leaves no one in any doubt that she regards the war as a mad pursuit by both sides. She takes a balanced view of the whole affair. War brings untold hardship to people and ought to be avoided at all costs. The leaders on both sides should have adopted a rational approach to a peaceful settlement. In her view secession hardly solves a political problem because "there was already oppression even before the young nation was able to stand on her feet." On the other hand, Nigerian soldiers should not have attacked Biafra with such brutal force. That only makes matters worse. Consideration ought to have been given to the close affinity between the two sides. . . .

In *One Is Enough* the novelist continues to show interest in home and family life. The emphasis here, as elsewhere, is on the disastrous effect on the woman of childlessness in marriage in a traditional society. Amaka gets into trouble not because she is a failure as a wife but because, after six years of marriage, she has not been able to produce a child. She obviously possesses the sterling qualities which should ordinarily endear a woman to a man. She is well domesticated and works hard to please Obiora and his people. She is successful in business and is willing to use her wealth to make her household comfortable. Furthermore, she is a good family woman and regards married life as honorable and sacred. . . . Unfortunately these qualities are not enough in the circumstances. Without a child, Amaka cannot command the respect of the villagers. Nor does she have their sympathy or consideration. She is, in fact, rated lower in their esteem than the woman who has two children for Obiora but who "did not know her right from her left" and who "behaved atrociously and embarrassed Obiora." This other woman is clearly idiotic and a total misfit. Even so, she is brought to the house to displace Amaka. When Obiora eventually realizes his folly and wants Amaka back, he is prevented by force of tradition from carrying out his legitimate wishes. So little importance is attached to the element of love in marriage. The marriage between Obiora and Amaka might have succeeded if the villagers had not held a childless woman to such merciless ridicule.

Oladele Taiwo. *Female Novelists of Modern Africa*
(New York: St. Martin's Press, 1984), pp. 47–48, 61–65

[In *One Is Enough*] Amaka . . . is apparently unable to have children after six years of marriage. One day, she discovers that her husband has been keeping a mistress who has already borne him two sons. . . . [She] decides to leave him and make a new life for herself; but Amaka . . . is sufficiently her own woman to realize a fully independent existence. In this she is supported by her mother and her aunt, both of whom inculcate in her a sense of her own worth as a woman. Even before Amaka gets married, her aunt puts her off an unsuitable prospect by reminding her that, "'What is important is not marriage as such, but children, being able to have children, being a mother. Have your children, be able to look after them, and you will be respected,'" and then proceeds to illustrate the truth of her claim by reference to her own experience. . . . And after Amaka leaves her husband, her mother recounts the good sense of her sister when she found herself in a similar predicament. . . . So Amaka travels to Lagos, sets herself up as a contractor, and makes a fortune. Eventually she meets a man she desires. It happens that he is a priest, but they consummate their relationship anyway and she becomes pregnant. He begs her to marry him but at first she refuses. He leaves the priesthood for her sake and mobilizes her family to plead on his behalf. She eventually yields; but before they can go through with the marriage, he rediscovers his vocation after he miraculously escapes death in a motor accident.

The convolutions of the plot in the second half of the novel are an unnecessary complication. There is no intrinsic reason why her lover should be a priest; there is even less reason why he should then go through fire in order to understand, at last, that he cannot marry the mother of his child. But the point about the affair is to make Amaka pregnant. We have it on the testimony of both Amaka's mother and her aunt that this is all that men are good for, a sentiment which Amaka herself, following her own disastrous marriage, takes sufficiently to heart to act in the way that she subsequently does. Almost any man would have sufficed, provided only that he met certain basic requirements. Why she should choose a priest for her purposes is itself a mystery; why she should then encourage his feelings towards her to the extent that he endures purgatory on her behalf is a betrayal of the moral universe the author has herself generated through the testimonies of the mother and the aunt.

"In her position, what does she want from a man?," Amaka's mother asks her rhetorically in respect to Ayo, the only one of her daughters with enough sense to take what she needs and then "gracefully" go her own way. Indeed, what did Amaka want from a man whose life was already complicated by the rigorous demands of a vocation which in any case precluded his assigned role in the scheme of things? In a word, nothing; and yet the author complicates what should have been a relatively straightforward story that achieves the same end towards which it was already moving. That said, however, *One Is Enough* . . . is among the few Nigerian novels which subvert the otherwise male-dominated view of the Nigerian society, at least as far as the majority of the novelists—male *and* female—are concerned.

Adewale Maja-Pearce. *A Mask Dancing: Nigerian Novelists of the Eighties* (London: Hans Zell, 1992), pp. 153–55

Flora Nwapa in *Women Are Different* dramatizes [the] notion of fulfillment as four female characters are portrayed through the presentation of their individual attitudes towards achieving self-satisfaction. The novel also enhances Nwapa's reputation, which a critic [Oladele Taiwo] points out when he says that "she has moved from the discussion of weighty traditional matters to topics relating to the social complications of modern life." This adherence to complications of modern life is not derogatory, for the society has evolved from the traditional to the modern and "the women we now meet in novels by women are often educated and have sophisticated expectations of life both in the town and country." The four major characters in *Women Are Different* are educated, and they possess sophisticated expectations. However, they occasionally contrast and even contradict themselves through their decisions, aims, and aspirations; but these contrasts coalesce to present those vital issues that militate against the mental and social development of women. . . .

Flora Nwapa has clearly worked out for herself a theory of life which explains the tribulations confronting women in the society. It may be too early [to expect] from her a consistently rational theory, since it may take time to evolve a theory of life, but it is clear that she has through this notion of fulfillment explained many of her convictions. The society may be unprincipled, but she is not prepared to accept a view which has been widely accepted if it contradicts the essence of womanhood. Moreover, Nwapa has shown that fulfillment can only be derived through the trust and honesty in human affairs which men have invariably lacked. The women who people the novel *Women Are Different* are thus portrayed as an exploited group of people whose ideals are often shattered by insensitive partners. The novelist thus insists that for the society to progress all instances of exploitation, even in emotional affairs, must be eliminated in order to douse the flash points of conflicts.

Ezenwa-Ohaeto. *Neohelicon.* 19, 1 (1992), pp. 323–24, 332

[Nwapa's] writing is situated outside of conventional male narrative history; she chooses to engage neither with the manly adventures and public displays of patriarchal authority described by male writers from her community nor with the narrative conventions of their accounts. Instead she concentrates, and at length, on what was incidental or simply contextual to male action—domestic matters, politics of intimacy.

In both *Efuru* and *Idu*, Nwapa's interest is in the routines and rituals of everyday life specifically within women's compounds. Women press into Nwapa's narrative as speakers, actors, decision-makers, brokers of opinion and market prices, and unofficial jurors in their communities. But Nwapa's specific intervention as a writer goes beyond her interest in women subjects. What also distinguishes her writing from others in the "Igbo school" are the ways in which she has used choric language to enable and to empower her representation, creating the effect of a women's verbal presence within her text, while bringing home her subject matter by evoking the vocality of women's everyday existence.

Though it may have attracted a certain amount of negative comment, the apparent lack of conventional novelistic complexity in *Efuru* and *Idu*, I would argue, far from being a deficiency, instead clears the space for the elaboration of another kind of narrative entirely—a highly verbalized collective women's biography—"transsubjective, anonymous," transgressive, a narrative method which bears comparison with Zora Neale Hurston's re-creation of porchside comment and of gossip on the road. . . .

Nwapa thus extends the boundaries of the African novel to include the women's side of the compound, a domain of village life which writers like [Elechi] Amadi have neglected for reasons not only of patriarchal lack of interest but also perhaps (a fact not given sufficient attention) of ignorance. Nwapa refracts a women's presence into her text through creating the conceit of women representing themselves in voice. Dialogue dominates in both novels, especially in *Idu*, as numbers of partly curious, partly phatic, and frequently anonymous women's voices meet, interact with, and interpellate one another. This vocality, rambling and seemingly unstoppable, pulls against the confinements of the women's lives—their market rivalries, their anxieties about husbands, families, and children. Therefore, if, as Nwapa portrays it, though not always overtly, male values in the society remain normative, women's talk can be interpreted not only as a way of life but as a mode of self-making. The impression of the fullness and autonomy of women's lives which Nwapa creates must remain partially qualified by their acquiescence in patriarchal views and values. Yet, at the same time, in their discourse, even as they speak, not only do the village women share their woes and confirm female bonds, they also transpose their lives into a medium which they control. The reader is made privy to the women representing and so, in effect, re-creating their lives in speech.

Elleke Boehmer. In Susheila Nasta, ed. *Motherlands*
(New Brunswick, N. J.: Rutgers University Press, 1992), pp. 11–12, 14–15

Nwapa's reflections on the role of women in both precolonial and modern Nigerian society place women at "the heart of the turmoil of their continent," as Maryse Condé notes. From rural women such as Efuru and Idu to the new urbanites Soha and Amaku, these women make choices about their lives, taking what they can from both the traditional and modern cultures to try to forge a life for themselves and their communities.

Of the early writers in anglophone African literature, Flora Nwapa has been perhaps the least acknowledged; probably this lack of attention has a simple explanation: Nwapa is a woman writing about the lives of women, a situation that makes her even further removed from the attention of the literary mainstream than the already marginalized male African writers. With new approaches to African literature and with more women critics, Nwapa's works—particularly her first two novels, *Efuru* and *Idu*—are receiving more of the recognition they deserve. She is continuing to work with her publishing house, Tana Press/Flora Nwapa and Company; and her novel *Women Are Different*, which further explores the place of women in Nigerian society, was published in 1986. She has also published *Cassava Song and Rice Song* and is working on a collection of short stories. For most contemporary critics of African literature, Nwapa's position as a foremother of modern African women's writings is secure, for through the voices of her classic novel *Efuru* and her other works, the previously undocumented women storytellers in African villages are heard.

Gay Wilentz. In Bernth Lindfors and Reinhard Sander, eds.
Dictionary of Literary Biography. 125 (1993), pp. 182–83

OGOT, GRACE (1930–   )

KENYA

[Grace] Ogot's writing deals mostly with aspects of traditional African society. Her novel *The Promised Land* . . . tells the story of the Western Kenyan Luo pioneer family, which seeks a more satisfactory life in Tanzania where conditions are better. The family is defeated when a curse is placed upon Nyapol, the hero of the novel, by an envious and vindictive neighbor. The novel is subtitled *A True Fantasy* not so much because the events of the novel are offered as historically accurate, but because the physical manifestations which result from the curse placed on Nyapol (his flesh breaks out in festering, painful, thornlike growths which drive him mad) are meant to show the force, the truth of the belief in indigenous religion. The novel fails to convince because there is too sharp a break between its two halves. The realistic and matter-of-fact evocation of domestic conditions of the first part gives way to passages describing Nyapol's hallucinations in his pain. There is as well a rather contrived eighth chapter interpolated into the text to show the utter inability of Western medicine (as practiced in a mission hospital) to cope with African medicine used by a pagan practitioner for nefarious purposes. The reader's credibility is too much strained. . . .

The stories in her *Land Without Thunder*, which offer themes dealing with traditional village occasions, events in mission hospitals in colonial days, the tragedy of young girls in contemporary Nairobi, and the problems of sophisticated Africans at an Egyptian airport, have an authenticity which is quite convincing and reveal a fine command and inventive use of the short-story form.

Douglas Killam. In Bruce King, ed. *Literatures of the World in English*
(London: Routledge & Kegan Paul, 1974), pp. 126–27

The nine stories contained in *The Other Woman: Selected Short Stories* are studies in common human problems and experiences, though their settings and almost all their characters are Kenyan. The same theme is explored in all but three of the other stories, but there are differences in the nature of action and in the predominance of various narrative devices. Thus "Pay Day" and "The Middle Door" deal with the theme of courage in the face of man's inhumanity to fellow man; "The Other Woman" and "The Honourable Minister" satirize marital infidelity and show it visited with nemesis; and "The Fisherman" and "The Ivory Trinket" depict the disastrous consequences of evil words addressed by husbands to their wives. Two of the three remaining stories, though they differ widely from these six in terms of experiential details, handle themes which are generally similar to two of those already indicated: "The Family Doctor" is about the need for perseverance in the face of a malignant illness; and "Fishing Village" deals with a despicable rogue who baptizes his thievery and duplicity *in nomine diaboli,* calling them "intelligence," and who justly falls victim to nemesis. Only the ninth and last story, "The Professor," deals with an entirely different theme: the shocking, inevitable capitulation of professional (academic) idealism before the forces of sociopolitical reality.

The success of most of the stories as works of art consists of Ogot's effective narrative skill, imagination, and language. Her masterly combination of the techniques of flashback, foreshadowing, and discovery makes for reading with breathless attention and sustained interest. The stories themselves are such terrific inventions with several layers of suggestiveness as can be the result only of a rare imaginative activity, and the language is lucid and fresh.

[R.] N. Egudu. *WLT*. 52, 1 (Winter 1978), p. 165

Grace Ogot is one of Africa's outstanding storytellers. She went into the lead early and has worked hard ever since to remain there. She has written several collections of short stories and full-length novels in English and Luo. *The Promised Land*, *Land Without Thunder*, *The Other Woman*, *Island of Tears*, and *The Graduate* are established and well received. The writings in Luo—*Ber Wat*, *Miaha*, *Aloo Kod Apul Apul*, *Simbi Nyaima*—may be new to many outside Kenya, but they have proved extremely popular at home. For example, a recent dramatization of *Miaha* in Luo-speaking areas of Kenya excited the people and showed to what extent drama could be used as a medium of transmitting indigenous culture. The drama version of two stories from *Land Without Thunder*—"The Rain Came" and "The White Veil"—staged by the Albert Wandago Production at the Cultural Center, Nairobi, was also well received and had almost twenty runs. So, not only has Grace Ogot been writing stories and novels, she has also been promoting creativity in other directions. A few of her books have been translated into several international languages, and some have been adopted for use as school texts . . . in Kenya.

In an interview she talked about her new books in the press, her motivation for writing, her craftsmanship, and the recognition that writing has brought her so far. She has three completed novels in the pipeline; two of them she has worked on for ten years. These two are historical novels. *In the Beginning* deals with the history of the Luo people from about 97 A.D. to about 1300 A.D when the people make a Wi-nam settlement, and what compels them to leave this settlement. For greater effectiveness the story . . . concentrates on three generations of one family. It hinges on a family spear, an inheritance of great cultural worth, which has to pass from one generation to another. At one stage a member of the family makes a mistake and an elephant walks away with the spear. The owner of the spear refuses compensation. So the man at fault goes in search of the spear. This action eventually leads to the separation of two brothers who later found two nations. The second novel, *Princess Nyilaak*, virtually continues the historical fiction where the first has left off. Nyilaak was born around 1517 A.D., and her story takes us up to about 1750 A.D She is the daughter of the ruler of the Luo people. In the absence of a male child she is designated to succeed her father. For this reason the oracles decree that she should not marry. Her mother does not like this decision and does everything in her power to oppose it. Nyilaak has an encounter with Ochak, a prince from another part of the land, marries him secretly, and becomes pregnant by him. Ochak is hunted down by Nyilaak's father, and is killed and cremated. Nyilaak is banished from the land, and her twin sons are to be killed. However, through the intervention of the elders, she is reprieved with her two sons and she later becomes a ruler. Nyilaak later founds the Alur society in Uganda, and one of her sons succeeds her as ruler.

The third novel, *A Call at Midnight* is different in texture and orientation from the first two. . . . It is a social comment on family life, especially the responsibility of the father to his wife and children. A father deserts his family, and ten years after he has left home there is a telephone call to his wife that her husband is critically ill in [a] hospital. The wife says she has no husband. The [nurse] . . . replies that dying men don't just call on any women in the city. All the time the man has been away from home he has maintained an illegal contact with another woman in a smuggling business. This woman dupes him of a large sum of money, dopes him, and leaves him unconscious by the roadside. This is why he goes to [the] hospital in the first place. He recovers from his illness, paralyzed, and returns to his matrimonial home. The wife is rather unhappy about his return, but the children feel it is much better to have a crippled father than not have any at all. When these three novels are published, they will confirm Grace Ogot's position as an outstanding female novelist in modern Africa. . . .

By her writing Grace Ogot has not only brought pleasure and satisfaction to many readers, she has also set a high standard of artistic performance from which young female writers can benefit. They will find her preoccupation with the African woman and family edifying, and her style lucid and attractive. She is particularly proficient in the use of verbal art. She integrates oral tradition into the living situations of her stories, especially in those scenes set in the rural areas. This gives her works the necessary authenticity. . . . Furthermore, her works are capable of reawakening in readers, especially female readers, the memory of the life they lived in infancy, and make them examine how firm their grasp of cultural matters is. Such an assessment is made easy by the fact that most of her heroines are ordinary people, sometimes gifted, but not fighters or revolutionaries. On city life she shows the experience of an observant woman. She puts her finger on items which make city life inferior in quality to rural life—avarice, greed, corruption, sexual laxity. Once she takes a fault she dramatizes it in such a way that the danger in that attitude of mind or approach to life becomes obvious. She combines realism with frankness in pointing out the foibles in society. In *The Graduate*, for example, all the difficulties put in the way of Jakoyo by Europeans and fellow Africans are realistic in the context and point to an unpardonable weakness in human nature. By consistently calling attention to these faults, she is directly advocating reform.

Oladele Taiwo. *Female Novelists of Modern Africa*
(New York: St. Martin's Press, 1984) pp. 128–29, 161

Questions of social morality and the quest for nationhood have preoccupied African writers dealing with postcolonial society. Novelists like Kofi Awoonor,

Ayi Kwei Armah, Chinua Achebe, Wole Soyinka, Ngugi wa Thiong'o, and Meja Mwangi have all examined these two dimensions of Africa's postcolonial reality. So has Grace Ogot. . . .

A study of Grace Ogot's fiction reveals that whereas problems of nationhood loom large in her short novel, *The Graduate*, problems of morality are more central in her short stories, especially such short stories as "The Middle Door," "The Honourable Minister," "Elizabeth," "The Professor," and "Pay Day." Nevertheless, her treatment of moral problems also suggests that postcolonial society's moral problems pose a deadly threat to its quest for national authenticity. . . .

[In *The Graduate*] Jakoyo encounters no ethnic obstacles on his way to answering the nation's call. Similarly, other potential sources of frustration are either glanced over or rendered as comedy. Thus, as his plane prepared to land [at] Nairobi's airport, "Jakoyo's heartbeat rose, as joy, fear, even pain settled upon him, shooting numerous questions in his mind." His misgivings are soon proved unfounded. His wife proves faithful and loving as ever. Though his daughter, Awino, who was born shortly after his departure for America, at first dislikes him, a lovely present soon wins her over. Even the clear evidence of culture shock and Jakoyo's alienation (he speaks Swahili with a Yankee accent) is underplayed. His dominant feeling is one of "a new life . . . a new beginning, a new era that would turn him into a new man." The break with the past is symbolized in his stuffing into his "air-sick bag" the dirty toilet tissue he had used in the plane, and dumping the bag "where it belonged."

Even nature smiles a warm welcome to Jakoyo. And the customs and immigration officials are all friendly, courteous, dutiful, and efficient. No one insults him. No one attempts to extort a bribe from him, as happens to his Nigerian counterpart in Achebe's *No Longer at Ease*, in which a corrupt customs official offers to let the hero Obi Okonkwo bring in his radiogram duty-free if Obu would give him a two-pound bribe. . . . An ideological issue (the opposition between Eastern-bloc socialism and the Western-dependent capitalism of most African countries) which provides the grit to Marxist writers like Ngugi wa Thiong'o and Sembène Ousmane is laughingly raised and dismissed. An official asks Jakoyo: "Any prohibited Marxist literature?" and accepts his crisp assurance that there is none.

Grace Ogot's short novel *The Graduate* has raised a number of problems facing African states in their quest for an authentic nationhood. This paper discusses only one of such problems, with specific reference to postcolonial Kenya. The paper shows that because most of Ogot's themes center on women, women's issues have also formed the matrix within which sociohistorical or sociopolitical phenomena are discussed. This applies naturally to her exploration of Kenya's quest for authentic nationhood.

Ify Achufusi. JCL. 26, 1 (1991), pp. 179–80, 186–87

Ogot is devoted to relating native Luo folktales to the younger generation of Kenyans. Many of her writings are also based on the day-to-day life of people she has known or read about. As a nurse she has been intrigued by the continuing use of traditional medical cures in Kenya. As Ogot explained to Bernth

Lindfors, "Stories of African traditional medicine and of the medicine man against the background of modern science and medicine fascinated me." This fascination led to the writing of *The Promised Land*; the short stories "The Old White Witch," "The Hero," and "Night Sister," in *Land Without Thunder*, and "The Family Doctor" and "The Professor" in *The Other Woman*. . . .

Ogot is well aware of the social, political, and economic changes taking place around her and continues to retain a respect and a close understanding of the traditional thought of her people. An understanding and appreciation of Luo traditional ways, customs, superstitions, and history are the strengths of Ogot's writing. Her close attention to an accurate recalling of details was exhibited when she changed the title of her story "Ayiembo's Ghost" to "The Ivory Trinket" . . . as soon as she learned that ghosts are not dead in Luo traditions. Another example is the recitation of the Nyamgondho legend in "The Fisherman." . . .

The tragic aspects of history and life fascinate Ogot: six stories in *Land Without Thunder*, three stories in *The Other Woman*, and two stories in *The Island of Tears* have an element of sadness in them. Ogot's belief is that "There are more tragic incidents in life than there are comic ones." To support her statement, Ogot has written about Tom Mboya's funeral in the title story of *The Island of Tears*; the death of Dr. Sserwadda from poliomyelitis in "The Hero"; the mother's desperate attempt to find a doctor to save her child's life in "The Family Doctor"; and the sacrifice of the life of Oganda, a king's daughter, for the survival of the village in "The Rain Came." In short, tragedy cuts across class lines and touches a cross-section of Kenyan rural and urban society.

Brenda F. Berrian. In Bernth Lindfors and Reinhard Sander, eds.
Dictionary of Literary Biography. 125 (1993), pp. 184–86

OKOT P'BITEK (1931–1982)

UGANDA

Few events in the development of modern African literature have been as dramatic as the appearance of [Okot p'Bitek's] *Song of Lawino*, late in 1966. From the very first line, the poem established a distinctive tone which appeared to owe nothing, and in fact did owe nothing, to any earlier African poetry in English, whether in East Africa or elsewhere. . . .

What are the sources of this extraordinary style, with the unfailing freshness and sharpness of its image, its range of mood, its ability to gather up and convey to us a whole distinctive way of life in work and play, in sorrow and in joy? Nothing remotely comparable had yet appeared in East Africa; but for the scale of its organization, *Song of Lawino* was also something new in anglophone Africa as a whole. The answer lies partly in the special nature of Okot's preparation as a poet. Born in 1931 at Gulu in the northwest of Uganda, he was in his youth an outstanding singer, dancer, and athlete. While still a schoolboy at King's College, Budo, he had composed and directed a full-length opera. At the age of twenty-two he published a novel in the Lwo language of Acoli, *Lak Tar Miyo Kinyero Wi Lobo*. In 1956 he wrote the first draft of the Lwo original, *Wer pa Lawino*, though he was then unable to find a publisher for anything so outspoken and uncompromising. Soon afterwards, he was playing football in England for Uganda's national team. This in turn led to his studies in education, law, and social anthropology, which culminated in his Oxford B.Litt. thesis, devoted to the oral literature of the Acoli and Lango. Thus Okot was occupied in both the study and practice of Lwo poetry for many years before he attempted to write in English. More important still, perhaps, he did not study English literature at the post-secondary level, which can be a distracting experience for a poet seeking to master his own tradition. . . .

To appreciate the extent of Okot's involvement in the stream of Acoli song, it is necessary only to look at his collection, *The Horn of My Love*, published in 1974. Equally revealing of the living context in which his song has grown is his more recent collection of Acoli folktales, *Hare and Hornbill*. Both collections will reveal the extraordinary strength and vigor of indigenous Acoli tradition, compared with the hesitations, apologies, or exaggerated justifications which often afflict those writing exclusively in English, or exclusively from an English literary stimulus. In the pages of *Song of Lawino*, we are never in any doubt that an African sensibility is in charge, a sensibility which will judge everything according to its own priorities and its own involvement with the struggle for articulation.

Gerald Moore. Twelve African Writers (Bloomington:
Indiana University Press, 1980), pp. 171–73, 175

As a poet Okot p'Bitek has several claims to importance. He was the first major East African poet in English; he has influenced a number of other poets; and he is a maker of abiding satiric myths. *Song of Lawino* not only showed that East African poetry could achieve more than the nonchalantly slight lyrics or brief graphic situation poems that had earlier appeared in periodicals and anthologies; it established that there was a readership for volumes of poetry in English by a single author. . . .

What is new [about the poem] is the sustained rhetoric of the complaint, the organized characterization and satire of the dramatic monologue, and the use of translation as a subject to make polemical and satiric points. Of Okot's four major poems, this is the one that lies closest to his own education in traditional culture, for which he was largely indebted to his mother, Lacwaa Cerina, "who first taught me to sing," as he says in the dedication to *Song of Ocol*. *Song of Lawino* is, indeed, named after her, for Lawino (meaning born with the umbilical cord wrapped around the neck) was one of his mother's names; and, like the fictional Lawino, his mother had been "chief of girls." It is also the poem closest to his academic studies in anthropology and religion; it contains a dramatic summary of some of the main positions taken up in his earlier study, *African Religions in Western Scholarship*. It has the most detailed characterization of any of his works and, in that Lawino is very much a woman who has been brought up in an identifiably Acoli culture, the narrowest frame of cultural reference. Lawino is, of course, also representative of the values of village life anywhere in Africa, as contrasted with those of European colonialism. She represents, too, the values of the African woman (or at least of a certain kind of African woman) faced with rivalry in love. But her quarrel with Ocol is more personal and more specific than one finds in Okot's later works. They spread out into cultural and political comment on the whole of black Africa in a way that would be quite foreign to the mind of the village-raised Lawino. . . .

Okot poured a great many of his own interests into the poem. Traditional dancing and singing, rites and ceremonies, education, religion, and other matters of cultural and anthropological interest; the role of the Christian church; and the two-party system of politics that operated early in Uganda's independence are all incorporated into the poem. His treatment of the church runs parallel to the more extended treatment he gives in his academic works. At the heart of his approach is the belief that in trying to relate their own religion to Acoli by translation, Christian missionaries misunderstood Acoli religion and distorted their own. They began with the assumption that the Acoli, clearly a polytheistic people, must believe in a Supreme Being or a High God. Okot considers this a gross error, not just about the Acoli but about all the peoples of the Upper Nile, that is, the Nilotes. . . .

If Okot is right in believing that the Acoli could not accommodate the Greco-Christian notion of God, it is difficult to see what he expected proselytizing missionaries to do, except to give up and go home. Even if their labor was ultimately vain, it seems a little harsh to blame them for trying, albeit misguidedly. The important point remains, though, that in Okot's view no accommodation was possible between two such dissimilar religions. It serves to strengthen Lawino's view that the two cultural systems—religious, educational, artistic, aesthetic, medical, culinary, sartorial, architectural, political, and linguistic—should be kept separate alongside each other.

K. L. Goodwin. *Understanding African Poetry*
(London: Heinemann, 1982), pp. 154–56, 159–61

When Okot p'Bitek surprised the world with *Song of Lawino* . . . he was recognized immediately as a major African poet. No other African writer—except possibly Christopher Okigbo of Nigeria—had made such an indelible impact with his first volume of verse, creating at one stroke a new poetic idiom so entirely his own. . . . When he sang, no European echoes could be heard in the background. His *Song of Lawino* was the first long poem in English to achieve a totally African identity. . . .

Throughout his busy academic and professional career, Okot p'Bitek never stopped writing. His enormously successful *Song of Lawino* was soon followed by three other long poems of the same genre: *Song of Ocol*, "Song of Prisoner" and "Song of Malaya" (the latter two were published together in *Two Songs*). He also published two scholarly works, *African Religions in Western Scholarship* and *Religion of the Central Luo*. . . . Another book, *Africa's Cultural Revolution*,

is a collection of some of the essays he wrote for East African periodicals, magazines, and newspapers between 1964 and 1971. Since these essays contain several of Okot's most candid statements on African culture, they provide an
excellent introduction to some of the ideas embedded in his poetry. . . .

Okot's strident style of satiric singing won him a wider audience than any
political propaganda would have done, and he achieved this immense popularity without pulling any of his punches. Indeed, his four outspoken songs compel
us to listen to voices we would not necessarily heed. Original in form, technique, and idea, these vivid lyrical soliloquies captivate the imagination and
provoke the intellect while advancing half-ironic arguments that radically challenge some of our basic cultural assumptions. Our immediate reaction to such
audacity may be to laugh in astonishment, but Okot has a talent for forcing us
to think as we laugh. He never lets us rest comfortably in mindless complacency. This makes him an unsettling writer, indeed a very revolutionary artist,
for his constant questioning teaches us entirely new ways of seeing ourselves
and others. By singing comically and occasionally off-key, he draws attention
to serious social disharmonies which require adjustment and correction. He
wrote not merely to amuse but to instruct and guide his people. He once said
that a truly African literature must have "deep human roots" and deal "honestly
and truthfully with the problems of the human situation." Okot p'Bitek, in striving to produce this kind of literature, has become one of Africa's major creative
writers. He was a serious clown who provoked regenerative laughter.

> Bernth Lindfors. In G. D. Killam, ed. *The Writing of East and*
> *Central Africa* (London: Heinemann, 1984) pp. 144–45, 157

[It] is clear that Okot p'Bitek uses style and themes to define the poet's relationship with the speakers of the poems. The mixture of romance and realism in
[*Song of*] *Lawino* and Lawino's knowledge in spite of her illiteracy, together
with her generally likable character, help to make her the most positive of the
three personae [Lawino, Ocol, and Prisoner]. She condemns copying alien ways
which are natural distortions and affirms the authenticity of her people's ways,
which she accepts may not be the best in the world. Ocol confirms Lawino's
portrayal of him as a cultural sellout. Having got Western education, Ocol's
eyes "opened," and he started to turn against his roots. . . . The poet suggests
that when the Western way of life is accepted by the African in its entirety
without consideration for relevant aspects, the receiver develops self-hatred.
Lawino has some weaknesses and there could be some truth in Ocol's statements, but his generalizations do not help to make convincing his case for
Africans copying Western ways. Ocol is the poet's mask, but only a mask to
avoid embarrassment and raise questions about what he unconvincingly sees as
the drawbacks of African peoples.

The poet, therefore, advocates authenticity among his people without
being obtusely xenophobic. He seems to be saying in ["Song of Prisoner"] that
as Africans rule themselves, he would like oppressive regimes to be removed,
but not by false revolutionaries riding on the waves of popular discontent to

satisfy their personal hunger for power. The three personae stand for ideas which are relevant in the discussion of the problems of contemporary Africa. They are, in a way, aspects of the poet's consciousness. The poet seems consistently concerned about his people as he endorses Lawino while he underscores the attitudes of Ocol and the Prisoner with irony and ambivalence respectively.

Tanure Ojaide. Callaloo. 9, 2 (Spring 1986), p. 382

Okot p'Bitek, the foremost opponent of the imitation of foreign cultures, criticizes educational institutions in East Africa, and he argues in his book, *Africa's Cultural Revolution*, that such institutions have been responsible for some kind of assimilation which he calls "apemanship." He wonders why, for instance, schools in East Africa should continue to teach songs like "Bobby Shaftoe" or "Baa Baa Black Sheep."

Yet in *Song of Lawino* and the *Song of Ocol*, [Okot] has used the same English language in which "Bobby Shaftoe" and "Baa Baa Black Sheep" are written. However, the *Song of Lawino* was first written in the Acoli language. [Okot] hates imitation of foreign cultures, and yet he has used a foreign language to express his ideas. The question now is how [Okot] has solved or tackled this language dilemma.

The clue to the answer lies in the following line, which appears in the first part of *Song of Lawino*: "Words cut more painfully than sticks." In Acoli traditional society this is a proverbial saying which carries several connotations. It suggests that [Okot] is going to rely, for his success, on the "right choice" of words and that it is not language as such that matters but the way in which one handles that language.

Ismael Mbise. In Emmanuel Ngara and Andrew Morrison, eds. Literature,
Language and the Nation (Harare: Baobab Books, 1989), pp. 83–84

Okot p'Bitek, the poet *par excellence*, is also a storyteller of moral and pedagogical significance. In the four long compelling "Songs" he wrote before his death in 1982, his story of a paradox revolves around the notion of freedom. He seems to be saying that freedom to the African did not mean a liberated mental condition but rather that the era of liberty in Africa unleashed a vicious circle of inferiority complex, slavishness, self-hatred, and confusion in her social and political systems. Okot, therefore, appears to have set out to dramatize Karl Popper's "paradox of freedom," in which the latter asserts that too much freedom leads to too little of it. The questions arising from Okot's ironic poetic tale would include such posers as: Was the African ready for independence at the time it came? Did he understand the true meaning of freedom? Could freedom have been a blessing to the African?

One had expected that the freedom derived from political independence would have ensured a new and progressive rationality. It did not. This is why all the characters in Okot's fictional world—Lawino, Ocol, Clementine, the prisoner (and those who imprisoned him) and the *malaya* (whore) [in "Song of Malaya"]— seem to be the shadows of their actual selves, somewhat propelled by a force other than an inner-directed one. . . . In various instances in Okot's poetry, either the persona is guilty of defeatism or he/she is accusing another of being afflicted by social malaise. The psychological aberration resulting from a subjugated consciousness—whether at the domestic level as in the case of Lawino or at the national and cultural level as in Ocol's case—is in itself an ailment of its own. . . .

Okot's protagonists appear to take the stance of spokespersons for or against Afro-tradition or Euro-culture, physical and spiritual torture, or societal hypocrisy, as in the case of the *malaya*. Sometimes, the mouthpiece syndrome may be a reflection of the function which poetry has always been known to fulfill in a typical African society. Nevertheless, morality is an important motif in Okot's poetry; at every stage he is asking us to pass some value judgment. His art is not one that you experience without feeling that you are being drawn into a moral battle. . . .

The fictional characters of Okot's "Songs" could not have made an impact on us as readers and observers of their actions if they had not been guilty of pawning either the freedom they earned from political independence or the private freedom which is their inalienable personal possession. Lawino, Ocol, Clementine, the prisoner (and his antagonists), and the *malaya* are evidently suffering from the afflictions of self-persecution. The common denominator for all the characters is that, when they are not promoting some defeatist tendency, they are themselves victims of it. . . .

As for the *malaya*, she is pinching everybody; she is making us realize the hypocrisy of our ostrich mentality. She is guilty herself, but she insists on showing that she is not alone—the teacher, the schoolboy, the sailor, the released detainee, the debauching Sikhs, the vegetarian Indian "breeding like a rat," Big Chief, the business executive, engineers, factory workers, shop assistants, party whips, and demagogues are all equally guilty. She knows our secrets and encourages us to remove our veil of pretense. Thus she seems to say that only when we have freed ourselves from our self-imposed imprisonment of guile and cant will we be able to breathe fresh air again. We may wish to continue our chosen way of life, for there is no one "who can command the sun not to rise in the morning," but we definitely need the *malaya*'s "Song" to purge us of our bondage to hypocrisy and self-deceit.

J. O. J. Nwachukwu-Agbada. *CE&S.* 12, 1 (Autumn 1989), pp. 95–96, 105

The oral literary features that Okot borrowed from Acoli traditional culture gave his poetry the distinctive oral song character that sets it apart from other written poetry. Nevertheless, Okot's songs can neither be sung nor fitted into the thematic classification of Acoli oral songs. Oral songs are composed in response to an immediate event or as a means of reflecting a localized issue within the village or clan. They are ephemeral, and their length is dictated by three factors: the creative ability of the composer-singer, the chosen theme, and the reaction of the audience. Other singers therefore have no obligation to perform the whole composition of any song. Modification of the original song gives it renewed life, and the audience's reaction depends on the quality of the performance.

In contrast, written poetry generally consists of fixed texts that have a certain number of lines per stanza. Its organization cannot be altered by anyone except the original poet. The images, symbols, and other literary qualities in it always remain the same, whereas the oral song can be modified to fit the specific performance situation. Once poetry has been written down, critics can only praise or blame the poet. . . .

Besides his creative borrowing of literary features from Acoli traditional culture, Okot has blended the different modes of Acoli oral songs in *Song of Lawino*. Satire dominates the early sections of the poem, which ends on a note of lament reminiscent of Acoli dirges. In the rest of the poem, Okot adopts the openly critical mode of the Bwola, Otole, and Apiti dance songs in which singers discard their satirical masks and directly confront the people they are satirizing. This approach is particularly appropriate for his criticism of politicians and Catholic missionaries. Although Lawino sometimes sings her own praises, she returns to the lament at the end of her Song. She laments the "death" of Ocol on two levels: the loss of a husband who can no longer consummate their marriage and the loss of a "Son of the Chief" who can no longer uphold his people's culture because he has assimilated Western values. . . .

The form of Okot's poetry is clearly derived from Acoli oral songs, which in many cases are inseparable from the dances during which they are performed. Viewed from this perspective, *Song of Lawino* falls into three overlapping parts. The satirical criticism in the first nine sections is directly related to the Orak dance songs that Okot classified in his . . . thesis as songs of "poetic justice." In section eleven, the mode is that of the political and topical songs that accompany the Bwola, Otole, and Apiti dances. The composer-singers of these songs do not wear the satirical masks of the Orak composer-singers, for their criticisms are collectively expressed by the participants in the dances; therefore, the lead singer cannot be held responsible for criticisms embedded in collectively performed songs. Sections twelve and thirteen are characterized by a mixture of modes, but the dominant one is that of lament: Lawino's attempt to dissuade Ocol has failed, and he has therefore died a cultural death. Their marriage has also ended, and her lament echoes the form and themes of an Acoli dirge.

Okot's poetic style is essentially vocal rather than visual; in fact, it is less concerned with the formal pattern on the written page than with breath. The mixture of humor, satire, and lament in *Song of Lawino* reflects Acoli oral poetic forms, which are interwoven with proverbs, similes, metaphors, symbols, and other figures of speech to constitute a powerful personal commentary on the social, political, religious, and economic situation in postindependence Uganda and, by extension, in the entire Third World.

Charles Okumu. RAL. 23, 3 (Fall 1992), pp. 55, 60–61, 64–65

OKRI, BEN (1959–   )

NIGERIA

With the possible exception of "What the Tapster Saw," which is more allegorical than the rest, [Ben] Okri's six stories [in *Stars of the New Curfew*] are all "true" reflections on life in Nigeria. The first goes back to the Biafran War; the rest are set in the present; all are vivid and frightening. The love story, "When the Lights Return," is like a guilt-ridden dream in which the heroine, white-clad Maria, is presented with Okri's consummate skill as the archetypal mistress of moral blackmail. In the background: the Lagos ghetto of Munshin, peopled with loathsome soldiers and a dead man who rises from a rubbish heap to preach revolt.

Okri's writing is suffused with helpless anger at the alienation of Nigerian society, the corruption not only of the rulers but also of the ruled who seem to connive at their own oppression. "The strongest fear in this town," one of his characters says, "is to be defenseless, to be without a powerful godfather, and therefore at the mercy of the drums. New starts are growing every day. They grow from the same powers, the same rituals . . ." The trouble with most people is that they cannot *see* the nature of the evil surrounding them. In "Worlds that Flourish," the hero, a clerk who is sacked without apparent reason, leaves his job without bitterness and tells his neighbor he feels "fine." This is "because you go around as if you don't have any eyes," the neighbor says. But even vision does not protect you in Okri's Nigeria. When the ex-clerk begins to see, he flees the city in horror, to end up in the village of the dead. There he rediscovers his neighbor who has been killed by a soldier who now displays *three* eyes.

Suzanne Cronje. New Statesman & Society. 1, 8 (July 29, 1988), pp. 43–44

In a short story the hero ought to discover some truth about himself, his fellow men, or society that has universal significance. Through him the reader achieves enlightenment, if not moral upliftment. For example, suffering makes us noble, we are our brother's keepers, labor makes us free, and so on.

The heroes in Ben Okri's collection of short stories [*Stars of the New Curfew*] do not have these simple consolations; they cannot find relief, much less salvation, in homilies. One hero hates suffering because it does not improve or ennoble, but sobers and hardens. The nightmares that they experience in life make them see life itself as nightmare. When it is discovered that reality is hallucination, the need for hardness and sobriety becomes obvious, and the experience of meaningless suffering becomes an epistemology of pain and illusion. . . .

Readers unfamiliar with the reality about which Okri writes will praise his fantastic imagination and wealth of invention. While not detracting from Okri's artistic powers, it is only fair to point out that what he writes about may appear hallucinatory and nightmarish but is nonetheless real. There is more description here—very accurate description—than invention. Okri holds up a mirror to actors in a neocolonial society who are incapable of distinguishing between tragedy and comedy. . . .

The style of these stories is lean, economical, almost claustrophobic. Floral embellishment would have destroyed the effects [it aims] to produce. The skeletal language—like clean-picked bones—allows us to see men, women, and children struggling viciously or gracefully for survival, then wondering if there is any purpose to it all, or whether survival is an end in itself.

P. F. Wilmot. WA. August 1, 1988, p. 1396

The Landscapes Within deals with the process of maturation of a young, bright, sensitive, and lonely artist as he tries to survive the general philistinism, corruption, and inhumanity that characterize big city life in Lagos. As a child, Omovo had moved with his parents from Igboland after the Nigeria-Biafra Civil War and had progressed quite well at school until he was prevented from taking the all-important school certificate examinations because of his father's failure to pay the necessary fees on time. Life becomes increasingly miserable for the young man when, not long after the death of his mother, his father remarries and, as a result of domestic tension, Omovo's elder brothers—Okur and Umeh—are kicked out of the family fold by their father.

After the struggle that usually accompanies a novel dealing with personal development, Omovo is finally able to find a job; and though he does have some friends (such as a painter called Dr. Okocha, Keme, the journalist, and Okoro, a veteran of the Nigerian Civil War), he becomes a lonely and sad person who finds solace only in painting and in the company of his lover-cum-friend Ifeyinwa, a married neighbor. Omovo and Ifeyinwa become attracted to each other because of some similar qualities (they are both sensitive, introverted, impressionable, intelligent, and great lovers of both literature and the visual arts), and also because they both feel trapped in a morally corrupt and physically degrading environment. Ifeyinwa has been forced into a life of misery because she was pushed into a loveless marriage after her father's suicide.

In scenes that clearly echo Ayi Kwei Armah's *The Beautyful Ones Are Not Yet Born* (on both the literal and symbolic levels), Okri shows how Omovo becomes more and more aware of the extensive malaise that pervades his society. But, unlike Armah's anonymous protagonist, who merely drifts aimlessly and helplessly in a sea of corruption, Omovo thinks that not only can he see through the wholly materialistic nature of the society, but that he can even depict the dirty quality of the corrupt society on canvas. He increasingly learns, however, that for his actions to be more meaningful he has to do more than merely express a symbolic disgust with corruption. Thus, by the end of *The Landscapes Within*, Omovo, who is often depicted as passive, nearly always given to reverie, has become capable of making down-to-earth assessments of events around him and able to act accordingly. After a series of terrible, even tragic, events (for example, he is forced to resign from his job because he dares display some modicum of integrity; Ifeyinwa, while trying to escape from her brutal husband, is senselessly killed in an insane war between her village and a neighboring village), the protagonist finally sees the need to forge a new vision of reality. Inspired by a poem written by his brother, Okur, Omovo suggests (albeit implicitly) that it is not enough for him as an artist to be merely cognizant of the filth around him; he should be ready to act.

Abioseh Michael Porter. WLWE. 28, 2 (Autumn 1988), pp. 203–4

"Little flowers in the shadows that's what we all are. Nobody knows what the larger shadows will do to the flowers; nobody knows what the flowers will become," says the mother to Jeffia, the protagonist of Ben Okri's novel *Flowers and Shadows*. The titular leitmotif iterates through the entire book, in variants spoken by different characters, as an omnipresent scorching sun beats down upon them all and surveys their actions.

Jeffia, an eighteen-year-old boy, suddenly starts noticing things about himself, as if the hushed, smooth life of his big home with its well-kept gardens, nicely furnished and air-conditioned rooms, servants, three cars, and other luxuries of well-to-do Nigerian society had ceased to exist. He is faced with the squalor of his surroundings, the filthy roads full of beggars and hungry people, the corrupt police, and suspicions about his father's integrity. The death of his best friend aggravates the situation even further and deepens his insight. . . .

Ben Okri was nineteen when he wrote *Flowers and Shadows*, and the acclaim it received was confirmed by the success of his second, *The Landscapes Within*. The short-story collections *Incidents at the Shrine* and *Stars of the New Curfew* offered further proof of his gifts. Okri has served as poetry editor of *West Africa* and in 1987 received the Commonwealth Writers Prize for Africa and the Aga Khan Prize for Fiction, sponsored by the *Paris Review*.

Nadezda Obradović. WLT. 64, 4 (Autumn 1990), p. 687

With *The Landscapes Within*, Ben Okri extends the line of novels (most notably by [Chinua] Achebe, Ngugi [wa Thiong'o], [Wole] Soyinka and [Ayi Kwei] Armah) which have sought to capture the disappointment and disillusion in postindependence Africa. And as the work of a stylist, the novel traces its line from works by Soyinka and Armah—whose writings it also recalls as a literary work in which the effort to imply, demonstrate, or posit aspects of the theory or practice of art is central or considerable. The novel paints the decline and decay, the materialism and corruption of a nation and the sense of loss and futility among the people; but it does all this so as to make conspicuous the sensitive character of its protagonist, Omovo, a young man aspiring to become a distinguished artist. In pursuing this primary interest, *The Landscapes Within* throws its spotlight on the turbulent, clustered mind of Omovo in order to make clear the lines of a mind's growth. . . .

The Landscapes Within is, above all else, a portrait of Omovo as a young man and artist, with special attention paid to his growing mind. He is shown picking his difficult way emotionally through the welter of life's experiences and intellectually through a clutter of ideas and concepts. His efforts to interfuse life and art, and to reach or grasp views and take attitudes on the aesthetics of art are also revealed. In these efforts, his ideals and models, as well as his preferences and affinities, underline the eclecticism of his mind. Out of the quarried pieces and fragments, however, Omovo is yet to build a coherent theory of art; but then, as he himself says: "I am still learning." It is to stress the education of his mind, to emphasize the point that the young man is still learning that, again and again, the author draws attention to the rather vast cultural background (African and European) from which Omovo seeks his inspiration in painting, literature, and music.

Ayo Mamudu. CE&S. 13, 2 (Spring 1991), pp. 85, 91

Ben Okri has been successful as a sensitive and careful [short-story] writer and poet. His short stories evoke the materially empty but mentally throbbing lives of people reduced to poverty in the ghettos of Lagos and other cities of Nigeria. His colorful characters fight themselves and their neighbors in a space that is forever narrowing physically; but they call forth another space, somewhere beyond the hand of poverty, and lay claim to it.

The Famished Road, his latest novel . . . teems with these dual spaces, these poor characters, these aspiring human beings who are forever defending their humanity against all forms of authority beginning with that of the slum landlord. Right from the beginning, the central character, Azaro, is captured in his duality, a being conscious of the world of his unborn companions who are forever wanting him back in their world and his poor parents, Mum and Dad, who tell him frankly that they have nothing to offer him except love and a promise of a good life. When those offerings are placed against the enticing images of the unborn, it is not always clear in the mind of Azaro which of the two worlds he should lean towards. The world of the living he enjoys through wandering in towns and in the forest, seeing double all the time and frightening his poor parents who sometimes react, not with the love they promise him, but with anger and frustration. In crossing a busy street, should Azaro allow himself to be knocked down by a car, thus permitting him to join the world of his unborn companion spirits who are anxiously awaiting his return [or] should he cross the road to the other side successfully and make his parents happy. . . .

This is not one story, but many stories. More than that, this is the story of the transition of many families from poverty through the ghettos of the cities to the posh areas of the town. It is the portrait of a world that stubbornly, perhaps because of the poverty of the people, clings to the superstitions and traditional healing devices of ancient Africa. It is also a narration of the failure of the modern state to effect for the better the lives of the majority of its citizens. It is also a successful portrait of the physical and mental world of the wretched of the earth.

The presentation of that spiritual world is not a gimmick of literary style borrowed from Latin America as a few writers from Africa are being deceived into practicing. Here, the mental image of the world of the traditional African is laid bare, side by side with the modern world brought into being as a result of the encounter with Europe. In this Ben Okri is being true to the world he depicts.

Kole Omotoso. *WA*. April 1–7, 1991, pp. 474–75

Ben Okri is the novelist of portents and of wonders. His last book, *The Famished Road*, had the Abiku-child Azaro wandering in from the world of the spirits, nosing the everyday world with his curiosity, exploring a terrain which, it gradually became clear, had more than a little in common with Nigeria on the brink of independence. In this environment Azaro the spirit-child existed as witness, interpreter, and victim: never quite in charge, never quite *savant*. Wonders took place before his astonished eyes, and we, the readers, participated in his astonishment.

In *Songs of Enchantment*, Azaro reappears, and so do the other members of the cast: the stalwart mother, energetic and wayward father, Madam Koto, bar owner and source both of mayhem and of strength. But this is very far from being a sequel. It is arguably a better novel since, riding on the back of its brother, it has no need to use its strength. Despite its relative shortness, the pace of this new book is leisurely, masterful. It takes its time and achieves its effects slowly. . . .

Okri shows us a society in the throes of convulsions familiar to those who contemplate the dilemmas facing Africa and the Third World. He is less concerned about the causes of these convulsions, or indeed the ways of ending them than the potential for transfiguration that lies inside the events. Okri shows us revolutions in the making, and the way that these evidences of instability hold within themselves the energy which may redeem them. It is why so many of his characters seem occupied in telling stories, since each story—a novel within a novel—is a paradigm of that sublime unpredictability of the phenomenal world which, seen through eyes alert to its magic, can mend the wounds of society even as it seems to rend them. Such novelists are needed because they teach us that, if we wish to progress and revive our forces, the very material for that revival may lie within the conditions of seeming defeat.

Robert Fraser. *WA*. April 12–18, 1993, p. 616

OSOFISAN, FEMI (1946–   )

NIGERIA

[*The Chattering and the Song* and *Once upon Four Robbers*] depict [Femi] Osofisan's radical approach to historical and social realities and the urgent need for a social revolution that will give birth to a socialist state in Nigeria. *The Chattering and the Song* deals with a revolt led by a group of enlightened radical youths challenging the forces of rot, corruption, and dictatorship, ending in the offer of a model for a new society that will replace autocracy in all its forms. This theme comes out positively in the central dramatic scene of the play, which is also a play-within-a-play. Here, Osofisan re-creates—even rewrites—the history of Oyo during the chaotic period of the rebellious Bashorun Gaha who overthrew the reigning Alafin and set up a reign of terror, killing all the princes of Oyo except Abiodun, who was crippled in one leg. Abiodun grew up to challenge and overthrow this despot, re-establishing law and order. But as . . . [Gerald] Moore rightly observes, Osofisan is against all forms of autocracy, however benevolent: for him, "heroism is a collective, not a kingly virtue." Osofisan throws his sympathy with Latoye, the rebel, to demonstrate the essence of a social revolution that will liberate society from the yoke of oppression. Latoye defies the Alafin by summoning his creative powers to raise the consciousness of the oppressed, represented in the play by the king's bodyguards (acted by the musicians). Instead of portraying the aspect of history where the old—the authoritative Alafin—uses his magical powers to subdue the young rebel, Osofisan depicts the successful challenge to traditional tyranny. . . .

But if Osofisan appropriates the historical past for his social vision in *The Chattering and the Song*, he confronts contemporary reality in *Once upon Four Robbers*, which is a metaphorical treatment of the phenomenon of armed robbery. His dialectic treatment of history . . . in the first play is continued in this new play, where he looks at the Nigerian condition from a purely Marxist viewpoint. He regards the armed robbers—Alhaja, Hassan, Angola, and Major—as products of an unjust social system. . . . In the program notes for the premiere of *Once upon Four Robbers*, Osofisan describes the robbers as a tiny part of the Nigerian masses who have been brutalized by social stratification—the existence of two extremely distinct social classes—in Nigeria. He attributes the violence of armed robbery to this social structure. . . .

The two plays . . . show Osofisan's employment of the revolutionary potential of theater to embody the political and ideological character of his work. Like his contemporaries, he aims to propose a socialist ethical perspective for Nigeria by first reawakening the people's consciousness to a reality beyond the decadence of the present. There are dangers inherent in such a commitment. As these young playwrights are aware, one of the grave dangers is that artistic depth might be sacrificed for political content; that the writers might resort to sheer propaganda as in the Farmers' Anthem in *The Chattering and the Song*. A more serious fault is Osofisan's inability, occasionally, to carry through a theatrical device set in motion in certain episodes. An example is the way Mokan's emotion gets in the way of his successful completion of his role as Aresa, the Alafin's chief bodyguard. His vindictiveness makes him reveal himself, for the first time, as a secret policeman. This sudden revelation of identity and his arrest of Sontri and Yajin, puzzlingly blurs the device and changes the mood of the play. A macabre dimension is thus attained from the position of a wedding entertainment play. But such faults are very few, as Osofisan appreciably succeeds in employing theatrical mechanics to harmonize the related arts of music, dance, mime, and verbal arts, achieving an impressive aesthetic quality which gives authenticity to his strong political bent. This must be the trend of a theater like Nigeria's, which is growing more and more revolutionary.

Olu Obafemi. In Eldred Durosimi Jones, ed.
African Literature Today. 12 (1982), pp. 121–24, 133–34

In *Morountodun*, Osofisan . . . uses the Agbekoya Farmers' Rebellion of 1968–1969 as the background for the portrayal of the individual's response to social change. Yet because he was commissioned to write a play celebrating the International Year of the Woman, he manipulates this event to examine the role of women in political activism. Additionally, he questions the function of myth in a contemporary setting. In accord with his aim to create a theater that encourages audiences to think, Osofisan begins with a group of actors onstage preparing for a performance, thereby calling attention at the outset to the role-playing, illusory nature of theater. But before these actors can even begin their production, the theater hall is invaded by a group of women traders demanding that the performance be cancelled. Hence, the audience is confronted almost immediately with community people altering theatrical production for attention to social issues. . . .

Osofisan incorporates traditional techniques into his drama: songs (sung in Yoruba), riddles, proverbs, and enacted parables. At other instances, also in accordance with traditional practices which call attention to the artificial, nonrealistic quality inherent in performance, Osofisan has Titubi stop the forward movement of the action to relate, by re-creating an event, the process by which she was won over to the farmers' perspective. Because all these devices represent familiar performance modes for the audience, they have the potential to lessen audience resistance to the political positions espoused. . . .

By exploiting traditional aesthetic structures while affirming and challenging his audience's abilities to exert positive control over their society, Femi Osofisan creates a theater with great potential to articulate his countrymen's aspirations and capture universal dreams of a just, sane world. How that potential is realized in the actual modes of production is another crucial consideration, which an extended discussion of his work would have to engage.

Sandra L. Richards. *Theatre Journal*. 39, 2 (1987), pp. 225–27

The Chattering and the Song and *Morountodun* both manifest Osofisan's concern with reinterpreting history in favor of the oppressed. The subject is history together with myth, and the issue, a reappraisal of the relevance of these to contemporary concrete reality.

In *The Chattering*, a casual celebration of a wedding eve ends up as a complex spectacle of re-enacted history merged with contemporary reality, and a proposition for the utilization of men and women's natural assets to surmount present and future social woes. For Sontri and Yajin's wedding eve, a play presumably written by Sontri is to be acted. Sontri is an angry young man through whom Osofisan denounces society's injustices. Sontri's play has its material in the so-called heroic deeds of an Alafin of Oyo, Abiodun. This play-within-[a]-play is actually a re-creation of history, not from the side of the so-called victors (the kings and the lords as is usually the case), but from that of the victims. Alafin Abiodun, like the present-day ruling class, feeds on the blood and sweat of others, yet his is the race of the "heroes." The "rebel" (played by Leje), arraigned before Abiodun (played by Sontri), rises to challenge, and succeeds in breaking the nerve center of Alafin's tyranny: the myth of a god-abetted subjugation of one human being by another. Herein lies Osofisan's point of departure. By reversing Latoye's and Abiodun's roles, Osofisan sides with the oppressed. Latoye becomes the true hero through his emancipation of the guards, while Abiodun becomes the villain because he has used his position to oppress and exploit.

The play-within-a-play does not end, but is arrested at a strategic point: when the people's awareness has been aroused and the people have been, like Brechtian spectators, inspired to take action for the improvement of their condition. Latoye has commanded that Abiodun be seized, but Mokan (playing Aresa, Abiodun's head of bodyguards) reveals his identity as a secret policeman on Sontri's trail. Sontri is arrested as an agitator—an action which gratifies

Mokan, who has been out to avenge Yajin's rejection of him. Sontri's arrest is to prove the point (to Nigeria's "angry young men"?) that the revolution needs not just anger but good organization and tact—a channeling of anger for results. Using masks, Leje who is Osongongon, the farmers' leader, is able to get close to the ruling class, know their plans and lay counter strategies to their oppressive measures against the progressive movement. . . .

Who's Afraid of Solarin? is parabolic mainly at a generalized, metaphorical level. This play, adapted from [Nikolai] Gogol's *The Inspector General*, shows a motley of social types. Ineptitude, indolence, indiscipline, gross misconduct—name the vice: the characters in the play depict a society at the nadir of depravity.

In the play, rumors of an impending visit of the Public Complaints Commissioner, Solarin, give everybody the jitters. The councillors and their chairman have shirked their various duties and have misappropriated public funds. The pastor of a church has also stolen the contributions of his congregation. As they all live in fear of the commissioner's wrath, they decide to seek the protection of Baba Fawomi, an Ifa priest. But Baba Fawomi is a mere charlatan, who merely plays on the gullibility of his clientele to enrich himself. Where the true Ifa priest divines without any mind to profit-making, Baba Fawomi taxes his clientele very heavily for services he is incapable of rendering. A rascal, Isola Oriebora, cashes in on the officials' ignorance and impersonates the commissioner. He swindles everyone: he seduces the pastor's daughter, extracts bribes from the officials, and then absconds. The arrival of the true commissioner is announced.

Osofisan's "revolutionary aesthetics" flag in *Who's Afraid?* This is partly because he merely throws the jabs at a decadent society without suggesting an alternative. He ridicules the vices and fails to show a way out. By arresting reality at an unsavory moment and failing to propel it forward, Osofisan's satire acquires a tinge of cynicism. The cynicism figures also in the characterization of Isola Oriebora. Like Efua Sutherland's Ananse [in *The Marriage of Anansewa*] and the trickster hero of the so-called moral fable, Oriebora gets away with his tricks. Oriebora's progress becomes a promotion of a negative ethic.

Modupe O. Olaogun. Okike. 27–28 (March 1988), pp. 46, 54–55

From the late 1970s, in such plays as *The Chattering and the Song* and *Morountodun and Other Plays*, as well as in his critical essays and interviews, Osofisan has consistently espoused the cause of a socialist revolution. To this end, he dedicated himself to the systematic destruction of all forms of social myths, whether religious as in *No More the Wasted Breed* in *Morountodun and Other Plays*, or the mystification of history in *The Chattering and the Song* or the mythification of "government power" in *Morountodun*. . . .

Osofisan's poetry in *Minted Coins* makes radical departures from views established in his earlier works—his view of the nature or philosophy of history and existence in general, as well as his view of traditional myths, legends, and history. There is an apparent shift from the basic materialist philosophy that informs his mature plays; [from] the materialist philosophy that "unmasks" all myths, to an idealist philosophy of life and history, which not only accepts the belief-contents of myths but accepts a philosophy of life (new in his artistic career) that is strongly underlined by traditional myths, the philosophy of the cyclical nature of existence. . . . "Minted coins" symbolize desires—for love, wealth or power—which are basically good but can be corrupted. Because of their passing from hand to hand, coins stand for "the meeting, parting and returning," that is the essence of all life. Moreover their roundness evokes the cyclical nature of time.

Aderemi Bamikunle. CE&S. 11, 1 (Autumn 1989), pp. 109–10

Femi Osofisan's reputation rests on a series of plays which have marked him as a leading figure among the younger generation of dramatists in Nigeria. Osofisan's first published work was not, however, a play, but a novel. This work, *Kolera Kolej*, appeared in 1975. It remains something of a maverick. . . . Yet there is more to *Kolera Kolej* than its neglect would suggest. In its manipulation of form and language, for instance, it is fairly adventurous. Further, an analysis of its structure reveals a way of thinking—a preoccupation with formal matters—that is dominant in those of Osofisan's works that are highly regarded. . . .

Kolera Kolej is an audacious piece of work. Its internal disjunctions are constantly stimulating: the narrative voice is one that can tease, lacerate, or turn blunt and earnest, within the space of a few lines. Clearly Osofisan's imagination is taken here with the possibility of creating novel form through the combination of dissimilar materials. In the plays that followed *Kolera Kolej*, this tendency emerges repeatedly: in the use of contrasting voices and language forms, in the notion of the play-within-[a]-play. The technique relates, of course, to the process of dialectic: argument progresses through the radical juxtaposition of unlike elements. In *Kolera Kolej*, however, Osofisan's technique has produced a dialectic that is not altogether coherent. . . . .

To date, more than a dozen of Osofisan's plays have appeared on stage. The two discussed below [*Morountodun* and *Once upon Four Robbers*] both demonstrate Osofisan's predilection for structuring contrasts: for those disjunctions in register and dramatic style which enable him to build his argument by a process of contradictions and which lead his audience towards a conclusion only by way of a series of revisions in the judgment-forming process.

The bulk of *Morountodun* is written in a clear, idiomatic English. Occasionally, however, the language shifts into a more intense, heightened register, to express especially forceful emotions, as in the heroine Titubi's comments on the historical figure Moremi; while, for a "Moremi play" inserted into the main action, Osofisan devises a more decorous and formal style. . . .

By contrast with the multistranded complexity of *Morountodun*, *Once upon Four Robbers* focuses with fierce concentration on a single idea, establishing armed robbery as an "apt metaphor" for life in contemporary Nigeria and the armed robber as both product of and moralizing commentator on an "unjust society." The public execution of these robbers may mean death and disgrace, "but so also does hunger, so does unemployment"; Osofisan reverses the orthodox

morality (that armed robbers are vile) in an attempt to provoke a sharper awareness of those injustices that the establishment prefers to ignore. The play
exposes a scandalous disjunction between the public recognition of a symptomatic evil and the systematic neglect of evils that are fundamental.

Osofisan's robbers pour scorn on the mentality of the rich and castigate a
system in which menial labor is equated to "respectability." The self-seeking
individualist is condemned, whether in the person of the army sergeant who
embezzles money recaptured after a theft, or in the case of Major—one of the
robbers, who betrays the others and is then immediately identified with the
absurd, ten-Mercedes-owning rich.

Major's betrayal places a moral gulf between him and his fellow robbers.
He is shown as having betrayed an ideal—the ideal of solidarity practiced by the
militantly antisocial. Osofisan succeeds in convincingly rendering the principle of
solidarity; it is, however, a weakness in the play that he never achieves a *categorical* distinction between Major's solitary acquisitiveness and the group acquisitiveness of the robbers; he never really establishes what the robbers mean by "justice"
or how, except in a sophistic sense, they can claim to be fighting for it. . . .

Osofisan's imagination is charged with the notion of conflict, with the
actual but often unspoken state of war existing between different social classes.
His work attempts to articulate this conflict and, in particular, to establish disjunctions—tangible contradictions—through which the *real* relationship
between opposing ideologies can be assessed.

The frequency with which Osofisan's work sets up these disjunctions
indicates the extent of his imaginative involvement in the dialectical process.
The technical expertise he has at his disposal is considerable; hence the variety
of means he is able to devise to provoke us into new recognitions: ranging from
shifts in language mode to songs that are, superrealistically, self-exposing, to
the creation of model, or the play-within-the-play. . . .

Osofisan's work very rarely dramatizes the life of the masses; it is the
dilemma of the leaders, their psychological development, that seems to preoccupy
Osofisan rather than the lives of the people they lead. *The Chattering and the
Song*, for example, succeeds as an exciting and inventive play partly because it is
a play about exceptionally exciting and inventive people. Further . . . in most cases
Osofisan is engaged in a process of special validation: the man in *Kolera Kolej*,
Titubi, and, to some extent, Sontri in *The Chattering and the Song* are very nearly
redundant, or even counterrevolutionary: each has to be shown to have a useful
role to play—a large part of the tension in Osofisan's work lies in the process by
which the apparent reactionary is revealed finally as a functioning revolutionary.
The one piece discussed above that does focus in some sense on the average man
is *Once upon Four Robbers*, in which the masses are approached only very
obliquely, as their condition is dramatized through the metaphor of armed robbery. This preoccupation with the leadership role may not be a weakness, but in
the work of an avowedly radical writer like Osofisan, it is a distinct peculiarity.

Chris Dunton. In Eldred Durosimi Jones, ed. *The Question of Language in African
Literature Today* (Trenton, N. J.: Africa World Press, 1991), pp. 81–82, 85, 88–89

The title play in Femi Osofisan's latest collection [*Birthdays Are Not for Dying and Other Plays*] is an ambivalent melodrama of corruption, strained moral rectitude, and calamity. Kunle Aremo is obsessed with carrying out his late father's wish that, at the age of thirty, he take sole control of the company his father built up. He stages a board meeting on his birthday at which his father's corrupt business associates are exposed and dismissed. These include his father-in-law, whose daughter Kunle condemns both as unfaithful and as the mere tool of a marriage of convenience. His own son, whose paternity he disclaims, falls ill and is left to be rushed to the hospital by his distraught wife. In his moment of triumph Kunle is rebuked for his righteous action by the only uncorrupted member of the board for humiliating his elderly associates. With a mysterious threatening gesture, concealed from the audience, Councillor Lekan Bamgbade reawakens in Kunle an old childhood trauma, which leads, with the crazed connivance of a wife just bereaved of her son, to a climax reminiscent of Greek tragedy. What promised to become a simple morality play shows righteous justice dashed on the rock of human passions and confounded by the confusing claims of compassion.

The second drama, *Fires Burn and Die Hard*, again focuses upon an entanglement of material and intangible moral values. A new market to replace one destroyed by fire is about to be opened, the marketwomen rejoicing at the prospect of regaining "a veritable home . . . a hive of comfort and companionship, for all who were born female, in a land where men are raised to be tyrants." Then the diviners foresee fresh disaster: one of the market women herself had set the fire; and, if no cleansing sacrifice is performed, the tragedy will recur. The incendiary, herself president of the Market Women's Association, confesses, learning "Profit is a demanding creed," for her son's righteous determination to report his discovery that she sold contraband goods had caused her to burn the evidence. Ironically, her illicit wealth had only been for him.

The short work *The Inspector and the Hero* is comparatively simplistic, a morality play whose message Nigeria doubtless needs, but it makes for weak drama. The plot is simply stated: a wealthy politician, on the brink of becoming state governor, is tracked down and exposed by a police inspector who resists all attempts to threaten or bribe him into silence. Whereas the politician makes his childhood poverty an alibi for his ruthless acquisition of "money and power," the inspector, of equally humble origins, lives by another "dream," that of a cleansed society.

Michael Thorpe. *WLT.* 65, 4 (Autumn 1991), pp. 754–55

A radical writer and critic with an articulated commitment to a materialist, socialist, and class perspective, Osofisan combines a radical ideology with a recognition of the importance of cultural traditions. He has consistently advocated and defended art that is anti-elitist, popular, and accessible. Like most leading Nigerian dramatists, Osofisan's dramaturgy often draws inspiration from traditional culture, but he is distinguished by the fact that he uses the devices of oral literature for far more radical purposes than any other Nigerian playwright. . . .

While the thematic interest of *The Chattering and the Song* and *Moroun-todun* derives from a revolutionary reinterpretation of history, myth, and legend, a number of Osofisan's plays attract our attention through their exploitation of the technical resources of folklore narrative. Oral narrative devices constitute the vehicle of plot and dramatic action in *Once upon Four Robbers*, *Farewell to a Cannibal Rage*, and *Morountodun*.

In these plays, Osofisan uses the traditional folktale approach of organizing moonlight stories and riddles around a storyteller or narrator. The storyteller usually places himself at the edge of an audience in circular formation and shouts out the traditional introductory formula, "*Alo o*" (meaning I have a riddle). And the audience responds "*Aalo!*" (meaning we are listening). This way the storyteller captures the attention of, and establishes a rapport with, the audience. This also generates full audience participation in the theater. . . .

There are hardly any of Osofisan's plays that do not employ the traditional Yoruba music, song, and dance. They possess participatory qualities because they evoke responses from the audience. They serve as means through which the audience actually partakes of the action on the stage. The playwright manipulates these elements not only to convey a sensually rich atmosphere but also to provide the Brechtian link between the action of the plot and the thematic horizon of the play. For example, the "Song of Khaki and Agbada" in *Esu and the Vagabond Minstrels* indicts both the military and civilian governments of corruption in Nigeria. . . .

Given his ideological orientation, it is not surprising that Osofisan consciously employs the devices of oral literature and the traditional performance mode in his plays. His conscious intention is to create a popular theater form with which the masses easily identify. Through this form, he is able to elicit responses from his audience and mobilize them to participate in the drama, thus breaking the "fourth wall" and bringing drama outside the stage to the level of the popular audience.

Osofisan also uses oral literature as a source of ideological attack that challenges and criticizes contemporary Nigeria, in which the social, political, and economic arrangements benefit only the ruling class. The desire for a new social order in which the masses shall be free from the existing oppression of the hegemony is implicit in his theater.

Muyiwa P. Awodiya. In Eldred Durosimi Jones, ed. *Orature in African Literature Today* (Trenton, N. J.: Africa World Press, 1992), pp. 105, 107, 112

OSUNDARE, NIYI (1947–   )

NIGERIA

Niyi Osundare's volume *Village Voices* reveals him as a rural lyricist, one who plucks poetic images from the fields of his youth, but without sentimentality or nostalgia. . . . He recalls how satirical songs were composed and used to shame wrongdoers; public humiliation was an effective social sanction. "This kind of creativity is a source of great inspiration. It has also sensitized me into the realization that poetry can never be divided from the society in which it has grown."

What Osundare calls "the poetry of abuse" arises directly from Ekiti tradition. . . . Osundare, whose first volume is entitled *Songs of the Marketplace*, says when he can't write, he takes a bus to market and returns to "mediate, not manipulate the experience, make it even more beautiful and give it back to society." . . .

Songs of the Marketplace opens with a definition: "Poetry is / the hawker's ditty / the eloquence of the gong / the lyric of the marketplace . . . man / meaning to / man." Such a definition is fundamentally communal, far from what Osundare called "the formalist and reified mentality of the European age of decadence." He says that "right from the beginning, I have been brought up to see the whole artistic enterprise as essentially socialized." For him . . . art is explicitly political. "I believe very strongly in socialist humanism. I believe that capitalism has not only failed us but ruined us, that we must share what we have. This is what the farmers are saying in *Village Voices*." In their words, then, "Let me be / an active grip / in a hand of equal fingers," and again, "Let no-one tell us again / that fingers are not equal / for we know / how the thumb grew fatter / than all the others."

Jane Bryce. WA. July 21, 1986, pp. 1524–25

[Osundare's] poetry has shown considerable development resulting in contrasting poetic practices in both [*Songs of the Marketplace* and *Village Voices*]. The contrast is clear at the level of form and content. Though many of the poems of *Songs of the Marketplace* are about Nigeria, a good proportion are about events in the Third World and on Third World personalities: the situations in Nicaragua ("The Fall of the Beast") and South Africa in "Soweto" and "Namibia Talks." . . . In *Village Voices* the focus shows complete concentration on the situation of the underprivileged in Nigeria. In *Songs of the Marketplace*, the poetic voice is still very much the voice of the poet as an individual as he roams the national and international political systems, satirically exposing the social contradictions, pretensions, oppression, and exploitations in the systems. In *Village Voices* the poetic voice has become the communal voice of the rural population of exploited peasants in their stand against their exploiters. Osundare's attitude towards this social group has undergone considerable change. In "Ignorance" in *Songs of the Marketplace*, the poet regards the oppressed as an ignorant lot, whose ignorance makes possible the rule of the oppressors. They are like the "sheep" that have "all agreed / to give their crown to a wolf." The result of a shift to a socialist perspective in *Village Voices* has led to a new confidence in the mass of underprivileged Nigerians and in their world-view and the art traditions that express that world-view. It is the explorations of the traditional world-view and relevant art tradition that is the special [quality] of Osundare's poetry.

There is quite a variety of themes in Osundare's poetry. Apart from the concern with international politics as it affects Third World nations in *Songs of the Marketplace*, there are the fascinating poems of "Songs of dawn and seasons," based on a close observation of the seasons of the year, climatic phenomena, and how they affect the cycles of human existence. These poems are very striking in their vivid images of nature that tickle the visual and aural senses. But they are more fascinating because of their subtle suggestion that the movement of the seasons is an analogy for the cycles of life moving from dryness and decay, with its discomforts and expectations, into the promise and fulfillment of hopes in the "Dawn." "Inchoate hour / soothtime / For straightening twisted word / for the ears of a waking day / Dawn / is time recall the future / foretell the past."

The most important preoccupation in both volumes of poetry is the politics of Nigeria, especially the marginalization of the peasantry and low-income workers in Nigerian society. . . .

If there is a general socialist/Marxist tendency in recent Nigerian literature, Osundare's poetry represents the most refined expression of the perspective's interpretation of contemporary politics. We are used to the elite addressing the system on behalf of the underprivileged. What we are not quite used to is the underprivileged's analyses of the social system they build but which they do not benefit from. This is what we see in poem after poem in *Village Voices*. Particularly in "The Land of Unease," "A Villager's Protest," "The New Farmer's Bank," "A Farmer on Seeing Cocoa House, Ibadan," and "Listen, Book Wizard" among others, the peasant, armed with the world-view of traditional life assesses [the] urban-based system run by the classes of politicians and their intellectuals and finds it wanting. In contrast with the inequitable distribution of the nation's resources, the peasantry shows its preference for egalitarianism that is the basis of [the] traditional social system.

Aderemi Bamikunle. *LitC*. 23, 1–2 (1988), pp. 81–84

As a critic, Osundare has not been prolific or, perhaps to be more accurate, he has not published many articles that can be found in North American university libraries. What is most remarkable about Osundare's very fine scholarship is its preoccupation with artistic quality. The Marxist is always in view, but he avoids the sociological rehashing of plot and the belabored paraphrasing of content and political arguments that are so common among Marxist critical writings. Implicit in all of Osundare's analyses is his conviction that a writer's first responsibility is to his/her craft. For example, the title of his article "'As Grasshoppers to Wanton Boys': The Role of the Gods in the Novels of Elechi Amadi" would lead one who knew that a Marxist had written it to expect an antireligion, antimysticism tract, ridiculing an author (not characters) for belief in the supernatural. Instead, we are treated to an erudite piece of scholarship which argues with other critics in an elegant, unstrident manner, and which demonstrates through comparison with a wide range of writers from many periods and places why Amadi is a third-rate writer; Amadi's deficiencies as a political thinker are subordinate to the point of being subliminal to this argument. . . .

Osundare is amazingly prolific as a poet. To date he has published two volumes, *Songs of the Marketplace* and *Village Voices*. A third volume is in press with Heinemann: *The Eye of the Earth*. A fourth, *A Nib in the Pond* is searching for a publisher, and two more volumes are near completion: *Requiem for the Second Republic* and *Daughter of the Rain* (love poems). All of the poems in these collections are produced separately from the average of two poems he writes each week "as a matter of policy and challenge" . . . for his extremely popular weekly Sunday column "Songs of the Season" in the national *Nigerian Tribune*. For about three years now he has been experimenting in this column with "verse journalism."

Stephen H. Arnold. WLWE. 29, 1 (Spring 1989), pp. 1–3

[Niyi Osundare is] a poet who mastered the technique of fusing oral traditions and modern poetic trends quite early in his career. In *Village Voices*, Osundare explores both the elasticity of poetic language and the intricate web of life in his society with a penetration unmatched by even the most notable poets. The personae in the poetry are varied and the thematic concerns multiple. If Chinweizu is the poet for the ordinary man, Osundare is the poet for the suffering man. His poetry confirms James Reeves's observation that "what poetry does to the mass of ordinary experience is to make permanent and memorable whatever in it is vital and significant." There are the parallelisms, adept use of vivid allusions, stark imagery, and pointillism of committed poetry. . . . With this mission Osundare commences a poetic exploration of the Nigerian social climate. The vision is that of a sensitive artist reluctant to allow his voice to become muzzled by rampant injustice. The division of the collection of poems illustrates the poet's sense of organization.

Metaphor is the idiom of this poetry. It is a technique that enables the poet to adopt abundant materials such as witty aphorisms and phrases from the Yoruba oral traditions. In addition, his poetry is highly political and social. It is not an attempt to beat the newspaper headline news of the day but a matter of effective generation of ideas related to stark realities. "A Dialogue of Drums" cautions reason as two drummers engage in dialogue to discover the effectiveness of their practice. Osundare uses dramatic language in this poem to capture humanity's weakness and predilection for sycophancy. . . . The voices who raise the songs are numerous. They include the street fighters, caricatured members of the ruling classes, farmers, politicians, and marketwomen. Osundare matches language with characters, and this technique necessitates the creation of appropriate patterns of linguistic behavior. In "Not in My Season of Songs" the language is that of a mature adult; in "Eating with All the Fingers" it is that of a troubled elder; and in "Feigning a Rebel" it is the language of a poor villager. Language is made a component part of his poetic art and illustrates his ability to mold the chosen character to suit the artistic creation.

In the highly lyrical poem "Akintunde Come Home," the poet creates a persona whose language indicates that he is a father. The frequency of proverbs and witty aphorisms are the marks of a wise father; and Osundare exploits these linguistic devices in this poem, which appeals to Akintunde to return home from the land where money is god, and since all men cannot be Irokos, stresses that, though the home may be full of meatless meals, it could still harbor amiable souls.

Ezenwa-Ohaeto. In Eldred Durosimi Jones, ed. The Question of Language in
African Literature Today (Trenton, N. J.: Africa World Press, 1991), pp. 160–61

In Osundare's ideal, "Poetry" is "man / meaning to / man." With this introduction, *Songs of the Marketplace* is meant to be popular poetry rendered in [a] "popular" art form shared by the community. His poetry is best appreciated as developing towards achieving this ideal.

The central preoccupation of his poetry is thus established in this first collection: the concern he feels for the suffering and deprivations of the masses; the disgust he feels for their exploiters and oppressors, the politicians; and the hope he harbors of the oppressed overturning the system to their own advantage. The subject matter of this collection is common enough, as the poet or his poetic persona quests through his society exposing one social malaise after another: the social suffering and deprivation of the masses ("Excursions"), large scale maladministration and mismanagement ("Sule Chase"), political fraud ("Rithmetic Ruse," "Siren"). Everywhere the poet goes, the university ("Publish or Perish"), the Railway Corporation ("The Nigerian Railway"), the civil service ("Excursions"), the story is the same: fraud on a pervasive large scale, inefficiency and mismanagement in high places with the masses bearing the burden of the fraudulent mismanagement of the leaders. . . .

In many respects it is in *Village Voices* that Osundare realizes his ideals in poetry. Here his social vision based on the socio-political values of the traditional village life (a vision which he juxtaposes with the urban-based "dog eat dog" contemporary socio-political system) finds perfect expression in the artistic forms of oral tradition. The organizing impulse for the poems is the revolutionary confrontation between rural man with his (somewhat idealized) vision of life and the oppressive, exploitative neocolonialist national political administration. By this confrontational juxtapositioning the poet uses tradition to assess the value of modern civilization and governance in order to condemn it. In order to allow the voice of tradition full scope to do this, Osundare adopts a poetic posture that modernists will call the posture of impersonality. His poetic voice is subsumed under the communal voice as he prefers to speak through various personae from the rural areas who adapt various forms of traditional art to denounce the national capitalist system. . . .

Osundare continues the celebration of traditional culture in *The Eye of the Earth*, but in a different mode from *Village Voices*. The most obvious difference is that in *The Eye of the Earth* he assumes his own poetic voice. He speaks as the prodigal, the alienated man, once "jilted from the farmstead" returning to the traditional society of his youth, to a stage of the traditional culture which was before the "Cancerous god called MONEY" from the West "smashed old customs." The organizing impulse of *The Eye of the Earth* is the journey motif. The substance of the collection is the "journey into these times [youth of the poet] and beyond," a journey "into the house of memory." The central preoccupation is to contrast what life meant in those times when "Earth was ours and we earth's," with what life means in contemporary times when after the destruction of the "Core of [their] ancient humanistic ethos," commercialism and "the god of money" have forced a desecration of the earth, the bedrock of ancient customs and culture. . . .

Osundare uses the oral traditions far more than many other writers. Not only has he used the many forms of art from the oral traditions as core elements in his poetic technique in *Village Voices* and to some extent, *The Eye of the Earth*, but he has also proved in the two books of poetry that the oral traditions can "provide for a meaningful critique of the contemporary problems." In his hands traditional social wisdom has become a weapon for very incisive criticism of contemporary political economy. Also his judicious use of elements of the African oral tradition has produced poetry that is distinctively African. There are definitely problems and limitations to attempts at transposing elements from the oral traditions to the written traditions in a non-African language. But the example of Osundare and the Ghanaian poetic experiments by Atukwei Okai and Kofi Anyidoho have proved that African poetry can gain in strength and distinctiveness by appropriating techniques and qualities from African performance poetry and dramatic ritual.

Aderemi Bamikunle. In Eldred Durosimi Jones, ed. Orature in African Literature Today (Trenton, N. J.: Africa World Press, 1992), pp. 51–54, 58, 60–61

Divided into four sections, *Waiting Laughters* uses the multiple situations of waiting in harsh times and places to explore poetically the "gloom and despair which seem to have gripped contemporary African society." Despite the current gloom, the poet looks forward to relief in "laughters." The formally organized and well-crafted volume gives a lie to the view, associated with Ken Goodwin and other critics of African literature, that the new generation of African poets tend to sacrifice form and craft for ideological commitment.

Two characteristic qualities of Osundare are intensified in the poems here: the linguist and the folklorist. A trained linguist, the poet plays with words, makes music with alliterations, assonances, and other forms of repetition, and creates startling images and figures, especially similes, metaphors, and personifications. In Osundare's poetry all things are personified, and they *live* actively. Sometimes the alliterations seem overused and contrived, but this is made up for by the variety of form, which assumes an Okigboesque quality in some parts of the book.

Osundare's use of Yoruba folklore enhances the vitality of the poems. The various segments of each section are chants to be accompanied by different African musical instruments. In the third section, where Osundare is at his best, his written orature combines traditional wisdom and form with sophisticated use of English to evoke instances of waiting. This results in exhilarating and memorable images. He turns experiences into fables for lasting impressions and uses apparently known folktales to express the contemporary African predicament of waiting painfully for succor from socioeconomic doom.

Thematically and stylistically, *Waiting Laughters* combines the strengths of two earlier works, *The Eye of the Earth* and *Moonsongs*. The poem ends with hope, not merely for relief as "A boil, time-tempered, / about to burst," but for action that will bring about positive change. Occasionally the lines seem overloaded with similes and metaphors, and the poet barely allows the reader time to reflect on one series of images before deluging the lines with more.

Sometimes, as in the second section, the formal experiment, though visually impressive on the page, does not seem to be effective when two distantly spaced words are set per line in order to reflect vocal emphasis.

Tanure Ojaide. *WLT*. 66, 1 (Winter 1992), p. 192

Selected Poems brings together samples of [Osundare's] verse issued by different publishers over almost a decade. The selection begins with poems from *A Nib in the Pond* . . . and ends with the Malthouse-produced *Waiting Laughters*, which earned the poet the Noma Prize. The volume easily accomplishes a major aim of a selected edition of a poet in his prime: it lets the reader follow the development of the poet from his first collection to the latest.

In *A Nib in the Pond*, as will be expected of a first work, the poetic rhythm is not as sure and smooth as in the later poems. At this point the poet is an activist, one who wants to "wake a slumbering world." The message appears more important than the form here. The poet is a spokesperson for the oppressed, as in "Promise Land" and "I Am the Common Man." These poems set the thematic and stylistic features that will characterize the later poetry. Osundare ranges on the side of the common people and uses cosmic images of the sun and moon to register his commitment. . . .

The Eye of the Earth and *Waiting Laughters* stand out as the most impressive collections represented in the selection. In these two works Osundare is at his best, celebrating, singing, and playing with words. He so fuses his message with the form that one goes through the poems marveling at the amazing lyricism in the poet's repertoire. *The Eye of the Earth* celebrates the earth but also warns that human beings should take care of the environment if they care about their future. . . .

Selected Poems confirms Osundare's place as a major African poet who uses the resources of the folklore of his people, his study of the English language, and his concern for the underprivileged and the destiny of Africa to bring passionate intensity, wit, musicality, and sensitivity to his writing.

Tanure Ojaide. *WLT*. 67, 4 (Autumn 1993), pp. 878–79

OUOLOGUEM, YAMBO (1940–   )

MALI

The most striking feature of the novel [*Le Devoir de violence*] is its style, the originality of which can only be compared with that of Amos Tutuola or perhaps Okot p'Bitek, both writing in English. While preserving the spontaneity of the oral tradition, [Yambo] Ouologuem's chronicle of oppression and debasement, of horror and violence, is told in a truly epic yet also sarcastic manner: his many parentheses, full of exclamations and Koranic formulas, give the sentences a broken, sinuous syntax which does not mar the novel's unity of tone. Unfortunately, those qualities are practically absent from the last part of the book, where the narrative rhythm becomes slow and heavy, and the tone pedantic.

The unique significance of *Le Devoir de violence* for the history of French African writing lies in the image it offers of the "Black Continent," an image as far removed from the romanticism of Négritude as from the anticolonial realism of the novelists. The work is clearly intended to offer the Western reader an alternative picture, less complacent, less imbued with anti-European rancor, presented as more faithful to the reality of Africa. . . .

By deliberately selecting from the African past only those elements which may debase it, Ouologuem created a myth different from, but as dangerous as, the one he was seeking to destroy. . . . It is worth noting that such ethical values as motherly love or the sense of solidarity and the social harmony inherent in the clan system, as well as such cultural values as dance and music, are all absent from Ouologuem's Africa. The legendary modesty of Muslim society is completely ignored. Ouologuem's image of black Africa is one of total permissiveness and generalized promiscuity. Do we have here "the true image of Africa"? The African reader does not hesitate to answer in the negative: Ouologuem's Africa is a myth born of what he himself called in his *Lettre à la France nègre*, "la gymnastique opératoire de l'écriture." . . .

This inverted interpretation of history seems to have been dictated by Ouologuem's wish to create an authentic African literature, for he considers that the works written before independence could not have been genuinely African. . . .

The literary influences that have entered into the service of Ouologuem's aesthetic purpose do not of themselves explain his approach to his subject. Political motives, namely, the bitter disappointment experienced by many African intellectuals since the end of colonial domination, must also be taken into account. During the struggle for independence, enthusiasm was at its highest; everyone aspired to a better world with plentiful opportunities for individual development. But those great expectations were ill-founded: the greater part of independent black Africa has since swayed between anarchy and dictatorship; its history is already ridden by civil wars and military coups, while its politics is too often the product of clan nepotism and shameful corruption.

J. Mbelolo Ya Mpiku. *Review of National Literatures.* 2, 2 (Fall 1971), pp. 140–45

There are reports that Ouologuem has written at least one other novel under a pseudonym, but it was, as a matter of fact, the wished-for next book published under Ouologuem's own name which began to cause many critics to have some nagging doubts, not because of the contents per se but because of its flimsiness of diction and weakness of structure. One critic, not yet aware of the full importance of foreign sources in the composition of *Le Devoir de violence*, put it bluntly but accurately when he exclaimed that "Disappointment came, however, when Ouologuem published his second book, *Lettre à la France nègre*, a pamphlet in every way inferior to his novel." The only way, in fact, that it is superior to *Le Devoir de violence* is in its authenticity, for there is no reason to think that this work is not fully the product of Ouologuem's own talents and abilities! Critics found it difficult to reconcile the novel and the book of essays. The discrepancy was disappointing, and it was so great that it could not simply be attributed to the "sophomore jinx" which has temporarily blighted many a career. A year or so after the publication of Ouologuem's first novel, disquieting charges of borrowings, extensive imitation, and outright plagiarism began to circulate as rumors and then in a series of articles which in turn drew two reactions: on the one hand, a number of people wrote to the authors and editors of these articles supplying further examples of stylistic indebtedness; and, on the other, some critics sought to minimize the significance of plagiarism in general and to defend Ouologuem in particular. . . .

The fact that *Le Devoir de violence* is largely a paste-up of unoriginal material which has been appropriately adapted to fit the book's general *structure d'accueil* does not mean that it is without significance. . . . If it is not deeply African in its contents, it may be that one or more major African impulses were nevertheless present in the attitude of the author with regard to the notion of plagiarism—even, perhaps, unbeknownst to him—as well as in the general characteristics emerging within the larger structure of his work. In other words, I contend that while the basic contents and method of composition are not spontaneously African, Ouologuem has—in opting for an episodic structure, contrived though it might be—remained faithful to at least one fundamental African impulse found expressed in the majority of Franco-African literary works from [Camara] Laye's *L'Enfant noir* to [Ahmadou] Kourouma's *Les Soleils des indépendances*. The African writer tends, by virtue of age-old traditions of the *khawaré* or *veillée poétique* and the oral folktale, to prefer to channel his creativity into short, self-contained episodes without undue attention to logical or smooth transitions. Within the larger *structure d'accueil* of the *khawaré* we have a variety of songs, dances, poetic chants, and musical renditions; and it was inevitable that African novels should either adopt compatible European forms like the diary, the collection of tales, and the series of salient memories neatly encapsulated in chapters, or else twist prose into an episodic structure.

Eric Sellin. *YFS*. 53 (1974–1976), pp. 142–43, 158–59

[Few literary works out of Africa have] attracted so much attention or aroused so much controversy as Yambo Ouologuem's first novel. The last word has yet to be said in this matter and the final judgment [is] still to be made. When *Le Devoir de violence* appeared in 1968, to be awarded the Prix Renaudot . . . it caused a sensation in France such as no other black writer's work—even including [René Maran's] *Batouala*—has ever known. The acclaim from France was followed by enthusiasm from the Anglo-Saxon world, particularly from America, on the publication of the English translation, under the title *Bound to Violence*. Glowing American reviews followed glowing French reviews. *Le Monde* greeted the work as "perhaps the first African novel worthy of the name." . . . One dissenting voice from the chorus of praise came from that usually percipient Nigerian critic, Abiola Irele, who denounced Ouologuem's novel as "a meandering succession of sordid happenings, excesses and extravagances, presented as a historical narrative of a fictitious but 'typical' African empire" and condemned the work for indicating that "the past has only bequeathed to the present generation of Africans a legacy of crime and violence." . . .

The storm, which brought red faces to the firm of Le Seuil and eventually to Heinemann, who were bringing out the English version in England, broke in 1971, when Eric Sellin . . . first challenged Ouologuem with plagiarism, proving by clear illustrations that the resemblances between the African novel and [André] Schwarz-Bart's *Le Dernier des justes* . . . was not simply one of categories, but were also textual. . . . But the echoes spread wider and the controversy became more bitter when the *Times Literary Supplement* of May 5, 1972, printed an article submitting the striking resemblance between two pages of Ouologuem's work and an extract from an early novel by Graham Greene—*It's a Battlefield*, published in 1934. . . . Schwarz-Bart expressed himself completely unconcerned by the use that the black writer had made of his work, in fact maintaining that he was "deeply touched, overwhelmed even" and "happy that his apples should be . . . taken and planted in different soil." Mr. Greene was somewhat less enchanted about the indirect flattery of [Ouologuem's] unacknowledged debt.

Dorothy S. Blair. *African Literature in French*
(Cambridge: Cambridge University Press, 1976), pp. 305–6

When [*Le Devoir de violence*] was first published in 1968, it was highly praised in Europe and America. However, it was received with mixed feelings in Africa. Ouologuem was hailed by non-Africans as the first African intellectual of international standing since [Léopold Sédar] Senghor. Speaking to journalists in France, he claimed that his book spoke of leaders who posed as "bawling revolutionaries while opening their tattered purses to capitalism." He concluded: "My aim is to do violence to the misconceptions of Africans so that we can realize what the real problems are. This is 'our duty of violence.'" This duty is necessitated by the need to reformulate the philosophies on which the African society is based, in view of centuries of brutalization through a three-pronged act of violence—slave-trading activities from the North and South, internecine wars and razzias, and colonization—which has created a new breed of humiliated Africans whom Ouologuem refers to in his novel as "the niggertrash." His duty of violence is based not on physical violence, for Africans have surfeited themselves with that, but on intellectual violence, a sort of brainstorming aimed at making the people aware of the necessity for revolutionary change. . . .

The sheer beauty of Ouologuem's art deepens our perception of the history of the blacks from about 1200 A.D. to the present day. His message is that violence, in all its ramifications, is a necessary evil, if true and lasting political freedom is to be achieved. . . . The reader is inevitably drawn into a vortex of words full of mystery, meaning and communication, right from the first paragraph of the novel. . . . Like the griot or chronicler retelling for the umpteenth time the tribe's history and explaining the more salient points of that history, Ouologuem sets off with lightning speed and draws us straight into a world of blood and tears in which, from century to century, we see the Saifs, rulers of Nakem, striving to aggrandize their empire or enrich themselves. Legends of the good and bad Saifs are used to describe events in those centuries when the written tradition had not yet superseded the oral.

Yusufu Maiangwa. In Kolawole Ogunbesan, ed.
New West African Literature (London: Heinemann, 1979), pp. 73, 76

One of the distinctive marks of Ouologuem's art . . . is his brilliant use of language. There can be no doubt of his mastery of his French medium which one suspects is even reflected in the excellent English translation [of *Le Devoir de violence*]. At times his prose exudes [a] tough intellectual quality. . . . It can [also] be lyrical, as in the description of the Tambira-Kassoumi love affair, and it can exude a poetic grandeur as in Sankolo's account of his experiences. Ouologuem also makes occasional attempts to modify the language and give it an African flavor, as in "May your path be straight" or "May God hear you and reward you." His superb descriptive power is partly due to his use of images. They are drawn largely from the world of traditional life as in "the members of that society who had no more courage than a wet hen" and "his face in anger turned as yellow as pepper." Appropriately, in a novel concerned with violence, most of the images are taken from the more repellent aspects of the animal kingdom as in "The crown forced men to swallow life as a boa swallows a stinking antelope," "That same night, at the hour when the jackals fill the bush with their howling, the emperor gathered together his whole court . . ." and "the Arab conquest . . . settled over the land like a she-dog baring her white fangs in raucous laughter."

Ouologuem's realization of his characters is also faultless. So many of them stand out in this motley throng because the author presents them in detail through thought and action. Apart from the superb portraits of the Saif, Raymond, Tambira, and Kassoumi, the reader is not likely to forget Sankolo, Bouremi, Chevalier, Awa, Wampoulo, Kratonga, Shrobenius, and even Kadidia. Ouologuem relies not so much on a complex plot and structure as on a full and detailed presentation of the experiences of his characters, thus achieving a novel of remarkable solidity and significance. His achievement is rare in the whole history of the African novel.

Eustace Palmer. *The Growth of the African Novel*
(London: Heinemann, 1979), pp. 218–20

The implications of Ouologuem's work are different as one moves from the world within the novel to the role of the novel in the world, but on each level the force of an *injunction* is evident. Within the fictive world which the novel projects, the Nakem empire is in subservient bondage to its rulers, held on a short leash: "Dans l'attente de ce grand jour de la proche éclosion du monde où le serf est l'égal du roi, la négraille—*court lien à méchant chien!*—accepta tout." [In his hope for that great day, the forthcoming blossoming of the world, when the serf will be equal to the king, the *négraille*—short leash for a bad dog!—accepts everything]. The "petit trait horizontal" [little horizontal leash] between Saif and *négraille* is the symbolic and real joint of a generalized injunction: political power. The populace is enjoined to efface itself before both the African notables and the incoming French. But if a false identity is forced on the *négraille* (through public education,

Christianity, etc.), the Saifs are equally false in their manner of adopting whatever identity suits their needs: the former thus become nothing, the latter everything. The bonds of power within the Nakem are bonds of violence by which bodies and identities are both made and broken—Ouologuem makes it amount to the same thing. . . . Violence is the language by which connections are made and therefore broken, no more apt to make sense than any other language. . . .

The "injunctive" nature of an author's work to which I first referred—that of binding an object and bringing it into the light—is radically disturbed by Ouologuem's negativism. What is brought to light is the fact that nothing can be brought to light; that which is bound is "bound to violence," torn apart like the two birds bound together. This may explain the impression shared by more than one reader of *Le Devoir de violence*, that they are reading strictly *n'importe quoi*, a brilliant mish-mash.

But it is on the outermost level, that of the politics of Ouologuem's literary practice, that his novel is at its most significant. As within the novel, there is a refusal of identity, but here it is the identity of the text, the author, and the genre which is negated. Ouologuem subverts the authoritative role of creator by pillaging European literature to compose "his" text. The whole notion of "text"—important not only to the legalities of copyright but also to modern criticism—is undermined, as if by sleight of hand. But most importantly, Ouologuem's act violates the national and continental boundaries by which integral bodies of literature are perceived. A "corpus," whole unto itself and distinct from all others, is generally assumed in the face-off between Europe, Africa, etc. It is here where dangerous metaphors get their foot in the door, metaphors which Ouologuem explodes: for if one body is distinct from another, one can or must be different, perhaps older and therefore better. This is the root of theories such as [Georg] Lukács's, which projects a hierarchy according to age, between "childlikeness" and "virile maturity," between epic and novel. But *Le Devoir de violence* is written in the excrescences, the orifices, and the intrusions between European and African literature, by an author without authority. Ouologuem's response to the condition of the African novel (if we can interpret his actions on such a plane) defies the rules of identity and injunction by which his work could be placed in a position of "childlikeness." Depicting all ties as destructive, Ouologuem strikes an uncompromising stance of pure negativity.

Christopher L. Miller. ECr. 23, 4 (Winter 1983), pp. 72–73

It is now possible to say that Dogon myths, West African traditions, form the core of *Le Devoir de violence*; but in Ouologuem's written transformation of the myths, they are generalized, spread out. In the narrative, the Dogon myths are interlaced with a variety and multiplicity of other texts. Without commenting on the ethical questions relevant to the patchwork of quotations that Ouologuem took from a wide variety of English, French, and African sources, and which he then stitched together to make up the fabric of the text, suffice it to say that this literary composite—what some critics have chosen to call an anthology—substantially contributes to the generalization of the narrative. The collection of fragments from oral literature, the Bible, Arab histories, [François] Villon, [Gustave] Flaubert, Graham Greene, André Schwarz-Bart, and on, and on; these fragments together, transformed, make up Ouologuem's picture of life. . . .

Ouologuem—along with many other African writers—is concerned with the problems of reconciling the past with a difficult present in an Africa going through an uncomfortable, often violent, period of transition. In *Le Devoir de violence* he explicitly rejects the romanticized histories of the Négritude writers and of the Europeans like [Leo] Frobenius—who appears in the text as Schrobenius—those histories which lead to complacency. In an attempt to deal with the realities of the present, and the possibilities of the future; instead of writing a chronological history, Ouologuem has united scattered fragments of the past and set them down, piecemeal, in the present. By combining fragments from different times, places, and cultures, Ouologuem places violence and evil in Africa in a larger perspective, which enables us to see it and understand it . . . and possibly deal with it.

Sandra Barkan. In Kofi Anyidoho, Abioseh M. Porter, Daniel [L.] Racine,
and Janice Spleth, eds. *Interdisciplinary Dimensions of African Literature*
(Washington, D. C.: Three Continents Press, 1985), pp. 110–11

Immediately hailed as "the first truly African novel," [*Le Devoir de violence*] was awarded institutional acclaim in France as the winner of the Prix Renaudot. The novel tells the epic history of a fictional African people from its precolonial origins to the contemporary present. Much of Ouologuem's success apparently came from the explicitly indigenous—that is, "original" as both primitive and new—nature of the text. It is written largely in the oral storytelling style of the traditional griots; it borrows heavily from traditional tales and folklore, is luridly savage in its depiction of violence and perverse sex, and responds in this way to the occidental taste for the exotic—the "real" Africa.

The problems start subsequent to the text's publication in English, whereupon a scandal erupted in the pages of the *Times Literary Supplement* when it was reported by an "anonymous critic" that the text included extensive "plagiarism" of Graham Greene's novel *It's a Battlefield*. Critic Eric Sellin had already discovered another instance of plagiarism in this "authentic" African text: it read like a rewrite of André Schwarz-Bart's novel *Les Dernier des justes*. These discoveries, as well as instigating a virulent polemic in and out of the *Times Literary Supplement*, jeopardized for a time the text's and the author's reputations, as Greene filed suit for plagiarism and the text was re-edited with the offending passages expurgated. The "anonymous critic" asks sarcastically if Ouologuem has discovered "a style of literary imperialism intended as a revenge for the much chronicled sins of territorial imperialists." Defenders claim, of course, that the accusations of plagiarism are no more than a thinly disguised racism, for the "authentic African novel" which borrows heavily from European sources is exposed as somehow neither authentic nor African. Ouologuem himself had maintained that the novel is "not traditional," is written with "references to international examples," and is "not just an African novel." In the same vein, its defenders maintain that the insistence on Africanness in its folkloric mode denies the essential reality of a contemporary Africa created by the assimilation of Western traditions imposed by those very colonial forces which continue to ghettoize the African by valorizing only traditional folklore. The irony, of course, is that the *real* Africa is precisely the one that the West rejects in the form of accusations of plagiarism. Formed by Western values and culture (Ouologuem was preparing a thesis in Paris at the time), modern African writers are as literate and as steeped in Western literature and cultural knowledge as are their Western counterparts. . . .

In the same year, 1968, Ouologuem published *Lettre à la France nègre*, a series of open letters to various sectors of French society. In one letter, addressed to "les pisse-copie Nègres d'écrivains célèbres" (to hack nigger-writers of famous authors), he ironically advises black writers to stick to the mystery or detective novel. . . . Ouologuem proposes a formula for producing an infinite number of assembly-line type novels by juggling in any order a number of passages stolen from major mystery writers. For demonstration purposes, he provides a number of these passages, rated according to their quotient of humor, suspense, violence, eroticism, and so on. Explicitly advocating a kind of wholesale plagiarism, Ouologuem points out the infinite possibilities available to the hack writer of second-rate fiction, the fate that he imputes to the black African writer. It is not coincidental that Ouologuem practices a form of this very strategy in his own "literary" novel. What appears as a rhetorical joke in the context of the political essay becomes a crime in the literary text.

Marilyn Randall. *NLH.* 22 (1991), pp. 536–37

PHELPS, ANTHONY (1928–   )

HAITI

Like brotherhood, the consciousness of the poet's mission (a long-standing tradition in French poetry) is a strong theme in [Anthony] Phelps's work. In his first novel [*Moins l'infini*], he fictionalizes the artist group who communicated in a kind of code through weekly broadcasts of poetry readings. There Phelps shows realistically the power of the word, the commitment of the engagement. . . .

For Phelps, words have power, strength, even physical form. . . . For words, lines, even the visual appearance of punctuation are all art-images for this poet. In an early love poem parentheses marks are two lovers inclining toward each other. Elsewhere parentheses form barriers against the outer world, protecting the lovers' union. He notices that tiny Haiti, a mere footnote in world power, nonetheless is marked by an asterisk star. Crossword puzzles are patterns of squares and spaces. The phrase "Points Cardinaux," both a volume title and the password for the revolutionaries in his novel, is graphically a cross or a plus. Algebra involves equation—equal signs, parallel lines—roads in the "algèbre des grandes villes." Phelps often signs with a flower sketched as part of his signature, an image more enduring than reality.

Besides form and shape, he finds that words have power of their own. They resist, they slip from grasp, they melt, they telescope, they subdue. . . .

In his word-joust with [René] Depestre over cross-words, Phelps shows himself reluctant but eager to believe in a better future. Despite the difficulties of his past, imprisonment, [and] exile, he is a poet of affirmation, even of happiness. And he finds strength in personal human relationships. He frequently affirms these ties in dedications or allusions. . . .

He also finds affirmation in a new country, with its new vocabulary, in new ideas of political organization, in solidarity with others of the Third World—faith for a future based on socialistic structure and love. . . . The title of his first novel, *Moins l'infini*, a phrase taken from the poetic theme song of the resistance poets, limits Haiti's tyranny as less than infinite, and looks beyond for a better future.

Charlotte [H.] Bruner. *The Gar.* 33 (February 1979), pp. 23–24

Anthony Phelps, poet, storyteller, novelist, is always a child of his island Haiti, even in exile in his adopted country Canada with his Canadian wife. He early wrote a poetic epic of his island's history, *Mon pays que voici.* His novels concern the Haiti of the 1960s, the period of his own activism and exile. His later stories and poems reflect his deep nostalgia for the island landscape and people. Only recently was he able to return to find again his identity, to rediscover his heritage (not African but Caribbean), to exorcise the hate and anguish of the past, to share with his wife the long-dreamed-of beloved's return, to bask today in the "unknown sun" of tomorrow's new hopes.

La Bélière caraïbe in its seven parts and brief epilogue symbolically leads the reader; the bellwether poet shows the way: "je nomme ma route / dans le vent veuf / Poète / Païen / en toute saison" [I choose my path / according to the widower-wind / Poet / Pagan / in all seasons]. He recasts past memories: "je corrige le brouillon de ma vie / au jardin extravagant de la mémoire" [I correct the rough draft of my life / in the wild garden of memory]. He has been a wanderer: "Nomade je fus" [I was a nomad]; now, returning, he has direction. After his "Vacances de paupières" [pun on "pauper's vacation" and "eyelids holiday" (sleep)], when he imagined a dream-like return, he will now experience the real "lente et savante caresse du recommencement" [slow and knowing embrace of beginning again]. It takes only a Proustian odor of sapotilla to roll back the years, to expose the child within the man: "Jamais l'homme en moi ne trahira l'enfant que j'étais" [the man in me will never betray the child that I was]. But he is no longer crippled by the past: "Béquilles sur l'épaule" [shouldering his crutches], he comes forth in "L'automme de l'oeil" [the autumn of the eye]. He has wandered ("j'ai honoré mon quota d'errance / et j'ai bien voyagé" [I have fulfilled my quota of wandering / and I have traveled well]), always with the shadow of the Caribbean at his back, ever reminded of its people, its foliage, its voices. He recognizes that the homeland has always mastered his thoughts, his sadness, been "Capitaine de mes douleurs" [captain of my griefs]. Now the wanderer must find again his roots and his identity from all his history: "Celui qui m'a acheté / et celui que je suis / l'acheteur et le vendeur en moi mêlés" [Who bought me and what I am / buyer and seller mixed into one]. Self-cognizant, he can discover "Non point le règne de cannibales / mais tendresse" [Not in the least the cannibal kingdom / but tenderness], and derive the present: "Père Caraïbe / Passé Piégé / Présent gagné" [Father Caribe / the past trapped / the present gained]. Though as a retourné he must observe the "Protocole du Midi," his heart can speak when words may not, and those who follow his meaning walk also in his path.

Anthony Phelps obliquely traces his struggle for self-knowledge—looking beneath his "patchwork" sin, through a maze of memories, to reveal the mature poet, strong in adversity, ever the islander, tender yet resolute.

Charlotte H. Bruner. WLT. 55, 2 (Spring 1981), pp. 363–64

Phelps is a master of psychological nuances. Unlike others, he does not give in to the temptation to turn his novels into a forum of exhibitionism for professional heroes who win every battle, regardless of how desperate the situation may be, because right and justice are supposed to triumph under all circumstances. Indeed, both Moins l'infini and Mémoire en Colin-Maillard end with the failure of the protagonists. The revolutionary project remains viable and valuable, though; despite themselves, Marco and Claude moved farther away from that project. No, this "Negro of capacity who will perform the indispensable deeds," whom they felt vibrate in themselves, no, it will be another, not they. In the course of the action they realize that the road to revolution is staked out with labyrinthine passages and that they, too, "not [as] a piece of wood" but like "other men" are subject to the same existential ambivalence. As Claude's mother said, "It is not like mathematics, where one and one are always two."

The structural organization of the narration also follows political uncertainty. Phelps does not mind using some writing devices from the *nouveau roman*: The linear discourse is rejected and the narrative time dislocated; the hero evolves inside a complex, multidimensional world where past, present, and future, dream and reality are superimposed, are juxtaposed and penetrate each other depending on the narrative situation. As in [Gérard] Etienne's *Le Nègre crucifié*, there exists an equalization between the substance and form of the discourse, which itself is in the image of the desperately ruined nation: "And the Building is fissured, criss-crossed with cracks, dislocated." There is the further image of the hero's impenetrable fate as it appears to Monsieur X in its almost Dedalean entanglement.

> Juris Silenieks. In William Luis, ed. *Voices from Under: Black Narrative in Latin America and the Caribbean* (Westport, Conn.: Greenwood Press, 1984), pp. 141–42

[Phelps] is a poet representative of that which is dying and which is being born in contemporary Haitian literature and society, someone who does his best to see the decline of certain aspects of traditional society and the difficult formation of new social traits. His poetry presents a sample of the ideology of a fraction of the Haitian diaspora of his time, an ideology marked by a tragic vision of the popular emigration. . . .

The poetry of Anthony Phelps includes a major theme, that of waiting. In Phelps's work, waiting is not only the title of a poem in the collection *Motifs pour le temps saisonnier*, it is very appropriately one of the key factors of the work. . . .

The theme of waiting is found in *Éclats de silence* and also in *Motifs pour le temps saisonnier*, but with an incomparably greater resonance.

Motifs pour le temps saisonnier, the most well-constructed and the most structured of the poetic books of Phelps, orders, arranges, and structures the poems in three categories: poems of completed time, poems of fragmented time, and poems of woven time. The leitmotif of time is correlated to the theme of waiting. In migrating from one collection to another and from one period to another, the theme of waiting moves from a personal dimension to a collective dimension. It becomes a political waiting.

That is because, in the meantime, Anthony Phelps became, from May 1964, a political exile, a refugee in Montreal, nurturing the nostalgia of return to his native country. While anticipating this return, he lives in waiting . . . in the living, active and impatient waiting for the end of the time of oppression that he believes rules his country. . . .

The dialectic of exile and the kingdom, along with the attendant exodus and nostalgia, plays from one end to the other in this poetry of waiting. . . .

Phelps's waiting is the hope for this "kingdom," this "city," symbols of his liberated country. . . .

Only, the time of liberation takes long to come and the light of hope surrenders to the dark night.

In the eyes of Phelps, the abomination of desolation is this exodus, this flight from hunger that pushes his people into so many foreign countries. . . .

Anthony Phelps is a poet from the left, but he is a complete stranger to the Négritude movement. His counter-Négritude is even the common denominator of the group Haiti-littéraire of which he is chief. . . .

Phelps's repudiation of Négritude is not without consequence on the level of social practice. If the blacks of the New World do not feel themselves to be sons of Africa, and if, as already asserted by Franklyn Frazier against Melville Herskovits, the blacks of the Americas do not maintain any ties with the blacks of Africa, then the umbilical cord which linked them to the alma mater is broken. Africa and its battles for liberation are strangers to them. . . .

The poetry of Anthony Phelps has an analogous social function in the Haitian migratory adventure of the second half of the twentieth century. His tragic vision of the phenomenon speaks of his social background, the interaction of social groups, and the economic stake of their conflict of interest.

Claude Souffrant. PA. 135 (1985), pp. 74–77, 82, 84, 89†

The [Haitian] poet who has emerged as the major voice among those who went into exile from the generation of the 1960s is Anthony Phelps. This is so because Phelps's poetry avoids the paralyzing self-pity and longing of the exile and explores, in the manner of a [Jacques] Roumain or a [René] Depestre, a poetics of "errance." . . . Feeling is structured in Phelps's poetry through a poetics of remoteness and restlessness. His early renunciations of indigenism and political engagement echo through his later writing in exile. Phelps reserves his political statements and overt references to Haiti for his novels. His poetry is one of absence, remoteness, wandering, of the suppressed referent. A poetic language emerges which is not the language of the tribe but a discourse whose symbolic values are "spread" to include a range of experiences. For instance, instead of using the Creole "poto-mitan," Phelps uses the expression "arbre milieu" to produce a special cluster of associations. In describing himself as "Poète / Païen / en toute saison" [Poet / Pagan / for all seasons], Phelps immerses himself in an elemental world of sun, salt, summer, dawn, wind, and earth. . . .

Phelps seems to have always privileged in his poetry moments and sites of intense feeling and of equilibrium. Words like été, Midi, seuil, and milieu have a special significance for Phelps. In order to attain these moments of vision, the poet must shed illusory identities: "une peau sans couture lisse et d'unique trame" [a skin seamless smoth and of unique texture]. Phelps's poetic strategy is to expose self ("la marche de l'écorché") and to expose text ("le texte nu") in order to discover self in relation to world. Indeed, he pushes the state of exile to extremes in La Bélière caraïbe in order to explore his rootlessness. . . . It is in such an exploration that the Caribbean emerges as the "Midi" for Phelps—a zone of intense encounter, of multiple unstable possibilities. It is not a land of nostalgia, trapped in memory but rather the "Lieu de mon métissage" where future possibilities become evident. . . . Through Phelps's poetic universe Haiti is reinserted in a process which is Caribbean and American, in the widest sense of the word.

J. Michael Dash. Callaloo. 15, 3 (Summer 1992), pp. 758–60

PHILLIPS, CARYL (1958–   )

ST. KITTS

[In Caryl Phillips's *A State of Independence*] Bertram Francis, a nineteen-year-old Island Scholarship winner (the island, maybe St. Kitts, maybe not, but certainly a symbolic social composite of all the anglophone Caribbean islands), leaves to study law in England, abandons his bursary after two years, works at odd jobs, saves wisely, and returns home a would-be businessman twenty years afterward, on the eve of independence. During his absence, Dominic, his only brother, whom he loved and who loved and doted on him, is killed by a hit-and-run motorist; Jackson Clayton, his best friend and a gifted schoolboy cricketer, has become deputy prime minister; Father Daniels, the teacher who had prepared him for the coveted scholarship, has died; and his mother has become seriously ill, embittered, and withdrawn. Bertram, who hadn't bothered to write his family or friends while he was away, is coldly rejected by his mother and by the deputy prime minister, who considers him a cheeky interloper, but not by Patsy Archibald, his former girlfriend, whom he gave up as soon as he had won his scholarship.

A very, *very* bleak novel indeed, allegorizing . . . accurately, a densely bleak Caribbean, socially and politically, where states of independence are, for the most part, neocolonial, dispiriting, and hopeless, and where true individual independence for the ignored, the poor, and the dispossessed continues to be beg-borrow-or-steal emigration to Britain or Canada or America. Caryl Phillips has written a well-modulated and sensitively focused novel of inconsolable Caribbean anguish. . . . His first book, *The Final Passage*, the story of a young Caribbean wife abandoned by her husband in London, left me creased by anger and wholehearted pity; this one, harrowed by personal recognition and near panic. I welcome this new, young miniaturist-realist, already the finest of his kind among Caribbean novelists.

Andrew Salkey. *WLT*. 61, 1 (Winter 1987), p. 145

In 1987, [Phillips] turned away from the Caribbean in order to explore his other nominal "home": Britain and, by extension, the rest of Europe. This time, he found fiction less suitable for his aims, explaining that "the tension between myself and my environment is so urgently felt that the fictional mold seems too delicate a vessel to hold it." Accordingly, *The European Tribe* documents a year of the author's wanderings, from Belfast to Gibraltar, Auschwitz to Moscow. Certainly it constitutes a kind of travel book, although one unlikely to appear with Arthur Frommer's signature on the cover: *Europe on Ten Dollars and Twenty Slurs a Day*.

No innocent abroad, Phillips quickly discovers the appalling extent of racism in Europe's most progressive nations. The French despise the Arabs, the Germans despise the Turks, and the British despise the Spanish and Moroccans (in Gibraltar) and just about everyone else (at home). Even Norway, with a non-white population of .35 percent, displays a toxic reaction to the handful of black people who have snuck, like trace elements, into the national bloodstream.

Taken strictly as a Baedeker, *The European Tribe* is a trifle thin. The countries flash by too quickly; there's a severe shortage of actual encounters with other people; and Phillips's prose, usually nimble and endowed with a winning, modest lyricism, falls here and there into chamber-of-commerce staleness (the black and red of a Spanish duenna's garb, for example, "seems to characterize Spain's proud and regal spirit"). But Phillips has more in mind than a verbal slide show. He wants to argue. And the arguments that gradually emerge from this grand tour are mostly corollaries of [Derek] Walcott's "homeless satellites."

One, which joins a fine portrait of James Baldwin to a discussion of Othello—two very different examples of "black European successes"—is the tricky notion of accommodation. Must a black man always pay for his integration into white society with the destruction of his identity? Is any success worth such a terrible price of admission? On his ten acres at St. Paul de Vence, a lily-white hill-village north of Nice, Baldwin retained his identity to the end; but there's a suggestion, in Phillips's portrait, that his isolation was lonely, even debilitating. Othello, on the other hand, adapted himself absolutely into "the mainstream of the European nightmare," going so far as to marry into the family, and earned nothing for his pains but a "European death—suicide."

Othello also points Phillips in another key direction: toward the Venetian ghetto and, a few chapters later, Auschwitz. Phillips admits his early sympathy for Jews: "As a child, in what seemed to me a hostile country, the Jews were the only minority group discussed with reference to exploitation and [racism], and for that reason, I naturally identified with them." The Jews, of course, are not only a despised minority but history's homeless people par excellence, and as such they're natural inhabitants of Phillips's universe of noncitizenship. At the same time, he can't move cogently beyond this initial sympathy. He deplores the cozy rapport between Israel and South Africa; he makes a dogged, inconclusive attempt to understand the sour relationship between Americans blacks and Jews. In fact, these issues—and Phillips's argument that the economies of Western Europe have been largely rebuilt on the backs of migrant labor pools—are simply too sprawling to fit comfortably into the wafer-thin chapters of *The European Tribe*. They nonetheless add to Phillips's composite of a black-and-white Europe, a continent that has by now incubated an entire, oxymoronic generation of native-born "foreigners."

James Marcus. *VV*. October 24, 1989, p. 57

The winner of Britain's Malcolm X Award . . . [Phillips's *The Final Passage*] concerns a young West Indian couple whose dissatisfactions with life on their small island eventually lead them to emigrate to London. Leila and Michael, unhappily matched, are shakily held together by custom, mutual lack of communication, and their infant son. A mulatto sometimes referred to on her island as "the white girl," Leila yearns in vain for a closer relationship with the taciturn mother who raised her alone. Michael, darker skinned and sullen, spends more time with cronies at the Day to Dawn Bar and with another woman (with whom he also has a child) than he does with his official family. When Leila's mother abruptly departs for England to seek medical treatment, Leila's desire to be near her coincides with Michael's vague ambitions and results in their leaving the island as well. Caryl Phillips . . . reveals his characters' muted existence in a narrative that shifts backward and forward in time. *The Final Passage* is at its best in long, carefully observed sequences like Leila and Michael's wedding, in which experience and emotion are made almost tangible through detailed descriptions of sights, speech and behavior. Less successful are passages in which the author spells out his principals' thoughts and feelings in an expository manner that clashes with the approach taken in the rest of the book. Finally, as husband and wife adapt individually to the dreary reality of life in London in the 1950s, the novel assumes a nearly unrelenting bleakness of scene and spirit. Michael and Leila's passage from the brightly colored foreground of a rural landscape to the cluttered background of a drab cityscape is depressingly complete.

Tom Nolan. *NYTBR*. April 29, 1990, p. 38

Higher Ground, a "novel in three parts," consists of three stories. "Heartland" . . . set on the African coast, is told by a slave acting as translator, brutally treated by his masters and rejected by his own. Beyond cruelty and degradation lie continuum and death—or the attempt to recover some self-respect and inner peace. The "profit" of a marginally privileged position proves finally unacceptable when set against the "loss" it entails, and the narrator himself is transported to the United States: his loss is now his profit. A brutal memoir, heightened by detail and dispassion: readers will understand, sympathize to a degree, and fight a recoil from the narrator.

"The Cargo Rap" . . . is made up of fifty letters written by "Rudy" Williams between January 1967 and August 1968 to his parents, sister, and two female lawyers who take an interest in his "case." At the age of nineteen, the armed Rudy tried (in his words) to persuade a shopkeeper to pay back a small portion of the collective historical debt owed by American whites to their black countrymen dating from the slave trade onward. Rudy's sentence is one to twenty years, depending on good (servile) behavior, and he spends most of his time in brightly lit solitary confinement. The parallels with the life and *The Prison Letters* of George Jackson are evident. Jackson died in a prison riot; Rudy's sanity flickers out, and his last letters are to generalized "Brothers and Sisters" and, poignantly, his mother, who had died a month earlier. The story is remarkable for the power with which it depicts the psychological and physical damage sustained by black Americans and for its character portrayal, bearing in mind its epistolary nature. Awareness comes too late to Rudy, and the reader, both involved and detached, notes the increasing disequilibrium.

"Higher Ground" . . . is about a Jewish girl hustled out of Poland by her parents to escape the Holocaust. The trauma of her experiences and the cold incomprehension she encounters in England drive her first inward to bleak loneliness, then to numb sexual experience and a loveless marriage, and finally to a breakdown and attempted suicide. The novel's epigraph is the traditional prayer, "Lord set my feet on higher ground," safe from the floodwaters of life; and the stories, though dealing with very different centuries, continents, and characters, are unified by this theme of individual lives damaged, if not destroyed, by cruel, man-made waters. Images of being marooned, of shipwrecked lives, of the impossibility of escape across the sea to another land, recur. It is not possible to deal adequately with Phillips's work within the space of a brief review; all I can do here is urge that it be read, for *Higher Ground* is a moving and disturbing book.

Charles [Ponnuthurai] Sarvan. *WLT*. 64, 3 (Summer 1990), p. 518

The journey behind his first novel, *The Final Passage*, was the one [Phillips] himself took part in, albeit unwittingly—the emigration [in] the postwar years from the Caribbean to this country. The journey that lies behind both [Phillips's] last novel, *Higher Ground*, and his new novel, *Cambridge*, is a more historic, more primal, and more terrible journey, the journey of the slave trade westwards from Africa.

[Phillips] has maintained, however, a keen interest in Europe or, to be more precise, in Europe's pretensions and delusions about the place of European civilization in the world. His book of essays, *The European Tribe*, was devoted to the subject. In *Higher Ground*, a novel in three parts, we travel from Africa in the slave trade days to North America at the time of the Black Power Movement, only to end up in a Europe still nursing its wounds from the last war. In *Cambridge*, [Phillips] has reversed the direction of this journey to bring a European consciousness face to face with Europe's global perpetrations. He does this through the person of Emily, a woman of the early nineteenth century who escapes an arranged marriage by traveling to her father's estate in the West Indies (her father being an absentee landlord), where she is exposed to and, indeed, exposed by the effects of slavery and colonialization.

Like its predecessor, *Cambridge* is a novel in three distinct parts, the first and longest of which is Emily's own account of her journey and her observations when she arrives. From what seems at first to be an inquisitive, self-consoling travelogue, there emerges a drama revolving around a handful of characters: Emily herself; Brown, an Englishman whom we understand has somehow ousted the previous manager of the estate; the Cambridge of the title, a Negro slave who has suffered the singular and equivocal fate of having lived in England and having been converted to Christianity; and another slave, Christiania, who, despite her name, indulges in decidedly un-Christian rites and appears to be on the verge of madness.

The second part of the book is Cambridge's own account of how he came to be Anglicized and Christianized. The third, written in the form of a report (which we guess to be far from reliable), describes how Cambridge comes to be executed for the murder of Brown. And the brief epilogue of the novel tells us the effect of all this on Emily. These last few pages are particularly astonishing. Coming at the end of a novel of enormous accumulative power, they pack a tremendous punch and, written in a prose of tense intimacy, they show how facile it is to assess either [Phillips's] work as a whole, or his heroine, by any crude cultural or racial analysis. [Phillips] is interested in human beings. Emily's plight at the end of the novel plainly has its cultural and racial dimension, but it's essentially one of personal trauma—psychological, sexual, moral, and . . . existential.

Graham Swift. *Kunapipi*. 13, 3 (1991), pp. 96–97

The European Tribe is, as Phillips describes it in his preface, a "narrative in the form of a notebook in which I have jotted various thoughts about a Europe I feel both of and not of," written on the occasion of his travels, over the span of nearly a year's time, "from Europe's closest neighbor, Morocco, to her furthest flung capital, Moscow." . . .

As I read it, *The European Tribe* performs a strategic (I am almost tempted to say "satirical") reversal of the traditional perspective and mode of operation of the (European) travel narrative: it "tribalizes" the European, decentering him/her from the self-ascribed position of "Universal Subject of Knowledge," and turning him/her into an object of study; in doing so, it "defamiliarizes" the European, and begins to supply a "mental framework and a set of practical directions for confronting the [as of now] unknown and different" (in a way, it begins to *break through* the established, "stereotypical" *self*-conceptions of Europe and its native people); this framework is built around a reconstituted knowledge of the history of complicity/culpability of different countries in colonial enterprises and the enslavement of others; this involves bringing to visibility the personal (hi)stories, subjectivities, and voices which "official history" had attempted to render invisible.

Phillips sets out across Europe to try and "understand" the Europeans, and thus himself (as, in part, a "product" of their culture—in which he has been raised—but also, importantly, of their history of colonization, expropriation and slave trading). In doing so, he is quite consciously setting out to reconstruct and recount the "other side" of the story that is normally told, by Europeans, about Europe, weaving historical information about the countries he visits, anecdotes, and personal reflections and meditations into the story of his own travels.

Hank Okazaki. *LitC.* 26, 3 (1991), pp. 38–41

Can Phillips be described as a British (or a black British) writer? In the bulk of [Joseph] Conrad's work, Poland—in terms of setting—is not significant, yet his Polish life shaped a part of his basic awareness. So too with Phillips, and even if little of his work thus far is set in England, his British years, from infancy to manhood, have given him great advantages. The term *advantages* may surprise, given the degree of racism—covert or overt, suave or crude—that pervades contemporary Britain. Still, I would argue that having grown up in Britain has heightened Phillips's awareness and fine (in the two meanings of *sharp* and *excellent*) sensitivity. This is not to suggest that Phillips is some bruised plant trembling delicately in unkind winds. His difference and exile have positively defined him; they make up his essential being, and, if often a source of hurt or anger, of alienation and loneliness, they also constitute his awareness and strength. It is the turning of what a hostile society and a denigrating culture would impose as misfortune and limitation into advantage and a wonderful broadening out of understanding and sympathy, a turning of prisons into castles (with acknowledgment to George Lamming and his novel *In the Castle of My Skin*), a moving from pain to knowledge and beyond to joy and pride, and thence to celebration.

To return to the question: Can Phillips be labeled "British" despite his "return" to the Caribbean? Not to do so would leave our taxonomic lust unsatisfied. If anything, his latest work, *Higher Ground*, shifting from the days of slavery somewhere on the coast of black Africa to a contemporary maximum-security prison cell in the United States and then to a Polish-Jewish woman suffering incomprehension, loneliness, and a breakdown in Britain during World War II, shows a liberated Phillips, a writer who can penetrate the inner being of people vastly different from himself in time, place, and gender, yet people very much like us all in the common and eternal human inheritance of pain and suffering. In a recent essay ["Living and Writing in the Caribbean: An Experiment"], Phillips writes that his "branches have developed, and to some extent continue to develop and grow, in Britain" but that his "roots are in Caribbean soil." Eluding labels that will seize and fix him, he finally remains Caryl Phillips.

Charles [Ponnuthurai] Sarvan and Hasan Marhama.
WLT. 65, 1 (Winter 1991), p. 40

Set firmly and with a sustained and vivid sensuous immediacy in the nineteenth century, and taking place mostly in the exotic world of the British West Indies though some scenes are set in London and the English countryside, *Cambridge* tells two stories that are closely related, indeed inextricably joined in time and place.

These two stories ought to be one (and are united in the novel), but prove to be more separate than the central characters are able to imagine, because of a multitude of assumptions, prejudices, and fundamental misapprehensions that isolate individuals not so much from one another as from the possibility of any clear and present understanding of others' motives, actions, or points of view. These personal and social misunderstandings lead inexorably to tragedy. At the center of the human tragedy is the institution of slavery, by then unlawful in Britain but still practiced legally in the West Indies.

Among many credible, well-realized characters, black and white, the two major figures are Emily Cartwright, a sensitive and thoughtful Englishwoman, unmarried and "almost thirty," and a proud and powerful slave called Cambridge, who lives on her father's plantation and whom Emily dubs Hercules in the privacy of her diary. In a story with layers of irony, it is ironic that Cambridge never knows about Emily's nickname for him. Nor can she ever know the names that he has had—his "true Guinea name, Olumide"; his first slave name, Thomas; his Christian name, under which he preached as a missionary in England, David Henderson. She, in fact, knows next to nothing of his personal history and she figures less in his life and thoughts than she imagines. Though both the central characters reveal themselves to be complex, ambiguous, and conflicted, they also come across (a triumph of Caryl Phillips's craft and art) as fundamentally good and decent people who try to be honest with themselves and who mean to do well, but who fail because of personal limitations and huge social forces beyond their control.

George Garrett. *NYTBR*. February 16, 1992, pp. 1, 24

The main body of Phillips's novel [*Crossing the River*] consists of four taut narratives—two white voices, two black; two male, two female. But its structure is poetic, built on a single refrain: "Why have you forsaken me?" The voices are richly counterpointed, and the forsakings are as various as the author's extraordinary imagination can make them.

In the prologue, a nameless African father, his crops having failed, sells his children to the master of a slave ship. Haunted for 250 years by "the chorus of a common memory," he discovers "among the sundry restless voices" those of his lost children: "My Nash. My Martha. My Travis." Gradually, as the stories in the main text unfold, we realize that this father has taken on the mythic proportions of the continent of Africa, that his abandonment represents the irreversible history of entire peoples. . . .

In the most spectacular accomplishment of the novel, Phillips produces the journal and letters home of one James Hamilton, captain of the slave ship Duke of York on its voyage from Liverpool to "the Windward Coast of Africa" and thence across "the river" that is the Atlantic.

Like Edward Williams, the twenty-six-year-old Hamilton has reason to go searching in Africa: his father died there, and the death is shrouded in mystery. The elder Hamilton was without religion, perceiving that his profession of slave ship captain was incompatible with a profession of faith. There are hints that he "traded not wisely" and that he "cultivated a passionate hatred, instead of a commercial detachment," toward his slaves. . . .

Throughout, Hamilton is perplexed by the mood of his cargo, who "appeared gloomy and sullen, their heads full of mischief." Just before departing from Africa, he is "approached by a quiet fellow" from whom he buys the "two strong man boys, and a proud girl," of the prologue. . . .

Identity, in both individuals and peoples, is composed of the story we tell ourselves of the past. That story is necessarily partial and selective, but if it deliberately omits significant events the resultant self is inauthentic. One of the values of fiction is that it can tell the story anew, can go back and include a neglected truth. *Crossing the River* does this and is therefore a book with an agenda. Phillips proposes that the diaspora is permanent, and that blacks throughout the world who look to Africa as a benevolent fatherland tell themselves a stunted story. They need not to trace but to put down roots.

The message, however, is neither simply nor stridently conveyed. Phillips's prologue strikes it as a stately note, and its resonance continues to deepen; only in the epilogue does it become uncomfortably literal. Phillips's theme sounds throughout, perhaps most poignantly in the laconic notation of Captain Hamilton:

"We have lost sight of Africa."

Janet Burroway. NYTBR. January 30, 1994, p. 10

RABÉARIVELO, JEAN-JOSEPH (1901–1937)

MADAGASCAR

One of the greatest French-speaking African poets is undoubtedly the Malagasy Jean-Joseph Rabéarivelo. His work has been much less boosted than that of some other French-speaking poets (he has been almost ignored by translators, so far), presumably because his writing does not seem to fit into the now fashionable Négritude movement.

Rabéarivelo died in 1937, which is two years before [Aimé] Césaire published his famous *Cahier d'un retour au pays natal*. The poet died tragically by taking his own life. His death came as a complete surprise to most of his friends, and the mystery that surrounded it has never really been solved. . . .

Nothing could be further removed from the themes and images of current French African poetry than the writing of Rabéarivelo. Colonialism and the African personality do not figure in it. There are no tom-toms, palm trees, and black nude women. There is no oppression and no revolution. In fact Rabéarivelo is not concerned with the everyday issues of here and now. . . .

The world Rabéarivelo describes is a strangely unreal world. There is an extremely tantalizing quality about these poems, because on the one hand he can make us see his visions so clearly—and on the other he destroys them again by removing them right out of our sphere of knowledge and experience. Thus he speaks of "blind light" or "insipid salt"; these are images that destroy themselves and produce a sudden shock in the reader. On the whole Rabéarivelo is careful to remove his poems from the sphere of everyday existence. Occasionally he mentions his native land, "Imerina," but more often he locates his action near the "frontiers of sleep." Nearly all of his images suggest that we move in strange, unexplored zones: "all seasons have been abolished in those unexplored zones that occupy half of the world," or "soil which is neither hot nor cold, like the skin of those who rest far from life and death." Rabéarivelo speaks of "leaves which no wind can shake" or "unidentified trees" or "unknown flowers of no climate." . . .

Rabéarivelo's poems are clear and precise visions of a strange and personal world. Like [Charles] Baudelaire, his favorite French poet, Rabéarivelo had a disgust of reality. In his poetry he has destroyed and dismembered reality. And out of the fragments he has built a new mythical world; it is a world of death and frustration, but also transcended by a sad beauty of its own.

Ulli Beier. *Introduction to African Literature* (Evanston, Ill.: Northwestern University Press, 1967), pp. 99–101

There is a distinct difference, both in quality and texture, between Rabéarivelo's early poetry and his mature poetry. The early poetry is technically competent, but it is based on the imitation of techniques and emotions reminiscent of late nineteenth-century French poetry. Nevertheless, the theme of departure—the poet's longing to break out of his prison—is present already in these early poems. His "Paroles de l'hiver," typical of this period, evokes "the distant mountains that speak my agony," the mountains that hold him prisoner on his island. Other early poems anticipate [Léopold Sédar] Senghor's lament that he is torn between his love for France and for Africa and finds himself unable to choose. On the one hand, Rabéarivelo wants to identify himself with French culture. . . . On the other, he regrets his loss of contact with traditional Malagasy culture. . . .

Although the personal themes of loneliness and despair are already present in Rabéarivelo's early poems, had he written nothing else they would have become merely literary curiosities. They still possess the impersonality of the borrowed language, so that the emotions are intellectual and therefore rhetorical.

The mature poems are dramatically different. They are written in a poetic language which is the poet's own, in spite of its antecedents, and they fully express the poet's experience of colonialism. His new language derives in part from [Jules] Supervielle, but he has assimilated the peculiar quality of the traditional Malagasy *hain-teny*. This new poetry is a direct product of the poet's despair, but instead of lamenting his despair, he uses it to create an imaginary paradise beyond it. His poetry becomes his escape from his prison, a substitute for the mental and physical freedom he will never know.

His paradise is a world remote from reality, but it is created out of the elements of nature which are at one and the same time typical of Madagascar and universal—the night sky, the stars, the sun, the moon, the prairies and the desert, birds and cattle, the wind and the rain. All these are transformed and molded by the poet's fantasy into a vision of joy and beauty. His poems invariably tell of the journey to this paradise, which is at the heart of the night, the opposite of the glaring light of day, representing reality. Inevitably there is a return to reality, but this return is not always, or even generally, seen as a loss so much as a triumph, for the poet returns with the poem. The paradise his imagination creates is synonymous with poetry. The experience is disguised in the image.

Clive Wake. *Review of National Literatures.* 2, 2 (Fall 1971), pp. 108–10

Rabéarivelo's first three books, *La Coupe de cendres*, *Sylves*, and *Volumes*, were published locally in Madagascar in very small editions. These collections of short poems are still imitative of the melancholy [Charles] Baudelaire and later minor French poets, the "Fantaisistes." One of these poets was a French colonial official, Pierre Camo, much older than Rabéarivelo, who became his great friend and literary mentor. Camo lived ten years in Madagascar, and his influence as a cultural leader extended to the French community on Mauritius as well. It was Camo's encouragement that gradually weaned Rabéarivelo from the "maudlin self-centeredness" of his early poetry to a mature style more strongly expressing his own inner world. The later volumes, *Presque-songes*, *Traduit de la nuit*, and *Chants pour Abéone*, are considered by critics to contain the Malagasy poet's finest work. Here, abandoning imitative rhymes and meter in favor of free verse, Rabéarivelo has mastered a sense of form and created dreamlike poems of strange and compelling imagery, drawn from his own fantasies as well as from a

Malagasy culture foreign to Western readers. Rabéarivelo's originality lies in the skillful blending of these elements. . . .

Vieilles chansons des pays d'Imerina, published in 1939 after the poet's death, is quite different in form and language from Rabéarivelo's other work. These are French renderings of traditional Malagasy *hain-teny*, formal love poems which are sometimes dialogues, sometimes monologues. Rabéarivelo also wrote poems directly in *hova*, and he sometimes translated into the musical Malagasy tongue poems he had originally written in French. . . .

Rabéarivelo was certainly a victim of the colonial situation as much as a beneficiary of it. The paradox was that the Western culture he had acquired with such effort and assimilated with such brilliance dazzled him with the riches of the wider world and at the same time continually denied him real access to its bounties, leaving him imprisoned on his island. He was a solitary, tormented person whose struggles with the real world were as much internal as external. In the end, they became overwhelming. The spectacular gesture of his suicide became both the poet's only way out and his most violent form of protest against endless poverty and humiliation.

Ellen Conroy Kennedy. *The Négritude Poets*
(New York: Thunder's Mouth Press, 1975), pp. 224–26

Rabéarivelo's early poetry is fairly obvious; there is little depth of feeling in it, and what feeling there is is mainly rhetorical. Neither the texture of the poetry nor its themes are particularly subtle or complex. The poet uses a borrowed literary language and style to express an experience of which he is not yet himself deeply conscious. However, between the publication of *Volumes* in 1928 and *Presque-songes* in 1934, Rabéarivelo's poetic sensibility underwent a profound transformation, and with it the quality and style of his poetry. During this period he abandoned the conventional meters, fixed-form poems, and borrowed language of his early poetry, substituting for them a masterly use of free verse and a totally new approach to imagery. Most significant of all, he was, suddenly (or so it seems), in possession of a subtly complex, rich, and vital personal poetic world, completely coherent and sure of itself. The explicitly stated tensions of his cultural exile gave way to the more complex insights of the poet's intuitive perception of himself and of his place in the world. . . .

In his mature poetry, Rabéarivelo uses his imagery in a way reminiscent of the contemporary surrealists, especially [Paul] Eluard, another poet fascinated by the *paysage intérieur*. Like Rabéarivelo, Eluard had a great predilection for nature imagery or, more specifically, for the image of the landscape. The image is always, or nearly always, the center of the poem. The object which provides the first element in the metaphor, the reality, is not mentioned. Only the image survives. The result is that the poem, through its imagery, is at one extra remove from the poet himself, since the element directly linking it with the poet is omitted. This creates a strangely remote, altogether independent world. Rabéarivelo draws nearly all his imagery from nature but, although his outlook is largely that of the romantic—self-centered, introspective—they are not affective images but nearer to objective symbols. The important thing about his nature imagery is that it is drawn entirely from his native Malagasy landscape, and it is therefore thoroughly real to his imagination. Indeed, on the visual level alone, his imagery gives the reader a remarkably vivid impression of the Malagasy countryside. . . .

Rabéarivelo was an individualist in the way the poets of [Léopold Sédar] Senghor's generation were not. Rabéarivelo's experience of colonialism produced a reaction of turning inward, since the poet could not break out of his prison in any other way. Senghor's generation were aware of themselves as the spokesmen of all black men, and their poetry was therefore outward-turning. The evolution of Senghor's poetry is totally different from Rabéarivelo's. The early Senghor was inclined towards introspection, driven to it by his initial sense of exile and loneliness in Paris, but very soon it turned outwards as his sense of responsibility towards other men increased. His poetry is self-centered, but he wants it this way, because he has chosen to be the ambassador of his people, who must keep their gaze turned on him. Rabéarivelo's early poetry shows signs of an objective concern with the cultural tensions created by colonialism, but he found it impossible within the narrow confines of his prison world to see beyond his own predicament and, in his mature poetry, had to create a freedom within himself. This could only exacerbate the tensions, with the final tragic result of suicide.

But Rabéarivelo's positive contribution to modern African poetry in French is nevertheless considerable. Before the doctrine of Négritude sought, by conscious practice, to create a specifically African poetry, Rabéarivelo had, unconsciously, welded together trends in modern French poetry and the traditional Malagasy *hain-teny*, and built his edifice on the solid ground of the Malagasy countryside, to produce poetry of striking originality.

Clive Wake. In Edgar Wright, ed. The Critical Evaluation of African
Literature (Washington, D. C.: INSCAPE, 1976), p. 157, 163, 172

Rabéarivelo's appearance alongside his fellow Malagasy, Flavien Ranaivo, in an anthology largely devoted to verse from West Africa and the French West Indies is not difficult to understand. In [Léopold Sédar] Senghor's eyes Rabéarivelo was significant both as precursor and as emblem, since, though from the other side of the continent and exempt from the more drastic excesses of the French educational system, his life bore witness to two essential elements in the black francophone predicament: a liege-bond to French literature and a countervailing desire to assert his local uniqueness through an imitation of indigenous forms. Like so many of the writers of French expression who were to follow in his stead, Rabéarivelo had been torn between two impulses. He wrote some early verse in *hova* and later, in his last published collection, followed the structures of the local Madagascan *hain-teny* or proverb poem. But at its most delicate and evocative his poetry reminds us most strongly of [Charles] Baudelaire, of his beloved [Arthur] Rimbaud, of the voluptuary lusciousness of [Stéphane] Mallarmé.

It has become customary to bewail Rabéarivelo's physical and cultural isolation, and also his lack of any clear commitment to a truly national identity. In practice both forms of commiseration are misplaced. When compared with . . . anglophone poets . . . Rabéarivelo enjoyed two supreme advantages. In the first place, though he never reached Paris, his acceptance among a small group of expatriate French writers resident in Madagascar had exposed him to recent developments in French literature. In the second, he possessed immediate access to an indigenous tradition which in his later French verse he learned to reproduce with a certain fidelity. All that he lacked compared with a later generation of more committed francophone writers was a cause, something which before the ideologically inflamed years of the late 1930s was not so mandatory a requirement for a self-respecting *indigène* as might now perhaps appear. When in the 1940s the banner of Négritude was raised aloft, Rabéarivelo was dead and the poetry of French-speaking Africa had changed decisively.

Robert Fraser. *West African Poetry*
(Cambridge: Cambridge University Press, 1986), pp. 43–44

It is very difficult for all men and especially a poet to avoid thinking about death. Rabéarivelo has left us, in his poems, in his journal, and by his suicide, irrefutable traces of this obsession. . . .

Presque-songes: The title of the collection of poems promises that we will remain on the threshold of dreams and the night and the threshold of death. . . .

The words of a living being in the world of the living, *Presque-songes* is rooted in the real world. Imerina, the native land which appeared in the poet's work with *Sylves*, became, in *Volumes*, one of the principal themes of inspiration, as the spectacle of hidden splendors and a pretext for expressing the uprooting of a colonized land. In *Presque-songes*, on the contrary, it emerges free, in the description of the twilight sceneries, in the scenes of the unpretentious picturesque genre, such as the hills of Iarivo, the zebus of the red lands, the women's clothing, *valiha* and dances, and the *makis* of the tropical forest. The thirst of the living is expressed here in the efforts of the inventor. . . . Thus, too, is the treatment of death transformed.

Faced with the dichotomy that the immediate experience of man has inscribed in language and which makes of life and death two contradictory realities in which the affirmation of one equals the negation of the other, the poet establishes in his refusal of the tragic, and by diverse strategies, a connection between that which was presented as absolutely incompatible. And this act favors life, because he summons the dead into our land of the living so that although dead, they are at the same time alive.

There are two kinds of dead in *Presque-songes*: the recently dead of the three parts of "Thrènes," whom he personally knew, even loved and whom he names or could name, and the anonymous collectivity of the ancestors whose evocation few poems ignore. The conscience of a radical rupture and of a tragic distance, which the poet tries to resolve, is associated with the former alone. The dead ancestors are presented from the start as being immanent to our world. . . .

One then understands that among all the poems, "Thrènes" offers to our senses the most crude material presentation of death. It is the scandal of the decomposition of the bodies and of their destruction. . . .

In the shock of the close encounter of a living being with death, the latter is experienced as discontinuity. It is the reverse, the inverse of life: the dead are "under the ground," in the night, in silence, in nothingness. . . .

Concretizing this schism between the living and the dead, with "Thrènes" and "Reconnaissance à Paul Gauguin," Rabéarivelo has demarcated, at the end of the work, a kind of enclosure reserved for the dead. Nevertheless, the choice of the appropriate poems already gives death a social character. . . .

The dialectic continues with socialized death becoming death salvaged and brought into the world of the living. This is predicted by the dedication, "A tous mes amis, morts et vivants" . . . the reduction of the opposition is accomplished through the jolts of the poem.

Marie-Christine Rochmann. *PA*. 145 (1988), pp. 165–67†

REED, ISHMAEL (1938–   )

UNITED STATES

A close reading of [Ishmael] Reed's works strongly suggests his concerns with the received form of the novel, with the precise rhetorical shape of the Afro-American literary tradition, and with the relation that the Afro-American tradition bears to the Western tradition. Reed's concerns, as exemplified in his narrative forms, seem to be twofold: the relation his own art bears to his black literary precursors, including [Zora Neale] Hurston, [Richard] Wright, [Ralph] Ellison, and James Baldwin; and the process of willing-into-being a rhetorical structure, a literary language, replete with its own figures and tropes, but one that allows the black writer to posit a structure of feeling that simultaneously critiques both the metaphysical presuppositions inherent in Western ideas and forms of writing and the metaphorical system in which the "blackness" of the writer and his experience have been valorized as a "natural" absence. In six demanding novels, Reed has criticized, through signifying, what he perceives to be the conventional structures of feeling that he has received from the Afro-American tradition. He has proceeded almost as if the sheer process of the analysis can clear a narrative space for the next generation of writers as decidedly as Ellison's narrative response to Wright and naturalism cleared a space for Leon Forrest, Toni Morrison, Alice Walker, James Alan McPherson, and especially for Reed himself.

By undertaking the difficult and subtle art of pastiche, Reed criticizes the Afro-American idealism of a transcendent black subject, integral and whole, self-sufficient and plentiful, the "always already" black signified, available for literary representation in received Western forms as would be the water dippered from a deep dark well. Water can be poured into glasses or cups or canisters, but it remains water just the same. Put simply, Reed's fictions argue that the so-called black experience cannot be thought of as a fluid content to be poured into received and static containers. For Reed, it is the signifier that both shapes and defines any discrete signified—and it is the signifiers of the Afro-American tradition with whom Reed is concerned.

Reed's first novel lends credence to this sort of reading and also serves to create a set of generic expectations for reading the rest of his works. *The Free-Lance Pallbearers* is, above all else, a parody of the confessional mode which is the fundamental, undergirding convention of Afro-American narrative, received, elaborated upon and transmitted in a chartable heritage from Briton Hammon's captivity narrative of 1760, through the antebellum slave narratives, to black autobiography, and into black fiction, especially the fictions of Hurston, Wright, Baldwin, and Ellison. The narrative of Reed's Bukka Doopeyduk is a pastiche of the classic black narrative of the questing protagonist's "journey into the heart of whiteness"; but it parodies that narrative form by turning it inside out, exposing the character of the originals and thereby defining their formulaic closures and disclosures. Doopeyduk's tale ends with his own crucifixion; as the narrator of his own story, therefore, Doopeyduk articulates, literally, from among the dead, an irony implicit in all confessional and autobiographical modes, in which any author is forced by definition to imagine him- or herself to be dead. More specifically, Reed signifies upon [Wright's] *Black Boy* and [Baldwin's] *Go Tell It on the Mountain* in a foregrounded critique which can be read as an epigraph to the novel: "read growing up in soulsville first of three installments—or what it means to be a backstage darky." Reed foregrounds the "scat-singing voice" that introduces the novel against the "other" voice of Doopeyduk, whose "second" voice narrates the novel's plot. Here, Reed parodies both Hurston's use of free indirect discourse in *Their Eyes Were Watching God* and Ellison's use in *Invisible Man* of the foregrounded voice in their prologue and epilogue that frame his nameless protagonist's picaresque account of his own narrative. In his second novel, *Yellow Back Radio Broke-Down*, Reed more fully, and successfully, critiques both realism and modernism. . . .

Reed's third novel, *Mumbo Jumbo*, is a novel about writing itself—not only in the figurative sense of the postmodern, self-reflexive text but also in a literal sense. . . . *Mumbo Jumbo* is both a book about texts and a book of texts, a composite narrative composed of sub-texts, pre-texts, post-texts and narratives-within-narratives. It is both a definition of Afro-American culture and its deflation. . . .

The text of *Mumbo Jumbo* is framed by devices characteristic of film narration. The prologue, situated in New Orleans, functions as a "false start" of the action: five pages of narration are followed by a second title page, a second copyright and acknowledgment page, and a second set of epigraphs, the first of which concludes the prologue. This prologue functions like the prologue of a film, with the title and credits appearing next, before the action continues. The novel's final words are "Freeze frame." The relative fluidity of the narrative structure of film, compared with that of conventional prose narrative, announces here an emphasis upon figural multiplicity rather than singular referential correspondence, an emphasis that Reed recapitulates throughout the text by an imaginative play of doubles. The play of doubles extends from the title and the double-Erzulie image of [Josephine] Baker on the novel's cover ("Erzulie" means "love of mirrors") to the double beginning implicit in every prologue, through all sorts of double images scattered in the text (such as the "two heads" of PaPa LaBas) and the frequently repeated arabic numerals 4 and 22), all the way to the double ending of the novel implied by its epilogue and "Partial Bibliography." The double beginning and double ending frame the text of *Mumbo Jumbo*, a book of doubles, from its title on. . . .

It is indeterminacy, the sheer plurality of meaning, the very play of the signifier itself, which *Mumbo Jumbo* celebrates. *Mumbo Jumbo* addresses the *play* of the black literary tradition and, as a parody, is a *play* upon that same tradition.

Henry Louis Gates, Jr. *Black Literature and Literary Theory*
(New York: Methuen, 1984), pp. 297–99, 305, 313

In a fundamental way it is pointless to evaluate Reed by conventional literary standards, since the cultural assumptions on which these standards are based are themselves his primary target. The pertinent question is whether he in fact creates and practices a new aesthetic or whether, like the black nationalist writers and critics he so often attacks, he turns literature into polemic. Like his opponents, he castigates, satirizes, and vilifies white cultural values; like them he views the dominant society as excremental, repressive, and death-driven. Both implicitly and explicitly, he sees blacks as allies of the life force and whites as death seekers. Unlike the nationalists, however, who emphasize present oppression, Reed seeks nothing less than the demystification and deconstruction of cultural history. He works backward to Egyptian myth to locate the source of the black-white conflict, which he sees as coinciding with the Osiris-Set conflict. From this primal struggle, apparently won by the forces of death, has come the underlying pattern of human experience, which is the effort of life, fertility, and creativity to assert themselves against the control of death, sterility, and repression. Through systemization and violence, the dominant culture has not only maintained its power, but has made itself appear as the true, beautiful, and natural. It presumes to be the only valid voice, the only Word. But because creativity is anarchic, individualistic, and irrepressible, it continually intrudes itself upon the controlling patterns. It is this intrusion, this breaking of the pattern, that Reed designates Neo-HooDoo. His fiction consistently operates dialectically: it exposes and denigrates the oppressive nature of Western culture so as to free the non-Western voices which express life and creativity. And this very act of exposure is the saying of the words which in voodoo practice give one access to the spirits. Thus, Reed serves the function not only of *Guedé*, but also of the *houngan* (priest) whose litany opens the way to an alternative world.

His six novels—*The Free-Lance Pallbearers, Yellow Back Radio Broke-Down, Mumbo Jumbo, The Last Days of Louisiana Red, Flight to Canada,* and *The Terrible Twos*—are variations on the theme of cultural conflict. Each presents some aspect of human history and makes clear the continuous character of the struggle by collapsing conventional literary time structures. In such simultaneity, as in the use of the forms of popular literature such as the western and the detective novel, Reed calls into question the dominant society's control of both history and language. His play with time and genre is a way of denaturalizing assumptions about these aspects of culture and revealing the underlying manipulative functions of both. In this, he resembles postmodernist white writers like John Barth and Donald Barthelme. However, his fictions differ from theirs in that his undercutting of literary and cultural values is premised on an alternative value system, Neo-HooDoo. The similarity to metafictional practice is clearest in the early nihilistic works, but, beginning with *Mumbo Jumbo*, he lays claim to a different mythology and aesthetic.

Keith E. Byerman. Fingering the Jagged Grain: Tradition and Form in Recent
Black Fiction (Athens: University of Georgia Press, 1985), pp. 218–19

Uppity, pretentious, pompous, sexist, and sophomoric are the most frequent if not the kindest names hurled by unsympathetic critics at Reed for the Neo-HooDoo aesthetic he develops between 1967 and 1983 in his four books of verse, five anthologies, and six novels.

At the heart of Reed's Neo-HooDoo aesthetic, which is largely constructed from residual elements of syncretistic African religions (Voodoo, Pocomania, Candomblé, Macumba, and Hoo-Doo) in the Caribbean and the Americas, especially Haiti, Brazil, and the United States, is a belief in the power of the unknown, particularly as expressed in artistic freedom and originality. In the prose poem "Neo-HooDoo Manifesto" he tells us that "Neo-HooDoo is a 'Lost American Church' updated," that "Neo-HooDoo borrows from Haiti Africa and South America. Neo-HooDoo comes in all styles and moods," and that "Neo-HooDoo believes that every man is an artist and every artist a priest." An incredibly eclectic mixture of ancient and contemporary techniques and forms of non-Western and Western cultures, Reed's six novels . . . challenge the reader to be as culturally egalitarian and imaginatively bold as the author.

Bernard W. Bell. The Afro-American Novel and Its Tradition
(Amherst: University of Massachusetts Press, 1987), pp. 330–31

Ishmael Reed's *Flight to Canada* presents the reader with many conundrums, all asking the rhetorical question, "Who is to say what is fact and what is fiction?" Through Uncle Robins's narrative, the amanuensis-cum-reflector . . . Raven Quickskill, demonstrates that the Afro-American, Ur-slave, is necessarily entrapped in slavehood concepts that contradict his experience. His experience tells him that he can choose either the slavehood concepts disseminated by his master or adopt the personal attitudes of those slaves who reject traditional slavehood values and attitudes. Whichever choice he makes leads to emotional conflict. Some of the slaves, however, use their knowledge of the slave community and the plantation society to grapple with and overcome the slavehood images of Southern society. Reed, through the pseudo slave narrative, elicits and evokes an image of the infernality of life in the South for Afro-Americans by re-creating the images that were so well-known to the slave community, the black freeman, and the whites who read slave narratives and heard blacks tell their tales. . . .

In spite of the rhetorical structure of *Flight to Canada*, the narrator-agent gives the reader several exposures from which to develop a composite picture of the major black characters. He does not, however, make the compositing process easy, for each exposure is influenced by the "witchery [which he puts] on the word," an influence which raises several questions: What effect does his necromancy have on the narrative, if any? (He admits he could not stand Uncle Robin when they were in slavery.) Does he manipulate the slavehood experiences and images of the slaves in the narrative? What are his relations with the other slaves really like? What do they actually think of him? Do the house slaves see themselves as the field slaves see them, and vice versa? How do the field slaves see each other? How do the house slaves see each other? These and many other questions about interpersonal relations among slaves, as well as their images of each other, are raised by this book.

Charles De Arman. *CLAJ.* 33, 2 (December 1989), pp. 157–59

Ishmael Reed extends the notion of syncretism into the level and texture he uses in his novels, thus creating a kind of contemporary bathetic language, whose principal rules of discourse are taken from the streets, popular music, and television. In Reed's novels, it is not uncommon to find the formal blend of language mixed with the colloquial, as it is Reed's contention that such an occurrence in the narrative is more in keeping with the ways contemporary people influenced by popular culture really speak. By purposely mixing the myriad aspects of language from different sources in popular culture, Reed pulls into individual *cardinal functions* (one closed set of narrative actions: [Roland] Barthes) words and expressions which create the fictive illusion of real speech. Though the emotive effect is bathetic, evoking interest and humor because of seeming incongruencies, the language Reed uses comes from concrete paroles (selected, individual utterances from the field of all available language usage [langúe]: [Ferdinand de] Saussure) of the present day. The involved reader in the text knows that contemporary language is not static, is in fact in tremendous flux, and that actual people mix levels of diction constantly to achieve the desired communicative effect; and the proof of the validity of Reed's artistic method is the ease with which his characters display bathetic discourse. . . .

All of Reed's books exhibit *dystaxy,* i.e., the disruption of linear narrative, but certainly the book which gives the best example of Reed's use of dystaxic, synchronic development in its various forms is *Flight to Canada.* The "time" of the novel is the antebellum period. But that time period overlaps with the present (1976) through the use of contemporary indices such as language lexicon, cardinal references, and the situational responses of the characters. For example, the characters make long-distance phone calls when in distress; Raven Quickskill, the crafty slave who escapes, joins the lecture circuit and uses a jet to travel through Canada, where he delivers his abolitionist speeches, reads his poetry, and collects his honoraria; Josiah Henson's spirit appears to lambast Harriet Beecher Stowe for stealing from Henson's slave narrative the plot for *Uncle Tom's Cabin.* Leechfield, another escaped slave, is making a fortune selling photographs of himself with women through an antebellum pornography magazine: "I'll be your slave for the night," one pictorial caption might read, not unlike the "personal" ads in the *Village Voice.* . . .

This narrative self-referentiality is not always so simple to decipher, as all of Reed's novels are readerly texts; he expects the reader to be familiar with past fiction and nonfictional events external to the particular novel at issue. Reed also expects the reader to "make" the text and its implications by way of understanding the narrative games being played. The fact that the 1976 publication of *Flight to Canada* is a direct response and a counterblast to the publishing of Alex Haley's *Roots*, and that both books can be appreciated much better with this knowledge, is something of which Reed expects the interested reader to be aware. Moreover, without a readerly knowledge of historical and contemporary personages, much of the satirical effect of any Reed novel is lost. A part of the cause of oppression, in Reed's scheme of things, is ignorance, and he will not accept ignorance from his readers; thus, an aspect of any Reed novel is didactic. Again, the point of syncretism as a literary method for Reed is that it pulls together from all existing language-level and discourse possibilities those utterances which he feels are most effective in illuminating the fictional situation he has created.

Reginald Martin. *MLS*. 20, 2 (Spring 1990), pp. 3, 7–9

In three novels, *The Free-Lance Pallbearers*, *The Terrible Twos*, and *The Terrible Threes*, Reed launches grotesque attacks on American social, economic, and political avatars of control. . . .

In *The Terrible Twos* and *The Terrible Threes*, Reed traces the tangled skeins of interconnection in American power centers, showing how broadcasters buy legislators, how advisers close to the president answer to backroom industrial interests, how the military can be influenced or bought, and how fake Hollywood glamour creates the illusion of reality. The reader learns how a tiny group of fanatics not answerable to any legal power could bring about the nuclear destruction of an African nation. Blackmail, drugs, the sale of information, secret societies, the manipulation of images: these are what *The Terrible Twos* and *The Terrible Threes* are about. Reed seems to fear that this degree of interconnectedness may make the system impervious to legal improvements. . . .

Control is also a helpful tool for understanding Reed's other novels. *Reckless Eyeballing* has confounded and revolted reviewers but makes some sense as a demonstration of how an alert and reasonably sophisticated individual persuades himself to submit to the forces of control. The results are nightmarish, though members of mainstream culture will not at first find them noteworthy: Ian Ball does not know his real self anymore. An island hex is the ostensible cause of his cloven personality, but magic only reinforces what his attempts to "make it" in New York have already effected: a split self with the inauthentic half dominant. . . .

Reed's works have often been treated as scattershot endeavors—*Reckless Eyeballing* as an attack on feminists; *Yellow Back Radio Broke-Down* as a western; *Mumbo Jumbo* as a HooDoo detective story; and *The Terrible Twos*, *The Terrible Threes*, and *The Free-Lance Pallbearers* as political satire. Most critics have found no stable core of concerns aside from a satiric attitude toward the world. I argue that Reed has an ongoing project in his explorations of control and that his grotesque vision of America resembles the visions of other artists sensitive to the workings of control. Reed and these other artists feel cheated of some lost element of the American dream and protest this betrayal with images of filth and violent perversion. The critique of America is flashy and is even compelling to readers disturbed by inequities in the country's treatment of its citizens. Reed's contribution to this strain in American thought becomes evident only when one looks at all his novels together. Examined individually, they are disparate and variably successful; however, the limitations of any one signify little in the series of hallucinatory portraits of America's soul. Each might be likened to a seance in which Reed depicts America as seen from the HooDoo spirit world. . . . The evils Reed attacks are not just African-American problems; his focus on control demonstrates that he belongs to a group of bitter satirists—female and male, black and white—whose experience with cultural lies appalls them. Their artistic violence aims at breaking through to vantages beyond those of ordinary social and literary consciousness. Such perspectives, they imply, reveal truths normally ignored by privileged members of society. Those ugly truths, not the bourgeois self-image that the contented have cultivated to protect their own comfort, are the reality.

Kathryn Hume. PMLA. 108, 3 (May 1993), pp. 508, 515–16

With his ninth novel, Ishmael Reed proves again that he is not afraid to plunge into the maelstrom. *Japanese by Spring* is full of contemporary issues plaguing the American consciousness: Rodney King, Anita Hill/Clarence Thomas, the United States attack on Iraq, and so on. As he moves through his fifties, has Reed lost his fictional abilities? No. For Reed, the novel is supreme. If you want to understand anything, put it into a novel and let the novel decide. And so Reed himself is also a character in the work: "He sometimes went around with a tacky beard in order to appear to be a man of the people. He sometimes wore clothes so long that they became ragged and his family would have to go to Macy's to buy him new clothes."

The protagonist is Benjamin Puttbutt, a black junior professor at white Jack London College. He is being nice to the English and Women's Studies departments and attacks black men for not shaping up—one of his heroes being Thomas Sowell—because he wants to get tenure. He even turns a blind eye to the outrageous racist actions against him by a student, Robert Bass, whose father is a rich contributor to the college. A radical in the 1960s, he will do anything that goes over: "Now that the writer was considered as obsolete as a 1960s computer, he could share in some of the profits of the growth industry of the 1980s and 1990s. Criticism. All you had to do was string together some quotes from [Walter] Benjamin, [Roland] Barthes, [Michel] Foucault and [Jacques] Lacan and you were in business. Even a New Critic like himself could make some cash." However, he is double-crossed and denied tenure.

Puttbutt has been studying Japanese because he sees it as the wave of the future. Suddenly, the college is bought by a Japanese group, and his Japanese teacher becomes acting president and makes him his right-hand man. While the Japanese do to the Eurocentrics what the latter have done to others, Puttbutt makes Crabtree, an English professor, teach Freshman Yoruba. Crabtree changes. "I have learned a language that transports me to a culture that's two thousand years old," he says. "Have they ever produced a Tolstoy? They have produced Tolstoys. Have they produced a Homer. They have hundreds of Homers. We were just too lazy and arrogant to find out."

Peter Nazareth. *WLT*. 67, 3 (Summer 1993), p. 610

In *Japanese by Spring* (the title comes from a short-course text used by our hero), Reed updates his ongoing quarrel with the world created by politicians and maintained by the denizens of Madison Avenue; he takes on, this time, the "groves of academe," especially the archaic silliness of tenure and all of its attendant quirkiness—teaching assistants, publish or perish departments, political infighting, assemblyline techniques. In his main character, "Chappie" Puttbutt, a schmoolike black, untenured professor at Jack London University and member of a long line of military officers (father a general, mother in military intelligence), Reed has created an alter ego who represents everything he objects to in academic life. Puttbutt, author of *Blacks, America's Misfortune* (his dissertation subject, an obscure 1920s poet, Nathan Brown), studies Japanese so as to be ready for the inevitable "invasion" of the West Coast. But plot is almost never as important as Reed's satiric intent; his great skill is to create topical scenes and characters to represent his favorite subjects of ridicule. He is most successful when he devastates them by revealing their true characters: academic hustlers, feminists, antifeminists, black supremacists, white supremacists, chiseling administrators, power brokers who use students for their own ends—in short, all that's wrong with higher education that could go so much higher but probably never will. Reed's very personal brand of satire is humor as classical as[François] Rabelais and [Johnathan] Swift, and as meaningful.

Jack Byrne. *RCF*. 13, 3 (Fall 1993), pp. 210–11

REID, V. S. (VIC) (1913–1987)

JAMAICA

[V. S. Reid's *New Day*] belongs to literary history in the Caribbean. When it appeared in 1949, it was a pioneering claim that a West Indian island could have its own national history and culture. By focusing on the life of the common people and on their popular idiom several years before Creole became "acceptable" in Jamaica, Reid foreshadowed important elements in the literary movement that was to follow. . . .

In this book Reid offers his own considered answers as to what constitutes "a people," as to what in terms of the human spirit was the justification for independence. His answers involve race, history, geography, sensations of touch, taste and sight, religion and politics. . . .

Reid also developed from the native Jamaican use of imagery. Popular imagery in the Caribbean . . . is concrete, down-to-earth, often witty. Reid goes further and makes it anthropomorphic: "green water walks fast past the prow" of a boat, and a flagpost "points empty finger at the sky." It is unlikely that any Jamaican countryman would use images just like this. But Reid has a justification, one that becomes even more fulfilled in his second novel, *The Leopard*. Reid creates a world that is personalized, dramatic, active. If wind and waves have human qualities, natural forces fuse with the lives of people: "gale wind was staring in his countenance," or "thunderhead opens in my Father's eyes." . . . Reid's imagery gives his action a heightened drama, and interpenetrates character and history with the natural life of his island. It must be pointed out that Reid does not claim this insight for all his characters.

Louis James. The Islands in Between: Essays on West Indian Literature
(London: Oxford University Press, 1968), pp. 64, 67

[*New Day*] rests upon a single proposition; that Jamaica has a history. This history is distinct from that of its various racial groups separately viewed. No group of people, however polyglot, can inhabit an island through 450 years of turbulence and change without forming a history and culture uniquely their own. It follows that there is such a creature as a Jamaican, and that we can only get to know him by looking at his island and following its story.

This central proposition is built into the structure of Reid's novel, for the life of a single man, his narrator, bridges the bloody Morant Bay Rebellion of 1865 and the new constitution of 1944. The first event signaled the abolition of representative government after more than two hundred years; the second announced its return. As the old man compares these events in his mind, relating them to one another and to the larger history of the island, the lineaments of Jamaica begin to emerge. . . .

Reid's book, written so soon after the latter event, is not concerned to ask whether that promise has been fulfilled. It announces by its very title a hope only, but a hope which had not been there before at any time in the island's history.

Yet the importance of *New Day* does not rest only on its central concern with Jamaica and its people. The same new confidence that dictated its theme extends into the style itself, for the whole book is couched in the form of a long monologue by the aged narrator as the crowds celebrating their new measure of freedom surge under his window. Hence it is written throughout in a style approximating Jamaican country dialect of the mid-nineteenth century. To use this style of speech even for dialogue, except to produce comical "quashi" (country bumpkin) effect, was effrontery enough to the delicate colonial sensibility which rotated around wistful connections with "Home" and garden parties at King's House. To write an entire book in this despised dialect, albeit spoken habitually by nine-tenths of the population, and in off-moments by the rest, was radical indeed.

Gerald Moore. The Chosen Tongue (New York: Harper & Row, 1969), pp. 3–4

Reid the novelist [in *New Day*] constructs his story not by going directly back to an earlier event like Emancipation, but by making use of possibilities of characterization and evocation of place, possibilities traditionally open to the novelist, to create for the reader a sense of the specific human and geographical context in which the riots took place. The parched soil of the parish of St. Thomas, which Reid makes us feel clutching at our throat, and white against our vision, is both a symbol of the condition of the people and a literal factor driving the black poor to despair. And Reid's use of historical document (quotation of part of the Queen's reply to the petition of the poor people of St. Ann's parish) is made acceptable novelistic by a choruslike presentation of the parishioners' different responses to it, thus partly suggesting the chronic nature of the discontent and enacting in dramatic language the different attitudes of the several economic and ethnic groups involved. . . .

Cutting across the differing class interests of the characters is the tension which Reid suggests between Pa John Campbell and his son, Davie. The psychological complexities inherent in the clash between generations—father and son, old and young—lend themselves naturally to Reid's presentation. Reid's success here lies in the way he makes use of this and at the same time consolidates our sense of the historical peculiarity of his individuals by relating the tension between them to the socio-economic situation. John Campbell bides his time, believing in justice and in the wrath of the Lord (behavior generally in keeping with the policy of the colored group which, however uneasily, accommodated itself to the wishes and intentions of the legally white plantocracy); his son Davie breaks from this pattern to associate himself with the revolutionary cause of the blacks led by Deacon Bogle. The relationship Reid builds out of this is one of the triumphs of the novel, and it is a novelist's triumph of characterization. The author interests us in father and son as unique contending individuals even while allowing their conflict to contain within it the essence of the broader socioeconomic class struggle. Finally, Reid's intuition allows us to understand not that Davie is "thinking black" whatever that means, but that to conceive of the historical conflict as basically socioeconomic is to absorb the black versus white formula in a more socially integrative, realistic, and humane theoretical framework.

Kenneth Ramchand. *An Introduction to the Study of West Indian Literature* (Sunbury-on-Thames: Nelson, 1976), pp. 34–36

[*The Leopard*] is a black Jamaican's imaginative rejection of anti-Mau Mau propaganda. In this novel the blacks are far from perfect, but they are fully human beings; they have a culture, history, morality, religion; they experience a wide range of human emotion. . . .

The emotional heart of the novel is the relationship between Nebu and Toto. Toto is not only physically deformed; psychologically and morally he is a cripple. He has never known a mother, and his father has been incredibly malicious. Toto's physical deformity has set him apart from other children, and he reveals his insecurity in overreaction: "'It is I who will not play with them, you black fool!' he shrieked at Nebu." A potential killer, he is deceitful, willing to feign piety or love according to the moment's need; like the cat's paw he is "the killer" that can seem "sheathed and innocuous." "The toto is false as a worm's skull." He is malignant, hateful at the core, unredeemed by the fact that he too can be made to suffer. In the American version of *The Leopard*, Nebu sums him up explicitly: "He hated so deeply that he would rather see his true father die than live himself." Toto is a sadist. He has enjoyed watching the house cat break the back of a mouse: "The boy shivered deliciously remembering. . . ." (But the memory prefigures his own death, struck down by a larger cat.) Toto enjoys the sight of pain. He is disappointed that Nebu is so impassive: "Suffering unmoved just like the dog long ago. And he was furious at Nebu for not exposing the pain., What thrill was there if it was not exposed?" He was happier with the stout Somali woman who used to lift him up and down stairs. "'We got along famously,'" he tells Nebu. "'She never reported me to my father but she often cried. Her face was not cut from lumber, as was the dog's and yours.'" . . .

Many readers have felt an allegorical dimension in the novel and particularly in the Nebu-Toto relationship. "It would not be fanciful to see the half-Bwana as a West Indian, having two fathers, the dead European . . . and the dying African." "*The Leopard* is in its finest aspect a parable on the relationship between alienated West Indian and embarrassing African ancestry." "Toto is symbolic of all cultures produced by a meeting of civilizations, whether in the Caribbean, or in Africa or India." Each of these judgments can be supported in detail. But Reid is anxious that readers also retain an awareness of the novel in its broadest significance, as it examines the ebb and flow of love and hate, between groups, between individuals and within a single person. In exploring a specific situation, Reid wishes to make us feel some human truths not limited by space and time.

Mervyn Morris. Introduction to V. S. Reid. *The Leopard*
(London: Heinemann, 1980), pp. vii, xiii–xiv

New Day, beginning with Paul Bogle and the rebellion at Morant Bay in 1865 and ending with Garth Campbell and the promise of internal self-government in 1944, is a largely imaginative reconstruction of the social and historical realities which shaped the identity of modern Jamaica. And if there are disparities between Reid's account of the Morant Bay rebellion (and its repercussions) and the accounts of historians, then such differences are explicable in terms of the different demands of history and fiction, and of Reid's view of what it means to be a Jamaican. For the novel is above all a powerful assertion of a genuinely felt experience: it powerfully reflects a landscape of real feeling, and therefore is an important landmark in the development of the Caribbean sensibility. It is the first West Indian novel written entirely in dialect form and, appropriately enough, is experienced by the reader directly through the eyes of a young boy, Johnny Campbell. The entire novel is concerned with the recollection of the aging John Campbell (on the eve of the New Constitution of 1944) of his childhood as the youngest member of the middle-class, near-white planter family out of which (as in the case of the Manley family) Jamaica's most famous leaders have come. But *New Day* is not mere "emotion recollected in tranquility": all the senses are evoked to present Johnny's childhood world as a *lived* experience. The use of natural imagery and metaphor, of a dialect-construction of strong, actively physical verbs, a vernacular syntax, contribute to the reality of the world of the novel.

Michael Gilkes. *The West Indian Novel* (Boston: Twayne, 1981), pp. 117–18

The Leopard may be seen in two lights. In the first place it is the West Indian novel of imaginary Africa and the African personality *par excellence*. . . .

By opting to narrate much of the novel through a series of flashbacks seen from Nebu's point of view, Reid commits himself to projecting his central character's personality from the inside. In doing so he utilizes stock ideas of romanticism and primitivism. Like [Léopold Sédar] Senghor, and like people who do not come from any of the countries of Africa, Reid refers to Nebu as an "African," and he uses this term in free variation with the word "Negro." Although we learn in chapter twenty-three that Nebu is "an effigy . . . fixed forever in gray stones," and in chapter thirteen that he is "a blue black god squatting quiet beyond comprehension," he is saved for humanity (and as we shall see below, for the *msabu* Gibson) by the "rich warm blood [that] was pumping along the African's veins." Indeed, even when asleep he is in rhythmic communion with the earth-force: "His eyes were closed and only the gentle heaving of the blanket showed that life was thereabout. His sleep was in rhythm with the land, and if the rain had ceased or the wind had died, he would have instantly waked." Little wonder that when, armed at last with a rifle, he runs to the bush, "the bush was waiting and drew him in with a hundred green arms in heat for him." Our response to one whole side of Reid is a response to a highly sensuous prose in the service of decadence.

Kenneth Ramchand. *The West Indian Novel and Its Background*
(London: Heinemann, 1983), p. 154

Throughout his career, Vic Reid has continued to write with the goal of helping Jamaicans, particularly young Jamaicans, to know themselves through an awareness of their rich and heroic history. In keeping with this goal, he wrote three novels especially for young readers: *Sixty-Five*, which treats the Morant Bay uprising; *The Young Warriors*, which focuses upon the Maroons; and *Peter of Mount Ephraim*, which is based on the Daddy Samuel Sharpe slave rebellion of 1831. *The Jamaicans*, which treats the valiant struggles of the seventeenth-century Jamaican guerrilla Juan de Bolas to preserve the freedom and dignity of his people, was motivated by the novelist's recognition that Jamaicans needed to know this aspect of their history. . . .

The Jamaicans focuses upon a band of escaped slaves who, under the leadership of de Bolas, establish a mountain stronghold above Guanaboa Vale and reach a truce with the Spaniards, who in return for not attempting to dislodge them are spared raids upon their haciendas. These guerrillas, who derive their sustenance and protection from the land, are well-nigh invincible when fighting in the jungles. . . . The alien Europeans (the occupying Spanish and the imperialistic British) have no such relationship with the land, and thus, despite their advantage in terms of weapons and men, they find themselves at the mercy of the blacks whenever they venture into the jungles. When the black warriors enter battle, they are also inspired and emboldened by their glorious history. Old Miguel often reminds his countrymen of the valiant deeds of five generations of mountain soldiers who had been "from the earliest landings of their African ancestors, fighting their way from the coast into the high country, linking up with and leading the few remaining Arawak Indians [in battle against the colonizers]." . . .

[De] Bolas, recognizing that the English are winning the war, determines that the guerrillas' goal should be to win the respect of whichever European power prevails. Thus, to force the conquering English to recognize the desirability of negotiating with them, de Bolas and his men audaciously attack and destroy the powerful English stronghold at St. Jago (Spanish Town). They win an easy victory over the English, who are consequently forced to deal with them on their own terms. Pablo regards Juan de Bolas's new alliance with the English as traitorous, however, and thus the two brave warriors are thrust into mortal combat, thereby effecting what no European ever could—the destruction of the two bravest and most indestructible of the guerrilla heroes. Reid suggests that their deaths are symbolic for the future of Jamaica, for in their final embrace they become one: as Old Miguel observes, "if they see now, they will know they are one . . . they know they are neither African, nor Spanish, nor English, but of the Jamaican earth." . . .

Reid has recently completed two works: *Nanny-Town*, a novel based on Nanny, a priestess-warrior who led the Blue Mountain Maroons against the English and forced them into signing a treaty which gave her people autonomy, and *The Horses of the Morning*, a biography of [Norman Washington] Manley, who was clearly the prototype for Garth of *New Day*. He is presently working on a novel, *The Naked Buck*, which will be more contemporary in its setting and will focus on ordinary Jamaicans, including the Rastafarians, who though they may not be "necessarily heroic in the accepted term . . . [are] people who are determined to use their folk intellect, and their folk understanding, and their own historical precedence to find a place for them[selves] in this world."

Daryl Cumber Dance. *Fifty Caribbean Writers*
(Westport, Conn.: Greenwood Press, 1986), pp. 383–86

Nanny-Town, Reid's last published novel, celebrates the priestess-warrior, Jamaica's aboriginal queen mother, who marshaled the Blue Mountain Maroons and led them to political and material independence from the English. If this work breaks new ground, it is in the depiction of a woman as hero. (Reid's admiring portrait of Edna Manley in [*The Horses of the Morning*] is notable as well.) . . .

In *Nanny-Town* there is a marked tension between the conviction that youth must learn to pull together as a group and that they should have the imagination and vigor to go their own ways, for the sake of progress. Even generically a conflict appears in Reid's work, since he writes historicized rather than historical fiction and writes fiction about a past time not for its own character nor even for its analogues with the present, but essentially for its argumentative, directive, developmental bearing on the future.

The teaching relationship that is pervasive in Reid's work expresses that aim, but it also clashes with his sense of the cyclic character of human time, embodied in his preoccupation with morning and evening. He was taken, he said, with "the commitment of the morning, and then the thinking-back of the evening," and his love of the countryside stemmed in part from his steady, palpable experience of the natural cycle. He felt that he enjoyed morning and evening, in the spirit of that cycle, "far more than most," and appropriately he expected to die "in the evening rather than morning." Yet he saw, throughout his work, how many things failed to square with one another. The untidy dynamism of events coming into conflict with the considered and desired ritual order of interpretation poured out of Reid's own perceptions and washed through the work he wrote about, and for, his country. Perhaps it is that split vision and split sympathy, caught in a nutshell in Nebu's existence as "half Kikuyu, half Masai," as well as half penitent and half avenger, that gives Reid's work its greatest interest and impact.

Michael G. Cooke. In Bernth Lindfors and Reinhard Sander, eds.
Dictionary of Literary Biography. 125 (1993), pp. 259–60

RIVE, RICHARD (1931–1989)

SOUTH AFRICA

[Richard Rive's play] *Make Like Slaves* is one fortunate example of a credible creative expression of the longing for humane resolution along the lines of reconciliation. But Richard Rive's resolution demands a reciprocal, intelligent understanding among the embattled parties. The play offers a mordant dissection of a specialized category of the . . . racial situation and reveals . . . some thread of hope for the breakdown of racial barriers. He does this by the paradox of confronting reality; indeed at the end it is possible to surmise that he suggests the impossibility of resolution. But the integrity of his treatment is revealed by the fact that he inscribes over this failure the fact of individual shortcomings. We are left to feel that, given a more sensitive white woman or a less abrasive (and guilt-ridden) colored man, given indeed time for the continuation of a process which has begun in the play—the process of self-examination and the recovery of the ability to see individuals as opposed to groups—a small part of the battle would be won. The strength of Richard Rive's writing is that he does not exaggerate the pace of this process, nor does he anywhere suggest that, if a negative, external event were interjected into this evolutionary process it would not, at least for the duration of that event, halt or distort the tempo of the positive development. And even that awareness, hovering in the background, its pity, gives more value to the gains that have been made.

Wole Soyinka. *Myth, Literature and the African World*
(Cambridge: Cambridge University Press, 1976), pp. 73–74

Much of Rive's work is strong stuff—the novel *Emergency* is a story of miscegenation set against the background of the Sharpeville episode—but his specialty, as in the stories in the present volume [*Selected Writings: Stories, Essays, Plays*], is the ironies inherent in racial relationships. In a Christmas story, for example, an Afrikaner hotelkeeper frets because his attempts to be broad-minded about the intellectual ability of "kaffirs" are costing him the business of white customers; meanwhile he gives refuge in his stable to an African couple and their infant and looks up for a "bright star" which is not there. Another story features an unresolved argument among "Coloreds" who cannot agree whether they should let a very dark friend into their soccer club. "Yes," says one, "but there are Coloreds and Coloreds." One of the essays describes a funny episode when Rive discovered that the waitress in an Oxford restaurant was giving him bad service not because of his race but because she thought he was an "Oxford snob." . . .

Rive knows that "liberal condescension" which overrates some black writers because they are black and the bigotry of holding a white writer "responsible for the wrongs of a regime he may very well oppose" are the two enemies of a true understanding of South African literature and experience. Though the stories and plays in this selection are probably of minor importance, the essays make the book a valuable South African document.

Robert L. Berner. *WLT*. 52, 2 (Spring 1978), p. 331

The main factual history of South Africa which forms the background of Rive's *Emergency* is the Sharpeville shootings of Monday, March 21, 1960. . . .

The main action of the novel takes place in Cape Town and focuses on the days March 28 to March 30, 1960. Structurally, the novel is divided into three parts. Each part is headed by a day of that three-day period, and each section describes roughly the events of that day in Andrew Dreyer's life. Thus, the narrative moves in a linear progression over a three-day period. But the novel is not completely chronological. There are a series of flashbacks which reconstruct Dreyer's early life.

Emergency is not, of course, history: it is fiction. Rive's problem is therefore how to reconcile history with fiction in a work of fiction and yet retain historical credibility. The method he adopts is to treat each day in a separate section, narrate historical events, mention names of historical places and organizations. But he also treats the events imaginatively, introduces fictional characters, and goes beyond the mere narration of the historical events into the hearts and feelings of both the blacks and whites who live in South Africa.

Okpure O. Obuke. In Eldred Durosimi Jones, ed.
African Literature Today. 10 (1979), pp. 192–93

Writing Black, an "essentially selective autobiography," is a stream of countless little episodes spiced with brief, often devastating sketches of unforgettable characters. Rive's design rarely abandons us to the singular beauty or horror of the individual episode or sketch. Beyond the significance of each episode, each finely-wrought character sketch, we find the larger patterns of converging significance. What Rive says of his memory of Paris is true of the book as a whole: a kaleidoscope of impressions.

There is a principle of recurrence at work in the structure of this book. Through this principle we experience a gradual accumulation of knowledge often culminating in important revelations. We move from slum to slum, from District Six in Cape Town through "the grimy heart of old Naples" and London and Paris, to the "ugly, sprawling ghetto in East Austin," Texas. . . . These slums lie smoldering in the shadow of the elegant sections of town. Perhaps it is true, as one artist-critic says, that "all civilization is built on a series of thefts." . . .

Racism and prejudice loom large in the background of Rive's narrative, yet he gives us delightful humor where one would expect bitterness and anger. In the end, however, *Writing Black* succeeds as more than an entertaining account of one black artist's growth into stardom. It is a thoughtful and efficiently organized recollection of how one talented, determined and singularly fortunate creator achieves maturity in a world where so many other potential creators must die so young.

Kofi Anyidoho. *WLT.* 56, 3 (Summer 1982), pp. 562–63

[Richard Rive's] first volume of stories, *African Songs*, appeared in 1963. Then, in the same year, came *Quartet*, his collection of stories by four writers, including himself. More recently he published his *Selected Writings*, which included seven short stories.

Although Rive says that he is a short-story writer rather than a novelist, he does bring some of the faults of the novel to his short fiction. There is a certain naiveté about his work which assumes that people will act in a certain way, and always do. The childlike character in "African Song," for example, comes to the city from the country without a pass and, as the police draw nearer to him at a meeting, has visions of love and joy while the people sing the Xhosa anthem. In "The Bench," Karlie is another innocent from the country who is so affected by hearing his first political speech about black being as good as white that he refuses to get up from a bench marked "whites only" and looks at the policeman who arrests him "with the arrogance of one who dared to sit on a 'European' bench." Rive's early promise of realism shown in "Willieboy" did not come to fruition.

We often know what the outcome of a story will be, which leads to lack of tension and makes the story appear contrived. One knows, for instance, that "No Room at Solitaire" will be an illustration of a South African version of the biblical tale. The story concerns a hotelkeeper, Fanie van der Merwe, who discusses Christianity with a customer and they wonder how one would "know Him when He comes again." A colored couple arrive at the back door and ask for shelter because the woman is about to give birth and is ill. The hotelkeeper refuses but the servant puts them up in the stable. When Fanie and his customer hear of this, the story inevitably ends.

Ursula A. Barnett. *A Vision of Order* (London: Sinclair Browne, 1983), pp. 194–95

Richard Rive's *Emergency* is the only novel to fictionalize political events in Cape Town in 1960. . . . His novel moves back and forth in time and encompasses the childhood years of the main protagonist, Andrew Dreyer, in District Six. These childhood sections are the liveliest parts of the book and recall [Es'kia] Mphahlele's *Down Second Avenue* and Peter Abrahams's *Tell Freedom*. This section of the novel brings District Six to life in the best tradition of Alex

La Guma, although Rive does not display La Guma's aptitude for reproducing dialect. There are autobiographical elements in the portrayal of Andrew Dreyer, who is darker than the rest of his family. As a result he is discriminated against. He distinguishes himself at school, proceeds to the University of Cape Town, where he graduates with a Bachelor of Arts degree, before taking up teaching. By following events in Andrew Dreyer's life, Rive takes the reader through some of the great [African National Congress] campaigns of the past such as the Defiance of Unjust Laws Campaign of 1952–1953, culminating in Sharpeville and Langa. The novel in its adult section contains lengthy political tracts, which are interesting in themselves but slow down action in the novel. . . .

    Emergency remains Rive's major work in fiction. He stayed on in South Africa, after most of his contemporaries had left, and took more to literary criticism, after *Emergency* and his earlier collection of short stories, *African Songs*, had been banned.

Mbulelo Vizikhungo Mzamane. Ariel. 16, 2 (April 1985), pp. 35–36

The novel [*"Buckingham Palace," District Six: A Novel of Cape Town*] is in three sections, dated 1955, 1960, and 1970, each of them introduced by an apparently autobiographical preface which relates Rive's own life as a resident of "Buckingham Palace" to that of the people whose lives he describes. His method resembles the romantic realism of [John] Steinbeck's *Tortilla Flat*: episodic, funny, unafraid of sentiment, but always able to balance it with a sometimes harsh vision of the social reality in which the stories take place. Considering that no character is seen for sustained periods in the novel, many of them are remarkably vivid: Zoot September, whose real name is Milton because his aunt studied poetry for her teaching certificate and "never recovered from the experience"; the Jungle-Boys, violent Muslim rugby players who enforce moral behavior in the neighborhood; Pretty-Boy, who judges a beauty contest in terms of the contestants' "sweet-melons"; and Katzen, the Jewish landlord who will not obey the official order to evict his tenants because he was himself a victim of persecution in Nazi Germany.

    Rive shows us that when a ruthless bureaucracy makes war on human values, its greatest ally is usually a perverted public opinion. When Katzen dies, his son Dieter (named after a friend murdered by the Nazis) sells his father's property to the local housing board—and thus helps evict the residents of District Six—with no apparent understanding of why his father believed that apartheid resembled the anti-Semitism from which he had suffered in Hitler's Germany.

Robert L. Berner. WLT. 61, 4 (Autumn 1987), p. 673

Richard Rive, in *Emergency*, takes the South African struggle itself for his subject matter, and adopts a straightforward news report-type narrative framework for his presentation of the events of 1960 in Langa and Cape Town during the campaign against the pass laws (the "Sharpeville" of the south). Though Rive avoids the romanticizing mythmaking pitfalls of [Peter] Abrahams's fictional subject matter, nevertheless he carries over his predecessor's concentration on the psychological development of the individual hero. The historical and social context of the novel—the march on Cape Town on March 28, the strike on March 29, the protest march against the arrests on March 30, the declaration of the state of emergency, and the resumé of the history of the liberation struggle—all function as a back-cloth against which Andrew Dreyer can work back over his childhood and youth, search out his political orientation and identify his priorities.

Consequently there is no conflict between the traditional novel framework Rive adopts and the work's thematic significance. Where the problem (that is the *literary* problem) does arise is in the long didactic passages where Abe, Braam, and Andrew hold long discussions on the issues at stake. Not only does Rive fail to evolve a sufficiently realistic dialogue—his characters speaking like university essays rather than heated human beings—but the discussions are intrusive and insufficiently related to the action of the novel to be accepted naturally by the reader. Hence they impede rather than push forward the functioning of the text as an instrument of the struggle, focusing the reader's attention on one character and his ethical dilemma rather than on the progress of the struggle. The literary conventions [Rive] adopts, though they may inhibit the novel's contribution to the struggle, nevertheless nicely convey the liberal education of the writer and his own hesitations concerning total commitment.

Jane Watts. *Black Writers from South Africa*
(New York: St. Martin's Press, 1989), pp. 213–14

The novel *"Buckingham Palace," District Six* travels back into the past in order to recall the defeats and the triumphs of a community that was broken up by the forces of apartheid in Cape Town. It is arguably Rive's best individual work. In it he manages, by means of chapters that focus closely on individual characters or small groups, to utilize one of his greatest talents: his ability as a short-story writer. The unity of the novel is achieved by means of the common destiny that faces all of his District Six characters. Rive later adapted the novel into a play, which was performed in Cape Town shortly after his death.

There is a great deal of potency in dealing with the destruction of a community such as District Six in the way that Rive does. He celebrates qualities in the district that are being ravaged by the policies of apartheid, such as trust between people of different backgrounds and the spirit of cooperation that exists among residents of a close-knit community. But there is no doubt whatsoever that the forces of violence ultimately have their way. District Six is finally destroyed by the authorities, and its residents are scattered. Yet out of this defeat a spirit of resistance has arisen, clearly illustrated in *"Buckingham Palace," District Six*, which brings to fruition many of his earlier treatments of the subject. . . .

Rive is not the only author to have dealt with the destruction of a vibrant South African community. Fellow writers of his from the Cape, such as [James] Matthews and [Alex] La Guma, have also paid homage to the community that was District Six. Further afield, Can Themba, Bloke Modisane, and Miriam Tlali have written about the similar destruction of Sophiatown in Johannesburg. Rive's stories and novels about District Six share much with the work of these authors. In this respect his works form part of a central stream of South African writing that deals with communal responses to the institutionalized violence of the state. Rive, like many of his fellow writers, finds an answer to this violence in the communal strength of the people in places such as District Six.

Rive's works of the 1980s indicate that there was little falling off in his powers as a writer. Indeed, after the long gap since his first works of fiction in the 1950s and early 1960s, there had been a renewal of creative energy in his more recent work. His death deprives South Africa of one of its most urbane writers.

Martin Trump. In Bernth Lindfors and Reinhard Sander, eds.
Dictionary of Literary Biography. 125 (1993), p. 263

ROBERT, SHAABAN (1909–1962)

TANZANIA

[Shaaban Robert] was the first assimilated Swahili African writer to write in a variety of genres, some from English models, in order that he should be read and not sung. He wrote to be published by English publishers. He was a master of traditional techniques. Like the earlier Swahili writers, he was very conservative, highly respected, and a guardian of conventional Islamic values, all factors that some might consider tend to mitigate against good creative writing. He was naturally averse to innovation in the conduct of society in general and of individuals in particular. Like so many other African writers in the vernacular, he liked to preach or sermonize. In the Koran the meaning of the Arabic word used for "heresy" is "innovation." Yet in a tentative way Shaaban Robert was a literary innovator.

His lifestyle and experience, most of all his religion, made him less of an innovator than the short story writers of the mid-1960s who wrote in vernacular papers, such as *Mwafrika* and *Tazama*, and who dealt only with the realistic seamier side of life in which religion is rejected or ignored. Shaaban Robert is the Swahili John Bunyan, whose characters often have names indicative of their moral character. At times the motives of his heroes are too good to be true, like the young clerk, Mr. Best Human Nature (Bw. Utubora), who is motivated to sacrifice a salary of unbelievable proportions in Zanzibar to go "back on the land" as a hired gardener on the mainland. In modern Tanzania, where the vast majority have never been off the land, "the simple life" is more often equated with a well-paid office job. But the cultivation of the soil is encouraged not only by the government but in Swahili literature, by other Muslim Africans, as the duty of the good citizen. The important thing for Shaaban Robert was to give his hero a motive that was not only relevant to the country's needs but also morally irreproachable. . . .

It can be said that the function of the writer in any society is to bring the contemporary mind to a new elevation of ideas and spirit, but the contemporary mind of Shaaban Robert's Africa was conditioned almost entirely by its African experience of comparative deep poverty in things material and intellectual. This is no criticism of the African way of life, but only a reminder that even Shaaban Robert shared the experience of his contemporaries. . . .

Shaaban Robert's writings are realistic only in the sense that they reflect a real situation in which the writer is not so far ahead of his readers as to lose them altogether. He was writing not for the educated elite but for people like himself who had received no higher education. This is one of the reasons for his great popularity in Tanzania, a country committed to the principles of *Ujamaa* or—for want of a better term in English—African socialism, by which any kind of intellectual capitalism unrelated to the life of the people is regarded as a hindrance to national development. Shaaban's desire to serve his people is in line not only with the political ideals of his country but also with the public preference for a writer who stays close to what in general people can understand.

Lyndon Harries. *Review of National Literatures.* 2, 2 (Fall 1971), pp. 45–46, 48

[Robert] is incomparable in the sense that there is no other Swahili writer with whom he can be compared for the range of his literary performance. His poetry can be compared with that of his contemporaries like Amri Abedi or [Mathias E.] Mnyampala, and his stories stand comparison with other Swahili stories, but he is alone in having also experimented in essay writing, allegory, prose-paraphrase of his own poetry, and autobiography. Comparison in a particular genre with works from another culture in some other language would no doubt place Shaaban at a disadvantage, but such a comparison would have to allow for the disadvantages Shaaban suffered from the literary poverty of his own environment.

He was an innovator who used the limited materials at his disposal in order to develop Swahili literature on a wider scale. His own limited education, which he freely acknowledged, kept him more firmly rooted in tradition than an innovator can afford to be. But he made a start in the direction that Swahili literature could be expected to go. The remarkable fact is that, in spite of the enhanced status of Swahili as the national language of Tanzania since independence, there has been practically no further advance in the literary situation from what it was when Shaaban left it. In spite of the high regard in which he is held, no Swahili writers have appeared to continue from where he left off. His ideal of a national literature representing the life and thought of the whole country, and not only of the Swahili coast, is still only a dream.

Lyndon Harries. *PA.* 93 (1975), pp. 198–99

Shaaban Robert's first wife, whose name was Amina, certainly inspired the poet with profound love which he expressed in a poem, "Amina," after she died. In Swahili literature most elegies were written for great men such as Mbaraka Ali Hinway . . . and Shaaban Robert himself. . . . Amina was perhaps the first woman to be so honored in Swahili literature. The poem was written presumably in the late 1940s. Although students of Western literature will find the poem an expression of restrained conventional poetic feelings, yet it is, by the standards of Swahili poetry and its tradition, an innovation in creative emotion, stronger than any others, less rigid and almost daring in its expressiveness. But Swahili poetry is never purely personal. Invariably the author has to extend his feelings to include those of his fellow townsmen, indeed of all the Swahili people. He speaks for the community and so he has to generalize his ideas. Thus the poem becomes a praise-song on marriage in general, rather than a personal lament on the end of his marriage. We should not see this as a loss of personal contact between the poet and his readers, who—if Western—would be interested in the unique expression of his individual agony, to find in it the reflection of their own sorrows. On the contrary, the Swahili poets elevate their own grief by lifting it above their narrow personal anxieties and raising it to the status of a mourning shared by all their fellow men, then making it into a lesson for all men. "In spite of this grief, marriage is still more than worth all the troubles I have seen." In this way, with religious devotion, grief is overcome and sublimated into a blessing for all members of the community. The traditional phrases and proverbs are already the shared property of the community, who expect to reap spiritual benefit from such proverbs, old and new, which are often repeated long after the poet, who is remembered as the author, has died. The audience of a Swahili poet still expects these variations on traditional themes. . . .

Shaaban Robert was the last poet—and one of the most famous—to write quatrains in Swahili. He translated the quatrains of Omar Khayyam into Swahili verse, but not directly. He used as intermediary the famous version by Edward Fitzgerald in English verse. In many respects, however, Shaaban has rendered the flavor of Omar Khayyam's oriental moods better than Fitzgerald; not because he knew Persian, but because he was a Muslim himself, and understood Omar better than Fitzgerald, the nineteenth-century Romanticist, ever could have. . . .

Shaaban Robert wrote several prose works, the finest of which [is] his autobiography *Maisha Yanga*. . . . His other prose works are mainly of an allegorical character, strongly oriental in setting and in flavor, like *Kufikirika* (*The Conceivable World*). They contain so many profound—if not moralistic—thoughts, that we might prefer to call them perhaps "philosophical tales." Two of his works, *Insha na Mashairi* (*Compositions and Poems*), and *Masomo yenye Adili* (*Noble Lessons* or perhaps *Righteous Readings*), contain a majority of poems interspersed with fables. He writes a moral lesson (*adili*) at the end of each of these prose as well as poetry passages. Here are some examples. "Our joys and misfortunes are mysteries in this world." "All our prosperity is attained by our actions." "Character is everything; a fine character is needed for scholarship, upbringing, independence and good manners." "A multitude of little people is better than the greatness of one."

Jan Knappert. Four Centuries of Swahili Verse: A Literary History and
Anthology (London: Heinemann, 1979), pp. 267–68, 270, 274

The decisive figure in the modernizing process that affected Swahili literature was Shaaban Robert from the Tanga area in Northern Tanganyika. Though he started writing poetry in the 1930s, his first volume, *Pambo la lugha*, did not appear until 1948, when it was issued in the "Bantu Treasury" series published in Johannesburg. This was the first of many works in prose and verse which made him, in the words of Wilfred Whiteley, "the most notable literary figure to have appeared on the Swahili scene in this century." Because of his exceptional position as a professional man of letters, because of the abundance and diversity of his literary output, and because of his deep knowledge and subtle handling of the Swahili language, he enjoys an exalted reputation among Tanzanian literates and Swahili scholars. He has even been called "the Shakespeare of Africa."

[Robert's] parents both belonged to the Yao tribe of present-day Malawi, but he himself was born on the northern coast of Tanganyika, and was obviously an intellectual product of Swahili culture. Because of this dual situation, he was very conscious of the desirability of striving for the cultural unification of the whole of East Africa through the spreading of the Swahili language, instead of limiting his concern, as classical Swahili writers had done, to the Swahili community in a narrow sense. . . .

The most important contribution of Shaaban to the modernization of Swahili literature is no doubt his addiction to prose writing. His first composition in this respect was probably the first part of his autobiography, *Maisha Yangu* . . . which won first prize in the 1936 East African Literary Competition, but did not reach print until 1949. The second part, entitled *Baada ya Miaka Hamsini* . . . was completed in 1960 and published in 1966. . . .

One of [Robert's] earliest prose stories *Kufikirika* (completed by 1946, printed 1967), is probably the first Swahili work that attempts to face the question raised by the intrusion of foreign innovation in a highly conservative state. The title is the name of an imaginary kingdom, whose rulers have to decide whether to follow their ancestral customs or to call upon the help of modern science, in this case medicine. The action is dominated by a mysterious character who appears in the guise of a soothsayer, a progressive teacher, and a wise peasant. Shaaban's attitude is that the law exists only for man's welfare: it should not be observed to the point of endangering his very survival.

Kusadikika, chi iliyo angani narrates the trial of a young man who is indicted for advocating the introduction of legal studies in the imaginary country of Kusadikika. In order to defend his views against the impressive public prosecutor, a die-hard reactionary bent on preserving the vested interests of the ruling hierarchy, he tells a parable about ministers of state sent to various foreign countries, whose reports, on their return, were completely ignored by the rulers. The very title shows that this is a companion piece to the earlier story. Shaaban has now enlarged his perspective: where modern medicine was the only paradigm of modernity, he now takes in wider problems of intellectual, social, and economic advance. As the accused is described as a commoner, and as the public prosecutor makes the point that the greatness of the kingdom has been due to people of nobler origins, there is an element of social criticism which may well refer, albeit ambiguously, to the aristocratic structure of Swahili society or to the inequality in colonial society.

Albert S. Gérard. African Language Literatures: An Introduction to the
Literary History of Sub-Saharan Africa (Washington, D. C.:
Three Continents Press, 1981), pp. 137, 139–40

Kusadikika is a story set in colonial Tanganyika disguised as a country floating somewhere in the sky. With this fantastic setting, Shaaban Robert managed so successfully to fool Her Royal Majesty's representatives in the then Tanganyika Territory that they allowed the novel to be circulated in the country.

Kusadikika tells the story of a people who have been turned into robots. They believe whatever their rulers tell them. Several Kusadikikans visit other planets, and when they come back to Kusadikika with the knowledge that could help change people's lives, they are suppressed and jailed by the oppressive aristocratic government in Kusadikika. Karama (Spiritual Talent) is one of the *Wajumbe* who have visited those other planets and who have witnessed so much development in those other countries—development which he would like to see taking place in Kusadikika. He decides to lead his people's struggle by defending his case in court. His major opponent is the Prime Minister of Kusadikika— Majivuno (Pride) who opposes everything that Karama says. Finally, however, Karama manages—through a long lecture in court—to convince the King about the truth behind the *Wajumbe's* demands. Consequently all the imprisoned *Wajumbe*—Buruhani (A Gift of God), Fadhili (Mercy), Kabuli (Acceptance), Auni (Help), Ridhaa (Gracious Thanksgiving), and Amini (Trust)—are set free; and the development plans are carried out by the *Wajumbe*. . . .

[One] must take into account the fact that *Kusadikika* belongs to the protest tradition in Swahili literature. It is, basically, about liberation struggle. Shaaban Robert lived and wrote at a time when contradictions between colonial governments and the colonized people in Africa were rapidly sharpening. These struggles were not without leaders, and the leaders are represented in the novel by Karama and the other political detainees—the *Wajumbe*.

F. E. M. K. Senkoro. In David F. Dorsey, Phanuel A. Egejuru, and
Stephen H. Arnold, eds. *Design and Intent in African Literature*
(Washington, D. C.: Three Continents Press, 1982), p. 65

Even though the writer completed it in 1946, [*Kufikirika*] did not appear until 1967, five years after [Shaaban Robert's] death, thanks to the cultural leadership of Tanzania that had by then won its independence. It can be assumed though that in the fifteen to sixteen years of his life between then and his death he must have reworked it more than once, polishing, improving, altering, and perfecting it. This can be seen from the exceptionally smooth flow of the writing, the almost unbroken line of the action as well as from a few features that could only have been introduced into the text under the influence of the ideals in the year following liberation.

Kufikirika (like *Kusadikika*) is also an imaginary land. In it, the idealized model of the traditional Swahili society (in some cases the East African society in the broader sense) is confronted with a confused, transitional path of development or one that appears from the outset to lead nowhere. Its figures in many respects recall the heroes of folk tales: their characteristics are unchanging, striking, and almost extreme. His heroes wrestle with (moral) black and white, good and bad, sober certainty and unthinking confusion. In the text itself the influence of the classic Swahili epic can be felt almost palpably in the linguistic means repeatedly used by the writer. . . .

Its origin can be placed in the period when the writer gradually moved away from poetry—although he never gave up poetry-writing completely—and rather chose prose forms to express his increasingly more complex thoughts that could no longer be contained within the framework of the traditional lyric and epic.

However, as a result the static picture of society formulated in the work and regarded as ideal, in the final analysis is made up of local semifeudal and partly free trading elements that cannot be linked to a concrete period of time, idealizing a newer and humanized combination of these elements. The essence of this is concern for people, in cases even in spite of their demands or even their will. As regards its extreme solutions, all this could even be described as the "gentle terror of wisdom and goodness." In certain respects this social ideal overlaps the Tanzanian social reality of one and a half to two decades later. Having acquired greater practical, political, and tactical experiences, these ideas can also be found in the social and political superstructure of *ujamaa socialism* that is sometimes also colored by naive aspirations and ideas. . . .

In his later works his notions of the workings of the social mechanisms acquire a more concrete and sounder form. . . .

[*Utobora mkulima* and *Siku ya watenzi wote*] are his last major works on an epic scale, written at the height of his creative powers. The literary policy background to the fate of these works has not yet been fully clarified, but it is certainly worth reflecting on the fact that they could not appear until six and seven years respectively after the death of Shaaban Robert. . . .

The novel *Siku ya watenzi wote* . . . contains perhaps the most pure essence of the author's idealized theory of society. In it, educated and simple people, lost and floundering in the dead end of a foreign civilization imposed on the local population from outside, work out and find for themselves a way out of their wretched situation holding out little hope. Ayabu, the hero of the novel, who quite clearly appears as the author's alter ego, is the well-intentioned and wise teacher of the people who also enjoys a certain prestige. It is he who, relying on the active assistance, or at least the passive goodwill of those who are weaker and less able to act than he is, organizes material and moral assistance for the unfortunates who have fallen victim to the colorful and tempting environment which holds many dangerous traps for them and is actually cruelly alienated. Sparing neither his material resources nor his material property, he goes almost to the limit of self-sacrifice to provide bread and work for the misfortunate with the help of his organization based on charity.

In the meantime dangerous pitfalls and promising possibilities alternate rhapsodically in his own life. The hero has to struggle with the hundred-headed hydra of alienating and harsh social reality in the field of his own chosen profession, while at the same time the fearful traps of the despised external world increasingly force their way into his private life too. He comes to the realization that the possibility for the individual's well-being cannot float in some kind of ethereal heights above the traps and mires of the surrounding world. He must free himself of all trace of the selfishness that inevitably lurks inside him before he can finally win his love and human happiness. This time the final outcome in Shaaban

Robert's novel is idyllic; the good man earns his well-deserved reward, but the path to improvement and prosperity is not closed irrevocably to the bad.

Géza Füssy Nagy. Neohelicon. 16, 2 (1989), pp. 51–55

ROTIMI, OLA (1938–   )

NIGERIA

[*The Gods Are Not to Blame*] is a reworking of *Oedipus Rex* in Yoruba terms, but it assumes an identity of its own, and is a remarkable piece of theater. The classic tale is given vivid life by its transposition to Africa, and some new dimensions. It is noticeable, for instance, that [Ola] Rotimi's play contains much humor—but it is not humor that detracts from the awfulness of the theme. Rather, in the tragicomic method of [Sean] O'Casey, Rotimi is able to maintain the integrity of the subject while exploring a wide range of human emotions and reactions. Rotimi's Oedipus is King Odewale, and Queen Ojuola his mother/wife. At the start of the play the Narrator introduces the Priest of Ifa to divine the future of the newborn son of Queen Ojuola and King Adetusa. . . . The priest gives the dreadful message of the gods: "This boy, he will kill his own father and then marry his own mother!". . . . From the mimed and ritualized opening, the play develops into immediate action with the inexorable working out of fate seen in ironic contrast to the strutting self-confidence of mortals. One of the most successful creations of this play is the character of Alaka, the old man who brings the supposedly good news of the death of Odewale's "parents" to him, and unwittingly reveals the horrific truth. Alaka is half clown, half philosopher, a man of rural wisdom, who reveals the true nature of the King's parenthood through a performance that is tantalizingly slow, warm with his goodness and innocence, enlivened by his country wit and manners, and finally exploded by his words. African theater accommodates this kind of character with particular understanding and response. Dramatically his presence is extraordinary, and his creation a triumph of theatrical craftsmanship and instinct.

Martin Banham and Clive Wake. African Theatre Today
(London: Pitman, 1976), pp. 43–44

In *Kurunmi* Rotimi achieves the twin objectives that he aims at in his first play [*The Gods Are Not to Blame*]. The career of Kurunmi (even as sketched in the historical note that accompanies the play) provides very suitable material for a tragic hero along the lines Rotimi subscribes to. Kurunmi is a man fighting a cause which he believes is just; he fails because he makes a fatal error of judgment but also because he is pitched against forces that he alone cannot withstand. Also, the historical background of a constitutional deadlock, unsuccessful peace moves, and eventual war is easily recognizable as a parallel to the Nigerian Civil War, and so the sociopolitical objective he intends in his first play comes out more clearly here. Altogether, Rotimi has been careful not to divert attention from the main concern of the play. The series of battles that take place in act three are all important as aspects of the historical event, but the playwright's intention is not to recount the facts of history. Rather, he is interested in the study of man caught up in a particular situation. The battles are important because they help to focus attention on Kurunmi's changing fortunes before the final blow that spells his doom. Rotimi therefore avoids needless details. Each scene in which there is an encounter between the armies of Ijaiye and Ibadan carries the action of the play a step forward. Great economy is effected through the diary records of the Manns (scenes five and nine), and the defeat of the combined army of Egba and Ijaiye marks the climax of the action and the downfall of Kurunmi.

Just as he has been careful in the selection of his material, Rotimi also pays greater attention to the appropriateness of language to the action which he depicts. There are still instances when the language provokes laughter, but these are moments calculated to effect comic interludes. Besides, such humor only serves to accentuate the tragic action, especially as most of the scorn comes ironically from Kurunmi himself and is directed at his enemies. . . . But quite apart from such instances Rotimi now takes greater pains to preserve the profundity of the traditional literary types he renders in English.

Akanji Nasiru. In Kolawole Ogunbesan, ed. *New West African Literature* (London: Heinemann, 1979), pp. 26–27

Rotimi's reputation was established by *The Gods Are Not to Blame*, a successful adaptation of the Oedipus legend which is innovative both on the level of the medium and in the development of the African theatre. It is his commitment to his audience which decided the distinctive character of the medium in this play. His intention was to reach a very wide, many-layered audience, hence his attempt to create a new idiom, a kind of language close to the rhythms and speech patterns of his native language but not deviating too radically from standard English and adequate to carry the weight of his themes. It is in these two areas—language and the African theater—as much as in the themes themselves that his significance as a new talent depends. . . .

In *Our Husband Has Gone Mad Again*, Rotimi has written a delightful, lighthearted satirical comedy which is more hilarious and farcical than satirical. The ingredients in this comedy are: an extravagant political figure rather than politics itself; the comic and absurd situations in a polygamous marriage with an attendant cultural conflict; the crucial but disruptive influence of women in politics; and well-known and accepted attitudes to politics, power, social prestige and society.

Alex C. Johnson. In Eldred Durosimi Jones, ed. *African Literature Today.* 12 (1982), pp. 137–38

Ovonramwen [Nogbaisi] is another play which is based on nineteenth-century events in Nigeria. It portrays the tragic consequences of the clash between the powerful Oba of Benin, Ovonramwen Nogbaisi, and the British colonialists who were scheming to control the source of trade. In theatrical terms Rotimi is doing what modern Nigerian historians such as Onwuka Dike and Obaro Ikime are doing: reconstructing African history, correcting false views of the clash between African nations and the colonists. In *Ovonramwen* Rotimi shows the fall of Benin as an effect of the British scheme to control African nations for economic reasons, not just of the Benin monarch's tyrannical rule. Phillips, the representative of the queen of England, affirms that they must disregard Benin tradition and enter Benin during the Ague festival, because "the conduct of trade in the colonies demands direct contact with the interior that produces the goods." Although the British intrusion into Benin plays an important role in directing the dramatic action toward its catastrophic end, the contradictions within the Benin kingdom aid the foreign element. . . .

If . . . A Tragedy of the Ruled also reveals Rotimi's personality and interest in contemporary history. His concern for the oppressed receives theatrical attention here, as the play exposes the exploitation of the people by the rich and powerful men of society. His concern for the masses and his insight into a possible means of solving that problem show in his recognition of group cohesion and franchise as viable tools that can be used for the liberation of the oppressed. However, the people fail to use this power to effect good leadership, and this leads to the tragic conclusion of the play. Thus, *If* is sociopolitical and ends on a pessimistic note, but through a powerful instrument of mass communication (theater) Rotimi succeeds in sensitizing the consciousness of the people. The fact that the dramatic personages fail to utilize their power properly served as a warning to the original audience, which was preparing for general elections at the time the play was first produced. The play therefore seemed to foreshadow the political reality of contemporary elections and politics in Nigeria and sounded a warning to the electorate.

In *If*, Rotimi once again shows his love for music, since songs and chants are dynamically integral to the action. For example, the contemporary music of Sunny Okosun, "Fire in Soweto," is not just a melodious element used for entertainment. The message of the music underlines Rotimi's intention of using the South African example to sensitize the audience to their own plight in Nigeria. In addition, the music is used as a basis for awakening the consciousness of the audience through the poignant dialogue between the then-ignorant Betty and the politically conscious Hamidu. Similarly, the children's song, which follows the rhythm of a religious catechism chanted by rote, contains a message which is directly relevant to them as future leaders of the nation. . . . In this way music becomes a dramatic technique that not only entertains but also serves a political purpose, for it rouses the political consciousness of the people at various levels.

It is in Rotimi's unpublished play, *Hopes of the Living Dead*, that the oppressed get what they failed to achieve in *If*, and it shows a new angle to Rotimi's historical plays. The issue of political struggle resurfaces here in the plight of the lepers and their struggle for redemption from their oppressors. As with *Kurunmi* and *Ovonramwen*, the source of *Hopes* is historical, in this case the experience of lepers in Port Harcourt in the late 1920s and early 1930s. Rotimi's treatment of the subject is serious; even though the play uses a good deal of music and humor, these do not diffuse the pathos of the action. The work does deviate, however, from the usual tragic denouement of Rotimi's plays, as the oppressed lepers triumph and the play concludes on a merely pessimistic note. . . .

Another work that uses the comic mode is *Holding Talks*, an absurdist play which employs humorous and absurd situations to explore the weariness and dissatisfaction resulting from inaction. Rotimi shows his impatience with the contemporary attitude toward events, demanding instant action. He admits that the play is a "reaction to a growing preference of our Age for talking even in the face of situations demanding action and obvious solutions." A barber is hungry. Nothing is done. He collapses and still nothing is done. Instead, his appalling situation becomes the subject of discussions and press photographs, at the end of which nothing has changed for him, as he continues to lie there naked. The plot consists of many strange incidents which appear unreal, illogical, and funny, yet on close appraisal we realize that they parody our very existence. For example, the policewoman engages in an argument with Man over the procedure for investigative interrogation instead of taking the dying or dead man to the hospital. Man and Apprentice also waste a lot of time arguing about whether the barber just collapsed or is actually dead. The illogicality of the situation and the triviality of the arguments evoke bitter laughter. It is in this seeming illogicality that the play's historical perspective can be gleaned, for the actions parody contemporary life's penchant for discourse and the application of bureaucratic red tape even when situations demand instant action.

Chinyere G. Okafor. *WLT*. 64, 1 (Winter 1990), pp. 26–27

Hopes of the Living Dead returns to one feature of the earlier plays in that it takes a historical incident as its inspiration, but with a firm allegorical intent, and with a sophistication of the dramaturgical experiments we have [seen] in *If*. The play is based on the life of Ikoli Harcourt Whyte. Harcourt Whyte has an enduring reputation as a composer of choral music, but the play is about Harcourt Whyte the leper. Together with forty other lepers Harcourt Whyte was, in 1924, being treated in Port Harcourt General Hospital in an experimental program initiated by a Scottish doctor, Dr. Fergusson. On his departure the experiment was discontinued and the colonial authorities attempted to disperse the lepers without any hope of continuing treatment. The lepers were led in their resistance to this move by Harcourt Whyte, despite attempts to bribe him away from their struggle by the offer of special privileges. He demanded from his fellow patients self-reliance and self-help; and the triumphant finale of the play is the establishment of the Uzuakoli Leper Settlement where the people could live in security, work for themselves, and receive appropriate treatment. The vulnerability amongst the patients that the authorities hoped to exploit was the diversity in their backgrounds and languages. The unity that Harcourt Whyte demanded meant surmounting the ignorance and prejudice created by these divisions. The parallel with the political unity of present-day Nigeria is clear.

There are many striking features about the play. The story is a genuinely exciting and moving one, made all the more effective by the fact that it is essentially true. Its pertinence in terms of today's "sick" society makes it constantly immediate and relevant, and its underlying message is instantly clear to its audience. Theatrically the play is energized by the cliffhanging action and by the skill of Rotimi's character-drawing, and is enriched not only by splendid moments of physical farce and verbal comedy but also by Harcourt Whyte's songs and music. A cast of about thirty performers plus singers indicates the scale of the production, and another scale of significance is that of the languages used. Rotimi observes that over fifteen languages are employed in the play. . . .

Niyi Osundare, reviewing the production of the play at Ibadan University (and importantly drawing our attention to the fact that in *Hopes of the Living Dead* we have for the first time in a Rotimi play a woman in a dominant position of community leadership in the character of Harcourt Whyte's co-leader Hannah), describes the language as "a vehicle for [the play's] thematic thrust. So many times the stage turns into a cacophony of tribes as each character shouts his desperation in his own language. At such moments, tension takes possession and communal unity receives a savage punch. It is part of the abiding optimism of the play, however, that 'though tribe and tongue may differ,' a common problem steers the people towards a unified goal." . . .

The play is a lesson in resourcefulness, accepting no obstacle as too great to be overcome. Typical of this is a scene where one inmate, an ex-army corporal, repulses efforts by the police to eject the patients from their ward. Frustrated at not being able to pick up a police rifle that he has knocked from its owner's grasp because he has no fingers on his hands to grip it with, he sees his leprous mutilation as his weapon and advances upon the police with his arms extended, causing them to flee in panic. The scene is moving, triumphant, and farcical, all at the same time.

Martin Banham. *MD*. 33, 1 (March 1990), pp. 74–76, 79

RUBADIRI, DAVID (1930–   )

MALAWI

[David Rubadiri] is the first novelist in East Africa to present a sympathetic, though critical, portrait of Indians in East Africa. The most damning comment [in *No Bride Price*] on Indians comes from an Indian, Sandra, the idealistic daughter of the Indian High Commissioner in East Africa. She criticizes them for not mixing more with Africans, for not taking out citizenship quickly, and for sending their money to India. . . .

By putting the criticism of Indians in the mouth of an Indian and discussing the problem as tragic, Rubadiri both criticizes Indians and reveals that Indians are not the stereotype "Asians" of the popular press. Of course, the ubiquitous Indian businessman is there in the novel, exploiting [the protagonist] Lombe's financial helplessness; but when Minister Chozo makes a speech about the "cancer of inward exploitation by a certain minority group . . . inwardly eating the nation and making it impotent," he is really thinking about Mr. Patel's frightening but legitimate bills!

In fact, Chozo and the other Ministers are revealed as the real cancer of the nation. Chozo is greedy, crude and lecherous. He wants to sleep with Sandra and he wants Lombe to "make a fixture," promising to make him his private secretary as a reward. When Lombe does not do this, the Minister suspends him for corruption, for taking bribes from an Indian businessman and for using his high office to sell confidential information to certain embassies.

Rubadiri contrasts the hollow, corrupting life of the city with the healing, communal power of life in the village. The village people are simple and everyone's problem is their problem. When Lombe first returns to the village, he is drawn inevitably into the communal dancing. . . .

Rubadiri satirically contrasts this communal life with the hollow "African socialism" preached by the big people in the big new government in the big city. . . .

Miria is a child of the village who has been spoiled by the city but [who still retains] her innocence and femininity. She loved Lombe and she had expressed this love by the way she had looked after him. Lombe did not realize how deep this love was until Miria left him. The novel becomes a search, Lombe's search for Miria. He discovers during the search that Sandra reminds him of Miria for Sandra too represents the subtle, mysterious, feminine element in life. (In contrast, the European woman who seduces Lombe is a predator, like a praying mantis, although we are made to feel a tinge of sympathy for her.) But Miria dies in childbirth after Lombe's child has been brought out piece by piece.

Peter Nazareth. Literature and Society in Modern Africa
(Nairobi: East African Literature Bureau, 1972), pp. 176–79

[In *No Bride Price*] Lombe never rises to the top of the civil service because foreigners are preferred by the insecure politicians at the top. The Minister finally destroys Lombe because the latter refuses to yield a girlfriend. . . .

No Bride Price . . . contains several key ideas. First there is a civilian organization that works to bring the government to power. This organization embraces the alienated educated who are debarred from work and who live the bar-cocktail-party route along with the seamier side of the top echelon of business and diplomacy. The implication here is that the educated who cannot get into the system will ally with the army to throw out uneducated bureaucrats and politicians from public life. More interesting is the idea Rubadiri puts forward when he argues that Gombe, the "father of independence" in this particular country and the one who had played the dominant political role in the ending of the colonial situation, is the head of the underground organization which allies itself with the army to bring about the coup. Rubadiri argues that the "father of the nation" had quit the government because it had become corrupt and his interest in the new order is to achieve good government. This suggests that the only way to get "good," that is to say noncorrupt, government is to use the young educated and the military. . . . The ideas expressed here are important because they point to the army as the savior of the nation from corruption and to the rejection of the domination of the politicians. It should be noted that Lombe, the civil servant, is rehabilitated into the new order. Perhaps the future may see more and more of this kind of alliance between the political bureaucracy, the intellectuals looking to the African past for the major values of society, and the military who by their very definition are professionals.

G-C. M. Mutiso. Socio-political Thought in African Literature
(New York: Barnes & Noble, 1974), pp. 35–38

The most exciting aspect of *No Bride Price* is to be found in the correlation between the images and the structure of the book. If it is true that the title of the book refers to the greedy new African elites who fail to pay voluntarily the very dear dowry of total sacrifice and to marry the best possibilities of a modern African country after independence, it is even more true that many African writers have failed to marry the viewing of their experience simultaneously from two opposing world-views. A number of African writers have joined Western writers in carefully delineating the existential pains of isolated individuals who succumb to the worst aspects of the materialistic West within the framework of Christian guilt. Only a few have taken the risk of embracing a usable African past in the midst of an African experience that will increasingly have to come to terms with a technological revolution growing geometrically and eventually touching every corner of the planet. Rubadiri is one of these.

A Western literary historian or critic dealing with the relationships and ideas of the main characters in *No Bride Price* would have to face the fact that life in Africa, traditionally, has been strikingly different from life in Western civilization. . . .

These differences in the mindset of Africans and Westerners become clearer and yet more complex as Lombe discusses them with his platonic Indian girlfriend, Sandra. She has witnessed and been moved by the power of the physical, social, and religious needs of Lombe's village answered in song, dance, and music without fully understanding the implications of that power. . . .

Rubadiri clearly uses a sympathetic non-African (Sandra) to demonstrate Lombe's total involvement in the communal African experience of dance, music, and song. . . . Forcing the English language to describe differences between an African and a Western world-view through the voices of Lombe and Sandra, the impersonal author introduces a continuum of viewpoints in which African and Western ways of thinking serve as the extremes. . . .

If anarchy is frightening for the West, it is much more terrifying for an African life revolving around closely knit communities. Like the falcon unable to hear the falconer, the African leaders of Lombe's country have forgotten the African tradition of concern for community and are like birds turning in the widening gyre of exploitation. Inevitably, then, as Chinua Achebe has realized in his first novel, "things fall apart." Lombe has left a village life and the "ceremony of innocence" to become that "urban African hung in the middle desperately trying to avoid the chasm below" with "the center no longer able to hold."

While the "worst are full of passionate intensity" in the novel, it is not entirely true that "the best lack all conviction." However, since conviction must be inspired by a firm rejection of neocolonial exploitation based upon a positive attraction to the best aspects of African traditions, Rubadiri directs the reader toward an appreciation of African traditions without harming the sense of "surface realism". . . . This he does subtly by embodying these African traditions in the structure and imagery of his novel.

Mark Shadle. PMQ. 6, 3–4 (July–October 1981), p. 123–25

The tumultuous disturbance of a thunderstorm is used in "An African Thunderstorm" to symbolize the effect on Africa of Western conquest and colonization. It is a symbolic poem, the implied meaning being hinted at only in the first line— "From the west," the direction where the storm originates. The western clouds are described in a series of suggestive, uniformly uncomplimentary images; they are "Like a plague of locusts," "Like a madman chasing nothing," and "Like dark sinister wings." The rhetorical figure of anaphora (in the repeated "Likes") is one that would become very familiar in later East and Central African poetry. Here it draws together the various similes used to describe the storm clouds. In the last verse-paragraph of the poem, the pace and confusion become more and more intense as the storm strikes. Now there is no time for the leisureliness of simile; the description has become literal and metaphorical: "the smell of fired smoke / In the rumbling belly of the storm." "Rumbling belly" is another uncomplimentary description of the West, suggestive perhaps of dyspepsia caused by the greedy ingestion of colonies. "Fired smoke" describes not just the smoke from undergrowth or stubble at harvest time but, more importantly, the smoke of firearms and of crops burnt deliberately by the invaders. The end of the poem, then, contains a last glance at the symbolic meaning.

A later poem, "The Tide That from the West Washes Africa to the Bone," discusses the same subject and once again uses a single overriding image. This time, however, the West is presented as a blood-red tide washing over Africa; Rubadiri is writing a more personal poem, for he admits that the tide of Western civilization and attitude has swept through him, dissolving the indigenous "bone and sinew." Where a more sanguine or ingenuous poet might have sought a vision of reintegration beyond this desolation, Rubadiri contents himself with a final riddling statement, beginning for the fourth time with his anaphoric formula: "The tide from the west / With blood washes Africa / Once washed a wooden cross." The primary meaning seems to be that it was the spirit of Western acquisitiveness and conquest that in an earlier age condemned a great spiritual leader to death on the cross. But the meaning may go beyond this to express a hope—rare in Rubadiri's poetry—that just as Christianity triumphed over the bloody death of its leader, so Africa will triumph over the Western tide of blood. Rubadiri avoids overt sentiment and hope. On the whole, however, his is poetry of vehement statement of what has happened and is happening; it is not a prophetic call for action. . . .

The contrast between old and new, hope and disappointed reality, runs through many of Rubadiri's poems. "Saaka Crested Cranes"—one of his few optimistic poems—contrasts the age-old crater lake with the eternal life symbolized by the crested cranes. "The Witch Tree at Mubende" has camera lenses "prying the old and the new." "Paraa Lodge" contrasts the elephants and hippos with noisy American tourists.

"Christmas 1967" represents a somewhat different style from most of Rubadiri's works. Instead of a single scene it presents a collage of incidents and memories joined together at an incongruous Western celebration of Christmas. It includes mercenaries in the Biafran War, famine and the dubious methods of Western relief agencies, a *coup d'état*, the queen's insensitive Christmas message ("all in the oral tradition"), Vietnam, a reminiscence of mercenaries in the Congo (Major Schramme), the Pope's Christmas message and legation to Nigeria and Biafra, death and birth, and a brief glance at "Journey of the Magi" again. But despite the jaggedness with which the fragmentary images are placed together, Rubadiri's control has not deserted him. The theme of Western mercenaries and power brokers interfering in former colonies and the theme of birth (initially the birth of Jesus) and death join the fragments together. Rubadiri has perhaps the most consistent control of any East [or] Central African poet. In this poem he has simply bent towards the darting, conversational fragmentariness that is a characteristic of much East African poetry.

[K. L.] Goodwin. In G. D. Killam, ed. *The Writing of East and Central Africa* (London: Heinemann, 1984), pp. 215–16

No Bride Price is a novel about the platonic relationship between an Indian woman and an African man. Their love is almost ethereal, to stress which the writer has employed the technique of contrasting it with other love episodes that the hero gets entangled into. But the Indian girl Sandra and the spiritual affinity between Lombe and herself remain central to the narration in the framework of the plot which deals with the problem of urbanization, the resulting alienation and their effects on the young people in a newly independent African country.

J. Lombe is more a type than an individual who represents those unfortunate ones who are caught in the predicament of changing values and changing circumstances in a newly independent African country.

The problem of survival has forced him to take up a job in the city and like many other young men of his generation, Lombe is suffering from the effects of alienation. His own village is like a haven for him but he has no place there as he has received university education and has lost his contact with the rural rhythm; his fate is to work in the city and live there whether he likes it or not. Lombe's mind finds a striking similarity between Miria, his housemaid and beloved (later discovered to be his step-sister) and Sandra, his Indian girlfriend whose father is the ambassador. Tensions of his job and the evils of city life lead him to have many sexual encounters with different city girls, but his soul is comforted by only these two. Chaudry, Sandra's brother is a friend of Lombe and it is in a party given by their father that Sandra and Lombe meet. Sandra's easy manners, spontaneity and her openmindedness draw Lombe towards her in no time. The author has been faithful to the reality in depicting the relationship between an African male and an Indian female, and so the maximum closeness Sandra and Lombe experience of one another is in their third meeting on the evening at Sandra's house in a veranda where they sit holding each other's hands and chat, while Sandra is trying to understand Lombe's troubles and offer him comfort and help. Sandra is depicted as a liberated woman for whom race or caste barriers do not exist, and she is aware of Lombe's attraction towards her; and yet, to have shown anything more than this would have been unrealistic and to this effect there is comment in the novel.

Yashoda Ramamoorthy. *AfrQ.* 24, 3–4 (1987), p.76

SALKEY, ANDREW (1928–   )

JAMAICA

Andrew Salkey's origins are urban middle class, which is unusual among West Indian writers. Perhaps it isn't surprising that his public comment on his first book should be in the nature of a cynical aside—that it was written to catch the market for "peasant" novels. For although the country is a tangible presence in any Jamaican town, including Kingston, the differences between townsman and countryman are self-consciously observed. They are for instance reflected in the emotional attitudes of the two parties that dominate the island's politics; and the term "bugguyaga" (bumpkin is as near as you can get to it in standard English) is capable of expressing a stringency of contemptuous reference. Therefore Salkey set his first novel, *A Quality of Violence*, in a rural setting not in contemporary Jamaica, but at the turn of the century. There is another possible reason why this precise period should be chosen. The Morant Bay uprising, which cost nearly five hundred Jamaican lives, took place in 1865, and the earthquake which razed Kingston occurred in 1907. Salkey has carefully chosen a period about which not a great deal is known and which is sufficiently free from the possessive clutch of modern Jamaican intellectuals to enable him to establish his drama on his own terms. He wants his readers to sense for themselves the presence of a defining history. . . .

A *Quality of Violence* emerges as a shapely, patterned fable on the conflicting possibilities—Mother Johnson or Brother Parkin—that ultimately make up the Jamaican consciousness. Salkey does not seek to provide confident "answers"—his concern is with the inherent possibilities of the real "question." The form of the book goes beyond reflecting the disordered violence that lies at its center. The action is choreographed, and the formal presentation of the book is intentionally reminiscent of the movement of dance, for the meaningful ordering of emotion is the true activity of the novelist.

Salkey's second novel, *Escape to an Autumn Pavement*, appeared in 1960. This time the setting is London and the theme is the by now conventional one of the experience of the West Indian migrant. But the central character is not the wittily resilient working-class or peasant migrant we associate with Samuel Selvon. Johnny Sobert is a middle-class Jamaican and to that extent is only a colored man in London. In Jamaica itself he is clearly defined as apart from the Negro mass of the population. I do not remember this being noticed when the book was reviewed in England. Most reviewers suggested that it was smart, or slick, or that it handled problems of sexuality and migrant bitterness in, finally, trivial and conventional ways. When I first read the book, this was in fact my own impression but, as with *A Quality of Violence*, experience of Jamaica obliges a positive shift in perspective. An essential difference between Johnny Sobert and a Selvon migrant is that the Selvon migrant is at the bottom, even in his own country. A man like Sobert, on the other hand, though he may feel a furtive guilt at the economic and social injustices which prevail in Jamaica itself, does not have any doubt that he really belongs in the respectable middle class. But London imposes an inferiority. The protective dikes of status and comparative affluence are eroded away. And it is, in significant measure, as a result of this that Sobert takes refuge in the consistently defensive sarcasm that reviewers in the main objected to.

Bill Carr. In Louis James, ed. *The Islands in Between: Essays on West Indian Literature* (London: Oxford University Press, 1968), pp. 101, 104–5

[*Escape to an Autumn Pavement*] is a fast-moving tale told with a slightly self-conscious toughness, the word "crap" being used with obsessive frequency. Sobert lives in a rooming house where he happens to be the only black resident, though there is an Indian girl whom he satirizes with pitiless intensity. He also works in a nightclub which is run by two English girls, and caters mainly [to] American servicemen. With all these people Johnnie has to achieve a more or less direct, individual relationship, since there is no warm, uncritical group into which he can retire whenever he gets hurt or confused. At first he moves through the days with a certain jazzy but cool insouciance, but soon he gets drawn into an affair with the insatiable Fiona, the wife of his landlord, who lives on the floor below. For a while he is flattered and sensually delighted by this involvement, but gradually Fiona begins to appear in the guise of a succubus, not merely available but inevitable and demanding. Johnnie has already felt himself attracted to Dick, a white chauffeur and fellow tenant whose apparent detachment makes him seem like an escape from the morass of female sexuality into which he feels himself sinking. The suspicion that Dick is a homosexual is one that Johnnie does not allow to rise very far in his mind; when Dick proposes that they move out and share a flat, he eagerly falls in with the arrangement, telling himself that it implies just that and no more. He breaks with Fiona and luxuriates for a while in the sense of relief this brings him. Resolutely averting his attention from the mounting strain in their relationship, he continues to treat Dick as a friend, confidant, and flatmate, while Dick patiently waits for a sign which never comes. For Dick believes that Johnnie is an unavowed homosexual who needs time to come to terms with himself and must not be hurried. His very agreement to share the flat was, in Dick's eyes, an admission of his real nature. But when Johnnie takes up with Fiona again and begins making assignations with her, Dick's patience finally snaps. He quits the flat and leaves a note telling Johnnie that he must now make a decision between them. The reader is left with the suspicion that neither Fiona nor Dick is really as important to Johnnie as they suppose, and that he will probably choose neither. He ends the book as he began it, alone. . . .

What is liberating about Johnnie Sobert is his relative self-sufficiency as a West Indian in London. He neither depends upon membership of an immigrant group which experiences and reacts to London collectively, nor does he play unduly the part of a professional black man. The last is a particular hazard for those with genuine personality and bounce, since the audience is always waiting and will soon clarify the limits within which the role is licensed to be played.

Johnnie's sexual ambiguity and stillborn rebelliousness are problems he must encounter as a man, an individual alone in a big city, but not specifically as a black immigrant. Too much dwelling upon the last can bring out something disturbingly like a Christ-complex, or a self-congratulatory mystique of Negro potency.

Gerald Moore. *The Chosen Tongue*
(New York: Harper & Row, 1969), pp. 105–7

The significance of [*In the Hills Where Her Dreams Live: Poems for Chile 1973–1978*] is its very existence: the Salkey-Cuba connection, which perhaps represents an important point of departure. It comes at a time of crisis in the Caribbean, where Jamaica, Cuba, and Haiti are all undergoing political transformations which have repercussions in Miami. The hurly-burly in the Third World seems to confuse the Western press, which gives only minimal coverage. But the revolt against imperialism is taking on new forms and spreading; new connections are being established. The ideas of [Salvador] Allende, [Frantz] Fanon and [Fidel] Castro are being used to give shape and force to this movement.

Andrew Salkey knows a good part of the world from his travels and studies. Currently teaching at a college in Massachusetts, he has written novels, poetry, short stories, radio plays, and travel journals in the new journalism tradition, has edited several volumes of Caribbean writing, and does interviews for the BBC. Much of his work shows a penetrating interest in the politics of the Caribbean and a dedication to the development of the Left. However, the specific nature of this commitment remains somewhat vague, even when dealing with Cuba. He seems to find it easier to attack the poverty, ignorance, and oppression associated with imperialism than to suggest new alternatives, though trade union organizing is shown as important in his novel *Riot*. . . .

Cuba has become perhaps the most controversial country in the world; the revolutionary regimes in Cuba and Chile are being intently studied by Third World peoples everywhere, to see how they happened, what went wrong, and what went right. Salkey expresses sympathy for both regimes but hesitates in making critical evaluations. Judgment is, however, necessary in order to reveal their meaning and relevance for other countries. Cannot a poem be lyrical, analytical, and dramatic at the same time? Mythic and historical? Salkey is to be commended for having made such great strides in doing political poetry and other writing; few have tried the way, and many of them have stumbled. In a world where literature is defined by bourgeois academies and journals which tend to frown at mixing politics and poetry, such a writer must struggle upstream. But in the day of decolonization, he may be moving with the mainstream of history.

Hal Wylie. *WLT*. 54, 4 (Fall 1980), pp. 686–87

The theme of Andrew Salkey's fourth volume of poetry is contained in the title *Away*. The poet has left home, Jamaica, in flight from colonial devastation, physical ("home was a dry river bed") and spiritual ("a flood man myself"). . . .

The protagonist has moved to the metropolis, living out an unending history ("his ill-chosen country of shopkeepers," a Napoleonic reference) which is a continuing conspiracy against the colonized. All roads lead to Rome—and all lead from Rome: in the centers the poet finds some of the pieces of the jigsaw puzzle: Haiti, Cuba, Vietnam, Martinique, Mexico, Brazil, Uganda, Guyana, Ethiopia, South Africa, and America (of the Indian and black American). Why didn't even radical Caribbean thinkers like [Marcus] Garvey, [George] Padmore and [Frantz] Fanon return? Because nothing fundamental has changed under "our kind of quick-sell independence / and brand-new, advertised nationhood." The man who returned found "the villagers clawed at him / and what little he'd brought back," so he had to leave again; the postcard from Uganda shows wildlife, but the real hunted are people, the hunters using modern tanks and equipment. So, as the last section says, "Only Change Will Do." . . .

Despite the pessimism of some poems, and the suspicion that change is frequently cosmetic, Salkey believes that real change can come about, that history can be made to boomerang, that Davids can defeat Goliaths because they have the raw materials to make the slingshots. And he celebrates the few Davids he remembers, like the barmaid who finds a way to keep the bar filled during the strike, so that the owner does not see "how far the ownership of the bar had changed; / it was now a repossessed *public* house." Here is Salkey's lyricism, in hints of the return home.

Peter Nazareth. *WLT*. 55, 2 (Spring 1981), p. 364

In Andrew Salkey's *Anancy's Score* he re-enters the *literary* folktale as the trickster hero of twenty stories with ancient and contemporary settings, all of which comment on present-day politics and society in the New World. . . . But in individual stories in the volume as well, traditional West African Anancy is placed at the center of contemporary events and incidents, and the implication throughout is that after the "fall," this tragic meeting of the two old worlds, New World man is forced to reenact in the present the brutalities and futilities engendered in him by his genesis and history. Like Barbadian novelist George Lamming, Salkey sees the perpetuation of this fall in the politics of imperialism in the contemporary world. Stories like "Vietnam Anancy and the Black Tulip" or "Soot, the Land of Billboards" make the implications of Caribbean history more generally applicable. . . .

The last tale in *Anancy's Score*, "New Man Anancy," points towards the reestablishment of community integrity through a rejection of the colonial obsession with other and better worlds (especially that of the European colonizing power), and with a concomitant forging of links between Caribbean man and his new land. In a postlapsarian world this is a slow and self-conscious choice and process; but it can be achieved, Salkey seems to suggest, by the next generation. . . . [It] is not Anancy alone who will effect this change, but a sort of Jeun Payee character helped by an old man (the Caribbean past) and a new love of the earth itself. . . .

While the two stories that enclose the other eighteen do seem to provide a structural and thematic framework that encompasses Old World fall and New World redemption, the overall effect of the volume is that of stasis. Insofar as Anancy stands for Caribbean man in *Anancy's Score*, he seems unable to move beyond an imprisoned present which, for all the forms in which he appears, denies his inherently transformative character and the apparent philosophical structure of the volume. It is in the work of Edward Brathwaite and Wilson Harris, where Anancy's protean character can simultaneously express negative past, static present, future possibility, and the mechanism by which these become the creative future, that he is a volatile metaphor and archetype rather than arbitrary equation in a series of set-piece satires.

Nevertheless, Anancy in Salkey's stories . . . is associated with Caribbean history, politics, and the attempt to transcend or reform the destructive contemporary political destiny that is the product of this history.

Helen Tiffin. In Robert Sellick, ed. Myth and Metaphor (Adelaide, Australia:
Center for Research in the New Literatures in English, 1982), pp. 26–29

Salkey's protagonists' aspiring, snobbish, middle-class backgrounds apparently . . . make it impossible for them to achieve any kind of meaningful relationship with people from the lower classes. Jerry Stover [in *The Late Emancipation of Jerry Stover*], for example, frequently makes love to his family's maid Miriam, but only when he is drunk—obviously when he is sober, he prefers to retain class distinctions. When she informs him that she is pregnant, he stifles a desire to laugh and gives her some money for an abortion. Further, even though Jerry seems sympathetic toward the lower-class Rastas, he regards them as inferiors and never comprehends their plans for revolution, nor does he have any faith in their envisioned revolutionary society.

Thus, unable to relate to people in any meaningful way, unable to find any avenue through which they can satisfactorily express themselves, unable to determine who they are, Salkey's lost middle-class seekers inevitably settle for seeking and asserting themselves through desperate, meaningless, uninhibited, often violent and perverted sexual acrobatics. Their lives, marked by incessant sexual activity, often described explicitly and titillatingly, might best be characterized through a phrase from [*The Adventures of Catallus Kelly*] as "a riot of fornication." Sex inevitably seems the only conscious option for action of which they are capable—even when they are "involved" in other apparent options such as Black Power Movements, political involvement, Rastafarian activity, and the like. Inevitably the field for action ends up the bed (or the car seat, the floor, whatever—the setting for copulation is often not a consideration among Salkey's characters).

Given the meaningless ritual of self-discovery that we witness with Salkey's protagonists, the emptiness of their beings, the inanities of their world, we are not surprised that there is nothing to discover and no meaningful world in which to discover it. We are neither surprised nor disappointed then in the outcomes of their quests: Catallus Kelly returns to Jamaica and is committed to an insane asylum; Johnny Sobert, still unable at the end of [*Escape to an Autumn Pavement*] to acknowledge his love for Dick or to end his brutalizing relationship with Fiona, is last seen agonizing over the fact that both of them are waiting for him to come to them. At the conclusion of *The Late Emancipation of Jerry Stover*, most of Jerry's cohorts (they are called the Termites) have been killed by a landslide, and we last view Jerry aimlessly wandering through the streets of Lower Kingston. Finally [in *Come Home, Malcolm Heartland*], Malcolm Heartland (who, though weak, is notable among Salkey's characteristically passive characters in these novels for taking *some* action on his own—he at least makes a decision to return to Jamaica and appears to be making some efforts to work toward it) meets his death as a result of his involvement with the black revolutionaries.

Unlike the lost, weak, undirected sons in Salkey's novels, the mothers are strong, determined women who know what they want, consistently strive for it, and attempt to give some direction to the lives of their sons. In these novels and in a few other instances in Salkey's works, there is, however, the implication that the power, strength, and domination of the women contribute to the ambivalence and emasculation of the men and are thus destructive.

Daryl Cumber Dance. *Fifty Caribbean Writers*
(Westport, Conn.: Greenwood Press, 1986), pp. 422–23

[From 1960 to 1967] Salkey devoted his energy to writing novels for children. He produced a quartet of books about Jamaica—*Hurricane, Earthquake, Drought*, and *Riot*. In 1966 he published *The Shark Hunters*, a reader for schools. The years after 1960 also saw the development of Salkey's work as an anthologist. *West Indian Stories, Stories from the Caribbean*, and *Caribbean Prose: An Anthology for Secondary Schools*, all edited by Salkey, bring together the works of a variety of West Indian writers. The anthologies are aimed at schoolchildren and no doubt were inspired by intentions similar to those that provoked his fiction for children: to provide West Indian youths with the opportunity to read about themselves, their landscape, and their societies so that they could develop a strong sense of who they were and so that they would not grow up to be like the lost heroes of Salkey's adult novels.

Hurricane, Earthquake, Drought, and *Riot*, all set in Jamaica, deal with children who have come to terms with disasters, both natural and man-made, which affect their societies. The incidents of the stories are from Jamaican history, and their settings are all specifically Jamaican. The language of the characters, however, does not always sound authentic. The children who are the central characters are lively and inquisitive but remarkably mature and understanding. They are helped at times of crisis in their lives by strong, loving relatives. Although some critics have accused these novels of being too nostalgic and sentimental, and although the books were not considered suitable for Jamaican children by the Jamaican Ministry of Education, Salkey's reputation as a children's novelist was established by this quartet. . . .

In 1969 Salkey published another novel for young people, *Jonah Simpson*. It is an attempt to familiarize the young Jamaican with the exotic past of the country while suggesting that the violent history of the town of Port Royal still has an effect on the present. . . .

Joey Tyson, the most explicitly political of Salkey's novels for children, deals with the turmoil caused in Jamaica by the government's decision to revoke the work permit of Walter Rodney, a lecturer at the University of the West

Indies, because the government disapproved of his involvement with the poor. A boy, Joey Tyson, has his eyes opened to the reality of Jamaican politics.

With *Come Home, Malcolm Heartland*, Salkey returned to the adult novel. The central character decides to leave his career as a lawyer in London to return to his home in Jamaica, where he wishes to make a contribution, but he is murdered because he disagrees with the attitudes of the black revolutionaries with whom he is associating. This novel, like those before it, expresses Salkey's growing disillusionment with the typical West Indian's ability to find himself.

Anthony Boxill. In Bernth Lindfors and Reinhard Sander, eds.
Dictionary of Literary Biography. 125 (1993), pp. 272, 74

Andrew Salkey's *Anancy's Score* was published two decades ago. The new volume [*Anancy, Traveller*] also consists of twenty stories that know the score, but in a much more complex world in which a near-invisible neocolonialism has tightened its tentacles. To help us catch on, and keep from being caught, Anancy is now traveling through space and time, on land, through the air, inside the oceans, and inside the mind. "For all we know," Anancy tells Brother Tacuma and Caribbea, "we might have to invent a brand new substance for the world, something that it never have before the happening of the thunderstorm of direct loss." Using the trickster form, and a Caribbean demotic, Salkey brings up everything: past/present history of exploitation; buried heroes such as Paul Bogle, Malcolm X, Marcus Garvey, and Nanny; and villains masquerading as heroes, including Columbus and Bartolomé de las Casas. Anancy tells us what is happening, using disguises which the agents of the mightiest imperialist power on earth will not be able to penetrate.

When colonialism put on the mask of freedom, it was an opportunity for many writers of the Caribbean and the Third World to be very creative to pull off the mask. However, when the mask has been removed only to reveal a series of masks, just the way each curtain parts on the new "Tonight Show" to reveal yet another curtain, Salkey's Anancy form shows itself to be endlessly inventive, for it has a goal: to help the people find real freedom. *Anancy, Traveller* is a complex and wise work, one to dip into constantly in order to strengthen one's nerve.

Peter Nazareth. *WLT*. 67, 2 (Spring 1993), p. 429

SANCHEZ, SONIA (1934–   )

UNITED STATES

There are few writers alive who have created a body of work that both teaches and celebrates life, even at its darkest moments. Sonia Sanchez does this and more throughout her many volumes of poetry, short stories, plays, and children's books. She is prolific and sharp-eyed. Her telescopic view of the world is seldom light, frivolous, or fraudulent. She is serious—serious to the point of pain and redemption. Her bottom line is this: she wants black people to grow and develop so that we can move toward determining our own destiny. She wants us not only to be responsible for our actions but to take responsible actions. This is the task she has set for herself, and indeed she believes that what she can do others can do. . . .

Sanchez writes poetry that is forever questioning black people's commitment to struggle. Much of her work intimately surveys the struggles between black people and black people, between blacks and whites, between men and women, between self and self, and between cultures. She is always demanding answers, questioning motives and manners, looking for the complete story and not the easy surface that most of us settle for. Her poetry cuts to the main arteries of her people, sometimes drawing blood, but always looking for a way to increase the heartbeat and lower the blood pressure. Her poetry, for the most part, is therapeutic and cleansing. Much of her work is autobiographical, but not in the limiting sense that it is only about Sonia Sanchez. She is beyond the problem of a consuming ego; and with her, unlike many autobiographical writers, we are not always aware of the protagonist's actual identity. Black experiences in America are so similar and the normal distinctions that set black people apart are not always obvious to outsiders. This is to note that, for the most part, her experiences are ours and vice versa. She is an optimistic realist searching the alleys for beauty and substance. . . .

All of Sanchez's books are significant: *Homecoming* for its pace-setting language, *We a BaddDDD People* for its scope and maturity. She [displays] an uncommon ability for combining words and music, content and approach. The longer poems are work songs, and she continues to be devastating in the shorter works. *Love Poems*, a book of laughter and hurt, smiles and missed moments, contains poems that expose the inner sides of Sanchez during the years 1964–73, in which she produces several masterworks. *A Blues Book for Blue Black Magical Women*, her black woman book, is a volume of sad songs and majestic histories. Her work becomes longer and balladlike. This book highlights black women as mothers, sisters, lovers, wives, workers, and warriors, an uncompromising commitment to the black family, and the black woman's role in building a better world. *I've Been a Woman: New and Selected Poems* contains more than a decade of important work; it is truly an earth-cracking contribution. This book not only displays the staying power of Sonia Sanchez but also confirms her place among the giants of world literature. Throughout the entire body of her work, never apologizing, she affirms and builds a magnificent case for the reality of being black and female, lashing out at all forms of racism, sexism, classism, just plain ignorance, and stupidity. It must be noted that she was taking these positions before it was popular and profitable.

Haki Madhubuti. In Mari Evans, ed., *Black Women Writers (1950–1980):*
A Critical Evaluation (New York: Doubleday, 1984), pp. 419–20, 422–23

The title of Sonia Sanchez's first collection, *Homecoming*, marks with delicate irony the departure point of a journey whose direction and destination can now be considered. *I've Been a Woman*, her most recent book, invites such an appraisal, including as it does a retrospective of her earlier work as well as an articulation of a newly won sense of peace: "shedding my years and / earthbound now, midnite trees are / more to my liking." These lines contain an explicit reworking of images that dominate "Poem at Thirty," one of the most personal statements in *Homecoming*. That early poem pulses with a terror rooted in a consciousness of age as debilitating. Midnight and traveling, images of perpetual transition, bracket the poem's fear. . . . In the new poems of *I've Been a Woman*, Sanchez re-evokes these images in order to establish her new sense of assurance. Midnight no longer terrifies; rootedness has succeeded sleepwalking as an emblematic image.

Correlating these poems in this way allows a useful perspective on the work of a poet whose development has been as much a matter of craft as it has been a widening and deepening of concerns. *Homecoming* largely satisfies [Amiri] Baraka's demand in *Black Art* for "assassin poems, Poems that shoot / guns"; but there is from the beginning an ironic vision in Sanchez's work that ensures that she differentiate between activist poetry and what she herself has labeled, in *We a BaddDDD People*, "black rhetoric." The difference is that between substance and shadow, between "straight / revolutionary / lines" and "catch / phrases." And it is clear from Sanchez's work in *Homecoming* that she believes that the ideal poetry demands the practice of a stringent discipline. The poems in that collection are characterized by an economy of utterance that is essentially dramatic, like language subordinated to the rhythms of action. The verse of *Homecoming* is speech heightened by a consciousness of the ironies implicit in every aspect of black existence. The poems read like terse statements intended to interrupt the silence that lies between perception and action. . . .

The new poems in *I've Been a Woman* benefit from the sense of continuity and evolution conferred by the earlier work. The impact of the section entitled "Haikus/Tankas & Other Love Syllables" is immeasurably enhanced by *Love Poems*, for instance; the new poems, drawing on a relatively limited stock of images (water in various forms, trees, morning, sun, different smells) are an accumulation of moments that define love, age, sorrow, and pride in terms of action. Particular configurations recur: the rhythms of sex, the bent silhouettes of old age, the stillness of intense emotion. But taken together, these poems are like the spontaneous eruptions that punctuate, geyserlike, the flow of experience.

The other new poems in *I've Been a Woman* consist of a series of eulogies, collectively titled "Generations," in which Sanchez explicitly claims her place among those who speak of and for black people. There is a schematic balance operating here: the individual poems respectively eulogize Sterling Brown (age), Gerald Penny (youth), Sanchez's father, and the idea and reality of mothers. The synthesis implied in this design is enacted in the poetry itself; the imagery and rhythms of the verse in this section convey an overwhelming sense of resolution and serenity.

David Williams. In Mari Evans, ed. *Black Women Writers (1950–1980): A Critical Evaluation* (New York: Doubleday, 1984), pp. 433–34, 446

Sonia Sanchez started writing plays because the longer dramatic form was useful when a poem could not contain her political message. The first published play by Sanchez appeared in *The Drama Review* special issue on black theater, edited by Ed Bullins. The short play *The Bronx Is Next* is set in Harlem in the midst of a racial revolution. Revolutionaries are burning all the buildings in a poor section to force the construction of livable housing units. A character called Old Sister, who is judged by the male leaders to be too attached to her oppressive past in Birmingham, is sent back to her apartment to go up in smoke with her possessions.

The play's other female character, called Black Bitch, projects the strident Sapphire stereotype so despised by male leaders of the movement as a threat to male superiority. The woman is devalued as both promiscuous, if not actually a professional prostitute, and nonseparatist. Not only is she caught in a compromising intimacy with a white policeman, but she spews forth condemnation of black men's abuse of black women, to which the male leader responds, "Oh shit. Another black matriarch on our hands." The leader immediately punishes and humiliates her with a brutal sexual assault and then sends her back to her apartment to burn in the holocaust. Although the Black Bitch character criticizes abusive men, she is portrayed as an enemy of the revolution who must be sacrificed for the future purity of the black nation. In the context of the dramatic piece, her complaints sound trivial and irrelevant if not downright black-hating.

Sanchez created her second play *Sister Son/ji* for *New Plays from the Black Theatre*, also edited by Ed Bullins. This dramatic monologue presents in flashbacks five periods in the life of a black revolutionary woman. Although the single speaking character does not present herself as a feminist, she acknowledges woman's frequent devaluation by abusive men intoxicated with self-importance. As Son/ji grows from her first act of resisting racism to a sense of betrayal by male revolutionaries who seduce and abandon women to maturity borne of loss and survival, the reader/ audience watches the character grow into solitary strength. . . .

The third revolutionary play published by Sanchez in the 1960s, *Uh, Huh; But How Do It Free Us?* presents three scenes which have no narrative connection but which illustrate the oppression created by power imbalance implicit in sexual polarity. The oppressed women in each scene suffer as a direct result of male selfishness and vanity. The male antagonists in the first and third scenes are portrayed as less pernicious than the female competitors for male attention.

The absurdist middle scene throws light on the power struggles in relationships dramatized more realistically in the framing first and third scenes. In the absurdist scene four (black) brothers and one white man ride rocking horses as a theatrical metaphor for their narcotic addictions. A black woman and a white woman, both called whores and costumed appropriately, cater to the sado-masochistic fantasies of the men by whipping them and bringing them cocaine upon demand. The scene concludes with a bizarre "queen contest" between the black whore and the character now called "white dude" prancing around the stage in drag and shouting, "See, I'm the real queen. I am the universe." Finally the white dude punches his opponent to the floor declaring, "Don't look at her. She's black. I'm white. The rightful queen." The scene suggests that all women are servants and caretakers for all men, regardless of race, but that only black men possess the true macho qualities inherent in the American masculine stereotype. White men easily degenerate into women.

The first and third scenes both centrally portray black revolutionary leaders whose vanity requires the sexual and nurturing attention of several women. Malik's two wives, both pregnant, are not sufficient to feed his insecurity. The reassurance of conquest is luring him on to pursue other women. The conservative homebody Waleesha contrasts with younger revolutionary activist wife Nefertia. Despite his past attentions, Malik has apparently tired of both of them by the time the play opens. Michele Wallace notes that the inordinate value placed on black masculinity tended to devalue black women's humanity to such an extent that young black women were dropping out of school because their boyfriends had convinced them that doing anything other than having babies and performing domestic chores was "counterrevolutionary."

Rosemary K. Curb. In Karelisa V. Hartigan, ed. The Many Forms of Drama
(Lanham, Md.: University Press of America, 1985), pp. 20–21, 24–25

Sanchez's finest poetry, perhaps her strongest artistic achievement until *homegirls & handgrenades*, is represented by *A Blues Book for Blue Black Magical Women.* . . . Dedicated to the poet's father and to Elijah Muhammad "who has labored forty-two years to deliver us up from this Western Babylon," the book carries an epigraph from the Koran. In five parts, it begins with "Introduction (Queens of the Universe)," addressed to black women, urging them to "embrace / Blackness as a religion / husband," and to turn away from acquired, false Western values. The voice is that of the poet as teacher, a guide at one with her audience yet standing a little apart in order to gain and share perspective.

The longest section, part two, "Past," details the poet's physical and spiritual growth, beginning with an address to the "earth mother," whose voice responds. . . .

Part three, "Present," lyrically affirms her position. She accepts the Nation of Islam as her faith. In part four, "Rebirth," the poet returns to an ancestral home, one imaginatively inspired by Sanchez's travels in the Caribbean (Bermuda, Jamaica, Guyana). She also traveled to the People's Republic of China before finishing the book. In "Rebirth," her plane trip becomes a metaphor for her spiritual odyssey, "roaming the cold climate of my mind where / winter and summer hold the same temperature of need." The poet states that she has destroyed her imperfection, has "become like a temple," made her form from the form of Allah, and is "trying to be worthy."

D. H. Melhem. MELUS. 12, 3 (Fall 1985), pp. 90–91

It is appropriate when analyzing a work such as *homegirls & handgrenades* to wonder about what might have been the motivation for its subject matter and form. It might be declared by some that this is just another in a long line of Sonia Sanchez's books of poems. . . . Part of Sanchez's early effort was to experiment with words in verse to create a new perspective on how blacks should perceive themselves within the context of a nation struggling to admit them into the fold of social equality. Although that task remains incomplete, one can nevertheless sense a development on the part of the poet as she advances her work to include the mystical *A Blues Book for Blue Black Magical Women* as well as *Love Poems* where there can be seen an attempt to reconcile all the various aspects of black culture for the benefit of progress. *I've Been a Woman* and *Under a Soprano Sky* are further examples of how the author has examined, in particular, the plight of black women as they strive toward freedom in a world not always conducive to that undertaking.

Nonetheless, it is in *homegirls* where Sanchez delivers what Henry Louis Gates has characterized as "the revising text . . . written in the language of the tradition, employing its tropes, its rhetorical strategies, and its ostensible subject matter, the so-called black Experience." . . . This tradition of signifying on what other writers have done is a deep-rooted feature of black writing that has as its origin the culture of blacks as a whole. It is, interestingly enough, the mark of black culture in its most creative posture, that of being able to play upon what is available, in terms of form and substance, and convert it into something new and unique.

Such is the achievement of Sanchez, who, in *homegirls*, has rendered a marvelous collage of thirty-two short stories, poems, letters, and sketches that often ring loudly with the truth of an autobiographical fervor.

James Robert Saunders. *MELUS*. 15, 1 (Spring 1988), pp. 73–74

The newest book by Sanchez, *Under a Soprano Sky*, is dedicated to her father and to her late brother, Wilson Driver, Jr. The new poetry carries forward the poet's lyricism, her political commitment, her confessional/moral declensions, and what may be called her transcendental imagery: sensory images infused with spiritual awareness. Three elegies set the tone. "A poem for my brother (reflections on his death from AIDS)" is a brave poem that identifies the poet's life journey with her brother's journey into death. Its nature imagery and transcendence of death take it into the grand precincts of pastoral elegy. . . .

The second of the three, "elegy (for MOVE and Philadelphia)," a strong, ambitious work in eight parts, treats of the "philadelphia [sic] based back to nature group" (as MOVE is described in a footnote) whose headquarters were bombed by the police, with the mayor's approval, on May 13, 1985, killing men, women, and children, and destroying a block of houses in the ensuing fire. The tragedy gained national notoriety. The poet relates the events with heavy irony, through which she weaves biblical lamentation: "who anointeth this city with napalm? / who giveth this city in holy infanticide?" She concludes, however, with traces of hope: since "there are people / navigating the breath of hurricanes," there may be "honor and peace. / one day." In the related third elegy, "Philadelphia: Spring, 1985," a Philadelphia fireman reflects on the carnage after seeing a decapitated body in the MOVE ruins, when "the city, lit by a single fire, / followed the air into disorder."

D. H. Melhem. *Heroism in the New Black Poetry*
(Lexington: The University Press of Kentucky, 1990), pp. 144–45

SCHWARZ-BART, SIMONE (1938–   )

GUADELOUPE

The problems of alienation and troubled consciousness; the awareness of past victimization, present disarray, and future uncertainty; and the urgency of the quest for self and group identity are themes that have been consistently explored by Simone Schwarz-Bart in her first two novels, *Un Plat de porc aux bananes vertes* and *Pluie et vent sur Télumée Miracle*. Her latest novel *Ti Jean l'horizon* mirrors her continuing concern with the cultural and psychic legacy accumulated in the history of her native Guadeloupe in particular, in the French Antilles in general and, by extension, in all the former European colonies of the Caribbean. But whereas *Un Plat de porc aux bananes vertes* and even more so *Pluie et vent sur Télumée Miracle* limit their perspective in space and time, *Ti Jean l'horizon*, beginning from a specific locus, explores the outer limits of the primordial. Taking its inspiration from the magical world of the Antillean stories, the novel, divided into nine books, follows the fabulous adventures of the mythical hero in his quest for lost identity and lost love.

The novel opens in Fond-Zombi, Guadeloupe. The inhabitants are polarized into two distinct groups, those living in the forested plateau (the "gens d'En-haut") and those on the neighboring lowlands (the "gens d'En-bas"). The forest dwellers, retaining almost intact their ancestral African culture and their tradition of revolt against plantation life, lead a rude, uncultured existence under the domination of Wademba, the last of the Maroons. The more "civilized" plains dwellers are despised by the mountain folk, who believe that they have lost their original identity as they continue a precarious existence as serfs of the plantation owners. However, the easy existence of the villagers proves attractive to some of the forest dwellers. Thus the companion of Wademba and later his daughter Awa leave the mountain hideout to settle on the lowlands. Ti Jean L'horizon, born of the union of Awa and a lowland dweller, represents a synthesis of the two polarized cultures.

Wilbert J. Roget. *WLT.* 55, 1 (Winter 1981), p. 163

In Schwarz-Bart's [*Ti Jean l'horizon*], the hero is at once an orphan (his mother's husband dies before he is born) and a divine son to Wademba (also known as "The Immortal"), the island's cultural protector. Wademba has overseen Guadeloupe's generations since the slave-trade crossing, and upon his death he entrusts the protection of their cultural legacy to Ti Jean. Furthermore, he confers upon him a mission to return to Africa and to restore the links to the cultural homeland. In taking on this spiritual and cultural enterprise, Ti Jean "orphans himself." As Jesus renounced his worldly parents in order to embrace his spiritual family, Ti Jean leaves his home and his wife-girlfriend in order to regain the larger family ties between his Caribbean people and their African homeland. . . .

In Schwarz-Bart's [*Pluie et vent sur Télumée Miracle*], the motif of flight is associated with the same spirit of strength and freedom as in *Ti Jean* and [Toni Morrison's *Song of Solomon*]. When misfortune sets in, Télumée feels "Le

maré-cage était sous mes pieds, c'était l'heure de me faire légère, adroite, ailée. . . ."
[The swamp was beneath my feet, it was time to become light, quick, winged.]
Flight in this novel, as in the others, does not always necessarily have positive value,
however, as when Lange Medard flies off with Télumée's adopted daughter, Sonore.
In [Morrison's] *Tar Baby*, the negative aspect of flight is evidenced in Jadine's final
flight from the island, from the daisy-tree women and from Ondine who would
envelop her in their arms. It is also a flight from Son who might have been her passport on a flight similar to Milkman's or Ti Jean's, had she been willing.

The most complex and perhaps the most fascinating flight to be found in
these novels is that of Ti Jean. His journey, like the others, is both internal and
external, both self-discovery and discovery of the outer world. But Ti Jean's journey is internal and external in another way as well. When Wademba dies, his
ghost soul slips through Ti Jean's lips and enters his body. Ti Jean's journey to
Africa, with which he has been charged, occurs inside the belly of the bird-beast—
or Wademba himself. Thus his journey is a cosmic voyage of a doubly internal
sort—both within himself (an existential self-searching) and within his "father's"
belly (an adventure backwards into Wademba's African legacy). The paradox of
the doubly inner voyage is that it leads to the outside world of present time and to
the discovery of the cultural legacy that each African descendant embodies. . . .

In *Pluie* [*et vent*], Télumée, who triumphs over affliction (the "rain" and
"wind" of the title), helps others in the community to endure and to overcome their
own painful struggles. She also has "witch powers" in the art of healing learned
from her grandmother. Her healing powers, as well as her personal integrity, lead
her to be regarded in her old age as the grandmother of the entire community:
"Maman Miracle, tu es l'arbre contre lequel s'appuie notre hameau, et que devien-
dra le morne sans toi, le sais-tu?" [Mother Miracle, you are the tree against which
we prop up our hamlet, and what would become of this little knoll without you, do
you know?] Ti Jean's life, perhaps more than Son's, resembles a black version of
the Christ story. He is born of a mysterious conception, fathered by the bird-god
Wademba. He goes on to make sense of the cosmos, indeed to regenerate it, and to
trace the history of his people. When he returns to Guadeloupe, the magic ring, the
perfect circle of the cosmos, given him by Wademba, comes to his aid, "telling
him the sign, and the path, and the way." From out of the belly of the beast, he
restores the sun to his people. . . . Ti Jean's return to his community inaugurates a
transformation, a new era of hope and strength; and his marriage to Égee—who is
likened to the damp, the sands, to the brilliance of flame itself—signifies a hierog-
amous union, a wedding between Guadeloupe and the cosmos itself.

Josie P. Campbell. CLS. 22, 3 (Fall 1985), pp. 397, 401–3

[*Pluie et vent sur Télumée Miracle*] opens and closes upon the same scene: an old
woman standing in her garden, dreaming of the past and waiting tranquilly for
death. The figure is that of the narrator, Télumée, who has received, late in life, the
admiring nickname "Télumée Miracle." Her upright posture suggests dignity,
strength, and a resolute will to resist adversity; these are the qualities to which the
narrative continually reverts, and which serve to create its prevailing moral

climate. Behind Télumée's vertical stance there is a second, latent image, that of a tree. Unexpressed at the start of the novel, this image becomes explicit as the story advances and she is successively compared to a bamboo, a poinciana or *flamboyant*, a coconut palm, and an acomat. The tree, with its stable roots and promise of upward growth, is a familiar presence in the work of [Aime] Césaire and [Jacques] Roumain: a symbol of constancy and harmonious integration, of triumphant recovery from the uprooting and alienation consequent on the fall of slavery. . . . In Simone Schwarz-Bart's [*Pluie et vent sur Télumée Miracle*] the tree . . . is above all associated with courage and tenacity. At the end of the novel, which tells the story of Télumée's life in early twentieth-century Guadeloupe, the image is specifically linked to the theme of her indomitable spirit by the tribute which her neighbors pay to her: "Mama Miracle, you are the tree our hamlet leans against." . . .

Critical discussions of this novel have stressed the way in which the narrator's life, like that of her female ancestors, falls into a recurrent pattern of ascent, ruin, and subsequent renaissance, in seeming obedience to a cyclical view of man's progression through time. The pattern is only lightly delineated in the case of Télumée's great-grandmother Minerva, the first of the Lougandor women: she is freed from a cruel master by the abolition of slavery in 1848, then is abandoned in a state of pregnancy by a transient lover, but is rescued by a tender and steadfast man who loves Minerva's child as if she were his own. It is more firmly sketched in when the narrator recounts the life of her mother, Victory, an unmarried girl struggling to bring up her first child, Regina, when she is abandoned by a faithless new lover from a neighboring island. She is rescued from months of alcoholic despair and degeneration by the gentle, compassionate Angebert, the future father of Télumée. Then Angebert's sudden, violent death casts her back into solitude; but two years later she meets the great love of her life, and soon sets sail with him for the island of Dominica. Briefly though they appear in the narrative, both Minerva and Victory have essential virtues in common with their respective daughters, Toussine (Télumée's grandmother) and Télumée herself. Minerva, the founder of the Lougandor line, who bears the name of the goddess of wisdom, is a woman who walks with her "head high" and has "an unshakable faith in life." Victory, whose slight body perhaps reflects her moral status as the most lightweight of the Lougandor women, is nonetheless a valiant fighter who also "carrie[s] her head high on a slender neck" and is moved by a "determination to stay serene however harshly the winds might blow." Forever singing at her work, keeping her griefs and disappointments to herself, she survives poverty, a miscarriage, the loss of her lovers, and the sole responsibility of two young children, without losing an innate knack of resilience and optimism; "not a fallen woman," she goes through life "with the same expectation, the same lightness she had when no man's hand had yet touched her." At some of the lowest moments of Télumée's life, Victory's example helps to sustain her: singing about her domestic tasks so as to distance herself from a faultfinding white employer, or mentally thanking her laundress mother for the "steel wrists" she has inherited, which enable her to endure the heavy labor of cutting cane.

Beverley Ormerod. *An Introduction to the French Caribbean Novel*
(London: Heinemann, 1985), pp. 108, 110

[The plot of *Ti Jean l'horizon*] follows the traditional thematic schema for quest literature, even down to the formal division of the story into seven episodes, each with a title announcing the adventure to come. The biological child of his good-natured Antillean father and the spiritual child of his African grandfather Wademba, Ti Jean moves in three spheres that make up the topography of his Guadeloupe: the hilly retreat of the Old Ancestors who remember and celebrate the heroism of runaway slaves; the village below inhabited by Guadeloupeans who discard the old in favor of the new and the modern; and the mysterious domain of spirits who roam the woods—the dead and the souls partially transformed into animals. The call to adventure comes when a huge cowlike beast appears on the island and swallows scores of inhabitants as well as the sun itself. When the Beast swallows Ti Jean's fiancée Egée, the young hunter returns to the Old Ancestors for counsel and his grandfather's magical arms: a belt of strength, a ring of wisdom, and an old musket from the times of the slave revolts. Once inside the Beast in search of Egée, Ti Jean journeys to other worlds: first to Wademba's homeland in Africa, then to the Kingdom of the Dead, then around the polar seas to France, and finally back to Guadeloupe. Ti Jean returns with a full measure of *connaissance*, a deep understanding of all three domains. Having learned the secret of the Beast, Ti Jean uses the musket to kill it and restore both his people and the sun to their proper place. Ti Jean himself undergoes a final transformation from an old man back into a youth who finds his lost love waiting for him and assumes the wisdom and the destiny of his island.

Ti Jean's journey is fascinating in that it leads the reader to the farthest possible limits in what is not just a quest but also a questioning of the Antillean search for identity. The young hero's passage to the inside of the Beast triggers an ironic, otherworldly look at ideas and cultural experience normally accepted as a matter of fact. In this case, that look, like the laser gaze of the Beast itself, deconstructs four myths traditionally associated with Antillean quest: the return to Africa, the power of the spirit world, the Promised Land of France, and the heroic, linear dimensions of machismo.

Kitzie McKinney. *FR.* 62, 4 (March 1989), pp. 654–55

Some works in Caribbean feminine expression can be viewed as breaking the chain of alienation. They propose images of women who find a voice to claim a parcel of power over reality and destiny. These works provoke interesting questions and uncover uncharted domains for women and the Caribbean as a whole. Such is the project of Simone Schwarz-Bart in *Pluie et vent sur Télumée Miracle*, strangely translated under the title *The Bridge of Beyond*. Schwarz-Bart affirms the forces of life against those of death and destruction. She articulates a poetry of presence and plenitude against absence and fragmentation. With her, the notions of Caribbean self and Caribbean history become thinkable. Télumée, her heroine, like the other women of the Lougandor family to which she belongs, expresses all that is possible to express in spite of the adverse conditions threatening her resolve to live. A system of liberating myths is elaborated in this novel, which celebrates the regenerating power of love and the possibility of conquering what in the brutal logic of realism seems impossible: freedom. To the reality of the plantation, of conditions of the Antilles, Schwarz-Bart opposes the indomitable spirit of women who refuse to be subjugated. Télumée draws her energy from the language and culture of the island, which mediates her entrance into the world of identity, presence, and continuity. Télumée is not extradited outside of her body, whose beauty she offers to her lover, Elie. She feels "right in her place where she is," that is, in the island. The island in Schwarz-Bart's fiction is not a place to be fled nor a prison in which one slowly dies; it is the locus of self-discovery and human realization. One can speak of Schwarz-Bart's aesthetic practice as a veritable "poetic of space." There is a certain solemnity in this novel, which celebrates the reappropriation by the islanders of their territory. Schwarz-Bart introduces her own Creolized language to take possession of the landscape. She selects a precise vocabulary to name familiar sites, trees, flowers, and plants of the island. It is as if the legitimate occupation of the Caribbean soil by its inhabitants depended on the act of naming. Time is reconquered as the Caribbean existence is replaced in its historical continuum. The quest for the African source is central in Schwarz-Bart's reconstruction of reality. Other dimensions are conquered as the author undertakes a bold exploration of the magical realm that lies beyond empirical reality. In this perilous enterprise, Schwarz-Bart never succumbs to sterile and factitious imagery. The point of departure and the point of arrival of her narrative is always the human experience.

In *Ti Jean l'horizon* . . . Schwarz-Bart executes one of the most accomplished Caribbean literary compositions. In this daring epic, history converges with the marvelous, playful notes alternating with grave tones, and vivacious spirit blends with an introspective mood. It is a polyphonic construct in which the author harmonizes different voices to tell a tale of indestructible love, the love of Ti Jean for Egée, a "négresse sans fard ni pose" [negress with neither makeup nor attitude], whom he calls his "Little Guadeloupe." It is also the fantastic tale of the hero's search for the sun, symbol of freedom, which has disappeared, swallowed by a monstrous Beast from "elsewhere." At the end of his long journey through the present and the past, the realms of reality and surreality, Ti Jean, the hero, feels "old as the mountains" but convinced that "everything is intact." The end, for him, is only the beginning because "already, life was being reinvented, passionately, in light of torches simply painted in the soil." Schwarz-Bart in her fiction brings to an apotheosis the creative force already illustrated in the remarkable works of Jacques Roumain, Jacques S. Alexis, and Edouard Glissant. Like these writers, she concretizes through a conscious aesthetic practice a *Weltanschauung* that recognizes the urgency of collective liberation. Her recently published play *Ton beau capitaine* also deserves mention here. In this piece, Schwarz-Bart, with an economy of words and brilliant insight, succeeds in relating the struggle of man and woman to forge a language to communicate over the waters that separate them. It is the story of a Haitian migrant worker in Guadeloupe and his wife, who remains in Haiti. It is a story of dreams shattered but unceasingly reformed, of truth emerging from lies, of desire indefinitely postponed, of two people searching for unknown words to formulate their love. A masterpiece of conciseness and vision, this play is significant not only because of the themes it explores but also because it suggests the development of a dialogue between the Caribbean societies. It signifies that Guadeloupe is aware of Haiti in an eminently urgent manner. It implies that a cross-discursive space has been created where a new debate on the destiny of the Caribbean is taking place.

Marie-Denise Shelton. In Selwyn R. Cudjoe, ed. Caribbean Women
Writers (Wellesley, Mass.: Calaloux Publications, 1990), pp. 354–56

Simone Schwarz-Bart's novels . . . attempt to treat the predicament of the woman and West Indian society at the level of the individual enduring life: self-esteem and self-worth are restored through a process of revalorizing of images and a heritage seen in negative terms by most *Antillais*. Schwarz-Bart reverses the connotations of the closed space and emphasizes only its positive, nurturing aspects. Her heroines' voyages are symbolic interior journeys. Coupled with the defeated, fettered figure is the other face of the islander, that of the hardy intrepid adventurer, braving the elements in order to survive, of the Maroon who lives by wits and is a figure of revolt and resourcefulness. This is the image evoked by the Guadeloupean novelist Simone Schwarz-Bart in the original title of her novel *The Bridge of Beyond* which, in the original French (*Pluie et vent sur Télumée Miracle*) means "Rain and Wind on Télumée, the Miracle woman." Télumée, indeed, is called *"marron sans bois"*—a testimony to her qualities of survival, self-sufficiency, and independence. Here the woman is a figure of strength and resistance and the island, hamlet, boat, or room becomes not a negative space but a positive one, not a restrictive enclosure, but a solid base from which to venture out to brave the waters of life, the open sea, that sea which at once protects and threatens, isolates and frees, gives and takes life.

Schwarz-Bart's vision does not deny either history or the realities of island life. Guadeloupe, Télumée's island, is described as "cette ile à volcans, à cyclones et moustiques, à mauvaise mentalité": battered by hurricanes, infected with mosquitos and with her share of people who as we say in Creole "have bad min" (are bad minded). It is a tiny speck on the map, but for Schwarz-Bart's heroines it is not a land with no past and no history. Schwarz-Bart makes explicit in her work that her concept of the island is at variance with the view of those who consider it unimportant or insignificant. Moreover, it is not necessary to look overseas to Europe or to Africa to find a sense of worth. Schwarz-Bart's heroines struggle resolutely to resist and reject the negative attitudes of the people around them and assert their power to remain afloat and upright in the waters of life. The Lougandor women journey not to France or to Guinea, but deep within themselves.

Télumée, an old lady, standing in her tiny garden, transcends the limitations of her island and her history and affirms her desire to relive her life, to suffer and to die in exactly the same circumstances. But one must come to terms with the reality in order to transcend it. Whatever hand life deals, one must play it. The Lougandor women, Télumée's clan, accept their destiny but refuse to be bowed by it. Télumée's life is rooted in positive values and in a belief in herself acquired at her grandmother's knee. It is a security conferred by a belief in an alternative vision of reality to which many *Antillais* do not subscribe or have access. Télumée has never "suffered from the exiguity" of her homeland, for, according to Télumée, "the country depends on the size of one's heart." One's reality is conditioned by one's point of view.

Elizabeth Wilson. In Carole Boyce Davies and Elaine Savory Fido, eds.
Out of the Kumbla: Caribbean Women and Literature
(Trenton, N. J.: Africa World Press, 1990), pp. 53–54

Simone Schwarz-Bart's novel *The Bridge of Beyond* is a celebration of life, manifest through a story told. The heroine, Télumée, has puzzled out a meaning for her life, and she shares it with us. It is the essential feature of Télumée's story that she tells it. In doing so she integrates the entire fabric of her life, by naming herself and each person in her life, and situating them all in time and place, on her island home of Guadeloupe. Throughout the text, and the life that the text embodies, words are a charged and living force, for good or ill, and silence can be tantamount to destruction or annihilation. Thus Télumée's story is a triumph simply because it exists as an ordered narrative. As a story told, it is a gift of life. . . .

Télumée learns to harness her words through an essential and insoluble spiritual union which reveals itself in the story through song and storytelling. The principal bonding relationship in this story is that between grandmother and grandchild, a tie reflected by the fact that, in the telling, Télumée's autobiography becomes at one and the same time her grandmother's biography. The fact that Télumée is situated in the text principally as storyteller serves to emphasize the grandmother's crucial role in her life, for within Télumée's own narrative, it is her grandmother who is presented as the storyteller. Thus it is Toussine who, by giving Télumée the comfort of words and the wisdom they contain, makes of Télumée a storyteller, and bequeaths to her the wisdom she finally transmits to us through autobiography. In a text wondrously conscious of the giving and receiving of words, Télumée's narrative teaches us to accept that there are words that separate, and words that bind. She passes on, as her legacy to us, that gift of metaphor which she herself received from her grandmother, and which served to liberate her own life. . . .

The Bridge of Beyond opens with the words "A man's country may be cramped or vast according to the size of his heart. I've never found my country too small." Two hundred pages later, the last sentences are "Sun risen, sun set, the days slip past and the sand blown by the wind will engulf my boat. But I shall die here, where I am, standing in my little garden. What happiness." Yet in between these two statements we have had a record of a great deal of suffering, a great deal of pain, a lot of betrayal. What matters to Télumée in the story of herself and her people, is that by the end she is sure of who she is, and where she is; and it is the grandmother who has helped her learn both, *and taught her how to tell us this*. The miraculous Télumée does manage to make sense of her world, and she tells us, and her narrative is a testimony to the bond between women for the articulation of liberty. Throughout the narrative, the guiding principle remains the same: to find the balance between alienation and annihilation. Both internal and external enslavement must be combatted. We must not be controlled either by our dreams, or by those of others. Life is beleaguered, but in the end, both its pains and its joys must be weathered, and it is this triumph which is manifest through narrative. Télumée has withstood the "rain and wind" upon her, and knows she is "not a statue of salt to be dissolved." She therefore leaves us, although unable to comfort the forlorn Elie, with a sense of joy in herself, and in her world.

Abena P. A. Busia. In Carole Boyce Davies and Elaine Savory Fido, eds.
Out of the Kumbla: Caribbean Women and Literature
(Trenton, N. J.: Africa World Press, 1990), pp. 289, 291–92, 299

Simone Schwarz-Bart's play *Ton beau capitaine* was inspired by the real-life circumstance of Haitian men who leave their native land in search of work. Set in 1985, it presents agricultural worker Wilnor Baptiste, who lives in Guadeloupe while his wife Marie-Ange remains behind in Haiti. During their years of separation they communicate by way of audiocassette. Wilnor's simultaneous absence from Haiti and presence in Guadeloupe are the subjects of this 1987 play. Consequently, patterns of isolation, separation, displacement, and exile are found throughout the text.

Even before the play opens, Schwarz-Bart underlines the poverty and isolation of Wilnor. All the action takes place in Wilnor's one-room shack, creating a claustrophobic atmosphere. Furnished with only a stool, an old crate, a stove, and a floor mattress, it resembles a prison cell. Far away from his family, he is indeed condemned to a life of loneliness. His clothes—one suit, one shirt, one tie, one pair of shoes—a few dishes, a plastic mirror, and a borrowed radio/cassette player complete the setting.

There are only two characters listed. Wilnor, described as a tall and thin thirty-year-old, and the tape player. Marie-Ange never appears onstage; her voice is heard only on the tape. That Wilnor is onstage alone throughout the play accentuates his isolation. He even dances two communal dances—the quadrille and the *lérose*—alone. Traditionally the quadrille is performed with a partner and three other couples. Here it functions paradoxically to reinforce his solitude and provide some consolation during his nostalgic moments. . . .

As a closing to his taped response, Wilnor repeats five times, "Ton beau capitaine," each time with a different intonation. The first time, while looking in the mirror, he says, "Ton beau capitaine. Wilnor." Dissatisfied with that sign-off, he removes his shirt and tie and repeats a second time, "Ton beau capitaine," but "sur un ton moins assuré" [in a less-confident tone of voice]. The "points de suspension" reflect his hesitancy. Still uncertain, he covers his mouth with his hand and hunches his shoulders in resignation as the third "Ton beau capitaine" audio signature is posed as a question. Then the music begins as Wilnor does a desperation dance. He stops and says, "Ton beau capitaine?" Then he dances to a drumbeat. Hands over his head, he reaches for the sky as if to fly away. This final gesture reflects Wilnor's desire to escape his prisonlike existence and rejoin his wife in Haiti. Then, in the darkness, one last ironic "Ton beau capitaine?" is heard. There is no happy ending here. The couple remain separated.

Renée Larrier. *WLT*. 64, 1 (Winter 1990), pp. 57–58

SEMBÈNE OUSMANE (1923–   )

SENEGAL

Sembène Ousmane is an exception in French-speaking West Africa. He is almost the only writer who started publishing novels during the colonial period, and still does, denouncing the evils of the postindependence era as he did for preindependence. He is the only one who, realizing the limitations of literature, especially literature written in French in largely illiterate societies, turned to another medium and made several films, thus becoming a pioneer in the field of African cinema. More important even, in our countries where the prestige of the so-called intellectual is so great, he constantly refused to be more than a man of the people close to his roots. . . .

Xala is set in Dakar, since the Senegalese society is what Sembène Ousmane seems to know best. The hero, El Hadji Abdou Kader Beye, belongs to the new class born after independence. He is a businessman just nominated as the Head of the Chamber of Commerce and Industry, the first Senegalese to occupy this seat. As the crowning of his happiness, he decides to marry a third wife, the young N'Gone. The story opens with the description of the wedding party, complete with male and female griots, champagne, and expensive gifts. As well as a car, El Hadji has promised 2,500 gallons of petrol to the new bride. The two other wives are also present at the ceremony and portrayed with great skill by Sembène Ousmane, who makes us aware of their different personalities through their behavior in the circumstances. But on his wedding night, El Hadji up to now so fortunate, discovers he has the *xala*—which means that he is suddenly impotent. This impotency is the writing on the wall. It is not only his physical manhood which is at stake, but his dignity and even his wealth. In his desperate attempts to cure his disease, he neglects his business which goes from bad to worse since in fact El Hadji was just a pretense of a businessman, living on credit and with no real financial power. This is, in my point of view, the most striking aspect of Sembène Ousmane's novel: the constant criticism, the constant demythification of the characters and aspects of society.

Maryse Condé. In Eldred Durosimi Jones, ed.
African Literature Today. 9 (1978), pp. 97–98

Sembène's work in both fiction and film, starting with the publication of his first novel, *Le Docker noir* . . . charts a steady progression away from a type of romantic individualism towards the communal struggle and communal consciousness celebrated in his later work. It is not that his work ever lacked an ideological content, of a generally radical tendency, but that the artistic means of expressing this content demanded many years and many experiments for their discovery.

The immaturity of *Le Docker noir* as a novel may also be attributed to what finally proved one of Sembène's strengths—his very lack of that sophistication in education and experience which severed many of his contemporary writers from the lot of their fellows. . . . One of the chief concerns of Diaw

Falla, the novel's hero, is to help [the black dockworkers] break out of [their] isolation, which is not only that of their blackness but that of the poverty they share with their white fellow workers. Instead of holding aloof from unionism and political action as "white men's business," they must throw themselves into both if they are to change their lot.

Here already is that insistence on the primacy of change which runs all through Sembène's work. But to some extent it runs counter to another tendency in *Le Docker noir*: Diaw's concern to change his own condition by the use of the pen. This brings him up against the perpetual dilemma of the artist; the need for isolation and withdrawal in order to create seems at times a betrayal of that very comradeship in suffering which he seeks to celebrate. Most dockers do not read novels and cannot hence feel liberated by them. . . .

Since the early 1960s, Sembène has been increasingly absorbed by his work as a filmmaker, and the fiction he has written since then (notably *Le Mandat* and *Xala*) has shown the signs of this absorption. Unlike many filmmakers of literary leanings, he has always recognized that the short novel provides the ideal basis for a film script, because the film can then develop and celebrate visually what is offered by the text, instead of having to cut and brutally condense a full-length novel. Hence he has not attempted to film any of his major novels. His major films to date, *Emitaï*, *The Money Order*, and *Xala*, all show this strong sense of visual and dramatic situation and all produce a result which is probably in many ways richer than the literary text (in the case of *Emitaï*, this is a speculation, as the original text has never been published). . . .

Xala is the closest of Sembène's novels to film form, and was clearly written with one eye already on the script. There is an abundance of dialogue and a relative absence of the sort of commentary or reflection which cannot be rendered visually. The plot concentrates solely upon the brief career of Abdou Kader Beye's third marriage, his immediate relapse into *xala* (impotence), and his eventual or supposed cure at the hands of the beggars.

Gerald Moore. *Twelve African Writers*
(Bloomington: Indiana University Press, 1980), pp. 70, 79–80

[Sembène Ousmane] evolved from fumbling beginnings as an autodidact to the full mastery of his art, producing five full-length novels, a collection of short stories, and two longish novellas in sixteen years. For nine years, he devoted himself to filmmaking, hoping by this medium . . . to reach people in the heartlands of Africa who are not yet—or are insufficiently—literate to be reached by the printed page, especially in French. . . .

Some of the facts of his life are reflected in his first novels, all written during the colonial era. He was born in a little Casamance fishing village, like the heroes of *Le Docker noir* and *O pays, mon beau peuple!* He earned a precarious living as a stevedore in Marseilles, where, like the hero of *Le Docker noir*, he supplemented his lack of formal education by wide reading and wrote his first novel as a passionate outcry against the hardships suffered by the black minorities in France, deploring in particular the conditions of the black dockworkers. His theses, more appropriate to a polemical tract than a novel, presented difficulties that the inexperienced Sembène proved, not surprisingly, unable to deal with satisfactorily. . . . Nevertheless, it is of great interest to trace his evolution as a novelist from this hesitant beginning where as an apprentice he tries out the tools of his trade.

Dorothy S. Blair. *Senegalese Literature: A Critical History*
(Boston: Twayne, 1984), p. 80

Two important observations may be made about the theme of growing consciousness in [*Les Bouts de bois de Dieu*, translated as *God's Bits of Wood*]. First, Sembène Ousmane has prophetically expressed in the art form of the novel what has since actually taken place in some liberation struggles in Africa. In Zimbabwe, women in the now-ruling ZANU-PF party became more and more outspoken about the oppression of women, not only in colonial and capitalist Rhodesia, but also in traditional Shona society, which was feudalistic and characterized by the subordination of woman to man. . . .

Secondly, the novel shows clearly that the workers and their women are not simply automatons acting under the spell of history. Theirs is "conscious activity of conscious men." The workers need the organizational skill of Lahbib and Bakayoko. To be successful they need the energy and intellectual acumen of Bakayoko. For the march of the women to succeed, the leadership qualities and untiring dedication of Penda are required. The exploited masses of French West Africa have indeed become conscious of their existence as a result of the relations of production, but they are not driven blindly to their success by the inexorable march of history. Individuals react to the situation differently according to their own being, talent, and level of political consciousness. Thus, while the majority of workers join in the strike, Sounkare, the watchman, chooses the opposite course; and privileged individuals like El Hadji Mabigué are used by the company and the state apparatus to frustrate the efforts of the strikers. These men and women are therefore not driven like robots by history. They also act upon and create history. . . .

[It] is important to emphasize that Sembène Ousmane is not only concerned with socio-political issues, that he is not only projecting socialist ideology, but is also alive to the need to project his social vision in a genuinely artistic form. . . .

On the sociological level, [Sembène Ousmane] successfully demonstrates that the strike has generated a new social psychology, marking a new level of sociopolitical awareness and a tendency towards democracy, justice, and progress. The workers have positively rejected the exploitation of man by man. The women have broken the chains of their psychological and social domination by men, and their men—Bakayoko included—have come to accept this. The masses of French West Africa have also come to the realization that their language and culture are not inferior to French language and culture—hence the emphasis on Ouolof and the return to old ceremonies and customs long forgotten. Indeed, the new awareness is an expression of the fact that "the masses do not want to go on living in the old way, that the existing conditions have become intolerable and should be changed."

Emmanuel Ngara. *Art and Ideology in the African Novel*
(London: Heinemann, 1985), pp. 65–66, 73

In ["Souleyman," translated as] "The Bilal's Fourth Wife" [collected in *Voltaïque*, translated as *Tribal Scars and Other Stories*], Sembène, with great humor, pokes fun at Senegalese attitudes toward divorce. He attacks the practice of double moral standards, which place women at a disadvantage. Sembène uses the character of Yacine to question and to disagree with the patriarchal Moslem marriage rules drawn up by males centuries ago. In spite of the rumors and intense external pressures, Yacine reveals a tremendous self-confidence. First, she refuses to be coerced by Suliman and her family into a divorce. Second, she is adamant about being treated on equal footing as a woman by the Cadi (special council of male elders called to review her case). Third, she questions why the woman is not free to take a lover when a man in a Moslem society can have four wives with the approval of the Koran and legal laws. These unyielding stances force the male elders to accept, with reluctance, the fact that there are two sides to every marital disagreement, and the woman's position is just as important as the man's. . . .

Sembène's short story, ["La Mère," translated as] "The Mother" is another example of the application of double moral standards in a Moslem society in Africa. This point is presented through the personage of the tyrannical king. The king, who has no intentions of cultivating the love and respect of his constituents, alienates himself and evokes the hatred and fear of his subjects to the point that they dream about seeing him burned alive. Meanwhile, these same subjects are passive and obey the king's orders to murder men over fifty years old. Thus, the king thinks that he owes no allegiance to anyone. He proceeds to pass a law that he will deflower every virgin before she is married. Over the years, only a few brave mothers succeed in saving their daughters from such a fate. When it is time for the king's daughter to marry, he repeals the law—separate rules for the poor and rich. . . .

Mores of another kind are explored in the short story, ["Ses trois jours," translated as] "Her Three Days," where one meets Noumbé, the third wife of Mustapha. When the story opens, Noumbé is preparing for her husband's visit during her allotted three days as dictated by the Koran. Drawing upon his filmmaking skills, Sembène zooms in on Noumbé to show her haggard face, her weakened body after the bearing of five children in rapid succession, her anxieties and fears of being replaced by the fourth wife, and her fight to handle a heart condition. Although Noumbé is still young, she looks older because of her full financial duties of providing for her children. . . .

Like Noumbé, Nafi in ["Lettres de France," translated as] "Letters from France" has been raised in a patriarchal society where man rules over woman, and one class over another. Viewed as a second-class citizen by her society and father, she is tricked into marrying a seventy-three-year-old man, who lives in Marseilles, France. The topic of love is not entertained, for marriage is based on loneliness, a wish to live in France, and an old man's desire to retain his lost youth. Nafi, the young wife, will serve Demba, her husband, be an instrument for his pleasure, bear his children, greet his friends, and care for him in his old age. By selecting a young wife, like Suliman in "The Bilal's Fourth Wife," Demba hopes that she will be easier to control and that he thereby will gain much from the unbalanced relationship. Unfortunately, the carefully laid plan backfires when Demba succumbs to cancer. . . .

Sembène's female characters are not losers. In the four short stories each woman triumphs no matter how small the victory. By presenting such women, Sembène opens up opportunities for African women to develop a more positive self-awareness and to draw upon capacities that have lain dormant within themselves. In order for Senegalese women to move forward, they must cast off outdated ideas and modes of behavior and view their plight realistically. In short, they must place themselves on the outside in order to look in. By doing so, they may begin to take steps to eliminate ignorance and mass illiteracy and improve their status in the twentieth century. All four women—Yacine, the mother, Noumbé, and Nafi—challenge the traditional order, which condemned them to a secondary role. They, as mothers, are believable as characters. They, as mothers and women, through the prism of social and political contexts, will turn their faces to the future with hope for the future generation, their children.

Brenda F. Berrian. In Carole Boyce Davies and Anne Adams Graves,

eds. *Ngambika: Studies of Women in African Literature*

(Trenton, N. J.: Africa World Press, 1986), pp. 196–98, 200, 202–4

Senegalese writer and filmmaker [Sembène Ousmane] is one African artist who, far from being reluctant to depict African traditions and scenes in his works, is pleased to point out, time and again, that many of the plots for his creative works come from real life. An analysis of his works also shows that African traditional beliefs and practices have a profound thematic, structural, or symbolic function in novels that are as far removed from each other in design and purpose as *O pays, mon beau peuple!*, *L'Harmattan*, and *Xala*. This same pattern applies to films like *Xala* and *Emitaï*. . . .

Sembène had several political aims in making *Emitaï*. One of these was to show that in black Africa there was no total passivity to colonialism but, instead, varying levels of resistance (just as there were in the United States, for example, slave uprisings and revolts, the news of which was often suppressed for fear of engendering others). The Jola resistance refuted a number of propagandist views like those of Dominique O. Mannoni, who suggested that Africans (including Senegalese sharpshooters) were looking for authority figures to whom they could attach themselves and found such models among European whites. Sembène shows in *Emitaï* a people, with a political will of their own tied to their religious beliefs, who achieve a moral victory at the very moment when they are defeated by a technologically greater adversary who uses their own young men as mercenaries. At the same time, the film eloquently shows the lack of political consciousness among the black soldiers who followed the orders of French officers unquestioningly and never once thought of rebelling against the whites.

Jonathan A. Peters. In Eileen Julien, Mildred [P.] Mortimer, and Curtis

Schade, eds. *African Literature in Its Social and Political Dimensions*

(Washington, D. C.: Three Continents, 1986), pp. 69, 71

In the search, during the late 1960s and early 1970s, for a more concretely committed, less elitist, more accessible African literature, the work of [Sembène Ousmane] of Senegal proved to be of pathbreaking significance. The real importance of Sembène's work lay in the daring simplicity of its overall conception. Even in his early work, dating back to the 1950s, Sembène had broken radically with the urban, intellectual biases prevailing in African literature. His most celebrated novel, *God's Bits of Wood*, had taken as its central focus a major railroad strike that had occurred in French West Africa in the late 1940s. Scrupulously avoiding abstraction or grand theorizing, it had devoted itself to a very close and concrete exploration of the material effect of the strike on the lives of a number of people—men, women, and children, strikers and strikebreakers, beggars and small traders, and proletarian activists—living and working in various communities along the thousand-mile rail line between Bamako and Dakar. Through this means, Sembène had been able to convey immediately and compellingly a sense of the movement of ideas in time, and of the intersection between thought and action in political events. Where other African writers might have spoken *about* the politicization of the laboring classes, Sembène, a self-proclaimed Marxist, had made this process the very subject of his novel, addressing it not simply as series of external events but phenomenologically . . . with an eye to its human and conceptual implications. . . .

In his subsequent work (he is also one of Africa's most acclaimed film directors), Sembène has continued to give prominence to the dispossessed strata of modern African society. His novels, stories, and films represent landless peasants, slum dwellers without work, beggars, and aged people for whom nothing is assured, not even their own survival. By drawing attention to the daily struggles of this "invisible" multitude—invisible, that is, to the architects of African "modernization"—Sembène is able not only to show that they are casualties of the existing order, but also, subtly but unmistakably, to hint at their potential revolutionary impact on society, latent in the first instance, in their sheer numbers.

Neil Lazarus. *Resistance in Postcolonial African Fiction*
(New Haven, Conn.: Yale University Press, 1990), pp. 207–9

The two novellas "Niiwam" and "Taaw" were originally published in French in a single volume by Présence Africaine in 1987. The preface to the new English edition, "Sembène Ousmane, Voice of the Voiceless," retraces the author's life and work through 1988, noting that "Taaw" was made into a film in 1970 (after *Le Mandat* made Sembène's international reputation). The "Commentary on the Translation" examines several problems: the audience aimed at by the Senegalese writer when he writes in French; the differences between standard French and that used in Senegal; Sembène's personal departures from standard French; the polyglossic quality of speech in Senegal; and the idiom of students and the young unemployed. Conclusion: it would be pointless to have the latter speaking like their counterparts in Cape Flats or Harlem. The English text serves its purpose if the reader gets the sense that English "can open and welcome other voices and other tongues."

"Niiwam" is very simply constructed. In Dakar, Thierno, an old and very poor man from the interior, leaves the morgue to go bury the corpse of his son Niiwam. Having no money, he and his wife have not eaten since the previous day. He leaves her weeping by the entrance (women do not go to the burial). An old ragman who washes corpses and buys their clothing tells Thierno that the cemetery is in the village of Yoff and pays his way on the bus. The remainder of the story details the actions and words of the driver, the conductor, and passengers as the bus crosses and exits the city. A fashionably-dressed, haughty Senegalese woman sitting by Thierno excites hysteria among the passengers on discovering that it is a corpse he is holding on his lap. However, an Islamic holy man takes up Thierno's defense, reminding the passengers of the respect due the dead. The two men descend from the bus and walk toward the burial ground amid the sand dunes. Meanwhile, the woman is now screaming because she has been robbed: a young man lifted her purse and passed it to an accomplice, now outside the bus. During the trip Thierno has been a mere spectator— guilty, nervous, unobtrusively swatting flies away from his son's corpse.

Taaw, the eldest son of Baye Tine and first wife Yaye Dabo, was once a good student. However, on [traveling] eleven kilometers four times a day to and from the secondary school and later being mistreated by an uncle's envious co-wives, he twice failed his classes and was forced to drop out. He has no job and his girlfriend is pregnant. As in "Niiwam," however, the title character does not undergo the greatest transformation. All her life Yaye Dabo has been quietly obedient to the men of her immediate family and her husband. She tries to make ends meet on the little money he gives her and to allay his violence against herself and her sons. When Taaw wins scholarship money, Baye Tine uses it to move the family to a *bidonville* near Dakar and buy a young second wife. He is particularly enraged at the insolent scorn of Taaw, who once stopped him from beating Yaye Dabo and broke one of his teeth while knocking him to the ground. For this Taaw received a six-month prison sentence from the council of old men. Back at home, he and his father do not speak to each other. Yaye Dabo grows in strength and independence, thinking about her husband, social customs, relatives, and co-wives. When Baye Tine, angered and frustrated by forced retirement, threatens to repudiate her, she shocks him by repudiating him in front of the neighborhood wives. She pushes him to the ground and steps over him, "an act violently condemned in Wolof society, particularly when done by a woman." Never again will Yaye Dabo be a woman of the past, seeing the world through other people's eyes.

Melvin B. Tolson, Jr. *WLT.* 67, 2 (Spring 1993), pp. 432–33

SENIOR, OLIVE (1941–   )

JAMAICA

The majority of tales [in *Summer Lightning and Other Stories*] feature a female character, but the dominant perspective is that of the child, and it is evocation of the child's world, an often mysterious jumble of magic and horror, that is [Olive] Senior's main achievement. The stories deal with threats from the external world, whether physical or emotional, and the half-understood and painful conflicts within.

Each story is fitted with a narrative language integrated into the dominant point of view; often, narrative language is the speaker's language and spans the Jamaican Creole continuum, stretching its resources to the full. . . .

Senior subtly exposes the repressiveness and self-sacrifice at the core of conventional morality as it has been applied to women, and the spiritual and emotional deformities which result. Only Bekkah, in "Do Angels Wear Brassieres?," has the inner resources to challenge the stultifying restrictions imposed by authority on the girl-child; Ma Bell, in "Country Of The One Eye God," representing the final phase of life, emerges as a victim whose complicity in her oppression is largely the result of a false value system inculcated by traditional religion.

Most of the stories, then, at once portray an almost idyllic community organically connected to the Jamaican landscape and reveal the frightening inadequacies in the society for the nurturing of the maturing individual.

Evelyn O'Callaghan. JCS. 6, 2 (Spring 1988), pp. 143–44

Senior's short stories and poetry are the work of a creative talent of great sensitivity which expresses tremendous understanding of the human condition, particularly that of poor people, both rural and urban. The attempt to categorize her writing into a particular genre immediately gives one an uncomfortable feeling. For the work is knit together by a common landscape and a recurring concern for humanity. Both poetry and prose bring the country paths of her childhood and the urban experiences of her young womanhood into focus. The themes of both concern the experiences of people in these environments who represent different points along a scale of social and financial privilege.

The point of view preferred, particularly in the prose published so far, is the child's eye view. . . .

The child's eye view is not childlike. It is a clear vision through which the irrationalities of adults, the inequities in society and, from time to time, the redeeming features in the environment, are expressed. The exploitation of the child's vision allows Senior space for the imaginative forays her readers find most engaging, and for the dramatic presentation of human foibles seen from the point of view of the little person looking and feeling from under. . . .

The narrative voice in fact records children's reaction to phenomena, to their own condition, and perhaps more critically, to the adults with whom they interact. "Bright Thursdays" for example describes a small girl's discomfort as she adjusts to the strange and demanding formality in the upper-class home of a newly acquired guardian (an unacknowledged grandmother), after the easy casualness of life with a working-class mother who had been a servant to a member of the family. In "Ballad" the child eulogizes her favorite adult, Miss Rilla, a woman of whose lifestyle her step-mother heartily disapproves and on whom she expects God to exact punishment. In "Confirmation Day" the young candidate is perplexed by the symbolism of the Anglican communion into which she is being inducted, is no less perplexed by the memory of another, more dramatic initiation (by water in the village river) into a less sophisticated flock, and finally rejects what both have to offer in the supreme indictment of the Christian religion: "I'd rather be a child of someone else, being a child of god is too frightening." . . .

Other thematic interests in Senior's work include historical matters reflecting Senior's personal research into the history of the Jamaican people at home and in countries to which they have migrated, especially Panama. . . . "Nansi 'Tory" is concerned with the Afro-Jamaican, the man who did not return to Africa; "Searching for My Grandfather" is about the Jamaican who did not return from Panama. "Arrival of the Snake-Woman" explores the Jamaican situation in which ex-African and ex-Asian strive to find a place in the postcolonial society.

The village is a microcosm of Jamaica. Senior gives a believable description of the integration of a postemancipation immigrant into a rural village. Through the child's eye, the author reveals early attitudes of the races to each other, the garbled versions of history available to the unlettered poor, and the interplay of Afro-Caribbean religion and American evangelism. Without implying any evaluation, the author allows the haphazard pattern of Jamaican family life and of community living to become part of the reader's consciousness.

Velma Pollard. Callaloo. 11, 3 (Summer 1988), pp. 540–41, 543

Olive Senior writes out of a clear awareness of a conflicted life which is only by effort brought into any kind of control and clarity. She spoke recently of her childhood lived between two homes, a village, "darkskin" one and a "lightskin," middle-class environment, where she was alone and being groomed for status and advancement. In her recent volume, *Talking of Trees*, she uses as a superscription to a section of the book [Bertolt] Brecht's statement, "What kind of period is it / when to talk of trees / is almost a crime / because it implies silence / about so many horrors?" and of course this is the source of the book's title as well. Similarly, she quotes Martin Carter, "But what the leaves hear / is not what the roots ask." Her vision is often one of solitude: "Alone I will walk through the glass." In "Cockpit Country Dreams," she speaks of father and mother saying different things as "Portents of a split future." . . . Poetry becomes the balancing point, the crossroads at which all directions have to meet. . . . Senior determines life through an awareness of many directions and contradictions facing the individual, and her poetry becomes the place where at least distances and schisms can be spoken of and accepted. . . . Part of the solution to these tensions is the control which poetry gives. In "To the Madwoman in My Yard," the poet speaks with an exasperated understanding and sisterhood but in the end they are divided by the certainty in the poet that "Life Equals Control." . . . [She] draws a good deal on a sense of African culture, of ancestors who are still present and of rituals, of the African past and its relation to the contemporary experience through family stretching back to slavery; and this provides an emotional base for much of her painful poetry of isolation and displacement.

Elaine Savory Fido. In Carole Boyce Davies and Elaine Savory Fido,
eds. Out of the Kumbla: Caribbean Women and Literature
(Trenton, N. J.: Africa World Press, 1990), pp. 33–35

Contemporary West Indian poetry includes both singers and storytellers, with no tidy distinction between the ways in which they bear witness to their experience as West Indians and to the past and future of the West Indies. The range of these experiences is very wide, as are their perspectives, and the languages and forms in which they write. Diversity is one of the most significant features of contemporary West Indian poetry, in fact, and has helped ensure that these experiences become part of the present heritage of West Indians and (almost as importantly) are not appropriated by somebody else.

This heritage, the heritage of slavery, is founded in loss—or what Edward Baugh once described as "the one grief of the world." For Baugh, West Indians are connected by the difficult grace that brought them together, and by the persistent, patient love that holds them together. At the heart of his own work is a love of language, and of his land and its people; and a conviction that literature can be both its most powerful expression and what Michael Smith called "a vehicle of giving hope." . . .

Olive Senior [writes] from the center of [her] people's lives, with a sure sense of the struggle that has shaped them. Senior grew up in rural Jamaica near the Cockpit Country, the refuge of the Maroons. She is best known as a writer of short stories, including *Summer Lightning* [*and Other Stories*] and *Arrival of the Snake-Woman*, though she has also written social and historical studies. For several years she was editor of the magazine, *Jamaica Journal*, in which capacity she drew from her own heritage to bring lively attention to all aspects of Jamaican life, landscape, and language. "Ancestral Poem," from her book *Talking of Trees*, tells of this heritage, the poet's hard-won freedom from its rituals and rigors, and its continuing hold on her imagination. This is a complex poem, its juxtapositions at first relatively untroubled, but quickly becoming very disturbing, as thoughts and emotions are intersected by the menace of ingrained ritual and encased memory, and then by the violence and betrayal that are their legacy. The second stanza, in parentheses, portrays one of those moments outside any frame of resolution—a moment of fierce and indelible irrationality, represented by the confusing of her father on earth with the Father in heaven, a confusion that intensifies the disabling bewilderment of the moment and of her memory. The irony of the final line of this whole passage, where the deeply ambivalent ritual of religious confirmation provides a gesture of freedom in a language that accumulates betrayal and abstraction, is hauntingly reminiscent of one of the themes of this book, for the ambiguous syntax is generated by the local use of the word "me" in a literary context. And the final word "freedom," with its rhetorical flourish, is as much a gesture of ill-fated defiance of her heritage as a description of any new liberation. . . .

The voices in "The Mother," another of Senior's poems, speak of the life of the West Indian poor, for whom the legacy of slavery has produced new forms of disgust and despair, and whose only hope may be in bearing witness to their own lives in their own words—words full of suffering and self-hatred and the sad ironies of self-conscious pretense and pathos.

J. Edward Chamberlin. *Come Back to Me My Language: Poetry and the West Indies* (Urbana: University of Illinois Press, 1993), pp. 248–51

The stories of *Summer Lightning*, [Senior] says, focus on the Jamaica of her childhood and emphasize the problems and perspectives of poor rural children, while those in *Arrival of the Snake-Woman* are more expansive, involving characters "of different races and classes," rich and poor, in both rural and urban settings. But both collections are explorations of Jamaican experience and identity within a larger network of competing cultures. . . . An awareness of that enveloping, sometimes corrosive larger culture is never very far in the background of Senior's stories precisely because the problematic relationship between the isolated, enclosed societies of the West Indies and the wider world is such a pervasive fact of Caribbean life. . . .

The major themes of *Summer Lightning*—the search for personal and cultural identities, the nurturing role of the West Indian mother in Creole society, the problematic and complex relationships between traditional ways and the wider world—are continued and expanded in *Arrival of the Snake-Woman*. "The View from the Terrace" takes up the question of identity most directly, focusing as it does on the lifelong struggle of its protagonist, Mr. Barton, to associate himself with what Senior has called "the colonial superstructure" that "determined everything." From early childhood, Barton has longed for "a world that somehow seemed rooted on its axis" and finds it in the literature of "daffodils and the downs and snow and damsels in distress"—the imagined world of England. Cultivated by teachers and "a succession of English bosses . . . who appreciated . . . his liking for things 'civilized,' i.e. English," he develops a distaste for black people (although he is himself darker than his first wife) and a deep-seated discomfort for his native country. But trips to Europe make him aware that he is not really English, either, and his second marriage, to an "incredibly vulgar" white Englishwoman, ends in divorce. . . .

The idea of home—where it is, what it is—is never very far from the center of Senior's attention. Barton's "European" house in "The View from the Terrace" is divided from Miss Vie's "Jamaican" hut by a deep ravine; in "The Tenantry of Birds," Senior attempts to bridge that gulf, bringing the two kinds of homes, with all their iconic associations, together. The "tenantry" of the title is a "rather bedraggled," somewhat wild-looking bird tree growing in an otherwise very formal, English garden belonging to a wealthy Kingston couple. For the wife, the tree represents a small part of the countryside where she spent many pleasant summers as a child. For her husband Philip, a university professor and political activist, the tree is an "unsightly" excrescence which he would like to cut down. Nolene, the wife, is particularly fond of watching "the star boarders . . . the pecharies" drive out the "rough, uncouth, chattering and uncaring" kling-klings when they attempt to take over. This detail provides the story with its governing metaphor and Nolene with the example she later needs to take similar action of her own. As Philip becomes more involved in politics (and acquires a black mistress), the marriage disintegrates. He sends Nolene to Miami with their children "for safety's sake," as he puts it. One of the most delicate points Senior makes is that Philip, who, like his wife, is a light-skinned Jamaican of the privileged social class, does not immerse himself in island politics because of any innate sensitivity to island culture. His political activity is motivated more by ambition and ego than by sympathetic understanding; and his behavior toward his wife is closely akin to that of master to servant—or of colonial power to colony.

Richard F. Patteson. *Ariel.* 24, 1 (January 1993), pp. 16, 23–25

SEPAMLA, SIPHO (1932–   )

SOUTH AFRICA

Over the past few years, there has been an upsurge in the publication of English poetry in South Africa . . . and a very important contribution has been by black poets, such as [Mongane] Serote, [Oswald] Mtshali, and others, to whom English is a second language. A new and already mature poetic voice, that of [Sipho] Sepamla, now rings out with an enviable sureness of diction [in the collection *Hurry Up to It!*]. Publication within South Africa probably obviates the shrillness that sometimes mars the poems of political exiles such as [Keorapetse] Kgositsile, but has not prevented Sepamla from mercilessly exposing the injustices of the white regime. . . .

The very first poem ("To Whom It May Concern") sets the tone. It is an ironical and Brechtian statement on the tragic situation of the black in South Africa—so tragic that it verges on the ridiculous; to keep his sanity he has to cultivate humor, black in both senses. . . . He has learned to accept the insults and indignities, but only for now, for the anger is always there, and the smoldering revolt: "God! where can the end lie / If not in me / I want you to trample the world once more / And I shall make it in your image." In an adaptation of a poem by the Colored Afrikaans poet Adam Small ("Feeling Small"), Sepamla exults over the white man for acting out of fear.

What is apparent is the directness and simplicity of the language, lit up with poetic insights, and the vividness of the very sparingly used images: "[his head] sways to the left and to the right / To allow only truths to pass." There are also a number of tender love poems, including one especially fine one in an e. e. cummings manner, expressing the awe and wonder of love in a stutter: "I am / None them they others / For I am / I know / Feel when I feel / Yours" ("In love").

Barend J. Toerien. *BA.* Summer 1976, pp. 707–8

Sipho Sepamla's collection [of poems], *The Soweto I Love*, is particularly interesting because his is an inside . . . view of the black struggle, suffering, and hopes for the future. It is no accident that a simple tabulation of the words used in his poems and their meanings would invariably have to do with fear, anger, stench, and humiliation. Thus I counted the following words and phrases which all link up, one way or the other, with the concept of fear: *terror, fleeing, cowed, scared, alarm, frantic, scare, cowardly, hounded, panic, scurry and scuttle, tremble.* . . .

Upon first reading his poetry, one tends to think of it as simple and naive. . . . A second and more thorough scrutiny teaches that the simplicity is singularly deceptive and hides a deeper, more profound meaning. The terror of his South African landscape is poignantly portrayed precisely through this simplicity of language: the at times inverted sentence structure further creates the impression of an awkwardness with the English language. Only when he abandons his special style, however, does he really sound awkward, as for example in the poem "I Saw This Morning" where the very direct "he was crippled by" and "he was wheeling round his teacher" jar. This simplicity, coupled with a staccato English and fairyesque quality—the Big Bad Wolf image—is hauntingly portrayed in "A Child Dies." His poem "Like a Hippo" must at first glance appear to the Western reader like the work of a child, an impression which quickly gives way to an understanding of the greater symbolism in the poem—again deceptively simple, like some of the oral stories with a tremendous sting in the tail. . . . The Hippo becomes the state = Afrikanerdom = apartheid.

Sepamla has hitherto successfully avoided writing "poetry conscripted for the victims." Like the Afro-American artist, the poet in South Africa can, to a large extent, function as a "guerrilla fighter who can talk Black English and ignore accepted aesthetics." There is after all the fundamental realization that while the language of the black artist in South Africa is Western, his idiom is definitely non-Western (black, if one wishes).

The poet's anger is contained with poise and does not spill over into a bitterness. . . . He seldom allows himself a comic ironic stance, yet when he does exploit humor as a device, the effect is clear, as for example in "Shop Assistant" which evokes images of another South African poet, Adam Small, who writes in Afrikaans, and his lampooning of white women in the poem "Oppie Parara." . . . Sepamla's "Civilization Aha" falls short of the reference to "Western Syphilization" by the Afro-American poet Jon Eckels. Although oral in tone at times, his poetry draws its strength from the urban proletariat environment which spawned him, the poet.

[Vernon] February. In Eldred Durosimi Jones, ed.
African Literature Today. 10 (1979), pp. 256–57

[*The Soweto I Love*] was written immediately after the harrowing events in Soweto in 1976 and these events still have Sepamla in their grip. In some of the poems, such as "I Saw This Morning," he describes and articulates the terror which the riots brought in their wake. In others, for instance "At the Dawn of Another Day" he gives an account of the actual uprising, and, with emphasis in printed pattern, explains the causes and aims. . . .

Besides the Soweto uprisings, he writes of suicide, murder, and rape in prison; and Robben Island is the metaphor for the authorities' attempts to break the black man's spirit. He has nothing but contempt for the white way of life, and he expresses pride in the action of the youth of today. The careful poet of the telling phrase, the subtle and witty lines, and well-constructed verse has given way to a writer standing too close to events, sick with abhorrence, and giving way to a need to let the words pour out of him. . . .

[Sepamla's novel *The Root Is One*] takes place during a six-day period in Johnstown, a black township whose citizens are about to be forcibly removed, and its adjacent white town, Bergersdorp. Berger is a phonetic spelling of *burger*, Afrikaans for citizen. The story concerns Juda, a young man who is involved first in organizing a strike and then in attempts to stop the removal. He is the son of a man known to be a "sell-out" (someone who plays along with the authorities), and who, in the course of a story, is killed by a mob when he advises them not to fight against the removal. Juda is terrified of arrest and through the six days we watch his moral disintegration, ending in a betrayal of his friend Spiwo to the authorities and his own suicide.

The Root Is One is a novel of unrelieved gloom and pain. It opens with the "dim, dull dawning" of the first day and a dream of "a terrible thing which is going to happen soon." It ends on the sixth day in a night of faint light cast by a horn-shaped moon which looked like a septic wound. The deepening night swallows up "the whole act and the people of Johnstown," and as they go away "unburdened their hearts of one's deeds; as they gesticulated in their talking, they hurled away the root of their agony."

This is not the work of the confident, witty, and satiric Sepamla who celebrated the purpose of living in his early poems. It is instead the poet of the 1977 volume *The Soweto I Love*, whose mood is one of total pessimism. Life is a nightmare. The brave who act against oppression, like the young man Spiwo, are arrested, tortured and perhaps killed, and those who succumb to fear and betray, like Juda, experience the same fate in their dreams. A crowd collects around the house in which Juda has hanged himself. . . . Sepamla provides no answer to the question which he poses in the novel. For the moment endurance is all. The pain which the people must endure must be "carried in the hearts of the living for days on end. The pain of suffering is like mist: it settles on every home," as one of the crowd puts it.

The Root Is One makes painful reading. Sepamla provides no relief, not in the theme, not in the story he wishes to tell, nor in the literary handling of the material. It is the work of a man in chains who has suffered so long that his vision of escape and freedom is dead.

Ursula A. Barnett. A Vision of Order
(London: Sinclair Browne, 1983), pp. 63–65, 156–57

Sipho Sepamla is a writer whose poetry makes the reader see and think: he has a gift for the precise, incisive stroke, and he knows how to find the words best suited to the description of his aspirations and those of his fellow blacks. As a satirical poet, he has a solid sense of irony and humor. As a lyric poet, he can be both fiery and tender; and he can rise above the demands of the "situation" to express the most universal human emotions.

Sepamla's activities are many and various. In his early forties, he is a man of the theater, a critic, and a poet. He also edits two literary reviews, *New Classic* and *Sketsh*. In the former he publishes both poets and short-story writers, white and black; in the second, more popular in appearance and content, he provides his readers with a review of the main theatrical events as well as extensive extracts from new plays. His editorials are inspired essentially by the daily life of the South African black, and it would be true to say that after the departure of [Oswald] Mtshali and [Mongane] Serote, along with [James] Matthews, he became one of the principal driving forces in his community. . . .

It can be seen that Sepamla's deep sense of commitment in no way interferes with his qualities as a poet. But this commitment, as unambiguous as it may be, extends well beyond the frontiers of his own community. For here is a man who is convinced that the South Africa of tomorrow will be built with the help of all its inhabitants. His poems constantly place the emphasis, not only on the common biological identity shared by all the people of his country, but also on the common destiny that binds all South Africans.

Jacques Alvarez-Pereyre. The Poetry of Commitment in South Africa
(London: Heinemann, 1984), pp. 215–16, 223

The images of black consciousness in Sepamla are not abstractions. The mere fact that a South African writer is against apartheid implies that he is against racial discrimination. If he happens to be a black writer then the motive becomes more pronounced because the black man in South Africa is on the lowest rung of the ladder of political acceptance. Moreover, Sepamla adds another dimension to this general aim when he concentrates on the tragic events that took place in the black township of Soweto. . . .

The wordiness in this poetry . . . is ameliorated by the subtle irony that is the foundation in Sepamla's art. He applies it to link history with [recent] events. There are no rough edges although it may be expected that such adherence to reality is prone to exhibit unpolished, scraggly, raw materials derived from memorable incidents. He definitely illustrates that "every poet is molded by his age, by the great events or Great Event that took place during his impressionable years." It is the intricate web of life that exploded in Soweto in 1976 which is the great event that informs this collection. . . .

Black consciousness is therefore illustrated as both a way of life and an attitude of mind in the poetry of Sepamla. The attitude of mind is reflected in the evocation of rioting men, women, and children who wish to assert their dignity and value systems. This evocation is typical of the eloquence of Soweto poetry which uses the imagery of the streets to incorporate its theme. . . .

When children become bold enough to show signs of rejecting the value systems that seek to make them strangers in their own country, it is an optimistic sign. The description of this incident justifies Sepamla as an eloquent poet who uses the eloquence of the streets to codify his poetic diction.

Ezenwa-Ohaeto. PA. 140 (1986), pp. 18, 20

A Ride on the Whirlwind downplays . . . sociological and historical concerns . . . without losing sight of them entirely. The action begins two days after the uprising with the arrival at Park Station of the guerrilla Mzi, sent by the Resistance Movement in Dar es Salaam to kill a brutal black policeman, Andries Batata. He meets with Uncle Ribs Mbambo, his contact man, and through him the student leader Mandla, who with a small group of followers is directing resistance in Soweto from the house of Sisi Ida. Mandla and Mzi form an alliance and together blow up a police station: Mzi subsequently assassinates Batata. Several of Mandla's followers, as well as Sisi Ida, are arrested after an accident with explosives at the house. Descriptions of their torture follow. The novel ends with Mandla fleeing into exile and Mzi attempting to persuade a white helper to drive him to Swaziland. . . .

[In the novel] a closeness to and identification with the action on the part of [Sepamla] can sometimes be noticed. The difference of views expressed by the characters does not, finally, constitute any basic challenge to the ideological thrust with which the reader is left. In *A Ride on the Whirlwind*, there is one incident of a far-ranging criticism being made of the organized resistance to the Sophiatown removals in the 1950s; but the person who makes them, the she-been owner Noah Witbaatjie . . . very quickly turns out to be a police spy. The [novel], therefore, [explicates and naturalizes] the inevitability and correctness of black political aspirations. While readers will identify with these aspirations, the manner in which liberation is supposed to happen and the way South African society is imagined are still worthy of attention.

Kelwyn Sole. *RAL*. 19, 1 (Spring 1988), pp. 67–70

Sipho Sepamla has been quietly building a reputation as one of the most percep-tive, ironic, and sensitive South African poets. He may lack the verbal outrage of Mongane Wally Serote or the violence of Mafika Paschal Gwala, but he cer-tainly exhibits a poetic quality undebased by his experiences in South Africa. *From Goré to Soweto* captures his peculiar reality with telling accuracy. . . .

Sepamla's observations on South Africa and other parts of the world serve as pedestals for an incisive condemnation of the dehumanization he has felt. The poetic portrayal of reality is achieved through the use of an ironic vision which enables him to imbue his poetry with succinct imagery and to engineer a reaction appropriate to the events described, as in the collection's very first poem. . . . A similar alienation or oppression of spirit emerges in "Wattville," with its implication of life as a prison for black South Africans: "we would be village / if only we were not crammed / into a crooked square mile / drawn by men drunk with power." Familiar thematic issues in South African verse are made fresh via subjection to his poetic furnace, as in "I love Soweto." . . .

The poet regards all natural human emotions as debased due to the debasement of life itself. An enormous bitterness forms his poems but is admirably controlled, as in "Moment Beyond Now." . . . Still, the reality of death is the reality of South Africa, with its constant riots. In "May Day," dedi-cated to the memory of dying youths, Sepamla warns "What we are saying so often / Some comfort can be gained from the trigger / But the real shit lies beyond / On the count of tomorrow's yield." That ominous warning also con-tains a hope that injustice will be eliminated in the poet's homeland, but this hope does not cause him to ignore the violence in real life. . . . A society which consumes its young, the poet implies, is making preparations for doom; but his special sorrow is that the extermination is directed only toward black babies, a primitive and savage practice for a society which prides itself on its civilized nature. The uncertainty of life effected by such savagery is illustrated in "28 July," where the speaker's loss of his home becomes a metaphor for his society's loss of the land: "I stand frozen in my house / Occupied territory / Taken over like the land yesteryears / No one tells me anything / but to keep my hands above my head." It is thus not surprising that in "A Man for the Land" the poet confirms that, despite the tragedy of their existence, the people will survive.

Ezenwa-Ohaeto. WLT. 64, 1 (Winter 1990), p. 184

SEROTE, MONGANE (WALLY) (1944–   )

SOUTH AFRICA

[With *Tsetlo*, Mongane Serote] emerges clearly as the most gifted, original, and intense of the black [South African] poets, and he penetrates the South African situation (and, indeed, the universal situation of the oppressed in ferment) in a way which I think is quite new in our literature.

His emotional burden is neither guilt nor anger—though these feelings are material to his vision—but a profoundly humane grief. . . .

It is necessary to make this bald affirmation because I want to guard against seeming to make the wrong emphasis when I claim that Serote's poetic sensibilities and passions have carried his political vision forward to a point morally in advance of anyone else's—in the South African context at least.

It takes boldness to invoke a vision of nemesis, yet many have done so—most whites reacting in a blur of fear or masochistic relish, most blacks in a red haze of revenge-lust. In either case the actors in the prophecy are dehumanized. Serote is exceptional in holding to a vision as direly purposive as any, but which sheds no shading of human complexity: on either side, people are both dangerous and desperately vulnerable—and retain an almost unbearable claim on that heart of his. . . . He shows, by a piling up of significant details from publicized events and from his own ranging observations of black lives misshapen by deprivation, humiliation and violence, what it is in our situation that could—perhaps must—eventually erupt in actions he starkly symbolizes by Lod Airport. But he does not gloss over the fact that such actions would be atrocities, as destructive of the doers' spirit as of the victims' flesh. At the end of "Introit," a poem on the bloody mission of emancipation, he says with apocalyptic despair: "I wonder where I'll cleanse my hands."

I know of no one else whose grief extends in this way and not only over the oppressed (he grieves for their violence and depravity as well as their sufferings in these "civilized times"), but also over those who have to be overthrown and over their blood-corrupted executioners.

Lionel Abrahams. Rand Daily Mail. June 17, 1974. Repub. in Michael
Chapman, ed. Soweto Poetry (Johannesburg: McGraw-Hill, 1982), pp. 74–75

[*No Baby Must Weep*] concerns the trajectory of the personal development of the subject/narrator of the poem. Starting from the earliest experiences that shape his subject's life, Serote is determined to show that none of the influences is random or chance, but rather that they embody all the contradictions of the circumstances and times in which the narrator is living. Further, the poem is inseparable from the current moment of the narrator's mental and emotional state, which is itself laden down with layer upon layer of turmoil inherited from the past.

The poetry itself seems to stem from the endless striving of the narrator for an understanding of the burden bequeathed to the current moment by the past. Serote tirelessly traces the connection between his subject's current anguish, the suffering of the past, and what there may be to hope for in the future.

Serote is not primarily concerned with writing about the overt political repression of the black man in South Africa. Instead he assumes this level, and leaves it behind in his search for some essential *meaning and significance* in the experience of dispossession and oppression. Serote journeys through the images and representations of the shared cultural experience of oppression of the black man in South Africa. It is in this sense that Serote's statement is a political work, an affirmation that there is meaning and significance behind the seemingly repetitive patterns of denigration that black South Africans have endured. Serote is determined to plumb the depths which hide in everyday realities, the greater realities that consume the past and embody the future. . . .

Serote's poem involves the reader in personally experiencing something of the pain inherent in traversing [the] distance between masses, history, and the personal realities of an individual subject. The irony and the pain in traversing this distance lies in the extraordinary loneliness that the subject, alone, has to endure once he has perceived the extent of the distance to be covered before liberation and the resolution of some of the contradictions of existence.

In this work Serote has isolated the essential political and psychological reality of Africa today, the double bind that in one breath separates the individual from the masses through the culture of oppression/exploitation and at the same time renders the individual's future in separation from the masses inconceivable.

Alex Levumo. Staffrider. 2, 1 (March 1979). Repub. in Michael Chapman,
ed. Soweto Poetry (Johannesburg: McGraw-Hill, 1982), pp. 76–77

Serote's poems, like [Oswald] Mtshali's, were first published in the literary journals *Purple Renoster, Bolt, New Coin,* and *Contrast,* during 1971 and 1972. Again it was *Purple Renoster* which introduced him, with what was in fact the first poem by a black contributor in these journals. It made its impact immediately, with its title "What's in this Black 'Shit'" and its graphically outspoken condemnation of white inhumanity to black. It is included in Serote's first collection, *Yakhal'inkomo,* also published by Renoster Books, in 1972. . . .

Critics naturally compared his work with that of Mtshali and generally found him the more accomplished poet, though it was felt that the work was very uneven. The title of the collection represents the cry of cattle at the slaughterhouse, as Serote explains in the preface and again in the August 1973 issue of

Bolt. It is based on a story told him by a sculptor friend who saw people kill a cow near a kraal, and in the kraal were cattle looking on and he heard them cry. . . . Serote compares the sound with the music of a tenor saxophone player, expressing the same cry of fear and rage. . . .

Tsetlo, his second collection, was published by Ad. Donker in Johannesburg in 1974. Whereas *Yakhal'inkomo* was the agonizing cry of the cattle watching their kind being slaughtered, *Tsetlo*, more subtly, is the tiny bird with the "weird sweet whistle which it plays while it flies from branch to branch in the bush, luring people to follow it. . . . And then it stops. It may lead you to sweet honey, to a very dangerous snake or to something very unusual." Serote's concept of the world has widened and the mood has deepened. Sadness is still predominant, but it has become firmer. He no longer speaks of returning to the bosom of Alexandra and lying amid the rubble, but mourns its passing and remembers it, in "Amen Alexandra," like " . . . a thunder clap / that froze in our hearts." There is less talk of tears and desolation. . . .

His probing continues in his subsequent two volumes, *No Baby Must Weep* and *Behold Mama, Flowers*. . . .

Serote's quest for truth and meaning takes on a new impetus in exile. He has walked far, and hopes that the road will lead him somewhere other than into nightmare, that it "can whisper wisdom" to him. . . . *No Baby Must Weep* is a single long poem on a theme of contrast between the darkness of life and the bright hope of birth. . . . The poem is strongly autobiographical. The first pages tell of his childhood in the township; this theme recurs, but later events take place within the poet himself. The world is real only insofar as he experiences it, and he expresses his experience symbolically. The mother becomes Africa; and the poet, if he can succeed in throwing off all physical trappings, even that of fear, will become one with the earth, with Africa. Black life is represented by a river, deep and dark, where the horrors of life and death form only little ripples on the surface. The sea represents a free Africa into which the poet longs to emerge. . . .

Neither this poem, nor the long title poem in the collection *Behold Mama, Flowers*, is entirely successful. . . . [There] are . . . too many banal passages and repetitions of phrases and moods that become monotonous. In *Behold Mama, Flowers*, Serote loses sight of the theme introduced in the foreword, of a child seeing pieces of human flesh and bones floating down a river and saying "behold mama, flowers," though he picks it up again at the end where the agony is tinged with hope. . . . The remaining poems in this collection are dedicated to various writers and friends. Most of the poems in this collection were written in the United States, but some were written in Botswana, where he was living at the time of [this] writing.

Ursula A. Barnett. *A Vision of Order* (London: Sinclair Browne, 1983), pp. 55–60

The most obvious problem that faces the reader in *To Every Birth Its Blood* is the relation between the two parts of the novel. The second part's sudden shift from first-person narration to third-person narration, the time shift, and the shift of focus to a set of characters referred to but never central in the first part, are initially disconcerting and bewildering. But gradually, on closer examination, significant patterns begin to emerge.

In relation to the second part, the first part of the novel reveals itself as the story of defeat and despair. This section is seen through the eyes of ex-journalist and unsuccessful actor, Tsi Molope. Personally defeated, Tsi registers the world as defeated too. For example, the members of his immediate family (the Molopes), are broken or damaged: one brother, Fix, has been detained; another brother, Ndo, is irrationally violent and constantly abuses his wife; his parents are old, empty and silenced, having fought to make a future for their children, and failed; and his sister Mary, initially bewildered by a frightening world and misguided by trashy escape fantasies, falls pregnant and is rejected by her parents.

More generally, the bitter realities of black experience in an apartheid society are felt with painful intensity. His home, Alexandra, is itself seen as a symbol of the defeat of the black man: it is the "Dark City," the polar opposite of the "Golden City" which is the symbol of the white man's success; and the two are understood as integrally related. There are the degrading incidents, too, which spell defeat: the permit raid, the humiliating visit to the police station to obtain a new permit, the insults of the liftman in Tsi's newspaper building—all the "shit" the black man resents, but has to put up with.

In the same way . . . the first section is pervaded by the uncertainties and fears surrounding Fix's detention, as well as the activity-in-exile of Tsi's friends, Anka, Boykie, Themba, and Tuki. Furthermore, the arbitrariness with which state power is employed is underlined by the central incident which dominates the first half of the novel. Responding to the news of further detentions, and reflecting on the way he could no longer bring himself to observe the "tumor" and "rot" of apartheid society as a reporter, Tsi thinks back to the experience of naked police intimidation and brutality that has fundamentally changed his life. This incident is related as a flashback, a point which tends to be missed in the complex interweavings of Tsi's thought processes. He recalls how, on the way back from a newspaper assignment in the Transkei, he and his photographer friend Boykie were stopped by police, physically assaulted, and held in solitary confinement for a week. According to Boykie, who had been driving, the ostensible reason for this police action was that there had been a dead body lying in the road. This incident galvanizes Boykie into furious hatred and opposition to the system, but Tsi's response is to feel undermined and emasculated: for him the incident serves to focus the black person's vulnerability and impotence. This is underscored by the response of Tsi's white-run newspaper. The incident is immediately made into a "story"—an insignificant story, moreover, "in some corner, on page two" in which Tsi is also racially categorized as a "black reporter." This is the point from which it becomes impossible for Tsi to report the "terrible township images," and from which his sense of defeat and despair takes over. It is thus inaccurate to respond to Tsi as simply a "feckless drunkard," as reviewers have tended to do. Rather, one should see that this series of traumatic events has wrenched him out of a relatively comfortable and stable position of social adjustment, and precipitated a severe state of psychological weariness and *anomie*.

Part one of the novel presents, through Tsi, an anatomy of a people's defeat. This defeat involves a world of experience which separates people from each other in their individual suffering, and is thus accurately portrayed through an isolated individual consciousness. From an epistemological viewpoint, what is captured here is the psychological response to a battering external world: it is an exploration of the way in which the environment acts upon and damages individuals. And it is precisely this subject-object relationship which is to be reversed in the second part of the novel.

Dorian Barboure. In M. J. Daymond, J. U. Jacobs, and Margaret Lenta, eds.
Momentum: On Recent South African Writing (Pietermaritzburg,
South Africa: University of Natal Press, 1984), pp. 172–74

In Serote's poetry traditional motifs do not occur, as in much of West African literature, as vestiges of a largely bygone culture, standing in contradistinction to and now being superseded by and wrestling with Western culture, but as examples of a living tradition, which the African growing up in the city takes in as completely as he absorbs Western culture. Serote's poetry, despite its urban setting, blends Western influences and traditional elements.

"Hell, Well, Heaven" is Serote's definitive statement in the "Who am I, Where did I come from, Where am I going" idiom. This poem sets the tone for the rest of his early poems, which have been collected in *Yakhal'inkomo* and *Tsetlo*. It describes the reawakening of the black people following the suppression of black cultural and political expression after the Sharpeville massacre of 1960. The poem celebrates the renaissance of the late 1960s, when a new generation of black artists, sculptors, musicians, dramatists, and poets blossomed throughout the country, against the tide of the most repressive legislation ever enacted by the South African racist regime. . . .

In "Alexandra," which first appeared in the last issue of *Classic*, the township is personified and presented in the guise of an unloving, uncaring mother. The mother image has reference to origin, to roots. Serote traces his roots to Alexandra township: "And Alexandra, / My beginning was knotted to you, / Just like you knot my destiny." The statement is intended to counteract government efforts to remove every African from the cities to resettle them in some impoverished "Homeland" or Bantustan. He is not renouncing his traditions, as such. He is simply asserting his right to live where he was born and became what he has become. . . .

At this stage in his development Serote was searching for an adequate vehicle to convey his African personality, for a poetic form that was consistent with black consciousness. This quest yielded its results in "Ofaywatcher-Blackwoman-Eternity," which appeared in 1974 in James Mathews's *Black Voices Shout*. "Ofaywatcher-Blackwoman-Eternity" is a tribute to black womanhood, after the manner of [Léopold Sédar] Senghor's "Black Woman." This poem represents an advance in Serote's technique. Where before his use of traditional oral motifs had been almost unconscious, he now handles them with conscious and consummate skill. The poem opens with a note of applause for black women: "Silent like a leaf falls to earth." His gestures manifest veneration, as when he describes his actions: "I bend, I bow my head." As in the opening line of "City Johannesburg," Serote's mode of address, which this time, he sustains to the end, is in the manner of *izibongo*. . . .

Towards the end of "Ofaywatcher-Blackwoman-Eternity," Serote strikes a note of celebration through his reference to dance and music: "You who dances to drums / Who dances to horns." The instruments used are traditional. They are in tune with the traditional form of the poem and attune the reader's mind to those virtues which are traditionally associated with women: their sympathy, patience, understanding, and endurance. "Ofaywatcher," a figure which appears in several of Serote's other early poems, derives from black American culture and refers to a black person who has set himself or herself up as the watchdog of the community, a role Serote has taken upon himself through his poetry.

Mbulelo Vizikhungo Mzamane. In Landeg White and Tim Couzens, eds.
Literature and Society in South Africa (New York: Longman, 1984), pp. 152–55

In spite of the disappointments recorded in *Tsetlo*, there is enough to justify the hope of a change, the responsibility for which lies in the hands of the younger generation, the children and the young men and women of the 1970s. They will not be afraid to address the white man on equal terms; they will not fear to hate the authors of their centuries-old suffering. They will regain the courage of their ancestors and hear from across the seas the message of liberation addressed to them by their brothers who have gone into exile in Europe and the United States. There would be nothing new here that was not already spoken of by [Oswald] Mtshali, except that Serote says directly, in his own voice, and *clearly*, what Mtshali hinted at or expressed by means of a fable. Serote—and this is the chief characteristic of black consciousness—dares to look the white man in the eye and, especially, to speak to him plainly.

He is, however, less anxious to speak to the white man or to reveal to him the "hidden face" of South African society than to speak to his fellow Africans, not in the language of the political militant, like Stokely Carmichael for instance, but by trying to bring about the cultural and psychological transformation that must necessarily precede political action proper. If we add that his work also shows his rejection of the white liberals, the prophecy of a retributive violence, and a stress on what is and is not to be done, we can say that Serote is the voice of the black consciousness movement, minus its didacticism but with the lyrical power of the poet. . . .

[If] we seek a poem to serve as a banner for black consciousness, a poem which bears the mark of the new relationship between the young generation of Africans and the whites, we must turn to "What's in this Black 'Shit.'" This poem is an expression of self-assertion and courage, in the metaphorical form suggested by the title: Serote implicitly returns to the dialogue idea only to leap immediately from servile or forced submission to the orders of the white man to categorical refusal. In both cases, there is denial of the other man's words; but in the second the roles are reversed, the only way, say the followers of black consciousness, for the African to regain his dignity and make an impression on the white man.

Jacques Alvarez-Pereyre. *The Poetry of Commitment in South Africa*
(London: Heinemann, 1984), pp. 190–91

What is Mongane Serote telling us? There are words and images that he uses and frequently returns to. Again, he does this relentlessly, compulsively, as if to extract the last drop of meaning from them. He returns to them like someone who repeats a call so that he may hear it echo in the hills, several times, to measure its quality and reach. . . .

In a sense they weave themselves into a refrain: a sad one, that sums up for us the anguish, the fear, the monstrous wound, that is this life, this odyssey. "Eyes are broken"; "mothers stare their babies in the eye"; "street lights look like wet eyes"; "the horrors of my stomach throb to my eyes"; "my heart bleeds through my eyes"; "droplets of tears as big as eyes"; "Thick footsteps pulsate on black shadows"; "the dark shadow wraps my heart"; "a bloody (Saturday) night whose shadows fall like blinking eyes"; "waste of resettlements screaming, forming ridged shadows over his body" (i.e. of a murdered man); "her eyes fell a cold shadow on my heart." . . .

These repeated images are turned around and inside out in a manner that quite clearly portrays a poet searching for meaning, up and down the vertical and horizontal planes. A man who has, since he was a child, been groping instinctively for a father figure, a mother's warmth and the intimacy of her body odor, for her hand, for a brother's reassurance. Even as a man, he seeks to reconnect with the mother. But, as in so much poetry of the black world, the mother figure does not stay at the physical level of femininity for long. Soon she takes on a symbolic meaning: she is by turn the biological mother, the protective maternal principle, love, Alexandra, Africa. This is particularly reminiscent of Léopold Sédar Senghor's poetry in its Négritude essence, of African-American poetry going as far back as the Langston Hughes of the 1920s.

Mongane Serote lives in exile in Botswana. But he will always return to his Alexandra in spirit, his beginnings. In *Yakhal'inkomo*, the township comes across raw, dusty, with its furrows alive with maggots. Later, in *Tsetlo*, Alexandra is still enveloped by the dust kicked up by traffic and bulldozers, but it is now refined in the memory, by an act of poetry. It is a "cruel memory," the memory of teardrops "as big as eyes."

Es'kia [Ezekiel] Mphahlele. The English Academy Review. 3 (1985), pp. 67–68

Mongane Wally Serote is . . . one of South Africa's leading poets of the post-Sharpeville generation, at a time when the rest of Africa has for the most part achieved independence, while South Africa's black population continues to bear the brunt of the apartheid policies of the white minority. Such has been the effect of these policies that the older generation of black writers had been virtually erased from the cultural memory of their people, through bannings and exile, when Serote began writing. Serote himself has described this: "When I started writing, it was as if there had never been writers before in my country. By the time I learned to write, many people—[Es'kia Mphahlele, Keorapetse] Kgositsile, Mazisi Kunene, Dennis Brutus—had left the country and were living in exile. We could not read what they had written, so it was as if we were starting right from the beginning." It was during this period that black consciousness came into being as the black South Africans' response to, and rejection of, white political and cultural domination. Like Négritude, with which it has close affinities in many respects, black consciousness sought to foster pride among black South Africans in their own cultural heritage and creativity and to establish an independent and free identity. Serote's own work is an expression of this movement.

Writing nearly forty years later than [Léopold Sédar] Senghor, in a situation in which colonizer and colonized have none of the closeness that Senghor felt bound him so closely to France in spite of their disagreement over the question of colonialism, their whole attitude to culture is worlds apart. Where Senghor sees the relationship between African and European culture in the form of equivalent and equal parallels, Serote sees it in the form of ironic contrast. The result for Serote is an emphasis on realism and the comment it makes on the relations between black and white in South Africa, while Senghor functions in the realm of idealism.

Clive Wake. RAL. 16, 1 (Spring 1985), p. 15

Mongane Serote, in his first novel, *To Every Birth Its Blood*, hurls himself literally into the pool of blood which envelops revolutionary South Africa. The novel is inspired in the first place by the Soweto student uprisings of 1976. Building on this revolutionary climate, Serote extends the battle to a people's war which must finally overthrow the apartheid system. Like [Alex] La Guma, Serote chooses his own suburb in Johannesburg, Alexandra Township, to depict the destruction of the minority regime. By choosing a place he knows well, the writer familiarizes the reader with the oppression of South Africa in a firsthand way. . . .

Mongane Serote's achievement in his first novel is remarkable. Themes related to the apartheid system are often difficult to present in an interesting, nondogmatic, and imaginative manner. The context of South African literature demands highly skilled writers, and Serote demonstrates in *To Every Birth Its Blood* that he is a bona fide member of such a group. His intimate and authentic understanding of the sociopolitical environment of black and white South Africa makes his story believable. He has the uncanny ability to extend South African writing beyond the mere reportage of current injustices to a realm in which many progressive South Africans are engaged in revolutionary struggle. He demonstrates that he is both an observer and participant in this ongoing human drama. We are not simply assaulted by the cruel, bare facts of South African life; these facts are interwoven beautifully with the authentic dialogue and realistic setting. The characters, both black and white, are real; and their demands are carved clearly on the reader's mind. We feel that we know the dilemma of Tsi Molope and David Horowitz, the white liberal journalist, and that we can fully understand the reasons for the revolutionary action that will bring the required change. Through Serote's observant eye and behind-the-scenes knowledge, we are given a magnificent tour of how meticulous revolutionaries plan their actions. As a poet first, the novelist provides us with stark, concrete imagery and metaphor, and he succeeds to orchestrate a flowing, rhythmic tale of woe and triumph. In the use of plaintive and defiant music by Miriam Makeba, John Coltrane, Hugh Masekela, and Dollar Brand, Serote not only melds artistic forms, but also pursues his historical theme of enslavement and defiance of the black man in Africa and America.

Cecil Abrahams. *Matatu*. 2, 3–4 (1988), pp. 34–35, 39–40

To Every Birth Its Blood "delves into the heart and soul of a nation heading for disaster and creates an awareness of why it is inevitable." Like his predecessors of the 1950s, Serote extensively examines the issues of economic deprivation and political oppression to illustrate this impending disaster. . . .

What distinguishes *To Every Birth Its Blood* . . . is the novel's uniquely dispassionate portrayal of underground political activity and the harassment of blacks by the police. The revolution that Serote anticipates in the title poem of *Behold Mama, Flowers*, is realized in the second part of the novel. The suffering, frustration, desperation, and despair that dominate the first part of the novel give way to the ever-growing influence of a political organization simply referred to as the Movement. Although the role of the collective is emphasized in relation to the activities of the Movement, Serote's method, unlike that of [Alex] La Guma's [*In the Fog of the Seasons' End*], is conventional. . . . In other sections of the book, the extensive influence of the Movement is compared to the wind and the sea. This all-embracing imagery and symbolism have much to do with Serote's background as a poet. In [Peter] Abrahams's *Night of Their Own* and La Guma's *In the Fog*, language is deceptive rather than poetic.

Serote does not romanticize revolution. Death in the struggle is portrayed in a calm and humane manner. Two of the outstanding members of the movement, Oupa (the protagonist's nephew) and Mandla, are captured and killed. The protagonist's attitude to their deaths, particularly to that of Oupa, is credible, moving, and unsensationalized. . . . Towards the end of the novel, the protagonist leaves South Africa for Botswana. He has hope for the future of blacks inside South Africa although the movement has been partly fragmented. The novel ends with the birth of a child, which—as in La Guma's *In the Fog*—symbolizes an optimistic future. Whereas La Guma's novel closes with an overt proclamation of impending, full-scale armed struggle, Serote's *To Every Birth Its Blood* ends with implied endorsement of the struggle.

Piniel Viriri Shava. *A People's Voice: Black South African Writing in the Twentieth Century* (London: Zed Books, 1989), pp. 84, 150–51

SERUMAGA, ROBERT (1939–1980)

UGANDA

Return to the Shadows, [Robert Serumaga's] first novel, deals with a military coup in an African country. To know who has grabbed power and from whom is irrelevant; even the new political leaders are no more than an impersonal voice on the radio, "the voice of the people of Adnagu." The country is in a state of complete chaos, which is not untypical; there have been enough coups in the past for Joe, the main character, to have his "drill." Whenever power changes hands, he runs to his country home, returning to the city only when he knows he can make a little profit on the confusion. But this time it is different. The novel opens with Joe and his ex-servant walking on a country road toward his mother's home. On the way a mysterious struggle is going on in Joe's mind; a hazy recollection of strange events the night before mixes with repressed feelings of guilt, resentment, and recurrent memories of certain "shadows" which went away without giving him answers. As the story goes on, flashbacks into Joe's past provide a clearer account of recent events and allow some insight into his slightly illegal transactions and political activities in the past. He had once tried to work toward getting his country out of the mess, but he had run into corruption everywhere. Now again it was chaos, the intellectuals were indifferent, and the population terrorized by soldiers and thugs.

The novel has a double theme: it goes back over the process by which this society has degraded itself, following a few minor characters in their decadence. But mostly it deals with the intellectual in a sick country, who tries first to escape by returning to the "shadows" beyond life, but gradually comes to forget his resentment and guilt, and slowly regains faith in action. It is a hard story, which places little confidence in idealism and efficiency; but it yields an interesting close-up view of the human effects of political unrest in Africa.

Marie-Claire Bue. *BA.* 44, 2 (Spring 1970), pp. 364–65

[Robert Serumaga] seems to be convinced that modern Africa has done so much to destroy itself that it is beyond redemption. In *Return to the Shadows,* he pictures an African society in a chronic state of political instability, with one military coup rapidly following another. His hero, a wealthy lawyer, economist, and businessman, has developed the habit of retreating to his home village whenever there are battles in the capital; but this time he arrives to find his mother raped and his nieces and cousins killed. He goes back to the city, witnesses more senseless brutality, recognizes the criminal greed and corruption of his closest friends, and debates frequently with an alter ego about the proper role of a moral man in an immoral society. "But what does a man do against the evil powers of the world? Fight? This way he is drawn into using the same means against which his soul is campaigning. He is pulled down to the level of the beasts who have made his blood boil in the first place. Evil drives out the good until the devil inhabits every corner of the world. What can one do?" After much agonizing, he decides that the only useful thing he can do is return to his village and bury his dead. He gives up all hope of reforming his society.

Bernth Lindfors. *Review of National Literatures* 2, 2 (Fall 1971), pp. 33–34

Serumaga, in addition to being a playwright, created the professional theater company, Theatre Limited, in Kampala; and under that name or that of the Abafumu Company, they have toured Serumaga's own drama *Renga Moi.*

Renga Moi draws upon song, music, and dance to present its story of [a] chief's defense of his village and the tragedy that surrounds him. Serumaga, like other African playwrights, draws increasingly upon the visual, and on dance and movement, to replace (or reinforce) the verbal. As we have noted in respect of some West African work, [Serumaga] . . . is increasingly aware of the strengths of indigenous theater forms and materials and increasingly confident in his use of them in his own work. Serumaga's plays in English are *A Play*, *Majangwa*, and *The Elephants*.

The last of these plays is a powerful study of a small group of people in an East African university who find themselves fighting for possession of each other—and for their sanity. David, a research fellow, has lost his parents in violent and horrifying circumstances as a child, as a result of which he went through—and still remains close to—a kind of madness. He takes into his home the artist Maurice, a refugee from a neighboring territory that has been attacked by mercenaries. He protects Maurice from the truth of the massacre of his own parents by deviously controlling the letters that Maurice sends home to produce apparently authentic replies. Maurice flourishes as an artist, increasingly drawing attention to himself; and in his growing assurance and confidence, David apparently finds a strength that enables him to keep his own horrors at bay. This precarious relationship is shattered by a young American Peace Corps girl whom Maurice has fallen in love with and wishes to marry. She discovers David's subterfuge, and the play comes to a powerful climax as David and the girl Jenny struggle over Maurice. Although such a plot outline suggests simply a lively and intriguing—perhaps melodramatic—drama of human relationships, in fact the play offers more. Maurice's status as a refugee is one that all the main characters share in one way or another: David fleeing from the traumas of his youth, and Jenny from the suffocatingly materialistic upbringing which she had had in the United States. . . .

Certainly all the characters in this play have the feeling of being consumed from within; and though some of Robert Serumaga's prose is a little forced, the overall impact of this play is very successful. In dramatic construction it illustrates both an eye and ear for theatrical rhythms, and a particular device used in this play—punctuating the action with the brief appearances of a bewildered old man looking for a hospital—is well conceived. The intrusion of this poor man's real sense of being outmaneuvered by events points the action of the play to a wider world than that presented on stage.

Martin Banham and Clive Wake. *African Theatre Today*
(London: Pitman, 1976), pp. 87–88

[The] impulse towards experiment is best seen in Robert Serumaga, who now dominates not just Uganda but the East African scene as a whole, in much the way that [Wole] Soyinka has come to dominate West Africa. When Serumaga's *A Play* appeared in 1968, the signs of a strongly individual talent were unmistakable. The nightmare of a guilty man on the anniversary of his wife's death, *A Play*, superficially, seemed highly derivative, with echoes of [Bertolt] Brecht, [Samuel] Beckett, Soyinka, and even [Christopher] Okigbo ghosting forth. Lines such as "this is a death cell not a theater," and "we must pass the time, some-how, before we die tomorrow," or "We are all just different kinds of germs. Different kinds of death," strike the authentic note of absurdist theater, not the note of *The Exodus* or any other kind of traditional piece. Yet despite derivative elements and occasional linguistic ineptness when a wrong register is used (see, for example, the Old Man's "undeniable cardiac contortions"), elemental forces are at work; and there is a sense of familiar viewpoints being expressed with originality and force. Serumaga's work now is far more maturely independent. As actor, producer, playwright, director of Theatre Limited and the Abafumi Company, he delights in unchained experimentation. *Majangwa* explores the life of an entertainer and his wife. Having failed to impress audiences with the tradi-tional arts of dancing and drumming, these two turn to obscenity as a desperate throw for success—rather as British cinemas in decline turned to pornography and wrestling. James Gibbs describes these obscenities as "startling salacious-ness," carrying the disturbing suggestion that "they constitute a symbol for the plight of the creative artist in a sick society." *Renga Moi*, Serumaga's most recent piece using music, ritual, dance, and four Ugandan vernaculars, is now in the repertoire of a company that has played to enthusiastic houses as far apart as Manila and Chicago. *Renga Moi* was particularly welcomed at the Belgrade International Festival; and a lengthy review in the newspaper *Politika* included the following comment: "a peculiar mixture of originality, the ancient and exotic, traditional and experimental, national and international." . . . Serumaga is boldly saying that language does not matter at all, and away with all those vexing problems of linguistic register and cultural transference. Four vernacu-lars are fine, and silence even better. Yet this is probably as much personal weakness as preferred philosophy. The texts of Serumaga's plays often suggest a slight discomfort with English, and his strengths are more technically theatri-cal than linguistic. *The Elephants* is a useful example of a play with a measure of psychological power, but which, stylistically, is rather vapid. Except in iso-lated cases, and despite Serumaga's claim in the introduction that "every word matters," there is neither rhythmic energy nor pungency of statement. Though stylistically it is a more even performance than *A Play*, the intensity of the author's account of city alienation is reduced by the nagging feeling that the rural world alternative is available only yards away beyond the city gate. But *The Elephants'* warm reception in Nairobi and elsewhere suggests how skillfully Serumaga has exploited those areas of his craft where he knows his strengths lie.

Adrian Roscoe. *Uhuru's Fire: African Literature East to South* (Cambridge: Cambridge University Press, 1977), pp. 262–64

After several well-received international tours of his plays by his own Theatre Limited-Abafumu Company, Robert Serumaga has probably become the East African dramatist best known to audiences outside the region. This is a result not only of his dedication to theater but of his extraordinary entrepreneurial ability, a commercial and publicity sense at least comparable to his acting and writing talents. . . .

Serumaga's most recent Abafumu Theatre Company production, *Renga Moi*, is an attempt to broaden the ethnic base of *Majangwa* and to reach into the nonverbal expressionism of African ritual, as perhaps sifted through the techniques of [Jerzy] Grotowski and Julian Beck. It is based on an Acholi myth from northern Uganda, in which the warrior chief of the village of the Seven Hills must choose between defending his people from an armed attack and completing the ceremony which will preserve the lives of his newly born twins. He leads his villagers into battle and sees his children sacrificed to propitiate demonic spirits, only to find that on returning home after successfully staying off the attackers, the villagers decline all responsibility for the deaths of the twins.

The story of Renga Moi and his village is dramatized through gestural acting, music, and the interweaving of four Ugandan languages, all directed by an English-speaking narrator-diviner on stage (played by Serumaga).

Andrew Horn. LHY. 19, 1 (January 1978), pp. 27, 33–34

Serumaga is concerned with both the agony of self-discovery and the tragic collapse of the gifted deceiver. But it is never the character's failure alone. Society is always shown to have betrayed him and forced him into compromise, deceit, and degradation; it is, therefore, civil community and its directive polities which Serumaga most condemns. It is this particular attack, not on specific social structures but on human community itself, which goes so abrasively against the grain of East African writing and theater. . . .

Renga Moi is based on an Acoli legend from northern Uganda, in which the warrior chief of the Village of the Seven Hills must choose between defending his people from armed attack and completing the ceremonies which will preserve the lives of his newly born twins, during which ritual he is expressly prohibited from shedding blood. Selflessly he decides for the common weal and leads the villagers into battle. But during his absence, grave privation strikes the village and, to propitiate the misfortune-bearing spirits, the powerful priest-diviner (who frames the action with an English commentary and was played by Serumaga), decrees that Renga Moi's twins will be sacrificially impaled. Upon returning home after successfully staving off the attackers, Renga Moi finds that the villagers decline all responsibility for the deaths of his twins. The warrior turns on the diviner and kills him; but this resolves nothing as the infants are already dead and their twin spirits will surely seek revenge on the father who abandoned them.

Renga Moi is Serumaga's clearest statement of the problem which has been his central concern from the beginning of his writing career. As he said in an interview during the play's London run, "we are posing a universal question about the choices an individual has to make, between himself and his social commitment." Renga Moi's choice is to act for the community; but, like Majangwa [in the play of that name], he discovers that the community not only undervalues his giving of himself, it ravenously demands more. Like the mob which drained Majangwa's life force and then burned his drum, the villagers of the Seven Hills accepted the warrior's self-abnegatory heroism and then destroyed his very flesh. Social commitment, Serumaga seems to be arguing, is an illusory ideal. The self-sacrificer is betrayed; the brave warrior, like the intellectual and the artist, is savaged by society and remains always an *isolato*—a man alone. . . .

Although the play's array of tongues, use of total theater and open staging techniques, inclusion of spectacular dances like *larakaraka* and *otole*, and adaptation of wrenching communal rituals elicits a greater visceral than intellectual response, it is wrong to conclude, as have some, that it lacks either design or programmatic purpose. Serumaga seems to be working towards the development of a nonverbal, theatrical objective correlative. . . .

In Serumaga's most recent work, he has continued to move away from the intellectualism of his earlier plays towards extraverbal expressive forms. A Kenyan review of the 1978 Abafumi production *Amanyakiriti* comments that the "cast became living sculptures" and that the play "appealed to the deepest emotions through mime, dance, and song, leaving the audience awestruck and in some cases in tears."

Although he is often clearly derivative and prone at times to neglect both idea and form for style, and his polished and startling surfaces may sometimes conceal confused or pedestrian thought, Serumaga does remain unique in East African theater: a man whose achievement is, admirably, more theatrical than literary and whose work shows a clear and logical development. He is, above all, sensitive to the gallops, lurches, and hiatuses of human speech, to the thrusts and hesitations of human action. The rhythms of his plays are always meticulously calibrated.

But, like his protagonists, Serumaga remains an *isolato* both professionally and ideologically. While so much of contemporary East African writing has been concerned with both a perception of community and a community of perception, Serumaga has persistently argued that community can only be destructive of the individual. Each of his embattled individualists—intellectual, politician, scholar, theatrical performer, and heroic warrior—is crushed by society, turning inwards in an implosive, nihilistic solipsism. Each becomes a strafed consciousness scrutinizing itself, its thoughts centripetal and distorted.

Andrew Horn. In Eldred Durosimi Jones, ed.
African Literature Today. 12 (1982), pp. 23, 36–39

Serumaga's concern is to dramatize the deterioration of society rather than to analyze why this has happened. A comparison with [Harold] Pinter is valid: Serumaga is creating a closed world in which society can be seen as absurd. In *Majangwa*, the traditional artistry of Majangwa and his wife, street entertainers, had degenerated into pornographic, live sex shows. His wife hates this, but he says that they have to survive and, after all, they still perform a social function: they give people some excitement and make it possible for them to continue living. But for Majangwa himself, death is as meaningless as an accident: "Death comes out of it [the road] in search of a victim or two. He comes out at night, but sometimes in the daytime. And each time the crack is repaired somebody dies. Killed by a passing car or a falling tree."

Serumaga's "writing of the absurd" is seen to best effect in his novel, *Return to the Shadows*. Serumaga, as Taban lo Liyong says, always was a royalist, and it might seem that his novel was a thinly-veiled attack on the Obote government for the crisis precipitated in 1966, particularly as the country in the novel is named Adnagu. Actually, this is not the case: the novel is about the nature of political violence and the involvement of the people themselves in creating the conditions of violence.

Peter Nazareth. In G. D. Killam, ed. *The Writing of East and Central Africa* (London: Heinemann, 1984), p. 17

SHANGE, NTOZAKE (1948–   )

UNITED STATES

Ntozake Shange gives voice to the ordinary experiences of black women in frank, simple, vivid language, telling the colored girl's story in her own speech patterns. Shange's gift is an uncanny ability to bring to life the experience of being black and a woman. Those who hear or read her choreopoem *for colored girls who have considered suicide/when the rainbow is enuf* may feel overwhelmed by so much reality, so much pain, so much resiliency, so much life force. They may even feel they have actually lived through the stories they have heard.

Like Adrienne Rich, Shange is acutely aware of the nothingness experienced by women in a society defined by men. But Shange is also aware of a double burden of pain and negation suffered by women who are black in a society defined by *white* men—where black women are not even granted the ambivalent recognition some white women receive for youth and beauty or for being wives and mothers of white men. Shange's poem also reflects the double strength black women have had to muster to survive in a world where neither being black nor being a woman is valued.

Though Shange's forte is the vivid recreation of experience, *for colored girls* is more than the simple telling of the black girl's story. It is also a search for the meaning of the nothingness experienced and a quest for new being. In Shange's poems, the experience of nothingness is born of the double burden of being black and a woman, but the stories she tells bring a shock of recognition to every woman who has given too much of herself to a man. The heart of the experience of nothingness in *for colored girls* is a woman's loss and debasement of self for love of a man. But what makes Shange's poems more than just another version of *Lady Sings the Blues*—a theme of sorrow and survival too familiar to black women (and white women)—is Shange's refusal to accept the black woman's sorrow as a simple and ultimate fact of life. She probes for a new image of the black woman that will make the old images of the colored girl obsolete. Shange envisions black women "born again" on the far side of nothingness with a new image of black womanhood that will enable them to acknowledge their history while moving beyond it to "the ends of their own rainbows."

[For] *colored girls* began as a series of separate poems, but as it developed Shange came to view "these twenty-odd poems as a single statement, a choreopoem." In the stage production, six actresses dressed in the colors of the rainbow—yellow, red, green, purple, blue, orange—and one dressed in the brown of earth and warm-toned skin alternately speak the twenty-odd poems, each a story. While one speaks, the others listen attentively or mime the story, their interest creating a sense of sisterhood and sharing. Often a story told by one woman evokes sympathetic "yeahs," or the telling of a related story, or even dancing from the other women. In a sense the dialogical form of Shange's play recreates the consciousness-raising group of the women's movement, wherein, sharing experiences and stories, women learn to value themselves, to recognize stagnant and destructive patterns in their lives, to name their strengths, and to begin to take responsibility for their lives. The sense of dialogue in Shange's choreopoem is an invitation to the women in the audience to tell their stories. What emerges is a tapestry of experiences, interwoven with a sense of plurality and commonality.

Carol P. Christ. *Diving Deep and Surfacing: Women Writers on Spiritual Quest* (Boston: Beacon Press, 1980), pp. 97–98

There are as many ways of looking at Ntozake Shange's *for colored girls who have considered suicide/when the rainbow is enuf* as there are hues in a rainbow. One can take it as an initiation piece, for instance, particularly with its heavily symbolic "Graduation Nite" and the girlhood perspectives of the mama's little baby/Sally Walker segment and in the voice of the eight-year-old narrator of "Toussaint." [*For*] *colored girls* also might be seen as a black feminist statement in that it offers a black woman's perspective on issues made prominent by the women's movement. Still another approach is to view it as a literary coming-of-age of black womanhood in the form of a series of testimonies which, in Shange's words, "explore the realities of seven different kinds of women." Indeed, the choreopoem is so rich that it lends itself to multiple interpretations which vary according to one's perspective and experiences. . . .

[*For*] *colored girls* is certainly woman's art, but it is also black art, or Third-World art, as Shange probably would prefer to have it designated. Its language and dialect, its geography, its music, and the numerous allusions to Third-World personalities make it an intensely cultural work. Much of these characteristics, however, are peculiar to Shange's upbringing, education, and experiences, with the result that the piece loses universality at points, as in the poem "Now I Love Somebody More Than." But even here, black audiences are sure to know which lady loved gardenias; they will know the Flamingoes and Archie Shepp and Imamu. Then there is the poem "Sechita," in which the dancer is linked to Nefertiti, hence to Africa and Olduvai Gorge, the "cradle of civilization"—all of which puts into perspective the cheapening of Sechita by the carnival audience. While "Sechita" speaks to the degradation of black womanhood, "Toussaint" speaks of the black woman's discovery of black pride. It also speaks, with subtle irony, of the black woman's awakening to the black man.

Sandra Hollin Flowers. *BALF.* 15, 2 (Summer 1981), pp. 51–52

That [*for colored girls who have considered suicide/when the rainbow is enuf*] is autobiographical is nowhere more evident than in the kind of women Shange wrote about and in the play's splendid isolation from the power poles of black culture: the extended family and the black church—and from salient aspects of black literary and political history as well. During the performance one does not notice what a narrow range of black women Shange portrays because, in part, Shange has converted her study of Afro-American dance, which taught her to accept "the ethnicity of my thighs and backside," into the body language of her choreopoem with dazzling effectiveness. Shange says, "dance as explicated by Raymond Sawyer and Ed Mock insisted that everything African, everything halfway colloquial, a grimace, a strut, an arched back over a yawn, waz mine. . . . I moved what waz my unconscious knowledge of being in a colored woman's body to my known everydayness." In *for colored girls*, we not only hear lines that real black women speak, delivered with acutely accurate inflections, but we also see familiar strides and shrugs and sweeps and recognize the grammar of black women's bodies. . . .

Shange speaks directly from and to the experience of a growing (but still small) section of African-American women who are born into the middle or upper middle class (or attain it through education or marriage), and are able to secure some college education and travel outside their neighborhoods in New York, Chicago, Atlanta, or Philadelphia to California, Europe, or the Caribbean. Though the black women in the audience may not have "considered suicide," they are familiar with the rootlessness, alienation, and isolation Shange portrays and are, to some extent, either as distanced as the ladies of the rainbow from the sustaining bedrock of black culture or as unable to work out a synthesis between traditional black culture and technocratic, impersonal, individualized, hectic, mobile, modern America. They have experienced . . . despair, loneliness, low self-esteem, and negative self-image . . . and this theater event offers them ways to understand, manage, and transcend that pain. A dimension of the play's appeal to white audiences also becomes clear. Alienation and despair are keystones of modernism. The individual angst of *for colored girls* (and Shange's resolutely apolitical solution) touches modernist themes familiar to educated whites since the beginning of the twentieth century, though its ending on a defiantly hopeful note is, like the vivid colors of the women's dresses, part of *African-American* spirit. The unanswerable question is how Shange fastened on troubles with black men as *the* roots of black women's pain. To do so, she had to ignore a range of other causes, including value conflicts between black parents and children, which provided so much of the fodder for black drama of the 1960s; the impact of the new sexual freedom on black women; the frustrations . . . come in the wake of expectations raised by the women's movement and the continued rejection of black women by the larger system; and the oppressive fist of white America keeping black men and black women on the bottom rung—together. If fastening on black men as the cause of black women's blues is inaccurate and unfair, it is also effective (because of the very real tensions between black women and black men), and safely apolitical.

Andrea Benton Rushing. *MassR.* 22, 3
(Autumn 1981), pp. 544–45, 547–48

In *spell #7*, subtitled a "quik magic trance manual for technologically stressed third world people," Shange tackles the iconography of "the nigger." Underneath a huge blackface minstrel mask, a master of ceremonies promises to perform a different kind of magic designed to reveal aspects of black life authentically. The minstrel performers move through the pain of dance steps and memories associated with black entertainment for white America on to the release of more private, improvisational party styles. In doing so, they banish the hideous mask along with their stage personae, thereby creating a safe space in which to expose secret hopes, fears, or dreams. But two confessions, coming at the end of each act, puncture the whimsical or contained quality of most of the fantasies to reveal an almost overwhelming anguish. . . .

Despite the public, political implications of contrariness, one may wonder how these pictures of wounded, stagnating women are an indication of Shange's combat breath. For an answer, one must examine the thrust which Shange's playwriting assumes, for most often she is not writing tidy plays in which a crisis is resolved within the structure of the play. Nowhere is the thrust beyond the theater clearer than in *spell #7*, for the play attempts to create a liberated stage space supportive of black self-expression. Because Sue-Jean's and Maxine's confessions threaten to reveal a pain almost beyond cure, the magician/master of ceremonies must halt the action in order to reassure his audience that it will indeed love his black magic. Under his spell, the cast takes up the refrain "bein colored & love it" and tries to manipulate it in order to conjure forth the joyous celebration of church. With the magician's defiant reaffirmation of the right of blacks to exist as they choose to define themselves, the minstrel mask returns, and the audience leaves.

To a certain extent, Shange, like her fictional magician, performs a sleight-of-hand which theoretically allows the drama to end on a positive note, provided that the communion between actors and audiences, brought into being by the refrain, becomes a sufficiently strong countervailing force against all the negativity represented by the minstrel mask. But given the earlier image of Sue-Jean and the final picture of a bejeweled Maxine, it is hard to imagine the actors ultimately being able to create a space for themselves and audiences. In a sense, in performance the play has two possible endings: It can culminate in hard-won triumph or in painful defeat, depending on the interaction of the energies of all those who have experienced the event.

Sandra L. Richards. *BALF*. 17, 2 (Summer 1983), pp. 74–75

In *Sassafrass, Cypress & Indigo*, Ntozake Shange, drawing from the personal realm of women's everyday experience and from the ancient or folk traditions of women's spirituality, incorporates a number of these "trivial" images, activities, and modes of expression—dolls, flowers, stones, feathers, apples, the moon, trees, the ocean, menstruation, dreams, spells, recipes, rituals for trance journeys, letters, journals, weaving, dancing, psychic healing—to depict the individual and the archetypal personalities of three sisters—Sassafrass, a weaver; Cypress, a dancer; and Indigo, a healer—and to evoke their world. . . .

Structurally, *Sassafrass, Cypress & Indigo* may be viewed as a circle of concentric rings, as Shange introduces Indigo first, then Sassafrass, then Cypress, then returns to Sassafrass, and finally to Indigo again. This structure suggests the circular *temenos* (sacred space) in practices of women's spirituality and so emphasizes the depth of the connection between the sisters, as well as their interrelatedness. This structure also reflects the extent to which each woman is connected to the transpersonal realm, with Indigo at the center as most psychic, then Sassafrass, and then Cypress as most worldly of the three at the outermost edge. In this sense, the circular structure suggests gradations in the similarities they share, as well as clarifying their unique and different personalities. The circle motif suggested by the overall structure of the novel appears, too, at the conclusion of the novel when Cypress and Indigo return home to celebrate the birth of Sassafrass's first child as the two women and their mother, Hilda Effania, circle around Sassafrass to be with her in support and encouragement. Here, the circle of women can be connected with themes of interconnection, healing, and empowerment.

While the structure of *Sassafrass, Cypress & Indigo* may very well be viewed as a circle of concentric rings, it can also be viewed as a textured weaving with various recurring strands/motifs—letters from Hilda Effania to her daughters, recipes for special occasions, images and rituals of transformation, manifestations of aspects of the immanent, archetypal Goddess. Personal and transpersonal, warp and woof, weaving together, creating new patterns, reclaiming the past, transforming the present. That the structure of the novel is suggestive of a weaving complements the facts that Hilda Effania is a weaver, as is her oldest daughter, Sassafrass; that the relationship of the three sisters evokes an allusion to the Greek Moerae, the Triple Goddess, the weavers of destiny; and that the archetypal Goddess is sometimes viewed in a global, contextual way as "the interwoven fabric of being . . . the web of connection . . . the pattern."

Jean Strandness. *JAC*. 10, 3 (Fall 1987), p. 11

In her plays, especially *for colored girls* and *spell #7*, Shange develops her narration primarily through monologues because monologic speech inevitably places the narrative weight of a play upon its spoken language and upon the performances of the individual actors. But she does not use this device to develop "character" in the same fashion as Maria Irene Fornes and other Method-inspired playwrights who turn toward monologic language in order more expressively to define and "embody" their characters both as woman and as individuals. Rather, Shange draws upon the uniquely "performative" qualities of monologue to allow her actors to take on *multiple* roles and therefore to emphasize the centrality of *storytelling* to her work. This emphasis is crucial to Shange's articulation of a black feminist aesthetic (and to the call to humanity to accept that "black women are inherently valuable") on two counts. First, the incorporation of role-playing reflects the ways that blacks (as "minstrels," "servants," "athletes," etc.) and women (as "maids," "whores," "mothers," etc.) are expected to fulfill such roles on a constant basis in Western society. Second, the space between our enjoyment of the "spectacle" of Shange's theater pieces (through the recitation of the monologues and through the dancing and singing which often accompany them), and our awareness of the urgency of her call for blacks/women to be allowed "selves" free of stereotypes, serves as a "rupturing" of the performance movement; it is the uncomfortableness of that space, that rupture, which moves and disturbs us. . . .

All of Shange's theater pieces, even *a photograph: lovers in motion* and *boogie woogie landscapes*, unfold before the audience as collections of stories rather than as traditionally linear narratives; the events are generated less from actual interactions as they unfold in the "present" of the play (except perhaps in *a photograph*) than from the internal storytellers' *recreations* of individual dramas. The implied privilege of the storyteller to create alternate worlds, as well as the fluidity of the stories themselves and the characters in them, relies heavily upon the immense power that African and Afro-American tradition have assigned to the spoken word. . . . Shange takes the notion of exchange and collectivity among storytellers even further in her use of the space in which her pieces are performed. Monologue creates "narrative space"; Shange depends upon the power and magic of the stories within her plays to create the scenes without the use of backdrops and other "theatrical" effects. [*For*] *colored girls* is the most "open" of the plays in this sense, as it calls for no stage set, only lights of different colors and specific places for the characters to enter and exit. [*B*]*oogie woogie landscapes* conjures up the mental images of the title within the confines of Layla's bedroom: "there is what furniture a bedroom might accommodate, though not too much of it. [The] most important thing is that a bedroom is suggested." Although the sets of both *spell #7* and *a photograph* are fairly specific (a huge minstrel mask as a backdrop and, later, a bar in lower Manhattan for the former; a photographer's apartment for the latter), they still call for this space to be reborn in different imaginary ways as the characters come forth and tell their stories. . . .

Unlike *for colored girls*, *spell #7* makes use of a central storyteller figure, Lou, who "directs" the monologues which are performed in the course of the play. It is appropriate that Lou is a magician, for even the title of *spell #7* (the subtitle of which is "geechee jibara quik magic trance manual for technologically stressed third world people") refers to magic-making. In his opening speech, though, Lou warns of the power (and danger) of "colored" magic. . . . The image of the narrator as "magician" implies that the storytellers themselves will be under the control of a certain "author"; yet as the actors perform their pieces, the stories seem at times to slip away from a guiding narratorial force and to become deeply personal. In a sense, the performers threaten to overpower the narrator in the same way that the third grader's request to be made white is beyond the power of Lou's magician father: the stories take on a kind of magic which is independent of their "director," and yet to enter this realm may be painful and perilous. Lou, then, is like a surrogate author who is responsible for the content of the play, but who also cannot fully control what happens to it once the performers begin to take part.

Deborah R. Geis. In Enoch Brater, ed. *Feminine Focus: The New Women Playwrights* (New York: Oxford University Press, 1989), pp. 211–13, 219–20

Shange's dramatic work, especially [*for colored girls*], represents a moment of crucial importance in black and American history. . . . Writers with whom she is often compared, such as Imamu Amiri Baraka and Nikki Giovanni, seem to speak of a different, earlier moment. Where these and other writers attacked the obstacles to black self-realization, Shange's dramas represent the tortured moment of becoming itself, *the* moment of emergence and discovery. Ambivalence and paradox mark this moment; a dynamic world full of potential inhabits the same sphere as an old dead world in which nothing can change. The future for Shange's characters fluctuates between a positive, realizable potential, such as [Karl] Marx envisioned, and a negative emptiness, such as [Walter] Benjamin envisioned, which must be filled by individual effort and suffering. The process of becoming is Shange's subject, "our struggle to become all that is forbidden by our environment, all that is forfeited by our gender, all that we have forgotten."

In *spell #7, boogie woogie landscapes*, and *colored girls*, there is no one outcome to the process of becoming, no one unifying end—but there is the process itself, in which all are engaged. What is more, communal expression may well be the only outlet for a certain range of feelings, according to Shange: "in addition to the obvious stress of racism in poverty / afro-american culture . . . has minimized its 'emotional' vocabulary to the extent that admitting feelings of rage, defeat, frustration is virtually impossible outside a collective voice." Again and again, Shange's dramas wander through a maze of personal and collective experience, only to coalesce in a chant that unites the subjective and the intersubjective. . . .

There is, however, a paradox about Shange's work. . . . [Her] works are inscribed with the tensions of a very specific time and place. Further, these pieces announce themselves as being "for" a particular audience, such as colored girls or technologically stressed Third-World people. Those pieces contain a great deal of aggression toward an oppressive white culture, an aggression that begins with an attack on white English: "i cant count the number of time i have viscerally wanted to attack deform n maim the language that i waz taught to hate myself in." "The mess of my fortune to be born black & English-speaking" has motivated her to cultivate nonwhite orthography, syntax, and what she has called verbal "distortions." Yet despite all this effort at exclusion, her works remain remarkably "open" texts—that is, they anticipate and welcome the indeterminacy of any dramatic text and the unavoidable variation of performance. As a result, these texts that are addressed to, dedicated to, and written for a particular audience nevertheless throw themselves open to a multiplicity of audiences and performances.

John Timpane. *Studies in American Drama, 1945–Present*. 4 (1989). Repub. in June Schlueter, ed. *Modern American Drama: The Female Canon* (Rutherford, N. J.: Fairleigh Dickinson University Press, 1990), pp. 198–200

Shange's *a photograph: lovers in motion* . . . contradicts her image as a feminist black-man-hater. Sean David, like Beau Willie Brown [in *for colored girls*], is Shange's effort to denounce what Erskine Peters calls Shange's portrayal of black man "basically as pasteboards or beasts." . . . Just as Beau Willie is presented with compassion, so too is Sean David. . . . And while Sean David exhibits the abusive behavior of *some* men, he is never close to being a "pasteboard." Instead, he dominates the action and wrestles continually with the complexities of success as a black artist, the complexities of real manhood, and the complexities of his relationship with his father.

Sean David is the first male character who takes center stage in a published play by Shange, and he is one of her most confused characters. We witness his complex social, physical, and psychological realms, particularly through his treatment of three confused female lovers. At a glance, Sean might seem the stereotypical male whose self-image is determined by his sexual prowess. And he boasts of his ability to juggle several female lovers while retaining complete control over each. Yet Shange undercuts his empty confidence by showing that Sean cannot keep his women apart any more than he can separate the suffering depicted in his Vietnam photographs. . . .

Sean's hostility subsides when he admits his need for real love, not just sex—which is precisely what Shange's colored girls discover and long for. Like Beau Willie, Sean David is not an abusive black man without redeeming qualities; he is confused. . . . What moves Sean away from the stereotypical black man is his ability to admit to himself that he is in pain and has been misguided in his move toward knowing who and what he is. . . .

Shange has described *From Okra to Greens/A Different Kind of Love Story: A Play/with Music & Dance* as a "feminist poem in motion," set within the framework of a variant of the boy-meets-girl love story. In the play, Okra (the black female) gives Greens (the black male) a gift—her sociopolitical views on the black women's existence within the local, national, and international arenas. In one sense, Greens represents Shange's ideal black male, though his coming to know the complex realities of female existence is a gradual process. Unlike Sean David, there is no question that Greens is what Shange argues every black woman needs and seeks in a black male companion. . . .

Significantly different from other black males in Shange's dramas, Greens acknowledges and celebrates the irresistible power of love that is both physical and spiritual. And unlike any other man in Shange's presentations, Greens recognizes the power play between male and female partners that manifests itself even in the intimacy of the bedroom. In "some men," one of the most poignant poem sequences in the play, Shange offers a feminist editorial on male behavior. Careful not to stereotype all men as insensitive and abusive, Shange signifies on the behavior of "some" men, like Sean David, who possess twisted definitions of manhood. In both the poetry collection *A Daughter's Geography* and the published booklet *Some Men*, in collaboration with Wopo Holup, Shange allows a single female persona to address males' behavior. As a participant in the exchange in this dramatic version, Greens offers an alternative male perspective to the one being condemned in the sequence. Greens represents those men who do not behave and think as *these* men.

Neal A. Lester. *African American Review* 26, 2 (Summer 1992), pp. 322–25

SOW FALL, AMINATA (1941–   )

SENEGAL

Aminata Sow Fall's first novel, *Le Revenant*, is less a character study than a comedy of manners. The urban Senegal that she depicts, like that of Ousmane Socé's *Karim* forty years before, is still dominated by the need for ostentatious display. Status is gained by external signs of wealth and unregarding generosity. A bride is won and a wife retained only by extravagant expenditure on gifts lavished on in-laws, friends, retainers, and opportunistic hangers-on. The hero, like Karim, is an amiable but weak young man who cannot withstand the pressures of this exacting society and, yielding to temptation, misappropriates large sums and lands in prison. He loses his wife and child, his family and friends reject him, and he sinks into degradation and despair until the very taste for ostentation which has been his undoing provides the means for his revenge. The author does not condemn her hero for embezzling millions of francs nor his wife for abandoning him when he has fallen on evil days. She attacks only the society that saps all moral integrity, those who exploit questionable customs and perpetuate wrong values, who are superficial, hypocritical, and lacking in human warmth. Her characters are divided into victims and exploiters. The wife is presented as the typical "investment" expected to give lifelong returns to her family who manipulates her and denies her the freedom to act on her love and loyalty to her husband. Bakar becomes a criminal because he has not the strength of character to withstand his in-laws' rapacity. His mother is oppressed by an autocratic, egoistic husband, confident that male superiority cannot be questioned. Even Bakar's loyal and admirable friend imposes on his wife and children by the extravagant hospitality he offers to a host of parasitical card players.

Dorothy S. Blair. *Senegalese Literature: A Critical History*
(Boston: Twayne, 1984), pp. 132–33

With this her third novel [*L'Appel des arènes*], Aminata Sow Fall provides yet another view of what is developing into a multifaceted portrait of contemporary Senegalese society. It constitutes, at the same time, a continuation of her acerbic criticism of that society and especially of its urbanized and privileged upper and middle bourgeoisie. While her first two books, *Le Revenant* and *La Grève des Bàttu*, depicted respectively the ruinous penchant of the Senegalese for ostentatious public generosity and the world of urban beggars harassed by self-important and hypocritical government officials, *L'Appel des arènes* is set against the backdrop of the milieu of traditional wrestling, an ancient national sport. The plot revolves around the conflict between the adolescent Nalla and his parents over Nalla's neglect of his studies in favor of an almost obsessive fascination with the world of wrestling and his adoring devotion to his newfound friend Malaw, champion of the arena. . . .

As if to underline the value of tradition, the author often assumes a distinctly oral tone: use of the present tense in descriptions, repetitions, conversations spiced with words in the original Wolof and traditional praise-songs interspersed throughout. Used with more consistency and smoother integration into the whole, these and other such techniques could put Sow Fall into the forefront of those writers who are forging European words and genres into an authentically modern African art form.

Fredric Michelman. *WLT*. 58, 1 (Winter 1984), pp. 153–54

Aminata Sow Fall's novelistic work consists of three texts, *Le Revenant*, *La Grève des Bàttu*, and *L'Appel des arènes*. As in the novels of Mariama Bâ, Islam is present in these novels except in the last one, but the manner in which it is presented is more general and social. . . .

[*Le Revenant*] depicts a certain Dakaran society, which under the pretext of respecting the customs and religion, leads a flashy and ostentatious lifestyle on which fortunes are spent. Throughout her text, Aminata Sow Fall denounces even more violently than does Mariama Bâ the ravages caused by this "pseudo-Islam," devoid of all humanity and spirituality. . . .

The novelist systematically presents great socioreligious moments which give rise to "folles depenses" each time.

During a baptism, the two families face each other like adversaries on a battlefield. The richness of the make-up and the jewelry foretells the generosity of the gifts. During the ceremony, the guests never think about the actual reason for their reunion. . . .

In the second novel of Aminata Sow Fall, *La Grève des Bàttu*, hardheartedness is placed at the center of the novel and serves as the criterion for distinguishing between the true and the false believer. The novelist indirectly poses the problem of the absence of charity through the collective confrontation of the beggar and the almsgivers.

In this novel, the false believer is no longer denounced by an individual, but by a whole class of penniless people. These people take action collectively when charity is put into question by the inhuman modernism of the administrators who nevertheless need to use the virtues of charity for their own personal ends.

Popular Islam presented in a human point of view, often malicious and always deeply rooted in traditional life, triumphs over unscrupulous egoism, camouflaged under the guise of modern progress.

A. C. Jaccard. *Nouvelles du Sud*. 6 (1986–1987), pp. 177–80†

Le Revenant is social satire, attacking the evils of today's inhumane, materialist society without reference to whites. The African nature of the work is limited almost exclusively to the social custom which demands the distribution of large sums of money at ritual baptisms. In [Sow Fall's] second novel, *La Grève des Bàttu*, three "patrons" are mentioned, only one of whom was white; and it is the vicious nature of a boss, not of a white, which is attacked. Selected for this study because of its ironic satire, this work is typical of current trends in the absence of racial issues. . . .

To recognize the satire of the work, the reader must share with the author the opinion that the system is bad. As it is theoretically possible that some readers might feel that breeding human children for food is a good solution for the problem of starvation, so there might be readers who feel that dumping beggars hundreds of kilometers outside the city, beating and killing them, is a good solution for their cluttering up the public streets. However, few among the African audience would fail to catch that the satirical intent is to demonstrate the grave faults in a system which, however humanely designed originally, has deteriorated in practice.

Elinor S. Miller. *French Literature Series* (Columbia: University of South Carolina Press, 1987), pp. 144–46

Through a first appraisal of Sow Fall's novels, readers are provided with a fairylike enchantment which seeks its essence from universal as well as specific patterns. In such a process, the readers may be led to follow a silver thread which carries them beyond Senegalese reality into a realm of dreams and fantasies. This enchantment enraptures from without and may even work as an escapist element. . . .

Although Fall's works are written, they bear the mark of Africa's oral literature. Since the novel is a genre imported to Africa, it is of necessity influenced by the original literary form of Africa: the oral tradition. Besides the many Wolof expressions which she uses, Sow Fall seems to take special interest in quoting such Wolof proverbs as the one reflected in Serigne Birama's answer concerning the beggars: "Ligééy de Mooy degg" (It is every man's duty to work). In *Le Revenant* a peddler tells Bakar: "Lu jongoma begg yal nay jamm . . ." (Woman's desire is . . . God's wish). Bakar also remembers: "Bañ Gatia nangoo dee" (Rather death than shame). This proverb is a line from a song his mother used to sing. This leads us to the musical element included by the griots to accompany their narration. Aminata Sow Fall includes a griot in *Le Revenant*, and she even gives us a translated Wolof rendition of the praises he addresses to Yama at the ball to chant her beauty. . . .

A modern griot, Aminata Sow Fall is a genuine voice of Africa. Her style emanates humor, and the content of her novels expresses wisdom, popular beliefs, and social criticism. Her narratives, based on fictitious events, provide useful universal truths and at the same time entertain and arouse curiosity. In the true tradition, her artistry and *divertissement* are functional. Her stories contain the moral element present in all African tales. Sow Fall discloses that those events that "go wrong" in life are mainly due to the very nature of man. The reader has to discover those truths as they occur in most tales, as opposed to fables, where the message is emphasized. *Le Revenant* indicates that selfishness and corruption are finally punished. *La Grève des Bàttu* shows that one cannot solely rely on magic forces to achieve success and that it is the fairness of one's previous actions which leads to a successful future. Both Bakar and Mour have "sinned" and are punished.

Françoise Pfaff. *CLAJ.* 31, 3 (March 1988), pp. 347, 357–58

Published in 1976, *Le Revenant* sets the stage for what could be called a vast *comédie humaine*. Here [Sow] Fall defines the milieu in which her characters evolve: the urban area of Dakar, capital of Senegal. It is a society at a cross-roads, caught in a process of rapid social change: "Tradition has been pierced to the heart, and what Bakar resented the most in that situation was the corruption of morals." Indeed, the old value system based on *ngor* (nobility), *jom* (dignity), and communal values has been replaced by only one criterion: money or material wealth. Under the impulse of that new divinity, all relationships have become a game, and society itself a stage ruled by money. The negative effect of money over collective and individual life is embodied in the corruption of social life and the drama of Bakar, the main character. . . .

On the surface, [*La Grève des Bàttu*, translated as *The Beggars' Strike*] appears as mere reportage on a Senegalese society faced with the dilemmas and traumas of economic development or "modernization." Confronting a severe cycle of drought that endangered their agriculturally based economics, public officials sought economic survival through the development of tourist industries. At the same time, hard-hit rural areas saw their population flee and invade the cities in a search for subsistence. With no formal education or skills, this displaced rural populace became beggars in the streets and public places, including those visited by the tourists. In order to maintain the flow of tourists from all over the world, public officials had to rid the city of its beggars. Therefore a campaign was launched to drive "the dregs of society" to a relocation area on the outskirts of the city.

[Sow] Fall's social vision goes beyond the issue of modernization to explore its implications for humans and their conduct. To reach such a depth of insight, she draws from an imagination fed by a strong knowledge of her countrymen and [countrywomen]. What would happen if, as a protest, the beggars decided to go on strike, thus depriving the entire population of the possibility of giving alms? In her fictional world [Sow] Fall brings to life a well-organized group of beggars—Salla Niang, Gorgui Diop, and Nugiraine Sarr—who decide to go on strike against the brutalities perpetrated by public officials, represented by the Director of Health and Hygiene, Mour Ndiaye, and his assistant, Keba Dabo. Exploring the consequences of this strike, [Sow] Fall highlights the collective and individual dramas generated by the contradictory demands of a changing society. . . .

Aminata Sow Fall was first a teacher and a specialist in education who participated in a committee for the reform of French programs in public schools. Education and the issues it raises in a changing society lie at the very heart of her third novel, *L'Appel des arènes*. Through the simple story of a schoolboy and his family in a small Senegalese town, [Sow] Fall stresses the disarray of a humanity confused by the content of an imposed educational system that does not correspond to its realities. Ndiogou and his wife Diattou are both professionally successful, Western-educated individuals of a type often referred to as "been-tos," people who have sojourned in Europe for their education. He has returned home with a degree in veterinary medicine, she with a degree in nursing.

Despite their professional success, however, both Ndiogou and Diattou have been victimized by their education abroad. Fascinated by the Western values of progress and civilization, and alienated from Africa, they reject the cultural realities of their country. Desiring to distance herself from everything that reminds her of her past, Diattou seeks a complete personal transformation: "Diattou concentrated on changing herself. She worked hard to domesticate her vocal cords and polish them. She learned to regulate her walk and gestures on the pace of the West. She became Toutou." What she draws from her Western experience is the intense desire to create an African aristocracy marked by progress and materialism. For her, progress comes to mean a total rejection of all that has belonged to her country's social values as well as to her own past values and cultural identity. . . .

L'Ex-père de la nation, deals with the hot topic of political life in an imaginary African country easily identifiable as Senegal. This reflection on political behavior is presented as the memoirs of Madiama Niang, former head of state, jailed after his dismissal from office. Through this flashback on his own past reign and personal tragedy, Madiama introduces the reader into the daily intrigues and vices of political life. . . .

Progressively, Madiama discovers himself to be a man trapped in a tragic situation, isolated from his relatives and stifled by power. The irony here is that he cannot even resign from the presidency that is killing his ideals of democracy and justice. He finds himself a hostage. Here [Sow] Fall goes beyond the sphere of domestic politics. The president, those around him, and the entire country are taken hostage by foreign powers through capital investment. As Madiama discovers later, dependence on foreign capital denies his nation its very foundation: the freedom to make choices and preside over its own destiny. This realization of his failure coincides with the last stage in Madiama's rule. The same hidden threads that brought him to power work to overthrow him. His very decision to find an honorable exit through resignation proves to be self-destructive. After an arranged public disturbance, a shadowy coup d'état topples him and he is thrown into jail, to be replaced by a more willing player.

L'Ex-père de la nation goes beyond the personal drama of an imaginary head of state to explore the tragedy of African political life. The nation Madiama presided over is like a confiscated ship in which, like worms, public officials greedily thrive on the sweat of the people. In this atmosphere of tension and competitiveness, freedom, humanity, and justice are replaced by hypocrisy as a way of life.

Samba Gadjigo. WLT. 63, 3 (Summer 1989), pp. 411–14

SOYINKA, WOLE (1934–   )

NIGERIA

The Nigerian Civil War, which was the culminating point of the series of political crises in that country since 1962, has provided some of the Nigerian poets with the opportunity of manifesting through art the nature of their feelings about life and human values. . . .

Wole Soyinka looks at war from a general point of view in "Idanre." In this poem, war is shown to be a two-sided sword cutting its owner as well as his enemy. The central character in this poem is Ogun, the ambivalent Yoruba god of creation and destruction, who indeed is himself a true symbol of the ambivalent nature of war as Soyinka sees it. Thus when men invited this god to lead them in a war against their enemies, he spared the enemies and destroyed his clients. . . . Because of this Soyinka feels he is "a guest no one / Can recall," just as war is an event no sane people can wish to experience twice. . . .

It is in his later poems, however, that Soyinka deals specifically with the Nigerian Civil War, which he feels was completely irrational. Thus in "When Seasons Change" the present generation made up of the organizers of the war is shown to have blindly refused to heed the lessons of the past (i.e., history). The ghosts of war ("Time's specters") "evade guardianship of predecessors" and come to the earth bringing with them old hints and old truths "up-held in mirrors of the hour." Instead of heeding these hints and truths, the "mind" remains "banked upon the bankrupt flow / of wisdom new." It becomes "a noble slave airborne on the cross" of two contradictory forces: its knowledge of the "futility" of "far ideas and urgent action" on one hand, and "fate" which compels response to the "present call" to war on the other. . . .

In another of his poems, "And what of it if thus he died?," Soyinka paints a picture of the wicked hearts of some fellow human beings. The victim of the hatred delineated in the poem is the artist, Soyinka himself or any artist of the same spirit, who refused to "be still" (against the orders of the sadists) "while winds of terror tore out shutters / Of his neighbor's home." For him "the wrongs of day / And cries of night burnt red fissures / In chambers of his mind." He endeavors to provide "a compass for bewildered minds," strives "to bring / Fleeting messages of time / To tall expression," and wishes to "regulate the turn of hours." Little does he know he is "seeking that whose plenitude / Would answer calls of hate and terror." For the reaction of the calloused hearts is of course: "What of it if thus he died / Burnt offering on the altar of fears?"

Because of Soyinka's outspoken advice for brotherly love instead of brotherly hate, for temperance instead of extremity, for reason instead of unreason, it would have mattered little to many "if thus he died." If he had "thus died" he would have been a mere victim of the fear that he might not have had good intentions for his nation. But from the evidence in his poem, he was genuinely concerned about the fate of his country and her values. The motivating force of his utterances has been a deep-rooted humanity which imbues his work with transcendent qualities.

R. N. Egudu. *Modern African Poetry and the African Predicament*
(New York: Barnes & Noble, 1978), pp. 104–5, 108–9

When Soyinka's first novel, *The Interpreters*, was published in 1965, practically all the early reviews were favorable, and some were downright adulatory. But critical opinion quickly settled against the novel; and although it is still sometimes mentioned, it is rarely read, even in the universities. How is one to explain this sudden decline in the fortune of a book which was once proclaimed as the African novel of the future? Virtually all the participants at a symposium on "The Novel and Reality in Africa and America," in Lagos in 1973, seemed to have agreed with Michael Echeruo that it was because Soyinka did not respond to the climate of opinion around him. "Nobody is bothered, I am afraid, by *The Interpreters*," Echeruo scorned. "It has not disturbed anybody as far as I know. It does not address itself to a general emotion." . . .

The Interpreters attempts to maintain a proper historic viewpoint. Egbo, the most "authorial" character, is most intimately connected with the past because of the choice he has to make between taking over the inheritance of his father's kingdom in the delta or becoming a bureaucrat in Lagos. Instead of being nostalgic, he is resentful of his traditional past, as he complains to Bandele and Sekoni: "If the dead are not strong enough to be ever-present in our being, should they not be as they are, dead?" When Sekoni replies that to make such distinctions would disrupt the dome of continuity, which is what life is, Egbo acknowledges that the past cannot be ignored, although it is tempting to do so, for "the present, equally futile, distinguishes itself only by a particularly abject lack of courage." So, where would morality come from? Egbo replies firmly: "A man's gift of life should be separate, an unrelated thing. All choice must come from within him, not from promptings of his past."

The contemporary reality which Soyinka dealt with in *The Interpreters* was highlighted in a paper on "modern black African theater," which he delivered at the First World Festival of Negro Arts in Dakar in 1966. The paper, subtitled "The Nigerian Scene, a Study of Tyranny and Individual Suppression," sums up the first five years of Nigerian political independence, 1960 to 1965. . . . *The Interpreters* deals with the problems of the intellectuals in the emerging African nations, a question of individual sensibility at war with the claims of society. The interpreters, the novel's composite "hero," are young intellectuals all of whom have had their visions frustrated by their society. . . .

Season of Anomy, unlike *The Interpreters*, is truly a political novel. It analyzes political motives, actions, and their consequences. However, because it deals with the world of action, where ideas as well as personalities become both polarized and simplified, it is inevitably less complex than *The Interpreters*. Clearly Soyinka means to subjugate art to social purpose. Here, he carries the war to his enemies. For it is Ofeyi who imbues the men of Aiyero (who constitute the progressive forces in the story) with his revolutionary ideas, and thereby initiates the fight against the Cartel which later provokes the massacre from the reactionary forces. But soon Ofeyi is forced to yield leadership of the progressive forces to the Dentist (Demakin), the apostle of violence whose morality is summed up by the professional ethics to extract the tooth of evil before it infects others. True, Ofeyi himself is not averse to violence. But the Dentist, the "selective assassinator," goes beyond Ofeyi's stated objective, the "need to protect the young seedling" of the revolution, and justifies the use of violence as a means of seizing the initiative from the Cartel, whose more efficient system of creating violence threatens to annihilate the Aiyero ideal. As the full dimension of the wanton destruction wrought by the Cartel becomes known, [the Dentist] wrests from Ofeyi the task of leading Aiyero against the Cartel. . . .

In the "season of anomy," violence becomes an inevitable prelude to political emancipation. But it remains only a means, to be used to achieve that higher ideal which it is the business of the man of vision to define. The Dentist himself acknowledges as much to Ofeyi: "Don't ask me what I envisage. Beyond the elimination of men I know to be destructively evil, I envisage nothing. What happens after is up to people like you."

Kolawole Ogungbesan. *New West African Literature*
(London: Heinemann, 1979), pp. 1–3, 6–7

During the Nigerian Civil War Soyinka was imprisoned in 1967 and held in solitary confinement for nearly two years by the government, which claimed that he had aided the Biafran secessionist movement. Much of his subsequent writing has treated of his experiences during these years or, by allusion, of the events connected with them. *The Man Died* is an autobiographical account of his arrest and imprisonment. Shortly after his arrest Soyinka is interrogated by Mallam D. "When the government has already laid down a policy, what makes you think you know better? You are intellectuals living in a dream world, yet you think you know better than men who have weighed out so many factors and come to a decision." . . .

Soyinka has claimed that his African mythic perspective provides a unified view of reality which has been lost to the West as a result of fragmentation proceeding from rationalist and materialistic thought. The power of his writing results from the obsessive vision permeating his work regardless of its explicit subject matter. In his prison poems, A *Shuttle in the Crypt*, the sequence "Chimes of Silence" in compressed form makes use of the analogy found in *The Man Died* between Ogun's passing through chaos and the author's will to survive imprisonment. Hezzy Maduakor has said: "Ogun's trials in the abyss of disintegration have their parallels in the private experience of every individual. Man must pass through the crucibles of experience like Ogun, and one's manhood is proven by the degree to which he summons the inner resources of his being to dare and overcome the abyss of dissolution." The early poems in the sequence both locate the experience in the prison and show the fatality of those who attempt to survive by prayer, compliance, or acceptance. "Purgatory" shows the absurdity of law with its supposed function of restoring man to society through punishment. Those who punish are themselves villains or perverts; the imprisoned include "the mad," "the damned": "Epileptics, seers and visionaries," all "Trudging the life-long road to a dread / Judicial sentence." Seeing the pain suffered by those who hope for reprieve, "The mind retreats behind a calloused shelter / Of walls, self-censor on the freedom of remembrance." The emasculation of hope and desire brings the "comfort of a gelded sanity." Where will such loneliness end? "Recession (*Mahapralaya*)" tells of the dissolution of the self from relationship with the world. Such negation or destruction is necessary before there can be liberation and renewal. Soyinka's footnote to *Mahapralaya* reads: "In Hindu

Metaphysics, the return of the universe to its womb; here, expressed as the consoling experience of man in the moment of death, the freeing of his being from the death of the world." The poems that follow speak of psychic renewal. Noah and the Dove are invoked in "Space": "His mind was boundless when out / He flew." Rebirth in "Seed" is suggested by "Roll away the stone," the reference to Lazarus, the images of "splitting wood-grains" and "gentle rain."

Bruce King. *The New English Literatures: Cultural Nationalism in a Changing World* (New York: St. Martin's, 1980), pp. 93–95

In *Season of Anomy*, Soyinka portrays a mythical community of Aiyéró as a foil to the anomic "Illosa" and "Cross-River" countries that are controlled by a cocoa cartel and characterized by brutality and slaughter, a carnage directed specifically toward an unnamed tribal group. Illosa and Cross-River, though undoubtedly universal in their implications, are clearly symbolic of Nigeria, the slaughter reminiscent of the historical events that led up to the Biafran secession and civil war, the unnamed tribal group its Igbo victims. Aiyéró, in contrast to the Illosa and Cross-River areas, is an idyllic community. . . .

In this portrayal of Aiyéró, Soyinka offers the traditional African spiritual-political ideal. Survival and spiritual continuity are inextricable. At the same time, the Religion of the Grain is not passive or pacifistic: Ogun is the god of gunmakers. It becomes obvious in *Season of Anomy* that the celebration of the past is not a retreat from political problems, but rather a potential source of strength in political battle. . . .

The power of Soyinka's myth derives from a specifically African circumstance and the affirmation of a traditional African concept of the sacred continuum. Simultaneously, however, Soyinka echoes the Western myth of Orpheus. Ofeyi, the musician, rescues his wife after crossing a river to the underworld of Cross-River, clearly divided into an outer Erebus and the Tartarus of the inner prison. He is guided toward the inner recesses of the prison by a deformed Charonlike guide who demands more than pennies for his pay. The prison is guarded by a mute who is consistently described in images of a monstrous Cerberus-like dog. Strengthening this parallel is the Yoruba echo of the names of these characters' Greek counterparts. Orpheus becomes Ofeyi; Eurydice becomes Iriyise. Charon becomes Karaun, and Cerberus, Subaru.

It is insufficient to note that Soyinka has Africanized a motif of Western literature. In a narrative that equates evil with the influence of the West, Soyinka's African analogue of a Western myth is used as a weapon, one that has been symbolically seized from the intruders and used against them. To see the analogue without simultaneously perceiving this irony is to falsify Soyinka's achievement.

Bonnie J. Barthold. *Black Time: Fiction of Africa, the Caribbean, and the United States* (New Haven, Conn.: Yale University Press, 1981), pp. 185–87, 194–95

Wole Soyinka is a leading writer in Nigeria, his own country, as well as in the rest of Africa, Europe, and America. Into his work he has integrated most facets of the African experience. Between the poles of tradition and change, he searches for essential human values, which he tries to make universally recognizable from an African perspective. Because he has most convincingly succeeded, and because interest in his work is growing throughout the world, it seems logical to give special attention to this playwright. . . .

Soyinka's work is filled with ideas from his African cultural heritage. He stands close to the "return to the sources" to which [Léopold Sédar] Senghor refers in his Négritude philosophy. According to the Senegalese poet, Négritude is the basis of the cultural heritage, values, and spirit of African civilization. The Négritude movement originated in reaction to colonial cultural domination. . . .

Soyinka kept a distance between himself and the Négritude writers, especially the French African writers. In his now famous dictum, he is as little concerned with meditating on his Africanness or his Négritude as the tiger has the need to talk about his "tigritude." In a discussion with American students at the University of Washington, he explained his point of view. He said that Négritude was the cause of a group of alienated people who had practically no contact with their own culture: Négritude is part of a European philosophy, which explains why intellectuals like [Jean-Paul] Sartre were enthusiastic about it. Essentially its concern is to place the African personality within a European frame of reference.

Mineke Schipper. *Theatre and Society in Africa*
(Johannesburg: Ravan Press, 1982), pp. 136, 142–43

Critics have claimed Soyinka's nonalignment to any specific ideology, but in *Season of Anomy* Soyinka comes very close to a commitment to socialist ideals. The author may not consider himself committed to socialism, but his work can certainly be given a socialist interpretation. . . . In *Season of Anomy* there is a definite antithesis between monopoly capitalism and repression on the one hand, and progressive communalism on the other. Monopoly capitalism is represented by the Cartel Corporation and the Mining Trust; and since monopoly capitalism must protect itself against the wrath of the exploited masses, we see an unholy alliance coming into existence, an alliance between "the purse and the gun." The regime running the affairs of the country (which could be Nigeria or any other African state) is a military regime. The Cartel itself is propped up by four distinguished personages: Chief Batoki, Chief Biga, Zaki Amuri, and the Commandant-in-Chief who declares that the hope for "national stability" is in "the alliance of the purse and the gun." The forces of progress are represented at the most elementary level by the communalist ideals of Aiyéró and on a higher level by Ofeyi's idea of a community of workers breaking down the artificial frontiers of tribe and region and undermining the exploitative activities of the Cartel. The idea is summarized in the following sentence: "The goals were clear enough, the dream a new concept of laboring hands across artificial frontiers, the concrete, affective presence of Aiyéró throughout the land, undermining the Cartel's superstructure of robbery, indignities and murder, ending the new phase of slavery." Ofeyi would like to work with the men of Aiyéró because "they live by an idea." Ofeyi's idea eventually merges with that of Demakin, the Dentist, who believes in the systematic elimination of the chief members of the group of exploiters. . . .

Soyinka's novel is stylistically difficult. It is not easy for the average reader to penetrate the complexities of symbol and verbal structure which characterize the novel. These difficulties will prevent many readers from enjoying one of Soyinka's most important artistic creations to date: *Season of Anomy* is not only a very accomplished novel, but it also marks a significant turning point in Soyinka's [career] as a writer. The theme of the novel is based on the dialectical relationship between exploitation and revolution, and Soyinka points to the inevitability of violence as a method of bringing about justice to the oppressed peoples of Africa. For thinking people like Ofeyi, the prevailing social conditions present a serious challenge. But the challenge applies no less to Soyinka than it does to Ofeyi, for Soyinka is certainly becoming a militant writer. . . . This recent commitment on the part of Soyinka is clearly stated in his introduction to *Ch'Indaba*, a journal of which he is the editor. There he expresses the view that it is not in the nature of man to sit idly while political events "roll over him."

Emmanuel Ngara. *Stylistic Criticism and the African Novel*
(London: Heinemann, 1982), pp. 99, 115

To enter the world of *Aké: The Years of Childhood* is to enter an enchanted world, [Léopold Sédar] Senghor's "Kingdom of Childhood," sometimes charmingly recreated by the adult Soyinka in some of his best prose to date. One of the most charming features of the work is the image of the boy which comes across—a precocious, mischievous but clever boy who is only too ready to become physically aggressive in an expression of an as yet unreached manhood: a denial of his inevitable youthful weakness. Another element is the child's perspective from which people, things, and events are seen and described. Soyinka is able to convey a child's sense of the magic and wonder of life—wonder at the incomprehensible world around him as in the early recapitulations, and the magic world of imagined demons and spirits, or "creatures," which people the world of children. Most charming and amusing of all is the child's sense of himself which Soyinka, the narrator, through his tongue-in-cheek prose, evokes admirably. This sense of self is very meaningful and serious for the child while it is only quixotic to adults. Hence the general indulgence of the boy, although this is partly due to his being male and a first-born son. Going to school, being choosy of women when he hasn't even reached puberty, his concern with his "wife," Mrs. Odufuwa—all these incidents come across humorously from the child's perspective so acutely presented in the older Soyinka's mocking tone. . . .

Soyinka succeeds in recreating the past from a child's perspective by his handling of focus—in an almost cinematic but verbal and structural way. It is best exemplified by the first chapter, in particular in the evocation of Bishop Ajayi Crowther. In Soyinka's past work, these characteristic techniques, employed in *The Interpreters*, and to our chagrin, in *A Dance of the Forests* and in parts of *Idanre* [& *Other Poems*] have aroused the cry of "obscurity" and "difficulty" among his readers. But in *Aké* these techniques are perfectly suited to the handling of a child's incomplete, imaginative and often surrealist view of life.

'Molara Ogundipe-Leslie. In Eldred Durosimi Jones, ed.
African Literature Today. 14 (1984), pp. 141, 143

Recent attacks on the writings of Wole Soyinka sound very similar to the earlier criticism of [Camara] Laye's *Dark Child*. . . . The critics involved may at first seem bothered by questions of obscurity in Soyinka's work, but what really angers them is their perception that Soyinka is a colonial writer. He does not deal directly with political issues, does not show any clear commitment to the problem of building Africa, politically and culturally, and thus sanctions a negative ideology. If these critics have had trouble with Soyinka's other works to date, they will undoubtedly find even mores to complain about in *Aké: The Years of Childhood*. After all, this work is not just a piece of literature; it is history. It chronicles the life of Soyinka from when he was two through roughly his eleventh year. These years corresponded with a significant era of colonialism, from the late 1930s through the mid-1940s; but only at the end do we see or hear about the colonial presence in any direct way. As is true of any piece of literature, it can be subjected to multiple readings (or deconstructive "misreadings"); and yet any close examination of rhetoric should reveal a definite ideological load and a very strong statement about a society in transition. . . .

Aké is not a work in which we can locate a clearly fixed center, or point to a single unified structure. One way of reading this work is to see it as a very nostalgic piece about lost innocence. We merely need to follow the chronological structure and the shape of the images. In the beginning, Aké is the child's world, physically and spiritually secure. If there are external threats such as the *àbikú*, the *iwin* and the *óró*, they serve only to give definition to boundaries and make the child more secure in his knowledge that he is within the safe area. But he must venture out, and he learns in his first experience of getting lost, that all compounds are not clearly connected with his own. Later he will have to come to terms with his mother's fear of his being poisoned outside the home, and he will learn to redefine snake as food. He will also be ritually treated by his grandfather. The treatment, a kind of initiation, is to insure he will be safe from the threatening powers of the outside world. All of this has to do with order versus disorder, apparently a central conflict in the work. Change always threatens one's ordered view of the world, and the young Soyinka discovers this is not just a matter of venturing away from one's compound. Change intrudes even inside the house in the form of a birth or a death, the rearrangement of furniture, the appearance of a "new" relative, the coming of electricity. Change, in a manner reminiscent of [Amos] Tutuola is made a palpable presence, personified and given capital letters: "CHANGE often acted inconsistently . . . I had believed that change was something that one or more of the household caught, then discarded—like Temperature." . . .

In the remainder of *Aké* [after chapter ten], we see the child moving out into the world, gaining in social awareness. His immediate concern, and the concern of his family, is with his formal education; and we see him enter Abeokuta Grammar School. At the end, he is about to go off to Government College, Ibadan. There is, however, another education he gets as he watches his mother and some other women become increasingly involved in a woman's movement. At first the women are only interested in helping women who are "socially backward,"

African women, for example, who do not know how to dress or act when they marry in a Christian/Western ceremony. There is, of course, no awareness on their part, or the young Soyinka observing them, that they are all engaged in "the depressing attempt to impose an outward covering—and an alien one—on a ceremony that lacked heart or love or indeed, identity." The women soon expand their area of "do gooding" to include women outside their elite economic and social circle, market women and farm women who are illiterate. At this point they become aware of problems they have never confronted before, and as a result become part of a much larger movement across the land. They see women exploited by a corrupt system of taxation, and they literally move to confront those traditional leaders immediately involved. Indirectly, they find themselves pitted against the entire colonial system. They are, through their action and experience, transformed from a ladies' social club to the Egba Woman's Union: "At some point, much later, we heard of the formation of the Nigerian Women's Union. The movement . . . begun over cups of tea and sandwiches to resolve the problem of newlyweds who lacked the necessary social graces, was becoming popular and nationwide. And it became all tangled in the move to put an end to the rule of white men in the country." In the final pages we see the mother developing a global awareness of the problems they face when she is on the phone verbally attacking the District Officer for the Western decision to drop atomic bombs on Japan. The racism in the decision is clear to her. More immediately, for the young Soyinka, that racism is somehow tied to even his clothing as he listens to his uncle on the subject of his not wearing shoes or having pockets in his shorts in secondary school. Moving out into the world has meant a progressive move from order to disorder, from the garden to the atomic bomb; and the tension of living in transition and change has intensified. The child at eleven feels "the oppressive weight of [his] years."

In these chapters subsequent to chapter ten we can see a very progressive view of Africa moving through the crisis of cultural and political transition. The position argues a way out for Africans from Western class stratification through their functional involvement in community education and political action. . . . [There] is little direct interpretation of events in these chapters. We merely see them through the eyes of the child trying to order his world.

Richard [K.] Priebe. In Stephen Arnold, ed. *African Literature Studies: The Present State/L'État présent* (Washington, D. C.: Three Continents Press, 1985), pp. 127, 130–33

As early as *A Dance of the Forests*, Soyinka had created Rola, who we learn had callously sent a stream of lovers to their deaths. It is here that the image of the femme fatale is set, and she reappears with amazing frequency in succeeding works. For the purposes of our discussion, Simi of *The Interpreters* is the first of these mysterious, quasi-mythical courtesans. Simi is a woman living and moving in the real world, but she is imbued with the characteristics of the river goddess. Simi is excessively beautiful, the "goddess of serenity" with the "skin of light pastel earth, Kano soil in the air." But there is a quality of danger and hypnotism in this beauty, for she is the "Queen Bee" who destroys the drones who are nevertheless attracted to her. . . .

Similarly, Segi of *Kongi's Harvest* is so beautiful, so alluring that she is, like Simi, the subject of praise songs. She too has hypnotic eyes (a physical feature which seems to fascinate the author) to which praises are sung, and nipples as "violent as thorns." She too is the "Mammy Watta" who "frolics by the sea at night." But this quality of danger is heightened in the description of Segi, for there is a beauty with viciousness expressed in the image of *agbadu* "the coiled black glistening snake."

Segi, Kongi's sometimes mistress, is by far Soyinka's most dangerous woman, but at least in this play her venom has a practical use. As the play climaxes and Daoudu is unable to carry through with the overthrow of Kongi, Segi resourcefully seizes the time and valorously sends the head of her executed father to Kongi. . . .

The depiction of Iriyise in *Season of Anomy* seems to take the positive woman's image created in Segi several steps backwards, as the characterization moves from woman as subject to woman as object [of] quest. Iriyise again has the characteristics of the goddess, the image of exceptional beauty that defines the Soyinka woman. She is "Celestial," "Iridescent," "the Cocoa Princess." But she can be moody and "bitchy" and one never knows if she is going to prepare breakfast for him or chase him with a stick. Iriyise is also the "Queen Bee" who actually lives in what the author explicitly describes as "a cell in a deep hive." Animal imagery again surrounds her portrayal. "Once in a while she unleashed the caged tigress in her at some trivial or imagined provocation . . . ".

Iriyise is mysterious too. She disappears and reappears at will without giving plausible explanations for her absence. Indeed her act as the Cocoa Princess involves her disappearance into the pod and reappearance as the new shoot. In this context, there is a definitive positive quality about her as expressed in her immersion into the life of Aiyéró, a context in which Ofeyi felt he knew little of her. Yet this quality of Iriyise is never developed by the author. Instead, her sexual attributes dominate as Ofeyi is caught in a trance admiring her beauty. . . .

Throughout Soyinka's works, one finds the kernel of positive portrayal of the female image which is never fully realized. The energy of Sadiku's victory song/dance [in *The Lion and the Jewel*] and Sidi's fire, Segi's organization of the prostitutes, the challenges of the chorus of women and the young girls in *Death and the King's Horsemen,* and Iriyise's brief involvement in Aiyéró, all provide the basis for a balanced image of women in this literature. But the author continuously abandons these potentially positive female characters or characteristics. Dehinwa, a realistic, modern African woman, is never developed in *The Interpreters*, for example. Instead, we find the idealization of physical attributes of women or the quest for the ideal, which limits the author's development of plausible female characters.

Carole Boyce Davies. In Kofi Anyidoho, Abioseh M. Porter, Daniel [L.] Racine, and Janice Spleth, eds. *Interdisciplinary Dimensions of African Literature* (Washington, D. C.: Three Continents Press, 1985), pp. 94–97

Soyinka has a primed sense of engagement and an abiding youthfulness of spirit. He has a wide range of imaginative sympathies. Those who see his initials as one of a few points of comparison with Shakespeare are right in the sense that . . . he has cast his dreams into the mold of a vast range of characters. And his writing is shot through with a rich inimitable poetry. Since Soyinka is a man of unique sensibilities, his circle of friends in Nigeria affectionately call him Kongi after one of his roguish creations. . . .

His versatility and sophistication [are] astounding. He has wrestled with almost every literary form, has written two novels, countless plays, sketches, reviews, has produced a film, and released an album of satiric songs, and published four volumes of poetry. Wole Soyinka represents to the younger generation of African writers the necessity of realizing the full potential of one's gifts and abilities. It is a remarkable living heritage. And it is more striking when one takes into consideration the fact that when he started he had no models. He represents imaginative fecundity, the ceaseless creation of self in constant interaction with the world. And the reason he can be like this is because he will not accept that there is only one mode of being. Existence, in his world, is necessarily creative. People cannot survive without myth, without religion. His desire to bring together, to reconcile the social with the mythic, the comic with the tragic, the condemnatory with the celebratory, makes of the corpus of his works something irreducible. Soyinka speaks of the creative process as a stream. In an interview I had with him two years ago, I asked if he had any influences or models. "No models," he said, pointedly. "My work has taken the form of creative experience and that includes not just the literary world. It could be, for instance, traditional art, music, architecture, pottery, cloth dyeing. I think people should learn to look at literature as extracts and summations of various aesthetic experiences, rather than looking in terms of direct models." . . .

Wole Soyinka has brought the center to Africa and it is fairly certain that there will be an explosion in our literature. The writers will have to rise to the challenge, and take the literary explorations farther on down the unending road. We have no choice but to have a larger vision of ourselves than we have shown over the last couple of years. Blaze open the arguments, debate not in rhetoric but in works of art, widen the range of our dialogues. We cannot afford to write as if we are in a corner, when in fact we inhabit one of the richest areas in the world in terms of literature. Pass me the casket of wine, brother; Wole Soyinka has inflamed us with joy.

Ben Okri. *WA*. October 27, 1986, pp. 2249–50

As in his collection of poems, *Idanre*, the authorial presence in *The Swamp Dwellers* and *The Strong Breed* [in *The Trials of Brother Jero, and The Strong Breed*] is clearly prophetic. Both plays, however, are rather straightforward, interesting in the evolution of Soyinka's dramatic talent, but lacking the force that the prophetic voice carries in the poetry. The origins of Soyinka's genius lie in Yoruba ritual and myth and none of these early plays demonstrates this so fully as *The Trials of Brother Jero*. More than anything else, Soyinka failed to endow the other two short plays with a sense of life, and above all Jero, that archetypal fantasist, is such an overwhelming success on stage because he is so entirely alive. To find the origins then is not enough; we must also see Soyinka's particular genius at work. He never again returned to the forms he experimented with in the three short plays, but he apparently learned that his forte is comedy. Though his interest is in "serious" writing, he must have found that his prophetic voice in drama was too sharp and brittle, that only by mellowing this voice with the fantastic could he achieve a roundness and suppleness in his plays.

Relatively little critical attention has been given to *Brother Jero* despite the fact that much of the action is generally considered quite successful as comedy. The play is usually dismissed as a rather conventional farce, saved somewhat by the effective interplay of Pidgin and conventional speech, but ruined by a weak ending.

Nevertheless, with the theater public, both in Nigeria and abroad, the play has proven to be one of the most popular Soyinka has written and possibly the most frequently produced. As an audience we become active participants in Jero's trials. The play opens with Jero speaking directly to us, telling us about himself. We learn that he is "a prophet by birth and by inclination" and has worked his way up against a lot of competition from others in his field as well as the modern diversions which keep his "wealthier patrons at home." In short, he tells us that he views his work as a profession that happens to be his chosen one by virtue of his extraordinary ability to gain money and power through his practice of it. Three of the five scenes in the play begin in a similar fashion with Jero addressing us and confiding in us secrets of his business. Since Brother Jero has told us much more than he would dare tell any of his usual patrons, this does more than merely set the point of view from which we are going to view the rest of the action. We are conned into letting him lead us through a day in his life, and even into conspiring with him as he moves his other pawns around. . . .

The question remains, how serious is Jero? Because he is such a perfect chameleon, it is difficult to say; but therein also lies our answer. He shifts from one role to another with ease, and as he does so we laugh with him. Nevertheless, there is more ambiguity here than just his role shifting. There are glimpses of Jero being absolutely serious in his desire to control the politician at the end of the play. In using a trickster figure as the central character in the play, Soyinka introduced a mechanism for controlling the temperature of the satire. Throughout, the satire stays at a mild level, never getting so hot that we are unable to laugh at the folly that we ourselves have become involved in. Yet it is, after all, this folly that has resulted in Chume's being led off to an insane asylum; and despite our intimate association with Jero, we see too much of ourselves in Chume to rest comfortably in our laughter.

Richard K. Priebe. *Myth, Realism, and the West African Writer*
(Trenton, N. J.: Africa World Press, 1988), pp. 129–30, 137

It should never be said that Wole Soyinka is unresponsive to criticism. Attacked by [the Nigerian critic] Chinweizu and others as a Eurocentric modernist out of touch with Africa, Soyinka responded with *Aké: The Years of Childhood*, a memoir that clarified his African roots and cultural allegiances. Attacked by the same critics for overly difficult and esoteric poetry, Soyinka now responds with *Mandela's Earth [and Other Poems]*, a new volume of poetry much less enigmatic than his earlier verse and overtly Africanist in its political commitments. However, not all responses are created equal, and though *Aké* is a superb work, possibly Soyinka's greatest achievement, *Mandela's Earth* is not nearly so successful. Soyinka is a great prose writer and dramatist, whether working in an esoteric or exoteric mode, but I have never found his poetry as powerful. *Mandela's Earth*, despite its greater directness, does not make me change my mind.

The volume opens with the sequence that gives it its title, and though the political sentiments expressed there are irreproachable, irreproachable political sentiments do not necessarily make for great poetry. The problem is that [Nelson] Mandela has been in prison for so long that for Soyinka he has become almost completely a symbol and affords nothing concrete for the poet to come to grips with. The only part of the sequence that rises above the tone of unexceptionable sentiments is "Like Rudolf Hess, the Man Said!," which takes off from Pik Botha's statement that "we keep Mandela for the same reason the Allied Powers are holding Rudolf Hess" into a fantasy that Mandela is really Hess or even [Joseph] Mengele in disguise. Here is the real Soyinka, superb at turning the rhetoric of dictators against themselves in savage and funny ways. However, as if thinking that he might be misunderstood, he retreats from this satire into the tepid pieties of the rest of the sequence.

Reed Way Dasenbrock. *WLT*. 63, 3 (Summer 1989), pp. 524–25

Isarà [A Voyage around Essay] stands in a particularly close relationship to *Aké*, but it is not in any usual sense a sequel or even a predecessor to that work. The times in which the volumes are set overlap. Soyinka was born in 1934, and *Aké* treats his early childhood, whereas *Isarà* ends in 1940 during World War II. Soyinka himself, moreover, is not a character in *Isarà* and is not at all an agent or object of narration. This constitutes the major difference between the two memoirs. Though Soyinka assures us that elements in both are fictional, *Aké* seems like a book based directly on childhood memories; *Isarà*, in contrast, is an attempt to imagine how the author's father must actually have been as a young man, how— for instance—he must have seemed to his coevals, not to his young son. . . .

Still, the greatest interest of *Isarà* for me is in how it thematically continues the project of *Aké*, not how it may generically contrast with it. *Aké* was in large measure a response to those critics, such as Chinweizu, who have attacked Soyinka as a Euromodernist without African roots, and its dense evocation of the author's childhood worked to show how little there was to that criticism. *Isarà* takes the discussion a stage further. Soyinka's father is portrayed throughout the book as the kind of modernizing intellectual Soyinka is attacked as being; but the climactic action concerns his involvement in the struggle over the appointing of a new king for Isarà, and a new face of "Teacher Soditan" is shown. Here the modernizing intellectual seems like a traditionalist, for he becomes intensely involved in the struggle, despite being told by a friend that such a kingship is outmoded in modern Nigeria. Soyinka's real point—here as elsewhere—is that these are falsely dichotomized choices. If African traditions are to survive, then they must also be transformed. However, as he tells his friend, there is no reason why the kingship of Isarà is an outmoded survival if the kingship of England is not. Those pretending to uphold African traditions do [themselves] a disservice by insisting that they have no connection to the modern world.

Reed Way Dasenbrock. WLT. 64, 3 (Summer 1990), pp. 517–18

A Nobel prizewinner and a dramatist to be reckoned with on three continents, Wole Soyinka remains the subject of intense debate. Is he fundamentally a satirist? Or a tragedian? A Yoruba traditionalist? Or a romantic individualist or modernist who appeals to a foreign bourgeoisie? There is some truth in each of these views. Against the satirical emphases of many plays—*The Lion and the Jewel, The Trials of Brother Jero, Kongi's Harvest, Madmen and Specialists, Jero's Metamorphosis, Opera Wonyosi, Requiem for a Futurologist*, and *A Play of Giants*—we can set the tragic emphases of others: *The Swamp Dwellers, A Dance of the Forests, The Strong Breed, The Bacchae of Euripides*, and *Death and the King's Horsemen*. In each of those plays, however, and especially in *The Road*, the satirical and the tragic are complementary. Nor can we separate Soyinka's traditionalism from his romantic modernism. The expressionist and absurdist strategies of *Madmen and Specialists* pay tribute to Yoruba folklore. The ritual pattern of *Death and the King's Horsemen* consorts with an Ibsenite realism. The revision of Euripides' *The Bacchae* into a post-Christian communion rite and the translation of [Bertolt] Brecht's *Threepenny Opera* into the Nigerian satire of *Opera Wonyosi* are exercises in yet bolder eclecticism. Soyinka's plays are so various in mode and style that they elude assessment from any narrow point of view.

Such variety also characterizes his work in other genres: the volumes of poetry from *Idanre* through *Ogun Abibimang*; the two novels, *The Interpreters* and *Season of Anomy*; the autobiographical works, *Aké: The Years of Childhood* and *Isarà: A Voyage around Essay*; and the lectures and essays in *Myth, Literature and the African World* and *Art, Dialogue and Outrage*. The eclecticism results from an evident belief that all peoples are now coming into a single conversation. But it also results from an imagination that, as Biodun Jeifo has noted in his introduction to *Art, Dialogue and Outrage*, is itself antinomic or dialectical. An early essay, "The Fourth Stage," pits the regenerative "will" against the tragic "abyss." A more recent essay finds in Aristophanes's *Lysistrata* both a satirical verve and an "idiom of fertility rites," and behind both a "Life impulse" that can be manifested in both comedy and tragedy. Such opposites inform Soyinka's own work. Indeed, the generative center of his most important plays can be described as a multiform "abyss" or field of transformation that promises both destruction and recreation.

Thomas R. Whitaker. In Bruce King, ed.
Post-Colonial English Drama: Commonwealth Drama Since 1960
(New York: St. Martin's Press, 1992), pp. 200–1

From Zia with Love is both a painful cry and a warning to those who perpetuate military buffoonery and selfishness in the Nigeria of the present and the very recent past. As is usual with Soyinka, especially since *A Play of Giants*, the main dramatic characters here are based on ousted military leaders—Generals Buhari and Idiagbon—and the event which is dramatized is the most topical in Nigeria's recent history. The central action is the macabre display of arrogance and the unbridled power show that culminated in the killing of several drug peddlers in the mid-1980s following the enactment of a retroactive decree. What is implicit in Soyinka's handling of this "national disgrace," as some have termed it, is not so much the killing of these "cocaine peddlers" as the absolute neglect of human rights which military dictatorships have brought on this country.

The story of *From Zia with Love* is simple enough. A group of megalomaniacs takes over power in Nigeria. This group transforms the nation's complex cultures into a massive cell for everyone, issues Draconian decrees, and converts the political system into a fascist outfit. This is only a facade, however, a show purely for public consumption. In "a session in the court of the commandant," with the dramatic dexterity for which he is known, and using music and satire, Soyinka dramatizes the childishness of these "leaders" as they prattle over unserious matters only to issue outrageous decrees. He portrays such characters as laughable, idiotic, and bloodthirsty shadow-chasers. The metaphor of Zia al-Haq, the late Pakistani leader, is clear, representing the misuse of power and the inevitable consequences of such misdeeds.

From the evidence of things seen, Soyinka has produced a living text, beautifully constructed around the *danse macabre* and the drama of Nigeria's recent past. It takes a Soyinka to produce a work such as this. On a very significant level, *From Zia with Love* furthers Soyinka's discourse of power and coloniality.

Onookome Okome. *WLT*. 67, 2 (Spring 1993), p. 432

ST. OMER, GARTH (1931–   )

ST. LUCIA

The structure of [Garth St. Omer's] novellas is largely fragmentary, consisting of incidents, memories, flashbacks in time, letters, dialogue, present and past thoughts, and similar devices which create rather mood and reflection than sequential, linear plot development. The general style is of concise economy, understatement, and episodes which are related by association rather than cause and effect. The focus of the narratives is more on the inner consciousness and observing the sensibility of the individual than on externalities. There is little action, few events; the focus rarely shifts from the consciousness of the characters, whose memories make up most of the narrative. Even dialogue seems observed rather than in itself dramatic. It is difficult to piece events together into a chronological sequence. Individual chapters begin with imprecise emotions, the object of which is not clear until later when some previous event is mentioned.

There is disillusionment, despair, introspection, and haunting immobility; often the main characters are unlikable, being in themselves both victims and exploiters. The effect is of carefully constructed, sensitive, artfully shaped brooding over memories rather than of story. This characteristic of guilty meditation is strengthened by the various characters and stories being analogous so that parts of the novellas could be moved to another book without seeming out of place. . . .

A Room on the Hill tells of the death of John Lestrade's mother, the long estrangement between mother and father, the death of a beautiful young woman, and the insanity of a local priest who has returned to the island. The central events are the suicide of Stephen, John's best friend, whose money to escape from the island was wasted by a callous father, and the rejection of John by Stephen's girlfriend. It is a record of isolation, drifting, lives without purpose, the young dying in accidents, heavy drinking, and premature aging. . . .

"The Lights on the Hill," the first of the two narratives [collected] in *Shades of Grey*, concerns Stephenson, twenty-eight-year-old drifter, who, ironically, because of favoritism given those from the smaller, backward islands, finds himself on a scholarship at the then University College of the West Indies. Despite his escape from the small island, Stephenson's life seems a continuation of John Lestrade's brooding aimlessness.

The central event of the novella is Eddie's death by lightning, an incident which in its effect parallels the suicide of Stephen in the previous novel. Stephenson had envied Eddie as someone who, unlike himself, can achieve, but the arbitrariness of death makes him realize that achievement in itself cannot be a goal: "human effort, in the end, if it did not benefit others, was futile." This realization depresses him further. He feels he has no special talents and is merely a spectator.

"Another Place Another Time," the second narrative in *Shades of Grey*, is somewhat more sociological in purpose. Derek (the name is also that of one of John's friends in *A Room on the Hill*) is another emotional cripple produced by history. Although the island is changing—elections, black faces replacing mulattos and whites at the college—his family is too poor to enjoy the benefits. Education is his only means upward in society. His mother, with whom he no longer can speak, works endlessly to pay for his schooling as that is the "only thing to save us poor people." He feels he should work to relieve her sufferings and he is guilty of losing contact with his childhood friends, but he must continue his education if his mother's efforts are not to be wasted. Although he does not want it and has no personal ambition, he must leave the island for further schooling. After winning the island scholarship to study abroad, he refuses to accept a teaching position at the local school, despite the headmaster's claim that Derek could help others of his race, as this would end his advancement.

St. Omer's third book, *Nor Any Country*, describes a successful young West Indian who, after being educated abroad, returns to his island feeling uprooted and alienated. He can no longer speak with his family; beyond exchanging memories, they have nothing in common. His father feels threatened both by Peter's achievement and by his brother's failure to succeed in a career. We learn that Peter had been trapped into a loveless marriage eight years before. If the marriage allowed his wife to escape from her family—she was an illegitimate child—Europe was Peter's escape from her. . . . The repetitive nature of the situation is shown when Peter makes his unloved wife pregnant again and, trying to be responsible, reluctantly takes her with him to his new job teaching at the university on a different island.

The fourth book, *J—, Black Bam and the Masqueraders*, is both a further development and a commentary on *Nor Any Country*. Here we see Peter's souring life as a lecturer at the university and his brother Paul's comments on his own, and implicitly Peter's, experience. The two lives, although apparently so different, are similar products of the same culture.

Bruce King. CE&S. 3 (1977–1978), pp. 56–58

It is, of course, true that his Catholic background is a central force in St. Omer's novels. The sin-guilt-punishment syndrome operates throughout the work and, though St. Omer does not preach, as [St. Lucian poet Robert] Lee puts it, "His tone is that of the confessional. . . ." In *A Room on the Hill*, as in all the novels, this air of the confessional pervades. It achieves its greatest heights in *J—, Black Bam and the Masqueraders*, where chapters headed "Paul" are confessions of one brother. There are also, of course, the Catholic Brothers who often appear in his work: successful as well as failed priests. One of the white characters—the headmaster—in part two of *Shades of Grey* is described as "a picture of colonial seediness," reminding Derek, the hero, of "Graham Greene's novels of expatriates in Africa and America." . . .

Within this framework, the theme of personal sin and public expiation (giving, as it were, a religious twist to the conflict between private sensibility and public function), St. Omer's characters are very tightly linked. In fact, characters in early books reappear (often in greater depth) in the later ones. We first meet Derek Charles, briefly, in *A Room on the Hill*. In part two of *Shades of Grey*, he is the main character. In part one of the same book, Dr. Peter Breville and his wife Phyllis and their violently unhappy marriage are mentioned peripherally. In *Nor Any Country* their relationship and Peter's sense of despair, of panic on his return to the island, are the central elements. His relationship with his brother Paul, who—"trapped on the island"—is becoming mentally unbalanced, is introduced. In *J—, Black Bam and the Masqueraders* the relationship between Peter and Paul is central; and Paul's voice, his own point of view, is more insistent. It is as if St. Omer is considering a particular group of characters—indeed a particular relationship between the homecoming intellectual and his less fortunate trapped brethren—in greater and greater depth. From a general, almost aerial survey of a society caught in the colonial mesh of poverty, guilt, and self-contempt (the world of "Syrop") St. Omer focuses, in successive novels, on the nature of the educated individual's relationship to his society and (with *J—, Black Bam and the Masqueraders*) on the divided intellectual's relationship with friend, brother, and finally, with himself. Exile, escape from a restricting, uncreative society leads to the inevitable return. But, if in St. Omer's work exile is seen primarily as a need to break out of the psychological prison of guilt and self-contempt, then the return—at its deepest level—suggests the equally vital need to live with the confusion and pain and frustration that a genuine at-one-ment involves.

Michael Gilkes. *The West Indian Novel* (Boston: Twayne, 1981), pp. 106–7

There is one representative figure behind St. Omer's four interlinked works of fiction, *A Room on the Hill, Shades of Grey, Nor Any Country,* and *J—, Black Bam, and the Masqueraders.* He is one of the first generation in his small island to make a breakthrough by way of secondary education and a scholarship which enables him to study abroad, and he is returning as the educated professional to take his "place" in the society. [*A Room on the Hill*] presents its protagonist, John Lestrade, prior to departure, in a kind of anticipatory disillusionment with the prospect of achievement; and in "Another Place Another Time," one of the two novellas in *Shades,* we go further back to the college days of Derek Charles to trace the growth of the single-minded determination to "escape" through education. Essentially these stories function as flashbacks in the total scheme, projecting the predestined course of one essential crisis—that of the professional returning home. The implicit effort to reconnect with his past environment is balked at every turn, and he returns to a sense of acute exile at home. From this condition of isolation, he assumes the role of spectator, this twofold motif being expressed in the first title, "room on the hill."

Thus, he becomes enmeshed in a close network of family relationships, friendships, past associations. He moves in the flesh, incapable of quite cutting himself off from the ties that bind; but in spirit he lives and inclines elsewhere. From his position as spectator, however, the St. Omer persona surveys the "several postures" of his small island with a clinical precision, which Gordon Rohlehr has aptly compared to [James] Joyce's "scrupulous meanness."

St. Omer has the rare novelistic skill of deploying an introspective drama through a texture of sheer, stark, social realism. He presents a full portrait of the social, cultural, moral condition of the St. Lucian environment, though the island is in fact never named. We get a close-up view of the small, cramped community of Castries, sharing its few, spare essentials—school, church and its various observances; of its narrow range of occupations, small vendors/domestics, civil servants, teachers. The milieu is pervaded by a sense of privation. The one cultural force binding all classes together is conformism to religious custom, the norms and codes of Christian morality—which makes for a prevailing atmosphere of constraint.

Patricia Ismond. *CarQ.* 28, 1–2 (1982), pp. 34–35

There can be little comfort in the utter despondency, the seemingly banal void with which Garth St. Omer concludes *J—, Black Bam and the Masqueraders* and, to a large extent, the quartet of which it is more the nadir than the climax. The petrification of both individual and society, the ceaseless repetition implicit in the novel's ending, these can go no further. This is not to say, however, that the characters have reached the end, since to have done so would at least be some consolation, and St. Omer's characters are not that fortunate! They

remain, on the contrary, totally unable to control either their social or psychological worlds, condemned to a common, endless, often directionless search for
identity, the victims of both their society and their lucidity.

We face, in the world created by St. Omer, the individual's struggle for
self-awareness and, as a seemingly inevitable corollary, his inability to fit into
his society—or, perhaps more precisely, the inability of that society to integrate
meaningfully the individual because it is itself static, chaotic, apparently meaningless. Little wonder, then, that St. Omer's protagonists are unable to define
themselves in terms of a positive existence when their every legitimate demand
(career, personal relationships, intellectual and spiritual quest) is thwarted.

St. Omer's analysis goes beyond this, however, and through the socio-cultural dimension he nudges his reader towards a growing awareness of the universal existential dilemma which, equally bleakly, accompanies it.

Peter Dunwoodie. CarQ. 29, 2 (June 1983), p. 30

From his earliest published novella, "Syrop," to his most recent, *J—, Black Bam
and the Masqueraders*, St. Omer's works reveal a familiar complex of themes,
conflicts, and even characters, consistently developed, elaborated upon, modified, and deepened effectively through an ever-increasing technical control and
formal sophistication. Organized in a manner comparable to the connected narratives of [William] Faulkner, [James] Joyce, [Marcel] Proust, and [Thomas]
Mann, his works constitute a trenchant, interrelated, multivolumed commentary
on the existential dilemmas inherent in colonial and postcolonial life in the West
Indies. Progressing in a style which tends to replace chronology and external reference with duplication and internal associations as formal determinants, these
slim volumes continue uniquely to mine the fundamental themes of exile, identity, and alienation implicit in the entire body of Caribbean writing.

"Syrop" is St. Omer's earliest novella and the first work to be published
outside the Caribbean. This story, with its classical overtones of man's untimely
but inevitable meeting with fate, is chronologically, stylistically, and thematically the best introduction to St. Omer's art. It contains many motifs employed
by the writer in later (and longer) works: madness, sibling rivalry, intergenerational conflict, religion, illegitimacy and its social responses, exile and return,
success, and responsibility for oneself and others. Graced by a subtly symbolic
pattern of imagery, highly descriptive language, and an astute manipulation of
point of view and temporal sequence, "Syrop" dramatizes the brief and ironic
passage of a young boy into manhood, achieved on the very day of his death. In
this tale of a divided house in which rejection, guilt, and the explosive violence
of internalized frustrations characterize family and social relationships, life as
imprisonment and death as a release are pervasive elements. . . .

The organizational method employed by St. Omer in his novellas reflects an
attempt to evoke an awareness of the whole in each narrative. It is a compositional
conception which, in its intention of totality, establishes an organic relationship
between individual volumes; that is, each novella becomes "associated" with those
that precede and those that follow. This is achieved through the repetitions

mentioned above (i.e., characters, themes, locales, imagery, and even tone). The protagonists of St. Omer's fiction, for example, are usually presented with psychological "doubles" (in order to emphasize how the characters are invaded from both the outside and the inside) and are presented as if fully developed. Since we have seen them before, it avoids the necessity for "overelaboration of individual character" found in the conventional narrative genres. In this way, St. Omer approximates the kind of "epic and revolutionary novel of associations" described by Wilson Harris, whereby the "characters are related within a personal capacity which works in a poetic and serial way so that a strange jigsaw is set in motion."

The correspondence between perspective and form is further reinforced by the open-ended nature of the plots. With this method of concluding his narratives, St. Omer emphasizes the ambiguity and inconclusiveness of life and also underscores the interconnectedness of the novellas; that is, the sense of inconclusiveness, the absence of a definite or certain resolution of conflict(s), functions as narrative interstices of a multivolumed work and also helps to sustain the anticipation of future installments. Moreover, along with the use of duplication and internal associations, this characteristic ending effects a style in which internal elements assume a greater importance than chronology and external reference.

Roland E. Bush. In Daryl Cumber Dance, ed. *Fifty Caribbean Writers*
(Westport, Conn.: Greenwood Press, 1986), pp. 406, 414

The large-scale tragedy of "Syrop," the experimentations in existential antiheroism of "The Lights on the Hill," the social realities in "Another Place Another Time," the concern over Catholicism found in *A Room on the Hill* are all ingredients welded together in *Nor Any Country*.

While it would be extreme to call *Nor Any Country* a work of reconciliation, the novella leaves the St. Omer reader with the impression that the author has finally gained control over his topic, his style, and his hero. Peter is the familiar educated West Indian who has left his island for England and who returns home with the potential for ordering his values.

St. Omer does not provide his reader with any forewarning that this time he is creating an existential antihero with a difference. Peter is like his predecessors in many ways: he exploits the women with whom he lives, he watches others rather like a scientist collecting specimens, he is generally self-indulgent. He takes a greater interest in the members of his family, however, and his accounts of his father, his mother, his brother, and his wife are more sympathetic than hitherto. Finally, Peter is able to listen to the fears and worries of a Roman Catholic clergyman. He allows Father Thomas time to explain his own sense of alienation as a dark-skinned clergyman assigned to labor among parishioners on his home island. In short, Peter has outgrown his solipsism enough to hear another's anxieties.

Peter's ability to open himself to Father Thomas's anxieties might well be the crack through which compassion for Phyllis enters. Once able to accept her love and to recognize her need for her husband, Peter is also able to extend his compassion to include Michael, his brother's little son. Peter, still a man of few words, may appear to be a stereotypic antihero, but he has grown beyond the protagonists of St. Omer's earlier works. He has redefined tragedy to include the angst of those who share his world.

Having achieved the ability to participate in the angst of those around him, Peter in *J—, Black Bam and the Masqueraders* is able to empathize with his brother's world view. Paul, not unlike Hamlet, declares himself mad. Paul's antic disposition enables him to countenance the disappointing turn his life has taken. An earlier Peter would have been too self-centered to share so much as bookspace with his brother. . . .

[John] Thieme believes that *J—, Black Bam and the Masqueraders* is St. Omer's most successful novel because the author is able to sustain the two parallel but separate points of view that Peter and Paul present. The point of view St. Omer elects is an interesting variant of the omniscient narrator. The St. Omer reader is so conditioned to accept the existential antihero's self-absorption that he or she assumes that Paul's narration is filtered through Peter's sensibility. In fact, it is not. Double, each narrative line is nevertheless distinct, enabling both Peter and Paul to delineate the details of their personal tragedies.

Whereas *Nor Any Country* offers promise of reconciliation, St. Omer's final West Indian novel plunges the reader back into the depths of modern alienation. This time, however, the degree of alienation is compounded by the doubling. Not one but two promising West Indians have succumbed to disillusionment and despair.

Elaine Campbell. In A. L. McLeod, ed., *Subjects Worthy Fame*
(New Delhi: Sterling Publishers, 1989), pp. 7–9

[St. Omer's novels] explore one single subject: the dilemma of the educated native son, returning home to take his place and make a contribution to his society. He finds this purpose thwarted by a society still trapped in the dearth of persisting poverty and alien religious values. He comes to face instead, his own personal paralysis and psychic disability. In a sensitive response to St. Omer's theme, [Derek] Walcott has described this dilemma as "homecomings without home." The St. Omer persona, who appears in all the various protagonists, sums up the problem thus: "From his memory he had exhumed corpses of his old self, probing them with the scalpel of his new awareness. . . . But the timidity and fear his discovery of himself had instilled and the paralysis they induced made any reconstruction in the future too daring for him to contemplate." Inclined toward self-withdrawal, he remains intimately enmeshed in the reality of . . . society, experiencing his past and continuing ties with it. He therefore reflects the predicament of the society in analyzing his own. . . .

What stands out especially in the community St. Omer presents is the rigid system of orthodox morality, which closely regulated its life. It dictated the prevailing codes, sanctions, and mores of the society. Among these, the most formidable was the sanction against illegitimacy. It imposed all kinds of double standards and constraints in a largely underprivileged class where the traditional pattern of unmarried mothers and fatherless homes obtained. Most expressive of the kind of authoritarianism the Church stood for was its policy for enforcing this sanction. Young men and women involved in pregnancies outside marriage had the choice of either getting married or losing their jobs in the teaching service and similar educational opportunities. . . .

One thing becomes quite clear about the society St. Omer recaptures: there were glaring gaps between its prescribed norms and its actual practices. . . . Most critically, its pressures and strains backfired to cause total disarray within the most private areas of human relationship. Family, married, and sexual life were all strangely disordered. Most of St. Omer's characters are casualties of one type or another of these abnormal relationships; and his final, most penetrating focus is on the toll in damaged psyches and ruined lives.

In his culminating novel, *J—, Black Bam and the Masqueraders*, St. Omer describes a situation that highlights the extreme reaches of just these violations. The novel juxtaposes the stories of two St. Lucian brothers, Paul and Peter Breville. Paul, the older brother who remained on the island, has ended up mad; Peter, who left the island on a scholarship, has just returned to a university post in one of "the larger islands to the north." The technique of the novel is both functional and thematic. Paul's letters to his brother, a desperate outpouring of his memories, alternate with snapshots of Peter's present life [on] the other island. The two brothers, in fact, emerge as alternate sides of the same coin: Paul, a victim of madness; Peter trapped in a violent, destructive marriage to a St. Lucian girl from his past. It is as if, in other words, neither had "escaped."

Behind their two contrasting circumstances lay two opposite choices. Both brothers had found themselves faced with the same problem, common enough: to conform to the Church's policy on extramarital pregnancies or lose their chances of a future through education. Paul, always confident of his own brilliance, had preferred to defy the system rather than enter into a marriage he did not want. Peter had married Phyllis, whom he later suspects of having deliberately trapped him, to preserve his chance of pursuing a career. To survive [on] the island, where he is doomed to remain, Paul dons a pose of madness. He is seduced into the role by egomaniac delusions of his own apartness, and contempt for his mean surroundings. The pose of madness becomes all too real. Peter, on the other side, pays an equally high price for his convenient conformism. His life with Phyllis is a mutually destructive affair, now down to a level of raw brutality and violence. He has nothing in common with the wife who had actually waited eight years in his mother's house during his absence. (Peter had left to take up the scholarship soon after marrying her). Phyllis embodies some of the worst hangovers of the past. She is devoid of ambition and is inarticulate, driven solely by her ambition to find her own salvation in someone, like Peter, who had achieved success. . . .

St. Omer singles out a portrait of St. Lucia which obviously has some personal urgency for him. Though there are other faces besides the one he shows, he does sound some of the key notes of the St. Lucian sensibility, and evokes strains and postures which also appear in Walcott. His images point to an authentic pull between two opposite strains of that sensibility—the one repressed, the other charged with a spirit and energy that will not stay harnessed.

Patricia Ismond. *WLWE*. 29, 2 (Autumn 1989), pp. 107–10

SUTHERLAND, EFUA (1924–   )

GHANA

Efua Sutherland founded the Ghana Drama Studio in Accra . . . and did much in the late 1950s and early 1960s to encourage experimental work in drama. Through her post in African literature and drama in the University of Ghana, she has been influential in the training of young dramatists and actors; and her own research on Ghanaian music theater and concert parties is of importance. In addition to her three major plays, *Foriwa*, *Edufa* and *The Marriage of Anansewa*, Efua Sutherland has written several plays for children. *The Marriage of Anansewa*, a play which uses music and dance to decorate and guide the action, is a witty and lighthearted story of a man who attempts to marry his daughter to several rich chiefs all at the same time, in order to raise money from them. When they all converge on his home together it takes all his ingenuity to resolve the situation. *Edufa*, by contrast, is the story of a man who gives his wife's life in place of his own. Edufa, a rich and successful businessman, respected in his hometown and greatly loved by his wife, learns from an oracle that he will die and that the only way to escape death is to find someone willing to die for him. To his horror, instead of being able to trap his old father into saying that he loves him well enough to die for him, his wife Ampoma states her affection for him in those terms, and is consequently made the victim of the charm Edufa has bought to save himself. The similarities to Euripides's *Alcestis* are acknowledged; but the play often seems rather static in construction and in dialogue, and the full impact of the story may be hindered by this.

Foriwa, however, has a lightness and a charm about it that make it probably Sutherland's most effective play. It is a simple moral tale, perhaps almost didactic in some ways, but not restricted by its morality and didacticism in any way. The play is set in a Ghanaian town, Kyerefaso, which is crumbling into dust through the neglect and inactivity of the elders. It takes a "stranger" (a Hausaman from northern Ghana) to come to Kyerefaso and revitalize it, helped by the Queen Mother of the town and her beautiful daughter Foriwa. The stranger, Labaran, clearly represents the new spirit of Ghana. He is a graduate, and yet lives simply and without ostentation. He is a stranger in the town, and yet makes the point that he is a Ghanaian, and though of different tribe is of the same nation. He represents the forces and the virtues of self-help—a respect for the tradition of the elders tempered by an awareness that tradition should be a creative force and not simply an exercise in placid nostalgia. Where others talk, Labaran acts. Often he attracts attention to himself not because of what he does, but of the way in which he does it. As he says: "If you want people to listen to you, do something that astounds them. They weren't astonished because I carried rubbish. It was because I wore a suit for the job." Labaran's first ambition is to build a bookshop in the town, and this he does through encouraging the local postmaster to extend his shop for this purpose. The symbol is obvious, and the care that Labaran takes to make his schemes seem to be the idea of the local people themselves is also quite clearly intended as a subtle lesson to the audience. Foriwa, who previously turned her back on her hometown because of its bickering and inertia, resolves to stay to support Labaran. All this takes place in the context of the town celebrating its annual festival. The elders see it as merely a ritual, devoid of meaning, simply perpetuating old ways. The Queen Mother, inspired perhaps by Labaran and Foriwa, challenges the elders and the townspeople to turn their thoughts to more positive ways and to hold their festival as a sign of regeneration. . . . The play ends on an optimistic note, and the moral is nicely made. This play has a charm and a functional quality about it, and is a good example of the conscious use of the drama in a social context.

Martin Banham and Clive Wake. *African Theatre Today*
(London: Pitman, 1976), pp. 52–54

In a discussion of the theater in Ghana, Efua Sutherland once declared that a truly vital theater should heed the example of oral literature by dealing directly with contemporary experience. Oral literature, she pointed out, "uses . . . experience artistically." By a similar token, a national theater should look at and utilize the repositories of a culture's experience, it should avoid the merely imitative art of "performing plays just because they exist in books already," and it therefore should depend on the willingness of the artist to create forms which can communicate both the contemporary experience and the historical process out of which it grew. In this sense, theater becomes a kind of immediate cultural exploration: "There are all sorts of exciting things to venture and I take a deep breath and venture forth . . . I'm on a journey of discovery. I'm discovering my own people." Sutherland's views and practice find a ready supporter in Ama Ata Aidoo: "What she conceives," Aidoo observes of Sutherland, "is that you take the narration—the traditional narration of a folktale. In the course of the narration, you get a whole lot of dramatic behavior which one should use, in writing plays even in English. . . . I believe with her that in order for African drama to be valid, it has to derive lots of its impetus, its strength, from traditional African dramatic forms." . . .

As writer, producer, and teacher, Sutherland has always been personally involved in the mechanics of theater, as well as the art of dramatic writing itself. Her career has enabled her to experiment with approaches to Ghanaian theater that explore the possible relevance of European models and the continuing vitality of indigenous folk drama and folktales. She has adapted Western drama (including her own adaptation of *Everyman*) to a Ghanaian context. At the same time, she has also been adapting Ghanaian tales to her contemporary theater. In fact, her career has been a "journey of discovery," to borrow her own words—a journey that has taken her from the adaptation of classical Greek drama, to the distinctive milieu of rural life in modern Ghana, to the reliance on indigenous folk forms. . . . Her other works [include *Odasani, Nyamekye,* and children's plays (*The Pineapple Child, Ananse and the Dwarf Brigade,* and *Vulture! Vulture!* and *Tahinta: Two Rhythm Plays*)]. But her three major, published plays exemplify at its best her continuing quest for certain dramatic forms—specifically, those forms which are analogous to the theme of sexual role-playing in the plays themselves.

Lloyd W. Brown. *Women Writers in Black Africa*
(Westport, Conn.: Greenwood Press, 1981), pp. 61, 65

Edufa, Efua Sutherland's adaptation of the Greek play *Alcestis*, is a study of the cultural conflicts of the transitional African who is torn between the differing values of the traditional tribal society and the modern industrialized world. But her play is also a folk art form which engages the mythic elements of Sutherland's Ghanaian society. It therefore relies on the oral tradition—folk art forms of song, language, and image—which plays an elemental role in an African historical past. Sutherland's adaptation of Greek classical forms establishes analogies between sexual and cultural conflicts in her society with those in Euripides's Greece. Both plays question the validity of certain social roles—the duties of husband, wife, parent, and citizen. From a broader thematic perspective, Euripides's complex, feminist-oriented portrait of Alcestis as woman, wife, and mother provides a functional backdrop for Sutherland's examination of the similarities of women's roles in various cultures: the limited role of women in society, entrenched male social privileges, and the vulnerability of women in relation to men. On an equally fundamental level, *Edufa* endeavors to express the tragic implications of African cultural rootlessness and the anxiety of assimilation. . . .

Sutherland explores Edufa's conflict of identity through the form of Greek drama because of its rootedness in the folklore that serves as the fundamental origin of Western cultural values. His African rootlessness stands in ironic contrast with the sense of roots represented by the Greek drama apropos of the West. The classical form in *Edufa*, with the prologue and choral mode as a representation of social mores, ironically contrasts with a return to traditional African values. But the play also incorporates African modes, such as the emphasis on communal values exemplified by Kankam's family ethic. Sutherland's use of Western dramatic forms and African modes amounts to an Afro-Western synthesis which draws upon the strengths of Western and African traditional values. This ideal synthesis is utilized successfully by Senchi, Sutherland's alter ego, in the guise of the Afro-Western intellectual/philosopher/poet. . . . This ideal synthesis, however, is external to a rootless African like Edufa. . . . His conflict as a transitional individual arises because of his own unresolved relationship to African cultural values. By manipulating the social conventions of the Greek cultural tradition, embodied by the chorus, Sutherland touches upon the brutalizing effects of Western influence and the exacting price inflicted upon the weak individual. Hence, on an equally fundamental level, the Afro-Western elements in *Edufa* function as signs of disorienting social transition.

Linda Lee Talbert. WLWE. 22, 2 (Autumn 1983), pp. 183, 188–89

The reputation of Efua Sutherland rests perhaps most firmly on her contribution to African theater. Since the 1950s, she has been involved with the theater as playwright, theater director, and founder of Ghana's foremost and most notable experimental theater group. Her emphasis on artistic dramatic form has been rightly noted. At times this emphasis seems so accomplished that the critic is misled into assuming that Sutherland's plays sacrifice thematic profundity for stylistic innovation. Her theatrical embellishment and inventiveness which comprise an overt use of stage props, the use of the Akan language and an emphasis on audience participation do not exclude authentic meanings for the reader or the audience. Sutherland's thematic concerns in her most popular plays, *Edufa*, *Foriwa*, and *The Marriage of Anansewa* range from an indictment of unscrupulous materialism to ideas on rural development, the uses of tradition, and an inquiry into the essence of true love. In all these plays, which are directed primarily towards Ghanaians, Sutherland's aims have been consistently didactic: teaching readers and audiences about the moralities of life, and how best to cope with their environment. She uses tradition and popular culture as the foundations of her plays, and through the dramatic process attempts to redefine and refine such traditions and cultures. Her plays reflect a conviction that through the play, the writer can actually monitor as well as influence a nation's cultural direction and taste. . . .

The theme of commitment and giving to others is the main concern in . . . *Foriwa*. In this play the theme is expanded into the conception of group self-help. *Foriwa* tells the story of a village, Kyerefaso, and its backward-looking and complacent people. The traditional ruler of the village, the Queen Mother, is herself progressive, but her ideas are always opposed by the more conservative elements of her council. This trend continues until Labaran, a visitor from the northern part of the country, throws in his lot with the Queen Mother and Foriwa, her daughter. The playwright's motive seems twofold: to show that group effort is the only really worthwhile way of achieving progress, and to demonstrate the true meaning of progress based on the proper use of tradition. She achieves the first by using not one, but three characters to advance the dramatic movement of the play. She makes the form of her play—the use of group protagonists in the persons of the Queen Mother, Labaran, and Foriwa—complement her main thematic concern—the need for group leadership and collective participation in societal development. In order to deal with the second issue of the appropriate approach to tradition and the past, Sutherland adopts an overly realistic mode in which her protagonists as simulated people are used to deliver her sermon. . . .

In *Foriwa*, Sutherland's idea of theater is fully realized. The play's structure is successfully integrated with the dominant themes of rebirth and communal involvement. Most of the play's action takes place in the vicinity of the four-branched god-tree. The tree, a symbol of vitality and change, dominates the town square, and thus indicates the vital role it has to play in the life of the village. The tree also imposes its presence on the language of the play—"the scattering of seeds like forest trees, and the picking of fruit from living branches." In addition, this tree of life is presented as related to the question of agricultural self-sufficiency and food for the sustenance of life, one of Labaran's major interests. The play achieves a similar synthesis with its other themes. The idea of the necessity to merge the old with the new, and the need to incorporate African values with Western ones for a rounded development, as well as the need for men and women from various tribes to work together are suggested formally through character representation. The Queen Mother, by virtue of her role as traditional ruler, belongs to the African past. Foriwa and Labaran, on the other hand, represent the new as well as the Western. In addition, Foriwa, a girl educated in Western values, represents emancipated woman. Labaran, being a university graduate, depicts the educated male elite with access to modern Western technology. Labaran is also used to represent the outsider from another ethnic group in the country. These characters who are not typical, but rather exemplary members of the class they represent, are used to demonstrate how the best from the old and the new, from Africa and the West can be utilized to achieve formidable progress. By using three characters of equal importance to carry her message, Sutherland uses the form of collective heroism to depict the idea of group leadership and participation of the community. The Queen Mother, Foriwa, and Labaran all start working for the good of Kyerefaso on an individual basis with little success. They begin to achieve real success when they team up with one another and with the entire village of Kyerefaso.

Adetokunbo Pearce. In Eldred Durosimi Jones, ed. Women in African
Literature Today (Trenton, N.J.: Africa World Press, 1987), pp. 71, 75–77

Efua Sutherland . . . is well known as one of Ghana's most active voices in utilizing traditional modes of theater to promote social change. Her goal has been to acknowledge traditional oral drama performed in villages, stimulate modern dramatic activities, and set up community theaters in rural areas. Moreover, she has been instrumental in fostering indigenous drama in both her theater groups and her plays. Sutherland's plays have been integral to her concept of theater as a means of revitalizing rural life in African communities, and her impact has been felt through her plays for children as well as for adults. Sutherland's best-known works, *Edufa*, *Foriwa*, and *The Marriage of Anansewa*, are all directed toward reconciling the conflict of Western and African cultural values in modern-day African society; the latter two plays also satisfy her objective that written drama serve the community as the oral tradition has done. . . .

Sutherland's play *Foriwa* is a later version of a short, allegorical tale called "New Life in Kyerefaso." Both pieces are based on the transformation of an African folktale used by mothers to warn their daughters away from unknown, handsome men. The folktale tells of a beautiful and proud girl who refuses to marry any young man chosen by her family but decides instead to marry a handsome stranger. Whether the man turns into a python, a spirit, or a skull, the moral taught is that young women who disobey their families and do not listen to the wisdom of their elders will eventually meet disaster. This folktale has been reworked by numerous West African writers, yet Sutherland is unique in that the moral of the folktale in *Foriwa* is a positive one. The choice of a stranger brings "new life" to the town of Kyerefaso rather than devastation, altering the meaning of the old tale. In this way Sutherland expands the message of the folktale to illustrate a different dilemma: how to build a nation out of the different ethnic groups in Ghana. . . .

In *Foriwa*, as in *The Marriage of Anansewa*, what is of real value is not necessarily material. The grandmother gives Anansewa advice in the form of a riddle, an aspect of the oral tradition. Moreover, her values come from the traditional culture that has been distorted, in the present generation, by Western materialistic values, illustrated by the trickery of her son, Ananse. So when the

Queen Mother asks Foriwa why she wants to refuse the present suitor, a man who "has salvaged his life from this decrepitude" by making a great success of his life materially, Foriwa answers that she will not join her life with a man who is interested merely in personal gain. She shudders at the kind of society he represents by ameliorating his own life at the expense of the community. She responds instead by approaching the subject of the town's deterioration and the Queen Mother's fights with the elders who care more for the words of the traditions than for what those words convey. . . .

In her three published plays for adults, Sutherland's aim has been to focus on the kinds of values that are being passed on the children: What will become of traditional culture, weakened by colonial domination, if the present generation does not continue their oral traditions and reform them to fit modern Ghanaian society? *Foriwa* works toward the resolution of these cultural conflicts by utilizing orature and literature as vehicles for the revitalization of rural communities. Sutherland's emphasis on women's role in "minding the culture" and bringing new life into old traditions, mirrors her own concern for and active participation in strengthening the bonds between the African past and future generations. Her performances and productions, her village education for children, and her plays themselves illustrate a playwright tied not only to the traditions and customs of the African continuum but secure in her place as an African woman passing on the values of her foremothers to the children.

Gay Wilentz. *RAL*. 19, 2 (Summer 1988), pp. 182–85, 194

TABAN LO LIYONG (1939–   )

UGANDA

Taban lo Liyong is an East African writer and critic who genuflects before no idols—European, Nigerian, or local—and who proves that he is right to exercise the prerogatives of genius. With this slim book of essays [*The Last Word*] he introduces himself as a powerful voice, a spectacular and audacious intelligence.

Finely and broadly educated but no pedant, [Taban] lo Liyong does not wear his learning on his sleeve. Instead, it is most visible where one is accustomed to its absence: at the business end of a set of brass knuckles. He writes with passion and a sense of humor, with a merciless contempt for cant and the wit and will to be devastating. His work is contentious, irreverent, and exciting. He writes on what interests him—and that, often, is what angers him: American arrogance, African self-indulgence, intellectual slackness, pettiness. He writes his own version of English, and, in a sentence of concentrated irony, has advised compatriots seeking a viable medium that "a domesticated East African English should be an obedient servant." . . .

He has no respect for the view that African writers should not be judged on the same scale as Homer and Shakespeare. He damns, equally, self-indulgent evaluations by Africans and the flattery of Africans by Europeans who may want to be encouraging but are in effect patronizing. He wants an African literature—above all an East African literature—which will move nobody to pat it on the head and say, "You're really very nice." In his view of writing, it is good *that* it's African (and he exhorts African schools to give encouragement of writing a high priority), but it's never good *because* it's African.

Basil Busacca. Africa Report. 15, 8 (November 1970), p. 34

It is as hard to write about Taban lo Liyong as it is to write about Amos Tutuola, for these two writers are Africa's greatest eccentrics. If, in Taban's phrase, the Yoruba writer is the true son of Zinjanthropus, then he himself is his delinquent nephew. Faced with either case, literary criticism is not sure where to start; and Taban's career . . . is deliberately designed to ensure that no critic ever will finally get at the truth about him. What Taban is or represents, what he wants to be or appears to be—these are as hard as deciding . . . into which pigeonhole his work should be squeezed. Teacher, researcher, marathon walker, polymath, eater of library books (and shelves), born cynic, utopian, bibliographer extraordinary, reformer, journalist, essayist, professional devil's advocate, catalyst, midwife, prophet, dabbler in riddles, poet, pop philosopher, brother to Ocol (secret lover of Lawino), Voltaire to [Okot p'Bitek's] Frederick the Great, Whitmanesque gadfly, modernist, traditionalist, sociologist, individualist, iconoclast, sententious elder of thirty-six. Which of all these is he, at heart? In which role would he like to be remembered? Chris Wanjala has rightly noted that "his works are full of the proud and grateful consciousness that he is a synthetic being," and perhaps this is as good a description as one could find. But whatever the answer, there is no doubt that Taban is the most chameleonlike figure in East Africa today. But of course all the critics say this, and it would be a relief simply to leave it there and get on with Ngugi [wa Thiong'o] or [Leonard] Kibera. Yet Taban's impact on the modern scene has been too great for so brief a dismissal: it won't do simply to label him as some weirdly synthetic chameleon. . . .

Like a prophet emerging from the desert, Taban returned home [from the United States] determined to do all in his power—by cajolery, coercion, provocation, and intellectual freedom-fighting —to transform East Africa and end its literary drought. After dipping his head deep into many wells of modern thought, he would, furthermore, return with no fixed position visible to readers, colleagues, or critics. His choice of a confessional strain, a stream-of-conscious-tell-it-all mode suggesting an honest mind's encounter with a myriad [of] viewpoints, looks like a quirk of temperament; but it was also a preferred way of releasing the maximum latent energy in the home scene and of placing before his community the widest possible range of ideas on which planning for the future might be based. Hence the persistent and deliberate contradictions; hence the love of paradox and Swiftian lists. Certainly East Africa's current position as the matrix of the continent's fiercest and most creative debates can be ascribed in generous measure to Taban's influence. His arrival from Iowa changed the local scene like magic. The words began to pour, essays, letters, poems, longer poems. Then books. First *The Last Word*, perversely titled because it was his first word (in book form) on African problems. Then came *Fixions* [& *Other Stories*], comprising work arising from research into oral tradition; *Eating Chiefs*, more work in oral literature; then *Frantz Fanon's Uneven Ribs*, a book of verse; and most recently, still more verse, *Another Nigger Dead*, and a potpourri, *Thirteen Offensives against Our Enemies*.

Initial response to Taban's writing mixed astonishment with disbelief. Astonishment at the jesting freshness of it all, disbelief at the violence of Taban's attacks on a herd of sacred cows including Négritude. There was a problem of appropriate response to writing whose viewpoint always shifted, never settling long enough to be pinned down or explained. The show kept moving at speed, and masks worn during the early period were thrown from the caravans as the circus headed up the road to a new pitch. A show over, what it had offered had to take its chance, either to live or die. The new reality, the current show, mattered most. Audience and disciples, gathering in droves, faced an impossible task trying to keep up and understand.

What emerges from behind the masks,and from writing that runs simultaneously in a dozen different directions, is a mind of Olympian independence, which refuses to be reduced to a formula, together with a comic attitude that cries plague on everyone's house, including the writer's own which he is just about to burn down. In the guessing game Taban's work sparked, it was fashionable to blame it all on [Friedrich] Nietzsche, especially when an adulatory Goethe Institute lecture by the author coincided with published work revealing dream visions of a super-modern Africa, a new economic and military giant. But it is not in Taban's nature to be the prisoner of one influence. A fuller picture emerges from seeing him partly as a gifted (and highly assimilative) child of Nietzsche, and partly as a child of an ancient tradition of world satire. The lineage is familiar enough. Beginning with Menippus, it comes down through [François] Rabelais, [John] Skelton, [Miguel] Cervantes, [Samuel] Butler, [Jonathan] Swift, [Alexander] Pope, [Laurence] Sterne . . . Voltaire, and [Thomas] Carlyle. Writers in this tradition often serve up satire in a narrative framework, despise—or appear to despise—formal principles, rejoice in rollicking wit, cock a snook at orthodox style, love exaggeration, delight in the grotesque and caricature, and work from values very hard to fix. It is the mad world of Jolly Rutterkin, Martinus Scriblerus, Gulliver, Tristram and Uncle Toby, Candide, and Professor Teufelsdrockh, a world where anything goes, or seems to go, except orthodoxy and stuffy conventionality.

Adrian Roscoe. *Uhuru's Fire: African Literature East to South*
(Cambridge: Cambridge University Press, 1977), pp. 114–16

Taban lo Liyong . . . in his poem "bless the african coups" blesses (ironically) the African coups, for according to him, "tragedy now means a thing." But it is with regard to tragedy as a physical and negative experience that it means something to the Africans. . . . To the extent that African coups bring about suffering and death and suppression of the "best ideas," they constitute a tragedy; but they fail to attain the overall status of tragedy because they do not effect spiritual regeneration or rebirth, and that knowledge and new awareness gained through experience.

For tragedy is like the fire that "burns the phoenix," from which it will emerge renewed; and is like the stage on which Proteus changes from shape to shape for more effective self-preservation. Tragedy is also like the process of reincarnation or metempsychosis in Hindu philosophy, whereby at death the soul leaves the body and finds a new and higher level of existence elsewhere; and is like the death of Jesus Christ which resulted in his resurrection and heavenly glorification. After establishing these parallels, [Taban lo] Liyong fervently prays that our own tragedy (the coups) may "also save us," teach us "that we are not the Lords of this world," make us "know our place in this world," teach us "final humility," open for us "the door by mistakes," and grant us "the tragic character's last self awareness."

R. N. Egudu. *Modern African Poetry and the African Predicament*
(New York: Barnes and Noble, 1978), pp. 95–96

The writings of Taban lo Liyong raise in an acute form the question of what poetry is. If poetry were solely lyrical, concerned with the songlike expression of emotions, then Taban would not be a poet, for his verse is made of gnomic philosophical utterances, rhetorical shouts, and repetitive lists. Where the Cameroonian poet Mbelle Sonne Dipoko will alter, and in particular condense, his prose utterances before presenting them as verse, Taban, who writes highly rhythmical prose, sometimes seems merely to divide it into lines or strophes and call it poetry. Where the Ghanaian poet Atukwei Okai seems aware of the danger of endlessly repeating a refrain or a structural formula of words in a rhetorical poem, Taban's tolerance of repetition sometimes knows no bounds.

Like Mazisi Kunene, Taban is a philosophical poet, prepared to make poetry directly out of belief. But his combination of substance (largely from Friedrich Nietzsche) and form (reminiscent of Heraclitean fragments, [William] Blake's gnomic sentences, Wyndham Lewis's "blasts," and, indeed, Nietzsche's own aphoristic style in *Human, All-Too-Human* and *Thus Spake Zarathustra*) is unique. His advocacy of Nietzsche's concepts of progress through the fusion of opposing tendencies (Taban's "syntheism"), the nature of frenzied creative energy, the elite Übermensch or Superman, and the dangers of rationalism (including orderly form) have made him an outsider to many literary circles. He is a person admired for his intellect and warmth of personality, but often deeply suspect because of his alien and uncongenial ideas. African poets in English are often expected to develop political ideas within a fairly narrow band of liberal or left-wing orthodoxy, whereas Taban conforms to no expectations, not even his own.

The cult of the Superman has made him quite shameless in talking about himself and his family in both prose and verse. He examines the meaning of his father's life and death, castigates his wife for infidelity, laments his loss of custody of his two sons, and discusses his own personal and literary ambitions. If the Freudian notion of creativity being the attempt to sublimate neurosis or the Jungian notion of it as an anodyne for inner distress and tension have any plausibility, it is in the work of people like Taban. And as an outstandingly intelligent and introspective person, he is aware of this. *Meditations [of Taban lo Liyong]* is "Dedicated to people with strong complexes of one kind or another"; and in it he justifies neurosis because it "lifts people up to another level, beyond society, *ahead* of society." He notes that "Somewhere in my make up, I share epicycles with the mad" and "It is madness of a sort." But it is not only in madness that he feels an affinity with Nietzsche; he also suggests that "Without syphilis, without malignant derangement, can a man ever amount to anything?" and announces that, in this sense, "Ladies and gentlemen, I have syphilis."

The short-breathed forms adopted by Taban allow him to try out propositions, even the most outrageous and shocking, to see where they lead. Because his senses of fact and of fiction are so intermingled, he sees no inconsistency between, for instance, advocating physical suicide, advocating metaphorical suicide by the cessation of writing, or advocating fortitude and resistance to depression. Each is a possibility, each an idea worth entertaining. As a result, when he seriously advocates practical policies (as, for instance, in *Thirteen Offensives against Our Enemies*) he is likely to be treated as a jester, prankster, impossible idealist, or self-appointed irritant rather than as an imaginative thinker of the unconventional and even the unthinkable.

K. L. Goodwin. *Understanding African Poetry*
(London: Heinemann, 1982), pp. 78–79

Taban lo Liyong is a unique figure in East African literature both in his thought and work. A highly individualistic poet, critic, short-story and folk literature writer, he draws his material from both traditional and modern life. The many facets of his character and work leave his critics and reviewers hiding behind such epithets as "stimulating," "prolific," and "controversial." However, his short stories fail to provoke much reaction and are all too often passed over as trivia in comparison with the longer, philosophical poems.

The short stories in Taban's two volumes, *Fixions* and *The Uniformed Man,* fall into three classes. There are the modern stories such as "A Traveller's Tale" and traditional tales like "Ododo pa Apwoyo Gin ki Lyech." Many of the stories, though, overlap into a third category in which a traditional story is brought up to date or a modern tale is told in the manner of a *lucak wer,* the traditional oral artist.

Elizabeth Knight. In Eldred Durosimi Jones, ed.
African Literature Today. 12 (1982), p. 104

There is no apparent consistency in the form of Taban's books. *Another Nigger Dead* is supposed to be a book of poems, but the last item, "Batsiary in Sanigraland," is a dissertation which could have fitted into *The Last Word. Fixions* is a book of short stories but most of the items in it are fables, which would have been in place in *Eating Chiefs,* a collection of folktales. *Thirteen Offensives against Our Enemies* is supposedly a program for development but contains some poems. *The Last Word* is meant to be literary criticism but contains autobiography. It is not that Taban cannot be a good critic. He shows profound insight into Ngugi [wa Thiong'o] when he says, before Ngugi wrote *Petals of Blood,* "This is a man who thinks (or used to think) in terms of 'Moses,' in terms of universalism, in terms of ideals: categorical imperatives. Obviously the whole Mau Mau war made him look at the Kikuyus as the oppressed children of Israel . . . When the Messianic Path was lost, James also got lost. . . . But that side of Ngugi which he had donated to the messiah to fulfill still yearned for actualization."

What Taban is doing is to deliberately break what he calls "categorical imperatives," linking together the apparently irreconcilable (for example, the American one-liner, Greek philosophy, television) because they unite in his consciousness. By breaking forms, Taban upsets our expectations. *Ballads of Underdevelopment* has in its table of contents not the conventional titles or first lines but several lines, even the complete poems we find in the text. In contrast, *Meditations in Limbo* has no table of contents. It is the uniform, the outward structure stifling the inner content, that Taban is seeking to smash: the Platonic vision of humanity and art is the enemy. For Plato, only content is fluid, while form is permanent; for Taban, form is changeable. For Plato, the good life is an escape from the world of the body; for Taban, the world is patently body, hence the numerous descriptions of his sexual escapades with "real" people.

Meditations in Limbo is Taban's most integrated work because it has the consistency of inconsistency. . . . Taban says, "In a sense, this is a novel." The antinovel as novel. The Taban "author" goes through many changes, sometimes becoming an all-seeing, timeless self, at other times earthbound; sometimes a critic, at other times a defendant. There is a shaping tension in this work: the changes are bounced off his father's expectations of him (tribal, success through monolithic education) and Plato's world-view (only content is fluid while form is permanent). Plato too is a character, just like Ngugi. . . .

The Uniformed Man, published shortly after, is an epilogue to the antinovel, equally successful, with Taban as author, hyperactive student, character, critic, and teller of folktales, bouncing off his father and Plato. Taban uses different forms and mixes forms. "The Education of Taban lo Liyong" is a counterpoint in a class of literature between the monovisioned professor and the multifarious, complex consciousness of the student, yoking disparate elements together. "Project X" . . . is a brief, do-it-yourself story, like something by Julio Cortázar of Argentina. The story that follows, "Asu the Great," is like a folktale, interrupted by philosophic one-line questions of historic and mythic figures, followed by an animal fable in which Shark talks to Monkey, the twist being that the shark has postgraduate degrees. Genres are deliberately mixed—*deus ex machinas* swoop in at the author's will, creating what Paul Holz calls metafiction. In "A Prescription for Idleness," there is a folktale within a folktale. The book ends with a chapter . . . containing a critique of Plato and his father, concluding with an episode of graphic, mindless violence whose meaning we must figure out, if there is one.

Peter Nazareth. In G. D. Killam, ed. *The Writing of East and Central Africa* (London: Heinemann, 1984), pp. 171–73

Taban lo Liyong is an exciting African avant-garde writer who refuses to be tied to any traditional literary models. Although he acknowledges his indebtedness to both [Amos] Tutuola and African oral literature from which he claims he draws inspiration, his attitude toward these sources is not slavish but creative. Basil Busacca aptly identifies the freedom of his creative spirit when he describes [Taban lo Liyong] as a writer who "genuflects before no idols—European, Nigerian or local—and who proves that he is right to exercise the prerogative of genius." Like most avant-garde artists, [Taban lo Liyong] proceeds in his writing from the premise that literary models existing before him are no longer adequate to express the reality of his time. An artist who accepts without question existing artistic traditions is not likely to create anything new. . . .

Among African writers Taban lo Liyong is perhaps the one who best understands the challenge of "a living literature." He perpetually experiments by synthesizing old and new methods with the hope of creating a style that is uniquely suited to his themes. In a story called "Sages and Wages," for example, there is a sentence with an unusual syntax covering sixteen lines. We may note here that this kind of experiment with syntax has been equalled and surpassed by the American writer, Donald Barthelme, whose story "Sentence" is a one-sentence story covering eight pages. What is important, however, is that, given [Taban's] independent approach to writing and his taste for avant-garde experimentation, it is only to be expected that he would explore the exciting artistic possibilities of the mode of the absurd. . . .

The title story in Taban lo Liyong's collection *Fixions* . . . paints a picture wherein a president of an African country receives in his secret chambers an envoy of a foreign nation in the middle of the night. This president had requested aid to build a road and a bridge to his home. The envoy now comes to report that the money for the project has arrived. The president concludes arrangements for the money to be diverted into his personal bank account. He is overjoyed for, as he says, "It will earn me quite a bit of interest." The envoy then proceeds in a studied fashion to inquire about the state of the president's national security. Thereafter the envoy discloses that a coup d'état is secretly being hatched by the leader of the opposition in collaboration with the deputy president and that the plotters aim to kill the president. Before departing, the envoy succeeds in putting the president in a state of seething rage. The story ends as the president is about to unleash a bloodthirsty, insane revenge on the supposed plotters.

All along the story strongly suggests that nobody is actually plotting a coup. Instead the calculated lie is told with the aim of destabilizing the African country. Furthermore, the reader is aware that the malicious envoy succeeds only because he is not dealing with an African leader of worth but with this greedy fool of a president, who appears to be even more gullible, and more naive than a child. This president is indeed no better than an animated cartoon being manipulated according to the wishes of the foreign envoy, his master. When a person—the more so a president—becomes a mere puppet, his life loses meaning. It becomes absurd. This story is an obvious satire on African heads of state. Furthermore, the situation which makes the reign of such ignorant, unpatriotic characters possible is exposed for its absurdity.

F. Odun Balogun. AfrSR. 27, 1 (March 1984), pp. 46–47, 50

[Taban lo Liyong] perceives black consciousness as part of the themes worth exploring in his poetry. Although his views have baffled numerous critics, he possesses that distinguishing mark of commitment required to create relevant works. He feels that English should be tamed and naturalized "so that it echoes local sentiments and figures of speech." The emergent synthesis does not, however, appear palatable, and he is given an original nomenclature as the creator of "Tabanic genre" that has no predecessor and [is] unlikely to possess a successor due to the frequency of its highly poetic variations. . . .

It appears that Taban poses a problem to critics, but that does not mean that he wraps his poetry in miscellaneous garbs of nonsense. It is, rather, a difficulty generated by an avidity for style due to the kind of books he read as a student. The style notwithstanding, his poetry gives the impression of a subject matter polished with digested ideas. One of these ideas is black consciousness, which indicates his concern with the nature of the black man in the world. . . .

The rousing call in this poetry is that the theme of black consciousness should be made substantial and practical. The black man must eliminate mouthing irrelevant slogans and assert his presence in world affairs. This is why the poet's preoccupation is the analysis of the collective experience of all black peoples. It appears that the message which this theme wishes to make persuasive to the reader is that the black man must and should solve his problems without waiting for international racial structures to be dismantled by liberating members of the dominating races.

Ezenwa-Ohaeto. PA. 140 (1986), pp. 12, 16

The seven stories in *The Uniformed Man* are a coordinated study in the cause and nature of violence as a pervasive reality of human existence. There is a deliberate plan in which our knowledge about the cause and nature of violence is gradually deepened by each successive story either by showing an increasingly intensified level of violence through a correspondingly intensified symbolism, or by demonstrating the pervasiveness of violence through an expanding variety of human participation. Also, each story is in itself a complete artistic unit that reveals three aspects of violence, namely, the personal, the societal, and the universal. . . .

It is obvious from the stories in this cycle that Taban lo Liyong has no illusions about human nature. Man, he correctly observes, "is not axiomatically human" and one cannot but agree with him when he says, "Pity, humanism, reverence for human life are not inherent in man: these are acquired characteristics." Human acts of gratuitous violence, the violence induced by selfishness, and the role of society in promoting robotism through mental enslavement—all of which are shown in this story cycle—reflect [Taban's] attempt to make us realize how much we have failed to transform ourselves from the "animal man" to the humane man. This is not pessimism but realism. If strong emphasis is laid throughout this cycle on the negative role of social institutions such as education, marriage, religion, and the army in promoting mental enslavement, robotism, and violence, we should not be misled into thinking that [Taban] is advocating nihilist individualism and anarchy. Clearly, [Taban's] objective is to alert us to the imperfections and negative characteristics of the institutions we operate so that we can better be able to organize a more humane, less violent society. This is a timely warning for Africa, his immediate audience, where violence has become a common feature, thanks to the aberrations of some of its leaders and the inhumanity of apartheid. It is similarly a timely warning for the world at large engulfed as it is in daily regional violence, any of which, unfortunately, might develop someday into the holocaust of a Third World War in spite of the periodic rapprochement of the superpowers (which are short-lived in any case) and in spite of, or perhaps because of, the even less frequent redrawing of the political map of the world.

F. Odun Balogun. *Tradition and Modernity in the African Short Story:*
An Introduction to a Literature in Search of Critics
(New York: Greenwood Press, 1991), pp. 150–51, 158–59

Another Last Word is profound, provocative, humorous, sarcastic, relaxed, anti-ideological, anticolonial, anti-Négritude, antistereotype, antifailure, the work of a gadfly. Only Taban could begin a book, "Good wine matures with age. So do good essays like these ones." Only Taban could say, "There was brooding James Ngugi, the committed Christian, who has now diversified into committed Christian Socialism. There was the publicly extroverted Okot p'Bitek, who, in private, was rather shy. And there was me; and this book is me." Yes, it is Taban, and it provides evidence that my interpretation . . . was right. I said that Taban is a transitional figure; Taban says, "There is something called transition." He adds that there were a "variety of styles" in his early books and wonders whether readers found that out. I did.

So, does the new book only confirm what I knew? Yes and no. There is a center to the work: "I regard this book as an essay in establishing a base for all our endeavors." This is a complex endeavor; there are many traps, one of which is mythifying other writers, particularly Ngugi [wa Thiong'o], whose socialism he finds dangerous because it is attractive to East African intellectuals who do not want to think. He is referring to Ngugi when he concludes, "Kuku is my tribe. Others have had their homecoming in Limuru. I had mine in Kajokaji." "Most of us entertain the false notion that our country needs us," Taban writes. "Some of us are needed, that's true. Some of us are also feared and hated. For others of us nobody really cares. The sooner we disabused ourselves of the sense of our self-importance, the better. Where your path is blocked at home, open up another elsewhere and fulfill yourself. Otherwise you might drink your talents to death, develop ulcers and cancer and neurosis." He then charges: "When the coups came through the barrels of the guns, we danced like little children for a day and cried thereafter. African so-called intellectual servants have been the blindest creatures among their peers in the world." A price must be paid for the blindness: exile, for "what we could not see at home because it was too immediate we might have the hindsight created by distance to put it in the proper perspective. And design better alternatives for the future." *Another Last Word* contains old steps, but the dance is new.

Peter Nazareth. *WLT.* 65, 2 (Spring 1991), pp. 354–55

TATI-LOUTARD, JEAN-BAPTISTE (1938–   )

CONGO

[Jean-Baptiste] Tati-Loutard's *Anthologie de la littérature congolaise d'expression française* is a well-conceived, well-constructed book of modern Congolese writing. Tati-Loutard is quite aware that other, more intensive, and more specialized anthologies will be needed as the literary activity of the Congo develops and expands, but he wisely sees that the present need is for the kind of book he has produced. His book introduces the reader to the lives and the thought and style of eighteen writers of the past quarter-century who have managed to have some of their work published. Most of the items included (except for a few tales and some short poems) are excerpts and can therefore only partially suggest their authors' literary virtues. Tati-Loutard's introductory comments for each writer cited, however, do much to overcome this limitation and help the reader to know whether he should look for the total work from which the excerpt has been made.

David K. Bruner. *WLT.* 52, 1 (Winter 1978), p. 162

Throughout nearly a dozen novels, Tati-Loutard illustrates with simplicity the fragility of man, but also his strength when faced with death. Each character has the privilege of escaping the present and being able to look at his life "du dehors." Thus emerge the memories, the joys, the deceptions . . . all that one calls a past, and which is nothing other than the path that one should have traveled to know how to live the present. For each person, it is a parenthesis which opens; and when it closes, one is no longer quite the same, without anything really being different in appearance in the meantime.

It is the theme of missed meetings which is most prominent in several novels. In *La Rendez-vous de la retraite*, Kotodi, crazy about his Peugeot 204, meets death on the road while getting ready to pick up his friend at the station. It is not only his friend that he missed, but also "les joies d'une retraite qu'il avait longtemps et soigneusement preparée" [the joys of retirement that he had meticulously planned for a long time]. A missed meeting, exactly like Alphonsine's, who at twenty-seven years had known nothing but pain and weariness. [One] Sunday, a car ride with a foreign diplomat made her see that life can be something other than the moments of terror spent with her brutal and unfaithful husband. But even when she is going to take advantage of this opportunity that she knows is unique, Alphonsine sees this parenthesis of her life close. In "le refuge," Matembélé, former political person-in-charge destroyed by prison, does not find his wife on his return home: after four years of solitude, she had asked for a divorce. . . .

Why don't these paths cross, why do these routes close, which have barely opened? The author does not bring any response to these questions; the reader, whoever he might be, will recognize this anxiety and will look for the answer in his own life.

The meetings of friendship, love, life . . . often fail in narratives filled with nostalgia; death, on the other hand, is present and points out to men their helplessness. . . .

Through all these nothings of existence, one begins to think that in the Congo or elsewhere, man has a need to think about his life, to meditate, and to judge that path that has been traveled.

Françoise Bureau. PA. 116 (1980), p. 220†

La Tradition du songe is Tati Loutard's last collection. It comprises three parts, and one could catalogue each one as follows: poetry, poetic prose, and "pensées" or reflections. Besides, the collection is literally divided into three parts: "Force et declin," "Force et destin," "Histoire," plus an appendix titled "Elements d'une vie poétique," which comprises essentially what we have named "pensées." . . .

In general, the texts are made up of reflections from the poet's own condition and reminiscences of friends who have disappeared, or of regions transfigured, not by dreams this time! . . .

At the level of language, what characterizes this collection is . . . the way in which the poet uses the natural elements of the African continent: fauna, flora, etc. What is also new is the entrance of the proverb, in a surreptitious manner, into poetry: "Le chacal vibre encore / Dans le chien" [The jackal still resonates / In the dog].

Willy Alante-Lima. PA. 142 (1987), pp. 179, 182†

The masculine/feminine opposition . . . which is part of an archaic, traditional perception of the world is . . . one of the major principles which structure

Tati-Loutard's poetry. . . . One finds it in the contrast between the sidereal immobility and fluidity of the night, between the constellations and the darkness, and between the sand and the sea. The sun, being from the beginning an element of male domination like fire, is seen in opposition to the feminine water although a distinction is imposed between the maternal sea and the gentle water which gives birth to the lover.

Man's environment is constituted by some great oppositions: sun/rain, afternoon/morning or evening, sea/land. These contrasts cover a more fundamental opposition between masculine and feminine principles or between paternal and maternal principles. . . .

The violence of the geographical and cosmic oppositions marks the imaginary world of the poet. Sun and rain, like day and night, alternate and follow each other, concretizing the cycle of time. The antithetical elements evoked suggest the dawn of life and a renaissance, the fruit of a transformation celebrated by the poet as the synthesis of extremes. But let us first envisage the elements in their divided opposition.

The sun, whose attributes are light and drought, is in opposition to both the moist night and the feminine rain. This dichotomy, from the first poems . . . to the most recent ones, reveals itself to be loaded with mythical significance, corresponding to the antithesis between sterility ("soleil de midi, étrange calvitie" [noonday sun, strange baldness]) and fertility. This image, the origin of which is linked to agrarian civilizations, has social connotations signifying economic misery as opposed to the desired prosperity. Light is experienced as an aggressive roughness, the sun rays in contrast to the softness ("la morbidezza") of the humid shade, the star opposing the nocturnal darkness, which is attractive, "inspiring," and rich in hidden life.

The tension is suggested in *Poèmes de la mer*, *Les Racines congolaises*, the collection written on the return to the country after studies in Europe. At the time of readaptation to local realities, this opposition becomes more noticeable. This opposition reaffirms itself with *L'Envers du soleil* and *Les Normes du temps*. Opposing the blinding and destructive solar values are the feminized night propitious to human flourishing, as well as the rain, the gentle water which has the same power. The place for the gestation of life is maternal like the warm and humid night and like the ground drenched by showers.

The harshness of the sun leads the prodigal son to refuse the seductiveness of African nature in order to turn his interest to human beings and their difficulties. The poet opposes a nostalgic romanticism of natural beauties with a humanism and social spirit: "Retourne vers l'homme, poète . . . l'homme d'une renaissante Afrique" [Return to man, poet . . . man of an Africa reborn]. Denouncing the "horror" of the sun is a way of turning away from the ideology of Négritude and from the themes that have become conventional with African poets from a certain time.

Arlette Chemain. PA. 145 (1988), pp. 117–19†

Jean-Baptiste Tati-Loutard has already distinguished himself as one of the foremost poets in the Congo. He is now being acclaimed as a master of the prose narrative. In fact, his is an exquisite poetic prose which maintains the originality and, to a degree, the high quality of his prizewinning *Le Récit de la mort*. The narrative's hero, Touazock, shares the author's preoccupation with death, "la lutte désespérée de son esprit contre le silence absolu" [the desparate struggle of his mind against absolute silence]. Death, as a central character in the book, is a capricious being which does not respect age, beauty, or intelligence and brings along with it at times a scandalous reminder of physical frailty, an acknowledgment of intellectual disappointment, or a shameful surrender to political disgrace. In his turn, the author informs us that death offers unsuspected traps in thousands of places and situations.

In addition to the protagonist's constant obsession with death as a lethal element against life, the author presents a number of disparate subjects, skillfully adjusting them to the somewhat dejected general theme of his narrative: the haunted citizens of contemporary Africa; revolution and torture; public health; national education; corruption and theft of public funds; the role of African women in society and politics; and allusions to recent African history, especially that of the Congo and Burkina-Faso. As an appropriate ending to the narrative, the last third of the book, entitled "Le Grand Exilé," is a text written by the hero, in which he introduces a study of the psychological trauma of a fallen ruler who is allowed to live in guarded exile: "L'homme n'est-il pas déjà mort à partir du moment où il ne peut plus former de projets?" [Isn't a man already dead from the moment he can no longer conceive?]. *Le Récit de la mort* is not a particularly fascinating story; however, the author seems to understand literature, and his storytelling craft makes the narrative more illuminating than depressing.

Robert P. Smith, Jr. *WLT*. 63, 1 (Winter 1989), p. 157

TCHICAYA U TAM'SI (1931—1988)

CONGO

Tchicaya U Tam'si is not only the most prolific of Africa's modern poets, but the one whose work displays the most sustained energy and intensity. He has been steadily engaged with development of his art for a period of nearly thirty years, during which he has published seven major collections of poetry. . . .

[His] initial move to France, no doubt well-intended on his father's part, left the deepest possible mark on his early poetry, which is charged with an overwhelming sense of loss. Whether literally or metaphorically, he feels deprived of his country, a mother, and even of a genealogical identity. These are some of the recurrent themes throughout the first collection, *Le Mauvais Sang*, [which he] published in 1955 at the age of twenty-four. All his poetry, however, is haunted by the figure of this "mère inconnue," and he reverts continually to the idea of something strange and alienated in his parentage. . . . Tchicaya had in fact been brought up in ignorance of his mother's identity, and even of her continued existence. The figure of the father in his poetry is also enigmatical, charged with tension and perhaps a sense of opposition. This is the father who brought the poet to Paris at the age of fifteen and who thus both connects him with Africa (by his existence) and separates him from it (by his action). . . . Tchicaya's second and third collections, *Feu de brousse* and *À triche-coeur*, are haunted by the figure of "the child" or "the orphan," who wanders everywhere seeking the tree or root of his origin, the source of his very being. . . .

The sense of isolation grows still deeper in *Epitomé*, when feelings in the West began to run high over the Congo tragedy, but in a direction absolutely contrary to those of any radical, informed African—more especially, any Congolese African. But these earlier lines give us already a powerful impression of the poet's inner exploration of a body, a physical "presence," which is his only link with the landscape and people of his own country. And since death is above all the process by which we mingle our elements with those from which we came, it is this process which dominates the opening stanza of the poem. But the impression is far from deathly, for the imagery of "breath of sperm," of "yeast" and of "rich suns" stresses that the path is more one of renewal than of disappearance. . . .

The poems in the main sequence of *Epitomé* each carry a superscription identifying them with particular phases or events of the struggle which raged on the banks of the Congo in 1959–1961. . . . The first part of *Epitomé* reads like a poetic diary of these events, in which their initial impact is recreated, their meaning sought in the deeper perspective of all other events suffered by the same or other colonized peoples. The vision nurtured during those perilous but heady days in Kinshasa was something very different from the American-dominated dictatorship which later rose upon the wrack of Lumumbist hopes. It could even be dreamed, as Tchicaya dreamed in some of those poems, that the Congo's five centuries of anguish since the Portuguese arrival might be resolved at last into freedom and unity for its peoples. The poet taunts Christ to share to the full the specific agony and division of his people, wrought by such "Christian" enslavers, colonizers, and intriguers. . . .

[The] poetry of *Epitomé* and *Le Ventre* is on the whole more public in its concerns than the intensely self-communing volumes that preceded it. And this more public orientation is matched, particularly in *Le Ventre*, by a slight simplification of style. A more stanzaic form reappears on the page, after the boiling cascades of images which pour through *Feu de brousse* or *À triche-coeur*, and there is a return to a limited use of punctuation, capitalization, and closed sentences within each poem.

Tchicaya continues to search for the tree of his origins, he pummels and dissects his own belly to find the meaning of rebirth within the giant fact of death in the Congo of those years; the great river flows as ever through his pages, carrying, changing and delivering up the burden of a tragic historic experience. Thus all the elements of continuity are present; only the poet's preoccupations begin to take on a more representative character; he is both literally and imaginatively closer to the experience of his people than the brilliant young Parisian poet of the 1950s.

Gerald Moore. *Twelve African Poets* (Bloomington:
Indiana University Press, 1980), pp. 147–49, 154, 157–58, 162

The first novel which the poet and playwright Tchicaya U Tam'si agreed to publish [*Les Cancrelats*] can definitely be stated as a combination of depth and density.

From the start, the narrative introduces us to the heart of a world so close and so troubled that no reader can remain indifferent to it. One is caught up in the web of a writing that mobilizes the symbols of a great richness and in the meanderings of so profound a story that one follows it as if it were a return to the origins. . . .

The narration introduces, into a world of mystery and darkness and into the depths of a being and his culture, the functioning of societies and of the human psyche at an obscure level. . . .

The novel gives us a cross-section of life, "tranche de vie," under colonial rule, in the region neighboring Loango, of a people with a touch of foreign culture, embedded in its traditions, hunted down in everyday life by the militia, and progressing toward an evolution of the situation in 1946, with the "pétition," title of the last chapter—which will lead to the elections.

But the novel, without concession to stereotypes, is much more than just a historic reconstruction.

The narration offers some chronological references, some landmarks which permit us to reconstruct the sequence of facts out of the multiple anachronisms, the flashbacks, the narrations within the narration and the "métalepses." The narration winds around itself even as it moves forward.

Two grids will help the reader to reestablish the logic from this dense romanesque fabric, a fabric inextricable from symbolic notations and allusions.

A family tree spreads its branches throughout the narration. It is opportunely summed up periodically in a way which complicates it further.

Ndundu, who followed his white employer to France in 1880, returns to the Congo twelve years later, with two children born in Grand-Bassan, where he had put into port and tried to found a family.

The novel focuses on the two—not the husband and wife but the brother and sister with symbolic names: Sophie, the wise, and Prosper, promise of prosperity—at the time of a second marriage. . . .

The other grid concerns dates and temporal references. . . .

The novel begins with the narration of the difficulty the steamboat experienced docking on the wharf. Past events are recaptured in an internal monologue.

Arlette Chemain. PA. 115 (1980), pp. 211–13†

Tchicaya's short stories [in *La Main sèche*], published the same year as his first novel, *Les Cancrelats*, have the same triple thrust as that novel. First, there is the surreal and fascinating style; second, there is the blend of Western Christianity and African tradition; and third, there is the proverbial tone to the diction. Particularly salient in these tales is the fascinating blend of Christian elements and the personal African optics of the narrator. A black baby who takes the place of the papier-mâché Jesus in a crèche has been abandoned by its mother. Or are we actually witnessing the Second Coming? In another story a talking mouth ("noire et lippue, bien sûr") retraces the evolution from sea organism to Homo sapiens.

Tchicaya has often been assimilated into the surrealist movement because of his unusual imagery and his interest in [Arthur] Rimbaud. Now, with the stories of *La Main sèche*, Tchicaya reinforces that association, especially in the oneiric passages of "Rebours" and on the plotless urgency of several other stories. These tales are not slices of life but rather slices of consciousness lent a palpable dimension. The major coordinates of Tchicaya's world are African and French conventions. If Tchicaya *is* a "surrealist," it his on his own terms. His devotion to the Rimbaudian tradition of the *hallucination simple* is embraced somewhat cynically, and his prime world-view remains African—namely natural rather than supernatural. Tchicaya brilliantly reverses one of Europe's most famous existentialist quotations when he speaks of people entering a judge's chambers, including "un certain Pascal qui, dit-on, enseignait aux arbres la mauvaise foi des humains" [a certain Pascal, who, it is said, taught trees the dishonesty of humans]. In this reversal lies the clue to the fundamental difference between European surrealism and African surreality.

Eric Sellin. *WLT*. 56, 1 (Winter 1982), pp. 162–63

In Tchicaya U Tam'si's second and last published play, *Le Destin glorieux du Maréchal Nnikon . . .* political satire in drama attains a level of originality and achievement only rarely seen in modern black francophone African theater. Central to the play is a poetic dislocation of nightmare and reality or of nightmare as reality. Within these unstable boundaries, Tchicaya transforms political oppression into a surrealistic vision whose semantic underpinning is supported by satire and its attendant ironies. This study examines the rhetorical devices of satire in *Destin* and how they function to demystify the archetype of the African tyrant and expand the text's literal meaning. Ultimately, the satirical mode serves to destabilize fixed conception and involves the audience in the cathartic deposing of the self-appointed "supreme guide," and president-dictator for life.

Katheryn Wright. *Ufahamu*. 19, 2–3 (1991), p. 80

Firmly convinced of the necessity, for Africa, to preserve its identity in a world that tends towards uniformization under the influence of the industrial culture of the masses, Tchicaya U Tam'si promoted the intelligent return to the original expressions of African theater. He saw in it one of the suitable means for the safeguarding, in our continent, of an art of living and simply of an art that achieves a syncretic harmony between tradition and modernity.

In an article published by *Le Monde diplomatique* and dealing with "the sacred origins of our theater," Tchicaya recognizes that "amongst the arts of speech," the theater is "the one that is the greatest collection of the founding myths." The judgment that he gives on "neo-theater africain" objectively takes things into account. On the one hand, he criticizes those who, under the pretext of originality for the sake of originality denature the entire theater; they present it "as a poor and strange juxtaposition of dance tracks (with uninspired choreography), of words and farces, the entire thing stuffed with the weight of a doubtful folklorism." On the other hand, he recognizes that this "neo-theater" is capable of "authentic successes" when the "most demanding"" of its creators know how to make use of the recourse "to the sources of ritual (among others).". . .

Tchicaya U Tam'si was "born"—perhaps without himself having complete awareness of the exceptional richness of all the registers of his dramatic range—for the theater. His poetic work has brought to his work as playwright an inestimable source of sensitivity and of images with which his characters are endowed. For example, some of his poetic collections (*Epitomé, Le Ventre*) are composed like funereal operas traversed by cries and tears causing alternately lulls and storms. *Epitomé*, a dramatic poem par excellence, which marks the passage of time through the breathless succession of the editions of the press, is a work that can be directly transposed onto the stage. Three characters— Lumumba, Christ, and the author himself confuse their silhouettes in a hallucinating superimpression—portray in it, in the strongest sense, Passion. Roger Godard, who has worked on Congolese poetry, has emphasized in Tchicaya U Tam'si the permanence of his poetic themes in his dramatic work.

Sylvain Bemba. *Europe*. 69, 750 (October 1991), pp. 124–26†

The death of Tchicaya U Tam'si on April 22, 1988, at the age of fifty-seven sent shock waves through the world of African literature. Tchicaya, the oldest of a generation of important Congolese writers, is one of the few whose reputation has reached beyond the confines of francophone Africa and France. During his lifetime, however, he never reached the wide audience that he deserved, not only as a poet, but also as novelist and playwright. . . . While recognizing him as one of the leading contemporary African poets, critics, and readers remain strangely reserved. In a recent publication Théophile Obenga puts his finger on one of the main reasons for this reticence: "U Tam'si n'est l'héritière de personne et de rien: à souhait, et non sans belle ironie" (U Tam'si inherits from nobody and nothing: by choice and not without beautiful irony). Tchicaya's writing defies classification. His intensely personal world view and poetic expression create his own individual mythology, which sets him apart from all neat literary categories. His poetry is often described as hermetic, which is, in reality, the literary critic's terminology for admitting that it is not easily understood. At the same time the poet's obvious mastery of his medium precludes his being dismissed as obscure or unintelligible. . . .

It is important to read [Tchicaya's] oeuvre not only as a whole but also chronologically, in the order of composition. His novels illustrate this very well; the first three . . . form a trilogy that paints a vast human and sociopolitical fresco of the Congo, although spanning only fifty-some years in the life of the main protagonists, Sophie and Prosper. In fact, it was conceived of as a single narrative and was divided into three in order to satisfy the editors. Thus, although each novel may be read and enjoyed in isolation, characters and events in one of the three may be alluded to in another or may reappear without explanation, with the result that the full significance is lost on the reader. Similarly, certain recurrent images become key symbols, an understanding of which is essential in order to release the full meaning of the text. One such image-symbol is that of the *cancrelat* or cockroach, which lends its name to the first novel, *Les Cancrelats*. The word first appears in the enigmatic proverb which introduces the novel: "Le cancrelat alla plaider une cause au tribunal des poules!" (The cockroach went to plead its cause before the hens' court). Both the proverb and the cockroach image reappear at significant points in the first and last of the three novels, illuminating the meaning of the text and themselves acquiring new connotative dimensions. . . .

In [Tchicaya's] writing, repetition and rhythm are not only semiologically but also structurally significant. The collection Le Ventre represents one of the most striking illustrations of this. . . . [It] is important to consider the *ventre* symbol in the context of the collection as a whole in order to appreciate how the contradictions and contrasts make up a synthetic unity. Space does not allow for the required detailed study of this high-frequency word. However, a chronological reading of the poems in the collection would reveal how the development of the referential value of the *ventre* symbol mirrors the organically integrated structure of the whole. This rhythmic pattern is a constant in [Tchicaya's] writing, a structural technique which can be found in his first collections of poems and which is developed to a striking degree in his later works. For example, repeated semiological and linguistic elements link the poems in Le Mauvais sang, and key recurrent images such as blood, water, the woman/mother/Africa, and the Christ are introduced. In later volumes the title of a poem is often anticipated in the preceding poem, thus reinforcing the sense of pattern in ideas and sounds. This repetition is not static; each reappearance of an image brings to it a new dimension, and its development can be traced through [Tchicaya's] work as a whole. It is significant that many of the key images in his verse are important signifiers in his prose. . . .

[Tchicaya's] work is of particular interest in this respect, for his highly integrated poetic universe reflects a holistic world view that stands in sharp contrast to the Manichean Western world-view. [Tchicaya's] thought processes are firmly rooted in a sense of rhythmic pattern, the cycles of life, and man's collective identity. His poetic discourse is strongly individualistic in terms of image and language, yet his concern is for understanding the meaning of "existential anguish," not for the individual alone but for the individual as part of a corporate body— past, present, and future. His poetry is the concrete expression of his conception of the poet-prophet, whose role in the life of society is as important as that of the mason or the carpenter: "The poet is above all a man, a man in the full meaning of the word, a conscious man. A conscious man is he who dreams, and the dream is only a projection into the future of what can be realized." The poet, like Christ and the political martyr, lays himself open to the conflicting forces of life. [Tchicaya's] creative writing constitutes the commitment of a life to this task.

Betty O'Grady. *WLT.* 65, 1 (Winter 1991), pp. 29–34

TLALI, MIRIAM (1933–   )

SOUTH AFRICA

Muriel at Metropolitan is largely autobiographical, based on [Miriam] Tlali's experiences in a hire purchase firm in Johannesburg. . . . [However], it has a theme which goes beyond the beginning and end of the contents.

Metropolitan, the H.P. firm, is a microcosm of South African life, with its variety of people and their relationship to each other. Muriel is unhappy there, not so much because of the way she is treated by the white staff but because she has to become part of the system of charging unduly high interest rates to black purchasers who can ill afford it. She hates having to ask for their particulars and passes and thus becoming identified with the establishment. Muriel is never in doubt, of course, where her loyalty lies. She would not defraud the firm herself and refuses to cooperate with another black employee who is doing so, but she would not dream of giving him away. Muriel's inner tensions increase. While she "knew the laws of this country" and did not want to "stage a one-man protest against them," the constant insults also tell on her eventually. Since the white clerical workers will not sit in the same office with Muriel, a workshop in the attic is cleared for her. Later she is moved downstairs into a section of the general office, separated from her white colleagues by cabinets and steel mesh wires. When the white women object to her using the same toilet, the boss promises to repair an outside toilet for her, but this never happens so she takes a leisurely stroll to the nearest public convenience.

Muriel needs the money, so she resigns only when she finds another job. This is with a garage concern, but ironically she later finds she cannot accept it after all, because the owner, an Italian immigrant, is less adept than her Jewish boss in bribing the authorities not to implement the apartheid laws governing the employment of blacks and therefore cannot obtain the necessary permission.

Irony is the moving force in the story. It sets the tone in which the absurd situations forming the action are told, and it underlies the description of the characters. It provides the humor with a sharp and serious undertone. The boss, Larry Bloch, is completely believable. Although we see only his business face, we can easily assume the rest to form a rounded picture. He is pleasant, he makes no bones about the fact that money is his god. Muriel looks on with amused tolerance. She accepts his brand of morality and never blames him for his system of doing business, only herself for being part of it. The three white women and the black characters also come to life. They are not an anonymous and interchangeable set of people identified by their color only. . . .

Miriam Tlali's second novel, *Amandla*, meaning "Power," was published by Ravan Press in 1980. The censors probably did not go further than the title and the picture of the clenched fist on the cover, both symbols of the struggle for freedom, before banning it. *Amandla* is a very different novel from *Muriel at Metropolitan* in every respect. Gone is most of the easy humor, the ironic approach, the tolerance. . . . [The] bitterness of . . . earlier writers and the hope which was emerging from it has given way to rage, frustration, and confrontation. The characters in *Amandla* and their creator have experienced the Soweto uprisings, and it has altered their outlook. Muriel did not want to stage a one-man protest. In *Amandla* almost all the characters know that they must be part of a combined protest against the system. The struggle is a hard and ruthless one, and it has transformed their lives. . . .

The racial ideas in *Amandla* concern the events in Soweto when schoolchildren rebelled against their inferior education, boycotted the schools, and were confronted by the police. The events are seen through the eyes of members of a family whom these events affect in various ways. Pholoso is a nineteen-year-old matriculated student. One of his friends is shot during a demonstration, which affects Pholoso enormously. He becomes a protest leader. Later he is arrested, tortured, and put into solitary confinement. While being transferred he manages to escape; as he is wandering from place to place evading further arrest, he and others organize large-scale demonstrations in Soweto and elsewhere. Eventually, when arrest seems inevitable, he leaves the country in secret. Pholoso is the central character around whom the events in the novel are built, but there are many others, members of his extended family and their friends; all their lives are disrupted by the events in Soweto.

In the course of the narrative we learn about every aspect of life in black townships in a period of crisis: how the students organize demonstrations and strikes, meeting literally underground (in a bunker under a church) and swearing oaths of secrecy based on traditional initiation formulas. We see the mourners at the graveside of children killed in confrontation with the police. There is fear, but the dominant mood is one of defiance. The liberation of women, in the black South African context, means that women must play their part and this they do courageously. The melodrama of violence . . . now comes to a head, and again it is the melodrama of real events. For art and psychology, and anything extraneous to the events, Tlali can find no place in literature; there is no place for it in life at such a time. At the end of the novel Pholoso's girlfriend, Felleng, has come to say farewell; and they are waiting for his transport across the border. He is telling her of an incident during the crisis when he tried in vain to protect a white man who had been taken hostage. The young couple only have a short while left together and Pholoso tries to change the subject: "Let us talk about more pleasant things, Felleng. Let us talk about ourselves." The girl replies: "But we are talking about ourselves, Pholoso. Talking about this land is talking about ourselves."

Ursula A. Barnett. *A Vision of Order*
(London: Sinclair Browne, 1983), pp. 157–58, 161–63

[Tlali] displays an incisive knowledge of the application of the vicious doctrine of apartheid to the blacks in South Africa. Her two novels concentrate on the inhumanity and cruelty of this system, the complete denial of human rights to the blacks, and the consequences of such a denial as manifested in the Soweto riots of 1976. She describes in detail the institutional arrangements which are designed to make the blacks second-class citizens in their own country and discusses the effectiveness of some of the measures Africans are taking to fight the obnoxious laws of apartheid. . . .

Muriel at Metropolitan discusses in great detail the depressing situation in South Africa where the system of apartheid has poisoned relations between the white and black communities, and made the achievement of racial harmony difficult. The policy of separate development for the two races is used as a smokescreen to oppress the blacks and keep them in perpetual bondage. The blacks cannot fend for themselves and have to depend on the whites for their livelihood.

They are treated as second-class citizens and are prevented from benefitting from an economy to which they make so much contribution. For the blacks South Africa is a place of physical and mental torture; for the whites it is a paradise. Yet without the sweat and labor of the black proletariat, the Republic cannot survive economically. It is to the hard work and perseverance of the blacks that "the Republic owes her phenomenal industrial development." A situation in which the white minority oppress the black majority is manifestly unjust. A political arrangement which proclaims the superiority of one culture to another is untenable. An attitude of mind which undermines a black man's ability and performance because of the color of his skin only helps to produce resentment and discontent. It kills initiative and destroys any sense of loyalty to the state. . . .

It is to this organized injustice, of which the blacks are the victims, that the author directs her attention in the novel. Attention is focused on the Metropolitan Radio to show how it reflects in [its] staff policy, methods of operation and attitude to customers the system of apartheid. Muriel is made to play a substantial part in the work of the company and react with the staff and customers in order to reveal the weaknesses in concept and organizational structure which exist in the establishment. . . .

In *Amandla* the author continues her assault on the iniquitous system of apartheid in South Africa. This is a more ample work than the previous novel. She brings in more details and uses these effectively by concentrating them on the Soweto riots of June 16, 1976. The riots are presented as the unavoidable outcome of the flagrant denial of human rights to the blacks. When oppression assumes the monstrous proportions that one reads about in this novel, then the reaction is bound to be violent.

Oladele Taiwo. Female Novelists of Modern Africa
(New York: St. Martin's Press, 1984), pp. 163, 175–76, 180

Miriam Tlali's most recent publication, *Mihloti* in many ways fits into the same generic pattern as [her] autobiographical works but with a variation in format. It is a collection of interviews, travelogues, an autobiographical account of her detention, and her classic story "Point of No Return." . . . The author's prefatory remarks locate the text's purpose. *Mihloti* means "teardrops" and each piece she writes presents various shades of the pain, grief, strength, and struggle that is black South African life. There are many painful pieces. Her "Detour into Detention," for example, reveals all the pathos connected to Steve Biko's death and the mass arrest and brutal treatment of people who were attempting to journey to the funeral. "Point of No Return," which anchors the collection, provides a dialogue on the need for self-sacrifice and commitment to a larger struggle than to individual satisfaction. Her first work, *Muriel at Metropolitan*, had detailed the experiences of a South African woman as she works in a store which is portrayed as a microcosm of the South African apartheid system. It is an autobiographical novel, and Tlali takes us through Muriel's unwitting collaboration with the dehumanizing system because of her work. Her position as a clerk in this department store places her in the uncomfortable position of being

caught between her people and the Jewish owner and staff. Not only is her relationship with them a challenge, but she has to participate in a system which
exploits. She constantly describes herself as feeling like a traitor; but except for
a few outbursts, continues throughout her career at Metropolitan to do her job
well. Muriel's final decision to leave Metropolitan is not an assertive resolution
to abandon the system but is prompted by the fact that she is offered a higher-
paying job with better conditions elsewhere. She discovers unfortunately that
she is not immune from apartheid's machinations as even in the promised new
position, the question of the African woman's place recurs. Interestingly, the
"toilet" metaphor figures prominently at the close of the novel as if to underline
her ambiguous position. Earlier in the text and at Metropolitan, the white
female co-workers had expressed indignation at her using their toilet facilities,
and she had been instructed to use one down the street. Her job at Continental
Scooter Repairs is delayed because a special toilet has to be constructed for her.

    Amandla, her second novel, describes the activities of Soweto youth in
their struggle against the system. We see the resourcefulness of the youth who
are now engaging in guerrilla warfare. The burning of an administrative building and the ceremony for the raising of a grandfather's tombstone, provide the
forum for ongoing debate and dialogue (largely by men) on the mode of dismantling apartheid. The work provides a vast canvas of characters and activities
which seems to mirror the turmoil of South African life.

Carole Boyce Davies. Ufahumu. 15, 1–2 (1986–1987), pp. 124–25

Muriel at Metropolitan is very largely autobiographical; it is, however, devoid
of all reference to the private life of the author beyond her work in the secretarial office of a white-owned firm in Johannesburg, Metropolitan Radio. In spite
of its name, the firm sells a bit of everything: radios and electrical appliances
certainly, but also the kind of coal-fired stove currently used by blacks in the
townships, carpets, and furniture such as sofas, tables, and armchairs. The boss,
Mr. Bloch, employs—apart from his own sister, Ms. Kuhn—a second white
woman, Ms. Stein, who is an Afrikaner, as well as some white and colored
mechanics and a number of black delivery men and [truck] drivers, who also
function as retrievers of merchandise. . . .

    Muriel/Miriam depicts her own feelings and the small world which gravi-
tates around her with considerable verve and sensibility. The minor occurrences
of everyday life reveal the characters in all their complexity, which she portrays, whoever they are, without Manichaeism. Reflections of a political nature,
when they appear, are not laid on thick in an artificial manner: Miriam Tlali
does not seek to convince, to "get a message across," but simply to show
human relationships as truthfully as possible as she sees them around her. Her
book is a sociological document of the first importance, not only because the
milieu portrayed lies at the point where the worlds of white and black meet, but
also, as far as the latter are concerned, because they form part of a culture going
through a process of change. *Muriel at Metropolitan* is no less a full-fledged literary work for that. One has difficulty in accepting the affirmation made by the

author/narrator as early as the fourth page of the text that she is not a writer and has no pretensions to authority in the study or the representation of human behavior—the opposite is the case.

Jacques Alvarez-Pereyre. *Matatu.* 2, 3–4 (1988), pp. 112–14

Amandla is constructed as an account of the lives of Soweto dwellers in the year after the uprising. The use of dialogue and the interweaving of several human-interest stories allows Tlali to present a number of areas of black discontent. . . .

After a brief prelude during the Israeli Embassy siege in Johannesburg in 1975, *Amandla* describes the events of the uprising mainly through the experiences and conversations of an extended family living in the Moroka area of Soweto. The love affair of Felleng and Pholoso, a high school student who becomes the leader of the Soweto Student Representative Council until his arrest, is one of the main areas of attention of the novel: *Amandla* ends with their parting and his departure into exile. Several other stories are interwoven with this: the death and funeral of Dumisani, shot by the police in the first clash between police and students; the attempts of Pholoso's grandmother, Mrs. Moeng (Gramsy), to save enough money to erect a tombstone on her husband's grave in Braamfontein Cemetery; the difficulties her niece Agnes experiences in her marriage to a drunk husband; the effect the dislocations of the Soweto uprisings have on her other niece, Nana, and her politically articulate husband, Moremi; an adulterous affair featuring a black policeman, Nicodemus; the political organization undertaken by a group of students under Pholoso; Pholoso's capture and escape from imprisonment and his subsequent exile. Into this web of familial experience Tlali places a number of other figures, historical events, and issues of discontent and political debate in Soweto at the time.

Kelwyn Sole. *RAL.* 19, 1 (Spring 1988), pp. 66–67

Muriel [in *Muriel at Metropolitan*] is undisguisedly Miriam [Tlali] herself. It is Tlali's experience in the white job market that concerns her. Her offense at the apartheid regime is personal. She makes the point about how unfair the system is to her as a black woman over and over again. She complains bitterly about how she is paid far less for often more work than her white female counterparts. But her personal offense against the racist and capitalist job market becomes a concerted economic analysis of the position of black labor, which is controlled entirely by white interests.

Muriel works in a white Afrikaans radio shop with a predominantly black clientele. When she first joins the establishment one of her black colleagues tells her: "the only thing I am not happy about is the rate of interest at this place. It's killing our people. Every time I introduce a person here, I know he'll pay and pay and pay. It makes me feel guilty, like I've brought him to be slaughtered." These conditions of extremely high interest exist only for the black consumer who makes one-third less in a comparable job than the white consumer does. These conditions are part of the economic system which first forced black people into urban communities by annexing their land through high taxation and then keeps them at the lowest economic level by mercilessly charging high interest for common household commodities.

There is something else which Tlali documents in her first . . . novel. This involves the herstories of Western women as well. For those of us who cherish "a dream of a common language," Tlali bursts the illusion of the universal sisterhood of women. Muriel records how colonialism and capitalism (both phenomena occurring at the same time) have eroded the possibility of a joint struggle. The very fact . . . that white Western women have economically benefited and are benefiting from the colonies precludes spontaneous cross-cultural solidarity between First- and Third-World women. As we all know, this problem was expressed in the split between black and white feminists in this country. In South Africa, as Tlali tells us, the split is very clear.

In Metropolitan Radio, the two white women, Mrs. Kuhn and Stein, are not only allowed to have better working space and conditions, but if Muriel is given more privileged work by the boss, they are up in arms against her: "Just because she knows a bit of English . . . she thinks she is like us, you know." . . . As long as Muriel has kept to the place prescribed for her by the Afrikaan women, the pretense of friendship could continue unhindered. This aspect of Third-World women's herstories is rooted in the actual betrayal by First-World women, and indeed places these personal testimonies in their political context.

Huma Ibrahim. In Carol Ramelb, ed. *Biography East and West*
(Honolulu: University of Hawaii Press, 1989), pp. 123–24

Amandla certainly captures the immediacy of events and draws the reader into the confused apprehensions which must be the lot of many of the participants in such a period of social turmoil. She allows the reader to stumble on events, on connections between characters, and on sequences of cause and effect in much the same state of bewildered ignorance as must have been the lot of many of the citizens of Soweto. This could have welded itself into a brilliant artistic play to draw the reader into significant experience of the action of the novel. But somehow it never does: it remains accident rather than design. The writer's rejection of Western structural devices may have been as deliberate as it was necessary; nevertheless the confusion of the action merely seems to reflect a confusion in the mind of the writer which is never resolved. It may be that the black South African reader, familiar with township relationships and interconnections, is less at a disadvantage here than the Western reader. And, after all, the novel is aimed at the black South African reader. However, there seems a low level of organizational awareness even on the part of the central characters, though their prototypes in the real event obviously constructed some loose organizational framework to control their activities and their destiny as much as they could in the teeth of accelerating events. Thus even for the black South African reader, there is a failure to transmit an important element of revolutionary consciousness.

Jane Watts. *Black Writers from South Africa*
(New York: St. Martin's Press, 1989), p. 222

Miriam Tlali is an African writer working within a Third-World context, and her aim is to represent her people and their aspirations. Her project is primarily political and humanistic, rather than aesthetic or formal. Tlali rejects what she terms "intellectualism" and in her writing often shows little respect for traditional generic categories of "novel" and "short story." In the case of *Muriel at Metropolitan* and *Amandla*, for example, she presents her texts as "novels" but interjects discursive and often seemingly tangential elements of history and social commentary. The result is not a well-crafted artifact, but rather a loosely woven rendering of the fabric of black experience from the perspective of a black woman. Her most recent offering, *Mihloti*, is a disparate collection of prose pieces that reflect on the lives of black women under apartheid. Any critical approach that aims to do justice to the character of her work must take into account that her purpose as a writer is to use her art as a weapon in a continuing political struggle. As Rebecca Matlou observes: "Her literature reflects life and it responds to the realities of the situation around her. She is committing her art to the needs of the people." Form, therefore, is determined by the imperatives of her project, which is didactic in nature, as she herself notes in an interview in 1981: "I regard the raising of the level of consciousness of blacks as my prime responsibility, I am personally committed to doing this . . . I must go deeper into them, their feelings, try to make them understand their hopes, desires and aspirations as a people."

Tlali's work has developed across the period of what is known as the "renaissance" of black writing, the 1970s and 1980s, and reflects the temper of the times by offering first social protest (in *Muriel at Metropolitan*) and then political resistance (in *Amandla*), always from a black woman's perspective. In the 1980s her interest in women's issues has intensified and *Mihloti* adds a feminist voice to the black writing in English. . . .

The writing of Miriam Tlali spans a period of almost twenty years. The fabric of black experience that she presents includes threads of history, both personal and communal; and her work covers the history of her people from Sophiatown in the 1950s, Sharpeville in the 1960s, Soweto in the 1970s and continuing into the early 1980s. She is shortly to edit an anthology of writing by black women in South Africa and also to publish her first collection of short stories with a British publishing house. She travels frequently to Europe and America to talk about her work, yet is not widely known here. Surely it is in the context of the developing critical interest in South African women writers . . . that Miriam Tlali deserves to be given wider recognition.

Cecily Lockett. In Cherry Clayton, ed.
Women and Writing in South Africa: A Critical Anthology
(London: Heinemann, 1989), pp. 276–77, 285

WALCOTT, DEREK (1930–   )

ST. LUCIA

While often concerned to define his identification with a specific region or a particular historical condition, Derek Walcott has always, in theory and in practice, been willing to draw on the total heritage available to him as an alert and inquiring human being. He was born in Castries, St. Lucia, on January 23, 1930, and he is racially mixed: "Mongrel as I am," he has written, "something prickles in me when I see the word Ashanti as with the word Warwickshire, both separately intimating my grandfathers' roots, both baptizing this neither proud nor ashamed bastard, this hybrid, this West Indian." But as a writer he has a wider ancestry than that; the whole world is his family, and he has argued that "maturity is the assimilation of the features of every ancestor." . . .

Walcott will draw on anything, and in discussion of his own work is often conscious of his attempt to fuse elements drawn from differing sources. "I am a kind of split writer: I have one tradition inside me going one way, and another tradition going another. The mimetic, the narrative, and dance element is strong on one side, and the literary, the classical tradition is strong on the other." With the Trinidad Theater Workshop which he formed in 1959 (and left in 1976), he tried to create "a theater where someone can do Shakespeare or sing Calypso with equal conviction."

Walcott has been consistently hostile to any force which seeks to limit his creativity or restrict access to anything which might feed it. "Most black writers," he has said, "cripple themselves by their separatism. You can't be a poet and believe in the division of man." Although so much of his own writing explores and dramatizes divisions within himself, the thrust is usually towards reconciliation, acceptance, compassion. Aware of history and the manifold cruelties it records, he has in recent years sought ways to avoid its uncreative traps. He has argued that "The truly tough aesthetic of the New World neither explains nor forgives history. It refuses to recognize it as a creative or culpable force." He finds in poets such as [Pablo] Neruda, [Aimé] Césaire, and [Saint-John] Perse an "awe of the numinous," the "elemental privilege of naming the new world which annihilates history. . . . They reject ethnic ancestry for faith in elemental man."

[*In a Green Night*] includes versions of six poems from Walcott's first book, *25 Poems*, and one from *Poems*, two volumes which, like *Epitaph for the Young*, were privately published. *In a Green Night* was followed by *Selected Poems* which has a selection from *In a Green Night* and a number of new poems. . . .

In the later Walcott, from *The Castaway* [*and Other Poems*] on, it is difficult to make a distinction between influence and allusion. Not so in the earlier books, where the poet is less confident in voice, trying on the manner of others. "Other men's voices, / other men's lives and lines."

Mervyn Morris. In Bruce King, ed. *West Indian Literature*
(Hamden, Conn.: Archon Books, 1979), pp. 144–47

Walcott's poems in *The Castaway* use the myth of [Robinson] Crusoe to suggest that the New World is a new beginning, a new Eden. Both white and black have been shipwrecked and, while those of African descent suffer an amnesia of their racial past, it is from such forgetfulness that a new culture began. Walcott sees himself in the line of such poets of the Americas as [Walt] Whitman, [Pablo] Neruda and [Saint-John] Perse. Art will give form and self-awareness to this new society. But in "Crusoe's Island" Walcott admits the limitations of art replacing belief. . . . Walcott has become increasingly conscious of the life of the St. Lucian community which he has left. Where others have sought their roots in Africa, or have identified with the black urban slum dweller, Walcott sees the poor, French-influenced, Catholic black community of St. Lucia as his home.

"What the Twilight Says: An Overture," which prefaces *Dream on Monkey Mountain and Other Plays*, is partly an analysis of West Indian culture from the period preceding independence until the Black Power Movement of the late 1960s. . . . The Black Power intellectuals mimic foreign revolutions in urging the people "to acquire pride which meant abandoning their individual dignity"; even the fury of the intellectual was "artificially generated" by an imitation of foreign "metropolitan anger." Thus Walcott angrily attacks politicians and intellectuals in *The Gulf* [*and Other Poems*] and *Sea Grapes*.

Bruce King. *The New English Literatures: Cultural Nationalism in a Changing World* (New York: St. Martin's Press, 1980), pp. 124–25

For those awakening to the nightmare of history, revenge—Walcott has conceded—can be a kind of vision, yet he himself is not vengeful. Nor is he simply a patient singer of the tears of things. His intelligence is fierce but it is literary. He assumes that art is a power and to be visited by it is to be endangered; but he also knows that works of art endanger nobody else, that they are benign. From the beginning he has never simplified or sold short. Africa and England beat messages along his blood. The humanist voices of his education and the voices from his elemental inarticulate place keep insisting on their full claims, pulling him in two different directions. He always had the capacity to write with the elegance of a [Philip] Larkin and make himself a ventriloquist's doll to the English tradition which he inherited, though that of course would have been an attenuation of his gifts, for he also has the capacity to write with the murky voluptuousness of a [Pablo] Neruda and make himself a romantic tongue, licking poetic good things off his islands. He did neither, but made a theme of the choice and the impossibility of choosing. And now [in *The Star-Apple Kingdom*] he has embodied the theme in the person of Shabine, the poor mulatto sailor of [the poem "The Schooner *Flight*"], a kind of democratic West Indian Ulysses, his mind full of wind and poetry and women. Indeed, when Walcott lets the sea breeze freshen in his imagination, the result is a poetry as spacious and heartlifting as the sea weather at the opening of [James] Joyce's *Ulysses*, a poetry that comes from no easy evocation of mood but from stored sensations of the actual. . . .

Walcott's poetry has passed the stage of self-questioning, self-exposure, self-healing to become a common resource. He is no propagandist. What he would propagate is magnanimity and courage, and I am sure that he would agree with [Gerard Manley] Hopkins's affirmation that feeling, and in particular love, is the great power and spring of verse. This book is awash with love of people and places and language: love as knowledge, love as longing, love as consummation, at one time the Sermon on the Mount, at another *Antony and Cleopatra.* . . . There is something risky about such large appropriations, but they are legitimate because Walcott's Caribbean and Cleopatra's Nile have the same sweltering awareness of the cynicism and brutality of political adventurers. He is not going beyond the field of his own imagery; he is appropriating Shakespeare, not expropriating him—the unkindest postcolonial cut of all.

Seamus Heaney. *Parnassus.* 8, 1 (Fall-Winter 1980), pp. 6, 9–10

Dream on Monkey Mountain and *Ti-Jean and His Brothers* mark the climax of Derek Walcott's mature, professional achievement as a dramatist. He makes, in these plays, his definitive statement on the seminal questions of West Indian liberation and identity. Subsequently (broadly speaking), his drama enters a new phase distinguished by certain interesting new trends, both in content and style. *The Joker of Seville* and *O Babylon!* . . . present various transitional features. . . .

The *Joker* and *O Babylon!*, the two musicals heading the post-*Dream* output, provide a useful introduction to these later developments. Each presents contrasts which serve to highlight the new trends. *The Joker*, outstanding in sheer theatrical scope, is in fact the culminating point of the characteristic style developed in *Dream*. Walcott's adaptation of the musical form grows organically out of the ritual structure employed in *Dream* and preserves its essential dynamic. That is, characters still function primarily as emblems, the action turns upon an internalized, metaphorical conception of theme, inner experience finds expression in physical enactment, and setting is essentially stylized.

Walcott is adapting, in this play, the story of the legendary seducer, Don Juan. In the Spanish original, he is the libertine who defies the codes of chastity and honor to make the most of it this side of the grave. Walcott's own portrait stresses the principle of moral freedom which Juan embodies. In satisfying the forbidden lusts of his women, he serves to release libido, denied by the prescribed norms of order and decorum. He frees them thereby to face the burden of choice. Walcott heightens the meaning of this quality of freedom in identifying it with the muse of the local Creole stick-fighter in whose guise the indigenized Juan appears. The watchword of the stick-fighting tradition, *sans humanité*, is thus adopted to affirm the principle of unflinching courage and affirmative purpose in strife. So that Walcott's Juan comes to personify, above all, that spirit which "can change to elation each grave situation," in the words of the theme song.

The focal point here is that the action materializes out of just this kind of ideation and mythicizing. Juan, although a vibrant personality in the play, is more of an animated force than a character, and action is realized in ritual modes. The plot thus moves through a series of major musical sequences, which present what are essentially moments of spiritual confrontation and recognition. They are enacted in powerful orchestrations of choral and physical performance.

Juan's climactic triumph over the dead system represented by the statuelike Don Gonzalo, for example, is extended in a ritual performance of the stick-fight.

O Babylon!, his next venture into a full-scale musical, is not so successful. It presents here the interesting case of a work uneasily strung between the two phases, which partly accounts for its weaknesses. On the one hand, the musical form links it with the preceding phase; on the other, it introduces the preoccupation with the current political, social climate, more subtly explored in *Pantomime* and *Remembrance*. This is, in fact, the only play of Walcott's explicitly and wholly devoted to public protest. The play presents the situation of the Rastafarian sect of Jamaica, oppressed by the corruption of the materialistic Establishment, and in rebellion against it. Walcott is on very solid, topical ground in speaking through a group that has emerged as the rallying point of militant antiestablishment posture, and with the equally strong appeal of an ideology aimed at a radical break with the Western value system. The Rastafarians are presented in a situation which shows a sympathetic engagement with both their crisis and their revolutionary cause. They face the threat of eviction from their area, which has been earmarked for a hotel construction site by the local politicians, who serve American big business. They appear, in the meantime, in a harmonious communal setting, practicing their pieties of brotherhood, love, and peace.

The play fails, however, for several related reasons. Many of the flaws show up in the plot itself: a number of issues, not sufficiently centered, seem to be going different ways. The Rastafarians are engaged in resisting the major threat of eviction; they are equally intent on pursuing the latest promise of African repatriation. When eviction comes, they retreat into a mountain hermitage to rebuild their ideal community—a fate which virtually obviates the revolutionary motive, and indeed protest. At the same time, Walcott allows one individual member of the community, his central figure Aaron, a symbolic gesture of rebellion against Babylon. Earl Lovelace, commenting on the play, sees Walcott's Rastas as a powerless bunch, with no clear, constructive direction.

Patricia Ismond. Ariel. 16, 3 (July 1985), pp. 89–91

Walcott had been drawn to art early by being "more deeply moved by the sight of works of art than by that of the things which they portray," as [André] Malraux wrote of Giotto. Walcott used Malraux's anecdote as an epigraph in *Another Life*, in which he wrote of his discovering art as if he were Saul, blinded with revelation of the true religion. His will alone could "transfigure" the mountain shacks of the poor into a "cinquecento fragment in gilt frame." He felt the power of art to re-create the world, to transcend the poverty of those shacks, to redeem his dispossessed people and their history. The task was as immense as that of Adam standing before his unnamed world, though Walcott had this advantage: in the books of his father's library, he had inherited the work of centuries of European masters.

The West Indian reverence for ancestors became for Walcott a need to assimilate tradition, to assume its features, to make it part of his visual vocabulary. He believed that his knowledge of tradition would augment his treatment of the island's watercolor seas, its vegetation ripe for oils. But where [Dunstan] St. Omer painted "with the linear elation of an eel," Walcott's own hand was "crabbed by that style, / this epoch, that school / or the next." Tradition proved too powerful a master; he was its sunstruck Caliban. . . .

The connection between poet and painter in Walcott lies deeper than eye level, being rooted in his early, most basic experience of the world. *Another Life* is the autobiography of his life as a young artist, an intimate odyssey in which he first experiences the primal facts of life and death through art. He undertakes the conventional epic journey to the underworld, the land of the dead, which he finds in books of paintings by the European masters. . . . Among the relics of art, he recognizes his father, who is not his natural father (also a painter, but who had died young) and not the liturgical Our-Father-who-art-in-heaven, but "Our father, / who floated in the vaults of Michelangelo." His spiritual father could be accessible only through art, wherein Walcott collects his true heritage and recognizes his future.

Robert Bensen. *LitR*. 29, 3 (Spring 1986), p. 257–58

Derek Walcott's recent poetry is one of traveling and mapping where history becomes the knowledge only places can give. "North and South," the central poem of his *The Fortunate Traveller* (a collection which, not incidentally, is divided into three sections, where two sections titled "North" straddle the central "South"), describes the tensions between the two poles. History becomes defined by the dialectic of these two places. Walcott foresees no resulting synthesis, except the holocaustic. The "white glare / of the white rose of inferno" merges the imagogical mystery of Dante's celestial white rose with imminent extinction. Yet, if the "North," with its history of colonialism and exploitation, is "sown with salt" and marked for a prefigured destruction, the "South" and Walcott's role as the voice of the place, is ambiguous: "I accept my function / as a colonial upstart at the end of an empire, / a single, circling, homeless satellite." The poetic process calls into question perceptions and the common assumptions that attend our perceptions. . . .

Midsummer, Walcott's most recent collection of poems, moves fully into the "South": "the sea glares like zinc. / Then, in the door light: not Nike loosening her sandal, / but a girl slapping sand from her foot, one hand on the frame." Walcott's line has expanded, usually carrying twelve or thirteen syllables, which extends even beyond the sustained pentameter of "The Spoiler's Return." Walcott's more expansive and traveled line, which is sustained throughout *Midsummer*, suggests another form of rupture or ambivalence toward the traditional poetics of the language he writes in, which is his mirror and map. Walcott increasingly seeks to site himself and history in the present, not to deconstruct or depoliticize the present, but to map its tensions traced in language. Yet, as Walcott creates a poetry of self-definition, he ironically moves away from any political recognition of the language used by the marginal, the exploited, or the other—the patois or demotic forms and tonal ranges. Earlier poems such as "Sainte Lucie" began to explore these possibilities; however, this was transformed into the more decorous mode of dramatic monologues or narrative poems such as "The Schooner *Flight*" and "The Spoiler's Return," where the language, like the narrator, is masked and thus mediated.

The poems of *Midsummer* arguably acquiesce to the conventions and poetics of the language of the colonialists in the rejection of the patois. One wonders if Walcott does not then become a "North" American poet rather than an Antillean poet. In turn, in what ways does the more personal (and self-defining) poetry of *Midsummer* abrogate the very process of self-definition in the acquisition and maintenance of the conventions of a colonialist's culture? One may ask for whom Walcott's maps are intended. Walcott may move geographically to the "South" in a poem like "Tropic Zone"; however, he has become not a resident but a displaced person, the radical version of the traveler.

James McCorkle. Ariel. 17, 2 (April 1986), pp. 3–4, 10–11

Derek Walcott's massive *Collected Poems, 1948–1984* has an edge of defiance, as if to say, "Dismiss me if you can." But who would want to dismiss him? Walcott's poems stand out from the wash of contemporary American poetry (so much of it so *mild*, like half-whispered, devious apologies) because they are so boldly eloquent. The writing is some of the most exquisite in the English language, resembling the Caribbean in its many voices—sometimes crisp, sometimes tough, sometimes sweetly lyrical, or clear and treacherous as water in a stream. The syntax is often elaborate, frustrating yet seductive in the way it both reveals and obscures. When a Walcott poem fails, the writing is rarely at fault.

A true Renaissance man, Walcott has consistently resisted being cubbyholed. He has rejected neither his Caribbean heritage nor his British education. Although in recent years he divides his time between Trinidad and Boston, for a while he lived exclusively in the West Indies as director of the Trinidad Theater Workshop. Although St. Lucia, his birthplace, forms his primary subject matter, he has also written about Manhattan and Mandelstam. In the eyes of the public, however, his unique position as the first English-speaking Caribbean poet of international renown threatens to make him " . . . a man no more / but the fervor and intelligence / of a whole country." And so the girth of this *Collected Poems* is also a demand to consider the whole man—not just his skin or age or prosody or heart or mind.

Rita Dove. Parnassus. 14, 1 (1987), pp. 49–50

A Branch of the Blue Nile, the most recent published play by Derek Walcott, the St. Lucian-born poet and playwright, wonderfully exemplifies [Mikhail] Bakhtin's notion of "heteroglossia." In the play Walcott draws upon his rich African, patois, French, English, and classical Latin linguistic legacy, his St. Lucian and Trinidadian heritage, and his long experience in the United States, to bring his mastery of heteroglotic language to a peak. He continues the sort of black/white, colonizer/colonized cultural reversals that he played with in his earlier drama, *Pantomime*, by means of his Crusoe/Friday role shifts. He also compounds his fascination with the Antony and Cleopatra legend, which configured several of his major poems, such as "Egypt, Tobago." Intertextual and intercultural references, woven through much of Walcott's poetry and drama, multiply exponentially in *A Branch of the Blue Nile*.

Stephen P. Breslow. *WLT.* 63, 1 (Winter 1989), p. 36

Derek Walcott has said, "schizoids, in a perverse way, have more personality than the normal person, and it is this conflict of our racial psyche that by irritation and a sense of loss continues to create artists." He further asserts in the same article that we are "deprived of what we cannot remember, or what, when we visit its origins never existed the way we imagined, or where we remain strangers, contemptible cousins, the children of indentured servants and slaves." The picaro in *The Fortunate Traveller* portrays this kind of "tormented ambiguity," to borrow a term from James Livingston. Because the term "ambiguity" is usually associated with meaning rather than with personal attitude, as intended here, "ambivalence" is chosen as the operative word for the purpose of this study.

Poet and persona share this ambivalence, and the artistic process which brings them together is marked by image patterns which map out a journey that simultaneously regresses to the past and advances inevitably into the future. History and memory frequently yield precedence to forward-moving time which eventually becomes apocalyptic vision. A brief consideration of the poet in relation to his consciousness of history, and a sketch of his artistic and psychological involvement with his persona should lead to a more informed analysis of Walcott's artistry in *The Fortunate Traveller*, an artistry that carries the imprint of the author's ambivalence expressed in the poem through a pattern of dual, ambiguous and paradoxical elements integrated by the complex personality of the traveler himself.

Despite Walcott's objections to the "masochistic recollection" of poets who look to the brutal history of the West Indies for inspiration, he presents in his main persona a quester who is ironically forced to confront his origins and the events of his past in the mirrored reflections of the present. His journey from the old to the new merely provides an unrelenting satire on the evils of the old. Put another way, in *The Fortunate Traveller*, a journey through the modern world of American and European civilization represented, among other things, by the passage across the Mason-Dixon line, is merely a repetition of the old order of victim and victimizer, conquered and conqueror, native dweller and foreign intruder. Walcott, consciously or unconsciously, is negating the statement made in "Laventville": "The middle passage never guessed its end." Instead, *The Fortunate Traveller* illustrates the counterclaim of [Edward Kamau] Brathwaite that the passage has guessed its end. Its end is inextricably bound up in its beginning. The process of the journey and of the quest is not only constructed from the racial memories of the past, but the outcome is shaped by and mirrored in this process.

Clement H. Wyke. *Ariel.* 20, 3 (July 1989), pp. 55–56

In writing a play where white characters are so much to the forefront and so sympathetically rendered, Walcott is certainly rare among his generation of West Indian writers. *The Last Carnival* is a revision of an earlier unpublished play *In a Fine Castle*. *In a Fine Castle*, written after *Dream on Monkey Mountain* and *Ti-Jean* and before *The Joker of Seville* and *O Babylon!*, shows Walcott already engaging in exploration of crises of identity among the educated and the urban. Issues of racial confrontation persist but are rendered so differently from the myth and symbol-laden *Dream*. *In a Fine Castle* too has leading roles for whites, which as Walcott had anticipated, drew him the ire of many local critics. But the center of focus is still the divided consciousness of Brown whose name captures his mixed racial inheritance. The white characters are sympathetically rendered, but Walcott's rendering of their predicament is somewhat hackneyed and melodramatic. . . .

Walcott's development as a playwright is in a sense his exploration of the many strategies that will allow him to most fully possess his environment in all its elements. First there is the matter of language. English has been the language of the master; Walcott wishes to claim it as his own. At the outset, for the young poet in love with the English language, come the heady imitations of blank verse. Walcott's great eloquence, his high English, is, however, at odds with the consciousness of characters he now chooses to represent. "You proffered silently the clarity of a language they could not speak, until your suffering, like the language, felt superior, estranged." In imitating [John Millington] Synge [in *The Sea at Dauphin*], he is also looking at Synge's rich poetic idiom crafted out of the dialect of his islands. He sets out to forge a "language that went beyond mimicry," that transformed his gift of English into something uniquely West Indian. The result is the moving poetic prose of this first volume—eloquent, accessible, yet clearly reflecting the idioms of West Indian speech. . . .

In *Omeros*, the playwright and poet come together in creating a narrative poem with characters as alive and vibrant as in any play. "Homeros" means hostage and, like the blind poet, Walcott too is in a sense a hostage of the past. We all are, but as survivors of this past we must learn to live with memories, all of them. The memories that Walcott appropriates in his work are not of one race but many races. The central characters of his poem—Helen, Achille, Hector—are ordinary people of St. Lucia, but in their lives are captured and renewed and refashioned many dimensions of the past. The poet's mind ranges from Antilles now to Greece of antiquity, to Africa of slavery, to the British Empire, to the America of the Indians, to America of today. The literary references are equally wide-ranging. There is nothing false about Walcott acknowledging Homer as his master or seeing Homer's song in the chants of the shaman: "I have always heard / your voice in that sea, master, it was the same song / of the desert shaman." In an interview with Robert Hamner, Walcott had said, "The more particular you get, the more universal you become." In writing about his Antillean characters and their particular experiences imagined with great temporal specificity, Walcott is also writing about the human condition. And like Homer, in this song about St. Lucia, London, Athens, and Boston, Walcott sings about what happened both to Trojans and to Greeks, to those who lost and those who won, to those who are black and those who are white. Experience of all is rendered with equal sympathy and understanding. This is how we can remember the past without becoming hostage to it.

Renu Juneja. In Bruce King, ed. *Post-Colonial English Drama: Commonwealth Drama Since 1960* (New York: St. Martin's Press, 1992), pp. 239, 247, 264

[In *Omeros*] Walcott aims for a Homeric scope of human conflict and visionary experience and, obviously, raises expectations for his language and characterization by comparing himself to such an illustrious predecessor. But *Omeros* is also ambitious in a second sense; for by raising the question of his relationship to Homer, Walcott defines himself against a primary Western paradigm of originality and mimetic power, and re-evaluates that paradigm as well as his own poetry. The "basic impulse of the Homeric style," as [Erich] Auerbach observes, is "to represent phenomena in a fully externalized form, visible and palpable in all their parts, and completely fixed in their spatial and temporal relations." Walcott's mimicry of Homer thus confronts mimesis at what we usually think of as both its root and its apex. Further, the series of parallels upon which *Omeros*, like [James] Joyce's *Ulysses*, stands presses us toward our own confrontations with mimesis. Our first impulse may be to compare Walcott's Helen to Homer's, Achille to Achilles, Philoctete to Philoctetes, and so on. But the continuous process of doing so will likely cause us to question our impulse to perceive, and hence to create, likenesses—especially when such questioning becomes an overt theme of the poem itself. When, for example, both Major Plunkett (a British veteran and colonist) and the persona of the poet struggle to grasp the St. Lucian Helen and then fail to determine her relation (if any) to her Greek counterpart, the validity of similitude falls into doubt.

Likewise, because Homer stands at or slightly before the beginning of Western poetic genealogy—at a distance at which genealogy evades the grasp—Walcott's rapprochement with Homer means a rapprochement with not just *a* poetic ancestor but with poetic ancestry. Walcott highlights this, too, first by making Omeros a character in the drama and casting his own persona as Omeros's poetic heir, and second by several times retelling the Odysseus-Telemachos story—a story that can be read as a parable of paternal, hence genealogical, mystery.

Omeros's two tiers of reference—Walcottian and Homeric—also complicate mimicry in new ways. I suggested at the outset that mimicry points to its own nonoriginality as well as to that of its model. *Omeros* does do this, in that "life" mimics "art" within the fiction of the poem. That is, the St. Lucian characters are ostensibly "real people" who yet appear to recall Homeric or other literary models. The character of Warwick Walcott, for example, the poet's father—who died of an ear infection at an early age—notices that his past echoes parts of Shakespeare's plays. . . . Walcott once again places literary models, representations—albeit tentatively—in positions usually reserved for originals. But given two fictional tiers, one will likely shine at the expense of the other. Odds are that figures in a painting gazing at another painting gain the appearance of verisimilitude in comparison to other figures inside the painting at which they gaze. Similarly, the rhetorical effects of Walcott's references to Homer's more distant poems is to vivify his own poem. By appearing to model "real" St. Lucians upon fictional Greeks, Walcott suggests that "life" imitates "art"—and thereby distracts the reader from the fact that what he calls "life" is already "art." In this sense *Omeros* actually *disguises* its own status as representation. If elsewhere in Walcott's work we learn that mimicry haunts mimesis, in *Omeros* a trompe-l'oeil mimesis returns to haunt mimicry.

Rei Terada. *Derek Walcott's Poetry: American Mimicry*
(Boston: Northeastern University Press, 1992), pp. 183–85

Walcott's poetry draws much of its energy from his uneasiness, his unrest, the hovering and hesitation that he characterizes as the stance of the poet—a detachment from the natural (men acting as men—though there is ambiguity in the word *acting*) and an acceptance of the artifice of another life, another way of seeing the world, a new frame for the familiar. His unease derives partly from his recognition of the ambivalences that define his being, not simply racial and historical but more profoundly imaginative, with allegiances both to piety and power, to the Old World and the New, to the condition of insider and outsider, to the particular and the universal, to the world as it is and the world as it might be. But partly also Walcott's unease comes from a deeper contradiction. "Where then is the nigger's home?" asks [Edward Kamau] Brathwaite. Like Odysseus, Walcott might answer—it is where I am going, which is where once I came from; but it is also where I am, for I am a wanderer, and have been one from the start. My cunning and good humor mask a sorrow that I must name; and then I will find peace. . . .

   Omeros represents a new kind of achievement, for despite its affiliations with the epic it does not come out [of] the literature and history of Europe; and despite its acceptance of the heritage of slavery it does not come out of Africa either. Rather, it emerges unmistakably from a West Indian literary tradition, one that Walcott has played a major role in shaping but that now has a broad reach and deep roots. *Omeros* would not be possible outside that tradition.

   Set in St. Lucia—called Iounalao, "where the iguana is found," by the Arawaks—it is a story about storytelling, contemplating the relationships between individual and collective histories, invoking figures of fact and fiction, proposing rhymes and half-rhymes across centuries and oceans and peoples and verse forms, a dense weave of metaphors and metonymys . . . and puns, for like all good poems it takes pleasure in its outrageousness and it takes liberties with its readers. *Omeros* is underwritten by a belief in the power of the imagination, and in real continuities—between the Mediterranean and the Caribbean, between suffering then and now, between all the experiences of men and women, even those that are shadowed by stereotypes. The territory of the poem is, in Walcott's phrase, a "reversible world," with the pun on verse being one of the least ostentatious in a poem whose exuberance is sometimes close to overwhelming. One of its most disconcerting extravagances is the number of voices and varieties of language in the poem—not untypical for Walcott, but developed with such irrepressible enthusiasm that ultimately the play becomes the thing and the parts are taken by whoever is next in line. And as so often in West Indian poetry, who is speaking is not nearly as important as who is listening.

J. Edward Chamberlin. *Come Back to Me My Language:*
Poetry and the West Indies (Urbana:
University of Illinois Press, 1993), pp. 167, 174–75

Walcott's epic perspective on history provides him with the necessary neutrality to perceive that glory does not necessarily follow from revolution, that all change is a mixed blessing. In his more recent poetry, in many poems from *The Fortunate Traveller, The Arkansas Testament,* and *Omeros,* Walcott has turned his attention often to the corruption and demise of the empire itself; and he links the waning of power of England and the United States to the final histories of Rome, Tyre, and Alexandria. From a cosmic or epic perspective, all civilizations follow many of the same patterns of rise, decline, and fall; the struggles of different peoples frequently resemble one another within the vast and ancient currents of human life around the world: "Albion too was once / A colony like ours." . . .

The Caribbean, as Walcott is so painfully and acutely aware, will forever remain quixotic among the world's annals. As a region, it may form the paradigm for postcolonial "antihistory," for the overturning of long-cherished myths and the brutal new chronicling of oppression, racism, and genocide. Its cultural history, which Walcott traces so accurately in the complex designs of his heteroglottic "multitexts," provides one of the world's richest models for true multiculturalism—a dense crossroads of human differences, sometimes tragic and sometimes hilarious in their juxtapositions and interrelationships.

If we are entering an era in which multiculturalism is our central ideology, Derek Walcott must be acclaimed as one of our greatest cultural leaders. He repeatedly demonstrates, in dozens of his plays and volumes of verse, the true meaning of "many cultures coexisting in dialogue" within the work of a single writer. His multiple voices with Joycean brilliance range not only among the numerous dialects and speech genres of the English- and French-patois-speaking Caribbean, but also move to the widest limits of our entire treasure house of Judeo-Christian, Greco-Roman, and European cultures. We may detect in Walcott's microcosmic Caribbean a paradigm for the most tolerant, mutually enriching coexistence of all the world's voices. Most wonderful of all, Walcott thoroughly exemplifies a "both/and" global political and cultural philosophy rather than an "either/or" divisive one. The Swedish Academy has certainly perceived this, and my congratulations go to its members for their choice, as well as to this profoundly accomplished, inspirational author whom they have lauded [as the 1992 Nobel Laureate in literature].

Stephen P. Breslow. *WLT.* 67, 2 (Spring 1993), p. 271

WALKER, ALICE (1944–   )

UNITED STATES

[Alice] Walker ends *The Third Life of Grange Copeland* with a focus on the voting-rights marches in Grange's town, but in *Meridian* she joins some of the younger black writers who came to prominence in the 1960s and who participated in the Civil Rights Movement; she makes the movement her primary subject. *Meridian* is perhaps the most memorable of the works in this vein; it depicts the involvement of the title character in civil rights activity both during the hey-day of the movement and when it was no longer fashionable. Walker draws upon her own experiences as a worker in voter registration and other activities in Mississippi and Georgia in the 1960s to portray Meridian's intense involvement in marches, voter registration, and desegregation of public facilities. Having deserted her child and husband to commit herself, paradoxically, to a life of improving conditions for black people, Meridian finds it hard to give up that pledge once the fervor of the movement has subsided. She therefore continues her solitary crusade against white Southern sheriffs and others who would stand in the way of progress. Strangely effective, indeed almost "touched in the head" in the manner of Harriet Tubman, Meridian not only has her small triumphs but succeeds in inspiring those who would prefer not to be inspired to follow in her footsteps. An exploration of the dissolution of the Civil Rights Movement, the novel is no less an exploration of its psychological impact upon a particular kind of committed individual. The movement, from one perspective, may have destroyed Meridian's homelife, but it represents the only fulfillment she finds in life; when it slows down, her dogged continuance successfully conveys Walker's point that the future in the South is possible only through constant vigilance.

Trudier Harris. In Louis D. Rubin, Jr, et al., eds. *The History of Southern Literature* (Baton Rouge: Louisiana State University Press, 1985), pp. 569–70

Alice Walker, in both short stories and novels, makes much more explicit use of history than [Toni Cade] Bambara, but ironically, she has a greater tendency to construct political solutions that run counter to the thrust of that very folk history. This history takes public and private forms. Whether re-creating the rural black South of the 1930s or the Civil Rights Movement of the 1960s, Walker seeks to place her narrative within the framework of the sociopolitical history of blacks in America. On the other hand, she gives her characters a very strong sense of their own pasts; in many cases, they are haunted by what has happened to them. Since she is, like Bambara, primarily concerned with black women, she writes stories that show these doubly oppressed figures searching for their own voices in the context of social and psychological conditioning that would deny them expression.

In her first novel, *The Third Life of Grange Copeland*, Walker's overt concern does not immediately seem to be with female characters. After all, the title character and his son Brownfield occupy center stage. Their development and inevitable conflict form the focus of the novel. In this sense the story resembles those by Ernest [J.] Gaines, who even in *The Autobiography of Miss Jane Pittman* concentrates on males. Walker, however, insists on testing the meaning of male development by its impact on female characters. The achieve-ment of self-consciousness or identity is thus doubly dialectical: it occurs in relation to both race and gender. In shaping the narrative, Walker uses folklore on both these subjects in showing the operation of the dialectical patterns.

The characterizations of both Grange and Brownfield draw on folk fig-ures, principally the bad man and the moral hard man. Brownfield lives out the selfish, violent, malevolent existence with which his father begins. In addition to being sexually promiscuous, he mistreats his wife and ultimately kills her, and he puts his newborn albino son outside on a winter night so that he will freeze to death. When his wife goes against his wishes in trying to create a more decent life for the family, he patiently and coldly calculates his revenge; he succeeds in returning the family to the barely human conditions from which they sought to rise. In all this, his attitudes resemble those of the bad man of black legend: the Great McDaddy, Billy Dupree, Stagolee. . . .

The stories in *In Love and Trouble* repeat the tension between folk wisdom and conventional systems of order. And again . . . black as well as white characters must be shown the limits and oppressiveness of those systems. "Strong Horse Tea," "The Revenge of Hannah Kemhuff," and "Everyday Use" provide the best examples of the working out of this theme. In each case a strong folk female figure must deal with the unbelief of a woman who has, either consciously or unconsciously, adopted an antifolk system of values. The validity of that system must be called into question and then the folk alternative given primacy. . . .

Meridian is Walker's most impressive effort to incorporate history, folk forms, and the conditions of women into fiction. While the time frame in which it operates is not extended, taking in only the period just before and during the Civil Rights Movement, the use of legends and folk tales adds historical depth in matters of race and gender. In addition, the technique of repetition moves it into the realm of cyclical time. As in *The Third Life of Grange Copeland,* the tension is between those who see that time as changelessness, which reduces people to ciphers, and those who see it as the pattern of growth and individuation. In *Meridian* . . . the powerful have a reductive, mechanistic vision, which is opposed by those who have or seek some connection with the folk in order to achieve an individual voice. The conflict in Walker's novel operates on three levels: gender, sexual politics, and race. These are not mutually exclusive categories, but rather dynamically related aspects of the basic quest for expression and, through it, power. . . .

The Color Purple, Walker's award-winning and much-praised novel, has achieved immense popularity. In part, this success can be explained because the book is, in essence, a "womanist" fairy tale. Like Snow White, Celie is poisoned (psychologically in the novel) by an evil stepparent; like Cinderella, she is the ugly, abused daughter who ultimately becomes the princess; like Sleeping Beauty, she is awakened from her death-in-life by the kiss of a beloved; and like them all, she and her companions, after great travails, live happily ever after. Moreover, the fairy-tale quality is more than metaphoric, since major plot elements are worked out with fairy-tale devices. The story is generated out of what Vladimir Propp calls interdiction and violation of interdiction. Celie is told by her evil stepfather, after he rapes her, that she must tell no one but God what he has done; she chooses to write her story, which . . . makes it a public text. Transformation from a life of shame to one of self-esteem occurs when Celie receives the physical embrace of the regal Shug Avery. Finally, the plot is resolved and the characters reunited through the exposure of villainy and the death of the primary villain, an event which reverses the dispossession of Celie and her sister Nettie.

Keith E. Byerman. *Fingering the Jagged Grain:*
Tradition and Form in Recent Black Fiction (Athens:
University of Georgia Press, 1985), pp. 128–29, 138, 146, 161

Possibly the most famous study of the interaction between the factors of gender, class, and race by a black woman writer is Alice Walker's *The Color Purple*. Despite the public acclaim the novel has received, certain of its features have proved highly controversial. Criticism has been leveled at Walker's treatment of the "unitary self"; at her celebratory depiction of the family unit (albeit an extended family and one which is not exclusively heterosexual); and at the element of "utopian fantasy" apparent in the novel's design. The plot, as Rachel Bowlby observes, is structured on a series of fortunate coincidences which provide the central character Celie with both personal fulfillment and economic security. Commenting on this particular feature of the novel, Bowlby complains that: "Rather than posing residual problems that thwart her growing aspirations, Celie's world falls into place to meet them, presenting her as in the best commercials with a dream house and a successful small business." The novel does have, however, a number of defenders. Anselma Jackson, replying to the criticism that Walker models her characters on the humanist concept of the unitary self, points to the strongly *collective* focus which she nonetheless achieves. Jackson claims, rightly in my view, that "the autobiographical element that informs the text is not one of individual singularity, but that of the black Western woman." And, in response to the accusation that Walker fails adequately to address the "determinants of patriarchy and capitalism as they work within the United States," she draws attention to her description of the cruelties of rape, incest, and forced marriage which the female characters suffer. These are, of course, crimes perpetrated by men—and the major part they play in the novel indicates Walker's interest in investigating the structures of male power. Her treatment of the theme is illuminated by [Audre] Lorde's analysis of the brutalizing effect which racial oppression has on black masculinity: "Exacerbated by racism and the pressures of powerlessness, violence against black women and children often becomes a standard within our communities, one by which manliness can be measured." Lorde's comments have obvious relevance to Walker's representation of the violent behavior of the male protagonists in the early stages of the novel. As Sofia laconically remarks: "A girl child ain't safe in a family of men."

Paulina Palmer. *Contemporary Women's Fiction: Narrative Practice and*
Feminist Theory (Jackson: University Press of Mississippi, 1989), pp. 82–83

The publication of *The Color Purple* transformed Alice Walker from an indubitably serious black writer whose fiction belonged to a tradition of gritty, if occasionally "magical," realism into a popular novelist, with all the perquisites and drawbacks attendant on that position. Unlike either *The Third Life of Grange Copeland* or *Meridian*, *The Color Purple* gained immediate and widespread public acceptance, winning both the Pulitzer Prize and the American Book Award for 1982–1983. At the same time, however, it generated immediate and widespread critical unease over what appeared to be manifest flaws in its composition. Robert Towers, writing in the *New York Review of Books*, concluded that on the evidence of *The Color Purple* "Alice Walker still has a lot to learn about plotting and structuring what is clearly intended to be a realistic novel," and his opinion was shared by many reviewers, who pointed out variously that in the last third of the book the narrator-protagonist Celie and her friends are propelled toward a fairy-tale happy ending with more velocity than credibility; that the letters from Nettie, with their disconcertingly literate depictions of life in an African village, intrude into the middle of the main action with little apparent motivation or warrant; and that the device of the letters to God is especially unrealistic inasmuch as it forgoes the concretizing details that traditionally have given the epistolary form its peculiar verisimilitude: the secret writing place, the cache, the ruses to enable posting letters, and especially the letters received in return.

Indeed, the violations of realist convention are so flagrant that they might well call into question whether *The Color Purple* "is clearly intended to be a realistic novel," especially as there are indications that at least some of those aspects of the novel discounted by reviewers as flaws may constitute its links to modes of writing other than Anglo-American nineteenth-century realism. For example, Henry Louis Gates, Jr., has recently located the letters to God within an Afro-American tradition deriving from slave narrative, a tradition in which the act of writing is linked to a powerful deity who "speaks" through scripture and bestows literacy as an act of grace. . . .

Gates's paradigm suggests how misleading it may be to assume that mainstream realist criteria are appropriate for evaluating *The Color Purple*. But the Afro-American preoccupation with voice as a primary element unifying both the speaking subject and the text as a whole does not deal with many of the more disquieting structural features of Walker's novel. For instance, while the letters from Nettie clearly illustrate Nettie's parallel acquisition of her own voice, a process that enables her to arrive at conclusions very like Celie's under very different circumstances, the Afro-American tradition sheds little light on the central *place* that these letters occupy in the narrative or on why the plot takes this sudden jump into geographically and culturally removed surroundings. And Gates's subtle explication of the ramifications of "voice" once Walker has reconstrued the term to designate a *written* discourse does not attempt to address the problematic ending, in which the disparate members of Celie's extended family come together, as if drawn by a cosmic magnet—and as if in defiance of the most minimal demands of narrative probability.

> Molly Hite. In Henry Louis Gates, Jr., ed. *Reading Black,*
> *Reading Feminist* (New York: Meridian, 1990), pp. 431–32

The context for Walker's meditations on the spirit is principally female and Afro-American: these are the chief elements in her cosmology, the chief sources of her inspiration. Although this interest in the particular doings of a particular group may strike some as insular, those who perceive this as a fault would do well to remember that it is Walker's intention to tell all of our stories, or some part of them, by recounting the adventures, mistakes, and triumphs of Afro-American women. We see our faces in the faces of Mem and Ruth Brownfield; we hear our voices in the voices of Meridian Hill and Celie. As indicated by my examples, I am principally interested in Walker's novels—*The Third Life of Grange Copeland, Meridian,* [and] *The Color Purple*—for it is in this narrative form that her commitment to spirituality, to our spiritual survival, is most apparent. It is here that she gives us her most instructive and most potent models.

The Third Life of Grange Copeland is, for many of us, an extremely difficult novel to read. The difficulty does not stem from Walker's selection and manipulation of language for she has consistently proven herself at least equal to the trials of the word. Nor does the difficulty stem from a young writer's—*The Third Life of Grange Copeland* is her first novel—mishandling of a deceptively facile, extremely complex form. The difficulty, and even the pain that we as readers initially avoid and then, perforce, face, stems from Walker's capacity to make us, in the spirit of Joseph Conrad, see the good and the evil in ourselves. Plainly, Walker believes that truth is the best medicine for an ailing spirit; but the truth is sometimes, since confabulations are often more appealing than facts, hard to bear. . . .

The Civil Rights Movement of the 1960s is the subject of Walker's second novel, *Meridian.* Here in a work that deserves a larger audience, Walker travels much farther than other novelists who have aided us in our re-examination of this important period in American history. Although [Ernest J.] Gaines's *The Autobiography of Miss Jane Pittman* and *In My Father's House,* powerful works in their own right, bring us to a point where we are able to engage the spirit of that volatile time, we do so only for a moment. In these novels Gaines's concerns are not defined by the Civil Rights Movement—this is not a flaw—but more by events that precede it, or by developments that occur alongside it. *Armies of the Night,* by Norman Mailer—another work of the imagination, although there is some debate about whether it is a novel—also treats the Civil Rights Movement. But Mailer seems more interested in documenting his own role in the events of history than in analyzing the events themselves. What sets *Meridian* apart from these texts is that the Civil Rights Movement is the subject, not an episode, backdrop, or mirror. The events of the time and the people who are caught in their pull are the poles between which an imagined, symbolic conflict achieves its resolution. . . .

In *The Third Life of Grange Copeland* the context for Walker's meditations on the spirit—on our spiritual survival and possibilities—is the home and the family. In *Meridian* her context is chiefly political and we are asked to consider the various ways in which we can assure the survival of that larger, greater family of which we are all members. In *The Color Purple,* her most controversial and most highly acclaimed novel, Walker returns to the home and to the family, for it is here that our first spiritual battles are fought. It is here that the spirit is most under siege. It is here that the spirit, when not respected and nurtured, is most in danger of being weakened and trivialized. . . .

The novels of Alice Walker contain the things of this world: pain and consolation, betrayal and reconciliation, love and transformation. They also contain the very thing we need to live in this world: models. It seems that Walker has always known what is essential for our survival because as a writer, as a womanist, and as an *artist* she has never failed to provide us with this vital resource. For Walker, models are essential spiritual aids with revelatory properties. Models reveal many things about ourselves and the world, but most importantly they reveal truth. This is why Walker shares with us situations in literature that are grounded in truth. Although we may sometimes wish to reject these situations, to dismiss them . . . as womanist propaganda, the force and purity of these situations, as well as our own knowledge of history and of human behavior, make such dismissals and rejections—if we love the truth—the greatest self-deception. But Walker's models reveal more than truth; they also reveal direction. Truth without direction is an oppression of the spirit. Without direction we flounder and agonize, but with it we apprehend not just a means of escape, but relief from spiritual suffering and an awareness not only of our fallibility but of our potentiality as well. In *The Third Life of Grange Copeland*, *Meridian*, and *The Color Purple*, Walker forces us, through her artful use of models, to face the truth; but she also, through these same models, provides direction. We celebrate Grange's transformation, Meridian's commitment, and Celie's triumph because each reveals what is true and possible.

Rudolph P. Byrd. In Joanne M. Braxton and Andrée Nicola McLaughlin, eds.
Wild Women in the Whirlwind: Afra-American Culture and the Contemporary Literary Renaissance (New Brunswick, N. J.: Rutgers University Press, 1990), pp. 364–65, 367, 373–74, 376–77

In *Meridian*, the individual experience of black motherhood within the context of historical black motherhood obliterates the souls of women and damages their children in an ever more serious cycle of destruction. Many critics have commented on this striking theme since Barbara Christian drew attention to it in *Black Women Novelists*. Gloria Wade-Gayles, for example, considers this resistance to motherhood as the sole defining element of black women's worthiness to be *Meridian*'s most original point. Christian explores contradictory social definitions of motherhood's paramount value and of black children as worthless, merely evidence of black women's promiscuity. Examining this issue further, Susan Willis proposes that, under these circumstances, mothers' impulses toward murder of their children or suicide "are the emotional articulation of social realities." In addition, *Meridian* "is less an indication of future possibilities and more a critique of the way heterosexual relationships have individualized a woman's relationship to *her* children, making them *her* property." *Meridian* simultaneously critiques traditional definitions of motherhood and implies more widely shared responsibility for children. In almost their only act of self-assertion, Saxon students riot when the college administration refuses to allow them to claim the Wild Child as one of their own. In focusing on the novel's opening scene—Meridian leading a "children's crusade" past a tank to desegregate a freak show—critics like Christian and Willis point to a politicized ideal of communal responsibility for children as central to Walker's vision in *Meridian*.

Accurate in itself, this critical focus has obscured another equally crucial component of the novel: the necessity for this rather abstract relationship of community and children to be manifested in an individual mother surrogate who provides emotional nurturance that the traditional role both demands and prevents. *Meridian* consistently focuses on both issues, on oppressive social structures and on the individual's capacity to resist them. Throughout, the novel emphasizes the power of individual example to rally opposition to injustice. The bereaved father testifying in church to the worth of his dead son's life, the minister who consciously imitates Martin Luther King, Jr.'s voice, Truman's inheritance of Meridian's role—all of these make a claim for the individual's power and worth. Both the harm done by oppressive institutions and the effectiveness of specific strategies of resistance are measured by their consequences for particular individuals. *Meridian* does not adopt a purely "quantitative" approach toward social change; that is, while continually emphasizing the need for social change, it values the rescue of each individual life, not only for its potential contributions toward social change, but in itself. With individuality such a strong underlying value, then, *Meridian* pushes beyond an abstract commitment of adults to the community's children and insists on one-to-one mothering nurturance for survival.

Missy Dehn Kubitschek. Claiming the Heritage: African-American Women
Novelists and History (Jackson: University Press of Mississippi, 1991), pp. 158–59

From the predominately Gothic vision in *The Third Life of Grange Copeland*, to the somewhat Camusian vision in *Meridian*, to the vision of the great gender divide-and-conquer in *The Color Purple*, Walker moves into T*he Temple of My Familiar* and creates a salutary vision, which points toward a monistic idealism in which humans, animals, and the whole ecological order coexist in a unique dynamic of pancosmic symbiosis.

Evidently, Walker must have been leery of the danger posed to her imagination by fragmentation—hence the urgency in the novel toward an ideal of unity—the unity of culture, moral truth, and imaginative thought and emotion. The best summation of this unity in *The Temple of My Familiar* is Lissie's long, moving story about the spirit of mutual dependence between humans and their animal cousins and Suwelo's reflections on its moral . . . and cultural implications, both for himself as well as for those with whom he has come in contact. . . .

With this vision clearly set before her, Walker proceeds to construct *The Temple of My Familiar* into six major parts, each consisting of diverse vignettes that project iconographic narrative movement (iconographic because Alice Walker not only tells a story in each movement, but also conveys its underlying metaphysical meaning by a carefully selected icon or mythic image, pretty much in the convention of African cosmological art and iconography). Behind the insistent particularity of each individual story is a serious quest, albeit unconscious, for the demonstrable values of oneness, wholeness, and unity as opposed to dialectical tension, exclusivity, and separateness. Insistently and consistently, characters in the novel are in motion, even when it appears they are in conflict, toward an underlying kinship that binds them with one another and with forces beyond themselves. For Walker this act of seeking means a basic freedom, which only a bird can enjoy, to range over all time, to employ any subtheme, to consecrate a limitless range of subject matter, to begin where she pleases, and to stop where she wishes.

The basic intent is to trace human life in its pancosmic and mythical dimensions through all its protean turns and twists, all its recesses, all its races and peoples. The watchword throughout the novel is communion, a communion forged through three distinct metaphysical contexts: Time, Nature, and Self.

Ikenna Dieke. *African American Review*. 26, 3 (Fall 1992), pp. 507–8

WARNER-VIEYRA, MYRIAM (n.d.)

GUADELOUPE

[*Le Quimboiseur l'avait dit*, translated as *As The Sorcerer Said*] is a short and touching first novel by a Guadeloupean woman. Myriam Warner-Vieyra ably raises the dilemma: is today's adolescent from the islands fated to a life of alienation and anguish in her search for education and a better life?

The author presents this dilemma through the literary device of the flashback. Zetou first appears in a state of shock, in a Parisian hospital ward for emotionally disturbed children. She is sixteen. Her plight and medical incarceration are explained as she relives in intervals of psychic, nostalgic retreat within herself the security of her island youth, her love of school successes, her hope to rise above the traditional life of the illiterate fisherman and their families. She remembers her idyllic dream of uniting with her first love, a bright neighbor boy, hoping that they might work together to benefit society. . . .

The exploitation of the promising child, rather than the themes of parental egoism and incestuous domination, provides the pathos and the originality of this novel. Certainly familiar elements appear: racial bigotry, hypocrisy in Parisian fringe societies, the irony of these islanders who are legally French but factually second-class citizens, escaping home poverty to survive abroad. The thrust, however, is a more universalized dilemma. Does the bright, industrious Antillean adolescent of today have a chance for a better life? Or, in today's developing and fluctuating social milieu, is she doomed, as the sorcerer said, to rejection and alienation, or even psychic disorientation?

Charlotte H. Bruner. *WLT*. 57, 2 (Spring 1983), p. 337

If one were simply interested in showing that [Warner-Vieyra's second novel] *Juletane* belongs to a certain genre of black African literature in Western languages, a summary of the novel would be sufficient to reveal what it has in common with other neo-African literary texts such as Ama Ata Aidoo's *The Dilemma of a Ghost* and Mariama Bâ's *Un Chant écarlate*: each one of them deals with the problem of a foreign woman who cannot fit well into her African husband's family. . . .

To dwell only on this point, however, would be to run the risk of missing the most striking feature of Warner-Vieyra's story: its insistent highlighting of the ways in which narrators and narratees relate to one another and how this, in turn, makes the text define "in quite specific and explicit terms its narrative situation and [describe] the conditions in which . . . it makes sense." This helps confirm the view that "every literary work *faces outward away from itself*" through narratees, toward real, flesh and blood listeners or readers, depending on whether we are in the oral or the written tradition. And to the extent that it does that, the text anticipates possible reactions to itself. As readers then we cannot help but come to a recognition that reading "is steered by two main structural components within the text: first, a repertoire of familiar literary patterns and recurrent literary themes, together with allusions to familiar social and historical contexts; second, techniques or strategies used to set the familiar against the unfamiliar." It is this second component that is of primary importance in the present essay. . . .

Narratees do play key roles in structuring the plurality of narratives in *Juletane*: they number at least three in a total of two narratives involving two different narrators. And insofar as two of the narratees are fictional characters themselves, they are internal to the stories under consideration and are easily identifiable. The overall structure of *Juletane* involves the embedding of a first-person narrative (by and essentially about the main character who gives her name to the novel) into a third-person narrative, and both of them are, in turn, prefaced by the authorial dedication and an epigraph on the same page. The third narratee, who is also the narratee of the novel as a whole, is external to the stories and is, in this respect, closer to actual readers of the text. The narrator of the third-person narrative is external to the events it relates and whereas its focus is on a female character who emerges as an unexpected reader of the first-person narrative, the author's function in writing the dedication is, as it were, to help provide the frame that makes it possible to contextualize the events of the novel.

Jonathan Ngate. Callaloo. 9, 4 (Fall 1986), pp. 553–55

Juletane is a frame-story narrative of cross-cultural marriage and tragedy. One Guadeloupean woman, Hélène, supposedly reads the diary of another, Juletane, and finds her heart touched and her sensibilities reawakened. Juletane wrote the diary in a month's time in 1961, but told in it the events of the last five years of her life. Orphaned early, she had left her island home to stay with her godmother in Paris. There she met a Senegalese charmer, Mamadou, whom she married. When she accompanied him to Africa, to her dismay she discovered that he already had a wife and child. She is only temporarily appeased when he promises to send his first wife, Awa, back to the village. Juletane keeps postponing her resolution to leave Mamadou and go back home. When she discovers she is pregnant, her husband avows his love for her, promising to live with her alone and to divorce Awa. An accident terminates the pregnancy, however, and saps Juletane's will. She begins to doubt her sanity. From that time on, a succession of frustrations (betrayals as she sees them) brings on her increasingly frequent periods of disorientation. Mamadou brings Awa back. Later Awa bears more children. Mamadou takes a cold, arrogant third wife who scorns Juletane and calls her a *toubabesse* (white woman). Juletane finally revenges herself on both wives and dies in a hospital for the criminally insane. . . .

When Juletane's story ends, Hélène closes the diary and weeps with compassion. Even Hélène's goal, however, is a conventional and not a radical one. Although she is a Paris career woman and expects to dominate her future husband, she is still marrying him in order to have a child. She believes she can find [in] motherhood the necessary fulfillment for her past life, which she now sees as empty. Perhaps the most insightful section of the novel, and the most original, is the gradual waning of Juletane's resolution to go home and reject a polygamous life. For many who wonder how a Western woman can accept the constraints of polygamy, *Juletane* provides some clues.

Charlotte H. Bruner. WLT. 62, 2 (Spring 1988), p. 323

A desire for oneness moves the feminine figures [in Warner-Vieyra's fiction] although they fail to define themselves. They seek refuge in madness, suicide, or symbolic self-annihilation. Zetou, the tragic character of Myriam Warner-Vieyra's *Le Quimboiseur l'avait dit*, recounts her tale of slow disintegration from her small Caribbean village of Karura to the psychiatric asylum in France where she has been committed. Uprooted, living under the constant fear of imminent catastrophe, Zetou, an adolescent abused by a cynical mother and her lover, unleashes her insane rage against the irrational order of life as she experiences it. . . . [*Juletane*] is in the form of an intimate diary. It recounts the "passion" in the sense of suffering and martyrdom of a Caribbean woman in Africa. Juletane, the protagonist, is married to an African whom she met in Paris and, when she arrives in Africa, she must share conjugal life with her husband's two other wives. The novel is a dark tale of the exile, solitude, and despair of a woman for whom madness becomes the principle of liberation and survival. She is known in the African community as "the mad one," and she herself dreams of "waking up in another world where insane people are not insane, but wise people who defend justice."

Marie-Denise Shelton. In Selwyn R. Cudjoe, ed. Caribbean Women
Writers (Wellesley: Calaloux Publications, 1990), pp. 350–51

Suzette and Juletane, the antiheroines of Miriam Warner-Vieyra's two companion novels (*Le Quimboiseur l'avait dit* and *Juletane*) are figures of dislocation, isolation, and alienation, victims of misguided efforts to escape from their initial restricted situations. Both are associated with closed spaces, severely circumscribed worlds. Suzette, a young West Indian girl, confined to her room in an insane asylum in Paris, looks back nostalgically to her island and what had once seemed to be a restricted environment comes to be in retrospect an idyllic paradise. Suzette's selective memory evokes an image of simple, communal life in a tiny village on an island "as big as two coconuts." In terms of the fate of woman's ambitions [Warner-Vieyra's] novels are pessimistic. Suzette affirms that she ought never to have left her village. The journeys to Europe [in *Le Quimboiseur l'avait dit*] and to Africa [in *Juletane*], attempts at self-actualization and escape, end in catastrophe. The woman who is not content to limit herself or to "be satisfied with the known domestic world," Suzette seems to suggest, is doomed to failure, to a last state worse than the first, partly because of her society's taboos, but also because of false, misplaced ambition. Juletane in Africa goes mad because she has been betrayed by her husband but also because she is unable to accept and be content with the sort of life typified by her husband's first wife, for whom "the entire universe was limited to a mat under a tree and three children around her."

Elizabeth Wilson. In Carole Boyce Davies and Elaine Savory Fido, eds.
Out of the Kumbla: Caribbean Women and Literature
(Trenton, N. J.: Africa World Press, 1990), pp. 48–49

Femmes échouées is a collection of nine stories by the Guadeloupean-born writer Myriam Warner-Vieyra, who has made Senegal her home for the last twenty years. The book is her third following the two novels *Le Quimboiseur l'avait dit* and *Juletane*. The stories are set in Guadeloupe, that beautiful French-speaking Caribbean island, and the rich mixture of its cultures permeates the stories with an exotic flavor, either through the local variety of the "fruit of passion" or through the lifestyles of its inhabitants.

The protagonist in each selection is a woman. A black servant girl dreams of winning the first prize at a Paris music academy when her gift for music is discovered by her (female) employers ("Premier Prix"); a married woman finds herself slowly dying from marriage to a cool, indifferent, uninterested husband, whom she calls "Wall" ("Le Mur, ou les charmes d'une vie conjugale"); a wheelchair-bound wife castrates her husband when she learns that their young maid is expecting his child ("Sidonie"). All the stories are written in a wholly realistic style except "Heure unique" (Unique Hour), in which the burial of a loved one triggers impressions of a revival of the love affair.

Nadezda Obradović. WLT. 64, 1 (Winter 1990), pp. 185–86

Juletane relies heavily on the principle of doubling, on both the levels of theme and structure. The text constructs a dialogue between Juletane's diary and Hélène's reading: it is thanks to the personal narrative of a fellow Guadeloupean that Hélène recognizes her own "face," and her own predicament in the mirror of the story. Doubling also occurs among the three co-wives, Juletane, Ndèye, and Awa, in a way that is suggestive of the echoing patterns of disfiguration, death, and castration that are at the center of Warner-Vieyra's works.

Feeling exiled in an inhospitable land, Juletane progressively loses her ability to function in the family compound that she shares with Awa and Ndèye, and literally shuts herself off from the community, depriving herself of food, and gradually sinking into mental illness: "Je restai enfermée dans notre chambre, sans boire ni manger" [I remain locked in our room without eating or drinking]. After a nervous breakdown and a violent outburst caused by her inability to adapt to her husband's polygamous culture, she spends time in a mental hospital, then has a miscarriage as a consequence of an accident, becomes sterile, and thus alienates herself completely from the household: "J'ai définitivement enterrétout ce qui se passe en dehors de cette maison. Ma vie se déroule dans une chambre de cinq pas sur quatre et sous le manguier de la cour où je prends mes repas" [I have buried once and for all everything that goes on outside this house. My life unfolds in a room five paces by four and under the mango tree in the yard where I eat my meals]. This "manguier stérile" [barren tree] is significant: it does not bear any fruit, and planted in the middle of the courtyard, it is a nagging reminder of Juletane's own "shortcomings" as a sterile wife. She begins to think of suicide, goes for days without food, shaves her head, begins to see Mamadou as a *monstre*, and displaces her fears onto every other human face she sees: "Je regardais les êtres humains qui m'entouraient; c'étaient des géants terrifiants, au visage monstreux" [I looked at the people who surrounded me; they were frightful giants, with monstrous faces]. She even harbors thoughts of murder against Mamadou: "Pour me venger, je l'imaginais mort, une belle dépouille de crapule puante sur laquelle je crachais" [To get revenge, I imagined him dead, nothing but a fine stinking corpse, on which I spat]. Her conflicts with Ndèye escalate to the point where the latter, calling her a *toubabesse* denies her the very identity she had come to Africa to claim: that of a black woman. Ndèye destroys Juletane's recording of Beethoven's Ninth Symphony, and violently slaps her face, propelling Juletane on a violent course of her own: "Cette gifle n'est que la goutte d'eau qui fait déborder ma coupe de passivité et transforme ma patience en torrent impétueux" [That slap in the face was the last drop that made my cup of passivity overflow and transformed my patience into a raging torrent]. Awa's children are found dead the following morning, and a week later, she literally disfigures Ndèye by pouring hot oil on her face, an incident that occurs after she had spent some time imagining herself sharpening the long kitchen knife, stabbing Ndèye to death, and watching her face become "un masque hieux aux yeux vitreux" [a hideous death mask, her eyes . . . glassy]. After being confined to a mental hospital, she dreams of visiting a cemetery with her father and seeing her own grave stone, with no name on it. Feeling ever more like a "zombie" from the Caribbean, she has the impression "d'être à la fois au-dessus et en dessu" [of being inside and outside the grave], of being a traveler between the world of the living and that of the dead. Narrative closure is finally provided by her actual death three months later in the hospital, a death that appears to redeem Hélène, the reader in the text, from her own coldness and unfeeling existence as a displaced Guadeloupean. . . .

If, as [Hélène] Cixous argues, the disfiguration and decapitation to which patriarchy subjects women is a displacement of male castration anxiety, then Myriam Warner-Vieyra's works constitute an interesting attempt to work out this problematic in structural as well as thematic terms. In her short story "Sidonie" [in *Femmes échouées*] there is a double crime which links both castration and disfiguration. The castrated husband musters enough strength to strangle his invalid wife, who is confined to a wheelchair. Here, it is Sidonie's brother, Septime, whose perspective dominates the third-person narrative. Warner-Vieyra uses free indirect discourse to enter the minds of all the protagonists. But it is Septime's interior monologue that frames the beginning and the end of the tale. His self-centered concerns for his personal loss at the death of his sister reveal a shallowness and a callousness, which are damning. There is an unequal and dissymmetrical presentation of perspectives which mirrors the relative power of the characters. Each character's interior monologue allows the reader some insight into Sidonie's life and feelings, into her reasons for writing: her jealous nature, her relationship with Bernard, the car accident that paralyzed her, and her feelings toward the young woman her husband has gotten pregnant. But we are never allowed into her own consciousness, and it is truly her silence that is resounding here. No one really knows her. She writes, but the reader does not have access to her notebooks. . . .

[There] is no interpretation of Bernard's own actions and reactions: only Sidonie's unruly behavior gets the benefit of each character's speculations and judgement. If the surface coherence of the texts thus strongly implies that Sidonie has gone mad, there is however an equally powerful countercoherence that emerges from the radical and disruptive force of the uninterpreted events of the story: it is up to the reader to examine these structural dissymmetries, and to understand the unstated social inequalities in the vision of each character. Sidonie is perhaps a "victim" gone mad, but, as with Juletane whose delusions make it hard to determine what degree of agency she is capable of having, it becomes clear that the very notion of agency needs to be redefined to accommodate those situations where extreme pain is *the* condition of subjectivity, of a "radical subjectivity" that imprisons humans in an utterly incommunicable experience. Juletane and Sidonie are locked in a private and painful world that remains largely inarticulate, and eruptions of violence are their only means of acting out their pain.

Thematically and textually, narrative closure is reached in death: the death of the title character. This is a very traditional way to provide closure and to restore order to the community. One might argue, then, that Warner-Vieyra's texts equivocate, that is, that they disown on a constructural level what they embrace on an ideological one. Since Juletane regrets that Mamadou has died before being able to read her journal, she appears to have reached a state of "rationality" and accommodation that allows her final reentry into the symbolic realm of patriarchal culture. She no longer wants to live . . . and it is suggested that Hélène becomes a more gentle, tender, accommodating, and "feminine" woman after reading the diary. In effect, the structure of the work reinforces traditional notions of femininity in the end, despite the strong ideological critique of female alienation it contains. Warner-Vieyra seems to want to do an about-face that will not antagonize traditional readers who constitute the majority of literate Africans capable of reading her works. . . . It is even clearer in "Sidonie" since Septime's point of view is more sympathetic to Bernard's awful "mutilation" than to his sister's crippled body and death. Male solidarity triumphs over female hysteria, and the social order remains intact.

Françoise Lionnet. *Callaloo.* 16, 1 (Winter 1993), pp. 139–43

WILSON, AUGUST (1945–   )

UNITED STATES

[If] August Wilson has wanted anything in his career as a playwright, it is to be recognized by the people of the ghetto as their voice, their bard. Wilson gives words to trumpeters and trash men, cabbies and conjurers, boarders and land-ladies, all joined by a heritage of slavery. Their patois is his poetry; their dreams are his dramas. And while Wilson's inspiration is contained—a few sloping blocks in Pittsburgh—his aspiration seems boundless. He intends to write a play about black Americans in every decade of this century, and he has already completed six of the projected ten.

Fences, a drama set in the 1950s . . . is the second of the cycle to reach Broadway. It was preceded by *Ma Rainey's Black Bottom*, which won the New York Drama Critics Circle Award as the best play of the 1984–85 season and . . . it established Wilson as "a major find for the American theater," a writer of "compassion, raucous humor and penetrating wisdom."

Fecundity, too, can be added to the list. *Joe Turner's Come and Gone*, written after *Fences* . . . may come to New York next season. *The Piano Lesson*, Wilson's most recent work, is on the 1987–88 schedule of the Yale Repertory. . . . It adds up to the most auspicious arrival of an American playwright since that of David Mamet some fifteen years ago.

Fences may prove the most accessible of Wilson's plays, faster-moving than *Ma Rainey* and less mystical than *Joe Turner*. Several critics have likened this family drama to Arthur Miller's *Death of a Salesman*, centering as it does on a proud, embittered patriarch, Troy Maxson, and his teenage son, Cory. Their immediate conflict is kindled when Cory is recruited to play college football and Troy, once a baseball star barred from the segregated big leagues, demands he turn down the scholarship because he cannot believe times have truly changed. Behind the narrative looms Wilson's concern with legacy. As Cory Maxson almost grudgingly discovers the value in his father's flawed life, he accepts his part in a continuum that runs from Pittsburgh to the antebellum South and finally to Mother Africa. . . .

Most of Wilson's plays concern the conflict between those who embrace their African past and those who deny it. "You don't see me running around in no jungle with no bone between my nose," boasts one character in *Ma Rainey*. Wilson's answer is that Africa remains a pervasive force, a kind of psychic balm available to twentieth-century blacks through blues songs, communal dances, tall tales. Wilson the mythologist coexists with Wilson the social realist. There is a broad historical truth to his characters—to Levee, the jazz musician who naively sells off his compositions to a white record company executive; to Troy Maxson, whose job prospects go no further than becoming the first black truck driver in the Pittsburgh Sanitation Department.

Samuel G. Freedman. NYTM.
March 15, 1987, pp. 36, 40

Every culture generates its own myths and superstitions, taboos and rituals of exorcism. To secure a glorious afterlife, Egyptians embalmed their deceased rulers. Ancient Greeks went to Delphi to worship divine wisdom and to learn about their fates. Most Chinese people still follow elaborate burial rites which commemorate the dead for forty-nine days with chants and incantation. Being a black American, August Wilson's heritage goes back to African traditions which are based on similar pantheistic views of celestial order ruling both the living and the dead. From *Joe Turner's Come and Gone*, through *Fences* to his present work *The Piano Lesson*, a seamless blend of Christianity with the inherent African cosmology defines the spiritual landscape within which the characters suffer and rejoice.

Set in small-scaled domestic environments, the three plays are immersed in a sense of mystery that transgresses the confinements of rigid realism. Wilson's central characters are all marvelous storytellers. In their fantastic tales, daily life takes on a subliminal cloak, transforming mundane facts into allegorical rituals.

Mei-Ling Ching. *Theater.* 19, 3 (Summer 1988), p. 70

The center of African-American playwright August Wilson's growing theatrical universe is conspicuously occupied by African-American men. They are the thinkers, the doers, the dreamers. Revolving around them in seemingly expendable supporting roles are wives, mistresses, sisters, children, and other relatives. As characters such as Levee [in *Ma Rainey's Black Bottom*], Troy Maxson [in *Fences*], Herald Loomis [in *Joe Turner's Come and Gone*], and Boy Willie [in *The Piano Lesson*], impose their authority, they overshadow the concerns of others. Most noticeable in their blind quest for omnipotence and wealth is that they place no stock in Christian dogma, adapting instead a purely secular ideology. Consequently, what emerges from their abandonment of Christianity is a more convenient, self-serving religion—one totally unaligned with the cultural reservoir provided by what many African-Americans have traditionally referred to as "good old-fashioned religion." While this good old-fashioned religion has, for centuries, provided inspiration, strength and moral principles for African-Americans, Wilson's men affirm that it has not and will not suit their needs. Therefore, they demonstrate their disavowal by challenging and withdrawing from the religion of their ancestors.

August Wilson has apparently chosen to focus on the African-American man's oppression in this country to symbolize the collective struggles of all African-Americans. Since the early 1980s, Wilson has committed himself to writing ten plays chronicling the history of his people in each decade of their existence in the United States. Often depicted on the verge of an emotional breakdown, Levee, Herald Loomis, Troy Maxson, and Boy Willie dominate center stage and become Wilson's primary spokesmen. Although the African-American woman appears in various supporting roles—devoted wife and mother, cranky blues singer, docile sex object, stubborn sister, etc.—the actions of the African-American man clearly convey the themes of each of the four plays Wilson has completed toward his ten-play mission. . . .

With a foreboding resonance, each of Wilson's four published plays addresses the difficulties the African-American man has had in accepting

Christianity as a moral frame of reference. Levee, Herald Loomis, Troy Maxson, and Boy Willie do not stop short of lambasting white society for their misfortunes. They blaspheme against Christianity with ease and run roughshod over any obstacle to their respective ambitions. But they are not above acknowledging themselves as villains. Having conceded this, they choose to pass over Christianity as practiced by fellow African-Americans in favor of less restrictive adaptations of their own brand of survival. Consequently, the language and actions associated with their makeshift ideals reflect a new means of compensating for their previously unquestioned belief in God.

Quite unlike the sorely tried though patient Job of the Old Testament, Wilson's African-American men have given up on their God. No longer content to "wait on the Lord," they make impetuous, often foolhardy decisions about their lives. They are no longer so easily appeased by spewing profanity and threats at white America or by finding solace in the word of God. Neither are they intimidated by the moral consequences of their infidelity. Where once the sanctity of Christianity may have been reinforced by a heavy hand like that extended by [Lorraine] Hansberry's uncompromising Lena Younger [in *A Raisin in the Sun*]: "In my mother's house there is still God," its ethics are being either challenged or totally ignored. Consigned to a life of subjugation, the African-American men who dominate Wilson's plays discard Christianity in favor of more flexible, manmade commandments.

Sandra G. Shannon. MELUS. 16, 3 (Fall 1989), pp. 127, 141–42

All of Wilson's plays spring from specific inspirations with widespread cultural implications; the genesis of [*Ma Rainey's Black Bottom*] was the first blues—a Bessie Smith record—he heard as a youth. He listened to the record twenty-two consecutive times, feeling that someone was speaking directly to him and that he understood instantly and emotionally. He came to see the blues as part of blacks' oral tradition: a way of passing on information that was given an emotional reference by music. The information Wilson received was that there was a nobility and beauty to blacks he hadn't seen.

This nobility and beauty he conveys in his plays in a style and tone that could be likened to a combination of Sophocles and Aristophanes: hauntingly poetic and raucously humorous, inexorable and irrepressible. Though Wilson's settings are realistic, his protagonists are larger than life; they are very much themselves and something more. His recurring themes and the stories embodying them (both those dramatized and those told by the characters) raise the black experience in America to epic stature. The dialogue, inspired by Wilson's longtime observation of black speech, is evocative stage poetry in what is said and not said. The pressure of characters struggling with a fate that is both within their own natures and a legacy of being black in America, the threat of being pushed beyond endurance into violence, gives the plays a sense of danger, dramatic tension and high theatricality. . . .

Though Wilson did not set out intending to write a cycle of plays, as *Fences* (set in 1957), *Joe Turner's Come and Gone* (set in 1911) and *The Piano Lesson* (set in 1936) were in various stages of development, he realized that he was creating a play for each decade of the [twentieth] century: "I'm taking each decade and looking at one of the most important questions that blacks confronted in that decade and writing a play about it. Put them all together and you have a history."

Fences began with the image of a man holding a baby in his arms—it was Wilson's reaction against the stereotype of the irresponsible black man. His protagonist, Troy Maxson, tries to hold closely what is his and keep out whatever threatens his control—he builds real and psychological fences in the play. . . .

The grandeur of Wilson's vision is most evident in *Joe Turner's Come and Gone.* The play's setting is a Pittsburgh boarding house in 1911, inspired by black artist Romare Bearden's painting of a boarding house scene that includes an abject man in a coat and hat. Wilson wondered why the man was so abject, and created the character of Herald Loomis—"Herald, because he's a herald. Loomis, because he's luminous," the playwright told a *New York Post* interviewer. Loomis is an ominous figure in a black coat and hat, a former church deacon pressed into seven years' labor by Joe Turner, whose villainous history W. C. Handy made into the blues song that is the play's title. . . .

August Wilson is a demanding playwright; the fabric of his plays is densely woven and speaks to attentive audiences. In the first scene of *Joe Turner*, Bynum describes a cleansing ritual that preceded his finding his song. That ritual is unwittingly repeated by Herald upon himself, and not only frees him from the past and sends him out to sing his own song, but gives Bynum the sanction of his life, for the last line of the play is "Herald Loomis, you shining! You shining like new money!" Wilson's language is incantatory, his story at once a spiritual allegory and a social document.

Holly Hill. In Bruce King, ed. Contemporary American Theatre
(New York: St. Martin's Press, 1991), pp. 88, 91, 93–94

In his newest play, *Two Trains Running*, August Wilson summons up . . . people and circumstances . . . from his own memory, reclaiming stories from the obscurity into which so much of the oral storytelling tradition has passed. The audience enters into the intimacy of the routine of these characters—stopping by for their morning coffee, checking on the numbers, commenting on the events of the street—just as Sterling Johnson, newly released from prison, breaks into the closed circle of the restaurant and provokes new performances of the stories and debates shared by Memphis and Holloway. . . .

The insistent rhythm of time and mortality pulses through the play. The restaurant is across the street from Lutz's Meat Market and West's Funeral Home—the characters travel between these three primitive sites of slaughter, consumption, and decay. People speculate about the last days of the world. The block the restaurant is on is scheduled to be levelled. West, the undertaker, goes about the ancient rituals of preparing the dead for the afterlife. He is a modern high priest officiating over the ceremonies of grief and valediction. Yet an impulse towards action emerges out of this desolation. Risa, Holloway, Sterling, and Memphis try to find their own ways to envisage a future through consulting prophets and oracles, playing with chance. Wolf, the numbers runner, offers new lives and different endings for the price of a ticket.

Playing the numbers is a way to try to control fate and get enough money to get ahead. There is no logic to the world: getting ahead happens only through a lucky number or a sudden contract. Working, particularly working according to standards imposed by white America, yields up only a slight variant on slavery. The real battle is revealed to be one not of language or attitude but of economics. Wilson tells stories of people inadequately recompensed for the work they've done, legal clauses written so a property owner can be bought out for a fraction of the price he paid, even lottery winnings that are cut in half. The only way to recover what has been lost or stolen is by following the dominant culture's tactics: robbery, burning buildings for insurance, carrying guns to assert power. But these people are arrested and imprisoned for actions that in the marketplace would be considered shrewd business. Wilson's characters are not innocent: they have already tried to make their lives work as the world dictates and lost. Their need to reclaim what has been taken from them, either in actual or symbolic terms—Herald Loomis's lost wife in *Joe Turner's Come and Gone*, the piano bought with a father's blood in *The Piano Lesson*, Memphis' farm— becomes the truest form of revolution and affirmation.

Lisa Wilde. *Theater.* 22 (Fall 1991), pp. 73–74

His 1984 play *Ma Rainey's Black Bottom* is a disturbing look at the consequences of waiting, especially as it relates to the precarious lot of black musicians during the pre-Depression era. Although the play features a still shot in the lives of several members of Ma Rainey's 1920s band, it is also suggestive of the many and varied oppressive forces under which the entire Afro-American population labored at that time. From education to employment, blacks got the smallest share of the American pie, while clinging to an often self-destructive ideology of tolerance. Through the actions and the dialogue of three crucial characters—the blues singer Ma Rainey, her piano player Toledo, and her trumpet player Levee—Wilson conveys the damage that prolonged periods of waiting have caused the Afro-American artist. . . .

While Ma Rainey tries the patience of her two promoters, her musicians waiting in the basement band room, all of whom are black males, bicker and taunt each other in deceptively simple repartee. Their conversations, which slip from the correct spelling of *music* to an existentialist discussion of black history, gradually intensify and unexpectedly erupt in a fatal stabbing. The self-made philosopher and pianist, Toledo, inadvertently steps on the new Florsheim shoes of the ambitious though disgruntled trumpet player Levee. In a gradual chain of events, this otherwise commonplace incident leads to murder. Apparently still angered by the recent refusal of one of Ma Rainey's promoters to launch his musical career, Levee, during several moments of extreme anger, stabs Toledo in the back. . . .

Because of the blatant image of a stabbing death, an unsympathetic viewer might perceive Levee's action to be monstrous. However, his conversations throughout the play give various reasons for a pre-existing cynicism. He brings with him to the recording session a history of negativism which spans his entire life. For example, as an eight-year-old, he watched white men rape his mother. In addition, his business arrangement with Sturdyvant is not proceeding as he had hoped. After agreeing to purchase lyrics Levee has composed, Sturdyvant squashes the trumpet player's ambitions to start a band of his own so that he can play his more upbeat, avant-garde arrangements. Added to these setbacks is Levee's incompatibility with Ma Rainey. He cannot yield his ambitious nature to the strict control that she exerts over her band and her promoters. He constantly rebels against the sovereignty that Ma Rainey has over what and how the band plays. Inevitably, because of their irreconcilable differences, Ma Rainey has no choice but to fire him. . . .

Despite Levee's genuine ambition to excel in the music industry, he is sucked under by the swirling vortex of oppression. If isolated and studied strictly in terms of his sociological relevance, Levee might easily serve as the basis for a viable case study on the root causes of black-on-black crime in the United States. His character mirrors the all-too-familiar results of the black male's battle to survive in a white-dominated society. No longer convinced that the Christian's God is the black man's ally, Levee resorts to annihilating members of his own race to appease his frustrations at having to wait for others in order to actualize his ambitions. Thus, Levee, like many one-time-ambitious, creative young black hopefuls, becomes disillusioned, self-defeating, and ultimately violent.

Each of August Wilson's four completed plays emphasizes "the choices that we as blacks in America have made." However, the playwright is also concerned about the oppressive forces which have precluded many of those choices. To this end, *Ma Rainey's Black Bottom* provides a provocative look into the world of several black musicians who have little or no control in determining the course of their professional lives. Even as they create and enjoy their music, the origins of which may be traced to their own African ancestry, they are forced to yield their primary rights of ownership to whites, who prey upon them. Waiting becomes the sedative that allows such predators to keep the personal aspirations of these black musicians forever in the balance. Waiting also stifles their "warrior spirit," the absence of which leads to noticeably neurotic compensations in their characters. Waiting becomes a dominant motif in the play, affecting each member of the band, as well as Ma Rainey, in some awkward manifestation. In addition to Ma Rainey's unrefined and boisterous personality, the extraordinary behavior of her pianist and her trumpet player suggests latent reactions to figurative roadblocks placed before them.

Sandra G. Shannon. BALF. 25, 1 (Spring 1991), pp. 135–36, 143–45

The question of self-identity seems to be the major force in [Wilson's] plays. In *Ma Rainey's Black Bottom* the play centers on black musicians who are exploited by white managers and record producers. . . . In a dispute over the arrangement of the music the blacks cease to argue only when the white manager Sturdyvant says what he wants. The piano player chides the others, saying, "As long as the colored man look to white folks to put the crown on what he say . . . as long as he looks to white folks for approval . . . then he ain't never gonna find who he is and what he's about." The title of the play is a type of pun: the Black Bottom was a dance popularized by Ma Rainey's song, but, of course, Ma Rainey also has a black bottom. The action of the play is very simple: the black musicians and the white managers are waiting for the arrival of the famous singer Ma Rainey. When she finally arrives she initially refuses to make the records, then finally agrees. She makes it clear throughout the play that she feels used by the white men who run the business. Saying that they care nothing about her, she concludes, "As soon as they get my voice down on them recording machines, then it's just like if I'd be some whore and they roll over and put their pants on." . . .

In *Fences* Wilson is dealing with the polarities of loving and dying. In *Beyond the Pleasure Principle* [Sigmund] Freud noted Eros and the death wish as the elementary powers whose counterpoint governs all the puzzles of life. Wilson establishes these two forces as the governing factors in the life of the protagonist. *Fences* deals with the failed dreams of Troy Maxson, a black ball player who played in the minority black leagues, but was barred from the major (all white) leagues because of his race. Wilson wrote the play to show the indignities which blacks in that generation suffered, but hid from their children. Set in the 1950s, the play presents conflicts familiar to blacks in the audience—indeed, one critic wrote that he was moved to tears because he seemed to see his own life on stage. . . .

In Wilson's next play, *Joe Turner's Come and Gone*, the question of identity is central. Into a boarding house in Pittsburgh comes a strange, lost man with a child, seeking his wife. Almost everyone in the play is seeking someone, and they appeal for assistance to two wondrously mythic types . . . the People Finder and the Binder of What Clings. The white man Selig is in a line of People Finders; but in contrast to his father who found runaway slaves for the plantation bosses, he is a beneficent figure who finds black people displaced after the end of slavery and reunites families. Bynum is in a line of African conjure men and works spells. He, however, is in search of his own song: in a vision his father revealed to him that if he could find a "shiny man"—a man who is One Who Goes Before and Shows the Way—"I would know that my song had been accepted and worked its full power in the world and I could lay down and die a happy man." In the course of the play it is revealed that the stranger, Loomis, was entrapped into seven years of indentured servitude by the notorious Joe Turner (an actual historical figure), and thereby lost not only his wife, but his whole sense of the world and his place in it. . . .

Wilson's latest play to open in New York has, like his others, first been performed at Yale, and then in a number of other cities. . . . *The Piano Lesson* is set in 1936. A group of blacks living in Pittsburgh are displaced from their roots and their acquaintances in Mississippi. Doaker and his niece Berneice are surprised by the unexpected arrival of Berneice's brother, the high-spirited Boy Willie, and his friend Lymon who have driven from Mississippi with a load of watermelons. Boy Willie hopes to make a large amount of money from the watermelons, so he will have part of the money he needs to buy a farm. He also hopes to persuade his sister Berneice to sell the family piano so that he can get the rest of the money he needs. The play becomes a struggle over the family inheritance, an elaborately decorated piano with pictures of family members carved on the legs. . . .

In a time when many American playwrights write about transitory problems, petty characters, and minor themes. Wilson seeks the great themes. . . . Although he feels very passionate about "the historical treatment of blacks in American society," his characters speak to both whites and blacks because they relate to archetypal themes and questions: What is true freedom? What is it to be a man? How does a family relate? What is the nature of responsibility? What, ultimately, is the purpose of life, and how does one "find one's own song?" How does one become (or find) a shiny man? In plays filled with poetic images, Wilson explores these questions.

Yvonne Shafer. *ZAA.* 39, 1 (1991), pp. 20–26

WYNTER, SYLVIA (1928–   )

JAMAICA

Sylvia Wynter's *The Hills of Hebron* documents the wide range of cults in the islands, including a Pocomania cult (corresponding to the Haitian voodoo worshippers): "the Believers" (corresponding to the Afro-Baptist cults which Philip Curtin and Orlando Patterson describe as having first formed themselves in the 1860s); and the "New Believers" (a cult invented from two related creeds— Marcus Garvey's Black God religion and the Jamaican Rastafarians' belief in the divinity of the Emperor of Ethiopia). When the Believers' movement collapses with the ignominious failure of their leader to take flight to heaven, some of the brethren join the orthodox Christian Church: "There was something atavistic about their singing as though they were shouting to recall lost gods from the primeval forests of Africa. And at times their singing stirred up secret urges in the Reverend's own heart which had been slumbering through centuries of civilization." Reverend Brooke's disturbance at his flock's hearts of darkness corresponds with the uneasiness of nineteenth-century missionaries at the incursions of rhythmic singing and other "African" manifestations into the orthodox Church.

Wynter comically deflates the cults depicted in her novel. A good illustration of the method used is Moses' confession to his first convert of how the Lord inspired him in a vision: "It was just a day like any other, Sister Edwards. No sign to mark it as different. I was watering the flowers. I came to a rhododendron bush that stood alone by itself. As I poured out water at the root, I see the whole bush light up with fire before my eyes. I step back, I stand still, I watch. The bush flamed orange and green fire. The presence of God was all round about me. I fall on my knees, I bow my head to the earth. I make to take off my shoes but as it wasn't Sunday I wasn't wearing any. And the ground on which I was standing, Sister Edwards, was holy, holy ground."

But the author does not simply make fun of her cultists. The novel shows a passionate concern about the void in the lives of the socially depressed cultists, and sees part of the solution as lying in socioeconomic adjustments. The socioeconomic leaning is given emphasis by Wynter's allowing Moses to become unnerved when a labor leader rouses the people to take stock of "the extent of their misery, the hopelessness of their poverty, the lack of any future for their children." He advises them to have nothing to do with churches ("All that is finished and done"); rather, they should believe in organized labor, and Man. The weight of the presentation leads the reader to think that this is Wynter's advice too.

Kenneth Ramchand. The West Indian Novel and Its Background
(London: Heinemann, 1983), pp. 127–29

[Wynter's] criticism alone would ensure her a place in the history of West Indian writing. Beginning in 1967, she published a series of articles and book reviews that would open, in her own words, "a new dimension for criticism."

In 1968 and 1969 she had published in two parts the monumentally titled "We Must Learn to Sit Down Together and Talk about a Little Culture: Reflections on West Indian Writing and Criticism." This was occasioned by her desire to express her disagreement with several works of criticism emerging from the university and to articulate what she saw as the radical difference between what she termed "acquiescent" criticism versus "challenging" criticism. For her, the "acquiescent" critic pretended to take an objective stance outside of the historical process which has molded his point of view. This "pretended objectivity and detachment" in fact resulted in a distorted perspective which merely served to bolster the status quo. The "challenging" critic, on the other hand, accepted and was aware that his point of view was molded by this historical process, and this awareness—Wynter felt—could lead to creative insights that could help to initiate conscious change. She expanded further on this in 1973, when in a note on her critique "Creole Criticism," she wrote, "Creole criticism . . . is merely literary criticism rehashed in brown or black face." Her attacks were wide-ranging and, at times, savage, aimed particularly at the work of W. I. Carr and Louis James (then lecturers in the Department of English at Mona) as well as at the work of Wayne Brown, John Hearne, Cameron King, and Mervyn Morris. As far as Wynter was concerned, all critics were too quick to come to terms with the "brilliant myth" of Europe as the "super culture which embraces all other cultures, and obliterates as it absorbs." In being enchained by this cultural myth, such "acquiescent" critics reflected and paralleled "the inauthenticity of the University and its society." Worse yet, since these critics were also the educators, Wynter felt that "the hostility that the West Indian writer meets with from university students comes directly from the concept of literature sold to them by [such] educators." Moreover, what she found is that the critics she examined almost all failed to understand that "when the creative instinct is stifled or driven into exile the critical faculty can survive only as maggots do—feeding on the decaying corpse of that which gives it a brief predatory life." The writing of criticism in the university had become like a "branch plant" industry, with the interpreter replacing the writer and the critic displacing the creator.

Sylvia Wynter's second major piece of literary criticism, "Creole Criticism: A Critique," reflected her belief that the folk culture represents "the only living tradition in the Caribbean" and that it is only by "drawing from, by feeding from [the West Indian peasant] that a truly national literature could begin." Indeed, it was that personality through "the reinvention of its culture against impossible odds, that made the West Indian novel possible." She also saw the culture of the folk as a kind of "guerrilla resistance against the market economy," and she posited the existence of a pervasive "African heritage which has been the crucible of the cultural deposits of the immigrant peoples." It was this recognition which motivated, in large measure, her attack on Kenneth Ramchand because she saw his mission as being "to negate, destroy, diminish, disguise the African centrality in the cultural dynamic of the Caribbean peoples." In opposition to this, she celebrated and emphasized the importance of the folk culture in such essays as "Jonkonnu in Jamaica," "Novel and History: Plot and Plantation," and "One Love: Aspects of Afro-Jamaicanism." In "Jonkonnu," for instance, she set out to prove the existence of "a pervasive African-descended folk culture in Jamaica, one that had . . . acted as a principle of revolt and a form of cultural resistance to the cultural superstructure brought by the colonizer."

From the viewpoint of the 1980s, when we have such magisterial and insightful criticism as Gordon Rohlehr's book on [Edward Kamau] Brathwaite's poetry, *Pathfinder*, and Bruce King's collection of critical essays on *West Indian Literature*, the controversy and heat generated by Wynter's articles in the 1970s, seem out of proportion. But her work was crucial because she was the first to articulate, and focus on, the problem, and she was ideally suited for it, being a creative writer herself, academically trained in literary criticism, and educated in the metropole. She was also an agitator, a stimulating lecturer, and a polemical writer who presented papers at numerous conferences expressing her point of view.

Whether West Indian criticism would have inevitably come of age and shed its dependent role is difficult to say. There is little doubt, however, that she helped to hasten the process by her provocative and stimulating articles.

Victor L. Chang. In Daryl Cumber Dance, ed. Fifty Caribbean Writers
(Westport Conn.: Greenwood Press, 1986), pp. 500–2

Where many Caribbean novels . . . indeed romanticize the image of woman as mother, in at least one Caribbean novel this very real mother-as-victim syndrome is dealt with. Jamaican Sylvia Wynter, as the first black woman novelist from the English-speaking Caribbean, creates, in her only novel, *The Hills of Hebron*, an indomitable woman figure, in the form of Gatha Randall Barton. But it is Gatha who falls desperately into the throes of this self-sacrificing motherdom. Like the mothering situation itself, Miss Gatha is a paradox. She is an ideal as a Caribbean black mother, the self-sacrificing, self-effacing woman parent to a young self-centered, ungrateful, partially crippled man-child. At the same time, Gatha Randall Barton, within the Hebron settlement, becomes an anomaly, a woman who is a pillar of fortitude, resourcefulness, and wisdom as the community's efficient leader. For most Caribbean women, the former role would certainly be the narrow enclosure from which there would be no easy means of escape, while the latter would not even be within the realm of consideration. Although for Miss Gatha both experiences are personal realities, she is caught fast in her narrow enclosure. Even with community acknowledgement, acceptance, and approval of her "more masculine" leadership attributes, Gatha, having so completely internalized her function as mother, never attempts to escape or even to obvert this most sacred of women-roles. Instead, this function becomes a prime motivation for everything else in her life; her every accomplishment rests on the fragile relationship she has with her son, Isaac, and her desire to see him as Hebron's leader. Gatha can never be an independent and individuated personality herself because of her almost fanatical commitment to her son's destiny which serves to entrap her in society's small enclosure of motherdom. This, indeed, is the tragic flaw in an otherwise self-assured Caribbean woman.

The primary thematic concern of *The Hills of Hebron* is certainly not with women, although women, as in nearly every facet of Caribbean life, play significant roles in the communication of the novel's theme. The rites of passage of a black community in the 1940s from postslavery oppression and poverty towards physical, psychological, and spiritual freedom is the basic concern of the novel. It is actually the story of Prophet Moses Barton, Gatha's husband, opportunist and visionary who, like the biblical Moses, leads his people out of a physical and psychological bondage. His Egypt is a small, decadent village called Cockpit Center. His exodus is to the hillside: to a landscape called Hebron where he will settle his Church of the New Believers of Hebron. Moses Barton, although depicted by Wynter with some farcical humor, is a forerunner of Jamaican "deliverers." Wynter tells us this; thus, we are never really expected to believe that Moses Barton's black God, whom he promises "would be on their side forever," will actually deliver the Hebronites from inequity. Through the brief glimpses of a young labor leader, the author hints to us that the movement to liberation which Moses Barton inspires will be evolutionary.

Janice Lee Liddell. In Carole Boyce Davies and Elaine Savory Fido, eds.
Out of the Kumbla: Caribbean Women and Literature
(Trenton, N. J.: Africa World Press, 1990), pp. 322–23

With *The Hills of Hebron* we enter the era of Black Power, black pride, and the quest for self-government. The novel heralds a time of radical reorientation, seemingly linking us with our past and taking us back where we began. For if, as Wynter suggests, slavery involved "the cutting off of a memory of the past, the denial of any indigenous history, and a kind of intellectual alienation from the self and society," *The Hills of Hebron* argues for the repossession of that past and the finding of a voice to express that denial and absence. And if, as Wynter insists, Caribbean people were oppressed first as natives, then as blacks, before the question of gender arose, the relative importance of gender has to be considered in that light. And even though Miss Gatha emerges as a powerful voice in the novel, she is powerful not so much because she is a woman but because of her status as a colonial person anxious to articulate this private sense of dispossession. . . .

In this novel, Wynter captures the vital instinct of Caribbean people to survive and to create. Although the novel may be much too long in parts and somewhat overbearing in its didacticism, it captures the sense of restlessness with the past and the need to break out of discourses and practices that are designed to keep us coffined within an alien ideology and culture. Structured in the anticolonialist struggle of the 1950s and 1960s, *The Hills of Hebron* brings to a closure the story of Mary Prince, coffined on her slave plantation and subjected to the brutality of the slave master, offered in 1831. *The Hills of Hebron* almost seems a response to Prince's plea for the recognition of her humanity. As she asked: "How can slaves be happy when they have the halter round their neck, and the whip upon their back? and are disgraced and thought nothing more of than beasts?—and are separated from their mothers, and husbands, and children, and sisters, just as cattle are sold and separated? Is it happiness for a driver in the field to take down his wife or sister or child, and strip them, and whip them in such a disgraceful manner?—women that have had children exposed in the open field to shame!"

Certainly, *The Hills of Hebron* reflects the movement toward the creation of a new day, a movement from the symbol of "the halter round their neck[s] and the whip upon their back[s]." Here, indeed, the spirits of the ancestors meet and ask that libation be given to soothe the transition from the old to the new, from the past to the present, from the public to the private sphere of discourse. The women writers of the contemporary era would explore new areas of concern, different continents of sensibility and feelings, and varied ways of speaking about their relationships with each other and with their men. Much of the work would be influenced by the Black Power, Rastafarian, and women's movements.

Selwyn R. Cudjoe. *Caribbean Women Writers*
(Wellesley, Mass.: Calaloux Publications, 1990), pp. 42–43

ZADI ZAOUROU, BERNARD (1938–   )

COTE D'IVOIRE

[Bernard] Zadi Zaourou has advocated a rehabilitation of African languages as the most valid vehicles for African thought and expression; in [his play] *L'Oeil*, he has moved in this direction in significant ways. There are four linguistic forms of expression: standard French, the language of officialdom and of the intellectuals (students); French slang, the language of intermediaries such as Django and Gringo; Pidgin French, a dialect of the People; African languages—principally Bambara, and several exclamations in Malinké. A fifth "language" of the play is that of the talking drum, the *attoungblan*, which uses a transcoded language, the mediated word. These linguistic codes dominate. Nonetheless, the author's use of mime must also be taken into account inasmuch as it represents a decision not to use language in favor of a form of non-verbal expression. . . .

Standard French is the dominant language of *L'Oeil*. It is dominant because the dramatic structure privileging the goal of the Ruling Class is dominant. Of the eighteen brief tableaux, eight are exclusively in standard French, and six contain varying combinations of standard French and other aforementioned forms of expression. In other words, government officials, and those like Djédjé who are aspiring to join them, speak standard French, both in public and private discourse. Students, whose sympathies are with the workers and the unemployed, speak standard French as well, accounting for two of the linguistically mixed tableaux.

Slang, essentially French, with American and Pidgin French traces, is used consistently by Django and Gringo, the two "strong-arm" men employed by Sôgôma Sangui.

The nameless workers and the unemployed, who are presented principally as a social class . . . speak what Zadi Zaourou calls Pidgin French. It does, in fact, conform to Webster's definition of the term: "a form of speech that usually has a simplified grammar and a limited often mixed vocabulary and is used principally for intergroup communication." The working class's use of Pidgin is not artificial (beyond the given fiction of a literary and scenic work). While [Côte d'Ivoire] is nowhere named, using the country of the author as a referent, there are sixty-odd African languages spoken within its borders. It is important to note, however, that in the three tableaux in which Pidgin is used, standard French occurs as well and often reiterates part of the discourse of the workers.

Finally, there are African languages called for, but *not* encoded, in the text in two sequences. This could conceivably have to do with the present state of linguistic research and the development of orthographies. But, based on [an] interview with Zadi Zaourou, it would appear that the lack of precise dialogue is linked to his concept of performance, specifically, a preference for improvisation in those sequences that call for group interaction, whether in a traditional or modern setting. One of the sequences in question is the meeting between the *marabout* (the Holy Man) and Sôgôma Sangui. The general theme of the tableau is developed in a dialogue in Pidgin and standard French, but Zadi Zaourou specifies that "ce tableau gagnerait à être joué en bambara. Ce texte n'est qu'indicatif du thème à traiter" [this scene would gain by being played in Bambara. The text is merely indicative of how to treat the theme]. And in the final tableau, when The People invade the home of the Governor General and confront his colleagues and guests, the unspecified slogans and cries of the crowd are called for 'en langue du pays."

There are two sequences that are basically non-verbal: the arrest of Sôgôma Sangui, a brief pantomime, and the final tableau, where language is minimal and mime is the medium. This all-important dénouement, dominated by mime, symbolic decor (the panoply), and the transcoded word—the talking drum that transmits a call to action—furnishes a network of signs that communicates a message of mythological or epic portent. . . .

[It] is quite evident from a reading of L'Oeil that the political and cultural conflict is greatly heightened by the clash of linguistic codes, which are the most crucial ones for the reader. Should this direction of linguistic authenticity lead eventually to a modern theater in the major languages of Africa (or the major languages of individual African countries), then, the Western spectator and/or reader of African theater has the challenge of learning a new language (or languages), if he/she is to follow. What is more, this is the goal of many African writers today, who recognize that other potential African authors are paralyzed by the historically imposed dilemma of creating works in an alienating linguistic form.

Louise M. Jefferson. FR. 55, 6 (May 1982), pp. 831–33

Zadi [Zaourou], who has been involved with the theater since he was a student, has developed in fairly characteristic fashion. After his return to the Ivory Coast in 1971, he continued to write plays on the classical model—for example, Les Sofas. But, in the light of the debates of the period, and perhaps encouraged by the experiments of La Griotique, he began to question his own approach. . . . The break began with L'Oeil et la tignasse. Zadi said he would henceforth base his writing on three principal elements: symbolism, rhythm, and narrative. Through them, he wanted to attack the evils bedeviling his country. He therefore opted for a political theater expressing itself in a host of symbols. The fact that his new company was called "Didiga" was no chance, and his latest play is an example of his new conception of the theater. The word didiga has, in fact, a symbolic origin. According to the author himself, it is a concept of hunting among the Bété people. It is the term used to refer to a kind of adventure story without an end which always features the same hero, Djergbeugbeu, the ideal hunter whom his more fallible brethren seek to emulate. As in most Bété legends and stories, the vision of the world portrayed by the didiga defies ordinary logic. The hunter stops on the bank of a river and starts to fish to amuse himself, intending to continue his hunting later. He casts a hook into the water, but instead of catching a large fish, he is surprised to pull up a wild guinea-fowl. It is the illogical aspect of this mystical world to which Zadi returns as the basis of his new approach to the theater. It is further enriched by the theoretical ideas developed by Aboubacar Touré.

His starting point is the use of symbolism. It works through the language of music (especially percussion), through bodily expression, and through the discourse of silence and the unspoken. The objects and animals he uses have an anthropomorphic quality, for among the Bété the panther, the elephant, and the buffalo are considered to be human beings. The hunter who kills them commits homicide and must undergo the ordeal of expiation. At this level, we enter the domain of ritual. These are all cultural elements deriving from the concept of *didiga*.

Unfortunately, in *La Termitière*, the spoken word is used sparingly, whereas the music, dance, and symbolic gesture which tell the story of a society in crisis are clearly dominant. But, while the gestures are transformed into ritual acts, the latter do not have any effective power; they are purely symbolic. . . .

[Although] Zadi is much more concerned with the theater as an art form, his discourse can fail to reach the listener as he does not always use the symbols present in the collective consciousness; or, when he does use symbols rooted in the culture, he sometimes detaches them from their context. This has led, for instance, to criticism over his giving a mask to a young girl to wear. Among the Dan, as well as among the Gouro and the Wê, women are forbidden to wear masks; not only does he, therefore, commit an error on the anthropological level, but he also goes against the rules of plausibility.

Barthélémy Kotchy. *TRI*. 9, 3, (1983–84), pp. 239–40

In Bété culture, the *didiga* is the art of the unthinkable, relating the adventures of an imaginary named Djerabeugbeu. It is by extension every narration, behavior, or act defying logic and physical laws.

The *didiga* creates a certain kind of relationship between beings, phenomena, and things, giving rise to the unusual and to a break in order to create a new consciousness. This technique suits a group who wish to defend a political or aesthetic notion of the theater by producing the constants of the African word: the symbolic, the poetry, and the rhythm. . . .

Zadi, in his dissertation "La Parole poétique dans la poésie africaine" favors this traditional form of African speech and has strived to present it in his theater, with all its dramatic force. This speech expresses itself by adopting the contours of melodic and rhythmic lines contrasted in a particular way in African languages, because of the varied and complex play of the tones.

The first speaker, master of the word, transmits a powerful and educative speech. A second speaker is composed of two elements: a musical instrument, a talking instrument like the musical bow [l'arc musical] or the "pédou," and the actor with the memory of the first speaker. Thereby results a new message thanks to the association of the actor and the talking instrument. The receiver of the message then needs a preliminary initiation.

Thus mediated speech can be conceived of as an instrumental language aimed at the reproduction of spoken sentences.

In Zadi's modern *didiga*, the mediated speech is translated by symbolic dances like the talking dance, through talking instruments like the musical bow, the tambour, the "pédou" and the double bell and finally through a "masked" language that the director introduces into the very structure of his plays. . . .

In *La Termitière*, the bow is especially well used and assures the intensity of the dramatic progression. Due to the fact that the bow has a sorrowful tone, it is used to transmit to the spectators a part of the anguish expressed. In the scene of the "jeu de la graine," the bow calls a musician with a "bissa" who undertakes the search of the hidden seed following the indications of the bow. It is the voice of the bow that tells the player if he is on the right track or not. The bow replies "oui" or "non" to the player's questions and the bow speaks so well that the player succeeds in finding the grain with the warm congratulations of his comrades.

The bow appears then as a character with a complete part who leads the whole scene. . . .

The songs are obviously accompanied by instruments. Just as the *didiga* does not require the public to decode the language of the musical arc, it does not demand that one understand the meaning of the words of its songs. One only expects from the public an emotional reaction on hearing the song, preceded naturally by a presentation and psychological preparation. The songs are never neutral, mere fillers, but portray a certain behavior, reinforce the depth of a certain character.

The poetic speech of Zadi Zaourou's *didiga* thus expresses itself under the most diverse forms, it is danced, proffered, sung, makes use of symbols, creates beauty from all angles. This speech enacted for the pleasure of the eyes and the ears, to promote awareness, is molded and molds in its turn by producing the richest images (rhythmic, melodic, visual). These word-spectacles which act upon our senses, present man under different aspects in order to help the spectator to understand the often contradictory situations and behavior. The poet, says Dibéro, is born with a "strong shadow" and the strength of that shadow is what gives strength to his words.

Zadi as a poet has been able to free, thanks to the theater, this poetic African speech, shackled today by writing; he knew how to draw from his cultural origin (orality) all the benefits that it could provide from the point of view of stylistic and dramatic rendition.

It is in pursuing the perfection of different possibilities of this speech that the theater of Zadi Zaourou will attain its originality and African specificity.

Marie-José Hourantier. Notre Librairie. 86 (1987), pp. 84–89†

As a specific imaginary structure, as a *significant human reality*, the *didiga* indicates at the outset, in the Bété cultural space of Zadi Zaourou, the art of the hunters in the form of oral narratives, relating to the accompaniment of a musical bow the strange experiences, mysterious, marvelous, and dangerous of the hunt, perceived as a singular experience—an experience which goes well beyond a simple work process, or routine economic activity.

In its nature and substance, the ancient *didiga* is a practice in which the process of signification is identical or homologous to literary art. It is the same way of constructing the signification as is practiced by poetic speech. . . .

The modern *didiga*, that of Zadi Zaourou, brings about a displacement, a transfer, a profound distortion in order to take the form and substance of a game, or a dramatic spectacle: the *didiga* becomes a spectacular ceremony of great amplitude, of a ludic, aesthetic, and secular nature. . . .

In the modern *didiga*, not only the constituent forces of the play and the sudden changes in fortune, but also the lighting, the colors—in one word, the dramatic apparatus—function as a universe, structured by a new subjective impetus. Instead of incitement to the esoteric initiation, it is a question hence-forth of introducing indirectly through the play the compassion and objectivity of the public to the level of comprehension and detection of political and ideo-logical mechanisms which regulate the functioning of today's societies. It is about our societies which, one knows, are characterized by new forms of domi-nation, oppression, and surveillance, in a perspective that is at once dialectic and Freudian. In theatrical writing, as well as in the spectacle, this perspective is continuously illustrated by the articulation "Répression-Résistance" in its reversals and complex modalities.

Koudou Aiko. *Imprévue*. 1 (1990), pp. 71–72†

ZOBEL, JOSEPH (1915–   )

MARTINIQUE

[Joseph] Zobel wishes to distinguish himself clearly from other black writers for whom the link between politics and art is both necessary and vital in the Third-World context. And behind this distinction lies the refusal to "sacrifice his indi-viduality" and the possible suggestion that he be placed in a special category and judged by different standards. Zobel seems to be making a discreet appeal for consideration as "un artiste tout court," fearing that classification as a disci-ple of Négritude might obscure the purely artistic qualities of his work. . . .

[In *Diab'là*, *La Rue cases-nègres*, and *La Fête à Paris*, one of Zobel's] chief preoccupations is the creation of heroes who symbolize the Negro's tri-umph over his destiny and the resultant pride in the black race. It is in this sense that we consider him to be a Négritude writer, aiming at black conscious-ness and black liberation. The picture of the Negro that eventually emerges from an overall examination of the novels in question is quite unlike the one usually painted by white Europeans. Against a background of misery, social injustice and suffering, the Negro stands out as a resourceful human being, an individual of dignity and honor, equal if not superior in status to his oppressors. In short, the myth of Negro inferiority is exploded by a display of qualities whose existence the European has refused to acknowledge, and which conse-quently the Negro does not easily recognize in himself. . . .

The simplicity of style and structure in Zobel's first novel, *Diab'là*, is in keeping with the simple nature of life in a small fishing village near Le Diamant on the Martinican South Coast. The story concerns the arrival of Diab'là, a peasant from a hillside village, Morne-Vent, and the use of his skill in agriculture not only to earn a living but to establish himself in the community as a leader and awaken in the inhabitants a spirit of cooperation and self-reliance. In essence, Diab'là's role is very similar to the one played by Manuel in [Jacques] Roumain's *Gouverneurs de la Rosée*, with the obvious difference that the former is a complete stranger to the scene of his operations. Zobel succeeds in capturing the frankness and simplicity of everyday life in rural Martinique through the use of a modified form of Creole dialogue and a direct, uncomplicated narrative style. He examines in great detail, and with considerable charm and appeal, the manners of the people, to the extent that in the early stages of the novel, we are tempted to place it in the category of the exotic novel devoted to "local color." As the story progresses, however, it becomes clear that the role of Diab'là and of his older, more experienced counterpart, Capitain'là, is to promote the interests of the underprivileged black Martinican and to serve as examples of the Negro's hope for the future emancipation of his race.

The real significance of Diab'là's achievements can be appreciated only in the light of the difficulties with which he is faced in the village of his adoption and his response to these pressures. He wins the early admiration of the villagers for his refusal to continue to place his services at the disposal of the white plantation owners and for his decision to rely on his own talents and initiative to attain a position of dignity. . . .

To experience the hardships of colonialist oppression is one thing. To fully appreciate its complex nature and draw up an effective plan for the liberation of the colonized Negro is a task which demands a careful analysis of the problems confronting the black man in his native society as well as in the "Mother" country. This is the task to which Zobel, after firing his first salvo in *Diab'là*, addresses himself in *La Rue cases-nègres* and *La Fête à Paris*. Together, the novels form a single unit in the sense that they trace the history and development of one character, José Hassam, from the period of his early childhood in a depressed rural area in Martinique to the time of his graduation from the Sorbonne. There is one real motivating force in José's life: his own liberation and that of his family. If we judge by José's itinerary, it is clear that Zobel considers education to be the key to the Negro's emancipation, the basic tool he needs to carve out for himself a new and meaningful destiny. For Zobel, however, the Negro's education ought not to be limited to the formal European-oriented type but must include an awareness of his relationship to the society and the development of an ability to apprehend and come to terms with his environment. On the other hand, it is in the very nature of the colonizer to wish to safeguard his position by perpetuating the status quo. To this end, he seeks to keep the colonized in a state of abject poverty and dependent on him for their survival. What is more, he provides limited opportunities for education and, whenever school places are made available, he ensures that the type of education offered is designed in such a way as to create individuals whose thinking and values are identical to his own. That is how the colonialist system operates. And what we see in *La Rue cases-nègres* and *La Fête à Paris* is an attempt to defeat the system.

Randolph Hezekiah. BlackI. 4, 3–4 (1975), pp. 44–45, 48–49

[*La Rue cases-nègres*, translated as *Black Shack Alley*] is divided into three almost equal sections. Part one deals with the early life of the narrator, José, as he grows up on the plantation and sees him through to the start of his primary school years. It is to the author's credit that he has avoided the pitfall of allowing the adult that is writing to filter through to the narrative of the young child. As a result, José's descriptions sound genuine and authentic, truly in keeping with the type a child would give and not at all inconsistent with the fact that beyond these it is the adult that is analyzing in retrospect.

It would, for example, be somewhat artificial to have the young José make certain telling comments on the state of the society—these are introduced gradually as José matures over the length of the novel—so these are put into the mouths of other characters. In this respect, Médouze's account of his father's troubles in the postslavery period is typical. In fact, it is this account that brings out one of the rare impulses to violence that we see in José: "I had this maddening desire to hit the first *béké* I set my eyes on," he concludes.

Part two shows José in primary school and takes us up to his preparation for and success in the examination that sends him to secondary school, the *lycée*. In order to take better care of him during this period, his grandmother, M'man Tine eventually leaves Petit Morne, and Zobel uses this occasion to introduce us to a wide variety of pen portraits of the typical plantation society in Martinique prior to World War II. José once more looks on at the adult world with eyes of innocence, allowing events to make, in a way, their own commentary. However, we witness the gradual awakening of the young narrator to the complexities of class distinctions and other social inequalities, an awakening that comes full circle in part three.

In this section, José is shown in the urban environment of Fort-de-France, where he is reunited with his mother Délia as he works his way up to the *baccalauréat*. It is a new type of life that José and his companions see in this setting. Contemporary Fort-de-France is shown in its vivid realism, one that comes from an eye for significant detail which Zobel obviously possesses. . . .

Inevitably, comparisons will be made with other novels of the same type. One of the more striking resemblances has to be with George Lamming's *In the Castle of My Skin*, set in Barbados and published in 1953. Lamming's novel is also about life in a village in colonial times, about poverty, about class and color, and about growth and change in a West Indian society. It too has an appeal that is both contemporary and universal.

Another comparison can be made with Camara Laye's *L'Enfant noir*, also published in 1953. The genesis of both novels is remarkably similar: the author alone in France, having problems of re-adaptation and thinking of his homeland, of his childhood and his loved ones. Since Zobel also wrote his novel while working in France . . . one can be tempted to ask the same question that some critics have asked with respect to Laye's novel: Does the author tailor what he says to suit the tastes of the French among whom and possibly for whom he was writing? In all fairness to Zobel, it does not appear so. And, of course, the *béké* was a different breed altogether, with a different sociopolitical background, so that the metropolitan white could easily divorce himself from Zobel's portrayals.

Zobel's impact in this novel can best be summed up by referring to the old saying that we can best know where we are going once we know where we have been. Zobel helps us see more clearly where we have been. In this respect, the novel takes its place alongside many of the fine autobiographical works that have made their mark on the West Indian literary landscape.

Keith Q. Warner. Introduction to Joseph Zobel.
Black Shack Alley (London: Heinemann, 1980), n. p.

[Zobel's] best known work, *La Rue cases-nègres*, is autobiographical; it describes the childhood of a young boy living alone first with his grandmother, who cuts cane six days a week and is prematurely old at age forty, then with his mother, who works as a servant in Fort-de-France. The child/grandmother or child/mother relationship is the seminal one in the life of many of Zobel's characters and seemingly in his own life. This relationship is rich and human, warm and loving, but is also seen as a kind of alienation—still one upon which the protagonist looks back with nostalgia. This key event seems to color all other aspects of Zobel's novelistic world: "Cet enfant s'est retranché dans une méfiance toujours en éveil sous une inébranlable placidité. . . .Ses joies les plus vraies lui viennent-elles de tout ce qu'il découvre dans ses livres. . . . Et sa revanche et son bonheur sont d'être presque invariablement le premier de sa classe. Ce que les autres ne lui pardonnent guère." [The child took refuge in an ever-alert mistrust, under an unflappable calmness. . . . His truest joys came from what he discovered in books. . . . And his revenge and his happiness were that he was almost always head of his class, for which the others scarcely forgave him.] This description of Mapiam in *Laghia de la mort* may be analogous to the author's own character. Mapiam gets by in an alienated world, feeling like an outsider but making his way into productive and responsible levels of society. Zobel apparently prefers to play a supporting role in the drama of Third-World development; he and his characters are not leaders, presidents, mayors, though they may be key social figures in the village (especially Cocotte in *Les Mains pleines d'oiseaux*). He and they do not present an abrupt alternative to the status quo; they seem to believe that progress in the condition of blacks and other Third-World peoples will be gradual and evolutionary. They are down-to-earth, practical, pragmatic people who seek solutions in a humanistic understanding of the problem, in return to smaller, decentralized structures (the village, etc.), in education, and in the development of pride and self-confidence. It seems that Zobel himself was slow in developing both as a writer and as a person, but he has put his great breadth of experience in many jobs and roles to good use in describing the world of formerly colonized peoples. His personal choices and his contribution to Third-World development are now clear; only his literary works remain to be better known. . . .

The alienation of the individual character becomes something of a symbol for the situation of the whole race. Alienation and disalienation are key themes in Zobel's novelistic world, where the psychological descriptions of the characters produce very true-to-life people, not ideal types. At first reading, the rather strong, obvious introversion of most of the male characters seems gratuitous and somewhat out of place. Then we see that this is meant as another documentary fact, and we see the objective correlations with other facts in the social milieu being described. . . .

Zobel is not a romantic spirit and practices a rather staid prose style based on the nineteenth-century novel. He offers neither the polemical fireworks of Négritude nor the magic of avant-garde formal experimentation or of "marvelous realism." Romantic love is not a concern. Zobel is not a revolutionary, another kind of romanticism. He preaches gradual reform and liberation, rooted in the understanding of the other and of foreign societies. Reform must be based on education and personal and social disalienation and the acceptance of responsibility.

Hal Wylie. WLT. 56, 1 (Winter 1982), pp. 62–64

[Zobel's] superb talent as a *conteur* . . . is revealed . . . in this delightful collection of short stories under the title of *Et si la mer n'était pas bleue*, which may have been neglected by reviewers at the time of publication.

It is the last story of the five, "Nardal," a type of postscript, which attracted me mostly to this book. "Nardal" is a panegyrical statement intended as a public compliment to the Nardal family of Martinique, especially to Paulette Nardal, who has been referred to as the godmother of Négritude. Zobel speaks of this family's love of knowledge and excellence and its pride of blackness. The title story, "Et si la mer n'était pas bleue," tells of a whole new world opened up to a young peasant boy during his first visit on foot to the seaside from his remote village, in the company of a mysterious aunt Oberline. In the second story, "Le Cahier d'Edouard Tanasio," the narrator gives an amusing account of his admiration for two childhood classmates, Eugène Tanasio for his macho image and Edouard Tanasio for his beautiful handwriting. In "Le Retour de Mamzelle Annette," the longest of the five stories, an industrious and obliging little peasant girl gives a child's view of the amorous and irreligious affair between Monsieur Ernest, the town barber, and his longtime housekeeper Mamzelle Annette. This third story also offers a quick look at the repugnant caste system based on the color of one's skin which has long plagued the French Antilles. The fourth story, "Le Cousin," gives credence to the old saying that it is often unwise and unsafe to judge a book by its cover. The "cousin," a fashionable young white gentleman, is none other than a relative of "Monsieur," a wealthy black man who, because he spurns ostentation, performs menial tasks and loves to work in his flower garden, is often mistaken for a lowly servant by those who happen to see him in action or visit his mansion.

Robert P. Smith, Jr. WLT. 57, 4 (Autumn 1983), p. 679

Zobel's *Black Shack Alley* is centered on an estate village in Martinique between the two world wars. . . . In Zobel's novel it is the black child José, born on the estate but too young at first to understand the frustration of the laborers and the quality of their despair, whose eyes are gradually opened to the interaction of color and class, first in rural Martinique and later in the Route Didier of the capital. This street with its rich *béké* villas and appendage of domestics' shacks mimics the contrast of the master's *grand'case* and the slaves' *cases-nègres* on the plantations, as the Rue Cases-Nègres itself, where José first lives—the "street of Negro huts" which gives the novel its French title—reminds the reader, by its very name, of the inequalities and injustices of slavery. . . .

The child narrator of Zobel's *Black Shack Alley* is largely unaware, during his first seven years, of the subtle class and color distinctions which are the heritage of plantation society. The divisions within José's own community are simpler, though no less rigidly hierarchical. On the one hand, there is the small and uniform group of black estate workers among whom he lives with his grandmother, M'man Tine, the canefield weeder. On the other hand, there are a few remote figures of authority whose power, in the child's eyes, derives principally from their adult status and their occupation on the estate. Their race is irrelevant to him; it is only in passing that he mentions that the overseer is a mulatto, and the care which he and his fellow urchins exercise in avoiding this man's attention during their forages into the canefields is due above all to their fear of parental punishment if they get into any trouble. In José's mind the distance between the management and the laborers is to be measured principally by the visible evidence of their dwelling places: the latter live in some three dozen ramshackle wooden huts perched on a hillside above the canefields; higher up the hill is the overseer's house; and at the very top stands the manager's larger house, tile-roofed and majestic, presiding over the *cases-nègres* and the great expanse of cane beyond them.

Beverley Ormerod. *An Introduction to the French Caribbean Novel*
(London: Heinemann, 1985), pp. 64–65

[*La Rue cases-nègres* is] based on myth. The child-hero leaves the bosom of his family and his closed world in order to go away little by little—towards the schools and villages and cities further and further away. Age, the degrees that he accumulates, and even the distance he travels are the ironic measures of his success because this road is also the road of separation from the ones he loves.

This is because the novel marches to two beats: that of an actual blocked sociohistorical state, where any progress seems impossible; and the personal one of the child who by nature moves, evolves, and develops progressively his vision and comprehension of the exterior world. It is this confrontation between the fixed and the dynamic, anchored in the characters of José and M'man Tine that appears to structure the reality of *La Rue cases-nègres*.

In the initial period it is the world of childhood that dominates. . . . *La Rue cases-nègres* poses the problem of an adult narrator who is at the same time the child subject. Zobel chooses to respect the progressive development of his character without distantiation and this results in the poetry of the novel. . . .

If the world of the child lends itself to the poetic language of the adult narrator because of its elementary temporality and happiness, it is also because of its subjectivity. This point of view which dominates the first part of the narration is also its subject because that which impresses the most is the sensitivity and emotion of the child viewing the colored frescoes that pass in front of his eyes, the meaning of which he is unable to decipher. The reader then is interested as much in childhood as in the real world in which the child lives. . . .

The first part of the narration is marked by the intimacy, mystery, and unique vision that is childhood. . . . In the second and third parts of the story, this vision gives way to another one of the cities. Life there is more noisy and varied; one finds there a cacaphony of voices and personalities. Although this society also passes through the eyes and thoughts of José, one no longer has the impression of regularity, stability, or harmony of the first part because the child himself notes the counter-currents, the tensions of social forces, the movement and the changing faces of the actors. The poetry of mystery and naïveté is exchanged for the poetry of the modern, dynamic, and vital swarming city. . . .

The principal agent of this progressive structuring of reality in *La Rue cases-nègres* is M'man Tine, who reflects the real world and structure in the imagination and nascent understanding of the child. She dominates the narration, because it is through her that José learns to see the world. It is thus that throughout the story M'man Tine lives this unfortunate reality and rejects it. The child, still very young, realizes this truth. M'man Tine is the reason of his success and also of his story. She is part of the real world and the mythical world, because she is the object of a closed society and yet she alone is capable of assuring the progress of the child. . . .

But, in José's text, M'man Tine is especially a narrative and poetic solution. She is the symbol of determination and of the will of metamorphosis.

Is it not the same metamorphosis that is carried out on the textual level? José's life is explained through literary forms such as the puzzles, the imaginary tales of Victor and Médouze, and by the fairy tales that help him see and understand his grandmother better. Literature nurtures his life and this metamorphosis is double because José, following the example of his grandmother, transforms the sad destiny of his grandmother and of the Cases-Nègres street into a novel of vision and poetic power.

Eileen Julien. *FR.* 60, 6 (1987), pp. 781–84, 786†

WORKS MENTIONED

Listed here, author by author, are all works mentioned in the critical selections. Each writer's works are arranged alphabetically, and the year of the first publication is given. The language of writers not publishing in English is given after their names, and their works are arranged alphabetically by the literal translation. Following each literal translation in parentheses are the original title and the date of first publication. If a published translation of a full-length work exists, its title and year of first publication is given after a colon. Individual poems, short stories, novellas, and other short works collected in works mentioned in the critical selections are indented and listed alphabetically beneath the title of the work in which they appear.

ACHEBE, CHINUA

Anthills of the Savannah, 1987
Arrow of God, 1964
A Man of the People, 1966
No Longer at Ease, 1960
Things Fall Apart, 1958

AIDOO, AMA ATA

Anowa, 1970
Birds and Other Poems, 1987
Changes: A Love Story, 1991
The Dilemma of a Ghost, 1965
The Eagle and the Chickens and Other
  Stories, 1986
"Last of the Proud Ones," 1964
No Sweetness Here, 1970
  "Other Versions"
Our Sister Killjoy, 1977
Someone Talking to Sometime, 1985
  "For Kinna II"
  "From the Only Speech That Was Not
    Delivered at the Rally"
  "Lorisnrudi"
  "Nation Building"
  "Of Love and Commitment"
  "A Salute to African Universities"

AMADI, ELECHI

The Concubine, 1966
Estrangement, 1986
The Great Ponds, 1969
The Slave, 1978
Sunset in Biafra, 1973

ANGELOU, MAYA

All God's Children Need Traveling Shoes,
  1986

Gather Together in My Name, 1974
The Heart of a Woman, 1981
I Know Why the Caged Bird Sings, 1970
Singin' and Swingin' and Gettin' Merry
  Like Christmas, 1976

ANTHONY, MICHAEL

All That Glitters, 1981
Cricket in the Road, and Other Stories, 1973
  "The Distant One"
  "Drunkard of the River"
  "Enchanted Alley"
  "The Girl and the River"
  "Hibiscus"
  "The Holiday by the Sea"
  "The Patch of Guava"
  "Sandra Street"
  "The Valley of Cocoa"
The Games Were Coming, 1963
Green Days by the River, 1967
King of the Masquerade, 1974
Streets of Conflict, 1976
The Year in San Fernando, 1965

ANYIDOHO, KOFI

AncestralLogic & CaribbeanBlues, 1993
  "Air Zimbabwe: En Route Victoria Falls"
  "DesertStorm"
  "Husago Dance"
  "Lolita Jones"
  "Santrofi"
Earthchild with Brain Surgery, 1985
  "Earthchild"
  "My Song"
  "The Rise of the New Patriot"
Elegy for the Revolution, 1978
  "Back to Memory"
  "Festival of Hopes"

"The Passion-Gulf"
"A Piece of Hope"
"Soul in Birthwaters"
"Upon the Harvest Moon"
A Harvest of Our Dreams, 1984
"Akofa"
"A Harvest of Our Dreams"
"Moments"
"Seedtime"

ARMAH, AYI KWEI

"African Socialism: Utopian or
    Scientific?," 1967
"Battle for the Mind of Africa," 1987
The Beautyful Ones Are Not Yet Born, 1968
"The Caliban Complex," 1985
"The Definitive Chaka," 1975–1976
"The Festival Syndrome," 1985
Fragments, 1970
The Healers, 1978
"Interview with Dimgba," 1986
"Larsony or Fiction as Criticism of
    Fiction," 1976
"The Lazy School of Literary Criticism,"
    1985
"One Writer's Education," 1985
Two Thousand Seasons, 1973
Why Are We So Blest?, 1972

AWOONOR, KOFI

The Breast of the Earth, 1975
Guardians of the Sacred Word, 1974
The House by the Sea, 1978
    "The Wayfarer Comes Home"
Night of My Blood, 1971
    "Desire"
    "Exiles"
    "Hymn to My Dumb Earth"
    "I Heard a Bird Cry"
    "Night of My Blood"
Rediscovery, and Other Poems, 1964
Ride Me, Memory, 1973
    "An American Memory of Africa"
"The Sea Eats the Land at Home," 1963
"Songs of Sorrow," 1963
"Song of War," 1963
This Earth, My Brother, 1971
Until the Morning After, 1987
    "All Men Are Brothers"

BÂ, MARIAMA (French)

A Scarlet Song (*Un Chant écarlate*, 1981):
    Scarlet Song, 1985
So Long a Letter (*Une Si Longue Lettre*,
    1979): *So Long a Letter*, 1981

BADIAN, SEYDOU (French)

The Blood of the Masks (*Le Sang des
    masques*, 1976)
The Death of Chaka (*La Mort de Chaka*,
    1962): *The Death of Chaka*, 1968
Sacred Wedding (*Noces sacrées*, 1977)
Under the Storm (*Sous l'orage*, part one,
    1957; reissued as *Sous l'orage
    (Kany)*, 1963)

BALDWIN, JAMES

Another Country, 1962
The Fire Next Time, 1963
Giovanni's Room, 1956
Go Tell It on the Mountain, 1953
If Beale Street Could Talk, 1974
Just Above My Head, 1979
Tell Me How Long the Train's Been Gone,
    1968

BAMBARA, TONI CADE

Gorilla, My Love, 1972
    "The Johnson Girls"
    "The Survivor"
The Salt Eaters, 1980
The Sea Birds Are Still Alive, 1977

BARAKA, AMIRI

Black Art, 1967
A Black Mass, 1966
The Dead Lecturer, 1964
Dutchman, 1964
The Eighth Ditch (Is Drama), 1961
Experimental Death Unit No. 1, 1965
"Expressive Language," 1973
Four Black Revolutionary Plays, 1969
Great Goodness of Life (A Coon Show),
    1967
Home on the Range, 1968
In the Tradition, 1982
Jello, 1970
Madheart, 1966
The Music, 1987
    "Greenwich Village and the African-
        American Music"
    "I Love Music"
Preface to a Twenty Volume Suicide Note,
    1961
    "In Memory of Radio"
    "The Screamers," 1963
Slave Ship: A Historical Pageant, 1965
The Toilet, 1966

BEBEY, FRANCIS (French)

The Ashanti Doll (*La Poupée ashanti*, 1973): *The Ashanti Doll*, 1977
Concert for an Old Mask (*Concert pour un vieux masque*, 1980)
Embarrassment and Company (*Embarras & Cie*, 1968)
Jimmy and Equality ("Jimmy et l'égalité")
The Marriage of Edda ("Le Mariage d'Edda")
King Albert of Effidi (*Le Roi Albert d'Effidi*, 1976): *King Albert*, 1982
The Son of Agatha Moudio (*Le Fils d'Agatha Moudio*, 1967): *Agatha Moudio's Son*, 1971

BEMBA, SYLVAIN (French)

Dormant Water (*Une Eau dormante*, 1975)
Eroshima (*Eroshima*, unpublished)
Hell Is Orpheus (*L'Enfer, c'est Orféo*, 1970)
The Last of the Cargonauts (*Le Dernier des cargonautes*, 1984)
Leopolis (*Léopolis*, 1984)
The Man Who Killed the Crocodile (*L'Homme qui tua le crocodile*, 1972)
Portable Dreams (*Rêves portatifs*, 1979)
A Screwed-Up World for a Too Honest Laundryman (*Un Foutu Monde pour un blanchisseur trop honnête*, 1979)
The Strange Crime of Mr. Pancrace Amadeus (*L'Étrange Crime de Monsieur Pancrace Amadeus*, 1986)
The Sun Has Left for M'Pemba (*Le Soleil est parti à M'Pemba*, 1982)
Traffic Jam (*Embouteillage*, 1975)

BENNETT, LOUISE

Jamaica Labrish, 1966
"Bans O' Killing"
"Bans O' Ooman!"
"Dry Foot Bwoy"
"Dutty Tough"
"Me Bredda"
"My Dream"
"Noh Lickle Twang!"
"Pinnacle"
"Solja Work"
"Uriah Preach"
"War-Time Grocery"

BETI, MONGO (French)

The Almost Laughable Downfall of a Buffoon (*La Ruine presque cocasse d'un polichinelle*, 1979)

Cruel Town (*Ville cruelle*, 1954)
The King Miraculously Healed (*Le Roi miraculé*, 1958): *King Lazarus*, 1960
Mission Accomplished (*Mission terminée*, 1957): *Mission Accomplished*, 1958
Perpétue and the Habit of Unhappiness (*Perpétue et l'habitude du malheur*, 1974): *Perpetua and the Habit of Unhappiness*, 1978
Plunder of Cameroon (*Main basse sur le Cameroun*, 1972)
The Poor Christ of Bomba (*Le Pauvre Christ de Bomba*, 1956): *The Poor Christ of Bomba*, 1971
Remember Ruben, 1974: *Remember Ruben*, 1980
The Revenge of Guillaume Ismaël Dzewatama (*La Revanche de Guillaume Ismaël Dzewatama*, 1984)
The Two Mothers of Guillaume Ismaël Dzewatama (*Les Deux Mères de Guillaume Ismaël Dzewatama*, 1982)

BRADLEY, DAVID

The Chaneysville Incident, 1981
South Street, 1975

BRATHWAITE, EDWARD KAMAU

The Arrivants: A New World Trilogy, 1973
Black + Blues, 1976
"The day the first snow fell," 1953
Days & Nights, 1975
Islands, 1969
"Jah"
Masks, 1968
"Adowa"
"The Making of the Drum"
Middle Passages, 1992
"Colombe"
"Duke"
"Flute(s)"
"How Europe underdeveloped Africa"
"Irae"
"Leopard"
"Letter Sycorax"
"Noom"
"The Sahell of Donatello"
"Soweto"
"Stone"
"Veridian"
"The Visibility Trigger"
Mother Poem, 1977
Odale's Choice, 1967
Other Exiles, 1975

Rights of Passage, 1967
Sun Poem, 1982
X/Self, 1987
"Julia"

BRODBER, ERNA

"Fiction in the Scientific Procedure," 1990
Jane and Louisa Will Soon Come Home,
　1980
Myal, 1988

BROOKS, GWENDOLYN

Annie Allen, 1949
"The Anniad"
"The Rites for Cousin Vit"
The Bean Eaters, 1960
"A Bronzeville Mother Loiters in
　Mississippi. Meanwhile a
　Mississippi Mother Burns Bacon"
"A Lovely Love"
Beckonings, 1975
Bronzeville Boys and Girls, 1956
"Ella"
Family Pictures, 1970
In the Mecca, 1968
Maud Martha, 1953
Primer for Blacks: Three Preachments, 1980
Riot, 1969
Selected Poems, 1963
A Street in Bronzeville, 1945
To Disembark, 1981

BRUTUS, DENNIS

"Berlin Notes," 1979
China Poems, 1975
"Crossing the Atlantic," 1979
"In Memoriam: Solomon Mahlangu," 1979
*Letters to Martha, and Other Poems from
　a South African Prison*, 1968
"Letters to Martha"
"Longing"
"The Mob"
"Nightsong: Country"
"No, I do not brim with sorrow"
"Postscripts"
"Train Journey"
Poems from Algiers, 1970
"And I am driftwood"
A Simple Lust, 1973
"For a Dead African"
"Lutuli: 10 December 1961"
Sirens, Knuckles, Boots, 1963
"At a Funeral"

"Autumn comes here with ostentation"
"Nightsong: City"
"A troubadour, I tráverse all my land"
Strains, 1975
Stubborn Hope, 1978
"For My Sons & Daughters"
"I remember the simple practicality of
　your reminiscences"
"I remembered in the tranquil Sunday
　afternoon"
"When they deprive me of the evenings"
Thoughts Abroad, 1970
"I might be a better lover I believe"
"When last I ranged and revelled"

CÉSAIRE, AIMÉ (French)

Discourse on Colonialism (*Discours sur le
　colonialisme*, 1950): *Discourse on
　Colonialism*, 1972
Me, Laminaire . . . (*Moi, Laminaire . . .*, 1982)
Notebook on a Return to My Native Land
　(*Cahier d'un retour au pays natal*,
　1939): *Return to My Native Land*, 1969
A Season in the Congo (*Une Saison au
　Congo*, 1966): *A Season in the
　Congo*, 1969
The Tragedy of King Christophe (*La
　Tragédie du roi Christophe*, 1963):
　The Tragedy of King Christophe, 1970

CHAMOISEAU, PATRICK (French)

Chronicle of the Seven Miseries
　(*Chronique des sept misères*, 1986)
Elegy of Creolism (*Éloge de la créolité*,
　1989 [with Jean Bernabé and
　Raphaël Confiant])
Manman Dlo vs. the Fairy Carabosse
　(*Manman Dlo contre la fée
　Carabosse*, 1982)
Past Childhood (*Antan d'enfance*, 1990)
Solibo Magnifique (*Solibo Magnifique*, 1988)
Texaco (*Texaco*, 1992)

CHENEY-COKER, SYL

The Blood in the Desert's Eyes, 1990
"Song on the Chinese Flute"
Concerto for an Exile, 1973
"Absurdity"
"Agony of the Dark Child"
"Environne"
"Freetown"
"Guinea"
"Hydropathy"
"I Throw Myself to the Crocodiles"

"The Masochist"
"Misery of the Converts"
"My Soul O Oasis!"
"Myopia"
"Storm"
"Toilers"
The Graveyard Also Has Teeth, 1980
"The Executed"
"Haemorrhage"
"Nausea"
"Putrefaction"
"Song for the Ravaged Country"
"Talons in the Flesh of My Country"
The Last Harmattan of Alusine Dunbar, 1990

CHILDRESS, ALICE

A Hero Ain't Nothin' But a Sandwich, 1973
Like One of the Family: Conversations from a Domestic's Life, 1956
A Short Walk, 1979
Trouble in Mind, 1955
Wedding Band, 1973
Wine in the Wilderness, 1969

CLARKE, AUSTIN C.

Amongst Thistles and Thorns, 1965
The Bigger Light, 1975
Growing Up Stupid under the Union Jack, 1980
The Meeting Point, 1967
Nine Men Who Laughed, 1986
The Prime Minister, 1977
Proud Empires, 1986
The Survivors of the Crossing, 1964
When Women Rule, 1985
"The Collector"

CLIFF, MICHELLE

Abeng, 1984
Bodies of Water, 1990
"Election Day"
"A Hanged Man"
"Screen Memory"
"A Woman Who Plays Trumpet Is Deported"
Claiming an Identity They Taught Me to Despise, 1980
No Telephone to Heaven, 1987

CLIFTON, LUCILLE

All Us Come Cross the Water, 1973
The Black BC's, 1970
Generations, 1976

Good News about the Earth, 1972
Good Times, 1969
An Ordinary Woman, 1974
"At Last We Killed the Roaches"
"In Salem"
The Times They Used to Be, 1974
Two-Headed Woman, 1980

COLLINS, MERLE

Angel, 1987
Because the Dawn Breaks!, 1985
"The Butterfly Born"
"Callaloo"
"The Lesson"

CONDÉ, MARYSE (French)

Death of Olowémi d'Ajumako (*Mort d'Olowémi d'Ajumako*, 1973)
God Gave It to Us (*Dieu nous l'a donné*, 1972)
Heremakhonon (*Hérémakhonon*, 1976): *Heremakhonon*, 1982
I, Tituba, Sorceress (*Moi, Tituba, sorcière*, 1986): *I, Tituba, Black Witch of Salem*, 1992
The Last Magi Kings (*Les Derniers Rois mages*, 1992)
Mangrove Crossing (*Traversée de la mangrove*, 1989)
A Season in Rihata (*Une Saison à Rihata*, 1981): *A Season in Rihata*, 1988
Ségou: The Walls of Earth (*Ségou: les murailles de terre*, 1984): *Segu*, 1987
Three Women in Manhattan ("Trois Femmes à Manhattan," unpublished)
Why Négritude? Négritude or Revolution? ("Pourquoi la négritude? Négritude ou révolution?," 1973)

DEPESTRE, RENÉ (French)

Black Ore (*Minerai noir*, 1956)
For the Revolution: For Poetry (*Pour la révolution: pour la poésie*, 1974)
Hadriana in All My Dreams (*Hadriana dans tous mes rêves*, 1988)
Hallelujah for a Woman-Garden (*Alléluia pour une femme-jardin*, 1973)
Hello and Goodbye to Négritude (*Bonjour et adieu à la négritude*, 1980)
The Adventures of a Black Man in Latin America ("Les Aventures du négrisme en Amérique latine")
Journal of a Sea Creature (*Journal d'un animal marin*, 1965)

Poet in Cuba (*Poète à Cuba*, 1976)
Poem to Be Screamed under the
  Windows of the White House
  ("Poème à hurler sous les fenêtres de
  la Maison Blanche")
The Pole of Plenty (*Le Mât de cocagne*,
  1979): *The Festival of the Greasy
  Pole*, 1990
A Rainbow for the Christian West (*Un
  Arc-en-ciel pour l'occident chrétien*,
  1967): *A Rainbow for the Christian
  West*, 1972
Sparks (*Etincelles*, 1945)
Spurting Blood (*Gerbe de sang*, 1946)
Translated from the High Seas (*Traduit du
  grand large*,1952)
Vegetations of Light (*Végétations de
  clarté*, 1951)

DIALLO, NAFISSATOU NIANG (French)

Awa, the Little Merchant (*Awa, la petite
  marchande*, 1981)
The Cursed Fort (*Le Fort maudit*, 1980)
Of Tilène on the Plateau: A Dakar
  Childhood (*De Tilène au plateau:
  une enfance dakaroise*, 1975): *A
  Dakar Childhood*, 1982

DOVE, RITA

Grace Notes, 1989
  "Arrow"
  "Ars Poetica"
  "Dialectical Romance"
  "Ozone"
  "Stitches"
Museum, 1983
  "Agosta the Winged Man and Rasha the
    Black Dove"
  "Anti-Father"
  "At the German Writers Conference in
    Munich"
  "Banneker"
  "Boccaccio: The Plague Years"
  "Catherine of Alexandria"
  "Catherine of Siena"
  "Fiammetta Breaks Her Peace"
  "Ike"
  "My Father's Telescope"
  "Nestor's Bathtub"
  "Roses"
  "Shakespeare Say"
  "Tou Wan Speaks to Her Husband, Liu
    Sheng"
Thomas and Beulah, 1986

"Jiving"
"Lightnin' Blues"
"One Volume Missing"
"Variations on Gaining a Son"
Through the Ivory Gate, 1992
The Yellow House on the Corner, 1980
  "Upon Meeting Don L. Lee, in a
    Dream"

EDGELL, ZEE

Beka Lamb, 1982

EMECHETA, BUCHI

The Bride Price, 1976
Destination Biafra, 1982
Double Yoke, 1982
The Family, 1989
Head above Water, 1986
In the Ditch, 1972
The Joys of Motherhood, 1979
Nowhere to Play, 1980
The Rape of Shavi, 1983
Second Class Citizen, 1974
The Slave Girl, 1977
Titch the Cat, 1979

FARAH, NURUDDIN

Close Sesame, 1983
From a Crooked Rib, 1970
Gifts, 1992
Maps, 1986
A Naked Needle, 1976
Sardines, 1981
Sweet and Sour Milk, 1979

FAUSET, JESSIE

The Chinaberry Tree, 1931
Comedy: American Style, 1933
Plum Bun, 1929
"The Sleeper Wakes," 1920
There Is Confusion, 1932

GAINES, ERNEST J.

The Autobiography of Miss Jane Pittman,
  1971
Bloodline, 1968
  "Just like a Tree"
  "A Long Day in November"
  "The Sky Is Gray"
Catherine Carmier, 1964
A Gathering of Old Men, 1983
In My Father's House, 1978
A Lesson Before Dying, 1993
Of Love and Dust, 1967

GILROY, BERYL

Boy-Sandwich, 1989
Frangipani House, 1986
Stedman and Joanna, 1991

GIOVANNI, NIKKI

Black Feeling, Black Talk/Black Judgement, 1970
"Beautiful Black Men"
"Dreams"
"Knoxville, Tennessee"
"Nikki-Rosa"
"Our Detroit Conference—For Don L. Lee"
"The True Impact of Present Dialogue, Black vs. Negro"
"Woman Poem"
Cotton Candy on a Rainy Day, 1978
"Forced Retirement"
"Woman"
Gemini, 1971
My House, 1972
"Categories"
"Legacies"
"My House"
"The Wonder Woman"
Re: Creation, 1970
"All I Gotta Do"
"Poem for Aretha"
"Revolutionary Dreams"
The Women and the Men, 1975
"The December of My Springs"
"The Life I Led"
"Something to Be Said for Silence"

GLISSANT, EDOUARD (French)

Antillean Discourse (*Le Discours antillais*, 1981): *Caribbean Discourse*, 1989
The Case of the Commander (*La Case du commandeur*, 1981)
The Crevice (*La Lézarde*, 1956): *The Ripening*, 1959
Foul Death (*Malemort*, 1975)
The Fourth Century (*Le Quatrième Siècle*, 1964)
Dreamed Country, Real Country (*Pays rêvé, pays réel*, 1985)
The Indies (*Les Indes*, 1956)
Mahogany (*Mahogany*, 1987)
Mr. Toussaint (*Monsieur Toussaint*, 1961): *Monsieur Toussaint*, 1981
The Poetic Intention (*L'Intention poétique*, 1969)
Shackles (*Boises*, 1979)

GOODISON, LORNA

Heartease, 1989
"Heartease I"
"Heartease II"
"Heartease III"
"My Last Poem (Again)"
I Am Becoming My Mother, 1986
"Bedspread"
"For My Mother (May I Inherit Half Her Strength)"
"For Rosa Parks"
"Garden of the Women Once Fallen"
"Guinea Woman"
"I Am Becoming My Mother"
"Jah Music"
"Jamaica 1980"
"Lullaby for Jean Rhys"
"Mulatta Song"
"Mulatta Song II"
"On Becoming a Mermaid"
"We Are the Women"
Selected Poems, 1992
"Mother the Great Stones Got to Move"
"On Becoming a Tiger"
"To Us, All Flowers Are Roses"
"The Woman Speaks to the Man Who Has Employed Her Son"
Tamarind Season, 1980
"The Day She Died"
"England Seen"
"For Don Drummond"
"For R & R in the Rain"
"Guyana Lovesong"
"Judges"
"Moonlongings"
"On Houses"
"Port Henderson 6 AM"
"Saggitarius"
"Sketches of Spain"
"Wedding in Hanover"
"Whose Is That Woman?"
"Xercise for Tony Mc"

HARPER, MICHAEL S.

Dear John, Dear Coltrane, 1970
"After the Operations"
"American History"
"Deathwatch"
"Reuben, Reuben"
"We Assume: On the Death of Our Son, Reuben Masai Harper"
Debridement, 1973
"Sambo's Mistakes: An Essay"

Healing Song for the Inner Ear, 1985
History Is Your Own Heartbeat, 1971
Images of Kin, 1977
  "Bristol: Bicentenary Remembrances of
    Trade"
  "Smoke"
  "Tongue-Tied in Black and White"
  "Uplift from a Dark Tower"
Nightmare Begins Responsibility, 1975
Song: I Want a Witness, 1972
  "The Families Album"

HARRIS, WILSON

Ascent to Omai, 1970
Black Marsden, 1972
Carnival, 1985
Companions of the Day and Night, 1975
*Da Silva da Silva's Cultivated Wilderness;
    and, Genesis of the Clowns*, 1977
Explorations, 1981
The Eye of the Scarecrow, 1965
The Far Journey of Oudin, 1961
Heartland, 1964
The Infinite Rehearsal, 1987
Palace of the Peacock, 1960
The Secret Ladder, 1963
Tradition, the Writer and Society, 1967
The Tree of the Sun, 1978
Tumatumari, 1968
The Waiting Room, 1967
The Whole Armour, 1962
*The Womb of Space: The Cross-Cultural
    Imagination*, 1983

HEAD, BESSIE

A Bewitched Crossroad, 1984
*The Collector of Treasures, and Other
    Botswana Village Tales*, 1977
  "Snowball: A Story"
A Gesture of Belonging, 1991
Maru, 1971
A Question of Power, 1973
Serowe: Village of the Rain Wind, 1981
Tales of Tenderness and Power, 1989
  "An African Story"
  "Chief Sekoto Holds Court"
  "The Deep River: A Story of Ancient
    Tribal Migration"
  "The General"
When Rain Clouds Gather, 1968
*A Woman Alone: Autobiographical
    Writings*, 1990

HEARNE, JOHN

The Autumn Equinox, 1959
The Faces of Love, 1957
Land of the Living, 1961
Stranger at the Gate, 1956
The Sure Salvation, 1981
Voices under the Window, 1955

HEATH, ROY A. K.

From the Heat of the Day, 1979
Genetha, 1981
*Kwaku; or, The Man Who Could Not
    Keep His Mouth Shut*, 1982
A Man Come Home, 1974
The Murderer, 1978
One Generation, 1981
Orealla, 1984
The Shadow Bride, 1988
Shadows Round the Moon, 1990

HODGE, MERLE

Crick Crack, Monkey, 1970

IYAYI, FESTUS

The Contract, 1982
Heroes, 1986
Violence, 1979

JAMES, C. L. R.

Beyond a Boundary, 1963
The Black Jacobins, 1938
  "La Divina Pastora," 1927
Minty Alley, 1936
  "Triumph," 1929

JOHNSON, CHARLES

Faith and the Good Thing, 1974
Middle Passage, 1990
Oxherding Tale, 1982

JOES, GAYL

Corregidora, 1975
Eva's Man, 1976
White Rat, 1977

JUMINER, BERTÈNE (French)

The Archduke Emerges from the Shadow
    (*Archiduc sort de l'ombre*, 1970)
The Bastards (*Les Bâtards*, 1961): *The
    Bastards*, 1989
Bozambo's Revenge (*La Revanche de
    Bozambo*, 1968): *Bozambo's
    Revenge*, 1976

Heirs to the Peninsular (*Les Héritiers de la presqu'île*, 1981)

On the Threshold of a New Cry (*Au seuil d'un nouveau cri*, 1963)

KINCAID, JAMAICA

Annie John, 1985

At the Bottom of the River, 1983
  "At the Bottom of the River"
  "Blackness"
  "Girl"
  "Holidays
  "In the Night"
  "My Mother"
  "Wingless"

Lucy, 1990

KOUROUMA, AHMADOU (French)

Monnè, Outrages and Defiances (*Monnè, outrages et défis*, 1990): *Monnew*, 1993

The Suns of the Independences (*Les Soleils des indépendances*, 1968): *The Suns of Independence*, 1981

The Teller of Truth (*Tougnatique*, unpublished)

KUNENE, MAZISI

The Ancestors & the Sacred Mountain, 1982

Emperor Shaka the Great: A Zulu Epic, 1979

Zulu Poems, 1970
  "Elegy for Msizi"
  "Elegy for My Friend E. Galo"
  "An Elegy to the Unknown Man Nicknamed Donda"
  "From the Ravages of Life We Create"
  "To the Killer"

LABOU TANSI, SONY (French)

The Antipeople (*L'Anté-peuple*, 1983): *The Antipeople*, 1988

I the Undersigned Cardiac (*Je Soussigné Cardiaque*, 1981)

Life and a Half (*La Vie et demie*, 1979)

The State of Shame (*L'État honteux*, 1981)

The Seven Solitudes of Lorsa Lopez (*Les Sept Solitudes de Lorsa Lopez*, 1985)

LA GUMA, ALEX

And a Threefold Cord, 1964

In the Fog of the Seasons' End, 1972

The Stone Country, 1967

Time of the Butcherbird, 1979

A Walk in the Night, 1962

LAMMING, GEORGE

"Birds of a Feather," 1948

The Emigrants, 1954

"The Illumined Graves," 1951

In the Castle of My Skin, 1953

Natives of My Person, 1972

Of Age and Innocence, 1958

The Pleasures of Exile, 1960
  "The Boy and the Sea"

Season of Adventure, 1960

Water with Berries, 1971

LIKING, WEREWERE (French)

African Orpheus (*Orphée-dafric*, 1981)

The Devil's Tail (*La Queue du diable*, 1979)

A New Earth (*Une Nouvelle Terre*, 1980)

The Power of Um (*La Puissance de Um*, 1979)

Ritual Spectacles (*Spectacles rituels*, 1987)
  The Hands Wish to Speak (*Les Mains veulent dire*)
  Rainbow Measles (*La Rougeole-arc-en-ciel*)

She Will Be Made of Jasper and Coral (*Elle sera de jaspe et de corail*, 1983)

The Unjust Sleep (*Du sommeil d'injuste*, 1980)

LOPES, HENRI (French)

The New Romance (*La Nouvelle Romance*, 1976)

On the Other Side (*Sur l'autre rive*, 1992)

To Cry, to Laugh (*Le Pleurer-rire*, 1982)

Tribal (*Tribaliques*, 1971)
  The Deputy ("Monsieur le député")
  The Flight of the Clever Hand ("La Fuite de la main habile")
  The Honest Man ("L'Honnête Homme")

Without Tam-Tam (*Sans tam-tam*, 1977)

LORDE, AUDRE

Between Our Selves, 1976

The Black Unicorn, 1978
  "125th Street and Abomey"
  "Chorus"
  "For Assata"
  "Harriet"
  "Meet"
  "The Women of Dan"

Cables to Rage, 1970
  "Bloodbirth"

Chosen Poems, Old and New, 1982

Coal, 1976

"And What About the Children"
"The Woman Thing"
The First Cities, 1968
From a Land Where Other People Live, 1973
"Dear Toni Instead of a Letter"
New York Headshop and Museum, 1974
"Blackstudies"
"Cables to Rage"
"To My Daughter The Junkie On A
    Train"
Our Dead Behind Us, 1986
"Diaspora"
"Every Traveler Has One Vermont Poem"
"Out to the Hard Road"
"Sisters in Arms"
Sister Outsider, 1984
Zami: A New Spelling of My Name, 1982
"Grenada Revisited"

LOVELACE, EARL

The Dragon Can't Dance, 1979
Jestina's Calypso, and Other Plays, 1984
    Jestina's Calypso
    My Name Is Village
    The New Hardware Store
The Schoolmaster, 1968
While Gods Are Falling, 1965
The Wine of Astonishment, 1982

MAILLU, DAVID

After 4:30, 1974
Dear Daughter, 1976
Dear Monika, 1976
The Equatorial Assignment, 1980
For Mbatha and Rabeka, 1980
Hit of Love, 1980
Jese Kristo, 1979
Kadosa, 1979
The Kommon Man, 1975–1976
My Dear Bottle, 1973
Tears of Sunset, unpublished
Troubles, 1974
Unfit for Human Consumption, 1973

MAIS, ROGER

Black Lightning, 1955
Brother Man, 1954
The Hills Were Joyful Together, 1953

MAPANJE, JACK

*The Chattering Wagtails of Mikuyu
    Prison*, 1993
"Kadango Village, Even Milimbo
    Lagoon Is Dry"

Of Chameleons and Gods, 1981
"An Elegy for Mangochi Fishermen"
"Epitaph for a Mad Friend"
"If Chiuta Were Man"
"In Memory of Matthew, 1976"
"Messages"
"The Palm Trees of Chigawe"
"Requiem to a Fallen Son"
"The Sweet Brew at Chitakale"
"These Too Are Our Elders"
"Visiting Zomba Plateau"
"We Wondered about the Mellow
    Peaches"

MARECHERA, DAMBUDZO

The Black Insider, 1990
"The Black Insider"
Black Sunlight, 1980
Cemetery of Mind, 1993
"Landscape Gardens"
The House of Hunger, 1978
"The Slow Sound of His Feet"
"The Writer's Grain"
Mindblast, or the Definitive Buddy, 1984

MARSHALL, PAULE

Brown Girl, Brownstones, 1959
The Chosen Place, the Timeless People,
    1969
Daughters, 1991
Praisesong for the Widow, 1983
Soul Clap Hands and Sing, 1961

MAXIMIN, DANIEL (French)

Lone Sun (*L'Isolé Soleil*, 1981): *Lone
    Sun*, 1989
Sulphur Mines (*Soufrières*, 1987)

MCMILLAN, TERRY

Disappearing Acts, 1989
Mama, 1987
Waiting to Exhale, 1992

MÉTELLUS, JEAN (French)

Anacaona (*Anacaona*, 1986)
Charles Honore Bonnefoy (*Charles
    Honoré Bonnefoy*, 1990)
An Etching (*Une Eau-forte*, 1983)
Jacmel at Dusk (*Jacmel au crépuscule*, 1981)
Louis Vortex (*Louis Vortex*, 1992)
The Men of Full Wind (*Hommes de plein
    vent*, 1981)
The Revolutionaries (*Les Cacos*, 1989)
The Vortex Family (*La Famille Vortex*, 1982)

The Year of Dessalines (*L'Année Dessalines*, 1986)

MORRISON, TONI

Beloved, 1987
The Bluest Eye, 1970
Jazz, 1992
Playing in the Dark, 1992
Song of Solomon, 1977
Sula, 1973
Tar Baby, 1981

MPHAHLELE, ES'KIA (EZEKIEL)

The African Image, 1962
Afrika My Music, 1984
Chirundu, 1979
Down Second Avenue, 1959
Father Come Home, 1984
In Corner B, 1967
The Living and Dead and Other Stories, 1961
  "We'll Have Dinner at Eight"
Man Must Live and Other Stories, 1946
Voices in the Whirlwind and Other Essays, 1972
The Wanderers, 1971

MTSHALI, OSWALD

Fireflames, 1980
Sounds of a Cowhide Drum, 1971
  "Boy on a Swing"
  "Handcuffs"
  "Pigeons at the Oppenheimer Park"
  "This Kid Is No Goat"
  "The Shepherd and His Flock"

MUDIMBE, V. Y. (French)

Between Tides (*Entre les eaux*, 1973): *Between Tides*, 1991
The Handsome Filthy One (*Le Bel Immonde*, 1976): *Before the Birth of the Moon*, 1989
Lacerations (*Déchirures*, 1971)
The Other Side of the Kingdom (*L'Autre Face du royaume*, 1973)
The Rift (*L'Écart*, 1979): *The Rift*, 1993
The Smell of the Father (*L'Odeur du père*, 1982)

MUGO, MICERE GITHAE

The Trial of Dedan Kimathi, 1984 (with Ngugi wa Thiong'o)

MUNONYE, JOHN

Bridge to a Wedding, 1978
A Dancer of Fortune, 1974

Obi, 1969
Oil Man of Obange, 1971
The Only Son, 1966
A Wreath for the Maidens, 1973

MWANGI, MEJA

The Bushtrackers, 1979
Carcase for Hounds, 1974
Going Down River Road, 1976
Kill Me Quick, 1973
Striving for the Wind, 1990
Taste of Death, 1975

NAYLOR, GLORIA

Bailey's Cafe, 1992
Linden Hills, 1985
Mama Day, 1988
The Women of Brewster Place, 1982

NDAO, CHEIK ALIOU (French)

Albouri's Exile (*L'Exil d'Albouri*, 1967)
Almamy's Son (*Le Fils de l'Almamy*, 1973)
Blood for a Throne or Gouye Ndiouli on Sunday (*Du sang pour un trône ou Gouye Ndiouli un dimanche*, 1983)
Buur Tilleen, King of Medina (*Buur Tilleen, roi de la Médina*, 1972)
Excellency, Your Wives! (*Excellence, vos épouses!*, 1983)
Kaïrée (*Kaïrée*, 1962)
  Guinté ("Guinté")
  Landscapes ("Paysages")
  "Poem for Laora"
  Tears of Flame for Lumumba ("Larmes de flammes pour Lumumba")
Mogariennes (*Mogariennes*, 1970)
  Africa II ("Afrique II")
  "Hello Joe"
  A Swan on the Sea ("Un Cygne sur la mer")

NDEBELE, NJABULO

Fools and Other Stories, 1983
  "Fools"
  "The Music of the Violin"
  "The Test"
  "Uncle"
"The Revolution of the Aged," 1982
"*Turkish Tales*, and Some Thoughts on South African Fiction," 1984

NETO, AGOSTINHO (Portuguese)

Poems (*Poemas*, 1961)
Sacred Hope (*Sagrada esperança*, 1974): *Sacred Hope*, 1974

Create ("Criar"): "Create"
Farewell at the Hour of Parting ("Adeus
    à hora da largada"): "Farewell at the
    Hour of Parting"
The Hoisting of the Flag ("O içar da ban-
    deira"): "The Hoisting of the Flag"
Mussunda Friend ("Mussunda amigo"):
    "Mussunda Friend"
Reconquest ("A reconquista"):
    "Reconquest"
Saturday in the Musseques ("Sábado
    nos musseques"): "Saturday in the
    Musseques"
We Shall Return ("Havemos de
    voltar"): "We Shall Return"
With Equal Voice ("A Voz Iqual"):
    "With Equal Voice"
With Dry Eyes (*Con occhi asciutti*, 1963)

NGUGI WA THIONG'O

Decolonising the Mind, 1986
Detained: A Writer's Prison Diary, 1981
Devil on the Cross, 1980; first published
    as *Caitaani Mutharaba-ni*, 1980
A Grain of Wheat, 1967
Matigari, 1989; first published as
    Matigari ma Njiruungi, 1986
I Will Marry When I Want; first published
    as *Ngaahika Ndeenda: Ithaako ria
    Ngerekano*, 1980
Petals of Blood, 1977
The River Between, 1965
Secret Lives, and Other Stories, 1975
Weep Not, Child, 1964

NTIRU, RICHARD

Tensions, 1971
    "Chorus of Public Men"
    "Flashback"
    "'Formula Two'"
    "The Happiness of a Mother"
    "Introduction"
    "The Latest Defector"
    "Morning Arrows"
    "Ojukwu's Prayer"
    "The Pauper"
    "Portrait of the Little Self"
    "The Prophecy"
    "The Secret of the Skeleton"
    "To a Late Rich Miser"

NWAPA, FLORA

Cassava Song and Rice Song, 1986
Efuru, 1966

Idu, 1970
Never Again, 1975
One Is Enough, 1981
This Is Lagos, and Other Stories, 1971
Wives at War, and Other Stories, 1980
Women Are Different, 1986

OGOT, GRACE

Aloo Kod Apul Apul, 1981
Ber Wat, 1981
A Call at Midnight, unpublished
The Graduate, 1980
In the Beginning, unpublished
Island of Tears, 1980
    "The Island of Tears"
Land Without Thunder, 1968
    "Elizabeth"
    "The Hero"
    "Night Sister"
    "The Old White Witch"
    "The Rain Came"
    "The White Veil"
Miaha, 1983
The Other Woman: Selected Short Stories,
    1976
    "The Family Doctor"
    "The Fisherman"
    "Fishing Village"
    "The Honourable Minister"
    "The Ivory Trinket"; first published as
        "Aiyembo's Ghost"
    "The Middle Door"
    "The Other Woman"
    "Pay Day"
    "The Professor"
Princess Nyilaak, unpublished
The Promised Land: A True Fantasy, 1966
Simbi Nyaima, unpublished

OKOT P'BITEK

African Religions in Western Scholarship,
    1971
Africa's Cultural Revolution, 1973
Are Your Teeth White? Then Laugh *(Lak
    Tar Miyo Kinyero Wi Lobo*, 1953):
    White Teeth, 1989
Hare and Hornbill, 1978
The Horn of My Love, 1974
Religion of the Central Luo, 1971
Song of Lawino *(Wer pa Lawino*, 1969):
    Song of Lawino, 1966
Song of Ocol, 1970
Two Songs, 1971
    "Song of Malaya"
    "Song of Prisoner"

OKRI, BEN

The Famished Road, 1991
Flowers and Shadows, 1980
Incidents at the Shrine, 1986
The Landscapes Within, 1981
Songs of Enchantment, 1993
Stars of the New Curfew, 1988
  "What the Tapster Saw"
  "When the Lights Return"
  "Worlds That Flourish"

OSOFISAN, FEMI

Birthdays Are Not for Dying and Other Plays, 1990
  Fires Burn and Die Hard
  The Inspector and the Hero
The Chattering and the Song, 1977
Esu and the Vagabond Minstrels, 1991
Farewell to a Cannibal Rage, 1986
Kolera Kolej, 1975
Minted Coins, 1987
Morountodun and Other Plays, 1982
  Morountodun
  No More the Wasted Breed
Once upon Four Robbers, 1980
Who's Afraid of Solarin?, 1978

OSUNDARE, NIYI

"'As Grasshoppers to Wanton Boys': The Role of the Gods in the Novels of Elechi Amadi," 1980
Daughter of the Rain, unpublished
The Eye of the Earth, 1986
Moonsongs, 1988
A Nib in the Pond, 1986
  "I Am the Common Man"
  "Promise Land"
Requiem for the Second Republic, unpublished
Selected Poems, 1992
Songs of the Marketplace, 1983
  "Dawn"
  "Excursions"
  "The Fall of the Beast"
  "Ignorance"
  "Namibia Talks"
  "The Nigerian Railway"
  "Publish or Perish"
  "Rithmetic Ruse"
  "Siren"
  "Soweto"
  "Sule Chase"
Village Voices, 1984

"Akintunde Come Home"
"A Dialogue of Drums"
"Eating with All the Fingers"
"A Farmer on Seeing Cocoa House, Ibadan"
"Feigning a Rebel"
"The Land of Unease"
"Listen, Book Wizard"
"The New Farmer's Bank"
"Not in My Season of Songs"
"A Villager's Protest"
Waiting Laughters, 1990

OUOLOGUEM, YAMBO (French)

Letter to Black France (*Lettre à la France nègre*, 1969)
The Wages of Violence (*Le Devoir de violence*, 1968): *Bound to Violence*, 1971

PHELPS, ANTHONY (French)

Blind-Man's-Buff Memory (*Mémoire en Colin-Maillard*, 1976)
Bursts of Silence (*Éclats de silence*, 1962)
The Caribbean Ram (*Le Bélière caraïbe*, 1980)
Minus the Infinite (*Moins l'infini*, 1973)
Motifs for Seasoned Time (*Motifs pour le temps saisonnier*, 1976)
This Country of Mine (*Mon pays que voici*, 1968)

PHILLIPS, CARYL

Cambridge, 1992
Crossing the River, 1994
The European Tribe, 1987
The Final Passage, 1985
Higher Ground, 1989
  "The Cargo Rap"
  "Heartland"
  "Higher Ground"
"Living and Writing in the Caribbean: An Experiment," 1989
A State of Independence, 1986

RABÉARIVELO, JEAN-JOSEPH (French)

The Cup of Ashes (*La Coupe de cendres*, 1924)
Near-Dreams (*Presque-songes*, 1934)
  Thrènes ("Thrènes")
  Recognition to Paul Gauguin ("Reconnaissance à Paul Gauguin")
Old Songs of Imerina (*Vieilles chansons des pays d'Imerina*, 1939)

Songs for Abéone (*Chants pour Abéone,*
    1937)
Translated from the Night (*Traduit de la nuit,*
    1935): *24 Poems* (1962)
Volumes (*Volumes,* 1928)
Woods (*Sylves,* 1927)
    Words of Winter ("Paroles de l'hiver")

REED, ISHMAEL

Flight to Canada, 1976
The Free-Lance Pallbearers, 1967
Japanese by Spring, 1993
The Last Days of Louisiana Red, 1974
Mumbo Jumbo, 1972
"Neo-HooDoo Manifesto," 1970
Reckless Eyeballing, 1986
The Terrible Threes, 1989
The Terrible Twos, 1982
Yellow Back Radio Broke-Down, 1969

REID, V. S. (VIC)

The Horses of the Morning, 1985
The Jamaicans, 1976
The Leopard, 1958
The Naked Buck, unpublished
Nanny-Town, 1983
New Day, 1949
Peter of Mount Ephraim, 1971
Sixty-Five, 1960
The Young Warriors, 1967

RIVE, RICHARD

African Songs, 1963
    "The Bench"
    "Willieboy"
"*Buckingham Palace," District Six,* 1986
Emergency, 1964
Make Like Slaves, 1973
Quartet, 1963 (with Alex La Guma, James
    Matthews, and Alf Wannenburgh)
    "No Room at Solitaire"
Selected Writings: Stories, Essays, Plays, 1977
    "African Song"
Writing Black, 1981

ROBERT, SHAABAN (Swahili)

After Fifty Years (*Baada ya Miaka
    Hamsini,* 1966)
Beauty of the Language (*Pambo la lugha,*
    1948)
Compositions and Poems (*Insha na
    Mashairi,* 1959)
The Day of All Workers (*Siku ya watenzi
    wote,* 1968)

Kufikirika (*Kufikirika,* 1967)
Kusadikika, a Country of Believers
    (*Kusadikika, chi iliyo angani,* 1951):
    Kusadikika: A Country in the Sky, 1973
My Life (*Maisha Yangu,* 1949)
    Amina ("Amina")
Noble Lessons (*Masomo yenye Adili,* 1959)
Utubora the Farmer (*Utobora mkulima,* 1968)

ROTIMI, OLA

The Gods Are Not to Blame, 1971
Holding Talks, 1979
Hopes of the Living Dead, 1988
If . . . A Tragedy of the Ruled, 1983
Kurunmi, 1971
Our Husband Has Gone Mad Again, 1977
Ovonramwen Nogbaisi, 1974

RUBADIRI, DAVID

"An African Thunderstorm," 1965
"Christmas 1967," 1968
No Bride Price, 1967
"Paraa Lodge," 1967
"Saaka Crested Cranes," 1967
"The Tide that from the West Washes
    Africa to the Bone," 1968
"The Witch Tree at Mubende," 1967

SALKEY, ANDREW

The Adventures of Catallus Kelly, 1969
Anancy, Traveller, 1988
Anancy's Score, 1973
    "New Man Anancy"
    "Soot, the Land of Billboards"
    "Vietnam Anancy and the Black Tulip"
Away, 1980
*Caribbean Prose: An Anthology for
    Secondary Schools,* 1967
Come Home, Malcolm Heartland, 1976
Drought, 1966
Earthquake, 1965
Escape to an Autumn Pavement, 1960
Hurricane, 1977
*In the Hills Where Her Dreams Live:
    Poems for Chile 1973–1978,* 1979
Joey Tyson, 1974
Jonah Simpson, 1969
The Late Emancipation of Jerry Stover,
    1968
A Quality of Violence, 1959
Riot, 1967
The Shark Hunters, 1966
Stories from the Caribbean, 1968
West Indian Stories, 1960

SANCHEZ, SONIA

*A Blues Book for Blue Black Magical
    Women*, 1973
The Bronx Is Next, 1968
Homecoming, 1969
    "Poem at Thirty"
homegirls & handgrenades, 1984
*I've Been a Woman: New and Selected
    Poems*, 1981
Love Poems, 1973
Sister Son/ji, 1969
Uh, Huh; But How Do It Free Us?, 1974
Under a Soprano Sky, 1987
    "elegy (for MOVE and Philadelphia)"
    "Philadelphia: Spring, 1985"
    "A poem for my brother (reflections on
        his death from AIDS)"
We A BaddDDD People, 1970

SCHWARZ-BART, SIMONE (French)

A Plate of Pork with Green Bananas (*Un
    Plat de porc aux bananes vertes*,
    1967), with André Schwarz-Bart
Rain and Wind on Télumée, the Miracle
    Woman (*Pluie et vent sur Télumée
    Miracle*, 1972): *The Bridge of
    Beyond*, 1981
Ti Jean the Horizon (*Ti Jean l'horizon*,
    1979): *Between Two Worlds*, 1981
Your Handsome Captain (*Ton beau capi-
    taine*, 1987): *Your Handsome
    Captain*, 1988

SEMBÈNE OUSMANE (French)

The Black Dockworker (*Le Docker noir*,
    1956): *Black Docker*, 1987
Emitaï (*Emitaï*, unpublished)
From Volta (*Voltaïque*, 1962): *Tribal
    Scars and Other Stories*, 1975
    Her Three Days ("Ses tois jours'): "Her
        Last Three Days"
    Letters from France ("Lettres de
        France"): "Letters from France"
    The Mother ("La Mère"): "The Mother"
    Souleymane ("Souleymane"): "The
        Bilal's Fourth Wife"
God's Bits of Wood (*Les Bouts de bois de
    Dieu*, 1960): *God's Bits of Wood*,
    1962
The Harmattan (*L'Harmattan*, 1964)
The Money Order (*Le Mandat*, 1965): *The
    Money Order*, 1972
"Niiwam," 1987

Oh Country, My Beautiful People (*O
    pays, mon beau peuple!*, 1957)
"Taaw," 1987
Xala (*Xala*, 1973): *Xala*, 1976

SENIOR, OLIVE

Arrival of the Snake-Woman, 1989
    "Arrival of the Snake-Woman"
    "The Tenantry of Birds"
    "The View from the Terrace"
Summer Lightning and Other Stories, 1986
    "Ballad"
    "Bright Thursdays"
    "Confirmation Day"
    "Country Of The One Eye God"
    "Do Angels Wear Brassieres?"
Talking of Trees, 1985
    "Ancestral Poem"
    "Cockpit Country Dreams"
    "The Mother"
    "Nansi 'Tory"
    "Searching for My Grandfather"
    "To the Madwoman in My Yard"

SEPAMLA, SIPHO

From Goré to Soweto, 1988
    "28 July"
    "I love Soweto"
    "A Man for the Land"
    "May Day"
    "Moment Beyond Now"
    "Wattville"
Hurry Up to It!, 1975
    "Feeling Small"
    "In Love"
    "To Whom It May Concern"
A Ride on the Whirlwind, 1984
The Root Is One, 1979
The Soweto I Love, 1977
    "At the Dawn of Another Day"
    "A Child Dies"
    "Civilization Aha"
    "I Saw This Morning"
    "Like a Hippo"
    "Shop Assistant"

SEROTE, MONGANE (WALLY)

Behold Mama, Flowers, 1978
No Baby Must Weep, 1975
"Ofaywatcher-Blackwoman-Eternity,"
    1974
To Every Birth Its Blood, 1981
Tsetlo, 1974
    "Amen Alexandra"

"Introit"
Yakhal'inkomo, 1972
   "Alexandra"
   "City Johannesburg"
   "Hell, Well, Heaven"
   "What's in this Black 'Shit'"

SERUMAGA, ROBERT

Amanyakiriti, unpublished
The Elephants, 1971
Majangwa, 1972
A Play, 1968
Renga Moi, unpublished
Return to the Shadows, 1969

SHANGE, NTOZAKE

boogie woogie landscapes, 1981
A Daughter's Geography, 1983
for colored girls who have considered sui-
   cide/when the rainbow is enuf, 1977
   "Graduation Nite"
   "Now I Love Somebody More Than"
   "Sechita"
   "Toussaint"
From Okra to Greens/A Different Kind of
   Love Story: A Play/ with Music &
   Dance, 1984
a photograph: lovers in motion, 1979: first
   published as *A Photograph:*
   A Still Life with Shadows/A
   Photograph: A Study of Cruelty, 1977
Sassafrass, Cypress & Indigo, 1982
Some Men, 1981
spell #7, 1979

SOW FALL, AMINATA (French)

The Beggars' Strike (*La Grève des Bàttu*,
   1979): *The Beggars' Strike*, 1981
The Call from the Arenas (*L'Appel des*
   arènes, 1982)
The Ex-Father of the Nation (*L'Ex-père*
   de la nation, 1987)
The Ghost (*Le Revenant*, 1976)

SOYINKA, WOLE

Aké: The Years of Childhood, 1981
Art, Dialogue and Outrage, 1988
   "The Fourth Stage"
The Bacchae of Euripides, 1973
A Dance of the Forests, 1963
Death and the King's Horsemen, 1975
From Zia with Love, 1992
Idanre & Other Poems, 1967
   "Idanre"

Isarà: A Voyage around Essay, 1989
The Interpreters, 1965
Jero's Metamorphosis, 1974
Kongi's Harvest, 1967
The Lion and the Jewel, 1963
Madmen and Specialists, 1971
The Man Died, 1972
Mandela's Earth and Other Poems, 1988
   "Like Rudolph Hess, the Man Said"
Myth, Literature and the African World,
   1976
Ogun Abibimang, 1976
Opera Wonyosi, 1981
A Play of Giants, 1984
Requiem for a Futurologist, 1985
The Road, 1965
Season of Anomy, 1973
A Shuttle in the Crypt, 1972
   "And what of it if thus he died?"
   "Crimes of Silence"
   "Purgatory"
   "Recession (*Mahapralaya*)"
   "Seed"
   "Space"
   "When Seasons Change"
The Swamp Dwellers, 1963
The Trials of Brother Jero, and The
   Strong Breed, 1969

ST. OMER, GARTH

J—, Black Bam and the Masqueraders, 1972
Nor Any Country, 1969
A Room on the Hill, 1968
Shades of Grey, 1968
   "Another Place Another Time"
   "The Lights on the Hill"
"Syrop," 1964

SUTHERLAND, EFUA

Ananse and the Dwarf Brigade, unpublished
Edufa, 1967
Foriwa, 1967
The Marriage of Anansewa, 1975
"New Life in Kyerefaso," 1960
Nyamekye, unpublished
Odasani, unpublished
The Pineapple Child, unpublished
Vulture! Vulture! [and *Tahinta*]: *Two*
   Rhythm Plays, 1968

TABAN LO LIYONG

Another Last Word, 1990
Another Nigger Dead, 1972
   "Batsiary in Sanigraland"

"bless the african coups"
Ballads of Underdevelopment, 1976
Eating Chiefs, 1970
Fixions & Other Stories, 1969
   "Ododo pa Apwoyo Gin ki Lyech"
   "Sages and Wages"
   "A Traveller's Tale"
Frantz Fanon's Uneven Ribs, 1971
The Last Word, 1969
Meditations of Taban lo Liyong, 1978
Meditations in Limbo, 1970
Thirteen Offensives against Our Enemies, 1973
The Uniformed Man, 1971
   "Asu the Great"
   "The Education of Taban lo Liyong"
   "A Prescription for Idleness"
   "Project X"

TATI-LOUTARD, JEAN BAPTISTE (French)

The Account of Death (*Le Récit de la mort*, 1987)
Anthology of Congolese Literature of French Expression (*Anthologie de la littérature congolaise d'expression française*, 1976)
The Congolese Roots (*Les Racines congolaise*, 1968)
New Congolese Chronicles (*Nouvelles Chroniques congolaises*, 1980)
The Rendezvous of the Retreat (*Le Rendez-vous de la retraite*)
The Norms of Time (*Les Normes du temps*, 1974)
Poems of the Sea (*Poèmes de la mer*, 1968): *Poems of the Sea*, 1990
The Tradition of the Dream (*La Tradition du songe*, 1985)
The Wrong Side of the Sun (*L'Envers du soleil*, 1970)

TCHICAYA U TAM'SI (French)

Bad Blood (*Le Mauvais Sang*, 1955)
The Belly (*Le Ventre*, 1964)
Brush Fire (*Feu de brousse*, 1957); *Brush Fire*, 1964
The Cockroaches (*Les Cancrelats*, 1980)
The Dry Hand (*La Main sèche*, 1980)
   Reverse ("Rebours")
Epitome (*Epitomé*, 1968)
A Game of Cheat-Heart (*À triche-coeur*, 1958)

The Glorious Destiny of Marshal Nnikon (*Le Destin glorieux du Maréchal Nnikon*, 1979): *The Glorious Destiny of Marshal Nnikon Nniku*, 1986

TLALI, MIRIAM

Amandla, 1980
Mihloti, 1984
   "Detour into Detention"
   "Point of No Return"
Muriel at Metropolitan, 1979

WALCOTT, DEREK

25 Poems, 1948
Another Life, 1973
The Arkansas Testament, 1987
A Branch of the Blue Nile, 1986
The Castaway and Other Poems, 1965
   "Crusoe's Island"
   "Crusoe's Journal"
   "Laventville"
Collected Poems, 1948–1984, 1986
Dream on Monkey Mountain and Other Plays, 1970
   "What the Twilight Says: An Overture"
Epitaph for the Young, 1949
The Fortunate Traveller, 1981
   "North and South"
   "The Spoiler's Return"
In a Fine Castle, 1971
In a Green Night, 1962
The Gulf, and Other Poems, 1969
The Joker of Seville, 1978
The Last Carnival, 1986
Midsummer, 1984
   "Tropic Zone"
O Babylon!, 1978
Omeros, 1990
Pantomime, 1980
Poems, 1951
Remembrance, 1980
Sea Grapes, 1976
   "Sainte Lucie"
Selected Poems, 1964
The Star-Apple Kingdom, 1979
   "Egypt, Tobago"
   "The Schooner *Flight*"
Ti-Jean and His Brothers, 1979

ALICE WALKER

The Color Purple, 1982
In Love and Trouble, 1973
   "Everyday Use"
   "The Revenge of Hannah Kemhuff"

"Strong Horse Tea"
Meridian, 1976
The Temple of My Familiar, 1989
The Third Life of Grange Copeland, 1970

WARNER-VIEYRA, MYRIAM (French)

As the Sorcerer Said (*Le Quimboiseur l'avait dit*, 1980): *As the Sorcerer Said*, 1982
Juletane (*Juletane*, 1982): *Juletane*, 1987
The Lost Women (*Femmes échouées*, 1988)
    First Prize ("Premier Prix")
    Sidonie ("Sidonie")
    Unique Hour ("Heure unique")
    The Wall, or The Charms of Married Life ("Le Mur, ou les charmes d'une vie conjugale")

WILSON, AUGUST

Fences, 1986
Joe Turner's Come and Gone, 1988
Ma Rainey's Black Bottom, 1985
The Piano Lesson, 1990
Two Trains Running, 1992

WYNTER, SYLVIA

"Creole Criticism: A Critique," 1973
The Hills of Hebron, 1962
"Jonkonnu in Jamaica," 1970
"Novel and History: Plot and Plantation," 1971
"One Love: Aspects of Afro-Jamaicanism," 1972

"We Must Learn to Sit Down Together and Talk about a Little Culture: Reflections on West Indian Writing and Criticism," part 1, 1968; part 2, 1969

ZADI ZAOUROU, BERNARD (French)

The Eye (*L'Oeil*, 1975)
The Eye and the Hair (*L'Oeil et la tignasse*, unpublished)
The Sofas (*Les Sofas*, 1975)
The Termite Nest (*La Termitière*, unpublished)

ZOBEL, JOSEPH (French)

And If the Sea Were Not Blue (*Et si la mer n'était pas bleue*, 1982)
And If the Sea Were Not Blue ("Et si la mer n'était pas bleue")
The Cousin ("Le Cousin")
Nardal ("Nardal")
The Notebook of Edouard Tanasio ("Le Cahier d'Edouard Tanasio")
The Return of Mamzelle Annette ("Le Retour de Mamzelle Annette")
The Devil (*Diab'là*, 1946)
The Hands Full of Birds (*Les Mains pleines d'oiseaux*, 1978)
Laghia of Death (*Laghia de la mort*, 1946)
Party in Paris (*La Fête à Paris*, 1953)
The Street of Black Houses (*La Rue cases-nègres*, 1950): *Black Shack Alley*, 1980

COPYRIGHT ACKNOWLEDGMENTS

AFRICAN AMERICAN REVIEW. For excerpts from articles by John F. Callahan on Harper. Reprinted from *African American Review*, Volume 13, Number 3, (Winter 1979). Copyright 1979 by Indiana State University; Sandra Hollin Flowers on Shange. Reprinted from *African American Review*, Volume 15, Number 2 (Summer 1981). Copyright 1981 by Indiana State University; Trudier Harris on Childress. Reprinted from *African American Review*, Volume 14, Number 1 (Spring 1980). Copyright 1980 by Indiana State University; Mary Jane Lupton on Fauset. Reprinted from *African American Review*, Volume 20, Number 4 (Winter 1986). Copyright 1986 by Indiana State University; Elinor S. Miller on Juminer. Reprinted from *African American Review*, Volume 11, Number 1 (Spring 1977). Copyright 1977 by Indiana State University; Carol E. Neubauer on Angelou. Reprinted from *African American Review*, Volume 17, Number 3 (1983). Copyright 1983 by Indiana State University; Sandra L. Richards on Shange. Reprinted from *African American Review*, Volume 17, Number 2 (Summer 1983). Copyright 1983 by Indiana State University; John W. Roberts on Gaines. Reprinted from *African American Review*, Volume 18, Number 3 (Fall 1984). Copyright 1984 by Indiana State University; Claudia C. Tate on Jones. Reprinted from *African American Review*, Volume 13, Number 4 (Winter 1979). Copyright 1979 by Indiana State University.

AFRICAN STUDIES REVIEW. For excerpts from articles by F. Odun Balogun on Taban lo Liyong; Charlotte [H.] Bruner on Emecheta; Chimalum Nwankwo on Cheney-Coker.

ALA BULLETIN. For excerpts from article by Ezenwa-Ohaeto on Marechera.

JACQUES ALVAREZ-PEREYRE. For excerpts from *The Poetry of Commitment in South Africa* (Brutus, Kunene, Mtshali, Sepamla, Serote).

AMERICAN IMAGO. For excerpts from "David Bradley's *The Chaneysville Incident*: The Belly of the Text" by Martin J. Gliserman. Reprinted from *American Imago*. Volume 43, Number 2, Summer 1986. Reprinted by permission of The Johns Hopkins University Press.

APPLAUSE BOOKS. For excerpts from article by Shelby Steele on Baraka in Errol Hill, ed., *The Theatre of Black Americans* (1987).

ARIEL. For excerpts from articles by Brian Crow on Mugo, Copyright © 1983, The Board of Governors, The University of Calgary; Lorna Down on Edgell, Copyright © 1987, The Board of Governors, The University of Calgary; Jean-Pierre Durix on Harris, Copyright © 1984, The Board of Governors, The University of Calgary; Simon Gikandi on Hodge, Copyright © 1989, The Board of Governors, The University of Calgary; John Haynes on Kunene, Copyright © 1987, The Board of Governors, The University of Calgary; Patricia Ismond on Walcott, Copyright © 1985, The Board of Governors, The University of Calgary; Anthony Kellman on Baraka, Copyright © 1990, The Board of Governors, The University of Calgary; Maria Helena Lima on Collins, Copyright © 1993, The Board of Governors, The University of Calgary; Mbulelo Vizikhungo Mzamane on Rive, Copyright © 1985, The Board of Governors, The University of Calgary; James McCorkle on Walcott, Copyright © 1986, The Board of Governors, The University of Calgary; Chikwenye Okonjo Ogunyemi on Brutus, Copyright © 1982, The Board of Governors, The University of Calgary; Tanure Ojaide on Brutus, Copyright © 1986, The Board of Governors, The University of Calgary; Virginia U. Ola on Head, Copyright © 1986, The Board of Governors, The University of Calgary; Richard F. Patteson on Senior, Copyright © 1993, The Board of Governors, The University of Calgary; Shalini Puri on Brodber, Copyright © 1993, The Board of Governors, The University of Calgary; Stephen Slemon on Harris, Copyright © 1988, The Board of Governors, The University of Calgary; Colin Style on Marechera, Copyright © 1985, The Board of Governors, The University of Calgary; Clement H. Wyke on Walcott, Copyright © 1989, The Board of Governors, The University of Calgary; A. Rasheed Yesufu on Ntiru, Copyright © 1987, The Board of Governors, The University of Calgary.

ASSOCIATED UNIVERSITY PRESSES. For excerpts from articles by John Timpane on Shange; Catherine Wiley on Childress in *Modern American Drama: The Female Canon* (1990), June Schlueter, ed.

BAOBAB BOOKS. For excerpts from articles by Anthony Chennells on La Guma; Ismael Mbise on Okot p'Bitek in *Literature, Language and the Nation* (1989), Emmanuel Ngara and Andrew Morrison, eds.

BARNES AND NOBLE. For excerpts from R. N. Egudu. *Modern African Poetry and the African Predicament* (Brutus, Soyinka, Taban lo Liyong).

BEACON PRESS. For excerpts from *Diving Deep and Surfacing: Women Writers on Spiritual Quest* by Carol P. Christ (Shange). Copyright © 1980 by Carol P. Christ. Reprinted by permission of Beacon Press.

ROBERT BENSEN. For excerpts from article on Walcott in *The Literary Review*.

BIM. For excerpts from article by Harold Barratt on Anthony.

BOWLING GREEN STATE UNIVERSITY POPULAR PRESS. For excerpts from articles by Angelita Reyes on Marshall; David Lionel Smith on Baraka in *Politics and the Muse: Studies in the Politics of Recent American Literature* (1989), Adam J. Sorkin, ed.

LLOYD W. BROWN. For excerpts from *West Indian Poetry* on Bennett, Brathwaite.

DIANA BRYDON. For excerpts from article on Clarke in *Canadian Literature*.

STEPHEN BUTTERFIELD. For excerpts from *Black Autobiography in America* (Angelou).

CALLALOO. For excerpts from "To W/rite in a New Language: Werewere Liking's Adaptation of Ritual to the Novel" by Anne Adams. Reprinted from *Callaloo*. Volume 16, Number 1, Winter 1993; "Chronicling Everyday Travails and Triumphs" by Michael Awkward on McMillan. Reprinted from *Callaloo*. Volume 11, Number 3, Summer 1988; "Their Long Scars Touch Ours: A Reflection on the Poetry of Michael Harper" by Joseph A. Brown, SJ. Reprinted from *Callaloo*. Volume 9, Number 1, Winter 1986; "Debrouya pa peche, or il y a toujours moyen de moyenner: Patterns of Opposition in the Fiction of Patrick Chamoiseau" by Richard D. E. Burton. Reprinted from *Callaloo*. Volume 16, Number 2, Spring 1993; "Reflections on Maryse Condé's *Traversée de la Mangrove*" by Patrick Chamoiseau. Reprinted from *Callaloo*. Volume 14, Number 2, Spring 1991; "Revisioning Our Kumblas: Transforming Feminist and Nationalist Agendas in Three Caribbean Women's Texts" by Rhonda Cobham on Hodge. Reprinted from *Callaloo*. Volume 16, Number 1, Winter 1993; "Scars and Wings: Rita Dove's *Grace Notes*" by Bonnie Costello. Reprinted from *Callaloo*. Volume 14, Number 2, Spring 1991; "Engagement, Exile and Errance: Some Trends in Haitian Poetry 1946–1986" by J. Michael Dash on Depestre and Phelps. Reprinted from *Callaloo*. Volume 15, Number 3, Summer 1992; "Race, Privilege, and the Politics of (Re)Writing History: An Analysis of the Novels of Michelle Cliff" by Belinda Edmondson. Reprinted from *Callaloo*. Volume 16, Number 1, Winter 1993; "Fictionalizing History: David Bradley's *The Chaneysville Incident*" by Klaus Ensslen. Reprinted from *Callaloo*. Volume 11, Number 2, Spring 1988; "Maximin's *L'Isolé Soleil* and Caliban's Curse" by John D. Erickson. Reprinted from *Callaloo*. Volume 15, Number 1, Winter 1992; "Rita Dove: Crossing Boundaries" by Ekaterini Georgoudaki. Reprinted from *Callaloo*. Volume 14, Number 2, Spring 1991; "Geographies of Pain: Captive Bodies and Violent Acts in the Fictions of Myriam Warner-Vieyra, Gayl Jones, and Bessie Head" by Françoise Lionnet on Warner-Vieyra. Reprinted from *Callaloo*. Volume 16, Number 1, Winter 1993; "The Assembling Vision of Rita Dove" by Robert [E.] McDowell. Reprinted from *Callaloo*. Volume 9, Number 1, Winter 1986; "Reading Warner-Vieyra's *Juletane*" by Jonathan Ngate. Reprinted from *Callaloo*. Volume 9, Number 4, Fall 1986; "Poetic Viewpoint: Okot p'Bitek and His Personae" by Tanure Ojaide. Reprinted from *Callaloo*. Volume 9, Number 2, Spring 1986; "An Introduction to the Poetry and Fiction of Olive Senior" by Velma Pollard. Reprinted from *Callaloo*. Volume 11, Number 3, Summer 1988; "The Poems of Rita Dove" by Arnold Rampersad. Reprinted from *Callaloo*. Volume 9, Number 2, Winter 1986; "A Shift Toward the Inner Voice and Créolité in the French Caribbean Novel" by Ann Armstrong Scarboro on Maximin. Reprinted from *Callaloo*. Volume 15, Number 1, Winter 1992; "Patrick Chamoiseau, *Solibo Magnifique*: From the

Escheat of Speech to the Emergence of Language" by Marie-Agnès Sourieau. Reprinted from *Callaloo*. Volume 15, Number 1, Winter 1992; "Cold Hearts and (Foreign) Tongues: Recitation and the Reclamation of the Female Body in the Works of Erna Brodber and Jamaica Kincaid" by Helen Tiffin on Kincaid. Reprinted from *Callaloo*. Volume 16, Number 3, Fall 1993. Reprinted by permission of The Johns Hopkins University Press.

CALALOUX PUBLICATIONS. For excerpts from articles by Selwyn R. Cudjoe on Bennett; Daryl Cumber Dance on Brodber; Laura Niesen de Abruna on Hodge, Kincaid; Marie-Denise Shelton on Schwarz-Bart, Warner-Vieyra; Ena V. Thomas on Hodge in *Caribbean Women Writers*, Selwyn R. Cudjoe, ed.

CAMBRIDGE UNIVERSITY PRESS. For excerpts from Dorothy S. Blair, *African Literature in French: A History of Writing in French from West and Equatorial Africa* (Badian, Bebey, Kourouma, Ndao, Ouologuem). Reprinted with the permission of Cambridge University Press; Robert Fraser, *West African Poetry* (Anyidoho, Awoonor, Rabéarivelo). Reprinted with the permission of Cambridge University Press; "Ethnos and the Beat Poets," by Steve Harney on Baraka, in *Journal of American Studies*, Vol. 25, No. 3 (1991). Reprinted with the permission of Cambridge University Press; Adrian Roscoe, *Uhuru's Fire: African Literature East to South* (Ntiru, Serumaga, Taban lo Liyong). Reprinted with the permission of Cambridge University Press; Wole Soyinka, *Myth, Literature and the African World* (Rive). Reprinted with the permission of Cambridge University Press.

CARIBBEAN QUARTERLY. For excerpts from articles by Selwyn R. Cudjoe on Juminer; Peter Dunwoodie on St. Omer; Patricia Ismond on St. Omer; Consuelo Lopez Springfield on James.

COLLEGE LITERATURE. For excerpts from article by Elizabeth Ammons on Fauset.

COMMONWEALTH ESSAYS & STUDIES. For excerpts from articles by Chidi Amuta on Iyayi; Aderemi Bamikunle on Osofisan; Alfred Kiema on Amadi; Bruce King on St. Omer; Ayo Mamudu on Okri; Alastair Niven on Anthony; J. O. J. Nwachukwu-Agbada on Okot p'Bitek; Roydon Salick on Gilroy; A. Rasheed Yesufu on Ntiru.

COMPARATIVE LITERATURE STUDIES. For excerpts from Josie P. Campbell, "To Sing the Song, to Tell the Tale: A Study of Toni Morrison and Simone Schwarz-Bart" on Schwarz-Bart, *Comparative Literature Studies*, Volume 22, Number 3, pp. 394–412. Copyright 1985 by The Pennsylvania State University. Reproduced by permission of The Pennsylvania State University Press.

CONTEMPORARY LITERATURE. For excerpts from articles by Henry Louis Gates, Jr. on Naylor; Catherine C. Ward on Naylor. Reprinted by permission of The University of Wisconsin Press.

CORNELL UNIVERSITY PRESS. For excerpts from Simon Gikandi, *Writing in Limbo: Modernism and Caribbean Literature* (Cliff, Edgell, James, Lamming, Marshall). Copyright © 1992 by Cornell University. Used by permission of the publisher, Cornell University Press.

THULANI DAVIS. For excerpt from article on McMillan in *The Village Voice*.

DOUBLEDAY. For excerpts from *Hopes and Impediments: Selected Essays* by Chinua Achebe on Awoonor, Baldwin. Copyright © 1988 by Chinua Achebe. Used by permission of Doubleday, a division of Bantam Doubleday Dell Publishing Group, Inc.; article by Melvin Dixon on Jones from *Black Women Writers* by Mari Evans. Copyright © 1983 by Mari Evans. Used by permission of Doubleday, a division of Bantam Doubleday Dell Publishing Group, Inc.; article by Paula Giddings on Giovanni from *Black Women Writers* by Mari Evans. Copyright © 1983 by Mari Evans. Used by permission of Doubleday, a division of Bantam Doubleday Dell Publishing Group, Inc.; article by George Kent on Brooks from *Black Women Writers* by Mari Evans. Copyright © 1983 by Mari Evans. Used by permission of Doubleday, a division of Bantam Doubleday Dell Publishing Group, Inc.; article by John O. Killens on Childress from *Black Women Writers* by Mari Evans. Copyright © 1983 by Mari Evans. Used by permission of Doubleday, a division of Bantam Doubleday Dell Publishing Group, Inc.; article by Haki Madhubuti on Sanchez from *Black Women Writers* by Mari Evans. Copyright © 1983 by Mari Evans. Used by permission of Doubleday, a division of Bantam Doubleday Dell Publishing Group, Inc.; article by Eleanor W. Traylor on Bambara from

JAMAICA JOURNAL. For excerpts from article by Pamela Mordecai on Goodison.

DIANNE JOHNSON-FEELINGS. For excerpt from article on Clifton in *The Children's Literature Association Quarterly*.

JOURNAL OF AMERICAN CULTURE. For excerpts from articles by Emmanuel S. Nelson on Brathwaite; Jean Strandness on Shange.

JOURNAL OF CARIBBEAN STUDIES AND O. R. DATHORNE. For excerpts from article by Evelyn O'Callaghan on Senior.

JOURNAL OF WEST INDIAN LITERATURE. For excerpts from articles by Steven R. Carter on Anthony; Michael G. Cooke on Brodber; Joyce Walker-Johnson on Brodber.

G. D. KILLAM. For excerpts from *An Introduction to the Writings of Ngugi* (Mugo, Ngugi wa Thiong'o); article on Ngugi wa Thiong'o in *The Writing of East and Central Africa*; article by Jacqueline Bardolph on Mwangi in *The Writing of East and Central Africa*; article by Angus Calder on Mwangi in *The Writing of East and Central Africa*; article by D. R. Ewen on Farah in *The Writing of East and Central Africa*; articles by [K. L.] Goodwin on Ntiru and Rubadiri in *The Writing of East and Central Africa*; article by Bernth Lindfors on Okot p'Bitek in *The Writing of East and Central Africa*; article by T. O. McLoughlin on Marechera in *The Writing of East and Central Africa*; articles by Peter Nazareth on Serumaga and Taban lo Liyong in *The Writing of East and Central Africa*.

JAN KNAPPERT. For excerpt from *Four Centuries of Swahili Verse* on Robert.

PETER LANG. For excerpts from Evelyn J. Hawthorne on Mais, *The Writer in Transition: Roger Mais and the Decolonization of Caribbean Culture* (1989); Dolly A. McPherson on Angelou, *Order Out of Chaos: The Autobiographical Works of Maya Angelou* (1990).

LANGUAGE QUARTERLY. For excerpts from article by Elerius Edet John on Bebey.

HANK LAZER. For excerpt from article on Clifton in *The Southern Review*.

LEGON JOURNAL OF THE HUMANITIES. For excerpts from article by J. Bekunuru Kubayanda on Anyidoho.

NEAL A. LESTER. For excerpts from article on Shange in *African American Review*.

THE LITERARY CRITERION. For excerpts from articles by Aderemi Bamikunle on Osundare; Ebele Keo on Amadi; Hank Okazaki on Phillips; Jasper A. Onuekwusi on Brutus.

THE LITERARY HALF-YEARLY. For excerpts from articles by David Olusegun Agbaje on Mtshali; Isaac I. Elimimian on Brutus; Andrew Horn on Serumaga.

CECILY LOCKETT. For excerpts from article on Tlali in Cherry Clayton, ed., *Women and Writing in South Africa*.

LONGMAN PUBLISHING GROUP. For excerpts from article by Mbulelo Vizikhungo Mzamane on Serote in *Literature and Society in South Africa*, White and Couzens, eds.

LOUISIANA STATE UNIVERSITY PRESS. For excerpts from article by Blyden Jackson on Gaines in *American Letters and the Historical Consciousness: Essays in Honor of Lewis P. Simpson*, edited by J. Gerald Kennedy and Daniel Mark Fogel. Copyright © 1987 by Louisiana State University Press. Used with permission; article by Trudier Harris on Walker in *The History of Southern Literature*, edited by Louis D. Rubin, Jr. Copyright © 1985 by Louisiana State University Press. Used with permission; article by Theodore R. Hudson on Gaines in *The History of Southern Literature*, edited by Louis D. Rubin, Jr. Copyright © 1985 by Louisiana State University Press. Used with permission.

MACMILLAN PUBLISHING COMPANY. For excerpts from Dorothy S. Blair, *Senegalese Literature: A Critical History* (Bâ, Diallo, Ndao, Sembène Ousmane, Sow Fall); Lloyd W. Brown, *West Indian Poetry* (Bennett, Brathwaite); Michael Gilkes, *The West Indian Novel* (Harris, James, Lamming, Mais, St. Omer); article by Deborah E. McDowell on Fauset in *Modern American Women Writers*, consulting editor, Elaine Showalter. Lea Baechler and A. Walton Litz, general editors. Copyright © 1991, Charles Scribner's Sons.

(February 16, 1992); "Women Together" by Annie Gottlieb on Naylor (August 22, 1982); "Chilling Out in Phoenix" by Susan Isaacs on McMillan (May 31, 1992); "McMillan's Millions" by Daniel Max on McMillan (August 9, 1992); "An Affair of Convenience" by Reginald McKnight on Mudimbe (April 30, 1989); "In Short" by Tom Nolan on Phillips (April 29, 1990); "Abandoned for Their Own Good" by Elizabeth Nunez-Harrell on Cliff (September 23, 1990); "Nothing Succeeds Like Virginia" by Geoff Ryman on Dove (October 11, 1992); "Someone To Walk Over Me" by Valerie Sayers on McMillan (August 6, 1989); "Dying Like a Man" by Carl Senna on Gaines (August 9, 1993). Copyright © 1982, 1987, 1989, 1990, 1991, 1992, 1993, 1994 by The New York Times Company. Reprinted by permission.'

EMMANUEL NGARA. For excerpts from *Stylistic Criticism and the African Novel* (Ngugi wa Thiong'o, Soyinka).

NORTHEASTERN UNIVERSITY PRESS. For excerpts from the foreword by Mae G. Henderson in the 1991 edition of *White Rat* by Gayl Jones. Reprinted with the permission of Northeastern University Press; *Derek Walcott's Poetry: American Mimicry* by Rei Terada. Copyright © 1992 by Rei Terada. Reprinted with the permission of Northeastern University Press, Boston.

OCTAGON BOOKS. For excerpts from Suzanne Juhasz, *Naked and Fiery Forms: Modern American Poetry by Women* (Brooks, Giovanni).

OCTOBER. For excerpts from article by Manthia Diawara on Mudimbe. Reprinted with permission of MIT Press.

OHIO UNIVERSITY PRESS. For excerpts from articles by Martin Trump on Ndebele in Martin Trump, ed. *Rendering Things Visible: Essays on South African Literay Culture*, (1990); Micahel Vaughan on Ndebele in Martin Trump, ed. *Rendering Things Visible: Essays on South African Literary Culture* (1990).

BEVERLEY ORMEROD. For excerpts from *An Introduction to the French Caribbean Novel* (Glissant, Schwarz-Bart, Zobel).

OXFORD UNIVERSITY PRESS. For excerpts from articles by Barthélémy Kotchy on Zadi Zaourou in *Theatre Research International*; Mineke Schipper on Bemba, Liking, in *Theatre Research International*; Gary Warner on Ndao in *Theatre Research International*; Harold A. Waters on Ndao in *Theatre Research International*.

PETERS FRASER & DUNLOP. For excerpts from Gerald Moore, *The Chosen Tongue* (Hearne, Mais, Reid, Salkey). Reprinted by permission of the Peters Fraser & Dunlop Group Ltd.

KENNETH RAMCHAND. For excerpts from *The West Indian Novel and Its Background* (Clarke, James, Reid, Wynter).

RANDOM HOUSE UK LIMITED. For excerpts from Edward [Kamau] Brathwaite's Introduction to *Brother Man* by Roger Mais. Jonathan Cape, publisher; Jean D'Costa's Introduction to *Black Lightning* by Roger Mais. Jonathan Cape, publisher.

RAVAN PRESS. For excerpts from Mineke Schipper, *Theatre and Society in Africa* (Soyinka)

REVIEW OF CONTEMPORARY FICTION. For excerpts from articles by Jack Byrne on Reed; Laura Frost on Cliff.

REVIEW OF NATIONAL LITERATURES. For excerpts from articles by Lyndon Harries on Robert; Bernth Lindfors on Serumaga; J. Mbelolo Ya Mpiku on Ouologuem; Clive Wake on Rabéarivelo.

REVISTA/REVIEW INTERAMERICANA. For excerpts from article by Henry Cohen on Depestre.

RODOPI. For excerpts from articles by Lucia Nankoe and Essa Reijmers on Marshall; Joseph Swann on Achebe in *Crisis and Creativity in the New Literatures in English*, Geoffrey V. Davis and Hena Maes-Jelinek, eds.

ROUTLEDGE & KEGAN PAUL. For excerpts from Henry Louis Gates, Jr., ed., *Black Literature and Literary Theory* (Brooks, Morrison, Reed); article by Douglas Killam on Ogot in *Literatures of the World in English*, Bruce King, ed.

CHARLES H. ROWELL. For excerpts from article on Gaines in *The Southern Review*.

ASHRAF H. A. RUSHDY. For excerpts from article on Johnson in *African American Review*.

RUTGERS UNIVERSITY PRESS. For excerpts from article by Abena P. A. Busia on Marshall in *Changing Our Own Words*, Cheryl A. Wall, ed.; Karla F. C. Holloway, *Moorings & Metaphors: Figures of Culture and Gender in Black Women's Literature* (Naylor); article by [Akasha] Gloria T. Hull on Lorde in *Changing Our Own Words*, Cheryl A. Wall, ed.; article by Toni Morrison on Bambara in *Literature and the Urban Experience*, Michael C. Jaye and Ann Chalmers Watts, eds.; articles by Barbara Smith on Naylor and Lorde in *Wild Women in the Whirlwind: Afra-American Culture and the Contemporary Literary Renaissance*, Joanne M. Braxton and Andrée Nicola McLaughlin, eds.; article by Susan Willis on Morrison in *Changing Our Own Words*, Cheryl A. Wall, ed.

ST. MARTIN'S PRESS. For excerpts from article by Pierrette M. Frickey on Lovelace in Bruce King, ed. *Post-Colonial English Drama: Commonwealth Drama since 1960*. Copyright © 1992 Bruce King. Reprinted with permission of St. Martin's Press, Incorporated; article by Holly Hill on Wilson in Bruce King, ed. *Contemporary American Theatre*. Copyright © 1991 Bruce King. Reprinted with permission of St. Martin's Press, Incorporated; article by Renu Juneja on Walcott in Bruce King, ed. *Post-Colonial English Drama: Commonwealth Drama since 1960*. Copyright © 1992 Bruce King. Reprinted with permission of St. Martin's Press, Incorporated; Bruce King, ed. *The New English Literatures: Cultural Nationalism in a Changing World* (Brathwaite, Harris, Soyinka, Walcott). Copyright © 1980 Bruce King. Reprinted with permission of St. Martin's Press, Incorporated; article by George Lamming on Hearne in Edward Baugh, ed. *Critics on Caribbean Literature*. Copyright © 1978 Edward Baugh. Reprinted with permission of St. Martin's Press, Incorporated; article by Mervyn Morris on Bennett in Edward Baugh, ed. *Critics on Caribbean Literature*. Copyright © 1978 Edward Baugh. Reprinted with permission of St. Martin's Press, Incorporated; Oladele Taiwo. *Female Novelists of Modern Africa* (Head, Nwapa, Ogot, Tlali). Copyright © 1984 Oladele Taiwo. Reprinted with permission of St. Martin's Press, Incorporated; Jane Watts. *Black Writers from South Africa: Towards a Discourse of Liberation* (La Guma, Mphahlele, Rive, Tlali). Copyright © 1989 Jane Watts. Reprinted with permission of St. Martin's Press, Incorporated; article by Thomas R. Whitaker on Soyinka in Bruce King, ed. *Post-Colonial English Drama: Commonwealth Drama since 1960*. Copyright © 1992 Bruce King. Reprinted with permission of St. Martin's Press, Incorporated; article by Bruce Woodcock on Goodison in Gina Wisker, ed. *Black Women's Writing*. Copyright © 1993 Gina Wisker. Reprinted with permission of St. Martin's Press, Incorporated.

SANDRA G. SHANNON. For excerpts from article on Wilson in *Black American Literature Forum* (now *African American Review*).

SOUTHERN HUMANITIES REVIEW. For excerpts from article by Sidonie Ann Smith on Angelou. Copyright *Southern Humanities Review*, 7.4 (1973): 367–68, 374–75. Published by Auburn University.

THE SOUTHERN QUARTERLY. For excerpts from "Alice Childress: Black Woman Playwright as Feminist Critic" by Gayle Austin. Reprinted from *The Southern Quarterly*, Volume 25, Number 3, Spring, 1987, pp. 53–65.

HORTENSE J. SPILLERS. For excerpts from article on Brooks in Henry Louis Gates, Jr., ed. *Reading Black, Reading Feminist*.

ROBERT B. STEPTO. For excerpts from article on Lorde in *Parnassus*.

STUDIES IN AMERICAN FICTION. For excerpts from article by Jonathan Little on Johnson.

STUDIES IN SHORT FICTION. For excerpts from Raymond A. Mazurek, "Gordimer's 'Something Out There' and Ndebele's *Fools and Other Stories*: The Politics of Literary Form." *Studies in Short Fiction*. 26 (1989): 71–79. Copyright © 1989 by Newberry College.

STUDIES IN TWENTIETH-CENTURY LITERATURE. For excerpts from articles by Janis L. Pallister on Neto; W. Curtis Schade on Bebey; Janice Spleth on Mudimbe.

UNIVERSITY OF HAWAII AT MANOA. For excerpts from "The Autobiographical Content in the Works of South African Women Writers: The Personal and the Political" (Tlali) by Huma Ibrahim in *Biography East and West*, Carol Remelb, ed.

UNIVERSITY OF ILLINOIS PRESS. For excerpts from article by Houston A. Baker, Jr. in *A Life Distilled: Gwendolyn Brooks, Her Poetry and Fiction*, Maria K. Mootry and Gary Smith, eds.; J. Edward Chamberlin, *Come Back to Me My Language: Poetry and the West Indies* (Bennett, Goodison, Senior, Walcott); article by Maria K. Mootry in *A Life Distilled: Gwendolyn Brooks, Her Poetry and Fiction*, Maria K. Mootry and Gary Smith, eds.

THE UNIVERSITY OF MASSACHUSETTS PRESS. For excerpts from Ursula A. Barnett, *A Vision of Order: A Study of Black South African Literature in English (1914–1980)* (Head, Kunene, Mphahlele, Mtshali, Rive, Sepamla, Serote, Tlali). Reprinted from *A Vision of Order: A Study of Black South African Literature in English (1914–1980)*, by Ursula A. Barnett (Amherst: University of Massachusetts Press, 1983), copyright © 1983 by Ursula Barnett; Bernard W. Bell, *The Afro-American Novel and Its Tradition* (Baldwin, Fauset, Morrison, Reed) (Amherst: The University of Massachusetts Press, 1987), copyright © 1987 by the University of Massachusetts Press; Joan Dayan's Introduction to *A Rainbow for the Christian West*, by René Depestre.

THE UNIVERSITY OF MICHIGAN PRESS. For excerpts from "Lucille Clifton: A Changing Voice for Changing Times" by Andrea Benton Rushing in *Coming to Light*. Diane Wood Middlebrook and Marilyn Yalom, eds. (Ann Arbor: The University of Michigan Press, 1985).

UNIVERSITY OF MINNESOTA PRESS. For excerpts from article by Françoise Lionnet on Cliff in *De/Colonizing the Subject*, Sidonie Smith and Julia Watson, eds. Copyright 1992 by the Regents of the University of Minnesota. Published by the University of Minnesota Press.

UNIVERSITY OF MISSOURI PRESS. For excerpts from Terry Otten, *The Crime of Innocence in the Fiction of Toni Morrison*.

UNIVERSITY OF NATAL PRESS. For excerpts from "Mongane Serote: Humanist and Revolutionary" by Dorian Barboure in *Momentum: On Recent South African Writing*. M. J. Daymond, J. U. Jacobs, and Margaret Lenta, eds. (1984).

UNIVERSITY OF NORTH CAROLINA PRESS. For excerpts from Elizabeth Fox-Genovese on Giovanni, "My Statue, My Self: Autobiographical Writings of Afro-American Women," in *The Private Self: Theory and Practice of Women's Autobiographical Writings*, edited by Shari Benstock. Copyright © 1988 by The University of North Carolina Press. Used by permission of the author and publisher. Reprinted in Henry Louis Gates, Jr., ed. *Reading Black, Reading Feminist* (1990).

UNIVERSITY OF PENNSYLVANIA PRESS. For excerpts from articles by Mary K. DeShazer on Lorde; Estella Lauter on Lorde in *Writing the Women Artist: Essays on Poetics, Politics, and Portraiture*, Suzanne W. Jones, ed.

UNIVERSITY OF SOUTH CAROLINA PRESS. For excerpts from article by Elinor S. Miller of Sow Fall in *French Literature Series*.

UNIVERSITY OF TENNESSEE PRESS. For excerpts from Jane Campbell, *Mythic Black Fiction: The Transformation of History* (Baldwin, Bradley).

UNIVERSITY OF WISCONSIN PRESS. For excerpts from Houston A. Baker, Jr. in *Afro-American Poetics* on Baraka.

UNIVERSITY PRESS OF KENTUCKY. For excerpts from D. H. Melhem on Brooks. Reprinted from D. H. Melhem, *Gwendolyn Brooks: Poetry and the Heroic Voice*, copyright © 1987 by D. H. Melhem, by permission of the publishers; D. H. Melhem on Sanchez and Baraka. Reprinted from D. H. Melhem, *Heroism in the New Black Poetry*, copyright © 1990 by D. H. Melhem, by permission of the publishers; Martha M. Vertreace on Bambara. Reprinted from Mickey Pearlman, ed., *American Women Writing Fiction: Memory, Identity, Family, Space*, copyright © 1989 by The University Press of Kentucky, by permission of the publishers.

INDEX TO CRITICS

Names of critics are cited on the pages given

ABRAHAMS, Cecil
Serote, 653

ABRAHAMS, Lionel
Serote, 645

ACHEBE, Chinua
Awoonor, 47; Baldwin, 65

ACHUFUSI, Ify
Ogot, 527

AGBAJE, David Olusegun
Mtshali, 449

AGOVI, Kofi
Anyidoho, 33

AIKO, Koudou
Zadi Zaourou, 763

AIRE, Victor O.
Mudimbe, 452

AIYEJINA, Funso
Brathwaite, 109; Lamming, 346

ALANTE-LIMA, Willy
Tati-Loutard, 708

ALVAREZ-PEREYRE, Jacques
Brutus, 130; Kunene, 327; Mtshali, 447;
Sepamla, 643; Serote, 650; Tlali, 720

AMANKULOR, J. Ndukaku
Badian, 61

AMMONS, Elizabeth
Fauset, 221

AMUTA, Chidi
Iyayi, 289; Neto, 501

ANGROSINO, Michael V.
Césaire, 135; Lamming, 348

ANYIDOHO, Kofi
Awoonor, 47; Rive, 591

APRONTI, E. O.
Maillu, 381

APRONTI, Jawa
Anyidoho, 31

ARMAH, Ayi Kwei
Ndao, 492

ARNOLD, Stephen H.
Osundare, 549

ASEIN, Samuel Omo
Brathwaite, 108

AUSTIN, Gayle
Childress, 149

AWKWARD, Michael
McMillan, 420

AWODIYA, Muyiwa P.
Osofisan, 546

BAKER, Houston A., Jr.
Baraka, 74; Brooks, 123

BALOGUN, F. Odun
Taban lo Liyong, 705, 706

BAMIKUNLE, Aderemi
Osofisan, 543; Osundare, 548, 551

BANHAM, Martin
Ndao, 486; Rotimi, 600, 604;
Serumaga, 655; Sutherland, 694

BARBOURE, Dorian
Serote, 649

BARDOLPH, Jacqueline
Farah, 216; Mwangi, 472

BARKAN, Sandra
Ouologuem, 558

BARNETT, Ursula A.
Head, 268; Kunene, 327; Mapanje, 391;
Mphahlele, 440 , 443; Mtshali, 445;
Rive, 591; Sepamla, 642; Serote, 647;
Tlali, 717

BARRATT, Harold
Anthony, 28, 29, 30; Lovelace, 370

BARTHOLD, Bonnie J.
Jones, 303; Soyinka, 675

BATTESTINI, S. M.
Badian, 56

BAUERLE, Richard F.
Awoonor, 46; Cheney-Coker, 144

BAUGH, Edward
Clarke, 153; Goodison, 249

BEIER, Ulli
Rabéarivelo, 571

BELL, Bernard W.
    Baldwin, 63; Fauset, 223; Morrison, 433; Reed, 579
BEMBA, Sylvain
    Tchicaya U Tam'si, 714
BENSEN, Robert
    Walcott, 727
BERNER, Robert L.
    Cheney-Coker, 141; Rive, 590, 592
BERRIAN, Brenda F.
    Ogot, 528; Sembène Ousmane, 633
BJORNSON, Richard
    Badian, 60; Bebey, 82, 83; Beti, 101; Liking, 354
BLAIR, Dorothy S.
    Bâ, 49; Badian, 57; Bebey, 78; Diallo, 188; Kourouma, 318; Ndao, 486, 490; Ouologuem, 555; Sembène Ousmane, 631; Sow Fall, 667
BLAU, Eleanor
    Johnson, 301
BOEHMER, Elleke
    Nwapa, 523
BOGLE, Enid
    Edgell, 201
BOURGEACQ, Jacques
    Badian, 59
BOXILL, Anthony
    Heath, 282; Salkey, 615
BRÁS, A. R.
    Neto, 500
BRATHWAITE, Edward Kamau
    Mais, 386
BRESLOW, Stephen P.
    Walcott, 729, 733
BRITWUM, Kwabena
    Kourouma, 319
BROWN, Joseph A., SJ
    Harper, 256
BROWN, Lloyd W.
    Aidoo, 10; Bennett, 91; Brathwaite, 107; Clarke, 152, 155; Emecheta, 205; Head, 266; Nwapa, 519; Sutherland, 694
BRUNER, Charlotte H.
    Bebey, 81; Condé, 171; Diallo, 189; Emecheta, 205, 207; Head, 267; Phelps, 560, 561; Warner-Vieyra, 741, 743
BRUNER, David K.
    Condé, 171; Emecheta, 205; Tati-Loutard, 707

BRYCE, Jane
    Osundare, 547
BRYDON, Diana
    Clarke, 154
BUE, Marie-Claire
    Serumaga, 654
BUREAU, Françoise
    Tati-Loutard, 708
BURNESS, Donald
    Neto, 498
BURROWAY, Janet
    Phillips, 570
BURTON, Richard D. E.
    Chamoiseau, 140
BUSACCA, Basil
    Taban lo Liyong, 699
BUSH, Roland E.
    St. Omer, 690
BUSIA, Abena P. A.
    Armah, 37; Bâ, 53; Marshall, 409; Schwarz-Bart, 628
BUTLER-EVANS, Elliott
    Bambara, 68; Morrison, 435
BUTTERFIELD, Stephen
    Angelou, 21
BYERMAN, Keith E.
    Bambara, 68; Gaines, 227; Jones, 306; Reed, 579; Walker, 736
BYRD, Rudolph P.
    Walker, 739
BYRNE, Jack
    Reed, 583
CAILLER, Bernadette
    Mudimbe, 455
CALDER, Angus
    Mapanje, 391; Mwangi, 473
CALLAHAN, John F.
    Harper, 255
CAMPBELL, Elaine
    Edgell, 199; St. Omer, 691
CAMPBELL, Jane
    Baldwin, 63; Bradley, 104
CAMPBELL, Josie P.
    Schwarz-Bart, 622
CARBY, Hazel V.
    Fauset, 222
CARR, Bill
    Salkey, 610

CARTER, Steven R.
  Anthony, 30
CÉSAIRE, Ina
  Labou Tansi, 331
CHAM, Mbye Baboucar
  Bâ, 51
CHAMBERLIN, J. Edward
  Bennett, 95; Goodison, 252; Senior,
  638; Walcott, 732
CHAMOISEAU, Patrick
  Condé, 175
CHANG, Victor L.
  Wynter, 756
CHEMAIN, Arlette
  Tati-Loutard, 709; Tchicaya U Tam'si,
  712
CHENNELLS, Anthony
  La Guma, 340
CHIMOMBO, Steve
  Mapanje, 393
CHING, Mei-Ling
  Wilson, 748
CHRIST, Carol P.
  Shange, 660
CHRISTIAN, Barbara
  Naylor, 480
COBHAM, Rhonda
  Bennett, 94; Collins, 168; Farah, 217;
  Hodge, 287
COHEN, Derek
  Marechera, 397
COHEN, Henry
  Depestre, 180
COLLIER, Eugenia
  James, 295
CONDÉ, Maryse
  Nwapa, 517; Sembène Ousmane, 629
COOKE, Michael G.
  Baldwin, 62; Bradley, 102; Brodber,
  116; Harper, 255; Hearne, 276 ; Jones,
  304; Reid, 589
COOPER, Carolyn
  Bennett, 92; Brodber, 114, 116
COOPER, Danielle Chavy
  Métellus, 428
CORNWELL, JoAnne
  Beti, 98
COSTELLO, Bonnie
  Dove, 197

COVI, Giovanna
  Kincaid, 315
CREARY, Jean
  Mais, 384
CRONJE, Suzanne
  Okri, 535
CROUCH, Stanley
  Johnson, 299
CROW, Brian
  Mugo, 459
CUDJOE, Selwyn R.
  Angelou, 25; Bennett, 93; Juminer, 308;
  Wynter, 758
CURB, Rosemary K.
  Sanchez, 619
DABYDEEN, Cyril
  Brathwaite, 112
DADA, Segun
  Cheney-Coker, 144
DAILLY, Christophe
  Badian, 58; La Guma, 339
D'ALMEIDA, Irène Assiba
  Bâ, 52
DAMATO, Diva Barbaro
  Glissant, 244
DANCE, Daryl Cumber
  Brodber, 115; Reid, 588; Salkey, 614
DASENBROCK, Reed Way
  Soyinka, 683, 684
DASH, J. Michael
  Brathwaite, 108; Depestre, 185; Phelps,
  563
DAVIES, Barrie
  Hearne, 275
DAVIES, Carole Boyce
  Cliff, 156; Kincaid, 314; Lorde, 363;
  Soyinka, 680; Tlali, 719
DAVIS, Angela Y.
  Condé, 175
DAVIS, Thulani
  McMillan, 422
DAYAN, Joan
  Depestre, 180, 184, 185
D'COSTA, Jean
  Mais, 389
DE ARMAN, Charles
  Reed, 580
DEGRAS, Priska
  Glissant, 245

DESCHAMPS, Alain
  Métellus, 426

DESHAZER, Mary K.
  Lorde, 361, 365

DHAIRYAM, Sagri
  Lorde, 369

DIAWARA, Manthia
  Mudimbe, 453

DIEKE, Ikenna
  Walker, 741

DINGOME, Jeanne N.
  Liking, 353

DIXON, Melvin
  Jones, 305

DOHARRIS, Brenda
  Collins, 169

DOUGHTY, Louise
  Cliff, 157

DOVE, Rita
  Walcott, 728

DOWN, Lorna
  Edgell, 200

DRAMÉ, Kandioura
  Beti, 97

DUNN, Margaret M.
  Cliff, 160

DUNTON, Chris
  Aidoo, 13; Liking, 351; Osofisan, 544

DUNWOODIE, Peter
  St. Omer, 689

DURIX, Jean-Pierre
  Harris, 262, 263

DUTTON, Wendy
  Kincaid, 312

EARLY, L. R.
  Awoonor, 46

EDMONDSON, Belinda
  Cliff, 161

EGBUJOR, Eronini E. C.
  Kourouma, 324

EGUDU, R. N.
  Brutus, 125; Ogot, 525; Soyinka, 672;
  Taban lo Liyong, 701

EILERSEN, Gillian Stead
  Head, 272

ELDER, Arlene A.
  Mugo, 459

ELIMIMIAN, Isaac I.
  Brutus, 131

EMENYONU, Ernest N.
  Emecheta, 209; Nwapa, 518

ENEKWE, Ossie Onuora
  Neto, 500

ENSSLEN, Klaus
  Bradley, 105

ERICKSON, John D.
  Maximin, 418

ETHERTON, Michael
  Aidoo, 10; Mugo, 457

EVANS, Jennifer
  Ngugi wa Thiong'o, 507

EWEN, D. R.
  Farah, 212

EZENWA-Ohaeto
  Marechera, 402; Nwapa, 522; Osundare,
  549; Sepamla, 643, 645; Taban lo
  Liyong, 705

FARAH, Nuruddin
  Achebe, 5

FATUNDE, Tunde
  Iyayi, 290

FEBRUARY, Vernon
  Sepamla, 641

FETTWEIS, Nadine
  Labou Tansi, 334

FIDO, Elaine Savory
  Emecheta, 210; Goodison, 249; Senior, 637

FLANNIGAN, Arthur
  Condé, 173

FLOWERS, Sandra Hollin
  Shange, 660

FOX-GENOVESE, Elizabeth
  Giovanni, 240

FRASER, Robert
  Anyidoho, 32, 33; Awoonor, 43; Okri,
  539; Rabéarivelo, 575

FREEDMAN, Samuel G.
  Wilson, 747

FRICKEY, Pierrette M.
  Lovelace, 376

FROST, Laura
  Cliff, 158

FUSSELL, Edwin
  Harper, 253

GADJIGO, Samba
  Sow Fall, 671

GAMARRA, Pierre
  Métellus, 427

GARDINER, Susan
    Head, 271
GARRETT, George
    Phillips, 569
GATES, Henry Louis, Jr.
    Naylor, 478; Reed, 578
GEIS, Deborah R.
    Shange, 664
GEORGOUDAKI, Ekaterini
    Dove, 196
GÉRARD, Albert S.
    Robert, 597
GIBBS, James
    Mapanje, 392, 396
GIDDINGS, Paula
    Giovanni, 238
GIKANDI, Simon
    Achebe, 8; Cliff, 158 ; Edgell, 203;
    Hodge, 285; James, 297; Lamming, 349;
    Marshall, 413; Mwangi, 475
GILKES, Michael
    Gilroy, 232; Harris, 261; James, 293;
    Lamming, 344; Mais, 388; Reid, 587;
    St. Omer, 688
GLEASON, William
    Johnson, 300
GLISERMAN, Martin J.
    Bradley, 104
GOODWIN, K. L.
    Awoonor, 42; Brutus, 127; Kunene,
    326; Ntiru, 514; Okot p'Bitek, 530 ;
    Rubadiri, 608; Taban lo Liyong, 702
GORDIMER, Nadine
    Mtshali, 444
GOTTLIEB, Annie
    Naylor, 476
GOULD, Jean
    Giovanni, 237
GRATIANT, Isabelle
    Juminer, 309
GRAVES, Anne Adams
    Liking, 356; Lopes, 358
GRIFFITHS, Gareth
    Mais, 387
GRIMES, Kyle
    Harper, 257
GRUESSER, John C.
    Angelou, 23
HAARHOFF, Dorian
    Mphahlele, 441

HALE, Thomas A.
    Césaire, 132
HARNEY, Steve
    Baraka, 77
HARRIES, Lyndon
    Robert, 595
HARRIS, Peter
    Dove, 194
HARRIS, Trudier
    Childress, 146; Walker, 734
HARRIS, Wilson
    Mais, 388
HARROW, Kenneth W.
    Labou Tansi, 332; Mudimbe, 451, 452
HAWTHORNE, Evelyn J.
    Kincaid, 316; Mais, 390
HAYNES, John
    Kunene, 329
HAYWARD, Jennifer
    Johnson, 300
HEANEY, Seamus
    Walcott, 725
HENDERSON, Mae G.
    Jones, 306
HEZEKIAH, Randolph
    Zobel, 764
HILL, Holly
    Wilson, 750
HILL-LUBIN, Mildred A.
    Aidoo, 11; Baldwin, 62
HITE, Molly
    Walker, 737
HOLLOWAY, Karla F. C.
    Naylor, 482
HORN, Andrew
    Serumaga, 657, 658
HORNE, Naana Banyiwa
    Aidoo, 15
HOURANTIER, Marie-José
    Zadi Zaourou, 762
HUDSON, Theodore R.
    Gaines, 227
HULL, [Akasha] Gloria T.
    Bambara, 67; Lorde, 362
HUME, Kathryn
    Reed, 582
IBRAHIM, Huma
    Tlali, 721
ILOEJE, Azubike F.
    Munonye, 464, 466

INGLEDEW, David
Hearne, 278

ISAACS, Susan
McMillan, 423

ISMOND, Patricia
St. Omer, 688, 692; Walcott, 726

JACCARD, A. C.
Sow Fall, 668

JACKSON, Blyden
Gaines, 229

JAMES, C. L. R.
Morrison, 432

JAMES, Louis
Bennett, 89; Reid, 584

JANMOHAMED, Abdul R.
La Guma, 338

JEFFERSON, Louise M.
Zadi Zaourou, 760

JOHN, Elerius Edet
Bebey, 82

JOHNSON, Alex C.
Rotimi, 601

JOHNSON-FEELINGS, Dianne
Clifton, 165

JOHNSON, Joyce
Mphahlele, 440

JONES, Gayl
Baraka, 76; Harper, 257

JONG, Erica
Clifton, 162

JOSEPH, Margaret Paul
Lamming, 350

JUHASZ, Suzanne
Brooks, 119; Giovanni, 236

JULIEN, Eileen
Labou Tansi, 335; Ngugi wa Thiong'o,
511; Zobel, 769

JUNEJA, Renu
Walcott, 730

KAMOCHE, Jidlaph
Ngugi wa Thiong'o, 509

KANKOLONGO, Mbuyamba
Mudimbe, 450

KATRAK, Ketu H.
Emecheta, 208

KELLMAN, Anthony
Baraka, 76

KENNEDY, Ellen Conroy
Depestre, 178; Rabéarivelo, 573

KENT, George
Brooks, 120

KEO, Ebele
Amadi, 16

KIEMA, Alfred
Amadi, 18

KILLAM, Douglas
Ogot, 524

KILLAM, G. D.
Mugo, 456; Ngugi wa Thiong'o, 503, 505

KILLENS, John O.
Childress, 147

KING, Bruce
Brathwaite, 108; Harris, 259; Soyinka,
675; St. Omer, 687; Walcott, 724

KLOOSS, Wolfgang
Achebe, 4

KNAPPERT, Jan
Robert, 596

KNIGHT, Elizabeth
Maillu, 377; Mwangi, 471; Taban lo
Liyong, 703

KNIPP, Thomas R.
Awoonor, 44

KNUTSON, April Ane
Césaire, 134

KOHN, Ingeborg
Juminer, 311

KOTCHY, Barthélémy
Zadi Zaourou, 761

KUBAYANDA, J. Bekunuru
Anyidoho, 34

KUBITSCHEK, Missy Dehn
Marshall, 411; Morrison, 437; Walker, 740

KUNDERA, Milan
Chamoiseau, 137

LAMMING, George
Hearne, 276

LARRIER, Renée
Schwarz-Bart, 628

LARSON, Charles R.
Mtshali, 446

LAUTER, Estella
Lorde, 366

LAZARUS, Neil
Ngugi wa Thiong'o, 508; Sembène
Ousmane, 634

LAZER, Hank
Clifton, 166

LESTER, Neal A.
    Shange, 666
LEVILAIN, Guy Viêt
    Césaire, 132
LEVIN, Tobe
    Ngugi wa Thiong'o, 506
LEVUMO, Alex
    Serote, 646
LEWIS, Ida
    Giovanni, 234
LEWIS, Vashti Crutcher
    Morrison, 436
LIDDELL, Janice Lee
    Wynter, 757
LIMA, Maria Helena
    Collins, 170
LINDFORS, Bernth
    Maillu, 379; Okot p'Bitek, 531;
    Serumaga, 654
LIONNET, Françoise
    Cliff, 161; Warner-Vieyra, 746
LITTLE, Jonathan
    Johnson, 299
LOCKETT, Cecily
    Tlali, 722
LUCE, Louise Fiber
    Labou Tansi, 336
LUPTON, Mary Jane
    Fauset, 220
LYAKHOVSKAYA, Nina D.
    Bemba, 86
MACKENZIE, Craig
    Head, 273
MADHUBUTI, Haki
    Clifton, 164; Sanchez, 616
MADUKA, Chidi
    Kunene, 328
MAES-JELINEK, Hena
    Harris, 258, 265
MAGEL, E. A.
    Mugo, 458
MAGNIER, Bernard
    Labou Tansi, 330
MAIANGWA, Yusufu
    Ouologuem, 556
MAJA-PEARCE, Adewale
    Iyayi, 292; Nwapa, 521
MAKANJUOLA, Bola
    Aidoo, 14

MAKHÉLÉ, Caya
    Bemba, 87
MAKWARD, Edris
    Bâ, 52
MALANDA, Ange-Séverin
    Bemba, 85
MAMUDU, Ayo
    Okri, 537
MARCUS, James
    Phillips, 565
MARHAMA, Hasan
    Phillips, 569
MARTIN, Reginald
    Reed, 581
MARTINHO, Fernando
    Neto, 499
MATUS, Jill L.
    Naylor, 481
MAX, Daniel
    McMillan, 423
MAZUREK, Raymond A.
    Ndebele, 494
MBISE, Ismael
    Okot p'Bitek, 532
McCLUSKEY, Audrey T.
    Clifton, 163
McCORKLE, James
    Walcott, 728
McDOWELL, Deborah E.
    Fauset, 219, 223
McDOWELL, Margaret B.
    Giovanni, 239
McDOWELL, Robert E.
    Dove, 192; Heath, 280
McKINNEY, Kitzie
    Schwarz-Bart, 624
McKNIGHT, Reginald
    Mudimbe, 453
McLEOD, A. L.
    Gilroy, 232; Heath, 282
McLOUGHLIN, T. O.
    Marechera, 398, 400
McPHERSON, Dolly A.
    Angelou, 24
McWATT, Mark A.
    Brathwaite, 110; Heath, 280, 281
MELHEM, D. H.
    Baraka, 75; Brooks, 124; Sanchez, 619,
    620

MICHELMAN, Fredric
  Labou Tansi, 332; Lopes, 360; Sow
  Fall, 668
MIDIOHOUAN, Guy Ossito
  Kourouma, 322
MILLER, Christopher L.
  Ouologuem, 557
MILLER, Elinor S.
  Juminer, 308 ; Sow Fall, 669
MOORE, Gerald
  Beti, 96; Hearne, 275; La Guma, 337;
  Mais, 385; Mphahlele, 439; Okot
  p'Bitek, 529; Reid, 584; Salkey, 611;
  Sembène Ousmane, 630; Tchicaya U
  Tam'si, 711
MOOTRY, Maria K.
  Brooks, 122
Mordecai, Pamela
  Goodison, 248
MORRIS, Ann R.
  Cliff, 160
MORRIS, Mervyn
  Bennett, 90, 93; Reid, 586; Walcott, 723
MORRISON, Toni
  Bambara, 66
MORTIMER, Mildred P.
  Glissant, 247; Kourouma, 321
MOURALIS, Bernard
  Maximin, 415
MPHAHLELE, Es'kia (Ezekiel)
  Serote, 651
MPIKU, J. Mbelolo Ya
  Ouologuem, 553
MSISKA, Mpalive-Hangson
  Mapanje, 395
MUNRO, Ian H.
  Heath, 284; Lamming, 342
MUSKE, Carol
  Clifton, 163
MUSWASWA, Makolo
  Lopes, 359
MUTISO, G-C. M.
  Rubadiri, 605
MZAMANE, Mbulelo Vizikhungo
  Marechera, 397; Rive, 592; Serote, 650
NAGY, Géza Füssy
  Robert, 600
NANKOE, Lucia
  Marshall, 410

NARINESINGH, Roy
  Hodge, 284
NASIRU, Akanji
  Rotimi, 601
NAZARETH, Peter
  Head, 273; Mwangi, 467; Reed, 583;
  Rubadiri, 605; Salkey, 612, 615;
  Serumaga, 659; Taban lo Liyong, 704,
  707
NELSON, Emmanuel S.
  Brathwaite, 111
NEUBAUER, Carol E.
  Angelou, 22
NEWSON, A. S.
  Gilroy, 234
NGARA, Emmanuel
  Achebe, 3; Armah, 36; Maillu, 382;
  Ngugi wa Thiong'o, 504, 506; Sembène
  Ousmane, 631; Soyinka, 677
NGATE, Jonathan
  Warner-Vieyra, 742
NGUGI WA THIONG'O
  Collins, 167
NÍ CHRÉACHÁIN, Fírinne
  Iyayi, 291, 292
NIESEN DE ABRUNA, Laura
  Hodge, 286; Kincaid, 313, 315
NIVEN, Alastair
  Anthony, 26
NNOLIM, Charles E.
  Munonye, 462
NOËL, Dexter
  Anthony, 26
NOLAN, Tom
  Phillips, 566
NOSS, Philip A.
  Lopes, 356
NUNEZ-HARRELL, Elizabeth
  Cliff, 157
NWACHUKWU-AGBADA, J. O. J.
  Bâ, 56; Okot p'Bitek, 533
NWANKWO, Chimalum
  Aidoo, 12; Amadi, 18; Cheney-Coker,
  145
OBAFEMI, Olu
  Osofisan, 540
OBRADOVIĆ, Nadezda
  Condé, 176; Marechera, 404; Okri, 537;
  Warner-Vieyra, 744

OBUKE, Okpure O.
  Rive, 590
O'CALLAGHAN, Evelyn
  Brodber, 113; Senior, 636
OFEIMUN, Odia
  Mwangi, 474
OGBAA, Kalu
  Maillu, 380
OGEDE, Ode S.
  Armah, 41
O'GRADY, Betty
  Tchicaya U Tam'si, 715
OGU, Julius N.
  Munonye, 463
OGUNDELE, Wole
  Amadi, 17
OGUNDIPE-LESLIE, 'Molara
  Soyinka, 677
OGUNGBESAN, Kolawole
  Soyinka, 674
OGUNYEMI, Chikwenye Okonjo
  Baraka, 70; Brutus, 128
OJAIDE, Tanure
  Anyidoho, 35; Brutus, 130; Marechera,
  404; Okot p'Bitek, 532; Osundare, 552
OJO-ADE, Femi
  Bâ, 48
OKAFOR, Chinyere G.
  Rotimi, 603
OKAZAKI, Hank
  Phillips, 568
OKOME, Onookome
  Soyinka, 685
OKONKWO, Juliet I.
  Farah, 213, 214
OKRI, Ben
  Soyinka, 681
OKUMU, Charles
  Okot p'Bitek, 534
OLA, Virginia, U.
  Achebe, 7; Head, 270; Munonye, 461
OLAOGUN, Modupe O.
  Osofisan, 542
OMOTOSO, Kole
  Okri, 538
ONUEKWUSI, Jasper A.
  Brutus, 131
ORMEROD, Beverley
  Glissant, 243; Schwarz-Bart, 623;
  Zobel, 768

OSOFISAN, Femi
  Munonye, 464
OSUNDARE, Niyi
  Amadi, 15
OTTEN, Terry
  Morrison, 434
PALLISTER, Janis L.
  Neto, 502
PALMER, Eustace
  Achebe, 2; Armah, 36; Cheney-Coker,
  142; Mwangi, 468, 470; Ouologuem, 556
PALMER, Paulina
  Walker, 736
PAQUET, Sandra Pouchet
  Lamming, 346
PATTESON, Richard F.
  Senior, 640
PEARCE, Adetokunbo
  Sutherland, 697
PETERS, Jonathan A.
  Sembène Ousmane, 633
PETERSEN, Kirsten Holst
  Emecheta, 211
PFAFF, Francoise
  Sow Fall, 669
PHILLIPS, K. J.
  Ndebele, 497
POLLARD, Velma
  Senior, 637
POLLER, Nidra
  Kourouma, 323
PORTER, Abioseh Michael
  Okri, 536
POVEY, John
  Mtshali, 445
PRIEBE, Richard K.
  Achebe, 5; Aidoo, 12; Armah, 39;
  Awoonor, 45; Soyinka, 679, 682
PURI, Shalini
  Brodber, 118
RACINE, Daniel L.
  Glissant, 246; Métellus, 425
RAHMING, Melvin B.
  Hearne, 277; Marshall, 407; Morrison,
  432
RAMAMOORTHY, Yashoda
  Rubadiri, 608
RAMCHAND, Kenneth
  Clarke, 154; James, 294; Lovelace, 369;
  Reid, 585, 587; Wynter, 755

RAMPERSAD, Arnold
Dove, 191
RAMRAJ, Victor J.
Clarke, 155
RANDALL, Marilyn
Ouologuem, 559
REIJMERS, Essa
Marshall, 410
REYES, Angelita
Marshall, 408
RICHARDS, Sandra L.
Osofisan, 541; Shange, 662
RIEMENSCHNEIDER, Dieter
Marechera, 403
ROBERTS, John W.
Gaines, 226
ROCHMANN, Marie-Christine
Rabéarivelo, 576
ROGET, Wilbert J.
Schwarz-Bart, 621
ROSCOE, Adrian
Mapanje, 395; Ntiru, 512; Serumaga,
656; Taban lo Liyong, 701
ROWELL, Charles H.
Gaines, 228
RUSHDY, Ashraf H. A.
Johnson, 302
RUSHING, Andrea Benton
Clifton, 165; Shange, 661
RYMAN, Geoff
Dove, 198
SABER, Ahmed
Armah, 40
SAHEL, André-Patrick
Diallo, 187
SALICK, Roydon
Gilroy, 233
SALKEY, Andrew
Gilroy, 231; Goodison, 251; Lovelace,
372; Phillips, 564
SALT, M. J.
Cheney-Coker, 143
SAMAD, Daizal R.
Hearne, 279
SAMPLE, Maxine
Amadi, 19
SANDER, Reinhard
Harris, 263
SAVIGNEAU, Josyane
Chamoiseau, 139

SARVAN, Charles Ponnuthurai
Bâ, 55; Head, 270; Phillips, 567, 569
SAUNDERS, James Robert
Sanchez, 620
SAYERS, Valerie
McMillan, 421
SCARBORO, Ann Armstrong
Césaire, 133; Depestre, 182; Maximin,
417
SCHADE, W. Curtis
Bebey, 79, 80
SCHIKORA, Rosemary G.
Kourouma, 320
SCHIPPER, Mineke
Bemba, 84; Liking, 351; Soyinka, 676
SCHULTZ, Elizabeth A.
Childress, 148; Johnson, 298
SEARLE, Chris
Collins, 166
SELLERS, Frances Stead
McMillan, 424
SELLIN, Eric
Ouologuem, 554; Tchicaya U Tam'si, 713
SENKORO, F. E. M. K.
Robert, 598
SENNA, Carl
Gaines, 230
SHADLE, Mark
Rubadiri, 606
SHAFER, Yvonne
Wilson, 754
SHANNON, Sandra G.
Wilson, 749, 752
SHAVA, Piniel Viriri
Mtshali, 447; Ndebele, 493; Serote, 653
SHELTON, Frank W.
Gaines, 224
SHELTON, Marie-Denise
Schwarz-Bart, 626; Warner-Vieyra, 743
SHOPTAW, John
Dove, 194
SILENIEKS, Juris
Césaire, 133; Chamoiseau, 136, 141;
Glissant, 242; Phelps, 562
SINGH, Raman
Achebe, 6
SKERRETT, Joseph T., Jr.
Marshall, 406
SLEMON, Stephen
Harris, 265

SMITH, Arlette M.
  Condé, 173
SMITH, Barbara
  Lorde, 364, 366; Naylor, 479
SMITH, David Lionel
  Baraka, 75
SMITH, Pamela J. Olubunmi
  Cheney-Coker, 145
SMITH, Robert P., Jr.
  Juminer, 310; Tati-Loutard, 710; Zobel,
  767
SMITH, Sidonie Ann
  Angelou, 20
SMITH, Valerie
  Bradley, 102
SMYER, Richard I.
  Anthony, 28
SOLE, Kelwyn
  Sepamla, 644; Tlali, 720
SOLLORS, Werner
  Baraka, 72
SOUFFRANT, Claude
  Phelps, 563
SOURIEAU, Marie-Agnès
  Chamoiseau, 138
SOYINKA, Wole
  Rive, 589
SPARROW, Fiona
  Farah, 215
SPEAR, Thomas C.
  Condé, 177
SPILLERS, Hortense J.
  Brooks, 124
SPLETH, Janice
  Mudimbe, 454
SPRINGFIELD, Consuelo Lopez
  James, 295, 296
SSENSALO, Bede M.
  Gaines, 225
STEELE, Shelby
  Baraka, 73
STEINMAN, Lisa M.
  Dove, 193
STEPTO, Robert B.
  Harper, 254; Lorde, 360
STOKLE, Norman
  Bebey, 79
STRANDNESS, Jean
  Shange, 663

STRATTON, Florence
  Bâ, 54; Emecheta, 209
STRINGER, Susan
  Diallo, 190
STYLE, Colin
  Marechera, 399
SUNITHA, K. T.
  Lovelace, 374
SWANN, Joseph
  Achebe, 7
SWIFT, Graham
  Phillips, 567
TABAN LO LIYONG
  Armah, 40
TAIWO, Oladele
  Head, 269; Nwapa, 520; Ogot, 526;
  Tlali, 718
TALBERT, Linda Lee
  Sutherland, 695
TANNER, Laura E.
  Naylor, 481
TATE, Claudia C.
  Jones, 303
TERADA, Rei
  Walcott, 732
THOMAS, Ena V.
  Hodge, 286
THOMAS, H. Nigel
  Baldwin, 64; Césaire, 134; Lovelace, 374
THOMAS, Sue
  Brathwaite, 111
THOMPSON, Paul L.
  Juminer, 307
THORPE, Marjorie
  Lovelace, 371, 372
THORPE, Michael
  Osofisan, 545
TIFFIN, Helen
  Kincaid, 317; Salkey, 613
TIMPANE, John
  Shange, 665
TOERIEN, Barend J.
  Sepamla, 640
TOLSON, Melvin B., Jr.
  Sembène Ousmane, 635
TRAYLOR, Eleanor W.
  Bambara, 66
TRUMP, Martin
  Ndebele, 495; Rive, 594

TSUCHIYA, Satoru
  Mwangi, 469
UMEH, Marie Linton
  Emecheta, 204, 207
VAIL, Leroy
  Mapanje, 394
VAN SERTIMA, Ivan
  Hearne, 274; Mais, 383
VAUGHAN, Michael
  Ndebele, 496
VEIT-WILD, Flora
  Marechera, 399, 401
VERTREACE, Martha M.
  Bambara, 69
VINSON, Audrey L.
  Gaines, 230
WAKE, Clive
  Beti, 100; Ndao, 486; Rabéarivelo, 572,
  574; Rotimi, 600; Serote, 652;
  Serumaga, 655; Sutherland, 694
WALKER-JOHNSON, Joyce
  Brodber, 113
WANGUSA, Timothy
  Ntiru, 511
WANIEK, Marilyn Nelson
  Marshall, 405
WARD, Catherine C.
  Naylor, 477
WARNER, Gary
  Ndao, 488
WARNER, Keith Q.
  Zobel, 766
WASHINGTON, Mary Helen
  Brooks, 121
WATERS, Harold A.
  Ndao, 489
WATTS, Jane
  La Guma, 341; Mphahlele, 442; Rive,
  593; Tlali, 721
WHITAKER, Thomas R.
  Soyinka, 684
WHITE, Emily
  Marshall, 412

WHITE, Landeg
  Mapanje, 394
WILDE, Lisa
  Wilson, 751
WILENTZ, Gay
  Naylor, 483; Nwapa, 523; Sutherland, 698
WILEY, Catherine
  Childress, 151
WILLIAMS, 'Bayo
  Munonye, 465
WILLIAMS, David
  Sanchez, 617
WILLIS, Susan
  Morrison, 430, 436
WILMOT, P. F.
  Okri, 535
WILSON, Anna
  Lorde, 368
WILSON, Elizabeth
  Condé, 174; Schwarz-Bart, 627;
  Warner-Vieyra, 744
WOOD, Michael
  Morrison, 438
WOODCOCK, Bruce
  Goodison, 250
WRIGHT, Derek
  Armah, 38; Farah, 218
WRIGHT, Katheryn
  Tchicaya U Tam'si, 713
WYKE, Clement H.
  Walcott, 729
WYLIE, Hal
  Bemba, 88; Beti, 97; Depestre, 181,
  182, 183; Métellus, 426, 429; Salkey,
  611; Zobel, 767
YESUFU, A. Rasheed
  Ntiru, 514, 516
YODER, Lauren W.
  Maximin, 420
YUMBA WA KIONI
  Lopes, 357
ZIMRA, Clarisse
  Maximin, 416